CHILTON'S GUIDE TO
FUEL INJECTION & ELECTRONIC ENGINE CONTROLS—1984-88
IMPORT CARS and TRUCKS

President	Lawrence A. Fornasieri
Vice President & General Manager	John P. Kushnerick
Editor-In-Chief	Kerry A. Freeman, S.A.E.
Managing Editor	Dean F. Morgantini, S.A.E.
Senior Editor	Richard J. Rivele, S.A.E.
Senior Editor	W. Calvin Settle Jr., S.A.E.

CHILTON BOOK COMPANY
Part of CAPITAL CITIES/ABC, INC.

Manufactured in USA
© 1988 Chilton Book Company
Chilton Way, Radnor, PA 19089
ISBN 0–8019–7818–1
Library of Congress Card Catalog No. 87–47940
1234567890   7654321098

SAFETY NOTICE

Proper service and repair procedures are vital to the safe, reliable operation of all motor vehicles, as well as the personal safety of those performing repairs. This manual outlines procedures for servicing and repairing vehicles using safe, effective methods. The procedures contain many NOTES, CAUTIONS and WARNINGS which should be followed along with standard safety procedures to eliminate the possibilty of personal injury or improper service which could damage the vehicle or compromise its safety.

It is important to note that the repair procedures and techniques, tools and parts for servicng motor vehicles, as well as the skill and experience of the individual performing the work vary widely. It is not possible to anticipate all of the conceivable ways or conditions under which vehicles may be serviced, or to provide cautions as to all of the possible hazards that may result. Standard and accepted safety precautions and equipment should be used when handling toxic or flammable fluids, and safety goggles or other protection should be used during cutting, grinding, chiseling, prying, or any other process that can cause material removal or projectiles.

Some procedures require the use of tools specially designed for a specific purpose. Before substituting another tool or procedure, you must be completely satisfied that neither your personal safety, nor the performance of the vehicle will be endangered

PART NUMBERS

Part numbers listed in this reference are not recomendations by Chilton for any product by brand name. They are references that can be used with interchange manuals and aftermarket supplier catalogs to locate each brand supplier's discrete part number.

Although information in this manual is based on industry sources and is complete as possible at the time of publication, the possibilty exists that some car manufacturers made later changes which could not be included here. While striving for total accuracy, Chilton Book Company cannot assume responsibility for any errors, changes or omissions that may occur in the compilation of this data.

CONTENTS

8803942

Basic Electricity

INDEX

FUNDAMENTALS OF ELECTRICITY

A good understanding of basic electrical theory and how circuits work is necessary to successfully perform the service and testing outlined in this manual. Therefore, this section should be read before attempting any diagnosis and repair.

All matter is made up of tiny particles called molecules. Each molecule is made up of two or more atoms. Atoms may be divided into even smaller particles called protons, neutrons and electrons. These particles are the same in all matter and differences in materials (hard or soft, conductive or non-conductive) occur only because of the number and arrangement of these particles. In other words, the protons, neutrons and electrons in a drop of water are the same as those in an ounce of lead, there are just more of them (arranged differently) in a lead molecule than in a water molecule. Protons and neutrons packed together form the nucleus of the atom, while electrons orbit around the nucleus much the same way as the planets of the solar system orbit around the sun.

The proton is a small positive natural charge of electricity, while the neutron has no electrical charge. The electron carries a negative charge equal to the positive charge of the proton. Every electrically neutral atom contains the same number of protons and electrons, the exact number of which determines the element. The only difference between a conductor and an insulator is that a conductor possesses free electrons in large quantities, while an insulator has only a few. An element must have very few free electrons to be a good insulator, and vice-versa. When we speak of electricity, we're talking about these free electrons.

In a conductor, the movement of the free electrons is hindered by collisions with the adjoining atoms of the element (matter). This hindrance to movement is called RESISTANCE and it varies with different materials and temperatures. As temperature increases, the movement of the free electrons increases, causing more frequent collisions and therefore increasing resistance to the movement of the electrons. The number of collisions (resistance) also increases with the number of electrons flowing (current). Current is defined as the movement of electrons through a conductor such as a wire. In a conductor (such as copper) electrons can be caused to leave their atoms and move to other atoms. This flow is continuous in that every time an atom gives up an electron, it collects another one to take its place. This movement of electrons is called electric current and is measured in amperes. When 6.28 billion, billion electrons pass a certain point in the circuit in one second, the amount of current flow is called one ampere.

The force or pressure which causes electrons to flow in any conductor (such as a wire) is called VOLTAGE. It is measured in volts and is similar to the pressure that causes water to flow in a pipe. Voltage is the difference in electrical pressure measured between two different points in a circuit. In a 12 volt system, for example, the force measured between the two battery posts is 12 volts. Two important concepts are voltage potential and polarity. Voltage potential is the amount of voltage or electrical pressure at a certain point in the circuit with respect to another point. For example, if the voltage potential at one post of the 12 volt battery is zero, the voltage potential at the other post is 12 volts with respect to the first post. One post of the battery is said to be positive (+); the other post is negative (-) and the conventional direction of current flow is from positive to negative in an electrical circuit. It should be noted that the electron flow in the wire is opposite the current flow. In other words, when the circuit is energized, the current flows from positive to negative, but the electrons actually move from negative to positive. The voltage or pressure needed to produce a current flow in a circuit must be greater than the resistance present in the circuit. In other words, if the voltage drop across the resistance is greater than or equal to the voltage input, the

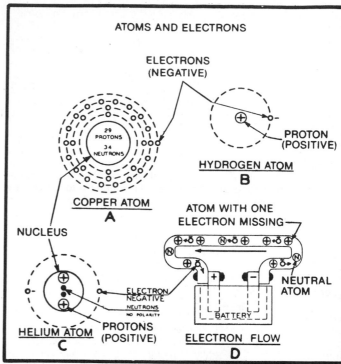

Typical atoms of copper (A), hydrogen (B) and helium (C). Electron flow in battery circuit (D)

voltage potential will be zero—no voltage will flow through the circuit. Resistance to the flow of electrons is measured in ohms. One volt will cause one ampere to flow through a resistance of one ohm.

Units Of Electrical Measurement

There are three fundamental characteristics of a direct-current electrical circuit: volts, amperes and ohms.

VOLTAGE in a circuit controls the intensity with which the loads in the circuit operate. The brightness of a lamp, the heat of an electrical defroster, the speed of a motor are all directly proportional to the voltage, if the resistance in the circuit and/

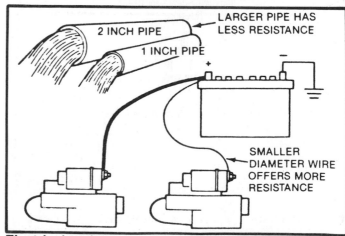

Electrical resistance can be compared to water flow through a pipe. The smaller the wire (pipe), the more resistance to the flow of electrons (water)

or mechanical load on electric motors remains constant. Voltage available from the battery is constant (normally 12 volts), but as it operates the various loads in the circuit, voltage decreases (drops).

AMPERE is the unit of measurement of current in an electrical circuit. One ampere is the quantity of current that will flow through a resistance of one ohm at a pressure of one volt. The amount of current that flows in a circuit is controlled by the voltage and the resistance in the circuit. Current flow is directly proportional to resistance. Thus, as voltage is increased or decreased, current is increased or decreased accordingly. Current is decreased as resistance is increased, however, and is increased as resistance is decreased. With little or no resistance in a circuit, current is high.

OHM is the unit of measurement of resistance, represented by the Greek letter Omega (Ω). One ohm is the resistance of a conductor through which a current of one ampere will flow at a pressure of one volt. Electrical resistance can be measured on an instrument called an ohmmeter. The loads (electrical devices) are the primary resistances in a circuit. Loads such as lamps, solenoids, and electric heaters have a resistance that is essentially fixed; at a normal fixed voltage, they will draw a fixed current. Motors, on the other hand, do not have a fixed resistance. Increasing the mechanical load on a motor (such as might be caused by a misadjusted track in a power window system) will decrease the motor speed. The drop in motor rpm has the effect of reducing the internal resistance of the motor because the current draw of the motor varies directly with the mechanical load on the motor, although its actual resistance is unchanged. Thus, as the motor load increases, the current draw of the motor increases, and may increase up to the point where the motor stalls (cannot move the mechanical load).

Circuits are designed with the total resistance of the circuit taken into account. Troubles can arise when unwanted resistances enter into a circuit. If corrosion, dirt, grease, or any other contaminant occurs in places like switches, connectors, and grounds, or if loose connections occur, resistances will develop in these areas. These resistances act like additional loads in the circuit and cause problems.

OHM'S LAW

Ohm's law is a statement of the relationship between the three fundamental characteristics of an electrical circuit. These rules apply to direct current (DC) only.

Ohm's law provides a means to make an accurate circuit analysis without actually seeing the circuit. If, for example, one wanted to check the condition of the rotor winding in a alternator whose specifications indicate that the field (rotor) current draw is normally 2.5 amperes at 12 volts, simply connect the rotor to a 12 volt battery and measure the current with an ammeter. If it measures about 2.5 amperes, the rotor winding can be assumed good.

An ohmmeter can be used to test components that have been removed from the vehicle in much the same manner as an ammeter. Since the voltage and the current of the rotor windings used as an earlier example are known, the resistance can be calculated using Ohms law. The formula would be:

If the rotor resistance measures about 4.8 ohms when checked with an ohmmeter, the winding can be assumed good. By plugging in different specifications, additional circuit information can be determined such as current draw, etc.

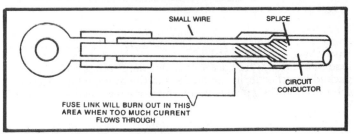

$$R = \frac{E}{I} \qquad \text{Where:} \quad E = 12 \text{ volts}$$
$$I = 2.5 \text{ amperes}$$
$$R = \frac{12 \text{ volts}}{2.5 \text{ amps}} = 4.8 \text{ ohms}$$

An example of calculating resistance (R) when the voltage (E) and amperage (I) is known.

Typical fusible link wire

SMALL WIRE · SPLICE · CIRCUIT CONDUCTOR · FUSE LINK WILL BURN OUT IN THIS AREA WHEN TOO MUCH CURRENT FLOWS THROUGH

Electrical Circuits

An electrical circuit must start from a source of electrical supply and return to that source through a continuous path. Circuits are designed to handle a certain maximum current flow. The maximum allowable current flow is designed higher than the normal current requirements of all the loads in the circuit. Wire size, connections, insulation, etc., are designed to prevent undesirable voltage drop, overheating of conductors, arcing of contacts, and other adverse effects. If the safe maximum current flow level is exceeded, damage to the circuit components will result; it is this condition that circuit protection devices are designed to prevent.

Protection devices are fuses, fusible links or circuit breakers designed to open or break the circuit quickly whenever an overload, such as a short circuit, occurs. By opening the circuit quickly, the circuit protection device prevents damage to the wiring, battery, and other circuit components. Fuses and fusible links are designed to carry a preset maximum amount of current and to melt when that maximum is exceeded, while circuit breakers merely break the connection and may be manually reset. The maximum amperage rating of each fuse is marked on the fuse body and all contain a see-through portion that shows the break in the fuse element when blown. Fusible link maximum amperage rating is indicated by gauge or thickness of the wire. Never replace a blown fuse or fusible link with one of a higher amperage rating.

── CAUTION ──
Resistance wires, like fusible links, are also spliced into conductors in some areas. Do not make the mistake of replacing a fusible link with a resistance wire. Resistance wires are longer than fusible links and are stamped "RESISTOR-DO NOT CUT OR SPLICE."

$$I = \frac{E}{R} \quad \text{or} \quad AMPERES = \frac{VOLTS}{OHMS}$$

$$R = \frac{E}{I} \quad \text{or} \quad OHMS = \frac{VOLTS}{AMPERES}$$

$$E = I \times R \quad \text{or} \quad VOLTS = AMPERES \times OHMS$$

Ohms Law is the basis for all electrical measurements. By simply plugging in two values, the third can be calculated using the illustrated formula.

8803942

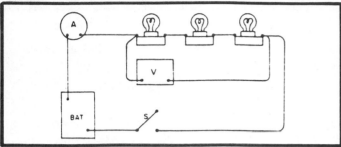

Example of a series circuit

Circuit breakers consist of two strips of metal which have different coefficients of expansion. As an overload or current flows through the bimetallic strip, the high-expansion metal will elongate due to heat and break the contact. With the circuit open, the bimetal strip cools and shrinks, drawing the strip down until contact is re-established and current flows once again. In actual operation, the contact is broken very quickly if the overload is continuous and the circuit will be repeatedly broken and remade until the source of the overload is corrected.

The self-resetting type of circuit breaker is the one most generally used in automotive electrical systems. On manually reset circuit breakers, a button will pop up on the circuit breaker case. This button must be pushed in to reset the circuit breaker and restore power to the circuit. Always repair the source of the overload before resetting a circuit breaker or replacing a fuse or fusible link. When searching for overloads, keep in mind that the circuit protection devices protect only against overloads between the protection device and ground.

There are two basic types of circuit; Series and Parallel. In a series circuit, all of the elements are connected in chain fashion with the same amount of current passing through each element or load. No matter where an ammeter is connected in a series circuit, it will always read the same. The most important fact to remember about a series circuit is that the sum of the voltages across each element equals the source voltage. The total resistance of a series circuit is equal to the sum of the individual resistances within each element of the circuit. Using ohms law, one can determine the voltage drop across each element in the circuit. If the total resistance and source voltage is known, the amount of current can be calculated. Once the amount of current (amperes) is known, values can be substituted in the Ohms law formula to calculate the voltage drop across each individual element in the series circuit. The individual voltage drops must add up to the same value as the source voltage.

A parallel circuit, unlike a series circuit, contains two or more branches, each branch a separate path independent of the others. The total current draw from the voltage source is the sum of all the currents drawn by each branch. Each branch of a parallel circuit can be analyzed separately. The individual branches can be either simple circuits, series circuits or combinations of series-parallel circuits. Ohms law applies to parallel

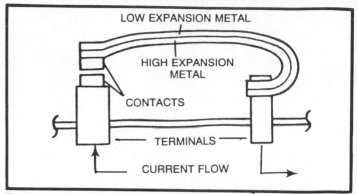

Typical circuit breaker construction

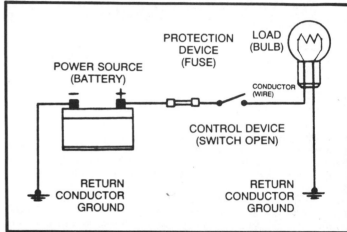

Typical circuit with all essential components

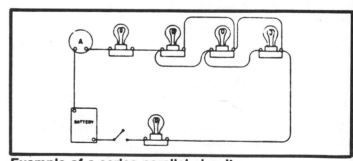

Example of a series-parallel circuit

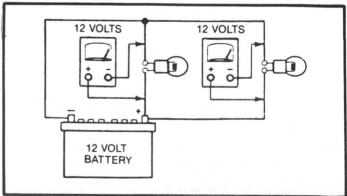

Voltage drop in a parallel circuit. Voltage drop across each lamp is 12 volts

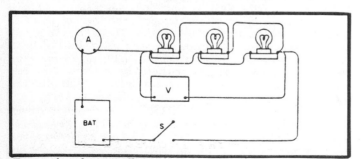

Example of a parallel circuit

circuits just as it applies to series circuits, by considering each branch independently of the others. The most important thing to remember is that the voltage across each branch is the same as the source voltage. The current in any branch is that voltage divided by the resistance of the branch. A practical method of determining the resistance of a parallel circuit is to divide the product of the two resistances by the sum of two resistances at a time. Amperes through a parallel circuit is the sum of the amperes through the separate branches. Voltage across a parallel circuit is the same as the voltage across each branch.

By measuring the voltage drops, you are in effect measuring the resistance of each element within the circuit. The greater the voltage drop, the greater the resistance. Voltage drop measurements are a common way of checking circuit resistances in automotive electrical systems. When part of a circuit develops excessive resistance (due to a bad connection) the element will show a higher than normal voltage drop. Normally, automotive wiring is selected to limit voltage drops to a few tenths of a volt. In parallel circuits, the total resistance is less than the sum of the individual resistances; because the current has two paths to take, the total resistance is lower.

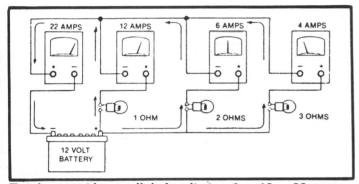

Total current in parallel circuit: 4 + 6 + 12 = 22 amps

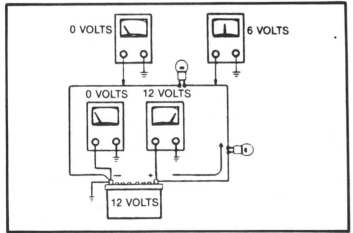

Voltage drop in a series circuit

Magnetism and Electromagnets

Electricity and magnetism are very closely associated because when electric current passes through a wire, a magnetic field is created around the wire. When a wire carrying electric current is wound into a coil, a magnetic field with North and South poles is created just like in a bar magnet. If an iron core is placed within the coil, the magnetic field becomes stronger because iron conducts magnetic lines much easier than air. This arrangement is called an electromagnet and is the basic princi-

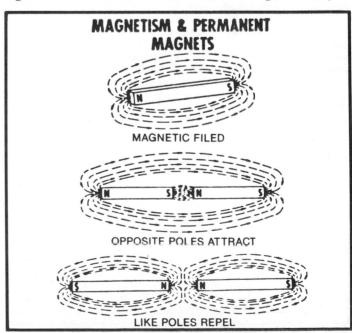

ELECTRO-MAGNETS

FORCE FIELD SURROUNDING A CURRENT CARRYING COIL
(WITHOUT IRON CORE)
ALL FORCE LINES ARE COMPLETE LOOPS

FORCE FIELD WITH SOFT IRON CORE
NOTE CONCENTRATION OF LINES IN IRON CORE

Magnetic field surrounding an electromagnet

ple behind the operation of such components as relays, buzzers and solenoids.

A relay is basically just a remote-controlled switch that uses a small amount of current to control the flow of a large amount of current. The simplest relay contains an electromagetic coil in series with a voltage source (battery) and a switch. A movable armature made of some magnetic material pivots at one end and is held a small distance away from the electromagnet by a spring or the spring steel of the armature itself. A contact point, made of a good conductor, is attached to the free end of the armature with another contact point a small distance away. When the relay is switched on (energized), the magnetic field created by the current flow attracts the armature, bending it until the contact points meet, closing a circuit and allowing current to flow in the second circuit through the relay to

MAGNETISM & PERMANENT MAGNETS

MAGNETIC FILED

OPPOSITE POLES ATTRACT

LIKE POLES REPEL

Magnetic field surrounding a bar magnet

the load the circuit operates. When the relay is switched off (de-energized), the armature springs back and opens the contact points, cutting off the current flow in the secondary, or controlled, circuit. Relays can be designed to be either open or closed when energized, depending on the type of circuit control a manufacturer requires.

A buzzer is similar to a relay, but its internal connections are different. When the switch is closed, the current flows through the normally closed contacts and energizes the coil. When the coil core becomes magnetized, it bends the armature down and breaks the circuit. As soon as the circuit is broken, the spring-loaded armature remakes the circuit and again energizes the coil. This cycle repeats rapidly to cause the buzzing sound.

A solenoid is constructed like a relay, except that its core is allowed to move, providing mechanical motion that can be used to actuate mechanical linkage to operate a door or trunk lock or control any other mechanical function. When the switch is closed, the coil is energized and the movable core is drawn into the coil. When the switch is opened, the coil is de-energized and spring pressure returns the core to its original position.

Basic Solid State

The term "solid state" refers to devices utilizing transistors, diodes and other components which are made from materials known as semiconductors. A semiconductor is a material that is neither a good insulator nor a good conductor; principally silicon and germanium. The semiconductor material is specially treated to give it certain qualities that enhance its function, therefore becoming either P-type (positive) or N-type (negative) material. Most semiconductors are constructed of silicon and can be designed to function either as an insulator or conductor.

Diodes

The simplest semiconductor function is that of the diode or rectifier (the two terms mean the same thing). A diode will pass current in one direction only, like a one-way valve, because it has low resistance in one direction and high resistance on the other. Whether the diode conducts or not depends on the polarity of the voltage applied to it. A diode has two electrodes, an anode and a cathode. When the anode receives positive (+) voltage and the cathode receives negative (-) voltage, current can flow easily through the diode. When the voltage is reversed, the diode becomes non-conducting and only allows a very slight amount of current to flow in the circuit. Because the semiconductor is not a perfect insulator, a small amount of reverse current leakage will occur, but the amount is usually too small to consider. The application of voltage to maintain the current flow described is called "forward bias."

A light-emitting diode (LED) is made of a particular type of crystal that glows when current is passed through it. LED's are used in display faces of many digital or electronic instrument clusters. LED's are usually arranged to display numbers (digital readout), but can be used to illuminate a variety of electronic graphic displays.

Like any other electrical device, diodes have certain ratings that must be observed and should not be exceeded. The forward current rating (or bias) indicates how much current can safely pass through the diode without causing damage or destroying it. Forward current rating is usually given in either amperes or milliamperes. The voltage drop across a diode remains constant regardless of the current flowing through it. Small diodes designed to carry low amounts of current need no special provision for dissipating the heat generated in any electrical device, but large current carrying diodes are usually mounted on heat sinks to keep the internal temperature from rising to the point where the silicon will melt and destroy the diode. When diodes are operated in a high ambient temperature environment, they must be de-rated to prevent failure.

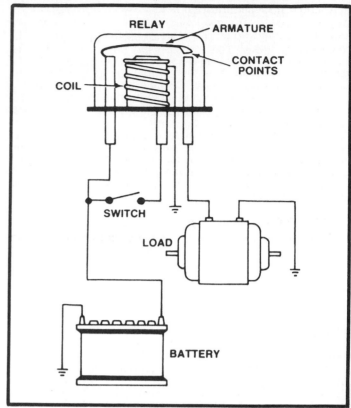

Typical relay circuit with basic components

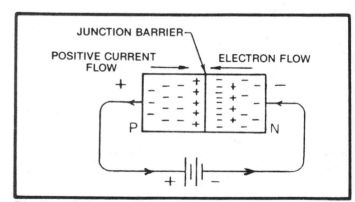

Diode with forward bias

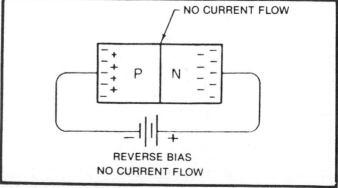

Diode with reverse bias

Another diode specification is its peak inverse voltage rating. This value is the maximum amount of voltage the diode can safely handle when operating in the blocking mode. This value can be anywhere from 50-1000 volts, depending on the diode, and if exceeded can damage the diode just as too much forward current will. Most semiconductor failures are caused by excessive voltage or internal heat.

One can test a diode with a small battery and a lamp with the same voltage rating. With this arrangement one can find a bad diode and determine the polarity of a good one. A diode can fail and cause either a short or open circuit, but in either case it fails to function as a diode. Testing is simply a matter of connecting the test bulb first in one direction and then the other and making sure that current flows in one direction only. If the diode is shorted, the test bulb will remain on no matter how the light is connected.

Transistors

The transistor is an electrical device used to control voltage within a circuit. A transistor can be considered a "controllable diode" in that, in addition to passing or blocking current, the transistor can control the amount of current passing through it. Simple transistors are composed of three pieces of semiconductor material, P and N type, joined together and enclosed in a container. If two sections of P material and one section of N material are used, it is known as a PNP transistor; if the reverse is true, then it is known as an NPN transistor. The two types cannot be interchanged.

Most modern transistors are made from silicon (earlier transistors were made from germanium) and contain three elements; the emitter, the collector and the base. In addition to passing or blocking current, the transistor can control the

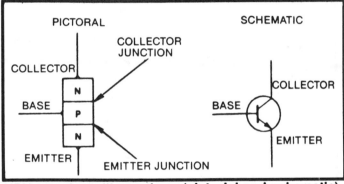

NPN transistor illustrations (pictorial and schematic)

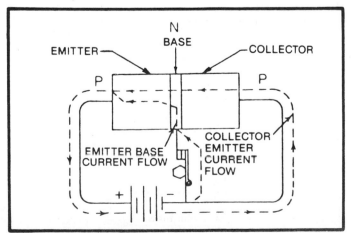

PNP transistor with base switch closed (base emitter and collector emitter current flow)

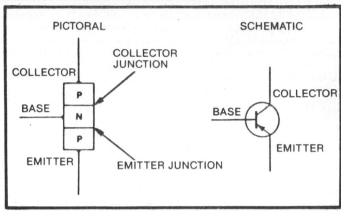

PNP transistor illustrations (pictorial and schematic)

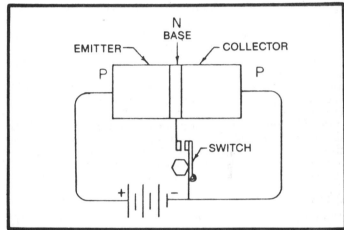

PNP transistor with base switch open (no current flow)

amount of current passing through it and because of this can function as an amplifier or a switch. The collector and emitter form the main current-carrying circuit of the transistor. The amount of current that flows through the collector-emitter junction is controlled by the amount of current in the base circuit. Only a small amount of base-emitter current is necessary to control a large amount of collector-emitter current (the amplifier effect). In automotive applications, however, the transistor is used primarily as a switch.

When no current flows in the base-emitter junction, the collector-emitter circuit has a high resistance, like to open contacts of a relay. Almost no current flows through the circuit and transistor is considered OFF. By bypassing a small amount of current into the base circuit, the resistance is low, allowing current to flow through the circuit and turning the transistor ON. This condition is known as "saturation" and is reached when the base current reaches the maximum value designed into the transistor that allows current to flow. Depending on various factors, the transistor can turn on and off (go from cutoff to saturation) in less than one millionth of a second.

Much of what was said about ratings for diodes applies to transistors, since they are constructed of the same materials. When transistors are required to handle relatively high currents, such as in voltage regulators or ignition systems, they are generally mounted on heat sinks in the same manner as diodes. They can be damaged or destroyed in the same manner if their voltage ratings are exceeded. A transistor can be checked for proper operation by measuring the resistance with an ohmmeter between the base-emitter terminals and then between the base-collector terminals. The forward resistance should be small, while the reverse resistance should be large. Compare the readings with those from a known good transistor. As a final check, measure the forward and reverse resistance between the collector and emitter terminals.

Integrated Circuits

The integrated circuit (IC) is an extremely sophisticated solid state device that consists of a silicone wafer (or chip) which has been doped, insulated and etched many times so that it contains an entire electrical circuit with transistors, diodes, conductors and capacitors miniaturized within each tiny chip. Integrated circuits are often referred to as "computers on a chip" and are largely responsible for the current boom in electronic control technology.

Microprocessors, Computers and Logic Systems

Mechanical or electromechanical control devices lack the precision necessary to meet the requirements of modern control standards, and the ability to respond to a variety of input conditions common to antilock brakes, climate control and electronic suspension operation. To meet these requirements, manufacturers have gone to solid state logic systems and microprocessors to control the basic functions of suspension, brake and temperature control, as well as other systems and accessories.

One of the more vital roles of microprocessor-based systems is their ability to perform logic functions and make decisions. Logic designers use a shorthand notation to indicate whether a voltage is present in a circuit (the number 1) or not present (the number 0), and their systems are designed to respond in different ways depending on the output signal (or the lack of it) from various control devices.

There are three basic logic functions or "gates" used to construct a microprocessor control system: the AND gate, the OR gate or the NOT gate. Stated simply, the AND gate works when voltage is present in two or more circuits which then energize a third (A and B energize C). The OR gate works when voltage is present at either circuit A or circuit B which then energizes circuit C. The NOT function is performed by a solid state device called an "inverter" which reverses the input from a circuit so that, if voltage is going in, no voltage comes out and vice versa. With these three basic building blocks, a logic designer can create complex systems easily. In actual use, a logic or decision making system may employ many logic gates and receive inputs from a number of sources (sensors), but for the most part, all utilize the basic logic gates discussed above.

Stripped to its bare essentials, a computerized decision-making system is made up of three subsystems:
  a. Input devices (sensors or switches)
  b. Logic circuits (computer control unit)
  c. Output devices (actuators or controls)

The input devices are usually nothing more than switches or sensors that provide a voltage signal to the control unit logic circuits that is read as a 1 or 0 (on or off) by the logic circuits. The output devices are anything from a warning light to solenoid-operated valves, motors, linkage, etc. In most cases, the

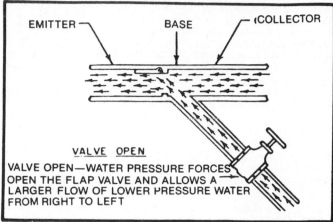

Hydraulic analogy to transistor function is shown with the base circuit energized

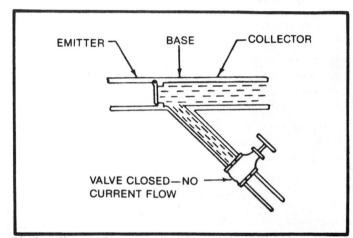

Hydraulic analogy to transistor function is shown with the base circuit shut off

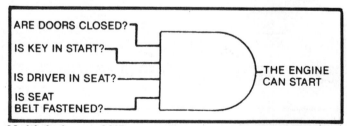

Multiple input AND operation in a typical automotive starting circuit

logic circuits themselves lack sufficient output power to operate these devices directly. Instead, they operate some intermediate device such as a relay or power transistor which in turn operates the appropriate device or control. Many problems diagnosed as computer failures are really the result of a malfunctioning intermediate device like a relay. This must be kept in mind whenever troubleshooting any microprocessor-based control system.

The logic systems discussed above are called "hardware" systems, because they consist only of the physical electronic components (gates, resistors, transistors, etc.). Hardware systems do not contain a program and are designed to perform specific or "dedicated" functions which cannot readily be changed. For many simple automotive control requirements, such dedicated logic systems are perfectly adequate. When more complex logic

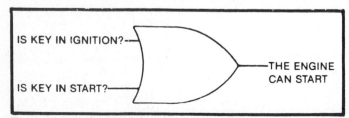

Typical two-input OR circuit operation

functions are required, or where it may be desirable to alter these functions (e.g. from one model car to another) a true computer system is used. A computer can be programmed through its software to perform many different functions and, if that program is stored on a separate integrated circuit chip called a ROM (Read Only Memory), it can be easily changed simply by plugging in a different ROM with the desired program. Most on-board automotive computers are designed with this capability. The on-board computer method of engine control offers the manufacturer a flexible method of responding to data from a variety of input devices and of controlling an equally large variety of output controls. The computer response can be changed quickly and easily by simply modifying its software program. The microprocessor is the heart of the microcomputer. It is the thinking part of the computer system through which all the data from the various sensors passes. Within the microprocessor, data is acted upon, compared, manipulated or stored for future use. A microprocessor is not necessarily a microcomputer, but the differences between the two are becoming very minor. Originally, a microprocessor was a major part of a microcomputer, but nowadays microprocessors are being called "single-chip microcomputers". They contain all the essential elements to make them behave as a computer, including the most important ingredient–the program.

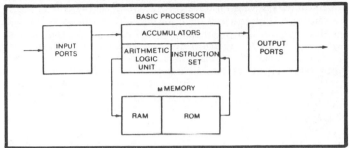

Schematic of typical microprocessor based on-board computer showing essential components

All computers require a program. In a general purpose computer, the program can be easily changed to allow different tasks to be performed. In a "dedicated" computer, such as most on-board automotive computers, the program isn't quite so easily altered. These automotive computers are designed to perform one or several specific tasks, such as maintaining the passenger compartment temperature at a specific, predetermined level. A program is what makes a computer smart; without a program a computer can do absolutely nothing. The term "software" refers to the program that makes the hardware do what you want it to do.

The software program is simply a listing in sequential order of the steps or commands necessary to make a computer perform the desired task. Before the computer can do anything at all, the program must be fed into it by one of several possible methods. A computer can never be "smarter" than the person programming it, but it is a lot faster. Although it cannot perform any calculation or operation that the programmer himself cannot perform, its processing time is measured in millionths of a second.

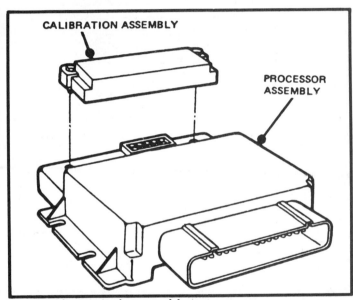

Electronic control assembly

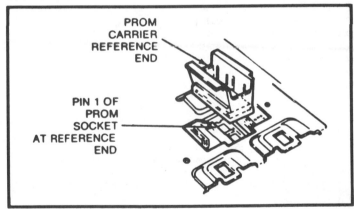

Installation of PROM unit

Because a computer is limited to performing only those operations (instructions) programmed into its memory, the program must be broken down into a large number of very simple steps. Two different programmers can come up with two different programs, since there is usually more than one way to perform any task or solve a problem. In any computer, however, there is only so much memory space available, so an overly long or inefficient program may not fit into the memory. In addition to performing arithmetic functions (such as with a trip computer), a computer can also store data, look up data in a table and perform the logic functions previously discussed. A Random Access Memory (RAM) allows the computer to store bits of data temporarily while waiting to be acted upon by the program. It may also be used to store output data that is to be sent to an output device. Whatever data is stored in a RAM is lost when power is removed from the system by turning off the ignition key, for example.

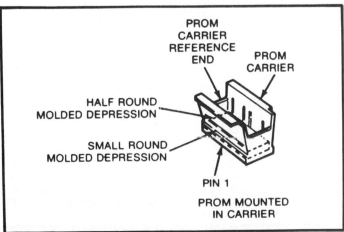

Typical PROM showing carrier refernce markings

Computers have another type of memory called a Read Only Memory (ROM) which is permanent. This memory is not lost when the power is removed from the system. Most programs for automotive computers are stored on a ROM memory chip. Data is usually in the form of a look-up table that saves computing time and program steps. For example, a computer designed to control the amount of distributor advance can have this information stored in a table. The information that determines distributor advance (engine rpm, manifold vacuum and temperature) is coded to produce the correct amount of distributor advance over a wide range of engine operating conditions. Instead of the computer computing the required advance, it simply looks it up in a pre-programmed table. However, not all electronic control functions can be handled in this manner; some must be computed. On an antilock brake system, for example, the computer must measure the rotation of each separate wheel and then calculate how much brake pressure to apply in order to prevent one wheel from locking up and causing a loss of control.

There are several ways of programming a ROM, but once programmed the ROM cannot be changed. If the ROM is made on the same chip that contains the microprocessor, the whole computer must be altered if a program change is needed. For this reason, a ROM is usually placed on a separate chip. Another type of memory is the Programmable Read Only Memory (PROM) that has the program "burned in" with the appropriate programming machine. Like the ROM, once a PROM has been programmed, it cannot be changed. The advantage of the PROM is that it can be produced in small quantities economi-

cally, since it is manufactured with a blank memory. Program changes for various vehicles can be made readily. There is still another type of memory called an EPROM (Erasable PROM) which can be erased and programmed many times. EPROM's are used only in research and development work, not on production vehicles.

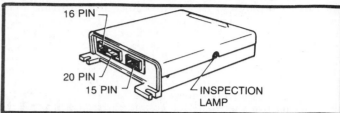

Typical automotive computer or electronic control unit (ECU). Except for pin connectors, all ECU assemblies look similar

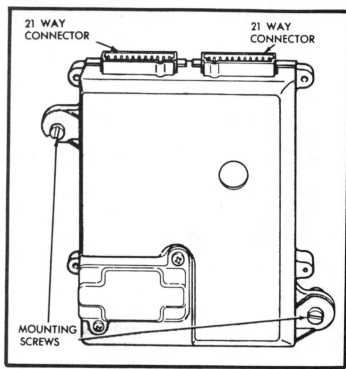

MFI system logic module with pin connectors

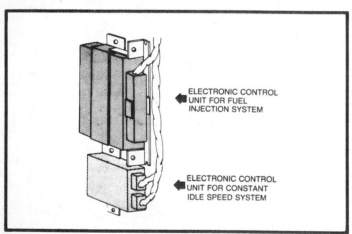

Typical control unit installations

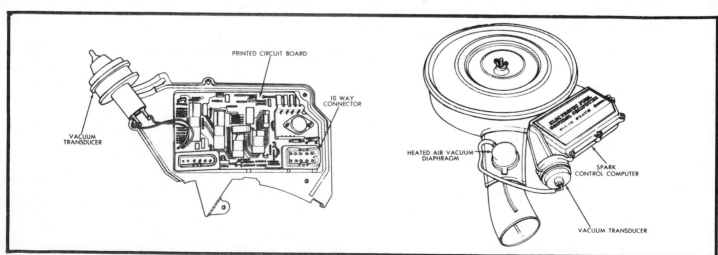

Typical combustion assembly showing air cleaner mounting

Troubleshooting and Diagnosis

INDEX

TROUBLESHOOTING AND DIAGNOSIS

Diagnostic Equipment and Special Tools

While we may think that with no moving parts, electronic components should never wear out, in the real world malfunctions do occur. The problem is that any computer-based system is extremely sensitive to electrical voltages and cannot tolerate careless or haphazard testing or service procedures. An inexperienced individual can literally do major damage looking for a minor problem by using the wrong kind of test equipment or connecting test leads or connectors with the ignition switch ON. Therefore, when selecting test equipment, make sure the manufacturers instructions state that the tester is compatible with whatever type of electronic control system is being serviced. Read all instructions carefully and double check all test points before installing probes or making any connections.

The following section outlines basic diagnosis techniques for dealing with computerized engine control systems. Along with a general explanation of the various types of test equipment available to aid in servicing modern electronic automotive systems, basic repair techniques for wiring harnesses and connectors is given. Read the basic information before attempting any repairs or testing on any computerized system, to provide the background of information necessary to avoid the most common and obvious mistakes that can cost both time and money. Likewise, the individual system sections for engine controls, fuel injection and feedback carburetors should be read from the beginning to the end before any repairs or diagnosis is attempted. Although the replacement and testing procedures are simple in themselves, the systems are not, and unless one has a thorough understanding of all components and their function within a particular fuel injection system (for example), the logical test sequence these systems demand cannot be followed. Minor malfunctions can make a big difference, so it is important to know how each component affects the operation of the overall electronic system to find the ultimate cause of a problem without replacing good components unnecessarily. It is not enough to use the correct test equipment; the test equipment must be used correctly.

Safety Precautions

CAUTION

Whenever working on or around any computer-based microprocessor control system, always observe these general precautions to prevent the possibility of personal injury or damage to electronic components:

• Never install or remove battery cables with the key ON or the engine running. Jumper cables should be connected with the key OFF to avoid power surges that can damage electronic control units. Engines equipped with computer controlled systems should avoid both giving and getting jump starts due to the possibility of serious damage to components from arcing in the engine compartment when connections are made with the ignition ON.

• Always remove the battery cables before charging the battery. Never use a high-output charger on an installed battery or attempt to use any type of "hot shot" (24 volt) starting aid.

• Exercise care when inserting test probes into connectors to insure good connections without damaging the connector or spreading the pins. Always probe connectors from the rear (wire) side, NOT the pin side, to avoid accidental shorting of terminals during test procedures.

• Never remove or attach wiring harness connectors with the ignition switch ON, especially to an electronic control unit.

• Do not drop any components during service procedures and

never apply 12 volts directly to any component (like a solenoid or relay) unless instructed specifically to do so. Some component electrical windings are designed to safely handle only 4 or 5 volts and can be destroyed in seconds if 12 volts are applied directly to the connector.

• Remove the electronic control unit if the vehicle is to be placed in an environment where temperatures exceed approximately 176°F (80°C), such as a paint spray booth or when arc- or gas-welding near the control unit location in the car.

Organized Troubleshooting

When diagnosing a specific problem, organized troubleshooting is a must. The complexity of a modern automobile demands that you approach any problem in a logical, organized manner. There are certain troubleshooting techniques that are standard:

1. Establish when the problem occurs. Does the problem appear only under certain conditions? Were there any noises, odors, or other unusual symptoms? Make notes on any symptoms found, including warning lights and trouble codes, if applicable.

2. Isolate the problem area. To do this, make some simple tests and observations; then eliminate the systems that are working properly. Check for obvious problems such as broken wires or split or disconnected vacuum hoses. Always check the obvious before assuming something complicated is the cause.

3. Test for problems systematically to determine the cause once the problem area is isolated. Are all the components functioning properly? Is there power going to electrical switches and motors? Is there vacuum at vacuum switches and/or actuators? Is there a mechanical problem such as bent linkage or loose mounting screws? Doing careful, systematic checks will often turn up most causes on the first inspection without wasting time checking components that have little or no relationship to the problem.

4. Test all repairs after the work is done to make sure that the problem is fixed. Some causes can be traced to more than one component, so a careful verification of repair work is important to pick up additional malfunctions that may cause a problem to reappear or a different problem to arise. A blown fuse, for example, is a simple problem that may require more than just replacing a fuse. If you don't look for a problem that caused a fuse to blow, a shorted wire may go undetected.

The diagnostic tree charts are designed to help solve problems by leading the user through closely defined conditions and tests so that only the most likely components, vacuum and electrical circuits are checked for proper operation when troubleshooting a particular malfunction. By using the trouble trees to eliminate those systems and components which normally will not cause the condition described, a problem can be isolated within one or more systems or circuits without wasting time on unnecessary testing. Experience has shown that most problems tend to be the result of a fairly simple and obvious cause, such as loose or corroded connectors or air leaks in the intake system. A careful inspection of components during testing is essential to quick and accurate troubleshooting. Frequent references to special test equipment will be found in the text and in the diagnosis charts. These devices or compatible equivalents are necessary to perform some of the more complicated test procedures listed, but many components can be functionally tested with the quick checks outlined in the "On-Car Service" procedures. Aftermarket testers are available from a variety of sources, as well as from the vehicle manufacturer, but care should be taken that any test equipment being used is designed to diagnose that particular system accurately without damaging the control unit (ECU) or components being tested.

NOTE: Pinpointing the exact cause of trouble in an electrical system can sometimes only be done using special test equipment. The following describes commonly used test equipment and explains how to put it to best use in diagnosis. In addition to the information covered below, the manufacturer's instructions booklet provided with the tester should be read and clearly understood before attempting any test procedures.

Jumper Wires

Jumper wires are simple, yet extremely valuable pieces of test equipment. Jumper wires are merely wires that are used to bypass sections of a circuit. The simplest type of jumper wire is merely a length of multistrand wire with an alligator clip at each end. Jumper wires are usually fabricated from lengths of standard automotive wire and whatever type of connector (alligator clip, spade connector or pin connector) that is required for the particular vehicle being tested. The well-equipped tool box will have several different styles of jumper wires in several different lengths. Some jumper wires are made with three or more terminals coming from a common splice for special-purpose testing. In cramped, hard-to-reach areas it is advisable to have insulated boots over the jumper wire terminals in order to prevent accidental grounding, sparks, and possible fire, especially when testing fuel system components.

Jumper wires are used primarily to locate open electrical circuits, on either the ground (−) side of the circuit or on the hot (+) side. If an electrical component fails to operate, connect the jumper wire between the component and a good ground. If the component operates only with the jumper installed, the ground circuit is open. If the ground circuit is good, but the component does not operate, the circuit between the power feed and component is open. You can sometimes connect the jumper wire directly from the battery to the hot terminal of the component, but first make sure the component uses 12 volts in operation. Some electrical components, such as fuel injectors, are designed to operate on about 4 volts and running 12 volts directly to the injector terminals can burn out the wiring. By inserting an in-line fuseholder between a set of test leads, a fused jumper wire can be used for bypassing open circuits. Use a 5 amp fuse to provide protection against voltage spikes. When in doubt, use a voltmeter to check the voltage input to the component and measure how much voltage is being applied normally. By moving the jumper wire successively back toward the power source, you can isolate the area of the circuit where the open is located. When the component stops functioning, or the power is cut off, the open is in the segment of wire between the jumper and the point previously tested.

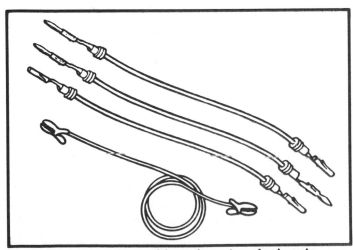

Typical jumper wires with various terminal ends

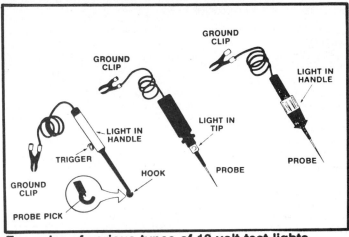

Examples of various types of 12 volt test lights

— CAUTION —

Never use jumpers made from wire that is of lighter gauge than used in the circuit under test. If the jumper wire is of too small gauge, it may overheat and possibly melt. Never use jumpers to bypass high-resistance loads (such as motors) in a circuit. Bypassing resistances, in effect, creates a short circuit which may, in turn, cause damage and fire. Never use a jumper for anything other than temporary bypassing of components in a circuit.

12 Volt Test Light

The 12 volt test light is used to check circuits and components while electrical current is flowing through them. It is used for voltage and ground tests. Twelve volt test lights come in different styles but all have three main parts; a ground clip, a probe, and a light. The most commonly used 12 volt test lights have pick-type probes. To use a 12 volt test light, connect the ground clip to a good ground and probe wherever necessary with the pick. The pick should be sharp so that it can penetrate wire insulation to make contact with the wire, without making a large hole in the insulation. The wrap-around light is handy in hard to reach areas or where it is difficult to support a wire to push a probe pick into it. To use the wrap around light, hook the wire to be probed with the hook and pull the trigger. A small pick will be forced through the wire insulation into the wire core.

— CAUTION —

Do not use a test light to probe electronic ignition spark plug or coil wires. Never use a pick-type test light to probe wiring on computer controlled systems unless specifically instructed to do so. Any wire insulation that is pierced by the test light probe should be taped and sealed with silicone after testing to weatherproof it.

Like the jumper wire, the 12 volt test light is used to isolate opens in circuits. But, whereas the jumper wire is used to bypass the open to operate the load, the 12 volt test light is used to locate the presence of voltage in a circuit. If the test light glows, you know that there is power up to that point; if the 12 volt test light does not glow when its probe is inserted into the wire or connector, you know that there is an open circuit (no power). Move the test light in successive steps back toward the power source until the light in the handle does glow. When it does glow, the open is between the probe and point previously probed.

NOTE: The test light does not detect that 12 volts (or any particular amount of voltage) is present; it only detects that some voltage is present. It is advisable before using the test light to touch its terminals across the battery posts to make sure the light is operating properly.

Self-Powered Test Light

The self-powered test light usually contains a 1.5 volt penlight battery. One type of self-powered test light is similar in design to the 12 volt test light. This type has both the battery and the light in the handle and pick-type probe tip. The second type has the light toward the open tip, so that the light illuminates the contact point. The self-powered test light is dual-purpose piece of test equipment. It can be used to test for either open or short circuits when power is isolated from the circuit (continuity test). A powered test light should not be used on any computer controlled system or component unless specifically instructed to do so. Many engine sensors can be destroyed by even this small amount of voltage applied directly to the terminals.

Open Circuit Testing

To use the self-powered test light to check for open circuits, first isolate the circuit from the vehicle's 12 volt power source by disconnecting the battery or wiring harness connector. Connect the test light ground clip to a good ground and probe sections of the circuit sequentially with the test light. (start from either end of the circuit). If the light is out, the open is between the probe and the circuit ground. If the light is on, the open is between the probe and end of the circuit toward the power source.

Short Circuit Testing

By isolating the circuit both from power and from ground, and using a self-powered test light, you can check for shorts to ground in the circuit. Isolate the circuit from power and ground. Connect the test light ground clip to a good ground and probe any easy-to-reach test point in the circuit. If the light comes on, there is a short somewhere in the circuit. To isolate the short, probe a test point at either end of the isolated circuit (the light should be on). Leave the test light probe connected and open connectors, switches, remove parts, etc., sequentially, until the light goes out. When the light goes out, the short is between the last circuit component opened and the previous circuit opened.

NOTE: The 1.5 volt battery in the test light does not provide much current. A weak battery may not provide enough power to illuminate the test light even when a complete circuit is made (especially if there are high resistances in the circuit). Always make sure that the test battery is strong. To check the battery, briefly touch the ground clip to the probe; if the light glows brightly the battery is strong enough for testing. Never use a self-powered test light to perform checks for opens or shorts when power is applied to the electrical system under test. The 12-volt vehicle power will quickly burn out the 1.5 volt light bulb in the test light.

Voltmeter

A voltmeter is used to measure voltage at any point in a circuit, or to measure the voltage drop across any part of a circuit. It can also be used to check continuity in a wire or circuit by indicating current flow from one end to the other. Voltmeters usually have various scales on the meter dial and a selector switch to allow the selection of different voltages. The voltmeter has a positive and a negative lead. To avoid damage to the meter, always connect the negative lead to the negative (−) side of circuit (to ground or nearest the ground side of the circuit) and connect the positive lead to the positive (+) side of the circuit (to the power source or the nearest power source). Note that the negative voltmeter lead will always be black and that the positive voltmeter will always be some color other than black (usually red). Depending on how the voltmeter is connected into the circuit, it has several uses.

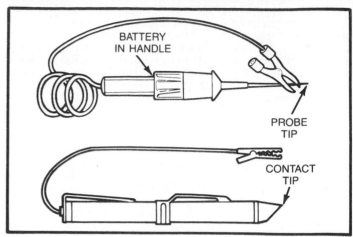

Two types of self-powered test lights

A voltmeter can be connected either in parallel or in series with a circuit and it has a very high resistance to current flow. When connected in parallel, only a small amount of current will flow through the voltmeter current path; the rest will flow through the normal circuit current path and the circuit will work normally. When the voltmeter is connected in series with a circuit, only a small amount of current can flow through the circuit. The circuit will not work properly, but the voltmeter reading will show if the circuit is complete or not.

Available Voltage Measurement

Set the voltmeter selector switch to the 20V position and connect the meter negative lead to the negative post of the battery. Connect the positive meter lead to the positive post of the battery and turn the ignition switch ON to provide a load. Read the voltage on the meter or digital display. A well-charged battery should register over 12 volts. If the meter reads below 11.5 volts, the battery power may be insufficient to operate the electrical system properly. This test determines voltage available from the battery and should be the first step in any electrical trouble diagnosis procedure. Many electrical problems, especially on computer controlled systems, can be caused by a low state of charge in the battery. Excessive corrosion at the battery cable terminals can cause a poor contact that will prevent proper charging and full battery current flow.

Normal battery voltage is 12 volts when fully charged. When the battery is supplying current to one or more circuits it is said to be "under load". When everything is off the electrical system is under a "no-load" condition. A fully charged battery

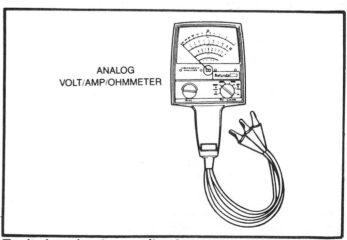

Typical analog-type voltmeter

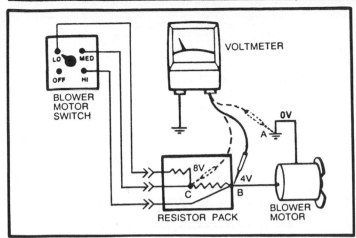

Measuring available voltage in a blower circuit

may show about 12.5 volts at no load; will drop to 12 volts under medium load; and will drop even lower under heavy load. If the battery is partially discharged the voltage decrease under heavy load may be excessive, even though the battery shows 12 volts or more at no load. When allowed to discharge further, the battery's available voltage under load will decrease more severely. For this reason, it is important that the battery be fully charged during all testing procedures to avoid errors in diagnosis and incorrect test results.

VOLTAGE DROP

When current flows through a resistance, the voltage beyond the resistance is reduced (the larger the current, the greater the reduction in voltage). When no current is flowing, there is no voltage drop because there is no current flow. All points in the circuit which are connected to the power source are at the same voltage as the power source. The total voltage drop always equals the total source voltage. In a long circuit with many connectors, a series of small, unwanted voltage drops due to corrosion at the connectors can add up to a total loss of voltage which impairs the operation of the normal loads in the circuit.

Indirect Computation of Voltage Drops

1. Set the voltmeter selector switch to the 20 volt position.
2. Connect the meter negative lead to a good ground.
3. Probe all resistances in the circuit with the positive meter lead.
4. Operate the circuit in all modes and observe the voltage readings.

Direct Measurement of Voltage Drops

1. Set the voltmeter switch to the 20 volt position.
2. Connect the voltmeter negative lead to the ground side of the resistance load to be measured.
3. Connect the positive lead to the positive side of the resistance or load to be measured.
4. Read the voltage drop directly on the 20 volt scale.
Too high a voltage indicates too high a resistance. If, for example, a blower motor runs too slowly, you can determine if there is too high a resistance in the resistor pack. By taking voltage drop readings in all parts of the circuit, you can isolate the problem. Too low a voltage drop indicates too low a resistance. If, for example, a blower motor runs too fast in the MED and/or LOW position, the problem can be isolated in the resistor pack by taking voltage drop readings in all parts of the circuit to locate a possibly shorted resistor. The maximum allowable voltage drop under load is critical, especially if there is

more than one high resistance problem in a circuit because all voltage drops are cumulative. A small drop is normal due to the resistance of the conductors.

High Resistance Testing

1. Set the voltmeter selector switch to the 4 volt position.
2. Connect the voltmeter positive lead to the positive post of the battery.
3. Turn on the headlights and heater blower to provide a load.
4. Probe various points in the circuit with the negative voltmeter lead.
5. Read the voltage drop on the 4 volt scale. Some average maximum allowable voltage drops are:
FUSE PANEL—7 volts
IGNITION SWITCH—5volts
HEADLIGHT SWITCH—7 volts
IGNITION COIL (+)—5 volts
ANY OTHER LOAD—1.3 volts

NOTE: Voltage drops are all measured while a load is operating; without current flow, there will be no voltage drop.

Ohmmeter

The ohmmeter is designed to read resistance (ohms) in a circuit or component. Although there are several different styles of ohmmeters, all will usually have a selector switch which permits the measurement of different ranges of resistance (usually the selector switch allows the multiplication of the meter reading by 10, 100, 1000, and 10,000). A calibration knob al-

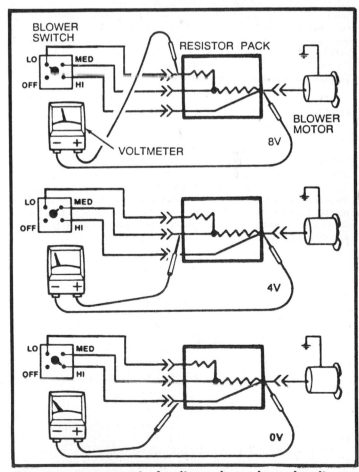

Direct measurement of voltage drops in a circuit

lows the meter to be set at zero for accurate measurement. Since all ohmmeters are powered by an internal battery (usually 9 volts), the ohmmeter can be used as a self-powered test light. When the ohmmeter is connected, current from the ohmmeter flows through the circuit or component being tested. Since the ohmmeter's internal resistance and voltage are known values, the amount of current flow through the meter depends on the resistance of the circuit or component being tested.

The ohmmeter can be used to perform continuity test for opens or shorts (either by observation of the meter needle or as a self-powered test light), and to read actual resistance in a circuit. It should be noted that the ohmmeter is used to check the resistance of a component or wire while there is no voltage applied to the circuit. Current flow from an outside voltage source (such as the vehicle battery) can damage the ohmmeter, so the circuit or component should be isolated from the vehicle electrical system before any testing is done. Since the ohmmeter uses its own voltage source, either lead can be connected to any test point.

NOTE: When checking diodes or other solid state components, the ohmmeter leads can only be connected one way in order to measure current flow in a single direction. Make sure the positive (+) and negative (-) terminal connections are as described in the test procedures to verify the one-way diode operation.

In using the meter for making continuity checks, do not be concerned with the actual resistance readings. Zero resistance, or any resistance readings, indicate continuity in the circuit. Infinite resistance indicates an open in the circuit. A high resistance reading where there should be none indicates a problem in the circuit. Checks for short circuits are made in the same manner as checks for open circuits except that the circuit must be isolated from both power and normal ground. Infinite resistance indicates no continuity to ground, while zero resistance indicates a dead short to ground.

Resistance Measurement

The batteries in an ohmmeter will weaken with age and temperature, so the ohmmeter must be calibrated or "zeroed" before taking measurements. To zero the meter, place the selector switch in its lowest range and touch the two ohmmeter leads together. Turn the calibration knob until the meter needle is exactly on zero.

NOTE: All analog (needle) type ohmmeters must be zeroed before use, but some digital ohmmeter models are automatically calibrated when the switch is turned on. Self-calibrating digital ohmmeters do not have an adjusting knob, but it's a good idea to check for a zero readout before use by touching the leads together. All computer controlled systems require the use of a digital ohmmeter with at least 10 megohms impedance for testing. Before any test procedures are attempted, make sure the ohmmeter used is compatible with the electrical system, or damage to the on-board computer could result.

To measure resistance, first isolate the circuit from the vehicle power source by disconnecting the battery cables or the harness connector. Make sure the key is OFF when disconnecting any components or the battery. Where necessary, also isolate at least one side of the circuit to be checked to avoid reading parallel resistances. Parallel circuit resistances will always give a lower reading than the actual resistance of either of the branches. When measuring the resistance of parallel circuits, the total resistance will always be lower than the smallest resistance in the circuit. Connect the meter leads to both sides of the circuit (wire or component) and read the actual measured ohms on the meter scale. Make sure the selector switch is set to

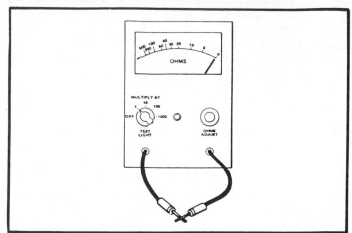

Analog ohmmeters must be calibrated before use by touching the probes together and adjusting the knob

the proper ohm scale for the circuit being tested to avoid misreading the ohmmeter test value.

CAUTION

Never use an ohmmeter with power applied to the circuit. Like the self-powered test light, the ohmmeter is designed to operate on its own power supply. The normal 12 volt automotive electrical system current could damage the meter.

Ammeters

An ammeter measures the amount of current flowing through a circuit in units called amperes or amps. Amperes are units of electron flow which indicate how fast the electrons are flowing through the circuit. Since Ohm's Law dictates that current flow in a circuit is equal to the circuit voltage divided by the total circuit resistance, increasing voltage also increases the current level (amps). Likewise, any decrease in resistance will increase the amount of amps in a circuit. At normal operating voltage, most circuits have a characteristic amount of amperes, called "current draw" which can be measured using an ammeter. By referring to a specified current draw rating, measuring the amperes, and comparing the two values, one can determine what is happening within the circuit to aid in diagnosis. An open circuit, for example, will not allow any current to flow so the ammeter reading will be zero. More current flows through a heavily loaded circuit or when the charging system is operating.

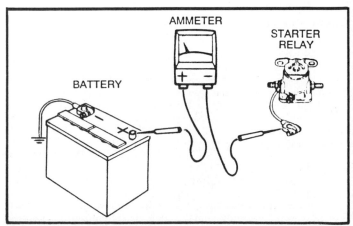

Battery current drain test

An ammeter is always connected in series with the circuit being tested. All of the current that normally flows through the circuit must also flow through the ammeter; if there is any other path for the current to follow, the ammeter reading will not be accurate. The ammeter itself has very little resistance to current flow and therefore will not affect the circuit, but it will measure current draw only when the circuit is closed and electricity is flowing. Excessive current draw can blow fuses and drain the battery, while a reduced current draw can cause motors to run slowly, lights to dim and other components not to operate properly. The ammeter can help diagnose these conditions by locating the cause of the high or low reading.

Multimeters

Different combinations of test meters can be built into a single unit designed for specific tests. Some of the more common combination test devices are known as Volt-Amp testers, Tach-Dwell meters, or Digital Multimeters. The Volt-Amp tester is used for charging system, starting system or battery tests and consists of a voltmeter, an ammeter and a variable resistance carbon pile. The voltmeter will usually have at least two ranges for use with 6, 12 and 24 volt systems. The ammeter also has more than one range for testing various levels of battery loads and starter current draw and the carbon pile can be adjusted to offer different amounts of resistance. The Volt-Amp tester has heavy leads to carry large amounts of current and many later models have an inductive ammeter pickup that clamps around the wire to simplify test connections. On some models, the ammeter also has a zero-center scale to allow test-

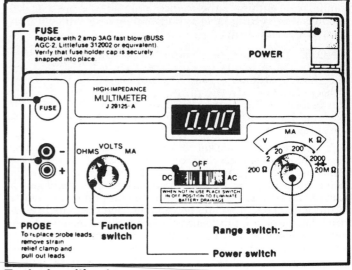

Typical multimeter

ing of charging and starting systems without switching leads or polarity. A digital multimeter is a voltmeter, ammeter and ohmmeter combined in an instrument which gives a digital readout. These are often used when testing solid state circuits because of their high input impedence (usually 10 megohms or more).

UF9

The tach-dwell meter combines a tachometer and a dwell (cam angle) meter and is a specialized kind of voltmeter. The tachometer scale is marked to show engine speed in rpm and the dwell scale is marked to show degrees of distributor shaft rotation. In most electronic ignition systems, dwell is determined by the control unit, but the dwell meter can also be used to check the duty cycle (operation) of some electronic engine control systems. Some tach-dwell meters are powered by an internal battery, while others take their power from the car battery in use. The battery powered testers usually require calibration much like an ohmmeter before testing.

Special Test Equipment

A variety of diagnostic tools are available to help troubleshoot and repair computerized engine control systems. The most sophisticated of these devices are the console-type engine analyzers that usually occupy a garage service bay, but there are several types of aftermarket electronic testers available that will allow quick circuit tests of the engine control system by plugging directly into a special connector located in the engine compartment or under the dashboard. Several tool and equipment manufacturers offer simple, hand-held testers that measure various circuit voltage levels on command to check all system components for proper operation. Although these testers usually cost about $300–500, consider that the average computer control unit (or ECM) can cost just as much and the money saved by not replacing perfectly good sensors or components in an attempt to correct a problem could justify the purchase price of a special diagnostic tester the first time it's used.

These computerized testers can allow quick and easy test measurements while the engine is operating or while the car is being driven. In addition, the on-board computer memory can be read to access any stored trouble codes; in effect allowing the computer to tell you where it hurts and aid trouble diagnosis by pinpointing exactly which circuit or component is malfunctioning. In the same manner, repairs can be tested to make sure the problem has been corrected. The biggest advantage these special testers have is their relatively easy hookups that

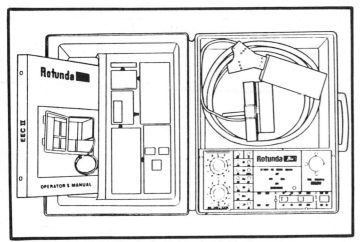

Typical electronic engine control tester

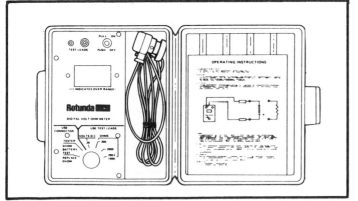

Digital volt-ohmmeter

minimize or eliminate the chances of making the wrong connections and getting false voltage readings or damaging the computer accidentally.

NOTE: It should be remembered that these testers check voltage levels in circuits; they don't detect mechanical problems or failed components if the circuit voltage falls within the preprogrammed limits stored in the tester PROM unit. Also, most of the hand-held testers are designed to work only on one or two systems made by a specific manufacturer.

A variety of aftermarket testers are available to help diagnose different computerized control systems. Owatonna Tool Company (OTC), for example, markets a device called the OTC Monitor which plugs directly into the assembly line diagnostic link (ALDL). The OTC tester makes diagnosis a simple matter of pressing the correct buttons and, by changing the internal PROM or inserting a different diagnosis cartridge, it will work on any model from full size to subcompact, over a wide range of years. An adapter is supplied with the tester to allow connection to all types of ALDL links, regardless of the number of pin terminals used. By inserting an updated PROM into the OTC tester, it can be easily updated to diagnose any new modifications of computerized control systems.

Hand-held aftermarket tester used to diagnosis electronic engine control systems

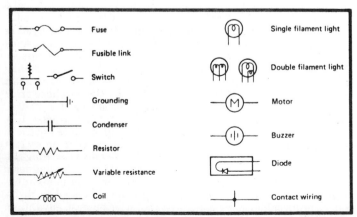

Typical adapter wiring harness for connecting tester to diagnostic terminal

Wiring Diagrams

The average automobile contains about ½ mile of wiring, with hundreds of individual connections. To protect the many wires from damage and to keep them from becoming a confusing tangle, they are organized into bundles, enclosed in plastic or taped together and called wire harnesses. Different wiring harnesses serve different parts of the vehicle. Individual wires are color-coded to help trace them through a harness where sections are hidden from view.

A loose or corroded connection or a replacement wire that is too small for the circuit will add extra resistance and an additional voltage drop to the circuit. A ten percent voltage drop can result in slow or erratic motor operation, for example, even though the circuit is complete. Automotive wiring or circuit conductors can be in any one of three forms:

1. Single strand wire
2. Multistrand wire

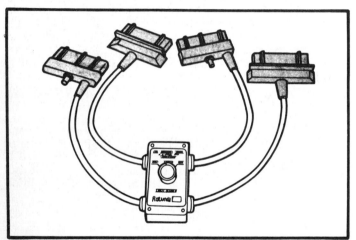

Typical electrical symbols found on wiring diagrams

Symbol	Name
	Fuse
	Fusible link
	Switch
	Grounding
	Condenser
	Resistor
	Variable resistance
	Coil
	Single filament light
	Double filament light
	Motor
	Buzzer
	Diode
	Contact wiring

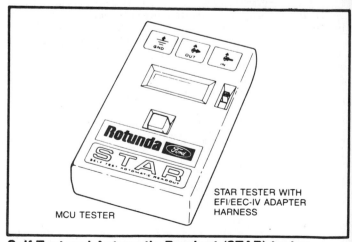

MCU TESTER

STAR TESTER WITH EFI/EEC-IV ADAPTER HARNESS

Self-Test and Automatic Readout (STAR) tester

3. Printed circuitry

Single strand wire has a solid metal core and is usually used inside such components as alternators, motors, relays and other devices. Multistrand wire has a core made of many small strands of wire twisted together into a single conductor. Most of the wiring in an automotive electrical system is made up of multistrand wire, either as a single conductor or grouped together in a harness. All wiring is color-coded on the insulator, either as a solid color or as a colored wire with an identification stripe. A printed circuit is a thin film of copper or other conductor that is printed on an insulator backing. Occasionally, a printed circuit is sandwiched between two sheets of plastic for more protection and flexibility. A complete printed circuit, consisting of conductors, insulating material and connectors for lamps or other components is called a printed circuit board. Printed circuitry is used in place of individual wires or harnesses in places where space is limited, such as behind instrument panels.

Wire Gauge

Since computer-controlled automotive electrical systems are very sensitive to changes in resistance, the selection of properly sized wires is critical when systems are repaired. The wire gauge number is an expression of the cross section area of the conductor. The most common system for expressing wire size is the American Wire Gauge (AWG) system.

Wire cross section area is measured in circular mils. A mil is one-thousandth of an inch (0.001); a circular mil is the area of a circle one mil in diameter. For example, a conductor $\frac{1}{4}$ inch in diameter is 0.250 in. or 250 mils. The circular mil cross section area of the wire is 250 squared or 62,500 circular mils. Imported car models usually use metric wire gauge designations, which is simply the cross section area of the conductor in square millimeters (mm^2).

Gauge numbers are assigned to conductors of various cross section areas. As gauge number increases, area decreases and the conductor becomes smaller. A 5 gauge conductor is smaller than a 1 gauge conductor and a 10 gauge is smaller than a 5 gauge. As the cross section area of a conductor decreases, resistance increases and so does the gauge number. A conductor with a higher gauge number will carry less current than a conductor with a lower gauge number.

NOTE: Gauge wire size refers to the size of the conductor, not the size of the complete wire. It is possible to have two wires of the same gauge with different diameters because one may have thicker insulation than the other.

12 volt automotive electrical systems generally use 10, 12, 14, 16 and 18 gauge wire. Main power distribution circuits and larger accessories usually use 10 and 12 gauge wire. Battery cables are usually 4 or 6 gauge, although 1 and 2 gauge wires are occasionally used. Wire length must also be considered when making repairs to a circuit. As conductor length increases, so does resistance. An 18 gauge wire, for example, can carry a 10 amp load for 10 feet without excessive voltage drop; however if a 15 foot wire is required for the same 10 amp load, a 16 gauge wire must be used.

An electrical schematic shows the electrical current paths when a circuit is operating properly. It is essential to understand how a circuit works before trying to figure out why it doesn't. Schematics break the entire electrical system down into individual circuits and show only one particular circuit. In a schematic, no attempt is made to represent wiring and components as they physically appear on the vehicle; switches and other components are shown as simply as possible. Face views of harness connectors show the cavity or terminal locations in all multi-pin connectors to help locate test points. The component locator in Chapter One will help in determining the exact location of various components in a particular model of vehicle.

If you need to backprobe a connector while it is on the component, the order of the terminals must be mentally reversed. The wire color code can help in this situation, as well as a keyway, lock tab or other reference mark.

Wiring Repairs

Soldering is a quick, efficient method of joining metals permanently. Everyone who has to make wiring repairs should know how to solder. Electrical connections that are soldered are far less likely to come apart and will conduct electricity much better than connections that are only "pig-tailed" together. The most popular (and preferred) method of soldering is with an electrical soldering gun. Soldering irons are available in many sizes and wattage ratings. Irons with higher wattage ratings deliver higher temperatures and recover lost heat faster. A small soldering iron rated for no more than 50 watts is recommended, especially on electrical systems where excess heat can damage the components being soldered.

There are three ingredients necessary for successful soldering; proper flux, good solder and sufficient heat. A soldering flux is necessary to clean the metal of tarnish, prepare it for soldering and to enable the solder to spread into tiny crevices. When soldering, always use a resin flux or resin core solder which is non-corrosive and will not attract moisture once the job is finished. Other types of flux (acid core) will leave a residue tht will attract moisture and cause the wires to corrode. Tin is a unique metal with a low melting point. In a molten state, it dissolves and alloys easily with many metals. Solder is made by mixing tin with lead. The most common proportions are 40/60, 50/50 and 60/40, with the percentage of tin listed first. Low priced solders usually contain less tin, making them very difficult for a beginner to use because more heat is required to melt the solder. A common solder is 40/60 which is well suited for general use, but 60/40 melts easier, has more tin for a better joint and is preferred for electrical work.

Soldering Techniques

Successful soldering requires that the metals to be joined be heated to a temperature that will melt the solder (usually 360–

COMMON SYMBOLS FOR AUTOMOTIVE COMPONENTS USED IN SCHEMATIC DIAGRAMS

Automotive service manuals use schematic diagrams to show how electrical and other types of components work, and how such components are connected to make circuits. Components that are shown whole are represented in full lines in a rectangular shape, and are identified by name; where only a part of a component is shown in a schematic diagram, the rectangular shape is outlined with a dashed line.

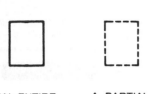

AN ENTIRE COMPONENT   A PARTIAL COMPONENT

COMPONENT CASE IS SHOWN DIRECTLY ATTACHED (GROUNDED) TO METAL PART OF CAR.

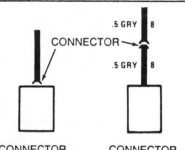

CONNECTOR

CONNECTOR ATTACHED TO COMPONENT   CONNECTOR ATTACHED TO LEAD WIRE

CIRCUIT BREAKER

PARK BRAKE SWITCH

SHOWN CLOSED WITH PARKING BRAKE ON

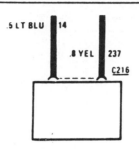

.5 LT BLU 14
.8 YEL 237
C216

TWO TERMINALS IN THE SAME CONNECTOR. DASHED LINE SHOWS A PHYSICAL CONNECTION BETWEEN PARTS.

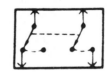

SWITCH CONTACTS THAT MOVE TOGETHER. DASHED LINE SHOWS A MECHANICAL CONNECTION BETWEEN SWITCH CONTACTS.

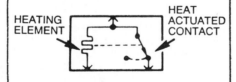

HEATING ELEMENT   HEAT ACTUATED CONTACT

HEAT-ACTUATED SWITCH

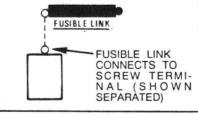

FUSIBLE LINK

FUSIBLE LINK CONNECTS TO SCREW TERMINAL (SHOWN SEPARATED)

"BRAKE" INDICATOR (RED)

LIGHTED INDICATOR

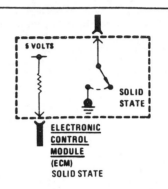

5 VOLTS   SOLID STATE

ELECTRONIC CONTROL MODULE (ECM) SOLID STATE

'SOLID STATE' IDENTIFIES MODULE AS ELECTRONIC. SIMPLIFIED COMPONENTS WITHIN THE MODULE SHOW HOW EACH CIRCUIT IS COMPLETED. (DO NOT MEASURE RESISTANCE OF CIRCUITS INSIDE SOLID STATE MODULES.)

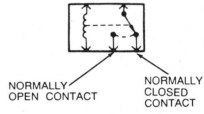

NORMALLY OPEN CONTACT   NORMALLY CLOSED CONTACT

RELAY SHOWN WITH NO CURRENT FLOWING THROUGH COIL. WHEN CURRENT FLOWS THROUGH COIL, CONTACT MOVES FROM NORMALLY OPEN POSITION.

5-CAVITY CONNECTOR WITH ALL CAVITIES IN USE

5-CAVITY CONNECTOR WITH ONLY 4 CAVITIES IN USE

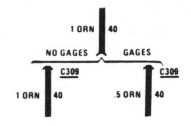

WIRE IS GROUNDED, AND GROUND IS NUMBERED FOR REFERENCE ON COMPONENT LOCATION TABLE.

FUSIBLE LINK SHOWS WIRE SIZE AND INSULATION COLOR.

WIRE CHOICES FOR OPTIONS OR DIFFERENT MODELS ARE SHOWN AND LABLED.

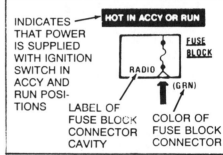

WIRE IS INDIRECTLY CONNECTED TO GROUND. (WIRE MAY HAVE ONE OR MORE SPLICES BEFORE IT IS GROUNDED.)

CURRENT PATH IS CONTINUED AS LABLED. THE ARROW SHOWS THE DIRECTION OF CURRENT FLOW, AND IS REPEATED WHERE CURRENT PATH CONTINUES.

INDICATES THAT POWER IS SUPPLIED WITH IGNITION SWITCH IN ACCY AND RUN POSITIONS

LABEL OF FUSE BLOCK CONNECTOR CAVITY

COLOR OF FUSE BLOCK CONNECTOR

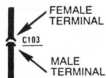

FEMALE TERMINAL

MALE TERMINAL

CONNECTOR REFERENCE NO. IS LISTED IN COMPONENT LOCATION TABLE, WHICH ALSO SHOWS TOTAL NO. OF TERMINALS POSSIBLE: C103 (6 CAVITIES).

A WIRE IS SHOWN WHICH CONNECTS TO ANOTHER CIRCUIT. THE WIRE IS SHOWN AGAIN ON THAT CIRCUIT.

DIODE

CURRENT CAN FLOW ONLY IN THE DIRECTION OF THE ARROW

INSULATION COLOR IS SHOWN AND LABLED

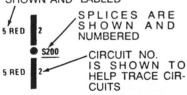

SPLICES ARE SHOWN AND NUMBERED

CIRCUIT NO. IS SHOWN TO HELP TRACE CIRCUITS

CIRCUITRY IDENTIFICATION

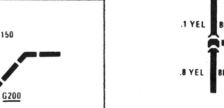

THE DASHED LINE INDICATES THAT THE CIRCUITRY IS NOT SHOWN IN COMPLETE DETAIL BUT IS COMPLETE ON THE INDICATED PAGE.

3 WIRES ARE SHOWN CONNECTED TOGETHER WITH A PIGGYBACK CONNECTOR

A WAVY LINE MEANS WIRE IS TO BE CONTINUED

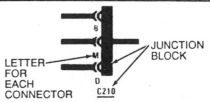

LETTER FOR EACH CONNECTOR

JUNCTION BLOCK

3 CONNECTORS ARE SHOWN CONNECTED TOGETHER AT A JUNCTION BLOCK. FOURTH WIRE IS SOLDERED TO COMMON CONNECTION ON BLOCK.

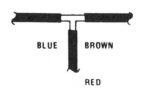

WIRE INSULATION IS ONE COLOR, WITH ANOTHER COLOR STRIPE (EXAMPLE: RED COLOR, WITH YELLOW STRIPE).

HOSE COLORS ARE SHOWN AT A VACUUM JUNCTION.

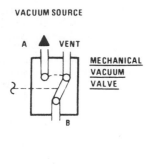

VACUUM SOURCE

MECHANICAL
VACUUM
VALVE

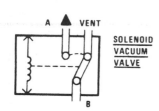

VACUUM SOURCE

SOLENOID
VACUUM
VALVE

2-POSITION VACUUM MOTORS

IN THE 'AT REST' POSITION SHOWN, THE VALVE SEALS PORT 'A' AND VENTS PORT 'B' TO THE ATMOSPHERE. WHEN THE VALVE IS MOVED TO THE 'OPERATED' POSITION, VACUUM FROM PORT 'A' IS CONNECTED TO PORT 'B'. THE SOLENOID VACUUM VALVE USES THE SOLENOID TO MOVE THE VALVE.

VACUUM MOTORS OPERATE LIKE ELECTRICAL SOLENOIDS, MECHANICALLY PUSHING OR PULLING A SHAFT BETWEEN TWO FIXED POSITIONS. WHEN VACUUM IS APPLIED, THE SHAFT IS PULLED IN. WHEN NO VACUUM IS APPLIED, THE SHAFT IS PUSHED ALL THE WAY OUT BY A SPRING.

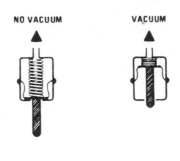

NO VACUUM   VACUUM

SINGLE-DIAPHRAGM MOTOR

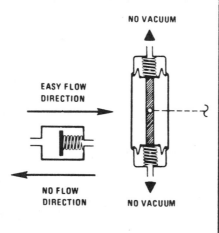

EASY FLOW
DIRECTION

NO FLOW
DIRECTION

NO VACUUM

NO VACUUM

VACUUM
CHECK
VALVE

DOUBLE
DIAPHRAGM
MOTOR

DOUBLE-DIAPHRAGM MOTORS CAN BE OPERATED BY VACUUM IN TWO DIRECTIONS. WHEN THERE IS NO VACUUM, THE MOTOR IS IN THE CENTER 'AT REST' POSITION.

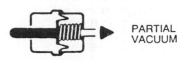

PARTIAL
VACUUM

SERVO MOTOR

SOME VACUUM MOTORS, SUCH AS THE SERVO MOTOR IN THE CRUISE CONTROL, CAN POSITION THE ACTUATING ARM AT ANY POSITION BETWEEN FULLY EXTENDED AND FULLY RETRACTED. THE SERVO IS OPERATED BY A CONTROL VALVE THAT APPLIES VARYING AMOUNTS OF VACUUM TO THE MOTOR. THE HIGHER THE VACUUM LEVEL, THE GREATER THE RETRACTION OF THE MOTOR ARM. SERVO MOTORS WORK LIKE THE TWO-POSITION MOTORS; THE ONLY DIFFERENCE IS IN THE WAY THE VACUUM IS APPLIED. SERVO MOTORS ARE GENERALLY LARGER AND PROVIDE A CALIBRATED CONTROL.

METRIC SIZE	AWG SIZES
.22	24
.35	22
.5	20
.8	18
1.0	16
2.0	14
3.0	12
5.0	10
8.0	8
13.0	6
19.0	4
32.0	2

Wire Size Conversion Table

460°F). Contrary to popular belief, the purpose of the soldering iron is not to melt the solder itself, but to heat the parts being soldered to a temperature high enough to melt the solder when it touches the work. Melting flux-cored solder on the soldering iron will usually destroy the effectiveness of the flux.

NOTE: Soldering tips are made of copper for good heat conductivity, but must be "tinned" regularly for quick transfer of heat to the project and to prevent the solder from sticking to the iron. To "tin" the iron, simply heat it and touch the flux-cored solder to the tip; the solder will flow over the hot tip. Wipe the excess off with a clean rag, but be careful as the iron will be hot.

After some use, the tip may become pitted. If so, simply dress the tip smooth with a smooth file and "tin" the tip again. An old saying holds that "metals well cleaned are half soldered." Flux-cored solder will remove oxides but rust, bits of insulation and oil or grease must be removed with a wire brush or emery cloth.

For maximum strength in soldered parts, the joint must start off clean and tight. Weak joints will result if there are gaps too wide for the solder to bridge.

If a separate soldering flux is used, it should be brushed or swabbed only on areas that are to be soldered. Most solders

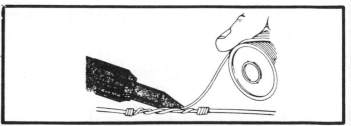

Proper soldering method. Allow the soldering iron to heat the wire first, then apply the solder as shown

contain a core of flux and separate fluxing is unnecessary. Hold the work to be soldered firmly. It is best to solder on a wooden board, because a metal vise will only rob the piece to be soldered of heat and make it difficult to melt the solder. Hold the soldering tip with the broadest face against the work to be soldered. Apply solder under the tip close to the work, using enough solder to give a heavy film between the iron and the piece being soldered, while moving slowly and making sure the solder melts properly. Keep the work level or the solder will run to the lowest part and favor the thicker parts, because these require more heat to melt the solder. If the soldering tip overheats (the solder coating on the face of the tip burns up), it should be retinned. Once the soldering is completed, let the soldered joint stand until cool. Tape and seal all soldered wire splices after the repair has cooled.

Wire Harness and Connectors

The on-board computer (ECM) wire harness electrically connects the control unit to the various solenoids, switches and sensors used by the control system. Most connectors in the engine compartment or otherwise exposed to the elements are protected against moisture and dirt which could create oxidation and deposits on the terminals. This protection is important because of the very low voltage and current levels used by the computer and sensors. All connectors have a lock which secures the male and female terminals together, with a secondary lock holding the seal and terminal into the connector. Both terminal locks must be released when disconnecting ECM connectors.

These special connectors are weather-proof and all repairs

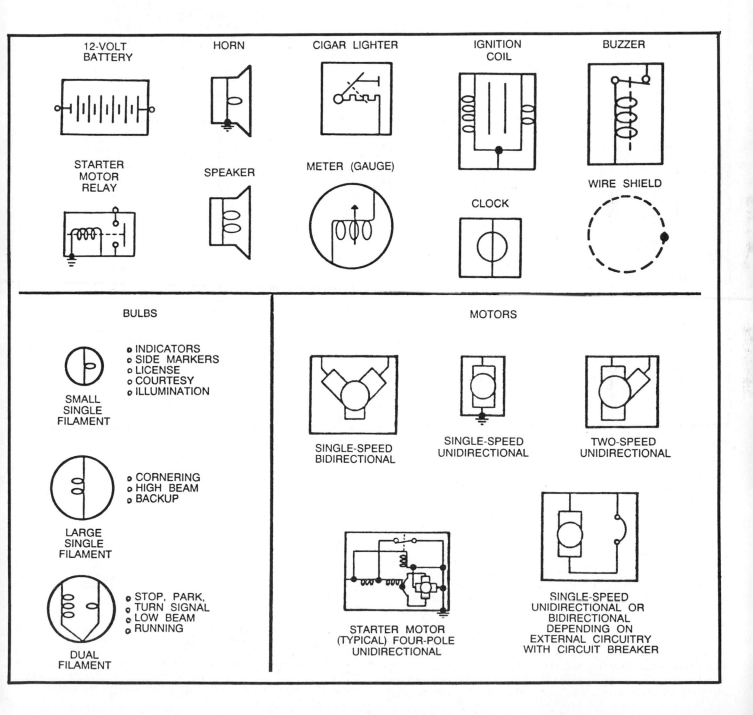

require the use of a special terminal and the tool required to service it. This tool is used to remove the pin and sleeve terminals. If removal is attempted with an ordinary pick, there is a good chance that the terminal will be bent or deformed. Unlike standard blade type terminals, these terminals cannot be straightened once they are bent. Make certain that the connectors are properly seated and all of the sealing rings in place when connecting leads. On some models, a hinge-type flap provides a backup or secondary locking feature for the terminals. Most secondary locks are used to improve the connector reliability by retaining the terminals if the small terminal lock tangs are not positioned properly.

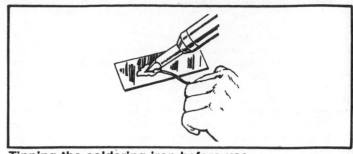

Tinning the soldering iron before use

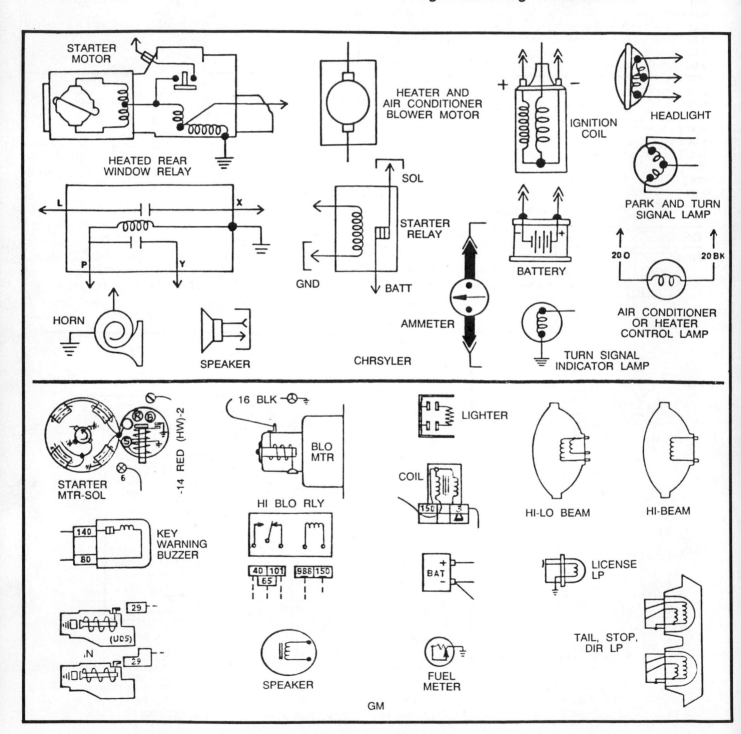

Various types of soldering guns

Molded-on connectors require complete replacement of the connection. This means splicing a new connector assembly into the harness. All splices in on-board computer systems should be soldered to insure proper contact. Use care when probing the connections or replacing terminals in them as it is possible to short between opposite terminals. If this happens to the wrong terminal pair, it is possible to damage certain components. Always use jumper wires between connectors for circuit checking and never probe through weatherproof seals.

Open circuits are often difficult to locate by sight because corrosion or terminal misalignment are hidden by the connectors. Merely wiggling a connector on a sensor or in the wiring harness may correct the open circuit condition. This should always be considered when an open circuit or a failed sensor is indicated. Intermittent problems may also be caused by oxidized or loose connections. When using a circuit tester for diagnosis, always probe connections from the wire side. Be careful not to damage sealed connectors with test probes.

All wiring harnesses should be replaced with identical parts, using the same gauge wire and connectors. When signal wires are spliced into a harness, use wire with high temperature insulation only. With the low voltage and current levels found in the system, it is important that the best possible connection at all wire splices be made by soldering the splices together. It is seldom necessary to replace a complete harness. If replacement is necessary, pay close attention to insure proper harness rout-

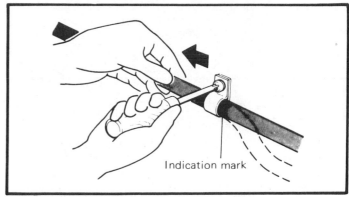

Indication mark

Secure the wiring harness at the indication marks, if used, to prevent vibrations from causing wear and a possible short

WIRE HARNESS REPAIR PROCEDURES

Condition	Location	Correction
Non-continuity	Using the electric wiring diagram and the wiring harness diagram as a guideline, check the continuity of the circuit in question by using a tester, and check for breaks, loose connector couplings, or loose terminal crimp contacts.	**Breaks**—Reconnect the point of the break by using solder. If the wire is too short and the connection is impossible, extend it by using a wire of the same or larger size. *Solder* *Be careful concerning the size of wire used for the extension* **Loose couplings**—Hold the connector securely, and insert it until there is a definite joining of the coupling. If the connector is equipped with a locking mechanism, insert the connector until it is locked securely. **Loose terminal crimp contacts**—Remove approximately 2 in. (5mm) of the insulation covering from the end of the wire, crimp the terminal contact by using a pair of pliers, and then, in addition, complete the repair by soldering. *Crimp by using pliers Solder*
Short-circuit	Using the electric wiring diagram and the wiring harness diagram as a guideline, check the entire circuit for pinched wires.	Remove the pinched portion, and then repair any breaks in the insulation covering with tape. Repair breaks of the wire by soldering.
Loose terminal	Pull the wiring lightly from the connector. A special terminal removal tool may be necessary for complete removal.	Raise the terminal catch pin, and then insert it until a definite clicking sound is heard. *Catch pin*

Note: There is the chance of short circuits being caused by insulation damage at soldered points. To avoid this possibility, wrap all splices with electrical tape and use a layer of silicone to seal the connection against moisture. Incorrect repairs can cause malfunctions by creating excessive resistance in a circuit.

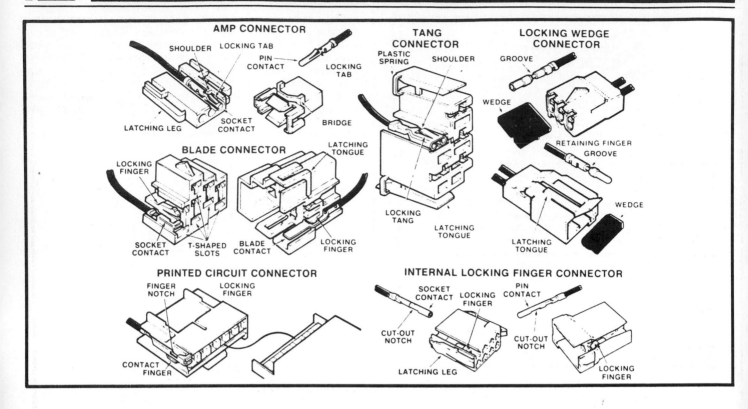

ing. Secure the harness with suitable plastic wire clamps to prevent vibrations from causing the harness to wear in spots or contact any hot components.

NOTE: Weatherproof connectors cannot be replaced with standard connectors. Instructions are provided with replacement connector and terminal packages.

Some wire harnesses have mounting indicators (usually pieces of colored tape) to mark where the harness is to be secured.

In making wiring repairs, it's important that you always replace damaged wires with wires that are the same gauge as the wire being replaced. The heavier the wire, the smaller the

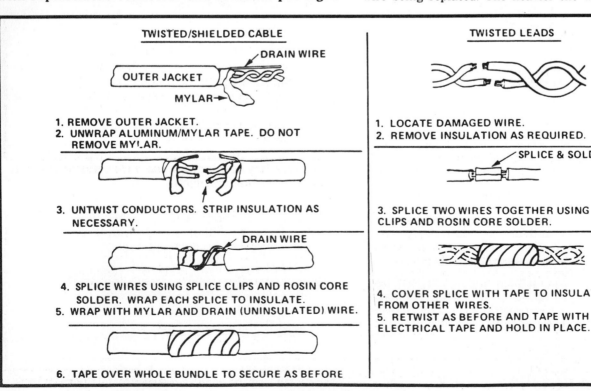

TWISTED/SHIELDED CABLE

1. REMOVE OUTER JACKET.
2. UNWRAP ALUMINUM/MYLAR TAPE. DO NOT REMOVE MYLAR.

3. UNTWIST CONDUCTORS. STRIP INSULATION AS NECESSARY.

4. SPLICE WIRES USING SPLICE CLIPS AND ROSIN CORE SOLDER. WRAP EACH SPLICE TO INSULATE.
5. WRAP WITH MYLAR AND DRAIN (UNINSULATED) WIRE.

6. TAPE OVER WHOLE BUNDLE TO SECURE AS BEFORE

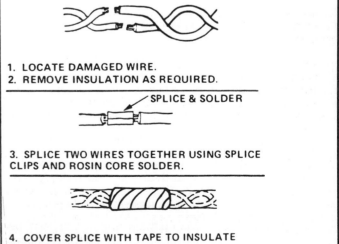

TWISTED LEADS

1. LOCATE DAMAGED WIRE.
2. REMOVE INSULATION AS REQUIRED.

3. SPLICE TWO WIRES TOGETHER USING SPLICE CLIPS AND ROSIN CORE SOLDER.

4. COVER SPLICE WITH TAPE TO INSULATE FROM OTHER WIRES.
5. RETWIST AS BEFORE AND TAPE WITH ELECTRICAL TAPE AND HOLD IN PLACE.

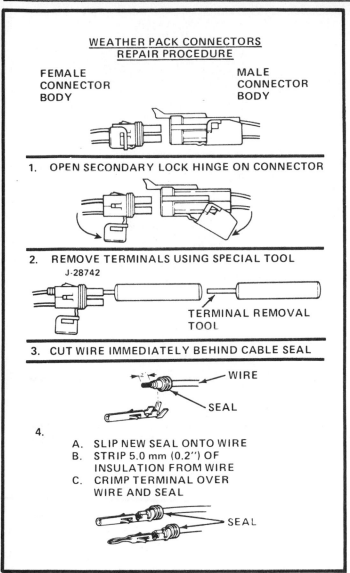

Repairing Weatherpak connectors. Note special terminal removal tools

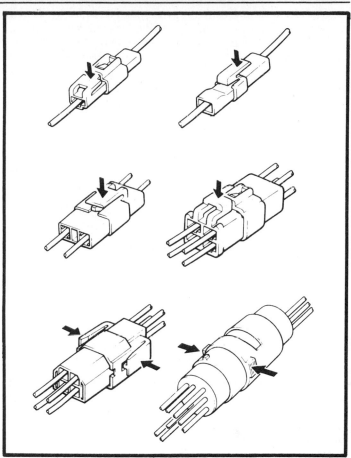

Various types of locking harness connectors. Depress the locks at the arrows to separate the connectors

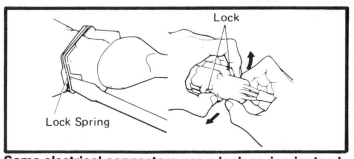

Some electrical connectors use a lock spring instead of the molded locking tabs

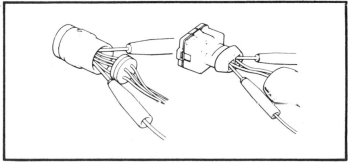

Correct method of testing weatherproof connectors. Do not pierce connector seals with test probes

gauge number. Wires are color-coded to aid in identification and whenever possible the same color coded wire should be used for replacement. A wire stripping and crimping tool is necessary to install solderless terminal connectors. Test all crimps by pulling on the wires; it should not be possible to pull the wires out of a good crimp.

Wires which are open, exposed or otherwise damaged are repaired by simple splicing. Where possible, if the wiring harness is accessible and the damaged place in the wire can be located, it is best to open the harness and check for all possible damage. In an inaccessible harness, the wire must be bypassed with a new insert, usually taped to the outside of the old harness.

When replacing fusible links, be sure to use fusible link wire, NOT ordinary automotive wire. Make sure the fusible segment is of the same gauge and construction as the one being replaced and double the stripped end when crimping the terminal connector for a good contact. The melted (open) fusible link segment of the wiring harness should be cut off as close to the harness as possible, then a new segment spliced in as described. In the case of a damaged fusible link that feeds two harness wires, the harness connections should be replaced with two fusible link wires so that each circuit will have its own separate protection.

Most of the problems caused in the wiring harness are due to bad ground connections. Always check all vehicle ground connections for corrosion or looseness before performing any power feed checks to eliminate the chance of a bad ground affecting the circuit.

Repairing Hard Shell Connectors

Unlike molded connectors, the terminal contacts in hard shell connectors can be replaced. Weatherproof hard-shell connectors with the leads molded into the shell have non-replaceable terminal ends. Replacement usually involves the use of a special terminal removal tool that depress the locking tangs (barbs) on the connector terminal and allow the connector to be removed from the rear of the shell. The connector shell should be replaced if it shows any evidence of burning, melting, cracks, or breaks. Replace individual terminals that are burnt, corroded, distorted or loose.

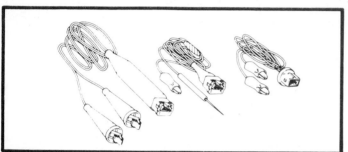

Special purpose test connections for use on some systems made up from factory connectors and jumper wires

NOTE: The insulation crimp must be tight to prevent the insulation from sliding back on the wire when the wire is pulled. The insulation must be visibly compressed under the crimp tabs, and the ends of the crimp should be turned in for a firm grip on the insulation.

The wire crimp must be made with all wire strands inside the crimp. The terminal must be fully compressed on the wire strands with the ends of the crimp tabs turned in to make a firm grip on the wire. Check all connections with an ohmmeter to insure a good contact. There should be no measurable resistance between the wire and the terminal when connected.

Mechanical Test Equipment
VACUUM GAUGE

Most gauges are graduated in inches of mercury (in. Hg), although a device called a manometer reads vacuum in inches of water (in. H_2O). The normal vacuum reading usually varies between 18 and 22 in. Hg at sea level. To test engine vacuum, the vacuum gauge must be connected to a source of manifold vacuum. Many engines have a plug in the intake manifold which can be removed and replaced with an adapter fitting. Connect the vacuum gauge to the fitting with a suitable rubber hose or, if no manifold plug is available, connect the vacuum gauge to any device using manifold vacuum, such as EGR valves, etc. The vacuum gauge can be used to determine if enough vacuum is reaching a component to allow its actuation.

HAND VACUUM PUMP

Small, hand-held vacuum pumps come in a variety of designs.

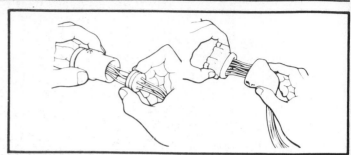

Slide back the weatherproof seals or boots on sealed terminals for testing

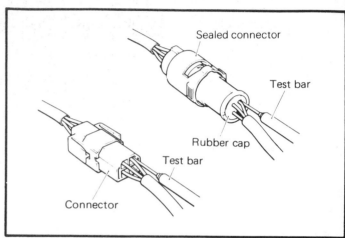

Probe all connectors from the wire side when testing

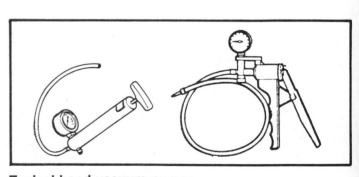

Typical hand vacuum pumps

Most have a built-in vacuum gauge and allow the component to be tested without removing it from the vehicle. Operate the pump lever or plunger to apply the correct amount of vacuum required for the test specified in the diagnosis routines. The level of vacuum in inches of Mercury (in. Hg) is indicated on the pump gauge. For some testing, an additional vacuum gauge may be necessary.

Intake manifold vacuum is used to operate various systems and devices on late model cars. To correctly diagnose and solve problems in vacuum control systems, a vacuum source is necessary for testing. In some cases, vacuum can be taken from the intake manifold when the engine is running, but vacuum is normally provided by a hand vacuum pump. These hand vacuum pumps have a built-in vacuum gauge that allow testing while the device is still attached to the car. For some tests, an additional vacuum gauge may be necessary.

Self-Diagnosis Systems

3

SECTION

INDEX

SELF-DIAGNOSTIC SYSTEMS

Acura/Sterling Programmed Fuel Injection (PGM-FI)
Diagnosis and Testing

SELF-DIAGNOSTIC SYSTEM

Self-Diagnosis Indicators

The quick reference chart(Section 6) covers the most common failure modes for the PGM-FI. The probable causes are listed in order of most-easily-checked first, then progressing to more difficult fixes. Run through all the causes listed. If problem is still unsolved, go on to the more detailed troubleshooting. Troubleshooting is divided into different LED displays. Find the correct light display and begin again.

For all the conditions listed, the PGM-FI warning light on the dashboard must be on (comes on and stays on). This indicates a problem in the electrical portion of the fuel injection system. At that time, check the LED display (self-diagnosis system) in the ECU.

On 1986–88 Acura Integra model, there is only one LED display. The LED will blink consecutively to indicate the trouble code. The ECU is located under the passenger's seat.

On 1986–88 Acura Legend and Sterling models, there are two LED displays. The yellow LED display is for idle speed adjustment check. The red LED display will blink consecutively to indicate the trouble code. The ECU is located under the passenger's seat on the 1986–88 Acura Legend Sedan and Sterling. On the 1987–88 Acura Legend Coupe, the ECU is located behind the floor kick panel in front of the passenger seat.

SELF-DIAGNOSIS INDICATOR BLINKS	SYSTEM INDICATED
0	ECU
1	FRONT OXYGEN CONTENT
2	REAR OXYGEN CONTENT
3	MANIFOLD ABSOLUTE PRESSURE
5	
6	COOLANT TEMPERATURE
7	THROTTLE ANGLE
8	CRANK ANGLE (TDC)
9	CRANK ANGLE (CYL)
10	INTAKE AIR TEMPERATURE
11	IMA
12	EXHAUST GAS RECIRCULATION SYSTEM
13	ATMOSPHERIC PRESSURE
14	ELECTRONIC IDLE CONTROL

Trouble codes and related systems—1986–88 Legend Sedan

SELF-DIAGNOSIS INDICATOR BLINKS	SYSTEM INDICATED
0	ECU
1	FRONT OXYGEN CONTENT
2	REAR OXYGEN CONTENT
3	MANIFOLD ABSOLUTE PRESSURE
5	
4	CRANK ANGLE
6	COOLANT TEMPERATURE
7	THROTTLE ANGLE
8	TDC POSITION
9	No.1 CYLINDER POSITION
10	INTAKE AIR TEMPERATURE
12	EXHAUST GAS RECIRCULATION SYSTEM
13	ATMOSPHERIC PRESSURE
14	ELECTRONIC IDLE CONTROL
15	IGNITION OUTPUT SIGNAL
17	VEHICLE SPEED PULSER
18	IGNITION TIMING ADJUSTMENT

Trouble codes and related systems—1987–88 Legend

SELF-DIAGNOSIS INDICATOR BLINKS	SYSTEM INDICATED
0	ECU
1	OXYGEN CONTENT
3	MANIFOLD ABSOLUTE PRESSURE
5	
6	COOLANT TEMPERATURE
7	THROTTLE ANGLE
8	CRANK ANGLE (TDC)
9	CRANK ANGLE (CYL)
10	INTAKE AIR TEMPERATURE
13	ATMOSPHERIC PRESSURE
14	ELECTRONIC IDLE CONTROL

Trouble codes and related systems—1986–88 Integra

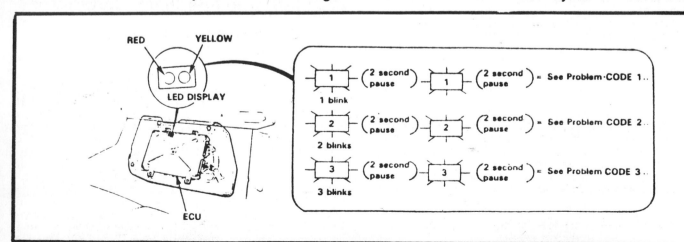

ECU location and self-diagnostic LED display—1987–88 Acura Legend Coupe

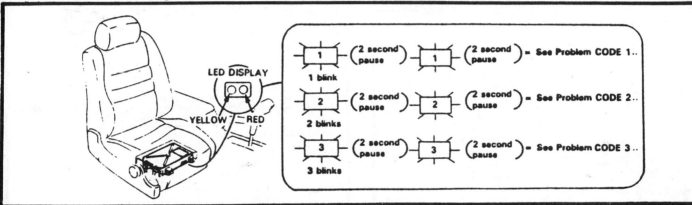

ECU location and self-diagnostic LED display—1986–88 Acura Integra

ECU location and self-diagnostic LED display—1986–88 Acura Legend Sedan and Sterling

Sometimes the dash warning light and/or ECU LED will come on, indicating a system problem, when, in fact, there is only a bad or intermittent electrical connection. To troubleshoot a bad connection, note the ECU LED pattern that is lit, refer to the diagnosis chart and check the connectors associated with the items mentioned in the "Possible Cause" column for that LED pattern (disconnect, clean or repair if necessary and reconnect those connections). Then, reset the ECU memory as described. Start the car and drive it for a few minutes and then recheck the LED(s). If the same pattern lights up, begin system troubleshooting; if it does not light up, the problem was only a bad connection.

The memory for the PGM-FI warning light on the dashboard will be erased when the ignition switch is turned off; however, the memory for the LED display will not be canceled. Thus, the warning light will not come on when the ignition switch is again turned on unless the trouble is once more detected. Troubleshooting should be done according to the LED display even if the warning light is off.

Other ECU information:
• After making repairs, disconnect the battery negative cable from the battery negative terminal for at least 10 seconds in order to reset the ECU memory. After reconnecting the cable, check that the LED display is turned off.
• Turn the ignition switch on. The PGM-FI warning light should come on for about 2 seconds. If the warning light won't come on, check for:
—Blown warning light bulb
—Blown fuse (causing faulty back up light, seat belt alarm, clock, memory function of the car radio)
—Open circuit in Yellow wire between fuse and gauge assembly

• After the PGM-FI warning light and self-diagnosis indicators have been turned on, turn the ignition switch off. If the LED display fails to come on when the ignition switch is turned on again, check for:
—Blown fuse
—Open circuit in wire between ECU A17 terminal and fuse
• Replace the ECU only after making sure that all couplers and connectors are connected securely.

Honda Programmed Fuel Injection (PGM-FI) and Feedback Carburetor

Diagnosis and Testing

SELF-DIAGNOSTIC SYSTEM

Many Honda's are equipped with a self-diagnosis function. When an abnormality is detected, the LED display on the ECU comes on. The location of the emission device control systems trouble can be diagnosed from the LED display pattern. Some of the models have four LED displays (they are numbered 1, 2, 4 and 8 as counted from right to left), while the others have a single LED that flashes the trouble code. The LED(s) are part of the control unit, which is inside the vehicle.

If there is no voltage from the control unit when there should be voltage or if there is voltage from the control unit when there should not be voltage, first observe the LED display on the control unit. If the LED display lights, note the LED pattern and isolate the problem according to the table. If the LED does not light, check the input signal sources.

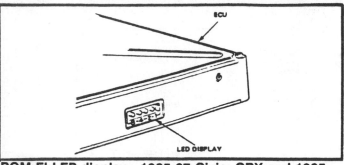

PGM-FI LED display—1985-87 Civic; CRX and 1985 Accord

On 1985-87 Civic/CRX EFI, 1986-87 CRX carbureted and Accord 1985 EFI models, there are four LED displays. The LED's are part of the ECU, which is located under the passenger's seat in the Accord and Civic/CRX for the years stated previously. They are numbered 1, 2, 4 and 8, as counted from right to left.

On 1986–88 Accord, 1986-87 Prelude, and 1988 Civic/CRX EFI models, there is only one LED. The LED will blink consecutively to indicate the trouble code. The ECU is located under the

SELF-DIAGNOSIS INDICATOR BLINKS	SYSTEM INDICATED
0	ECU
1	OXYGEN CONTENT
3	MANIFOLD ABSOLUTE PRESSURE
5	
6	COOLANT TEMPERATURE
7	THROTTLE ANGLE
8	CRANK ANGLE (TDC)
9	CRANK ANGLE (CYL)
10	INTAKE AIR TEMPERATURE
12	EXHAUST GAS RECIRCULATION SYSTEM
13	ATMOSPHERIC PRESSURE

Trouble codes and related systems—1986–87 Accord Fuel Injected

driver's seat on the 1986-88 Accord and in the left side panel beside the rear seat on the 1986-87 Preludes. The 1988 Prelude's (carbureted and fuel injected) ECU is under the carpet of the passenger's floor. This also has only one LED indicator.

Sometimes the dash warning light and/or ECU LED(s) will come on, indicating a system problem, when, in fact, there is

LED Display	Possible Cause
○ ○ ○ ○ (Dash Warning Light ON only)	· Loose or poorly connected power line to ECU · Short circuit in combination meter or warning light wire · Faulty ECU
○ ○ ○ ★ (1)	· Disconnected oxygen sensor coupler · Spark plug mis-fire · Short or open circuit in oxygen sensor circuit · Faulty oxygen sensor
○ ○ ★ ○ (2)	· Faulty ECU
○ ○ ★ ★ (2 1)	· Disconnected manifold air pressure sensor coupler · Short or open circuit in manifold air pressure sensor wire · Faulty manifold air pressure sensor
○ ★ ○ ○ (4)	· Faulty ECU
○ ★ ○ ★ (4 1)	· Disconnected manifold air pressure sensor piping
○ ★ ★ ○ (4 2)	· Disconnected coolant temperature sensor coupler · Open circuit in coolant temperature sensor wire · Faulty coolant temperature sensor (thermostat housing)
○ ★ ★ ★ (4 2 1)	· Disconnected throttle angle sensor coupler · Open or short circuit in throttle angle sensor wire · Faulty throttle angle sensor
★ ○ ○ ○ (8)	· Short or open circuit in crank angle sensor wire · Crank angle sensor wire interfering with high tension cord · Crank angle sensor at fault
★ ○ ○ ★ (8)	Same as above
★ ○ ★ ○ (8 2)	· Disconnected intake air temperature sensor · Open circuit in intake air temperature sensor wire · Faulty intake air temperature sensor
★ ○ ★ ★ (8 2 1)	· Disconnected idle mixture adjuster sensor coupler · Shorted or disconnected idle mixture adjuster sensor wire · Faulty idle mixture adjuster sensor
★ ★ ○ ○ (8 4)	· Disconnected EGR control system coupler · Shorted or disconnected EGR control wire · Faulty EGR control system
★ ★ ○ ★ (8 4 1)	· Disconnected atmospheric pressure sensor coupler · Shorted or disconnected atmospheric pressure sensor wire · Faulty atmospheric pressure sensor
★ ★ ★ ○ (8 4 2)	· Faulty ECU
★ ★ ★ ★ (8 4 2 1)	Same as above

Trouble codes and related systems—1985 Accord Fuel Injected

LED Display	Possible Cause
○ ○ ○ ○ (Dash warning light off)	· Loose or poorly connected power line to ECU · Disconnected control unit ground wire · Faulty ECU
○ ○ ○ ○ (Dash warning light on)	· Disconnected control unit ground wire · Short circuit in combination meter or warning light wire · Faulty ECU
○ ○ ○ ★ (1)	· Disconnected oxygen sensor connector · Spark plug mis-fire · Short or open circuit in oxygen sensor circuit · Faulty oxygen sensor
○ ○ ★ ○ (2)	· Faulty ECU
○ ○ ★ ★ (2 1)	· Disconnected MAP sensor connector · Short or open circuit in MAP sensor wire · Faulty MAP sensor
○ ★ ○ ○ (4)	· Faulty ECU
○ ★ ○ ★ (4 1)	· Disconnected MAP sensor piping
○ ★ ★ ○ (4 2)	· Disconnected TW sensor connector · Open circuit in TW sensor wire · Faulty TW sensor
○ ★ ★ ★ (4 2 1)	· Disconnected throttle angle sensor connector · Open or short circuit in throttle angle sensor wire · Faulty throttle angle sensor
★ ○ ○ ○ (8 1)	· Short or open circuit in crank angle sensor wire · Crank angle sensor wire interfering with spark plug wires · Faulty crank angle sensor
★ ○ ○ ★ (8 1)	Same as above
★ ○ ★ ○ (8 2 1)	· Disconnected TA sensor connector · Open circuit in TA sensor wire · Faulty TA sensor
★ ○ ★ ★ (8 2 1)	· Disconnected IMA sensor connector · Open or short circuit in IMA sensor wire · Faulty IMA sensor
★ ★ ○ ○ (8 4)	· Faulty ECU
★ ★ ○ ★ (8 4 1)	· Disconnected PA sensor connector · Open or short circuit in PA sensor wire · Faulty PA sensor
★ ★ ★ ○ (8 4 2)	· Faulty ECU
★ ★ ★ ★ (8 4 2 1)	Same as above

Trouble codes and related systems—1985–87 Civic; CRX EFI

only a bad or intermittent electrical connection. To troubleshoot a bad connection, note the ECU LED code that is lit, refer to the diagnosis chart and check the connectors associated with the items mentioned in the "Possible Cause" column for that LED pattern (disconnect, clean or repair if necessary and reconnect those connections). Then, reset the ECU memory as described. Start the car and drive it for a few minutes and then recheck the LED(s). If the same code lights up, begin system troubleshooting; if it does not light up, the problem was only a bad connection.

To clear the ECU memory after making repairs, disconnect the negative battery cable from the battery negative terminal for at least 10 seconds. After reconnecting the cable, check that the LED display is turned off. Turn the ignition switch ON and all LED displays should come on for about 2 seconds and then go out.

Isuzu (I-TEC) Diagnosis and Testing

I-MARK, PICK-UP AND TROOPER II

SYSTEM MALFUNCTION LAMP

This system utilizes a dashboard mounted malfunction indicator lamp which, for some failure modes will inform the driver of the need for unscheduled maintenance. In the event of a system malfunction the legend "CHECK ENGINE" will light and re-

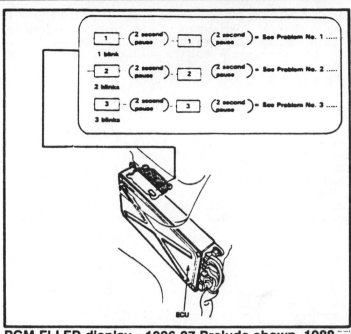

PGM-FI LED display—1986-87 Prelude shown, 1988 Prelude beneath right front carpet. 1986-88 Accord ECU under driver's seat

No. of LED Blinks between 2 second pauses		Symptom	Possible cause
0	Warning light off	• Engine will not start	• Disconnected ECU ground wire • Faulty ECU
	Warning light on	• Engine will not start • No particular symptom shown	• Loose or poorly connected power line to ECU • Disconnected ECU ground wire • Short circuit in combination meter or warning light wire • Faulty ECU
1		• No particular symptom shown • Erratic idling (Erratic injector, connector and wiring Insufficient fuel)	• Disconnected O2 sensor connector • Spark plug mis-fire • Short or open circuit in O2 sensor ciruct • Faulty O2 sensor • Faulty fuel system
2		• No particular symptom shown or system does not operate	• Faulty ECU
3		• Fuel fouled plug • Frequent engine stalling • Hesitation	• Disconnected MAP sensor connector • Short or open circuit in MAP sensor wire • Faulty MAP sensor
4		• No particular symptom shown or system does not operate	• Faulty ECU
5		• Hesitation • Fuel fouled plug • Frequent engine stalling	• Disconnected MAP sensor piping
6		• High idle speed during warm-up • High idle speed • Hard starting at low temp	• Disconnected TW sensor connector • Open or short circuit in TW sensor wire • Faulty TW sensor (thermostat housing)
7		• Poor engine response to opening throttle rapidly • High idle speed • Engine does not rev up when cold	• Disconnected throttle angle sensor connector • Open or short circuit in throttle angle sensor wire • Faulty throttle angle sensor
8		• Engine does not rev up • High idle speed • Erratic idling	• Short or open circuit in crank angle sensor wire • Crank angle sensor wire interfering with spark plug wires • Crank angle sensor at fault
9		• Same as above	• Same as above
10		• High idle speed • Erratic idling when very cold	• Disconnected TA sensor connector • Open or short circuit in TA sensor wire • Faulty TA sensor
11		• No particular symptom shown or system does not operate	• Faulty ECU
12		• Frequent engine stalling • Erratic or unstable running at low speed • No particular symptom shown	• Disconnected EGR control system connector • Shorted or disconnected EGR control wire • Faulty EGR control system
13		• Poor acceleration at high altitude • Hard starting at high altitude when cold	• Disconnected PA sensor connector • Shorted or disconnected PA sensor wire • Faulty PA sensor

Trouble codes and related systems—1986–87 Prelude Fuel Injected

main on as long as the fault function occurs and the engine is running. The electronic control unit incorporates a diagnostic program which will assist in diagnosing the closed loop control system discrepancies. When activated the diagnostic program will flash a code through the malfunction lamp which isolates the source of the system discrepancy.

DIAGNOSIS CIRCUIT CHECK

The diagnostic circuit check makes sure that the self-diagnostic system works, determines that the trouble codes will display and guides diagnosis to other problem areas. When the engine is running and a problem develops in the system which the self diagnosis can evaluate, the "CHECK ENGINE" light will come on and a trouble code will be stored in the ECM trouble code memory. The light will remain on with the engine running as long as there is a problem. If the problem is intermittent the

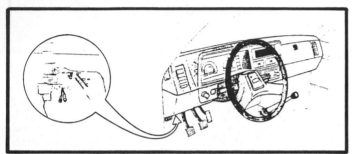

Location of the trouble code TEST lead(s) — Pick-Up

Location of the trouble code TEST lead(s) — I-Mark RWD

"CHECK ENGINE" light will go out, but the trouble codes will be stored in the ECM trouble code memory.

With the ignition turned on and the engine stopped, the "CHECK ENGINE" lamp should be on. This is a bulb check to indicate the light is working properly. The trouble code test leads are located as follows:

1. I-MARK RWD — The trouble code "TEST" leads are usually taped to the wiring harness under the instrument panel, to the right of the steering column and just above the accelerator pedal.

2. I-MARK FWD — A three terminal connector, is located near the ECM connector, this connector is used to actuate the trouble code system in the ECM. This connector is also known as the ALDL (assembly line diagnostic link) or the ALCL (assembly line communications link). Two terminals of this connector (A & C) are used to activate the trouble code system in the ECM.

3. PICK-UP and TROOPER II — A trouble code "TEST" lead (white cable) and a ground lead (black cable) are branched from a harness at a distance of eight inches from the ECM connector. On some later Trooper II vehicles, the trouble code test leads may located under the instrument panel behind the radio.

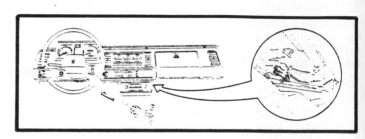

SELF-DIAGNOSIS INDICATOR BLINKS	SYSTEM INDICATED
1	OXYGEN CONTENT
2	VEHICLE SPEED PULSER
3	MANIFOLD ABSOLUTE PRESSURE
4	VACUUM SWITCH SIGNAL
5	MANIFOLD ABSOLUTE PRESSURE
6	COOLANT TEMPERATURE
8	IGNITION COIL SIGNAL
10	INTAKE AIR TEMPERATURE
14	ELECTRONIC AIR CONTROL

Trouble codes and related systems — 1988 Prelude Carbureted

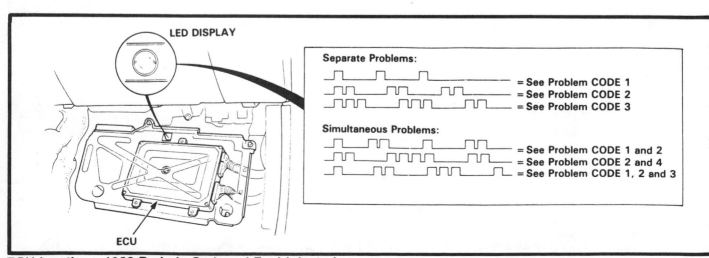

ECU location — 1988 Prelude Carb and Fuel Injected

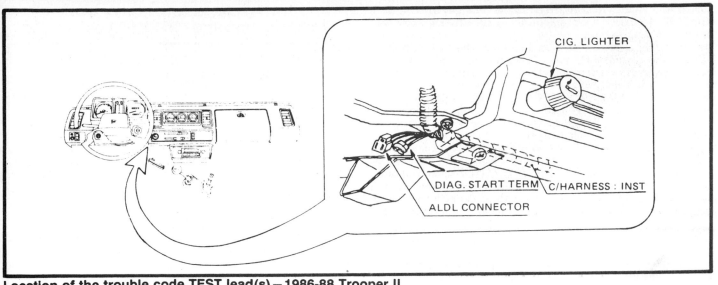

Location of the trouble code TEST lead(s) — 1986-88 Trooper II

On all models except the I-Mark FWD, the trouble code memory is activated by placing the ignition switch in the ON position and connecting the trouble code "TEST" lead to the ground lead. On the I-Mark FWD vehicles, the trouble code memory is activated by placing the ignition switch in the ON position and running a jumper wire between terminals A and C of the ALDL.

The "CHECK ENGINE" light will begin to flash a trouble code "12". Code "12" consists of one flash , a short pause and then two flashes. There will be a longer pause and a code "12" will repeat two more times. The check indicates that the self-diagnostic system is working. This cycle will repeat itself until the engine is started and the ignition switch is turned OFF. If more than one fault code is stored in the memory, the lowest number code will flash three times followed by the next highest code number until all the codes have been flashed. The faults will then repeat in the same order. In most cases, codes will be checked with the engine running since no codes other than code 12 or 51 will be present on the initial "KEY ON". Remove the ground from the test terminal before starting the engine.

A trouble code indicates a problem in a given circuit. For example a trouble code 14 indicates a problem in the coolant sensor circuit, this includes the coolant sensor, connector harness and ECM. The procedure for finding the problem can be found by using the proper troubleshooting charts. When the engine is

I-TEC DIAGNOSTIC CODES AND TROUBLESHOOTING CHART 1984-88 IMPULSE

DIAGNOSED ITEM	DIAGNOSED CONTENT		CODE NO.
	FAULT MODE	MICRO-COMPUTER INPUT	
Power transistor system for ignition	Output terminal shorted with ground.	—	23
	Harness open	—	35
	Defective transistor or grounding system	—	54
Vacuum switching valve system	Output terminal shorted with ground or harness open	—	25
	Defective transistor or grounding system.	—	53
Fuel injector system	Output terminal shorted with ground or harness open	—	33
	Defective transistor or grounding system.	—	64
Throttle position sensor system TURBO CONTROL SYSTEM	Abnormal signal	Insufficient signal	71
EGR vacuum switching valve system	Output terminal shorted with ground or harness open	—	72
	Defective transistor or grounding system	—	73

I-TEC DIAGNOSTIC CODES AND TROUBLESHOOTING CHART 1984-88 IMPULSE

DIAGNOSED ITEM		DIAGNOSED CONTENT		CODE NO
		FAULT MODE	MICRO-COMPUTER INPUT	
Engine is not started		—	Engine speed less than 200 rpm	12
O₂ sensor system		Harness open Sensor deterioration	Intermediate voltage	13
		Incorrect signal (Lean)	Lean signal (Low voltage)	44
		Incorrect signal (Rich)	Rich signal (High voltage)	45
Water temperature sensor system		Shorted with ground	Insufficient signal	14
		Incorrect signal	Signal is less than 0°C (32°F) even after the engine is warmed up sufficiently	15
		Harness open	Excessive signal	16
Throttle valve switch system	Both idle contact and full contact	Both idle contact and full make contact simultaneously	Both contacts make simultaneously	21
	Idle contact	Normally make contact	Signal is sent continuously (Not diagnosed when the air flow sensor system is defective)	43
	Full contact	Normally make contact	Signal is sent continuously	65

started the "CHECK ENGINE" light will go OFF. If the "CHECK ENGINE" light remains ON, the self-diagnostic system has detected a fault.

If a trouble code can be obtained when the "CHECK ENGINE" light is OFF with the engine running, the trouble code must be evaluated. A determination must be made to see if the fault is intermittent or if the engine must be at certain operating conditions to turn the "CHECK ENGINE" light ON. Faults indicated by trouble codes 13, 31, 44 and 45 require engine operation at part throttle for up to five minutes after the engine has reached normal operating temperature before the "CHECK ENGINE" light will come on and store a trouble code.

The fault indicated by trouble code 15 takes five minutes of engine operation before it will display. The diagnostic charts (section 6) for trouble codes 13, 31, 44 and 45 should be used if any of these trouble codes can be obtained. Be sure to remove the ground from the test terminal before starting the engine.

CLEARING THE TROUBLE CODE MEMORY

The trouble code memory is fed a continuous 12 volts even with the key in the OFF position. After a fault has been corrected, it will be necessary to remove the voltage for 10 seconds to clear any stored codes. The quickest way to remove the voltage is to remove the "ECM" fuse from the fuse block for 10 seconds. The voltage can also be removed by disconnecting the negative battery cable, but this will mean if the vehicle is equipped with electronic instrumentation, such as a clock and radio, they would have to be reset.

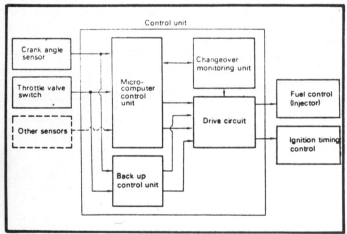

I-TEC Back Up control system

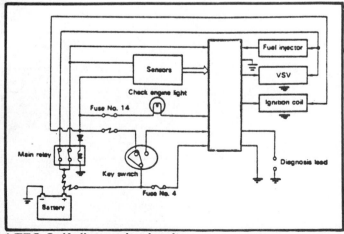

I-TEC Self-diagnosis circuit

I-TEC DIAGNOSTIC CODES AND TROUBLESHOOTING CHART 1984-88 IMPULSE

DIAGNOSED ITEM	DIAGNOSED CONTENT		CODE NO.
	FAULT MODE	MICRO-COMPUTER INPUT	
Starter signal system	Normally open	Signal is not input	22
Crank angle sensor system	· No signal arrives · Faulty signal	· No angle sensor signal is input · Idling speed is lower than the actual speed	41
Air flow sensor system	Harness open, shorting with ground, or broken hot wire	Insufficient signal	61
	Broken cold wire	Excessive signal	62
Car speed sensor system	No signal arrives	No signal is input (Not diagnosed when the air flow sensor system is defective)	63
Knocking sensor system	Harness open or shorting with ground.	Excessive or insufficient signal	66
Micro-computer unit	Abnormal LSI (1)	—	51
	Abnormal LSI (2)	—	52
	Abnormal LSI (3)	—	55

DRIVER COMMENTS

After performing the Diagnostic Circuit Check, and there is no "CHECK ENGINE" light with a warm running engine, then refer to the Driver Comments for an emission non-compliance problem or an engine performance problem (odor, surge, fuel economy, etc.). This ultimately will lead to the System Performance Check which is also used after a repair had been made.

Mazda Electronic Gasoline Injection (EGI)

CONTROL UNIT INSPECTION WITH SYSTEM CHECKER 83

NOTE: The system checker 83 (part # 49–G030–920) can be used to detect and indicate any problems of each sensor, damaged wiring, poor contact or a short circuit between each of the sensor-control units. Trouble is indicated by a red lamp and a buzzer.

If there are more than two problems at the same time, the indicator lamp lights in the numerical order of the code number. Even if the problem is corrected during indication, one cycle will be indicated. If after a malfunction has occured and the ignition key is switched off, the malfunction indicator for the feedback system will not be displayed on the checker.

Mitsubishi Self-Diagnosis System

The Mitsubishi self-diagnosis system monitors the various input signals from the engine sensors and enters a trouble code in the on-board computer memory if a problem is detected. There are nine monitored items, including the "normal operation" code. Because the computer memory draws its power directly from the battery, the trouble codes are not erased when the ignition is switched OFF. The memory can only be cleared (trouble codes erased) if a battery cable is disconnected or the main ECU wiring harness connector is disconnected from the computer module for more than 15 seconds.

DIAGNOSTIC CODES 1987—88 VAN/WAGON MPI 1987 GALANT MPI

Malfunction No.	Diagnosis item
1	Oxygen sensor
2	Crankshaft angle sensor
3	Air flow sensor (AFS)
4	Atmospheric pressure sensor
5	Throttle position sensor (TPS)
6	Motor position sensor (MPS)
7	Engine coolant temperature sensor
8	No. 1 cylinder TDC sensor

Nissan Electronic Controlled Carburetor (ECC) System

The self-diagnostic system determines malfunctions of signal systems such as sensors, actuators, and wire harnesses based on the status of the input signals received by the EFI control unit. A malfunction is displayed by both the red and green LED's (Light Emitting Diodes).

Nissan Electronic Fuel Injection (EFI)

Basically, self-diagnosis is always performed when the power is furnished to the EFI control unit. The self-diagnosis results are retained in the memory chip of the EFI control unit and are displayed only when the diagnosis mode selector (located on the side of the control unit) is turned ON.

The self-diagnostic system is provided with functions which display malfunctions being checked as well as those which are stored in the memory. In this sense, it is very effective in determining an "intermittent" malfunction. The results which is or was stored in the memory can be erased by following the steps specified.

DIAGNOSTIC CODES 1986 GALANT MPI

Code No.	Diagnosis item
1	Oxygen sensor
2	Ignition pulse
3	Air flow sensor
4	Barometric pressure sensor
5	Throttle position sensor
6	ISC motor position sensor
7	Coolant temp. sensor
8	No. 1 cylinder pulse
9	Normal

Code No.	Location problem
01	Crank angle sensor
02	Air flow meter
03	Water thermo sensor
04	Intake air temperature sensor (Air flow meter)
05	Oxygen (O2) sensor
06	Throttle sensor
07	Boost sensor
09	Atmospheric pressure sensor
12	Coil with igniter (Trailing side)
15	Intake air temperature sensor

Trouble codes and related systems 86—88 Mazda RX7

DIAGNOSTIC CODES 1988 GALANT MPI

Malfunction code	Diagnosis item	Malfunction code	Diagnosis item
11	Oxygen sensor	23	TDC sensor (No.1 cylinder)
12	Air-flow sensor (AFS)	24	Vehicle-speed reed switch
13	Intake air temperature sensor	25	Barometric pressure sensor
14	Throttle position sensor	41	Injector
21	Coolant temperature sensor	42	Fuel pump
22	Crank angle sensor	43	EGR*

The diagnosis item marked • is applicable to vehicles for California only.

DIAGNOSTIC CODES 1984—86 MIRAGE AND STARION; 1985—88 CORDIA/TREDIA

Code No.	Diagnosis item
1	Oxygen sensor & Computer
2	Ignition pulse
3	Air flow sensor
4	Pressure sensor
5	Throttle position sensor
6	ISC motor position switch
7	Coolant temp. sensor

DIAGNOSTIC CODES 1987—88 STARION ECI MIRAGE ECI

Malfunction No.	Diagnosis item
1	Oxygen sensor
2	Ignition pulse (engine speed sensor)
3	Air flow sensor
5	Throttle position sensor
6	ISC motor position sensor
7	Coolant temperature sensor

DIAGNOSTIC CODES 1984 CORDIA/TREDIA

Code No.	Diagnosis item
1	Oxygen sensor & Computer
2	Ignition pulse
3	Air flow sensor
4	Pressure sensor
5	Throttle position sensor
6	ISC motor position switch
7	Coolant temp. sensor
8	Vehicle speed

	Red L.E.D.	Green L.E.D.	Faulty part or circuit
Case 1	ON	ON / OFF	• Vacuum sensor • *Barometric pressure sensor • Water temperature sensor • Air temperature sensor
Case 2	ON	ON / OFF	• Mixture heater relay • Air-fuel ratio solenoid valve • *Richer solenoid valve • Fuel cut solenoid valve • Air injection control solenoid valve • *Vacuum control modulator • E.G.R. & Canister control solenoid valve
			• **Idle-up solenoid valve
Case 3	OFF	ON	No problem

*: Non-California model only
**: California & Canada model only

Trouble codes and related systems 1984—88 Carbureted Models

A malfunctioning area is determined by the number of blinks of both the red and green LED's. First, the red LED blinks and then the green blinks. The red LED refers to the tenth digit while the green one refers to the unit digit. For example, when the red LED blinks three times and the green LED blinks twice, this implies number "32". In this way, all problems are classified by code numbers.

Items Displayed All The Time

When performing the self-diagnosis, the items listed below are displayed by the EFI control unit as a malfunction even though they are working. Therefore, whenever performing the self-diagnosis, enter the appropriate signals for the items.

INPUT PROCEDURE

1. Throttle Valve Switch (Idle Switch) Circuit And Air Conditioner Switch Circuit—After the ignition switch is turned ON and "ON-OFF" signal from each switch are entered.
2. Start Signal—After the engine has started and when start signal "ON" and then "OFF" are entered.
3. Load Signal—After load signal is turned "ON", a signal is entered.

Items Retained In Memory

The following items will be retained in the memory from the time of detection until erased:
• Air Flow Meter Circuit—When the air flow meter produces an abnormally high output voltage with the engine off or low output voltage with the engine running

• Water Temperature Sensor Circuit—When the circuit is shorted or open
• Ignition Signal—When an ignition signal is not produced on the primary winding of the ignition coil after the engine has started
• Fuel Pump Circuit—When current flowing through the control unit to drive the fuel pump is too small or too large while the engine is operating
• Air Temperature Sensor Circuit—When the circuit is shorted or open

TESTING PRECAUTIONS

1. Before connecting or disconnecting control unit ECU harness connectors, make sure the ignition switch is OFF and the negative battery cable is disconnected to avoid the possibility of damage to the control unit.
2. When performing ECU input/output signal diagnosis, remove the pin terminal retainer from the 20 and 16-pin connectors to make it easier to insert tester probes into the connector.
3. When connecting or disconnecting pin connectors from the ECU, take care not to bend or break any pin terminals. Check that there are no bends or breaks on ECU pin terminals before attempting any connections.
4. Before replacing any ECU, perform the ECU input/output signal diagnosis to make sure the ECU is functioning properly or not.
5. After performing the Electronic Control System Inspection, perform the EFI self-diagnosis and driving test.
6. When measuring supply voltage of ECU controlled components with a circuit tester, separate one tester probe from another. If the two tester probes accidentally make contact with each other during measurement, a short circuit will result and damage the power transistor in the ECU.

DIAGNOSTIC CODES

1984 STANZA, 200SX AND 1986 STANZA WAGON 4WD WITH CA20E ENGINE
CODE 12...Air flow meter
CODE 13...Water temperature sensor
CODE 21...Ignition signal
CODE 22...Fuel pump
CODE 23...Throttle valve(Idle switch)
CODE 24...Transmission switch
CODE 31 (w/ac)...F.I.C.D. system
CODE 31 (w/o ac)...Items checked in self diagnosis o.k.
CODE 32...Starter signal
CODE 33...Exhaust gas sensor
CODE 41...Air temperature sensor
CODE 44...No malfunction

1984-88 200SX WITH CA18ET ENGINE
CODE 11...Crank angle sensor
CODE 12...Air flow meter
CODE 13...Water temperature sensor
CODE 21...Ignition signal
CODE 22...Fuel pump
CODE 23...Throttle valve
CODE 31(w/ac)...F.I.C.D. system
CODE 31(w/o ac)...Items checked in self-diagnosis o.k.
CODE 32...Starter signal
CODE 34...Detonation sensor
CODE 44...No malfunction

1985-86 200SX, STANZA, AND STANZA WAGON, WITH CA20E ENGINE
CODE 12...Air flow meter
CODE 13...Water temperature sensor

CODE 21...Ignition signal
CODE 22...Fuel pump
CODE 23...Throttle valve(Idle switch)
CODE 24...Transmission switch
CODE 31(w/ac)...F.I.C.D. system
CODE 31(w/o ac)...Items checked in self-diagnosis o.k.
CODE 32...Starter signal
CODE 41...Air temperature sensor
CODE 44...No malfunction

1984-86 300ZX, 1985-86 MAXIMA

CODE 11...Crank angle sensor
CODE 12...Air flow meter
CODE 13...Cylinder head temperature sensor
CODE 14...Vehicle speed sensor
CODE 21...Ignition signal
CODE 22...Fuel pump
CODE 23...Throttle valve(Idle switch)
CODE 24...Neutral/Park switch (VG30ET engine)
CODE 31...Load signal
CODE 32...Starter signal
CODE 34...Detonation sensor(VG30ET engine)
CODE 41...Fuel temperature sensor
CODE 44...No malfunction

1987-88 200SX, STANZA WAGON, WITH CA20E ENGINE

CODE 11...Crank angle sensor
CODE 12...Air flow meter
CODE 13...Water temperature sensor
CODE 21...Ignition signal
CODE 22...Fuel pump
CODE 41...Air temperature sensor
CODE 44...No malfunction

1087-88 300ZX, 200SX, MAXIMA, WITH VG30E OR VG30ET ENGINE

CODE 11...Crank angle sensor
CODE 12...Air flow meter
CODE 13...Cylinder head temperature sensor
CODE 21...Ignition signal
CODE 22...Fuel pump
CODE 34...Detonation sensor(VG30ET engine)
CODE 41...Fuel temperature sensor
CODE 44...No malfunction

1987-88 PULSAR NX, SENTRA, 4WD, WITH E16i ENGINE

CODE 11...Crank angle sensor
CODE 12...Air flow meter
CODE 13...Water temperature sensor
CODE 21...Ignition signal
CODE 22...Idle speed control slips out
CODE 33...Exhaust gas sensor
CODE 41...Air temperature sensor
CODE 42...Throttle sensor
CODE 43...Mixture ratio feedback control slips out
CODE 44...No malfunction

1987-88 VAN

CODE 11...Crank angle sensor
CODE 12...Air flow meter
CODE 13...Water temperature sensor
CODE 21...Ignition signal
CODE 33...Exhaust gas sensor

CODE 42...Throttle sensor
CODE 43...Injector
CODE 44...No malfunction

1987-88 TRUCK, PATHFINDER

CODE 11...Crank angle sensor
CODE 12...Air flow meter
CODE 13...Cylinder/Water temperature sensor
CODE 21...Ignition signal
CODE 33...Exhaust gas sensor(VG30i)
CODE 42...Throttle sensor
CODE 43...Injector
CODE 44...No malfunction

1987-88 PULSAR NX WITH CA16DE ENGINE

CODE 11...Crank angle sensor
CODE 12...Air flow meter
CODE 13...Water temperature sensor
CODE 21...Ignition signal
CODE 34...Detonation sensor
CODE 44...No malfunction

1986 TRUCK

CODE 11...Crank angle sensor
CODE 12...Air flow meter
CODE 13...Water temperature sensor
CODE 21...Ignition signal
CODE 23...Idle switch
CODE 24...Neutral/Clutch switch
CODE 32...Start signal
CODE 42...Throttle sensor
CODE 43...Injector
CODE 44...No malfunction

1984 PULSAR WITH E15ET (CANADA) ENGINE

CODE 11...Crank angle sensor
CODE 12...Air flow meter
CODE 13...Water temperature sensor
CODE 14...Vehicle speed sensor
CODE 21...Ignition signal
CODE 23...Idle switch
CODE 31(w/ac)...F.I.C.D. system
CODE 31(w/o ac)...Items checked in self-diagnosis o.k.
CODE 32...Starter signal
CODE 33...Exhaust gas sensor
CODE 34...Detonation sensor
CODE 41...Air temperature sensor
CODE 42...Barometric pressure sensor
CODE 43...Battery voltage incorrect
CODE 44...No malfunction

Toyota Self-Diagnostics

The ECU contains a built in self diagnosis system by which troubles with the engine signal the engine signal network are detected and a "Check Engine" warning light on the instrument panel flashes code numbers 12, 13, 14, 21, 22, 31, 32, 42, 52 and 53 (these code numbers vary from model to model). The "Check Engine" light on the instrument panel informs the driver that a malfunction has been detected. The light goes out automatically when the malfunction has been cleared.

The diagnostic code can be read by the number of blinks of the "Check Engine" warning light when the proper terminals of the check connector are short-circuited. If the vehicle is equipped with a super monitor display, the diagnostic code is indicated on the display screen.

DIAGNOSTIC CODES
1984–85 CAMRY
1984 TRUCK AND 4 RUNNER
1984–85 VAN; 1984 CELICA

Code No.	Number of "CHECK ENGINE" blinks	System
1		Normal
2		Air flow meter signal (Vc)
3		Air flow meter signal (Vs)
4		Water thermo sensor signal (THW)
5 *		Oxygen sensor signal
6		Ignition signal
7		Throttle position sensor signal

* NOTE Code No.5 is applicable to USA only.

DIAGNOSTIC CODES 1986 CAMRY

Code No.	Number of "CHECK ENGINE" blinks	System
1		Normal
2		Air flow meter signal (Vc)
3		Air flow meter signal (Vs)
4		Water temp. sensor signal (THW)
6		Ignition signal
7		Throttle position sensor signal

DIAGNOSTIC CODES
1985–88 COROLLA RWD
1987–88 COROLLA FWD,
1986–88 MR2

Code No.	Number of blinks "CHECK ENGINE"	System
1		Normal
2		Air flow meter signal
3		Ignition signal
4		Water temp. sensor signal
5		Oxygen sensor signal
6		RPM signal
7		Throttle position sensor signal
8		Intake air temp. sensor signal
10		Starter signal
11		Switch signal

DIAGNOSTIC CODES
1984 STARLET

Code No.	Number of blinks "CHECK ENGINE"	System
1		Normal
2		Air flow meter signal (Vc)
3		Air flow meter signal (Vs)
4		Water thermo senser signal (THW)
5		O₂ sensor signal
6		Ignition signal
7 *		Throttle position sensor signal

DIAGNOSTIC CODES
1987–88 SUPRA

Code No.	System	Code No.	System
—	Normal	32	(7M-GE) Air Flow Meter Signal (7M-GTE) HAC Sensor Signal
11	ECU (+B)		
12	RPM Signal	34	Turbocharger pressure
13	RPM Signal	41	Throttle Position Sensor Signal
14	Ignition Signal	42	Vehicle Speed Sensor Signal
21	Oxygen Sensor Signal	43	Starter Signal (+B)
22	Water Temp. Sensor Signal	51	Switch Signal
24	Intake Air Temp. Sensor Signal	52	Knock Sensor Signal
31	Air Flow Meter Signal	53	Knock Control Part (ECU)

DIAGNOSTIC CODES
1985–86 SUPRA
1985–88 CRESSIDA

Code No.	System	Code No.	System
22	Water Temp. Sensor Signal	42	Vehicle Speed Sensor Signal
23	Intake Air Temp. Sensor Signal	43	Starter Signal (+ B)
31	Air Flow Meter Signal	51	Switch Signal
32	Air Flow Meter Signal	52	Knock Sensor Signal
41	Throttle Position Sensor Signal	53	Knock Sensor Signal

DIAGNOSTIC CODES 1985 CELICA

Code	Number of blinks "CHECK ENGINE"	System
1		Normal
2		Air flow meter signal
3		Ignition signal
4		Water thermo sensor signal
5		Ox sensor signal
6		RPM signal (crank angle pulse)
7		Throttle position sensor signal
8		Intake air thermo sensor signal
10		Starter signal
11		Switch signal
12		Knock control sensor signal
13		Knock control CPU (ECU)

DIAGNOSTIC CODES 1986 CELICA; 1986—88

Code No.	Number of "CHECK ENGINE" blinks	System
1	ON ON ON ON ON / OFF OFF OFF OFF F10840	Normal
2	F10841	Air flow meter signal
3	F10842	Ignition signal
4	F10843	Water temp. sensor signal
5	F10844	Oxygen sensor signal
6	F10845	RPM signal
7	F10846	Throttle position sensor signal
8	F10847	Intake air temp. sensor signal
9	F10848	Vehicle speed sensor signal
10	F10849	Starter signal
11	F10850	Switch signal

DIAGNOSTIC CODES 1986 CELICA 1984 CRESSIDA, SUPRA

Code No.	Number of "CHECK ENGINE" blinks	System
—	ON / OFF F11401	Normal
11	F11388	ECU (+B)
12	F11389	RPM signal
13	F11390	RPM signal
14	F11391	Ignition signal
21	F11140	Oxygen sensor signal
22	F11392	Water temp. sensor signal
23	F11393	Intake air temp. sensor signal
31	F11394	Air flow meter signal
32	F11395	Air flow meter signal
41	F11396	Throttle position sensor signal
42	F11397	Vehicle speed sensor signal
43	F11398	Starter signal
51		Switch signal

DIAGNOSTIC CODES 1985—86 SUPRA 1985—88 CRESSIDA

Code No.	System
	Normal
11	ECU (+ B)
12	RPM Signal
13	RPM Signal
14	Ignition Signal
21	Oxygen Sensor Signal

DIAGNOSTIC CODES
1987–88 CELICA, CAMRY

Code No.	Number of "CHECK ENGINE" blinks	System
–	ON _ⅢⅢⅢ_ OFF (F11401)	Normal
11	(F11388)	ECU (+B)
12	(F11389)	RPM signal
13	(F11390)	RPM signal
14	(F11391)	Ignition signal
21	(F11400)	Oxygen sensor signal
22	(F11392)	Water temp. sensor signal
24	(F11611)	Intake air temp. sensor signal
31	(F11394)	Air flow meter signal
32	(F11395)	Air flow meter signal
41	(F11396)	Throttle position sensor signal
42	(F11397)	Vehicle speed sensor signal
43	(F11398)	Starter signal
51	(F11399)	Switch signal

DIAGNOSTIC CODES
1985 TRUCK AND 4 RUNNER

Code	Number of blinks "CHECK ENGINE"	System
1		Normal
2		Air flow meter signal
3		Ignition signal
4		Water thermo sensor signal
5		Ox sensor signal
6		RPM signal (crank angle pulse)
7		Throttle position sensor signal
8		Intake air thermo sensor signal
10		Starter signal
11		Switch signal
12		Knock control sensor signal
13		Knock control CPU (ECU)

DIAGNOSTIC CODES 1986–88
TRUCK AND 4 RUNNER

Code	Number of blinks "CHECK ENGINE"	System
1		Normal
2		Air flow meter signal
3		Ignition signal
4		Water temp. sensor signal
5		Oxygen sensor signal
6		RPM signal (crank angle pulse)
7		Throttle position sensor signal
8		Intake air temp. sensor signal
10		Starter signal
11		Switch signal
12		Knock sensor signal
13		Knock control Part (ECU)
*1 14		Turbocharger pressure

*1 22R-TE only
*2 Abnormalities in the air flow meter may also be detected.

Fuel Injection Systems

INDEX

ACURA/STERLING

ENGINE CONTROL SYSTEM APPLICATION CHART

Year	Model	Engine cc (liter)	Engine VIN	Fuel System	Ignition System
1986	Integra RS,LS	1590 (1.6)	D16A1	PGM-FI	Electronic
	Legend LX	2494 (2.5)	C25A1	PGM-FI	Electronic
	Sterling 825	2494 (2.5)	P	PGM-FI	Electronic
1987	Integra RS,LS	1590 (1.6)	D16A1	PGM-FI	Electronic
	Legend Sedan	2494 (2.5)	C25A1	PGM-FI	Electronic
	Legend Coupe	2675 (2.7)	C27A1	PGM-FI	PGM-IG
	Sterling 825	2494 (2.5)	P	PGM-FI	Electronic
1988	Integra RS,LS	1590 (1.6)	D16A1	PGM-FI	Electronic
	Legend Sedan	2675 (2.7)	C27A1	PGM-FI	PGM-IG
	Legend Coupe	2675 (2.7)	C27A1	PGM-FI	PGM-IG
	Sterling 825	2494 (2.5)	P	PGM-FI	Electronic

PGM-FI Programmed Fuel Injection
PGM-IG Programmed Ignition

PROGRAMMED FUEL INJECTION (PGM-FI) SYSTEM

General Description

Programmed Fuel-Injection (PGM-FI) System consists of three sub-systems: Air intake, electronic control, idle control, fast idle control and fuel supply.

Air Intake System

The system supplies air for all engine needs. It consists of the air cleaner, air intake pipe, throttle body, electronic idle control valve (EICV) system, fast idle mechanism, and intake manifold. A resonator in the air intake pipe provides additional silencing as air is drawn into the system.

THROTTLE BODY

The throttle body is a single- or two-barrel side-draft type. The lower portion of the throttle valve is heated by engine coolant which is led from the cylinder head. The idle adjusting screw which increases/decreases bypass air and the canister/purge port are located on the top of the throttle body. On cars equipped with a manual transmission, a dashpot is used to slow the throttle as it approaches the closed position.

IDLE CONTROL SYSTEM

The idle speed of engine is controlled by the electronic idle control valve (EICV) and the fast idle valve. The valve changes the amount of air bypassing into the intake manifold in response to

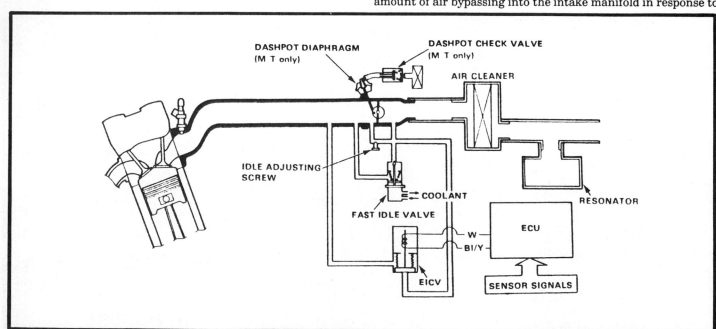

Air intake system—Acura Integra shown, others similar

electric current sent from the ECU. When the EICV is activated, the valve opens to maintain thes proper idle speed.

After the engine starts, the EICV opens for a certain time. The amount of air is increased to raise the idle speed about 0–150 rpm. When the coolant temperature is low, EICV is opened to obtain the proper fast idle speed. The amount of bypassed air is thus controlled in relation to the coolant temperature. When the coolant temperature reaches 86°F (30°C), it also activates the fast idle valve to prevent the idle speed from dropping.

FAST IDLE CONTROL SYSTEM

To prevent erratic running when the engine is warming up, it is necessary to raise the idle speed. The air bypass valve is controlled by a thermowax plunger. When the thermowax is cold, the valve is open. When the thermowax is heated, the valve is closed. With the engine cold and the thermowax consequently cold, additional air is bypassed into the intake manifold so that the engine idles faster than normal. When the engine reaches operating temperature, the valve begins to close, reducing the amount of air bypassing into the manifold.

BYPASS CONTROL SYSTEM

On 1987–88 Acura Legend Coupe and 1988 Legend Sedan use a bypass control system, which utilized two air intake paths are provided in the intake manifold to allow the selection of the intake path length most favorable for a given engine speed.

Satisfactory power performance is achieved by switching the paths. High torque at low rpm is achieved by using the long intake path, whereas high power at high rpm is achieved by using the intake path.

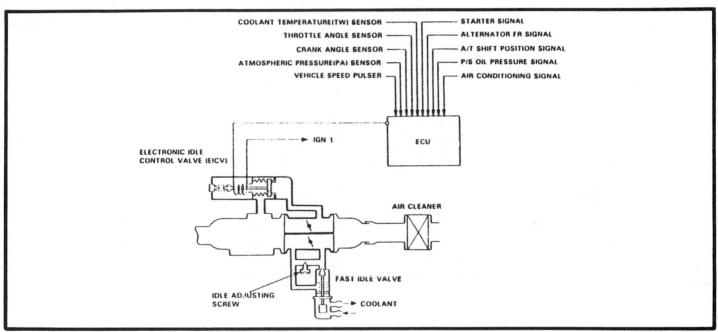

Idle control system—Acura Legend Sedan and Sterling shown, others similar

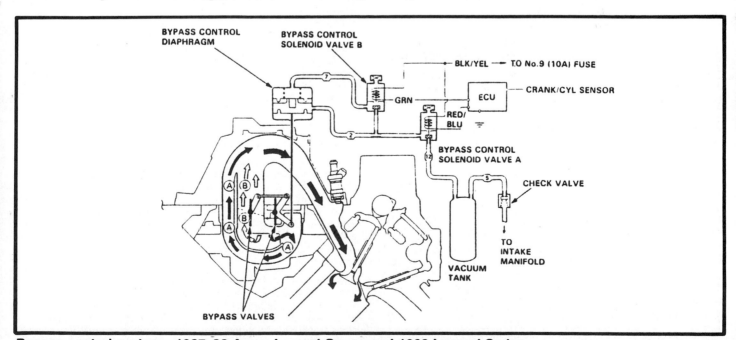

Bypass control system—1987–88 Acura Legend Coupe and 1988 Legend Sedan

Electronic Control System

CONTROL SYSTEM

In order to get fuel into the cylinders at the correct instant and in correct amount, the control system must perform various separate functions. The ECU (Electronic Control Unit), the heart of the PGM-FI, uses an eight-bit microcomputer and consists of a CPU (Central Processing Unit), memories, and I/O (Input/Output) ports. Basic data stored in the memories are compensated by the signals sent from the various sensors to provide the correct air/fuel mixture for all engine needs.

ELECTRONIC CONTROL UNIT (ECU)

The unit contains memories for the basic discharge duration at various engine speeds and manifold pressures. The basic discharge duration, after being read out from the memory, is further modified by signals sent from various sensors to obtain the final discharge duration. Other functions also include:

- Starting Control—The fuel system must vary the air/fuel ratio to suit different operating requirements. For example, the mixture must be rich for starting. The memories also contain the basic discharge durations to be read out by signals from the starter switch, and engine speed and coolant temperature sensors, thereby providing extra fuel needed for starting.
- Fuel Pump Control—When the speed of the engine falls below the prescribed limit, electric current to the fuel pump is cut off, preventing the injectors from discharging fuel.
- Safety—A fail-safe system monitors the sensors and detects any abnormality in the ECU, ensuring safe driving even if one or more sensors are faulty, or if the ECU malfunctions.

CRANK ANGLE SENSOR (TDC/CYL SENSORS)

The sensors are designed as an assembly to save space and weight. The entire unit consist of a pair of rotors, TDC and CYL, and a pickup for each rotor. Since the rotors are coupled to the camshaft, they turn together as a unit as the camshaft rotates. The CYL sensor detects the position of the No. 1 cylinder as the base for the Sequential Injection whereas the TDC sensor serves to determine the injection timing for each cylinder. The TDC sensor is also used to detect engine speed to read out the basic discharge duration for different operating conditions.

MANIFOLD AIR PRESSURE SENSOR (MAP SENSOR)

The sensor converts manifold air pressure readings into electrical voltage signals and sends them to the ECU. This information with signals from the crank angle sensor is then used to read out the basic discharge duration from the memory.

ATMOSPHERIC PRESSURE SENSOR (PA SENSOR)

Like the MAP sensor, the unit converts atmospheric pressures into voltage signals and sends them to the ECU. The signals then modify the basic discharge duration to compensate for changes in the atmospheric pressure.

COOLANT TEMPERATURE SENSOR (TW SENSOR)

The sensor uses a temperature-dependent diode (thermistor) to measure differences in the coolant temperature. The basic discharge duration is read out by the signals sent from this sensor through the ECU. The resistance of the thermister decreases with a rise in coolant temperature.

INTAKE AIR TEMPERATURE SENSOR (TA SENSOR)

This device is also a thermistor and is placed in the intake manifold. It acts much like the water temperature sensor but with a reduced thermal capacity for for quicker response. The basic discharge duration read out from the memory is again compensated for different operating conditions by the signals sent from this sensor through the ECU.

THROTTLE ANGLE SENSOR

This sensor is essentially a variable resistor. In construction, the rotor shaft is connected to the throttle valve shaft such that, as the throttle valve is moved, the resistance varies, altering the output voltage to the control unit.

OXYGEN SENSOR

The oxygen sensor, by detecting the oxygen content in the exhaust gas, maintains the stoichiometric air/fuel ratio. In operation, the ECU receives the signals from the sensor and changes the duration during which fuel is injected. The oxygen sensor is located in the exhaust manifold.

The sensor is a hollow shaft of zirconia with a closed end. The inner and outer surfaces are plated with platinum, thus forming a platinum electrode. The inner surface or chamber is open to the atmosphere whereas the outer surface is exposed to the exhaust gas flow through the manifold.

Voltage is induced at the platinum electrode when there is any difference in oxygen concentration between the two layers of air over the surfaces. Operation of the device is dependent upon the fact that voltage induced changes sharply as the stoichiometric air/fuel ratio is exceeded when the electrode is heated above a certain temperature.

IDLE MIXTURE ADJUSTER SENSOR (IMA SENSOR)

The sensor is located in the control box. The primary objective of this unit is to maintain the correct air/fuel ratio at idling. No adjustment of the IMA sensor is necessary as the feedback control is performed by the oxygen sensors even during idling.

Fuel System

FUEL PUMP

On Acura Integra models, the fuel pump is an in-line, direct drive type. Fuel is drawn into the pump through a filter, flows around the armature through the one-way valve and is delivered to the engine compartment. A baffle is provided to prevent fuel pulsation. The fuel pump has a relief valve to prevent excessive pressure. It opens if there is a blockage in the discharge side. When the relief valve opens, fuel flows from the high pressure to the low pressure side. A check valve is provided to maintain fuel pressure in the line after the pump is stopped. This is to ease restarting.

The pump section is composed of a rotor, rollers and pump spacer. When the rotor turns, the rollers turn and travel along the inner surface of the pump spacer by centrifugal force. The volume of the cavity enclosed by these three parts changes, drawing and pressurizing the fuel.

On Acura Legend and Sterling models, the fuel pump is a compact impeller design and is installed inside the fuel tank, thereby saving space and simplifying the fuel line system.

The fuel pump is comprised of a DC motor, a circumference flow pump, a relief valve for protecting the fuel line systems, a check valve for retaining residual pressure, an inlet port, and a discharge port. The pump assembly consists of the impeller (driven by the motor), the pump casing (which forms the pumping chamber), and cover of the pump.

PRESSURE REGULATOR

The fuel pressure regulator maintains a constant fuel pressure to the injectors. The spring chamber of the pressure regulator is connected to the intake manifold to constantly maintain the fuel pressure at 36–41 PSI (250–279 kPa) higher than the pressure in the manifold. When the difference between the fuel pressure and manifold pressure exceeds 36–41 PSI (250–279 kPa), the diaphragm is pushed upward, and the excess fuel is fed back into the fuel tank through the return line.

INJECTOR

The injector is of the solenoid-actuated constant-stroke pintle type consisting of a solenoid, plunger, needle valve and housing. When current is applied to the solenoid coil, the valve lifts up and pressurized fuel fills the inside of the injector and is injected close to the intake valve. Because the needle valve lifts and the fuel pressure are constant, the injection quantity is determined by; the length of time that the valve is open, i.e., the duration the current is supplied to the solenoid coil. The injector is sealed by an O-ring and seal ring at the top and bottom. These seals also reduce operating noise.

RESISTOR

The injector timing, which controls the opening and closing intervals, must be very accurate since it dictates the air/fuel mixture ratio. The injector must also be durable. For the best possible injector response, it is necessary to shorten the current rise time when voltage is applied to the injector coil. Therefore, the number of windings of the injector coil is reduced to reduce the inductance in the coil. This, however, makes low resistance in the coil, allowing a large amount of current to flow through the coil. As a result, the amount of heat generated is high, which compromises the durability of the coil. Flow of current in the coil is therefore restricted by a resistor installed in series between the electric power source and the injector coil.

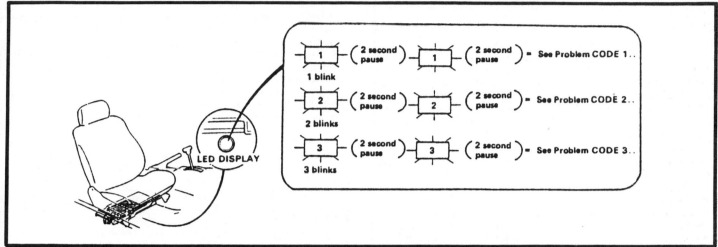

ECU location and self-diagnostic LED display—1986–88 Acura Integra

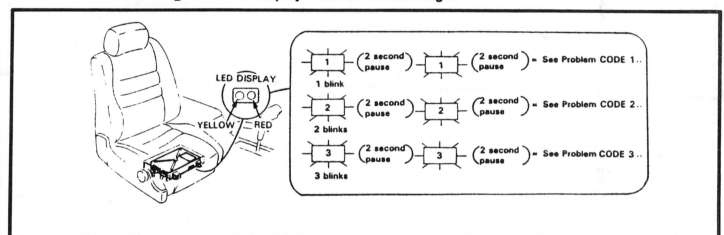

ECU location and self-diagnostic LED display—1986–88 Acura Legend Sedan and Sterling

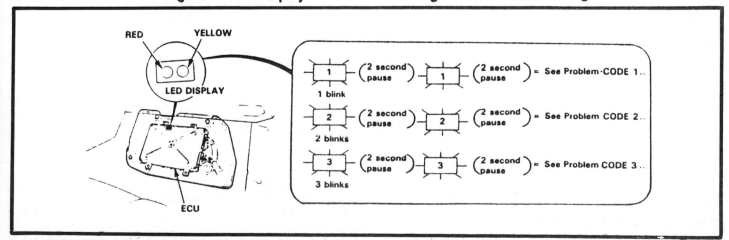

ECU location and self-diagnostic LED display—1987–88 Acura Legend Coupe

MAIN RELAY

The main relay is a direct coupler type which contains the relays for the electronic control unit power supply and the fuel pump power supply. This relay is installed behind the fuse box.

SELF-DIAGNOSIS INDICATOR BLINKS	SYSTEM INDICATED
0	ECU
1	OXYGEN CONTENT
3	MANIFOLD ABSOLUTE PRESSURE
5	
6	COOLANT TEMPERATURE
7	THROTTLE ANGLE
8	CRANK ANGLE (TDC)
9	CRANK ANGLE (CYL)
10	INTAKE AIR TEMPERATURE
13	ATMOSPHERIC PRESSURE
14	ELECTRONIC IDLE CONTROL

ECU self-diagnostic code identification—1986–88 Acura Integra

SELF-DIAGNOSIS INDICATOR BLINKS	SYSTEM INDICATED
0	ECU
1	FRONT OXYGEN CONTENT
2	REAR OXYGEN CONTENT
3	MANIFOLD ABSOLUTE PRESSURE
5	
6	COOLANT TEMPERATURE
7	THROTTLE ANGLE
8	CRANK ANGLE (TDC)
9	CRANK ANGLE (CYL)
10	INTAKE AIR TEMPERATURE
11	IMA
12	EXHAUST GAS RECIRCULATION SYSTEM
13	ATMOSPHERIC PRESSURE
14	ELECTRONIC IDLE CONTROL

ECU self-diagnostic code identification—1986–87 Acura Legend Sedan and 1986–88 Sterling

SERVICE PRECAUTIONS

- Do not operate the fuel pump when the fuel lines are empty.
- Do not reuse fuel hose clamps.
- Make sure all ECU harness connectors are fastened securely. A poor connection can cause an extremely high surge voltage in the coil and condenser and result in damage to integrated circuits.
- Keep ECU all parts and harnesses dry during service.
- Before attempting to remove any parts, turn off the ignition switch and disconnect the battery ground cable.
- Always use a 12 volt battery as a power source.
- Do not attempt to disconnect the battery cables with the engine running.
- Do not depress the accelerator pedal when starting.
- Do not rev up the engine immediately after starting or just prior to shutdown.
- Do not apply battery power directly to injectors.

SELF-DIAGNOSIS INDICATOR BLINKS	SYSTEM INDICATED
0	ECU
1	FRONT OXYGEN CONTENT
2	REAR OXYGEN CONTENT
3	MANIFOLD ABSOLUTE PRESSURE
5	
4	CRANK ANGLE
6	COOLANT TEMPERATURE
7	THROTTLE ANGLE
8	TDC POSITION
9	No.1 CYLINDER POSITION
10	INTAKE AIR TEMPERATURE
12	EXHAUST GAS RECIRCULATION SYSTEM
13	ATMOSPHERIC PRESSURE
14	ELECTRONIC IDLE CONTROL
15	IGNITION OUTPUT SIGNAL
17	VEHICLE SPEED PULSER
18	IGNITION TIMING ADJUSTMENT

ECU self-diagnostic code identification—1987–88 Acura Legend Coupe and 1988 Legend Sedan

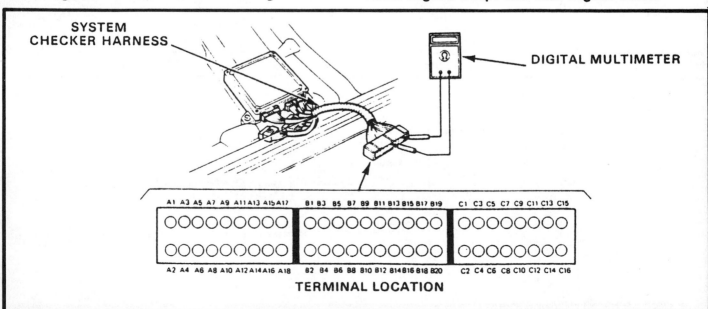

ECU terminal identification and diagnostic tools

Diagnosis and Testing

SELF-DIAGNOSTIC SYSTEM

Self-Diagnosis Indicators

The quick reference chart covers the most common failure modes for the PGM-FI. The probable causes are listed in order of most-easily-checked first, then progressing to more difficult fixes. Run through all the causes listed. If problem is still unsolved, go on to the more detailed troubleshooting. Troubleshooting is divided into different LED displays. Find the correct light display and begin again.

For all the conditions listed, the PGM-FI warning light on the dashboard must be on (comes on and stays on). This indicates a problem in the electrical portion of the fuel injection system. At that time, check the LED display (self-diagnosis system) in the ECU.

On 1986–88 Acura Integra model, there is only one LED display. The LED will blink consecutively to indicate the trouble code. The ECU is located under the passenger's seat.

On 1986–88 Acura Legend and Sterling models, there are two LED displays. The yellow LED display is for idle speed adjustment check. The red LED display will blink consecutively to indicate the trouble code. The ECU is located under the passenger's seat on the 1986–88 Acura Legend Sedan and Sterling. On the 1987–88 Acura Legend Coupe, the ECU is located under the floor kick panel in front of the passanger seat.

Sometimes the dash warning light and/or ECU LED will come on, indicating a system problem, when, in fact, there is only a bad or intermittent electrical connection. To troubleshoot a bad connection, note the ECU LED pattern that is lit, refer to the diagnosis chart and check the connectors associated with the items mentioned in the "Possible Cause" column for that LED pattern (disconnect, clean or repair if necessary and reconnect those connections). Then, reset the ECU memory as described, restart the car and drive it for a few minutes and then recheck the car and drive it for a few minutes and then recheck the LED(s). If the same pattern lights up, begin system troubleshooting; if it does not light up, the problem was only a bad connection.

The memory for the PGM-FI warning light on the dashboard will be erased when the ignition switch is turned off; however, the memory for the LED display will not be cancelled. Thus, the warning light will not come on when the ignition switch is again turned on unless the trouble is once more detected. Troubleshooting should be done according to the LED display even if the warning light is off.

Other ECU information:

• After making repairs, disconnect the battery negative cable from the battery negative terminal for at least 10 seconds and reset the ECU memory. After reconnecting the cable, check that the LED display is turned off.

• Turn the ignition switch on. The PGM-FI warning light should come on for about 2 seconds. If the warning light won't come on, check for:
— Blown warning light bulb
— Blown fuse (causing faulty back up light, seat belt alarm, clock, memory function of the car radio)
— Open circuit in Yellow wire between fuse and combination meter

• After the PGM-FI warning light and self-diagnosis indicators have been turned on, turn the ignition switch off. If the LED display fails to come on when the ignition switch is turned on again, check for:
— Blown fuse
— Open circuit in wire between ECU A17 terminal and fuse

• Replace the ECU only after making sure that all couplers and connectors are connected securely.

DIAGNOSTIC TREE CHARTS

ECU DIAGNOSTIC CHART—1986–88 ACURA INTEGRA

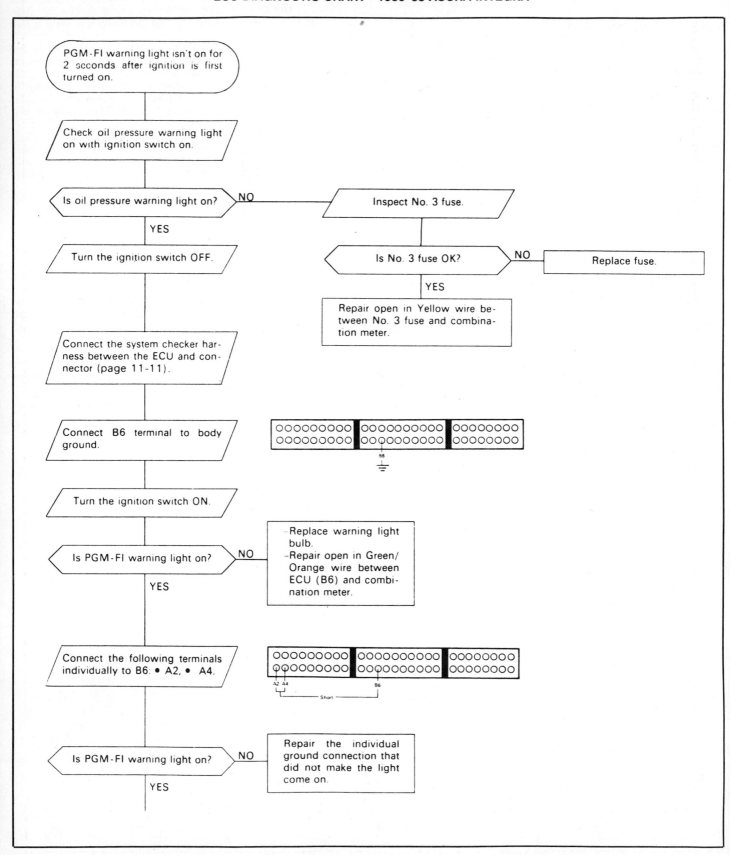

PGM-FI warning light isn't on for 2 seconds after ignition is first turned on.

Check oil pressure warning light on with ignition switch on.

Is oil pressure warning light on? — NO → Inspect No. 3 fuse.

YES

Turn the ignition switch OFF.

Is No. 3 fuse OK? — NO → Replace fuse.

YES

Repair open in Yellow wire between No. 3 fuse and combination meter.

Connect the system checker harness between the ECU and connector (page 11-11).

Connect B6 terminal to body ground.

Turn the ignition switch ON.

Is PGM-FI warning light on? — NO → - Replace warning light bulb.
- Repair open in Green/Orange wire between ECU (B6) and combination meter.

YES

Connect the following terminals individually to B6: • A2, • A4.

Is PGM-FI warning light on? — NO → Repair the individual ground connection that did not make the light come on.

YES

ECU DIAGNOSTIC CHART—1986–88 ACURA INTEGRA

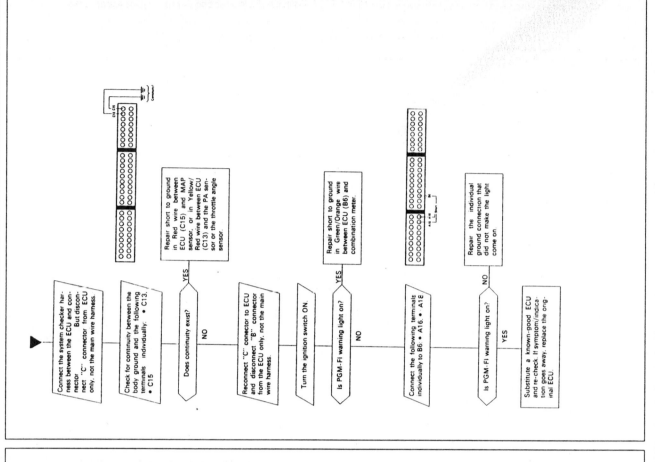

ECU DIAGNOSTIC CHART—1986–88 ACURA INTEGRA

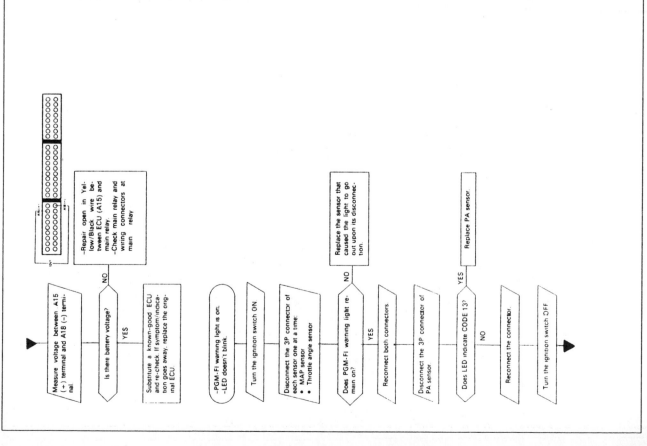

OXYGEN SENSOR DIAGNOSTIC CHART—1986–88 ACURA INTEGRA

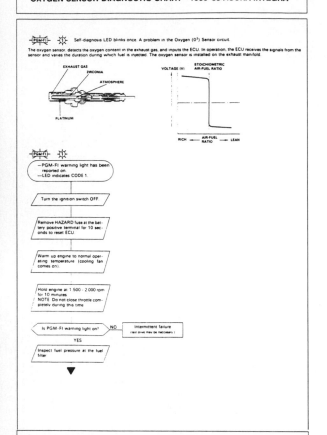

MAP SENSOR DIAGNOSTIC CHART—1986–88 ACURA INTEGRA

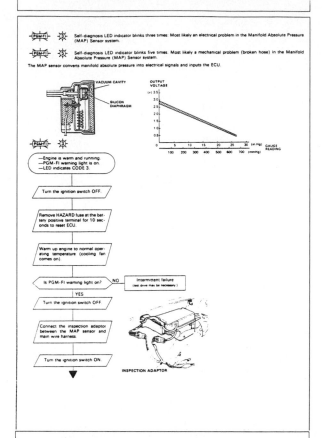

OXYGEN SENSOR DIAGNOSTIC CHART—1986–88 ACURA INTEGRA

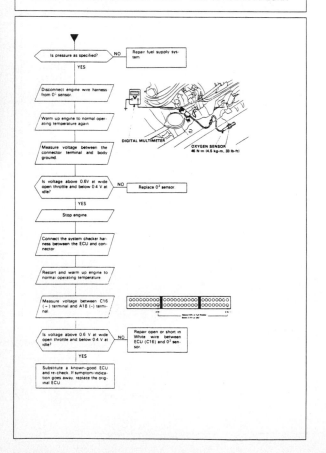

MAP SENSOR DIAGNOSTIC CHART—1986–88 ACURA INTEGRA

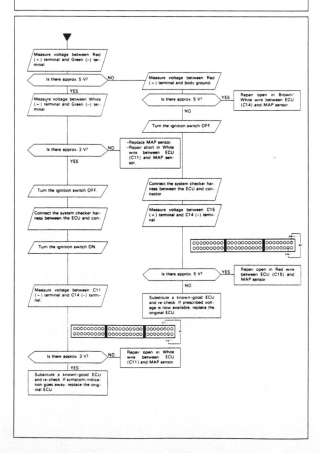

MAP SENSOR DIAGNOSTIC CHART – 1986–88 ACURA INTEGRA

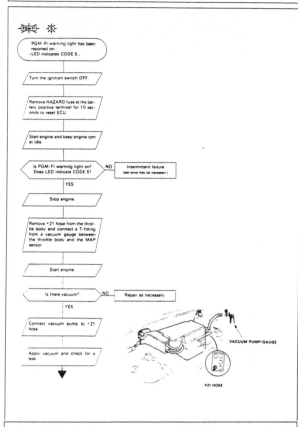

[PGM-FI] [☀]

PGM-FI warning light has been reported on.
-LED indicates CODE 5.

Turn the ignition switch OFF.

Remove HAZARD fuse at the battery positive terminal for 10 seconds to reset ECU.

Start engine and keep engine rpm at idle.

Is PGM-FI warning light on? Does LED indicate CODE 5? — NO → Intermittent failure (test drive may be necessary)

YES

Stop engine.

Remove #21 hose from the throttle body and connect a T-fitting from a vacuum gauge between the throttle body and the MAP sensor.

Start engine.

Is there vacuum? — NO → Repair as necessary.

YES

Connect vacuum pump to #21 hose.

Apply vacuum and check for a leak.

VACUUM PUMP/GAUGE

#21 HOSE

MAP SENSOR DIAGNOSTIC CHART – 1986–88 ACURA INTEGRA

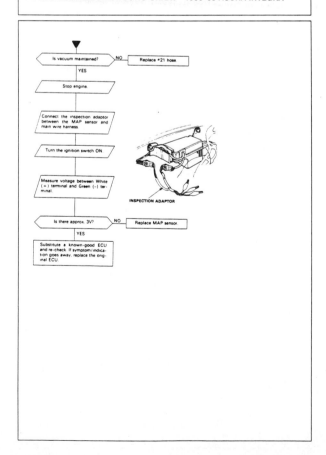

Is vacuum maintained? — NO → Replace #21 hose

YES

Stop engine.

Connect the inspection adaptor between the MAP sensor and main wire harness.

Turn the ignition switch ON.

Measure voltage between White (+) terminal and Green (-) terminal.

INSPECTION ADAPTOR

Is there approx. 3V? — NO → Replace MAP sensor.

YES

Substitute a known-good ECU and re-check. If symptom/indication goes away, replace the original ECU.

TW SENSOR DIAGNOSTIC CHART – 1986–88 ACURA INTEGRA

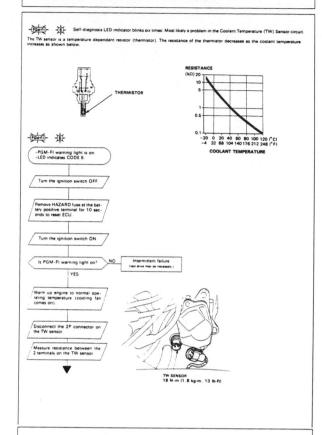

[PGM-FI] [6] Self-diagnosis LED indicator blinks six times: Most likely a problem in the Coolant Temperature (TW) Sensor circuit.
The TW sensor is a temperature dependant resistor (thermistor). The resistance of the thermistor decreases as the coolant temperature increases as shown below.

THERMISTOR

RESISTANCE (kΩ) 20 10 5 1 0.5 0.1
-20 0 20 40 60 80 100 120 (°C)
-4 32 68 104 140 176 212 248 (°F)
COOLANT TEMPERATURE

[PGM-FI] [6]

PGM-FI warning light is on.
-LED indicates CODE 6.

Turn the ignition switch OFF.

Remove HAZARD fuse at the battery positive terminal for 10 seconds to reset ECU.

Turn the ignition switch ON.

Is PGM-FI warning light on? — NO → Intermittent failure (test drive may be necessary)

YES

Warm up engine to normal operating temperature (cooling fan comes on).

Disconnect the 2P connector on the TW sensor.

Measure resistance between the 2 terminals on the TW sensor.

TW SENSOR
18 N·m (1.8 kg-m, 13 lb-ft)

TW SENSOR DIAGNOSTIC CHART – 1986–88 ACURA INTEGRA

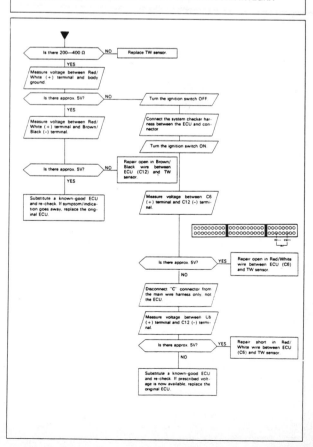

Is there 200—400 Ω? — NO → Replace TW sensor.

YES

Measure voltage between Red/White (+) terminal and body ground.

Is there approx. 5V? — NO → Turn the ignition switch OFF.

YES

Measure voltage between Red/White (+) terminal and Brown/Black (-) terminal.

Is there approx. 5V? — NO → Connect the system checker harness between the ECU and connector.

Turn the ignition switch ON.

Repair open in Brown/Black wire between ECU (C12) and TW sensor.

Substitute a known-good ECU and re-check. If symptom/indication goes away, replace the original ECU.

Measure voltage between C6 (+) terminal and C12 (-) terminal.

Is there approx. 5V? — YES → Repair open in Red/White wire between ECU (C6) and TW sensor.

NO

Disconnect "C" connector from the main wire harness only, not the ECU.

Measure voltage between Lb (+) terminal and C12 (-) terminal.

Is there approx. 5V? — YES → Repair short in Red/White wire between ECU (C6) and TW sensor.

NO

Substitute a known-good ECU and re-check. If prescribed voltage is now available, replace the original ECU.

THROTTLE ANGLE SENSOR DIAGNOSTIC CHART
1986–88 ACURA INTEGRA

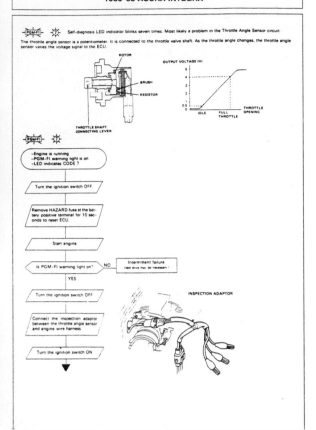

PGM-FI — Self-diagnosis LED indicator blinks seven times. Most likely a problem in the Throttle Angle Sensor circuit.

The throttle angle sensor is a potentiometer. It is connected to the throttle valve shaft. As the throttle angle changes, the throttle angle sensor varies the voltage signal to the ECU.

ROTOR
BRUSH
RESISTOR
THROTTLE SHAFT CONNECTING LEVER

OUTPUT VOLTAGE (V)

IDLE / FULL THROTTLE / THROTTLE OPENING

PGM-FI —
- Engine is running
- PGM-FI warning light is on
- LED indicates CODE 7

Turn the ignition switch OFF.

Remove HAZARD fuse at the battery positive terminal for 10 seconds to reset ECU.

Start engine.

Is PGM-FI warning light on? — NO → Intermittent failure (test drive may be necessary.)

YES

Turn the ignition switch OFF.

INSPECTION ADAPTOR

Connect the inspection adaptor between the throttle angle sensor and engine wire harness.

Turn the ignition switch ON.

CRANK ANGLE SENSOR DIAGNOSTIC CHART
1986–88 ACURA INTEGRA

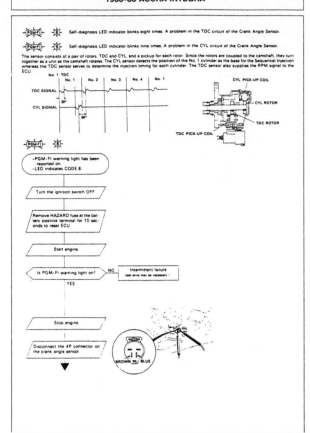

PGM-FI — 8 — Self-diagnosis LED indicator blinks eight times. A problem in the TDC circuit of the Crank Angle Sensor.

PGM-FI — 9 — Self-diagnosis LED indicator blinks nine times. A problem in the CYL circuit of the Crank Angle Sensor.

The sensor consists of a pair of rotors, TDC and CYL, and a pickup for each rotor. Since the rotors are coupled to the camshaft, they turn together as a unit as the camshaft rotates. The CYL sensor detects the position of the No. 1 cylinder as the base for the Sequential Injection whereas the TDC sensor serves to determine the injection timing for each cylinder. The TDC sensor also supplies the RPM signal to the ECU.

No. 1 TDC
TDC SIGNAL
CYL SIGNAL
CYL PICK-UP COIL
CYL ROTOR
TDC PICK-UP COIL
TDC ROTOR

PGM-FI —
- PGM-FI warning light has been reported on.
- LED indicates CODE 8.

Turn the ignition switch OFF.

Remove HAZARD fuse at the battery positive terminal for 10 seconds to reset ECU.

Start engine.

Is PGM-FI warning light on? — NO → Intermittent failure (test drive may be necessary.)

YES

Stop engine.

Disconnect the 4P connector on the crank angle sensor.

BROWN / BLUE

THROTTLE ANGLE SENSOR DIAGNOSTIC CHART
1986–88 ACURA INTEGRA

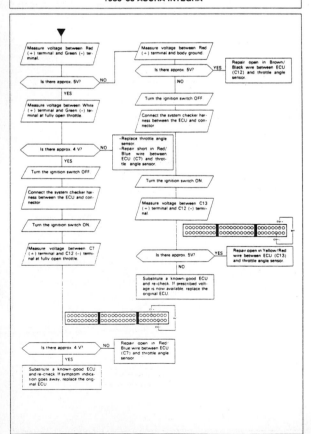

Measure voltage between Red (+) terminal and Green (−) terminal.

Is there approx. 5V? — NO →

Measure voltage between Red (+) terminal and body ground.

Is there approx. 5V? — YES → Repair open in Brown/Black wire between ECU (C12) and throttle angle sensor.

NO

Turn the ignition switch OFF.

Connect the system checker harness between the ECU and connector.

Turn the ignition switch ON.

Measure voltage between C13 (+) terminal and C12 (−) terminal.

YES

Measure voltage between White (+) terminal and Green (−) terminal at fully open throttle.

Is there approx. 4 V? — NO →

- Replace throttle angle sensor.
- Repair short in Red/Blue wire between ECU (C7) and throttle angle sensor.

YES

Turn the ignition switch OFF.

Connect the system checker harness between the ECU and connector.

Turn the ignition switch ON.

Measure voltage between C7 (+) terminal and C12 (−) terminal at fully open throttle.

Is there approx. 5V? — YES → Repair open in Yellow/Red wire between ECU (C13) and throttle angle sensor.

Substitute a known-good ECU and re-check. If prescribed voltage is now available, replace the original ECU.

Is there approx. 4 V? — NO → Repair open in Red/Blue wire between ECU (C7) and throttle angle sensor.

YES

Substitute a known-good ECU and re-check. If symptom indication goes away, replace the original ECU.

CRANK ANGLE SENSOR DIAGNOSTIC CHART
1986–88 ACURA INTEGRA

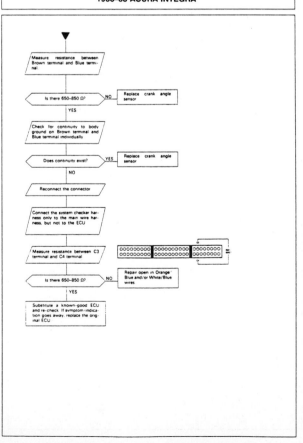

Measure resistance between Brown terminal and Blue terminal.

Is there 650–850 Ω? — NO → Replace crank angle sensor.

YES

Check for continuity to body ground on Brown terminal and Blue terminal individually.

Does continuity exist? — YES → Replace crank angle sensor.

NO

Reconnect the connector.

Connect the system checker harness only to the main wire harness, but not to the ECU.

Measure resistance between C3 terminal and C4 terminal.

Is there 650–850 Ω? — NO → Repair open in Orange/Blue and/or White/Blue wires.

YES

Substitute a known-good ECU and re-check. If symptom indication goes away, replace the original ECU.

CRANK ANGLE SENSOR DIAGNOSTIC CHART
1986–88 ACURA INTEGRA

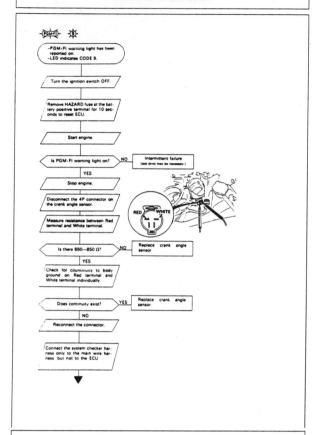

-PGM-FI- 🔆

- PGM-FI warning light has been reported on.
- LED indicates CODE 9.

→ Turn the ignition switch OFF.

→ Remove HAZARD fuse at the battery positive terminal for 10 seconds to reset ECU.

→ Start engine.

→ Is PGM-FI warning light on? —NO→ Intermittent failure (test drive may be necessary)

↓ YES

→ Stop engine.

→ Disconnect the 4P connector on the crank angle sensor.

→ Measure resistance between Red terminal and White terminal.

→ Is there 650—850 Ω? —NO→ Replace crank angle sensor

↓ YES

→ Check for continuity to body ground on Red terminal and White terminal individually.

→ Does continuity exist? —YES→ Replace crank angle sensor

↓ NO

→ Reconnect the connector.

→ Connect the system checker harness only to the main wire harness but not to the ECU.

CRANK ANGLE SENSOR DIAGNOSTIC CHART
1986–88 ACURA INTEGRA

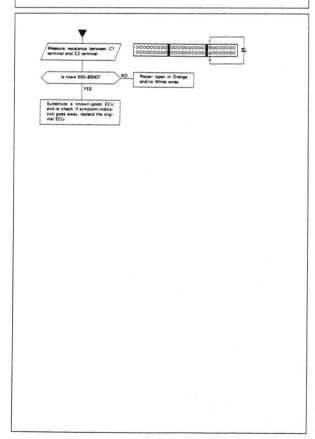

→ Measure resistance between C1 terminal and C2 terminal.

→ Is there 650–850Ω? —NO→ Repair open in Orange and/or White wires.

↓ YES

Substitute a known-good ECU and re-check. If symptom/indication goes away, replace the original ECU.

TA SENSOR DIAGNOSTIC CHART
1986–88 ACURA INTEGRA

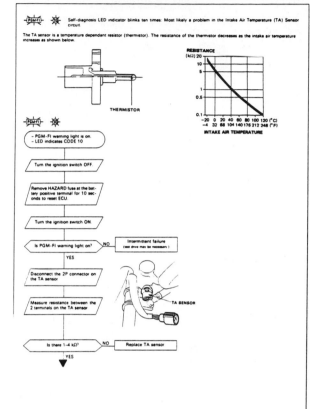

-PGM-FI- 🔆 Self-diagnosis LED indicator blinks ten times: Most likely a problem in the Intake Air Temperature (TA) Sensor circuit.

The TA sensor is a temperature dependant resistor (thermistor). The resistance of the thermistor decreases as the intake air temperature increases as shown below.

THERMISTOR

RESISTANCE (kΩ)

INTAKE AIR TEMPERATURE

-PGM-FI- 🔆

- PGM-FI warning light is on.
- LED indicates CODE 10.

→ Turn the ignition switch OFF.

→ Remove HAZARD fuse at the battery positive terminal for 10 seconds to reset ECU.

→ Turn the ignition switch ON.

→ Is PGM-FI warning light on? —NO→ Intermittent failure (test drive may be necessary)

↓ YES

→ Disconnect the 2P connector on the TA sensor.

TA SENSOR

→ Measure resistance between the 2 terminals on the TA sensor.

→ Is there 1–4 kΩ? —NO→ Replace TA sensor

↓ YES

TA SENSOR DIAGNOSTIC CHART – 1986–88 ACURA INTEGRA

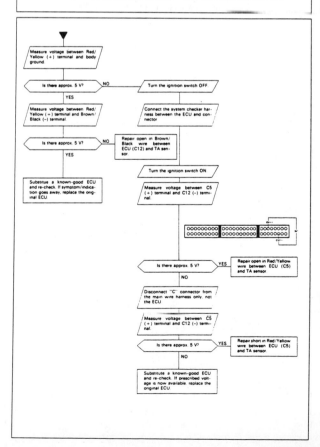

→ Measure voltage between Red/Yellow (+) terminal and body ground.

→ Is there approx. 5 V? —NO→ Turn the ignition switch OFF.

↓ YES

→ Measure voltage between Red/Yellow (+) terminal and Brown/Black (–) terminal.

↓   → Connect the system checker harness between the ECU and connector

→ Is there approx. 5 V? —NO→ Repair open in Brown/Black wire between ECU (C12) and TA sensor

↓ YES

Substitute a known-good ECU and re-check. If symptom/indication goes away, replace the original ECU.

→ Turn the ignition switch ON.

→ Measure voltage between C5 (+) terminal and C12 (–) terminal.

→ Is there approx. 5 V? —YES→ Repair open in Red/Yellow wire between ECU (C5) and TA sensor.

↓ NO

→ Disconnect "C" connector from the main wire harness only, not the ECU.

→ Measure voltage between C5 (+) terminal and C12 (–) terminal.

→ Is there approx. 5 V? —YES→ Repair short in Red/Yellow wire between ECU (C5) and TA sensor.

↓ NO

Substitue a known-good ECU and re-check. If prescribed voltage is now available, replace the original ECU.

PA SENSOR DIAGNOSTIC CHART—1986–88 ACURA INTEGRA

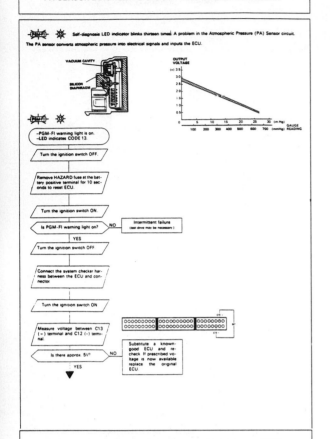

EICV DIAGNOSTIC CHART—1986–88 ACURA INTEGRA

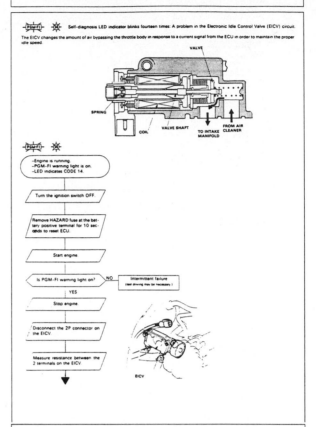

PA SENSOR DIAGNOSTIC CHART—1986–88 ACURA INTEGRA

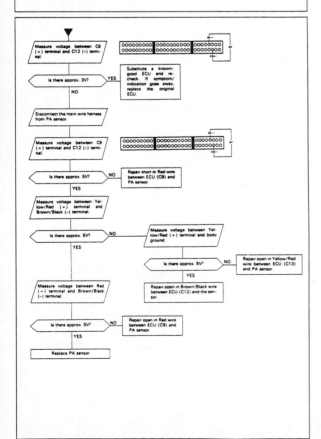

EICV DIAGNOSTIC CHART—1986–88 ACURA INTEGRA

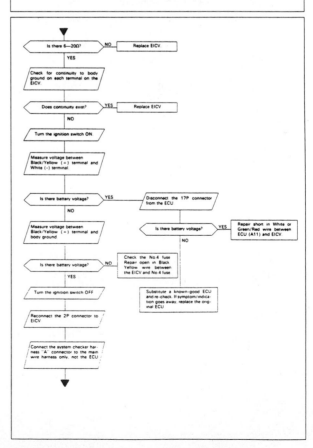

EICV DIAGNOSTIC CHART—1986–88 ACURA INTEGRA

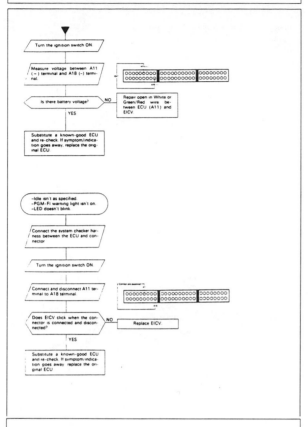

Turn the ignition switch ON.

Measure voltage between A11 (–) terminal and A18 (–) terminal.

Is there battery voltage? → NO → Repair open in White or Green/Red wire between ECU (A11) and EICV.

YES

Substitute a known-good ECU and re-check. If symptom/indication goes away, replace the original ECU.

–Idle isn't as specified.
–PGM-FI warning light isn't on.
–LED doesn't blink.

Connect the system checker harness between the ECU and connector.

Turn the ignition switch ON.

Connect and disconnect A11 terminal to A18 terminal.

Does EICV click when the connector is connected and disconnected? → NO → Replace EICV.

YES

Substitute a known-good ECU and re-check. If symptom/indication goes away, replace the original ECU.

STARTER SIGNAL DIAGNOSTIC CHART—1986–88 ACURA INTEGRA

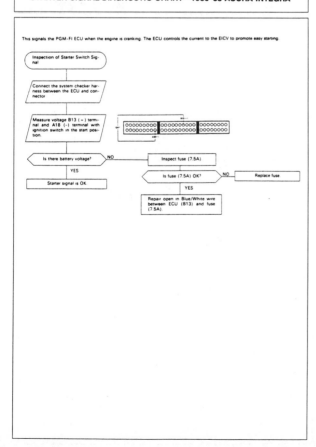

This signals the PGM-FI ECU when the engine is cranking. The ECU controls the current to the EICV to promote easy starting.

Inspection of Starter Switch Signal.

Connect the system checker harness between the ECU and connector.

Measure voltage B13 (+) terminal and A18 (–) terminal with ignition switch in the start position.

Is there battery voltage? → NO → Inspect fuse (7.5A).

YES

Starter signal is OK.

Is fuse (7.5A) OK? → NO → Replace fuse.

YES

Repair open in Blue/White wire between ECU (B13) and fuse (7.5A).

ALTERNATOR FR SIGNAL DIAGNOSTIC CHART
1986–88 ACURA INTEGRA

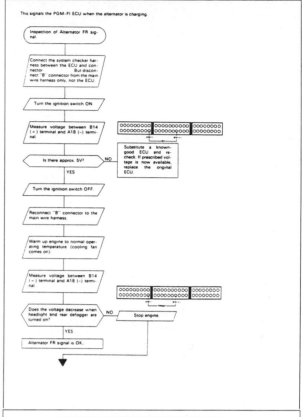

This signals the PGM-FI ECU when the alternator is charging.

Inspection of Alternator FR signal.

Connect the system checker harness between the ECU and connector. But disconnect "B" connector from the main wire harness only, not the ECU.

Turn the ignition switch ON.

Measure voltage between B14 (+) terminal and A18 (–) terminal.

Is there approx. 5V? → NO → Substitute a known-good ECU and re-check. If prescribed voltage is now available, replace the original ECU.

YES

Turn the ignition switch OFF.

Reconnect "B" connector to the main wire harness.

Warm up engine to normal operating temperature (cooling fan comes on).

Measure voltage between B14 (–) terminal and A18 (–) terminal.

Does the voltage decrease when headlight and rear defogger are turned on? → NO → Stop engine.

YES

Alternator FR signal is OK.

ALTERNATOR FR SIGNAL DIAGNOSTIC CHART
1986–88 ACURA INTEGRA

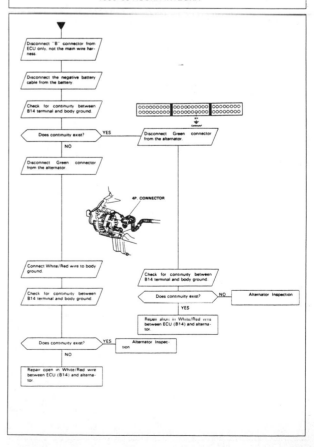

Disconnect "B" connector from ECU only, not the main wire harness.

Disconnect the negative battery cable from the battery.

Check for continuity between B14 terminal and body ground.

Does continuity exist? → YES → Disconnect Green connector from the alternator.

NO

Disconnect Green connector from the alternator.

4P. CONNECTOR

Connect White/Red wire to body ground.

Check for continuity between B14 terminal and body ground.

Check for continuity between B14 terminal and body ground.

Does continuity exist? → NO → Alternator Inspection.

YES

Repair short in White/Red wire between ECU (B14) and alternator.

Does continuity exist? → YES → Alternator Inspection.

NO

Repair open in White/Red wire between ECU (B14) and alternator.

A/T SHIFT POSITION SIGNAL DIAGNOSTIC CHART
1986–88 ACURA INTEGRA

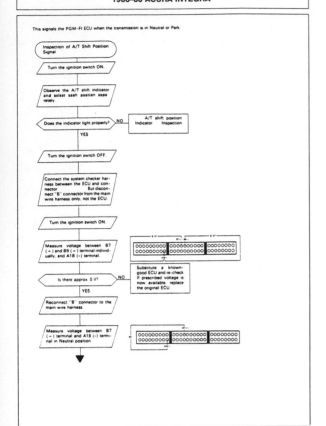

A/T SHIFT POSITION SIGNAL DIAGNOSTIC CHART
1986–88 ACURA INTEGRA

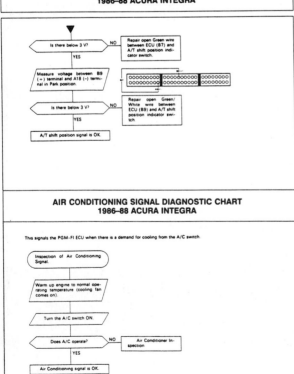

AIR CONDITIONING SIGNAL DIAGNOSTIC CHART
1986–88 ACURA INTEGRA

VEHICLE SPEED SIGNAL DIAGNOSTIC CHART
1986–88 ACURA INTEGRA

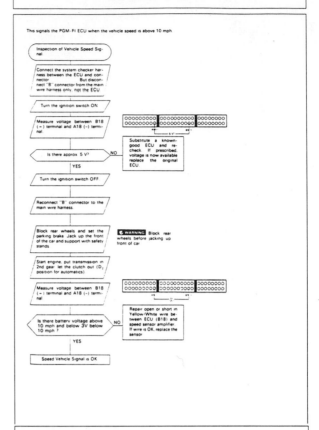

ECU DIAGNOSTIC CHART
1986–87 ACURA LEGEND SEDAN AND 1986–88 STERLING

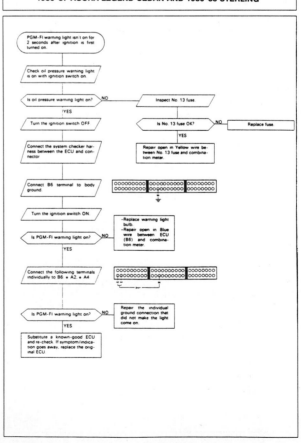

ECU DIAGNOSTIC CHART
1986–87 ACURA LEGEND SEDAN AND 1986–88 STERLING

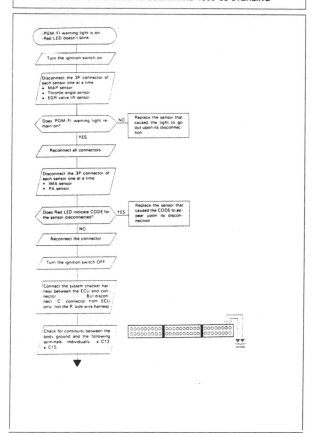

- PGM-FI warning light is on
- Red LED doesn't blink

Turn the ignition switch on

Disconnect the 3P connector of each sensor one at a time
- MAP sensor
- Throttle angle sensor
- EGR valve lift sensor

Does PGM-FI warning light remain on? — NO → Replace the sensor that caused the light to go out upon its disconnection.

YES

Reconnect all connectors

Disconnect the 3P connector of each sensor one at a time
- IMA sensor
- PA sensor

Does Red LED indicate CODE for the sensor disconnected? — YES → Replace the sensor that caused the CODE to appear upon its disconnection.

NO

Reconnect the connector

Turn the ignition switch OFF

Connect the system checker harness between the ECU and connector. But disconnect 'C' connector from ECU only not the R side wire harness

Check for continuity between the body ground and the following terminals individually • C13. • C15.

OXYGEN SENSOR DIAGNOSTIC CHART
1986–87 ACURA LEGEND SEDAN AND 1986–88 STERLING

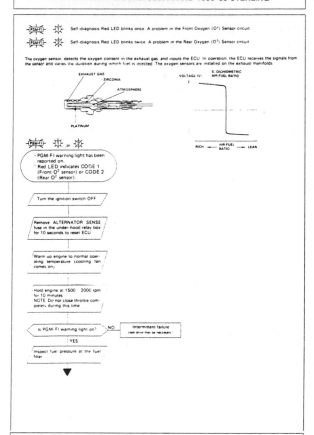

Self-diagnosis Red LED blinks once A problem in the Front Oxygen (O_2) Sensor circuit

Self-diagnosis Red LED blinks twice A problem in the Rear Oxygen (O_2) Sensor circuit

The oxygen sensor, detects the oxygen content in the exhaust gas, and inputs the ECU. In operation, the ECU receives the signals from the sensor and varies the duration during which fuel is injected. The oxygen sensors are installed on the exhaust manifolds

- PGM-FI warning light has been reported on.
- Red LED indicates CODE 1 (Front O_2 sensor) or CODE 2 (Rear O_2 sensor).

Turn the ignition switch OFF

Remove ALTERNATOR SENSE fuse in the under-hood relay box for 10 seconds to reset ECU

Warm up engine to normal operating temperature (cooling fan comes on).

Hold engine at 1500–2000 rpm for 10 minutes
NOTE Do not close throttle completely during this time

Is PGM-FI warning light on? — NO → Intermittent failure (test drive may be necessary)

YES

Inspect fuel pressure at the fuel filter

ECU DIAGNOSTIC CHART
1986–87 ACURA LEGEND SEDAN AND 1986–88 STERLING

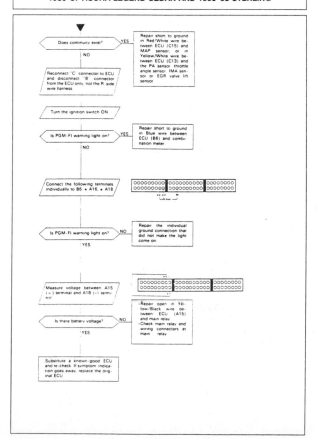

Does continuity exist? — YES → Repair short to ground in Red/White wire between ECU (C15) and MAP sensor, or in Yellow/White wire between ECU (C13) and the PA sensor throttle angle sensor, IMA sensor or EGR valve lift sensor

NO

Reconnect 'C' connector to ECU and disconnect 'B' connector from the ECU only, not the R side wire harness

Turn the ignition switch ON

Is PGM-FI warning light on? — YES → Repair short to ground in Blue wire between ECU (B6) and combination meter.

NO

Connect the following terminals individually to B6 • A16, • A18

Is PGM-FI warning light on? — NO → Repair the individual ground connection that did not make the light come on.

YES

Measure voltage between A15 (–) terminal and A18 (–) terminal

Is there battery voltage? — NO → Repair open in Yellow/Black wire between ECU (A15) and main relay. Check main relay and wiring connectors at main relay.

YES

Substitute a known-good ECU and re-check. If symptom indication goes away. replace the original ECU.

OXYGEN SENSOR DIAGNOSTIC CHART
1986–87 ACURA LEGEND SEDAN AND 1986–88 STERLING

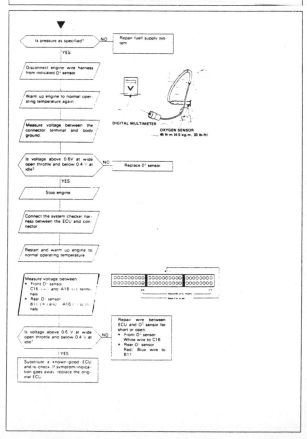

Is pressure as specified? — NO → Repair fuel supply system

YES

Disconnect engine wire harness from indicated O_2 sensor

Warm up engine to normal operating temperature again

Measure voltage between the connector terminal and body ground.

Is voltage above 0.6V at wide open throttle and below 0.4 V at idle? — NO → Replace O_2 sensor

YES

Stop engine

Connect the system checker harness between the ECU and connector

Restart and warm up engine to normal operating temperature

Measure voltage between:
- Front O_2 sensor C16 (–) and A18 (–) terminals
- Rear O_2 sensor B11 (–) and A16 (–) terminals

Is voltage above 0.6 V at wide open throttle and below 0.4 V at idle? — NO → Repair wire between ECU and O_2 sensor for short or open
- Front O_2 sensor White wire to C16
- Rear O_2 sensor Red: Blue wire to B11

YES

Substitute a known-good ECU and re-check. If symptom indication goes away, replace the original ECU.

MAP SENSOR DIAGNOSTIC CHART
1986–87 ACURA LEGEND SEDAN AND 1986–88 STERLING

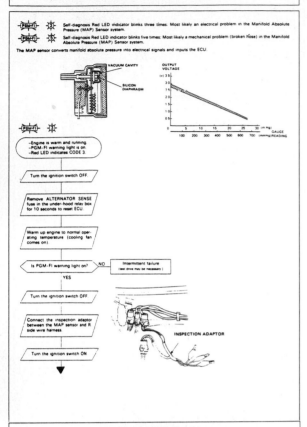

MAP SENSOR DIAGNOSTIC CHART
1986–87 ACURA LEGEND SEDAN AND 1986–88 STERLING

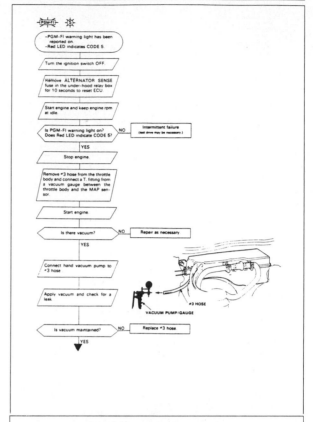

MAP SENSOR DIAGNOSTIC CHART
1986–87 ACURA LEGEND SEDAN AND 1986–88 STERLING

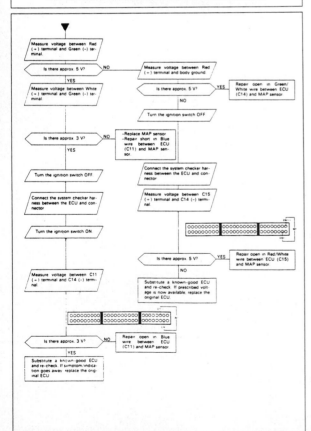

MAP SENSOR DIAGNOSTIC CHART
1986–87 ACURA LEGEND SEDAN AND 1986–88 STERLING

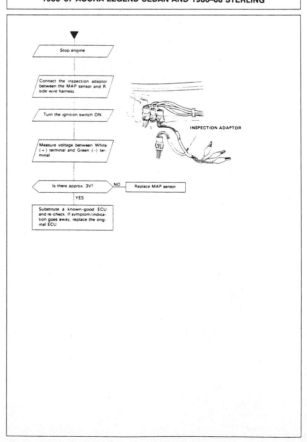

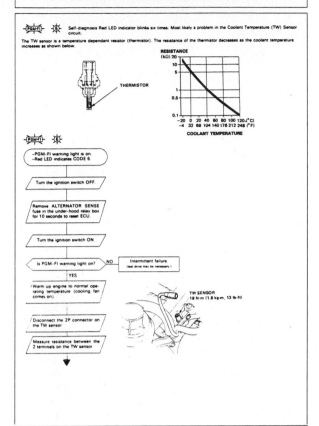

TW SENSOR DIAGNOSTIC CHART
1986–87 ACURA LEGEND SEDAN AND 1986–88 STERLING

[PGM-FI] [⚙] Self-diagnosis Red LED indicator blinks six times. Most likely a problem in the Coolant Temperature (TW) Sensor circuit.

The TW sensor is a temperature dependant resistor (thermistor). The resistance of the thermistor decreases as the coolant temperature increases as shown below.

— THERMISTOR

RESISTANCE (kΩ)
COOLANT TEMPERATURE

[PGM-FI] [⚙]

- PGM-FI warning light is on.
- Red LED indicates CODE 6.

↓

Turn the ignition switch OFF.

↓

Remove ALTERNATOR SENSE fuse in the under-hood relay box for 10 seconds to reset ECU.

↓

Turn the ignition switch ON.

↓

Is PGM-FI warning light on? — NO → Intermittent failure (test drive may be necessary)

↓ YES

Warm up engine to normal operating temperature (cooling fan comes on).

↓

Disconnect the 2P connector on the TW sensor.

↓

Measure resistance between the 2 terminals on the TW sensor.

TW SENSOR
18 N·m (1.8 kg·m, 13 lb·ft)

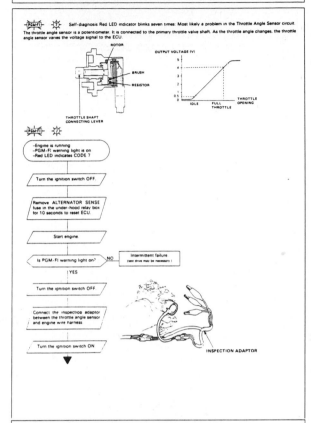

THROTTLE ANGLE SENSOR DIAGNOSTIC CHART
1986–87 ACURA LEGEND SEDAN AND 1986–88 STERLING

[PGM-FI] [⚙] Self-diagnosis Red LED indicator blinks seven times. Most likely a problem in the Throttle Angle Sensor circuit.

The throttle angle sensor is a potentiometer. It is connected to the primary throttle valve shaft. As the throttle angle changes, the throttle angle sensor varies the voltage signal to the ECU.

ROTOR — BRUSH — RESISTOR

THROTTLE SHAFT CONNECTING LEVER

OUTPUT VOLTAGE (V)
IDLE FULL THROTTLE THROTTLE OPENING

[PGM-FI] [⚙]

- Engine is running.
- PGM-FI warning light is on.
- Red LED indicates CODE 7

↓

Turn the ignition switch OFF.

↓

Remove ALTERNATOR SENSE fuse in the under-hood relay box for 10 seconds to reset ECU.

↓

Start engine.

↓

Is PGM-FI warning light on? — NO → Intermittent failure (test drive may be necessary)

↓ YES

Turn the ignition switch OFF.

↓

Connect the inspection adaptor between the throttle angle sensor and engine wire harness.

↓

Turn the ignition switch ON.

INSPECTION ADAPTOR

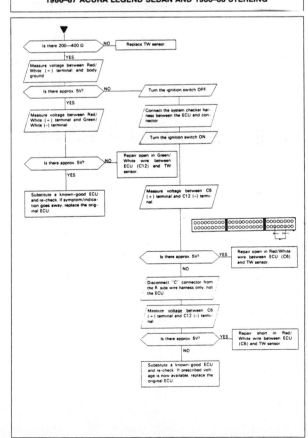

TW SENSOR DIAGNOSTIC CHART
1986–87 ACURA LEGEND SEDAN AND 1986–88 STERLING

Is there 200–400 Ω — NO → Replace TW sensor.

↓ YES

Measure voltage between Red/White (+) terminal and body ground.

↓

Is there approx. 5V? — NO → Turn the ignition switch OFF.

↓ YES

Measure voltage between Red/White (+) terminal and Green/White (–) terminal.

↓

Is there approx. 5V? — NO → Connect the system checker harness between the ECU and connector.

↓ YES

Substitute a known-good ECU and re-check. If symptom/indication goes away, replace the original ECU.

Turn the ignition switch ON.

↓

Repair open in Green/White wire between ECU (C12) and TW sensor.

Measure voltage between C6 (+) terminal and C12 (–) terminal.

↓

Is there approx. 5V? — YES → Repair open in Red/White wire between ECU (C6) and TW sensor.

↓ NO

Disconnect "C" connector from the R side wire harness only, not the ECU.

↓

Measure voltage between C6 (+) terminal and C12 (–) terminal.

↓

Is there approx. 5V? — YES → Repair short in Red/White wire between ECU (C6) and TW sensor.

↓ NO

Substitute a known-good ECU and re-check. If prescribed voltage is now available, replace the original ECU.

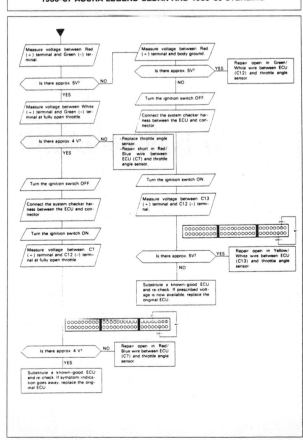

THROTTLE ANGLE SENSOR DIAGNOSTIC CHART
1986–87 ACURA LEGEND SEDAN AND 1986–88 STERLING

Measure voltage between Red (+) terminal and Green (–) terminal. → Measure voltage between Red (+) terminal and body ground.

↓

Is there approx. 5V? — NO → Is there approx. 5V? — YES → Repair open in Green/White wire between ECU (C12) and throttle angle sensor.

↓ YES

Measure voltage between White (+) terminal and Green (–) terminal at fully open throttle.

↓ NO

Turn the ignition switch OFF.

↓

Is there approx. 4 V? — NO → Connect the system checker harness between the ECU and connector.

- Replace throttle angle sensor.
- Repair short in Red/Blue wire between ECU (C7) and throttle angle sensor.

↓ YES

Turn the ignition switch ON.

↓

Turn the ignition switch OFF.

↓

Measure voltage between C13 (+) terminal and C12 (–) terminal.

Connect the system checker harness between the ECU and connector.

↓

Turn the ignition switch ON.

↓

Measure voltage between C7 (+) terminal and C12 (–) terminal at fully open throttle.

↓

Is there approx. 5V? — YES → Repair open in Yellow/White wire between ECU (C13) and throttle angle sensor.

↓ NO

Substitute a known-good ECU and re-check. If prescribed voltage is now available, replace the original ECU.

↓

Is there approx. 4 V? — NO → Repair open in Red/Blue wire between ECU (C7) and throttle angle sensor.

↓ YES

Substitute a known-good ECU and re-check. If symptom/indication goes away, replace the original ECU.

CRANK ANGLE SENSOR DIAGNOSTIC CHART
1986–87 ACURA LEGEND SEDAN AND 1986–88 STERLING

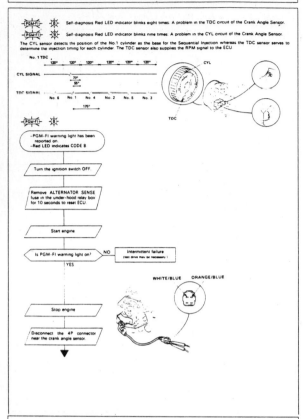

CRANK ANGLE SENSOR DIAGNOSTIC CHART
1986–87 ACURA LEGEND SEDAN AND 1986–88 STERLING

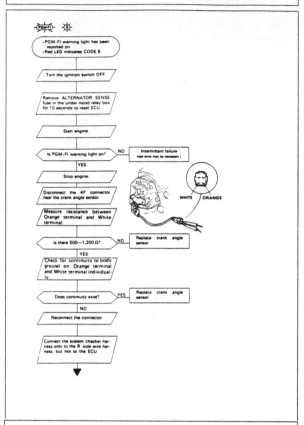

CRANK ANGLE SENSOR DIAGNOSTIC CHART
1986–87 ACURA LEGEND SEDAN AND 1986–88 STERLING

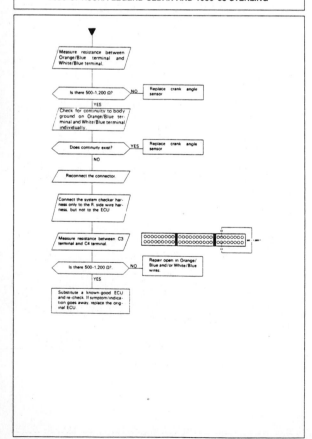

CRANK ANGLE SENSOR DIAGNOSTIC CHART
1986–87 ACURA LEGEND SEDAN AND 1986–88 STERLING

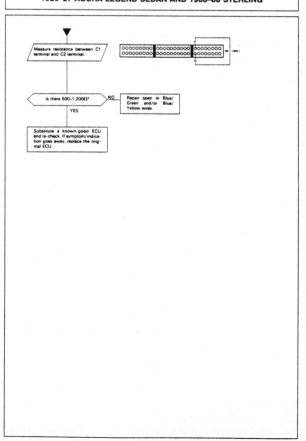

TA SENSOR DIAGNOSTIC CHART
1986–87 ACURA LEGEND SEDAN AND 1986–88 STERLING

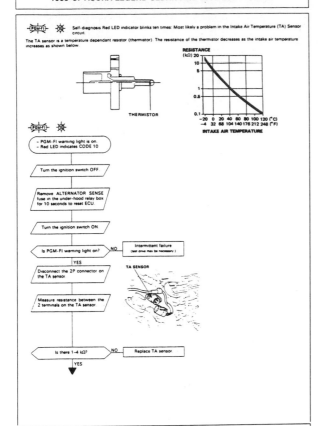

-PGM-FI-   Self-diagnosis Red LED indicator blinks ten times: Most likely a problem in the Intake Air Temperature (TA) Sensor circuit.

The TA sensor is a temperature dependant resistor (thermistor). The resistance of the thermistor decreases as the intake air temperature increases as shown below.

THERMISTOR

RESISTANCE (kΩ)
INTAKE AIR TEMPERATURE

-PGM-FI-

- PGM-FI warning light is on.
- Red LED indicates CODE 10

Turn the ignition switch OFF.

Remove ALTERNATOR SENSE fuse in the under-hood relay box for 10 seconds to reset ECU.

Turn the ignition switch ON.

Is PGM-FI warning light on? —NO→ Intermittent failure (test drive may be necessary)

↓ YES

Disconnect the 2P connector on the TA sensor.

TA SENSOR

Measure resistance between the 2 terminals on the TA sensor.

Is there 1–4 kΩ? —NO→ Replace TA sensor

▼

IMA SENSOR DIAGNOSTIC CHART
1986–87 ACURA LEGEND SEDAN AND 1986–88 STERLING

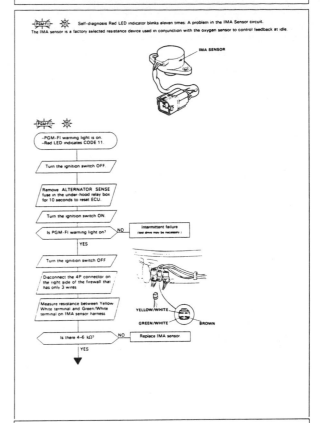

-PGM-FI-   Self-diagnosis Red LED indicator blinks eleven times: A problem in the IMA Sensor circuit.

The IMA sensor is a factory selected resistance device used in conjunction with the oxygen sensor to control feedback at idle.

IMA SENSOR

-PGM-FI-

- PGM-FI warning light is on.
- Red LED indicates CODE 11.

Turn the ignition switch OFF.

Remove ALTERNATOR SENSE fuse in the under-hood relay box for 10 seconds to reset ECU.

Turn the ignition switch ON.

Is PGM-FI warning light on? —NO→ Intermittent failure (test drive may be necessary)

↓ YES

Turn the ignition switch OFF.

Disconnect the 4P connector on the right side of the firewall that has only 3 wires.

YELLOW/WHITE
GREEN/WHITE   BROWN

Measure resistance between Yellow White terminal and Green/White terminal on IMA sensor harness.

Is there 4–6 kΩ? —NO→ Replace IMA sensor

↓ YES

TA SENSOR DIAGNOSTIC CHART
1986–87 ACURA LEGEND SEDAN AND 1986–88 STERLING

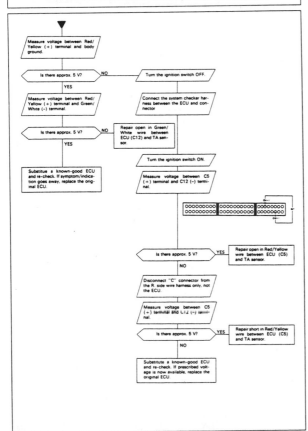

▼

Measure voltage between Red/Yellow (+) terminal and body ground.

Is there approx. 5 V? —NO→ Turn the ignition switch OFF.

↓ YES

Measure voltage between Red/Yellow (+) terminal and Green/White (−) terminal.

Connect the system checker harness between the ECU and connector

Is there approx. 5 V? —NO→ Repair open in Green/White wire between ECU (C12) and TA sensor.

↓ YES

Substitute a known-good ECU and re-check. If symptom/indication goes away, replace the original ECU.

Turn the ignition switch ON.

Measure voltage between C5 (+) terminal and C12 (−) terminal.

Is there approx. 5 V? —YES→ Repair open in Red/Yellow wire between ECU (C5) and TA sensor.

↓ NO

Disconnect "C" connector from the R. side wire harness only, not the ECU.

Measure voltage between C5 (+) terminal and C12 (−) terminal.

Is there approx. 5 V? —YES→ Repair short in Red/Yellow wire between ECU (C5) and TA sensor.

↓ NO

Substitute a known-good ECU and re-check. If prescribed voltage is now available, replace the original ECU.

IMA SENSOR DIAGNOSTIC CHART
1986–87 ACURA LEGEND SEDAN AND 1986–88 STERLING

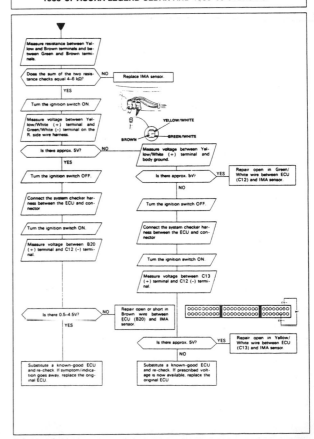

▼

Measure resistance between Yellow and Brown terminals and between Green and Brown terminals.

Does the sum of the two resistance checks equal 4–6 kΩ? —NO→ Replace IMA sensor.

↓ YES

Turn the ignition switch ON.

Measure voltage between Yellow/White (+) terminal and Green/White (−) terminal on the R. side wire harness.

YELLOW/WHITE
BROWN   GREEN/WHITE

Is there approx. 5V? —NO→ Measure voltage between Yellow/White (+) terminal and body ground.

↓ YES

Turn the ignition switch OFF.

Is there approx. 5V? —YES→ Repair open in Green/White wire between ECU (C12) and IMA sensor.

↓ NO

Connect the system checker harness between the ECU and connector

Turn the ignition switch OFF.

Turn the ignition switch ON.

Connect the system checker harness between the ECU and connector

Measure voltage between B20 (+) terminal and C12 (−) terminal.

Turn the ignition switch ON.

Measure voltage between C13 (+) terminal and C12 (−) terminal.

Is there 0.5–4.5V? —YES→ Repair open or short in Brown wire between ECU (B20) and IMA sensor.

↓ YES

Is there approx. 5V? —YES→ Repair open in Yellow/White wire between ECU (C13) and IMA sensor.

↓ NO

Substitute a known-good ECU and re-check. If symptom/indication goes away, replace the original ECU.

Substitute a known-good ECU and re-check. If prescribed voltage is now available, replace the original ECU.

PA SENSOR DIAGNOSTIC CHART
1986–87 ACURA LEGEND SEDAN AND 1986–88 STERLING

-PGM-FI- ☀ Self-diagnosis Red LED indicator blinks thirteen times: A problem in the Atmospheric Pressure (PA) Sensor circuit.

The PA sensor converts atmospheric pressure into electrical signals and inputs the ECU.

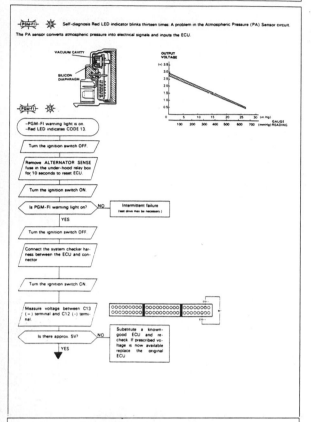

-PGM-FI- ☀

-PGM-FI warning light is on.
-Red LED indicates CODE 13.

↓

Turn the ignition switch OFF.

↓

Remove ALTERNATOR SENSE fuse in the under-hood relay box for 10 seconds to reset ECU.

↓

Turn the ignition switch ON.

↓

Is PGM-FI warning light on? —NO→ Intermittent failure (test drive may be necessary)

↓ YES

Turn the ignition switch OFF.

↓

Connect the system checker harness between the ECU and connector

↓

Turn the ignition switch ON.

↓

Measure voltage between C13 (+) terminal and C12 (−) terminal.

↓

Is there approx. 5V? —NO→ Substitute a known-good ECU and re-check. If prescribed voltage is now available replace the original ECU

↓ YES

PA SENSOR DIAGNOSTIC CHART
1986–87 ACURA LEGEND SEDAN AND 1986–88 STERLING

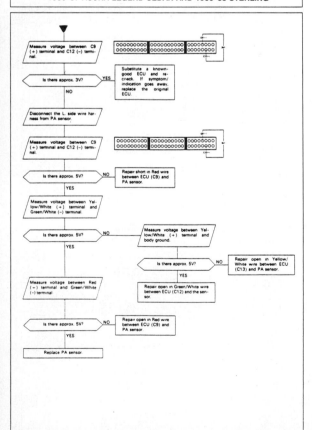

Measure voltage between C9 (+) terminal and C12 (−) terminal.

↓

Is there approx. 3V? —YES→ Substitute a known-good ECU and re-check. If symptom/indication goes away, replace the original ECU.

↓ NO

Disconnect the L. side wire harness from PA sensor.

↓

Measure voltage between C9 (+) terminal and C12 (−) terminal.

↓

Is there approx. 5V? —NO→ Repair short in Red wire between ECU (C9) and PA sensor.

↓ YES

Measure voltage between Yellow/White (+) terminal and Green/White (−) terminal.

↓

Is there approx. 5V? —NO→ Measure voltage between Yellow/White (+) terminal and body ground.

↓ YES

Is there approx. 5V? —NO→ Repair open in Yellow/White wire between ECU (C13) and PA sensor.

Measure voltage between Red (−) terminal and Green/White (−) terminal.

Repair open in Green/White wire between ECU (C12) and the sensor.

↓

Is there approx. 5V? —NO→ Repair open in Red wire between ECU (C9) and PA sensor.

↓ YES

Replace PA sensor.

EICV DIAGNOSTIC CHART
1986–87 ACURA LEGEND SEDAN AND 1986–88 STERLING

-PGM-FI- ☀ Self-diagnosis Red LED indicator blinks fourteen times: A problem in the Electronic Idle Control Valve (EICV) circuit.

The EICV changes the amount of air bypassing the throttle body in response to a current signal from the ECU in order to maintain the proper idle speed.

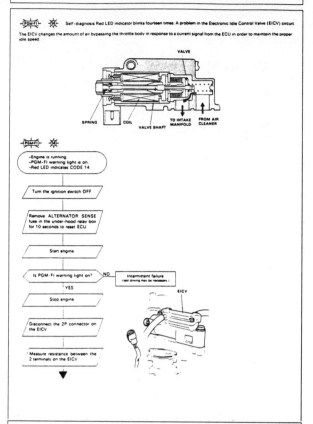

-PGM-FI- ☀

-Engine is running.
-PGM-FI warning light is on.
-Red LED indicates CODE 14.

↓

Turn the ignition switch OFF.

↓

Remove ALTERNATOR SENSE fuse in the under-hood relay box for 10 seconds to reset ECU.

↓

Start engine

↓

Is PGM-FI warning light on? —NO→ Intermittent failure (test driving may be necessary)

↓ YES

Stop engine

↓

Disconnect the 2P connector on the EICV.

↓

Measure resistance between the 2 terminals on the EICV.

EICV DIAGNOSTIC CHART
1986–87 ACURA LEGEND SEDAN AND 1986–88 STERLING

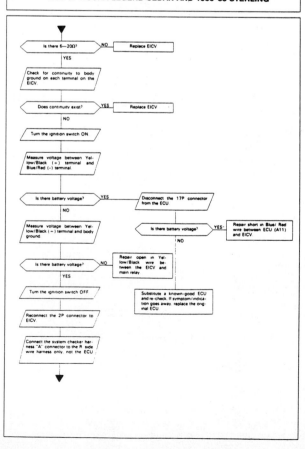

Is there 6—20Ω? —NO→ Replace EICV

↓ YES

Check for continuity to body ground on each terminal on the EICV.

↓

Does continuity exist? —YES→ Replace EICV

↓ NO

Turn the ignition switch ON

↓

Measure voltage between Yellow/Black (+) terminal and Blue/Red (−) terminal.

↓

Is there battery voltage? —YES→ Disconnect the 17P connector from the ECU.

↓ NO

Measure voltage between Yellow/Black (−) terminal and body ground.

Is there battery voltage? —YES→ Repair short in Blue/Red wire between ECU (A11) and EICV.

↓ NO

Is there battery voltage? —NO→ Repair open in Yellow/Black wire between the EICV and main relay

↓ YES

Turn the ignition switch OFF

Substitute a known-good ECU and re-check. If symptom/indication goes away, replace the original ECU.

↓

Reconnect the 2P connector to EICV.

↓

Connect the system checker harness "A" connector to the R side wire harness only, not the ECU.

EICV DIAGNOSTIC CHART
1986–87 ACURA LEGEND SEDAN AND 1986–88 STERLING

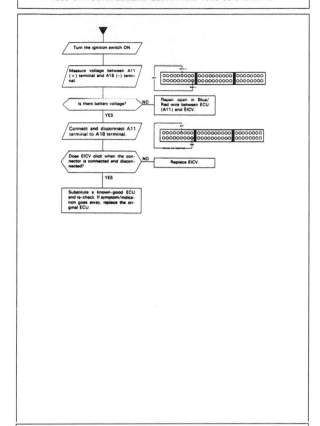

ALTERNATOR FR SIGNAL DIAGNOSTIC CHART
1986–87 ACURA LEGEND SEDAN AND 1986–88 STERLING

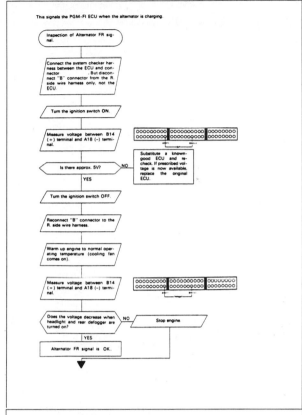

STARTER SIGNAL DIAGNOSTIC CHART
1986–87 ACURA LEGEND SEDAN AND 1986–88 STERLING

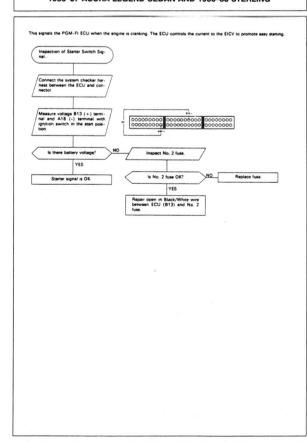

ALTERNATOR FR SIGNAL DIAGNOSTIC CHART
1986–87 ACURA LEGEND SEDAN AND 1986–88 STERLING

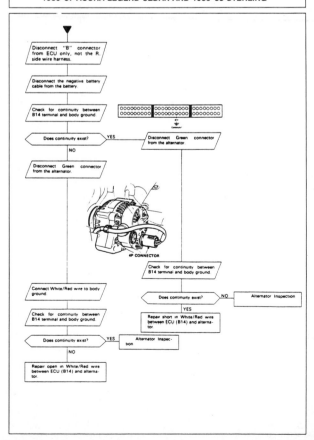

A/T SHIFT POSITION SIGNAL DIAGNOSTIC CHART
1986–87 ACURA LEGEND SEDAN AND 1986–88 STERLING

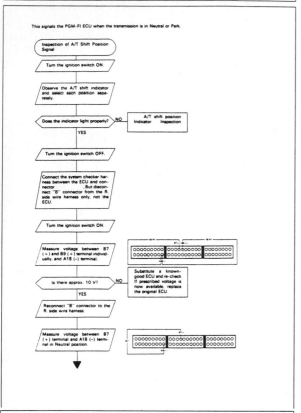

VEHICLE SPEED SIGNAL DIAGNOSTIC CHART
1986–87 ACURA LEGEND SEDAN AND 1986–88 STERLING

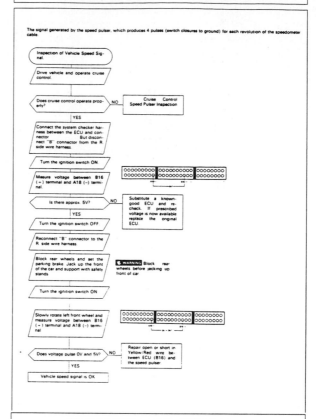

A/T SHIFT POSITION SIGNAL DIAGNOSTIC CHART
1986–87 ACURA LEGEND SEDAN AND 1986–88 STERLING

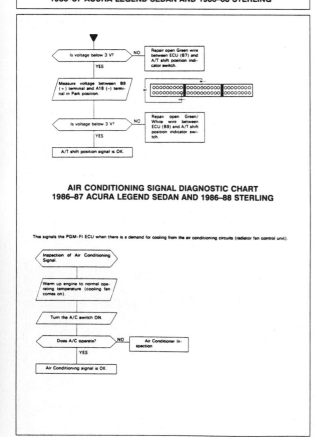

AIR CONDITIONING SIGNAL DIAGNOSTIC CHART
1986–87 ACURA LEGEND SEDAN AND 1986–88 STERLING

P/S OIL PRESSURE SIGNAL DIAGNOSTIC CHART
1986–87 ACURA LEGEND SEDAN AND 1986–88 STERLING

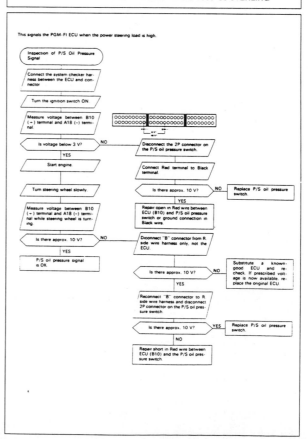

EGR SYSTEM DIAGNOSTIC CHART
1986–87 ACURA LEGEND SEDAN AND 1986–88 STERLING

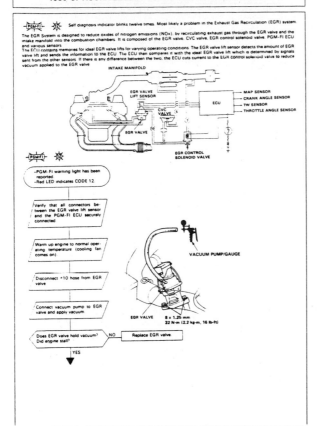

PGM-FI — Self diagnosis indicator blinks twelve times. Most likely a problem in the Exhaust Gas Recirculation (EGR) system.

The EGR System is designed to reduce oxides of nitrogen emissions (NOx), by recirculating exhaust gas through the EGR valve and the intake manifold into the combustion chambers. It is composed of the EGR valve, CVC valve, EGR control solenoid valve, PGM-FI ECU and various sensors.

The ECU contains memories for ideal EGR valve lifts for varying operating conditions. The EGR valve lift sensor detects the amount of EGR valve lift and sends the information to the ECU. The ECU then compares it with the ideal EGR valve lift which is determined by signals sent from the other sensors. If there is any difference between the two, the ECU cuts current to the EGR control solenoid valve to reduce vacuum applied to the EGR valve.

INTAKE MANIFOLD

EGR VALVE LIFT SENSOR
CVC VALVE
EGR VALVE
ECU
- MAP SENSOR
- CRANK ANGLE SENSOR
- TW SENSOR
- THROTTLE ANGLE SENSOR
EGR CONTROL SOLENOID VALVE

PGM-FI
-PGM-FI warning light has been reported.
-Red LED indicates CODE 12

Verify that all connectors between the EGR valve lift sensor and the PGM-FI ECU securely connected

Warm up engine to normal operating temperature (cooling fan comes on).

VACUUM PUMP/GAUGE

Disconnect #10 hose from EGR valve

Connect vacuum pump to EGR valve and apply vacuum.

EGR VALVE — 8 x 1.25 mm / 22 N·m (2.2 kg-m, 16 lb-ft)

Does EGR valve hold vacuum? Did engine stall? — NO → Replace EGR valve.

YES ↓

EGR SYSTEM DIAGNOSTIC CHART
1986–87 ACURA LEGEND SEDAN AND 1986–88 STERLING

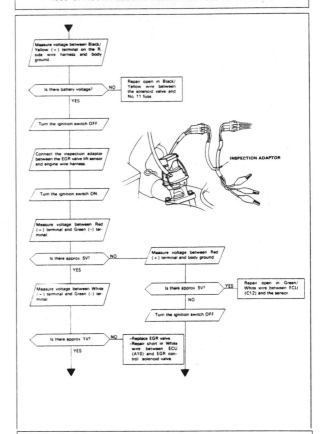

Measure voltage between Black/Yellow (+) terminal on the R. side wire harness and body ground.

Is there battery voltage? — NO → Repair open in Black/Yellow wire between the solenoid valve and No. 11 fuse.

YES ↓

Turn the ignition switch OFF.

Connect the inspection adaptor between the EGR valve lift sensor and engine wire harness.

INSPECTION ADAPTOR

Turn the ignition switch ON.

Measure voltage between Red (+) terminal and Green (–) terminal.

Is there approx. 5V? — NO → Measure voltage between Red (+) terminal and body ground.

YES ↓

Measure voltage between White (–) terminal and Green (–) terminal.

Is there approx. 5V? — YES → Repair open in Green/White wire between ECU (C12) and the sensor.

NO ↓

Turn the ignition switch OFF

Is there approx. 1V? — NO → -Replace EGR valve. -Repair short in White wire between ECU (A10) and EGR control solenoid valve.

YES ↓

EGR SYSTEM DIAGNOSTIC CHART
1986–87 ACURA LEGEND SEDAN AND 1986–88 STERLING

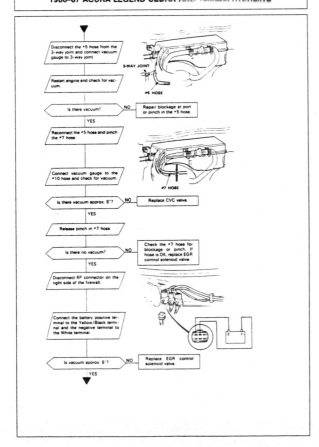

Disconnect the #5 hose from the 3-way joint and connect vacuum gauge to 3-way joint

3-WAY JOINT
#5 HOSE

Restart engine and check for vacuum.

Is there vacuum? — NO → Repair blockage at port or pinch in the #5 hose.

YES ↓

Reconnect the #5 hose and pinch the #7 hose.

#7 HOSE

Connect vacuum gauge to the #10 hose and check for vacuum.

Is there vacuum approx. 8"? — NO → Replace CVC valve.

YES ↓

Release pinch in #7 hose.

Is there no vacuum? — NO → Check the #7 hose for blockage or pinch. If hose is OK, replace EGR control solenoid valve.

YES ↓

Disconnect 6P connector on the right side of the firewall.

Connect the battery positive terminal to the Yellow/Black terminal and the negative terminal to the White terminal.

Is vacuum approx. 8"? — NO → Replace EGR control solenoid valve.

YES ↓

EGR SYSTEM DIAGNOSTIC CHART
1986–87 ACURA LEGEND SEDAN AND 1986–88 STERLING

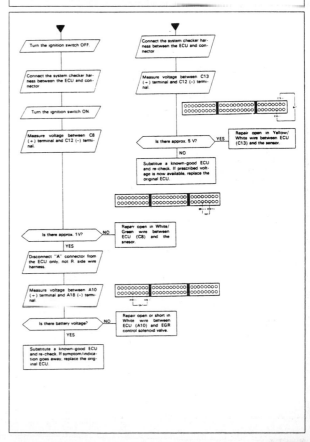

Turn the ignition switch OFF.

Connect the system checker harness between the ECU and connector

Turn the ignition switch ON

Measure voltage between C8 (+) terminal and C12 (–) terminal.

Connect the system checker harness between the ECU and connector

Measure voltage between C13 (+) terminal and C12 (–) terminal.

Is there approx. 5 V? — YES → Repair open in Yellow/White wire between ECU (C13) and the sensor.

NO ↓

Substitute a known-good ECU and re-check. If prescribed voltage is now available, replace the original ECU.

Is there approx. 1V? — NO → Repair open in White/Green wire between ECU (C8) and the sensor.

YES ↓

Disconnect "A" connector from the ECU only, not R. side wire harness.

Measure voltage between A10 (+) terminal and A18 (–) terminal.

Is there battery voltage? — NO → Repair open or short in White wire between ECU (A10) and EGR control solenoid valve.

YES ↓

Substitute a known-good ECU and re-check. If symptom/indication goes away, replace the original ECU.

ECU DIAGNOSTIC CHART
1987–88 ACURA LEGEND COUPE AND 1988 LEGEND SEDAN

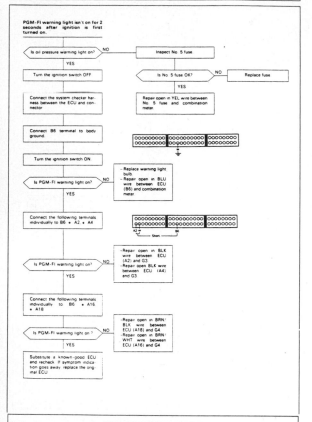

ECU DIAGNOSTIC CHART
1987–88 ACURA LEGEND COUPE AND 1988 LEGEND SEDAN

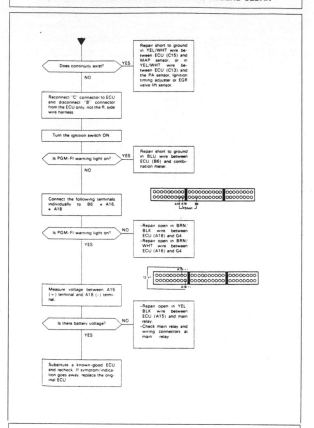

ECU DIAGNOSTIC CHART
1987–88 ACURA LEGEND COUPE AND 1988 LEGEND SEDAN

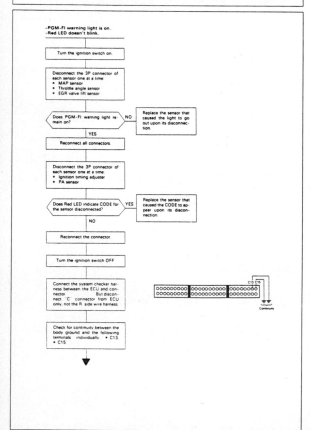

OXYGEN SENSOR DIAGNOSTIC CHART
1987–88 ACURA LEGEND COUPE AND 1988 LEGEND SEDAN

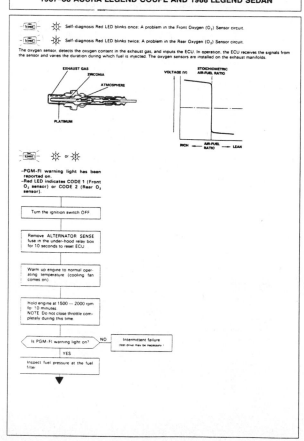

OXYGEN SENSOR DIAGNOSTIC CHART
1987–88 ACURA LEGEND COUPE AND 1988 LEGEND SEDAN

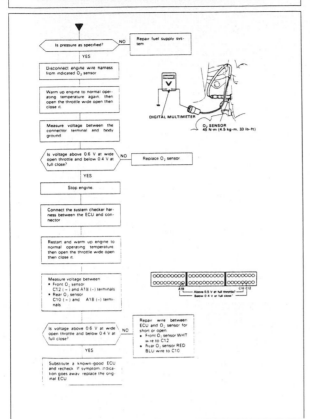

MAP SENSOR DIAGNOSTIC CHART
1987–88 ACURA LEGEND COUPE AND 1988 LEGEND SEDAN

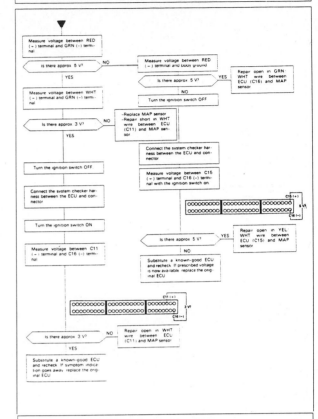

MAP SENSOR DIAGNOSTIC CHART
1987–88 ACURA LEGEND COUPE AND 1988 LEGEND SEDAN

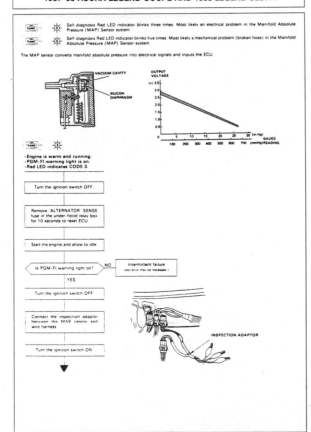

MAP SENSOR DIAGNOSTIC CHART
1987–88 ACURA LEGEND COUPE AND 1988 LEGEND SEDAN

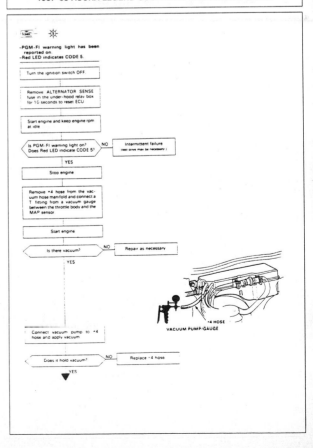

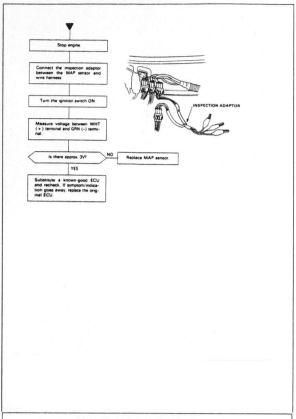

MAP SENSOR DIAGNOSTIC CHART
1987–88 ACURA LEGEND COUPE AND 1988 LEGEND SEDAN

Stop engine.

Connect the inspection adaptor between the MAP sensor and wire harness.

Turn the ignition switch ON.

Measure voltage between WHT (+) terminal and GRN (−) terminal.

Is there approx. 3V? — NO → Replace MAP sensor.

YES

Substitute a known-good ECU and recheck. If symptom/indication goes away, replace the original ECU.

INSPECTION ADAPTOR

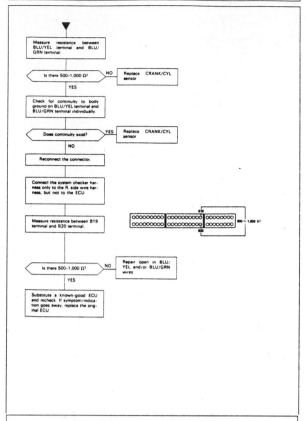

CRANK/CYL SENSOR DIAGNOSTIC CHART
1987–88 ACURA LEGEND COUPE AND 1988 LEGEND SEDAN

Measure resistance between BLU/YEL terminal and BLU/GRN terminal.

Is there 500–1,000 Ω? — NO → Replace CRANK/CYL sensor.

YES

Check for continuity to body ground on BLU/YEL terminal and BLU/GRN terminal individually.

Does continuity exist? — YES → Replace CRANK/CYL sensor.

NO

Reconnect the connector.

Connect the system checker harness only to the R. side wire harness, but not to the ECU.

Measure resistance between B19 terminal and B20 terminal.

Is there 500–1,000 Ω? — NO → Repair open in BLU/YEL and/or BLU/GRN wires.

YES

Substitute a known-good ECU and recheck. If symptom/indication goes away, replace the original ECU.

CRANK/CYL SENSOR DIAGNOSTIC CHART
1987–88 ACURA LEGEND COUPE AND 1988 LEGEND SEDAN

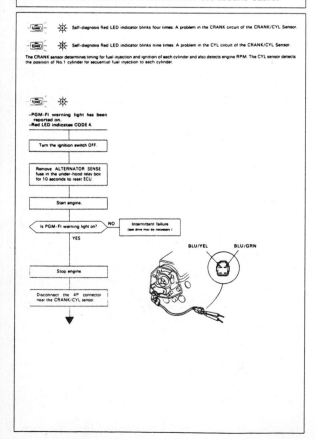

Self-diagnosis Red LED indicator blinks four times: A problem in the CRANK circuit of the CRANK/CYL Sensor.

Self-diagnosis Red LED indicator blinks nine times: A problem in the CYL circuit of the CRANK/CYL Sensor.

The CRANK sensor determines timing for fuel injection and ignition of each cylinder and also detects engine RPM. The CYL sensor detects the position of No.1 cylinder for sequential fuel injection to each cylinder.

–PGM-FI warning light has been reported on.
–Red LED indicates CODE 4.

Turn the ignition switch OFF.

Remove ALTERNATOR SENSE fuse in the under-hood relay box for 10 seconds to reset ECU.

Start engine.

Is PGM-FI warning light on? — NO → Intermittent failure (test drive may be necessary.)

YES

Stop engine.

Disconnect the 4P connector near the CRANK/CYL sensor.

BLU/YEL   BLU/GRN

CRANK/CYL SENSOR DIAGNOSTIC CHART
1987–88 ACURA LEGEND COUPE AND 1988 LEGEND SEDAN

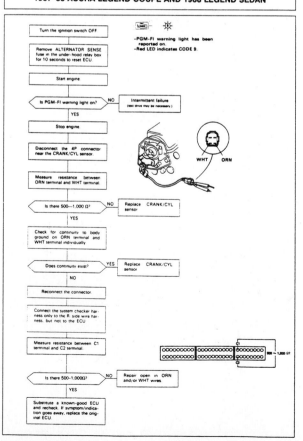

Turn the ignition switch OFF.

–PGM-FI warning light has been reported on.
–Red LED indicates CODE 9.

Remove ALTERNATOR SENSE fuse in the under-hood relay box for 10 seconds to reset ECU.

Start engine.

Is PGM-FI warning light on? — NO → Intermittent failure (test drive may be necessary.)

YES

Stop engine.

Disconnect the 4P connector near the CRANK/CYL sensor.

WHT   ORN

Measure resistance between ORN terminal and WHT terminal.

Is there 500–1,000 Ω? — NO → Replace CRANK/CYL sensor.

YES

Check for continuity to body ground on ORN terminal and WHT terminal individually.

Does continuity exist? — YES → Replace CRANK/CYL sensor.

NO

Reconnect the connector.

Connect the system checker harness only to the R. side wire harness, but not to the ECU.

Measure resistance between C1 terminal and C2 terminal.

Is there 500–1,000 Ω? — NO → Repair open in ORN and/or WHT wires.

YES

Substitute a known-good ECU and recheck. If symptom/indication goes away, replace the original ECU.

TW SENSOR DIAGNOSTIC CHART
1987–88 ACURA LEGEND COUPE AND 1988 LEGEND SEDAN

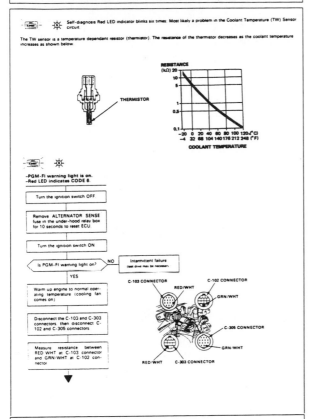

Self-diagnosis Red LED indicator blinks six times: Most likely a problem in the Coolant Temperature (TW) Sensor circuit.

The TW sensor is a temperature dependant resistor (thermistor). The resistance of the thermistor decreases as the coolant temperature increases as shown below.

THERMISTOR

RESISTANCE (kΩ)
COOLANT TEMPERATURE

-PGM-FI warning light is on.
-Red LED indicates CODE 6.

Turn the ignition switch OFF

Remove ALTERNATOR SENSE fuse in the under-hood relay box for 10 seconds to reset ECU.

Turn the ignition switch ON

Is PGM-FI warning light on? —NO→ Intermittent failure (test drive may be necessary)

YES

Warm up engine to normal operating temperature (cooling fan comes on)

Disconnect the C-103 and C-303 connectors, then disconnect C-102 and C-305 connectors

Measure resistance between RED/WHT at C-103 connector and GRN/WHT at C-102 connector

C-103 CONNECTOR   C-102 CONNECTOR
RED/WHT   GRN/WHT
C-305 CONNECTOR
GRN/WHT
RED/WHT   C-303 CONNECTOR

THROTTLE ANGLE SENSOR DIAGNOSTIC CHART
1987–88 ACURA LEGEND COUPE AND 1988 LEGEND SEDAN

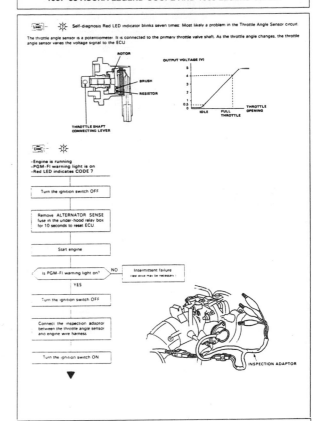

Self-diagnosis Red LED indicator blinks seven times: Most likely a problem in the Throttle Angle Sensor circuit.

The throttle angle sensor is a potentiometer. It is connected to the primary throttle valve shaft. As the throttle angle changes, the throttle angle sensor varies the voltage signal to the ECU.

ROTOR
BRUSH
RESISTOR
THROTTLE SHAFT CONNECTING LEVER

OUTPUT VOLTAGE (V)
IDLE   FULL THROTTLE   THROTTLE OPENING

-Engine is running
-PGM-FI warning light is on
-Red LED indicates CODE 7

Turn the ignition switch OFF

Remove ALTERNATOR SENSE fuse in the under-hood relay box for 10 seconds to reset ECU

Start engine

Is PGM-FI warning light on? —NO→ Intermittent failure (test drive may be necessary)

YES

Turn the ignition switch OFF

Connect the inspection adaptor between the throttle angle sensor and engine wire harness

Turn the ignition switch ON

INSPECTION ADAPTOR

TW SENSOR DIAGNOSTIC CHART
1987–88 ACURA LEGEND COUPE AND 1988 LEGEND SEDAN

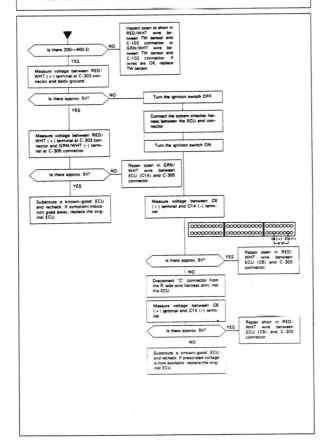

Is there 200–400 Ω —NO→ Inspect open or short in RED/WHT wire between TW sensor and C-103 connector or GRN/WHT wire between TW sensor and C-102 connector. If wires are OK, replace TW sensor

YES

Measure voltage between RED/WHT (+) terminal at C-303 connector and body ground.

Is there approx. 5V? —NO→ Turn the ignition switch OFF.

YES

Connect the system checker harness between the ECU and connector

Turn the ignition switch ON.

Measure voltage between RED/WHT (+) terminal at C-303 connector and GRN/WHT (-) terminal at C-305 connector.

Is there approx. 5V? —NO→ Repair open in GRN/WHT wire between ECU (C14) and C-305 connector.

YES

Substitute a known-good ECU and recheck. If symptom/indication goes away, replace the original ECU.

Measure voltage between C6 (+) terminal and C14 (-) terminal.

C6 (+) C14 (-)
(-6 V?)

Is there approx. 5V? —YES→ Repair open in RED/WHT wire between ECU (C6) and C-303 connector.

NO

Disconnect "C" connector from the R side wire harness only, not the ECU.

Measure voltage between C6 (+) terminal and C14 (-) terminal.

Is there approx. 5V? —YES→ Repair short in RED/WHT wire between ECU (C6) and C-303 connector.

NO

Substitute a known-good ECU and recheck. If prescribed voltage is now available, replace the original ECU.

THROTTLE ANGLE SENSOR DIAGNOSTIC CHART
1987–88 ACURA LEGEND COUPE AND 1988 LEGEND SEDAN

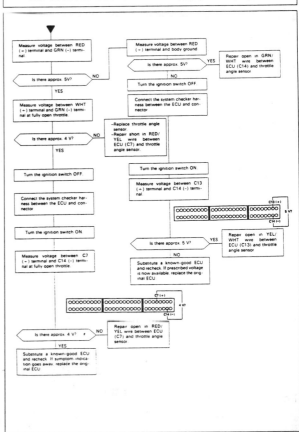

Measure voltage between RED (+) terminal and GRN (-) terminal.

Measure voltage between RED (-) terminal and body ground.

Is there approx. 5V? —YES→ Repair open in GRN/WHT wire between ECU (C14) and throttle angle sensor

NO

Turn the ignition switch OFF

Connect the system checker harness between the ECU and connector

Is there approx. 5V? —NO→

YES

Measure voltage between WHT (+) terminal and GRN (-) terminal at fully open throttle

-Replace throttle angle sensor.
-Repair short in RED/YEL wire between ECU (C7) and throttle angle sensor

Is there approx. 4 V? —NO→

YES

Turn the ignition switch OFF.

Connect the system checker harness between the ECU and connector

Turn the ignition switch ON

Turn the ignition switch ON.

Measure voltage between C13 (+) terminal and C14 (-) terminal.

C13 (+)
C14 (-) 5 V?

Is there approx. 5 V? —YES→ Repair open in YEL/WHT wire between ECU (C13) and throttle angle sensor

Measure voltage between C7 (+) terminal and C14 (-) terminal at fully open throttle

NO

Substitute a known-good ECU and recheck. If prescribed voltage is now available, replace the original ECU.

C7 (+) 4 V?
C14 (-)

Is there approx. 4 V? —NO→ Repair open in RED/YEL wire between ECU (C7) and throttle angle sensor

YES

Substitute a known-good ECU and recheck. If symptom indication goes away, replace the original ECU.

TDC SENSOR DIAGNOSTIC CHART
1987–88 ACURA LEGEND COUPE AND 1988 LEGEND SEDAN

Self-diagnosis LED indicator blinks eight times. A problem in the TDC sensor

The TDC sensor determines ignition timing at start-up (cranking) and when crank angle signal is abnormal.

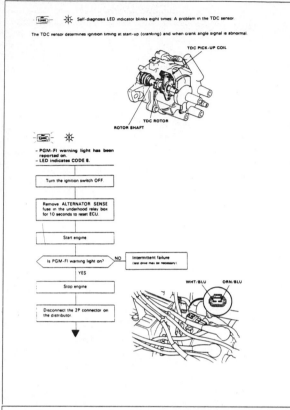

TDC PICK-UP COIL
TDC ROTOR
ROTOR SHAFT

– PGM-FI warning light has been reported on.
– LED indicates CODE 8.

↓

Turn the ignition switch OFF.

↓

Remove ALTERNATOR SENSE fuse in the underhood relay box for 10 seconds to reset ECU.

↓

Start engine

↓

Is PGM-FI warning light on? → NO → Intermittent failure *(test drive may be necessary)*

↓ YES

Stop engine

↓

Disconnect the 2P connector on the distributor.

WHT/BLU   ORN/BLU

↓

TDC SENSOR DIAGNOSTIC CHART
1987–88 ACURA LEGEND COUPE AND 1988 LEGEND SEDAN

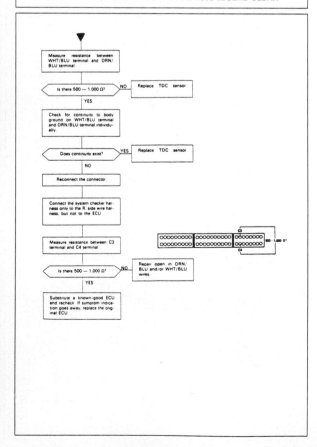

Measure resistance between WHT/BLU terminal and ORN/BLU terminal.

↓

Is there 500 — 1,000 Ω? → NO → Replace TDC sensor

↓ YES

Check for continuity to body ground on WHT/BLU terminal and ORN/BLU terminal individually.

↓

Does continuity exist? → YES → Replace TDC sensor

↓ NO

Reconnect the connector.

↓

Connect the system checker harness only to the R. side wire harness, but not to the ECU.

↓

Measure resistance between C3 terminal and C4 terminal.

500 - 1,000 Ω?

↓

Is there 500 — 1,000 Ω? → NO → Repair open in ORN/BLU and/or WHT/BLU wires.

↓ YES

Substitute a known-good ECU and recheck. If symptom indication goes away, replace the original ECU.

TA SENSOR DIAGNOSTIC CHART
1987–88 ACURA LEGEND COUPE AND 1988 LEGEND SEDAN

Self-diagnosis Red LED indicator blinks ten times: Most likely a problem in the Intake Air Temperature (TA) Sensor circuit.

The TA sensor is a temperature dependant resistor (thermistor). The resistance of the thermistor decreases as the intake air temperature increases as shown below.

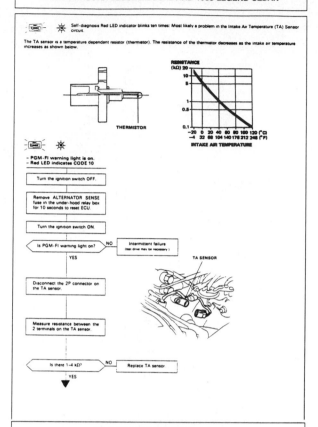

THERMISTOR

RESISTANCE (kΩ) 20 10 5 1 0.5 0.1
−20 0 20 40 60 80 100 120 (°C)
−4 32 68 104 140 176 212 248 (°F)
INTAKE AIR TEMPERATURE

– PGM-FI warning light is on.
– Red LED indicates CODE 10.

↓

Turn the ignition switch OFF.

↓

Remove ALTERNATOR SENSE fuse in the under-hood relay box for 10 seconds to reset ECU.

↓

Turn the ignition switch ON.

↓

Is PGM-FI warning light on? → NO → Intermittent failure *(test drive may be necessary)*

↓ YES

Disconnect the 2P connector on the TA sensor.

TA SENSOR

↓

Measure resistance between the 2 terminals on the TA sensor.

↓

Is there 1–4 kΩ? → NO → Replace TA sensor

↓ YES

TA SENSOR DIAGNOSTIC CHART
1987–88 ACURA LEGEND COUPE AND 1988 LEGEND SEDAN

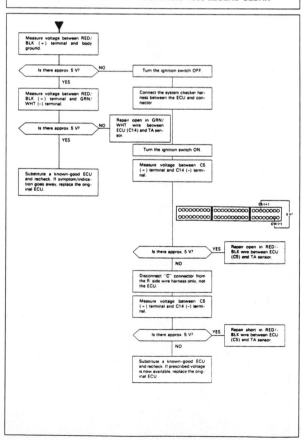

Measure voltage between RED/BLK (+) terminal and body ground.

↓

Is there approx. 5 V? → NO → Turn the ignition switch OFF.

↓ YES

Measure voltage between RED/BLK (–) terminal and GRN/WHT (–) terminal.

Connect the system checker harness between the ECU and connector

↓

Is there approx. 5 V? → NO → Repair open in GRN/WHT wire between ECU (C14) and TA sensor.

↓ YES

Substitute a known-good ECU and recheck. If symptom/indication goes away, replace the original ECU.

Turn the ignition switch ON.

↓

Measure voltage between C5 (–) terminal and C14 (–) terminal.

C5 (+)
5 V
C14 (–)

↓

Is there approx. 5 V? → YES → Repair open in RED/BLK wire between ECU (C5) and TA sensor.

↓ NO

Disconnect "C" connector from the R. side wire harness only, not the ECU.

↓

Measure voltage between C5 (–) terminal and C14 (–) terminal.

↓

Is there approx. 5 V? → YES → Repair short in RED/BLK wire between ECU (C5) and TA sensor

↓ NO

Substitute a known-good ECU and recheck. If prescribed voltage is now available, replace the original ECU.

PA SENSOR DIAGNOSTIC CHART
1987–88 ACURA LEGEND COUPE AND 1988 LEGEND SEDAN

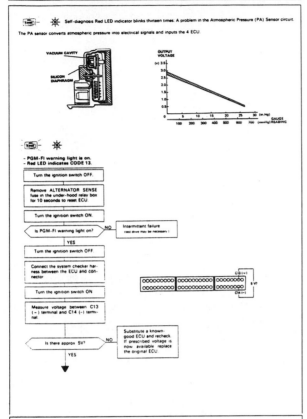

IGNITION OUTPUT SIGNAL DIAGNOSTIC CHART
1987–88 ACURA LEGEND COUPE AND 1988 LEGEND SEDAN

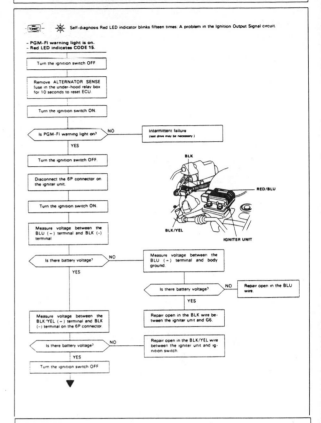

PA SENSOR DIAGNOSTIC CHART
1987–88 ACURA LEGEND COUPE AND 1988 LEGEND SEDAN

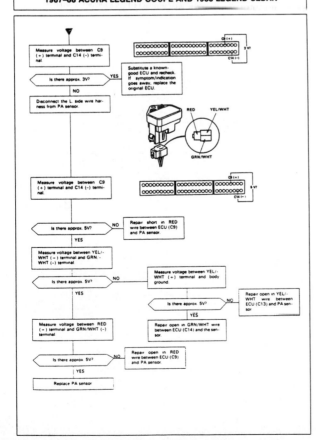

IGNITION OUTPUT SIGNAL DIAGNOSTIC CHART
1987–88 ACURA LEGEND COUPE AND 1988 LEGEND SEDAN

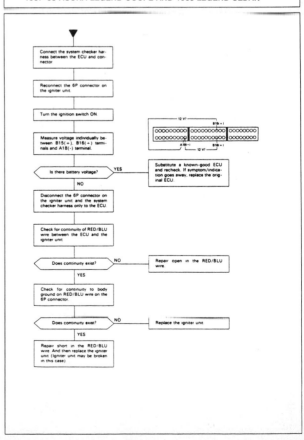

VEHICLE SPEED PULSER DIAGNOSTIC CHART
1987–88 ACURA LEGEND COUPE AND 1988 LEGEND SEDAN

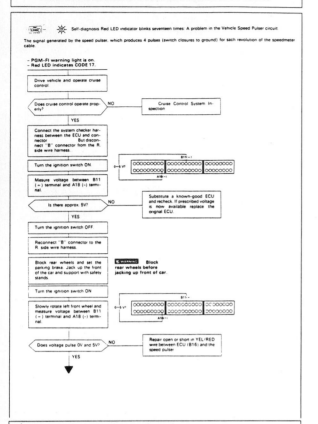

Self-diagnosis Red LED indicator blinks seventeen times: A problem in the Vehicle Speed Pulser circuit.

The signal generated by the speed pulser, which produces 4 pulses (switch closures to ground) for each revolution of the speedmeter cable.

IGNITION TIMING ADJUSTER DIAGNOSTIC CHART
1987–88 ACURA LEGEND COUPE AND 1988 LEGEND SEDAN

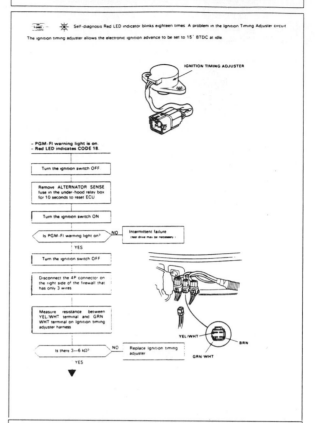

Self-diagnosis Red LED indicator blinks eighteen times: A problem in the Ignition Timing Adjuster circuit.

The ignition timing adjuster allows the electronic ignition advance to be set to 15° BTDC at idle.

VEHICLE SPEED PULSER DIAGNOSTIC CHART
1987–88 ACURA LEGEND COUPE AND 1988 LEGEND SEDAN

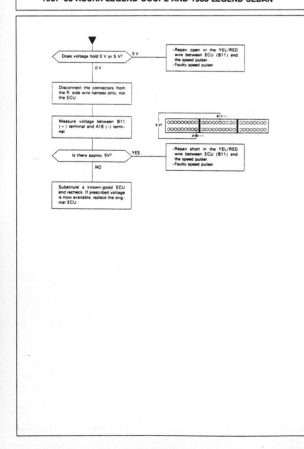

IGNITION TIMING ADJUSTER DIAGNOSTIC CHART
1987–88 ACURA LEGEND COUPE AND 1988 LEGEND SEDAN

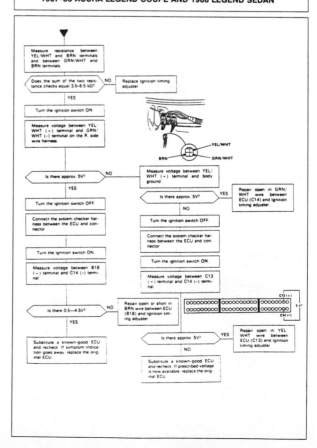

EICV DIAGNOSTIC CHART
1987–88 ACURA LEGEND COUPE AND 1988 LEGEND SEDAN

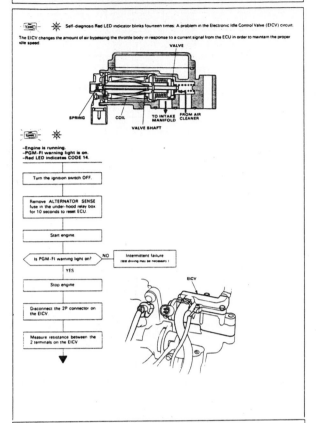

- Self-diagnosis Red LED indicator blinks fourteen times. A problem in the Electronic Idle Control Valve (EICV) circuit.

The EICV changes the amount of air bypassing the throttle body in response to a current signal from the ECU in order to maintain the proper idle speed.

-Engine is running.
-PGM-FI warning light is on.
-Red LED indicates CODE 14.

Turn the ignition switch OFF.

Remove ALTERNATOR SENSE fuse in the under-hood relay box for 10 seconds to reset ECU.

Start engine.

Is PGM-FI warning light on? — NO → Intermittent failure (test driving may be necessary)

YES

Stop engine.

Disconnect the 2P connector on the EICV.

Measure resistance between the 2 terminals on the EICV.

EICV DIAGNOSTIC CHART
1987–88 ACURA LEGEND COUPE AND 1988 LEGEND SEDAN

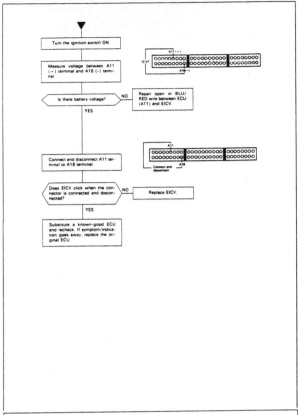

Turn the ignition switch ON

Measure voltage between A11 (–) terminal and A18 (–) terminal

Is there battery voltage? — NO → Repair open in BLU/RED wire between ECU (A11) and EICV.

YES

Connect and disconnect A11 terminal to A18 terminal.

Does EICV click when the connector is connected and disconnected? — NO → Replace EICV.

YES

Substitute a known-good ECU and recheck. If symptom/indication goes away, replace the original ECU.

EICV DIAGNOSTIC CHART
1987–88 ACURA LEGEND COUPE AND 1988 LEGEND SEDAN

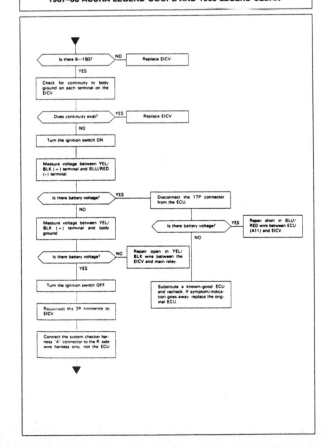

Is there 8—15Ω? — NO → Replace EICV.

YES

Check for continuity to body ground on each terminal on the EICV.

Does continuity exist? — YES → Replace EICV.

NO

Turn the ignition switch ON.

Measure voltage between YEL/BLK (+) terminal and BLU/RED (–) terminal.

Is there battery voltage? — YES → Disconnect the 17P connector from the ECU.

NO

Measure voltage between YEL/BLK (+) terminal and body ground

Is there battery voltage? → Repair short in BLU/RED wire between ECU (A11) and EICV.

NO

Is there battery voltage? — NO → Repair open in YEL/BLK wire between the EICV and main relay.

YES

Turn the ignition switch OFF.

Reconnect the 2P connector to EICV.

Connect the system checker harness "A" connector to the R. side wire harness only. not the ECU.

Substitute a known-good ECU and recheck. If symptom/indication goes away. replace the original ECU.

STARTER SIGNAL DIAGNOSTIC CHART
1987–88 ACURA LEGEND COUPE AND 1988 LEGEND SEDAN

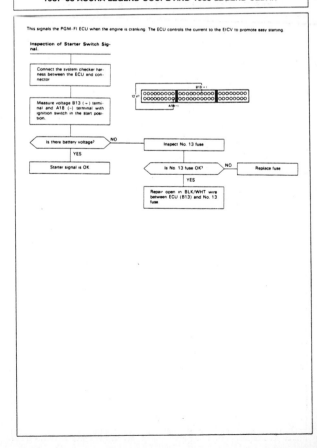

This signals the PGM-FI ECU when the engine is cranking. The ECU controls the current to the EICV to promote easy starting.

Inspection of Starter Switch Signal.

Connect the system checker harness between the ECU and connector

Measure voltage B13 (+) terminal and A18 (–) terminal with ignition switch in the start position.

Is there battery voltage? — NO → Inspect No. 13 fuse

YES

Starter signal is OK

Is No. 13 fuse OK? — NO → Replace fuse

YES

Repair open in BLK/WHT wire between ECU (B13) and No. 13 fuse

ALTERNATOR FR SIGNAL DIAGNOSTIC CHART
1987–88 ACURA LEGEND COUPE AND 1988 LEGEND SEDAN

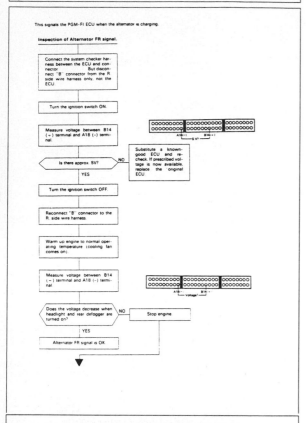

A/T SHIFT POSITION SIGNAL DIAGNOSTIC CHART
1987–88 ACURA LEGEND COUPE AND 1988 LEGEND SEDAN

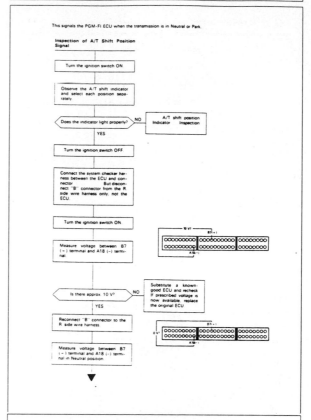

ALTERNATOR FR SIGNAL DIAGNOSTIC CHART
1987–88 ACURA LEGEND COUPE AND 1988 LEGEND SEDAN

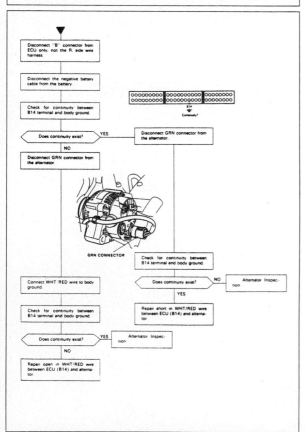

A/T SHIFT POSITION SIGNAL DIAGNOSTIC CHART
1987–88 ACURA LEGEND COUPE AND 1988 LEGEND SEDAN

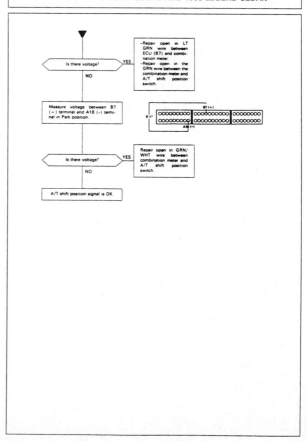

P/S OIL PRESSURE SIGNAL DIAGNOSTIC CHART
1987–88 ACURA LEGEND COUPE AND 1988 LEGEND SEDAN

This signals the PGM-FI ECU when the power steering load is high.

Inspection of P/S Oil Pressure Signal

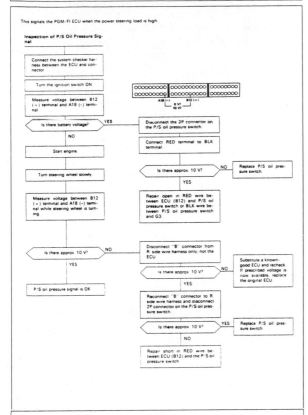

CLUTCH SWITCH SIGNAL DIAGNOSTIC CHART
1987–88 ACURA LEGEND COUPE AND 1988 LEGEND SEDAN

This signals the PGM-FI ECU when the clutch is engaged.

Inspection of clutch switch signal

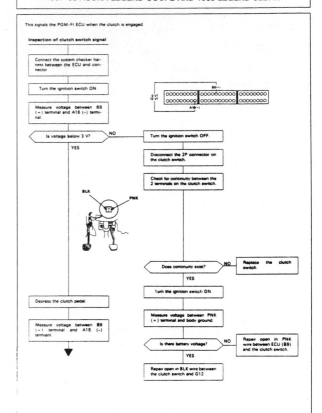

M/T NEUTRAL SWITCH SIGNAL DIAGNOSTIC CHART
1987–88 ACURA LEGEND COUPE AND 1988 LEGEND SEDAN

This signals the PGM-FI ECU when the transmission is in Neutral.

Inspection of M/T Neutral Switch Signal

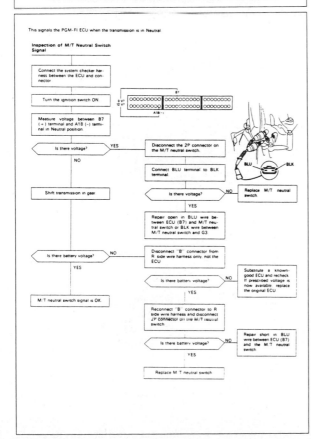

CLUTCH SWITCH SIGNAL DIAGNOSTIC CHART
1987–88 ACURA LEGEND COUPE AND 1988 LEGEND SEDAN

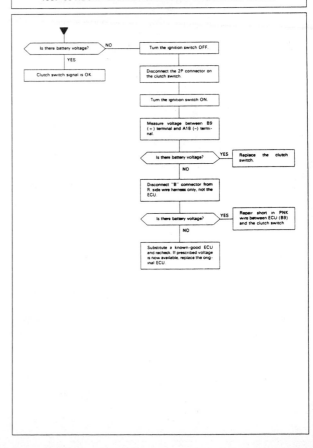

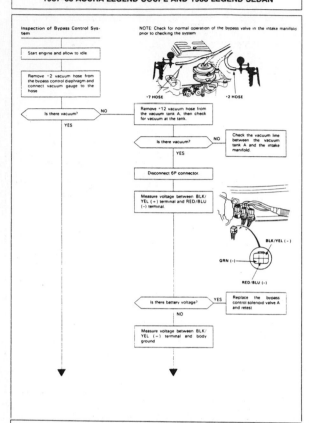

BYPASS CONTROL SYSTEM DIAGNOSTIC CHART
1987–88 ACURA LEGEND COUPE AND 1988 LEGEND SEDAN

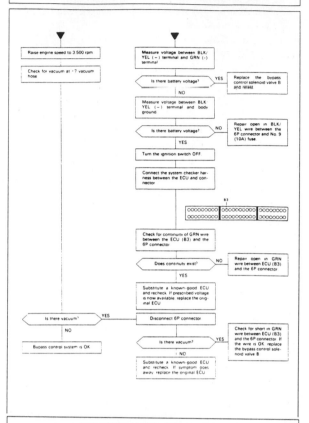

BYPASS CONTROL SYSTEM DIAGNOSTIC CHART
1987–88 ACURA LEGEND COUPE AND 1988 LEGEND SEDAN

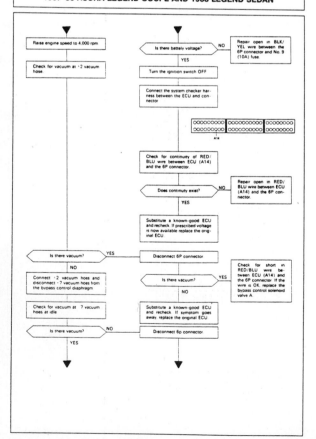

BYPASS CONTROL SYSTEM DIAGNOSTIC CHART
1987–88 ACURA LEGEND COUPE AND 1988 LEGEND SEDAN

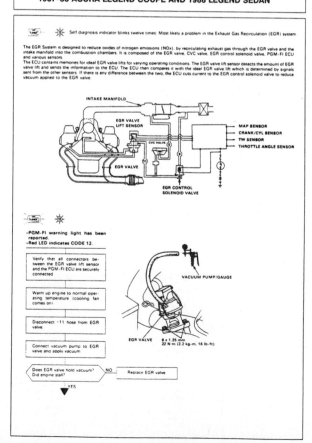

EGR SYSTEM DIAGNOSTIC CHART
1987–88 ACURA LEGEND COUPE AND 1988 LEGEND SEDAN

EGR SYSTEM DIAGNOSTIC CHART
1987–88 ACURA LEGEND COUPE AND 1988 LEGEND SEDAN

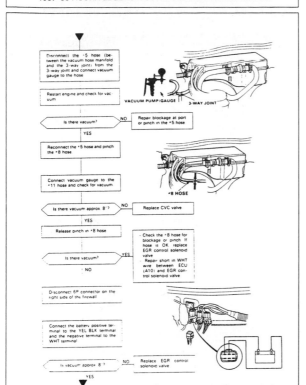

EGR SYSTEM DIAGNOSTIC CHART
1987–88 ACURA LEGEND COUPE AND 1988 LEGEND SEDAN

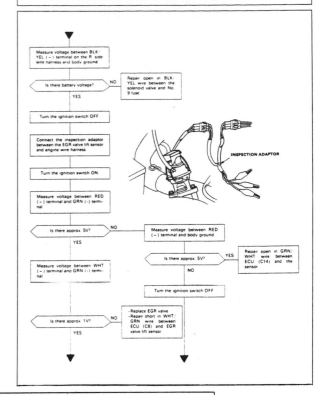

EGR SYSTEM DIAGNOSTIC CHART
1987–88 ACURA LEGEND COUPE AND 1988 LEGEND SEDAN

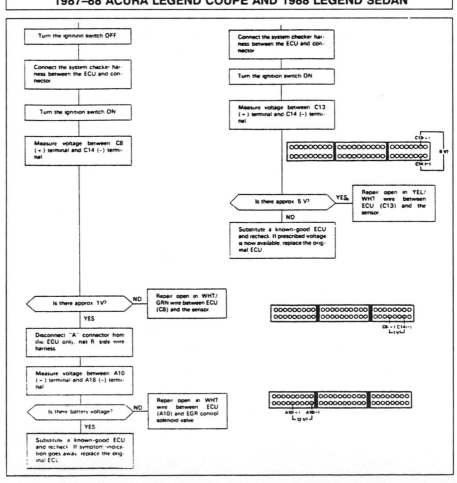

FAST CHECK DIAGNOSTIC CHART—1986–88 STERLING

IMPORTANT

A fault with the oxygen sensors will be indicated by the illuminated 'CHECK ENGINE' warning lamp on the instrument panel. These cannot be checked by the Fast Check. If a fault is suspected in this area, refer to the Repair Manual for diagnosis.

CODE DISPLAYED	COMPONENT UNDER TEST	CODE DISPLAYED	COMPONENT UNDER TEST
01	Injector 1	20	Manifold absolute pressure (MAP) sensor
02	Injector 2	21	Atmospheric pressure (PA) sensor
03	Injector 3	22	Throttle angle sensor
04	Injector 4	23	Idle mixture adjustment (IMA) sensor
05	Injector 5	24	Exhaust gas recirculation (EGR) lift sensor
06	Injector 6	25	Water temperature (TW) sensor
07	Electronic idle control valve (EICV)	26	Manifold air temperature (TA) sensor
08	Exhaust gas recirculation (EGR) solenoid	*27	Front oxygen sensor
09	Convertor lock up solenoid	*28	Rear oxygen sensor (EXKPRO sensor on non emission controlled vehicle)
10	Pressure regulator solenoid	29	Alternator
11	Ignition control solenoid A	30	Power steering switch
12	Ignition control solenoid B	31	Automatic transmission park switch
*13	Air suction control solenoid	32	Automatic transmission neutral switch
*14	Air conditioning clutch relay	33	Radiator fan control switch
*15	Fascia warning lamp	34	Speed transducer
16	Fuel pump	35	Earth
17	Cranking signal		
18	Crank angle sensor 1		
19	Crank angle sensor 2		

* EMISSION CONTROLLED VEHICLES ONLY

Ignition off   Disconnect harness from ECU

FAST CHECK DIAGNOSTIC CHART—1986–88 STERLING

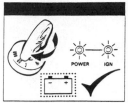

Switch ignition on   IGNITION LED off — refer to possible causes

IGNITION LED on — OK to proceed

POSSIBLE CAUSES	ACTION
Fuse 'H' (50A) under bonnet fusebox open circuit	Check fuse — renew
Fuse 'U' (15A) under bonnet fusebox open circuit	Check fuse — renew
Fuse '13' (10A) passenger compartment fusebox open circuit	Check fuse — renew
Open circuit between battery and ECU connector	With ignition switched on, check the following wires on the main relay base for battery voltage. Light green/orange wire, Blue/light green wire, Brown wire, Yellow/black wire, Yellow/black wire pin A15 ECU connector, Rectify above as necessary
Main relay faulty	Renew — retest

FAST CHECK DIAGNOSTIC CHART—1986–88 STERLING

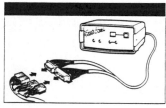
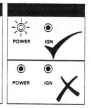

Connect Fast Check harness to ECU harness POWER LED on — OK to proceed

POWER LED off — refer to possible causes

POSSIBLE CAUSES	ACTION
Battery below nominal charge	If battery below 12V charge or renew
Fuse 'S' (10A) under bonnet fusebox open circuit	Check fuse — renew
Open circuit between passenger compartment fusebox and ECU connector. Pin A17. Brown/black wire	Check for battery voltage — rectify as necessary

---

FAST CHECK DIAGNOSTIC CHART—1986–88 STERLING

IMPORTANT

Tests 01–06 are individual injector tests and share the same diagnostic routine, with the exception of wire colours and ECU connector pins

CODE DISPLAYED	INJECTOR	WIRE COLOUR	ECU CONNECTOR PIN No
01	1	Brown	A1
02	2	Red	A3
03	3	Orange	A5
04	4	White/blue	A7
05	5	Black/red	A13
06	6	Yellow	A6

A common red/black wire supplies all 6 injectors

Press PROCEED button code displayed Audible clicking from injector — OK to proceed FAIL LED continuously on or flashing — refer to possible causes

PASS LED on

FAST CHECK DIAGNOSTIC CHART – 1986–88 STERLING

POSSIBLE CAUSES	ACTION
Open circuit in yellow/black wire between main relay and harness connector to resistor pack	With ignition on check for battery voltage — rectify as necessary
IMPORTANT Disconnect ECU connector from Fast Check harness, resistor pack from harness and injector connectors from injectors	
Open/short circuit resistor in resistor pack	Check for a resistance of 5-7 ohms between the red wire and each black wire on the resistor pack connector, renew — retest
Open circuit between resistor pack connector and each injector connector (red/black wire)	Check for continuity — rectify as necessary
Open circuit between injector connectors and ECU connector. Wire colours and ECU pin numbers relate to injectors shown in table above	Check for continuity — rectify as necessary
Short circuit between wires in injector connector	Check resistance of each connector above 1M ohm — OK — or rectify as necessary

POSSIBLE CAUSES	ACTION
Short circuit between wires in harness connector to resistor pack	Check resistance between each red/black wire and the yellow/black wire and every red/black wire with the others. Above 1M ohm — OK — or rectify as necessary
Injector faulty	Check resistance of each injector between 1.5 - 2.5 ohms — OK — or renew — retest

---

FAST CHECK DIAGNOSTIC CHART – 1986–88 STERLING

Exhaust Gas Re-Circulation (EGR) Solenoid Test

Press PROCEED button 08 displayed

PASS LED on

Audible clicking from solenoid — OK to proceed

FAIL LED continuously on or flashing refer to possible causes

POSSIBLE CAUSES	ACTION
Open circuit in green/orange wire between passenger compartment fuse box and harness connector to solenoid control box	Check for battery voltage rectify as necessary
IMPORTANT Ignition off. Disconnect ECU connector from Fast Check harness and harness connection from solenoid control box	
Open circuit between blue/red wire on harness connector to control box and ECU connection pin A1C	Check for continuity — rectify as necessary
Short circuit between green/orange wire and blue/red wire or harness connection to control box	Check resistance — above 1M ohm — OK — or rectify as necessary
Short circuit between blue/red wire on harness connector to control box and earth	Check resistance — above 1M ohm — OK — or rectify as necessary
Control solenoid faulty	Renew — retest

FAST CHECK DIAGNOSTIC CHART – 1986–88 STERLING

Electronic Idle Control Valve (EICV) Solenoid Test

 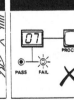

Press PROCEED button 07 displayed

PASS LED on

Audible clicking from solenoid — OK to proceed

FAIL LED continuously on or flashing — refer to possible causes

POSSIBLE CAUSES	ACTION
Open circuit between main relay base and EICV connector (yellow/black wire)	With ignition on check for battery voltage on the EICV connector
IMPORTANT Ignition off. Disconnect ECU connector from Fast Check harness and connector from EICV	
Open circuit between blue/red wire on EICV connector and ECU connector Pin A11	Check for continuity — rectify as necessary
Short circuit between yellow/black wire and blue/red wire on EICV connector	Check resistance, above 1M ohm — OK — or rectify as necessary
Short circuit between yellow/black wire on EICV connector and earth	Check resistance above 1M ohm — OK — or rectify as necessary
Short circuit between blue/red wire on EICV connector and earth	Check resistance, above 1M ohm — OK — or rectify as necessary
EICV solenoid faulty	Renew — retest

FAST CHECK DIAGNOSTIC CHART – 1986–88 STERLING

Convertor Lock-up Solenoid Test (Auto only)

  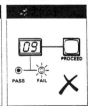

Press PROCEED button 09 displayed

PASS LED on

Audible clicking from solenoid — OK to proceed

FAIL LED continuously on or flashing — refer to possible causes

POSSIBLE CAUSES	ACTION
IMPORTANT Ignition off. Disconnect harness ECU connector from Fast Check harness and solenoid connector from solenoid	
Open circuit between green/orange wire on passenger compartment fuse box and black/yellow wire on solenoid connector	Check for continuity — rectify as necessary
Open circuit between solenoid connector and ECU connector pin A14 (blue/yellow wire)	Check for continuity — rectify as necessary
Short circuit between yellow/black wire and blue/yellow wire on solenoid connector	Check resistance — above 1M ohm — UK — or rectify as necessary
Short circuit between blue/yellow wire on solenoid connector and earth	Check resistance — above 1M ohm — OK — or rectify as necessary
Solenoid faulty	Renew — retest

FAST CHECK DIAGNOSTIC CHART – 1986–88 STERLING

IMPORTANT

Tests 10-13 are individual solenoid tests and share the same diagnostic routine, with the exception of wire colours and ECU connector pins

CODE DISPLAYED	CONTROL SOLENOID VALVE	WIRE COLOUR	ECU PIN No
10	Pressure regulator	Blue green	B17
11	Ignition A	Orange	A8
12	Ignition B	Green/slate	B2
13	Air suction	Pink (emission controlled vehicles only)	B15

A common orange green wire supplies all four solenoids

Press PROCEED button 10 displayed

PASS LED on

Audible clicking from solenoid – OK to proceed

FAIL LED continuously on or flashing – refer to possible causes

---

FAST CHECK DIAGNOSTIC CHART – 1986–88 STERLING

Press PROCEED button 13 displayed

PASS LED on

Audible clicking from solenoid – OK to proceed

FAIL LED continuously on or flashing – refer to possible causes

POSSIBLE CAUSES	ACTION
Open circuit in green/orange wire between passenger compartment fusebox and harness connector to solenoid control box	Check for battery voltage – rectify as necessary
IMPORTANT Ignition off. Disconnect ECU connector from Fast Check harness and harness connector from solenoid control box	
Open circuit between harness connector to control box and ECU connector. Wire colours and pin numbers to solenoid in the table above	Check for continuity – rectify as necessary
Short circuit between green/orange wire and harness connector and each of the wire colours listed in table above	Check resistance – above 1M ohm – OK – or rectify as necessary
Apart from green orange wire short circuit between each of the wires on the harness connector and earth	Check resistance – above 1M ohm – OK – or rectify as necessary
Control solenoid faulty	Renew – retest

FAST CHECK DIAGNOSTIC CHART – 1986–88 STERLING

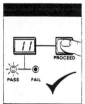

Press PROCEED button 11 displayed

PASS LED on

Audible clicking from solenoid – OK to proceed

FAIL LED continuously on or flashing – refer to possible causes

 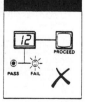

Press PROCEED button 12 displayed

PASS LED on

Audible clicking from solenoid – OK to proceed

FAIL LED continuously on or flashing – refer to possible causes

---

FAST CHECK DIAGNOSTIC CHART – 1986–88 STERLING

Air Conditioning Clutch Relay Test (Air Con. only)

Press PROCEED button 14 displayed

PASS LED on

Audible clicking from relay – OK to proceed

PASS LED on – OK to proceed

FAIL LED continuously on or flashing – refer to possible causes

POSSIBLE CAUSES	ACTION
Fuse No. '16' (10A) passenger compartment fuse box open circuit	Check fuse – renew
Open circuit between green/yellow wire passenger compartment fusebox and relay base pin 85	With ignition on check for battery voltage on pin 85
IMPORTANT Ignition off. Disconnect ECU harness connector from Fast Check harness and relay from relay base	
Open circuit between black/yellow wire on relay base pin 86 and ECU connector pin B19	Check continuity – rectify as necessary
Short circuit between black/yellow wire on relay base pin 86 and earth	Check resistance – above 1M ohm – OK – or rectify as necessary
Relay faulty	Renew – retest

FAST CHECK DIAGNOSTIC CHART – 1986–88 STERLING

Instrument Panel Warning Lamp Test

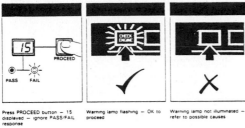

Press PROCEED button – 15 displayed – ignore PASS/FAIL response

Warning lamp flashing – OK to proceed

Warning lamp not illuminated – refer to possible causes

POSSIBILE CAUSES	ACTION
IMPORTANT Ignition off – Disconnect ECU connector from Fast Check harness and white 10 pin connector from fuel/temperature gauge side of instrument pack	
Bulb blown	Renew bulb
Open circuit between white connector and ECU harness connector Pin B6 – blue wire	Check for continuity – rectify as necessary
Short circuit between ECU harness connector pin B6 and earth	Check resistance – above 1M ohm OK – or rectify as necessary
Fault not found	Use Analogue Fast Check SMD 4060 to diagnose fault

---

FAST CHECK DIAGNOSTIC CHART – 1986–88 STERLING

Cranking Signal Test

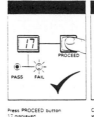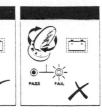

Press PROCEED button 17 displayed

FAIL LED continuously on

Crank engine – PASS LED on while engine is cranking OK to proceed

FAIL LED continuously on during cranking – refer to possible causes

POSSIBLE CAUSES	ACTION
Fuse '12' (10A) passenger compartment fuse box open circuit	Check fuse – renew
IMPORTANT Ignition off – Disconnect ECU connector from Fast Check harness	
Open circuit between passenger compartment fusebox connector and ECU Pin B13 (white red wire)	Check for continuity – rectify as necessary
Short circuit between red white wire ECU connector Pin B13 and earth	Check resistance – above 1M ohm – OK – or rectify as necessary

---

FAST CHECK DIAGNOSTIC CHART – 1986–88 STERLING

Fuel Pump Test

Press PROCEED button 16 displayed

PASS LED on

Pump runs (pulsed) – OK to proceed

FAIL LED continuously on or flashing – refer to possible causes

POSSIBLE CAUSES	ACTION
IMPORTANT Ignition off. Disconnect ECU connector from Fast Check harness, main relay from relay base and harness connector from fuel pump	
Open circuit between main relay base and fuel pump connector (black/yellow wire)	Check for continuity – rectify as necessary
Open circuit between main relay base and ECU connector pin A12 (green/black wire)	Check for continuity – rectify as necessary
Open circuit between black wire on fuel pump connector and earth	Check for continuity – rectify as necessary
Short circuit between black/yellow wire on fuel pump connector	Check resistance – if above 1M ohm OK – or rectify as necessary
Short circuit between black/yellow wire on fuel pump connector and earth	Check resistance – if above 1M ohm OK – or rectify as necessary
Short circuit between green/black wire on main relay base and earth	Check resistance – if above 1M ohm OK – or rectify as necessary
Main relay faulty	Renew – retest
Fuel pump faulty	Renew – retest

FAST CHECK DIAGNOSTIC CHART – 1986–88 STERLING

Crank Angle Sensor 1 Test

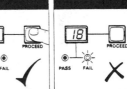

Crank angle sensor 1 test

Press PROCEED button 18 displayed

PASS LED on – OK to proceed

FAIL LED continuously on or flashing – refer to possible causes

POSSIBLE CAUSES	ACTION
IMPORTANT Ignition off. Disconnect ECU harness connector from Fast Check harness and crank angle harness connector from sensor	
Open circuit between harness connector to sensor and ECU pin C1 (blue wire)	Check for continuity – rectify as necessary
Open circuit between harness connector to sensor and ECU pin C2 (white wire)	Check for continuity – rectify as necessary
Short circuit between blue wire and white wire on harness connector to sensor	Check resistance – above 1M ohm – OK – or rectify as necessary
Short circuit between blue wire on harness connector to sensor and earth	Check resistance – above 1M ohm – OK – or rectify as necessary
Short circuit between white wire on harness connector to sensor and earth	Check resistance – above 1M ohm – OK – or rectify as necessary
Sensor faulty	Renew – retest

FAST CHECK DIAGNOSTIC CHART — 1986–88 STERLING

Crank Angle Sensor 2 Test

Crank angle sensor 2 test

Press PROCEED button
19 displayed

PASS LED on — OK to proceed

FAIL LED continuously on or
flashing — refer to possible
causes

POSSIBLE CAUSES	ACTION
IMPORTANT Ignition off. Disconnect ECU harness connector from Fast Check harness and crank angle harness connector from sensor	
Open circuit between harness connector to sensor and ECU pin C3 (orange/blue wire)	Check for continuity — rectify as necessary
Open circuit between harness connector to sensor and ECU pin C4 (white/blue wire)	Check for continuity — rectify as necessary
Short circuit between orange/blue wire and white/blue wire on harness connector to sensor	Check resistance — above 1M ohm — OK — or rectify as necessary
Short circuit between orange/blue wire on harness connector to sensor and earth	Check resistance — above 1M ohm — OK — or rectify as necessary
Short circuit between white/blue wire on harness connector to sensor and earth	Check resistance — above 1M ohm — OK — or rectify as necessary
Sensor faulty	Renew — retest

FAST CHECK DIAGNOSTIC CHART — 1986–88 STERLING

Manifold Absolute Pressure (MAP) Sensor Test

 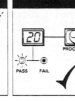 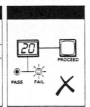

Manifold absolute pressure
(MAP) sensor test

Press PROCEED button
20 displayed

PASS LED on — OK to proceed

FAIL LED continuously on or
flashing — refer to possible
causes

POSSIBLE CAUSES	ACTION
IMPORTANT Ignition off. Disconnect ECU harness connector from Fast Check harness and harness connector from MAP sensor	
Open circuit between the following wires on harness connector to sensor and ECU pins	Check for continuity — rectify as necessary
Blue wire to pin C11 Green/orange wire to pin C14 Red/white wire to pin C15	
Short circuit between the following wires on harness connector to sensor	Check resistance — above 1M ohm — OK — or rectify as necessary
Blue wire and green/orange wire Blue wire and red/white wire Green/orange wire and red/white wire	
Short circuit between the following wire on harness connector to sensor and earth	Check resistance — above 1M ohm — OK — or rectify as necessary
Blue wire and earth Green/orange wire and earth Red/white wire and earth	
Sensor faulty	Renew — retest

FAST CHECK DIAGNOSTIC CHART — 1986–88 STERLING

IMPORTANT
Tests 21–26 are individual sensor tests and share the same diagnostic routine, with the exception of wire colours and ECU connector pins. To achieve correct results all six sensors should be tested and responses noted before diagnosis is carried out.

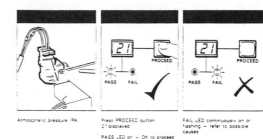

CODE DISPLAYED	SENSOR	WIRE COLOUR	ECU PIN No
21	Atmospheric pressure (PA)	Red	C0
22	Throttle angle	Red/blue	C7
23	Idle mixture adjustment (IMA)	Brown/orange	B20
24	EGR lift	White/green	C8
25	Water temperature (TW)	Red/white	C6
26	Manifold air temperature (TA)	Red/yellow	C5

A common green/white wire supplies all 6 sensors and is connector to pin C12 ECU connector.

Sensors 21–24 also share a common yellow/white wire which is connected to pin C13 ECU connector.

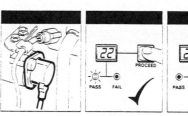

Atmospheric pressure (PA)

Press PROCEED button
21 displayed

PASS LED on — OK to proceed

FAIL LED continuously on or
flashing — refer to possible
causes

FAST CHECK DIAGNOSTIC CHART — 1986–88 STERLING

Throttle angle

Press PROCEED button
22 displayed

PASS LED on — OK to proceed

FAIL LED continuously on or
flashing — refer to possible
causes

Throttle Potentiometer Calibration	
FAIL LED flashing Throttle potentiometer out of calibration	Slacken retaining screw, turn throttle potentiometer clockwise through 'pass' band until fail LED flashes. Reverse direction and attain mid point in 'pass' band — OK to proceed
FAIL LED remains flashing	Refer to possible causes
FAIL LED continuously on Throttle potentiometer out of calibration	Slacken retaining screws, turn throttle potentiometer anti-clockwise through 'pass' band until fail LED continuously on. Reverse direction and attain mid point in 'pass' band — OK to proceed
FAIL LED remains continuously on	Refer to possible causes

FAST CHECK DIAGNOSTIC CHART—1986–88 STERLING

Idle mixture adjustment (IMA)

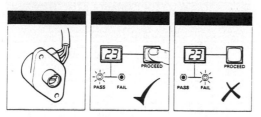

Press PROCEED button
23 displayed

PASS LED on — OK to proceed

FAIL LED continuously on or
flashing — refer to possible
causes

EGR lift

Press PROCEED button
24 displayed

PASS LED on — OK to proceed

FAIL LED continuously on or
flashing — refer to possible
causes

FAST CHECK DIAGNOSTIC CHART—1986–88 STERLING

POSSIBLE CAUSES	ACTION
IMPORTANT Ignition off. Disconnect ECU harness connector from Fast Check harness and harness connectors from all sensors	
Open circuit between harness connector to sensor and ECU connector pin C12 (green/white wire)	Check for continuity — rectify as necessary
Open circuit between harness connector to sensor and ECU connector pin C13 where applicable (yellow/white wire)	Check for continuity — rectify as necessary
Open circuit between ECU connector pin No. and wire to sensor connector under test, as listed in table above	Check for continuity — rectify as necessary
Short circuit between wire to sensor under test and green/white wire on harness connector sensor	Check resistance — above 1M ohm — OK — or rectify as necessary
Short circuit between wire to sensor under test and yellow/white wire on harness connector to sensor where applicable	Check resistance — above 1M ohm — OK — or rectify as necessary

POSSIBLE CAUSES	ACTION
Short circuit between wire to sensor under test and earth	Check resistance — above 1M ohm — OK — or rectify as necessary
Short circuit between green/white wire on harness connector to sensor and earth	Check resistance — above 1M ohm — OK — or rectify as necessary
Short circuit between yellow/white wire on harness connector to sensor and earth	Check resistance — above 1M ohm — OK — or rectify as necessary
Sensor faulty	Renew — retest

FAST CHECK DIAGNOSTIC CHART—1986–88 STERLING

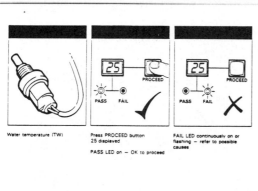

Water temperature (TW)

Press PROCEED button
25 displayed

PASS LED on — OK to proceed

FAIL LED continuously on or
flashing — refer to possible
causes

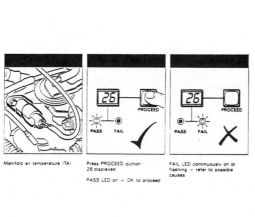

Manifold air temperature (TA)

Press PROCEED button
26 displayed

PASS LED on — OK to proceed

FAIL LED continuously on or
flashing — refer to possible
causes

FAST CHECK DIAGNOSTIC CHART—1986–88 STERLING

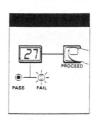

Press PROCEED button
27 displayed

SPARE CODE FOR FUTURE DEVELOPMENTS—
IGNORE TEST RESPONSE

Press PROCEED button
28 displayed

SPARE CODE FOR FUTURE DEVELOPMENTS—
IGNORE TEST RESPONSE

FAST CHECK DIAGNOSTIC CHART — 1986–88 STERLING

POSSIBLE CAUSES — ACTION

IMPORTANT
Ignition off. Disconnect ECU connector from Fast Check harness and alternator connector from alternator

Possible Causes	Action
Open circuit between white/red wire on alternator connector and ECU connector pin B14 (brown/red wire)	Check for continuity — rectify as necessary
Short circuit between white/red wire on alternator connector and earth	Check resistance — above 1M ohm — OK — or rectify as necessary
Alternator faulty	Refer to repair manual for alternator diagnosis

Alternator Test

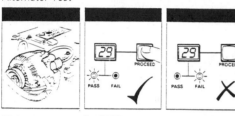

Alternator test

Press PROCEED button
29 displayed

PASS LED on — OK to proceed

FAIL LED continuously on —
refer to possible causes

FAST CHECK DIAGNOSTIC CHART — 1986–88 STERLING

POSSIBLE CAUSES — ACTION

IMPORTANT
Ignition off. Disconnect ECU connector from Fast Check harness connector and harness connector from power steering switch

Possible Causes	Action
Open circuit between harness connector to switch and ECU connector pin B10 (red wire)	Check for continuity — rectify as necessary
Open circuit between black wire on harness connector to switch and earth	Check for continuity — rectify as necessary
Short circuit between red wire and black wire on harness connector to switch	Check resistance — above 1M ohm — OK — or rectify as necessary
Short circuit between red wire on harness connector and earth	Check resistance — above 1M ohm — OK — or rectify as necessary
Switch faulty	Renew — retest

Auto Transmission Park Switch Test (Auto only)

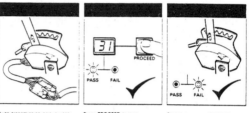

Auto transmission park switch test

IMPORTANT
Ensure gear selector is in park position

Press PROCEED button
31 displayed

PASS LED on

Select reverse — FAIL LED on
— OK to proceed

FAST CHECK DIAGNOSTIC CHART — 1986–88 STERLING

Power Steering Switch Test

 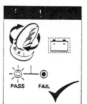

Power steering switch test

Press PROCEED button
30 displayed

FAIL LED on

Crank engine and turn steering wheel — PASS LED on

NOTE The PASS LED may only be on briefly

Stop cranking and turning —
FAIL LED on

FAIL LED on throughout — refer
to possible causes

FAST CHECK DIAGNOSTIC CHART — 1986–88 STERLING

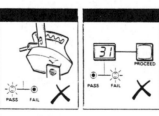

Select reverse — PASS LED on
— refer to possible causes

FAIL LED continuously on or
flashing — refer to possible
causes

IMPORTANT
Ensure gear selector is in park position

POSSIBLE CAUSES — ACTION

IMPORTANT
Ignition off. Disconnect ECU connector from Fast Check harness; 2 pin and 7 pin connectors from selector switch

Possible Causes	Action
Open circuit between green/white wire on 2 pin harness connector to switch and ECU harness connector pin B9	Check for continuity — rectify as necessary
Open circuit between black wire on 7 pin harness connector to switch and earth	Check for continuity — rectify as necessary
Short circuit between green/white wire on 2 pin harness connector to switch and earth	Check resistance — above 1M ohm — OK — or rectify as necessary
Inhibitor switch faulty	Renew — retest

FAST CHECK DIAGNOSTIC CHART – 1986–88 STERLING

Auto Transmission Neutral Switch Test (Auto only)

Auto transmission neutral switch test

IMPORTANT
Ensure gear selector is in neutral position

Press PROCEED button 32 displayed

PASS LED on

Select any gear – FAIL LED on – OK to proceed

Select any gear – PASS LED on – refer to possible causes

FAIL LED on continuously on or flashing – refer to possible causes

IMPORTANT
Ensure gear selector is in park position

FAST CHECK DIAGNOSTIC CHART – 1986–88 STERLING

POSSIBLE CAUSES	ACTION
IMPORTANT Ignition off. Disconnect ECU connector from Fast Check harness and connector from dual pressure switch	
Open circuit between blue/red wire on dual pressure switch connector and ECU connector pin B8	Check for continuity – rectify as necessary
Short circuit between blue/red wire on dual pressure switch and earth	Check resistance – above 1M ohm – OK – or rectify as necessary
Air condition circuit faulty	Use Air Conditioning Fast Check to diagnose fault

Speed Transducer Test

Speed transducer test

Press PROCEED button 34 displayed

PASS or FAIL LED on

Raise either front wheel off the ground

Rotate wheel

PASS/FAIL LEDs should illuminate alternately – OK to proceed

PASS or FAIL LED remains on continuously during wheel rotation – refer to possible causes

---

FAST CHECK DIAGNOSTIC CHART – 1986–88 STERLING

POSSIBLE CAUSES	ACTION
IMPORTANT Ignition off. Disconnect ECU connector from Fast Check harness. 2 pin and 7 pin connectors from selector switch	
Open circuit between green/white wire on 2 pin harness connector to switch and ECU harness connector pin B7	Check for continuity – rectify as necessary
Open circuit between black wire on 7 pin harness connector to switch and earth	Check for continuity – rectify as necessary
Short circuit between green/white wire on 2 pin harness connector to switch and earth	Check resistance – above 1M ohm – OK – or rectify as necessary
Inhibitor switch faulty	Renew – retest

Radiator Fan Control Switch (Air Con. only)

Air conditioning switch

Press PROCEED button 33 displayed

FAIL LED on

Press air con. switch – PASS LED on – OK to proceed

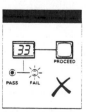

FAIL LED on after switch pressed – refer to possible causes

FAST CHECK DIAGNOSTIC CHART – 1986–88 STERLING

POSSIBLE CAUSES	ACTION
Speedometer not functioning	Use Instrument Fast Check to diagnose fault
Speedometer functioning:	
IMPORTANT Ignition off. Disconnect ECU connector from Fast Check harness and black connector from instrument pack	
Open circuit between black connector on instrument pack and ECU harness connect pin B16 (black/orange wire)	Check continuity – rectify as necessary
Short circuit between black/orange wire on instrument pack connector and earth	Check resistance – above 1M ohm OK – rectify as necessary
No signal out of instrument pack	Use Instrument Fast Check to diagnose fault

Earth Test

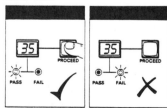

Press PROCEED button 35 displayed

PASS LED on – OK to proceed – END OF TESTS

FAIL LED continuously on – refer to possible causes

POSSIBLE CAUSES	ACTION
Open circuit between the following ECU harness connector pins and earth	Check for continuity – rectify as necessary
Black/slate wire pin A2 and earth Black wire pin A4 and earth Blue/brown wire pin A16 and earth Brown/green wire pin A18 and earth	

COMPONENT TEST PROCEDURES

Fast Idle Valve

ALL MODELS

NOTE: Fast idle valve is factory adjusted, it should not be disassembled.

1. Start engine.
2. Remove cover of fast idle valve.
3. Make sure that there is air flow with engine cold (coolant temperature below 86°F (30°C)). It can be detected by putting your finger on valve seat area.
4. If no air flow, replace fast idle valve.
5. Warm up to normal operating temperature (cooling fan comes on).
6. Check that valve is completely closed. If not, air is being sucked from valve seat area. It can be detected by putting your finger on valve seat area.
7. If any suction sound is heard, valve is leaking. Replace fast idle valve.

Dashpot

ALL MODELS

1. Check vacuum line for leaks, blockage or disconnected hose.

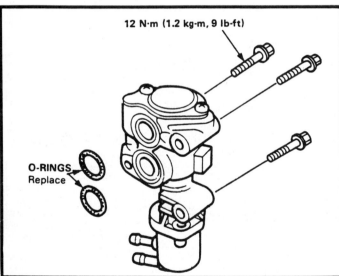

Fast idle valve

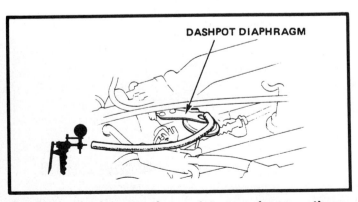

Dashpot diaphragm—Acura Integra shown, others similar

2. Disconnect vacuum hose (#6 on Integra and #8 on 1986–88 Legend Sedan and Sterling and #10 on 1987–88 Legend Coupe) from dashpot diaphragm, and connect a vacuum pump/gauge to hose.
3. Apply vacuum. Vacuum should leak out slowly.
4. If vacuum holds or leaks out quickly, replace dashpot check valve.
5. Connect a vacuum pump to dashpot diaphragm.
6. Apply vacuum and check that rod pulls in and vacuum holds. Rod should pull in and vacuum should hold.
7. If vacuum does not hold or rod does not move, replace dashpot diaphragm.

Injector Test

ALL MODELS

NOTE: Check following items before testing idle speed, ignition timing, valve clearance and idle CO%.

1. If engine will run, disconnect injector couplers with engine idling, and inspect change in idling speed. Idle should drop the same for each cylinder.
2. Check clicking sound of each injector by means of a stethoscope when engine is idling.
3. If any injector fails to make typical clicking sound, check wiring between ECU and injector. Voltage at injector coupler should fluctuate between 0–2 volts. If voltage is OK, replace injector.
4. If engine can not be started, remove coupler of injector, and measure resistance between terminals of injector. Resistance should be 1.5–2.5 ohms.
5. If resistance is not as specified, replace injector. If resistance is normal, check wiring between resistor and injector, wiring between resistors and control unit, and resistors.

Fuel System Resistor

ALL MODELS

1. Disconnect resistor coupler.

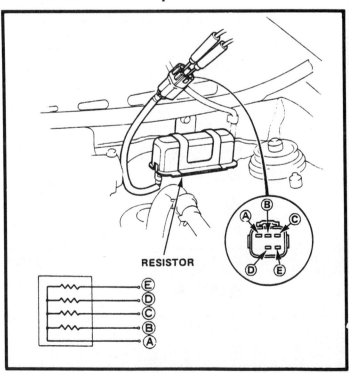

Fuel injector resistor pin identification and location—1986–88 Acura Integra

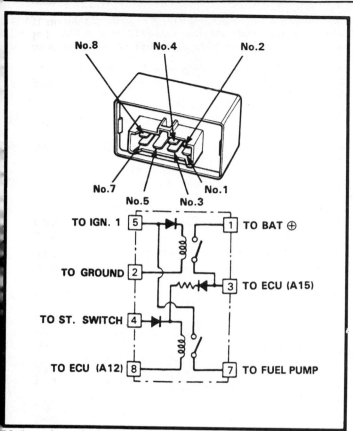

Main relay pin identification

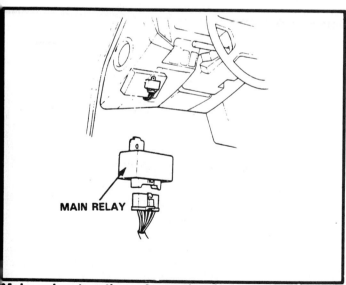

Main relay location—Acura Legend shown, others similar

2. On Integra models, check for resistance between each of resistor terminals (E, D, C and B) and power terminal (A). Resistance should be 5–7 ohms.

3. On Legend and Sterling models, check for resistance between each of resistor terminals (g, f, e, d, c and b) and power terminal (a). Resistance should be 5–7 ohms.

4. Replace resistor with a new one if any of resistances are outside of specification.

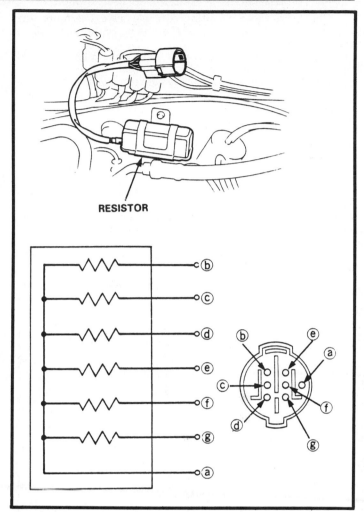

Fuel injector resistor pin identification and location— 1986–88 Acura Legend and Sterling

Fuel Pressure Testing

ALL MODELS

1. Relieve fuel pressure.
2. Remove service bolt and attach fuel pressure gauge.
3. Start engine. Measure fuel pressure with engine idling and vacuum hose of pressure regulator disconnected. Pressure should be 36–41 psi (250–279 kPa).
4. If fuel pressure is not as specified, first check fuel pump. If pump is OK, check following:
    a. If pressure is higher than specified, inspect for pinched or clogged fuel return hose or piping, and faulty pressure regulator.
    b. If pressure is lower than specified, inspect for clogged fuel filter, pinched or clogged fuel hose from fuel tank to fuel pump, pressure regulator failure, leakage in fuel line, or pinched, broken or disconnected regulator vacuum hose.

Main Relay Testing

ALL MODELS

1. Remove main relay, near under-dash fuse box.
2. Connect battery positive terminal to No. 4 terminal and battery negative terminal to No. 8 terminal of main relay.
3. Check for continuity between No. 5 terminal and No. 7 terminal of main relay. If no continuity, replace main relay.
4. Connect battery positive terminal to No. 5 terminal and battery negative terminal to No. 2 terminal of main relay.

5. Check that there is continuity between No. 1 terminal and No. 3 terminal of main relay. If there is no continuity, replace main relay.

6. Connect battery positive terminal to No. 3 terminal and battery negative terminal to No. 8 terminal of main relay.

7. Check that there is continuity between No. 5 terminal and No. 7 terminal of main relay. If there is no continuity, replace main relay.

Harness Testing

1986–88 ACURA INTEGRA

1. Keep ignition switch in off position.
2. Disconnect main relay connector.
3. Check continuity between Black wire in connector and body ground.
4. Connect positive probe of circuit tester to Yellow/White wire and negative probe of tester to Black wire. Tester should read battery voltage.
5. If there is no voltage, check wiring between battery and main relay as well as 15A fuse.

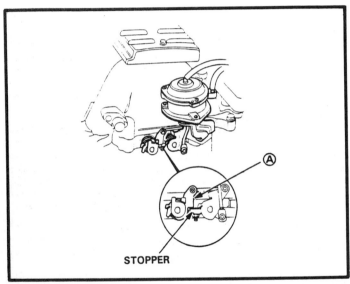

Bypass valve lever A and lever stopper—1987–88 Acura Legend Coupe and 1988 Legend Sedan

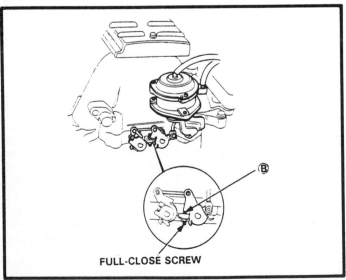

Bypass valve lever B and full-close screw—1987–88 Acura Legend Coupe and 1988 Legend Sedan

6. Connect positive probe of tester to Black/Yellow wire of connector and ground negative probe of tester to Black wire.
7. Turn ignition switch on. Tester should read battery voltage.
8. If no voltage, check wiring from ignition switch and main relay as well as fuse No. 4.
9. Connect positive probe of tester to Blue/White wire and negative probe to Black wire.
10. Turn ignition switch to START position. Tester should read battery voltage.
11. If no voltage, check wiring between ignition switch and main relay as well as fuse (7.5A).
12. Connect a jumper wire between Black/Yellow and Yellow wire in connector. Turn ignition switch ON. Fuel pump should work.
13. If pump does not work, check wiring between battery and fuel pump and wiring from fuel pump to ground (Black wire).

1986–87 LEGEND SEDAN AND STERLING

1. Keep ignition switch in off position.
2. Disconnect main relay connector.
3. Check continuity between Black wire in connector and body ground.
4. Connect positive probe of circuit tester to Yellow/Black wire and negative probe of tester to Black wire. Tester should read battery voltage.
5. If there is no voltage, check wiring between battery and main relay as well as ECU (15A) fuse.
6. Connect positive probe of tester to Black/Yellow wire of connector and ground negative probe of tester to Black wire.
7. Turn ignition switch on. Tester should read battery voltage.
8. If no voltage, check wiring from ignition switch and main relay as well as fuse No. (11 on Legend Sedan and Sterling and 9 on Legend Coupe).
9. Connect positive probe of tester to Black/White wire and negative probe to Black wire.
10. Turn ignition switch to START position. Tester should read battery voltage.

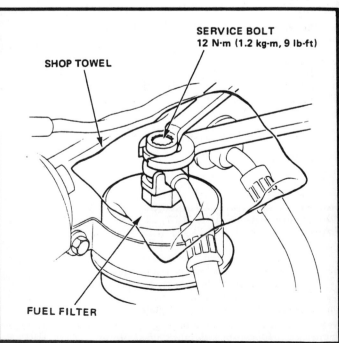

Fuel pressure relief—Acura Integra shown, others similar

11. If no voltage, check wiring between ignition switch and main relay as well as No. (2 fuse (10A) on Legend Sedan and Sterling and 13 (7.5A) on Legend Coupe).

12. Connect a jumper wire between two Black/Yellow wires in connector. Turn ignition switch ON. Fuel pump should work.

13. If pump does not work, check wiring between battery and fuel pump and wiring from fuel pump to ground (Black wire).

Bypass Valve Test

1987-88 ACURA LEGEND COUPE AND 1988 ACURA LEGEND SEDAN

NOTE: Do not adjust the bypass valve full-close screw. It was preset at the factory.

1. Check bypass valve shaft for binding or sticking.
2. Check bypass valve for smooth movement.
3. Check that lever A of bypass valve is in close contact with stopper when bypass valve is fully open.
4. Check that lever B of bypass valve is in close contact with full-close screw when valve is fully closed.
5. If any fault is found, clean linkage adn shafts with carburetor cleaner. If problem still exists after cleaning, disassemble intake manifold and check bypass valve.

Component Replacement

Fuel System Pressure Relieving

ALL MODELS

CAUTION

Keep open flames or sparks from work area. Do not smoke while working on fuel system. Be sure to relieve fuel pressure while engine is off.

NOTE: Before disconnecting fuel pipes or hoses, release pressure from system by loosen 6mm service bolt at top of fuel filter.

1. Disconnect battery negative cable from battery negative terminal.
2. Use a box end wrench on 6mm service bolt at top of fuel filter, while holding special banjo bolt with another wrench.
3. Place a rag or a shop towel over 6mm service bolt.
4. Slowly loosen 6mm service bolt one complete turn.

NOTE: A fuel pressure gauge can be attached at 6mm service bolt hole. Always replace washer between service bolt and Special Banjo Bolt, whenever service bolt is loosened to relieve fuel pressure. Replace all washers whenever bolts are removed to disassemble parts.

IDLE SPEED

Adjustment

1986-88 ACURA INTEGRA

1. Start engine and warm up to normal operating temperature; cooling fan will come on.
2. Connect a tachometer.
3. With engine idling, disconnect connector at EICV.
4. With all accessories off, check idle speed. Idle speed should be 550 ± 50 rpm (in neutral). Adjust idle speed, if necessary, by turning idle adjusting screw.
5. After adjustment, reconnect connector at EICV.
6. Disconnect hazard fuse at battery positive terminal for at least 10 seconds to reset ECU memory.

7. Start engine and warm it up to normal operating temperature (cooling fan comes on).
8. With all accessories off, check idle speed. Idle speed should be 800 ± 50 rpm (in neutral).
9. Check idle speed with headlights (HI) and rear window defogger ON. Idle should remain stable at 800 ± 50 rpm.
10. Check idle speed with air conditioner compressor on. Idle should remain stable at 800 ± 50 rpm.
11. If equipped with automatic transmission, check idle speed with transmission in gear. Idle should remain stable at 800 ± 50 rpm.

1986-88 LEGEND AND STERLING

1. Start engine and warm up to normal operating temperature; cooling fan will come on.
2. Connect a tachometer.
3. Set steering in straight forward condition, and check idling in no-load conditions in which all accessories are turned off and/or not operating.
4. Check idle speed. Idle speed should be:
1986-87 Legend Sedan and 1986-88 Sterling – 720 ± 50 rpm (in neutral).
1987-88 Legend Coupe and 1988 Legend Sedan – 680 ± 50 rpm (in neutral).
5. Check yellow LED display at ECU under passanger's seat.
   a. If yellow LED is OFF, do not adjust idle adjusting screw.
   b. If yellow LED is BLINKING, adjust idle screw ¼ turn clockwise.
   c. If yellow LED is ON, adjust idle screw ¼ turn counterclockwise.

NOTE: The yellow LED display may by lit at earlier stages, for example, when the distance covered is within 310 miles (500 km). However, no adjustment should be made. Check that the yellow LED goes off after approximately 30 seconds. If it does not go off, rotate the idle adjusting screw by ¼ turn in the same direction, and repeat teh same operation until the yellow LED goes off.

6. Check idle speed with headlights (HI) and rear window defogger ON. Idle should remain stable at specified idle speed.
7. Check idle speed with air conditioner compressor on. Idle should remain stable at specified idle speed.
8. If equipped with automatic transmission, check idle speed with transmission in gear. Idle should remain stable at specified idle speed.

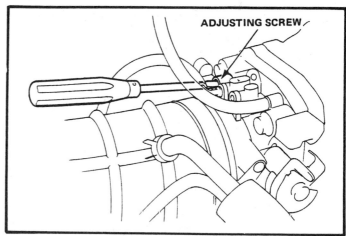

ADJUSTING SCREW

Idle speed adjusting screw—1986-88 Acura Integra

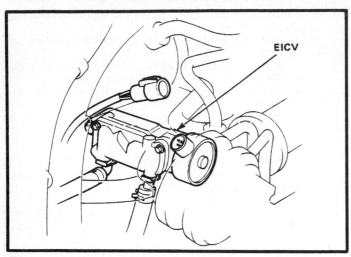

Electronic idle control valve (EICV)—1986–88 Acura Integra shown, others similar

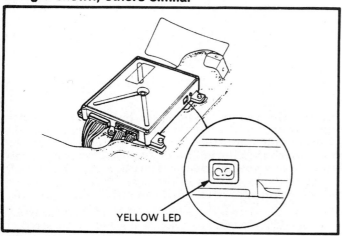

ECU yellow LED display—1986–87 Acura Legend Sedan and 1986–88 Sterling shown, Acura Legend Coupe and 1988 Legend Sedan similar

CRANK ANGLE SENSOR/ CRANK/CYL SENSOR

Removal and Installation

1986–88 ACURA INTEGRA

1. Disconnect connector from crank angle sensor.
2. Remove 3 bolts and remove sensor.
3. To install, reverse removal procedure. Make sure to use new O-ring with installing.

1986–88 ACURA LEGEND AND STERLING

1. Remove cruise control actuator.
2. Remove upper cover at front side of timing belt.
3. Remove timing belt.
4. Remove 3 bolts and detach pulley.
5. Remove 4 bolts and detach front side cover plate of timing belt.
6. To install, place sensor on cylinder head.
7. Align cam pulley pin with cam shaft hole to install cam pulley.
8. Complete installation by reversing removal procedure. Make sure cam pulley is aligned properly before install timing belt.

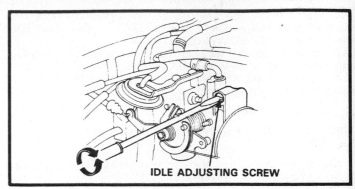

Idle speed adjusting screw—1986–87 Acura Legend Sedan and 1986–88 Sterling

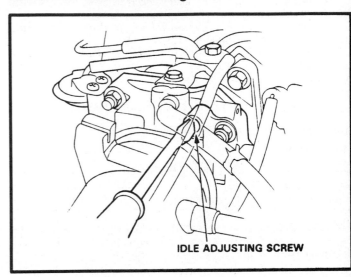

Idle speed adjusting screw—1987–88 Acura Legend Coupe and 1988 Legend Sedan

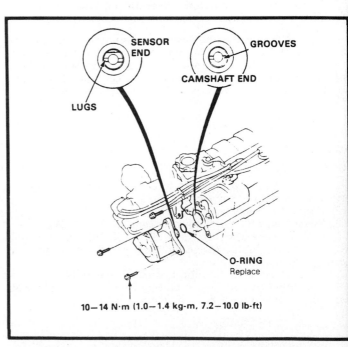

Crank angle sensor servicing—1986–88 Acura Integra

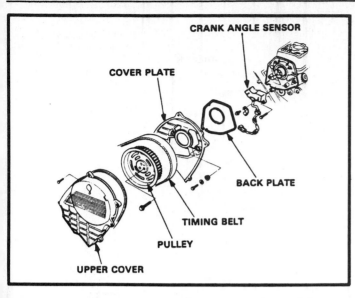

Crank angle sensor (Crank/CYL sensor) servicing—1986–88 Acura Legend and Sterling

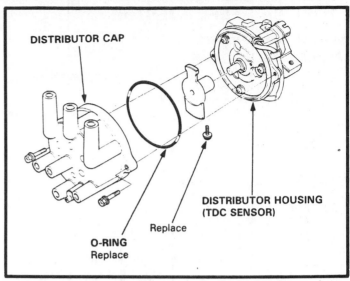

Top dead center (TDC) sensor—1987–88 Acura Legend Coupe and 1988 Legend Sedan

TOP DEAD CENTER (TDC) SENSOR

Removal and Installation

1987–88 LEGEND COUPE AND 1988 LEGEND SEDAN

1. Remove distributor.
2. Remove distributor cap from distributor housing (TDC sensor).
3. To install, reverse removal procedure. Be sure to use new O-ring.

THROTTLE BODY

Removal and Installation

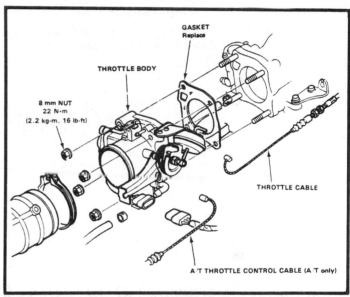

Throttle body servicing—1986–88 Acura Integra

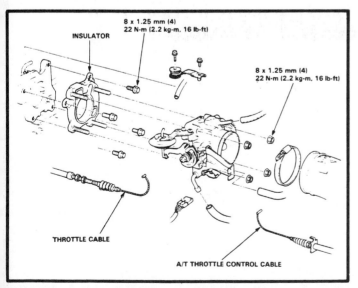

Throttle body servicing—1987–88 Acura Legend Coupe and 1988 Legend Sedan

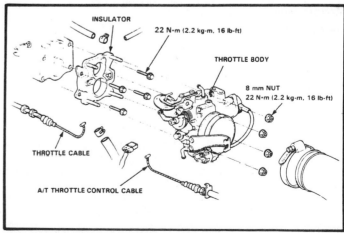

Throttle body servicing—1986–87 Acura Legend Sedan and 1986–88 Sterling

FUEL INJECTOR

Removal and Installation

1986–88 ACURA INTEGRA

1. Disconnect battery negative cable from battery negative.
2. Relieve fuel pressure.
3. Disconnect connector of injectors.
4. Disconnect vacuum hose and fuel return hose from pressure regulator.

NOTE: Place a rag or shop towel over hose and tube before disconnecting.

5. Remove pulsation damper.
6. Remove connector holder.
7. Loosen retainer nuts on fuel pipe.
8. Disconnect fuel pipe.
9. Remove injector from intake manifold.
10. Slide new cushion onto injector.
11. Coat new O-rings with clean engine oil and put O-rings on injectors.
12. Insert injectors into fuel pipe first.
13. Coat new seal rings with clean engine oil and press into intake manifold.
14. Install injector and fuel pipe assembly in manifold.

NOTE: To prevent damage to O-ring, install injectors in fuel pipe first, then install in intake manifold.

15. Align center line on connector with mark on fuel pipe.
16. Install and tighten retainer nuts.
17. Install pulsation damper.
18. Connect vacuum hose ad fuel return hose to pressure regulator.
19. Install connectors on injectors.
20. Turn ignition switch ON but do not operate starter. After fuel pump runs for approximately two seconds, fuel pressure in fuel line rises. Repeat this two or three times, then check whether there is any fuel leakage.

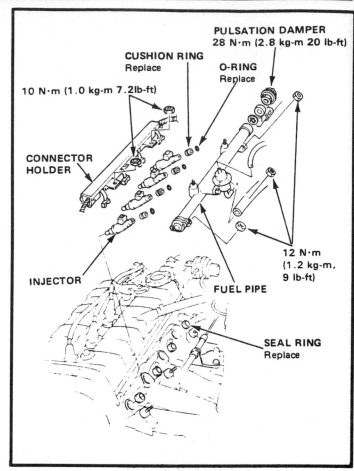

Fuel injector servicing—1986–88 Acura Integra

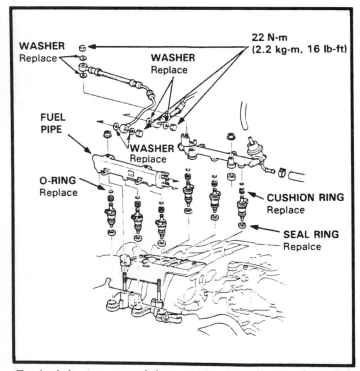

Fuel injector servicing—1987–88 Acura Legend Coupe and 1988 Legend Sedan

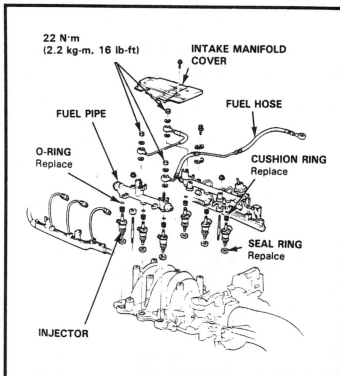

Fuel injector servicing—1986–87 Acura Legend Sedan and 1986–88 Sterling

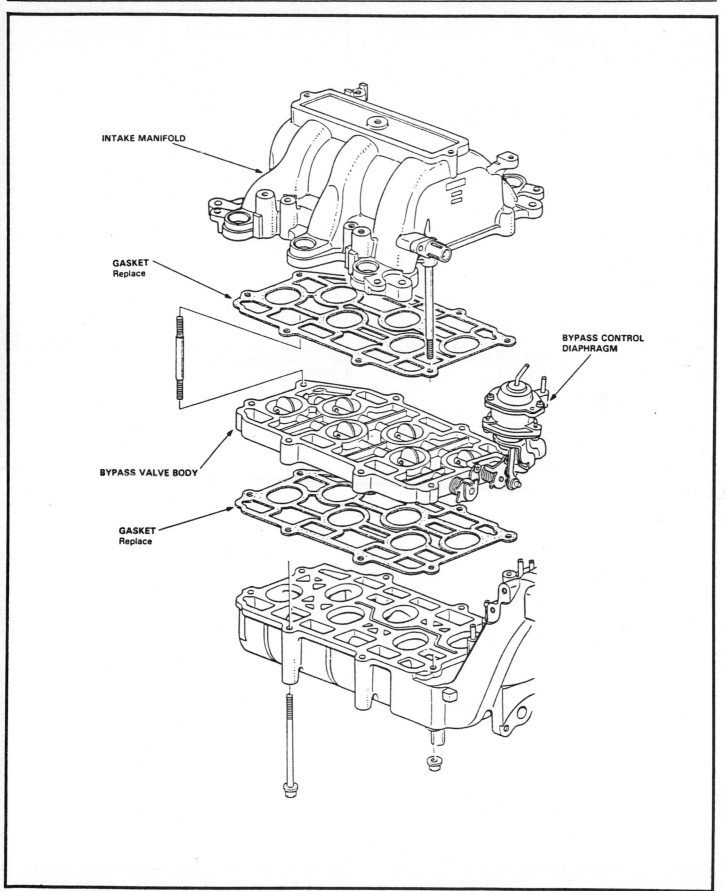

INTAKE MANIFOLD

GASKET
Replace

BYPASS CONTROL
DIAPHRAGM

BYPASS VALVE BODY

GASKET
Replace

Bypass valve body, exploded view—1987-88 Legend Coupe and 1988 Legend Sedan

1986–88 LEGEND AND STERLING

1. Disconnect battery negative cable from battery negative.
2. Relieve fuel pressure.
3. Disconnect connector of injectors.
4. Disconnect vacuum hose and fuel return hose from pressure regulator.

NOTE: Place a rag or shop towel over hose and tube before disconnecting.

5. On 1986–87 Legend Sedan and 1986–88 Sterling, remove intake manifold cover.
6. Disconnect fuel hose from fuel pipe.
7. Loosen retainer nuts on fuel pipe and harness holder.
8. Disconnect fuel pipe.
9. Remove injector from intake manifold.
10. Slide new cushion onto injector.
11. Coat new O-rings with clean engine oil and put O-rings on injectors.
12. Insert injectors into fuel pipe first.
13. Coat new seal rings with clean engine oil and press into intake manifold.
14. Install injector and fuel pipe assembly in manifold.

NOTE: To prevent damage to O-ring, install injectors in fuel pipe first, then install in intake manifold.

15. Align center line on connector with mark on fuel pipe.
16. Install and tighten retainer nuts.

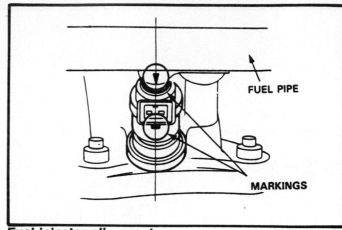

Fuel injector alignment

17. Connect vacuum hose ad fuel return hose to pressure regulator.
18. On 1986–87 Legend Sedan and 1986–88 Sterling, install intake manifold cover.
19. Install connectors on injectors.
20. Turn ignition switch ON but do not operate starter. After fuel pump runs for approximately two seconds, fuel pressure in fuel line rises. Repeat this two or three times, then check whether there is any fuel leakage.

PROGRAMMED FUEL INJECTION (PGM-FI) SYSTEM

ENGINE CONTROL SYSTEM APPLICATION CHART

Year	Model	Engine cc (liter)	Engine VIN	Fuel System	Ignition System
1984	Accord, S, STD, LX	1830 (1.8)	ES2	2 bbl	Electronic
	Civic	1342 (1.3)	EV1	2 bbl	Electronic
	Civic	1488 (1.5)	EW1	2 bbl	Electronic
	Prelude	1830 (1.8)	ES1	Dual 1 bbl ①	Electronic
1985	Accord S,STD,LX	1830 (1.8)	ES2	2 bbl	Electronic
	Accord Sei	1830 (1.8)	ES3	PGM-FI	Electronic
	Civic	1342 (1.3)	EV1	2 bbl	Electronic
	Civic	1488 (1.5)	EW1	2 bbl	Electronic
	Civic CRX HF	1488 (1.5)	EW1	2 bbl	Electronic
	Civic CRX Si	1488 (1.5)	EW3	PGM-FI	Electronic
	Prelude	1830 (1.8)	ET2	Dual 1 bbl ①	Electronic
1986	Accord DX,LX	1995 (2.0)	BS	2 bbl	Electronic
	Accord LXi	1995 (2.0)	BT	PGM-FI	Electronic
	Civic	1342 (1.3)	EV1	2 bbl	Electronic
	Civic Si	1342 (1.3)	EV1	PGM-FI	Electronic
	Civic	1488 (1.5)	EW1	2 bbl	Electronic
	Civic CRX DX	1488 (1.5)	EW1	2 bbl	Electronic
	Civic CRX HF	1488 (1.5)	EW1	2 bbl	Electronic
	Civic CRX Si	1488 (1.5)	EW3	PGM-FI	Electronic
	Prelude	1829 (1.8)	ET2	Dual 1 bbl ①	Electronic
	Prelude	1955 (2.0)	BT	PGM-FI	Electronic
1987-88	Accord DX,LX	1955 (2.0)	A20A1	2 bbl	Electronic
	Accord LXi	1955 (2.0)	A20A3	PGM-FI	Electronic
	Civic	1342 (1.3)	D13A2	2 bbl	Electronic
	Civic	1488 (1.5)	D15A2	2 bbl	Electronic
	Civic	1488 (1.5)	D15A3	PGM-FI	Electronic
	Civic CRX STD	1488 (1.5)	D15A2	2 bbl	Electronic
	Civic CRX HF	1488 (1.5)	D15A2	2 bbl	Electronic
	Civic CRX Si	1488 (1.5)	D15A3	PGM-FI	Electronic
	Prelude	1829 (1.8)	A18A1	Dual 1 bbl ①	Electronic
	Prelude	1955 (2.0)	A20A3	PGM-FI	Electronic

BBL Barrel Carburetor
PGM-FI Programmed Fuel Injection
① Sidedraft Carburetor

General Description

Programmed Fuel Injection (PGM-FI) System consists of three sub-systems: Air intake, electronic control, and fuel.

Air Intake System

The system supplies air for all engine needs. It consists of the air cleaner, air intake pipe, throttle body, idle control system, fast idle mechanism, and intake manifold. A resonator in the air intake pipe provides additional silencing as air is drawn into the system.

THROTTLE BODY

The throttle body, is a two-barrel side-draft type with the primary air horn at the top. To prevent icing of the throttle valves and air horn walls, under certain atmospheric conditions of the throttle valves air air horn walls the lower portion of the throttle body is heated by engine coolant. A throttle sensor is attached to the primary throttle valve to sense changes in throttle opening. A dashpot is used to slow the throttle as it approaches the closed position.

IDLE CONTROL SYSTEM

The air/fuel ratio during idling is controlled by the electronic control unit and various solenoid valves such as idle control, fast idle and A/C idle control solenoid valves. With the exception of the A/C idle control solenoid valve, these change the amounts of air bypassing into the air intake manifold. The A/C control solenoid valve opens the throttle when the air conditioner is turned on by signals sent from the ECU.

Idle Control Solenoid Valve is used to compensate for idle speed reduction due to electrical, or other loads on the engine. The valve does this by bypassing additional air into the intake manifold. This additional air will allow the idle speed to increase to its normal speed (750 ± 50 rpm). The operation depends upon changes in the voltage at the FR terminal of the alternator for quick response. The valve also lowers the fast idle speed in steps during warm-up, after the coolant temperature has researched 131°F (55°C). To prevent erratic running after the engine first fires, the valve is opened during cranking and immediately after starting to provide additional air into the intake manifold.

Fast Idle Control Solenoid Valve prevents erratic running when the engine is warming up, a higher idle speed is needed. When the atmospheric pressure is 660mm Hg or less, the valve opens to bypass additional air into the intake manifold.

A/C Idle Control Solenoid Valve maintains an idle speed of 750 ± 50 rpm when the air conditioner is turned on. The valve causes the A/C idle control diaphragm to open the throttle valve which raises the idle speed. The valve is also opened when coolant temperature is low (immediately after starting) thereby ensuring stable idling regardless of position of the A/C switch.

IDLE ADJUSTER (BYPASS CIRCUIT)

Fuel cut-off takes place at a set position or angle of the throttle valve. If the throttle valve is moved to adjust idle speed, this position or angle will be changed and the system may not cut off fuel supply. To solve this problem, the throttle body contains an adjustable bypass circuit. This circuit is designed to control the amount of air bypassing into the intake manifold without changing the position of throttle valve. The idle speed usually does not require the idle control system is in operation, the idle screw has no effect on the idle speed.

Usually it does not require to adjust idle speed by idle adjust screw since idle speed is adjusted automatically by the operation of idle control system. Idle speed does not change by turning the idle adjust screw while idle control system is in operation.

FAST IDLE MECHANISM

To prevent erratic running when the engine is warming up, it is necessary to raise the idle speed. The air bypass valve is controlled by a thermowax plunger. When the thermowax is cold,

the valve is open. When the thermowax is heated, the valve is closed. With the engine cold and the thermowax consequently cold, additional air is bypassed into the intake manifold so that the engine idles faster than normal. When the engine reaches operating temperature, the valve begins to close, reducing the amount of air bypassing into the manifold.

Electronic Control System

CONTROL SYSTEM

In order to get fuel into the cylinders at the correct instant and in correct amount, the control system must perform various separate functions. The ECU (Electronic Control Unit), the heart of the PGM-FI, uses an eight-bit microcomputer and consists of a CPU (Central Processing Unit), memories, and I/O (Input/Output) ports. Basic data stored in the memories are compensated by the signals sent from the various sensors to provide the correct air/fuel mixture for all engine needs.

ELECTRONIC CONTROL UNIT (ECU)

The unit contains memories for the basic discharge duration at various engine speeds and manifold pressures. The basic discharge duration, after being read out from the memory, is further modified by signals sent from various sensors to obtain the final discharge duration. Other functions also include:

- Starting Control — The fuel system must vary the air/fuel ratio to suit different operating requirements. For example, the mixture must be rich for starting. The memories also contain the basic discharge durations to be read out by signals from the starter switch, and engine speed and coolant temperature sensors, thereby providing extra fuel needed for starting.
- Fuel Pump Control — When the speed of the engine falls below the prescribed limit, electric current to the fuel pump is cut off, preventing the injectors from discharging fuel.
- Fuel Cut-Off Control — During deceleration with the throttle valve nearly closed, electric current to the injectors is cut off at speeds over 900 rpm, contributing to improved fuel economy. Fuel cut-off action also takes place when engine speed exceeds 7000 rpm regardless of the position of the throttle valve.
- Safety — A fail-safe system monitors the sensors and detects any abnormality in the ECU, ensuring safe driving even if one or more sensors are faulty, or if the ECU malfunctions.

CRANK ANGLE SENSOR (TDC/CYL SENSORS)

The sensors and distributor are designed as an assembly to save space and weight. The entire unit consist of a pair of rotors, TDC and CYL, and a pickup for each rotor. Since the rotors are coupled to the camshaft, they turn together as a unit as the camshaft rotates. The CYL sensor detects the position of the No. 1 cylinder as the base for the Sequential Injection whereas the TDC sensor serves to determine the injection timing for each cylinder. The TDC sensor is also used to detect engine speed to read out the basic discharge duration for different operating conditions.

MANIFOLD AIR PRESSURE SENSOR (MAP SENSOR)

The sensor converts manifold air pressure readings into electrical voltage signals and sends them to the ECU. This information with signals from the crank angle sensor is then used to read out the basic discharge duration from the memory.

ATMOSPHERIC PRESSURE SENSOR (PA SENSOR)

Like the MAP sensor, the unit converts atmospheric pressures into voltage signals and sends them to the ECU. The signals then modify the basic discharge duration to compensate for changes in the atmospheric pressure.

COOLANT TEMPERATURE SENSOR (TW SENSOR)

The sensor uses a temperature-dependent diode (thermistor) to measure differences in the coolant temperature. The basic discharge duration is read out by the signals sent from this sensor through the ECU. The resistance of the thermister decreases with a rise in coolant temperature.

INTAKE AIR TEMPERATURE SENSOR (TA SENSOR)

This device is also a thermistor and is placed in the intake manifold. It acts much like the water temperature sensor but with a reduced thermal capacity for for quicker response. The basic discharge duration read out from the memory is again compensated for different operating conditions by the signals sent from this sensor through the ECU.

THROTTLE ANGLE SENSOR

This sensor is essentially a variable resistor. In construction, the rotor shaft is connected to the throttle valve shaft such that, as the throttle valve is moved, the resistance varies, altering the output voltage to the control unit.

OXYGEN SENSOR

The oxygen sensor, by detecting the oxygen content in the exhaust gas, maintains the stoichiometric air/fuel ratio. In operation, the ECU receives the signals from the sensor and changes the duration during which fuel is injected. The oxygen sensor is located in the exhaust manifold.

The sensor is a hollow shaft of zirconia with a closed end. The inner and outer surfaces are plated with platinum, thus forming a platinum electrode. The inner surface or chamber is open to the atmosphere whereas the outer surface is exposed to the exhaust gas flow through the manifold.

Voltage is induced at the platinum electrode when there is any difference in oxygen concentration between the two layers of air over the surfaces. Operation of the device is dependent upon the fact that voltage induced changes sharply as the stoichiometric air/fuel ratio is exceeded when the electrode is heated above a certain temperature.

IDLE MIXTURE ADJUSTER SENSOR (IMA SENSOR)

The sensor is located in the control box. The primary objective of this unit is to maintain the correct air/fuel ratio at idling. No adjustment of the IMA sensor is necessary as the feedback control is performed by the oxygen sensor even during idling.

STARTER SWITCH

The air/fuel mixture must be rich for starting. During cranking, the ECU detects signal from the starter switch and increases the amount of fuel injected into the manifold according to the engine temperature. The amount of fuel injected is gradually reduced when the starter switch is turned off.

Fuel System

FUEL PUMP

The fuel pump is an in-line, direct drive type. Fuel is drawn into the pump through a filter, flows around the armature through the one-way valve and is delivered to the engine compartment. A baffle is provided to prevent fuel pulsation. The fuel pump has a relief valve to prevent excessive pressure. It opens if there is a blockage in the discharge side. When the relief valve opens, fuel flows from the high pressure to the low pressure side. A check valve is provided to maintain fuel pressure in the line after the pump is stopped. This is to ease restarting.

The pump section is composed of a rotor, rollers and pump spacer. When the rotor turns, the rollers turn and travel along the inner surface of the pump spacer by centrifugal force. The volume of the cavity enclosed by these three parts changes, drawing and pressurizing the fuel.

PRESSURE REGULATOR

The fuel pressure regulator maintains a constant fuel pressure to the injectors. The spring chamber of the pressure regulator is connected to the intake manifold to constantly maintain the fuel pressure at 36 PSI (2.55 kg/cm^2) higher than the pressure in the manifold. When the difference between the fuel pressure and manifold pressure exceeds 36 PSI (2.55 kg/cm^2), the diaphragm is pushed upward, and the excess fuel is fed back into the fuel tank through the return line.

INJECTOR

The injector is of the solenoid-actuated constant-stroke pintle type consisting of a solenoid, plunger, needle valve and housing. When current is applied to the solenoid coil, the valve lifts up and pressurized fuel fills the inside of the injector and is injected close to the intake valve. Because the needle valve lifts and the fuel pressure are constant, the injection quantity is determined by; the length of time that the valve is open, i.e., the duration the current is supplied to the solenoid coil. The injector is sealed by an O-ring and seal ring at the top and bottom. These seals also reduce operating noise.

RESISTOR

The injector timing, which controls the opening and closing intervals, must be very accurate since it dictates the air/fuel mixture ratio. The injector must also be durable. For the best possible injector response, it is necessary to shorten the current rise time when voltage is applied to the injector coil. Therefore, the number of windings of the injector coil is reduced to reduce the inductance in the coil. This, however, makes low resistance in the coil, allowing a large amount of current to flow through the coil. As a result, the amount of heat generated is high, which compromises the durability of the coil. Flow of current in the coil is therefore restricted by a resistor installed in series between the electric power source and the injector coil.

MAIN RELAY

The main relay is a direct coupler type which contains the relays for the electronic control unit power supply and the fuel pump power supply. This relay is installed at the back of the fuse box.

SERVICE PRECAUTIONS

- Do not operate the fuel pump when the fuel lines are empty.
- Do not reuse fuel hose clamps.
- Make sure all ECU harness connectors are fastened securely. A poor connection can cause an extremely high surge voltage in the coil and condenser and result in damage to integrated circuits.
- Keep ECU all parts and harnesses dry during service.
- Before attempting to remove any parts, turn off the ignition switch and disconnect the battery ground cable.
- Always use a 12 volt battery as a power source.
- Do not attempt to disconnect the battery cables with the engine running.
- Do not depress the accelerator pedal when starting.
- Do not rev up the engine immediately after starting or just prior to shutdown.
- Do not apply battery power directly to injectors.

Diagnosis and Testing

SELF-DIAGNOSTIC SYSTEM

Self-Diagnosis Indicators

The quick reference chart covers the most common failure modes for the PGM-FI. The probable causes are listed in order of most-easily-checked first, then progressing to more difficult fixes. Run through all the causes listed. If problem is still unsolved, go on to the more detailed troubleshooting. Troubleshooting is divided into different LED displays. Find the correct light display and begin again.

For all the conditions listed, the PGM-FI warning light on the dashboard must be on (comes on and stays on). This indicates a problem in the electrical portion of the fuel injection system. At that time, check the LED display (self-diagnosis system) in the ECU.

On all Civic models and 1985 Accord models, there are four

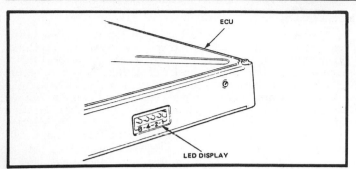

ECU

LED DISPLAY

PGM-FI LED display—1985–88 Civic and 1985 Accord

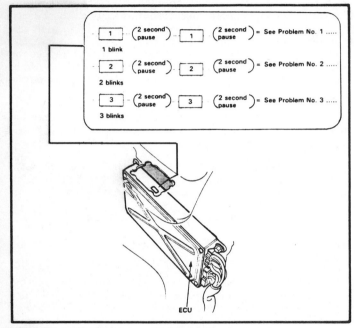

PGM-FI LED display—1986–88 Prelude shown, 1986–88 Accord ECU under driver's seat

LED displays. They are part of the ECU, which is located under the passenger's seat in the Accord and Civic and in the left side panel beside the rear seat on Prelude. They are numbered 1, 2, 4 and 8, as counted from right to left.

On 1986–88 Accord and Prelude models, there is only one LED display. The LED will blink consecutively to indicate the trouble code. The ECU is located under the driver's seat on the Accord and in the left side panel beside the rear seat on the Prelude.

Sometimes the dash warning light and/or ECU LED(s) will come on, indicating a system problem, when, in fact, there is only a bad or intermittent electrical connection. To troubleshoot a bad connection, note the ECU LED pattern that is lit, refer to the diagnosis chart and check the connectors associated with the items mentioned in the "Possible Cause" column for that LED pattern (disconnect, clean or repair if necessary and reconnect those connections). Then, reset the ECU memory as described, restart the car and drive it for a few minutes and then recheck the car and drive it for a few minutes and then recheck the LED(s). If the same pattern lights up, begin system troubleshooting; if it does not light up, the problem was only a bad connection.

The memory for the PGM-FI warning light on the dashboard will be erased when the ignition switch is turned off; however, the memory for the LED display(s) will not be cancelled. Thus, the warning light will not come on when the ignition switch is again turned on unless the trouble is once more detected. Troubleshooting should be done according to the LED display(s) even if the warning light is off.

Other ECU information:
- After making repairs, disconnect the battery negative cable from the battery negative terminal for at least 10 seconds and reset the ECU memory. After reconnecting the cable, check that the LED display is turned off.
- Turn the ignition switch on. The PGM-FI warning light should come on for about 2 seconds. If the warning light won't come on, check for:
—Blown warning light bulb
—Blown No. 3 fuse (causing faulty back up light, seat belt alarm, clock, memory function of the car radio)
—Open circuit in Yellow wire between No. # 3 fuse and combination meter
—Open circuit in Green/Orange wire between combination meter and control unit
- After the PGM-FI warning light and self-diagnosis indicators have been turned on, turn the ignition switch off. If the LED display fails to come on when the ignition switch is turned on again, check for:
—Blown No. 10 fuse·
—Open circuit in White/Green wire between ECU A17 terminal and No. 10 fuse
- Replace the ECU only after making sure that all couplers and connectors are connected securely.

PGM-FI LED DISPLAY QUICK REFERENCE CHART 1986-88 ACCORD AND PRELUDE

No. of LED Blinks between 2 second pauses	Symptom	Possible cause
0 — Dash warning light off	Engine will not start	· Disconnected control unit ground wire · Faulty ECU
0 — Dash warning light on	Engine will not start · No particular symptom shown	· Loose or poorly connected power line to ECU · Disconnected control unit ground wire · Short circuit in combination meter or warning light wire · Faulty ECU
1	· No particular symptom shown · Erratic idling (Erratic injector, coupler and wiring Insufficient fuel)	· Disconnected oxygen sensor coupler · Spark plug mis-fire · Short or open circuit in oxygen sensor circuit · Faulty oxygen sensor · Faulty fuel system
2	· No particular symptom shown or system does not operate	· Faulty ECU
3	· Fuel fouled plug · Frequent engine stalling · Hesitation	· Disconnected manifold absolute pressure sensor coupler · Short or open circuit in manifold absolute pressure sensor wire · Faulty manifold absolute pressure sensor
4	· No particular symptom shown or system does not operate	· Disconnected manifold absolute pressure sensor piping · Faulty ECU
5	· Hesitation · Fuel fouled plug · Frequent engine stalling	· Disconnected manifold absolute pressure sensor piping
6	· High idle speed during warm-up · High idle speed · Hard starting at low temp	· Disconnected coolant temperature sensor coupler · Open or short circuit in coolant temperature sensor wire · Faulty coolant temperature sensor (thermostat housing)
7	· Poor engine response to opening throttle rapidly · High idle speed · Engine does not rev up when cold	· Disconnected throttle angle sensor coupler · Open or short circuit in throttle angle sensor wire · Faulty throttle angle sensor
8	· Engine does not rev up · High idle speed · Erratic idling	· Short or open circuit in crank angle sensor wire · Crank angle sensor wire interfering with spark plug wires · Crank angle sensor at fault
9	· Same as above	· Same as above
10	· High idle speed · Erratic idling when very cold	· Disconnected intake air temperature sensor · Open or short circuit in intake air temperature sensor wire · Faulty intake air temperature sensor
11	· No particular symptom shown or system does not operate	· Faulty ECU
12	· Frequent engine stalling · Erratic or unstable running at low speed · No particular symptom shown	· Disconnected EGR control system coupler · Shorted or disconnected EGR control wire · Faulty EGR control system
13	· Poor acceleration at high altitude · Hard starting at high altitude when cold	· Disconnected atmospheric pressure sensor coupler · Shorted or disconnected atmospheric pressure sensor wire · Faulty atmospheric pressure sensor

NOTE:
- If the number of blinks between 2 second pauses exceeds 13, or if the LED indicator stays on, the ECU is faulty.
- Some failure indications (such as, one blink) require the full test procedures on the following pages to confirm that the failure has or has not been eliminated.

PGM-FI LED DISPLAY QUICK REFERENCE CHART 1985-88 CIVIC and 1985 ACCORD

LED Display	Symptom	Possible Cause
(Dash warning light off)	· Engine will not start.	· Loose or poorly connected power line to ECU main relay resistor · Disconnected control unit ground wire · Faulty ECU
(Dash warning light on)	· Engine will not start. · No particular symptom shown	· Disconnected control unit ground wire · Faulty ECU · Short circuit in combination meter or warning light wire
1	· No particular symptom shown · Erratic idling (Erratic injector, coupler and wiring) Insufficient fuel	· Disconnected oxygen sensor coupler · Spark plug mis-fire · Short or open circuit in oxygen sensor circuit · Faulty oxygen sensor
2	· No particular symptom shown or system does not operate	· Faulty ECU
3	· Wet-plug · Frequent engine stalling · Engine fails to pick up speed	· Disconnected manifold air pressure sensor coupler · Short or open circuit in manifold air pressure sensor wire · Faulty manifold air pressure sensor
4	· No particular symptom shown or system does not operate	· Disconnected manifold air pressure sensor piping · Faulty ECU
5	· Engine fails to pick up speed · Wet-plug · Frequent engine stalling	· Disconnected manifold air pressure sensor piping
6	· High idle speed during warm-up · High idle speed · Hard starting at low temp	· Disconnected coolant temperature sensor coupler · Open circuit in coolant temperature sensor wire · Faulty coolant temperature sensor (thermostat housing)
7	· Poor engine response to opening throttle rapidly · High idle speed · Engine does not rev up when cold	· Disconnected throttle angle sensor coupler · Open or short circuit in throttle angle sensor wire · Faulty throttle angle sensor
8	· Engine does not rev up · High idle speed · Erratic idling	· Short or open circuit in crank angle sensor wire · Crank angle sensor wire interfering with high tension cord · Crank angle sensor at fault
8	· Same as above	· Same as above
8	· High idle speed · Erratic idling when very cold	· Disconnected intake air temperature sensor · Open circuit in intake air temperature sensor wire · Faulty intake air temperature sensor
8	· No particular symptom shown · High idle speed	· Disconnected idle mixture adjuster sensor coupler · Shorted or disconnected idle mixture adjuster sensor wire · Faulty idle mixture adjuster sensor
8	· No particular symptom shown or system does not operate at all.	· Faulty ECU
8	· Poor acceleration at high altitude · Hard starting at high altitude when cold	· Disconnected atmospheric pressure sensor coupler · Shorted or disconnected atmospheric pressure sensor wire · Faulty atmospheric pressure sensor
8	· No particular symptom shown or system does not operate at all	· Faulty ECU
8	Same as above	Same as above

NOTE: Some failure indications (such as when only the No. 1 indication is lit) require the full test procedures on the following pages to confirm that the failure has or has not been eliminated.

ECU DIAGNOSTIC CHART—1985 ACCORD

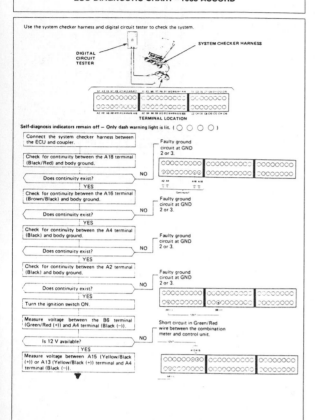

Use the system checker harness and digital circuit tester to check the system.

DIGITAL CIRCUIT TESTER

SYSTEM CHECKER HARNESS

TERMINAL LOCATION

Self-diagnosis indicators remain off — Only dash warning light is lit. (○ ○ ○ ○)

Connect the system checker harness between the ECU and coupler.

Check for continuity between the A18 terminal (Black/Red) and body ground.

Does continuity exist? — NO → Faulty ground circuit at GND 2 or 3.

YES

Check for continuity between the A16 terminal (Brown/Black) and body ground.

Does continuity exist? — NO → Faulty ground circuit at GND 2 or 3.

YES

Check for continuity between the A4 terminal (Black) and body ground.

Does continuity exist? — NO → Faulty ground circuit at GND 2 or 3.

YES

Check for continuity between the A2 terminal (Black) and body ground.

Does continuity exist? — NO → Faulty ground circuit at GND 2 or 3.

YES

Turn the ignition switch ON.

Measure voltage between the B6 terminal (Green/Red (+)) and A4 terminal (Black (−)).

Is 12 V available? — NO → Short circuit in Green/Red wire between the combination meter and control unit.

YES

Measure voltage between A15 (Yellow/Black (+)) or A13 (Yellow/Black (+)) terminal and A4 terminal (Black (−)).

▼

ECU DIAGNOSTIC CHART—1985 ACCORD

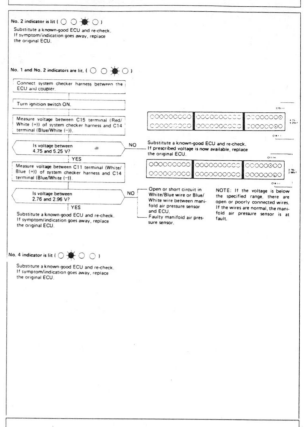

No. 2 indicator is lit (○ ○ ☀ ○)

Substitute a known-good ECU and re-check. If symptom/indication goes away, replace the original ECU.

No. 1 and No. 2 indicators are lit (○ ○ ☀ ○)

Connect system checker harness between the ECU and coupler.

Turn ignition switch ON.

Measure voltage between C15 terminal (Red/White (+)) of system checker harness and C14 terminal (Blue/White (−)).

Is voltage between 4.75 and 5.25 V? — NO → Substitute a known-good ECU and re-check. If prescribed voltage is now available, replace the original ECU.

YES

Measure voltage between C11 terminal (White/Blue (+)) of system checker harness and C14 terminal (Blue/White (−)).

Is voltage between 2.76 and 2.96 V? — NO → Open or short circuit in White/Blue wire or Blue/White wire between manifold air pressure sensor and ECU. Faulty manifold air pressure sensor.

Substitute a known-good ECU and re-check. If symptom/indication goes away, replace the original ECU.

NOTE: If the voltage is below the specified range, there are open or poorly connected wires. If the wires are normal, the manifold air pressure sensor is at fault.

No. 4 indicator is lit (○ ☀ ○ ○)

Substitute a known-good ECU and re-check. If symptom/indication goes away, replace the original ECU.

ECU DIAGNOSTIC CHART—1985 ACCORD

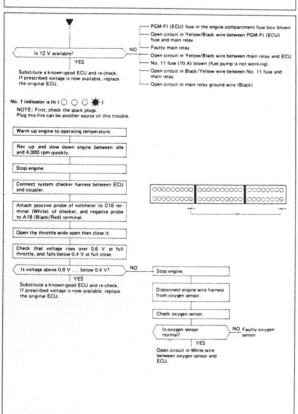

▼

Is 12 V available? — NO →
— PGM-FI (ECU) fuse in the engine compartment fuse box blown
— Open circuit in Yellow/Black wire between PGM-FI (ECU) fuse and main relay
— Faulty main relay
— Open circuit in Yellow/Black wire between main relay and ECU
— No. 11 fuse (10 A) blown (fuel pump is not working)
— Open circuit in Black/Yellow wire between No. 11 fuse and main relay
— Open circuit in main relay ground wire (Black)

YES

Substitute a known-good ECU and re-check. If prescribed voltage is now available, replace the original ECU.

No. 1 indicator is lit (○ ○ ○ ☀)

NOTE: First, check the spark plugs. Plug mis-fire can be another source of this trouble.

Warm up engine to operating temperature.

Rev up and slow down engine between idle and 4,000 rpm quickly.

Stop engine.

Connect system checker harness between ECU and coupler.

Attach positive probe of voltmeter to C16 terminal (White) of checker, and negative probe to A18 (Black/Red) terminal.

Open the throttle wide open then close it.

Check that voltage rises over 0.6 V at full throttle, and falls below 0.4 V at full close.

Is voltage above 0.6 V . . . below 0.4 V? — NO → Stop engine.

YES

Substitute a known-good ECU and re-check. If prescribed voltage is now available, replace the original ECU.

Disconnect engine wire harness from oxygen sensor.

Check oxygen sensor.

Is oxygen sensor normal? — NO → Faulty oxygen sensor

YES

Open circuit in White wire between oxygen sensor and ECU.

ECU DIAGNOSTIC CHART—1985 ACCORD

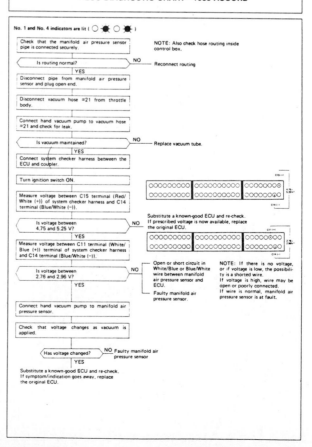

No. 1 and No. 4 indicators are lit (○ ☀ ○ ☀)

Check that the manifold air pressure sensor pipe is connected securely.

NOTE: Also check hose routing inside control box.

Is routing normal? — NO → Reconnect routing

YES

Disconnect pipe from manifold air pressure sensor and plug open end.

Disconnect vacuum hose #21 from throttle body.

Connect hand vacuum pump to vacuum hose #21 and check for leak.

Is vacuum maintained? — NO → Replace vacuum tube.

YES

Connect system checker harness between the ECU and coupler.

Turn ignition switch ON.

Measure voltage between C15 terminal (Red/White (+)) of system checker harness and C14 terminal (Blue/White (−)).

Is voltage between 4.75 and 5.25 V? — NO → Substitute a known-good ECU and re-check. If prescribed voltage is now available, replace the original ECU.

YES

Measure voltage between C11 terminal (White/Blue (+)) terminal of system checker harness and C14 terminal (Blue/White (−)).

Is voltage between 2.76 and 2.96 V? — NO → Open or short circuit in White/Blue or Blue/White wire between manifold air pressure sensor and ECU. Faulty manifold air pressure sensor.

NOTE: If there is no voltage, or if voltage is low, the possibility is a shorted wire. If voltage is high, wire may be open or poorly connected. If wire is normal, manifold air pressure sensor is at fault.

YES

Connect hand vacuum pump to manifold air pressure sensor.

Check that voltage changes as vacuum is applied.

Has voltage changed? — NO → Faulty manifold air pressure sensor

YES

Substitute a known-good ECU and re-check. If symptom/indication goes away, replace the original ECU.

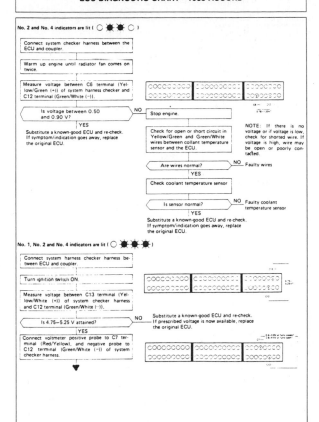

ECU DIAGNOSTIC CHART—1985 ACCORD

No. 2 and No. 4 indicators are lit (○ ● ● ○)

Connect system checker harness between the ECU and coupler.

Warm up engine until radiator fan comes on twice.

Measure voltage between C6 terminal (Yellow/Green (+)) of system harness checker and C12 terminal (Green/White (−)).

Is voltage between 0.50 and 0.90 V? — NO → Stop engine.

YES

Substitute a known-good ECU and re-check. If symptom/indication goes away, replace the original ECU.

Check for open or short circuit in Yellow/Green and Green/White wires between collant temperature sensor and the ECU.

NOTE: If there is no voltage or if voltage is low, check for shorted wire. If voltage is high, wire may be open or poorly contacted.

Are wires normal? — NO → Faulty wires

YES

Check coolant temperature sensor

Is sensor normal? — NO → Faulty coolant temperature sensor

YES

Substitute a known-good ECU and re-check. If symptom/indication goes away, replace the original ECU.

No. 1, No. 2 and No. 4 indicators are lit (○ ● ● ●)

Connect system harness checker harness between ECU and coupler.

Turn ignition switch ON.

Measure voltage between C13 terminal (Yellow/White (+)) of system checker harness and C12 terminal (Green/White (−)).

Is 4.75—5.25 V attained? — NO → Substitute a known-good ECU and re-check. If prescribed voltage is now available, replace the original ECU.

YES

Connect voltmeter positive probe to C7 terminal (Red/Yellow), and negative probe to C12 terminal (Green/White (−)) of system checker harness.

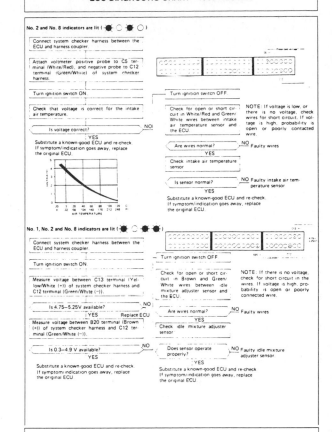

ECU DIAGNOSTIC CHART—1985 ACCORD

No. 2 and No. 8 indicators are lit (● ○ ● ○)

Connect system checker harness between the ECU and harness coupler.

Attach voltmeter positive probe to C5 terminal (White/Red), and negative probe to C12 terminal (Green/White) of system checker harness.

Turn ignition switch ON.

Check that voltage is correct for the intake air temperature.

Is voltage correct? — NO

YES

Substitute a known-good ECU and re-check. If symptom/indication goes away, replace the original ECU.

Turn ignition switch OFF.

Check for open or short circuit in White/Red and Green/White wires between intake air temperature sensor and the ECU.

NOTE: If voltage is low, or there is no voltage, check wires for short circuit. If voltage is high, probability is open or poorly contacted wire.

Are wires normal? — NO → Faulty wires

YES

Check intake air temperature sensor

Is sensor normal? — NO → Faulty intake air temperature sensor

YES

Substitute a known-good ECU and re-check. If symptom/indication goes away, replace the original ECU.

No. 1, No. 2 and No. 8 indicators are lit (● ● ○ ●)

Connect system checker harness between the ECU and harness coupler.

Turn ignition switch ON.

Measure voltage between C13 terminal (Yellow/White (+)) of system checker harness and C12 terminal (Green/White (−)).

Is 4.75—5.25V available? — NO → Replace ECU

YES

Measure voltage between B20 terminal (Brown (+)) of system checker harness and C12 terminal (Green/White (−)).

Is 0.3—4.9 V available? — NO

YES

Check idle mixture adjuster sensor

Does sensor operate properly? — NO → Faulty idle mixture adjuster sensor

YES

Turn ignition switch OFF.

Check for open or short circuit in Brown and Green/White wires between idle mixture adjuster sensor and the ECU.

NOTE: If there is no voltage, check for short circuit in the wires. If voltage is high, probability is open or poorly connected wire.

Are wires normal? — NO → Faulty wires

YES

Substitute a known-good ECU and re-check. If symptom/indication goes away, replace the original ECU.

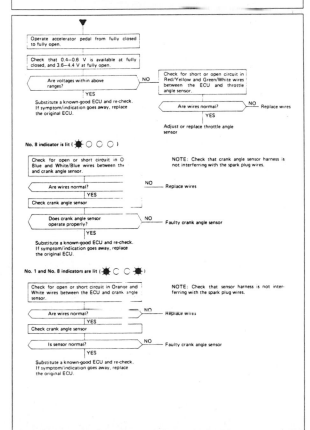

ECU DIAGNOSTIC CHART—1985 ACCORD

Operate accelerator pedal from fully closed to fully open.

Check that 0.4—0.6 V is available at fully closed, and 3.6—4.4 V at fully open.

Are voltages within above ranges? — NO

YES

Substitute a known-good ECU and re-check. If symptom/indication goes away, replace the original ECU.

Check for short or open circuit in Red/Yellow and Green/White wires between the ECU and throttle angle sensor.

Are wires normal? — NO → Replace wires

YES

Adjust or replace throttle angle sensor

No. 8 indicator is lit (● ○ ○ ○)

Check for open or short circuit in Orange/Blue and White/Blue wires between the ECU and crank angle sensor.

Are wires normal? — NO → Replace wires

YES

Check crank angle sensor

NOTE: Check that crank angle sensor harness is not interfering with the spark plug wires.

Does crank angle sensor operate properly? — NO → Faulty crank angle sensor

YES

Substitute a known-good ECU and re-check. If symptom/indication goes away, replace the original ECU.

No. 1 and No. 8 indicators are lit (● ○ ○ ●)

Check for open or short circuit in Orange and White wires between the ECU and crank angle sensor.

NOTE: Check that sensor harness is not interfering with the spark plug wires.

Are wires normal? — NO → Replace wires

YES

Check crank angle sensor

Is sensor normal? — NO → Faulty crank angle sensor

YES

Substitute a known-good ECU and re-check. If symptom/indication goes away, replace the original ECU.

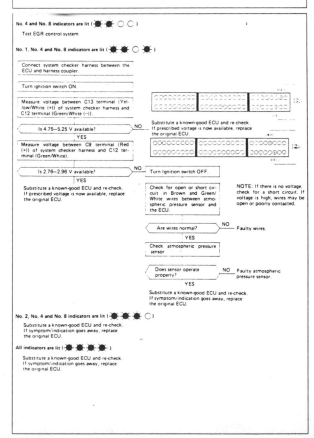

ECU DIAGNOSTIC CHART—1985 ACCORD

No. 4 and No. 8 indicators are lit (● ● ○ ○)

Test EGR control system

No. 1, No. 4 and No. 8 indicators are lit (● ● ○ ●)

Connect system checker harness between the ECU and harness coupler.

Turn ignition switch ON.

Measure voltage between C13 terminal (Yellow/White (+)) of system checker harness and C12 terminal (Green/White (−)).

Is 4.75—5.25 V available? — NO → Substitute a known-good ECU and re-check. If prescribed voltage is now available, replace the original ECU.

YES

Measure voltage between C9 terminal (Red (+)) of system checker harness and C12 terminal (Green/White).

Is 2.76—2.96 V available? — NO

YES

Substitute a known-good ECU and re-check. If prescribed voltage is now available, replace the original ECU.

Turn ignition switch OFF.

Check for open or short circuit in Brown and Green/White wires between atmospheric pressure sensor and the ECU.

NOTE: If there is no voltage, check for a short circuit. If voltage is high, wires may be open or poorly contacted.

Are wires normal? — NO → Faulty wires.

YES

Check atmospheric pressure sensor

Does sensor operate properly? — NO → Faulty atmospheric pressure sensor

YES

Substitute a known-good ECU and re-check. If symptom/indication goes away, replace the original ECU.

No. 2, No. 4 and No. 8 indicators are lit (● ● ● ○)

Substitute a known-good ECU and re-check. If symptom/indication goes away, replace the original ECU.

All indicators are lit (● ● ● ●)

Substitute a known-good ECU and re-check. If symptom/indication goes away, replace the original ECU.

ECU DIAGNOSTIC CHART — 1985 ACCORD

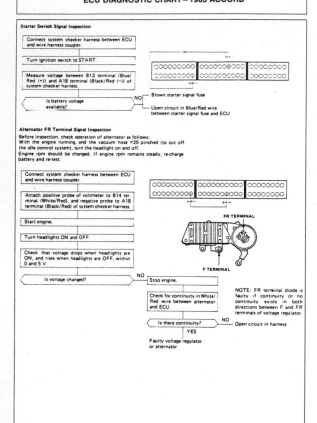

Starter Switch Signal Inspection

Connect system checker harness between ECU and wire harness coupler.

Turn ignition switch to START.

Measure voltage between B13 terminal (Blue/Red (+)) and A18 terminal (Black/Red (−)) of system checker harness.

Is battery voltage available? — NO → Blown starter signal fuse
— Open circuit in Blue/Red wire between starter signal fuse and ECU

Alternator FR Terminal Signal Inspection

Before inspection, check operation of alternator as follows:
With the engine running, and the vacuum hose =26 pinched (to cut off the idle control system), turn the headlight on and off. Engine rpm should be changed. If engine rpm remains steady, re-charge battery and re-test.

Connect system checker harness between ECU and wire harness coupler.

Attach positive probe of voltmeter to B14 terminal (White/Red), and negative probe to A18 terminal (Black/Red) of system checker harness.

Start engine.

Turn headlights ON and OFF.

Check that voltage drops when headlights are ON, and rises when headlights are OFF, within 0 and 5 V.

Is voltage changed? — NO → Stop engine.

Check for continuity in White/Red wire between alternator and ECU.

Is there continuity? — NO → Open circuit in harness
↓ YES

Faulty voltage regulator or alternator

NOTE: FR terminal diode is faulty if continuity or no continuity exists in both directions between F and FR terminals of voltage regulator.

FR TERMINAL
F TERMINAL

ECU DIAGNOSTIC CHART — 1985 ACCORD

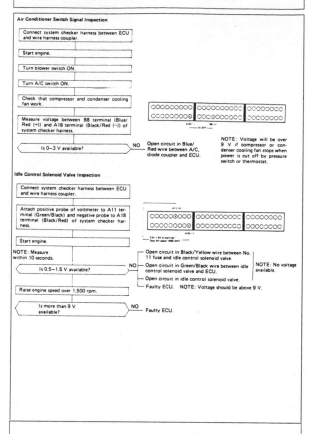

Air Conditioner Switch Signal Inspection

Connect system checker harness between ECU and wire harness coupler.

Start engine.

Turn blower switch ON.

Turn A/C switch ON.

Check that compressor and condenser cooling fan work.

Measure voltage between B8 terminal (Blue/Red (+)) and A18 terminal (Black/Red (−)) of system checker harness.

Is 0−3 V available? — NO → Open circuit in Blue/Red wire between A/C, diode coupler and ECU

NOTE: Voltage will be over 9 V if compressor or condenser cooling fan stops when power is cut off by pressure switch or thermostat.

Idle Control Solenoid Valve Inspection

Connect system checker harness between ECU and wire harness coupler.

Attach positive probe of voltmeter to A11 terminal (Green/Black) and negative probe to A18 terminal (Black/Red) of system checker harness.

Start engine.

NOTE: Measure within 10 seconds.

Is 0.5−1.5 V available? — NO →
— Open circuit in Black/Yellow wire between No. 11 fuse and idle control solenoid valve.
— Open circuit in Green/Black wire between idle control solenoid valve and ECU.
— Open circuit in idle control solenoid valve.
— Faulty ECU. NOTE: Voltage should be above 9 V.
NOTE: No voltage available.

Raise engine speed over 1,500 rpm.

Is more than 9 V available? — NO → Faulty ECU.

ECU DIAGNOSTIC CHART — 1985 ACCORD

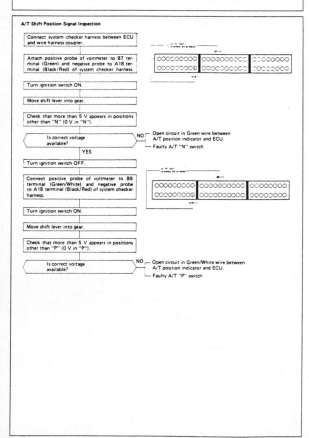

A/T Shift Position Signal Inspection

Connect system checker harness between ECU and wire harness coupler.

Attach positive probe of voltmeter to B7 terminal (Green) and negative probe to A18 terminal (Black/Red) of system checker harness.

Turn ignition switch ON.

Move shift lever into gear.

Check that more than 5 V appears in positions other than "N" (0 V in "N").

Is correct voltage available? — NO →
— Open circuit in Green wire between A/T position indicator and ECU.
— Faulty A/T "N" switch
↓ YES

Turn ignition switch OFF.

Connect positive probe of voltmeter to B9 terminal (Green/White) and negative probe to A18 terminal (Black/Red) of system checker harness.

Turn ignition switch ON.

Move shift lever into gear.

Check that more than 5 V appears in positions other than "P" (0 V in "P").

Is correct voltage available? — NO →
— Open circuit in Green/White wire between A/T position indicator and ECU.
— Faulty A/T "P" switch

ECU DIAGNOSTIC CHART — 1985 ACCORD

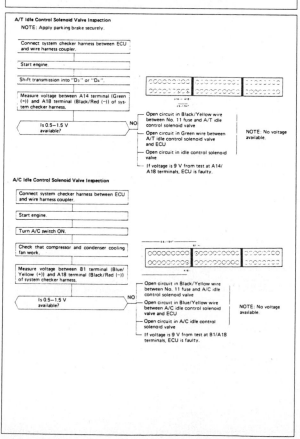

A/T Idle Control Solenoid Valve Inspection

NOTE: Apply parking brake securely.

Connect system checker harness between ECU and wire harness coupler.

Start engine.

Shift transmission into "D3" or "D4".

Measure voltage between A14 terminal (Green (+)) and A18 terminal (Black/Red (−)) of system checker harness.

Is 0.5−1.5 V available? — NO →
— Open circuit in Black/Yellow wire between No. 11 fuse and A/T idle control solenoid valve
— Open circuit in Green wire between A/T idle control solenoid valve and ECU
— Open circuit in idle control solenoid valve
— If voltage is 9 V from test at A14/A18 terminals, ECU is faulty.
NOTE: No voltage available.

A/C Idle Control Solenoid Valve Inspection

Connect system checker harness between ECU and wire harness coupler.

Start engine.

Turn A/C switch ON.

Check that compressor and condenser cooling fan work.

Measure voltage between B1 terminal (Blue/Yellow (+)) and A18 terminal (Black/Red (−)) of system checker harness.

Is 0.5−1.5 V available? — NO →
— Open circuit in Black/Yellow wire between No. 11 fuse and A/C idle control solenoid valve
— Open circuit in Blue/Yellow wire between A/C idle control solenoid valve and ECU
— Open circuit in A/C idle control solenoid valve
— If voltage is 9 V from test at B1/A18 terminals, ECU is faulty.
NOTE: No voltage available.

ECU DIAGNOSTIC CHART — 1985 ACCORD

Fast Idle Control Solenoid Valve Inspection

Connect system checker harness between ECU and wire harness coupler.

Start engine.

Measure voltage between B4 terminal (Blue/Black (+)) and A18 terminal (Black/Red (−)) of system checker harness.

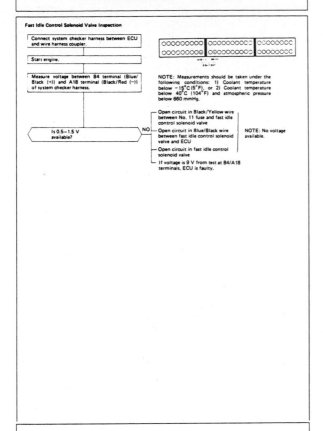

NOTE: Measurements should be taken under the following conditions: 1) Coolant temperature below −15°C (5°F), or 2) Coolant temperature below 40°C (104°F) and atmospheric pressure below 660 mmHg.

Is 0.5−1.5 V available? — NO →
- Open circuit in Black/Yellow wire between No. 11 fuse and fast idle control solenoid valve
- Open circuit in Blue/Black wire between fast idle control solenoid valve and ECU
- Open circuit in fast idle control solenoid valve
- If voltage is 9 V from test at B4/A18 terminals, ECU is faulty.

NOTE: No voltage available.

ECU DIAGNOSTIC CHART — 1985 CIVIC

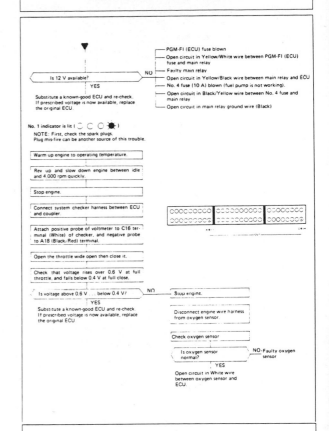

Is 12 V available? — NO →
- PGM-FI (ECU) fuse blown
- Open circuit in Yellow/White wire between PGM-FI (ECU) fuse and main relay
- Faulty main relay
- Open circuit in Yellow/Black wire between main relay and ECU
- No. 4 fuse (10 A) blown (fuel pump is not working).
- Open circuit in Black/Yellow wire between No. 4 fuse and main relay
- Open circuit in main relay ground wire (Black)

YES

Substitute a known-good ECU and re-check. If prescribed voltage is now available, replace the original ECU.

No. 1 indicator is lit ( )
NOTE: First, check the spark plugs. Plug mis-fire can be another source of this trouble.

Warm up engine to operating temperature.

Rev up and slow down engine between idle and 4,000 rpm quickly.

Stop engine.

Connect system checker harness between ECU and coupler.

Attach positive probe of voltmeter to C16 terminal (White) of checker, and negative probe to A18 (Black/Red) terminal.

Open the throttle wide open then close it.

Check that voltage rises over 0.6 V at full throttle, and falls below 0.4 V at full close.

Is voltage above 0.6 V ... below 0.4 V? — NO → Stop engine.

YES

Substitute a known-good ECU and re-check. If prescribed voltage is now available, replace the original ECU.

Disconnect engine wire harness from oxygen sensor.

Check oxygen sensor

Is oxygen sensor normal? — NO - Faulty oxygen sensor

YES

Open circuit in White wire between oxygen sensor and ECU.

ECU DIAGNOSTIC CHART — 1985 CIVIC

Use the system checker harness and digital circuit tester to check the system.

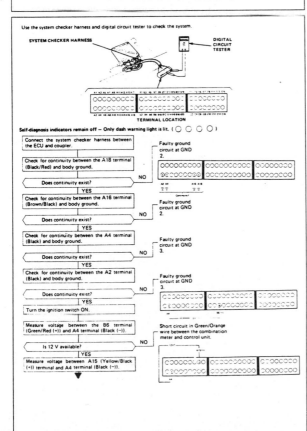

SYSTEM CHECKER HARNESS

DIGITAL CIRCUIT TESTER

TERMINAL LOCATION

Self-diagnosis indicators remain off — Only dash warning light is lit. ( )

Connect the system checker harness between the ECU and coupler.

Check for continuity between the A18 terminal (Black/Red) and body ground.

Does continuity exist? — NO → Faulty ground circuit at GND 2.

YES

Check for continuity between the A16 terminal (Brown/Black) and body ground.

Does continuity exist? — NO → Faulty ground circuit at GND 2.

YES

Check for continuity between the A4 terminal (Black) and body ground.

Does continuity exist? — NO → Faulty ground circuit at GND 3.

YES

Check for continuity between the A2 terminal (Black) and body ground.

Does continuity exist? — NO → Faulty ground circuit at GND 3.

YES

Turn the ignition switch ON.

Measure voltage between B6 terminal (Green/Red (+)) and A4 terminal (Black (−)).

Is 12 V available? — NO → Short circuit in Green/Orange wire between the combination meter and control unit.

YES

Measure voltage between A15 (Yellow/Black (+)) terminal and A4 terminal (Black (−)).

ECU DIAGNOSTIC CHART — 1985 CIVIC

No. 2 indicator is lit ( )
Substitute a known-good ECU and re-check. If symptom/indication goes away, replace the original ECU.

No. 1 and No. 2 indicators are lit. ( )

Connect system checker harness between the ECU and coupler.

Turn ignition switch ON.

Measure voltage between C15 terminal (Red/White (+)) of system checker harness and C14 terminal (Blue/White (−)).

Is voltage between 4.75 and 5.25 V? — NO →

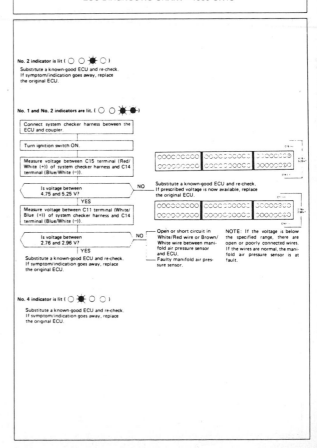

Substitute a known-good ECU and re-check. If prescribed voltage is now available, replace the original ECU.

YES

Measure voltage between C11 terminal (White/Blue (+)) of system checker harness and C14 terminal (Blue/White (−)).

Is voltage between 2.76 and 2.96 V? — NO →
- Open or short circuit in White/Red wire or Brown/White wire between manifold air pressure sensor and ECU.
- Faulty manifold air pressure sensor.

NOTE: If the voltage is below the specified range, there are open or poorly connected wires. If the wires are normal, the manifold air pressure sensor is at fault.

YES

Substitute a known-good ECU and re-check. If symptom/indication goes away, replace the original ECU.

No. 4 indicator is lit ( )

Substitute a known-good ECU and re-check. If symptom/indication goes away, replace the original ECU.

ECU DIAGNOSTIC CHART—1985 CIVIC

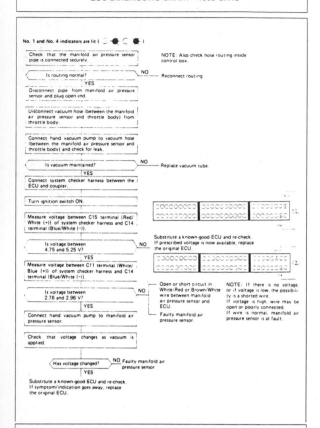

ECU DIAGNOSTIC CHART—1985 CIVIC

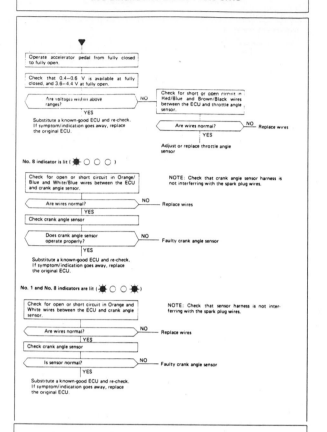

ECU DIAGNOSTIC CHART—1985 CIVIC

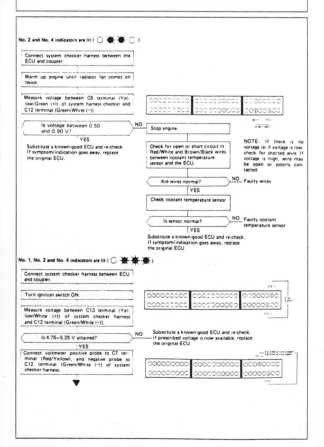

ECU DIAGNOSTIC CHART—1985 CIVIC

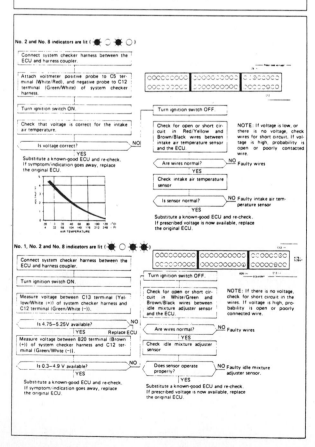

ECU DIAGNOSTIC CHART—1985 CIVIC

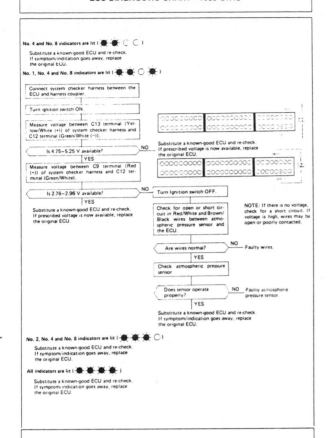

No. 4 and No. 8 indicators are lit (● ● ○ ○)

Substitute a known-good ECU and re-check.
If symptom/indication goes away, replace
the original ECU.

No. 1, No. 4 and No. 8 indicators are lit (● ● ○ ●)

Connect system checker harness between the
ECU and harness coupler.

Turn ignition switch ON.

Measure voltage between C13 terminal (Yellow/White (+)) of system checker harness and
C12 terminal (Green/White (−)).

Is 4.75–5.25 V available? —NO→ Substitute a known-good ECU and re-check.
If prescribed voltage is now available, replace
the original ECU.

YES

Measure voltage between C9 terminal (Red
(+)) of system checker harness and C12 terminal (Green/White).

Is 2.76–2.96 V available? —NO→ Turn ignition switch OFF.

YES

Substitute a known-good ECU and re-check.
If prescribed voltage is now available, replace
the original ECU.

Check for open or short circuit in Red/White and Brown/Black wires between atmospheric pressure sensor and the ECU.

NOTE: If there is no voltage,
check for a short circuit. If
voltage is high, wires may be
open or poorly contacted.

Are wires normal? —NO→ Faulty wires.

YES

Check atmospheric pressure sensor

Does sensor operate properly? —NO→ Faulty atmosphere
pressure sensor.

YES

Substitute a known-good ECU and re-check.
If symptom/indication goes away, replace
the original ECU.

No. 2, No. 4 and No. 8 indicators are lit (● ● ● ○)

Substitute a known-good ECU and re-check.
If symptom/indication goes away, replace
the original ECU.

All indicators are lit (● ● ● ●)

Substitute a known-good ECU and re-check.
If symptom/indication goes away, replace
the original ECU.

ECU DIAGNOSTIC CHART—1985 CIVIC

Air Conditioner Switch Signal Inspection

Connect system checker harness between ECU
and wire harness coupler.

Start engine.

Blower switch ON.

A/C switch ON.

Check that compressor and condenser cooling
fan work.

Measure voltage between B8 terminal (Blue/
Red (+)) and A18 terminal (Black/Red (−)) of
system checker harness.

Is 0–3 V available? —NO→ Open circuit in Blue/
Red wire between A/C
diode coupler and ECU.

NOTE: Voltage will be over
9 V if compressor or condenser cooling fan stops when
power is cut off by pressure
switch or thermostat.

Idle Control Solenoid Valve Inspection

Connect system checker harness between ECU
and wire harness coupler.

Attach positive probe of voltmeter to A11 terminal (Green/Black) and negative probe to A18
terminal (Black/Red) of system checker harness.

Start engine.

NOTE: Measure
within 10 seconds.

Is 0.5–1.5 V available? —NO→

Raise engine speed over 1,500 rpm.

Is more than 9 V available? —NO→ Faulty ECU.

— Open circuit in Black/Yellow wire between No.
4 fuse and idle control solenoid valve.

— Open circuit in Green/White wire between idle
control solenoid valve and ECU.

— Open circuit in idle control solenoid valve.

— Faulty ECU. NOTE: Voltage should be above 9 V.

NOTE: No voltage
available.

ECU DIAGNOSTIC CHART—1985 CIVIC

Starter Switch Signal Inspection

Connect system checker harness between ECU
and wire harness coupler.

Turn ignition switch to START.

Measure voltage between B13 terminal (Blue/
Red (+)) and A18 terminal (Black/Red (−)) of
system checker harness.

Is battery voltage available? —NO→

— Blown starter signal fuse.

— Open circuit in Blue/White wire
between starter signal fuse and ECU.

Alternator FR Terminal Signal Inspection

Before inspection, check operation of alternator as follows:
With the engine running, and the vacuum hose #10 pinched (to cut off
the idle control system), turn the headlight on and off.
Engine rpm should be changed. If engine rpm remains steady, re-charge
battery and re-test.

Connect system checker harness between ECU
and wire harness coupler.

Attach positive probe of voltmeter to B14 terminal (White/Red), and negative probe to A18
terminal (Black/Red) of system checker harness.

Start engine.

Turn headlights ON and OFF.

Check that voltage drops when headlights are
ON, and rises when headlights are OFF, within
0 and 5 V.

Is voltage changed? —NO→ Stop engine.

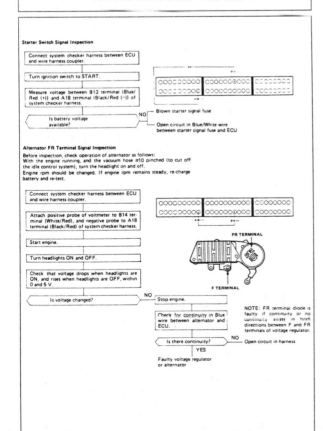

FR TERMINAL

F TERMINAL

Check for continuity in Blue
wire between alternator and
ECU.

Is there continuity? —NO→ Open circuit in harness

YES

Faulty voltage regulator
or alternator.

NOTE: FR terminal diode is
faulty if continuity or no
continuity exists in both
directions between F and FR
terminals of voltage regulator.

ECU DIAGNOSTIC CHART—1985 CIVIC

Fast Idle Control Solenoid Valve Inspection

Connect system checker harness between ECU
and wire harness coupler.

Start engine.

Measure voltage between B4 terminal (Blue/
Black (+)) and A18 terminal (Black/Red (−))
of system checker harness.

NOTE: Measurements should be taken when the
atmospheric pressure is below 660 mmHg.

Is 0.5–1.5 V available? —NO→

— Open circuit in Black/Yellow wire
between No. 4 fuse and fast idle
control solenoid valve

— Open circuit in Green/Yellow wire
between fast idle control solenoid
valve and ECU

— Open circuit in fast idle control
solenoid valve

— If voltage is 9 V from test at B4/A18
terminals, ECU is faulty.

NOTE: No voltage
available.

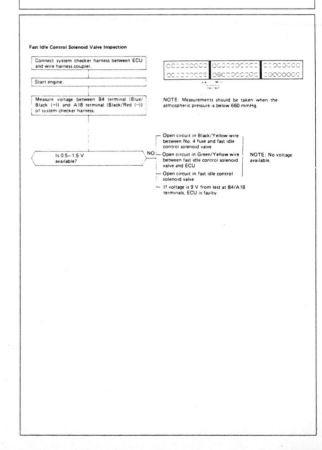

ECU DIAGNOSTIC CHART — 1986 ACCORD

Use the system checker harness and digital circuit tester to check the system.

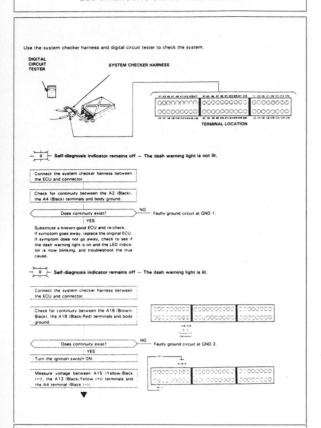

DIGITAL CIRCUIT TESTER

SYSTEM CHECKER HARNESS

TERMINAL LOCATION

0 — Self-diagnosis indicator remains off — The dash warning light is not lit.

Connect the system checker harness between the ECU and connector.

Check for continuity between the A2 (Black), the A4 (Black) terminals and body ground.

Does continuity exist? — NO → Faulty ground circuit at GND 1.
YES

Substitute a known-good ECU and re-check. If symptom goes away, replace the original ECU. If symptom does not go away, check to see if the dash warning light is on and the LED indicator is now blinking, and troubleshoot the true cause.

0 — Self-diagnosis indicator remains off — The dash warning light is lit.

Connect the system checker harness between the ECU and connector.

Check for continuity between the A16 (Brown/Black), the A18 (Black/Red) terminals and body ground.

Does continuity exist? — NO → Faulty ground circuit at GND 2.
YES

Turn the ignition switch ON.

Measure voltage between A15 (Yellow/Black (+)), the A13 (Black/Yellow (+)) terminals and the A4 terminal (Black (−)).

ECU DIAGNOSTIC CHART — 1986 ACCORD

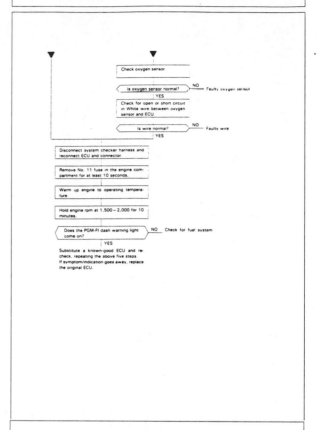

Check oxygen sensor

Is oxygen sensor normal? — NO → Faulty oxygen sensor
YES

Check for open or short circuit in White wire between oxygen sensor and ECU.

Is wire normal? — NO → Faulty wire
YES

Disconnect system checker harness and reconnect ECU and connector.

Remove No. 11 fuse in the engine compartment for at least 10 seconds.

Warm up engine to operating temperature.

Hold engine rpm at 1,500 − 2,000 for 10 minutes.

Does the PGM-FI dash warning light come on? — NO → Check for fuel system
YES

Substitute a known-good ECU and re-check, repeating the above five steps. If symptom/indication goes away, replace the original ECU.

ECU DIAGNOSTIC CHART — 1986 ACCORD

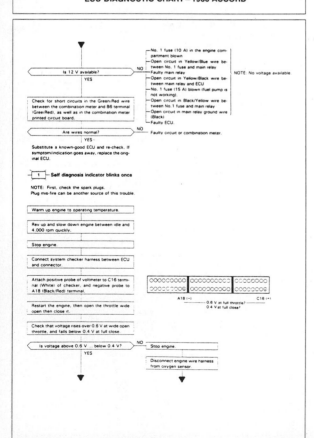

Is 12 V available? — NO →
- No. 1 fuse (10 A) in the engine compartment blown
- Open circuit in Yellow/Blue wire between No. 1 fuse and main relay
- Faulty main relay
- Open circuit in Yellow/Black wire between main relay and ECU
- No. 1 fuse (15 A) blown (fuel pump is not working)
- Open circuit in Black/Yellow wire between No. 1 fuse and main relay
- Open circuit in main relay ground wire (Black)
- Faulty ECU.

NOTE: No voltage available.

YES

Check for short circuits in the Green/Red wire between the combination meter and B6 terminal (Gree/Red), as well as in the combination meter printed circuit board.

Are wires normal? — NO → Faulty circuit or combination meter.
YES

Substitute a known-good ECU and re-check. If symptom/indication goes away, replace the original ECU.

1 — Self diagnosis indicator blinks once

NOTE: First, check the spark plugs. Plug mis-fire can be another source of this trouble.

Warm up engine to operating temperature.

Rev up and slow down engine between idle and 4,000 rpm quickly.

Stop engine.

Connect system checker harness between ECU and connector.

Attach positive probe of voltmeter to C16 terminal (White) of checker, and negative probe to A18 (Black/Red) terminal.

Restart the engine, then open the throttle wide open then close it.

Check that voltage rises over 0.6 V at wide open throttle, and falls below 0.4 V at full close.

Is voltage above 0.6 V ... below 0.4 V? — NO → Stop engine.
YES

Disconnect engine wire harness from oxygen sensor.

A18 (−)   C16 (+)
0.6 V at full throttle?
0.4 V at full close?

ECU DIAGNOSTIC CHART — 1986 ACCORD

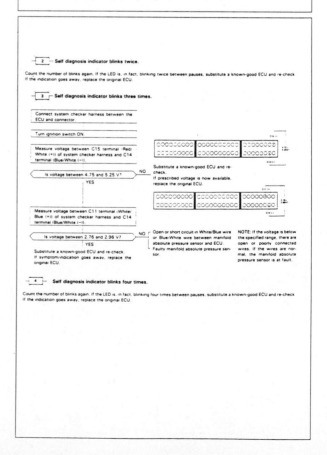

2 — Self diagnosis indicator blinks twice.

Count the number of blinks again. If the LED is, in fact, blinking twice between pauses, substitute a known-good ECU and re-check. If the indication goes away, replace the original ECU.

3 — Self diagnosis indicator blinks three times.

Connect system checker harness between the ECU and connector.

Turn ignition switch ON.

Measure voltage between C15 terminal (Red/White (+)) of system checker harness and C14 terminal (Blue/White (−)).

Is voltage between 4.75 and 5.25 V? — NO → Substitute a known-good ECU and re-check. If prescribed voltage is now available, replace the original ECU.
YES

Measure voltage between C11 terminal (White/Blue (+)) of system checker harness and C14 terminal (Blue/White (−)).

Is voltage between 2.76 and 2.96 V? — NO → Open or short circuit in White/Blue wire or Blue/White wire between manifold absolute pressure sensor and ECU. Faulty manifold absolute pressure sensor.
YES

Substitute a known-good ECU and re-check. If symptom/indication goes away, replace the original ECU.

NOTE: If the voltage is below the specified range, there are open or poorly connected wires. If the wires are normal, the manifold absolute pressure sensor is at fault.

4 — Self diagnosis indicator blinks four times.

Count the number of blinks again. If the LED is, in fact, blinking four times between pauses, substitute a known-good ECU and re-check. If the indication goes away, replace the original ECU.

ECU DIAGNOSTIC CHART—1986 ACCORD

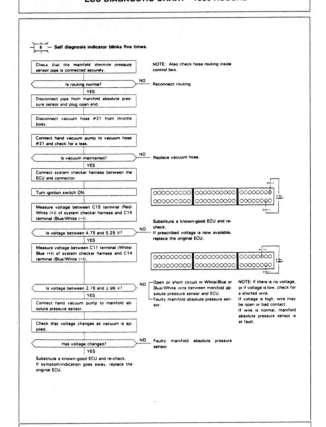

5 — Self diagnosis indicator blinks five times.

Check that the manifold absolute pressure sensor pipe is connected securely.

NOTE: Also check hose routing inside control box.

Is routing normal? → NO → Reconnect routing
↓ YES

Disconnect pipe from manifold absolute pressure sensor and plug open end.

Disconnect vacuum hose #21 from throttle body.

Connect hand vacuum pump to vacuum hose #21 and check for a leak.

Is vacuum maintained? → NO → Replace vacuum hose.
↓ YES

Connect system checker harness between the ECU and connector.

Turn ignition switch ON.

Measure voltage between C15 terminal (Red/White (+)) of system checker harness and C14 terminal (Blue/White (−)).

Is voltage between 4.75 and 5.25 V? → NO → Substitute a known-good ECU and re-check. If prescribed voltage is now available, replace the original ECU.
↓ YES

Measure voltage between C11 terminal (White/Blue (+)) of system checker harness and C14 terminal (Blue/White (−)).

Is voltage between 2.76 and 2.96 V? → NO → – Open or short circuit in White/Blue or Blue/White wires between manifold absolute pressure sensor and ECU.
– Faulty manifold absolute pressure sensor.
↓ YES

NOTE: If there is no voltage, or if voltage is low, check for a shorted wire. If voltage is high, wire may be open or bad contact. If wire is normal, manifold absolute pressure sensor is at fault.

Connect hand vacuum pump to manifold absolute pressure sensor.

Check that voltage changes as vacuum is applied.

Has voltage changed? → NO → Faulty manifold absolute pressure sensor
↓ YES

Substitute a known-good ECU and re-check. If symptom/indication goes away, replace the original ECU.

ECU DIAGNOSTIC CHART—1986 ACCORD

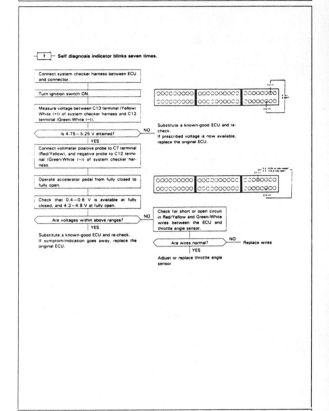

7 — Self diagnosis indicator blinks seven times.

Connect system checker harness between ECU and connector.

Turn ignition switch ON.

Measure voltage between C13 terminal (Yellow/White (+)) of system checker harness and C12 terminal (Green/White (−)).

Is 4.75 – 5.25 V attained? → NO → Substitute a known-good ECU and re-check. If prescribed voltage is now available, replace the original ECU.
↓ YES

Connect voltmeter positive probe to C7 terminal (Red/Yellow), and negative probe to C12 terminal (Green/White (−)) of system checker harness.

Operate accelerator pedal from fully closed to fully open.

Check that 0.4 – 0.6 V is available at fully closed, and 4.3 – 4.8 V at fully open.

Are voltages within above ranges? → NO → Check for short or open circuit in Red/Yellow and Green/White wires between the ECU and throttle angle sensor.
↓ YES

Substitute a known-good ECU and re-check. If symptom/indication goes away, replace the original ECU.

Are wires normal? → NO → Replace wires
↓ YES

Adjust or replace throttle angle sensor

ECU DIAGNOSTIC CHART—1986 ACCORD

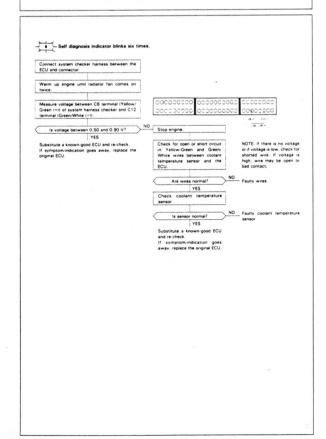

6 — Self diagnosis indicator blinks six times.

Connect system checker harness between the ECU and connector.

Warm up engine until radiator fan comes on twice.

Measure voltage between C6 terminal (Yellow/Green (+)) of system harness checker and C12 terminal (Green/White (−)).

Is voltage between 0.50 and 0.90 V? → NO → Stop engine.
↓ YES

Substitute a known-good ECU and re-check. If symptom/indication goes away, replace the original ECU.

Check for open or short circuit in Yellow/Green and Green/White wires between coolant temperature sensor and the ECU.

NOTE: If there is no voltage or if voltage is low, check for shorted wire. If voltage is high, wire may be open or bad contact.

Are wires normal? → NO → Faulty wires
↓ YES

Check coolant temperature sensor

Is sensor normal? → NO → Faulty coolant temperature sensor
↓ YES

Substitute a known-good ECU and re-check. If symptom/indication goes away, replace the original ECU.

ECU DIAGNOSTIC CHART—1986 ACCORD

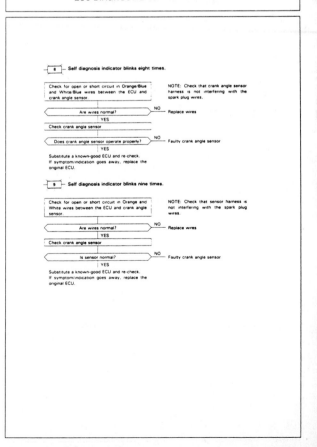

8 — Self diagnosis indicator blinks eight times.

Check for open or short circuit in Orange/Blue and White/Blue wires between the ECU and crank angle sensor.

NOTE: Check that crank angle sensor harness is not interfering with the spark plug wires.

Are wires normal? → NO → Replace wires
↓ YES

Check crank angle sensor

Does crank angle sensor operate properly? → NO → Faulty crank angle sensor
↓ YES

Substitute a known-good ECU and re-check. If symptom/indication goes away, replace the original ECU.

9 — Self diagnosis indicator blinks nine times.

Check for open or short circuit in Orange and White wires between the ECU and crank angle sensor.

NOTE: Check that sensor harness is not interfering with the spark plug wires.

Are wires normal? → NO → Replace wires
↓ YES

Check crank angle sensor

Is sensor normal? → NO → Faulty crank angle sensor
↓ YES

Substitute a known-good ECU and re-check. If symptom/indication goes away, replace the original ECU.

ECU DIAGNOSTIC CHART—1986 ACCORD

10 — Self diagnosis indicator blinks ten times.

Connect system checker harness between the ECU and harness connector.

Attach voltmeter positive probe to C5 terminal (White/Red), and negative probe to C12 terminal (Green/White) of system checker harness.

Turn ignition switch ON.

Check that voltage is correct for the intake air temperature.

Is voltage correct? — NO → Turn ignition switch OFF.

YES

Substitute a known-good ECU and re-check. If symptom/indication goes away, replace the original ECU.

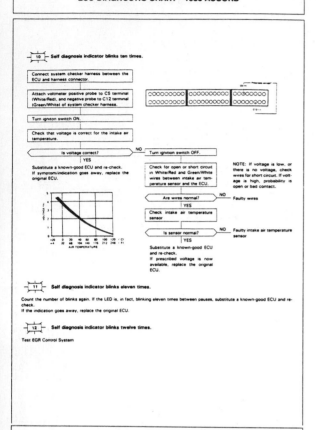

Check for open or short circuit in White/Red and Green/White wires between intake air temperature sensor and the ECU.

NOTE: If voltage is low, or there is no voltage, check wires for short circuit. If voltage is high, probability is open or bad contact.

Are wires normal? — NO → Faulty wires

YES

Check intake air temperature sensor

Is sensor normal? — NO → Faulty intake air temperature sensor

YES

Substitute a known-good ECU and re-check. If prescribed voltage is now available, replace the original ECU.

11 — Self diagnosis indicator blinks eleven times.

Count the number of blinks again. If the LED is, in fact, blinking eleven times between pauses, substitute a known-good ECU and re-check.
If the indication goes away, replace the original ECU.

12 — Self diagnosis indicator blinks twelve times.

Test EGR Control System

ECU DIAGNOSTIC CHART—1986 ACCORD

Starter Switch Signal Inspection

Connect system checker harness between ECU and wire harness connector.

Attach positive probe of voltmeter to B13 terminal (Blue/Red), and negative probe to A18 terminal (Black/Red) of system checker harness.

Turn ignition switch to START.

Is battery voltage available? — NO → Blown No. 10 fuse (7.5 A)
Open circuit in Blue/Red wire between No. 10 fuse and ECU

Alternator FR Terminal Signal Inspection

Before inspection, check operation of alternator as follows:
With the engine running, and the upper vacuum hose of idle control solenoid valve pinched (to cut off the idle control system), turn the headlights on and off.
Engine rpm should be changed. If engine rpm remains steady, re-charge battery and re-test.

Connect system checker harness between ECU and wire harness connector.

Attach positive probe of voltmeter to B14 terminal (White/Red) and negative probe to A18 terminal (Black/Red) of system checker harness.

Start engine.

Turn headlights ON and OFF.

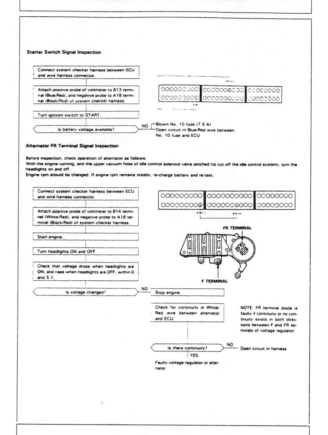

FR TERMINAL

F TERMINAL

Check that voltage drops when headlights are ON and rises when headlights are OFF, within 0 and 5 V.

Is voltage changed? — NO → Stop engine.

Check for continuity in White/Red wire between alternator and ECU.

NOTE: FR terminal diode is faulty if continuity or no continuity exists in both directions between F and FR terminals of voltage regulator.

Is there continuity? — NO → Open circuit in harness

YES

Faulty voltage regulator or alternator

ECU DIAGNOSTIC CHART—1986 ACCORD

13 — Self diagnosis indicator blinks thirteen times.

Connect system checker harness between the ECU and harness connector.

Turn ignition switch ON.

Measure voltage between C13 terminal (Yellow/White (+)) of system checker harness and C12 terminal (Green/White (−)).

Is 4.75—5.25 V available? — NO → Substitute a known-good ECU and re-check. If prescribed voltage is now available, replace the original ECU.

YES

Measure voltage between C9 terminal (Red (+)) of system checker harness and C12 terminal (Green/White).

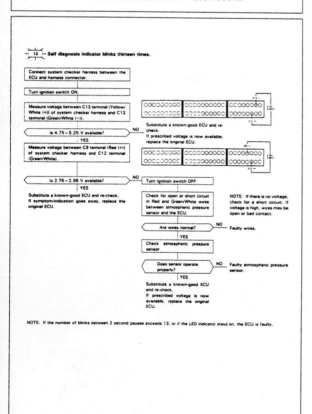

Is 2.76—2.96 V available? — NO → Turn ignition switch OFF.

YES

Substitute a known-good ECU and re-check. If symptom/indication goes away, replace the original ECU.

Check for open or short circuit in Red and Green/White wires between atmospheric pressure sensor and the ECU.

NOTE: If there is no voltage, check for a short circuit. If voltage is high, wires may be open or bad contact.

Are wires normal? — NO → Faulty wires

YES

Check atmospheric pressure sensor

Does sensor operate properly? — NO → Faulty atmospheric pressure sensor

YES

Substitute a known-good ECU and re-check. If prescribed voltage is now available, replace the original ECU.

NOTE: If the number of blinks between 2 second pauses exceeds 13, or if the LED indicator stays on, the ECU is faulty.

ECU DIAGNOSTIC CHART—1986 ACCORD

A/T Shift Position Signal Inspection

Connect system checker harness between ECU and wire harness connector.

Attach positive probe of voltmeter to B7 terminal (Green) and negative probe to A18 terminal (Black/Red) of system checker harness.

Turn ignition switch ON.

Move shift lever into gear.

Check that more than 5 V appears in positions other than "N" (0 V in "N").

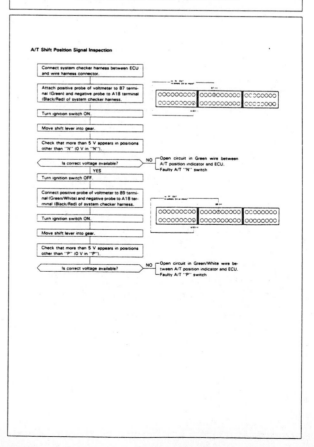

Is correct voltage available? — NO → Open circuit in Green wire between A/T position indicator and ECU.
Faulty A/T "N" switch

YES

Turn ignition switch OFF.

Connect positive probe of voltmeter to B9 terminal (Green/White) and negative probe to A18 terminal (Black/Red) of system checker harness.

Turn ignition switch ON.

Move shift lever into gear.

Check that more than 5 V appears in positions other than "P" (0 V in "P").

Is correct voltage available? — NO → Open circuit in Green/White wire between A/T position indicator and ECU.
Faulty A/T "P" switch

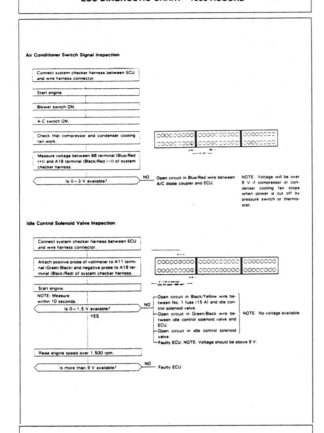

ECU DIAGNOSTIC CHART — 1986 ACCORD

Air Conditioner Switch Signal Inspection

- Connect system checker harness between ECU and wire harness connector.
- Start engine.
- Blower switch ON.
- A·C switch ON.
- Check that compressor and condenser cooling fan work.
- Measure voltage between B8 terminal (Blue/Red (+)) and A18 terminal (Black/Red (−)) of system checker harness.

Is 0 − 3 V available? — NO → Open circuit in Blue/Red wire between A/C diode coupler and ECU.

NOTE: Voltage will be over 9 V if compressor or condenser cooling fan stops when power is cut off by pressure switch or thermostat.

Idle Control Solenoid Valve Inspection

- Connect system checker harness between ECU and wire harness connector.
- Attach positive probe of voltmeter to A11 terminal (Green/Black) and negative probe to A18 terminal (Black/Red) of system checker harness.
- Start engine.
- NOTE: Measure within 10 seconds.

Is 0 − 1.5 V available? — NO →
- Open circuit in Black/Yellow wire between No. 1 fuse (15 A) and idle control solenoid valve.
- Open circuit in Green/Black wire between idle control solenoid valve and ECU.
- Open circuit in idle control solenoid valve.
- Faulty ECU. NOTE: Voltage should be above 9 V.

NOTE: No voltage available.

YES

- Raise engine speed over 1,500 rpm.

Is more than 9 V available? — NO → Faulty ECU.

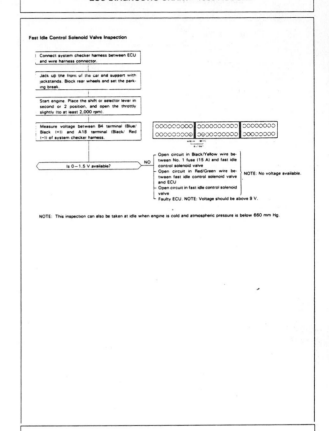

ECU DIAGNOSTIC CHART — 1986 ACCORD

Fast Idle Control Solenoid Valve Inspection

- Connect system checker harness between ECU and wire harness connector.
- Jack up the front of the car and support with jackstands. Block rear wheels and set the parking brake.
- Start engine. Place the shift or selector lever in second or 2 position, and open the throttle slightly (to at least 2,000 rpm).
- Measure voltage between B4 terminal (Blue/Black (+)) and A18 terminal (Black/Red (−)) of system checker harness.

Is 0 − 1.5 V available? — NO →
- Open circuit in Black/Yellow wire between No. 1 fuse (15 A) and fast idle control solenoid valve.
- Open circuit in Red/Green wire between fast idle control solenoid valve and ECU.
- Open circuit in fast idle control solenoid valve.
- Faulty ECU. NOTE: Voltage should be above 9 V.

NOTE: No voltage available.

NOTE: This inspection can also be taken at idle when engine is cold and atmospheric pressure is below 660 mm Hg.

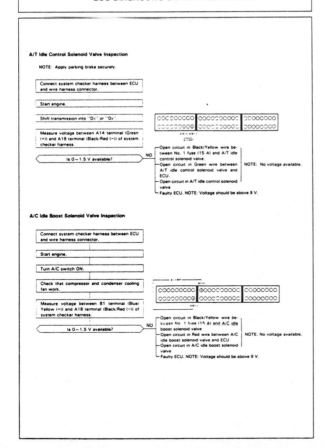

ECU DIAGNOSTIC CHART — 1986 ACCORD

A/T Idle Control Solenoid Valve Inspection

NOTE: Apply parking brake securely.

- Connect system checker harness between ECU and wire harness connector.
- Start engine.
- Shift transmission into "D3" or "D4".
- Measure voltage between A14 terminal (Green (+)) and A18 terminal (Black/Red (−)) of system checker harness.

Is 0 − 1.5 V available? — NO →
- Open circuit in Black/Yellow wire between No. 1 fuse (15 A) and A/T idle control solenoid valve.
- Open circuit in Green wire between A/T idle control solenoid valve and ECU.
- Open circuit in A/T idle control solenoid valve.
- Faulty ECU. NOTE: Voltage should be above 9 V.

NOTE: No voltage available.

A/C Idle Boost Solenoid Valve Inspection

- Connect system checker harness between ECU and wire harness connector.
- Start engine.
- Turn A/C switch ON.
- Check that compressor and condenser cooling fan work.
- Measure voltage between B1 terminal (Blue/Yellow (+)) and A18 terminal (Black/Red (−)) of system checker harness.

Is 0 − 1.5 V available? — NO →
- Open circuit in Black/Yellow wire between No. 1 fuse (15 A) and A/C idle boost solenoid valve.
- Open circuit in Red wire between A/C idle boost solenoid valve and ECU.
- Open circuit in A/C idle boost solenoid valve.
- Faulty ECU. NOTE: Voltage should be above 9 V.

NOTE: No voltage available.

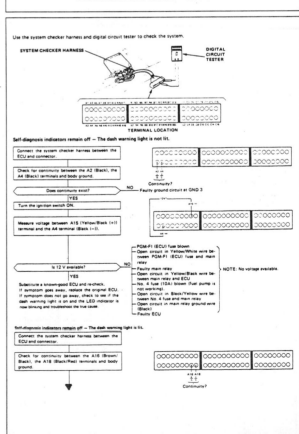

ECU DIAGNOSTIC CHART — 1986 CIVIC

Use the system checker harness and digital circuit tester to check the system.

SYSTEM CHECKER HARNESS

DIGITAL CIRCUIT TESTER

TERMINAL LOCATION

Self-diagnosis indicators remain off — The dash warning light is not lit.

- Connect the system checker harness between the ECU and connector.
- Check for continuity between the A2 (Black), the A4 (Black) terminals and body ground.

Does continuity exist? — NO → Faulty ground circuit at GND 3

YES

- Turn the ignition switch ON.
- Measure voltage between A15 (Yellow/Black (+)) terminal and the A4 terminal (Black (−)).

Is 12 V available? — NO →
- PGM-FI (ECU) fuse blown
- Open circuit in Yellow/White wire between PGM-FI (ECU) fuse and main relay
- Faulty main relay
- Open circuit in Yellow/Black wire between main relay and ECU
- No. 4 fuse (10A) blown (fuel pump is not working)
- Open circuit in Black/Yellow wire between No. 4 fuse and main relay
- Open circuit in main relay ground wire (Black)
- Faulty ECU

NOTE: No voltage available.

YES

Substitute a known-good ECU and re-check. If symptom goes away, replace the original ECU. If symptom does not go away, check to see if the dash warning light is on and the LED indicator is now blinking and troubleshoot the true cause.

Self-diagnosis indicators remain off — The dash warning light is lit.

- Connect the system checker harness between the ECU and connector.
- Check for continuity between the A16 (Brown/Black), the A18 (Black/Red) terminals and body ground.

Continuity?

ECU DIAGNOSTIC CHART—1986 CIVIC

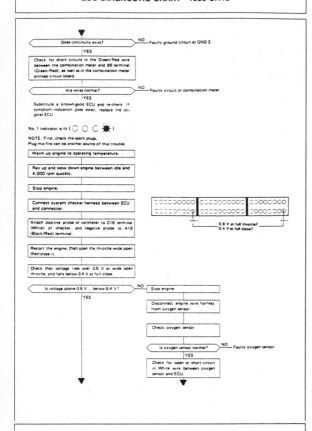

ECU DIAGNOSTIC CHART—1986 CIVIC

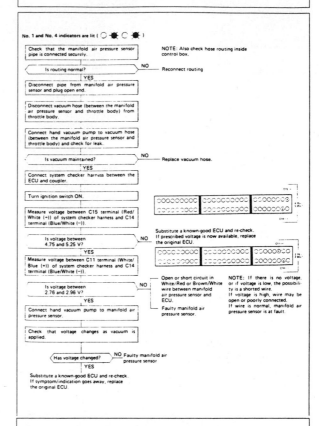

ECU DIAGNOSTIC CHART—1986 CIVIC

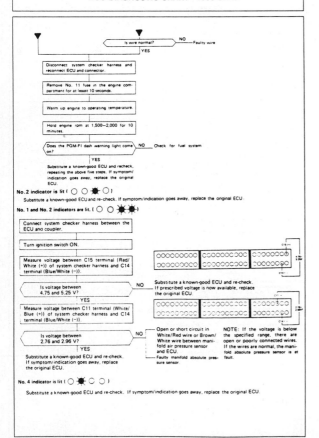

ECU DIAGNOSTIC CHART—1986 CIVIC

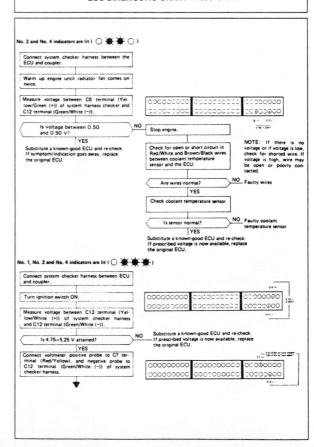

ECU DIAGNOSTIC CHART—1986 CIVIC

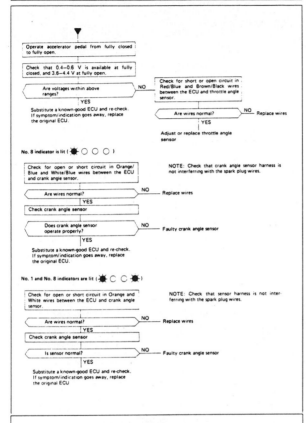

Operate accelerator pedal from fully closed to fully open.

Check that 0.4–0.6 V is available at fully closed, and 3.6–4.4 V at fully open.

Are voltages within above ranges? → NO → Check for short or open circuit in Red/Blue and Brown/Black wires between the ECU and throttle angle sensor.

YES

Substitute a known-good ECU and re-check. If symptom/indication goes away, replace the original ECU.

Are wires normal? → NO → Replace wires

YES

Adjust or replace throttle angle sensor

No. 8 indicator is lit (●○○○)

Check for open or short circuit in Orange/Blue and White/Blue wires between the ECU and crank angle sensor.

NOTE: Check that crank angle sensor harness is not interfering with the spark plug wires.

Are wires normal? → NO → Replace wires

YES

Check crank angle sensor

Does crank angle sensor operate properly? → NO → Faulty crank angle sensor

YES

Substitute a known-good ECU and re-check. If symptom/indication goes away, replace the original ECU.

No. 1 and No. 8 indicators are lit (●○○●)

Check for open or short circuit in Orange and White wires between the ECU and crank angle sensor.

NOTE: Check that sensor harness is not interfering with the spark plug wires.

Are wires normal? → NO → Replace wires

YES

Check crank angle sensor

Is sensor normal? → NO → Faulty crank angle sensor

YES

Substitute a known-good ECU and re-check. If symptom/indication goes away, replace the original ECU

ECU DIAGNOSTIC CHART—1986 CIVIC

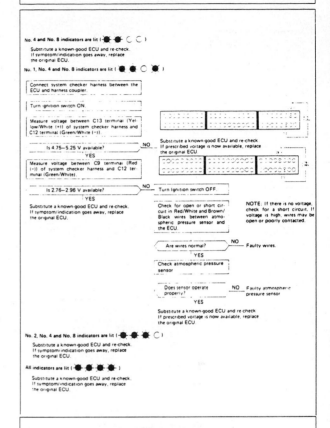

No. 4 and No. 8 indicators are lit (●●○○)

Substitute a known-good ECU and re-check. If symptom/indication goes away, replace the original ECU.

No. 1, No. 4 and No. 8 indicators are lit (●●○●)

Connect system checker harness between the ECU and harness coupler.

Turn ignition switch ON.

Measure voltage between C13 terminal (Yellow/White (+)) of system checker harness and C12 terminal (Green/White (–)).

Is 4.75–5.25 V available? → NO → Substitute a known-good ECU and re-check. If prescribed voltage is now available, replace the original ECU.

YES

Measure voltage between C9 terminal (Red (–)) of system checker harness and C12 terminal (Green/White).

Is 2.76–2.96 V available? → NO → Turn ignition switch OFF.

YES

Substitute a known-good ECU and re-check. If symptom/indication goes away, replace the original ECU.

Check for open or short circuit in Red/White and Brown/Black wires between atmospheric pressure sensor and the ECU.

NOTE: If there is no voltage, check for a short circuit. If voltage is high, wires may be open or poorly contacted.

Are wires normal? → NO → Faulty wires.

YES

Check atmospheric pressure sensor

Does sensor operate properly? → NO → Faulty atmospheric pressure sensor

YES

Substitute a known-good ECU and re-check. If prescribed voltage is now available, replace the original ECU.

No. 2, No. 4 and No. 8 indicators are lit (●●●○)

Substitute a known-good ECU and re-check. If symptom/indication goes away, replace the original ECU.

All indicators are lit (●●●●)

Substitute a known-good ECU and re-check. If symptom/indication goes away, replace the original ECU.

ECU DIAGNOSTIC CHART—1986 CIVIC

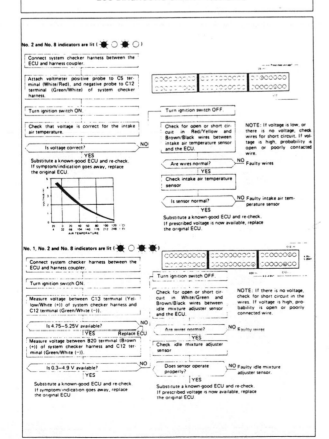

No. 2 and No. 8 indicators are lit (●○●○)

Connect system checker harness between the ECU and harness coupler.

Attach voltmeter positive probe to C5 terminal (White/Red), and negative probe to C12 terminal (Green/White) of system checker harness.

Turn ignition switch ON.

Check that voltage is correct for the intake air temperature.

Is voltage correct? → NO

YES

Substitute a known-good ECU and re-check. If symptom/indication goes away, replace the original ECU.

Turn ignition switch OFF.

Check for open or short circuit in Red/Yellow and Brown/Black wires between intake air temperature sensor and the ECU.

NOTE: If voltage is low, or there is no voltage, check wires for short circuit. If voltage is high, probability is open or poorly contacted wire.

Are wires normal? → NO → Faulty wires

YES

Check intake air temperature sensor

Is sensor normal? → NO → Faulty intake air temperature sensor

YES

Substitute a known-good ECU and re-check. If prescribed voltage is now available, replace the original ECU.

No. 1, No. 2 and No. 8 indicators are lit (●○●●)

Connect system checker harness between the ECU and harness coupler.

Turn ignition switch ON.

Measure voltage between C13 terminal (Yellow/White (+)) of system checker harness and C12 terminal (Green/White (–)).

Is 4.75–5.25 V available? → NO → Replace ECU

YES

Measure voltage between B20 terminal (Brown (+)) of system checker harness and C12 terminal (Green/White (–)).

Is 0.3–4.9 V available? → NO

YES

Substitute a known-good ECU and re-check. If symptom/indication goes away, replace the original ECU

Turn ignition switch OFF.

Check for open or short circuit in White/Green and Brown/Black wires between idle mixture adjuster sensor and the ECU.

NOTE: If there is no voltage, check for short circuit in the wires. If voltage is high, probability is open or poorly connected wire.

Are wires normal? → NO → Faulty wires

YES

Check idle mixture adjuster sensor

Does sensor operate properly? → NO → Faulty idle mixture adjuster sensor

YES

Substitute a known-good ECU and re-check. If prescribed voltage is now available, replace the original ECU.

ECU DIAGNOSTIC CHART—1986 CIVIC

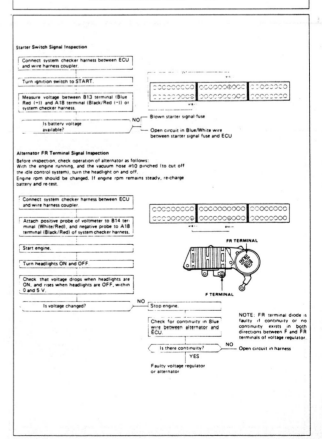

Starter Switch Signal Inspection

Connect system checker harness between ECU and wire harness coupler.

Turn ignition switch to START.

Measure voltage between B13 terminal (Blue/Red (+)) and A18 terminal (Black/Red (–)) of system checker harness.

Is battery voltage available? → NO → Blown starter signal fuse

→ Open circuit in Blue/White wire between starter signal fuse and ECU

Alternator FR Terminal Signal Inspection

Before inspection, check operation of alternator as follows:
With the engine running, and the vacuum hose #10 pinched (to cut off the idle control system), turn the headlight on and off. Engine rpm should be changed. If engine rpm remains steady, re-charge battery and re-test.

Connect system checker harness between ECU and wire harness coupler.

Attach positive probe of voltmeter to B14 terminal (White/Red), and negative probe to A18 terminal (Black/Red) of system checker harness.

Start engine.

Turn headlights ON and OFF.

Check that voltage drops when headlights are ON, and rises when headlights are OFF, within 0 and 5 V.

Is voltage changed? → NO → Stop engine.

YES

Faulty voltage regulator or alternator

Check for continuity in Blue wire between alternator and ECU.

Is there continuity? → NO → Open circuit in harness

YES

Faulty voltage regulator or alternator

NOTE: FR terminal diode is faulty if continuity or no continuity exists in both directions between F and FR terminals of voltage regulator.

FR TERMINAL

F TERMINAL

ECU DIAGNOSTIC CHART — 1986 CIVIC

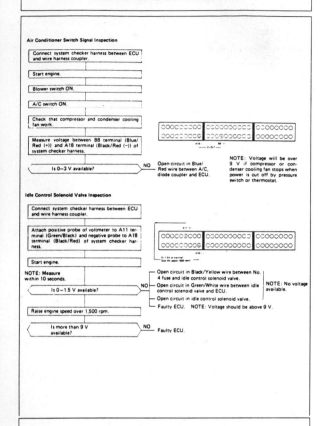

Air Conditioner Switch Signal Inspection

Connect system checker harness between ECU and wire harness coupler.

Start engine.

Blower switch ON.

A/C switch ON.

Check that compressor and condenser cooling fan work.

Measure voltage between B8 terminal (Blue/Red (+)) and A18 terminal (Black/Red (−)) of system checker harness.

Is 0–3 V available? — NO → Open circuit in Blue/Red wire between A/C, diode coupler and ECU.

NOTE: Voltage will be over 9 V if compressor or condenser cooling fan stops when power is cut off by pressure switch or thermostat.

Idle Control Solenoid Valve Inspection

Connect system checker harness between ECU and wire harness coupler.

Attach positive probe of voltmeter to A11 terminal (Green/Black) and negative probe to A18 terminal (Black/Red) of system checker harness.

Start engine.

NOTE: Measure within 10 seconds.

Is 0–1.5 V available? — NO →
- Open circuit in Black/Yellow wire between No. 4 fuse and idle control solenoid valve.
- Open circuit in Green/White wire between idle control solenoid valve and ECU.
- Open circuit in idle control solenoid valve.
- Faulty ECU. NOTE: Voltage should be above 9 V.

NOTE: No voltage available.

Raise engine speed over 1,500 rpm.

Is more than 9 V available? — NO → Faulty ECU.

ECU DIAGNOSTIC CHART — 1987–88 ACCORD

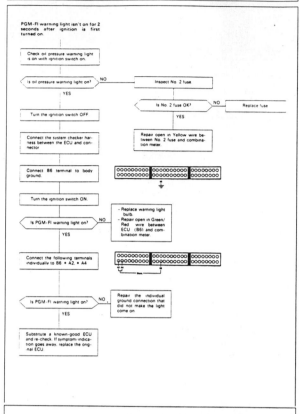

PGM-FI warning light isn't on for 2 seconds after ignition is first turned on.

Check oil pressure warning light is on with ignition switch on.

Is oil pressure warning light on? — NO → Inspect No. 2 fuse

Is No. 2 fuse OK? — NO → Replace fuse

YES → Repair open in Yellow wire between No. 2 fuse and combination meter.

Turn the ignition switch OFF.

Connect the system checker harness between the ECU and connector.

Connect B6 terminal to body ground.

Turn the ignition switch ON.

Is PGM-FI warning light on? — NO →
- Replace warning light bulb.
- Repair open in Green/Red wire between ECU (B6) and combination meter.

Connect the following terminals individually to B6 • A2 • A4

Is PGM-FI warning light on? — NO → Repair the individual ground connection that did not make the light come on

Substitute a known-good ECU and re-check. If symptom/indication goes away, replace the original ECU.

ECU DIAGNOSTIC CHART — 1986 CIVIC

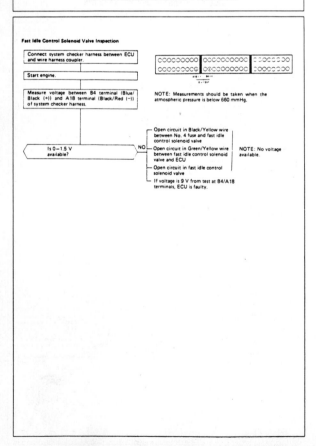

Fast Idle Control Solenoid Valve Inspection

Connect system checker harness between ECU and wire harness coupler.

Start engine.

Measure voltage between B4 terminal (Blue/Black (+)) and A18 terminal (Black/Red (−)) of system checker harness.

NOTE: Measurements should be taken when the atmospheric pressure is below 660 mmHg.

Is 0–1.5 V available? — NO →
- Open circuit in Black/Yellow wire between No. 4 fuse and fast idle control solenoid valve
- Open circuit in Green/Yellow wire between fast idle control solenoid valve and ECU
- Open circuit in fast idle control solenoid valve
- If voltage is 9 V from test at B4/A18 terminals, ECU is faulty.

NOTE: No voltage available.

ECU DIAGNOSTIC CHART — 1987–88 ACCORD

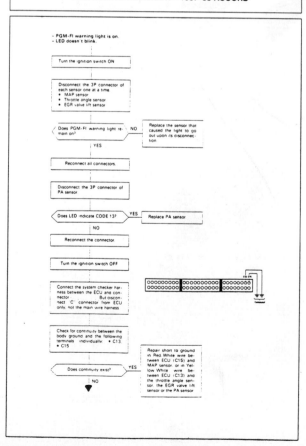

- PGM-FI warning light is on.
- LED doesn't blink.

Turn the ignition switch ON

Disconnect the 3P connector of each sensor one at a time.
- MAP sensor
- Throttle angle sensor
- EGR valve lift sensor

Does PGM-FI warning light remain on? — NO → Replace the sensor that caused the light to go out upon its disconnection

Reconnect all connectors.

Disconnect the 3P connector of PA sensor

Does LED indicate CODE 13? — YES → Replace PA sensor

NO

Reconnect the connector.

Turn the ignition switch OFF

Connect the system checker harness between the ECU and connector. But disconnect 'C' connector from ECU only, not the main wire harness

Check for continuity between the body ground and the following terminals individually • C13 • C15

Does continuity exist? — YES → Repair short to ground in Red/White wire between ECU (C15) and MAP sensor, or in Yellow/White wire between ECU (C13) and the throttle angle sensor, the EGR valve lift sensor or the PA sensor.

NO

ECU DIAGNOSTIC CHART—1987–88 ACCORD

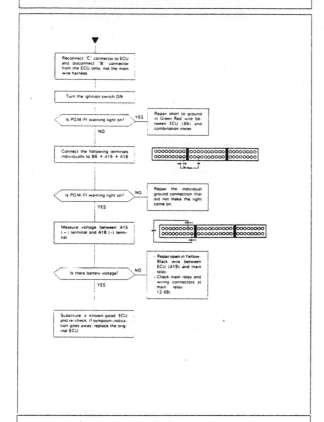

▼

Reconnect "C" connector to ECU and disconnect "B" connector from the ECU only, not the main wire harness

↓

Turn the ignition switch ON

↓

Is PGM-FI warning light on? — YES → Repair short to ground in Green/Red wire between ECU (B6) and combination meter

NO ↓

Connect the following terminals individually to B6 • A16 • A18

↓

Is PGM-FI warning light on? — NO → Repair the individual ground connection that did not make the light come on.

YES ↓

Measure voltage between A15 (−) terminal and A18 (−) terminal.

↓

Is there battery voltage? — NO → - Repair open in Yellow/Black wire between ECU (A15) and main relay.
- Check main relay and wiring connectors at main relay (12-68)

YES ↓

Substitute a known-good ECU and re-check. If symptom indication goes away, replace the original ECU.

ECU DIAGNOSTIC CHART—1987–88 ACCORD

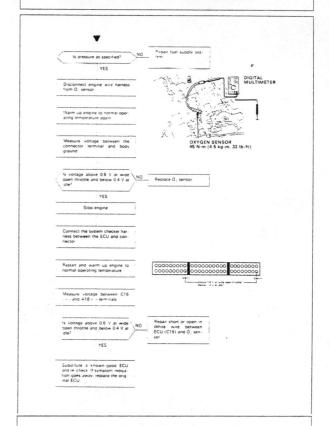

▼

Is pressure as specified? — NO → Repair fuel supply system

YES ↓

Disconnect engine wire harness from O₂ sensor

↓

Warm up engine to normal operating temperature again

↓

Measure voltage between the connector terminal and body ground

↓

Is voltage above 0.6 V at wide open throttle and below 0.4 V at idle? — NO → Replace O₂ sensor

YES ↓

Stop engine

↓

Connect the system checker harness between the ECU and connector

↓

Restart and warm up engine to normal operating temperature

↓

Measure voltage between C16 (−) and A18 (−) terminals

↓

Is voltage above 0.6 V at wide open throttle and below 0.4 V at idle? — NO → Repair short or open in White wire between ECU (C16) and O₂ sensor

YES ↓

Substitute a known-good ECU and re-check. If symptom indication goes away, replace the original ECU.

OXYGEN SENSOR
45 N·m (4.5 kg-m, 33 lb-ft)

DIGITAL MULTIMETER

ECU DIAGNOSTIC CHART—1987–88 ACCORD

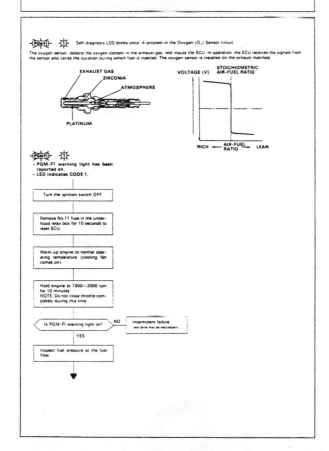

[PGM-FI] ☼ Self-diagnosis LED blinks once. A problem in the Oxygen (O₂) Sensor circuit.

The oxygen sensor detects the oxygen content in the exhaust gas, and inputs the ECU. In operation, the ECU receives the signals from the sensor and varies the duration during which fuel is injected. The oxygen sensor is installed on the exhaust manifold.

EXHAUST GAS
ZIRCONIA
ATMOSPHERE
PLATINUM

VOLTAGE (V)
STOICHIOMETRIC AIR-FUEL RATIO
RICH — AIR-FUEL RATIO — LEAN

[PGM-FI] ☼
- PGM-FI warning light has been reported on.
- LED indicates CODE 1.

↓

Turn the ignition switch OFF

↓

Remove No.11 fuse in the underhood relay box for 10 seconds to reset ECU.

↓

Warm up engine to normal operating temperature (cooling fan comes on).

↓

Hold engine at 1500–2000 rpm for 10 minutes.
NOTE: Do not close throttle completely during this time.

↓

Is PGM-FI warning light on? — NO → Intermittent failure (test drive may be necessary)

YES ↓

Inspect fuel pressure at the fuel filter

▼

ECU DIAGNOSTIC CHART—1987–88 ACCORD

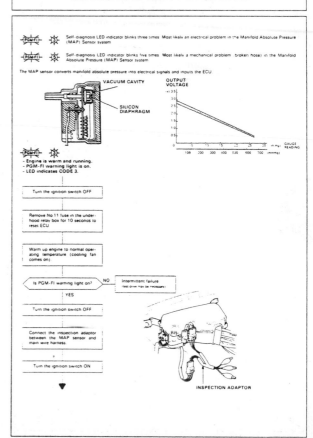

[PGM-FI] ☼ Self-diagnosis LED indicator blinks three times. Most likely an electrical problem in the Manifold Absolute Pressure (MAP) Sensor system.

[PGM-FI] ☼ Self-diagnosis LED indicator blinks five times. Most likely a mechanical problem (broken hose) in the Manifold Absolute Pressure (MAP) Sensor system.

The MAP sensor converts manifold absolute pressure into electrical signals and inputs the ECU.

VACUUM CAVITY
SILICON DIAPHRAGM

OUTPUT VOLTAGE
GAUGE READING

[PGM-FI] ☼
- Engine is warm and running.
- PGM-FI warning light is on.
- LED indicates CODE 3.

↓

Turn the ignition switch OFF

↓

Remove No.11 fuse in the underhood relay box for 10 seconds to reset ECU.

↓

Warm up engine to normal operating temperature (cooling fan comes on).

↓

Is PGM-FI warning light on? — NO → Intermittent failure (test drive may be necessary)

YES ↓

Turn the ignition switch OFF

↓

Connect the inspection adaptor between the MAP sensor and main wire harness

↓

Turn the ignition switch ON

▼

INSPECTION ADAPTOR

ECU DIAGNOSTIC CHART — 1987–88 ACCORD

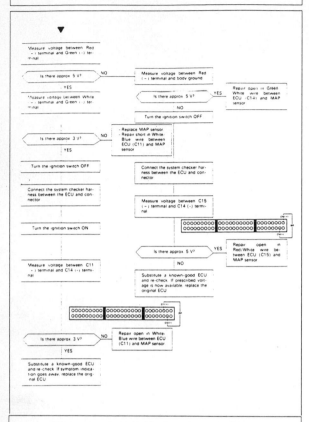

ECU DIAGNOSTIC CHART — 1987–88 ACCORD

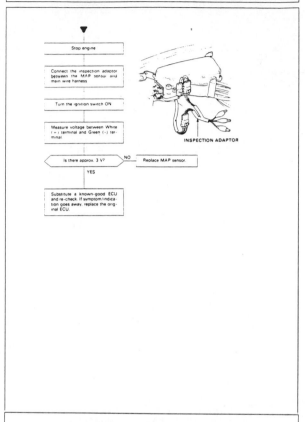

ECU DIAGNOSTIC CHART — 1987–88 ACCORD

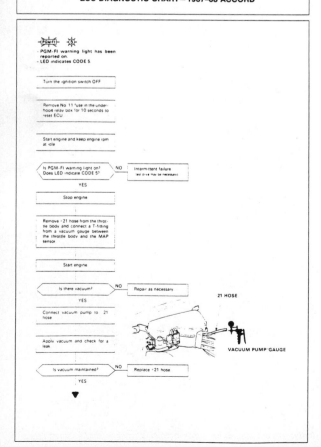

ECU DIAGNOSTIC CHART — 1987–88 ACCORD

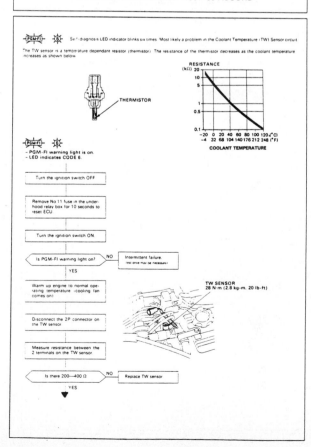

ECU DIAGNOSTIC CHART—1987–88 ACCORD

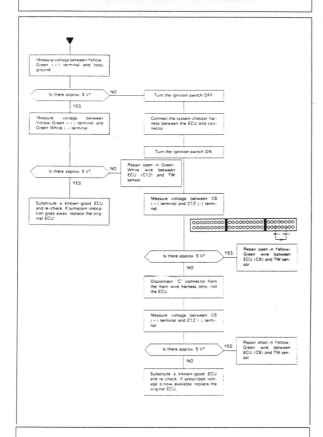

Measure voltage between Yellow/Green (–) terminal and body ground

Is there approx 5 V? — NO → Turn the ignition switch OFF

↓ YES

Measure voltage between Yellow/Green (–) terminal and Green/White (–) terminal

↓ Connect the system checker harness between the ECU and connector

↓ Turn the ignition switch ON

Is there approx 5 V? — NO → Repair open in Green/White wire between ECU (C12) and TW sensor

↓ YES

Substitute a known-good ECU and re-check. If symptom indication goes away, replace the original ECU

Measure voltage between C5 (–) terminal and C12 (–) terminal

Is there approx 5 V? — YES → Repair open in Yellow/Green wire between ECU (C6) and TW sensor

↓ NO

Disconnect "C" connector from the main wire harness only, not the ECU.

Measure voltage between C5 (–) terminal and C12 (–) terminal

Is there approx 5 V? — YES → Repair short in Yellow/Green wire between ECU (C6) and TW sensor

↓ NO

Substitute a known-good ECU and re-check. If prescribed voltage is now available, replace the original ECU

ECU DIAGNOSTIC CHART—1987–88 ACCORD

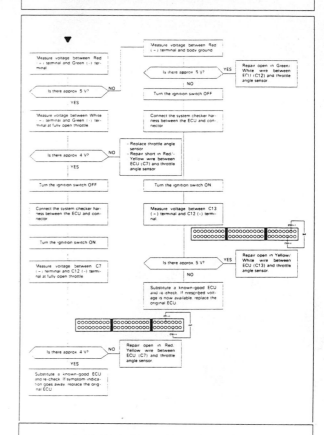

Measure voltage between Red (–) terminal and Green (–) terminal

Measure voltage between Red (–) terminal and body ground

Is there approx 5 V? — YES → Repair open in Green/White wire between ECU (C12) and throttle angle sensor

↓ NO

Is there approx 5 V? — NO → Turn the ignition switch OFF

↓ YES

Measure voltage between White (–) terminal and Green (–) terminal at fully open throttle

↓ Connect the system checker harness between the ECU and connector

Is there approx 4 V? — NO → • Replace throttle angle sensor • Repair short in Red/Yellow wire between ECU (C7) and throttle angle sensor

↓ YES

Turn the ignition switch OFF

↓ Turn the ignition switch ON

Connect the system checker harness between the ECU and connector

Measure voltage between C13 (–) terminal and C12 (–) terminal

↓ Turn the ignition switch ON

Is there approx 5 V? — YES → Repair open in Yellow/White wire between ECU (C13) and throttle angle sensor

Measure voltage between C7 (–) terminal and C12 (–) terminal at fully open throttle

↓ NO

Substitute a known-good ECU and re-check. If prescribed voltage is now available, replace the original ECU

Is there approx 4 V? — NO → Repair open in Red/Yellow wire between ECU (C7) and throttle angle sensor

↓ YES

Substitute a known-good ECU and re-check. If symptom indication goes away, replace the original ECU

ECU DIAGNOSTIC CHART—1987–88 ACCORD

PGM-FI — Self-diagnosis LED indicator blinks seven times. Most likely a problem in the Throttle Angle Sensor circuit.

The throttle angle sensor is a potentiometer. It is connected to the primary throttle valve shaft. As the throttle angle changes, the throttle angle sensor varies the voltage signal to the ECU.

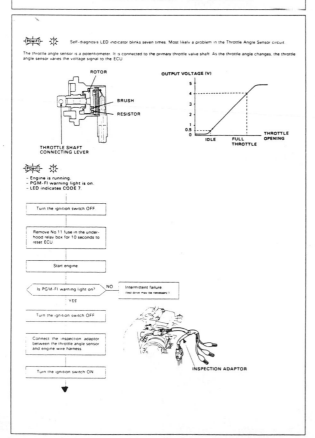

PGM-FI
- Engine is running.
- PGM-FI warning light is on.
- LED indicates CODE 7.

↓ Turn the ignition switch OFF

↓ Remove No.11 fuse in the under-hood relay box for 10 seconds to reset ECU

↓ Start engine

Is PGM-FI warning light on? — NO → Intermittent failure (test drive may be necessary)

↓ YES

Turn the ignition switch OFF

↓ Connect the inspection adaptor between the throttle angle sensor and engine wire harness

↓ Turn the ignition switch ON

INSPECTION ADAPTOR

ECU DIAGNOSTIC CHART—1987–88 ACCORD

PGM-FI — Self-diagnosis LED indicator blinks eight times. A problem in the TDC circuit of the Crank Angle Sensor.

PGM-FI — Self-diagnosis LED indicator blinks nine times. A problem in the CYL circuit of the Crank Angle Sensor.

The sensor consists of a pair of rotors, TDC and CYL, and a pickup for each rotor. Since the rotors are coupled to the camshaft, they turn together as a unit as the camshaft rotates. The CYL sensor detects the position of the No. 1 cylinder as the base for the Sequential Injection, whereas the TDC sensor serves to determine the injection timing for each cylinder. The TDC sensor also supplies the RPM signal to the ECU.

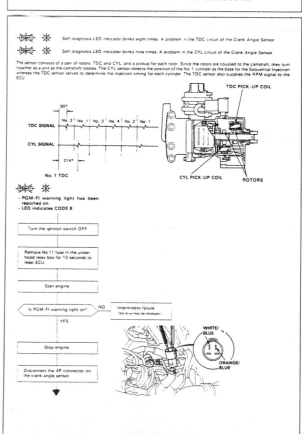

PGM-FI
- PGM-FI warning light has been reported on.
- LED indicates CODE 8.

↓ Turn the ignition switch OFF

↓ Remove No.11 fuse in the under-hood relay box for 10 seconds to reset ECU

↓ Start engine

Is PGM-FI warning light on? — NO → Intermittent failure (test drive may be necessary)

↓ YES

Stop engine

↓ Disconnect the 4P connector on the crank angle sensor

ECU DIAGNOSTIC CHART—1987–88 ACCORD

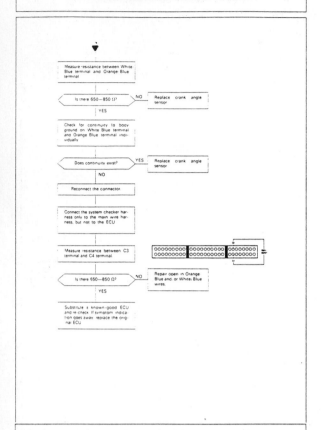

Measure resistance between White-Blue terminal and Orange-Blue terminal

Is there 650—850 Ω? → NO → Replace crank angle sensor

↓ YES

Check for continuity to body ground on White-Blue terminal and Orange-Blue terminal individually.

Does continuity exist? → YES → Replace crank angle sensor

↓ NO

Reconnect the connector.

Connect the system checker harness only to the main wire harness, but not to the ECU.

Measure resistance between C3 terminal and C4 terminal.

Is there 650—850 Ω? → NO → Repair open in Orange-Blue and/or White-Blue wires.

↓ YES

Substitute a known-good ECU and re-check. If symptom indication goes away replace the original ECU.

ECU DIAGNOSTIC CHART—1987–88 ACCORD

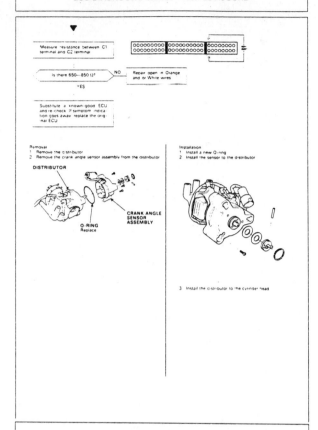

Measure resistance between C1 terminal and C2 terminal

Is there 650—850 Ω? → NO → Repair open in Orange and/or White wires

↓ YES

Substitute a known-good ECU and re-check. If symptom indication goes away replace the original ECU.

Removal
1. Remove the distributor.
2. Remove the crank angle sensor assembly from the distributor.

DISTRIBUTOR

O-RING Replace

CRANK ANGLE SENSOR ASSEMBLY

Installation
1. Install a new O-ring.
2. Install the sensor to the distributor.

3. Install the distributor to the cylinder head.

ECU DIAGNOSTIC CHART—1987–88 ACCORD

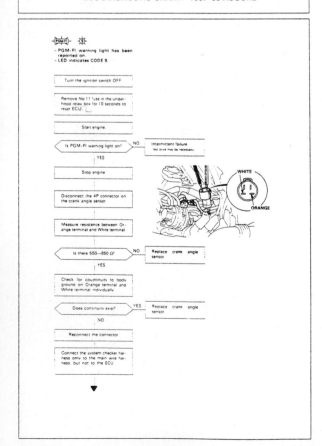

PGM-FI 9

- PGM-FI warning light has been reported on.
- LED indicates CODE 9.

Turn the ignition switch OFF

Remove No. 11 fuse in the underhood relay box for 10 seconds to reset ECU.

Start engine.

Is PGM-FI warning light on? → NO → Intermittent failure
Test drive may be necessary.

↓ YES

Stop engine.

Disconnect the 4P connector on the crank angle sensor.

WHITE

ORANGE

Measure resistance between Orange terminal and White terminal.

Is there 650—850 Ω? → NO → Replace crank angle sensor

↓ YES

Check for continuity to body ground on Orange terminal and White terminal individually.

Does continuity exist? → YES → Replace crank angle sensor

↓ NO

Reconnect the connector.

Connect the system checker harness only to the main wire harness, but not to the ECU.

ECU DIAGNOSTIC CHART—1987–88 ACCORD

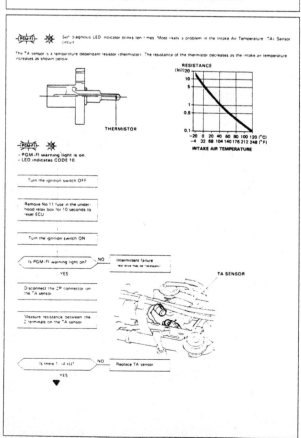

PGM-FI 10 Self-diagnosis LED indicator blinks ten times. Most likely a problem in the Intake Air Temperature (TA) Sensor circuit.

The TA sensor is a temperature dependant resistor (thermistor). The resistance of the thermistor decreases as the intake air temperature increases as shown below.

THERMISTOR

RESISTANCE (kΩ) 20

INTAKE AIR TEMPERATURE

PGM-FI 10

- PGM-FI warning light is on.
- LED indicates CODE 10.

Turn the ignition switch OFF

Remove No. 11 fuse in the underhood relay box for 10 seconds to reset ECU

Turn the ignition switch ON

Is PGM-FI warning light on? → NO → Intermittent failure
Test drive may be necessary.

↓ YES

Disconnect the 2P connector on the TA sensor.

TA SENSOR

Measure resistance between the 2 terminals on the TA sensor.

Is there 1—4 kΩ? → NO → Replace TA sensor

↓ YES

ECU DIAGNOSTIC CHART — 1987-88 ACCORD

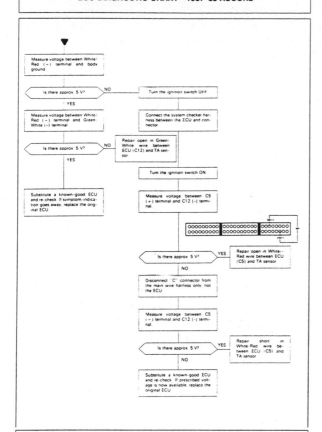

ECU DIAGNOSTIC CHART — 1987-88 ACCORD

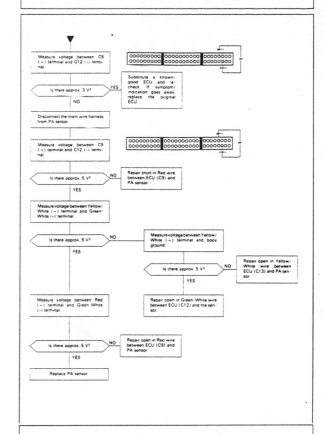

ECU DIAGNOSTIC CHART — 1987-88 ACCORD

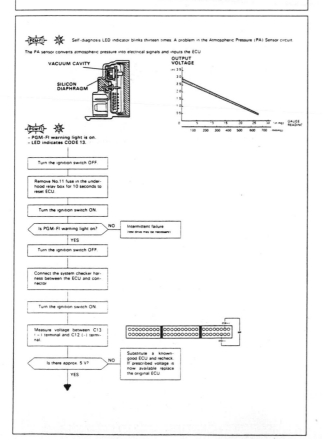

ECU DIAGNOSTIC CHART — 1987-88 ACCORD

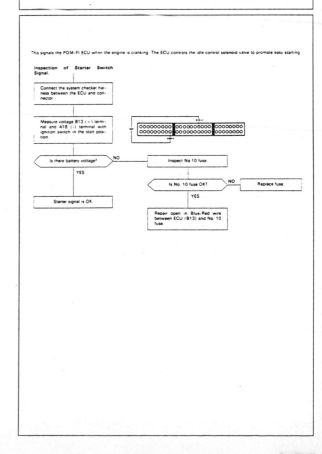

ECU DIAGNOSTIC CHART—1987–88 ACCORD

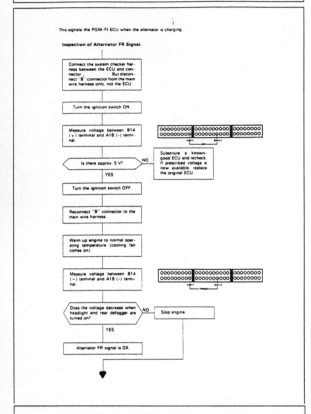

This signals the PGM-FI ECU when the alternator is charging.

Inspection of Alternator FR Signal.

Connect the system checker harness between the ECU and connector. But disconnect "B" connector from the main wire harness only, not the ECU.

Turn the ignition switch ON.

Measure voltage between B14 (+) terminal and A18 (−) terminal.

Is there approx. 5 V? — NO → Substitute a known-good ECU and recheck. If prescribed voltage is now available, replace the original ECU.

YES

Turn the ignition switch OFF.

Reconnect "B" connector to the main wire harness.

Warm up engine to normal operating temperature (cooling fan comes on).

Measure voltage between B14 (−) terminal and A18 (−) terminal.

Does the voltage decrease when headlight and rear defogger are turned on? — NO → Stop engine.

YES

Alternator FR signal is OK.

ECU DIAGNOSTIC CHART—1987–88 ACCORD

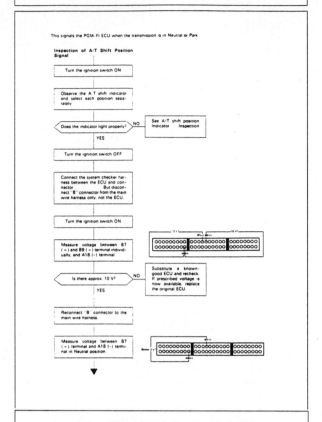

This signals the PGM-FI ECU when the transmission is in Neutral or Park.

Inspection of A/T Shift Position Signal

Turn the ignition switch ON.

Observe the A/T shift indicator and select each position separately.

Does the indicator light properly? — NO → See A/T shift position Indicator Inspection

YES

Turn the ignition switch OFF.

Connect the system checker harness between the ECU and connector. But disconnect "B" connector from the main wire harness only, not the ECU.

Turn the ignition switch ON.

Measure voltage between B7 (−) and B9 (−) terminal individually, and A18 (−) terminal.

Is there approx. 10 V? — NO → Substitute a known-good ECU and recheck. If prescribed voltage is now available, replace the original ECU.

YES

Reconnect "B" connector to the main wire harness.

Measure voltage between B7 (−) terminal and A18 (−) terminal in Neutral position.

ECU DIAGNOSTIC CHART—1987–88 ACCORD

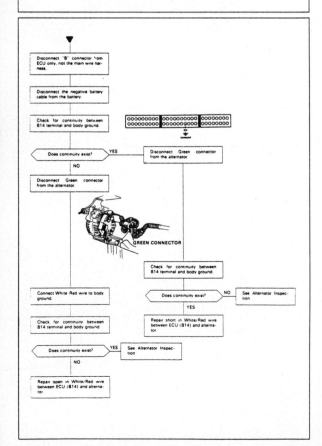

Disconnect "B" connector from ECU only, not the main wire harness.

Disconnect the negative battery cable from the battery.

Check for continuity between B14 terminal and body ground.

Does continuity exist? — YES → Disconnect Green connector from the alternator.

NO

Disconnect Green connector from the alternator.

GREEN CONNECTOR

Check for continuity between B14 terminal and body ground.

Does continuity exist? — NO → See Alternator Inspection

YES

Connect White/Red wire to body ground.

Repair short in White/Red wire between ECU (B14) and alternator.

Check for continuity between B14 terminal and body ground.

Does continuity exist? — YES → See Alternator Inspection

NO

Repair open in White/Red wire between ECU (B14) and alternator.

ECU DIAGNOSTIC CHART—1987–88 ACCORD

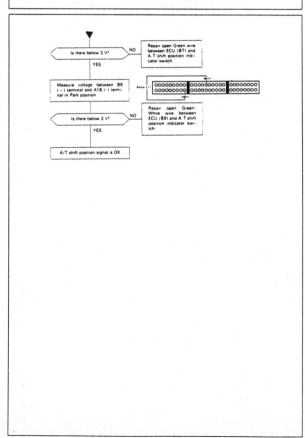

Is there below 3 V? — NO → Repair open Green wire between ECU (B7) and A.T. shift position indicator switch

YES

Measure voltage between B9 (−) terminal and A18 (−) terminal in Park position.

Is there below 3 V? — NO → Repair open Green-White wire between ECU (B9) and A.T. shift position indicator switch

YES

A/T shift position signal is OK.

ECU DIAGNOSTIC CHART—1987–88 ACCORD

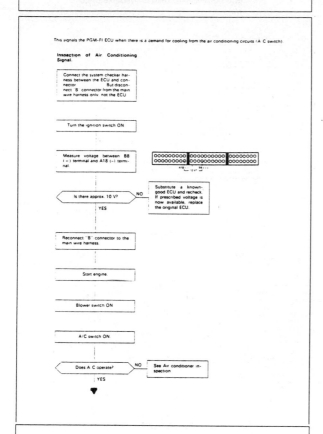

ECU DIAGNOSTIC CHART—1987–88 ACCORD

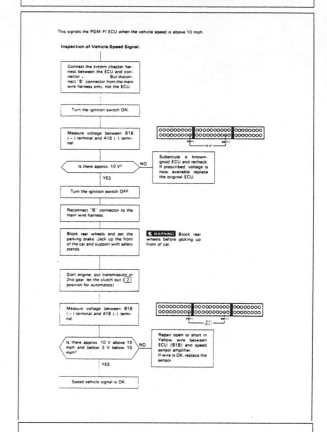

ECU DIAGNOSTIC CHART—1987–88 ACCORD

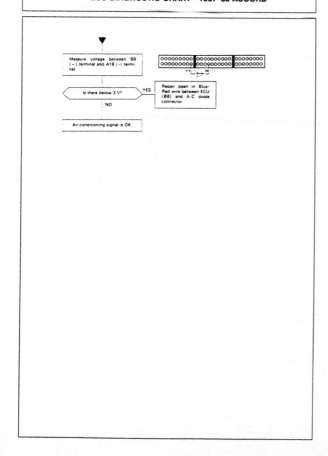

ECU DIAGNOSTIC CHART—1987–88 CIVIC

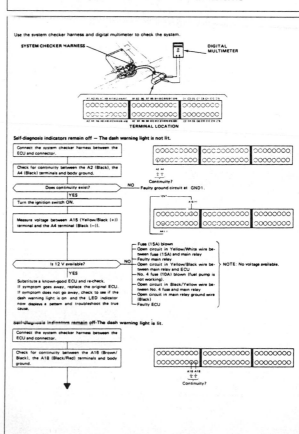

ECU DIAGNOSTIC CHART—1987–88 CIVIC

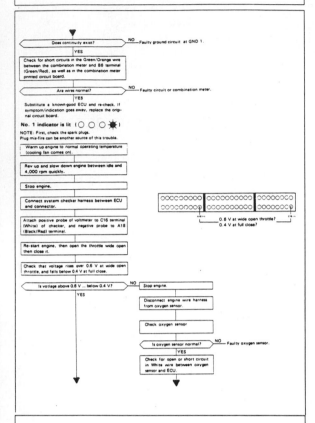

ECU DIAGNOSTIC CHART—1987–88 CIVIC

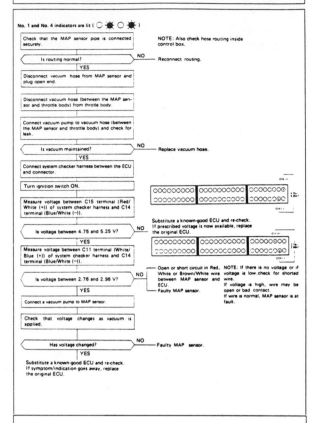

ECU DIAGNOSTIC CHART—1987–88 CIVIC

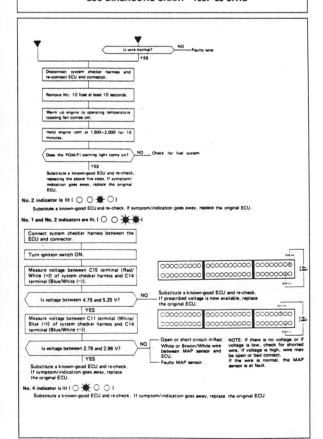

ECU DIAGNOSTIC CHART—1987–88 CIVIC

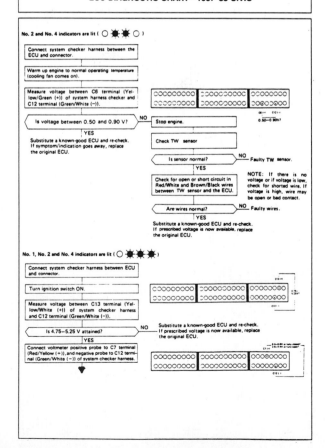

ECU DIAGNOSTIC CHART – 1987–88 CIVIC

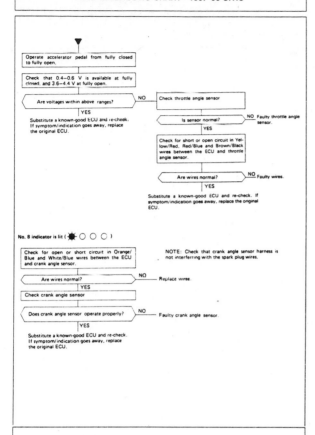

Operate accelerator pedal from fully closed to fully open.

Check that 0.4–0.6 V is available at fully closed, and 3.6–4.4 V at fully open.

Are voltages within above ranges? — NO → Check throttle angle sensor

Is sensor normal? — NO → Faulty throttle angle sensor.

YES → Substitute a known-good ECU and re-check. If symptom/indication goes away, replace the original ECU.

Check for short or open circuit in Yellow/Red, Red/Blue and Brown/Black wires between the ECU and throttle angle sensor.

Are wires normal? — NO → Faulty wires.

YES → Substitute a known-good ECU and re-check. If symptom/indication goes away, replace the original ECU.

No. 8 indicator is lit ( )

Check for open or short circuit in Orange/Blue and White/Blue wires between the ECU and crank angle sensor.

NOTE: Check that crank angle sensor harness is not interfering with the spark plug wires.

Are wires normal? — NO → Replace wires.

YES → Check crank angle sensor

Does crank angle sensor operate properly? — NO → Faulty crank angle sensor.

YES → Substitute a known-good ECU and re-check. If symptom/indication goes away, replace the original ECU.

ECU DIAGNOSTIC CHART – 1987–88 CIVIC

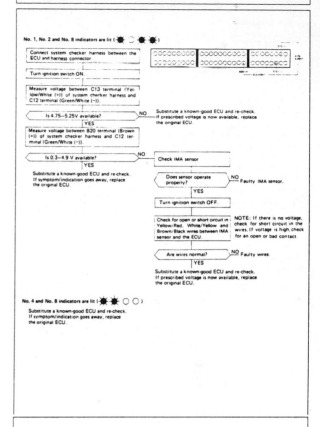

No. 1, No. 2 and No. 8 indicators are lit ( )

Connect system checker harness between the ECU and harness connector.

Turn ignition switch ON.

Measure voltage between C13 terminal (Yellow/White (+)) of system checker harness and C12 terminal (Green/White (–)).

Is 4.75–5.25V available? — NO → Substitute a known-good ECU and re-check. If prescribed voltage is now available, replace the original ECU.

YES → Measure voltage between B20 terminal (Brown (+)) of system checker harness and C12 terminal (Green/White (–)).

Is 0.3–4.9 V available? — NO → Check IMA sensor

YES → Does sensor operate properly? — NO → Faulty IMA sensor.

YES → Turn ignition switch OFF.

Check for open or short circuit in Yellow/Red, White/Yellow and Brown/Black wires between IMA sensor and the ECU.

NOTE: If there is no voltage, check for short circuit in the wires. If voltage is high, check for an open or bad contact.

Are wires normal? — NO → Faulty wires.

YES → Substitute a known-good ECU and re-check. If prescribed voltage is now available, replace the original ECU.

No. 4 and No. 8 indicators are lit ( )

Substitute a known-good ECU and re-check. If symptom/indication goes away, replace the original ECU.

ECU DIAGNOSTIC CHART – 1987–88 CIVIC

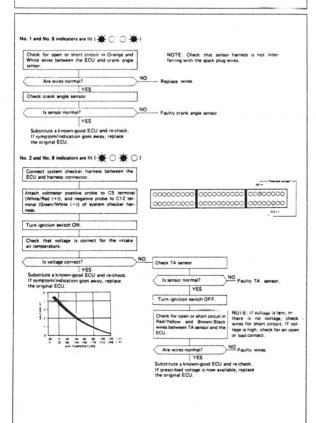

No. 1 and No. 8 indicators are lit ( )

Check for open or short circuit in Orange and White wires between the ECU and crank angle sensor.

NOTE: Check that sensor harness is not interfering with the spark plug wires.

Are wires normal? — NO → Replace wires.

YES → Check crank angle sensor

Is sensor normal? — NO → Faulty crank angle sensor.

YES → Substitute a known-good ECU and re-check. If symptom/indication goes away, replace the original ECU.

No. 2 and No. 8 indicators are lit ( )

Connect system checker harness between the ECU and harness connector.

Attach voltmeter positive probe to C5 terminal (White/Red (+)), and negative probe to C12 terminal (Green/White (–)) of system checker harness.

Turn ignition switch ON.

Check that voltage is correct for the intake air temperature.

Is voltage correct? — NO → Check TA sensor

YES → Substitute a known-good ECU and re-check. If symptom/indication goes away, replace the original ECU.

Is sensor normal? — NO → Faulty TA sensor.

YES → Turn ignition switch OFF.

Check for open or short circuit in Red/Yellow and Brown/Black wires between TA sensor and the ECU.

NOTE: If voltage is low, or there is no voltage, check wires for short circuit. If voltage is high, check for an open or bad contact.

Are wires normal? — NO → Faulty wires.

YES → Substitute a known-good ECU and re-check. If prescribed voltage is now available, replace the original ECU.

ECU DIAGNOSTIC CHART – 1987–88 CIVIC

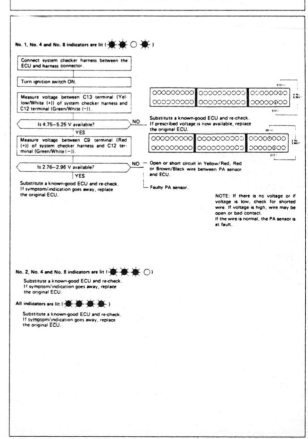

No. 1, No. 4 and No. 8 indicators are lit ( )

Connect system checker harness between the ECU and harness connector.

Turn ignition switch ON.

Measure voltage between C13 terminal (Yellow/White (+)) of system checker harness and C12 terminal (Green/White (–)).

Is 4.75–5.25 V available? — NO → Substitute a known-good ECU and re-check. If prescribed voltage is now available, replace the original ECU.

YES → Measure voltage between C9 terminal (Red (+)) of system checker harness and C12 terminal (Green/White (–)).

Is 2.76–2.96 V available? — NO → Open or short circuit in Yellow/Red, Red or Brown/Black wire between PA sensor and ECU.

— Faulty PA sensor.

YES → Substitute a known-good ECU and re-check. If symptom/indication goes away, replace the original ECU.

NOTE: If there is no voltage or if voltage is low, check for shorted wire. If voltage is high, wire may be open or bad contact. If the wire is normal, the PA sensor is at fault.

No. 2, No. 4 and No. 8 indicators are lit ( )

Substitute a known-good ECU and re-check. If symptom/indication goes away, replace the original ECU.

All indicators are lit ( )

Substitute a known-good ECU and re-check. If symptom/indication goes away, replace the original ECU.

ECU DIAGNOSTIC CHART – 1987–88 CIVIC

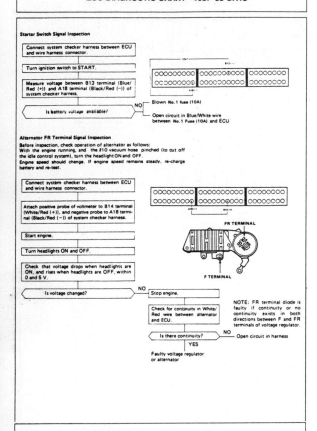

Starter Switch Signal Inspection

Connect system checker harness between ECU and wire harness connector.

Turn ignition switch to START.

Measure voltage between B13 terminal (Blue/ Red (+)) and A18 terminal (Black/Red (−)) of system checker harness.

Is battery voltage available? → NO → Blown No.1 fuse (10A)

Open circuit in Blue/White wire between No.1 Fuse (10A) and ECU

Alternator FR Terminal Signal Inspection

Before inspection, check operation of alternator as follows:
With the engine running, and the #10 vacuum hose pinched (to cut off the idle control system), turn the headlight ON and OFF.
Engine speed should change. If engine speed remains steady, re-charge battery and re-test.

Connect system checker harness between ECU and wire harness connector.

Attach positive probe of voltmeter to B14 terminal (White/Red (+)), and negative probe to A18 terminal (Black/Red (−)) of system checker harness.

Start engine.

Turn headlights ON and OFF.

Check that voltage drops when headlights are ON, and rises when headlights are OFF, within 0 and 5 V.

Is voltage changed? → NO → Stop engine.

Check for continuity in White/ Red wire between alternator and ECU.

NOTE: FR terminal diode is faulty if continuity or no continuity exists in both directions between F and FR terminals of voltage regulator.

Is there continuity? → NO → Open circuit in harness

YES

Faulty voltage regulator or alternator

FR TERMINAL

F TERMINAL

ECU DIAGNOSTIC CHART – 1987–88 CIVIC

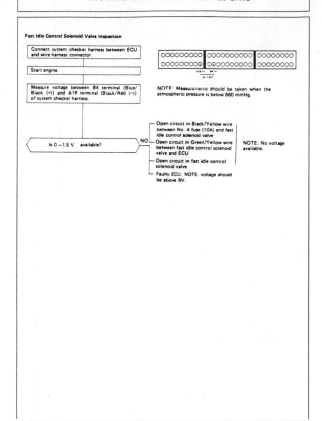

Fast Idle Control Solenoid Valve Inspection

Connect system checker harness between ECU and wire harness connector.

Start engine.

Measure voltage between B4 terminal (Blue/ Black (+)) and A18 terminal (Black/Red (−)) of system checker harness.

NOTE: Measurements should be taken when the atmospheric pressure is below 660 mmHg.

Is 0 – 1.5 V available? → NO →
- Open circuit in Black/Yellow wire between No. 4 fuse (10A) and fast idle control solenoid valve
- Open circuit in Green/Yellow wire between fast idle control solenoid valve and ECU
- Open circuit in fast idle control solenoid valve
- Faulty ECU. NOTE: voltage should be above 9 V.

NOTE: No voltage available.

ECU DIAGNOSTIC CHART – 1987–88 CIVIC

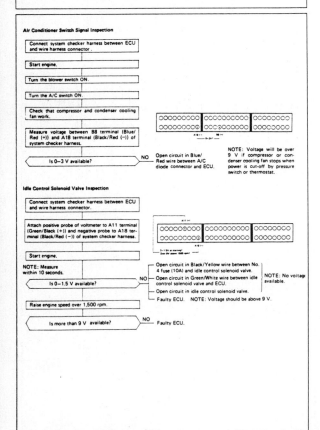

Air Conditioner Switch Signal Inspection

Connect system checker harness between ECU and wire harness connector.

Start engine.

Turn the blower switch ON.

Turn the A/C switch ON.

Check that compressor and condenser cooling fan work.

Measure voltage between B8 terminal (Blue/ Red (+)) and A18 terminal (Black/Red (−)) of system checker harness.

Is 0–3 V available? → NO → Open circuit in Blue/ Red wire between A/C diode connector and ECU.

NOTE: Voltage will be over 9 V if compressor or condenser cooling fan stops when power is cut-off by pressure switch or thermostat.

Idle Control Solenoid Valve Inspection

Connect system checker harness between ECU and wire harness connector.

Attach positive probe of voltmeter to A11 terminal (Green/Black (+)) and negative probe to A18 terminal (Black/Red (−)) of system checker harness.

Start engine.

NOTE: Measure within 10 seconds.

Is 0–1.5 V available? → NO →
- Open circuit in Black/Yellow wire between No. 4 fuse (10A) and idle control solenoid valve.
- Open circuit in Green/White wire between idle control solenoid valve and ECU.
- Open circuit in idle control solenoid valve.
- Faulty ECU. NOTE: Voltage should be above 9 V.

NOTE: No voltage available.

Raise engine speed over 1,500 rpm.

Is more than 9 V available? → NO → Faulty ECU.

ECU DIAGNOSTIC CHART – 1986–88 PRELUDE

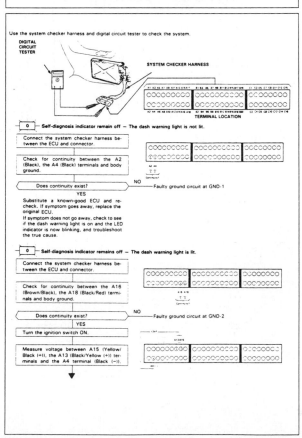

Use the system checker harness and digital circuit tester to check the system.

DIGITAL CIRCUIT TESTER

SYSTEM CHECKER HARNESS

TERMINAL LOCATION

0 — Self-diagnosis indicator remain off — The dash warning light is not lit.

Connect the system checker harness between the ECU and connector.

Check for continuity between the A2 (Black), the A4 (Black) terminals and body ground.

Does continuity exist? → NO → Faulty ground circuit at GND-1

YES

Substitute a known-good ECU and re-check. If symptom goes away, replace the original ECU.
If symptom does not go away, check to see if the dash warning light is on and the LED indicator is now blinking, and troubleshoot the true cause.

0 — Self-diagnosis indicator remains off — The dash warning light is lit.

Connect the system checker harness between the ECU and connector.

Check for continuity between the A16 (Brown/Black), the A18 (Black/Red) terminals and body ground.

Does continuity exist? → NO → Faulty ground circuit at GND-2

YES

Turn the ignition switch ON.

Measure voltage between A15 (Yellow/ Black (+)), the A13 (Black/Yellow (+)) terminals and the A4 terminal (Black (−)).

ECU DIAGNOSTIC CHART—1986–88 PRELUDE

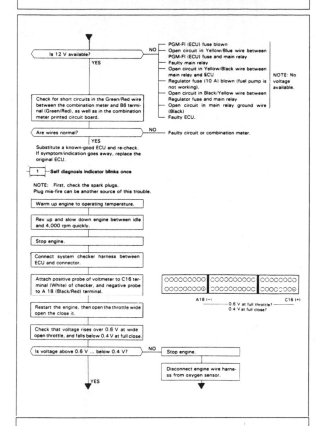

Is 12 V available? — **NO** →
- PGM-FI (ECU) fuse blown
- Open circuit in Yellow/Blue wire between PGM-FI (ECU) fuse and main relay
- Faulty main relay
- Open circuit in Yellow/Black wire between main relay and ECU
- Regulator fuse (10 A) blown (fuel pump is not working).
- Open circuit in Black/Yellow wire between Regulator fuse and main relay
- Open circuit in main relay ground wire (Black)
- Faulty ECU.

NOTE: No voltage available.

YES

Check for short circuits in the Green/Red wire between the combination meter and B6 terminal (Green/Red), as well as in the combination meter printed circuit board.

Are wires normal? — **NO** → Faulty circuit or combination meter.

YES

Substitute a known-good ECU and re-check. If symptom/indication goes away, replace the original ECU.

1 — Self diagnosis indicator blinks once

NOTE: First, check the spark plugs.
Plug mis-fire can be another source of this trouble.

Warm up engine to operating temperature.

Rev up and slow down engine between idle and 4,000 rpm quickly.

Stop engine.

Connect system checker harness between ECU and connector.

Attach positive probe of voltmeter to C16 terminal (White) of checker, and negative probe to A 18 (Black/Red) terminal.

A18 (−)   C16 (+)
0.6 V at full throttle?
0.4 V at full close?

Restart the engine, then open the throttle wide open the close it.

Check that voltage rises over 0.6 V at wide open throttle, and falls below 0.4 V at full close.

Is voltage above 0.6 V ... below 0.4 V? — **NO** →
Stop engine.
Disconnect engine wire harness from oxygen sensor.

YES

ECU DIAGNOSTIC CHART—1986–88 PRELUDE

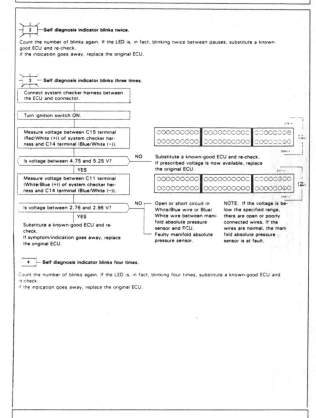

2 — Self diagnosis indicator blinks twice.

Count the number of blinks again. If the LED is, in fact, blinking twice between pauses, substitute a known-good ECU and re-check.
If the indication goes away, replace the original ECU.

3 — Self diagnosis indicator blinks three times.

Connect system checker harness between the ECU and connector.

Turn ignition switch ON.

Measure voltage between C15 terminal (Red/White (+)) of system checker harness and C14 terminal (Blue/White (−)).

Is voltage between 4.75 and 5.25 V? — **NO** → Substitute a known-good ECU and re-check. If prescribed voltage is now available, replace the original ECU.

YES

Measure voltage between C11 terminal (White/Blue (+)) of system checker harness and C14 terminal (Blue/White (−)).

Is voltage between 2.76 and 2.96 V? — **NO** →
- Open or short circuit in White/Blue wire or Blue/White wire between manifold absolute pressure sensor and ECU.
- Faulty manifold absolute pressure sensor.

NOTE: If the voltage is below the specified range, there are open or poorly connected wires. If the wires are normal, the manifold absolute pressure sensor is at fault.

YES

Substitute a known-good ECU and re-check.
If symptom/indication goes away, replace the original ECU.

4 — Self diagnosis indicator blinks four times.

Count the number of blinks again. If the LED is, in fact, blinking four times, substitute a known-good ECU and re-check.
If the indication goes away, replace the original ECU.

ECU DIAGNOSTIC CHART—1986–88 PRELUDE

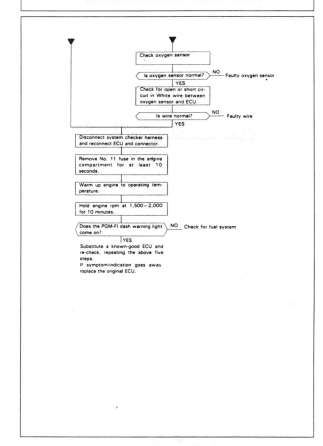

Check oxygen sensor

Is oxygen sensor normal? — **NO** → Faulty oxygen sensor

YES

Check for open or short circuit in White wire between oxygen sensor and ECU.

Is wire normal? — **NO** → Faulty wire

YES

Disconnect system checker harness and reconnect ECU and connector.

Remove No. 11 fuse in the engine compartment for at least 10 seconds.

Warm up engine to operating temperature.

Hold engine rpm at 1,500–2,000 for 10 minutes.

Does the PGM-FI dash warning light come on? — **NO** → Check for fuel system

YES

Substitute a known-good ECU and re-check, repeating the above five steps.
If symptom/indication goes away replace the original ECU.

ECU DIAGNOSTIC CHART—1986–88 PRELUDE

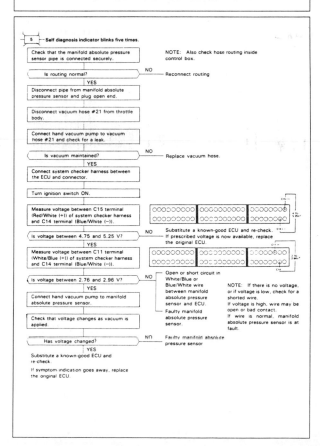

5 — Self diagnosis indicator blinks five times.

Check that the manifold absolute pressure sensor pipe is connected securely.

NOTE: Also check hose routing inside control box.

Is routing normal? — **NO** → Reconnect routing

YES

Disconnect pipe from manifold absolute pressure sensor and plug open end.

Disconnect vacuum hose #21 from throttle body.

Connect hand vacuum pump to vacuum hose #21 and check for a leak.

Is vacuum maintained? — **NO** → Replace vacuum hose.

YES

Connect system checker harness between the ECU and connector.

Turn ignition switch ON.

Measure voltage between C15 terminal (Red/White (+)) of system checker harness and C14 terminal (Blue/White (−)).

Is voltage between 4.75 and 5.25 V? — **NO** → Substitute a known-good ECU and re-check. If prescribed voltage is now available, replace the original ECU.

YES

Measure voltage between C11 terminal (White/Blue (+)) of system checker harness and C14 terminal (Blue/White (−)).

Is voltage between 2.76 and 2.96 V? — **NO** →
- Open or short circuit in White/Blue or Blue/White wire between manifold absolute pressure sensor and ECU.
- Faulty manifold absolute pressure sensor.

NOTE: If there is no voltage, or if voltage is low, check for a shorted wire.
If voltage is high, wire may be open or bad contact.
If wire is normal, manifold absolute pressure sensor is at fault.

YES

Connect hand vacuum pump to manifold absolute pressure sensor.

Check that voltage changes as vacuum is applied.

Has voltage changed? — **NO** → Faulty manifold absolute pressure sensor

YES

Substitute a known-good ECU and re-check.
If symptom indication goes away, replace the original ECU.

ECU DIAGNOSTIC CHART—1986–88 PRELUDE

6 — Self diagnosis indicator blinks six times.

Connect system checker harness between the ECU and connector.

Warm up engine until radiator fan comes on twice.

Measure voltage between C6 terminal (Yellow/Green (+)) of system harness checker and C12 terminal (Green/White (−)).

Is voltage between 0.50 and 0.90 V? — NO → Stop engine.

YES

Substitute a known-good ECU and re-check. If symptom/indication goes away, replace the original ECU.

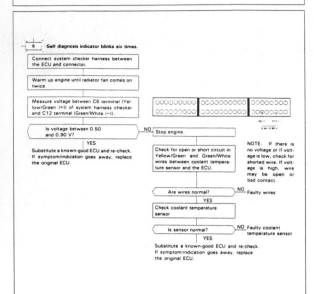

Check for open or short circuit in Yellow/Green and Green/White wires between coolant temperature sensor and the ECU.

NOTE: If there is no voltage or if voltage is low, check for shorted wire. If voltage is high, wire may be open or bad contact.

Are wires normal? — NO → Faulty wires

YES

Check coolant temperature sensor

Is sensor normal? — NO → Faulty coolant temperature sensor

YES

Substitute a known-good ECU and re-check. If symptom/indication goes away, replace the original ECU.

ECU DIAGNOSTIC CHART—1986–88 PRELUDE

8 — Self diagnosis indicator blinks eight times.

Check for open or short circuit in Orange/Blue and White/Blue wires between the ECU and crank angle sensor.

NOTE: Check that crank angle sensor harness is not interfering with the spark plug wires.

Are wires normal? — NO → Replace wires

YES

Check crank angle sensor

Does crank angle sensor operate properly? — NO → Faulty crank angle sensor

YES

Substitute a known-good ECU and re-check. If symptom/indication goes away, replace the original ECU.

9 — Self diagnosis indicator blinks nine times.

Check for open or short circuit in Orange and White wires between the ECU and crank angle sensor.

NOTE: Check that sensor harness is not interfering with the spark plug wires.

Are wires normal? — NO → Replace wires

YES

Check crank angle sensor

Is sensor normal? — NO → Faulty crank angle sensor

YES

Substitute a known-good ECU and re-check. If symptom/indication goes away, replace the original ECU.

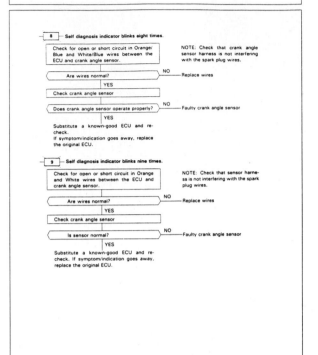

ECU DIAGNOSTIC CHART—1986–88 PRELUDE

7 — Self diagnosis indicator blinks seven times.

Connect system checker harness harness between ECU and connector.

Turn ignition switch ON.

Measure voltage between C13 terminal (Yellow/White (+)) of system checker harness and C12 terminal (Green/White (−)).

Is 4.75–5.25 V attained? — NO → Substitute a known-good ECU and re-check. If prescribed voltage is now available, replace the original ECU.

YES

Connect voltmeter positive probe to C7 terminal (Red/Yellow), and negative probe to C12 terminal (Green/White (−)) of system checker harness.

Operate accelerator pedal from fully closed to fully open.

Check that 0.4–0.6 V is available at fully closed, and 4.3–4.8 V at fully open.

Are voltages within above ranges? — NO → Check for short or open circuit in Red/Yellow and Green/White wires between the ECU and throttle angle sensor.

YES

Substitute a known-good ECU and re-check. If symptom/indication goes away, replace the original ECU.

Are wires normal? — NO → Replace wires

YES

Adjust or replace throttle angle sensor

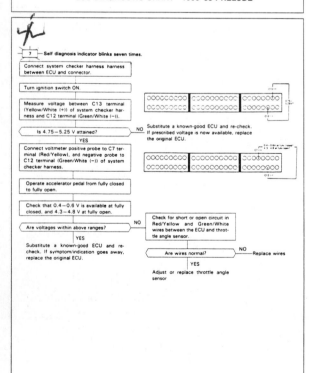

ECU DIAGNOSTIC CHART—1986–88 PRELUDE

10 — Self diagnosis indicator blinks ten times.

Connect system checker harness between the ECU and harness connector.

Attach voltmeter positive probe to C5 terminal (White/Red), and negative probe to C12 terminal (Green/White) of system checker harness.

Turn ignition switch ON.

Check that voltage is correct for the intake air temperature.

Is voltage correct? — NO → Substitute a known-good ECU and re-check. If symptom/indication goes away, replace the original ECU.

YES

Turn ignition switch OFF.

Check for open or short circuit in White/Red and Green/White wires between intake air temperature sensor and the ECU.

NOTE: If voltage is low, or there is no voltage, check wires for short circuit. If voltage is high, probability is open or bad contact.

Are wires normal? — NO → Faulty wires

YES

Check intake air temperature sensor

Is sensor normal? — NO → Faulty intake air temperature sensor

YES

Substitute a known-good ECU and re-check. If prescribed voltage is now available, replace the original ECU.

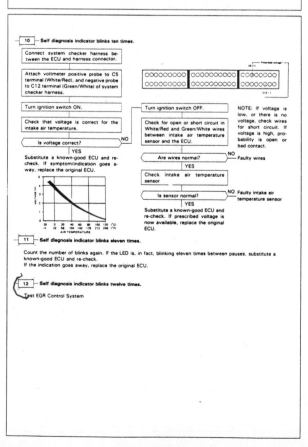

11 — Self diagnosis indicator blinks eleven times.

Count the number of blinks again. If the LED is, in fact, blinking eleven times between pauses, substitute a known-good ECU and re-check. If the indication goes away, replace the original ECU.

12 — Self diagnosis indicator blinks twelve times.

Test EGR Control System

ECU DIAGNOSTIC CHART—1986-88 PRELUDE

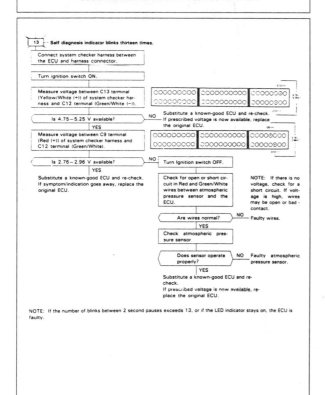

13 — Self diagnosis indicator blinks thirteen times.

Connect system checker harness between the ECU and harness connector.

Turn ignition switch ON.

Measure voltage between C13 terminal (Yellow/White (+)) of system checker harness and C12 terminal (Green/White (−)).

Is 4.75—5.25 V available? — NO → Substitute a known-good ECU and re-check. If prescribed voltage is now available, replace the original ECU.

YES

Measure voltage between C9 terminal (Red (+)) of system checker harness and C12 terminal (Green/White).

Is 2.76—2.96 V available? — NO → Turn ignition switch OFF.

YES

Substitute a known-good ECU and re-check. If symptom/indication goes away, replace the original ECU.

Check for open or short circuit in Red and Green/White wires between atmospheric pressure sensor and the ECU.

NOTE: If there is no voltage, check for a short circuit. If voltage is high, wires may be open or bad - contact.

Are wires normal? — NO → Faulty wires.

YES

Check atmospheric pressure sensor

Does sensor operate properly? — NO → Faulty atmospheric pressure sensor.

YES

Substitute a known-good ECU and re-check.
If prescribed voltage is now available, replace the original ECU.

NOTE: If the number of blinks between 2 second pauses exceeds 13, or if the LED indicator stays on, the ECU is faulty.

ECU DIAGNOSTIC CHART—1986-88 PRELUDE

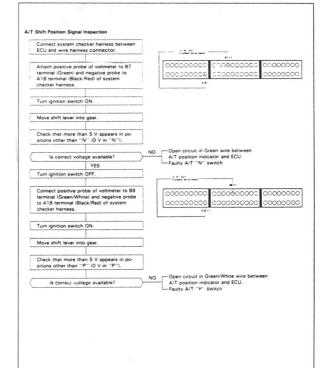

A/T Shift Position Signal Inspection

Connect system checker harness between ECU and wire harness connector.

Attach positive probe of voltmeter to B7 terminal (Green) and negative probe to A18 terminal (Black/Red) of system checker harness.

Turn ignition switch ON.

Move shift lever into gear.

Check that more than 5 V appears in positions other than "N" (0 V in "N").

Is correct voltage available? — NO → Open circuit in Green wire between A/T position indicator and ECU. Faulty A/T "N" switch

YES

Turn ignition switch OFF.

Connect positive probe of voltmeter to B9 terminal (Green/White) and negative probe to A18 terminal (Black/Red) of system checker harness.

Turn ignition switch ON.

Move shift lever into gear.

Check that more than 5 V appears in positions other than "P" (0 V in "P").

Is correct voltage available? — NO → Open circuit in Green/White wire between A/T position indicator and ECU. Faulty A/T "P" switch

ECU DIAGNOSTIC CHART—1986-88 PRELUDE

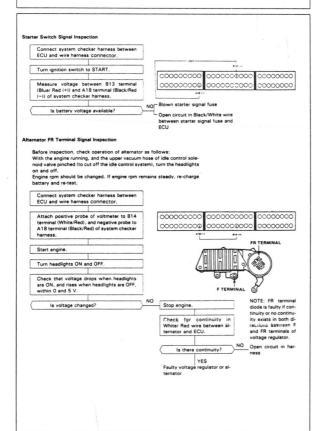

Starter Switch Signal Inspection

Connect system checker harness between ECU and wire harness connector.

Turn ignition switch to START.

Measure voltage between B13 terminal (Blue/Red (+)) and A18 terminal (Black/Red (−)) of system checker harness.

Is battery voltage available? — NO → Blown starter signal fuse
— Open circuit in Black/White wire between starter signal fuse and ECU

Alternator FR Terminal Signal Inspection

Before inspection, check operation of alternator as follows:
With the engine running, and the upper vacuum hose of idle control solenoid valve pinched (to cut off the idle control system), turn the headlights on and off.
Engine rpm should be changed. If engine rpm remains steady, re-charge battery and re-test.

Connect system checker harness between ECU and wire harness connector.

Attach positive probe of voltmeter to B14 terminal (White/Red), and negative probe to A18 terminal (Black/Red) of system checker harness.

Start engine.

Turn headlights ON and OFF.

Check that voltage drops when headlights are ON, and rises when headlights are OFF, within 0 and 5 V.

Is voltage changed? — NO → Stop engine.

Check for continuity in White/Red wire between alternator and ECU.

NOTE: FR terminal diode is faulty if continuity or no continuity exists in both directions between F and FR terminals of voltage regulator.

Is there continuity? — NO → Open circuit in harness

YES

Faulty voltage regulator or alternator

FR TERMINAL

F TERMINAL

ECU DIAGNOSTIC CHART—1986-88 PRELUDE

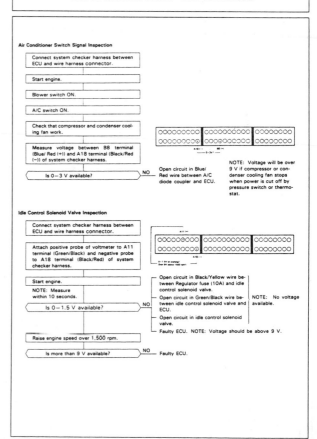

Air Conditioner Switch Signal Inspection

Connect system checker harness between ECU and wire harness connector.

Start engine.

Blower switch ON.

A/C switch ON.

Check that compressor and condenser cooling fan work.

Measure voltage between B8 terminal (Blue/Red (+)) and A18 terminal (Black/Red (−)) of system checker harness.

Is 0—3 V available? — NO → Open circuit in Blue/Red wire between A/C diode coupler and ECU.

NOTE: Voltage will be over 9 V if compressor or condenser cooling fan stops when power is cut off by pressure switch or thermostat.

Idle Control Solenoid Valve Inspection

Connect system checker harness between ECU and wire harness connector.

Attach positive probe of voltmeter to A11 terminal (Green/Black) and negative probe to A18 terminal (Black/Red) of system checker harness.

Start engine.

NOTE: Measure within 10 seconds.

Is 0—1.5 V available? — NO → - Open circuit in Black/Yellow wire between Regulator fuse (10A) and idle control solenoid valve.
- Open circuit in Green/Black wire between idle control solenoid valve and ECU.
- Open circuit in idle control solenoid valve.
- Faulty ECU. NOTE: Voltage should be above 9 V.

NOTE: No voltage available.

Raise engine speed over 1,500 rpm.

Is more than 9 V available? — NO → Faulty ECU.

ECU DIAGNOSTIC CHART—1986–88 PRELUDE

ECU DIAGNOSTIC CHART—1986–88 PRELUDE

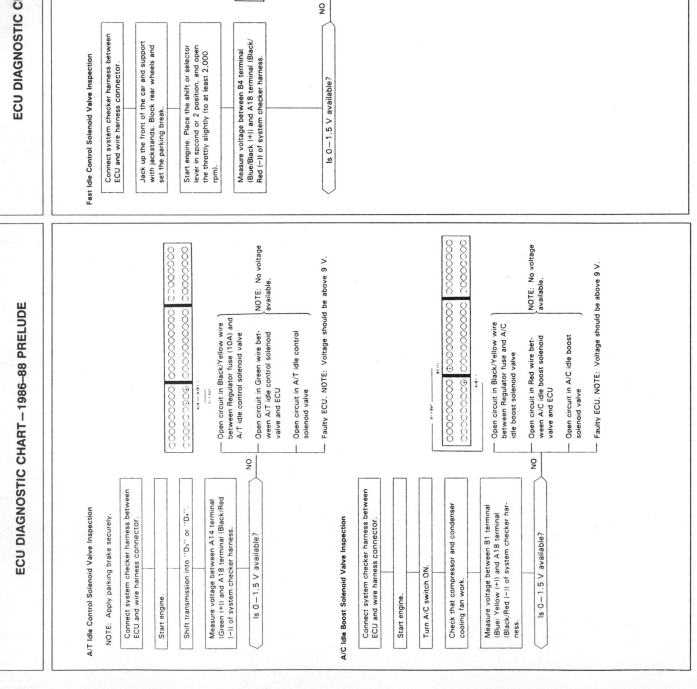

Fast Idle Control Solenoid Valve Inspection

Connect system checker harness between ECU and wire harness connector.

Jack up the front of the car and support with jackstands. Block rear wheels and set the parking brake.

Start engine. Place the shift or selector lever in second or 2 position, and open the throttle slightly (to at least 2,000 rpm).

Measure voltage between B4 terminal (Blue/Black (+)) and A18 terminal (Black/Red (−)) of system checker harness.

Is 0 − 1.5 V available?

NO

Open circuit in Black/Yellow wire between Regulator fuse and fast idle control solenoid valve

Open circuit in Red/Green wire between fast idle control solenoid valve and ECU — NOTE: No voltage available.

Open circuit in fast idle control solenoid valve

Faulty ECU. NOTE: Voltage should be above 9 V.

NOTE: This inspection can also be taken at idle when engine is cold and atmospheric pressure is below 660 mm Hg.

A/T Idle Control Solenoid Valve Inspection

NOTE: Apply parking brake securely.

Connect system checker harness between ECU and wire harness connector.

Start engine.

Shift transmission into "D₃" or "D₄".

Measure voltage between A14 terminal (Green (+)) and A18 terminal (Black/Red (−)) of system checker harness.

Is 0 − 1.5 V available?

NO

Open circuit in Black/Yellow wire between Regulator fuse (10A) and A/T idle control solenoid valve

Open circuit in Green wire between A/T idle control solenoid valve and ECU — NOTE: No voltage available.

Open circuit in A/T idle control solenoid valve

Faulty ECU. NOTE: Voltage should be above 9 V.

A/C Idle Boost Solenoid Valve Inspection

Connect system checker harness between ECU and wire harness connector.

Start engine.

Turn A/C switch ON.

Check that compressor and condenser cooling fan work.

Measure voltage between B1 terminal (Blue/Yellow (+)) and A18 terminal (Black/Red (−)) of system checker harness.

Is 0 − 1.5 V available?

NO

Open circuit in Black/Yellow wire between Regulator fuse and A/C idle boost solenoid valve

Open circuit in Red wire between A/C idle boost solenoid valve and ECU — NOTE: No voltage available.

Open circuit in A/C idle boost solenoid valve

Faulty ECU. NOTE: Voltage should be above 9 V.

COMPONENT TEST PROCEDURES

Oxygen Sensor

1985–86 ACCORD, 1985–88 CIVIC AND 1986–88 PRELUDE

1. Disconnect connector of oxygen sensor.
2. Start engine and warm up for two minutes at 3000 rpm under no load. Raise engine speed to 4000 rpm and release throttle suddenly at least 5 times.
3. Within on minute after engine has been warmed up, measure voltage between connector terminal and body ground as described in in Steps 4 and 5.

4. Raise engine speed to 5000 rpm, then lower to 2000 rpm by operating accelerator pedal, immediately turn ignition switch off. Voltage should be below 0.4 volts.
5. Disconnect vacuum tube (between MAP sensor and throttle body on Civic models and hose #21 on Accord models) from throttle body; plug opening in throttle body. Connect a hand vacuum pump to open end of vacuum tube and apply 12 in. Hg (300mm Hg), and raise engine speed to 4000 rpm. Voltage should be above 0.6 volts.
6. Replace oxygen sensor if voltages are out of ranges.

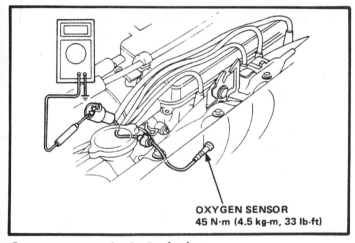

OXYGEN SENSOR
45 N·m (4.5 kg-m, 33 lb-ft)

Oxygen sensor test – typical

Manifold Air Pressure (MAP) Sensor

1985–86 ACCORD AND CIVIC, AND 1986 PRELUDE

1. Disconnect vacuum hose (between MAP sensor and throttle body on Civic models and hose #21 on Accord models) from throttle body; plug opening in throttle body. Connect a vacuum hand pump to open end of vacuum tube.
2. Disconnect connector from control unit. Connect system checker harness (07999–PD6000A or equivalent) between control unit and wire harness connector.
3. Turn ignition switch on. Connect a digital voltmeter positive probe to C11 terminal of system checker harness and negative probe to C14 terminal. Measure voltage between two terminals. Voltmeter should indicate between 0.5 volts at 4 in. Hg (100mm Hg) of vacuum and 4.5 volts at 45 in. Hg (1200mm Hg).
4. If voltage is incorrect, check vacuum tube for leakage, and wires between control unit and sensor for open or short circuit. Replace sensor if wires are normal.

Atmospheric Pressure (PA) Sensor

1985–86 ACCORD AND CIVIC

1. Disconnect connector from control unit. Connect system

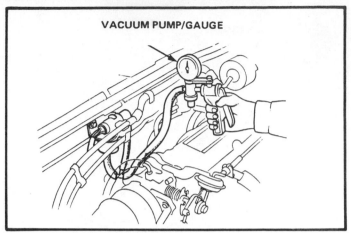

VACUUM PUMP/GAUGE

Manifold air pressure (MAP) sensor check – 1985–86 Civic shown, 1985 Accord similar

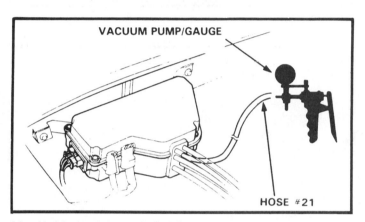

VACUUM PUMP/GAUGE

HOSE #21

Manifold air pressure (MAP) sensor check – 1986 Accord and Prelude

checker harness (07999–PD6000A or equivalent) between control unit and wire harness connector.
2. Turn ignition switch on. Connect a digital voltmeter positive probe to C9 terminal of system checker harness and negative probe to C12 terminal. Measure voltage between two terminals. Voltmeter should indicate 2.76–2.96 volts.
3. If voltage is outside ranges, check for open or short circuit between ECU and PA sensor. Replace PA sensor with a new one if wires are in good condition.

Idle Mixture Adjuster (IMA) Sensor

1985–88 CIVIC

1. Measure resistance between Green terminal and Yellow terminal (Yellow/White and Black terminal on 1987–88 models) of control box coupler. Resistance should be 0.25–6.2 kilo ohm (kΩ).
2. Replace IMA sensor if resistance are out of range.

1985 ACCORD

1. Open No. 1 control box lid and remove rivets attaching IMA sensor.
2. Disconnect IMA sensor 3P coupler.
3. Measure resistance between Brown terminal and Green terminal of IMA sensor while turning adjuster. Resistance should be 0.25–6.2 kilo ohm (kΩ).
4. Replace IMA sensor if resistance are out of range.

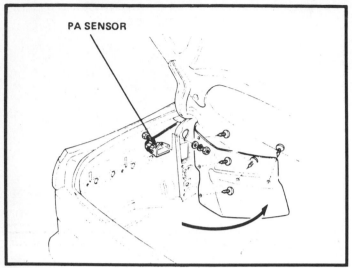

Atmospheric pressure sensor location — 1985 Accord

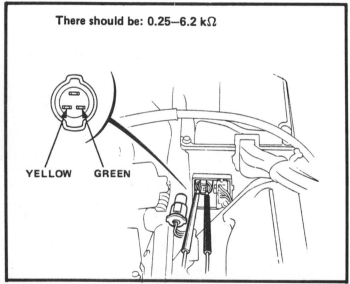

Idle mixture adjuster (IMA) sensor resistance check — 1985 Civic

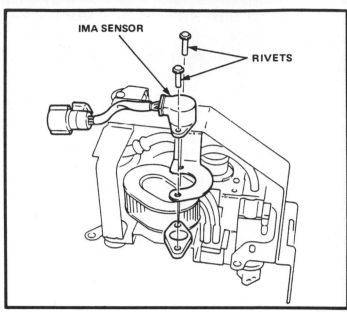

Idle mixture adjuster (IMA) sensor servicing — 1985–88 Civic

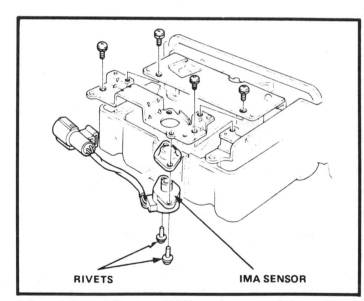

Idle mixture adjuster (IMA) sensor servicing — 1985 Accord

Intake Air Temperature (TA)/Coolant Temperature (TW) Sensor

1985 ACCORD AND 1985–88 CIVIC

1. Disconnect connector and remove TA/TW sensor from inlet manifold/cylinder head.

2. To test a sensor, suspend it in cold water and heat water slowly. Measure resistance between terminals. Measurements should be 0.98–1.34 kilo ohm (kΩ) at 95°F (40°C) and 0.22–0.35 kilo ohm (kΩ) at 176°F (80°C).

3. Replace sensor if resistance is outside of range.

Intake Air Temperature (TA) Sensor

1986 ACCORD AND 1986–88 PRELUDE

1. Disconnect connector and remove TA sensor from intake manifold.

2. To test a sensor, suspend it in cold water and heat water slowly. Measure resistance between terminals. Measurements should be 0.98–1.34 kilo ohm (kΩ) at 104°F (40°C) and 0.22–

0.35 kilo ohm (kΩ) at 176°F (80°C).

3. Replace sensor if resistance is outside of range.

Coolant Temperature (TW) Sensor

1986 ACCORD AND 1986–88 PRELUDE

1. Disconnect connector and remove TW sensor from thermostat housing.

2. To test a sensor, suspend it in cold water and heat water slowly. Measure resistance between terminals. Measurements should be 0.98–1.34 kilo ohm (kΩ) at 95°F (40°C) and 0.22–0.35 kilo ohm (kΩ) at 176°F (80°C).

3. Replace sensor if resistance is outside of range. On installing sensor, torque to 20 ft. lbs. (28 Nm).

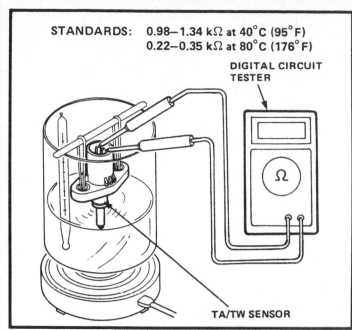

Intake air temperature (TA)/coolant temperature (TW) sensor resistance test—1985–88 Civic and 1985 Accord

Crank Angle Sensor (CYL Sensor)

1985–86 ACCORD, 1985–88 CIVIC AND 1986–88 PRELUDE

NOTE: If either CYL or TDC sensor tests bad, replace as an assembly.

1. Disconnect connector of crank angle sensor.
2. Measure resistance between (White and Red on 1985–88 Civic and 1985 Accord and White and Orange on 1986 Accord and 1986–88 Prelude) terminal at sensor. Resistance should be 0.65–0.85 kilo ohm (kΩ).
3. Measure insulation resistance between (White and Red on 1985–88 Civic and Accord and White and Orange on 1986 Accord and 1986–88 Prelude) terminal of sensor and crank angle sensor housing. Resistance should be 100 kilo ohm (kΩ) or more.

Crank Angle Sensor (TDC Sensor)

1985–86 ACCORD, 1985–88 CIVIC AND 1986–88 PRELUDE

NOTE: If either CYL or TDC sensor tests bad, replace as an assembly.

1. Disconnect connector of crank angle sensor.
2. Measure resistance between (Brown and Blue on 1985–88 Civic and Orange/Blue and White/Blue on 1986 Accord and 1986–88 Prelude) terminal at sensor. Resistance should be 0.65–0.85 kilo ohm (kΩ).
3. Measure insulation resistance between (Brown and Blue on 1985–88 Civic and Orange/Blue and White/Blue on 1986 Accord and 1986–88 Prelude) terminal of sensor and crank angle sensor housing. Resistance should be 100 kilo ohm (kΩ) or more.

Throttle Angle Sensor

1985 ACCORD AND 1985–88 CIVIC

NOTE: Do not adjust throttle valve stop screw since it is preset at factory.

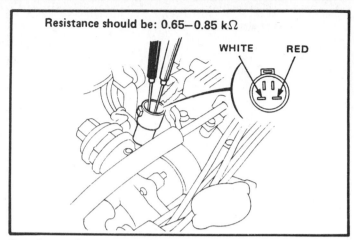

Crank angle sensor-CYL sensor resistance test—1985 Civic shown, others similar

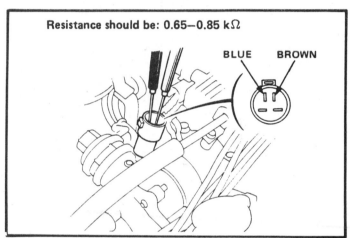

Crank angle sensor-TDC sensor resistance test—1985 Civic shown, others similar

1. Disconnect connector of throttle angle sensor.
2. Measure full resistance between Brown/Black (Yellow on Accord models) terminal and Yellow/Red (Green on Accord models) terminal at sensor. Resistance should be 3.2–7.2 kilo ohm (kΩ).

1986 ACCORD AND 1986–88 PRELUDE

NOTE: Do not adjust throttle valve stop screw since it is preset at factory.

1. Disconnect connector of throttle angle sensor.
2. Measure full resistance between Yellow/White terminal and Green/White terminal at sensor. Resistance should be 4–6 kilo ohm (kΩ).

Idle Control Solenoid Valve

1985–88 CIVIC

The idle control solenoid valve is activated by commands from the ECU. When the solenoid valve opens, this causes vacuum in the vacuum hose (between the air filter and the solenoid valve) and increases idle speed under the following conditions:

● For a short period after starting the engine.
● Whenever electrical loads are turned on (vacuum will disappear when engine rpm is raised over 1700 rpm by operating the throttle).

While the solenoid valve is being activated, 9 volts or higher

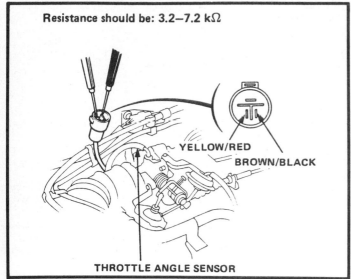

Resistance should be: 3.2—7.2 kΩ

YELLOW/RED

BROWN/BLACK

THROTTLE ANGLE SENSOR

Throttle angle sensor resistance check—1985–86 Civic shown, others similar

should be available between the Black (Black/Yellow on 1987–88 model) terminal (+) and Light Green (Green/White on 1987–88 models) terminal (–) of the valve leads.

1. Open control box lid and disconnect wire harness from control box.
2. Disconnect vacuum hose between idle control solenoid valve and the No. 10 vacuum hose (upper vacuum hose of idle control solenoid valve from 3-way joint on 1987–88 models) and connect vacuum pump to hose.
3. Apply vacuum to the hose. It should hold vacuum.
4. Connect battery positive terminal to Black terminal of control box and negative battery terminal to Light Green terminal.
5. Apply vacuum to hose. It should not hold vacuum. If vacuum holds, replace solenoid valve.

1985 ACCORD

The idle control solenoid valve is activated by commands from the ECU. When the solenoid valve opens, this causes vacuum in the vacuum hose (#26 on 1985 models and upper hose on 1986 models) and increases idle speed under the following conditions:

- For a short period after starting the engine.
- Whenever electrical loads are turned on (vacuum will disappear when engine rpm is raised over 1500 rpm by operating the throttle).

While the solenoid valve is being activated, 9 volts or higher should be available between the Black/Yellow terminal (+) and Green/Black terminal (–) of the valve leads.

1. Disconnect wire harness from idle control solenoid valve.
2. Disconnect vacuum hose (#26 from air flow tube on 1985 models and upper hose from intake manifold on 1986 models).
3. Pump air into hose #26. There should not be air flow.
4. Connect battery positive terminal to Black/Yellow terminal of solenoid valve and negative battery terminal to Green/Black terminal.
5. Disconnect vacuum hose #28 from intake manifold.
6. Pump air into vacuum hose #26. There should be air flow.

1986 ACCORD AND 1986–88 PRELUDE

The idle control solenoid valve is activated by commands from the ECU. When the solenoid valve opens, this causes vacuum in the upper vacuum hose of the solenoid valve (from the intake manifold) and increases idle speed under the following conditions:

- For a short period after starting the engine.
- Whenever electrical loads are turned on (vacuum will disap-

pear when engine rpm is raised over 1500 rpm by operating the throttle).

While the solenoid valve is being activated, 9 volts or higher should be available between the Black/Yellow terminal (+) and Green/Black terminal (–) of the valve leads.

1. Disconnect wire harness from idle control solenoid valve.
2. Disconnect upper vacuum hose of solenoid valve from intake manifold.
3. Apply vacuum to hose. Vacuum should hold steady. If vacuum is not steady, replace valve.
4. Connect battery positive terminal to Black/Yellow terminal of solenoid valve and negative battery terminal to Green/Black terminal.
5. Apply vacuum to hose. Vacuum should not hold. If valve holds vacuum, replace valve.

Idle Control Test

1987–88 ACCORD

1. Check vacuum line for proper connection, cracks, blockage or disconnected hoses.
2. Disconnect lower vacuum hose of idle control solenoid valve from air chamber and connect a vacuum gauge to vacuum hose.
3. Start engine and check for vacuum. Make check within 10 seconds. Vacuum should be present.
4. If no vacuum, go to IDLE CONTROL SOLENOID VALVE TEST I. If vacuum is present, raise engine speed above 1500 rpm and check vacuum. Vacuum should not be present.
5. If vacuum is present, go to IDLE CONTROL SOLENOID VALVE TEST II.

Idle Control Solenoid Valve Test I

1987–88 ACCORD

1. Start engine and allow to idle.
2. Disconnect upper vacuum hose of idle control solenoid valve from intake manifold and check vacuum. Vacuum should be present.
3. If no vacuum, check vacuum port.
4. Stop engine.
5. Disconnect 2P connector on idle control solenoid valve.
6. Attach positive probe of voltmeter to Black/Yellow terminal and negative probe to Green/Black terminal.
7. Within 10 seconds after restarting engine, check voltage at idle.
8. If voltage is present, replace solenoid valve.
9. If no voltage, attach positive probe of voltmeter to Black/Yellow terminal of connector, and negative probe to body ground. Within 10 seconds after restarting engine, check voltage.
10. If no voltage, repair open in Black/Yellow wire between solenoid valve and fuse No. 1.
11. If voltage is present, inspect for an open in Green/Black wire between solenoid valve and ECU. If wire is OK, check ECU.

Idle Control Solenoid Valve Test II

1987–88 ACCORD

1. Start engine.
2. Disconnect 2P connector on idle control solenoid valve.
3. Attach positive probe of voltmeter to Black/Yellow terminal, and negative probe to Green/Black terminal.
4. Hold engine above 1500 rpm and check voltage.
5. If voltage is present, inspect for a short in Green/Black wire between solenoid valve and ECU. If wire is OK, check ECU.
6. If no voltage, replace solenoid valve.

Fast Idle Control Solenoid Valve

1985–88 CIVIC

The fast idle control solenoid valve is open when the atmospher-

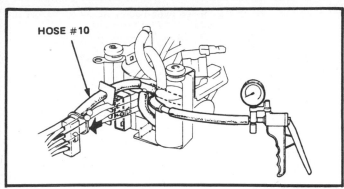

Idle control solenoid valve vacuum check — 1985–86 Civic shown

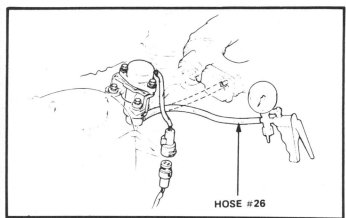

Idle control solenoid valve vacuum check — 1985 Accord

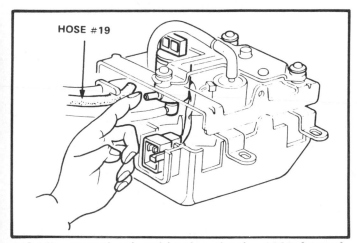

A/C idle control solenoid valve check — 1985 Accord

ic pressure is 660mm Hg. or less. Vacuum is produced in the vacuum hose (between the solenoid valve and air filter).

When the valve is open, 9 volts or more should be available between the Black terminal (+) and Yellow terminal (–) (Black/Yellow terminal (+) and Green/Yellow terminal (–) on 1987–88 models) of the wire harness of the control box.

1. Open control box lid and disconnect wire harness from control box.

2. Disconnect vacuum hose between fast idle control solenoid valve and No. 10 vacuum hose (lower vacuum hose of fast idle control solenoid valve from 3-way joint on 1987–88 models) and connect vacuum pump.

3. Apply vacuum to hose. It should hold vacuum.

4. Connect battery positive terminal to Black terminal of control box coupler, and battery negative terminal to Yellow terminal.

5. Apply vacuum to hose. It should not hold vacuum. If vacuum hold, replace valve.

1985 ACCORD

The fast idle control solenoid valve is open when the coolant temperature is below 5°F (-15°C). If the coolant temperature is below 104°F (40°C), it is energized only when the atmospheric pressure is 660mm Hg or less. In either case, vacuum is produced in the vacuum hose #18 between the solenoid valve and air flow tube.

When the valve is open, 9 volts or more should be available between the Black/Yellow terminal (+) and Blue/Black terminal (–) of the wire harness of the No. 1 control box.

1. Disconnect wire harness from No. 1 control box.

2. Disconnect vacuum hose #18 from air flow tube.

3. Pump air into vacuum hose #18. There should be no air flow.

4. Connect battery positive terminal to Black terminal of No. 1 control box coupler, and battery negative terminal to Orange terminal.

5. Disconnect vacuum hose #23 from intake manifold.

6. Pump air into vacuum hose #18. There should be air flow.

1986 ACCORD AND 1986–88 PRELUDE

The fast idle control solenoid valve is open when the coolant temperature is below 5°F (-15°C). If the coolant temperature is below 104°F (40°C), it is energized only when the atmospheric pressure is 660mm Hg or less. In either case, vacuum is produced in the vacuum hose #18 between the solenoid valve and air flow tube. Also, the solenoid valve opens with the vehicle speed more than 10 mph and the engine speed more than 2000 rpm. When the valve is open, 9 volts or more should be available between the Black/Yellow terminal (+) and Red/Green terminal (–) of the main harness at the control box.

1. Disconnect 6 cavity rectangle connector from control box.

2. Disconnect vacuum hose #23 from vacuum hose manifold.

3. Apply vacuum to hose #23. Vacuum should hold. If valve does not hold vacuum, replace valve.

4. Connect battery positive terminal to Black/Yellow terminal of control box coupler, and battery negative terminal to Orange terminal.

5. Apply vacuum to hose #23. Valve should not hold vacuum. If valve holds vacuum, replace valve.

1987–88 ACCORD

1. Check vacuum line for proper connection, cracks, blockage or disconnected hoses.

2. Start engine and allow to idle.

3. Disconnect #23 vacuum hose from; intake manifold and check vacuum.

4. If no vacuum, check vacuum port.

5. Turn ignition switch OFF.

6. Connect system checker harness (07999–PD6000A or equivalent) B connector to main wire harness only, not ECU.

7. Disconnect #23 vacuum hose from vacuum hose manifold and connect a vacuum pump to hose.

8. Apply vacuum to hose. Vacuum should hold.

9. If vacuum does not hold, replace solenoid valve.

10. Turn ignition switch ON and apply vacuum to hose. Vacuum should hold.

11. If vacuum does not hold, repair short in Red/Green wire between solenoid valve and ECU.

NOTE: On cars with automatic transmission, also inspect short in Green wire between A/T idle control solenoid valve and ECU.

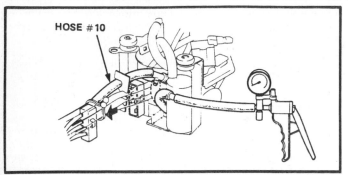

Fast idle control solenoid valve—1985-86 Civic shown

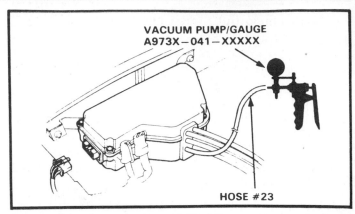

Automatic transmission (A/T) idle control solenoid valve and fast idle control solenoid valve vacuum check—1986 Accord and Prelude

12. Connect B4 terminal to A18 terminal and apply vacuum to hose. Vacuum should not hold.

13. If vacuum holds, turn ignition switch OFF. Disconnect 6P connector, then attach positive probe of voltmeter to Black/Yellow terminal, and negative probe to Red/Green terminal. Turn ignition switch ON.

14. If voltage is present, replace solenoid valve.

15. If no voltage, attach positive probe of voltmeter to Black/Yellow terminal, and negative probe to body ground.

16. If no voltage, repair open in Black/Yellow wire between solenoid valve and No. 1 fuse.

17. If voltage is present, repair open in Red/Green wire between solenoid valve and ECU.

Automatic Transmission (A/T) Idle Control Solenoid Valve

1985 ACCORD

The A/T idle control solenoid valve is energized when the A/T shift lever is in D4, D3, 2 and R.

When the solenoid valve is energized, it opens, causing vacuum in the vacuum hose #18 between the valve and air flow tube.

While the valve is energized, 9 volts or higher should be available between the Black/Yellow terminal (+) and Green terminal (−) of the No. 1 control box harness.

1. Disconnect wire harness from No.1 control box.

2. Disconnect vacuum hose #18 from air flow tube.

3. Pump air into vacuum hose #18. There should be no air flow.

4. Connect battery positive terminal to Black terminal of No. 1 control box coupler and battery negative terminal to Yellow/Black terminal.

5. Disconnect vacuum hose #23 from intake manifold.

6. Pump air into vacuum hose #18. There should be air flow.

1986 ACCORD AND 1986-88 PRELUDE

The A/T idle control solenoid valve is energized when the A/T shift lever is in gear, allowing air to bypass the throttle valve and maintain the specified idle speed.

While the valve is energized, 9 volts or higher should be available between the Black/Yellow terminal (+) and Green terminal (−) of the main harness at the control box.

1. Disconnect 6 cavity rectangular connector from control box.

2. Disconnect vacuum hose #23 from vacuum hose manifold.

3. Apply vacuum to hose #23. Valve should hold vacuum. If valve does not hold vacuum, replace valve.

4. Connect battery positive terminal to Black/Yellow terminal of control box coupler and battery negative terminal to Blue terminal.

6. Apply vacuum to hose #23. Valve should not hold vacuum. If valve holds vacuum, replace valve.

1987-88 ACCORD

1. Check vacuum line for proper connection, cracks, blockage or disconnected hoses.

2. Warm up engine normal operating temperature (cooling fan comes on).

NOTE: Apply parking brake securely.

3. Disconnect #18 vacuum hose from air flow tube and connect a vacuum gauge to hose. Vacuum should not be present.

4. If vacuum is present, go to AUTOMATIC TRANSMISSION (A/T) IDLE CONTROL SOLENOID VALVE TEST II.

5. Shift transmission into D3 or D4. Vacuum should be present.

6. If no vacuum, go to AUTOMATIC TRANSMISSION (A/T) IDLE CONTROL SOLENOID VALVE TEST I.

Automatic Transmission (A/T) Idle Control Solenoid Valve Test I

1987-88 ACCORD

1. With parking brake applied, start engine and allow to idle.

2. Disconnect #23 vacuum hose from intake manifold and check for vacuum.

3. If no vacuum, check vacuum port.

4. Disconnect 6P connector.

5. Attach positive probe of voltmeter to Black/Yellow terminal, and negative probe to Green terminal.

6. Shift transmission into D3 or D4.

7. If voltage is present, replace solenoid valve.

8. If no voltage, attach positive probe of voltmeter to Black/Yellow terminal, and negative probe to body ground. Check voltage.

9. If no voltage, repair open in Black/Yellow wire between solenoid valve and No. 1 fuse.

10. If voltage is present, inspect for an open in Green wire between solenoid valve and ECU. If wire is OK, check ECU.

Automatic Transmission (A/T) Idle Control Solenoid Valve Test II

1987-88 ACCORD

1. With parking brake applied, start engine.

2. Disconnect 6P connector.

3. Attach positive probe of voltmeter to Black/Yellow terminal, and negative probe to Green terminal.

4. If voltage is present, inspect for a short n Green wire between solenoid valve and ECU. If wire is OK, check ECU.

5. If no voltage, replace solenoid valve.

Air Conditioning (A/C) Idle Control Solenoid Valve

1985 ACCORD

The A/C idle control solenoid valve is activated when the A/C switch is turned on. When the solenoid valve is activated, vacuum is generated in the vacuum hose #19 between the solenoid valve and idle diaphragm.

9 volts or high should be detected between the Black/Yellow terminal (+) and Blue/Yellow terminal (–) of the No.2 control box harness.

1. Disconnect wire harness from No. 2 control box.
2. Disconnect vacuum hose #19 from air flow tube.
3. Start engine and feel for vacuum at opening of solenoid valve. There should be no vacuum.
4. Connect battery positive terminal to Black/Yellow terminal of control box coupler and battery negative terminal to Blue/Yellow terminal.
5. Start engine and feel vacuum at opening of solenoid valve. There should be vacuum.

1986 ACCORD AND 1986–88 PRELUDE

When the solenoid valve is energized, vacuum is directed from vacuum hose #12 to the A/C idle boost valve through vacuum hose #19

9 volts or high should be detected between the Black/Yellow terminal (+) and Red terminal (–) of the main harness at the control box.

1. Open control box lid and disconnect 6 cavity rectangular connector form control box.
2. Disconnect lower vacuum hose of A/C idle boost solenoid valve (between valve and check valve) from check valve.
3. Apply vacuum to hose. Vacuum should hold. If no vacuum, check for check valve. If check valve is OK, replace solenoid valve.
4. Connect battery positive terminal to Black/Yellow terminal of control box coupler and battery negative terminal to Red terminal.
5. Apply vacuum to hose. Vacuum should not hold. If vacuum holds, check check valve. If check valve is OK, replace solenoid valve.

1987–88 ACCORD

1. Check vacuum line for improper connection, cracks, blockage or disconnected hoses.
2. Start engine and allow to idle.
3. Disconnect vacuum hose between A/C idle boost valve and air chamber from A/C idle boost valve and connect a vacuum gauge to valve. No vacuum should be present.
4. If vacuum is present, disconnect #19 vacuum hose from A/C idle boost valve and connect vacuum gauge to hose.
5. If no vacuum, replace A/C idle boost valve. If vacuum is present, go to AIR CONDITIONING IDLE BOOST SOLENOID VALVE TEST II.
6. Turn A/C switch and blower switch ON, then check that compressor and condenser cooling fan work. Vacuum should be present.
7. If no vacuum, disconnect #19 vacuum hose from A/C idle boost valve and connect vacuum gauge to hose.
8. If vacuum is present, replace A/C idle boost valve. If no vacuum, go to AIR CONDITIONING IDLE BOOST SOLENOID VALVE TEST I.

Air Conditioning Idle Boost Solenoid Valve Test I

1987–88 ACCORD

1. With parking brake applied, start engine and allow to idle.
2. Disconnect #12 vacuum hose from intake manifold and check for vacuum.
3. If no vacuum, check vacuum port.
4. Disconnect 6P connector.
5. Attach positive probe of voltmeter to Black/Yellow terminal, and negative probe to Red terminal.

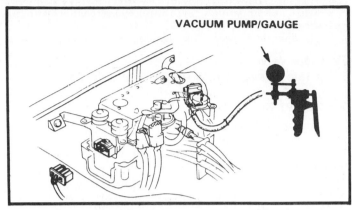

Air conditioning (A/C) idle boost solenoid valve vacuum check – 1986 Accord and Prelude shown, others similar

6. Turn A/C switch and blower switch ON, then check that compressor and condenser cooling fan work.
7. If voltage is present, replace solenoid valve.
8. If no voltage, attach positive probe of voltmeter to Black/Yellow terminal, and negative probe to body ground. Check voltage.
9. If no voltage, repair open in Black/Yellow wire between solenoid valve and No. 1 fuse.
10. If voltage is present, inspect for an open in Red wire between solenoid valve and ECU. If wire is OK, check ECU.

Air Conditioning Idle Boost Solenoid Valve Test II

1987–88 ACCORD

1. Start engine.
2. Disconnect 6P connector.
3. Attach positive probe of voltmeter to Black/Yellow terminal, and negative probe to Red terminal.
4. If voltage is present, inspect for a short in Red wire between solenoid valve an ECU. If wire is OK, check ECU.
5. If no voltage, replace solenoid valve.

Fast Idle Valve (Idle Speed Too High After Warm Up)

1985–88 ACCORD AND CIVIC
1986–88 PRELUDE

NOTE: Fast idle valve is factory adjusted, it should not be disassembled. Check PCV (engine breather) circuit tubing for breakage, disconnection, clogging, etc. Check that throttle valve are fully closed.

1. Confirm that engine is adequately warmed up.
2. Check whether idling control function is normal.
3. Remove cover of fast idle valve.
4. Check that valve is completely closed. If not, air is being sucked from valve seat area. It can be detected by putting your finger on valve seat area.
5. If any suction sound is heard, valve is leaking. Replace fast idle valve and adjust idle speed.

Fast Idle Valve (Idle Speed Too Low After Warm Up)

1985–88 ACCORD AND CIVIC
1986–88 PRELUDE

NOTE: Fast idle valve is factory adjusted, it should not be disassembled. Check PCV (engine breather) circuit tubing for breakage, disconnection, clogging, etc. Check that throttle valve are fully closed.

1. Remove idle adjusting screw.

2. Wash idle adjusting screw and air bypass channel with carburetor cleaner.

3. Readjust idle speed after cleaning.

Fast Idle Valve
(Fast Idle Speed Is Low When Engine Is Cold)

1985–88 ACCORD AND CIVIC
1986–88 PRELUDE

NOTE: Fast idle valve is factory adjusted, it should not be disassembled. Fast idle speed should be 1250–2250 rpm for Civic models and 1000–1800 rpm for Accord models.

1. Remove fast idle valve assembly from throttle body.
2. Apply cold water and cool down wax part of fast idle valve to 41–86°F (5–30°C).
3. Blow through part A of fast valve, and check that a fairly large amount of air flows without resistance.
4. If air does not flow or resistance is large, replace fast idle valve and adjust idle speed.

Dashpot

1985–86 ACCORD, 1987–88 CIVIC AND 1986–88 PRELUDE

1. With engine off, slowly open throttle arm until dashpot rod is raised up as far as it will go.
2. Release throttle arm and measure time until throttle arm contacts stop screw. Time should be less than 2 seconds.
3. If time is over 2 seconds, replace dashpot check valve.
4. If rod does not operate, check for bound linkage, or for clogged check valve or vacuum line. If OK, replace dashpot.

1987–88 ACCORD

1. Check vacuum line for leaks, blockage or disconnected hose.
2. Disconnect #6 vacuum hose from dashpot diaphragm, and connect a vacuum pump/gauge to hose.
3. Start engine.
4. Raise engine speed to 3500 rpm. Vacuum should appear on gauge.
5. If no vacuum, check that vacuum port on throttle body.
6. Release throttle. Vacuum should go out slowly.
7. If vacuum holds or goes out quickly, replace dashpot check valve.
8. Connect a vacuum pump to dashpot diaphragm.
9. Apply vacuum and check that rod pulls in and vacuum holds. Rod should pull in and vacuum should hold.
10. If vacuum does not hold or rod does not move, replace dashpot diaphragm.

Injector Test

1985–88 ACCORD AND CIVIC
1986–88 PRELUDE

NOTE: Check following items before testing idle speed, ignition timing, valve clearance and idle CO%.

1. If engine will run, disconnect injector couplers with engine idling, and inspect change in idling speed. Idle should drop the same for each cylinder.
2. Check clicking sound of each injector by means of a stethoscope when engine is idling.
3. If any injector fails to make typical clicking sound, check wiring between ECU and injector. Voltage at injector coupler should fluctuate between 0–2 volts. If voltage is OK, replace injector.
4. If engine can not be started, remove coupler of injector, and measure resistance between terminals sf injector. Resistance should be 1.5–2.5 Ω.
5. If resistance is not as specified, replace injector. If resis-

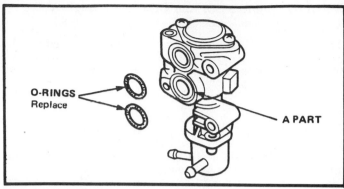

Fast idle valve assembly—typical

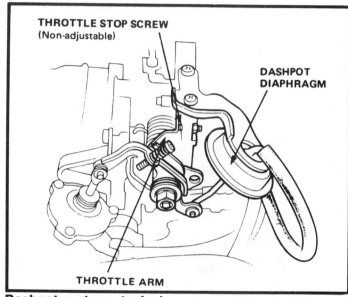

Dashpot system—typical

tance is normal, check wiring between resistor and injector, wiring between resistors and control unit, and resistors.

Fuel System Resistor

1985–88 ACCORD AND CIVIC
1986–88 PRELUDE

1. Disconnect resistor coupler.
2. Check for resistance between each of resistor terminals (E, D, C and B) and power terminal (A). Resistance should be 5–7 Ω.
3. Replace resistor with a new one if any of resistances are outside of specification.

Fuel Pressure Testing

1985–88 ACCORD AND CIVIC
1986–88 PRELUDE

1. Relieve fuel pressure.
2. Remove service bolt and attach fuel pressure gauge.
3. Start engine. Measure fuel pressure with engine idling and vacuum hose of pressure regulator disconnected. Pressure should be 36 ± 3 psi (255 ± 20 kPa).
4. If fuel pressure is not as specified, first check fuel pump. If pump is OK, check following:
   a. If pressure is higher than specified, inspect for pinched or clogged fuel return hose or piping, and faulty pressure regulator.
   b. If pressure is lower than specified, inspect for clogged

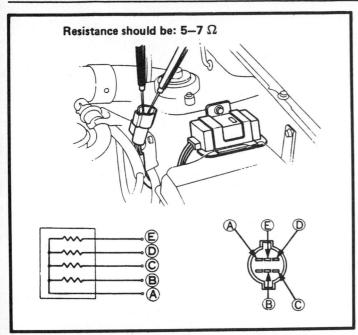

Fuel system resistor testing—1985 Civic shown, others similar

fuel filter, pinched or clogged fuel hose from fuel tank to fuel pump, pressure regulator failure, leakage in fuel line, or pinched, broken or disconnected regulator vacuum hose.

Main Relay Testing

1985–88 ACCORD AND CIVIC
1986–88 PRELUDE

1. Remove main relay, near under-dash fuse box.
2. Connect battery positive terminal to No. 4 terminal and battery negative terminal to No. 8 terminal of main relay.
3. Check for continuity between No. 5 terminal and No. 7 terminal of main relay. If no continuity, replace main relay.
4. Connect battery positive terminal to No. 5 terminal and battery negative terminal to No. 2 terminal of main relay.
5. Check that there is continuity between No. 1 terminal and No. 3 terminal of main relay. If there is no continuity, replace main relay.
6. Connect battery positive terminal to No. 3 terminal and battery negative terminal to No. 8 terminal of main relay.
7. Check that there is continuity between No. 5 terminal and No. 7 terminal of main relay. If there is no continuity, replace main relay.

Harness Testing

1985 ACCORD AND 1985–88 CIVIC

1. Keep ignition switch in off position.
2. Disconnect main relay connector.
3. Connect positive probe of circuit tester to Yellow/White wire for 1985–86 Civic (Yellow/Blue wire for 1985 Accord) in coupler and ground negative probe of tester to body ground. Tester should read battery voltage.
4. If there is no voltage, check wiring between battery and main relay as well as ECU fuse in engine compartment.
5. Connect positive terminal of tester to Black/Yellow wire of coupler and ground negative terminal of tester to body ground.
6. Turn ignition switch on. Tester should read battery voltage.
7. If no voltage, check wiring from ignition switch and main relay as well as fuse No. 4 for 1985–86 Civic (fuse No. 11 for 1985 Accord).

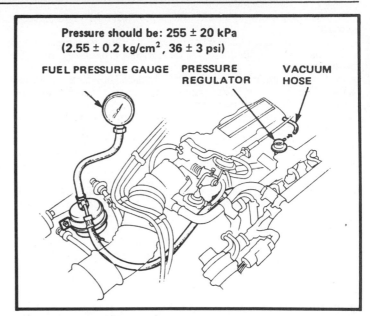

Pressure regulator testing—Civic shown, Prelude and Accord similar

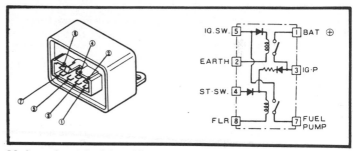

Main relay pin identification—typical

8. Connect positive terminal of tester to Blue/White wire for 1985–86 Civic (Blue/Red wire for 1985 Accord) in coupler and ground negative terminal to body.
9. Turn ignition switch to start position. Tester should read battery voltage.
10. If no voltage, check wiring between ignition switch and main relay as well as starter fuse No. 1 for 1985–86 Civic (fuse No. 21 for 1985 Accord).
11. Connect a jumper wire between Yellow/White wire and Yellow wire for 1985–86 Civic (Black/Yellow wire and Yellow wire on 1987–88 Civic) (Yellow/Blue and Black/Yellow wire for 1985 Accord) in coupler. Fuel pump should work.
12. If pump does not work, check wiring between battery and fuel pump and wiring from fuel pump to ground (Black wire).

1986–88 ACCORD AND PRELUDE

1. Keep ignition switch in off position.
2. Disconnect main relay coupler.
3. On 1987–88 models, check continuity between Black wire in connector and body ground.
4. Connect positive probe of circuit tester to Yellow/Blue wire in coupler and ground negative probe of tester to body ground (on 1987–88 models, Black wire). Tester should read battery voltage.
5. If there is no voltage, check wiring between battery and main relay as well as No. 1 fuse in engine compartment.
6. Connect positive terminal of tester to Black/Yellow wire of coupler and ground negative terminal of tester to body ground (on 1987–88 models, Black wire).

7. Turn ignition switch on. Tester should read battery voltage.

8. If no voltage, check wiring from ignition switch and main relay as well as fuse No. 1 for Accord (regulator fuse for Prelude).

9. Connect positive terminal of tester to Blue/Red for Accord (Black/White for Prelude) wire in coupler and ground negative terminal to body ground (on 1987–88 models, Black wire).

10. Turn ignition switch to start position. Tester should read battery voltage.

11. If no voltage, check wiring between ignition switch and main relay as well as fuse No. 10 for Accord (starter signal fuse for Prelude).

12. Connect a jumper wire between Yellow/Blue (Black/Yellow on 1987–88) and Yellow wire for Accord (Yellow/Blue and Yellow/Black wire for 1986 Prelude and Black/Yellow and Yellow/Black for 1987–88 Prelude) in connector. Fuel pump should work.

13. If pump does not work, check wiring between battery and fuel pump and wiring from fuel pump to ground (Black wire).

Component Replacement

Fuel System Pressure Relieving

1985–88 ACCORD AND CIVIC
1986–88 PRELUDE

―――――――――― CAUTION ――――――――――

Keep open flames or sparks from work area. Do not smoke while working on fuel system. Be sure to relieve fuel pressure while engine is off.

――――――――――――――――――――――――――――――

NOTE: Before disconnecting fuel pipes or hoses, release pressure from system by loosen 6mm service bolt at top of fuel filter.

1. Disconnect battery negative cable from battery negative terminal.

2. Use a box end wrench on 6mm service bolt at top of fuel filter, while holding special banjo bolt with another wrench.

3. Place a rag or a shop towel over 6mm service bolt.

4. Slowly loosen 6mm service bolt one complete turn.

NOTE: A fuel pressure gauge can be attached at 6mm service bolt hole. Always replace washer between service bolt and Special Banjo Bolt, whenever service bolt is loosened to relieve fuel pressure. Replace all washers whenever bolts are removed to disassemble parts.

IDLE SPEED

Adjustment

1985 ACCORD AND 1985–88 CIVIC

1. Start engine and warm up to normal operating temperature; cooling fan will come on.

2. Connect tachometer.

3. Check idle speed with all accessories off.

NOTE: To prevent idle control system from operating, pinch vacuum hose (#10 on 1985–88 Civic and #27 on 1985 Accord)

4. Idle speed should be 750 ± 50 rpm (in neutral). Adjust idle speed, if necessary, by turning idle adjusting screw, check fast idle valve.

5. Check idle controller boosted speed with A/C on. Idle speed should be:

1985–86 Civic – 750 ± 50 rpm (in neutral)
1985 Accord – 800 ± 50 rpm (in neutral)
Adjust idle speed, if necessary, by turning adjusting screw B.

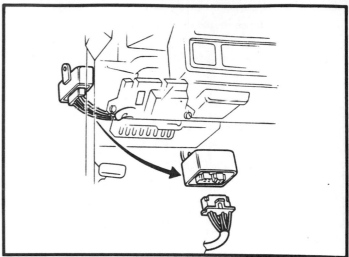

Harness and main relay location – typical

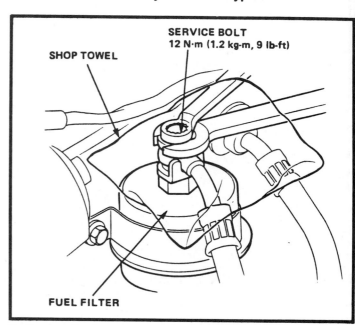

Relieving fuel pressure – typical

1986–88 ACCORD AND PRELUDE

1. Start engine and warm up to normal operating temperature; cooling fan will come on twice.

2. Connect tachometer.

3. Disconnect upper vacuum hose of idle control solenoid valve (between valve and intake manifold) from intake manifold.

4. Cap end of hose and intake manifold.

5. With all accessories off, check idle speed. Idle speed should be 750 ± 50 rpm (in neutral). Adjust idle speed, if necessary, by turning idle adjusting screw.

6. Check idle speed with heater fan switch at HI and A/C on. Idle speed should be 750 ± 50 rpm (in neutral). Adjust idle speed, if necessary, by turning adjusting bolt on A/C idle boost valve.

7. After adjustment, connect idle control solenoid valve vacuum hose.

8. On automatic transmission model, after adjusting idle speed, check that it remains within specified limit when shifted in gear. Idle speed should be 750 ± 50 rpm.

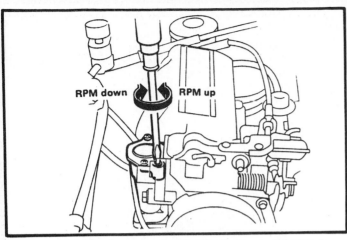

Idle speed adjustment—1985–88 Civic and 1985 Accord

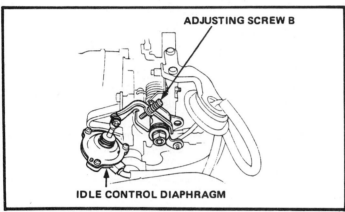

Idle controller boost speed adjustment—1985–88 Civic

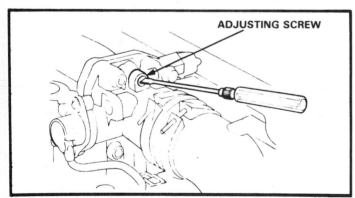

Idle speed adjust—1986–88 Accord and Prelude

9. Check idle speed with all accessories on and A/C off. Idle should remain 750 ± 50 rpm.

THROTTLE ANGLE SENSOR

Adjustment

1985–86 ACCORD AND CIVIC, AND 1986 PRELUDE

1. Disconnect control unit connectors and connect System Checker Harness (07999–PDF6000A or equivalent).
2. Connect a digital voltmeter positive probe to C7 terminal of System Checker Harness and negative probe to C12 terminal.

3. With ignition switch turned on, adjust sensor to a position in which throttle stopper lever contacts between stop screw. Voltage measurement should read 0.48–0.52 volts. If replacement and/or adjustment is necessary, remove the shear screws, adjust sensor and install new shear screws. Tighten till hex head twist off.

FUEL INJECTOR

Removal and Installation

1985–86 CIVIC

1. Disconnect battery negative cable from battery negative.
2. Relieve fuel pressure.
3. Disconnect coupler of injector.
4. Disconnect vacuum hose and fuel return hose from pressure regulator.

NOTE: Place a rag or shop towel over hose and tube before disconnecting.

5. Loosen retainer nuts.
6. Disconnect fuel pipe.
7. Remove injector from intake manifold.
8. Slide new cushion onto injector.
9. Coat new O-rings with clean engine oil and put O-rings on injectors.
10. Insert injectors into fuel pipe.

NOTE: To prevent damage to O-ring, insert injector into fuel pipe squarely and carefully.

11. Coat new seal rings with clean engine oil and press into intake manifold.
12. Install injector and fuel pipe assembly in manifold.

NOTE: To prevent damage to O-ring, install injectors in fuel pipe first, then install in intake manifold.

13. Tighten retainer nuts.
14. Connect vacuum hose ad fuel return hose to pressure regulator.
15. Install couplers of injectors.
16. Turn ignition switch on but do not operate starter. After fuel pump runs for approximately two seconds, fuel pressure in fuel line rises. Repeat this two or three times, then check whether there is any fuel leakage.

1985 ACCORD

1. Disconnect battery negative cable from battery negative.
2. Relieve fuel pressure.
3. Remove air cleaner case.
4. Disconnect coupler of injector.
5. Disconnect vacuum hose and fuel return hose from pressure regulator.

NOTE: Place a rag or shop towel over hose and tube before disconnecting.

6. Disconnect two ground cables from intake manifold.
7. Disconnect fuel lines.
8. Remove injector from intake manifold.

NOTE: Use new O-rings, seal rings and cushion rings whenever disassembled. When installing injector, check O-ring and seal ring are installed properly. Coat new O-rings and seal rings with clean engine oil before assembly. Install injector with center line of coupler aligned with index mark on intake manifold.

9. Slide new cushion onto injector.
10. Put O-ring onto injector.
11. Press seal ring into intake manifold, and install injector and fuel pipe assembly on manifold. Tighten retainer nuts securely.

12. Connect two ground cables.

13. Connect vacuum hose and fuel return hose to pressure regulator.

14. Install couplers of injectors.

15. Turn ignition switch on but do not operate starter. After fuel pump runs for approximately two seconds, fuel pressure in fuel line rises. Repeat this two or three times, then check whether there is any fuel leakage.

1986–88 ACCORD AND PRELUDE

1. Disconnect battery negative cable from battery negative.
2. Relieve fuel pressure.
3. Disconnect coupler of injector.
4. Disconnect vacuum hose and fuel return hose from pressure regulator.

NOTE: Place a rag or shop towel over hose and tube before disconnecting.

5. Loosen retainer nuts on fuel pipe.
6. Disconnect fuel pipe.
7. Remove injector from intake manifold.
8. Slide new cushion onto injector.
9. Coat new O-rings with clean engine oil and put O-rings on injectors.
10. Insert injectors into fuel pipe first.

NOTE: To prevent damage to O-ring, insert injector into fuel pipe squarely and carefully, then install them in intake manifold.

11. Coat new seal rings with clean engine oil and press into intake manifold.
12. Install injector and fuel pipe assembly in manifold.

NOTE: To prevent damage to O-ring, install injectors in fuel pipe first, then install in intake manifold.

13. Align center line on coupler with mark on fuel pipe.
14. Install and tighten retainer nuts.
15. Connect vacuum hose ad fuel return hose to pressure regulator.
16. Install couplers of injectors.
17. Turn ignition switch on but do not operate starter. After fuel pump runs for approximately two seconds, fuel pressure in fuel line rises. Repeat this two or three times, then check whether there is any fuel leakage.

1987–88 CIVIC

1. Disconnect battery negative cable from battery negative.
2. Relieve fuel pressure.
3. Disconnect connector of injectors.
4. Disconnect vacuum hose and fuel return hose from pressure regulator.

NOTE: Place a rag or shop towel over hose and tube before disconnecting.

5. Remove fuel line and pulsation damper.
6. Loosen retainer nuts on fuel pipe.
7. Disconnect fuel pipe.
8. Remove injector from intake manifold.
9. Slide new cushion onto injector.
10. Coat new O-rings with clean engine oil and put O-rings on injectors.
11. Insert injectors into fuel pipe first.
12. Coat new seal rings with clean engine oil and press into intake manifold.
13. Install injector and fuel pipe assembly in manifold.

NOTE: To prevent damage to O-ring, install injectors in fuel pipe first, then install in intake manifold.

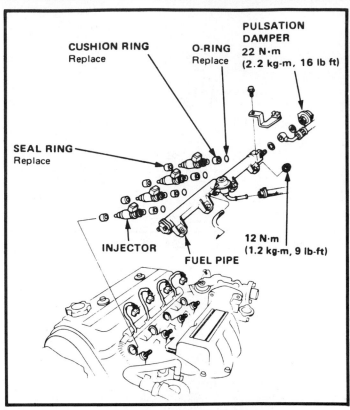

Fuel injector servicing—1985–88 Civic

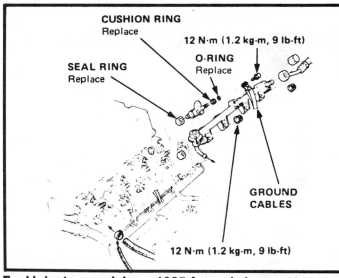

Fuel injector servicing—1985 Accord shown, 1986–88 Accord and Prelude similar

14. Align center line on connector with mark on fuel pipe.
15. Install and tighten retainer nuts.
16. Install fuel line and pulsation damper.
17. Connect vacuum hose ad fuel return hose to pressure regulator.
18. Install couplers of injectors.
19. Turn ignition switch on but do not operate starter. After fuel pump runs for approximately two seconds, fuel pressure in fuel line rises. Repeat this two or three times, then check whether there is any fuel leakage.

ISUZU

ENGINE CONTROL SYSTEM APPLICATION CHART

Year	Model	Engine cc (liter)	Engine VIN	Fuel System	Ignition System
1984	I-Mark	1816 (1.8)	G-108Z	2 bbl	Electronic
	Impulse	1949 (1.9)	G-200Z	EFI	Electronic
	Pick-Up	1949 (1.9)	G-200Z	2 bbl	Electronic
1985	I-Mark (RWD)	1816 (1.8)	G-108Z	2 bbl	Electronic
	I-Mark (FWD)	1471 (1.5)	4XC1-U	2 bbl	Electronic
	Impulse	1949 (1.9)	G-200Z	EFI	Electronic
	Impulse (Turbo)	1983 (2.0)	4ZC1-T	EFI	Electronic
	Pick-Up	1949 (1.9)	G-200Z	2 bbl	Electronic
	Tropper II	1949 (1.9)	G-200Z	2 bbl	Electronic
1986	I-Mark (FWD)	1471 (1.5)	4XC1-U	2 bbl	Electronic
	Impulse	1949 (1.9)	G-200Z	EFI	Electronic
	Impulse (Turbo)	1983 (2.0)	4ZC1-T	EFI	Electronic
	Pick-Up	1949 (1.9)	G-200Z	2 bbl	Electronic
	Pick-Up	2261 (2.3)	4ZD1	2 bbl	Electronic
	Trooper II	2261 (2.3)	4ZD1	2 bbl	Electronic
1987-88	I-Mark (FWD)	1471 (1.5)	4XC1-U	2 bbl	Electronic
	I-Mark (FWD)	1471 (1.5)	4XC1-U	2 bbl	Electronic
	Impulse	1949 (1.9)	G-200Z	EFI	Electronic
	Impulse (Turbo)	1983 (2.0)	4ZC1-T	EFI	Electronic
	Pick-Up	1949 (1.9)	G-200Z	2 bbl	Electronic
	Pick-Up	2261 (2.3)	4ZD1	2 bbl	Electronic
	Trooper II	2261 (2.3)	4ZD1	2 bbl	Electronic

FUEL INJECTION SYSTEM

All Impulse Models
I-TEC SYSTEM

The I-TEC control system constantly monitors and controls engine operation, which in turn helps lower emissions while maintaining the fuel economy and driveability. The Electronic Control Unit (ECU) controls the fuel injection system, the ignition system and the turbocharger control system (if so equipped).

The ignition system consists of the following components; the crank angle sensor, the throttle valve switch, the vehicle speed sensor, the coolant temperature sensor, air flow sensor, knock sensor, a transistorize ignition coil and the ECU.

The fuel injection system consists of the following components; the crank angle sensor, the throttle valve switch, the vehicle speed sensor, the coolant temperature sensor, air flow sensor, oxygen sensor, four injectors and the ECU.

The turbocharger system consists of the following components; the throttle valve switch, the throttle position sensor, the knock sensor, the coolant temperature sensor, air flow sensor, oxygen sensor, the stepping motor, the turbocharger controller and the ECU.

DATA SENSORS

The sensors used in this system, provide electrical impulses to the ECU by monitoring the pressure, temperature, vacuum and other engine operating conditions.

Air Flow Sensor

The air flow sensor is usually located in the air cleaner housing assembly. The purpose of the air flow sensor id to measure the volume (rate) of air that is coming into the engine.

Back-Up Control System

This system is used in case there is a malfunction with the microcomputer within the ECU, the back-up control system works to maintain the necessary functions of the control unit to permit continuous operation of the vehicle.

Coolant Temperature Sensor

This sensor is usually located on the engine block, under the intake manifold. It sends the coolant temperature information back to the ECU. The ECU then uses this information to determine the engine temperature for calculating the required air/fuel mixture.

Crank Angle Sensor

The crank angle sensor is usually located inside the distributor housing, it is used to detect the engine speed and relative position of each piston in its cylinder. Using these parameters, the ECU calculates the proper ignition timing and dwell angle. The ECU then sends a signal to the transistorized ignition coil, to create a spark.

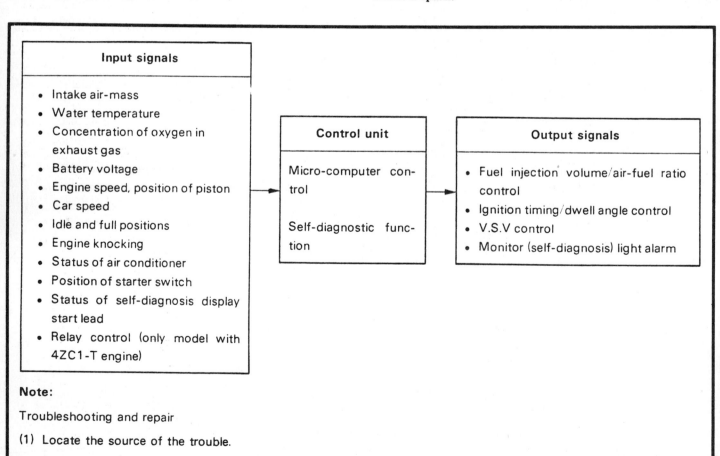

Input signals	Control unit	Output signals
• Intake air-mass • Water temperature • Concentration of oxygen in exhaust gas • Battery voltage • Engine speed, position of piston • Car speed • Idle and full positions • Engine knocking • Status of air conditioner • Position of starter switch • Status of self-diagnosis display start lead • Relay control (only model with 4ZC1-T engine)	Micro-computer control Self-diagnostic function	• Fuel injection volume/air-fuel ratio control • Ignition timing/dwell angle control • V.S.V control • Monitor (self-diagnosis) light alarm

Note:

Troubleshooting and repair

(1) Locate the source of the trouble.

(2) Before replacing any parts, check to see that the related connector are properly attached and positioned. Perform this check by removing and reinstalling each of the connectors.

I-TEC control system flow chart

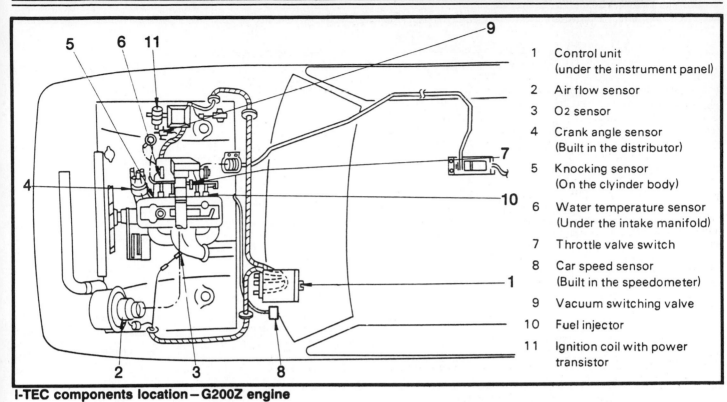

1   Control unit
    (under the instrument panel)

2   Air flow sensor

3   O2 sensor

4   Crank angle sensor
    (Built in the distributor)

5   Knocking sensor
    (On the clyinder body)

6   Water temperature sensor
    (Under the intake manifold)

7   Throttle valve switch

8   Car speed sensor
    (Built in the speedometer)

9   Vacuum switching valve

10 Fuel injector

11 Ignition coil with power
    transistor

I-TEC components location – G200Z engine

Turbocharger Control System wiring diagram

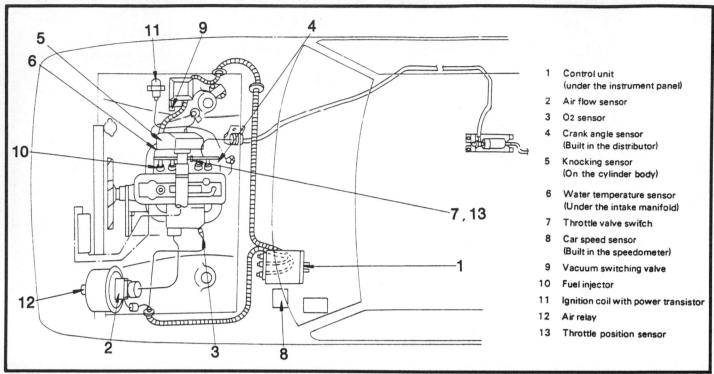

I-TEC components location—4ZC1-T engine

1	Control unit (under the instrument panel)
2	Air flow sensor
3	O2 sensor
4	Crank angle sensor (Built in the distributor)
5	Knocking sensor (On the cylinder body)
6	Water temperature sensor (Under the intake manifold)
7	Throttle valve swifch
8	Car speed sensor (Built in the speedometer)
9	Vacuum switching valve
10	Fuel injector
11	Ignition coil with power transistor
12	Air relay
13	Throttle position sensor

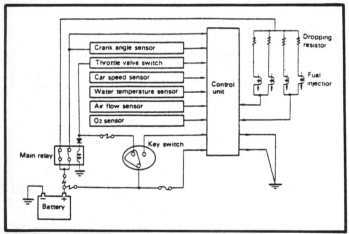

I-TEC fuel injection volume control

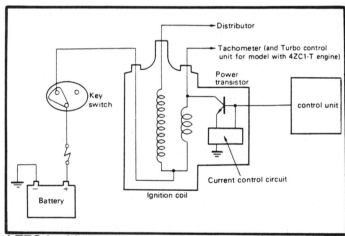

I-TEC ignition coil and power transistor circuit

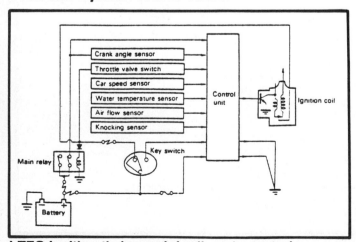

I-TEC ignition timing and dwell angle control

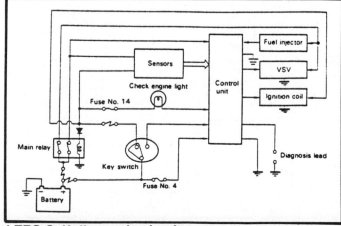

I-TEC Self-diagnosis circuit

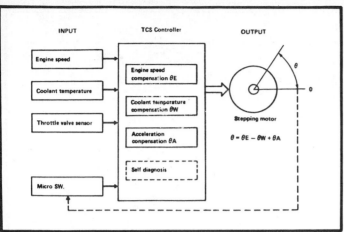

Turbocharger Control System flow chart

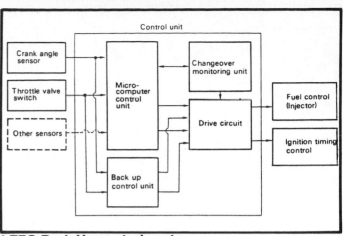

I-TEC Back-Up control system

Electronic Control Unit

The ECU is usually located under the instrument panel. The ECU analyzes all electrical data signals from the sensor. It controls the fuel injection system, the ignition system and the turbocharger control system (is so equipped). The ECU has a built in back-up, diagnostic and fail safe control systems.

Fuel Injector

The fuel injector is controlled by the ECU and injects fuel when ever it is energized by the ECU.

Knock Sensor

This sensor is usually located in the cylinder head. The purpose of this sensor is to send electrical impulses to the ECU when ever engine "knocking" occurs. The ECU uses these impulses to retard the ignition timing.

Oxygen Sensor

This sensor is usually threaded into the exhaust manifold. The oxygen sensor measures and produces an electrical signal proportional to the amount of the oxygen sensor present in the exhaust gases.

Throttle Position Sensor

The throttle position sensor (TPS) is used on turbocharged models only. The sensor controls the fuel cut system.

Throttle Valve Switch

The throttle position switch is usually located on the throttle body. It is used to detect the throttle valve position at engine idle, part throttle and wide open throttle.

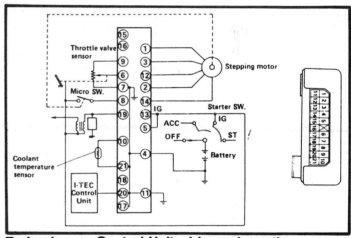

Turbocharger Control Unit wiring schematic

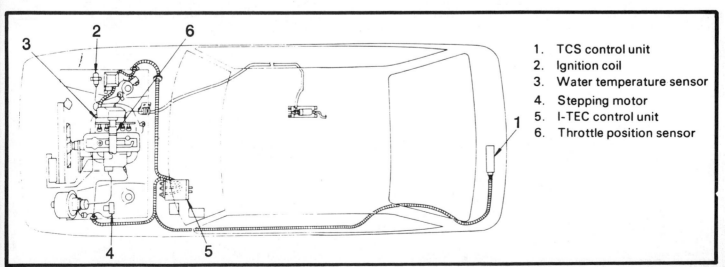

1. TCS control unit
2. Ignition coil
3. Water temperature sensor
4. Stepping motor
5. I-TEC control unit
6. Throttle position sensor

Turbocharger Control System component location

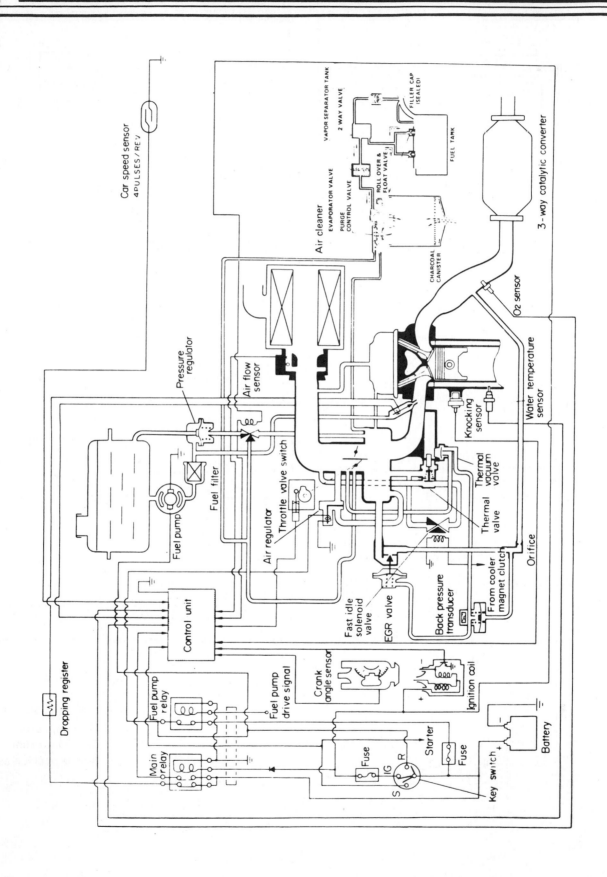

Emission control system for the G200Z engine

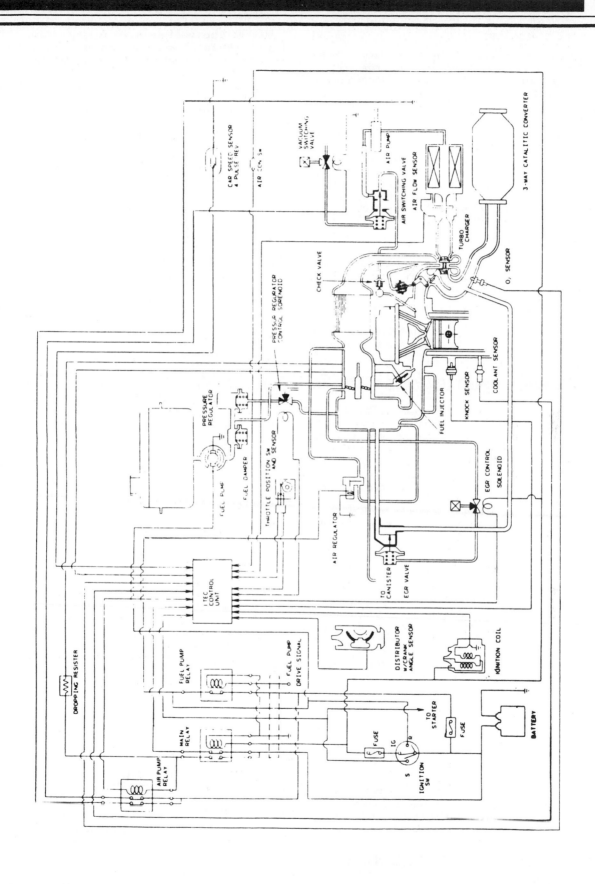

Emission control system for the 4ZC1-T engine

Turbocharger Control Unit

This control unit is usually located in the rear of the vehicle, behind the driver's side tail light cover in the luggage compartment. The turbocharger control unit, controls the operation of the turbocharger system.

Stepper Motor

The stepper motor is used on turbocharged vehicles only. The stepper motor is rotated by a voltage pulse sent to it by the turbocharger control unit. The stepper motor is able to rotate 90 degrees, depending on the number of pulses it receives from the turbocharger control unit. A microswitch inside the stepper motor unit tells the turbocharger control unit when the stepper motor is at zero degree angle. 250 pulses from the turbocharger control unit are required to move the stepper motor 90 degrees.

Vacuum Switching Valve

The vacuum switching valve is controlled by a signal from the ECU. This valve controls the fuel pressure according to the vacuum developed in the intake manifold.

Vehicle Speed Sensor

The vehicle speed sensor is incorporated into the speedometer. The ECU receives electrical impulses from the vehicle speed sensor.

SERVICE PRECAUTIONS

Be careful not to get water on the I-TEC system. Pay close attention to the relay box and throttle valve switch connector. The connector is not water proofed and will be damaged by water.

When charging the battery be sure to remove it from the vehicle first. Never disconnect the battery cable from the battery why the engine is running. The generation of surge voltage may damage the control unit and other electrical parts such as the multi-drive monitor.

When replacing parts of the I-TEC system or checking the I-TEC system, make sure to set the starter switch to the OFF position. When measuring voltage at the control unit harness connector, disconnect all the control unit harnesses first, then set the starter switch to the on position.

When checking the electrical terminals of the control unit with a tester, do not apply the probe to terminal directly but insert a pin into the terminal from the harness side and perform the measurement through the pin. If the tester probe is held against the terminal directly, the terminal will be deformed, causing poor contact. Connect each harness correctly and firmly to ensure a good contact.

The wiring connectors for the fuel injector, throttle valve switch, air regulator and water temperature sensor are provided with locked wires. To unlock the connector, pull and shake it gently.

I-TEC cables must be placed at least 4 in. away from the tension cables. Be careful not to apply any shock to the I-TEC components such as the air flow sensor, crank angle sensor, and control unit. Component parts of the I-TEC system are precisely set. Even a slight distortion or dent will seriously affect performance.

The fuel pump must not be operated without fuel since fuel lubricates the pump. Otherwise noise or other serious problems such as parts seizure will result. It is also prohibited to use any other fuel other than gasoline.

COMPONENT TEST PROCEDURES

Fuel Pressure Test

1. Loosen the clip on the fuel hose between the pressure regulator and the fuel hose carefully.

NOTE: The fuel line is still under pressure. When pulling out the fuel hose, cover up the joint with a shop towel to prevent the gasoline from spraying.

2. Connect a suitable fuel pressure gauge (J-33945 or equivalent) across the fuel pressure regulator and fuel distributor pipe correctly. Disconnect the vacuum switching valve at the harness connector.

3. Start the engine and measure the fuel pressure under the four different conditions as listed below:

a. With the vacuum hose of the pressure regulator disconnected (intake manifold side end of the hose plugged), the pressure should be, 35.6 psi on G200Z engines and 42.6 psi on the 4ZC1-T engine.

b. With the vacuum hose of the pressure regulator connected (and an idle speed of 900 rpm), the pressure should be, 28.4 psi on the G200Z engine and 35.6 On the 4ZC1-T engine.

c. Engine stopped and vacuum hose disconnected, the pressure should be 28.4 psi on the G200Z engine and 35.6 psi on the 4ZC1-T engine.

d. Battery voltage applied directly to the vacuum switching valve under condition B above. The pressure should be, 35.6 psi on the G200Z engine and 42.6 psi on the 4ZC1-T engine. If the fuel pressure remains unchanged through the check in Step D, replace the vacuum switching valve.

NOTE: The following method can be used to operate the fuel pump without running the engine. Operate the fuel pump by applying battery voltage directly to cable 2BR connected to the fuel pump relay within the relay box. The measurement as described in Step B, can not be obtained when this method of measurement is employed.

3. Remove the fuel pressure gauge and reconnect the fuel lines. Start the engine and check for fuel leaks.

4. If the fuel pressure was to low use the following procedure (be sure to check the fuel pressure with battery voltage applied directly to the fuel pump using suitable jumper wires:

a. If the fuel pressure does not reach normal level, check the fuel pump circuit and correct as necessary or the fuel pump relay may be defective.

b. If the fuel pressure remains unchanged, check for a restriction in the hose on the intake side of the fuel pump. The pressure regulator may be defective or the fuel pump is malfunctioning, replace parts as necessary.

5. If the fuel pressure is too high, the pressure regulator may be defective, replace as necessary. There could be a restriction if the fuel return circuit, clean or replace. The fuel pump may be defective, replace as necessary.

6. If the fuel pump pressure lowers immediately after the fuel pump stops, the fuel pump may be defective, replace as necessary. The pressure regulator may be defective, replace as necessary. The fuel injector is leaking , check or replace as necessary.

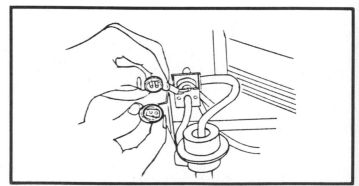

Disconnecting the vacuum switching valve harness at the connector

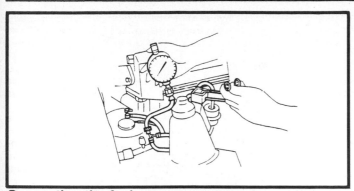

Connecting the fuel pressure gauge

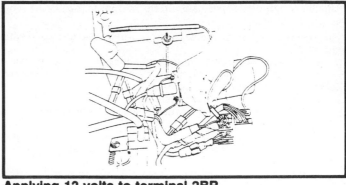

Applying 12 volts to terminal 2BR

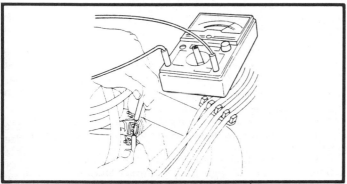

Measuring the fuel injector resistance

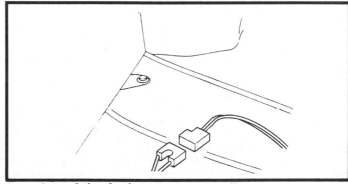

Location of the fuel pump connector

Fuel Injector Inspection

1. Disconnect the fuel injector harness at the connector. Using a suitable ohmmeter, measure the resistance across the terminals.

2. The standard resistance should be 2–3 ohms.

3. If the injector resistance deviates from the specified range, replace the injector.

4. With the engine running, check the fuel injector operating noise using a metal bar or stethoscope.

   a. Normal operation of the injector is indicated when a regular click is heard which varies with engine speed.

   b. If a regular click is not heard, the injector is malfunctioning and must be replaced.

5. Test for leakage as follows:

   a. Remove the common chamber assembly. Remove all the injectors with the fuel hoses still connected.

   b. Check for fuel leakage by operating the fuel pump with the battery voltage applied directly to the fuel pump relay terminal 2BR.

   c. The leakage should be less then 2 drop per minute.

   d. If the amount of leakage is beyond the set limit, replace the injector.

   e. Install the parts in the reverse order of the removal.

Dropping Resistor Inspection

1. Disconnect the wiring connector from the dropping resistor.

2. Using a suitable ohmmeter, measure the resistance across the center terminal of the dropping resistor side connectors and other terminals.

3. The standard resistance should be 5–7 ohms.

4. If the measured resistance deviates from the specified range, replace the dropping resistor assembly.

Air Regulator Fast Idle Inspection

The engine must be cold to perform this inspection.

1. The engine idling speed must be slightly higher than normal immediately after starting the engine.

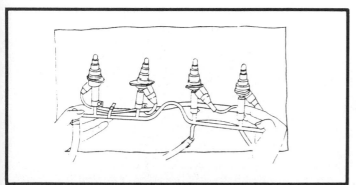

Checking for a fuel injector leak down

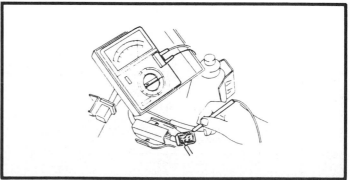

Measuring the reisistance at the dropping resistor

2. The engine idle speed should normalize as the engine temperature increases.

3. When fast idle speed is not obtained, use the following procedure:

    a. Disconnect the air regulator harness at the connector.

    b. Using a suitable ohmmeter, measure the resistance across the air regulator terminals.

    c. The standard resistance should be 38–42 ohms.

    d. If the measured resistance deviates from the specified range, replace the air regulator assembly.

4. Turn the ignition switch to the ON position and using a suitable voltmeter, check for voltage at the air regulator connectors.

    a. When voltage is present, check the wiring leading to the air regulator and correct as necessary. The fuel pump may be defective, replace as necessary.

    b. When voltage is present, the air regulator is defective and should be replaced.

Air Regulator Leakage Inspection

Check for leakage after allowing the engine to warm up throughly.

1. Disconnect the hose between the air regulator and throttle valve body at the throttle valve body side.

2. Close the hole in the throttle valve body. Start the engine.

3. Check for variation in the engine speed by closing and opening the end of the air regulator hose (this test is made to determine the function of the air regulator).

4. The variation of the engine speed should be less than 50 rpm. If the variation in engine speed is more than specified, replace the air regulator assembly.

Throttle Valve Switch & Throttle Position Sensor Inspection

1. Check that the operation of the accelerator pedal and control cable is smooth.

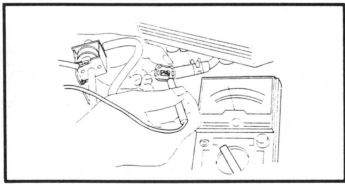

Measuring the air regulator resistance

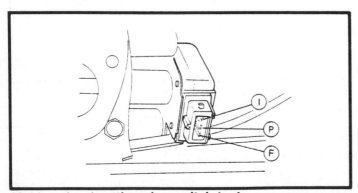

Making the throttle valve switch test

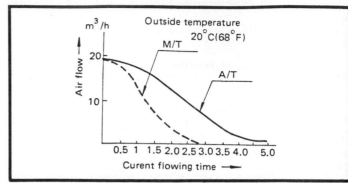

Air regulator fast idle air flow graph chart

2. Check that the valve stopper returns and makes a firm contact with the throttle valve stopper screw when the throttle valve is released.

NOTE: The throttle valve stopper screw is factory set and sealed with paint. Setting of the screw should not be disturbed unless absolutely necessary.

3. Test the throttle switch as follows:

    a. Disconnect the throttle valve switch harness connector.

    b. Using a suitable ohmmeter, make a continuity test across the terminals with the accelerator pedal depressed in the Steps.

    c. With the accelerator pedal NOT depressed, the resistance should be 0 ohms at idle contact and infinity ohms at full contact when testing terminals I and P.

    d. With the accelerator pedal slightly depressed, the resistance should be infinity ohms at idle contact and infinity ohms at full contact when testing terminals I,P and P,F.

    e. With the accelerator pedal fully depressed, the resistance should be infinity ohms at idle contact and 0 ohms at full contact when testing terminals P and P.

Throttle Switch Adjustment

1. Check that the throttle valve is completely closed. Loosen the throttle valve switch mounting screws slightly.

2. Using an ohmmeter and while checking the continuity across the terminals, turn the switch body in the clockwise direction until a continuity is obtained.

3. When a continuity is obtained, further turn the switch one degree in the clockwise direction and lock in that position.

NOTE: Turning of the switch body one degree is equivalent to approximately 0.6 mm of a stroke of the throttle valve stopper bolt.

Throttle Position Sensor Inspection

1. Turn the ignition switch to the ON position. Remove the water shield cover.

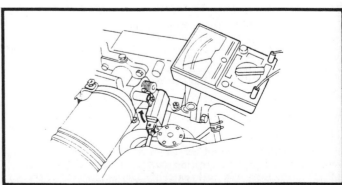

Making the throttle valve switch adjustment

2. Using a suitable voltmeter, place the positive probe into the white color wire harness.

3. Measure the voltage between the white color harness of the throttle position sensor.

NOTE: The throttle position sensor has three leads, red for 5 volt power source, white for output and black for ground.

4. The voltage should be higher then 4 volts at idle contact and lower than 2 volts at full contact.

NOTE: Make sure that 5 volts (± 0.5 volts) is measured at the red colored harness before making the voltage check in Step 4.

5. Confirm the difference in the voltage of the idle contact and full contact is 3.6 ± 1 volt.

6. If the throttle position sensor fails any part of this inspection, replace it with a new one.

Idle Speed Adjustment

1. Place the vehicle in Park or Neutral, block the drive wheels and apply the emergency brake.

2. Make sure the throttle valve is completely closed and the idle contact is on.

3. Turn off the air conditioner, if so equipped. Disconnect the harness of the pressure regulator vacuum switching valve.

4. Connect a tachometer. Start the engine and allow it to reach normal operating temperature. Check that the idle speed is within specifications.

5. If the idle speed is out of specification, adjust the idle speed by turning the idle speed adjusting screw. (900–950 rpm). Stop the engine.

6. After the adjustment connect the vacuum switching valve harness at the connector securely.

NOTE: Check and clean the idle port(s) as necessary as restriction in the port(s) will cause fluctuation in the idle speed.

Dashpot Adjustment

1. Set the engine speed to 2000 rpm with the throttle lever.

2. Tighten the adjusting screw until it just makes contact with the dash pot shaft head.

3. Lock the adjusting screw in position with the lock nut.

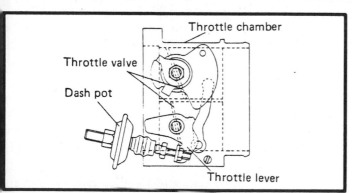

Making the dash pot adjustment

Fuel Cut Off System Inspection

G200Z ENGINE

1. Start the engine and let it run to reach normal operating temperature. Turn the ignition switch to the OFF position.

2. Disconnect the throttle valve switch harness at the connector, insert a fine wire into the idle terminal (upper), then make

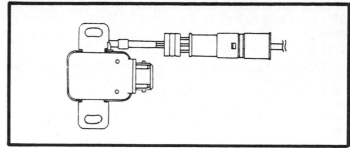

Testing the throttle position sensor

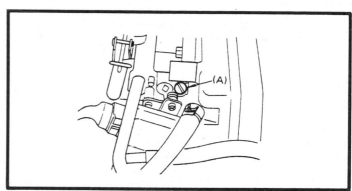

Location of the idle speed screw

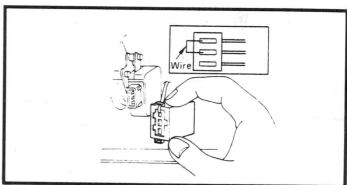

Placing the jumper wire into the throttle valve switch harness

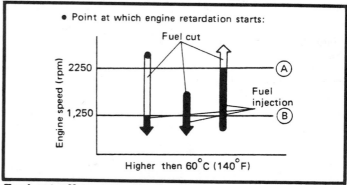

Fuel cut off system graph chart

the connections at the connector with the wire pulled part way out.

3. Start the engine and keep the engine running at 2500–3000 rpm. Check to make sure the engine speed drops to approximately 1250 rpm when battery voltage is applied to the wire extending from the idle terminal.

NOTE: An engine shake may occur at the speed of 1250 rpm or so, but it does not indicate abnormal conditions.

4ZC1-T ENGINE

1. Start the engine and let it run to reach normal operating temperature. Turn the ignition switch to the OFF position.

2. Disconnect the throttle valve switch harness at the connector, insert a fine wire into the idle terminal (upper), then make the connections at the connector with the wire pulled part way out.

3. Disconnect the throttle position sensor at the connector. Use a suitable jumper wire to connect the harness side connector terminals.

NOTE: Do not connect the harness side connector and throttle position sensor with the piece of wire in place. Shorting will result.

4. Start the engine and keep the engine running at 2500–3000 rpm. Check to make sure the engine speed drops to approximately 1250 rpm when battery voltage is applied to the wire extending from the idle terminal.

NOTE: Engine hunting may occur at the speed of 1250 rpm or so, but it does not indicate abnormal conditions.

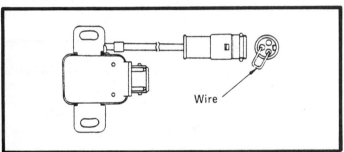

Placing the jumper wire into the throttle position sensor

SELF-DIAGNOSIS SYSTEM

The self-diagnosis system is so designed that the circuits handling the input signals from the sensors and output signals for the driving actuator are continuously monitored by the control unit. In the event of a failure, the control unit stores it in memory and operates the check engine light on the instrument panel when the nature of trouble is important, to warn the operator of failure.

NOTE: The self-diagnosis system is capable of troubleshooting the electrical circuits in the I-TEC system only and does not cover the trouble in the sensors, actuators or the engine itself.

When a failure has developed in the following systems while driving, the check engine light within the instrument panel is operated to warn the driver of a system failure.
1. Air Flow Sensor System.
2. Coolant Temperature Sensor.
3. Fuel Injection System.
4. Knock Sensor System.
5. Micro Computer.
6. Oxygen Sensor.
7. Vehicle Speed Sensor.

Code Number Display

When the diagnosis lean (usually located near the control unit) is connected to the ignition switch in the On position, the trouble code stored in memory is displayed in the check engine light.

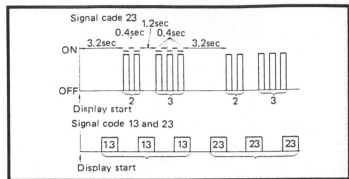

Trouble code display signals

A maximum of three kinds of trouble codes are storable in memory and will be displayed in numerical sequence regardless of sequence in which troubles had occur.

The display of a trouble code is switched to another after repeated display of the same code three times and this action will be repeated as long as the diagnosis lead is connected to the ignition switch in the ON position.

Clearing The Memory

After completion of the service operation, clear the trouble codes stored in memory by disconnecting the number four fuse (ECM) in the fuse junction block, then check that only code 12 is displayed.

NOTE: All the codes stored in memory will be cleared automatically when the 13-pole connector in the control unit is disconnected. Since all the memory will be cleared when number four fuse is disconnected, it will be necessary to reset the clock and other electrical equipment.

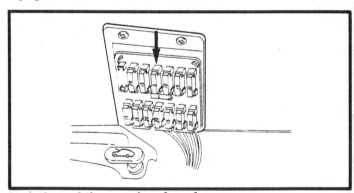

Location of the number four fuse

Tools Needed For Inspection

1. Ohmmeter.
2. Voltmeter.
3. Test Light.
4. 1.5V Dry Cell Battery.
5. A3 Meter Conductor Wire Fitted At Ends With Pin And Alligator Clip.
6. 4 Jumper Wire(s).

How To Read The Code Number On The Control Unit Harness Connector Terminals

The control unit harnesses are connected with three types of connectors each of which has specific numbers. In the following, inspection procedures will be described with reference to the specific numbers.

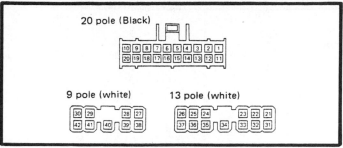

Control unit harness connectors terminal identification

NOTE: When checking the system, note the numbers carefully to avoid the wrong connection since battery power is applied to some terminals only when the ignition switch is in the ON position.

Inspection Procedure

The inspection based on the monitor codes should be performed in the following steps:

1. When trouble is not found through checks in Steps 1 and 2, proceed as follows:

    a. Clear the memory.

    b. Reconnect the circuit properly.

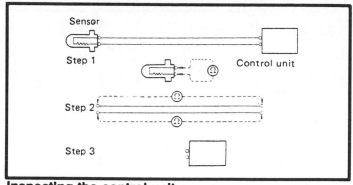

Inspecting the control unit

    c. Road test the vehicle.

    d. Obtain the code display to see if the trouble has been corrected.

    e. If the trouble persists, replace the control unit.

2. When making a continuity test or a short out test on the circuit, disconnect the wiring at the control unit, sensor or actuator.

3. When checking the control unit harness connector terminals, make the connection by inserting the pin at the end of the lead. Avoid connecting the tester probe directly to the control unit terminal.

I-TEC DIAGNOSTIC CODES AND TROUBLESHOOTING CHART 1984-88 IMPULSE

DIAGNOSED ITEM	DIAGNOSED CONTENT FAULT MODE	DIAGNOSED CONTENT MICRO-COMPUTER INPUT	CODE NO.	CODE MEMORY	FAIL-SAFE FUNCTION OF MICRO-COMPUTER	ENGINE CONDITION	VEHICLE CONDITION
Engine is not started		Engine speed less than 200 rpm	12	No	None	Normal	Normal
O₂ sensor system	Harness open, Sensor deterioration	Intermediate voltage	13	Yes	Fuel is not compensated by O₂ signal	Exhaust is worsened	No noticeable abnormal operation
	Incorrect signal (Lean)	Lean signal (Low voltage)	44	Yes			
	Incorrect signal (Rich)	Rich signal (High voltage)	45	Yes			
Water temperature sensor system	Shorted with ground	Insufficient signal	14	Yes	Coolant temperature is assumed to be 85°C (185°F)	• The engine does not operate normally when temperature is low and signal is insufficient, or when temperature is high and signal is excessive. Or the engine cannot be started. • The engine does not operate smoothly when temperature is low after the fail-safe function is actuated	
	Incorrect signal	Signal is less than 0°C (32°F) even after the engine is warmed up sufficiently	15	Yes			
	Harness open	Excessive signal	16	Yes			
Throttle valve switch system	Both idle contact and full contact	Both idle contact and full make contact simultaneously	Both contacts make simultaneously	21	Yes	Both signals are assumed to be OFF.	Fuel is not cut after the fail-safe function is actuated, and lean fuel is resulted when the throttle valve is fully opened	Fuel consumption rate is worsened after the fail-safe function is actuated. Fuel tends to be lean when the throttle valve is fully opened.
	Idle contact	Normally make contact	Signal is sent continuously (Not diagnosed when the air flow sensor system is defective)	43	Yes	Assumed to be OFF.	• Fuel cut range appears during running. • Fuel is not cut after the fail-safe function is actuated.	• The vehicle does not run smoothly. • Fuel consumption rate is worsened after the fail-safe function is actuated.
	Full contact	Normally make contact	Signal is sent continuously	65	Yes	Assumed to be OFF.	• Air-fuel ratio is high when partially loaded • Fuel tends to be lean when the throttle valve is fully opened after the fail-safe function is actuated.	• Fuel consumption rate and exhaust are worsened. The spark plugs are carboned or the engine stalls depending on the condition. • Fuel tends to be lean when the throttle valve is fully opened after the fail-safe function is actuated.

I-TEC DIAGNOSTIC CODES AND TROUBLESHOOTING CHART
1984-88 IMPULSE

DIAGNOSED ITEM	DIAGNOSED CONTENT — FAULT MODE	DIAGNOSED CONTENT — MICRO-COMPUTER INPUT	CODE NO.	CODE MEMORY	FAIL-SAFE FUNCTION OF MICRO-COMPUTER	ENGINE CONDITION	VEHICLE CONDITION
Starter signal system	Normally open	Signal is not input	22	Yes	None	Normal	No abnormality is felt
Crank angle sensor system	· No signal arrives. · Faulty signal.	· No angle sensor signal is input. · Idling speed is lower than the actual speed.	41	Yes	None	· The engine stalls. The engine cannot be started. · Air-fuel ratio tends to be high.	· Stalls or cannot be started · Both fuel consumption rate and exhaust are worsened.
Air flow sensor system	Harness open, shorting with ground, or broken hot wire.	Insufficient signal	61	Yes	Injection pulse is changed over at throttle valve position.	· The engine stalls depending on the condition. · The engine may be slightly unstable after the fail-safe function is actuated.	· The engine stalls depending on the condition. · The accelerator response is worsened after the fail-safe function is actuated. The engine may not operate smoothly.
	Broken cold wire	Excessive signal	62	Yes			
Car speed sensor system	No signal arrives	No signal is input (Not diagnosed when the air flow sensor system is defective)	63	Yes	None	The fuel cut operates even when running under a low speed.	Does not run smoothly and shakes.
Knocking sensor system	Harness open or shorting with ground.	Excessive or insufficient signal	66	Yes	Ignition timing is delayed.	· Engine knocking. · Output drops after the fail-safe function is actuated.	· Engine knocking. · Output drops after the fail-safe function is actuated.
Micro-computer unit	Abnormal LSI (1)	—	51	Yes		· In the worst case, the engine stalls, or the engine does not operate smoothly at a certain time. · The engine does not stall but it does not satisfy the specification	· In the worst case, the engine stalls, or the engine does not operate smoothly at a certain time. · The exhaust and running performance deviate from the specification.
	Abnormal LSI (2)	—	52	Yes	· Injection pulse is changed over at throttle valve position. · Fixed ignition timing.		
	Abnormal LSI (3)	—	55	Yes			

I-TEC DIAGNOSTIC CODES AND TROUBLESHOOTING CHART 1984-88 IMPULSE

DIAGNOSED ITEM	DIAGNOSED CONTENT — FAULT MODE	DIAGNOSED CONTENT — MICRO-COMPUTER INPUT	CODE NO.	CODE MEMORY	FAIL-SAFE FUNCTION OF MICRO-COMPUTER	ENGINE CONDITION	VEHICLE CONDITION
Power transistor system for ignition	Output terminal shorted with ground.	—	23	Yes	None	· The engine stalls. · Cannot be started.	· The engine stalls. · Cannot be started.
	Harness open	—	35	Yes			
	Defective transistor or grounding system	—	54	Yes			
Vacuum switching valve system	Output terminal shorted with ground or harness open	—	25	Yes	None	Output terminal shorted with ground. · Fuel pressure rises continuously when the engine is cold, causing fuel to be rich. · When the engine is warmed up, automatically corrected as the O_2 sensor compensates	Output terminal shorted with ground. · Fuel consumption rate and exhaust gas level are worsened when the engine is cold or when accelerated rapidly.
	Defective transistor or grounding system	—	53	Yes	None	Same as below for harness open.	Same as below for harness open.
Fuel injector system.	Output terminal shorted with ground or harness open	—	33	Yes	None	When the engine is over-heated, air-fuel ratio tends to be lean. No problem when the engine is warmed up normally.	The engine cannot be restarted smoothly when coolant temperature is high.
	Defective transistor or grounding system.	—	64	Yes	None	· The engine stalls. · Cannot be started.	· The engine stalls. · Cannot be started.
Throttle position sensor system TURBO CONTROL SYSTEM	Abnormal signal	Insufficient signal	71	Yes	None	The engine stalls depending on the condition	The engine stalls depending on the condition
EGR vacuum switching valve system	Output terminal shorted with ground or harness open	—	72	Yes	None	Exhaust is worsened	No noticeable abnormal operation
	Defective transistor or grounding system	—	73				

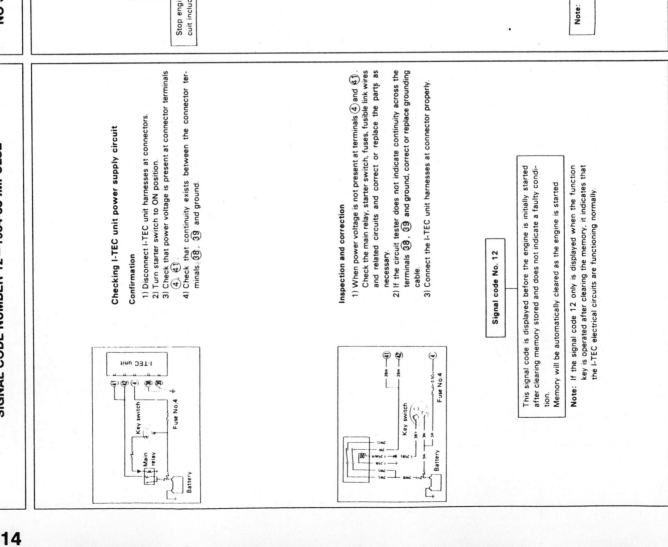

SIGNAL CODES NUMBER 13, 44 and 45 NO SIGNALS OR ABNORMAL SIGNAL FROM THE OXYGEN SENSOR 1984-88 IMPULSE

Code No.13

Start engine. 2 minutes after start (also after engine is completely warmed up), operate for one minute longer.

Is Code 13 displayed?

No / Yes

Stop engine. Inspect circuit including connector.

Replace O₂ sensor.

END

Stop engine.

Inspect circuit including connector for I-TEC unit and O₂ sensor.

Replace I-TEC unit.

OK?

No → Replace or adjust.

Yes → Disconnect O₂ sensor connector. Instead, add a charge of 1-1.5 volts.

Note: Trouble shooting procedure
Â : 1st step B̂ : 2nd step Ĉ : 3rd step

SIGNAL CODE NUMBER 12 – 1984-88 IMPULSE

Checking I-TEC unit power supply circuit

Confirmation

1) Disconnect I-TEC unit harnesses at connectors.
2) Turn starter switch to ON position.
3) Check that power voltage is present at connector terminals ④ ④.
4) Check that continuity exists between the connector terminals ㊳, ㊴ and ground.

Inspection and correction

1) When power voltage is not present at terminals ④ and ④. Check the main relay, starter switch, fuses, fusible link wires and related circuits and correct or replace the parts as necessary.
2) If the circuit tester does not indicate continuity across the terminals ㊳, ㊴ and ground, correct or replace grounding cable.
3) Connect the I-TEC unit harnesses at connector properly.

Signal code No. 12

This signal code is displayed before the engine is initially started after clearing memory stored and does not indicate a faulty condition.
Memory will be automatically cleared as the engine is started

Note: If the signal code 12 only is displayed when the function key is operated after clearing the memory, it indicates that the I-TEC electrical circuits are functioning normally.

INSPECTION FOR SIGNAL CODES NUMBER 13, 44 and 45 1984-88 IMPULSE

Inspection for signal code No. 13, 44 and 45

Inspection and correction

1) Check that continuity exists between the control unit harness connector terminal 30 and O_2 sensor harness connector terminal.

2) If the tester does not indicate continuity, correct or replace the harness assembly.

3) If the harness and connections are found to be normal, repeat the test with a new O_2 sensor installed, road test the vehicle and see if the same trouble coce is displayed.

Inspection of O_2 sensor

The output voltage of the O_2 sensor can be checked with a voltmeter having a minimum input resistance of one megohm.

1) Disconnect the O_2 sensor from the vehicle harness.

2) Insert a jumper with exposed wire between the sensor and vehicle harness connectors.

3) Set the voltmeter to the approximately two volt range.

4) Connect the positive (+) lead of the voltmeter to the jumper and the negative (−) lead to vehicle ground.

5) Start the engine and run at elevated speed until the emission system has gone "closed loop". The meter should move between approximately 0.50 and 0.80 volts.

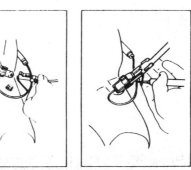

SIGNAL CODES NUMBER 44 AND 45 — 1984-88 IMPULSE

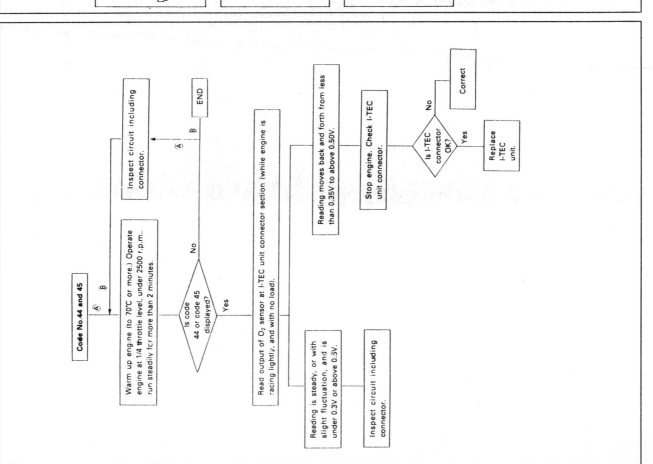

Code No. 44 and 45

Warm up engine (to 70°C or more.) Operate engine at 1/4 throttle level, under 2500 r.p.m... run steadily for more than 2 minutes.

Is code 44 or code 45 displayed?

Inspect circuit including connector.

END

Read output of O_2 sensor at I-TEC unit connector section (while engine is racing lightly, and with no load).

Reading is steady, or with slight fluctuation, and is under 0.3V or above 0.5V.

Inspect circuit including connector.

Reading moves back and forth from less than 0.35V to above 0.50V.

Stop engine. Check I-TEC unit connector.

Is I-TEC connector OK?

Correct

Replace I-TEC unit.

SIGNAL CODES NUMBER 15 AND 16 — 1984-88 IMPULSE

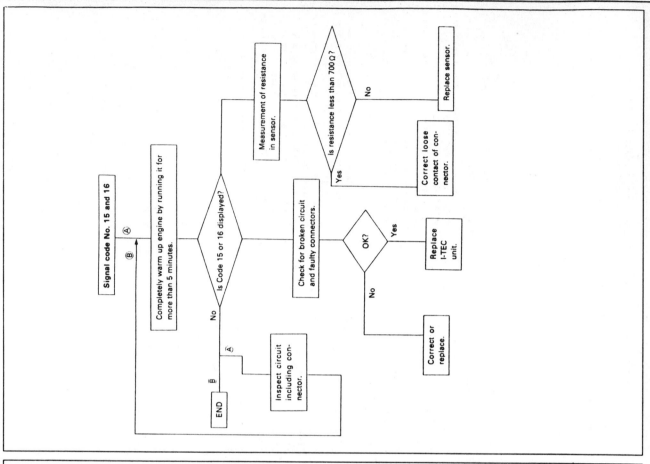

SIGNAL CODE NUMBER 14 — 1984-88 IMPULSE

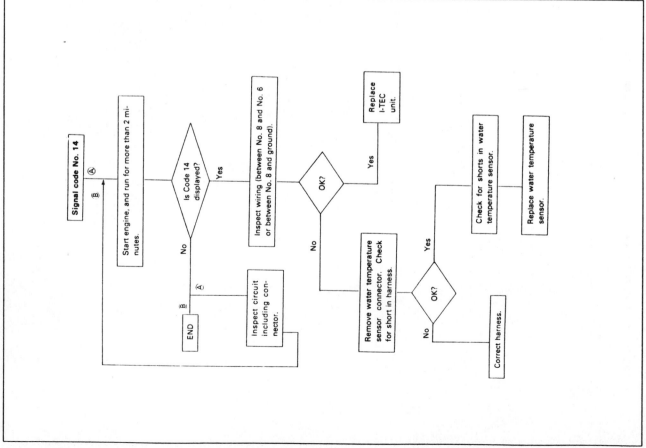

SIGNAL CODE NUMBER 21 — 1984-88 IMPULSE

Signal code No. 21

Ⓐ
Ⓑ

Start engine and idle it for 5 seconds, then run engine for 5 more seconds of continuous wide open throttle running.

Is Code 21 displayed?

— No → Ⓐ Ⓑ → Inspect circuit including connector. → END

— Yes → Inspect throttle switch and circuit. → OK?

— Yes → Replace I-TEC unit.

— No → Correct or replace

INSPECTION FOR SIGNAL CODES NUMBER 14, 15 and 16 1984-88 IMPULSE

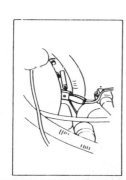

Inspection for signal code No. 14, 15 and 16

Measurement of resistance in sensor

Disconnect sensor harnesses at connector and measure the resistance across the sensor terminals.

Note: Although the resistance varies with the engine coolant temperature, normal condition is indicated when measured resistance falls within the range shown in the following table:

Coolant temperatue °C (°F)	Normal resistance KΩ
−10 (14)	7 — 12
10 (50)	3 — 5
20 (68)	2 — 3
50 (122)	0.7 — 1
80 (176)	0.2 — 0.4

If measured resistance deviates from the specified range, replace water temperature sensor.

Wiring

Signal code No.	Wiring		Ω
14	⑧ — B		∞
	⑧ — Ground		∞
	⑧ — GY		0
15, 16	⑥ — B		0
	⑥ — Ground		∞

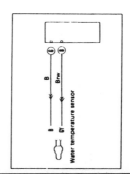

Water temperature sensor

When abnormal condition is indicated, correct or replace applicable harnesses.

THROTTLE SWITCH INSPECTION—1984-88 IMPULSE

Throttle switch

Refer to "Throttle switch" for throttle valve inspection procedure.

Accelerator pedal position	Idle contact	Full contact	Termianl No.
Not depressed	0 Ω	∞ Ω	① and ℗
Slightly depressed	∞ Ω	∞ Ω	①, ℗ and, ℗, ℉
Fully depressed	∞ Ω	0 Ω	℗ and ℉

Note: Trouble-shooting will not be performed for troubles indicated by the signal code No. 43 and 65 when air flow sensor circuit is malfunctioning.

Circuits

When throttle switch is functioning properly.

Signal code No.	Wiring		Ω
21, 43	② — LR		∞
21, 65	⑬ — LR		∞

When circuit is found to be at fault, correct or replace applicable harness assembly.

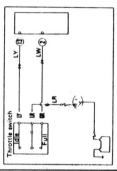

SIGNAL CODES NUMBER 43 AND 65—1984-88 IMPULSE

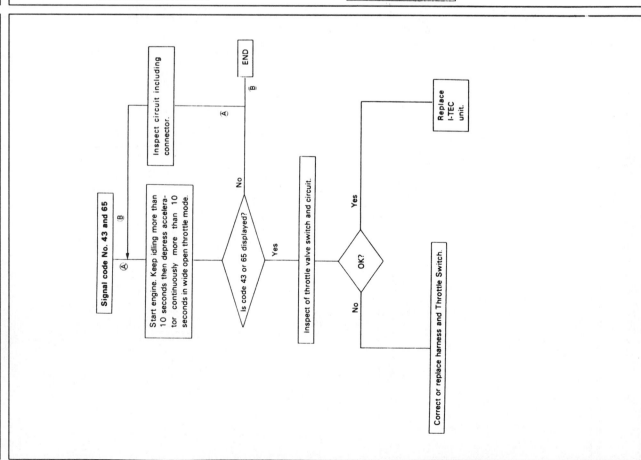

Signal code No. 43 and 65

Ⓑ

Ⓐ

Start engine. Keep idling more than 10 seconds then depress accelerator or continuously more than 10 seconds in wide open throttle mode.

Is code 43 or 65 displayed?

No → Inspect circuit including connector.

Ⓐ

Ⓑ → END

Yes → Inspect of throttle valve switch and circuit.

OK?

No → Correct or replace harness and Throttle Switch.

Yes → Replace I-TEC unit.

SIGNAL CODE NUMBER 41 – 1984-88 IMPULSE

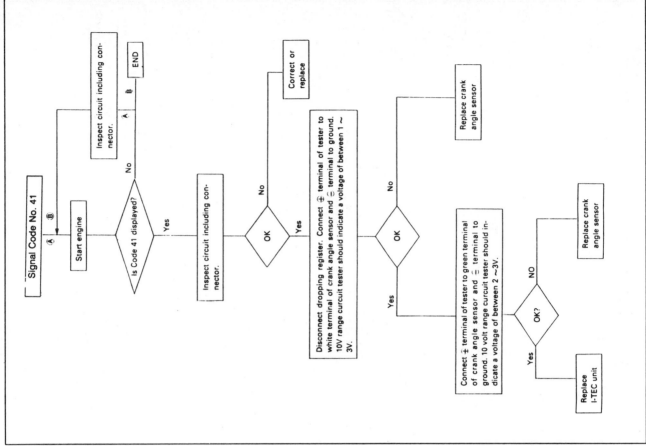

SIGNAL CODE NUMBER 22 – 1984-88 IMPULSE

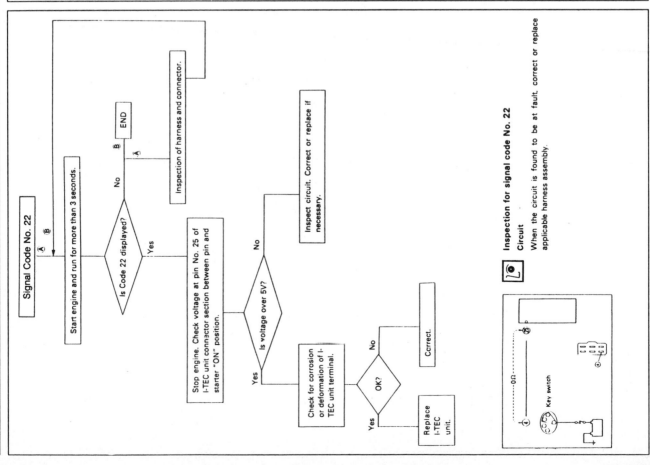

Inspection for signal code No. 22 Circuit

When the circuit is found to be at fault, correct or replace applicable harness assembly.

SIGNAL CODES NUMBER 61 AND 62 — 1984-88 IMPULSE

Signal code No. 61 and 62

Start engine and idle for several seconds.

Is Code 61 or 62 displayed?

- No → Stop engine. Inspect circuit including connector. → END

- Yes → Start engine and idle it. Check terminal voltage of Air flow sensor connector of Engine Harness: Body side, after sliding water-proof connector cap partially off, with ⊕ Rod of DC 50V range tester at red terminal and ⊝ Rod at black terminal, it should read 8V or more.

OK?

- No → Inspect circuit including connector. → OK?
  - Yes → Replace I-TEC unit.
  - No → Repair or replace.

- Yes → While engine is idling, check voltage, with DC5V range tester setting, with ⊕ tester at white terminal and with ⊝ at black terminal.

Is indicator below 0.3V or above 5V?

- Yes → Inspect circuit including connector. → OK?
  - Yes → Replace air flow sensor.
  - No → Repair or replace.

- No →

INSPECTION FOR SIGNAL CODES NUMBER 22 AND 41 1984-88 IMPULSE

Inspection for signal code No. 22 and 41

Circuit

1) Remove the relay box cover.
2) Disconnect crank angle sensor harnesses at connector.
3) Disconnect 20 pole and 9 pole connectors at I-TEC unit.
4) Turn ignition on.

Wiring	Ω	V
⑫ —— W	0	—
① —— G	0	—
R —— Ground	—	10—14
B —— Ground	0	—

5) Measure resistances and voltage shown in chart above. When circuit is found to be at fault, correct or replace applicable harness assembly.
6) Install the relay box cover and connect harness at connector securely.

When circuit is found to be in normal condition, replace distributor assembly.

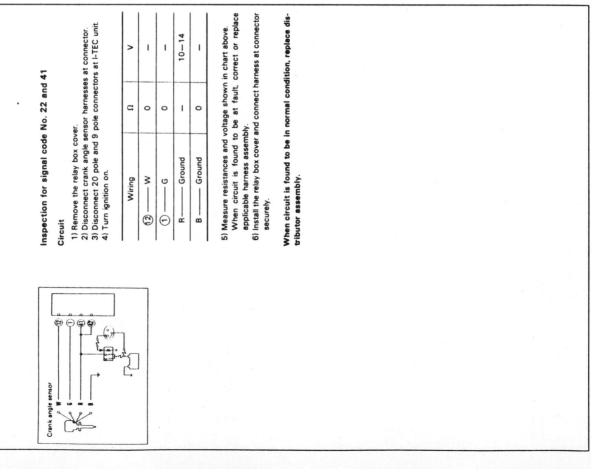

Crank angle sensor

SIGNAL CODE NUMBER 63 – 1984-88 IMPULSE

Signal code No. 63

Start engine, running for more than 3 minutes under 1/2 throttle.

Is Code 63 displayed?

- No → Inspect circuit including connector. → Ⓐ → END Ⓑ
- Yes → Inspect sensor and equipment. → OK?
  - Yes → Replace I-TEC unit.
  - No → Inspect circuit including connector. → OK?
    - Yes → Inspect car speed sensor. Replace sensor if necessary.
    - No → Correct or replace.

INSPECTION FOR SIGNAL CODES NUMBER 61 AND 62 1984-88 IMPULSE

Inspection for signal code No. 61 and 62

Removal of air flow sensor

1) Remove bolts attaching air flow sensor.
2) Loosen the clamp bolt and remove air flow sensor from the air cleaner.

Inspection of air flow sensor

Partly raise the sealing gasket on the air flow sensor side of the harness connector.

Wiring	Ignition switch	Condition	V	Ω
A. Red-Ground	ON	—	10—14	—
B. White-Ground	ON	—	0.2—0.6(IG200Z) Less than 0.2(4ZC1)	—
	ON	When breathing	1.0—2.0(IG200Z) 0.5—1.5(4ZC1)	—
C. Black-Ground	—	—	—	0

When A. and C. are abnormal, check circuit and correct as necessary.
When A. and C. are normal but B. is abnormal, replace air flow sensor.

Installation of air flow sensor

Install the air flow sensor assembly in the reverse order of removal.

Circuits

Wiring	Ω
W —⑦—	0
W —Ground	∞
R —㉑—	0
R —Ground	∞
B —⑯—	0

When circuit is found to be at fault, correct or replace applicable harness assembly.

Note: If the air flow sensor has been removed, check by-pass circuit (A) for contamination and clean with carburetor cleaner as necessary.

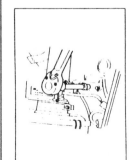

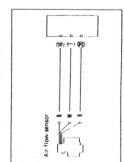
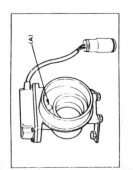

Air flow sensor

SIGNAL CODE NUMBER 66 — 1984-88 IMPULSE

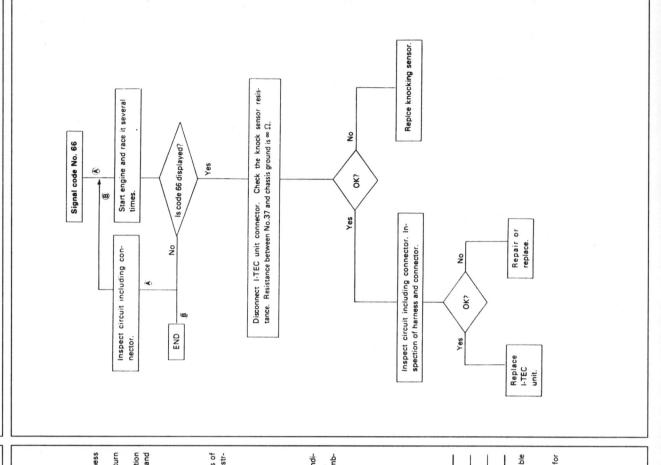

Signal code No. 66

Ⓐ

Start engine and race it several times.

Ⓑ

Is code 66 displayed? — No → Inspect circuit including connector. → Ⓐ / END Ⓑ

Yes ↓

Disconnect I-TEC unit connector. Check the knock sensor resistance. Resistance between No.37 and chassis ground is ∞ Ω.

OK? — No → Replce knocking sensor.

Yes ↓

Inspect circuit including connector. Inspection of harness and connector.

OK? — No → Repair or replace.

Yes → Replace I-TEC unit.

INSPECTION FOR SIGNAL CODES NUMBER 63 — 1984-88 IMPULSE

Inspection for signal code No. 63

Sensor and equipment

1) Connect a circuit tester between the control unit harness connector terminal ⑤ and ground.

2) Disconnect speedometer cable at transmission end and turn the inner cable slowly.

3) If the tester indicates continuity and open circuit condition alternately as the cable is turned. the car speed sensor and circuit are operating normally.

Car speed sensor

1) Remove the meter assembly

2) Connect the leads of a circuit tester across the terminals of the connector at rear face of the meter assembly as illustrated.

3) Turn the inner shaft slowly and check that the tester indicates a continuity and open circuit condition alternately. If speedometer is inoperative, replace speedometer assembly.

Circuits

Wiring		Ω
Y —— ⑤		O
Y —— Ground		∞

When circuit is found to be at fault, correct or replace applicable harness assembly.

2) Install the speedometer assembly. Refer to "Meters" in Section "Chassis electrical" for installation procedure.

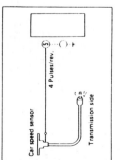

Car speed sensor
4 Pulses/rev.
Transmission side

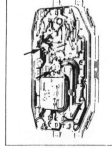

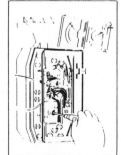

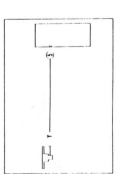

INSPECTION FOR SIGNAL CODE NUMBER 66—1984-88 IMPULSE

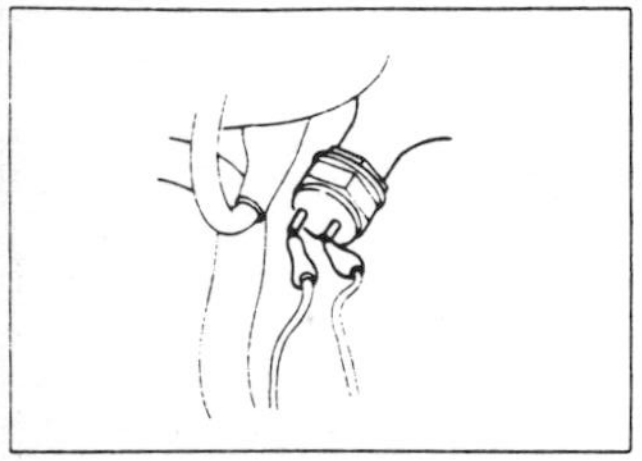

Inspection for signal code No. 66

Measurement of resistance

1) Disconnect knocking sensor harnesses at connector.
2) Measure the resistance across the terminals of the knocking sensor.

Standard resistance (Ω)	More than 1M Ω

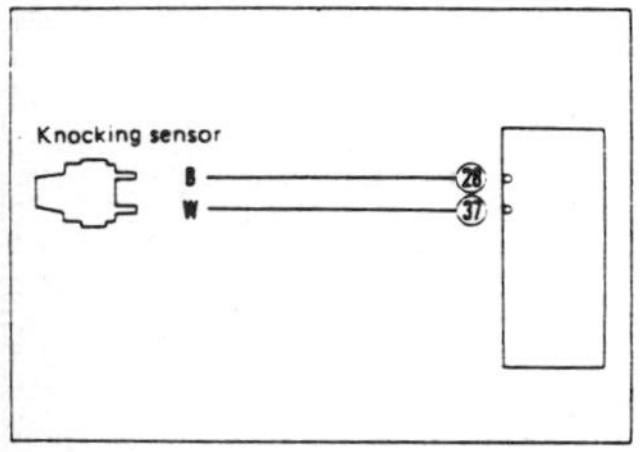
Knocking sensor
B
W
28
37

Circuits

Wiring	Ω
37 — W	0
37 — Ground	∞
28 — B	0

When circuit is found to be at fault, correct or replace applicable harness assembly.

Note: Replace the knocking sensor if the ignition timing is correct but the engine produces serious knocking.
If the trouble persists, replace the control unit.

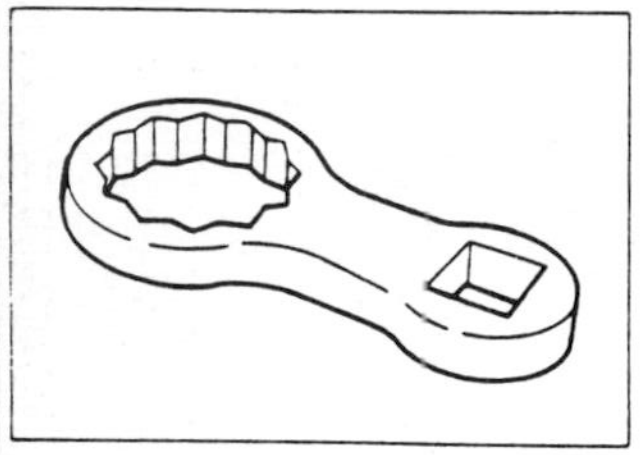

Knocking sensor installation procedure

When installing, tighten the knocking sensor to specification carefully.

Tightening torque kg·m(ft.lbs.)	2—3 (14.5—21.7)

Wrench:
Knocking sensor : J-22898-A

SIGNAL CODES NUMBER 51, 52 AND 55—1984-88 IMPULSE

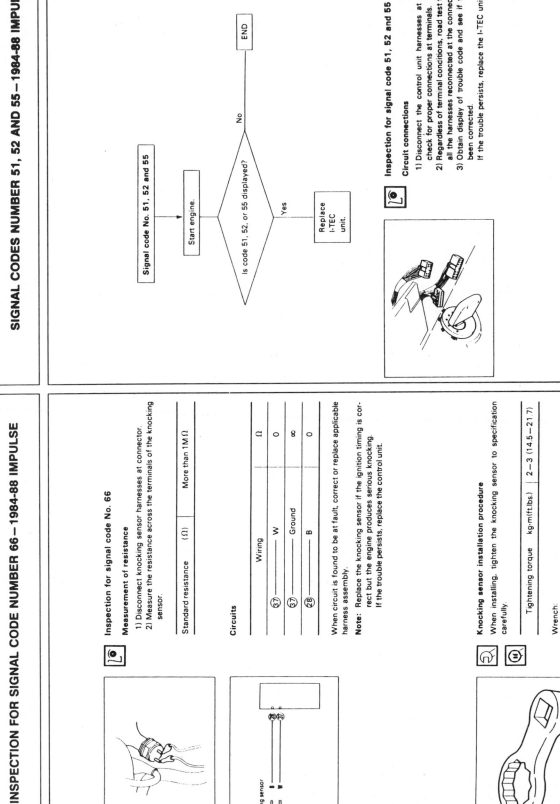

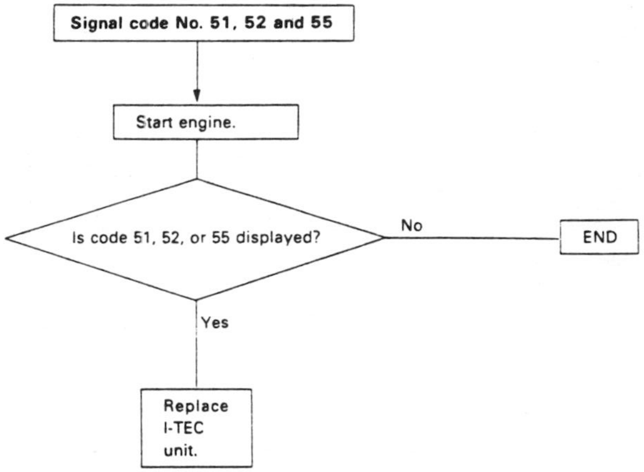
Signal code No. 51, 52 and 55
Start engine.
Is code 51, 52, or 55 displayed?
No
END
Yes
Replace I-TEC unit.

Inspection for signal code 51, 52 and 55

Circuit connections

1) Disconnect the control unit harnesses at connector and check for proper connections at terminals.
2) Regardless of terminal conditions, road test the vehicle with all the harnesses reconnected at the connector.
3) Obtain display of trouble code and see if the trouble has been corrected.
If the trouble persists, replace the I-TEC unit.

INSPECTING THE POWER TRANSISTOR – 1984-88 IMPULSE

Power transistors

1) Disconnect power transistor harnesses at connector.
2) Disconnect high-tension cable between the ignition coil and distributor at distributor sice.
3) Hold end of disconnected high-tension cable 5 to 6 mm (0.2 to 0.24 in.) apart from metal parts.

Note: To prevent electrical shock, hold the cable via an effective insulation.

4) Turn starter switch to ON position.
6) Connect positive side (+) of a 1.5V dry battery to Y terminal of the power transistor and negative side (–) to ground.
7) Disconnect dry battery lead and check that a spark jumps across the gap between end of the high-tension cable and ground.

Repeat the test several times.

Spark does not occur, replace power transistor together with bracket.

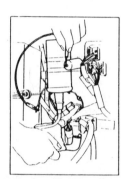

Circuits

If the power transistor is found to be normal, check wiring by refering to the illustration and wiring diagram.

Signal code No.	Wiring		Ω
23	24 —— Ground		∞
35	24 —— L		0
54	23 —— Ground		0

Ignition coil

If any abnormal condition was found, correct or replace faulty parts.

SIGNAL CODES NUMBER 23, 35 AND 54 – 1984-88 IMPULSE

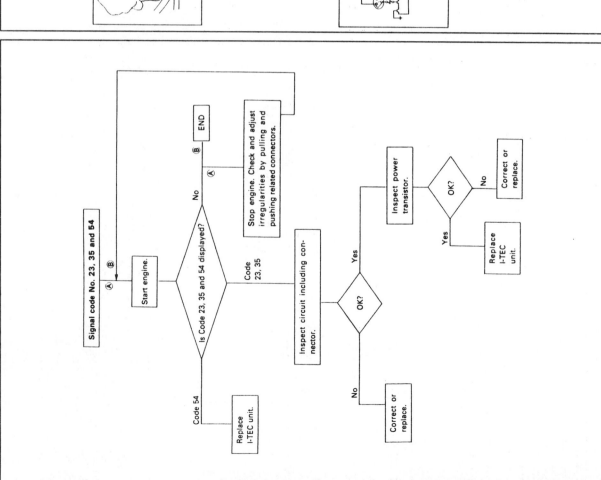

Signal code No. 23, 35 and 54

Ⓐ Ⓑ → Start engine.

Is Code 23, 35 and 54 displayed?

No → Ⓐ → Stop engine. Check and adjust irregularities by pulling and pushing related connectors. → Ⓑ → END

Code 23, 35 → Inspect circuit including connector. → OK?
  No → Correct or replace.
  Yes → Inspect power transistor. → OK?
    Yes → Replace I-TEC unit.
    No → Correct or replace.

Code 54 → Replace I-TEC unit.

INSPECTION FOR SIGNAL CODES NUMBER 25 AND 53 984-88 IMPULSE

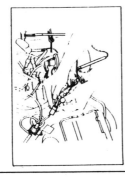

Inspection for signal code No. 25 and 53

Checking operation of vacuum switching valve

1) Check operation of vacuum switching valve by applying battery voltage directly to the vacuum switching valve.
Replace vacuum switching valve if found to be defective.

Note:

Standard resistance in vacuum switching valve	(Ω)	Approx. 35

Circuits

Signal code No.	Wiring	Ω	V
25	Bw —— Ground	—	12
	LgY —— ⑮	0	—
53	㉓ —— Ground	0	—

If any abnormal condition was found, correct or replace applicable harness assembly.

Note: Normal operation of the entire vacuum switching valve system including control unit is indicated if the vacuum switching valve operates properly when the starter switch is turned to ON position with the engine stationary and with the diagnosis lead connected.

Vacuum switching valve

SIGNAL CODES NUMBER 25 AND 53 — 1984-88 IMPULSE

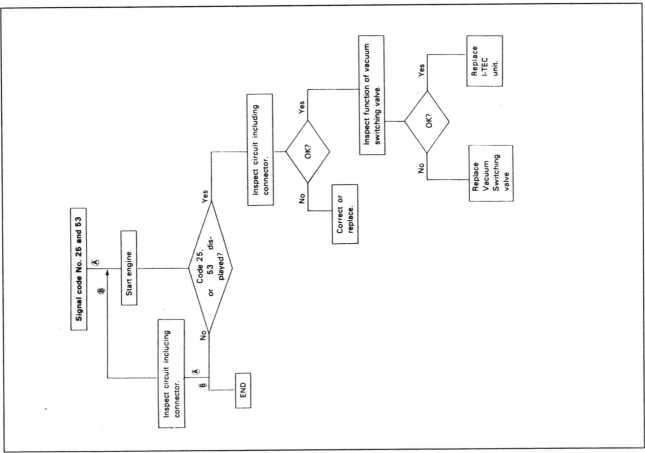

INSPECTION FOR SIGNAL CODE NUMBER 33 — 1984-88 IMPULSE

Voltage in fuel injector circuit

1) Turn the starter switch to ON position and see if the battery voltage is being applied to the terminals 21 and 22 of the control unit harness connector.

2) If the battery voltage is not present, disconnect the fuel injector harnesses at connector and check that voltage is present at either terminals of the connectors. If voltage is not present, correct or replace dropping resistor, main relay or starter switch assembly.

Circuits

When voltage is being applied to circuit leading to fuel injector.

Wiring		Ω
21 —	A B	0
21 —	Ground	∞
22 —	C D	0
22 —	Ground	∞

If any abnormal condition was found, correct or replace faulty parts.

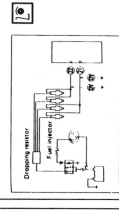

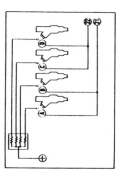

Dropping resistor — Fuel injector

SIGNAL CODE NUMBER 33 — 1984-88 IMPULSE

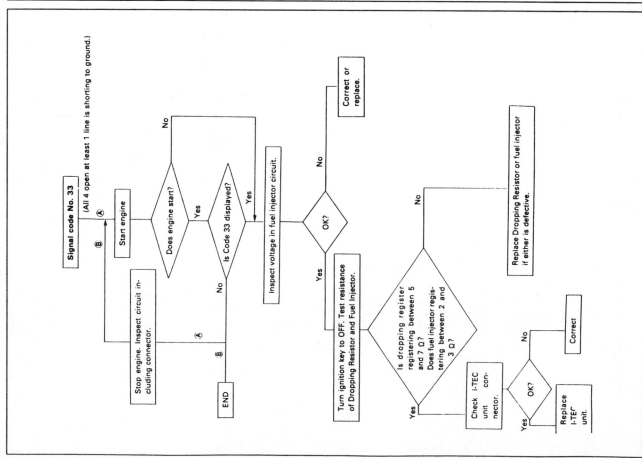

Signal code No. 33
(All 4 open at least 1 line is shorting to ground.)

- A
- B → Start engine → Does engine start?
  - No → Stop engine. Inspect circuit including connector. → A
  - Yes → Is Code 33 displayed?
    - No → END (B)
    - Yes → Inspect voltage in fuel injector circuit. → OK?
      - No → Correct or replace.
      - Yes → Turn ignition key to OFF. Test resistance of Dropping Resistor and Fuel Injector. → Is dropping register registering between 5 and 7 Ω? Does fuel injector registering between 2 and 3 Ω?
        - No → Replace Dropping Resistor or fuel injector if either is defective.
        - Yes → Check I-TEC unit connector. → OK?
          - No → Correct
          - Yes → Replace I-TEC unit.

SIGNAL CODE NUMBER 71 – 1984-88 IMPULSE

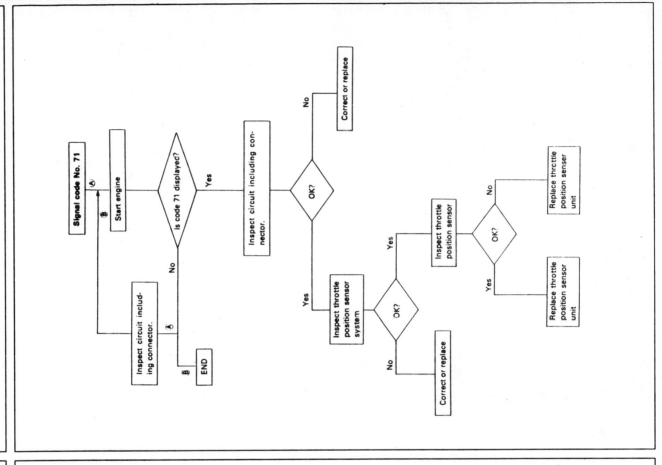

SIGNAL CODE NUMBER 64 – 1984-88 IMPULSE

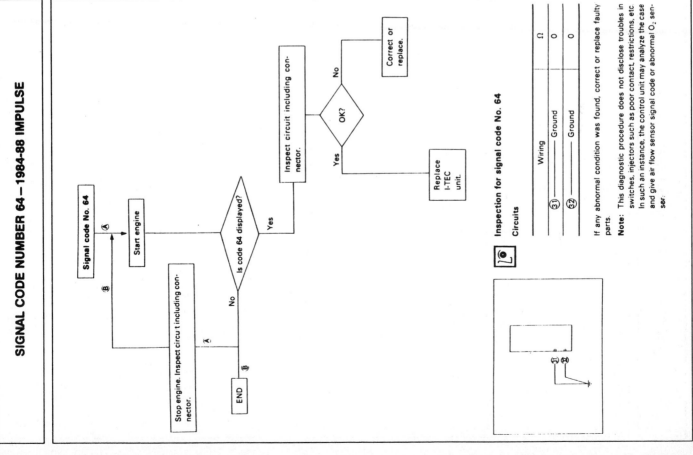

INSPECTION FOR SIGNAL CODES NUMBER 71, 72 AND 73 1984-88 IMPULSE

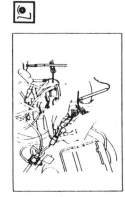

Inspection for signal code No. 71, 72 and 73

Checking operation of vacuum switching valve

1) Check operation of vcuum switching by applying battery voltage directly to the vacuum switching vavle.
2) Replace vacuum switching valve if found to be defective.

Standard resistance in vacuum switching valve	(Ω)	Approx. 35

Circuits

Signal code No.	Wiring	Ω	V
72	Vb —— Ground	—	12
	LgY —— 55	0	—
73	23 —— Ground	0	—

If any abnormal condition was found, correct or replace applicable harness assembly.

Note: Normal operation of the entire vacuum switching valve system including control unit is indicated if the vacuum switching valve operates properly when the starter switch is turned to ON position with the engine stationary and with the diagnosis lead connected.

Vacuum swiching valve

SIGNAL CODES NUMBER 72 AND 73—1984-88 IMPULSE

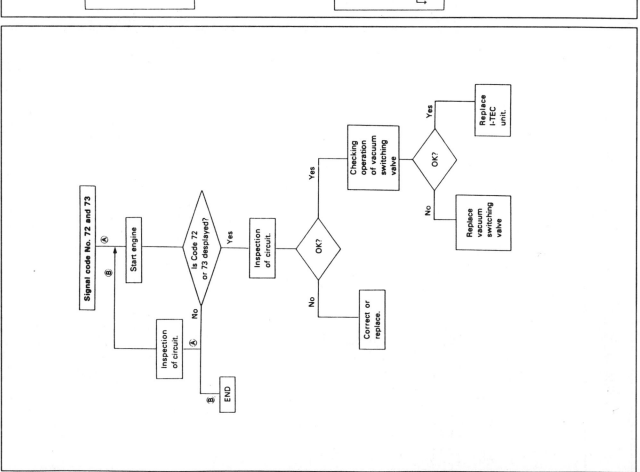

TURBOCHARGER CONTROL SYSTEM DIAGNOSTIC CODES AND TROUBLESHOOTING CHART — 1984-88 IMPULSE

Diagnosis item	Trouble assessing conditions	System operation	LED display
Knock control circuit	Abnormal knock control signal	Stopped	1
Ignition signal circuit	No input of ignition signal for about 0.3 sec. or more.	Stopped	2
Water temperature sensor circuit	Short or open circuit between Terminal ⑩ and ㉑ (water temperature) sensor.	Water temperature correction; fixed to θw = 250	3
Stepping motor circuit (micro switch circuit)	0V of voltage between Terminals ⑧ and ④ when the control unit is not driving the stepping motor.		4
	More than 0V voltage between Terminals ⑧ and ④ when the operating stepping motor.	During assessement; Operatec After assessement; Stopped	
Throttle sensor circuit	Shortcircuiting or disconnection between terminal ⑥ and ④ (throttle sensor output terminal).	Stopped	5
Throttle sensor circuit	No voltage variance or abnormal voltage between terminals ⑥ (throttle sensor output) and ④.	Stopped	6
	No wide open throttle operation since engine was started.	Operated	
Power supply voltage	Less than 10V or more than 16V power supply voltage.	Stopped	7

Note: The numbers in the circles refer to the controller's pin numbers. The controller's pin numbers are as follows.

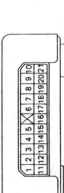

Herness side connector

TCS controller side conector

TURBOCHARGER CONTROL SYSTEM SELF—DIAGNOSIS AND TROUBLESHOOTING PROCEDURES 1985-88 IMPULSE

Signal code No. display

1) For items which are abnormal, the LEDs flash quickly.
2) When all items are normal, the LEDs turn off.
3) The shown in the diagram is for item 3 (coolant temperature sensor).

TROUBLESHOOTING PROCEDURE

1) Turn the starter switch to the "ON" position. Signal codes "2" and "6" (stored in memory) displayed.
2) Depress the accelerator pedal fully then let return. Signal code "6" (stored in memory) cleared.
3) Start the engine. Signal code "2" (stored in memory) cleared.
4) If there is a problem, the abnormal code is displayed.

Note: After repairs are completed, perform steps 1, 2, and 3 above and check that the LEDs do not light.

System inspection

1) Warm up the engine.
2) Depress the accelerator pedal quickly (less than 0.35 seconds) and check that the stepping motor function properly.
3) If it is abnormal, check the self-diagnosis items.

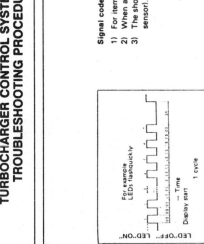

For example
LEDs flashquickly
Display start
1 cycle
— Time
LED "OFF", LED "ON".

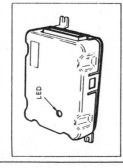

LED

SIGNAL CODE NUMBER 66—1984-88 IMPULSE

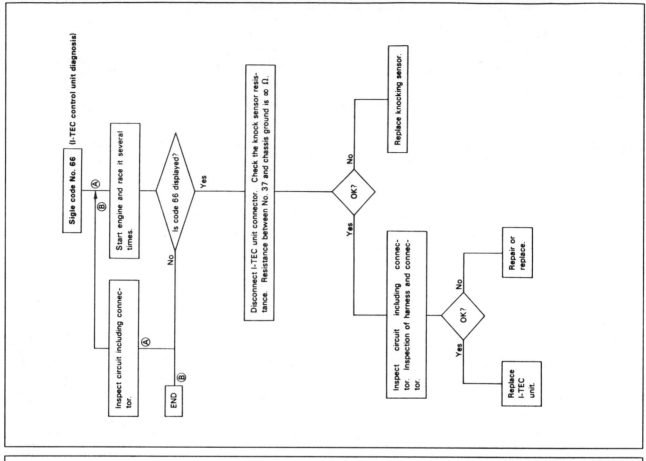

TROUBLE CODE NUMBER 1—1985-88 IMPULSE TURBO MODELS

INSPECTION OF THE TURBO CONTROL AND I-TEC CONTROL UNIT CIRCUIT 1985-88 IMPULSE TURBO MODELS

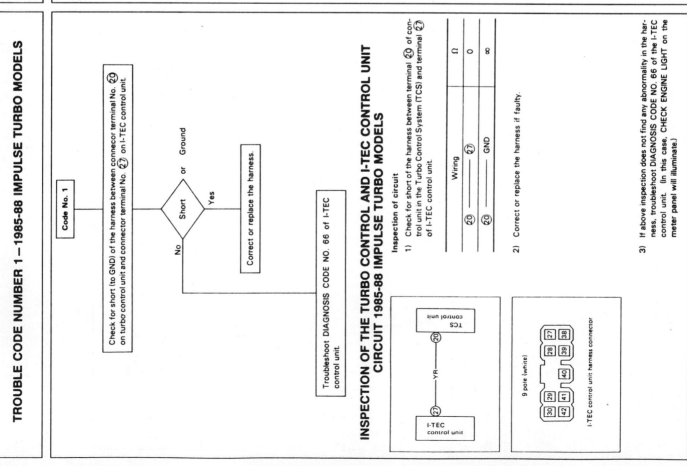

TROUBLE CODE NUMBER 2 — 1985-88 IMPULSE TURBO MODELS

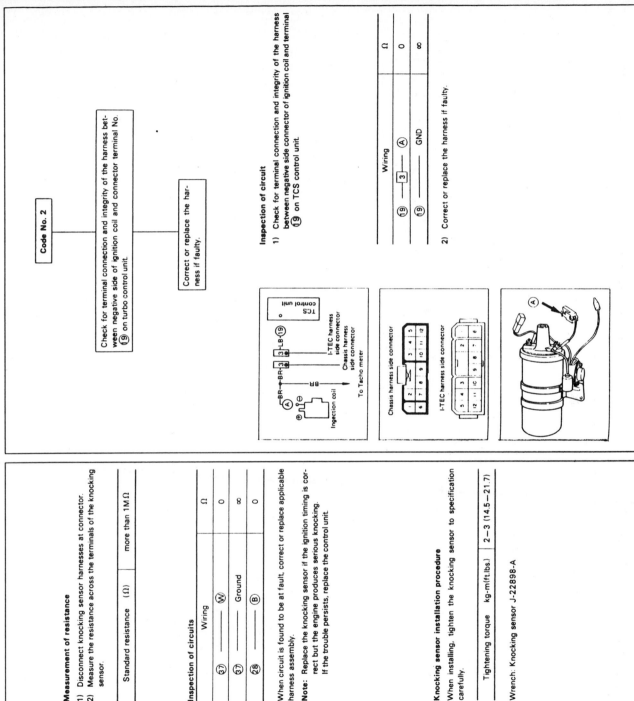

Code No. 2

Check for terminal connection and integrity of the harness between negative side of ignition coil and connector terminal No. ⑲ on turbo control unit.

Correct or replace the harness if faulty.

Inspection of circuit

1) Check for terminal connection and integrity of the harness between negative side connector of ignition coil and terminal ⑲ on TCS control unit.

Wiring			Ω
⑲ —	3 —	Ⓐ	0
⑲ —		GND	∞

2) Correct or replace the harness if faulty.

INSPECTING THE KNOCK SENSOR AND KNOCK SENSOR CIRCUIT 1985-88 IMPULSE TURBO MODELS

Measurement of resistance

1) Disconnect knocking sensor harnesses at connector.
2) Measure the resistance across the terminals of the knocking sensor.

Standard resistance (Ω)	more than 1MΩ

Inspection of circuits

Wiring		Ω
㉗ —	Ⓦ	0
㉗ —	Ground	∞
㉘ —	Ⓑ	0

When circuit is found to be at fault, correct or replace applicable harness assembly.

Note: Replace the knocking sensor if the ignition timing is correct but the engine produces serious knocking. If the trouble persists, replace the control unit.

Knocking sensor installation procedure

When installing, tighten the knocking sensor to specification carefully.

Tightening torque	kg-m(ft.lbs.)	2—3 (14.5—21.7)

Wrench. Knocking sensor J-22898-A

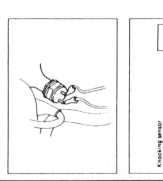

Knocking sensor

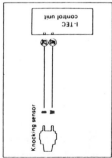

I-TEC control unit

Knocking sensor

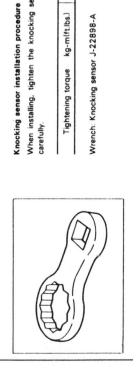

TROUBLE CODE NUMBER 3 – 1985-88 IMPULSE TURBO MODELS

Code No. 3

Check for open, short, or terminal connection of the harness between connector terminal No. 10 and 21 on turbo control unit and coolant temperature sensor.

OK?

No → Correct or replace the harness.

Yes → Check coolant temperature sensor. → Replace coolant temperature sensor.

INSPECTING THE CIRCUIT OF TROUBLE CODE NUMBER 3 1985-88 IMPULSE TURBO MODELS

Inspection of circuit

1) Check for open, short or terminal connection of the harness between terminal No. 10 and 21 on TCS control unit and coolant temperature sensor.

Wiring		Ω
10 — 106		0
10 — GND		∞
21 — 109		0
21 — GND		∞

2) Correct or replace the harness if faulty.

Inspection of coolant temperature sensor

3) Measure the coolant temperature sensor resistance.

Coolant temperature °C (°F)	Resistance (KΩ)
20 (68)	2.45 ± 0.24
30 (86)	1.65 ± 0.08
60 (140)	0.58 ± 0.03

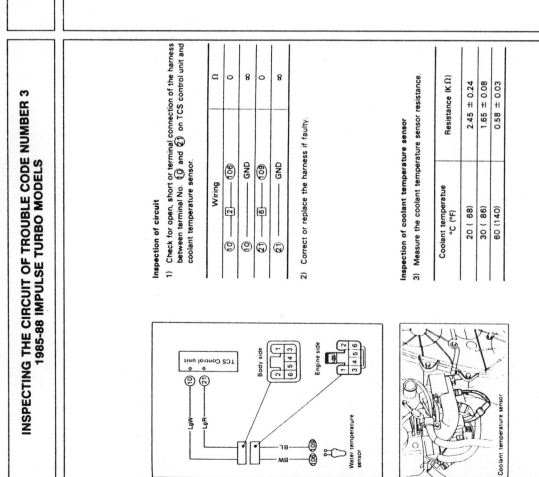

Water temperature sensor

Coolant temperature sensor

INSPECTING THE CIRCUIT OF TROUBLE CODE NUMBER 4
1985-88 IMPULSE TURBO MODELS

Inspection of circuit

1) Check for continuity between connector terminal No. ⑧ and ⑬ on the TCS control unit with home position switch (micro-switch) on the Stepping Motor assembly in ON state. Check is to be carried out, with TCS control unit and Engine body harness being connected.

2) If continuity is not confirmed between terminals ⑧ and ⑬, check terminal connection and integrity of the harness between connector terminals ⑧ and ⑬ on the TCS control unit harness side and micro-switch terminals.

Wiring		Ω
⑧	101	0
⑧	GND	∞
⑬	141	0
⑬	GND	∞

Correct or replace the harness if faulty.
In addition, replace the Stepping Motor assembly unless the harness is faulty.

3) If continuity is confirmed between terminals ⑧ and ⑬ in step 1) above, make sure that continuity is not obtained when releasing the contact between the micro-switch and lever, by turning the Stepping Motor manually.

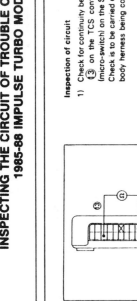
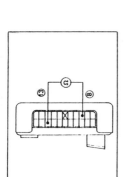
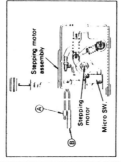
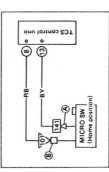
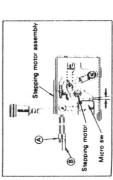
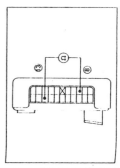

TROUBLE CODE NUMBER 4 — 1985-88 IMPULSE TURBO MODELS

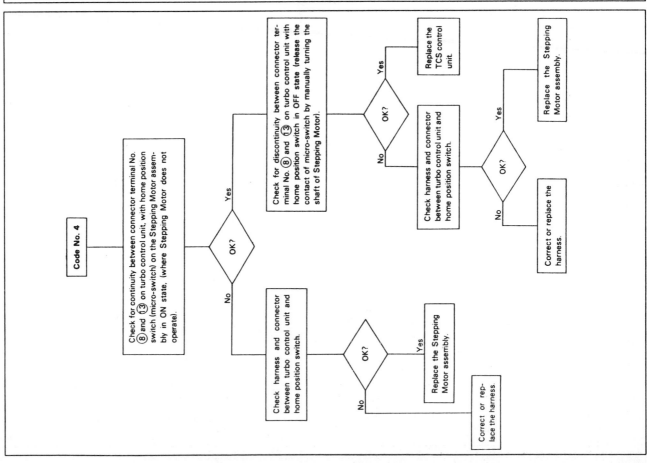

Code No. 4

Check for continuity between connector terminal No. ⑧ and ⑬ on turbo control unit, with home position switch (micro-switch) on the Stepping Motor assembly in ON state. (where Stepping Motor does not operate).

OK?
- No → Check harness and connector between turbo control unit and home position switch.
  - OK?
    - Yes → Replace the Stepping Motor assembly.
    - No → Correct or replace the harness.
- Yes → Check for discontinuity between connector terminal No. ⑧ and ⑬ on turbo control unit with home position switch in OFF state (release the contact of micro-switch by manually turning the shaft of Stepping Motor).
  - OK?
    - Yes → Replace the TCS control unit.
    - No → Check harness and connector between turbo control unit and home position switch.
      - OK?
        - Yes → Replace the Stepping Motor assembly.
        - No → Correct or replace the harness.

TROUBLE CODE NUMBER 7 – 1985-88 IMPULSE TURBO MODELS

Throttle position sensor test

1) Turn the starter switch to the "ON" position.
2) Remove the water shield cover as shown in the illustration. Do not remove the connector.
3) Place the circuit tester positive probe in white color harness.

Note: The throttle position sensor has three leads, red for 5V power source, white for output, and black for GND.

4) Measure the voltage between white color harness and black color harness.

Note: Make sure that 5V (± 0.5V) is measured at the red color harness before measurement of step 4).

Throttle position	Idle contact	Full contact
Voltage (V)	Higher than 4	Lower than 2

5) Confirm that difference in voltage of idle contact and full contact is 3.6 ± 1V.

	(V)	
Voltage difference between idle contact and full contact		3.6 ± 1

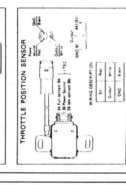

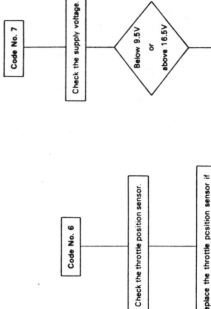

THROTTLE POSITION SENSOR

WIRING DESCRIPTION

5V	Red	
Output	White	
GND	Black	

2♂ Full contact SW
3♂ Power Source
2♀ Idle contact SW

```
Code No. 7 ──── Check the supply voltage. ──── ◇ Below 9.5V or above 16.5V ◇ ──── Check the voltage regulator.
```

```
Code No. 6 ──── Check the throttle position sensor. ──── Replace the throttle position sensor if faulty.
```

TROUBLE CODE NUMBER 5 – 1985-88 IMPULSE TURBO MODELS

4) If continuity is obtained in step 3), check the harness between connector terminals ⑧ and ⑬ on the TCS control unit harness side and micro-switch terminals.

Wiring		Ω
⑧	10	0
⑬	141	∞
⑧	141	∞

Correct or replace the harness if faulty.
In addition, replace the Stepping Motor assembly unless the harness is faulty.

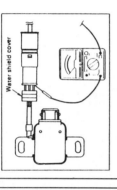

TCS control unit

⑧ ⑬

RB   BY

141

MICRO SW
(Home position)

10

B

TROUBLE CODE NUMBER 6 – 1985-88 IMPULSE TURBO MODELS

Check for short or open of the harness between terminals given below on turbo control unit and throttle position sensor.

Throttle position sensor side	Turbo control unit side
Output (A)	10
Power source (B)	9
Ground (C)	7

Correct or replace the harness if faulty.

Inspection of circuit

1) Check for short, open, or terminal connection of the harness between terminals given below on the turbo control unit and throttle position sensor.

Wiring		Ω
⑨	9	B	0
⑨	GND		∞
⑥	10	A	0
⑥	GND		∞
⑦	4	C	0

Correct or replace the harness if faulty.

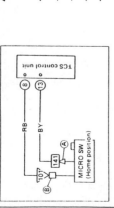

⑨ ⑥ ⑦

Body side

```
2 1
8 7 6 5
4 3
10 9 8 7 6 5
```

Engine side

```
1 2
5 6 7 8 9 10
3 4
```

BY
LgB
BY

BG
BR
RG

C B A

MAZDA

ENGINE CONTROL SYSTEM APPLICATION CHART

Year	Model	Engine cc (liter)	Engine VIN	Fuel System	Ignition System
1984	GLC	1490 (1.5)	E5	2-BBL	Electronic
	626	1998 (2.0)	FE	2-BBL	Electronic
	RX-7	1146 (1.1)	12A	2-BBL	Electronic
	RX-7	1308 (1.3)	13B	EGI	Electronic
	B2000, B2200	1970 (2.0)	MA	2-BBL	Electronic
1985	GLC	1490 (1.5)	E5	2-BBL	Electronic
	626	1998 (2.0)	FE	2-BBL	Electronic
	RX-7	1146 (1.1)	12A	2-BBL	Electronic
	RX-7	1308 (1.3)	13B	EGI	Electronic
	B2000, B2200	1970 (2.0)	MA	2-BBL	Electronic
1986	323	1597 (1.6)	B	2-BBL	Electronic
	323	1597 (1.6)	B	EGI	Electronic
	626	1998 (2.0)	FE	EGI	Electronic
	626 Turbo	1998 (2.0)	RF	EGI	Electronic
	RX-7	1308 (1.3)	13B	EGI	Electronic
	RX-7	1308 (1.3)	13B	EGI	Electronic
	B2000	1998 (2.0)	FE	2-BBL	Electronic
1987-88	323	1597 (1.6)	B	2-BBL	Electronic
	323	1597 (1.6)	B	EGI	Electronic
	626	1998 (2.0)	FE	EGI	Electronic
	626 Turbo	1998 (2.0)	RF	EGI	Electronic
	RX-7	1308 (1.3)	13B	EGI	Electronic
	RX-7	1308 (1.3)	13B	EGI	Electronic
	B2600, B2200	1998 (2.0)	FE	2-BBL	Electronic

ELECTRONIC GASOLINE INJECTION (EGI) SYSTEM

MAZDA 323

General Information

The fuel injection system supplies the necessary fuel to the injectors to achieve combustion at constant pressure. Fuel is metered and injected into the intake manifold according to the signals from the EGI control unit. The injection system consists of the fuel pump, fuel filter, distribution pipe, pulsation dampener, pressure regulator, injectors, air flow meter, air valve, and solenoid resistor.

The EGI control unit (ECU), through various input sensors, monitors battery voltage, engine rpm, amount of air intake, cranking signal, intake temperature, coolant temperature, oxygen concentration in the exhaust gases, throttle opening, atmospheric pressure, gearshift position, clutch engagement, braking, power steering operation and A/C compressor operation.

The ECU controls operation of the fuel injection system, idle-up system, fuel evaporation system and ignition timing. The ECU has a built in fail-safe mechanism. If a fault occurs while driving, the ECU will substitute pre-programmed values. Driving performance will be affected, but the vehicle will still be driveable.

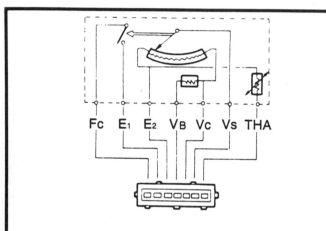

Inspecting the air flow meter

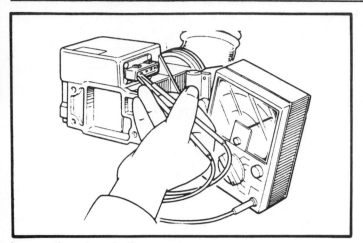

Terminal	Resistance (Ω)
E2 ↔ Vs	20 to 400
E2 ↔ Vc	100 to 300
E2 ↔ VB	200 to 400
E2 ↔ THA (Air temp sensor)	−20°C (−4°C) 10,000 to 20,000 0 (0°F) 4,000 to 7,000 20°C (68°F) 2,000 to 3,000 40°C (104°F) 900 to 1,300 60°C (140°F) 400 to 700
E1 ↔ Fc	∞

Air flow meter terminal resistance specifications

Diagnosis and Testing

AIR FLOW METER

Inspection

1. Inspect the air flow meter body for cracks. Using a suitable ohmmeter, check the resistance between the terminals.

2. Using a suitable tool press open the measuring plate. Measure the resistance between E1 and FC (fuel pump switch) and between E2 and VS.

3. The resistance between E1 and FC should be infinity when the measuring plate is fully closed and 0 ohms when fully opened.

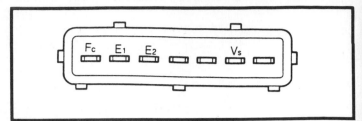

Measuring the resistance between the fuel pump switch connector

4. The resistance between E2 and VS should be 20–400 ohms when the measuring plate is fully closed and 20–1000 ohms when fully opened.

5. If the air flow meter fails to meet these specifications, replace it.

Removal and Installation

1. Disconnect the negative battery cable. Remove the high tension lead and connectors.

2. Loosen the hose band and remove the intake hose.

3. Remove the air flow meter attaching bolts.

4. Turn the air cleaner cover upside down and remove the attaching nuts, remove the air flow meter.

5. Installation is the reverse order of the removal procedure.

AIR VALVE

Inspection

1. Start the engine and let it run at idle speed. Pinch the air valve air hose and check if the engine slows down.

NOTE: When the engine is still cold the engine speed will reduce. After the engine has warmed up the engine sped will drop within 200 rpm.

2. Using a suitable ohmmeter, check the resistance between the terminals. The standard resistance is 30–50 ohms.

3. Check the valve for proper operation as follows:

   a. When the engine temperature is 68° or lower the air valve should be open.

   b. When the engine temperature is 68° or above the air valve should be closed.

4. If the air valve fails any of these tests, replace it.

Removal and Installation

1. Disconnect the negative battery cable. Disconnect the by-pass air hose.

2. Disconnect and plug the water hoses.

3. Disconnect the air valve connector and remove the air valve assembly.

4. Installation is the reverse order of the removal procedure.

THROTTLE BODY

Inspection

1. Check for smooth operation. Check the free play of the accelerator cable. It should be 0.039–0.118 in. (1–3mm).

Removal and Installation

1. Disconnect the negative battery cable. Disconnect the accelerator cable from the throttle linkage.

2. Disconnect the air funnel. Disconnect the hoses and tubes from the throttle body.

3. Disconnect the throttle position sensor connector. Remove the throttle body retaining screws and remove the throttle body assembly.

4. Installation is the reverse order of the removal procedure.

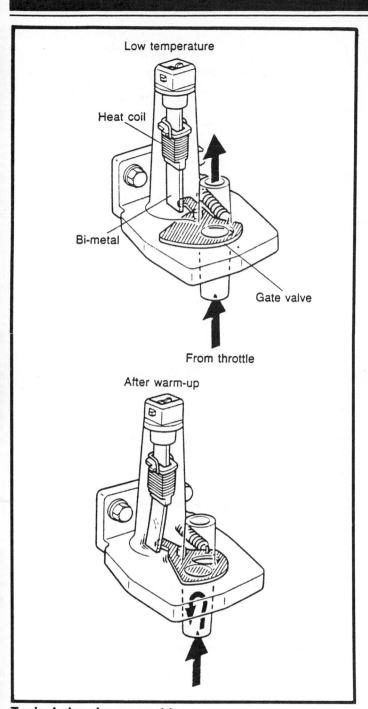

Typical air valve assembly

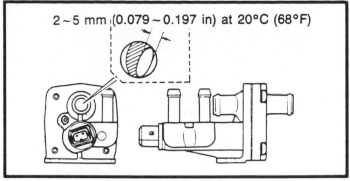

2~5 mm (0.079~0.197 in) at 20°C (68°F)

Inspecting the air valve assembly

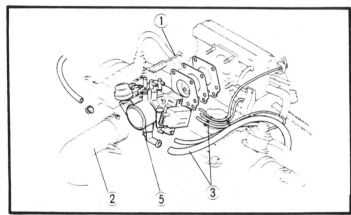

Throttle body removal and installation

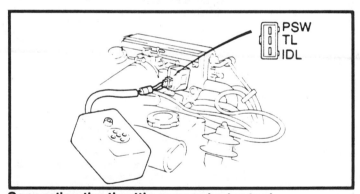

PSW
TL
IDL

Connecting the throttle sensor tester tool

THROTTLE POSITION SENSOR

Inspection

1. Disconnect the connector from the throttle position sensor.

2. Connect the throttle position sensor tester (49-9200-165) and adapter (49-9200-166) or equivalent in the throttle position sensor or connect a suitable ohmmeter.

3. Insert a feeler gauge between the throttle stop screw and stop lever.

4. Note the operation of the buzzer or continuity between terminals.

Adjustment

1. Disconnect the connector from the throttle position sensor and connect a throttle position sensor tester (49-9200-165) and adapter (49-9200-166) or equivalent in the throttle position sensor or connect a suitable ohmmeter.

2. Insert a 0.020 in. (0.5mm) feeler gauge between the throttle stop screw and throttle lever.

3. Loosen the two attaching screws. Rotate the throttle position sensor clockwise approximately 30°, then rotate it back counterclockwise until the buzzer sounds.

4. Replace the feeler gauge with a 0.027 in. (0.7mm) feeler gauge. Check that the buzzer does not sound. If the buzzer sounds, repeat Steps 3 and 4.

5. Tighten the two attaching screws. Be sure not to move the throttle position sensor from the set position when tightening the screw.

6. Open the throttle valve fully a few times, then recheck the adjustment of the throttle position sensor, by performing the inspection over again.

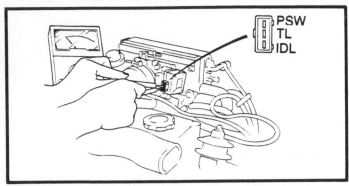

Inspecting the throttle sensor with an ohmmeter

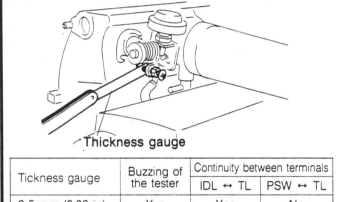

Using a feeler gauge to test the throttle sensor

Tickness gauge	Buzzing of the tester	Continuity between terminals	
		IDL ↔ TL	PSW ↔ TL
0.5 mm (0.02 in)	Yes	Yes	No
0.7 mm (0.027 in)	No	No	No
Fully open throttle lever	Yes	No	Yes

WATER THERMO SENSOR

Inspection

1. Remove the water thermo sensor from the intake manifold.
2. Place the water thermo sensor in a container of water with a thermometer and heat up the water gradually.
3. Using a ohmmeter, check the calibration of the sensor as follows;
–4° F. 16.2–1.6 kilo-ohms
68° F. 2.45–0.24 kilo-ohms
176° F. 0.322–0.032 kilo-ohms.
4. If the water thermo sensor does not fall within specifications during this test, remove and replace the sensor.

WATER TEMPERATURE SWITCH

Inspection

1. Remove the water temperature switch from the radiator.
2. Place the water temperature switch in a container of water with a thermometer and heat up the water gradually.
3. Using a ohmmeter, check that the switch opens and stays open at a temperature of 63°F or higher.

OXYGEN SENSOR

Inspection

1. Warm the engine up to normal operating temperature and let the engine idle.

2. Disconnect the oxygen sensor connector at the wiring harness. Attach a voltmeter between the oxygen sensor connector and a body ground.
3. Run the engine at 4000 rpm until the voltmeter reads 0.7 volts.
4. Increase and decrease the engine speed quickly several times. When the engine speed is increased the volt meter should read between 0.5–1.0 volts.
5. When the engine speed is decreased the volt meter should read between 0–0.3 volts.
6. If the oxygen sensor fails to meet these specifications, replace the sensor.

ATMOSPHERIC PRESSURE SENSOR

Inspection

1. Connect a voltmeter to the (D) terminal of the atmospheric pressure sensor.
2. Turn the ignition switch to the ON position and take a voltage reading.
3. The voltage reading should be as follows:
   a. 4 ± 0.5 volts at sea level.
   b. 3 ± 0.5 volts at high altitude (6500 ft.).
4. If the sensor fails to meet these specifications, replace the sensor.

RELIEVING FUEL PRESSURE

The fuel in the fuel system remains under high pressure even when the engine is not running. So before disconnecting any fuel lines, release the fuel pressure to reduce the risk of injury or fire. Relieve the fuel pressure as follows:
1. Remove the rear seat cushion. Start the engine.
2. Dusconnect the fuel pump connectors with the engine running.
3. After the engine stalls from lack of fuel, turn the ignition switch off.
4. Use a shop rag to cover the fuel lines when disconnecting and plug all fuel lines after they have been disconnected.

FUEL PUMP

Inspection

1. Turn the ignition switch to the ON position.
2. Use a jumper wire and connect the (GW) and (B) terminals of the fuel pump check connector and check that the fuel pump operates.
3. If there is no opertional sound from the fuel pump, check the circuit opening relay. Turn the ignition switch to the ON and OFF position at the same time the circuit opening relay should click.

NOTE: The circuit opening relay is mounted under the EGI control unit.

4. If the relay does not operate, use a suitable ohmmeter and check the resistance between the terminals.
5. If the circuit opening relay is normal, check the voltage at the fuel pump connector (GR) terminal. With the ignition switch on, and the jumper wire still connected, there should be 12 volts at the fuel pump connector terminal.
6. If the voltage is normal, remove the jumper wire and replace the fuel pump.

Removal and Installation

1. With the rear seat cushion removed, relieve the fuel pressure from the fuel system.
2. Remove the filler cap and remove the fuel pump cover.
3. Disconnect and plug the fuel main and return lines from the fuel pump.

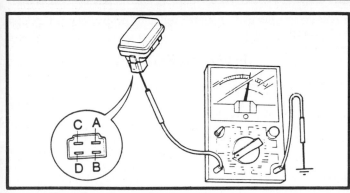

Inspecting the atmospheric pressure sensor

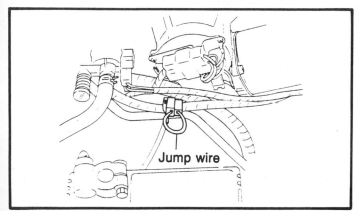

Jump wire

Jumping the fuel pump check connector terminals

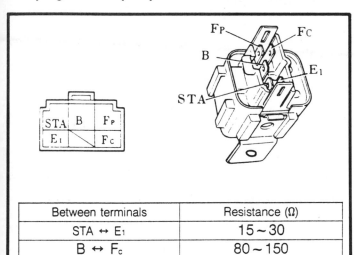

Between terminals	Resistance (Ω)
STA ↔ E_1	15 ~ 30
B ↔ F_c	80 ~ 150
B ↔ F_p	∞

Inspecting the circuit opening relay

4. Remove the fuel pump and fuel tank gauge as an assembly.
5. Replace the fuel pump.
6. Installation is the reverse order of the removal procedure.

FUEL PRESSURE

Pump Outlet Pressure Inspection

1. With the rear seat cushion removed, relieve the fuel pressure from the fuel system.
2. Disconnect the negative battery cable. Disconnect the fuel line from the fuel filter.

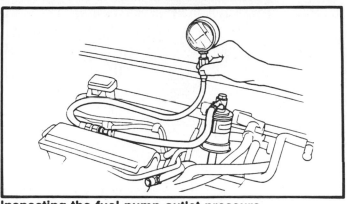

Inspecting the fuel pump outlet pressure

3. Connect a fuel pressure gauge to the fuel filter. Reconnect the negative battery cable.
4. Turn the ignition switch to the ON position. Use a jumper wire and connect the (GW) and (B) terminals of the fuel pump check connector and check that the fuel pump pressure.
5. The fuel pump outlet pressure should be 64.0–85.3 psi.
6. If the fuel pressure is not within specifications, replace the fuel pump.

Fuel Line Pressure Inspection

1. With the rear seat cushion removed, relieve the fuel pressure from the fuel system.
2. Disconnect the negative battery cable. Connect the multi-pressure tester (49-9200-750) or equivalent to the fuel line.
3. Reconnect the negative battery cable. Start the engine and measure the fuel pressure at idle. The fuel pressure (regulating pressure) should be 28.4–31.3 psi.

NOTE: The fuel pressure is indicated on the lower LED line (fuel pressure line) at any ranges.

4. Disconnect the vacuum hose connected to the pressure regulator and plug it off. The fuel pressure (regulating pressure) should be 34.8–40.5 psi.
5. If not within specifications, check the following:
   a. Fuel pump outlet pressure.
   b. Fuel filter clog.
   c. If these items check out, replace the pressure regulator.

PRESSURE REGULATOR

Removal and Installation

1. With the rear seat cushion removed, relieve the fuel pressure from the fuel system. Disconnect the negative battery cable.
2. Remove the surge tank in the order as follows:
   a. Accelerator cable.
   b. Air funnel.
   c. Air hoses.
   d. Vacuum tubes.
   e. Water hoses.
   f. Retaining nuts and bolts.
   g. Surge tank.
3. Disconnect the fuel return hose.
4. Remove the pressure regulator.
5. Installation is the reverse order of the removal procedure. Be sure to replace the O-ring(s) and after installation check for fuel leaks with fuel pressure applied.

FUEL FILTER

The fuel filter should be replaced every 30,000 miles. Replace the filter as follows:

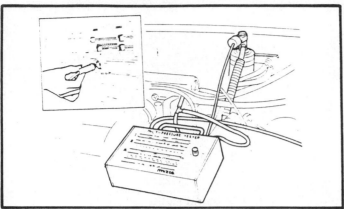

Connecting the multi-pressure tester

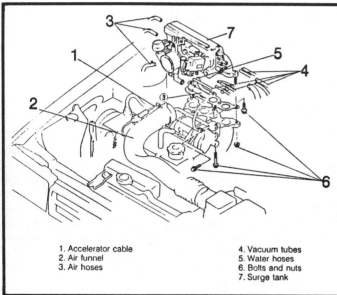

1. Accelerator cable
2. Air funnel
3. Air hoses
4. Vacuum tubes
5. Water hoses
6. Bolts and nuts
7. Surge tank

Surge tank removal and Installation

Pressure regulator removal

1. With the rear seat cushion removed, relieve the fuel pressure from the fuel system. Disconnect the negative battery cable.

2. Disconnect and plug the fuel lines. Remove the fuel filter with bracket as an assembly.

3. Install a new filter ind reconnect the fuel lines.

4. Replace the copper washer with a new one and torque it to 18–25 ft.lbs. When installing the fuel filter make sure that the

fuel lines are pushed on as far up as possible. Secure the hose with clamps.

FUEL INJECTORS

Injection Fuel Pressure Inspection

1. With the rear seat cushion removed, relieve the fuel pressure from the fuel system.

2. Disconnect the negative battery cable. Connect the multi-pressure tester (49-9200-750) or equivalent to the fuel line.

3. Reconnect the negative battery cable. Start the engine and measure the fuel pressure at the III range of the multi pressure tester. The fuel pressure (injection pressure) should be 34.8–40.5 psi.

NOTE: The fuel pressure is indicated on the lower LED line (fuel pressure line) at any ranges.

4. If the injection pressure is lower than specifications, check the following:
   a. Fuel pump outlet pressure.
   b. Fuel line pressure.
   c. Fuel filter clog.

5. If the injection pressure is higher than specifications, check the following:
   a. Fuel return pipe clogged.
   b. fuel line pressure.

Injector Inspection

Check the operating sound of the injector, using a sound scope, check that operating sounds are produced from each injector at idle and at acceleration.

1. If the injectors do not operate, check the following:
   a. Check the fuel injection system main fuse (40 amp).
   b. Turn the ignition switch ON and OFF, verify that the main relay clicks.

2. If the clicking sound is not heard at the main relay, when the ignition switch is turned ON, use a voltmeter and check for 12 volts at the main relay connector (BW) terminal wire.

Removal and Installation

1. With the rear seat cushion removed, relieve the fuel pressure from the fuel system. Disconnect the negative battery cable.

2. Remove the surge tank in the order as follows:
   a. Accelerator cable.
   b. Air funnel.
   c. Air hoses.
   d. Vacuum tubes.
   e. Water hoses.
   f. Retaining nuts and bolts.
   g. Surge tank.

3. Disconnect the fuel hose and pipe. Disconnect the injector connector.

4. Remove the pressure regulator and distribution pipe.

5. Remove the injector. Once the injector is removed, use an ohmmeter and measure the resistance at the injector connector (on the injector). The resistance should be 1.5–3.0 ohms.

6. Installation is the reverse order of the removal procedure. Be sure to replace the O-ring(s) and after installation check for fuel leaks with fuel pressure applied.

Injector Fuel Leak Test

1. With the rear seat cushion removed, relieve the fuel pressure from the fuel system.

2. Remove the surge tank in the order as follows:
   a. Accelerator cable.
   b. Air funnel.
   c. Air hoses.
   d. Vacuum tubes.

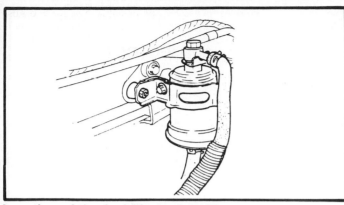

Location of the fuel filter assembly

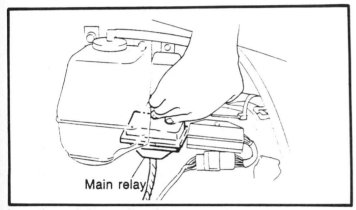

Location of the main relay

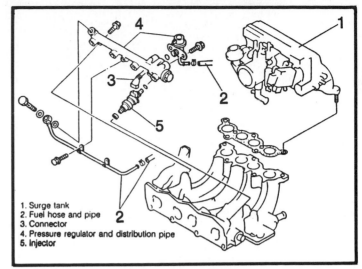

1. Surge tank
2. Fuel hose and pipe
3. Connector
4. Pressure regulator and distribution pipe
5. Injector

Fuel injector removal and installation

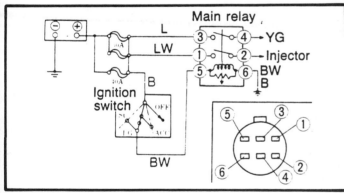

Inspecting the main relay

e. Water hoses.
f. Retaining nuts and bolts.
g. Surge tank.

3. Loosen the distribution pipe attaching bolts. Afix the injectors to the distribution pipe with some suitable wire.

NOTE: Affix the injectors firmly to the distribution pipe so no movement of the injectors is possible.

4. Turn the ignition switch to the ON position. Use a jumper wire and connect the (GW) and (B) terminals of the fuel pump check connector. Make sure that the fuel does not leak from the injector nozzles.

5. After approximately five minutes, a very small (slight) amount of fuel leakage from the injectors is acceptable.

6. If the injector leaks fuel at a fast rate, replace the injector. If the injectors do not leak, remove all test equipment and install the removed components in the reverse order of the removal procedure.

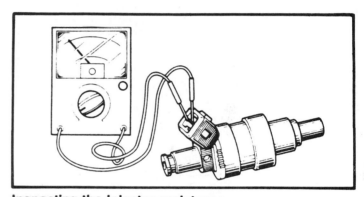

Inspecting the injector resistance

Injector Volume Test

1. With the rear seat cushion removed, relieve the fuel pressure from the fuel system.

2. Connect a suitable hose to the injector. Connect injector checker (49-9200-040) or equivalent to the injector.

3. Turn the ignition switch to the ON position. Use a jumper wire and connect the (GW) and (B) terminals of the fuel pump check connector. Make sure that the fuel does not leak from the injector nozzles.

4. Apply battery voltage to the injector checker and measure the injector volume with a graduated cylinder (measuring container).

NOTE: Do not apply battery voltage directly to the injector. The injector checker must be used or the injector will be damaged.

Solenoid Resistor Inspection

1. Using a suitable ohmmeter, measure the resistance between the (B) terminal and terminals 1 through 4 with the solenoid resistor connector disconnected. The solenoid resistor is usually located next to the main relay on the left fender well.

2. The standard resistance should be 5–7 ohms. If the resistance is not within specifications, replace the resistor.

IDLE SYSTEM

Idle Speed Adjustment

Before adjusting the idle speed and idle mixture, be sure the ig-

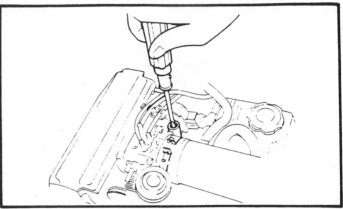

Performing the fuel injector leak test

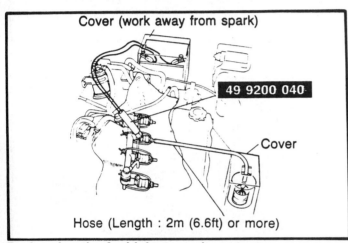

Cover (work away from spark)

49 9200 040

Cover

Hose (Length : 2m (6.6ft) or more)

Performing the fuel injector volume test

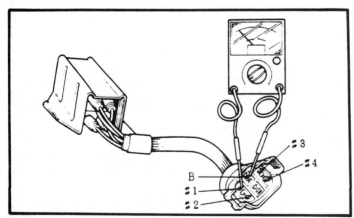

Inspecting the solenoid resistance

Making the idle speed adjustment

Dashpot Adjustment

1. Push lightly on the dash pot rod and make sure the rod goes into the dash pot slowly. Release the pressure and make sure the rod comes out quickly.

2. Start the engine and let it run to reach normal operating temperature. Stop the engine and connect a suitable tachometer to the engine.

3. Start the engine and slowly increase to the engine speed to 3000 rpm.

4. Slowly reduce the engine speed and make sure that the dash pot rod touches the lever at 2650–2950 rpm.

5. If the function is not correct, loosen the lock nut and adjust by turning the dash pot.

Idle-Up System Adjustment

ELECTRICAL LOAD SOLENOID

This adjustment is unecessary unless the solenoid valve has been replaced or the engine is running rough when the system is operating.

1. Start the engine and let it run to reach normal operating temperature. Stop the engine and connect a suitable tachometer to the engine.

2. Ground the (L) terminal of the solenoid valve with a suitable jumper wire. Start the engine and let it run at idle.

--- **CAUTION** ---

Do not ground the (YG) terminal, this will cause the ignition system fuse to blow.

3. Confirm that the engine speed is within specifications:
   a. 900–950 rpm — Manual transmission models.
   b. 1050–1100 rpm — Automatic transmission models.

NOTE: Make sure that all the accessories are off.

4. If the engine speed is not within specifications, remove the screw cap from the solenoid valve and turn the valve adjusting screw to obtain the correct speed.

POWER STEERING SWITCH

1. Start the engine and let it run to reach normal operating temperature. Stop the engine and connect a suitable tachometer to the engine.

2. Disconnect the power steering switch connector and ground the disconnected connector directly with a jumper wire.

3. Start the engine and let it run at idle. Confirm that the engine speed is within specifications:
   a. 1000–1100 rpm — Manual transmission models.
   b. 1150–1250 rpm — Automatic transmission models.

NOTE: Make sure that all the accessories are off.

4. If the engine speed is not within specifications, turn the valve adjusting screw to obtain the correct speed.

nition timing, spark plugs, etc., are all in normal operating condition. Turn off all lights and other unnecessary electrical loads.

1. Connect a tachometer to the engine.

2. After warming up the engine, check that the choke valve has fully opened.

3. Check the idle speed. If necessary, turn the throttle adjust screw and set the idle speed to specifications.
   a. 800–900 rpm — Manual transmission models.
   b. 950–1050 rpm — Automatic transmission models.

NOTE: After adjusting the idle speed, the dashpot should be adjusted.

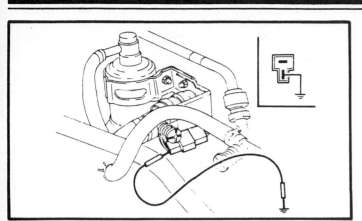

Grounding the L terminal of the solenoid valve

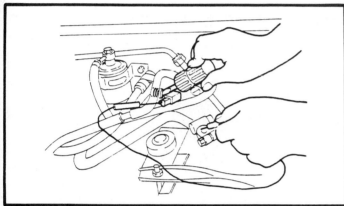

Using the solenoid valve adjusting screw

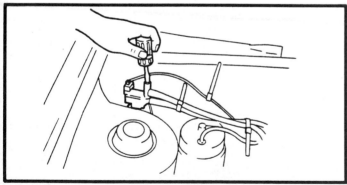

Using the power steering switch adjusting screw

A/C IDLE-UP SOLENOID

1. Start the engine and let it run to reach normal operating temperature. Stop the engine and connect a suitable tachometer to the engine.

2. Disconnect the connector from the A/C idle-up solenoid. Apply battery power to the solenoid.

3. Start the engine and let it run at idle. Confirm that the engine speed is within specifications:
   a. 1250–1350 rpm — Manual transmission models.
   b. 1450–1550 rpm — Automatic transmission models.

NOTE: Make sure that all the accessories are off.

4. If the engine speed is not within specifications, turn the valve adjusting screw to obtain the correct speed.

EGI CONTROL UNIT

The EGI control unit (ECU), through various input sensors,

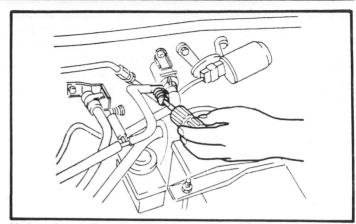

Using the A/C solenoid valve adjusting screw

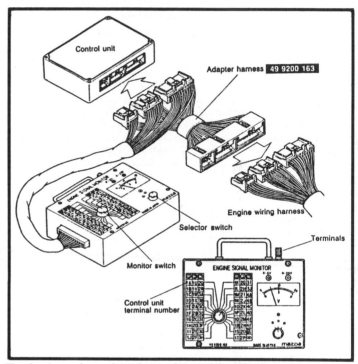

Typical engine signal monitor with adapter

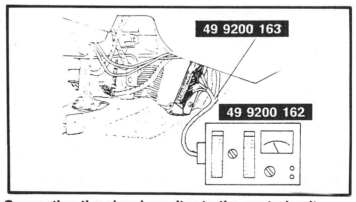

Connecting the signal monitor to the control unit

monitors battery voltage, engine rpm, amount of air intake, cranking signal, intake temperature, coolant temperature, oxygen concentration in the exhaust gases, throttle opening, atmospheric pressure, gearshift position, clutch engagement, braking, power steering operation and A/C compressor operation.

Terminal	Connection to	Voltage with ignition ON	Voltage when idling
1A (output)	Check connector	12 – 13V	12 – 13V
1D (output)	Check connector	12 – 13V	repeat 12 – 13V & CV
1E (input)	T.P. sensor (IDL)	0V (12 – 13V: depress accelerator)	CV
1G (input)	Clutch and neutral switch	0v (neutral)	0V
1H (input)	Water temp. switch	12 – 13V (in-gear, release clutch pedal)	0V
		0V (12 – 13V: below 17°C (63°F)	0V
1I (input)	T.P. sensor (PCW)	12 – 13V (0V: depress accelerator)	12 – 13V
1M (input)	Ignition — terminal	12 – 13V	12 – 13V
1S (output)	A/C cut relay	12 – 13V	12 – 13V
1U (output)	Igniter (Black connector)	12 – 13V	12 – 13V
1V (output)	Idle up solenoid (E/L)	12 – 13V	12 – 13V
1W (output)	Check connector	12 – 13V	12 – 13V
2A (output)	Atmosperhic P. sensor	approx. 5V	approx. 5V
2B (input)	A.F.M. VC terminal	approx. 8V	approx. 8V
2C	Ground	0V	0V
2D (input)	O2 sensor	0V	0.2 – 0.7V (racing)
2E (input)	A.F.M. VS terminal	approx. 1.8V	approx. 4.5
2H (input)	Atmosperic P. sensor	approx. 4V	approx. 4
2I (input)	Water thermo sensor	approx. 0.5V (normal operating temp.)	approx. 0.5V
2J (input)	A.F.M. THA terminal	approx. 1.6V	approx. 1.8V
2K (output)	Solenoid No. 2 (Evapo.)	12 – 13V	12 – 13V
2P (output)	Solenoid (Evapo.)	12 – 13V	12 – 13V
2R	Ground	0V	0
3A	Ground	0V	0
3B (input)	Starter ST terminal	0V (approx. 10V: cranking)	0
3C (output)	Injector No. 3, No. 4	12 – 13V	12 – 13V
3D (input)	Inhibitor switch (ATX)	0V ("N" & P range 12 – 13V (other range)	
3E (output)	Injector No. 1, No. 2	12 – 13V	12 – 13V
3G	Ground	0V	0V
3I (output)	A.F.M. VB terminal	12 – 13V	12 – 13V
3J (input)	Battery	12 – 13V	12 – 13V

EGI control unit connector

3I	3G	3E	3C	3A	2Q	2D	2M	2K	2I	2G	2E	2C	2A	1W	1U	1S	1Q	1O	1M	1K	1I	1G	1E	1C	1A
3J	3H	3F	3D	3B	2R	2P	2N	2L	2J	2H	2F	2D	2B	1X	1V	1T	1R	1P	1N	1L	1J	1H	1F	1D	1B

EGI control unit connector terminal identification

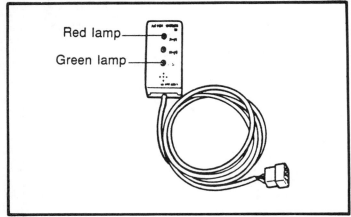

Red lamp
Green lamp

Typical system checker 83

The ECU controls operation of the fuel injection system, idle-up system, fuel evaporation system and ignition timing. The ECU has a built in fail-safe mechanism. If a fault occurs while driving, the ECU will substitute pre-programmed values. Driving performance will be affected, but the vehicle will still be driveable.

EGI Control Unit Inspection

To inspect the control unit, special tool Engine Signal Monitor (49-9200-162) and Adapter (49-9200-163) will be needed. If this tool is not available, a suitable voltmeter can be used in its place. The engine signal monitor has been developed to check the EGI control unit terminal voltage. The monitor easily inspects the terminal voltage by setting the monitor switch. Make sure the engine is at normal operating temperatures before proceeding with this inspection.

1. Connect the engine signal monitor between the EGI control unit and engine harness using the adapter.
2. Turn the select switch and monitor switch to select the terminal number and check the terminal voltage.

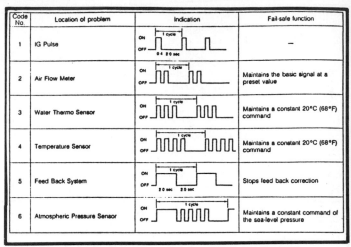

Code No.	Location of problem	Indication	Fail-safe function
1	IG Pulse		—
2	Air Flow Meter		Maintains the basic signal at a preset value
3	Water Thermo Sensor		Maintains a constant 20°C (68°F) command
4	Temperature Sensor		Maintains a constant 20°C (68°F) command
5	Feed Back System		Stops feed back correction
6	Atmospheric Pressure Sensor		Maintains a constant command of the sea-level pressure

Trouble code indication chart - 1985-86 B2000

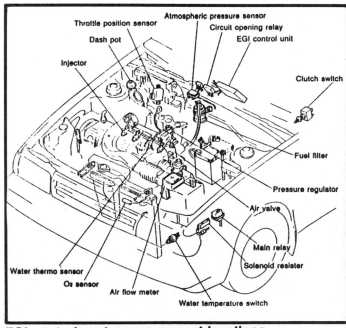

Connecting the system checker 83 to the control unit

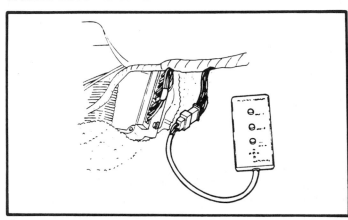

Throttle position sensor
Atmospheric pressure sensor
Circuit opening relay
EGI control unit
Dash pot
Clutch switch
Injector
Fuel filter
Pressure regulator
Air valve
Main relay
Solenoid resister
Water thermo sensor
O2 sensor
Air flow meter
Water temperature switch

EGI control system component locations

— CAUTION —

Do not apply voltage to terminals (A) and (B) of the engine signal monitor.

TROUBLE CODE TROUBLESHOOTING CHARTS (CONT.)

TROUBLE CODE TROUBLESHOOTING CHARTS

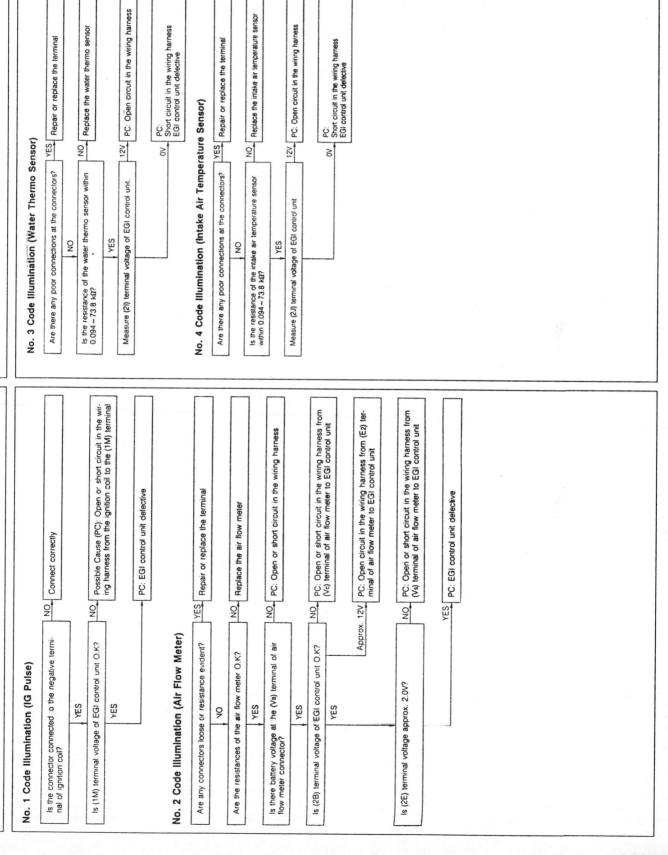

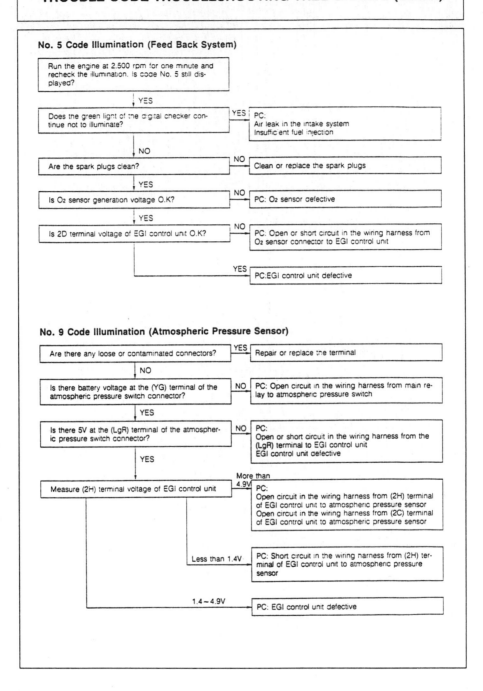

TROUBLE CODE TROUBLESHOOTING TREE CHARTS (CONT.)

No. 5 Code Illumination (Feed Back System)

Run the engine at 2.500 rpm for one minute and recheck the illumination. Is code No. 5 still displayed?

YES

Does the green light of the digital checker continue not to illuminate? — YES → PC: Air leak in the intake system / Insufficient fuel injection

NO

Are the spark plugs clean? — NO → Clean or replace the spark plugs

YES

Is O₂ sensor generation voltage O.K? — NO → PC: O₂ sensor defective

YES

Is 2D terminal voltage of EGI control unit O.K? — NO → PC: Open or short circuit in the wiring harness from O₂ sensor connector to EGI control unit

YES → PC: EGI control unit defective

No. 9 Code Illumination (Atmospheric Pressure Sensor)

Are there any loose or contaminated connectors? — YES → Repair or replace the terminal

NO

Is there battery voltage at the (YG) terminal of the atmospheric pressure switch connector? — NO → PC: Open circuit in the wiring harness from main relay to atmospheric pressure switch

YES

Is there 5V at the (LgR) terminal of the atmospheric pressure switch connector? — NO → PC: Open or short circuit in the wiring harness from the (LgR) terminal to EGI control unit / EGI control unit defective

YES

Measure (2H) terminal voltage of EGI control unit

More than 4.9V → PC: Open circuit in the wiring harness from (2H) terminal of EGI control unit to atmospheric pressure sensor / Open circuit in the wiring harness from (2C) terminal of EGI control unit to atmospheric pressure sensor

Less than 1.4V → PC: Short circuit in the wiring harness from (2H) terminal of EGI control unit to atmospheric pressure sensor

1.4 ~ 4.9V → PC: EGI control unit defective

NOTE: If the engine signal monitor is not available, check the control unit terminals with a suitable voltmeter as follows; connect a voltmeter to the control unit, which in most cases is located under the (center) dash panel. Turn the ignition switch to the ON position (do not start the engine) and measure the voltage at each terminal with the aid of the chart provided.

3. If the proper voltage is not indicated on the monitor or the voltmeter, check all wiring, connections and finally check the involved component.

TROUBLESHOOTING WITH THE SELF–DIAGNOSIS CHECKER

The system checker 83 (part # 49–G030–920) can be used to detect and indicate any problems of each sensor, damaged wiring, poor contact or a short circuit between each of the sensor-control units. Trouble is indicated by a red lamp and a buzzer.

If there is more than two problems at the same time, the indicator lamp lights on in the numerical order of the code number. Even if the problem is corrected during indication, one cycle will be indicated. If after a malfunction has occured the ignition key is switched off, the malfunction indicator for the feedback system will not be displayed on the checker.

The control unit has a built in fail-safe mechanism. If a malfunction occurs during driving, the control unit will on its own initiative send out a command and driving performance will be affected.

Inspection

1. Warm up the engine to the normal operating temperature and run it at idle. The engine speed should be below 4000 rpm, while warming up.

2. Connect the system checker 83 to the control unit service (check) connector. Be sure that the system checker 83 is working properly. The buzzer should sound for approximately three seconds after the ignition is turned ON.

3. Check whether the trouble-indication lamp illuminates. If the lamp lights up, check for the cause of the problem using the code charts.

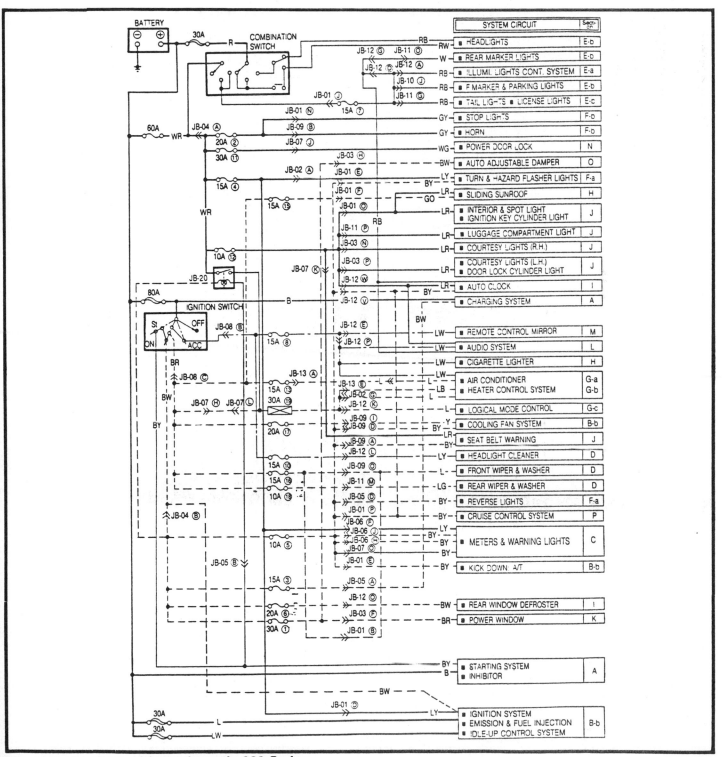

EGI control system wiring schematic 323 Sedan

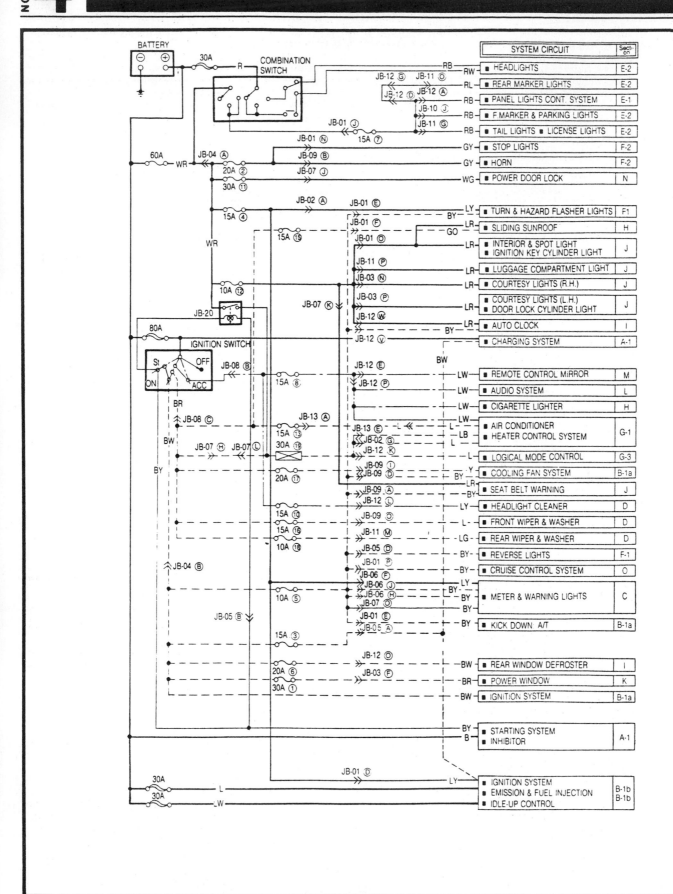

SYSTEM CIRCUIT	Section
■ HEADLIGHTS	E-2
■ REAR MARKER LIGHTS	E-2
■ PANEL LIGHTS CONT. SYSTEM	E-1
■ F.MARKER & PARKING LIGHTS	E-2
■ TAIL LIGHTS ■ LICENSE LIGHTS	E-2
■ STOP LIGHTS	F-2
■ HORN	F-2
■ POWER DOOR LOCK	N
■ TURN & HAZARD FLASHER LIGHTS	F1
■ SLIDING SUNROOF	H
■ INTERIOR & SPOT LIGHT ■ IGNITION KEY CYLINDER LIGHT	J
■ LUGGAGE COMPARTMENT LIGHT	J
■ COURTESY LIGHTS (R.H.)	J
■ COURTESY LIGHTS (L.H.) ■ DOOR LOCK CYLINDER LIGHT	J
■ AUTO CLOCK	I
■ CHARGING SYSTEM	A-1
■ REMOTE CONTROL MIRROR	M
■ AUDIO SYSTEM	L
■ CIGARETTE LIGHTER	H
■ AIR CONDITIONER ■ HEATER CONTROL SYSTEM	G-1
■ LOGICAL MODE CONTROL	G-3
■ COOLING FAN SYSTEM	B-1a
■ SEAT BELT WARNING	J
■ HEADLIGHT CLEANER	D
■ FRONT WIPER & WASHER	D
■ REAR WIPER & WASHER	D
■ REVERSE LIGHTS	F-1
■ CRUISE CONTROL SYSTEM	O
■ METER & WARNING LIGHTS	C
■ KICK DOWN A/T	B-1a
■ REAR WINDOW DEFROSTER	I
■ POWER WINDOW	K
■ IGNITION SYSTEM	B-1a
■ STARTING SYSTEM ■ INHIBITOR	A-1
■ IGNITION SYSTEM ■ EMISSION & FUEL INJECTION ■ IDLE-UP CONTROL	B-1b B-1b

EGI control system wiring schematic 323 Station Wagon

MAZDA 626

Non-Turbocharged and Turbocharged Engines

General Information

The fuel injection system supplies the necessary fuel to the injectors to achieve combustion at constant pressure. Fuel is metered and injected into the intake manifold according to the signals from the EGI control unit. The injection system consists of the fuel pump, fuel filter, distribution pipe, pulsation dampener, pressure regulator, injectors, fuel pump switch (incorporated into the air flow meter), and the circuit opening relay.

The EGI control unit (ECU), through various input sensors, monitors battery voltage, engine rpm, amount of air intake, cranking signal, No. 1 cylinder ignition timing, intake temperature, coolant temperature, oxygen concentration in the exhaust gases, EGR amount, throttle opening, atmospheric pressure, gearshift position, clutch engagement, braking, power steering operation and A/C compressor operation.

The ECU governs operation of the fuel injection system, bypass air control system, fuel evaporation system and EGR control system. The ECU has a built in fail-safe mechanism. If a fault occurs while driving, the ECU will substitute pre-programmed values. Driving performance will be affected, but the vehicle will still be driveable.

The injectors are supplied with battery voltage directly through the main relay. The electrical connectors on the injectors are color coded to distinguish the non-turbocharged injector from the turbocharged injector. The non-turbocharged injectors use a yellow connector while the turbocharged injectors use a purple connector.

SERVICE PRECAUTIONS

The following are examples of safety precautions to adhere to when performing maintenance on the fuel injection system. They will be repeated throughout the text for emphasis where appropriate.
- Fuel injector lines are subjected to high pressure even when the engine is not operating. Exercise extreme caution when disconnecting and relieving pressure from fuel lines to avoid the possibility of injury or fire.
- Ensure that eye protection is worn when performing maintenance on pressurized fuel injection components. DO NOT allow hands and face to come in contact with fuel or fuel spray.
- DO NOT allow fuel or fuel spray to come in contact with any open flame or sparks. Prior to disconnecting and removing fuel injection system components, ensure that the negative battery terminal is disconnected. Have a fire extinguisher in the vicinity of the work area, and post "No Smoking" signs an adequate distance from the vehicle.
- If any fuel leakage or spillage occurs, ensure that all traces of fuel are removed from engine and/or floor surfaces.
- Exercise care during removal, installation and handling of the fuel injectors. The fuel injectors are precision components that are susceptible to damage if dropped or mishandled.

Diagnosis and Testing

AIR FLOW METER (AFM)

Terminal Voltage Test

1. Remove the rubber boot from the AFM connector.

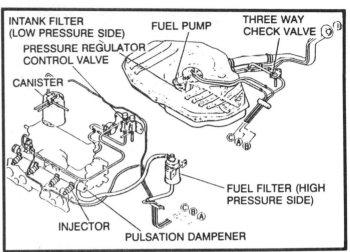

Mazda 626 fuel injection system components—1986-87 (non-turbocharged and turbocharged engines)

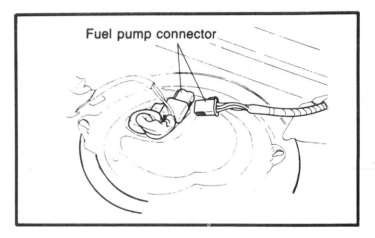

2. Turn the ignition switch to the On position.
3. With a voltmeter, measure the voltage between the indicated terminals and ground.
4. If the voltage readings are not within the specified range, check the main fuse, main relay resistance in the AFM, or wiring harnesses.
5. Reinstall the rubber boot onto the connector.

Resistance Test

1. Disconnect the AFM connector.
2. With an ohmmeter, measure the resistance between the indicated terminals.
3. Remove the air cleaner upper case assembly.
4. Press the measuring plate open.

NOTE: Inspect the measuring plate for sticking or resistance when moving the plate. If resistance is encountered, clean the measuring plate and sensor wall interior with low pressure compressed air.

5. With an ohmmeter, measure the resistance between the indicated terminals.
6. If the resistance readings are not within the specified ranges, replace the AFM assembly.
7. Reinstall the air cleaner upper case assembly and reconnect the AFM connector.

Fuel injection system dianosis

Is the terminal (Fp) voltage of the circuit opening relay OK? — **NO** → Check the circuit opening relay, main fuse and wiring harness.

YES

Is the fuel pressure, regulated by the pressure regulator or the injection pressure OK?

YES .... **NO**

Is the fuel pump outlet pressure OK? — **NO** → Check the fuel pump.

YES → Check the pressure regulator, fuel filter, and for fuel leaks in the fuel line.

Is there an operating sound in each injector? — **NO** → Check the control unit, wiring harness and the injector(s).

YES

Is the engine speed decreased equally by disconnecting each injector connector? — **NO** → Check the injectors.

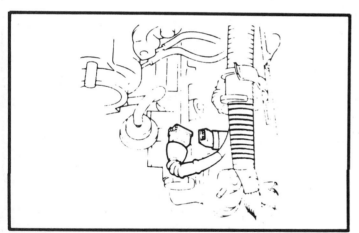

Disconnecting the fuel injector connector

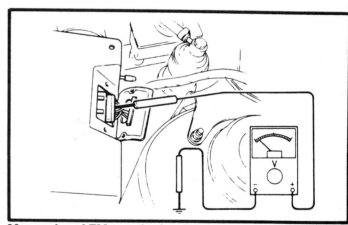

Measuring AFM terminal voltage

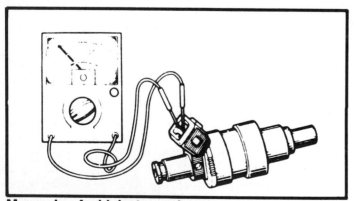

Measuring fuel injector resistance

Removal and Installation

1. Disconnect the AFM connector.
2. Loosen the clamps or clips then disconnect the main air hose, secondary air hoses ind air control valve vacuum hoses.
3. Remove the accelerator cable bracket.
4. Remove the air cleaner upper case.

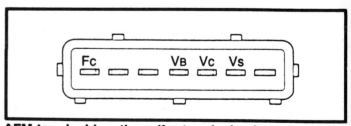

AFM terminal locations (for terminal voltage test)

5. Remove the AFM and seal rubber from the air cleaner upper case.
6. Install the new AFM into the air cleaner upper case, then install a new seal rubber.
7. Reinstall the air cleaner upper case; reconnect the hoses and tighten the clamps (clips).
8. Reinstall the accelerator cable bracket.
9. Reconnect the AFM connector.
10. Start the engine and warm up to normal operating temperature.
11. Check the idle speed, adjust if necessary.

Terminal	Voltage
Vs	0.7 ~ 2.7 V
Vc	6 ~ 10 V
VB	Approx. 12 V
Fc (fuel pump switch)	Approx. 12 V

AFM terminal voltage specifications

Terminal	Resistance (Ω)
E2 ↔ Vs	More than 20
E2 ↔ Vc	100 to 300
E2 ↔ VB	200 to 400
E2 ↔ THA (Intake air temperature sensor)	
E1 ↔ Fc	∞

AFM resistance specfications

Intake Air Temperature	Resistance
−20°C (−4°F)	13.6 ~ 18.4 kΩ
20°C (68°F)	2.205 ~ 2.695 kΩ
60°C (140°F)	0.493 ~ 0.667 kΩ

Intake air temperature sensor resistance specifications

Moving the measuring plate

THROTTLE SENSOR

Terminal Voltage Test

1. Remove the rubber boot from the throttle sensor connector.
2. Turn the ignition switch to the On position.
3. Measure the voltage between each terminal and ground with the throttle in the closed position.
4. Move the throttle valve to the fully open position and re-check the voltage between each terminal and ground.
5. If all the voltage readings, except the D terminal, are within the specified ranges; check the throttle sensor setting.
6. If the remaining terminals are not within specifications, measure the resistances of the throttle sensor terminals (2A, 2C, 2E and 1G) located in the EGI control unit and wiring harness.

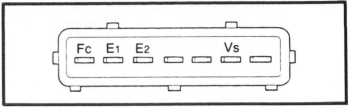

AFM terminal locations (for resistance test after moving the measuring plate)

Terminals	Resistance (Ω)
E2 ↔ Vs	Less than 400
E1 ↔ Fc	0 (continuity)

AFM resistance specifications

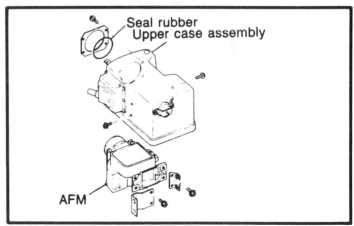

1. AFM connector
2. Air hose
3. Secondary air hose
4. Air control and duty solenoid valve vacuum hoses
5. Accelerator cable bracket
6. Air cleaner upper case

Air flow meter assembly

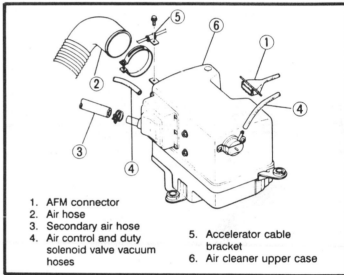

Removing the AFM from the upper case assembly

7. Reinstall the rubber boot onto the throttle sensor connector.

Setting Inspection

1. Disconnect the throttle sensor connector.
2. Connect a Throttle Sensor Tester (No. 49 9200 165) to the throttle sensor or connect an ohmmeter across the B and D terminals of the throttle sensor connector.

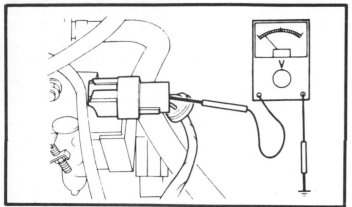

Measuring throttle sensor terminal voltage

Condition Terminal	Closed	Fully opened
A (V$_T$)	0.4 ~ 0.6V	Approx. 4.0V
B (GND)	Below 1.5 V	
C (V$_5$)	4.5 ~ 5.5 V	
D (IDL)	Below 1.5 V	Approx. 12 V

Throttle sensor terminal voltage specifications

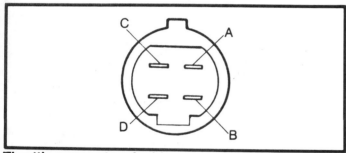

Throttle sensor terminal locations

3. Insert a 0.028 in. (0.7mm) feeler gauge between the throttle lever and the throttle stop screw. Ensure that the tester buzzer sounds or the ohmmeter reads continuity between the A and B terminals.

NOTE: The throttle stop screw is pre-set and has been anti-tampered to retain the adjustment. DO NOT attempt to adjust the throttle stop screw.

4. If the results of the test are not as described, refer to the Setting Adjustment section to adjust the throttle sensor.

Setting Adjustment

1. Disconnect the throttle sensor connector.
2. Connect a Throttle Sensor Tester (49 9200 165) to the throttle sensor.
3. Insert a 0.016 in. (0.4mm) feeler gauge between the throttle lever and the throttle stop screw.
4. Loosen, but do not remove, the two throttle sensor attaching screws.
5. Rotate the throttle sensor clockwise 30° then counterclockwise 30° until the tester buzzer sounds.
6. Replace the feeler gauge with a 0.022 in. (0.55mm) feeler gauge.
7. Ensure that the tester buzzer does not sound.
8. If the tester buzzer sounds, repeat Steps 5–7 until the tester buzzer does not sound.

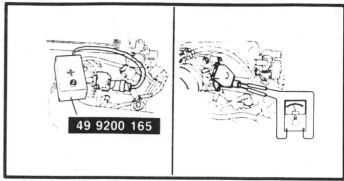

Testing throttle sensor using Throttle Sensor Tester and ohmmeter methods

Thickness gauge	0 mm (0 in)	0.7 mm (0.028 in)
Buzzer	Sounds	Does not sound
Lamp	ON	OFF
Continuity	YES	NO

Throttle stop screw clearance specifications

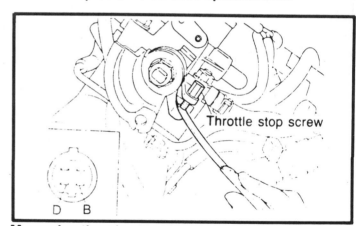

Measuring throttle stop screw clearance

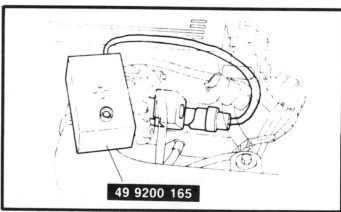

Connecting throttle sensor tester

9. When the proper adjustment is obtained, hold the throttle sensor stationary and tighten the two throttle sensor attaching screws.

NOTE: DO NOT disturb the throttle sensor position when tightening the attaching screws.

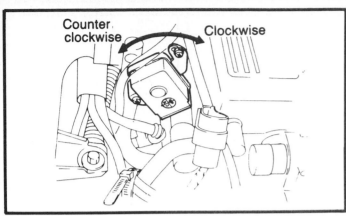

Rotating throttle sensor to obtain adjustment

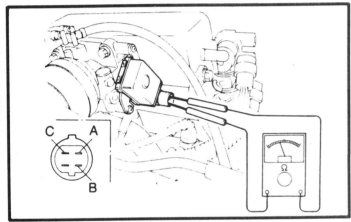

Measuring throttle sensor resistance

Terminal \ Condition	Closed	Fully opened
A ↔ B	Approx. 500 Ω	Approx. 4.5 kΩ
B ↔ C	4~6 kΩ	

Throttle sensor resistance specifications

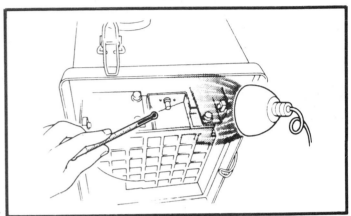

Heating the air intake temperature sensor

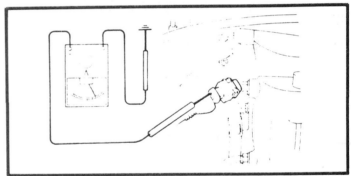

Measuring water thermo sensor terminal voltage

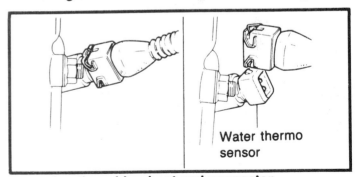

Water thermo sensor

Removing the rubber boot and connector

10. Recheck the throttle sensor adjustment by performing the procedures described in the Setting Inspection section.

11. Disconnect the Throttle Sensor Tester and reconnect the throttle sensor connector.

Resistance Test

1. Disconnect the throttle sensor connector.
2. With an ohmmeter, measure the resistance between terminals A and B and terminals B and C with the throttle in the closed position.
3. Move the throttle valve to the fully open position and recheck the resistance.
4. If the resistance readings are not within the specified ranges, replace the throttle sensor.

INTAKE AIR TEMPERATURE SENSOR

Resitance Test

1. Remove the air cleaner upper cover assembly.
2. With a suitable heat source, heat the intake air temperature and monitor the temperature.
3. With an ohmmeter, measure the resistance between the THA and E2 terminals.
4. If the resistance is not within the specified range (over the indicated temperature range), replace the air flow meter assembly.
5. Reinstall the air cleaner assembly.

WATER THERMO SENSOR

Terminal Voltage Test

1. Start the engine and warm up to normal operating temperature, then stop the engine. Engine speed should not exceed 4000 rpm during the warm up period.

2. Remove the rubber boot from the water thermo sensor connector and disconnect the connector.

CAUTION

Do not disconnect the water thermo switch connector when the ignition switch is in the On position because the fan will turn.

3. Turn the ignition switch to the On position.
4. Measure the voltage between the LR terminal and ground. The voltage reading should be approximately 0.5(V).

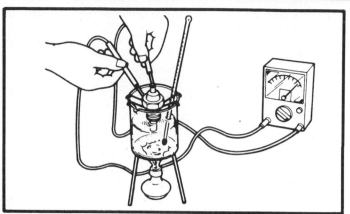

Measuring water thermo sensor resistance

5. If the voltage reading is not as specified, proceed to the Resistance Test section and also check the wiring harness for open and short circuits.

Resistance Test

1. Remove the rubber boot from the water thermo sensor connector and disconnect the connector.

— CAUTION —

Do not disconnect the water thermo switch connector when the ignition switch is in the On position because the fan will turn and may cause injury.

2. Drain the coolant.
3. Loosen and remove the water thermo sensor switch from the thermostat cover.
4. Place the water thermo switch into a container of water and heat the container.
5. Connect an ohmmeter to the water thermo switch and measure the resistance over the specified temperature ranges.
6. If the resistance readings are not within the specified ranges, replace the water thermo switch.

NOTE: Prior to reinstalling the water thermo switch, replace the old O-ring with a new O-ring to ensure proper sealing. Do not use any form of sealing tape on the water thermo switch threads.

7. Reinstall and tighten the water thermo switch into the thermostat cover opening.
8. Refill the coolant.
9. Reconnect the water thermo switch connector and reinstall the rubber boot.
10. Start the engine and check for coolant leaks. Repair all leaks as necessary.

ATMOSPHERIC PRESSURE SENSOR (APS)

Terminal Voltage Test

1. Remove the rubber cap and connect a vacuum pump to the sensor port.
2. Turn the ignition switch to the On position.
3. Measure the voltage between each terminal and ground by creating and releasing vacuum to the sensor.
4. If the voltage readings at terminals A, C or D are not within the specified range, check the wiring harness.
5. If the voltage readings at terminals A, C and D are correct, but the voltage reading at terminal B is not within the specification, replace the atmospheric pressure sensor.

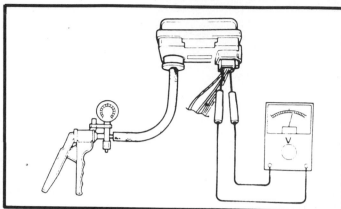

Measuring APS terminal voltage

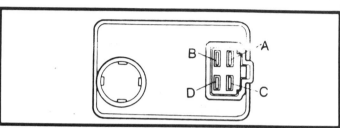

APS terminal locations

Terminal (Color)	Voltage
A (YG)	Approx. 12V
B (Lg)	1.4 ~ 4.9V
C (LgR)	Below 1.5V
D (LgW)	4.5 ~ 5.5V

APS terminal voltage specifications

WATER TEMPERATURE SWITCH
Resistance Test

1. Drain the coolant.
2. Disconnect the water temperature switch connector.
3. Loosen and remove the water temperature switch from the radiator.
4. Place the water temperature switch into a container of water and heat the container.
5. Connect an ohmmeter to the water temperature switch and measure the resistance at a number of temperatures.
6. If no resistance can be measured at the temperatures selected, replace the water temperature switch.

NOTE: Prior to reinstalling the water temperature switch, replace the old O-ring with a new O-ring to ensure proper sealing. Do not use any form of sealing tape on the water thermo switch threads.

7. Reinstall and tighten the water temperature switch into the radiator opening.
8. Refill the coolant.
9. Reconnect the water temperature switch connector.
10. Start the engine and check for coolant leaks. Repair all leaks as necessary.

OXYGEN SENSOR
Terminal Voltage Test

1. Start the engine and warm up to normal operating temperature at idle speed.

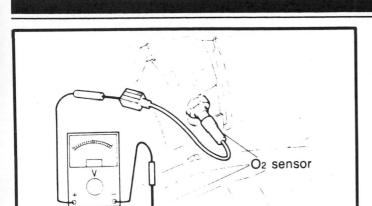

Measuring O₂ sensor terminal voltage

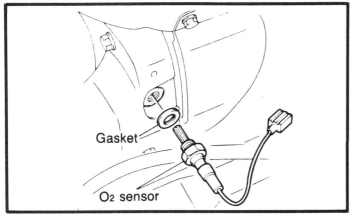

Installation view of the O₂ sensor

2. Disconnect the oxygen sensor connector from the wiring harness.

3. Connect a voltmeter between the oxygen sensor connector terminal and ground.

4. Run the engine at 4000 rpm until the voltmeter reads approximately 0.55(V).

5. Increase and decrease the engine speed suddenly several times while observing the voltage meter. When the engine speed is increased, the meter should read between 0.5(V)-1.0(V). When the engine speed is decreased, the meter should read between 0-0.4(V).

6. If the voltage readings are not within the specified ranges, replace the oxygen sensor.

Removal and Installation

1. Disconnect the oxygen sensor connector from the wiring harness.

2. Loosen and remove the oxygen sensor with gasket.

3. Install a new gasket onto the the new oxygen sensor.

4. Reinstall and tighten the oxygen sensor.

5. Reconnect the oxygen sensor connector to the wiring harness.

NUMBER 1 CYLINDER SENSOR (TURBOCHARGED ENGINES ONLY)

Terminal Voltage Test

1. Remove the rubber boot from the No.1 cylinder distributor connector.

2. Turn the ignition switch to the On position.

3. With a voltmeter, ensure there is battery voltage present at the d terminal (R).

4. Start the engine and increase the engine speed.

5. Measure the voltage at the D terminal (LgB). The voltage reading should be within the range of 2(V)-3(V).

6. If the voltage reading is not within the specified range, replace the No. cylinder sensor.

7. Reinstall the rubber boot.

PRESSURE SWITCH

Terminal Voltage

1. Disconnect the pressure switch connector.

2. Disconnect the hose from the pressure switch port.

3. Connect a Pressure Tester (No. 49 H080 740) or equivalent to the pressure switch port. Connect a source of low pressure air to the Pressure Tester.

4. Connect a voltmeter between the BrW terminal and ground.

NOTE: Ensure the Pressure Tester output does not exceed 14 psi.

5. Apply an air signal of 10-11 psi to the pressure switch while measuring the voltage across the BrW terminal. At this pressure, the reading should be less than 1.5(V).

6. Decrease the air signal to 9 psi or below and recheck the voltage. At this pressure, the reading should be approximately 12(V).

7. If the voltage readings are not as specified, replace the pressure switch.

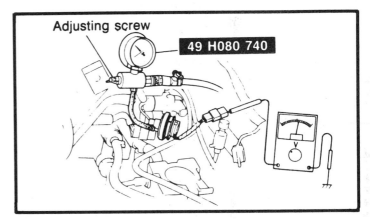

Measuring pressure switch terminal voltage

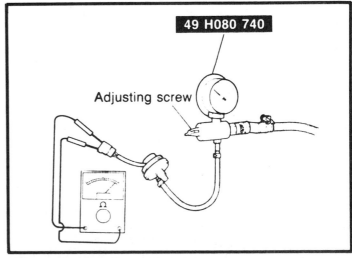

Measuring pressure switch resistance

Resistance Test

1. Disconnect the pressure switch connector.
2. Disconnect the hose from the pressure switch port and remove the pressure switch.
3. Connect a Pressure Tester (No. 49 H080 740) or equivalent to the pressure switch port. Connect a source of low pressure air to the Pressure Tester.
4. Connect a ohmmeter across the pressure switch connector terminals.

NOTE: Ensure the Pressure Tester output does not exceed 14 psi.

5. Apply an air signal of 10-11 psi to the pressure switch while measuring the resistance across the connector terminals. At this pressure, there should be continuity across the pressure switch.
6. Decrease the air signal to 9 psi or below and recheck the resistance. At this pressure, there should be no continuity.
7. If the continuity across the switch is not as specified, replace the pressure switch.

MAIN RELAY

Terminal Voltage Test

1. Turn the ignition switch to the On position.
2. With a voltmeter, measure the voltage between each terminal and ground.
3. If the voltage readings are not within the specified ranges, proceed to the Resistance Test section.

Resistance Test

1. Disconnect and remove the main relay.
2. With a multimeter, measure the resistance between the A and B terminals. The resistance reading should be approximately 70 Ohms.
3. Apply battery power to the A terminal and ground the B terminal.
4. Check for continuity between the A and B terminals.
5. If the resistance reading is not as specified or there is no continuity, replace the main relay.

RELIEVING FUEL SYSTEM PRESSURE

──── CAUTION ────

Fuel injector lines are subjected to high pressure even when the engine is not operating. Exercise exterme caution when disconnecting and relieving pressure from fuel lines to avoid the possibilty of injury or fire.

Ensure that eye protection is worn when performing maintenance on pressurized fuel injection components. DO NOT allow hands and face to come in contact with fuel or fuel spray.

DO NOT allow fuel or fuel spray to come in contact with any open flame or sparks. Prior to disconnecting and removing fuel injection system components, ensure that the negative battery terminal is disconnected. Have a fire extinguisher in the vicinity of the work area, and post "No Smoking" signs an adequate distance from the vehicle.

1. Start the engine and warm up to normal operating temperature at idle speed.
2. Disconnect the fuel pump connector while the engine is running.
3. Allow the engine to stall, then turn the ignition switch to the Off position.
4. Disconnect the negative battery terminal.

NOTE: Allow adequate time for the engine to cool down prior to disconnecting or removing fuel hoses and fuel injection system components.

5. Carefully loosen, but do not remove, the fuel hose clamp located at the distribution pipe inlet.

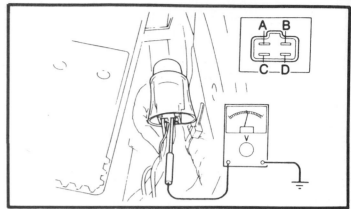

Measuring main relay terminal voltage

Terminal	Voltage
A	Approx. 12V
B	0V
C	Approx. 12V
D	Approx. 12V

Main relay terminal voltage specifications

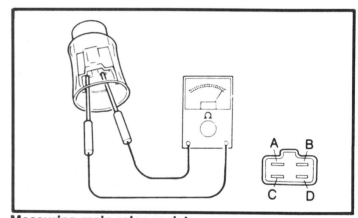

Measuring main relay resistance

6. Place a rag around the end of the fuel inlet hose and slide the clamp away from the distribution pipe inlet opening.
7. With the rag still in place, carefully work the fuel hose from the inlet opening to relieve any system pressure. Drain all residual fuel into a suitable waste container.
8. If further disassembly is required, ensure that all component or hose openings are plugged or covered.
9. Reconnect and tighten the fuel hose to the distribution pipe. Reconnect the fuel pump connector and the negative battery terminal.

FUEL PUMP

Outlet Pressure Test

NOTE: Allow adequate time for the engine to cool down prior to disconnecting or removing fuel hoses and fuel injection system components.

1. Disconnect the negative battery terminal.
2. Relieve the fuel system pressure as described in the Relieving Fuel Pressure section.
3. Loosen the clip and disconnect the fuel hose from the fuel

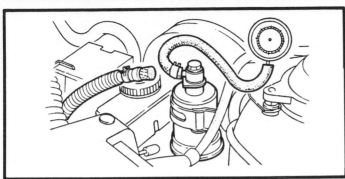

Measuring fuel pump output pressure with gauge connected to the fuel filter

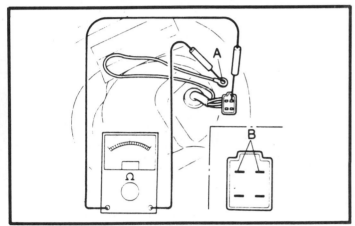

Measuring fuel pump resistance

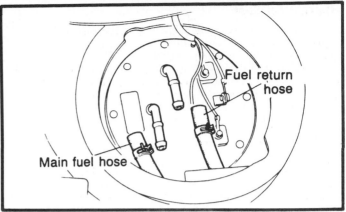

Disconnecting fuel pump hoses

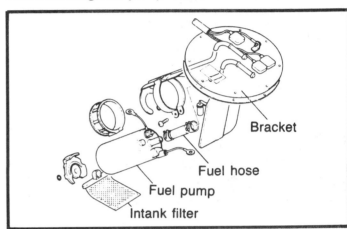

Exploded view of the fuel pump assembly

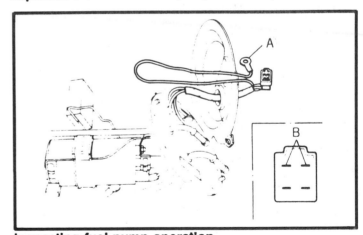

Inspecting fuel pump operation

filter outlet connection (high pressure side). Ensure all residual fuel is drained into a suitable waste container. Plug or clamp the fuel hose opening.

4. Connect and tighten a suitable 0-100 psi (0-700 kPA) gauge to the fuel filter outlet connection.

5. Connect a jumper wire across both terminals of the fuel pump check connector.

6. Connect the negative battery terminal and turn the ignition switch to the On position.

7. Ensure that the fuel pump outlet pressure is within the range of 64-85 psi (440-590 kPA).

8. If the fuel pump outlet pressure is not within the specified range, then check the fuel pump operation, circuit opening relay and main fuse.

9. Turn the ignition switch to the Off position and remove the jumper wire. Remove the gauge and reconnect and tighten the fuel hose to the fuel filter outlet connection.

Resistance Test

1. Remove the rear seat cushion.
2. Disconnect the fuel pump connector.
3. With an ohmmeter, measure the resistance between the A and B terminals. The resistance reading should be approximately 0.3 Ohms.
4. If the resistance reading is as specified, replace the fuel pump.

Removal and Installation

1. Remove the rear seat cushion and the filler cap.
2. Disconnect the fuel pump connector.
3. Remove the service hole cover.
4. Relieve the fuel system pressure as described in the RELIEVING THE FUEL SYSTEM PRESSURE section.

5. Loosen the clips and disconnect the fuel return and main fuel hoses. Plug or cover the hose openings.

NOTE: To ensure proper installation; prior to disconnecting the fuel pump electrical wires, identify each wire with its respective connecting terminal.

6. Disconnect and remove the electrical wires.
7. Loosen the clip and disconnect the hose from the fuel pump discharge connection.
8. Loosen the bracket screws and remove the fuel pump with the intank filter from the bracket.
9. Install a new fuel pump and intank filter into the bracket and tighten the bracket screws.
10. Installation is the reverse of the removal procedure.

Operational Test

1. Remove the rear seat cushion and the filler cap.
2. Disconnect the fuel pump connector.
3. Remove the service hole cover.
4. Relieve the fuel system pressure as described in the RE-LIEVING FUEL SYSTEM PRESSURE section.
5. Loosen the clips and disconnect the fuel return and main fuel hoses. Plug or cover the hose openings.
6. Briefly apply battery power to the B terminal and connect the A terminal to ground.
7. If the fuel pump does not operate, replace the fuel pump.

FUEL LINE PRESSURE TEST

NOTE: Allow adequate time for the engine to cool down prior to disconnecting or removing fuel hoses and fuel injection system components.

1. Disconnect the negative battery terminal.
2. Relieve the fuel system pressure as described in the Relieving Fuel System Pressure section.
3. Loosen the clip and disconnect the fuel hose from the fuel filter outlet connection (high pressure side). Ensure all residual fuel is drained into a suitable waste container. Plug or clamp the fuel hose opening.
4. Attach the special Multi-Pressure Tester (49 9200 750) to the fuel filter outlet connection.
5. Connect a jumper wire across both terminals of the fuel pump check connector.
6. Connect the negative battery terminal and turn the ignition switch to the On position.
7. Ensure that the fuel line pressure is within the range of 35-41 psi (245-280 kPA) as shown on the Multi-Pressure Tester diplay.
8. Start and operate the engine at idle speed.
9. Ensure that the fuel line pressure is within the range of 27-33 psi (186-226 kPA) as shown on the Multi-Pressure Tester display.
10. If the fuel line pressure is not within the specified ranges, check the fuel filter and the fuel pump pressure.
11. If the fuel filter is not clogged and the fuel pump pressure is within specifications, replace the pressure regulator.
12. Turn the ignition switch to the Off position and remove the jumper wire. Disconnect the Multi-Pressure Tester and reconnect and tighten the fuel hose to the fuel filter outlet connection.

PRESSURE REGULATOR SOLENOID VALVE

Removal and Operational Test

1. Disconnect the pressure regulating valve connector and vacuum hoses. Remove the valve.
2. Connect one of the lengths of vacuum hose (A) to the port below the air filter.
3. Blow air through the hose (A) and ensure that the air exits through port (B).
4. Connect a jumper wire from the negative terminal to ground and apply battery voltage.
5. Blow air through the hose (A) and ensure that the air exits through the air filter port.
6. If the air does not flow in the directions described, replace the valve.
7. Installation is the reverse of the removal procedure.

FUEL FILTER

Removal and Installation

1. Relieve the fuel system pressure as described in the Relieving Fuel System Pressure section.

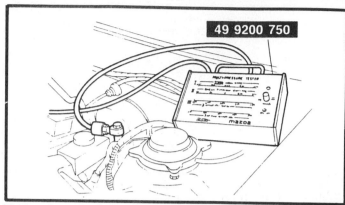

Measuring fuel line pressure with Multi-Pressure Tester

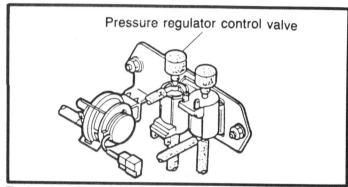

Pressure regulator control valve

Turbocharged engine shown—non-turbocharged engine similar

2. Loosen the clips and disconnect the fuel filter inlet and outlet hoses.
3. Loosen and remove the bracket retaining nuts and remove the bracket with the fuel filter.
4. Loosen the bracket screw and remove the fuel filter.
5. Remove the bolts, connectors and copper washers from the existing fuel filter. Discard the filter and copper washers.
6. Reinstall the bolts and connectors with new copper washers into the new fuel filter. Position the fuel filter into the bracket and reinstall the bracket.
7. Reconnect the fuel filter inlet and outlet hoses and tighten the clips.
8. Torque the bolts to 18-25 ft. lbs..

FUEL INJECTOR SYSTEM

Fuel Injectors On-Vehicle Inspection

1. Start the engine and warm up to normal operating temperature at idle speed.
2. Apply a sound scope or equivalent to the injector and check for operating sound.
3. If no sound is detected, check the injector resistance, circuit opening relay, fuses, wiring harness, or control unit.
4. Connect a tachometer to the engine.
5. Disconnect the electrical connector from the injector and observe the engine idle speed with the tachometer. Verify that the idle speed decreases 100-200 rpm with the connector removed.
6. If the idle speed does not decrease within the specified range, check the injector resistance, injection volume and fuel pressure.
7. Repeat Steps 1 through 5 for the remaining fuel injectors.

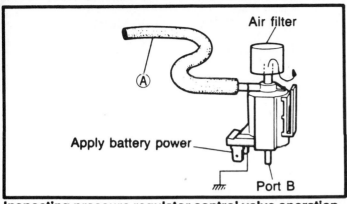

Inspecting pressure regulator control valve operation

Removing the reed valve housing

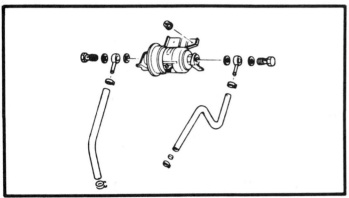

Exploded view of the fuel filter assembly

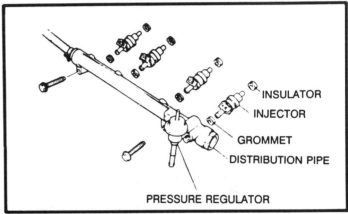

Distribution pipe assembly with fuel injectors

Resistance Test

1. Disconnect the electrical connector from the fuel injector.
2. With an ohmmeter, measure the resistance across the fuel injector connector terminals. The resistance reading should be within the range of 12-16 Ohms.
3. If the resistance is not within the specified range, replace the fuel injector.
4. Repeat Steps 1 through 3 for the remaining fuel injectors.

Injector Volume and Leak Test Preparation

—— CAUTION ——

Fuel injector lines are subjected to high pressure even when the engine is not operating. Exercise extreme caution when disconnecting and relieving pressure from fuel lines to avoid the possibility of injury or fire.

—— CAUTION ——

DO NOT allow fuel or fuel spray to come in contact with any open flame or sparks. Prior to disconnecting and removing fuel injection system components, ensure that the negative battery terminal is disconnected. Have a fire extinguisher in the vicinity of the work area, and post "No Smoking" signs an adequate distance from the vehicle.

NOTE: Allow adequate time for the engine to cool down prior to disconnecting or removing fuel hoses and fuel injection system components.

1. Disconnect the negative battery terminal.
2. Relieve the fuel system pressure as described in the Relieving Fuel System Pressure section.
3. Loosen the clips and disconnect the fuel hoses from the fuel filter outlet connection and pressure regulating valve inlet and outlet connections. Ensure that all residual fuel is drained into a suitable waste container. Temporarily plug or clamp all hose openings.

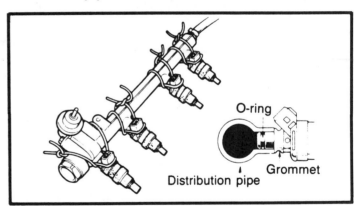

Attaching fuel injectors to the distribution pipe with wire

4. Disconnect the electrical connector from each fuel injector and route the the connectors with wiring away from the distribution pipe.
5. Remove the reed valve housing.

—— CAUTION ——

Exercise care during the removal, installation and handling of the fuel injectors. The fuel injectors are precision components that are susceptible to damage if dropped or mishandled.

6. Loosen and remove the bolts that attach the distribution pipe to the intake manifold. Carefully lift the distribution pipe, with injectors, away from the intake manifold.
7. Remove the insulators from the injector tips and firmly attach each injector to the distribution pipe with a piece of wire. Ensure that the injectors are not allowed to move or rotate on the distribution pipe.

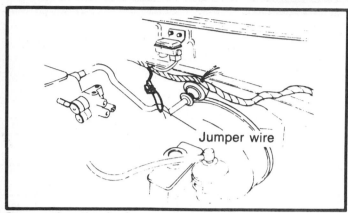

Connecting the fuel pump jumper wire

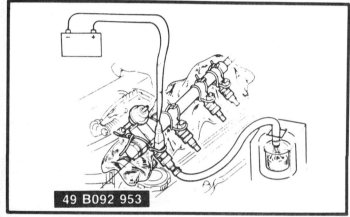

49 B092 953

Mearsuring fuel injector volume

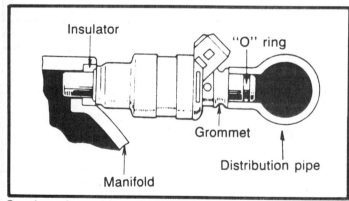

Section view of installed fuel injector

8. Reconnect the fuel filter and pressure regulating valve fuel hoses and reinstall and tighten the clips.

9. Reconnect the negative battery terminal.

Leak Test

Ensure that eye protection is worn when performing maintenance on pressurized fuel injection components. DO NOT allow hands and face to come in contact with the fuel or fuel spray. DO NOT allow fuel or fuel spray to come in contact with any open flame or sparks. If any fuel leakage or spillage occurs, ensure that all traces of fuel are removed from engine and/or floor surfaces.

1. Connect a jumper wire across both terminals of the fuel pump check connector.

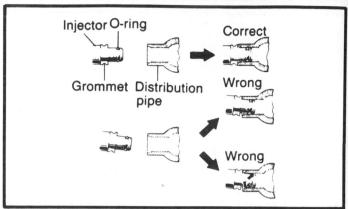

Proper fuel injector/distribution pipe installation

2. Position a suitable waste container under the fuel injectors.

3. Turn the ignition switch to the On position.

4. Inspect each fuel injector for leakage for 5 minutes.

NOTE: After the 5 minute period, a small amount of leakage is acceptable.

5. Replace injector(s) that leak excessively.

6. Turn the ignition switch to the Off position and remove the jumper wire.

Volume Test

1. Connect and tighten a 39 inch (or more) length of vinyl hose to the end of the injector. Place the end of the hose into a suitable measuring container or graduated cylinder.

2. Connect a jumper wire across both terminals of the fuel pump check connector.

3. Connect an Injector Checker (No. 49 B0902 953) between the battery and the injector.

4. Turn the ignition switch to the On position to apply battery voltage to the injector for 15 seconds. The volume discharged from the injector should be within the range of 3.8-5.2 cu. in. (63-85 cc).

5. If the volume is not within the specified range, replace the injector.

6. Repeat Steps 1–5 for the remaining injectors.

7. Turn the ignition switch to the Off position and disconnect the Injector Checker from the battery. Remove the jumper wire. Remove the vinyl hose.

8. Remove the wire and remove the injectors from the distribution pipe openings.

9. Remove the existing O-rings from the end of each injector and discard. Apply a light coating of clean fuel to each new O-ring and install. Replace worn grommets and insulators as required.

NOTE: Ensure that the injectors are installed straight into the distribution pipe openings. Do not allow the injectors to become cocked or uneven. Ensure that the connectors are accessible during installation.

10. Reinstall the injectors into the distribution pipe. Install the distribution pipe onto the intake manifold in the reverse order of removal.

Injection Pressure Test

Conduct the injection pressure test when the engine is experiencing poor acceleration or hesitation.

NOTE: Allow adequate time for the engine to cool down prior to disconnecting or removing fuel hoses and fuel injection system components.

1. Disconnect the negative battery terminal.

2. Relieve the fuel system pressure as described in the RELIEVING FUEL SYSTEM PRESSURE section.

3. Loosen the clip and disconnect the fuel hose from the fuel filter outlet connection (high pressure side). Ensure all residual fuel is drained into a suitable waste container. Plug or clamp the fuel hose opening.

4. Attach a Multi-Pressure Tester (49 9200 750) to the fuel filter outlet connection.

5. Connect a jumper wire across both terminals of the fuel pump check connector.

6. Connect the negative battery terminal and turn the ignition switch to the On position.

7. Start and operate the engine at idle speed.

8. Rotate the Multi-Pressure Tester range selector knob to the "Range III" position and measure the injection pressure as shown on the "Range III" display. The injection pressure should be within the range of 35-41 psi (245-280 kPA).

9. If the injection pressure is lower than the specified range, check the following:
   a. Fuel pump outlet pressure
   b. Fuel line pressure
   c. Fuel filter clogging

10. If the injection pressure is higher than the specified range, check the following:
   a. Fuel return pipe clogging
   b. Fuel line pressure

12. Turn the ignition switch to the Off position and remove the jumper wire. Disconnect the Multi-Pressure Tester and reconnect and tighten the fuel hose to the fuel filter outlet connection.

CIRCUIT OPENING RELAY

Terminal Voltage Test

1. With a voltmeter, measure the voltage between each terminal and ground.

2. If the voltage reading at B terminal is not as specified, check the fuses or wiring harness from the ignition switch.

3. If the voltage reading at STA terminal is not as specified, check the wiring harness at the ignition switch.

4. If the voltage reading at E_1 terminal is not as specified, check the ground harness.

5. If the voltage reading at Fc terminal is not as specified, check the air flow meter or test on the circuit opening relay resistance.

6. If the voltage reading at Fp terminal is not as specified, check the circuit opening relay resistance.

Resistance Test

1. With an ohmmeter, measure the resistance across the indicated terminals.

2. If the resistance readings are not within the specified ranges, replace the circuit opening relay.

IDLE SPEED

Inspection

1. Inspect the general condition of the engine. Ensure that hoses are sound and all hose connections are tight. Repair as necessary.

2. Turn all the vehicle's accessories off.

3. Apply the emergency brake and place the transmission in Neutral.

4. Start the engine and warm up to normal operating temperature at 2,500-3,000 rpm for 3 minutes.

5. Check the ignition timing and adjust if necessary.

Terminal / Condition	Fp	Fc	B	STA	E_1
IG SW: ON	0V	12V	12V	0V	0V
Measuring plate: opened	12V	0V	12V	0V	0V
IG SW: ST	12V	0V	12V	12V	0V

Circuit opening relay terminal voltage specifications

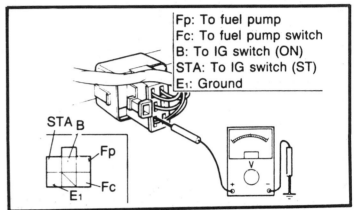

Fp: To fuel pump
Fc: To fuel pump switch
B: To IG switch (ON)
STA: To IG switch (ST)
E_1: Ground

Measuring circuit opening relay terminal voltage

Between terminals	Resistance (Ω)
STA ↔ E1	15~30
B ↔ Fc	80~150
B ↔ Fp	∞

Circuit opening relay resistance specifications

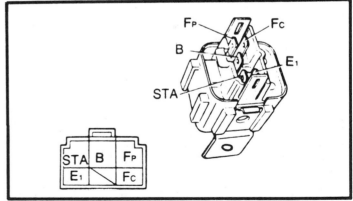

Circuit opening relay terminal locations

Adjustment

NOTE:If adjusting the idle speed at sea level (altitudes less than 3,280 feet), disconnect the air bypass solenoid valve connector prior to performing adjustment procedures.

1. Start the engine and warm up to normal operating temperature. If the electric cooling fan operates, allow the engine to run at idle speed until the cooling fan stops.

2. Connect a tachometer to the engine.

3. With the tachometer, check that the idle speed is within the following ranges:

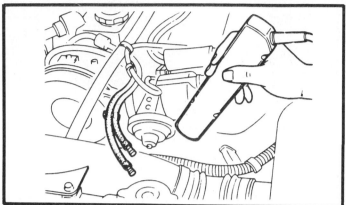

Checking the idle speed

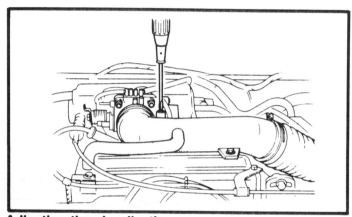

Adjusting the air adjusting screw

- 800-850 rpm for turbocharged and non-turbocharged engines with manual transmissions.
- 900-950 rpm for non-turbocharged engines with automatic transmissions.

4. If the idle speed is not within the specified ranges, adjust by rotating the air adjusting screw clockwise or counter-clockwise until the correct idle speed is obtained.

EGI CONTROL UNIT

Service Precautions

When testing the EGI control unit, the following precautions should be observed.

- Never place the test probe of a circuit tester into the connectors from the EGI control unit side.
- Before attempting to check the EGI control unit, use the Digital Code Checker (No. 49 B018 9A0) to eliminate all possible component malfunctions.
- If the EGI unit terminal voltage is not within specification(s), check the components, wiring harnesses and terminal contacts related to the out of specification terminal before replacing the EGI control unit.

Terminal Voltage Test

1. Start the engine and warm up to normal operating temperature at idle speed, then stop the engine.
2. Disconnect the engine wiring harness connectors from the EGI control unit.
3. Connect the Adaptor (No. 49 9200 163) between the engine wiring harness connectors and the EGI control unit.
4. Connect the Engine Signal Monitor (No. 49 9200 163) to the adaptor.

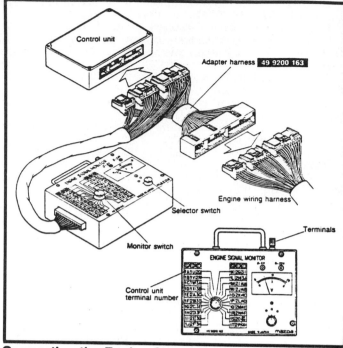

Connecting the Engine Signal Monitor

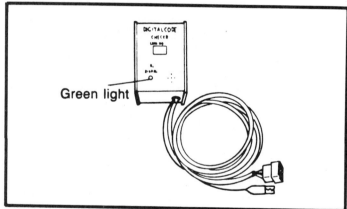

Digital Code Checker

5. Turn the ignition switch to the On position.
6. Rotate the selector switch to the desired terminal number and read the voltage shown on the signal meter.

EGI CONTROL SYSTEM

Fault Diagnosis Using The Digital Code Checker

The Digital Code Checker (No. 49 G018 9A0) is a special diagnostic tool used to detect and indicate sensor malfunctions, damaged wiring, faulty connections, and short circuits between each sensor-control unit. Faults detected within the control system are indicated by a code number and a buzzer. When conducting fault diagnosis, the the following should be considered.

- The Digital Code Checker incorporates a green light that is used to indicate the operation of the oxygen sensor. This feature enables the technician to determine whether or not the oxygen sensor is feeding information back to the EGI control unit. The light will illuminate when the air/fuel mixture is rich and go out when the air/fuel mixture is lean.
- If more than one fault exists, the fault with the lowest code number will be indicated first.

EGI CONTROL SYSTEM TERMINAL FAULT ANALYSIS (TURBOCHARGED ENGINES)

Terminal	Connected to	Voltage when operating properly	Checking of the function
1A (Output)	Digital code checker	Below 1.5 V or approx. 12 V depending on signal	—
1C (Output)	Air bypass solenoid valve (C)	Approx. 12 V	Vacuum applying to the atmospheric pressure sensor is more than 155 mmHg (6.1 inHg): Below 1.5 V
1D (Output)	Digital code checker	—	—
1E (Input)	Idle switch in throttle sensor	Below 1.5 V at idle position	—
1G (Input)	Neutral and clutch switch	Approx. 12 V in neutral / Below 1.5 V in gear	—
1H (Input)	Water temperature switch	Below 1.5 V	—
1I (Input)	Pressure switch	Approx. 12 V when depressing pedal	—
1J (Input)	Brake switch	Below 1.5 V when switch is turned off	—
1L (Input)	Air conditioner magnetic clutch circuit	Approx. 12 V	—
1M (Input)	Ignition coil negative terminal	Approx. 12 V	—
1S (Output)	Turbocharge indicator light	Below 1.5 V	—
1U (Output)	Knock control unit	Approx. 12 V	—
1V (Output)	Air bypass solenoid valve (B)	Approx. 12 V	Vacuum applying to the atmospheric pressure sensor is more than 85 mmHg (3.3 inHg): Below 1.5 V
1W (Not used)		Approx. 12 V	—
2A (Power supply)	Throttle sensor, EGR position sensor, Atmospheric pressure sensor	4.5 – 5.5 V	—
2B (Input)	Air flow meter Vc terminal	6 – 10 V	—
2C (Ground)	Air flow meter, Throttle sensor, Water thermo sensor, Atmospheric pressure sensor, EGR position sensor	Below 1.5 V	—
2D (Input)	O2 sensor	0V	—
2E (Input)	Air flow meter Vs terminal	0.7 – 2.7 V	—
2F (Input)	EGR position sensor	0 – 1.5 V	—
2G (Input)	Throttle sensor	0.4 – 0.6 V	—
2H (Input)	Atmospheric pressure sensor	Approx. 4 V at sea level	—
2I (Input)	Water thermo sensor	Approx. 0.5 V	—
2J (Input)	Intake air temperature sensor	Approx. 2.3 V at 20°C (68°F)	—
2K (Output)	Pressure regulator control valve	Approx. 12 V	2 minutes after starting when intake air temperature is more than 55°C (137°F): Below 1.5 V
2M (Output)	Duty solenoid valve (Vent)	Approx. 12 V	Engine speed increased: reduce voltage
2N (Output)	Duty solenoid valve (Vacuum)	Approx. 12 V	Engine speed increased: reduce voltage
2P (Output)	Three way solenoid valve for No.3 purge control valve	Approx. 12 V	Acceleration at 1500 rpm or above: Below 1.5 V
2R (Ground)	Engine ground	Below 1.5 V	—
3A (Ground)	Engine ground	Below 1.5 V	—
3B (Input)	Ignition switch ST position	Below 1.5 V	Approx. 12 V during cranking
3C (Output)	No.2 & No.4 injectors	Approx. 12 V	Engine speed increased, reduce voltage
3E (Output)	No.1 & No.3 injectors	Approx. 12 V	Engine speed increased, reduce voltage
3G (Ground)	Engine ground	Below 1.5 V	—
3J (Battery power)	Main relay	Approx. 12 V	—

EGI CONTROL SYSTEM TERMINAL FAULT ANALYSIS (NON-TURBOCHARGED ENGINES)

Terminal	Connected to	Voltage when operating properly	Checking of the function
1A (Output)	Digital code checker	Below 1.5 V or approx. 12 V depending on signal	—
1C (Output)	Air bypass solenoid valve (C)	Approx. 12 V	Vacuum applying to the atmospheric pressure sensor is more than 155 mmHg (6.1 inHg): Below 1.5 V
1D (Output)	Digital code checker	Below 1.5 V or approx 12 V depending on signal	—
1E (Input)	Idle switch in throttle sensor	Below 1.5 V at idle position	—
1G (Input)	Neutral and clutch switch	Approx. 12 V in neutral / Below 1.5 V in gear	—
1H (Input)	Water temperature switch	Below 1.5 V	—
1I (Input)	5th gear switch	Approx. 12 V in 5th gear	—
1J (Input)	Brake switch	Approx. 12 V when depressing pedal	—
1L (Input)	Air conditioner magnetic clutch circuit	Below 1.5 V when switch is turned off	—
1M (Input)	Ignition coil negative terminal	Approx. 12 V	—
1S (Output)	Shift indicator light	Below 1.5 V	Idle: Approx. 12V. Engine speed is 2000 rpm or above with the neutral switch being short-circuited: Below 1.5V
1V (Output)	Air bypass solenoid valve (B)	Approx. 12 V	Vacuum applying to the atmospheric pressure sensor is more than 85 mmHg (3.3 inHg): Below 1.5 V
1W (Not used)		Approx. 12 V	—
2A (Power supply)	Throttle sensor, Atmospheric pressure sensor	4.5 – 5.5 V	—
2B (Input)	Air flow meter Vc terminal	6 – 10 V	—
2C (Ground)	Air flow meter, Throttle sensor, Water thermo sensor, Atmospheric pressure sensor	Below 1.5 V	—
2D (Input)	O2 sensor	0V	—
2E (Input)	Air flow meter Vs terminal	0.7 – 2.7 V	—
2G (Input)	Throttle sensor	0.4 – 0.6 V	—
2H (Input)	Atmospheric pressure sensor	Approx. 4 V at sea level	—
2I (Input)	Water thermo sensor	Approx. 0.5 V	—
2J (Input)	Intake air temperature sensor	Approx. 2.3 V at 20°C (68°F)	—
2K (Output)	Pressure regulator control valve	Approx. 12 V	2 minutes after starting when intake air temperature is more than 55°C (131°F): Below 1.5 V
2N (Output)	Three way solenoid valve for EGR control valve	Below 1.5 V	—
2P (Output)	Three way solenoid valve for No.3 purge control valve	Approx. 12 V	Acceleration at 1500 rpm or above Below 1.5 V
2R (Ground)	Engine ground	Below 1.5 V	—
3A (Ground)	Engine ground	Below 1.5 V	—
3B (Output)	No 2 & No 4 injector	Below 1.5 V	Engine speed increased, reduce voltage
3C (Input)	Ignition switch ST position	Below 1.5 V	Approx. 12V during cranking
3D (Input)	Inhibitor switch	Below 2.0 V in "N" or "P" / Approx 12 V in others	—
3E (Output)	No.1 & No.3 injectors	Approx. 12 V	Engine speed increased, reduce voltage
3G (Ground)	Engine ground	Below 1.5 V	—
3J (Battery power)	Main relay	Approx. 12 V	—

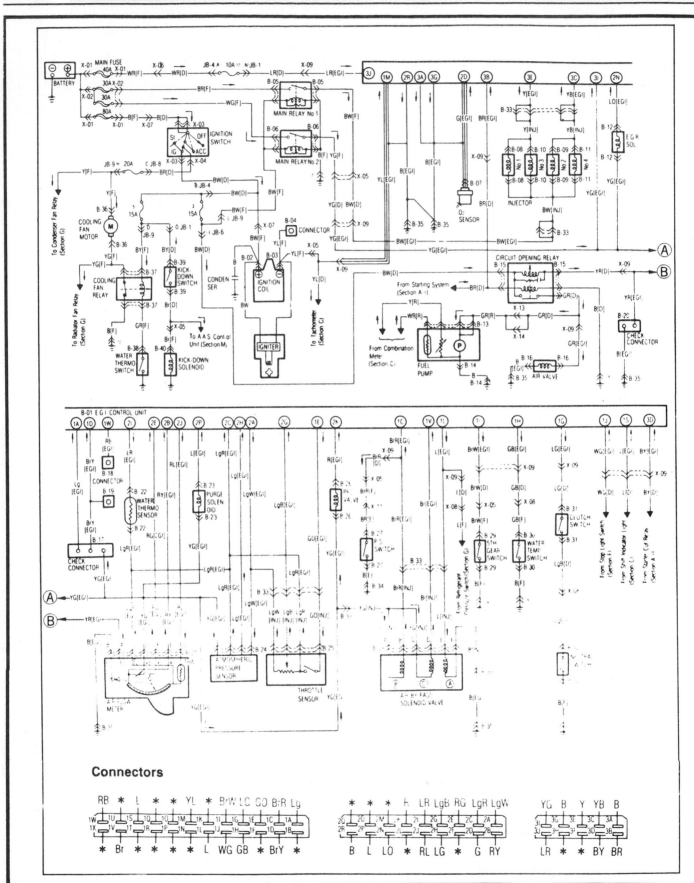

Wiring diagram for non-turbocharged engines

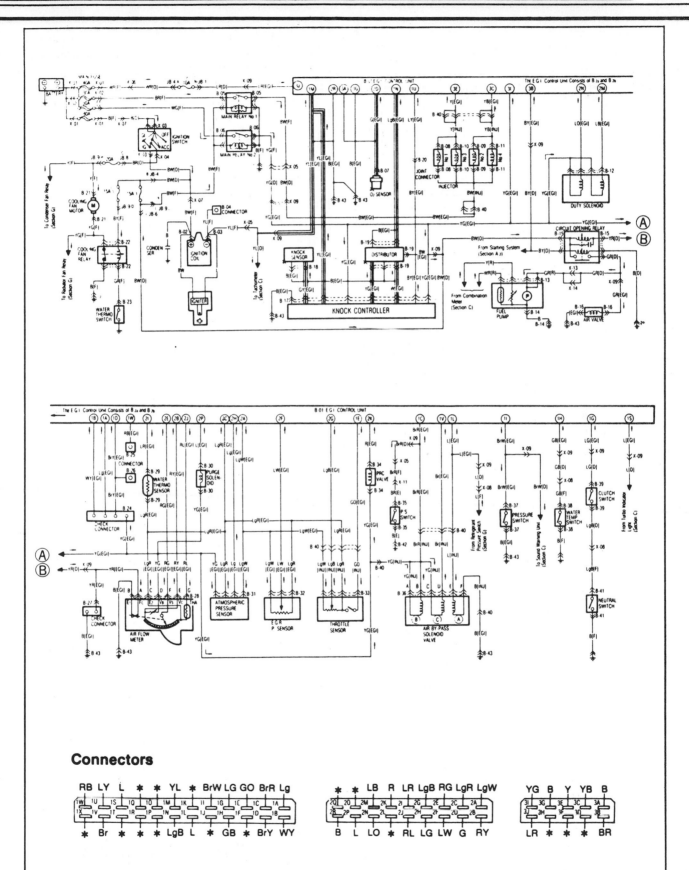

Wiring diagram for turbocharged engines

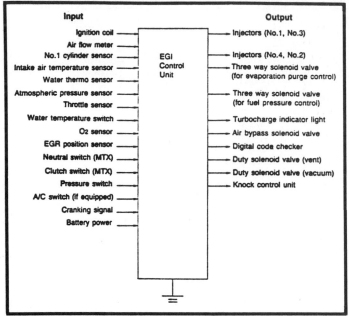

Control system construction for non-turbocharged engines

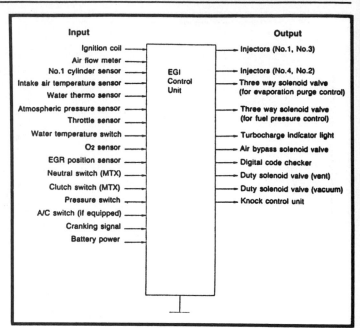

Control system construction for turbocharged engines

● If the ignition key is turned to the Off position after a fault has taken place, the fault indication will not be displayed on the Digital Code Checker.

● The control unit incorporates a built-in fail-safe device. If a fault occurs while driving, the control unit will sense the fault and substitute fail-safe function values for the normal operating values. The vehicle may be driven in the fail-safe mode; however, vehicle performance will be affected.

Diagnosis Procedure

1. Start the engine and warm up to normal operating temperature, then stop the engine. Engine speed should not exceed 4000 rpm during the warm up period.

2. Connect the Digital Code Checker to the check connector and attach the ground wire.

3. Start the engine and wait three minutes.

4. If a code number is displayed, refer to the proper fault diagnosis flowchart provided in this section.

CODE NUMBER FAULT ANALYSIS FOR NON-TURBOCHARGED ENGINES

Code Number	Location of problem	Buzzer	Fail-safe function
1	IG Pulse	1 cycle — 0.4 s 2.0 s	—
2	Air Flow Meter	1 cycle — 0.4 s 0.8 s 2.0 s	Maintains the basic signal at a preset value.
3	Water Thermo Sensor	1 cycle — 0.4 s 1.6 s 2.0 s	Maintains a constant 35°C(95°F) command.
4	Intake Air Temperature Sensor	1 cycle — 2.0 s 2.4 s 2.0 s	Maintains a constant 20°C(68°F) command.
5	Feedback System	1 cycle — 2.0 s 2.0 s	Dose not take in the feed-back.
6	Throttle Sensor	1 cycle — 2.0 s 0.8 s 2.0 s	Maintains a constant command opened the throttle valve fully
9	Atomspheric Pressure Sensor	1 cycle — 2.0 s 3.2 s 2.0 s	Maintains a constant command of the sea level pressure

TROUBLE CODE TROUBLESHOOTING CHARTS

No. 2 code display (Air flow meter)

Are there any poor connections at the connectors?
— **YES** → Repair or replace the terminal
— **NO** →

Is the resistance of the air flow meter OK? (Refer to page 4A—13)
— **NO** → Replace air flow meter
— **YES** →

Is there battery voltage at the V8 terminal of air flow meter connector? (Refer to page 4A—12)
— **NO** → Possible Cause (PC): Open or short circuit in the wiring harness
— **YES** →

Measure 2B terminal voltage of EGI control unit. (Refer to page 4A—44)
— **0V** → PC: Open or short circuit in the wiring harness from Vc terminal of air flow meter to 2B terminal of EGI control unit
— **6~10V** / **Approx. 12V** → PC: Open circuit in the wiring harness from E2 terminal of air flow meter to EGI control unit

Is 2E terminal voltage of EGI control unit within **0.7~2.7V?** (Refer to page 4A—44)
— **NO** → PC: Open or short circuit in the wiring harness from Vs terminal of air flow meter to EGI control unit
— **YES** → PC: EGI control unit faulty

No. 3 code display (Water thermo sensor)

Are there any poor connections at the connector?
— **YES** → Repair or replace the terminal
— **NO** →

Is the resistance of water thermo sensor within **0.094~73.8kΩ?**
— **NO** → Replace the water thermo sensor
— **YES** →

Measure 2I terminal voltage of EGI control unit.
— **12V** → Possible Cause (PC): Open circuit in the wiring harness
— **0V** → PC: Short circuit in the wiring harness from 2I terminal to the water thermo sensor / EGI control unit faulty

CODE NUMBER FAULT ANALYSIS FOR TURBO-CHARGED ENGINES

Code No.	Location of problem	Buzzer	Fail-safe function
1	IG Pulse	—1 cycle / 0.4 s 2.0 s	—
2	Air Flow Meter	—1 cycle / 0.4 s 0.8 s 2.0 s	Maintains the basic signal at a preset value.
3	Water Thermo Sensor	—1 cycle / 0.4 s 1.6 s 2.0 s	Maintains a constant 35°C(95°F) command.
4	Intake Air Temperature Sensor	—1 cycle / 2.0 s 2.4 s 2.0 s	Maintains a constant 20°C(68°F) command.
5	Feedback system	—1 cycle / 2.0 s 2.0 s	Does not take in the feed-back correction
6	Throttle Sensor	—1 cycle / 2.0 s 0.8 s 2.0 s	Maintains a constant command opened the throttle valve fully
8	EGR Position Sensor	—1 cycle / 2.0 s 2.4 s 2.0 s	Cuts off EGR
9	A.omspheric Pressure Sensor	—1 cycle / 2.0 s 3.2 s 2.0 s	Maintains a constant command of the sea level pressure
22	No.1 cylinder sensor	—1 cycle / 0.4 s 2.0 s	Injects fuel at the same time (1 time/2 revolutions)

No. 1 code display (IG pulse)

Is the connector connected to the negative terminal of ignition coil C.K?
— **NO** → Connect the terminal.
— **YES** →

Is 1M terminal voltage of EGI control unit OK? (Refer to page 4A—44)
— **NO** → Possible Cause (PC): Open or short circuit in the wiring harness from the ignition coil to the 1M terminal
— **YES** → PC: EGI control unit faulty

TROUBLE CODE TROUBLESHOOTING CHARTS TURBOCHARGED ENGINES ONLY

No. 6 code display (Throttle sensor)

- Are there any poor connections at the connectors?
  - **YES** → Repair or replace the terminal.
  - **NO** → Is the resistance of the throttle sensor OK?
    - **NO** → Replace the throttle sensor
    - **YES** → Is there **4.5 – 5.5V** at the Vs terminal of the throttle sensor connector?
      - **NO** → Possible Cause (PC): Open or short circuit in the wiring harness from the Vs terminal of the throttle sensor to EGI control unit. EGI control unit faulty
      - **YES** → Measure 2G terminal voltage of EGI control unit. (Refer to page 4A—44)
        - **More than 4.5V** → PC: Open circuit in the wiring harness from A terminal of throttle sensor to EGI control unit. Open circuit in the wiring harness of ground
        - **Less than 0.4V** → PC: Short circuit in the wiring harness from the A terminal of throttle sensor to EGI control unit
        - **0.4V – 4.5V** → PC: EGI control unit faulty

(EGR position sensor)

- Are there any poor connections at the connectors?
  - **YES** → Repair or replace the terminal
  - **NO** → Is the resistance in the EGR position sensor O.K? (Refer to page 4B—65)
    - **NO** → Replace the EGR position sensor
    - **YES** → Is there **4.5 – 5.5V** at the A terminal of the EGR position sensor connector? (Refer to page 4B—65)
      - **NO** → Possible Cause (PC), Open or short circuit in the wiring harness from A terminal to the EGI control unit
      - **YES** → Measure 2F terminal voltage of the EGI control unit (Refer to page 4B—47)
        - **More than 4.5V** → PC: Open circuit in the wiring harness of ground. Open circuit in the wiring harness from the C terminal to 2F terminal of EGI control unit
        - **0V** → PC: Short circuit in the wiring harness from the C terminal to 2F terminal of EGI control unit. EGI control unit faulty
        - **0.23 – 1.1V** → PC: EGI control unit faulty

TROUBLE CODE TROUBLESHOOTING CHARTS (CONT.)

No. 4 code display (Intake air temperature sensor)

- Are there any poor connections at the connectors?
  - **YES** → Repair or replace the terminal
  - **NO** → Is the resistance of the intake air temperature sensor within **0.094 – 73.8kΩ**?
    - **NO** → Replace the intake air temperature sensor
    - **YES** → Measure 2J terminal voltage of EGI control unit. (Refer to page 4A—44)
      - **12V** → Possible Cause (PC): Open circuit in the wiring harness
      - **0V** → PC: Short circuit in the wiring harness. EGI control unit faulty

No. 5 code display (Feedback system)

- Run the engine at **2500 rpm for one minute** and recheck the illumination. Is No. 5 code still displayed?
  - **YES** → Does the green light of the digital code checker not illuminate at idle?
    - **NO** → Possible Cause (PC): Air leak in the intake air system. Insufficient fuel injection
    - **YES** → Are the spark plugs clean?
      - **NO** → Clean or replace the spark plugs
      - **YES** → Is the O₂ sensor generated voltage OK?
        - **NO** → PC: O₂ sensor faulty
        - **YES** → Is 2D terminal voltage of EGI control unit OK?
          - **NO** → PC: Open or short circuit in the wiring harness from O₂ sensor connector to EGI control unit
          - **YES** → PC: EGI control unit faulty

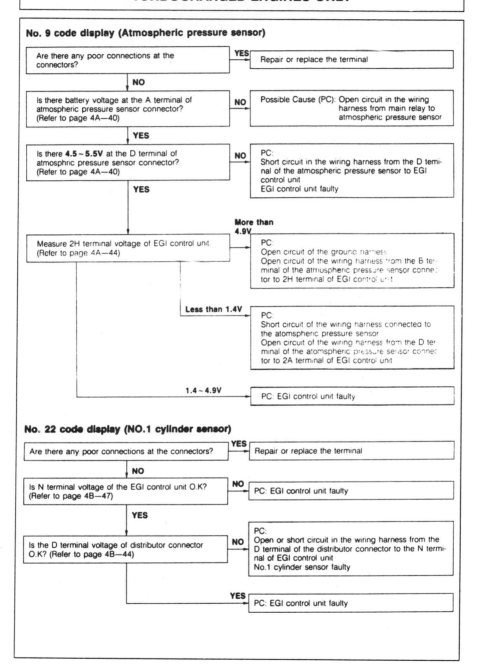

TROUBLE CODE TROUBLESHOOTING CHARTS
TURBOCHARGED ENGINES ONLY

No. 9 code display (Atmospheric pressure sensor)

Are there any poor connections at the connectors? **YES** → Repair or replace the terminal

NO

Is there battery voltage at the A terminal of atmospheric pressure sensor connector? (Refer to page 4A—40) **NO** → Possible Cause (PC): Open circuit in the wiring harness from main relay to atmospheric pressure sensor

YES

Is there **4.5 ~ 5.5V** at the D terminal of atmosphric pressure sensor connector? (Refer to page 4A—40) **NO** → PC: Short circuit in the wiring harness from the D teminal of the atmospheric pressure sensor to EGI control unit. EGI control unit faulty

YES

Measure 2H terminal voltage of EGI control unit. (Refer to page 4A—44)

More than 4.9V → PC: Open circuit of the ground harness. Open circuit of the wiring harness from the B terminal of the atmospheric pressure sensor connector to 2H terminal of EGI control unit

Less than 1.4V → PC: Short circuit of the wiring harness connected to the atomspheric pressure sensor. Open circuit of the wiring harness from the D terminal of the atomspheric pressure sensor connector to 2A terminal of EGI control unit

1.4 ~ 4.9V → PC: EGI control unit faulty

No. 22 code display (NO.1 cylinder sensor)

Are there any poor connections at the connectors? **YES** → Repair or replace the terminal

NO

Is N terminal voltage of the EGI control unit O.K? (Refer to page 4B—47) **NO** → PC: EGI control unit faulty

YES

Is the D terminal voltage of distributor connector O.K? (Refer to page 4B—44) **NO** → PC: Open or short circuit in the wiring harness from the D terminal of the distributor connector to the N terminal of EGI control unit. No.1 cylinder sensor faulty

YES → PC: EGI control unit faulty

MAZDA RX-7 ELECTRONIC GASOLINE INJECTION (EGI) SYSTEM

General Information

RX-7 with 13B Engine

This system is broken down into three major systems. The Fuel System, Air Induction System and Electronic Control System.

FUEL SYSTEM

The fuel injection system supplies the necessary fuel to the injectors to achieve combustion at constant pressure. Fuel is metered and injected into the intake manifold according to the signals from the EGI control unit. The injection system consists of the fuel pump, fuel filter, distribution pipe, pulsation dampener, pressure regulator, injectors, air flow meter, air valve, and solenoid resistor.

AIR INDUCTION SYSTEM

The air induction system provides sufficient air for the engine operation.

ELECTRONIC CONTROL SYSTEM

The EGI control unit (ECU), through various input sensors, monitors battery voltage, engine rpm, amount of air intake, cranking signal, intake temperature, coolant temperature, oxygen concentration in the exhaust gases, throttle opening, atmospheric pressure, gearshift position, clutch engagement, braking, power steering operation and A/C compressor operation.

The ECU controls operation of the fuel injection system, idle-up system , fuel evaporation system and ignition timing. The ECU has a built in fail-safe mechanism. If a fault occurs while driving, the ECU will substitute pre-programed values. Driving performance will be affected, but the vehicle will still be driveable.

Diagnosis and Testing

SERVICE PRECAUTIONS

- Do not operate the fuel pump when the fuel lines are empty.
- Do not reuse fuel hose clamps.
- Make sure all EGI harness connectors are fastened securely. A poor connection can cause an extremely high surge voltage in the coil and condenser and result in damage to integrated circuits.
- Keep the EGI harness at least 4 in. away from adjacent harnesses to prevent an EGI system malfunction due to external electronic "noise."
- Keep EGI all parts and harnesses dry during service.
- Before attempting to remove any parts, turn off the ignition switch and disconnect the battery ground cable.
- Always use a 12 volt battery as a power source.
- Do not attempt to disconnect the battery cables with the engine running.
- Do not depress the accelerator pedal when starting.
- Do not rev up the engine immediately after starting or just prior to shutdown.
- Do not attempt to disassemble the EGI control unit under any circumstances.
- If installing a two-way or CB radio, keep the antenna as far as possible away from the electronic control unit. Keep the antenna feeder line at least 8 in. away from the EGI harness and do not let the two run parallel for a long distance. Be sure to ground the radio to the vehicle body.
- Do not apply battery power directly to injectors.
- Handle air flow meter carefully to avoid damage.
- Do not disassemble air flow meter or clean meter with any type of detergent.

TESTING PRECAUTIONS

1. Before connecting or disconnecting control unit ECU harness connectors, make sure the ignition switch is OFF and the negative battery cable is disconnected to avoid the possibility of damage to the control unit.
2. When performing ECU input/output signal diagnosis, remove the pin terminal retainer from the connectors to make it easier to insert tester probes into the connector.
3. When connecting or disconnecting pin connectors from the ECU, take care not to bend or break any pin terminals. Check that there are no bends or breaks on ECU pin terminals before attempting any connections.
4. Before replacing any ECU, perform the ECU input/output signal diagnosis to make sure the ECU is functioning properly or not.
5. After checking throught EGI troubleshooting, perform the EFI self-diagnosis and driving test.
6. When measuring supply voltage of ECU controlled components with a circuit tester, separate one tester probe from another. If the two tester probes accidentally make contact with each other during measurement, a short circuit will result and damage the power transistor in the ECU.

Diagnosis, Testing and Component Replacement

AIR FLOW METER

Inspection

1. Inspect the air flow meter body for cracks.
2. Using a suitable ohmmeter, check the resistance between the terminals and check the resistance on the charts below.

Operational Check

1. Using a suitable tool press open the measuring plate. Measure the resistance between E_1 and Fc (fuel pump switch) and between E_2 and Vs.
2. The resistance should be within the specifications shown in the following charts.
3. If the air flow meter fails to meet these specifications, replace it.

Removal and Installation

1. Disconnect the negative battery cable. Remove the high tension lead and connectors.
2. Loosen the hose band and remove the intake hose.
3. Remove the air flow meter attaching bolts.
4. Turn the air cleaner cover upside down and remove the attaching nuts, remove the air flow meter.
5. Installation is the reverse order of the removal procedure.

THROTTLE BODY

Checking the No. 1 Secondary Throttle Valve

1. The No. 1 secondary throttle valve starts to open when the

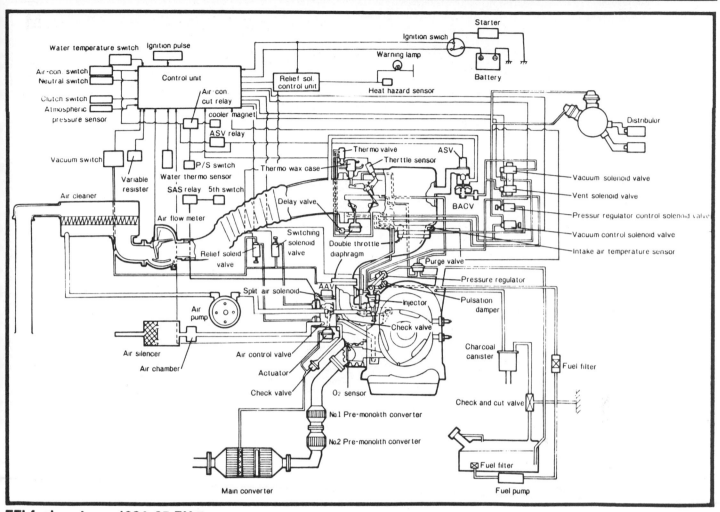

EFI fuel system – 1984–85 RX-7

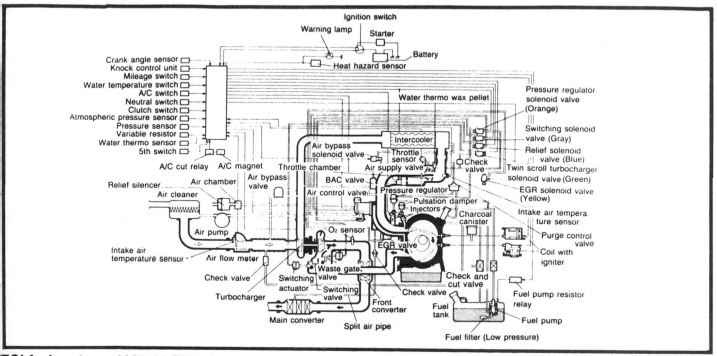

EGI fuel system – 1987–88 RX-7 Turbo

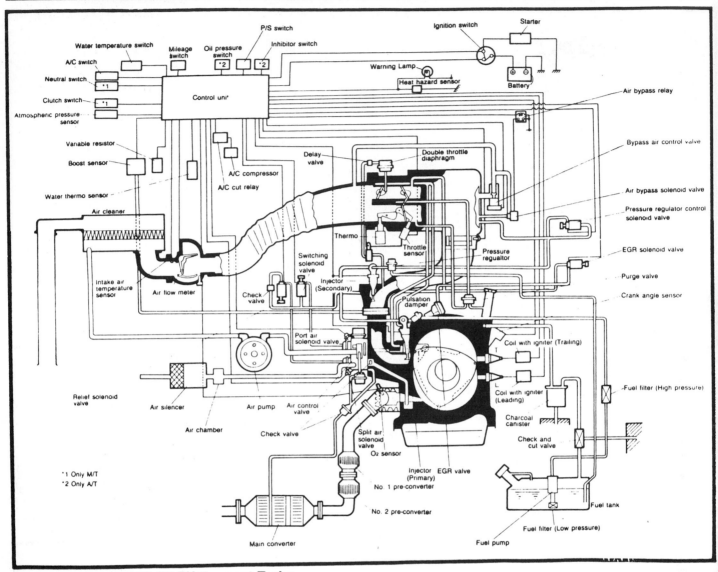

EFI fuel system—1986–88 RX-7 except Turbo

primary throttle valve opens to (15° 1984-85 and 1987–88 Turbo), (12° M/T, 8° A/T 1986–88) and completely opens at the same time when the primary throttle valve fully opens.

2. Check the clearance between between the primary throttle valve and the wall of the throttle bore when the No. 1 secondary throttle valve starts to open.

3. If the clearance is not within the specification shown below, bend the tab until the proper clearance is obtained.

Standard Clearance:
- 1984–85 RX-7 — 0.43–0.67 in. (1.1–1.7mm)
- 1986–88 RX-7 except Turbo — M/T 0.02–0.03 in. (0.5–0.7mm), A/T 0.03–0.06 in. (0.8–1.4mm)
- 1987–88 RX-7 Turbo — 0.43–0.67 in. (1.1–1.7mm)

Checking fast idle operation

In order to perform this operation properly the vehicle and the throttle chamber must be at 77°F (25°C).

1. For proper fast idle operation the matching mark on the fast idle cam must be aligned with the center of the cam roller.

2. If the matching mark and the center of the cam roller do not align, turn the cam roller do not align, turn the cam adjusting screw until the proper alignment is obtained.

NOTE: Fast idle adjustment is unnecessary unless it has been tampered with.

3. Once the correct matching mark aligns with the center of the cam roller check the clearance (throttle chamber — primary throttle valve), turn the fast idle adjusting screw to the correct specification.

Standard clearance: 0.016–0.02 in. (0.4–0.5mm)

Removal and Installation

1. Disconnect the negative battery cable. Disconnect the accelerator cable from the throttle linkage.

2. Disconnect the air funnel. Disconnect the hoses and tubes from the throttle body.

3. Disconnect the throttle position sensor connector. Remove the throttle body retaining screws and remove the throttle body assembly.

4. Installation is the reverse order of the removal procedure.

THROTTLE POSITION SENSOR
Inspection

1. Disconnect the throttle sensor connector.

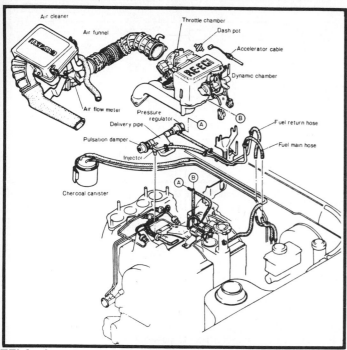

EFI fuel system components—1984–85 RX-7

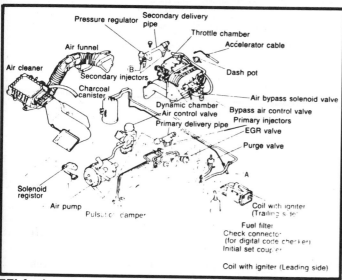

EFI fuel system components—1986–88 RX-7 except Turbo

2. Connect a suitable ohmmeter to the sensor as shown in the illustration.

3. Open the throttle valve and observe the resistance readings:
Throttle opening

A to B
- A–B Idle position: approximately 1 kΩ
- Full open position: approximately 4–6 kΩ

A to C
- A–B Idle position: approximately 4–6 kΩ
- Full open position: approximately 4–6 kΩ
4. Reconnect the connector.

Adjustment

1. Warm up the engine to operating temperature, then turn it OFF.

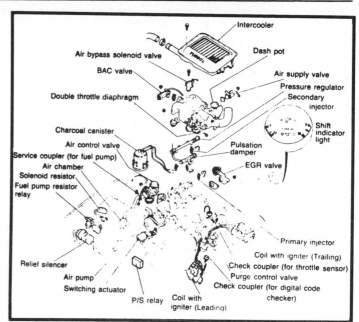

EGI fuel system components—1987–88 RX-7 Turbo

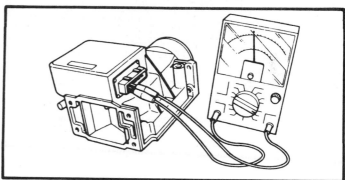

Air flow meter resistance check

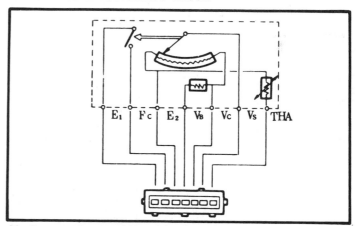

Air flow meter terminal locations—1984–85 RX-7

2. Disconnect the connector from the throttle position sensor.

3. Connect the throttle position sensor tester (49 F018 001) to the check connector (green) or connect a two ohmmeters.

4. Turn the ignition switch on and check whether one of the tester lamps illuminates.

5. If both lamps illuminate or if neither does, turn the throttle sensor adjusting screw until one of the lamps illuminates.

Terminal	Resistance (Ω)	
$E_2 \leftrightarrow V_S$	20 ~ 400	
$E_2 \leftrightarrow V_C$	100 ~ 300	
$E_2 \leftrightarrow V_B$	200 ~ 400	
$E_2 \leftrightarrow$ THA (Intake air temperature sensor)	$-20°C$ ($-4°F$)	10,000 ~ 20,000
	$0°C$ ($32°F$)	4,000 ~ 7,000
	$20°C$ ($68°F$)	2,000 ~ 3,000
	$40°C$ (104°F)	900 ~ 1,300
	$60°C$ (140°F)	400 ~ 700
$E_1 \leftrightarrow F_C$	∞	

Air flow meter resistance values — 1984–85 RX-7

Terminal	Resistance (Ω)	
$E_2 \leftrightarrow V_S$	200 ~ 600	
$E_2 \leftrightarrow$ Vref	200 ~ 400	
$E_2 \leftrightarrow$ THA (Intake air temperature sensor)	$-20°C$ ($-4°F$)	10,000 ~ 20,000
	$0°C$ ($32°F$)	4,000 ~ 7,000
	$20°C$ ($68°F$)	2,000 ~ 3,000
	$40°C$ (104°F)	900 ~ 1,300
	$60°C$ (140°F)	400 ~ 700
$E_1 \leftrightarrow F_C$	∞	

Air flow meter resistance values — 1987–88 RX-7 Turbo

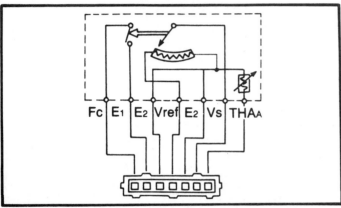

Air flow meter terminal locations — 1986–88 RX-7 except Turbo

Conditions	Measuring plate	
Terminals	Fully closed	Fully open
$E_1 \leftrightarrow F_C$	∞	0
$E_2 \leftrightarrow V_S$	20 to 400Ω	20 to 1,000Ω

Air flow meter operational resistance values 1984–85 RX-7

Terminal	Resistance (Ω)	
$E_2 \leftrightarrow V_S$	50 ~ 500	
$E_2 \leftrightarrow$ Vref	200 ~ 500	
$E_2 \leftrightarrow$ THA (Intake air temperature sensor)	$-20°C$ ($-4°F$)	10,000 ~ 20,000
	$0°C$ ($32°F$)	4,000 ~ 7,000
	$20°C$ ($68°F$)	2,000 ~ 3,000
	$40°C$ (104°F)	900 ~ 1,300
	$60°C$ (140°F)	400 ~ 700
$E_1 \leftrightarrow F_C$	∞	

Air flow meter resistance values — 1986–88 RX-7 except Turbo

Condition	Measuring plate	
Terminal	Fully closed	Fully open
$E_1 \leftrightarrow F_C$	∞	0
$E_2 \leftrightarrow V_S$	50 ~ 500	50 ~ 500

Air flow meter operational resistance values 1986–88 RX-7 except Turbo

Condition	Measuring plate	
Terminal	Fully closed	Fully open
$E_1 \leftrightarrow F_C$	∞	0
$E_2 \leftrightarrow V_S$	200 ~ 600	20 ~ 1,000

Air flow meter operational resistance values 1987–88 RX-7 Turbo

    a. If both lamps illuminate turn the adjusting screw counter-clockwise.

    b. If both lamps do not illuminate turn the adjusting screw clockwise.

    6. Reinstall the cap on the adjusting screw after adjustment.

NOTE: Do not apply excessive pressure on the adjusting screw, as it may cause incorrect adjustment.

RELIEVING FUEL PRESSURE

The fuel in the fuel system remains under high pressure even when the engine is not running. So before disconnecting any fuel lines, release the fuel pressure to reduce the risk of injury or fire. Relieve the fuel pressure as follows:

    1. Start the engine.

    2. Disconnect the fuel pump connector with the engine running.

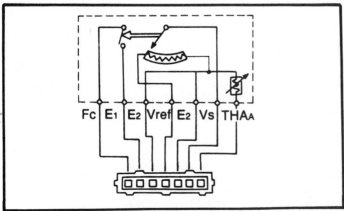

Air flow meter terminal locations — 1987–88 RX-7 Turbo

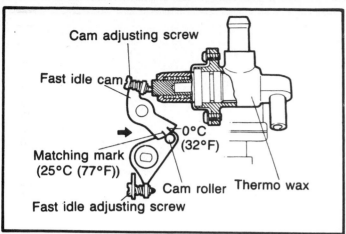

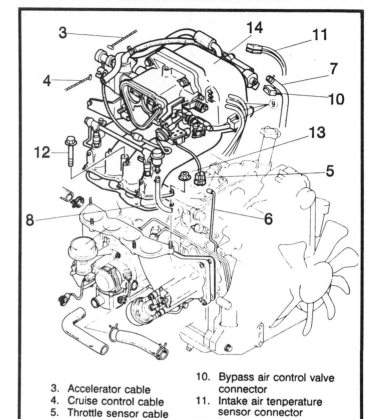

3. Accelerator cable
4. Cruise control cable
5. Throttle sensor cable
6. Metering oil pump connecting rod
7. Water hoses
8. Fuel hoses
10. Bypass air control valve connector
11. Intake air tenperature sensor connector
12. Bolts
13. Nuts
14. Dynamic chamber with throttle body

Throttle body assembly (Dynamic Chamber)

Fast idle adjustment

3. After the engine stalls from lack of fuel, turn the ignition switch off.

4. Use a shop rag to cover the fuel lines when disconnecting and plug all fuel lines after they have been disconnected.

FUEL PUMP

Inspection

1. Relieve the fuel system pressure.
2. Disconnect the negative battery cable.
3. Disconnect the main fuel hose from the main fuel line.
4. Connect a suitable fuel pressure gauge.
5. Connect the negative battery cable.
6. Connect the terminals of the check connector with a jumper wire. Turn on the ignition switch to operate the fuel pump.
7. Obsere that the fuel pressure is within the following specifications:

Fuel Pump Pressure:
- 1984–85 RX-7 – 49.8–71.1 psi (350–500 kPa)
- 1986–88 RX-7 except Turbo – 64–85.3 psi (441–588 kPa)
- 1987–88 RX-7 Turbo – 49.8–71.1 psi (350–500 kPa)

Removal and Installation

1984–85

1. Relieve the fuel pressure from the fuel system.
2. Remove the storage compartment located behind the driver's seat.
3. Disconnect the fuel pump wiring connector.
4. Disconnect and plug the fuel main and return lines from the fuel pump.
5. Remove the fuel pump and fuel tank gauge as an assembly.
6. Replace the fuel pump.
7. Installation is the reverse order of the removal procedure.

1986–88

1. Relieve the fuel pressure from the fuel system.
2. Lift up the rear mat and remove the fuel pump cover.
3. Disconnect the fuel pump wiring connector.
4. Disconnect and plug the fuel main and return lines from the fuel pump.
5. Remove the fuel pump and fuel tank gauge as an assembly.
6. Replace the fuel pump.
7. Installation is the reverse order of the removal procedure.

PRESSURE REGULATOR

Fuel Line Pressure Inspection

1. Relieve the fuel pressure from the fuel system.

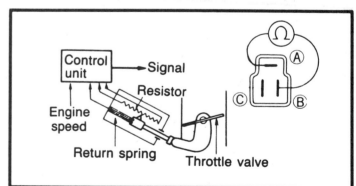

Throttle position sensor inspection

2. Disconnect the negative battery cable. Connect the multipressure tester (49-9200-750) or equivalent to the fuel line.
3. Reconnect the negative battery cable. Start the engine.
4. Disconnect the vaccumm hose from the pressure regulator (non-turbo models), or connect a jumper wire to the pressure regulator solenoid valve (LO) terminal and ground (turbo models).
5. Measure the fuel pressure at idle. The fuel pressure (regulating pressure) should be 35.6–37.0 psi.

NOTE: The fuel pressure is indicated on the lower LED line (fuel pressure line) at any ranges.

6. Reconnect the vacuum hose connected to the pressure regulator (non-turbo models), or connect a jumper wire to the pressure regulator solenoid valve (LO) terminal and ground (turbo

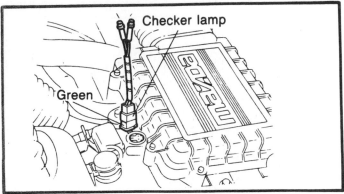

Throttle position sensor adjustment

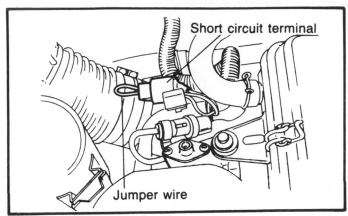

Jumper wire connection

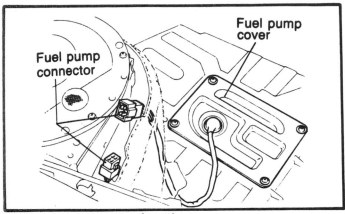

Fuel pump connecter location

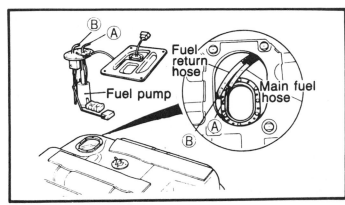

Fuel pump removal

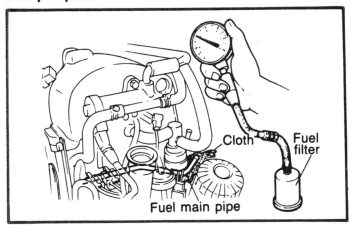

Fuel pressure gauge connection

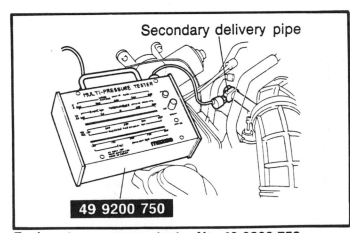

Fuel system pressure tester No. 49 9200 750

models). The fuel pressure (regulating pressure) should be 28.4 psi.

7. If not within specifications, replace the pressure regulator.

Removal and Installation

1. Relieve the fuel pressure from the fuel system. Disconnect the negative battery cable.
2. Remove the throttle chamber (dynamic chamber).
3. Disconnect the fuel return hose.
4. Remove the pressure regulator.
5. Installation is the reverse order of the removal procedure. Be sure to replace the O-ring(s) and after installation check for fuel leaks with fuel pressure applied.

FUEL FILTER

The fuel filter should be replaced every 30,000 miles. Replace the filter as follows:

1. Relieve the fuel pressure from the fuel system. Disconnect the negative battery cable.
2. Raise the front of the front of the car and support it with jack stands.
2. Disconnect and plug the fuel lines. Remove the fuel filter with bracket as an assembly.
3. Install a new filter and reconnect the fuel lines.
4. Replace the copper washer with a new one and torque it to 18–25 ft.lbs. When installing the fuel filter make sure that the fuel lines are pushed on as far up as possible. Secure the hose with clamps.

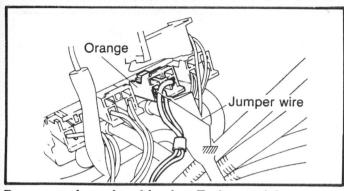

Pressure wire solenoid valve, Turbo models

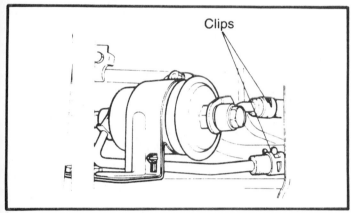

RX-7 fuel filter assembly

FUEL INJECTORS

Injection Fuel Pressure Inspection

1. Relieve the fuel pressure from the fuel system.
2. Disconnect the negative battery cable. Connect the multi-pressure tester (49-9200-750) or equivalent to the fuel line.
3. Reconnect the negative battery cable. Start the engine and measure the fuel pressure at the "III" range of the multi pressure tester. The fuel pressure (injection pressure) should be 35.6–37.0 psi.

NOTE: The fuel pressure is indicated on the lower LED line (fuel pressure line) at any ranges.

4. If the injection pressure is lower than specified, check the following:
   a. Fuel pump outlet pressure.
   b. Fuel line pressure.
   c. Fuel filter clog.
5. If the injection pressure is higher than specifications, check the following:
   a. Fuel return pipe clogged.
   b. fuel line pressure.

Injector Inspection

Check the operating sound of the injector, using a sound scope, check that operating sounds are produced from each injector at idle and at acceleration.

1. If the injectors do not operate, check the following:
   a. Check the fuel injection system main fuse (40 amp).
   b. Turn the ignition switch ON and OFF, verify that the main relay clicks.
2. If the clicking sound is not heard at the main relay, when the ignition switch is turned ON, use a voltmeter and check for 12 volts at the main relay connector (BW) terminal wire.

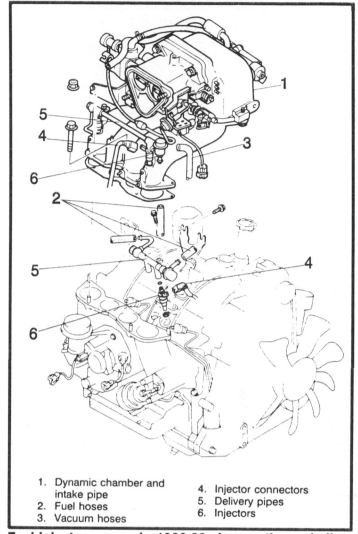

1. Dynamic chamber and intake pipe
2. Fuel hoses
3. Vacuum hoses
4. Injector connectors
5. Delivery pipes
6. Injectors

Fuel injector removal—1986-88 shown others similar

Removal and Installation

1. Relieve the fuel pressure from the fuel system. Disconnect the negative battery cable.
2. Remove the throttle body (dynamic chamber) as described eariler.
3. Disconnect the fuel hose and pipe. Disconnect the injector connector.
4. Remove the pressure regulator and distribution pipe.
5. Remove the injector. Once the injector is removed, use an ohmmeter and measure the resistance at the injector connector (on the injector). The resistance should be 1.5–3.0 ohms.
6. Installation is the reverse order of the removal procedure. Be sure to replace the O-ring(s) and after installation check for fuel leaks with fuel pressure applied.

Injector Fuel Leak Test

1. Relieve the fuel pressure from the fuel system.
2. Remove the throttle body unit (Dynamic Chamber).
3. Loosen the distribution pipe attaching bolts. Afix the injectors to the distribution pipe with some suitable wire.

NOTE: Affix the injectors firmly to the distribution pipe so no movement of the injectors is possible.

4. Turn the ignition switch to the ON position. Use a jumper wire and connect the shot circuit terminals of the fuel pump

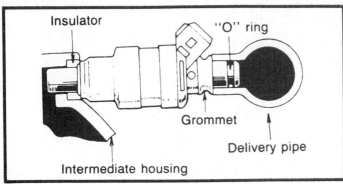
Side view of injector mounting

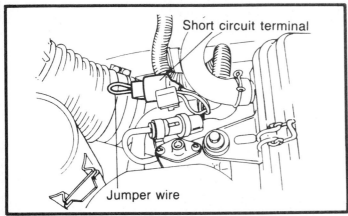
Fuel pump shortcircuit connector

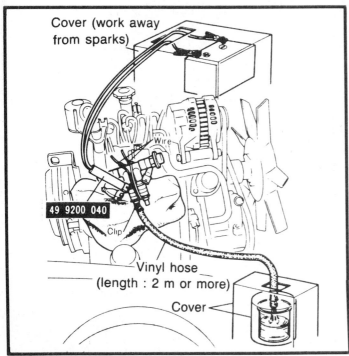
Fuel injector volume test

check connector. Make sure that the fuel does not leak from the injector nozzles.

5. After approximately five minutes, a very small (slight) amount of fuel leakage from the injectors is acceptable.

6. If the injector leaks fuel at a fast rate, replace the injector. If the injectors do not leak, remove all test equipment and in-

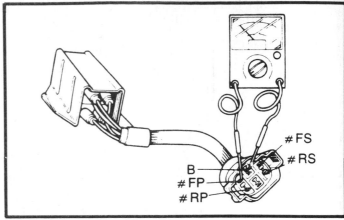
Testing the solenoid resistor

stall the removed components in the reverse order of the removal procedure.

Injector Volume Test

1. Relieve the fuel pressure from the fuel system.
2. Connect a suitable hose to the injector. Connect injector checker (49-9200-040) or equivalent to the injector.
3. Turn the ignition switch to the ON position. Use a jumper wire and connect the terminals of the fuel pump check connector. Make sure that the fuel does not leak from the injector nozzles.
4. Apply battery voltage to the injector checker and measure the injector volume with a graduated cylinder (measuring container).

NOTE: Do not apply battery voltage directly to the injector. The injector checker must be used or the injector will be damaged.

Solenoid Resistor Inspection

1. Using a suitable ohmmeter, measure the resistance between the (B) terminal and the other four terminals with the solenoid resistor connector disconnected. The solenoid resistor is usually located next to the main relay on the left fender well.

2. The standard resistance should be 5–7 ohms. If the resistance is not within specifications, replace the resistor.

IDLE SYSTEM

Idle Speed Adjustment

Before adjusting the idle speed and idle mixture, be sure the ignition timing, spark plugs, etc., are all in normal operating condition. Turn off all lights and other unnecessary electrical loads.

1. Connect a tachometer to the engine.
2. After warming up the engine, check that the choke valve has fully opened.
3. Check the idle speed. If necessary, turn the throttle adjust screw and set the idle speed to specifications.
- 1984–85 – 800 rpm
- 1986–88 – 725–775 rpm

EGI CONTROL UNIT

The EGI control unit (ECU), through various input sensors, monitors battery voltage, engine rpm, anount of air intake, cranking signal, intake temperature, coolant temperature, oxygen concentration in the exhaust gases, throttle opening, atmospheric pressure, gearshift position, clutch engagement, braking, power steering operation and A/C compressor operation.

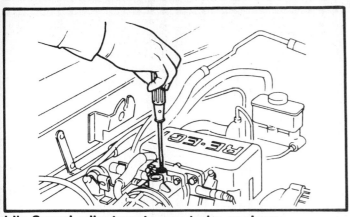

Idle Speed adjustment—non-turbo engines

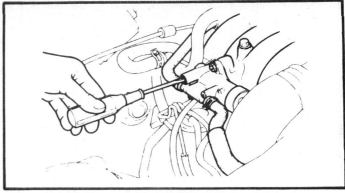

Idle Speed adjustment—turbo engines

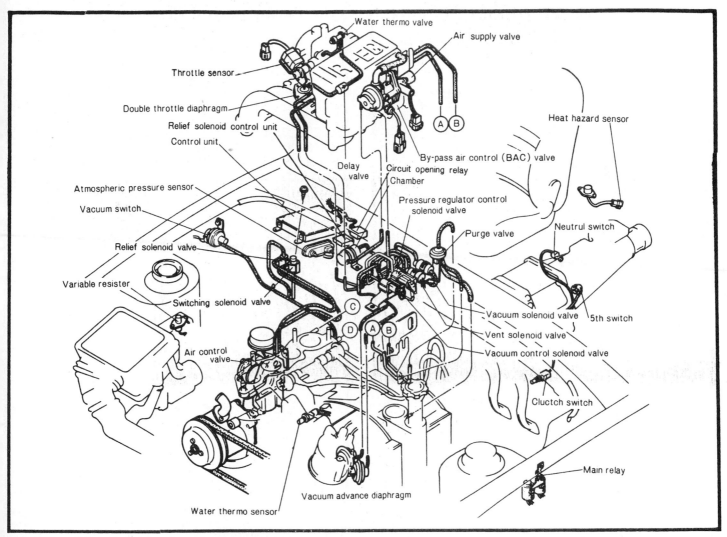

Control unit input device locations—1984–85

The ECU controls operation of the fuel injection system, idle-up system, fuel evaporation system and ignition timing. The ECU has a built in fail-safe mechanism. If a fault occurs while driving, the ECU will substitute pre-programmed values. Driving performance will be affected, but the vehicle will still be driveable.

EGI Control Unit Inspection

Inspection of the control unit requires a suitable voltmeter for 1984–85 models, or special tool "Engine Signal Monitor" (No.49-9200-162) and Adapter (49-9200-163) for 1986–88 models. If this tool is not available, a suitable voltmeter can be used

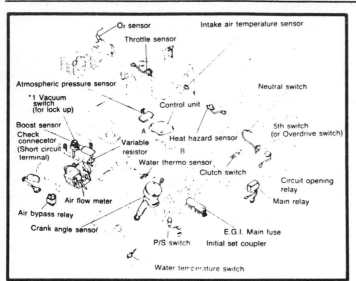

Control unit input device locations–1986–88 except Turbo

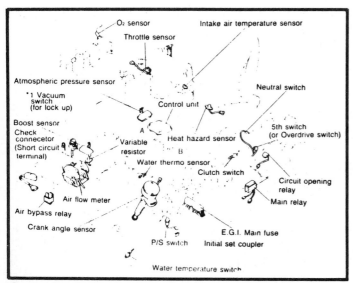

Control unit input device locations–1987–88 Turbo

Terminal	Connection to	Voltage with ignition ON (when functioning properly)
A	Main relay	approx. 12V
B	Ground	0V
C	Water thermo sensor	1 ~ 2V (warm engine)
D	Ground	0V
E	Air flow meter	4 ~ 6V . . . at 20°C 1.5 ~ 3.5V . . . at 50°C
F	Injector (#20)	approx. 12V
G	Throttle sensor & Atmospheric pressure sensor	4.5 ~ 5.5V
H	Injector (#10)	approx. 12V
I	Throttle sensor	approx. 1V
J	Vacuum switch	approx. 12V
L	Variable resistor (V/R)	0 ~ 12V (Varies according to the V/R adjustment)
M	Ignition switch "START" terminal	below 1.5V
N	O₂ sensor	0V
O	Air flow meter	approx. 12V
P	Atmospheric pressure sensor	approx. 4V
Q	Air flow meter	approx. 2V
R	Air flow meter	approx. 7.5V
S	Ground	0V
T	Ground	0V
U	Ignition coil (T) – terminal	approx. 12V
V	Main relay	approx. 12V
a	Switching solenoid valve	approx. 12V
b	Relief solenoid valve control unit	approx. 12V
c	Checking connector	0V
d	Vacuum control solenoid valve (T/L)	approx. 12V
e	Pressure regulator control valve	below 1.5V
f	Checking connector	0V
h	Vent solenoid valve	below 1.5V (throttle sensor is adjusted properly)
i	Clutch switch	below 1.5V . . . pedal released / approx. 12V . . . pedal depressed
j	Neutral switch	below 1.5V . . . in neutral approx. 12V . . . in gear
k	Water temperature switch	below 1.5V . . . above 15°C
l	Intake air temperature sensor	8.5 ~ 10.5V . . . at 20°C 5 ~ 7V . . . at 50°C
m	Air-con. switch	below 1.5V . . . air-con. switch OFF
n	Vacuum control valve	approx. 12V (throttle sensor is adjusted properly)

Control unit connector

Control unit pin locations and test voltages and control unit connector–1984–85 models

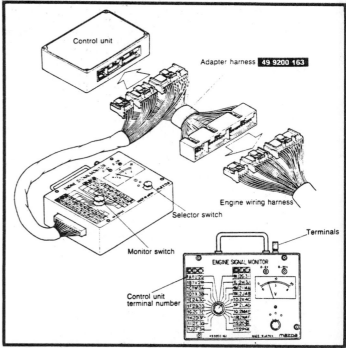

Engine signal monitor tool

in its place. The engine signal monitor has been developed to check the EGI control unit terminal voltage. The monitor easily inspects the terminal voltage by setting the monitor switch. Make sure the engine is at normal operating temperatures before proceeding with this inspection.

1. Connect the engine signal monitor between the EGI control unit and engine harness using the adapter.

2. Turn the select switch and monitor switch to select the terminal number and check the terminal voltage.

NOTE: If the engine signal monitor is not available, check the control unit terminals with a suitable voltmeter as follows; connect a voltmeter to the control unit, which in most cases is located under the (center) dash panel. Turn the ignition switch to the ON position (do not start the engine) and measure the voltage at each terminal with the aid of the chart provided.

3. If the proper voltage is not indicated on the monitor or the voltmeter, check all wiring, connections and finally check the involved component.

Troubleshooting with the System Checker 83 – Diagnosis Checker

1984–85 Models

The System Checker '83 (part # 49–G030–920) can be used to detect and indicate any problems of each sensor, damaged wiring, poor contact or a short circuit between each of the sensor-control units. Trouble is indicated by a red lamp and a buzzer.

If there is more than two problems at the same time, the indi-

CONTROL UNIT PIN LOCATIONS AND TEST VOLTAGES — 1986-88 MODELS EXCEPT TURBO

Terminal	Input	Output	Connection to	Voltage (after warming up) Ignition switch: ON	Idle	Remark
1S		O	Port air solenoid valve	below 2.5V		
1T	O		Crank angle sensor Ne ①	below 1.0V		
1U		O	Coil with igniter (Trailing) IGs-T (Select signal)	approx. 4.4V	approx. 2.2V	
1V		O	Coil with igniter (Leading) IGT-L (Ignition timing signal)	0V	approx. 0.8V	
1W	O		Heat hazard sensor	below 1.5V	approx. 12V	Floor Temp. below 110°C (230°F)
1X		O	Coil with igniter (Trailing) IGT-T (Ignition timing signal)	0V	approx. 0.8V	
2A		O	V ref	4.5~5.5V		
2B	O		Boost sensor	3.5~4.0V		Disconnect the vacuum hose
2C		—	Ground	0V		
2D	O		O2 sensor	below 1.0V		
2E	O		Air flow meter (Vs)	approx. 4V	2.5~3.5V	
2F	O		Variable resistor	1~4V (Varies according to the variable resistor adjustment)		
2G	O		Throttle sensor (TVO)	approx. 1V (Throttle sensor adjusted properly)		
2H	O		Atmospheric pressure sensor	3.5~4.5V (at sea level) 2.5~3.5V (at 2,000 m (6,500ft))		
2I	O		Water thermo sensor	approx. 0.4~1.8V		
2J	O		Air flow meter (Intake air temperature sensor)	2~3V at 20°C (68°F)		
2K		O	Split air solenoid valve	approx. 12V (M/T: Neutral, A/T: N,P range)		
2L	O		Intake air temperature sensor (dynamic chamber)	1~2V at 80°C (176°F)		
2M		O	Pressure regulator control solenoid valve	below 2.0V	approx. 12V	
2N		O	EGR solenoid valve	approx. 12V		
2O		O	Switching solenoid valve	approx. 12V (Throttle sensor is adjusted properly)	approx. 12V	
2P		O	Relief solenoid valve	below 2.0V (Throttle sensor is adjusted properly)	below 2.0V	
2Q		O	Bypass air control valve	8~12V		
2R	—		Ground	0V		
3A	—	—	Ground	0V		
3B	O		Starter switch	below 1.5V	approx. 12V (at cranking)	
3C		O	Injector (rear primary)	approx. 12V		
3D		O	Inhibitor switch	below 1.5V (A/T: N,P range, M/T: others)	approx. 12V (A/T; others)	

CONTROL UNIT PIN LOCATIONS AND TEST VOLTAGES — 1986-88 MODELS EXCEPT TURBO

Terminal	Input	Output	Connection to	Voltage (after warming up) Ignition switch: ON	Idle	Remark
1A		O	Digital code checker	Ignition switch OFF → ON for 3 sec. below 5V, after 3sec. approx 12V		with digital code checker
1B		O	Digital code checker	Ignition switch OFF → ON for 3 sec. below 5V, after 3 sec. approx. 12V		with digital code checker
1C		O	Air bypass relay	approx. 12V		
1D		O	Digital code checker (Green lamp)	Ignition switch OFF → ON for 3 sec. below 5V, after 3 sec. approx. 12V		with digital code checker
1E	O		A/C switch	below 2.5V (A/C: ON), approx. 12V (A/C: OFF)		Blower motor ON
1F		O	A/C main relay	approx. 12V (A/C: OFF)		Blower motor ON
1G	O		Neutral switch	below 1.5V (in neutral: A/T) approx. 12V (others)		
1H	O		Water temperature switch	below 1.5V (Radiator coolant temperature above 17°C (62.6°F))		
1I	O		5th switch	approx. 12V (M/T: 5th gear, A/T: others) below 1.5V (M/T others, A/T: over drive)		
1J	O		Initial set coupler	approx. 4~7V (Initial set coupler: OFF), below 1.5V (Initial set coupler: ON)		
1K		O	Shift indicator light	below 1.5V	approx. 12V	
1L	O		Clutch switch	below 1.5V (clutch pedal: released) approx. 12V (clutch pedal: depressed, A/T)		
1M		O	Coil with igniter (Trailing) IGT-T	below 2V		
1N	O		Crank angle sensor G ①	below 1.0V		G
1O	O		Mileage switch	approx. 12V (below 20,000 miles) below 1.5V (above 20,000 miles)		
1P	O		Crank angle sensor G ②	below 1.0V		B
1Q	O		Crank angle sensor Ne ②	below 1.0V		W
1R	O		P/S switch	10~12V	below 1.5V (Steering wheel turned) approx. 12V (Straight ahead)	

CONTROL UNIT PIN LOCATIONS AND TEST VOLTAGES – 1987-88 TURBO MODELS

Terminal	Input	Output	Connection to	Ignition switch: ON	Idle	Remark
1U		O	Coil with igniter (Trailing) IGs-T (Select signal)	approx. 4.4V	approx. 2.2V	
1V		O	Coil with igniter (Leading) IGT-L (Ignition timing signal)	0V	approx. 0.8V	
1W	O		Heat hazard sensor	below 1.5V	approx. 12V	Floor Temp.: below 110°C (230°F)
1X		O	Coil with igniter (Trailing) IGT-T (Ignition timing signal)	0V	approx. 0.8V	
2A		O	V ref	4.5~5.5V		
2B	O		Pressure sensor	2.3~2.7V		Disconnect the vacuum hose
2C	-	-	Ground	0V		
2D	O		O2 sensor	below 1.0V		
2E	O		Air flow meter (Vs)	approx. 4V	2.5~3.5V	
2F	O		Variable resistor	1~4V (Varies according to the variable resistor adjustment)		
2G	O		Throttle sensor (TVO)	approx. 1V (Throttle sensor adjusted properly)		
2H	O		Atmospheric pressure sensor	3.5~4.5V (at sea level) 2.5~3.5V (at 2,000 m (6,500 ft))		
2I	O		Water thermo sensor	approx. 0.4~1.8V		Warm engine
2J	O		Air flow meter (Intake air temperature sensor)	2~3V at 20°C (68°F)		
2K		O	Twin scroll turbocharger solenoid valve	below 2.0V		
2L	O		Intake air temperature sensor (Inlet air pipe)	1~2V at 80°C (176°F)		
2M		O	Pressure regulator control solenoid valve	below 2.0V	approx. 12V	
2N		O	EGR solenoid valve	approx. 12V		
2O		O	Switching solenoid valve	approx. 12V (Throttle sensor is adjusted properly)	approx. 12V	
2P		O	Relief solenoid valve	below 2V (Throttle sensor is adjusted properly)	below 2.0V	
2Q		O	Bypass air control (BAC) valve	8~12V		
2R	-	-	Ground	0V		
3A	-	-	Ground	0V		
3B	O		Starter switch	below 1.5V	approx. 12V (at cranking)	Cranking: below 2.0V
3C		O	Injector (Rear primary)	approx. 12V		
3D		O	Fuel pump resistor relay	approx. 12V	below 2.0V	
3E		O	Injector (Front primary)	approx. 12V		
3F		O	Injector (Rear secondary)	approx. 12V		

CONTROL UNIT PIN LOCATIONS AND TEST VOLTAGES – 1986-88 MODELS EXCEPT TURBO

Terminal	Input	Output	Connection to	Ignition switch: ON	Idle	Remark
3E		O	Injector (front primary)	approx. 12V	approx. 12V	
3F		O	Injector (rear secondary)	approx. 12V	approx. 12V	
3G	-	-	Ground	0V	0V	
3H		O	Injector (front secondary)	approx. 12V	approx. 12V	
3I	-	-	Main relay	approx. 12V	approx. 12V	
3J		O	Battery	approx. 12V	approx. 12V	

CONTROL UNIT PIN LOCATIONS AND TEST VOLTAGES – 1987-88 TURBO MODELS

Terminal	Input	Output	Connection to	Ignition switch: ON	Idle	Remark
1A		O	Digital code checker	Ignition switch OFF → ON for 3 sec. 5V, after 3sec. approx. 12V	below approx. 12V	with digital code checker
1B		O	Digital code checker	Ignition switch OFF → ON for 3 sec. 5V after 3 sec. approx. 12V	below approx. 12V	with digital code checker
1C		O	Air bypass solenoid valve	Approx. 12V		
1D		O	Digital code checker (Green lamp)	Ignition switch OFF → ON for 3 sec. 5V after 3 sec. approx. 12V	below approx. 12V	with digital code checker
1E			A/C switch	below 2.5V (A/C: ON), approx. 12V (A/C: OFF)		Blower motor ON
1F		O	A/C main relay	approx. 12V (A/C: OFF)		
1G	O		Neutral switch	below 1.5V (in neutral), approx. 12V (others)		
1H	O		Water temperature switch	below 1.5V (water temperature; above 17°C (62.6°F)		
1I	O		5th switch	below 1.5V; (5th gear), approx. 12V (others)		
1J	O		Initial set coupler	approx. 4~7V (Initial set coupler: OFF), below 1.5V (Initial set coupler: ON)		
1K		O	Shift indicator light	below 1.5V	approx. 12V	
1L	O		Clutch switch	below 1.5V (clutch pedal: released) approx. 12V (clutch pedal: depressed)		
1M	O		Coil with igniter (Trailing) IGt-T	below 2V		
1N	O		Crank angle sensor G ①	below 1.0V		G
1O	O		Mileage switch	approx. 12V (below 20,000 miles), below 1.5V (above 20,000 miles)		
1P	O		Crank angle sensor G ②	below 1.0V		B
1Q	O		Crank angle sensor Ne ②	below 1.0V		W
1R	O		Knock control unit	3~5V		
1S		O	Port air solenoid valve	approx. 12V		Mileage switch ON: below 1.5V
1T	O		Crank angle sensor Ne ①	below 1.0V		R

CONTROL UNIT PIN LOCATIONS AND TEST VOLTAGES – 1987-88 TURBO MODELS

Terminal	Input	Output	Connection to	Voltage (after warming up) Ignition switch: ON	Idle	Remark
3G	—	—	Ground	0V		
3H		O	Injector (Front secondary)	approx. 12V		
3I	—	—	Main relay	approx. 12V		
3J	O		Battery	approx. 12V		

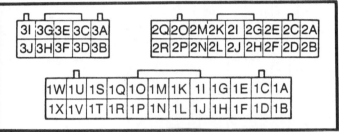

Control Unit Connecter – 1986–88 models

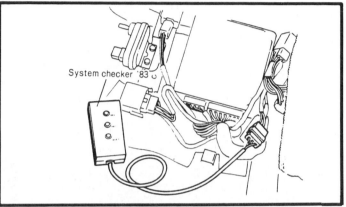

System checker '83 hookup – 1984–85 models

cator lamp lights on in the numerical order of the code number. Even if the problem is corrected during indication, one cycle will be indicated. If after a malfunction has occurred the ignition key is switched off, the malfunction indicator for the feedback system will not be displayed on the checker.

The control unit has a built in fail-safe mechanism. If a malfunction occurs during driving, the control unit will on its own initiative send out a command and driving performance will be affected.

Inspection

1. Warm up the engine to the normal operating temperature and run it at idle. The engine speed should be below 4000 rpm, while warming up.
2. Connect the system checker 83 to the control unit service (check) connector. Be sure that the system checker 83 is working properly. The buzzer should sound for approximately three seconds after the ignition is turned ON.
3. Check whether the trouble-indication lamp illuminates. If the lamp lights up, check for the cause of the problem using the code charts.

Troubleshooting with the Digital Code Checker

1986–88 Models

The Digital Code Checker (part # 49–G018–9A0) can be used to

detect and indicate any problems of each sensor, damaged wiring, poor contact or a short circuit between each of the sensor-control units. Trouble codes are indicated directly on the tool.

The control unit has a built in fail-safe mechanism. If a malfunction occurs during driving, the control unit will on its own initiative send out a command and driving performance will be affected.

Inspection

1. Warm up the engine to the normal operating temperature and run it at idle.
2. Connect the Digital Code Checker (49 G018 9A0) to the control unit service (check) connector. Be sure that the checker is working properly. The buzzer should sound for approximately three seconds after the ignition is turned ON.
3. Check for a code number indication.
4. If a code number is indicated, check for the cause of the problem as shown in the following charts:

TROUBLE CODE TROUBLESHOOTING CHARTS

No. 1 code illumination

Are there any poor connections at the connectors? — Yes → Repair or replace the connector terminal.

↓ No

Is the resistance of the crank angle sensor OK? — No → Replace the crank angle sensor.

↓ Yes

Is there continuity between crank angle sensor and control unit.

Crank angle sensor	Control unit
G ①	1N
G ②	1P
Ne ①	1T
Ne ②	1Q

No → PC: Open or short circuit in the wiring harness.

Yes → PC: Control unit malfunction.

No. 2 code illumination

Are there any poor connections at the connectors? — Yes → Repair or replace the connector terminal.

↓ No

Is the resistance of the air flow meter OK? — No → Replace the air flow meter.

↓ Yes

Is there Vref at the (Br/W) terminal of the air flow meter connector? (Vref 4.5~5.5V) — No → PC: • Open or short circuit in the wiring harness. • Control unit malfunction.

↓ Yes

Is there continuity between air flow meter and control unit.

Air flow meter	Control unit
Vs	2E
E₂	2₂

No → PC: Open or short circuit in the wiring harness from air flow meter to control unit.

Yes → PC: Control unit malfunction.

RED LAMP AND BUZZER INDICATIONS—SYSTEM CHECKER '83

Code No.	Location of problem	Indication	Checking procedure
1	Engine speed		Disconnect the trailing coil – terminal crank engine at least 1.5 seconds, with IG "ON" code should be heard.
2	Air flow meter		Disconnect air flow meter connector, turn IG "ON" code should be heard.
3	Water thermo sensor		Disconnect the water thermo sensor connector, turn IG "ON" code should be heard.
4	Oxygen (O₂) sensor		Refer to page 4B–72.
5	Throttle sensor		Disconnect throttle sensor connector, turn IG "ON" code should be heard.
6	Atmospheric pressure sensor		Disconnect the atmospheric pressure sensor, turn IG "ON" code should be heard.

GREEN LAMP INDICATIONS—SYSTEM CHECKER '83

Green Lamp	Air-Fuel Ratio
Turns ON	Richer than the stoichiometric air/fuel ratio.
Turns ON and OFF	O₂ sensor signal is fed back to the control unit.
Turns OFF	Leaner than the stoichiometric one.

DIGITAL CODE CHECKER TROUBLE CODES

Code No.	Location problem	Fail safe function
01	Crank angle sensor	
02	Air flow meter	Maintains the basic signal at a preset value.
03	Water thermo sensor	Maintains a constant 80°C (176°F) command.
04	Intake air temperature sensor (Air flow meter)	Maintains a constant 20°C (68°F) command.
05	Oxygen (O₂) sensor	Stop the feedback correction
06	Throttle sensor	Maintains a constant 100% (approx.18°) command.
07	Boost sensor	Maintains a constant –96 mmHg (3.78 inHg) command.
09	Atmospheric pressure sensor	Maintains a constant command of the sea-level pressure
12	Coil with igniter (Trailing side)	Stop the operation of ignition system (only trailing side)
15	Intake air temperature sensor (Dynamic chamber)	Maintains a constant 20°C (68°F) command.

TROUBLE CODE TROUBLESHOOTING CHARTS (CONT.)

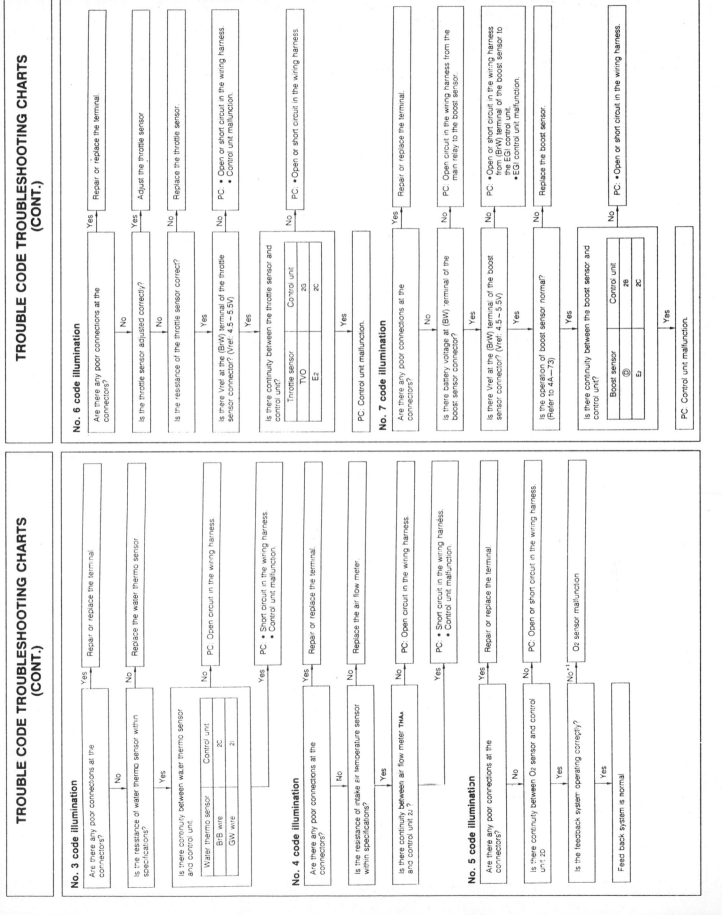

No. 3 code illumination

- Are there any poor connections at the connectors?
  - Yes → Repair or replace the terminal.
  - No →
- Is the resistance of water thermo sensor within specifications?
  - No → Replace the water thermo sensor
  - Yes →
- Is there continuity between water thermo sensor and control unit.

Water thermo sensor	Control unit
B/B wire	2C
G/W wire	2I

  - No → PC: Open circuit in the wiring harness
  - Yes → PC: • Short circuit in the wiring harness. • Control unit malfunction.

No. 4 code illumination

- Are there any poor connections at the connectors?
  - Yes → Repair or replace the terminal.
  - No →
- Is the resistance of intake air temperature sensor within specifications?
  - No → Replace the air flow meter.
  - Yes →
- Is there continuity between air flow meter THAA and control unit 2I ?
  - No → PC: Open circuit in the wiring harness.
  - Yes → PC: • Short circuit in the wiring harness. • Control unit malfunction.

No. 5 code illumination

- Are there any poor connections at the connectors?
  - Yes → Repair or replace the terminal.
  - No →
- Is there continuity between O2 sensor and control unit 2D
  - No → PC: Open or short circuit in the wiring harness.
  - Yes →
- Is the feedback system operating correctly?
  - No*1 → O2 sensor malfunction
  - Yes →
- Feed back system is normal.

No. 6 code illumination

- Are there any poor connections at the connectors?
  - Yes → Repair or replace the terminal.
  - No →
- Is the throttle sensor adjusted correctly?
  - No → Adjust the throttle sensor
  - Yes →
- Is the resistance of the throttle sensor correct?
  - No → Replace the throttle sensor.
  - Yes →
- Is there Vref at the (Br/W) terminal of the throttle sensor connector? (Vref: 4.5~5.5V)
  - No → PC: • Open or short circuit in the wiring harness. • Control unit malfunction.
  - Yes →
- Is there continuity between the throttle sensor and control unit?

Throttle sensor	Control unit
TVO	2G
E2	2C

  - No → PC: • Open or short circuit in the wiring harness.
  - Yes → PC: Control unit malfunction.

No. 7 code illumination

- Are there any poor connections at the connectors?
  - Yes → Repair or replace the terminal.
  - No →
- Is there battery voltage at (BW) terminal of the boost sensor connector?
  - No → PC: Open circuit in the wiring harness from the main relay to the boost sensor.
  - Yes →
- Is there Vref at the (Br/W) terminal of the boost sensor connector? (Vref: 4.5~5.5V)
  - No → PC: • Open or short circuit in the wiring harness from the (Br/W) terminal of the boost sensor to the EGI control unit. • EGI control unit malfunction.
  - Yes →
- Is the operation of boost sensor normal? (Refer to 4A—73)
  - No → Replace the boost sensor.
  - Yes →
- Is there continuity between the boost sensor and control unit?

Boost sensor	Control unit
(D)	2B
E2	2C

  - No → PC: • Open or short circuit in the wiring harness.
  - Yes → PC: Control unit malfunction.

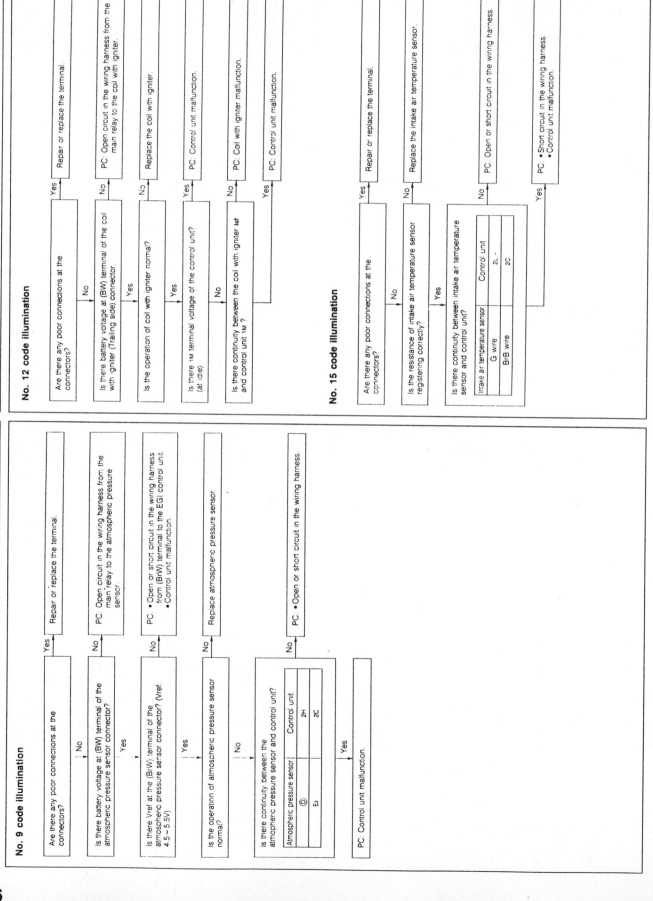

TROUBLE CODE TROUBLESHOOTING CHARTS (CONT.)

No. 12 code illumination

Are there any poor connections at the connectors? → Yes → Repair or replace the terminal.

↓ No

Is there battery voltage at (BW) terminal of the coil with igniter (Trailing side) connector? → No → PC: Open circuit in the wiring harness from the main relay to the coil with igniter.

↓ Yes

Is the operation of coil with igniter normal? → No → Replace the coil with igniter.

↓ Yes

Is there 1M terminal voltage of the control unit? (at idle) → Yes → PC: Control unit malfunction.

↓ No

Is there continuity between the coil with igniter 1af and control unit 1M? → No → PC: Coil with igniter malfunction.

↑ Yes → PC: Control unit malfunction.

No. 15 code illumination

Are there any poor connections at the connectors? → Yes → Repair or replace the terminal.

↓ No

Is the resistance of intake air temperature sensor registering correctly? → No → Replace the intake air temperature sensor.

↓ Yes

Is there continuity between intake air temperature sensor and control unit?

Intake air temperature sensor	Control unit	
G wire	2L	
BrB wire	2C	

→ No → PC: Open or short circuit in the wiring harness.

↑ Yes → PC: • Short circuit in the wiring harness.
• Control unit malfunction.

TROUBLE CODE TROUBLESHOOTING CHARTS (CONT.)

No. 9 code illumination

Are there any poor connections at the connectors? → Yes → Repair or replace the terminal.

↓ No

Is there battery voltage at (BW) terminal of the atmospheric pressure sensor connector? → No → PC: Open circuit in the wiring harness from the main relay to the atmospheric pressure sensor.

↓ Yes

Is there Vref at the (BrW) terminal of the atmospheric pressure sensor connector? (Vref. 4.5~5.5V) → No → PC: • Open or short circuit in the wiring harness from (BrW) terminal to the EGI control unit.
•Control unit malfunction.

↓ Yes

Is the operation of atmospheric pressure sensor normal? → No → Replace atmospheric pressure sensor.

↓ No

Is there continuity between the atmospheric pressure sensor and control unit?

Atmospheric pressure sensor	Control unit	
D	2H	
E2	2C	

→ No → PC: • Open or short circuit in the wiring harness.

↓ Yes

PC: Control unit malfunction.

MITSUBISHI

ENGINE CONTROL SYSTEM APPLICATION CHART

Year	Model	Engine cc (liter)	Engine VIN	Fuel System	Ignition System
1984	Tredia	1997 (2.0)	G63B	FBC	Electronic
		1795 (1.8)	G62B	ECI	ESC
	Cordia	1997 (2.0)	G63B	FBC	Electronic
		1795 (1.8)	G62B	ECI	ESC
	Starion	2555 (2.6)	G54B	ECI	ESC
	Montero	2555 (2.6)	G54B	FBC	Electronic
	Truck	1997 (2.0)	G63B	FBC	Electronic
		2555 (2.6)	G54B	FBC	Electronic
1985	Tredia	1997 (2.0)	G63B	FBC	Electronic
		1795 (1.8)	G62B	ECI	ESC
	Cordia	1997 (2.0)	G63B	FBC	Electronic
		1795 (1.8)	G62B	ECI	ESC
	Starion	2555 (2.6)	G54B	ECI	ESC
	Galant	2350 (2.4)	G64B	ECI	Electronic
	Mirage	1468 (1.5)	G15B	FBC	Electronic
		1597 (1.6)	G32B	ECI	ESC
	Montero	2555 (2.6)	G54B	FBC	Electronic
	Truck	1997 (2.0)	G63B	FBC	Electronic
		2555 (2.6)	G54B	FBC	Electronic
1986	Tredia	1997 (2.0)	G63B	FBC	Electronic
		1795 (1.8)	G62B	ECI	ESC
	Cordia	1997 (2.0)	G63B	FBC	Electronic
		1795 (1.8)	G62B	ECI	ESC
	Starion	2555 (2.6)	G54B	ECI	ESC
	Galant	2350 (2.4)	G64B	ECI	Electronic
	Mirage	1468 (1.5)	G15B	FBC	Electronic
		1597 (1.6)	G32B	ECI	ESC
	Montero	2555 (2.6)	G54B	FBC	Electronic
	Truck	1997 (2.0)	G63B	FBC	Electronic
		2555 (2.6)	G54B	FBC	Electronic
1987	Tredia	1997 (2.0)	G63B	FBC	Electronic
		1795 (1.8)	G62B	ECI	ESC
	Cordia	1997 (2.0)	G63B	FBC	Electronic
		1795 (1.8)	G62B	ECI	ESC
	Starion	2555 (2.6)	G54B	ECI	ESC
	Galant	2350 (2.4)	G64B	MPI	ECITS
	Mirage	1468 (1.5)	G15B	FBC	Electronic
		1597 (1.6)	G32B	ECI	ESC
	Montero	2555 (2.6)	G54B	FBC	Electronic

ENGINE CONTROL SYSTEM APPLICATION CHART

Year	Model	Engine cc (liter)	Engine VIN	Fuel System	Ignition System
1987	Truck	1997 (2.0)	G63B	FBC	Electronic
		2555 (2.6)	G54B	FBC	Electronic
	Van/Wagon	2350 (2.4)	G64B	MPI	ECITS
1988	Tredia	1997 (2.0)	G63B	FBC	Electronic
		1795 (1.8)	G62B	ECI	ESC
	Cordia	1997 (2.0)	G63B	FBC	Electronic
		1795 (1.8)	G62B	ECI	ESC
	Starion	2555 (2.6)	G54B	ECI	ESC
	Galant	2972 (3.0)	6G72	MPI	ECITS
	Mirage	1468 (1.5)	G15B	FBC	Electronic
		1597 (1.6)	G32B	ECI	ECS
	Precis	1468 (1.5)	G15B	FBC	Electronic
	Montero	2555 (2.6)	G54B	FBC	Electronic
	Truck	1997 (2.0)	G63B	FBC	Electronic
		2555 (2.6)	G54B	FBC	Electronic
	Van/Wagon	2350 (2.4)	G64B	MPI	ECITS

ECI   Electronic Controlled Injection
ECITS   Electronic Control Ignition Timing System

ESC   Electronic Spark Control
FBC   Feedback Carburetor
MPI   Multi-Point Injection

ELECTRONICALLY CONTROLLED INJECTION (ECI) SYSTEM

General Information

The Mitsubishi Electronically Controlled Injection (ECI) system is basically a standard throttle body system with some variations in operation and components. The fuel control system consists of an electronic control unit (ECU), one or two solenoid-type fuel injectors, an air flow sensor and several engine sensors. The ECU receives voltage signals from the engine sensors on operating conditions, then sends out impulses to the injectors to constantly adjust the fuel mixture. In addition, the ECU controls starting enrichment, warm-up enrichment, fast idle, deceleration fuel cut-off and overboost fuel cut-off on turbocharged models.

One of the primary components is the air flow sensor with its device for generating Karman vortexes. Ultrasonic waves are transmitted across the air flow containing the Karman vortexes, which are generated in proportion to the air flow rate. The greater the number of vortexes, the more the frequency of the ultrasonic waves are changed (modulated). These modulated ultrasonic waves are picked up by the receiver in the air flow sensor and converted into a voltage signal for the ECU. The ECU uses this signal to measure air flow and control fuel delivery and secondary air management. An intake air temperature sensor is used to provide a signal so that air density changes due to temperature can be calculated.

Other components in the system are common to all throttle body systems. During closed loop operation, the ECU monitors the oxygen sensor to determine the correct fuel mixture according to the oxygen content of the exhaust gases. In the open loop mode, fuel mixture is preprogrammed into the control unit memory.

When the ECI system is activated by the ignition switch, the fuel pump is energized by the ECU. The pump will only operate for about one second unless the engine is running or the starter is cranking. When the engine starts, the fuel pump relay switches to continuous operation and all engine sensors are activated and begin providing input for the ECU. The ISC motor will control idle speed (including fast idle) if the throttle position switch is in the idle position, and the ignition advance shifts from base timing to the preprogrammed ignition advance curve. The fuel pressure regulator maintains system pressure at approximately 14.5 psi (1 bar) by returning excess fuel provided by the fuel pump to the tank.

The ECU provides a ground for the injectors to precisely control the open and closing time (pulse width) to deliver exact amounts of fuel to the engine, continuously adjusting the air/fuel mixture while monitoring signals from the various engine sensors including:

- Engine coolant temperature
- Intake manifold air temperature and volume
- Barometric pressure
- Intake manifold absolute pressure
- Engine speed (rpm)
- Idle speed
- Detonation
- Boost pressure (turbo models only)
- Throttle position
- Exhaust gas content (oxygen level)

OPERATION OF ECI SYSTEM

Air/Fuel Ratio Control System

The air/fuel ratio control is achieved by controlling the driving time of one or two injectors installed to the injection mixer. After passing through the in-tank filter, fuel is force-fed by the in-tank fuel pump so as to be sent to the injectors on the injection mixer through the main pipe and fuel filter. The fuel pressure applied to the injector is maintained at a fixed level by the fuel pressure regulator so that it may be 36 psi (250 kPa) higher than the internal pressure of the injection mixer where fuel injection takes place. After pressure regulation, excess fuel is returned to the fuel tank through the return hose. When the injector is energized, the valve inside the injector opens fully to inject the fuel. Since the fuel pressure is kept at a fixed level, supply of fuel injected from the injectors into the injection mixer varies with the energized time.

Fuel Injection Control

The amount of fuel injection is basically determined by the air flow sensor (AFS) output frequency corresponding to the amount of intake air. With the increase of air flow sensor output frequency, the amount of fuel injection increases and as the air flow sensor output frequency decreases, the amount of fuel injection decreases. When the air flow sensor is in trouble, the backup control is made by driving the injectors by means of engine speed sensor signal.

AIR FLOW SENSOR (AFS)

The AFS measures the intake air volume. It makes use of Karman vortex to detect the air flow rate and sends it to the ECU as the intake air volume signal. The ECU uses this intake air volume signal to decide the basic fuel injection duration.

ATMOSPHERIC PRESSURE SENSOR

The atmospheric pressure sensor installed on the AFS senses the atmospheric pressure and converts it into a voltage which is sent to the ECU. The ECU uses this signal to compute the altitude at which the vehicle is running and corrects accordingly the air/fuel ratio to the optimum and also corrects the ignition timing, thus improving driveability at high altitude at which the vehicle is running and corrects accordingly the air/fuel ratio to the optimum and also corrects the ignition timing, thus improving driveability at high altitude.

INTAKE AIR TEMPERATURE SENSOR

The intake air temperature sensor, located at the illustrated position on AFS, is a resistor-based sensor for detecting the intake air temperature. According to the intake air temperature information from the sensor, the ECU provides necessary fuel injection amount control.

ENGINE COOLANT TEMPERATURE SENSOR

The engine coolant temperature sensor installed in the engine coolant passage of the intake manifold is a resistor-based sensor. The ECU judges engine warm-up state by the sensor output voltage and provides optimum fuel enrichment when the engine is cold.

THROTTLE POSITION SENSOR (TPS)

The TPS is a rotating type variable resistor that rotates together with the injection mixer throttle shaft to sensor the throttle valve angle. As the throttle shaft rotates, the output voltage of

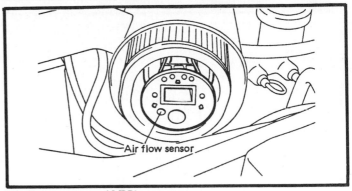

Air flow sensor (AFS)

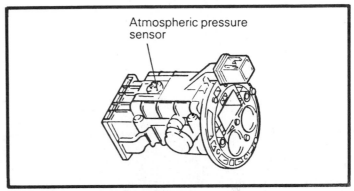

Atmospheric pressure sensor

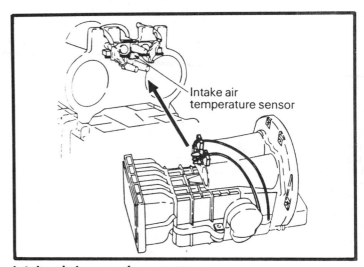

Intake air temperature sensor

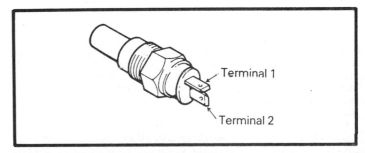

Engine coolant temperature sensor

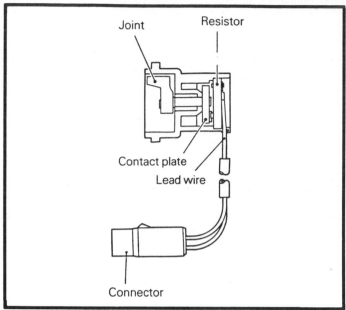

Throttle position sensor (TPS)

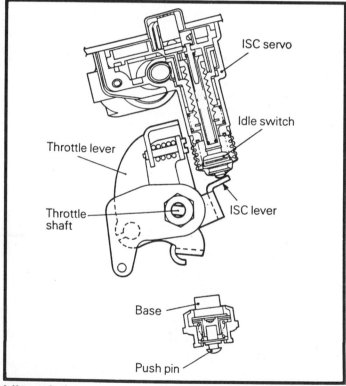

Idle switch

the TPS changes and the ECU detects the throttle valve opening based on the change of the voltage. Based on this output voltage, the ECU computes throttle valve opening change (output voltage change) and judges the engine acceleration/deceleration state and accordingly corrects fuel injection amount during acceleration/deceleration.

IDLE SWITCH

The idle switch, which is a contact type switch, senses accelera-

tor operation. The switch is installed at the tip of the ISC servo. When the throttle valve is at idle opening, the ISC lever pushes the push pin to turn on the contact.

MOTOR POSITION SENSOR (MPS)

The MPS, a variable resistor sensor, is installed in the ISC servo. Its sliding pin is in contact with the plunger end and as the plunger moves, the internal resistance of the MPS changes (namely, the output voltage changes). The MPS senses the ISC servo plunger position and sends the signal to the ECU. The ECU controls the valve opening, and consequently, the idle speed by using the MPS signal, idle signal, engine coolant temperature signal, load signal (automatic transmission and air conditioner) and vehicle speed signal.

ENGINE SPEED SENSOR (IGNITION NEGATIVE TERMINAL VOLTAGE SENSOR)

The ignition coil negative terminal voltage makes sudden increase twice per engine revolution synchronously with ignition timing. By sensing this ignition coil negative terminal voltage change and measuring the time between peak voltages, the ECU computes the engine speed, judges the engine operating mode and controls the air/fuel ratio and idle speed.

OXYGEN SENSOR

The oxygen sensor installed in the exhaust pipe makes use of the principles of solid electrolyte oxygen concentration cell. It is characterized by sharp change of the output voltage in the vicinity of the 14:1 air/fuel ratio.

Using such characteristics, the oxygen sensor senses the oxygen concentration in the exhaust gas and feeds it back to the ECU. The ECU then judges if the air/fuel ratio is richer of leaner as compared to the 14:1 air/fuel ratio and provides feedback control to adjust the air/fuel ratio to the 14:1 ratio where the emission purification rate of the three-catalyst converter is the optimum.

VEHICLE SPEED SENSOR

The vehicle speed sensor uses a reed switch. The speed sensor built in the speedometer converts the transaxle speedometer gear revolution (vehicle speed) into pulse signals, which are sent to the ECU.

INHIBITOR SWITCH (VEHICLES WITH AUTOMATIC TRANSAXLE)

This switch detects whether the select lever is currently positioned at NEUTRAL or PARK. Based on this signal, the ECU senses the automatic transaxle load and drives the ISC servo to keep optimum idle speed.

AIR CONDITIONER SWITCH

When the air conditioner is turned on, the air conditioner ON signal is sent to the ECU. Based on this signal, the ECU drives the ISC servo to keep optimum idle speed.

DETONATION SENSOR

Installed on the cylinder block, the detonation sensor converts vibration into voltage by its piezoelectric element. When detonation occurs, it resonates with cylinder block vibration to generate high voltage which is sent to the igniter as the detonation signal. Based on this signal, the igniter retards the ignition timing to prevent detonation.

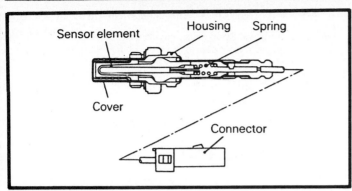

Oxygen sensor

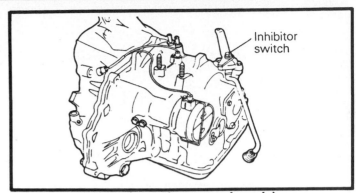

Inhibitor switch (automatic transaxle only)

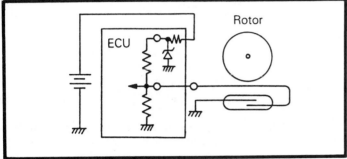

Vehicle speed sensor

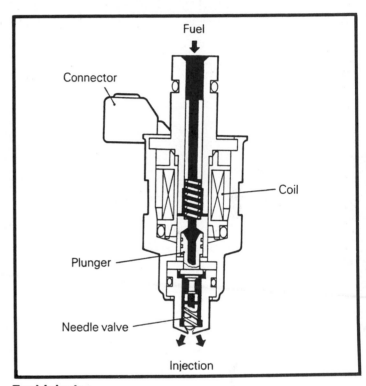

Fuel injector

INJECTORS

The injector, which is an injection nozzle with solenoid valve, injects fuel based on the injection signal from the ECU. The injectors are installed on the injection mixer and inject fuel upstream of the throttle valve. When the solenoid coil is energized, the plunger is attracted. The needle valve integral with the plunger is then pulled to the full open position with the plunger and fuel is injected through the valve so opened. As the injection nozzle opening is fixed and the fuel pressure is also fixed, the injection amount is determined by the duration during which the needle valve is open, namely, by the time during which the solenoid coil is energized.

FUEL PRESSURE REGULATOR

The fuel pressure regulator keeps the injector fuel pressure at a level 36 psi (250 kPa) higher than the injection mixer inside pressure. By doing so, the fuel injection amount is kept constant even when the mixer inside pressure changes. The spring chamber is connected by vacuum hose to the mixer nipple so that the mixer inside intake pressure always acts in the spring chamber. Therefore, when the fuel pressure becomes higher than the spring tension plus intake air pressure in the mixer, the diaphragm is forced up and excess fuel is returned through the return pipe to the fuel tank.

RESISTOR

The resistor limits the electric current flowing to the injector coil. The injector is required to respond quickly to the fuel injection signal. This fast response is achieved by reducing the number of turns of the injector coil and thus improving current rise when the coil is energized. This smaller number of turns, however, draws more current and generates more heat. In order to prevent this, a resistor is provided between the power supply (+) and the injector to limit current flowing to the coil.

IDLE SPEED CONTROL (ISC) SERVO

The ISC servo consists of a motor, worm gear, worm wheel and plunger. Also are incorporated, the motor position sensor (MPS) to detect plunger position and the idle switch to detect idle position. The worm gear, installed on the motor shaft, transmits motor rotation to the worm wheel. The worm wheel is meshed with worm on the plunger so that the plunger extends or retracts as the worm wheel rotates. As the motor rotates according to the signal from the ECU, the plunger extends or retracts depending on the direction of rotation of the motor to actuate the throttle valve via the ISC lever. In this way, the idle speed is controlled by adequately changing the throttle valve opening.

IGNITER

The igniter has the section to judge severity of detonation and the section to control the ignition timing. Based on the signal from the detonation sensor, the igniter judges detonation and controls the ignition timing. The igniter incorporates a fail-safe feature which retards the ignition timing by a fixed angle (except when the engine is at idle) to protect the engine in the event of detonation sensor failure.

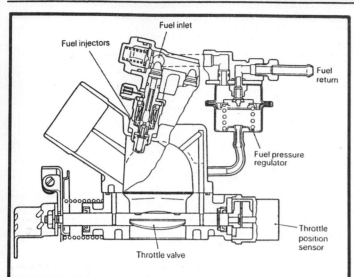

Injection mixer assembly

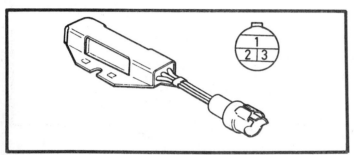

Injector resistor

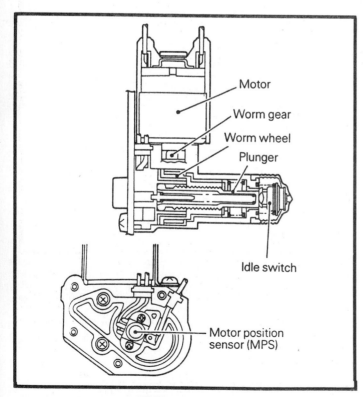

Idle speed control (ISC) servo

ELECTRONIC CONTROL UNIT (ECU)

Based on the information from various sensors, the ECU determines (computes) an optimum control for varying operating conditions and accordingly drives the output actuators. The ECU consists of an 8-bit microprocessor, random access memory (RAM), read only memory (ROM) and input/output (I/O) interface.

Diagnosis and Testing

SELF-DIAGNOSIS SYSTEM

The Mitsubishi self-diagnosis system monitors the various input signals from the engine sensors and enters a trouble code in the on-board computer memory if a problem is detected. There are nine monitored items, including the "normal operation" code which can be read by using a special ECI tester and adapter. The adapter connects the ECI tester to the diagnosis connector located on the right cowl, next to the control unit. Because the computer memory draws its power directly from the battery, the trouble codes are not erased when the ignition is switched OFF. The memory can only be cleared (trouble codes erased) if a battery cable is disconnected or the main ECU wiring harness connector is disconnected from the computer module.

NOTE: The trouble codes will not be erased if the battery cable or harness connector is reconnected with 15 seconds.

If two or more trouble codes are stored in the memory, the computer will read out the codes in order beginning with the lowest number. The needle of the ECI tester will sing back and forth between 0 and 12 volts to indicate the trouble code stored. There is no memory for code No. 1 (oxygen sensor) once the ignition is switched OFF, so it is necessary to perform this diagnosis with the engine running. The oxygen sensor should be allowed to warm up for testing (engine at normal operating temperature) and the trouble code should be read before the ignition is switched OFF. All other codes will be read out with the engine ON or OFF. If there are no trouble codes stored in the computer (system is operating normally), the ECI tester will indicated a constant 12 volts on the meter. Consult the instructions supplied with the test equipment to insure proper connections for diagnosis and testing of all components.

If there is a problem stored, the meter needle will swing back and forth ever 0.4 seconds. Trouble codes are read by counting the pulses, with a two second pause between different codes. If the battery voltage is low, the self-diagnosis system will not operate properly, so the battery condition and state of charge should be checked before attempting any self-diagnosis inspection procedures. After completing service procedures, the computer trouble code memory should be erased by disconnecting the battery cable or main harness connector to the control unit for at least 15 seconds.

NOTE: Installation of CB or other two-way radio equipment may affect the operation of the electronic control unit. Antennas and other radio equipment should be installed as far away from the ECU as possible.

INSPECTION OF ECI SYSTEM

If ECI system components (sensors, ECU, injector, etc.) fail, interruption of fuel supply (injection) or failure to supply proper amount of fuel for engine operating conditions will result. Therefore, the following situations will be encountered.
  1. Engine is hard to start or does not start at all.
  2. Unstable idle.
  3. Poor driveability.

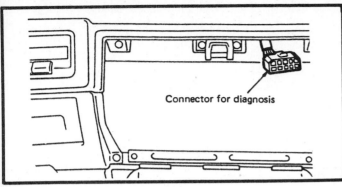

Diagnostic connector location

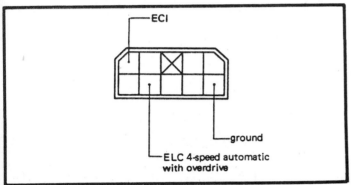

Diagnostic connector terminal identification

Code No.	Diagnosis item
1	Oxygen sensor & Computer
2	Ignition pulse
3	Air flow sensor
4	Pressure sensor
5	Throttle position sensor
6	ISC motor position switch
7	Coolant temp. sensor
8	Vehicle speed

Diagnostic code chart—1984 Cordia/Tredia and Starion

Code No.	Diagnosis item
1	Oxygen sensor & Computer
2	Ignition pulse
3	Air flow sensor
4	Pressure sensor
5	Throttle position sensor
6	ISC motor position switch
7	Coolant temp. sensor

Diagnostic code chart—1985–86 Mirage and Starion, 1985 Galant, and 1985–88 Cordia/Tredia

Malfunction No.	Diagnosis item
1	Oxygen sensor
2	Ignition pulse (engine speed sensor)
3	Air flow sensor
5	Throttle position sensor
6	ISC motor position sensor
7	Coolant temperature sensor

Diagnostic code chart—1987–88 Starion and Mirage

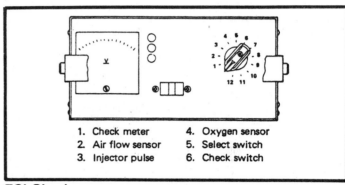

1. Check meter
2. Air flow sensor
3. Injector pulse
4. Oxygen sensor
5. Select switch
6. Check switch

ECI Checker

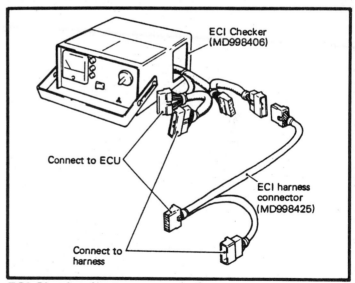

ECI Checker harness connections

If any of above conditions is noted, first perform inspection by self-diagnosis and subsequent basic engine checks (ignition system malfunctions, incorrect engine adjustment, etc.), and then inspect the ECI system components by ECI Checker.

The ECI system can be checked by use of the ECI Checker, Diagnosis Harness Connector and Adapter.

SERVICE PRECAUTIONS

1. Before battery terminals are disconnected, make sure that

ignition switch is set to OFF. If battery terminals are disconnected while engine is running or when ignition switch is in ON position, malfunction of ECU or damage to semi-conductors could result.

2. Disconnect battery cables before charging battery.

3. When battery is reconnected, be sure not to reverse polarity.

4. Make sure that harness connectors are securely connected. Use care not to allow entry of water or oil into connectors.

INSPECTION PROCEDURE BY SELF-DIAGNOSIS

1. Turn ignition switch to OFF.

2. Open glove compartment and pull out connector for diagnosis.

3. Connect a volt meter between terminal for "ECI" and terminal for ground.

4. Turn ignition switch to ON, and indication of ECU memory contents will immediately start. If system is in normal condition, pointer of volt meter constantly indicates 12 volts. If any abnormality is in memory, pointer of volt meter will deflect, indicating abnormal item as described in "Indication Method". Abnormal item can be known from voltage waveform that is, number of pointer deflections shown in "Diagnosis Chart". After recording abnormal item, check and repair each part according to check items in "Diagnosis Chart".

5. Turn ignition switch to OFF.

6. If defective parts have been repaired, disconnect ground cable for 15 seconds or more from negative terminal of battery and connect it again to make sure that abnormal code has been erased.

AIR FLOW SENSOR

Inspection

Check following and replace if defective:

1. Check air cleaner element for contamination and damage.

2. Check air cleaner case and cover for damage and cracks.

3. Check intake air temperature sensor by measuring resistance. Resistance should be 2.5 kilo ohms (kΩ) at 20F°C (68°F).

FUEL INJECTOR

Flow Test

1. Set ignition switch to OFF.

2. Disconnect high tension cable from ignition coil.

3. Remove air intake pipe from air intake port of injection mixer to make visual inspection of injection condition.

4. Check to make ensure that when ignition is placed to "ST" position, injection from each injector is in good condition.

5. Check to ensure that after ignition switch has been set to OFF, there is no fuel leakage from nozzle of injectors.

6. Reconnect high tension cable to ignition coil.

Injector Coil Test

1. Set ignition switch to OFF.

2. Disconnect connectors from injectors.

3. Check injector coil for continuity with a circuit tester (ohm range). Coil resistance should be 0.8 ohms (Ω). If resistance is 0 ohms (Ω) or abnormally large, short or open circuit is in coil. Therefore, replace fuel injector.

4. Reconnect connectors to injectors.

IDLE SWITCH

Test

1. Set ignition switch to OFF.

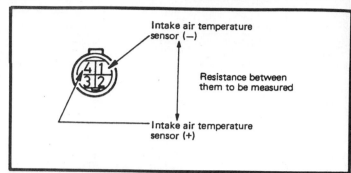

Air flow sensor inspection

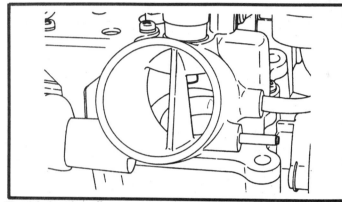

Fuel injection flow test

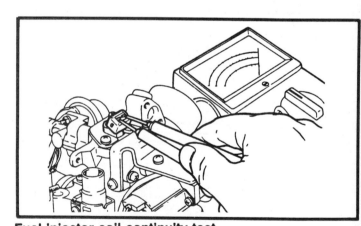

Fuel injector coil continuity test

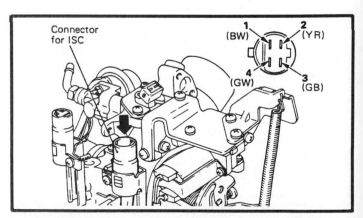

Idle switch test

ECI SYSTEM CHECK PROCEDURE CHART 1984 CORDIA/TREDIA AND STARION

Select switch	Check switch	Check item	Condition	Check meter reading when normal	Terminal location of computer
A	1	Power supply	Ignition switch OFF → ON	11 – 13V	B-1
	2	Secondary air control solenoid valve	Ignition switch OFF → ST after warming up the engine	0.2 – 1V 30 seconds 13 – 15V	A-10
	3	Throttle position switch	Accelerator closed	0.4 – 1.5V	A-1
			Accelerator wide opened	4.5 – 5.0 V	
	4	Coolant temperature sensor	Ignition switch OFF → ON 0°C (32°F)	3.5V	A-3
			20°C (68°F)	2.6V	
			40°C (104°F)	1.8V	
			80°C (176°F)	0.6V	
	5	Intake air temperature sensor	Ignition switch OFF → ON 0°C (32°F)	3.5V	A-4
			20°C (68°F)	2.6V	
			40°C (104°F)	1.8V	
			80°C (176°F)	0.6V	
	6	Idle position switch	Ignition switch OFF → ON Accelerator closed	0 – 0.4V	A-5
			Accelerator wide opened	11 – 13V	
	7	ISC motor position switch	Ignition switch OFF → ON	11 – 18V *1	A-14
	8	EGR control solenoid valve	Ignition switch OFF → ON	0 – 0.6V after 1 second	B-4
	9	ISC motor for extension	Ignition switch OFF → ON	Needle swings momentarily*2	B-6
	10	*3 A/C relay	Ignition switch OFF → ON A/C switch OFF → ON	11 – 13V	B-12
	11	Lead switch for vehicle speed	Start engine, transaxle in first and operate vehicle slowly	0.2 – 1V Flashing 4 – 5V	A-15
	12	ISC motor for retraction	Ignition switch OFF → ON	Needle swings momentarily*2	B-11
B	1	Cranking signal	Ignition switch OFF → ST	Over 8V	A-13
	2	Control relay	Idling	0 – 1V	B-5
	3	ISC motor position switch	Idling	11 – 13V	A-14
	4	Ignition pulse	Idling	12 – 15V	A-8
			3000 rpm	11 – 13V	
	5	Air flow sensor	Idling	2.7 – 3.2V	A-7
			3000 rpm		
	6	Injector No. 1	Idling	13 – 15V	B-9
			3000 rpm	12 – 13V	

ECI SYSTEM CHECK PROCEDURE CHART 1985–86 MODELS EXCEPT INTERCOOLED ENGINES

Select switch	Check switch	Check item	Condition	Check meter reading when normal	Terminal location of computer
B	7	Injector No. 2	Idling	13 – 15V	B-10
			3000 rpm	12 – 13V	
	8	Oxygen sensor	Keep 1300 rpm after warming up the engine	0 – 1V ↓ Flashing 2.7V	A-6
	9	EGR control solenoid valve	Keep idling after warming up the engine	13 – 15V	B-4
	10	Pressure sensor	Ignition switch: OFF → ON	1.5 – 2.6V	A-17
	11	ISC motor for extension	Idling	0.2 – 1.2V	B-6
			A/C switch: OFF → ON	Over 6V *4	
	12	ISC motor for retraction	Idling A/C switch: ON → OFF	Over 6V *4	B-11

NOTE:
*1: If ON for 15 seconds or longer, will change to 1 V or less.
*2: The needle may not always swing back and forth If it doesn't, switch OFF and ON several times.
*3: AC = air conditioner
*4: 6 V will be indicated for only a moment; if the indication is difficult to read, switch the A/C switch ON and OFF several times so that the voltmeter needle swings back and forth.

Select switch	Check switch	Check item	Condition	Check meter reading when normal	Terminal location of computer
A	1	Power supply	Ignition switch OFF → ON	11 – 13V	B-1
	2	Secondary air control solenoid valve	Ignition switch OFF → ST after warming up the engine	After 15 seconds 0 – 0.5V ↓ 13 – 15V	A-10
	3	Throttle position sensor	Accelerator closed	0.4 – 1.5V	A-1
			Accelerator wide opened	4.5 – 5.0V	
	4	Coolant temperature sensor	Ignition switch OFF → ON 0°C (32°F)	3.5V	A-3
			20°C (68°F)	2.6V	
			40°C (104°F)	1.8V	
			80°C (176°F)	0.6V	
	5	Intake air temperature sensor	Ignition switch OFF → ON 0°C (32°F)	3.5V	A-4
			20°C (68°F)	2.6V	
			40°C (104°F)	1.8V	
			80°C (176°F)	0.6V	
	6	Idle position switch	Ignition switch OFF → ON Accelerator closed	0 – 0.4V	A-5
			Accelerator wide opened	11 – 13V	
	7	ISC motor position switch	Ignition switch OFF → ON	11 – 13V *1	A-14
	8	—	—	—	—
	9	—	—	—	—
	10	A/C (Air conditioner) relay	Ignition switch OFF → ON A/C switch OFF	0 – 0.5V	B-12
			A/C switch ON	11 – 13V	

ECI SYSTEM CHECK PROCEDURE CHART — 1986 STARION WITH INTERCOOLED ENGINE

Select switch	Check switch	Check item	Condition		Check meter reading when normal	Terminal location of computer
A	6	Idle position switch	Ignition switch OFF → ON	Accelerator closed	0~0.5V	A-7
				Accelerator opened	11~13V	A-8
	7	ISC motor position switch (MPS)	Ignition switch OFF → ON	—	11~13V *1	—
	8			—	—	—
	9			—	—	—
	10	A/C relay *2	Ignition switch OFF → ON	A/C switch OFF	0~0.5V	B-6
				A/C switch ON	11~13V	—
	11	Lead switch for vehicle speed	Start engine, transmission in first or D and operate vehicle slowly		0~0.5V 1 Pulses Over 2V	A-19
	12			—	—	—
B	1	Cranking signal	Ignition switch OFF → ON		Over 8V	B-5
	2	Control relay	Idling		0~0.5V	A-22
	3			—	—	—
	4	Ignition pulse	Idling		12~14V	A-1
			3,000 rpm		11~13V	—
	5	Air flow sensor	Idling		2.7~3.2V	A-2
			3,000 rpm		—	—
	6	Injector No. 1	Idling		13~15V	B-10
			3,000 rpm		12~14V	—
	7	Injector No. 2	Idling		13~15V	B-12
			3,000 rpm		12~14V	—
	8	Oxygen sensor	Keep 1,300 rpm after warming up the engine		0.4~1V 1 Pulses 2.7V	A-11
	9	EGR control solenoid valve	Keep idling after warming up the engine		13~15V	B-4
			Raise the engine speed 3,500 rpm		0~0.5V	—
	10	Pressure sensor	Ignition switch OFF → ON		1.5~2.6V	A-9
			Idling		0.2~1.2V *3	—
	11	ISC motor for extension	Idling		0~2V	B-9
			Idling A/C switch OFF → ON		Momentarily Over 6V	—
	12	ISC motor for retraction	Idling		0~2V	B-11
			Idling A/C switch ON → OFF		Momentarily Over 6V	—

NOTE:
*1: If ignition switch is turned to ON for 15 seconds or more, the reading drops below 5V momentarily.
*2: A/C stands for air conditioner.
*3: The reading rises to 1.5~2.6V every 2 minutes momentarily.

Check item	Checking with voltmeter	Condition			Check meter reading when normal	Terminal location of computer
Spark advance signal		Idling			Over 5V	A-12
Intake air temperature sensor "B"			Coolant temp below 35°C (95°F)		0~0.5V	—
			Coolant temp above 35°C (95°F)	Altitudes below 3,900 ft	Over 5V	—
				Altitudes above 3,900 ft		—
		Ignition switch OFF → ON	0°C (32°F)		3.5V	A-17
			20°C (68°F)		2.6V	
			40°C (104°F)		1.8V	
			80°C (176°F)		0.6V	

ECI SYSTEM CHECK PROCEDURE CHART — 1985–86 MODELS EXCEPT INTERCOOLED ENGINES

Select switch	Check switch	Check item	Condition		Check meter reading when normal	Terminal location of computer
B	11	Lead switch for vehicle speed	Start engine, transaxle in first and operate vehicle slowly		Flashing 0~0.5V 1 Over 2V	A-15
	1	Cranking signal	Ignition switch OFF → ST		Over 8V	A-13
	2	Control relay	Idling		0~0.5V	B-5
	3			—	—	—
	4	Ignition pulse	Idling		12~14V	A-8
			3,000 rpm		11~13V	—
	5	Air flow sensor	Idling		2.7~3.2V	A-7
			3,000 rpm		—	—
	6	Injector No. 1	Idling		13~15V	B-9
			3,000 rpm		12~14V	—
	7	Injector No. 2	Idling		13~15V	B-10
			3,000 rpm		12~14V	—
	8	Oxygen sensor	Keep 1,300 rpm after warming up the engine		Flashing 0.4V 1 2.7V	A-6
	9	EGR control solenoid valve	Keep idling after warming up the engine		13~15V	B-4
			Raise the engine speed to 3,500 rpm		0~0.5V	—
	10	Pressure sensor	Ignition switch OFF → ON		1.5~2.6V	A-17
			Idling		0.2~1.2V *2	—
	11	ISC motor for extension	Idling	A/C switch OFF → ON	0.2V	B-6
			Idling		Momentarily Over 6V	—
	12	ISC motor for retraction	Idling	A/C switch ON → OFF	0.2V	B-11
			Idling		Momentarily Over 6V	—

NOTE:
*1: If ignition switch is turned to ON for 15 seconds or more, the reading drops below 5V momentarily.
*2: The reading rises to 1.5~2.6V every 2 minutes momentarily.

Select switch	Check switch	Check item	Condition		Check meter reading when normal	Terminal location of computer
A	1	Power supply	Ignition switch OFF → ON		11~13V	B-1
	2	Secondary air control solenoid valve	Restart the engine after warming up		After 15 secs. 0~0.5V ← 13~15V	A-23
	3	Throttle position sensor	Ignition switch OFF → ON	Accelerator closed	0.4~1.5V	A-15
				Accelerator wide opened	4.5~5.0V	—
	4	Coolant temperature sensor	Ignition switch OFF → ON	0°C (32°F)	3.5V	A-6
				20°C (68°F)	2.6V	
				40°C (104°F)	1.8V	
				80°C (176°F)	0.6V	
	5	Intake air temperature sensor "A"	Ignition switch OFF → ON	0°C (32°F)	3.5V	A-5
				20°C (68°F)	2.6V	
				40°C (104°F)	1.8V	
				80°C (176°F)	0.6V	

ECI SYSTEM CHECK PROCEDURE CHART 1987–88 CORDIA/TREDIA

Select switch	Check switch	Check item	Condition	Check meter reading when normal	Terminal number of computer
A	1	Power supply	Ignition switch OFF → ON	SV	51
	2	Secondary air control solenoid valve	Ignition switch OFF → ST after warming up the engine	After 15 seconds 0~0.5V → SV	10
	3	Throttle position switch	Accelerator closed / Ignition switch OFF → ON	0.4~1.5V	1
			Accelerator wide opened	4.5~5.0V	
	4	Coolant temperature sensor	Ignition switch OFF → ON	0°C (32°F) 3.5V; 20°C (68°F) 2.6V; 40°C (104°F) 1.8V; 80°C (176°F) 0.6V	3
	5	Intake air temperature	Ignition switch OFF → ON	0°C (32°F) 3.5V; 20°C (68°F) 2.6V; 40°C (104°F) 1.8V; 80°C (176°F) 0.6V	4
	6	Idle position switch	Accelerator closed / Ignition switch OFF → ON	0~0.4V	5
			Accelerator wide opened	SV	
	7	ISC motor position switch	Ignition switch OFF → ON	SV	14
	8	–	–	–	–
	9	–	–	–	–
	10	A.C (Air conditioner) relay	A/C switch OFF / Ignition switch OFF → ON / A/C switch ON	0~0.5V; SV	62
	11	Lead switch for vehicle speed	Start engine, transaxle in first and operate vehicle slowly	Flashing 0~0.5V ↕ Over 2V	15
	12	–	–	–	–
B	1	Cranking signal	Ignition switch OFF → ST	Over 8V	13
	2	Control relay	Idling	0~0.5V	55
	3	–	–	–	8
	4	Ignition pulse	Idling / 3000 rpm	12~14V; SV	
	5	Air flow sensor	Idling / 3000 rpm	2.2~3.2V	7
	6	Injector No. 1	Idling / 3000 rpm	SV; 12~14V	59

ECI SYSTEM CHECK PROCEDURE CHART 1987–88 CORDIA/TREDIA

Select switch	Check switch	Check item	Condition	Check meter reading when normal	Terminal number of computer
B	7	Injector No. 2	Idling	SV	60
			3000 rpm	12~14V	
	8	Oxygen sensor	Keep 1300 rpm after warming up the engine	Flashing 0.4~1V ↕ 2.7V	6
	9	EGR control solenoid valve	Keep idling after warming up the engine	SV	54
			Raise the engine 3500 rpm	0~0.5V	
	10	Pressure sensor	Ignition switch: OFF → ON	1.5~2.6V	17
	11	ISC motor for extension	Idling	0.2~1.2V*2	56
			Idling	0~2V	
	12	ISC motor for retraction	Idling	A/C switch: OFF → ON Momentarily Over 6V	61
			Idling	0~2V	
				A/C switch: ON → OFF Momentarily Over 6V	

NOTE: *1 If ignition switch is turned to ON for 15 seconds or more, the reading drops below 5V momentarily.
*2 The reading rises to 1.5~2.6V every 2 minutes momentarily.

Checking with voltmeter		Check item	Condition	Check meter reading when normal	Terminal location of computer
		Spark advance signal	Idling	Coolant temp. below 35°C (95°F) Altitudes below 3,900 ft.	Over 5V	12
				Coolant temp. above 35°C (95°F) Altitudes above 3,900 ft.	0~0.5V / Over 5V	
		Inhibitor switch	Ignition switch OFF → ON / Select lever in "P" or "N"	0~0.5V	11
			Select lever in "D"	SV	11

SV : System Voltage

ECI Checker Operation

Select Switch	Check Switch	Check item	Condition	ECU Terminal # Checked	Test Specification
1	1	Power supply	Ignition switch "LOCK" → "ON"	51	11V~13V
	2	Ignition pulse	Ignition switch "LOCK → START"	1	4V~10V
	3	Intake air temperature sensor	Ignition switch "LOCK" → "ON"	5	0°C (32°F) 3.4V~3.6V; 20°C (68°F) 2.5V~2.7V; 40°C (104°F) 1.7V~1.9V; 80°C (176°F) 0.6V~0.8V

ECI SYSTEM CHECK PROCEDURE CHART (PART 1) — 1987–88 MIRAGE AND STARION

ECI Checker Operation Select Switch	Check Switch	Check Item	ECU Terminal # Checked	Condition	Test Specification
"A"	4	Engine coolant temperature sensor	6	Ignition switch "LOCK" → "ON"	0°C (32°F) 3.4V – 3.6V
					20°C (68°F) 2.5V – 2.7V
					40°C (104°F) 1.5V – 1.7V
					80°C (176°F) 0.5V – 0.7V
	5	Power supply for sensor	10	Ignition switch "LOCK" → "ON"	4.5V – 5.5V
	6	Throttle position sensor	15	Ignition switch "LOCK" → "ON" (Warm engine)	Accelerator fully closed 0.4V – 0.7V
					Accelerator fully opened 4.5V – 5.5V
	7	Motor position sensor	3	Ignition switch "LOCK" → "ON"	After 15 seconds 0.8V – 1.2V
	8	Idle position switch	7	Ignition switch "LOCK" → "ON"	Accelerator fully closed 0V – 0.6V
					Accelerator fully opened 8V – 13V
	9	Cranking signal	55	Ignition switch "LOCK" → "START"	Over 8V
	10	Vehicle speed sensor reed switch	19	Start engine and operate vehicle slowly in 1st or DRIVE range	0V – 0.6V (pulsates) Over 2V
	11	Air conditioner switch	56	Ignition switch "LOCK" → "ON"	Air conditioner switch "OFF" 0V – 0.6V
					Air conditioner switch "ON" *1 11V – 13V
	12	Inhibitor switch	58	Ignition switch "LOCK" → "ON"	At "P" or "N" range 0V – 0.6V
					At "D" range 11V – 13V
"B"	1				
	2				
	3				
	4	Spark advance signal	13	Idling	Engine coolant temperature less than 35°C (95°F) Over 5V
					Engine coolant temperature 35°C (95°F) or higher, altitude up to approx. 1,200 m (3,900 ft.) 0 – 0.6V
					Engine coolant temperature 35°C (95°F) or higher, altitude approx. 1,200 m (3,900 ft.) or above Over 5V
	5	Air flow sensor	2	Idling	2.2 – 3.2V
				3,000 rpm	
	6				
	7	EGR control solenoid valve	54	Hold engine at a speed less than 3,500 rpm after warming up	13V – 15V
				Hold engine at a speed 3,500 rpm or higher	0V – 0.6V
	8	Oxygen sensor	11	Hold engine at a constant speed above 1,300 rpm, after 30 seconds from start of warm engine	0V – 0.6V *2 (pulsates) 2V – 3V

ECI SYSTEM CHECK PROCEDURE CHART (PART 2) — 1987–88 MIRAGE AND STARION

ECI Checker Operation Select Switch	Check Switch	Check Item	ECU Terminal # Checked	Condition	Test Specification
"B"	9				
	10				
	11				
	12				

Failure of parts other than the oxygen sensor can also cause deviation from the specifications. Therefore, check other parts related to air-fuel ratio control.

NOTE
*1: ON means compressor clutch engaged.

ECI Checker Operation Select Switch	Check Switch	Check Item	ECU Terminal # Checked	Condition	Test Specification
"A"	1				
	2	Secondary air control solenoid valve	20	Hold engine over 1,500 rpm, 15 seconds after start of warm engine	0V – 0.6V then 13V – 15V
	3				
	4				
	5				
	6				
	7				
	8				
	9				
	10				
	11				
	12				
"B"	1	ISC motor for extension	23	Idling, Air conditioner switch OFF → ON *1	Momentarily over 4V, then 0V – 2V *2
	2	ISC motor for retraction	12	Idling, Air conditioner switch ON → OFF *1	Momentarily over 4V, then 0V – 2V *2
	3	Air conditioner cutoff relay	24	Idling, Air conditioner switch OFF → ON *1	12V – 15V, then 0V – 0.6V
	4	Control relay	22	Ignition switch "LOCK" → "ON"	11V – 13V
				Idling	0V – 0.6V
	5				
	6	Boost meter	59	Idling	12V – 14V
				Quick acceleration from idling to above 2,000 rpm in "N" or "P" position	Slight drop
	7	Injector No. 1 pulse	60	Idling	12V – 14V
				Quick acceleration from idling to above 2,000 rpm in "N" or "P" position	Slight drop

ECI SYSTEM CHECK PROCEDURE CHART
(PART 2) – 1987–88 MIRAGE AND STARION

ECI Checker Operation		Check Item	ECU Terminal # Checked	Condition		Test Specification
Select Switch	Check Switch					
	8					
	9	Detonation retard signal	61	Idling		Over 5V
				Quick acceleration from idling to above 2,000 rpm in "N" or "P" position		0V – 0.6V
	10					
	11	Injector No. 2 pulse	62	Idling		12V – 15V
				Quick acceleration from idling to above 2,000 rpm in "N" or "P" position		Slight drop
	12	Heater relay	17	Idling, 3 seconds after start of engine	Engine coolant temperature less than 70°C (158°F)	0V – 0.6V
					Engine coolant temperature 70°C (158°F) or higher	13V – 15V

NOTE
*1: ON means compressor clutch engaged
*2: Pointer indicates over 6V momentarily. If it is hard to read indication, repeat OFF → ON or ON → OFF operation of air conditioner switch several times. If the pointer of voltmeter deflects, ISC motor is normal.

ECU terminal

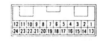

View from front as installed in ECU

2. Disconnect connector of ISC servo.

3. Check for continuity with a circuit tester (ohm range) between pole 2 and injection mixer body.

4. If there is continuity when throttle valve is placed in idle position and if there is no continuity when throttle valve is opened (to extent that lever leaves idle switch), then switch is good. If there is continuity wen throttle valve is in either condition, contacts are bound together. If there is no continuity with throttle valve in either condition, grounding is defective. Therefore, replace ISC servo assembly.

5. Reconnect ISC servo connector.

IDLE SPEED CONTROL (ISC) SERVO

Voltage Test

1. Connect voltmeter between terminal 3 and injection mixer body. Do not disconnect ISC servo connector.

NOTE: Use voltmeter which has good response.

2. Set ignition switch to OFF and then to ON. While keeping it in ON position for more then 15 seconds, note needle of voltmeter. If voltmeter needle indicates 11–13 volts with ignition switch set to ON and after momentary indication of 5 volts or less, it returns to indicate about 11–13 volts, ISC servo and position switch are operating normally.

3. Turn ignition switch to OFF and remove voltmeter.

Continuity Test

1. Set ignition switch to OFF.

2. Disconnect connector of ISC servo.

3. Check motor for continuity with a circuit tester (ohm range) between terminal 1 and 4. Resistance should be 7–10 ohms (Ω). If resistance is 0 ohm (Ω) or abnormally large, open or short circuit is in motor coil. Therefore, replace ISC servo assembly.

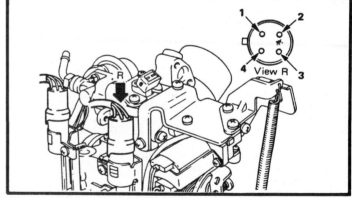

Idle speed control (ISC) test

4. Make sure that there is no continuity between terminal 1 or 4 and injection mixer body. If there is continuity, short circuit is in coil. Therefore, replace ISC servo assembly.

THROTTLE POSITION SENSOR (TPS)

Continuity Test

1. Set ignition switch to OFF.

2. Disconnect sensor connector.

3. Check resistance across poles 1 and 3. Total resistance of throttle position sensor should be 4–6 kilo ohms (kΩ)

4. Connect a circuit tester across poles 1 and 2 or 2 and 3, and check to ensure that when throttle valve is slowly operated from idle to fully opened position, resistance changes smoothly.

5. Fasten connector firmly.

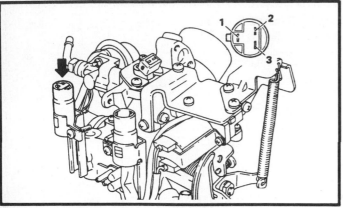

Throttle position sensor (TPS) test

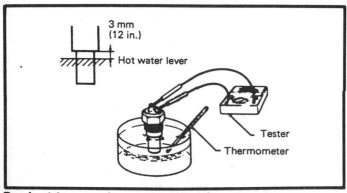

Coolant temperature sensor testing

COOLANT TEMPERATURE SENSOR

Inspection

1. Remove coolant temperature sensor from intake manifold.
2. With temperature sensing portion of coolant temperature sensor immerse in hot water, measure resistance. Do not allow temperature sensing portion to directly touch heated portion of hot water container. Stir hot water continuously. Connector terminal portion of sensor should be held 0.12 in. (3mm) above hot water level. Resistance should be:

16.2 kilo ohms (kΩ) at −20°C (−4°F)
2.45 kilo ohms (kΩ) at 20°C (68°F)
296 ohms (Ω) at 80°C (176°F)

3. If resistance meets specifications, sensor is good. If anything abnormal is evident, replace sensor.

INTAKE AIR TEMPERATURE SENSOR B

Inspection

1. Disconnect harness connector of intake air temperature sensor.
2. Check resistance across terminals in connector of sensor. Resistance should be 2.45 kilo ohms (kΩ) at 68°F (20°C).
3. If resistance is abnormally small or large, sensor is short or open-circuited. Therefore, replace sensor.
4. Fasten harness connector of sensor firmly.

ECU CONTROL RELAY

Inspection

1. Test continuity between terminals 1 and 7 and between terminals 3 and 7. If there is no continuity, control relay is good. If there is continuity, replace control relay.

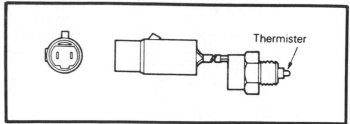

Intake air temperature sensor B—intercooled models

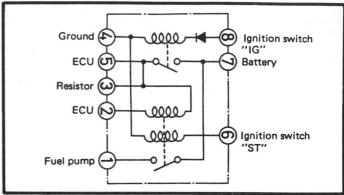

ECI control relay terminal identification

2. Apply 12 volts across terminals 8 and 4 while testing continuity between terminals 3 and 7. If there is continuity, control relay is good.
3. Apply 12 volts across terminals 6 and 4 while testing continuity between terminals 1 and 7. If there is continuity, control relay is good. Similarly, apply 12 volts across terminals 5 and 2 while testing continuity between terminals 1 and 7. If there is continuity, control relay is good.

INJECTOR RESISTOR

Inspection

1. Disconnect harness connector of resistor.
2. Measure resistance across terminals 1 and 2 and across terminals 1 and 3. Resistance should be 6 ohms (Ω).
3. If resistance is within standard value, resistor is good. If resistance is 0 or abnormally large, resistor is short-or open-circuited. Replace resistor.
4. Fasten connector of resistor firmly.

Component Replacement

INJECTION MIXER

Removal and Installation

1. Disconnect battery ground cable.
2. Drain coolant down to intake manifold level or below.
3. Disconnect air intake hose from injection mixer.
4. Disconnect throttle cable from throttle lever of injection mixer.
5. Disconnect fuel inlet pipe and fuel return hose from injection mixer.
6. Disconnect harness connectors at injectors.
7. Disconnect connectors for ISC servo and throttle position sensor.
8. Disconnect vacuum hoses from nipple of mixer.

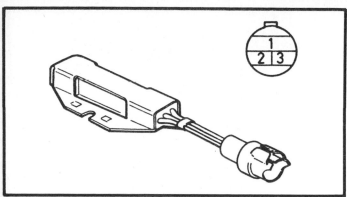

Fuel resistor terminal identification

9. Remove four bolts and remove injection mixer from intake manifold.

10. Reinstall injection mixer in reverse order of removal, paying special attention to following items:

  a. When replacing throttle position sensor or ISC servo, output voltage or engine speed should be adjusted.

  b. Start and run engine, and check for fuel leakage.

Overhaul

NOTE: When a cross-recessed screw is to be loosened, use a cross-recessed screwdriver of proper size for cross recess, as screws are held tightly.

1. Clamp injection mixer in a vise with soft jaws.

2. Disconnect rubber hose from fuel pressure regulator and mixing body.

3. Remove injector retainer tightening screws and remove retainer.

4. Remove fuel pressure regulator from retainer.

5. Remove pulsation damper cover from retainer, and then take out spring and diaphragm.

6. Pull injectors from mixing body. Do not clamp injector by pliers. Then remove gaskets from body.

7. Remove throttle return spring and damper spring.

8. Remove connector bracket.

9. Remove ISC servo mounting bracket retaining bolts and remove ISC servo and bracket.

NOTE: Do not remove ISC servo except when replacement is required.

10. Remove two screws and then remove mixing body and seal ring from throttle body.

11. Remove throttle position sensor.

NOTE: Do not remove throttle position sensor except when replacement is required.

12. When cleaning injection mixer parts, do not immerse parts in cleaning solvent. Immersing ISC servo, throttle position sensor and injector will damage insulation. Wipe these parts with a cloth only.

13. Do not immerse injectors and fuel pressure regulator in cleaning solvent.

14. Check vacuum parts and passages for clogging. Clean vacuum passage and fuel passage with compressed air.

CAUTION

Always wear eye protection when using compressed air.

---

15. To reassemble, insert joint A of throttle position sensor to joint B and install throttle position sensor to throttle body. Then temporarily tighten screws.

NOTE: After installing injection mixer assembly to engine, adjust throttle position sensor.

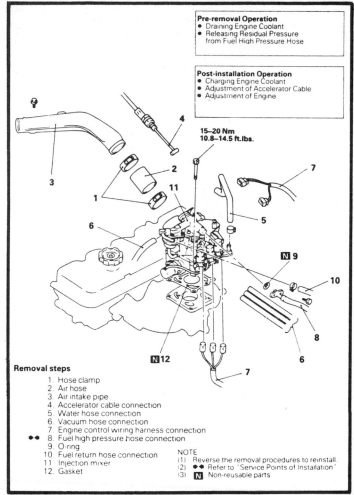

Pre-removal Operation
- Draining Engine Coolant
- Releasing Residual Pressure from Fuel High Pressure Hose

Post-installation Operation
- Charging Engine Coolant
- Adjustment of Accelerator Cable
- Adjustment of Engine

15–20 Nm
10.8–14.5 ft.lbs.

Removal steps
1. Hose clamp
2. Air hose
3. Air intake pipe
4. Accelerator cable connection
5. Water hose connection
6. Vacuum hose connection
7. Engine control wiring harness connection
◆◆ 8. Fuel high pressure hose connection
9. O-ring
10. Fuel return hose connection
11. Injection mixer
12. Gasket

NOTE
(1) Reverse the removal procedures to reinstall.
(2) ◆◆ Refer to "Service Points of Installation"
(3) N Non-reusable parts

Injection mixer removal and installation — 1987–88 Starion

16. Clamp connector into bracket.

17. Check for proper installation of throttle position sensor. Measure resistance value between terminals 1 and 2 or 3 and 4, while moving throttle lever from open to close. If resistance value changes, throttle position sensor is properly installed.

18. Install new seal ring into groove of throttle body.

19. Install mixing body into throttle body and tighten screws firmly.

20. Install ISC servo and bracket, and tighten screws firmly.

NOTE: If ISC has been replaced, be sure to adjust it correctly.

21. Install connector bracket to throttle body, and clamp ISC connector into bracket.

22. Install throttle return spring and damper spring.

23. Insert new seal rings into mixing body. When installing seal ring, be sure to install with flat face side up.

24. Install new O-ring onto injectors.

25. Install injectors into mixing body. Push injector down firmly by finger.

26. Insert pulsation damper diaphragm into injector retainer.

27. Install pulsation damper spring and cover, and then tighten screws.

28. Install new O-rings onto regulator, and then install fuel pressure regulator to injector retainer.

29. Check filters in retainer for clogging or damage. Replace as necessary.

30. Install injector retainer and push down firmly.

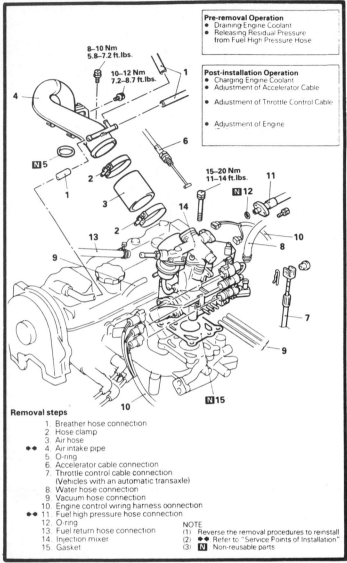

Removal steps
1. Breather hose connection
2. Hose clamp
3. Air hose
◆◆ 4. Air intake pipe
5. O-ring
6. Accelerator cable connection
7. Throttle control cable connection (Vehicles with an automatic transaxle)
8. Water hose connection
9. Vacuum hose connection
10. Engine control wiring harness connection
◆◆ 11. Fuel high pressure hose connection
12. O-ring
13. Fuel return hose connection
14. Injection mixer
15. Gasket

NOTE
(1) Reverse the removal procedures to reinstall
(2) ◆◆ : Refer to "Service Points of Installation"
(3) N : Non-reusable parts

Injection mixer removal and installation — 1987–88 Mirage

31. Tighten screws alternately a little at a time, and then tighten them to specified torque.

IDLE SPEED CONTROL (ISC) SERVO AND THROTTLE POSITION SENSOR (TPS)

Adjustment

If ISC servo, throttle position sensor, throttle body or injectors have been removed or replaced, following adjustments should be made. These adjustments are important to driveability.
1. Start engine and allow it to reach operating temperature.
2. Disconnect accelerator cable from throttle lever of injection mixer.
3. Loosen throttle position sensor mounting screws and turn throttle position sensor clockwise as far as it will go, then temporarily tighten screws.
4. Set ISC Servo position by turning ignition ON for 15 seconds, then turn ignition OFF.
5. Disconnect ISC servo harness connector.
6. Start engine and check idle speed. Idle speed should 600 rpm. If necessary, by turning adjusting screw clockwise to increase rpm or counterclockwise to decrease rpm.
7. Stop engine.

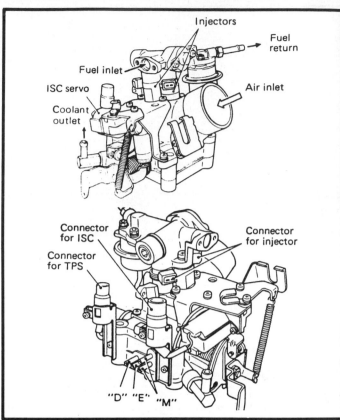

Injection mixer component identification

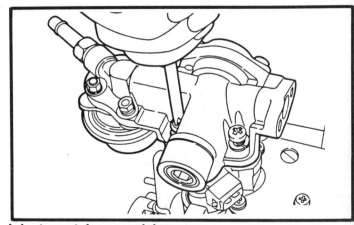

Injector retainer servicing

8. In order to read output voltage of TPS, insert digital voltmeter test probe from rubber cap side of TPS connector and bring it into contact with pins in connector. Insert test probes along GW lead (TPS output) and B lead (Ground) of body side harness.
9. Turn ignition switch ON but do not start engine.
10. Read throttle position sensor output voltage on digital voltmeter. If voltage is not 0.48 ± 0.03 volts, loosen throttle position sensor mounting screws and turn sensor until reading is within specified range, then tighten mounting screws.
11. Open throttle fully and confirm that output voltage is correct when throttle valve s returned to idle position.
12. Remove digital voltmeter connections and recheck idle speed.

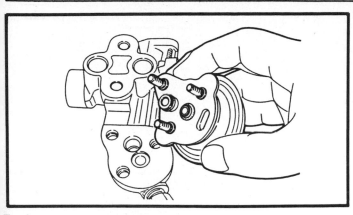

Fuel pressure regulator

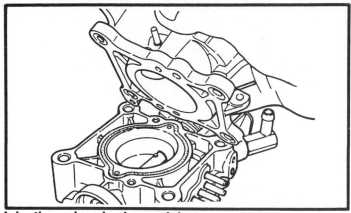

Injection mixer body servicing

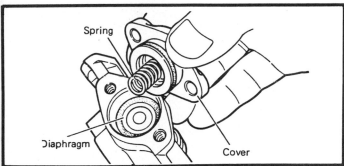

Pulsation damper servicing

Spring

Diaphragm

Cover

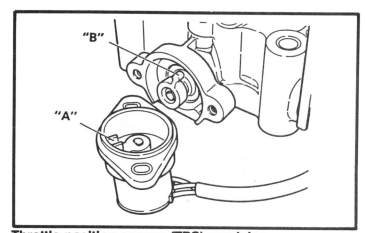

"B"

"A"

Throttle position sensor (TPS) servicing

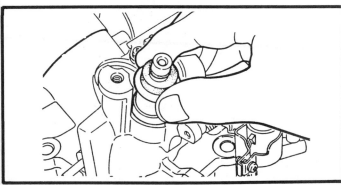

Fuel injector servicing

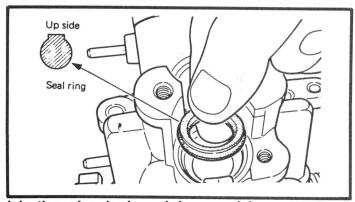

Up side

Seal ring

Injection mixer body seal rings servicing

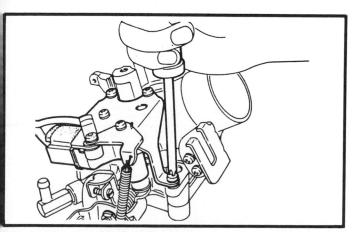

Idle speed control (ISC) servo and bracket servicing

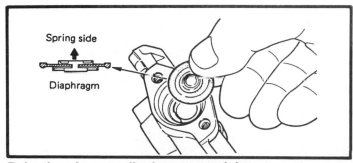

Spring side

Diaphragm

Pulsation damper diaphragm servicing

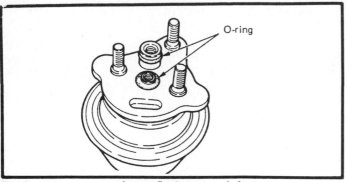

Fuel pressure regulator O-ring servicing

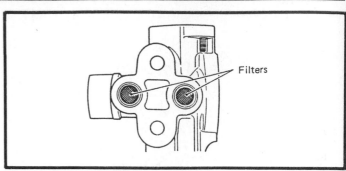

Injector retainer filter location

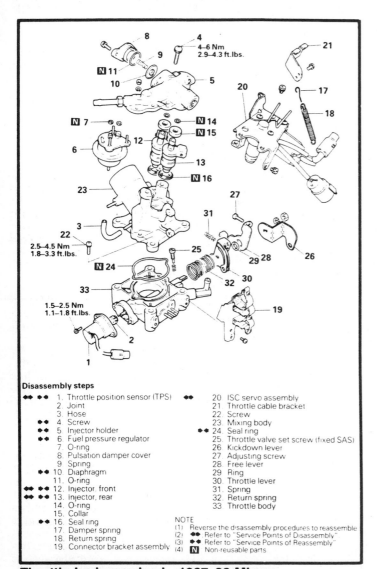

Disassembly steps

1. Throttle position sensor (TPS)	20.	ISC servo assembly
2. Joint	21.	Throttle cable bracket
3. Hose	22.	Screw
4. Screw	23.	Mixing body
5. Injector holder	24.	Seal ring
6. Fuel pressure regulator	25.	Throttle valve set screw (fixed SAS)
7. O-ring	26.	Kickdown lever
8. Pulsation damper cover	27.	Adjusting screw
9. Spring	28.	Free lever
10. Diaphragm	29.	Ring
11. O-ring	30.	Throttle lever
12. Injector, front	31.	Spring
13. Injector, rear	32.	Return spring
14. O-ring	33.	Throttle body
15. Collar		
16. Seal ring	NOTE	
17. Damper spring	(1) Reverse the disassembly procedures to reassemble	
18. Return spring	(2) ◆◆ Refer to "Service Points of Disassembly"	
19. Connector bracket assembly	(3) ◆◆ Refer to "Service Points of Reassembly"	
	(4) [N] Non-reusable parts	

Throttle body overhaul—1987–88 Mirage

13. Turn ignition switch from OFF to ON position, and after lapse of 15 seconds, return it to OFF position.

14. Connect accelerator cable to throttle lever of injection mixer and adjust accelerator cable.

AIR FLOW SENSOR

Removal and Installation

1. Disconnect air flow sensor connector.

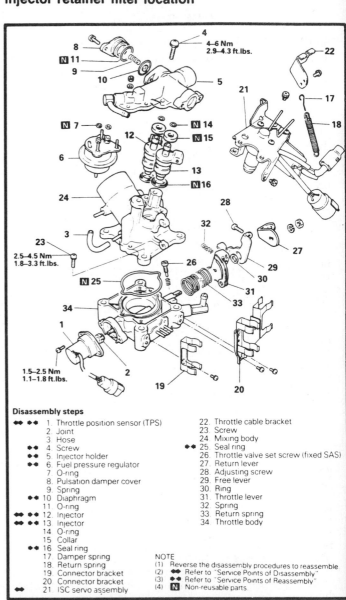

Disassembly steps

1. Throttle position sensor (TPS)	22.	Throttle cable bracket
2. Joint	23.	Screw
3. Hose	24.	Mixing body
4. Screw	25.	Seal ring
5. Injector holder	26.	Throttle valve set screw (fixed SAS)
6. Fuel pressure regulator	27.	Return lever
7. O-ring	28.	Adjusting screw
8. Pulsation damper cover	29.	Free lever
9. Spring	30.	Ring
10. Diaphragm	31.	Throttle lever
11. O-ring	32.	Spring
12. Injector	33.	Return spring
13. Injector	34.	Throttle body
14. O-ring		
15. Collar		
16. Seal ring	NOTE	
17. Damper spring	(1) Reverse the disassembly procedures to reassemble	
18. Return spring	(2) ◆◆ Refer to "Service Points of Disassembly"	
19. Connector bracket	(3) ◆◆ Refer to "Service Points of Reassembly"	
20. Connector bracket	(4) [N] Non-reusable parts	
21. ISC servo assembly		

Throttle body overhaul—1987–88 Starion

NOTE: Connector must be disconnected before removing air cleaner cover and air cleaner body.

2. Unsnap finger clip and remove air cleaner cover.

3. Remove filter element from air cleaner body.

4. Remove air flow sensor.

5. Installation is reverse of removal. Make sure connector is correctly fastened.

MULTI-POINT INJECTION (MPI) SYSTEM

General Information

The MPI (Multi-Point Injection) system controls the fuel flow, idle speed, and ignition timing. The basic function of the MPI system is to control the air/fuel ratio according to operational conditions through the Electronic Control Unit (ECU), based on data from various sensors. The MPI System is roughly divided into three areas such as the fuel system, intake system, and control system.

FUEL SYSTEM

The fuel is press-fed through the in-tank filter by the in-take fuel pump and is distributed to the respective injectors via the main pipe and fuel filter. The fuel pressure applied to the injector is a continuous 335 kPa (47.6 psi), higher than the pressure in the intake manifold. The pressure is controlled by the pressure regulator. The excess fuel, after being pressure-adjusted, is returned to the fuel tank through the return pipe.

When an electric current flows in the injector, the injector valve is fully opened to inject the fuel. Since the fuel pressure is a continuous constant, the amount of the fuel injected from the injector into the manifold is increased or decreased in proportion to the time the electric current flows. Based on ECU signals, the injectors inject fuel to the cylinder manifold ports in firing order.

INTAKE SYSTEM

The flow rate of the air drawn through the air cleaner is measured by the air flow sensor (AFS). The air enters the air intake plenum through the throttle body.

The air is distributed to each cylinder manifold from the air intake plenum. In the manifold, the air is mixed with the fuel from the injectors and is drawn into the cylinder. The air flow rate is controlled according to the degree of the throttle valve and the stepper motor openings.

The amount of air drawn during idling is adjusted by the idle speed control (ISC) servo controlled by the ECU. Further, the amount of air drawn during warm-up and deceleration is also controlled by the ISC servo.

CONTROL SYSTEM

The control system is composed of a sensor section, which monitors engine conditions, and an Electronic Control Unit (ECU), which calculates the injection timing and rate according to the signals from the sensors. The sensors convert such conditions as the amount of intake air, amount of oxygen in the exhaust gas, coolant temperature, intake air temperature, engine revolution speed, and driving speed into electric signals, which are sent to the ECU.

Analyzing these signals, the ECU determines the amount of fuel to inject according to driving conditions and drives the injectors. The fuel injection is by sequential injection type, in which four or six injectors are sequentially driven.

During idling, the ISC Servo is driven according to the load to assure stable idling.

SYSTEM OPERATION

Air/Fuel Ratio Control System

The air fuel ratio control is achieved by controlling the driving time of each injector installed at each intake air port. After passing through the in-tank filter, fuel is force-fed by the in-tank pump so as to be sent to the delivery pipe through the main pipe and fuel filter, and is distributed to each injector by the delivery pipe. The fuel pressure applied to the injector is maintained at a fixed level by the fuel pressure regulator so that it may be 250 kPa (36.26 psi) higher than the internal pressure of the intake manifold where fuel injection takes place. After pressure regulation, excess fuel is returned to the fuel tank through the return hose. When the injector is energized, the valve inside the injector opens fully to inject the fuel. Since the fuel pressure is kept at a fixed level, supply of fuel injected from the injectors into the intake manifold varies with the energizing time. The injectors inject fuel to each manifold port, in the sequential firing order of each cylinder, according to ECU signals.

Fuel Injection Control

The fuel injection amount is basically determined by the number of injector activations, which corresponds to the engine rpm, and by the injector activation time, which corresponds to the amount of intake air during each cycle.

Injector activation occurs for each cylinder, and is one time for each two engine rpm.

Injector Drive (Fuel Injection) Timing
SIMULTANEOUS INJECTION (NON-SYNCHRONEOUS INJECTION)

During engine starting (during cranking), there are two fuel injections (for each engine rpm) simultaneously for each of the four cylinders. In addition, when acceleration, fuel in an amount proportionate to the magnitude of the acceleration during a certain fixed time (10 milliseconds) is injected to certain cylinders (2 cylinders) in the intake and exhaust strokes.

SEQUENTIAL INJECTION (SYNCHRONOUS INJECTION)

After the engine is started, the injectors are activated at the exhaust stroke of each cylinder, one cylinder after another. Injection is, therefore, synchronized to the signals of the crankshaft angle sensor.

The No. 1 cylinder signal is the standard reference signal for sequential injection; thus, using this signal as the standard reference, the cylinder for fuel injection is determined, and the fuel injection occurs in synchronization with the crankshaft angle sensor signals. For each cylinder, there is one injection for each two rotations of the crankshaft, in the order of cylinders.

Injector Drive Time

Injector activation occurs one time per cycle for each cylinder, and the injector activation time (amount of fuel injection), which is the theoretical air/fuel mixture ratio relative to the amount of intake air, is called the basic activation time.

The ECU functions to, first of all, calculate this basic activation time according to air-flow sensor (AFS) signals and crankshaft angle sensor signals.

When starting (cranking) the engine, the map value determined by the engine coolant temperature sensor signal is used as the basic drive time. During the deceleration, the basic driving time is set as zero. The injector driving time is obtained by making the following corrections on the above-mentioned basic driving time.

● Oxygen sensor feedback correction (Closed loop control correction)—In normal operation (including idling) after engine warming up, air/fuel ratio is corrected to theoretical air/fuel ratio by using oxygen sensor signals. The three-way catalytic converter gives best degree of purification at theoretical air/fuel ratio.

- air/fuel ratio map correction (Open loop control correction) – Correction to the optimum air/fuel ratio is made by the map values set by engine speed and amount of intake air.
- Engine coolant temperature correction – To maintain operability of cold engine, correction is so made that the lower the engine coolant, the more the amount of fuel injection.
- Intake air temperature correction – Change in air/fuel ratio due to difference in intake air density caused by intake air temperature is corrected.
- Barometric pressure correction – Change in air/fuel ratio due to difference in intake air density caused by charge in barometric pressure is corrected.
- Acceleration/deceleration correction – In accordance with change in amount of intake air, fuel amount is corrected, improving operability at acceleration and deceleration.
- Dead time correction – The injectors opened by the driving signal from ECU have operation lag which changes according to difference due to battery voltage. This means that actual injector valve opening time becomes less than injector driving signal, failing to provide expected air/fuel ratio. Therefore, battery correction time corresponding to the battery voltage is added.

Ignition Timing Control System

The ignition timing control system controls the ignition timing by making the ignition coil's primary current intermittent, by ON/OFF control of the power transistor.

CONTROL DURING STARTING

During engine starting, there is synchronization to the crankshaft angle sensor's signals, thus resulting in a fixed ignition timing.

CONTROL DURING ORDINARY DRIVING

For each engine revolution and intake of air, and with the present map value as the reference ignition spark advance, the engine coolant temperature correction value or the atmospheric pressure correction value, whichever is greater relative to the reference ignition spark advance, is applied as the correction value, thus regulating to the optimum ignition spark advance.

- Engine coolant temperature correction – In order to improve driveability when the engine is cold, the spark is advanced when the engine coolant temperature is low.
- Barometric pressure correction – In order to maintain good driveability at high altitude, the spark is advanced when the barometric pressure is low.

CONTROL DURING IGNITION TIMING ADJUSTMENT

When the ignition timing adjustment terminal is grounded, there is synchronization with the crankshaft angle sensor's signal, thus resulting in the fixed ignition timing, and in this condition the reference ignition timing is adjusted. Note, however, that the spark advance becomes the same as control during ordinary drive if the engine rpm becomes the set rpm (1,200 rpm) or higher.

CONTROL DURING A MALFUNCTION OF THE AIR-FLOW SENSOR

If there occurs a malfunction of the air-flow sensor, there is control to the greatest load of the map value set to each engine revolution and intake air amount. This is, in other words, equivalent to the centrifugal spark-advance characteristic of the conventional type of distributor.

Idle Speed Control (ISC) System

The ISC system provides the following four modes of control:

START CONTROL

The throttle valve opening is controlled to optimum position for start according to the engine coolant temperature and the altitude (atmospheric pressure).

FAST IDLE CONTROL

When the idle switch is on, the engine speed is controlled to a target rpm according to the engine coolant temperature (rpm feedback control). When the idle switch is off, the ISC servo is actuated to move the throttle valve to a target opening position (throttle valve opening position) according to the engine coolant temperature (target opening control).

IDLE CONTROL

When the air conditioner switch is turned on or when the transmission is shifted from N to D, the system causes the idle speed to increase to the target rpm according to the load (rpm feedback control).

DASH POT CONTROL

The system provides dash pot control according to deceleration conditions to alleviate shock at deceleration

Air Conditioner Relay Control

When the air conditioner switch is turned on while the engine is at idle, the ISC servo operates to increase the engine speed. However, there is some delay before the engine speed actually increases. To maintain the engine free from the air conditioner load during that delay period, the ECU keeps the power transistor off for a fixed time (about 0.5 seconds) to open the air conditioner power relay circuit. As a result, even if the air conditioner switch is on, the air compressor is not driven instantly, preventing engine speed drop due to compressor load.

Fuel Pressure Control System

Ordinarily, the intake manifold negative pressure (vacuum) is caused to act upon the fuel-pressure regulator, the fuel pressure is maintained at a constant fixed level relative to the pressure within the intake manifold, and the amount of fuel injection is thus regulated to a constant fixed amount; however, during starting when the temperature of the intake air is high (50°C (122°F) or higher), and when the temperature of the engine coolant is also high (90°C (194°F or higher), the ECU switches ON the power transistor for a certain fixed time (approximately 2 minutes), thus making the fuel-pressure solenoid valve conductive. As a result, the atmospheric pressure is caused to act upon the fuel-pressure regulator, the fuel pressure becomes high relative to the pressure within the intake manifold, and the amount of fuel injection is increased, thus maintaining idling stability immediately after restarting at high temperature.

INJECTORS

Injectors are electromagnetic type injection nozzles which function to inject fuel according to injection signals calculated and provided by the ECU.

Injector Operation

When there is continuity at the solenoid coil, the plunger and the needle valve unified with it are pulled and, as a result, fuel is sprayed from the nozzle. Because the stroke of the needle valve is always constant, the amount of fuel spray (injection) is determined by the continuity time of the solenoid coil.

PRESSURE REGULATOR

The pressure regulator functions to maintain the fuel injection amount at a certain fixed amount relative to fuel injection time. As a means to improve the precision of the checking of the amount, the pressure regulator controls the fuel pressure applied to the injectors at a constant pressure relative to the surge tank negative pressure.

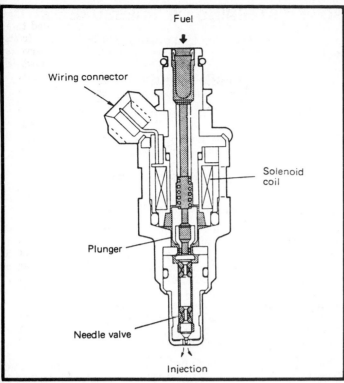

Fuel injector

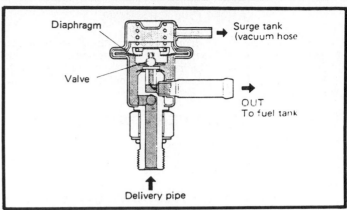

Pressure regulator

Pressure Regulator Operation

Surge tank negative pressure is applied to the diaphragm chamber of the pressure regulator, when the fuel pressure within the pressure regulator reaches a pressure of approximately 250 Kpa (36.26 psi) or higher, extra fuel is by-passed to the return hose and is returned to the fuel tank.

FUEL PULSATION DAMPER

The fuel pulsation damper functions to absorbs the slight fluctuations of the fuel pressure which occur when the injectors inject the fuel.

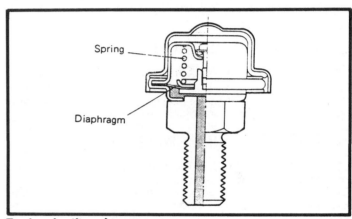

Fuel pulsation damper

Pulsation Damper Operation

The fuel pressure is constantly maintained, by the pressure regulator at a pressure of approximately 250 Kpa (36.26 psi) relative to manifold negative pressure, but slight fluctuations of the fuel pressure do occur when the injector sprays the fuel. The fuel pulsation damper, through the action of this diaphragm, absorbs these minor fluctuations of the fuel pressure.

RESISTOR

The resistor is used to lower the source voltage to a level suitable for the injector. The dropping resistor is connected in series with the injector. It reduces the voltage to approximately ¼ of the source voltage. These resistors protect the injectors from alternator voltage surges and the effects of other components in the vehicle's electrical system.

SPARK-ADVANCE SWITCHING SOLENOID DRIVE

The spark-advance switching solenoid is activated in order to advance the ignition timing at high altitudes where the atmospheric pressure is low or during cold weather.

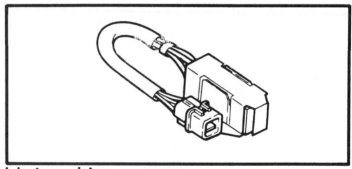

Injector resistor

At a barometric pressure of less than 660mm Hg or a water temperature of less than 95°F (35°C), the spark-advance control solenoid is driven, and, by leading the surge tank negative pressure to the boost control, the ignition timing is advanced 5°.

AIR CONDITIONER RELAY CONTROL

The air cleaner relay is switched OFF, even when the air conditioner switch is switched ON, according to the engine rpm and the throttle opening.

● The air conditioner rely is switched OFF at an engine rpm of 400 rpm or less.

● The air contioner relay is switched OFF for 5 seconds, if a judgment is made, according to the throttle opening, that acceleration is full acceleration.

AIRFLOW SENSOR

This measures the input airflow; utilizing the Karman vortex phenomenon, it counts the number of vortices and converts this data to electric pulses, at the modulator, which are then sent to the ECU. The ECU uses these signals to determine the basic injection time.

INTAKE AIR TEMPERATURE SENSOR

This sensor detects the temperature of the intake air, and converts this data to voltage which is sent to the ECU. The ECU, based on these signals, performs air/fuel ratio feedback control.

BAROMETRIC PRESSURE SENSOR

This sensor detects the barometric pressure, and converts this data to voltage which is sent to the ECU. The ECU uses these signals for correct the fuel injection amount and the ignition timing.

THROTTLE POSITION SENSOR (TPS)

The TPS detects the degree of throttle valve opening; this data is converted to voltage and is sent to the ECU. The ECU uses these signals to calculate the changes in the degree of throttle opening and to sense the variable speed condition.

IDLE SWITCH

This switch detects the fact that the throttle valve opening is in the idling condition, and sends this data as signals to the ECU. The ECU, based on these signals, senses that the engine idling condition exists, and then functions to control the fuel injection amount, the ignition timing, the ISC servo, etc.

COOLANT TEMPERATURE SENSOR

This sensor detects the temperature of the engine's coolant, and converts this data to voltage which is sent to the ECU. The ECU uses these signals for correction of the fuel injection amount and the ignition spark advance.

OXYGEN SENSOR

This sensor measures the temperature of the oxygen in the exhaust gas, and sends these signals to the ECU. The ECU, based on these signals, performs air/fuel ratio feedback control.

TOP DEAD CENTER (TDC) SENSOR

This sensor identifies the reference signal applicable to each cylinder; the disc slit is read by the light-emitting diode and the photo diode, and this data is sent from the unit assembly to the ECU as electrical pulses. The ECU uses these signals and the signals from the crankshaft angle sensor to determine the injection timing.

CRANKSHAFT ANGLE SENSOR

This sensor detects at which position the crankshaft (in other words, the piston) is the 360 slits in the disc are read by the light-emitting diode and the photo diode , and this data is sent from the unit assembly to the ECU as electrical pulses.

VEHICLE SPEED SENSOR

This sensor converts the rotation of the transaxles speedometer gear to electrical pulses and sends them to the ECU.

POWER STEERING OIL PRESSURE SWITCH

Whether a power steering load exists or not is detected by the contact type switch.

INHIBITOR SWITCH (VEHICLES WITH AN AUTOMATIC TRANSAXLE)

Whether the transaxle is in neutral or drive position is detected, and the result is used as the idle speed control signal.

Diagnosis and Testing

SELF-DIAGNOSIS

Self-diagnosis is a system in which the input signal from each sensor is monitored by the ECU and, should any abnormality happen in the input signal, the abnormal item is memorized by the ECU. Nine items are diagnosed including that for normal condition and can be confirmed using a volt meter.

The abnormality-diagnosis memory is kept by direct power supply from the battery. Therefore, the memory of diagnosis result is not erased by turning off the ignition switch. However, it is erased if the back-up power supply is turned off by disconnection of battery cable or ECU connector.

NOTE: The memory is not erased if the power supply is restored within 15 seconds after turning off the power supply to the ECU.

Diagnosis Item

The abnormality-diagnosis items are the following nine items. If there are two or more items found abnormal, they are indicated in the order of increasing code numbers.

INDICATION METHOD

Indication is made by deflection of the pointer of volt meter. Connect a voltmeter to the connector for self-diagnosis in the glove box.

TROUBLESHOOTING

When checking and correcting engine troubles, it is important to start with inspection of the basic systems in case you have such troubles as engine start failure, unstable idling or poor acceleration, therefore, you should first check the following basic systems:

1. Power supply
   a. Battery
   b. Fusible link
   c. Fuse
2. Body ground
3. Fuel supply
   a. Fuel line
   b. Fuel filter
   c. Fuel pump
4. Ignition system
   a. Spark plugs
   b. High tension cable
   c. Distributor
   d. Ignition coil
5. Emissin control system
   a. PCV system
   b. EGR system
   c. Vacuum leak
6. Others
   a. Ignition timing
   b. Idle speed

Troubles with the MPI system are often caused by poor contact

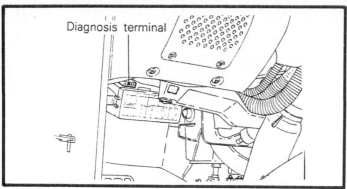

MPI diagnosis connector location—1987–88 models

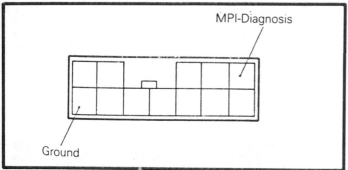

MPI diagnosis connector terminal identification

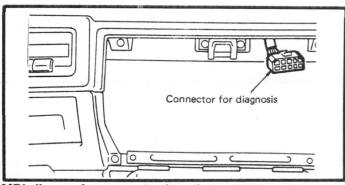

MPI diagnosis connector location—1986 models

Malfunction code	Diagnosis item	Malfunction code	Diagnosis item
11	Oxygen sensor	23	TDC sensor (No.1 cylinder)
12	Air-flow sensor (AFS)	24	Vehicle-speed reed switch
13	Intake air temperature sensor	25	Barometric pressure sensor
14	Throttle position sensor	41	Injector
21	Coolant temperature sensor	42	Fuel pump
22	Crank angle sensor	43	EGR*

* The diagnosis item marked • is applicable to vehicles for California only.

MPI diagnostic codes—1988 Galant

of harness connector. It is, therefore, important to check harness connector contact.

System Inspection

1. Before removing or installing a part, read diagnosis code and then disconnect the battery (−) terminal cable.

Code No.	Diagnosis item
1	Oxygen sensor
2	Ignition pulse
3	Air flow sensor
4	Barometric pressure sensor
5	Throttle position sensor
6	ISC motor position sensor
7	Coolant temp. sensor
8	No. 1 cylinder pulse
9	Normal

MPI diagnostic codes—1986 Galant

Malfunction No.	Diagnosis item
1	Oxygen sensor
2	Crankshaft angle sensor
3	Air flow sensor (AFS)
4	Atmospheric pressure sensor
5	Throttle position sensor (TPS)
6	Motor position sensor (MPS)
7	Engine coolant temperature sensor (MPS)
8	No. 1 cylinder TDC sensor

MPI diagnostic codes—1987–88 Van/Wagon and 1987 Galant

2. Before disconnecting the cable from battery terminal, turn the ignition switch to OFF. Removal or connection of battery cable during engine operation or while the ignition switch is ON could cause erroneous operation of the ECU or damage to semiconductors.

3. The control harness between the ECU and oxygen sensor are shielded wires with shield grounded to the body in order to prevent influences of ignition noise and radio interference. When the shielded wire is faulty, therefore, the control harness must be replaced.

4. When ECI check is used, pay attention to the following.
● Avoid rough operation of switches.
● Do not subject ECI checker to shock and other external forces, heat, etc.
● Keep the checker away from water and oil.

SERVICE PRECAUTION

1. When battery voltage is low, no detection of failure is possible. Be sure to check battery for voltage and other conditions before starting the test.

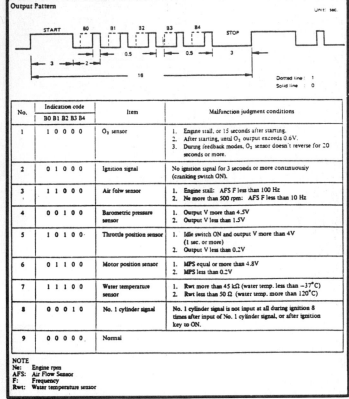

Output Pattern   UNIT: sec.

Dotted line : 1
Solid line : 0

No.	Indication code B0 B1 B2 B3 B4	Item	Malfunction judgment conditions
1	1 0 0 0 0	O₂ sensor	1. Engine stall, or 15 seconds after starting. 2. After starting, until O₂ output exceeds 0.6V. 3. During feedback modes, O₂ sensor doesn't reverse for 20 seconds or more.
2	0 1 0 0 0	Ignition signal	No ignition signal for 3 seconds or more continuously (cranking switch ON).
3	1 1 0 0 0	Air flow sensor	1. Engine stall: AFS F less than 100 Hz 2. Ne more than 500 rpm: AFS F less than 10 Hz
4	0 0 1 0 0	Barometric pressure sensor	1. Output V more than 4.5V 2. Output V less than 1.5V
5	1 0 1 0 0	Throttle position sensor	1. Idle switch ON and output V more than 4V (1 sec. or more) 2. Output V less than 0.2V
6	0 1 1 0 0	Motor position sensor	1. MPS equal or more than 4.8V 2. MPS less than 0.2V
7	1 1 1 0 0	Water temperature sensor	1. Rwt more than 45 kΩ (water temp. less than −37°C) 2. Rwt less than 50 Ω (water temp. more than 120°C)
8	0 0 0 1 0	No. 1 cylinder signal	No. 1 cylinder signal is not input at all during ignition 8 times after input of No. 1 cylinder signal, or after ignition key to ON.
9	0 0 0 0 0	Normal	

NOTE
Ne: Engine rpm
AFS: Air Flow Sensor
F: Frequency
Rwt: Water temperature sensor

MPI system diagnosis chart — 1986 Galant

2. Diagnosis item is erased if the battery or the ECU connector is disconnected. Do not disconnect the battery before the diagnosis result is completely read.

3. Warm up engine and drive a good distance before oxygen sensor is diagnosed. Do not set ignition switch to OFF after driving. If set to OFF, the result in memory is erased.

4. After check and correction are over, disconnect ground cable for 15 seconds or more from negative terminal of battery and connect it again to make sure that failure code is erased.

MPI SYSTEM

Inspection Procedure

1. Turn ignition switch to OFF.

2. Open the glove compartment and pull out the connector for diagnosis.

3. Connect a volt meter between terminal for "MPI" and terminal for ground.

4. Turn ignition switch to ON, and indication of ECU memory contents will immediately start. If the system is in normal condition, pointer of voltmeter indicates normal pattern. If any abnormality is in memory, the pointer of volt meter will deflect. Abnormal item can be known from voltage waveform that is, long/short pulse.

5. Turn ignition switch to OFF.

6. If the defective parts have been repaired, disconnect ground cable for 15 seconds or more from negative terminal of battery and connect it again to make sure that abnormal code has been erased.

MPI SYSTEM INSPECTION USING ECI CHECKER

The electric system of MPI system can be quickly inspected and

maintained if the electric input and output signals of ECU are checked by ECI checker and the component whose abnormality is indicated by the signal and the harness connected between ECU and the component is checked as well.

1. Turn ignition switch to LOCK.

2. Take out the seat belt retractor at the driver's seat, and pull out the electronic control unit.

3. Disconnect the large test harness and small test harness from the ECU.

4. Set check switch of the ECI checker to OFF.

5. Set select switch of the ECI checker to A.

6. Connect white color connectors labeled "CHECKER" of the test harness to the ECI checker connectors. Then connect test harness to the ECU and body harness.

7. Perform checks.

8. Turn ignition switch to LOCK.

9. Set check switch of the ECI checker to OFF.

10. Disconnect white color connectors labeled "CHECKER" of the test harness from the ECI checker. Then connect green color connectors labeled "CHECKER" of the test harness to the connectors of ECI checker.

11. Perform checks.

12. If checker shows any deviation from specifications, check the corresponding sensor and related electrical wiring. Repair or replace if necessary.

13. After repair or replacement, recheck with the ECI checker to confirm that the repair has removed the problem.

14. Set the ignition switch to LOCK.

15. Set the check switch of the ECI checker to OFF.

16. Disconnect the connectors of the ECI checker and test harness from the ECU and body side test harness. Make certain that the power supply has been removed from ECU for at least 15 seconds. This will erase the memory.

17. Connect the body side test harness to the ECU.

18. After completion of the above test, perform a road test to be sure that the trouble has been eliminated.

FUEL PRESSURE

Check

1. Make the following operations to release the pressure remaining in fuel pipe line so that fuel will not flow out.

   a. Disconnect the fuel pump harness connector at the fuel tank side.

   b. Start the engine and after it stops by itself, turn the ignition switch to OFF.

   c. Disconnect the battery (−) terminal.

   d. Connect the fuel pump harness connector.

2. Disconnect the fuel high pressure hose at the delivery pipe side.

— CAUTION —

Cover the hose connection with rage to prevent splash of fuel that could be caused by some residual pressure in the fuel pipe line.

3. Using the special tool, install the fuel-pressure gage to the delivery pipe. Tighten the bolt at a torque of 18–25 ft. lbs. (25–35 Nm).

4. Connect the battery's negative (−) terminal.

5. Apply battery voltage to the terminal for fuel pump drive and activate the fuel pump; then, with fuel pressure thus applied, check to be sure that there is no fuel leakage from the pressure gage or the special tool connection part.

6. Disconnect the vacuum hose from the pressure regulator, and plug the hose end. Measure the fuel pressure during idling. Standard value: 35.6–38.4 psi (245–264 kPa).

7. Measure the fuel pressure when the vacuum hose is connected to the pressure regulator. Standard value: 28.4 psi (196 kPa).

8. If the results of the measurements made in Steps 6 and 7

above are not within the standard value, determine the probably cause, and then make the necessary repair.

9. Stop the engine and check change of fuel pressure gage indication, which should not drop.

10. Release residual pressure from the fuel pipe line.

11. Disconnect the fuel-pressure gage from the delivery pipe.

────────── CAUTION ──────────

Cover the hose connection with rags to prevent splash of fuel that could be caused by some residual pressure in the fuel pipe line.

────────────────────────────

12. Using a new gasket, connect the fuel high-pressure hose, and tighten at the specified torque.

13. Check for fuel leaks.

    a. Apply battery voltage to the fuel pump drive terminal to operate the fuel pump.

    b. With fuel pressure acting, check the fuel line for leaks.

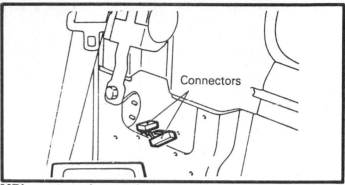

MPI system inspection connector location—1986 Galant

AIR FLOW SENSOR (AFS)

Inspection

NOTE: If the air flow sensor fails, the intake air volume cannot be measured and as a result, normal fuel injection control is no longer available. The vehicle can be run, however, by the backup function.

1. Disconnect the air flow sensor connector.

2. Connect the special tool (test harness) between the unattached connectors.

3. Warm the engine and bring it to a normal idle.

4. Measure the voltage of terminals red 5 (AFS output) and black 4 (sensor ground). Voltage at 3000 rpm should be 2.2–3.2 volts

BAROMETRIC PRESSURE SENSOR

Inspection

1. Disconnect the air flow sensor connector.

2. Connect the special tool (test harness) between the unattached connectors.

3. Warm the engine and bring it to a normal idle.

4. Connect a voltmeter between the terminals (3) (green, barometric sensor output) and (4) (black, sensor ground).

5. Slowly cover above half of the air cleaner air intake, watching the change in voltage. Voltage should fall as pressure falls (0.79 volts at 2.9 psi–4.00 volts at 14.7 psi).

6. If not good, replace the air flow sensor assembly.

INTAKE AIR TEMPERATURE SENSOR

Inspection

1. Disconnect the air flow sensor connectors.

2. Measure resistance between terminals 2 and 4. Resistance should be 6.0 kilo ohms at 32°F (0°C)–0.4 kilo ohms at 176°F (80°C).

3. Measure resistance while heating the sensor using a hair drier. Resistance should become smaller as temperature become higher.

4. If the value deviates from the standard value or the resistance remains unchanged, replace the air flow sensor assembly.

ENGINE COOLANT TEMPERATURE SENSOR

Inspection

1. Remove engine coolant temperature sensor from the intake manifold.

2. With temperature sensing portion of engine coolant tem-

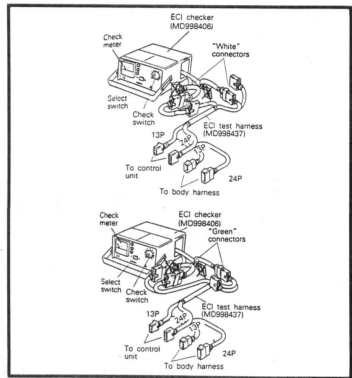

ECI Checker and harness

perature sensor immersed in hot water check resistance. The sensor should be held with its housing 3mm (0.12 in.) away from the surface of the hot water. Resistance should be 5.9 kilo ohms at 32°F (0°C) to 0.3 kilo ohms at 176°F (80°C).

3. If the resistance deviates from the standard value greatly, replace the sensor.

THROTTLE POSITION SENSOR (TPS)

Inspection

1. Disconnect the throttle position sensor connector.

2. Measure resistance between terminal 1 (sensor ground) and terminal 3 (sensor power). Standard value: 3.5–6.5 kilo ohms.

3. Connect a pointer type ohmmeter between terminal 1 (sensor ground terminal) and terminal 2 (sensor output terminal).

4. Operate the throttle valve slowly from the idle position to the full open position and check that the resistance changes smoothly from inproportion with the throttle valve opening angle.

MPI SYSTEM CHECK PROCEDURE CHART (STEP 2) — 1987–88 VAN/WAGON AND 1987 GALANT

ECI Checker Operation (Select Switch / Check Switch)	Check Item	ECU Terminal Checked	Condition	Test Specification
Set to "A" — 1				
2	Atmospheric pressure sensor	20	Ignition switch "LOCK→ON" — at sea level	3.8V to 4.2V
			Idling	
3				
4				
5				
6				
7				
8				
9				
10				
11				
12				
Set to "B" — 1	ISC motor for extension	23	Idling — A/C switch OFF→ON[1]	Momentarily over 4V, then 0V to 2V[2]
2	ISC motor for retraction	12	Idling — A/C switch OFF→ON[1]	Momentarily over 4V, then 0V to 2V[2]
3	A/C cutoff relay	24	Idling — A/C switch OFF→ON[1]	Over 12V, then 0V to 6V
4	Control relay	22	Ignition switch "LOCK→ON"	11V to 13V
			Idling	0V to 0.6V
5				
6	Injector No 1 pulse	59	Idling	12V to 14V
			Quick acceleration from idling to above 2000 rpm with "N" or "P" position	Slight drop
7	Injector No 2 pulse	60	Idling	12V to 14V
			Quick acceleration from idling to above 2000 rpm with "N" or "P" position	Slight drop
8				
9	Injector No 3 pulse	61	Idling	12V to 14V
			Quick acceleration from idling to above 2000 rpm with "N" or "P" position	Slight drop
10				
11	Injector No 4 pulse	62	Idling	12V to 14V
			Quick acceleration from idling to above 2000 rpm with "N" or "P" position	Slight drop
12	Purge control solenoid valve	17	Idling (warm engine) — A/C switch OFF	12V to 15V
			A/C switch ON	0V to 0.6V

NOTE:
[1] ON means compressor clutch engaged.
[2] Pointer indicates over 6V momentarily. If it is hard to read indication, repeat the OFF→ON or ON→OFF operation of A/C switch several times. If the pointer of voltmeter deflects, ISC motor is normal.

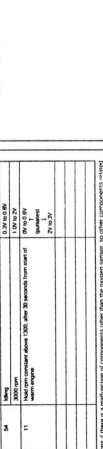

ECU Terminal

View from front as installed in ECU

MPI SYSTEM CHECK PROCEDURE CHART (STEP 1) — 1987–88 VAN/WAGON AND 1987 GALANT

ECI Checker Operation (Select Switch / Check Switch)	Check Item	ECU Terminal Checked	Condition	Test Specification
Set to "A" — 1	Power supply	51	Ignition switch "LOCK→ON"	11V to 13V
2	Crank angle sensor	1	Ignition switch "LOCK→START"	1.8V to 2.5V
			3000 rpm	
3	Intake air temperature sensor	5	Ignition switch "LOCK→ON" — 0°C (32°F)	3.4V to 3.6V
			20°C (68°F)	2.5V to 2.7V
			40°C (104°F)	1.7V to 1.9V
			80°C (176°F)	0.6V to 0.8V
4	Coolant temperature sensor	6	Ignition switch "LOCK→ON" — 0°C (32°F)	3.4V to 3.6V
			20°C (68°F)	2.5V to 2.7V
			40°C (104°F)	1.5V to 1.7V
			80°C (176°F)	0.5V to 0.7V
5	Power supply for sensor	10	Ignition switch "LOCK→ON"	4.5V to 5.5V
6	Throttle position sensor	15	Ignition switch "LOCK→ON" (Warm engine) — Accelerator fully closed	0.4V to 0.7V
			Accelerator fully opened	4.5V to 5.5V
7	Motor position sensor	3	Ignition switch "LOCK→ON" — After 15 seconds	0.8V to 1.2V
8	Idle position switch	7	Ignition switch "LOCK→ON" — Accelerator fully closed	0V to 0.6V
			Accelerator fully opened	8V to 13V
9	Cranking signal	55	Ignition switch "LOCK→START"	Over 8V
10	Reed switch for vehicle speed	19	Start engine, transmission in first or drive and operate vehicle slowly	0V to 0.6V (pulsates) ↕ Over 2V
11	A/C switch	56	Ignition switch "LOCK→ON" — A/C switch OFF	0V to 0.6V
			A/C switch ON	11V to 13V
12	Inhibitor switch	58	Ignition switch "LOCK→ON" — Transaxle in "P" or "N"	0V to 0.6V
			Transaxle in "D"	11V to 13V
Set to "B" — 1	Fuel pressure exchange solenoid valve	8	Ignition switch "LOCK→START" — Coolant temp less than 90°C (194°F) or air temp less than 50° (122°F)	Over 8V
			Coolant temp more than 90°C (194°F) or air temp more than 50° (122°F)	0V to 0.6V
2				
3				
4	No.1 cylinder sensor	13	Ignition switch "LOCK→START"	0.2V to 1.5V (oscillating)
			3000 rpm	0.8V to 1.2V
5	Air flow sensor	2	Idling	2.2V to 3.2V
			3000 rpm	
6				
7	Ignition control signal	54	Idling	0.3V to 0.8V
			3000 rpm	1.0V to 2V
8	Oxygen sensor[1]	11	Hold rpm constant above 1300, after 30 seconds from start of warm engine	0V to 0.6V (pulsates) ↕ 2V to 3V
9				
10				
11				
12				

[1] There may also be differences from specifications. If there is a malfunction of components other than the oxygen sensor, so other components related to air/fuel mixture control should also be checked.
[2] ON means compressor clutch engaged.

MPI SYSTEM CHECK PROCEDURE CHART (WITH WHITE CONNECTOR) – 1986 GALANT

Select switch	Check switch	Check item	Condition		Check meter reading when normal	Terminal location of computer
A	1	Battery	Ignition switch OFF → ON		11-13V	B-1
	2	Ignition pulse	Idling		9-14V	A-1
		Coil (−) terminal	3000 rpm		8-13V	
	3	Intake air temperature sensor	Ignition switch OFF → ON	0°C (32°F)	3.5V	A-5
				20°C (68°F)	2.6V	
				40°C (104°F)	1.8V	
				80°C (176°F)	0.6V	
	4	Coolant temperature sensor	Ditto	0°C (32°F)	3.5V	A-6
				20°C (68°F)	2.6V	
				40°C (104°F)	1.8V	
				80°C (176°F)	0.6V	
	5	Sensor power supply	Ditto		4.5-5.5V	A-10
	6	Throttle position sensor	After warming up. Ignition switch OFF → ON	Accelerator closed	0.4-0.7V	A-15
				Accelerator wide opened	4.5-5.0V	
	7	ISC motor position sensor	Ditto		0.9-2.0V	A-3
	8	Idle position switch	Ignition switch OFF → ON	Accelerator closed	0-0.5V	A-7
				Accelerator opened	11-13V	
	9	Cranking signal	Ignition switch OFF → ST		Over 8V	B-5
	10	Vehicle speed	Start engine, transmission in 1st or D and move vehicle slowly		0-0.5V ↑ Pulsates ↓ Over 2V	A-19
	11	A/C relay	Ignition switch OFF → ON	A/C switch OFF	0-0.5V	B-6
				A/C switch ON	11-13V	
	12	Inhibitor switch	Ditto	Select lever in	0-0.5V	B-8
				Select lever in	11-13V	
B	1	—	—		—	—
	2	—	—		—	—
	3	—	—		—	—
	4	No. 1 cylinder signal (SGC)	Idling		0.5-1.0V	A-13
			3000 rpm		0.8-1.2V	
	5	Air flow sensor output	Idling		2.7-3.2V	A-2
			3000 rpm		—	—
	6	—	—		—	—
	7	—	—		—	—

MPI SYSTEM CHECK PROCEDURE CHART (CRANKING CHECK) – 1988 GALANT

Select switch	Check switch	Check item	Condition		Check meter reading when normal	Terminal location of computer
	8	Oxygen sensor	Maintain 1300 rpm after warming up		0.4-1V ↑ Pulsates ↓ 2.7V	A-11
	9				—	—
	10				—	—
	11				—	—
	12				—	—
B	1	ISC servo motor (extention)	Idling		0.2V	A-23
			Idling. A/C switch OFF → ON		momentarily over 6V	
	2	ISC servo motor (retraction)	Idling		0.2V	A-12
			Idling. A/C switch ON → OFF		momentarily over 6V	
	3	A/C relay	Idling. A/C switch OFF → ON		momentarily 13-15V ↓ 0-0.5V	A-24
	4	Fuel pump relay	Ignition switch OFF → ON		11-13V	A-22
			Idling		0-0.5V	
	5	—	—		—	—
	6	Injector No 1	Idling		13-15V	B-9
			Idling, quick acceleration		momentarily 9-10V	
	7	Injector No 2	Same as check switch "6"		—	B-10
	8	—	—		—	—
	9	Injector No 3	Same as check switch "6"		—	B-11
	10	—	—		—	—
	11	Injector No 4	Same as check switch "6"		—	B-12
	12	High-altitude vacuum advance sol.	Idling	Coolant temp. below 35°C (95°F)	0-0.5V	A-17
				Coolant temp above 35°C (95°F) — Altitudes below 3,900 ft	13-15V	
				Altitudes above 3,900 ft	0-0.5V	

MPI SYSTEM CHECK PROCEDURE CHART (ENGINE CONTROL SYSTEM CHECK) 1988 GALANT

Check item (item No.)	Tester mode	Condition		Test specification	Troubleshooting when outside the test specifications
Power steering oil pressure switch (27)		Engine: After warming up idle the engine	Steering wheel in neutral (forward direction)	OFF	• Check the power steering oil pressure switch • Check the oil pressure switch circuit
			The steering wheel is turned a half turn	ON	
Air conditioner switch (28)	Data transfer	Engine: After warming up idle the engine	Air conditioner switch "OFF"	OFF	• Check the air conditioner system
			Air conditioner switch "ON"	ON	
Inhibitor switch (29)		Ignition switch ON NOTE: Automatic transaxle only	Shift lever "P" or "N"	N	• Check the inhibitor switch • Check the inhibitor circuit • Adjustment of the control cable between the shift lever and the inhibitor switch
			Shift lever "D", "2", "L" or "R"	D	

Check item (item No.)	Tester mode	Condition		Test specification		Troubleshooting when outside the test specifications
Injector (16)	Actuator forced drive	Engine: After warming up idle the engine	Injector No.	Engine	Idling state varies unstably	• If there is a cylinder in which the idling state does not vary, check the injector and the spark plug of the cylinder
			1			
			2			
			3			
			4			
			5			
			6			
Oxygen sensor (11)	Data transfer	Engine: Warming up	Engine condition	Voltage (mV)		• When low voltage continues during idling check the intake air for leakage • When the voltage is higher than 1,000 mV check the oxygen sensor circuit • When the voltage is low during racing check the oxygen sensor and the oxygen sensor circuit
			Idling	400 or less (pulsates)		
			2,000 rpm	600 - 1,000		
			Rapid deceleration from 4,000 rpm	200 or less		
			Rapid racing is repeated	600 - 1,000		
EGR temperature sensor (43)		Engine: Warming up NOTE: Engine is maintained in a constant state for 2 minutes or more	Engine revolution speed	Voltage (V)		• Check the EGR temperature sensor • Check the EGR control system • Check the EGR valve • Check the thermo valve • Check the EGR valve control negative pressure
			700 (idling)	2.5 or more		
			3,000	1.5 or more		
Purge control solenoid valve (8)	Actuator forced drive	Ignition switch ON (Engine stop) Disconnect the purge hose (red stripe) from the throttle body, and connect the hand vacuum pump to the hose end	Actuator is not driven	Negative pressure is maintained		• Check the purge control solenoid valve • Check the purge hose for leakage • Check the purge control solenoid valve drive circuit
			Actuator forced drive	Negative pressure leaks		

Check item (item No.)	Tester mode	Condition			Test specification		Troubleshooting when outside the test specifications

Stepper motor (45)		Engine: After warming up idle the engine.
		NOTE: The compressor clutch operates when the air conditioner switch is turned on
			Air conditioner switch	Engine revolution speed (rpm)	Step		• When the step is large during idling
							  (1) Dispose sticks to the throttle valve area
							  (2) EGR valve may leak.
							• When the step is small during idling, check the intake air for leakage
							• Adjust the speed adjusting screw
							• If engine revolution speed does not increase when the air conditioner switch is turned on, check the stepper motor and the circuit

			OFF	700 (idling)			
			ON	900			
					4 - 14		
					45 - 55		

MPI SYSTEM CHECK PROCEDURE CHART (SENSOR CHECK) – 1988 GALANT

Check item (item No.)	Tester mode	Condition		Test specification	Troubleshooting when outside the test specifications
Power supply (16)	Data transfer	Ignition switch ON		11 - 13V	• Measure the battery voltage • Check the circuit that supplies the ECI power
Throttle position sensor (14)		Ignition switch ON Throttle valve: Idle position		400 - 600mV	• Check the throttle position sensor • Check the sensor circuit • Adjust the throttle position sensor
Malfunction code read out	Self-diagnosis	Execute cranking for 4 seconds or more Ignition switch ON		Malfunction code is not output	• Check the check items (Refer to the self diagnosis section.)
Fuel pump (07)	Actuator forced drive	Ignition switch ON Actuator drive	Squeeze the return hose	Feel the fuel pulse with a finger	• Check the fuel pump • Check the circuit that supplies power to the fuel pump
			Listen near the fuel tank	Pump driving sound is heard	
TDC sensor (22)	Data transfer	Engine: Cranking Tachometer Connect	Cranking revolution speed (rpm)	Approx. 200	• Check the power transistor and the ignition coil (The tachometer reading is not proper.) • Check the TDC sensor circuit. If the circuit is proper, replace the distributor assembly and recheck the system
Ignition switch-ST (18)		Ignition switch ON	Engine stop	OFF	• Check the ignition switch ST circuit • Check the ignition switch
			Cranking	ON	

Check item (item No.)	Tester mode	Condition		Test specification	Troubleshooting when outside the test specifications
Intake air temperature sensor (13)	Data transfer	Ignition switch ON	Intake air temperature (°C (°F))	Voltage (V)	• Check the air intake temperature sensor • Check the sensor circuit
			0 (32)	3.4 - 3.6	
			20 (68)	2.5 - 2.7	
			40 (104)	1.7 - 1.9	
			80 (176)	0.6 - 0.8	
Coolant temperature sensor (21)		Ignition switch ON	Coolant temperature (°C (°F))	Voltage (V)	• Check the engine coolant temperature sensor • Check the sensor circuit
			0 (32)	3.4 - 3.6	
			20 (68)	2.5 - 2.7	
			40 (104)	1.5 - 1.7	
			80 (176)	0.5 - 0.7	
Barometric pressure sensor (25)	Data transfer	Ignition switch ON	Altitude (m (ft))	Pressure (mmHg)	• Check the barometric pressure sensing circuit. If the circuit is proper, replace the flow sensor assembly and recheck the system
			0 (sea level)	760	
			600 (1,970)	710	
			1,200 (3,940)	660	
			1,800 (5,910)	610	
Ignition switch ST (18)		Ignition switch ON		OFF	• Check the ignition switch ST circuit • Check the ignition switch
Throttle position sensor (14)		Ignition switch ON	Throttle valve	Voltage (mV)	• Check the throttle position sensor • Check for traces that the idle switch (it used SAS) has moved. If traces are found, adjust the idle switch (used SAS) • Adjust the throttle position sensor
			Fully closed	480 - 520	
			Gradually open	The pressure increases according to the degree of opening of the valve	
			Fully opened	4,500 - 5,500	

Check item (item No.)	Tester mode	Condition		Test specification	Troubleshooting when outside the test specifications
Idle switch (06)		Ignition switch ON	Throttle valve idle position	ON	• Check the idle switch • Check the idle switch circuit • Adjustment of the accelerator cable • Adjustment of the automatic speed-control cable
			Slightly open the throttle valve	OFF	
TDC sensor (22)	Data transfer	Engine: After warming up idle the engine. Tachometer Connect	Engine revolution speed (rpm)	Revolution speed (rpm)	• Check the TDC sensor circuit. If the circuit is proper, replace the distributor assembly and recheck the system
			700	700	

**MPI SYSTEM CHECK PROCEDURE CHART
(ENGINE CONTROL SYSTEM CHECK)
1988 GALANT**

Check item (Item No.)	Tester mode	Condition		Test specification	Troubleshooting when outside the test specifications
Power transistor (44)	Data transfer	Engine: Warming up Timing light: set NOTE 1. Even though the ignition timing varies during idling, no problem occurs 2. At high altitude, the farther advancing angle value (approximately 5 degrees) is indicated	Engine revolution speed (rpm)	Ignition timing (BTDC)	• Adjust the ignition timing
			700 (Idling)	13 - 20	
			2,000	27 - 31	
Air-flow sensor (12)		Engine: Warming up	Engine revolution speed (rpm)	Frequency (Hz)	• If both frequency and drive time are large, (1) Engine resistance may increase (2) EGR valve may leak (3) Compression pressure may leak
			700 (Idling)	30 - 45	
			2,000	95 - 115	
Injector (41)		Engine: Warming up	Engine revolution speed (rpm)	Drive time (ms)	
			700 (Idling)	2.7 - 3.2	
			2,000	2.4 - 2.9	

Fuel pump operation connector location

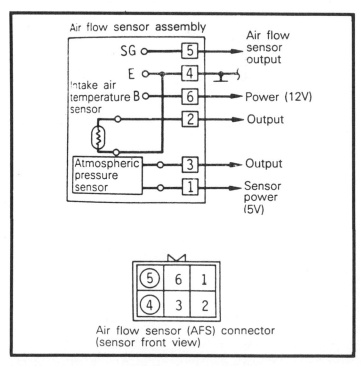

Fuel pressure gauge connection location

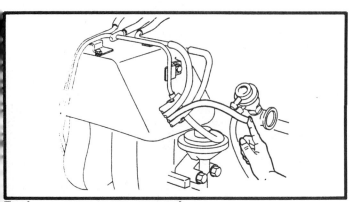

Fuel pressure measurement

NOTE: The resistance changes within the range from approximately 0.5 kilo ohms to the value measured at Step 2.

5. If the resistance is out of specification, or fails to change smoothly, replace the TPS.

IDLE SWITCH

Inspection

1. Disconnect the ISC motor connector.
2. Check continuity between terminal 2 and body ground. Ac-

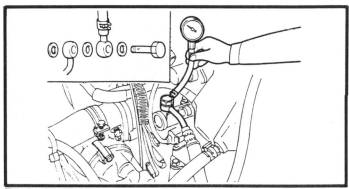

Air flow sensor terminal identification

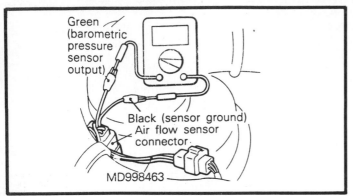

Barometric pressure sensor check

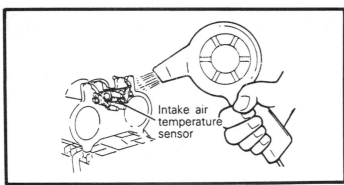

Intake air temperature sensor connector identification

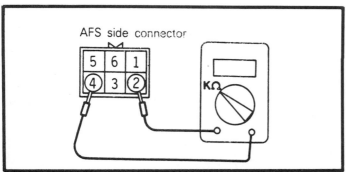

Intake air temperature sensor testing

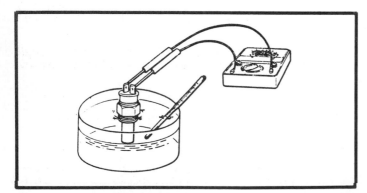

Engine coolant temperature sensor testing

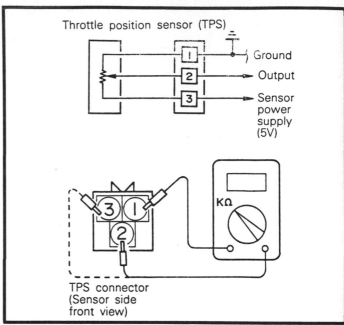

Throttle position sensor testing

celerator depressed — no continuity, accelerator released — continuity.

3. If out of specification, replace the ISC servo assembly.

MOTOR POSITION SENSOR (MPS)

Inspection

1. Disconnect the motor position sensor connector.
2. Connect the special tool (test harness) to the disconnected MPS connector.
3. Disconnect the ISC motor connector.
4. Connect the special tool (test harness) to the disconnected connector's ISC motor end.

NOTE: Be sure not to connect the harness (ECU side) connector.

5. Measure the resistance between terminals 3 (white, sensor power) and 4 (black, sensor ground) of the motor position sensor connector. Standard value: 4–6 kilo ohms.
6. Connect resistance gauge between terminals 1 (red, MPS output) and 4 (black, sensor ground) of the motor position sensor connector.
7. Connect 6 volts DC batteries (4 dry batteries) between terminals 1 (red) and 4 (black) of the ISC motor connector and check to see that resistance change smoothly when the ISC motor is activated.

NOTE: Resistance will change from 0.5 kilo ohms to somewhere within the angle measured in Step 5.

8. If the standard value is not achieved, or a smooth change is not obtained, replace the ISC servo assembly.

NO. 1 CYLINDER TDC SENSOR AND CRANKSHAFT ANGLE SENSOR

Inspection

1. Disconnect the spark plug wires from the ignition coil.
2. Disconnect the crankshaft angle sensor connector.
3. Connect the special tool (test harness) between the disconnected connectors.

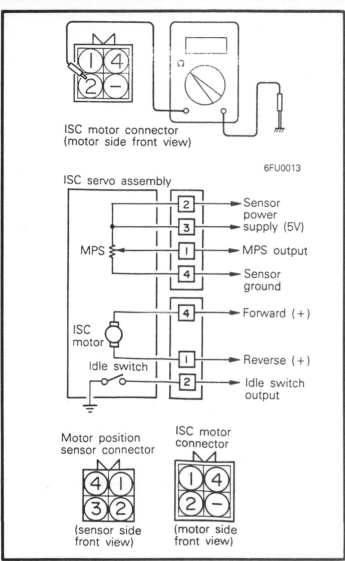

6FU0013

Idle switch testing

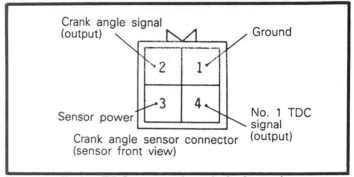

No. 1 cylinder TDC sensor/crankshaft angle sensor connector identification

POWER STEERING OIL PRESSURE SWITCH

Inspection

1. Disconnect the power steering oil pressure switch connector.

2. Start the engine and check continuity between the pressure switch terminal body ground when the steering wheel is at straightforward position and when it is turned. Steering wheel straight — no continuity, steering wheel turned — continuity.

3. If the check result is otherwise than specified, check the oil pump assembly.

INJECTORS

Operation Sound Check

Using a sound scope, check operation sound (tick, tick) during idling or cranking. Check that the sound is produced at shorter intervals as the engine speed increases.

NOTE: Check carefully. Other injectors may produce sound as they operate even if the injector under checking does not operate.

Resistance Between Terminals Measurement

1. Disconnect the injector connector.
2. Measure the resistance between terminals. Standard value: 2–3 ohms at 68°F (20°C).
3. Install the injector connector.

IDLE SPEED CONTROL (ISC) MOTOR

Inspection

1.

Disconnect the ISC motor connector.
2. Check continuity of the ISC motor coil.
3. Connect 6 volt DC between terminal 1 and terminal 4 of the ISC motor connector and check to be sure that the ISC servo operates.

NOTE: Apply only a 6 volts DC or lower voltage. Application of higher voltage could cause locking of the servo gears.

4. If not, replace ISC servo as an assembly.

THROTTLE POSITION SENSOR (TPS)

Inspection

1. Measure resistance between terminals 1 and 3 of the throttle position sensor using a circuit tester. Standard value: 3.5–6.5 kilo ohms.
2. Check sensor body for cracks and damages.

4. Measure the output voltage between terminals 2 and 1 (crank angle signal) and 4 and 1 (No. 1 TDC signal) while cranking the engine. No. 1 cylinder TDC sensor should be 0.5–1 volt and crankshaft angle sensor should be 2–2.5 volts.

5. When the voltage is abnormal, check the sensor power and ground circuit, and where nothing unusual is found here, disassemble the distributor and check it.

OXYGEN SENSOR

Inspection

NOTE: Before checking, warm up the engine until engine coolant temperature reaches 185–205°F (85–95°C). Use an accurate digital voltmeter.

1. Disconnect the oxygen sensor connector and connect a voltmeter to the oxygen sensor connector.

2. While repeating engine racing, measure the oxygen sensor output voltage. Oxygen sensor output should be approximately 1 volt.

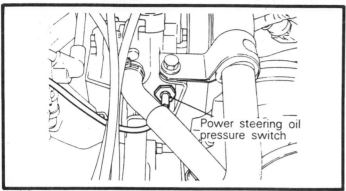

Power steering oil pressure switch location

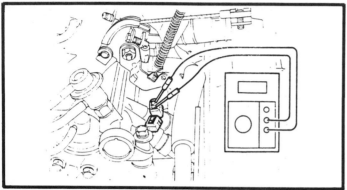

Fuel injector continuity testing

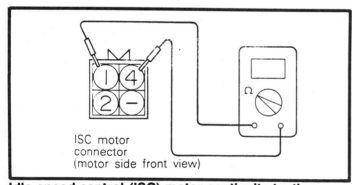

Idle speed control (ISC) motor continuity testing

ISC SERVO

Continuity Check

Measure resistance between terminals 1 and 4 using a circuit tester. Standard value: 5–35 ohms at 68°F (20°C).

Component Replacement
THROTTLE BODY

Removal and Installation

IDLE SPEED

Check Procedure

NOTE: The improper setting (throttle valve opening) will increase exhaust gas temperature at deceleration, reducing catalyst life greatly and deteriorating exhaust

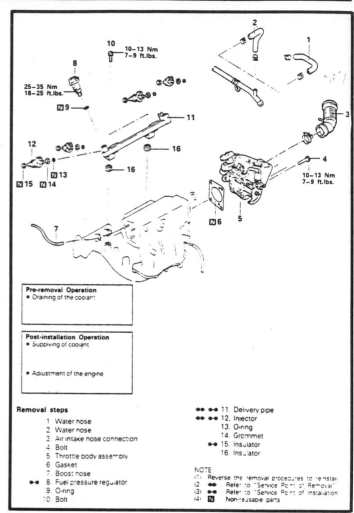

Injector and throttle body removal and installation— 1988 Galant

gas cleaning performance. It also has effect on fuel consumption and engine braking. Checking conditions: Engine coolant temperature – 185–205°F (85–95°C); lights, electric cooling fan and accessory drive – OFF; transmission – in NEUTRAL or PARK; steering wheel – straight forward position (vehicles with power steering)

1. Set the timing light and tachometer.
2. Start the engine and let it idle.
3. Check the basic ignition timing and adjust if necessary.

NOTE: When checking the basic ignition timing at high altitude, stop the engine and disconnect the waterproof female connector from the ignition timing connector. Connect a lead wire with an alligator clip to the ignition timing adjusting terminal to ground it.

4. Run the engine for more than 5 seconds at an engine speed of 2,000–3,000 rpm.
5. Run the engine at idle for 2 minutes.
6. Take idle speed reading. Curb idle speed: 750 ± 100 rpm. If outside specified limits, readjust the speed to the nominal specification. The idle speed adjustment is unnecessary since this system controls the idle speed. If necessary, check the ISC system.

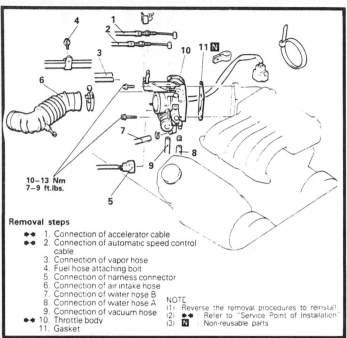

Removal steps

- ◆◆ 1. Connection of accelerator cable
- ◆◆ 2. Connection of automatic speed control cable
- 3. Connection of vapor hose
- 4. Fuel hose attaching bolt
- 5. Connection of harness connector
- 6. Connection of air intake hose
- 7. Connection of water hose B
- 8. Connection of water hose A
- 9. Connection of vacuum hose
- ◆◆ 10. Throttle body
- 11. Gasket

NOTE
(1) Reverse the removal procedures to reinstall
(2) ◆◆ : Refer to "Service Point of Installation"
(3) N : Non-reusable parts

Injector and throttle body removal and installation— 1987 Galant

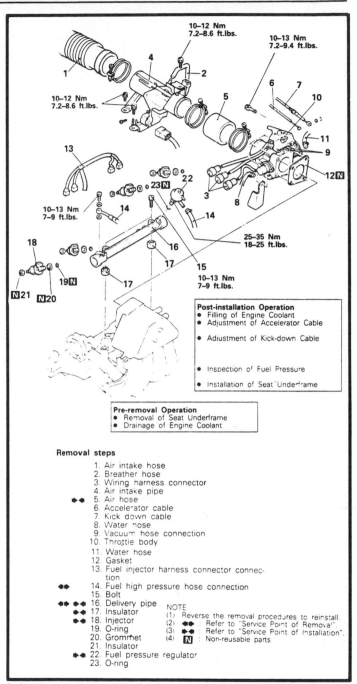

Post-installation Operation
- Filling of Engine Coolant
- Adjustment of Accelerator Cable
- Adjustment of Kick-down Cable
- Inspection of Fuel Pressure
- Installation of Seat Underframe

Pre-removal Operation
- Removal of Seat Underframe
- Drainage of Engine Coolant

Removal steps

- 1. Air intake hose
- 2. Breather hose
- 3. Wiring harness connector
- 4. Air intake pipe
- ◆◆ 5. Air hose
- 6. Accelerator cable
- 7. Kick down cable
- 8. Water hose
- 9. Vacuum hose connection
- 10. Throttle body
- 11. Water hose
- 12. Gasket
- 13. Fuel injector harness connector connection
- ◆◆ 14. Fuel high pressure hose connection
- 15. Bolt
- ◆◆ ◆◆ 16. Delivery pipe
- ◆◆ 17. Insulator
- ◆◆ 18. Injector
- ◆◆ 19. O-ring
- 20. Grommet
- 21. Insulator
- ◆◆ 22. Fuel pressure regulator
- 23. O-ring

NOTE
(1) Reverse the removal procedures to reinstall.
(2) ◆◆ : Refer to "Service Point of Removal".
(3) ◆◆ : Refer to "Service Point of Installation".
(4) N : Non-reusable parts

Injector and throttle body removal and installation— 1987–88 Van/Wagon

IDLE SPEED CONTROL (ISC) AND THROTTLE POSITION SENSOR (TPS)

Adjustment

NOTE: Before testing, engine coolant temperature must be 185–205°F (85–95°C), all accessories off, electric fan off and transaxle in PARK OR NEUTRAL.

1. Slacken the accelerator cable enough.
2. Disconnect the TPS connector.
3. Connect the special tool (Test harness) between the detached connectors.
4. Connect a digital voltmeter between the blue and black terminals of the special tool.

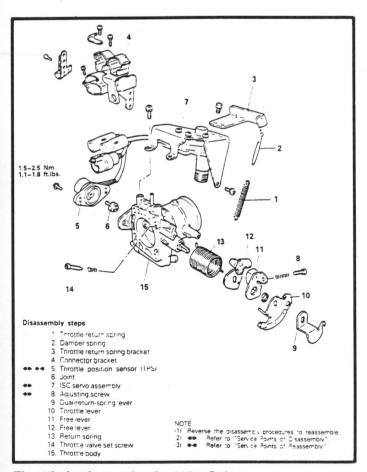

Disassembly steps

1. Throttle return spring
2. Damper spring
3. Throttle return spring bracket
4. Connector bracket
- ◆◆ ◆◆ 5. Throttle position sensor (TPS)
6. Joint
- ◆◆ 7. ISC servo assembly
- ◆◆ 8. Adjusting screw
9. Dual-return-spring lever
10. Throttle lever
11. Free lever
12. Free lever
13. Return spring
14. Throttle valve set screw
15. Throttle body

NOTE
(1) Reverse the disassembly procedures to reassemble
(2) ◆◆ : Refer to "Service Points of Disassembly"
(3) ◆◆ : Refer to "Service Points of Reassembly"

Throttle body overhaul—1987 Galant

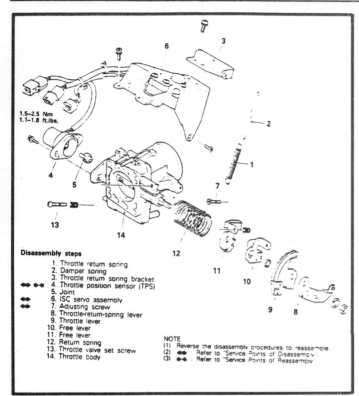

Disassembly steps
1. Throttle return spring
2. Damper spring
3. Throttle return spring bracket
4. Throttle position sensor (TPS)
5. Joint
6. ISC servo assembly
7. Adjusting screw
8. Throttle-return-spring lever
9. Throttle lever
10. Free lever
11. Free lever
12. Return spring
13. Throttle valve set screw
14. Throttle body

NOTE
(1) Reverse the disassembly procedures to reassemble
(2) ➡➡ : Refer to "Service Points of Disassembly"
(3) ➡◄ : Refer to "Service Points of Reassembly"

Throttle body overhaul — 1987–88 Van/Wagon

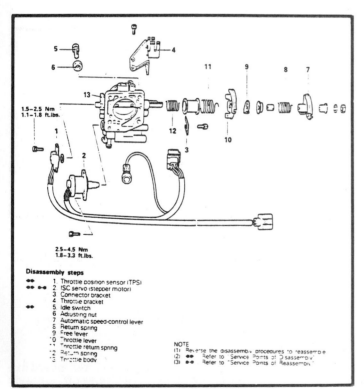

Disassembly steps
1. Throttle position sensor (TPS)
2. ISC servo (stepper motor)
3. Connector bracket
4. Throttle bracket
5. Idle switch
6. Adjusting nut
7. Automatic speed-control lever
8. Return spring
9. Free lever
10. Throttle lever
11. Throttle return spring
12. Return spring
13. Throttle body

NOTE
(1) Reverse the disassembly procedures to reassemble
(2) ➡➡ : Refer to "Service Points of Disassembly"
(3) ➡◄ : Refer to "Service Points of Reassembly"

Throttle body overhaul — 1988 Galant

5. Insert a paper clip to the connector (2 pin) of the harness for short-circuit, and connect an tachometer.

NOTE: Connector contact should not be separated. The paper clip can be inserted along terminal surface.

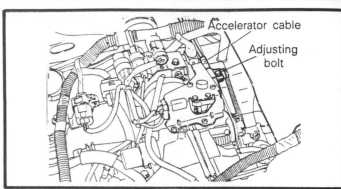

Idle speed control (ISC) and Throttle position sensor (TPS) adjustment

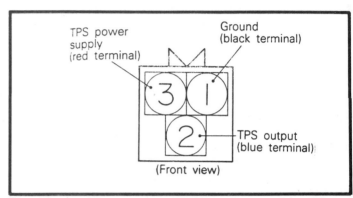

Throttle position sensor (TPS) connector identification

Idle speed check connector location

6. Turn the ignition switch to ON (do not start the engine) and hold the switch in that position for 15 seconds or more to check that the ISC motor is set at the initial position (idle point).

NOTE: When the ignition switch is turned to ON, the ISC motor extends to the fast idle position opening and in 15 seconds, it retracts and stops at the initial position.

7. Disconnect the ISC servo connector and fix the ISC servo at the initial position.
8. In order to prevent binding of the throttle valve, open the throttle valve by hand to a half or more opening two or three times and then release it to allow to return with a snap. Then, loosen the fixed SAS enough.
9. Start the engine and run idle.
10. Check that the engine speed is as specified. Standard value: 750 rpm.

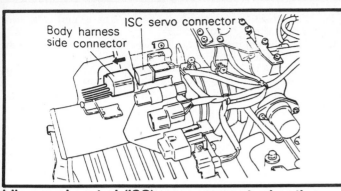

Idle speed control (ISC) servo connector location

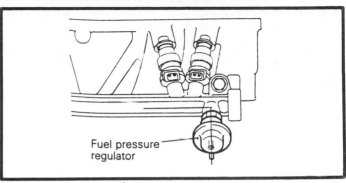

Fuel pressure regulator

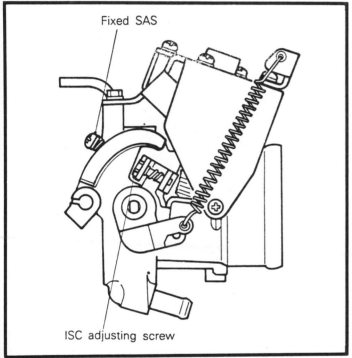

Idle speed adjusting screws

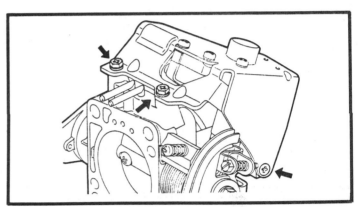

Idle speed control (ISC) servo servicing

NOTE: It may happen, when test driving is not sufficient, that the engine speed will be 20–100 rpm low, but adjustment is not necessary. If, even though test driving is sufficient, the engine stalls or the engine speed is low, there may be deposits adhered at the throttle valve, and for this reason the throttle valve should be cleaned.

11. If the engine speed is not as specified, adjust by the ISC adjusting screw for the standard rpm.

NOTE: When turning the ISC adjusting screw, use hexagon wrench whenever possible. To prevent the screw from becoming loose due to backlash of the screw, make the adjustment only when it is turned in the tightening direction.

12. Tighten the fixed SAS until the engine speed starts to increase. Then, loosen it until the engine speed ceases to drop (touch point) and then loosen a half turn from the touch point.
13. Stop the engine.
14. Turn the ignition switch to ON (engine does not start) and check that the TPS output voltage is as specified. Standard value: 0.48–0.52 volts.

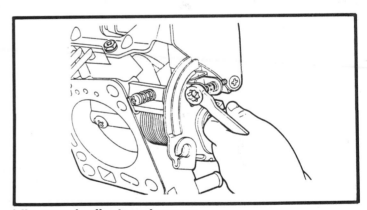

Idle speed adjustment screw

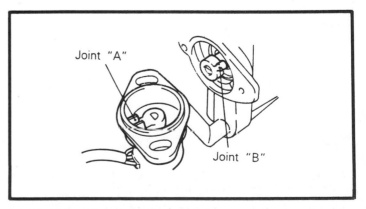

Throttle position sensor servicing

15. If it is out of specification, loosen TPS mounting screws and adjust by turning the TPS.

NOTE: Turning the TPS clockwise increases the output voltage. Tighten the screws securely after adjustment.

16. Turn ignition switch to OFF.
17. Adjust the accelerator cable play.
18. Connect the ISC servo connector.

19. Disconnect the special tool (Test harness) and voltmeter, and connect the TPS connector.
20. Start the engine and check to be sure that the idling speed is correct. Standard value: 750 ± 100 rpm.
21. Turn the ignition switch to OFF and disconnect the battery terminal for 5–6 seconds and then reconnect. (This erases the data stored in diagnosis memory during the ISC adjustment.)

NISSAN

ENGINE CONTROL SYSTEM APPLICATION CHART

Year	Model	Engine cc (liter)	Engine VIN	Fuel System	Ignition System
1984	Maxima	2393 (2.4)	L24E	EFI	Electronic
	Pulsar	1488 (1.5)	E15ET	ECCS ①③	ECCS
	Pulsar	1597 (1.6)	E16	ECC	Electronic
	Sentra	1597 (1.6)	E16	ECC	Electronic
	Stanza	1974 (2.0)	CA20E	EFI	Electronic
	Truck	1952 (2.0)	Z20	ECC	Electronic
	Truck	2389 (2.40	Z24	ECC	Electronic
	200SX	1974 (2.0)	CA20E	EFI	Electronic
	200SX	1809 (1.8)	CA18ET	ECCS ①③	ECCS
	300ZX	2960 (3.0)	VG30E	ECCS ③	ECCS
	300ZX	2960 (3.0)	VG30ET	ECCS ①③	ECCS
1985	Maxima	2960 (3.0)	VG30E	ECCS ③	ECCS
	Pulsar	1597 (1.6)	E16	ECC	Electronic
	Sentra	1597 (1.6)	E16	ECC	Electronic
	Stanza	1974 (2.0)	CA20E	EFI	Electronic
	Truck	1952 (2.0)	Z20	ECC	Electronic
	Truck	2389 (2.4)	Z24	ECC	Electronic
	200SX	1974 (2.0)	CA20E	EFI	Electronic
	200SX	1809 (1.8)	CA18ET	ECCS ①③	ECCS
	300ZX	2960 (3.0)	VG30E	ECCS ③	ECCS
	300ZX	2960 (3.0)	VG30ET	ECCS ①③	ECCS
1986	Maxima	2960 (3.0)	VG30E	ECCS ③	ECCS
	Pulsar	1597 (1.6)	E16	ECC	Electronic
	Sentra	1597 (1.6)	E16	ECC	Electronic
	Stanza	1974 (2.0)	CA20E	EFI	Electronic
	Truck	1952 (2.0)	Z20	ECC	Electronic
	Truck	2389 (2.4)	Z24	ECC	Electronic
	200SX	1974 (2.0)	CA20E	EFI	Electronic
	200SX	1809 (1.8)	CA18ET	ECCS ①③	ECCS
	300ZX	2960 (3.0)	VG30E	ECCS ③	ECCS
	300ZX	2960 (3.0)	VG30ET	ECCS ①③	ECCS
1986½	Truck	2389 (2.4)	Z24i	ECCS ②	ECCS
	Truck	2960 (3.0)	VG30i	ECCS ②	ECCS
1987-88	Maxima	2960 (3.0)	VG30E	ECCS ③	ECCS
	Pulsar	1597 (1.6)	E16i	ECCS ②	ECCS
	Pulsar	1597 (1.6)	CA16DE	ECCS ③	ECCS
	Sentra	1597 (1.6)	E16	ECC	Electronic
	Sentra	1597 (1.6)	E16i	ECCS ②	ECCS
	Stanza	1974 (2.0)	CA20E	ECCS ③	ECCS

ENGINE CONTROL SYSTEM APPLICATION CHART

Year	Model	Engine cc (liter)	Engine VIN	Fuel System	Ignition System
1987-88	Truck/Pathfinder	2389 (2.4)	Z24i	ECCS ②	ECCS
	Truck/Pathfinder	2960 (3.0)	VG30i	ECCS ②	ECCS
	Van	2389 (2.4)	Z24i	ECCS ②	ECCS
	200SX	1809 (1,8)	CA18ET	ECCS ①③	ECCS
	200SX	1974 (2.0)	CA20E	ECCS ③	ECCS
	200SX	2960 (3.0)	VG30E	ECCS ③	ECCS
	300ZX	2960 (3.0)	VG30E	ECCS ③	ECCS
	300ZX	2960 (3.0)	VG30ET	ECCS ①③	ECCS

ECC Electronic Carburetor Control
ECCS Electronic Concentrated Control
System
EFI Electronic Fuel Injection
① Turbocharged engine
② Throttle body fuel injection
③ Port fuel injection

ELECTRONIC FUEL INJECTION (EFI)

General Information

The Nissan Electronic Fuel Injection (EFI) is an air flow controlled, port fuel injection system. The EFI electronic control unit consists of a microcomputer, inspection lamps, a diagnostic mode selector and connectors for signal input and output and for power supply. The electronic control unit, or ECU, controls the following functions:

- Amount of injected fuel
- IC ignition unit
- Mixture ratio feedback
- Idle speed control
- Fuel pump operation
- Air regulator control
- Self-diagnostics
- Spark plug switching control (if equipped)
- Auto transmission lock-up (models with Auto trans)

Air Flow Meter

The air flow meter measures the quantity of intake air and sends a signal to the control unit. The air flow meter is provided with a flap in the air passage. During idling operation, when the amount of intake air is extremely small, the air flows parallel with the flap through the by-pass port so that the specified intake air flow can be provided correctly. An air temperature sensor is installed in the air passage.

The by-pass port has the air by-pass screw which regulates the idle mixture ratio. The air by-pass screw is preset and sealed at the factory.

Water Temperature Sensor

The water temperature sensor, built into the water outlet, monitors changes in coolant temperature and transmits a signal to the ECU. The temperature sensing unit employs a thermistor which is sensitive to the change in temperature. Electrical resistance of the thermistor decreases in response to the temperature rise.

Exhaust Gas Sensor

The exhaust gas sensor, which is built into the exhaust manifold, monitors the density of oxygen in the exhaust gas. It consists of a closed-end tube made of ceramic zirconia and other components. Porous platinum electrodes cover the tubes inner and outer surfaces. The closed-end of the tube is exposed to the exhaust gas in the exhaust manifold. The outer surface of the tube contacts the exhaust gas while the inner surface contacts the air.

Throttle Valve Switch

The throttle valve switch is attached to the throttle chamber and operates in response to accelerator pedal movement. The switch has an idle contact and a full throttle contact. The idle contact closes when the throttle valve is positioned at idle and opens when it is in any other position.

Air Regulator

A bimetal, heater and rotary shutter are built into the air regu-

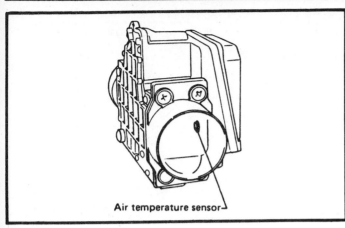

Air flow meter (EFI)

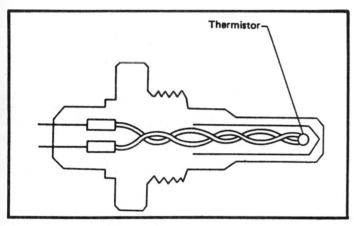

Water temprature sensor

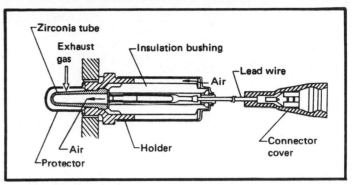

Exhaust gas sensor

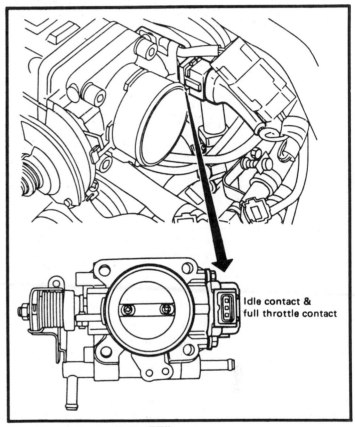

Throttle valve switch (EFI)

lator. When the bimetal temperature is low, the air by-pass port is open. As the engine starts and electric current flows through a heater, the bimetal begins to rotate the shutter to close off the by-pass port. The air passage remains closed until the engine is stopped and the bimetal temperature drops.

Fuel Injector

The fuel injector is a small, precision solenoid valve. As the EFI control unit output an injection signal to each fuel injector, the coil built into the injector pulls the needle valve back, and fuel is injected through the nozzle to intake manifold. The amount of fuel injected is controlled by the EFI control unit as an injection pulse duration.

IC Ignition Unit

The ignition signal is sent to the EFI control unit to control the injected fuel digitally by monitoring the engine revolution. The signal from the EFI control unit switches the spark plugs and control the spark timing (for automatic transmission models).

Idle-Up Solenoid Valve

The idle-up solenoid valve is attached to the intake manifold. The solenoid valve actuates to stabilize idle speed when engine load is heavy because of electric load, power steering oil pump, etc.

SERVICE PRECAUTIONS

● Do not operate the fuel pump when the fuel lines are empty.

● Do not reuse fuel hose clamps.
● Make sure all EFI harness connectors are fastened securely. A poor connection can cause an extremely high surge voltage in the coil and condenser and result in damage to integrated circuits.
● Keep the EFI harness at least 4 in. away from adjacent harnesses to prevent an EFI system malfunction due to external electronic "noise."
● Keep EFI all parts and harnesses dry during service.
● Before attempting to remove any parts, turn off the ignition switch and disconnect the battery ground cable.
● Always use a 12 volt battery as a power source.
● Do not attempt to disconnect the battery cables with the engine running.
● Do not depress the accelerator pedal when starting.
● Do not rev up the engine immediately after starting or just prior to shutdown.

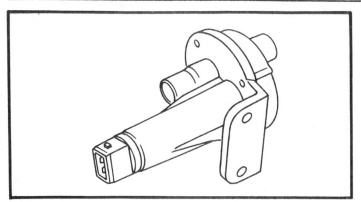

Air regulator

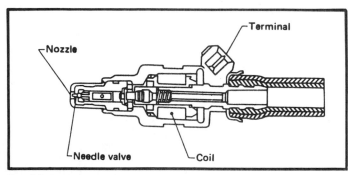

Fuel injector

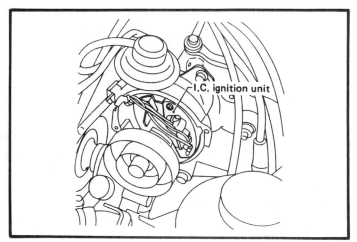

EFI distributor

• Do not attempt to disassemble the EFI control unit under any circumstances.
• If installing a two-way or CB radio, keep the antenna as far as possible away from the electronic control unit. Keep the antenna feeder line at least 8 in. away from the EFI harness and do not let the two run parallel for a long distance. Be sure to ground the radio to the vehicle body.
• Do not apply battery power directly to injectors.
• Handle air flow meter carefully to avoid damage.
• Do not disassemble air flow meter or clean meter with any type of detergent.

SELF-DIAGNOSTIC SYSTEM

The self-diagnostic system determines malfunctions of signal

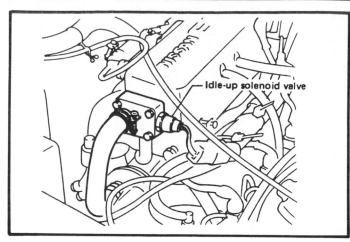

Idle-up solenoid valve

systems such as sensors, actuators, and wire harnesses based on the status of the input signals received by the EFI control unit. A malfunction is displayed by both the red and green LED's (Light Emitting Diodes).

Basically, self-diagnosis is always performed when the power is furnished to the EFI control unit. The self-diagnosis results are retained in the memory chip of the EFI control unit and are displayed only when the diagnosis mode selector (located on the side of the control unit) is turned ON.

The self-diagnostic system is provided with functions which display malfunctions being checked as well as those which are stored in the memory. In this sense, it is very effective in determining an "intermittent" malfunction. The results which is or was stored in the memory can be erased by following the steps specified.

A malfunctioning area is determined by the number of blinks of both the red and green LED's. First, the red LED blinks and the green follows. The red LED refers to the tenth digit while the green one refers to the unit digit. For example, when the red LED blinks three times and the green LED blinks twice, this implies number "32". In this way, all problems are classified by code numbers.

Items Displayed All The Time

Whenever performing the self-diagnosis, input the signals regarding the following items because when performing self-diagnosis the following items are displayed by EFI control unit as a malfunction even though it is working properly.

INPUT PROCEDURE

1. Throttle Valve Switch (Idle Switch) Circuit And Air Conditioner Switch Circuit—After the ignition switch is turned ON and "ON-OFF" signal from each switch are entered.
2. Start Signal—After the engine has started and when start signal "ON" and then "OFF" are entered.
3. Load Signal—After load signal is turned "ON", a signal is entered.

Items Retained In Memory

The following items will be retained in the memory from the time of detection until erased:
• Air Flow Meter Circuit—When the air flow meter produces an abnormally high output voltage with the engine off or low output voltage with the engine running
• Water Temperature Sensor Circuit—When the circuit is shorted or open
• Ignition Signal—When an ignition signal is not produced on the primary winding of the ignition coil after the engine has started

- Fuel Pump Circuit—When current flowing through the control unit to drive the fuel pump is too small or too large while the engine is operating
- Air Temperature Sensor Circuit—When the circuit is shorted or open

TESTING PRECAUTIONS

1. Before connecting or disconnecting control unit ECU harness connectors, make sure the ignition switch is OFF and the negative battery cable is disconnected to avoid the possibility of damage to the control unit.

2. When performing ECU input/output signal diagnosis, remove the pin terminal retainer from the 20 and 16-pin connectors to make it easier to insert tester probes into the connector.

3. When connecting or disconnecting pin connectors from the ECU, take care not to bend or break any pin terminals. Check that there are no bends or breaks on ECU pin terminals before attempting any connections.

4. Before replacing any ECU, perform the ECU input/output signal diagnosis to make sure the ECU is functioning properly or not.

5. After performing the Electronic Control System Inspection, perform the EFI self-diagnosis and driving test.

6. When measuring supply voltage of ECU controlled components with a circuit tester, separate one tester probe from another. If the two tester probes accidentally make contact with each other during measurement, a short circuit will result and damage the power transistor in the ECU.

MAINTENANCE REMINDER LIGHTS

Exhaust gas sensor should be checked after every 30,000 miles (48,000 km) of operation. At this time, the exhaust gas sensor warning lamp will come on to indicate that the sensor should be inspected. After inspecting and/or replacing the sensor, the sensor warning lamp should be reset. On 1984, most 1985 and Canada models, the sensor light connector is disconnected and further maintenance is not required. On 1985 Maxima and most 1986–88 models, a warning light hold relay must be located and reset at the 30,000 mile (48,000 km) and 60,000 mile (96,000 km) intervals. At 90,000 miles (144,000 km), the sensor warning light is disabled by disconnecting the sensor light connector.

SENSOR LIGHT CONNECTOR LOCATION

- 1984–86 Stanza—Behind left kick panel
- 1984 200SX—Under right side dash
- 1985–88 200SX—Above fuse box
- 1984–88 Maxima—Near hood release
- 1986 Stanza Wagon—Above fuse box

SENSOR LIGHT HOLD RELAY LOCATION

- 1986 Stanza—Behind right kick panel
- 1986–88 200SX—Center console
- 1985–88 Maxima—Behind left kick panel
- 1986 Stanza Wagon—Under right seat

ELECTRONIC CONTROL UNIT (ECI) LOCATION:

- 1984–86 Stanza—Behind left (driver) kick panel
- 1984–87 200SX—Behind left (driver) kick panel
- 1984–87 Maxima—Under right (passenger) seat
- 1986 Stanza Wagon—Under left (driver) seat

EFI DIAGNOSTIC CHART—1984 MAXIMA

AIR FLOW METER TESTS

Test No. 1 Air flow meter resistance

Tester	Leads to Pins (+)	Leads to Pins (−)	Notes	Should Read
Ohmmeter	33	34		100 to 400Ω

Component check

If test is O.K., go to Test No. 2.   If test is not O.K., perform component check.

Measure the resistance between terminals ③ and ④. The standard resistance is 100 to 400 ohms.
If test is O.K., check harness.
If test is not O.K., replace component.

Test No. 2 Air flow meter resistance

Tester	Leads to Pins (+)	Leads to Pins (−)	Notes	Should Read
Ohmmeter	34	35		200 to 500Ω

Component check

If test is O.K., go to Test No. 3.   If test is not O.K., perform component check.

Measure the resistance between terminals ④ and ⑤. The standard resistance is 200 to 500 ohms.
If test is O.K., check harness.
If test is not O.K., replace component.

EFI DIAGNOSTIC CHART—1984 MAXIMA

Test No. 3 Air flow meter resistance

Tester	Leads to Pins (+)	Leads to Pins (−)	Notes	Should Read
Ohmmeter	32	34		Except 0 and ∞Ω

Component check

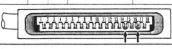

If test is O.K., go to Test No. 4.   If test is not O.K., perform component check.

While sliding flap, measure resistance between terminals ③ and ④. If resistance is at any value other than 0 and ∞ ohm, air flow meter is normal.
If test is O.K., check harness.
If test is not O.K., replace component.

Test No. 4 Insulation resistance

Tester	Leads to Pins (+)	Leads to Pins (−)	Notes	Should Read
Ohmmeter	32 33 34 35	Body ground		∞Ω

Component check

If test is O.K., go to Test No. 5.   If test is not O.K., perform component check.

Check insulation resistance between the air flow meter body and any one of the terminals ③, ③, ④ and ⑤. If continuity exists, the air flow meter is out of order.
If test is O.K., check harness.
If test is not O.K., replace component.

Test No. 5 air flow meter flap.

Fully open the flap by hand to check that it opens smoothly without binding. If it doesn't, it is out of order.
If test is O.K., air flow meter is O.K.
If test is not O.K., replace air flow meter.

EFI DIAGNOSTIC CHART—1984 MAXIMA

AIR TEMPERATURE SENSOR TESTS

Test No. 1 Air Temperature Sensor

Tester	Leads to Pins (+)	Leads to Pins (−)	Notes		Should Read
Ohmmeter	25	34	Intake air temperature		
			20°C (68°F) or above		Below 2.9 kΩ
			Below 20°C (68°F)		2.1 kΩ or above

Component check

1. Measure the outside air temperature.
2. Measure resistance between terminals ② and ④ of the air flow meter connector.
If test is O.K., check harness.
If test is not O.K., replace component.

Test No. 2 Insulation Resistance

Tester	Leads to Pins (+)	Leads to Pins (−)	Notes	Should Read
Ohmmeter	25	Body ground		∞Ω

Component check

If test is O.K., air temperature sensor is O.K.   If test is not O.K., perform component check.

Check insulation resistance between terminal ② and air flow meter body.
If test is O.K., check harness.
If test is not O.K., replace component.

EFI DIAGNOSTIC CHART—1984 MAXIMA

CYLINDER HEAD TEMPERATURE SENSOR TEST

Cylinder head temperature sensor test

Tester	Leads to Pins (+)	Leads to Pins (−)	Notes	Should Read
Ohmmeter	14	Body ground	20°C (68°F) or above	Below 2.9 kΩ
			Below 20°C (68°F)	2.1 kΩ or above

If test is O.K., test is complete.
If test is not O.K., perform component check.

Dip the sensor into water maintained at a temperature of 20°C (68°F), 80°C (176°F), etc. and read its resistance.

Component check

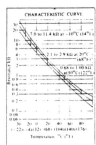

CHARACTERISTIC CURVE

If test matches curve, sensor is O.K. Check harness.
If test does not match curve, replace sensor.

EXHAUST GAS SENSOR CIRCUIT TEST

Exhaust gas sensor circuit test

Tester	Leads to Pins (+)	Leads to Pins (−)	Notes	Should Read
Ohmmeter	31	Body ground	Disconnect exhaust gas sensor harness connector, and connect EFI harness terminal for exhaust gas sensor to ground with a jumper wire.	0Ω

If test is O.K., exhaust gas sensor circuit is O.K. For performing component check, refer to MIXTURE RATIO FEEDBACK SYSTEM.

EFI DIAGNOSTIC CHART—1984 MAXIMA

THERMOTIME SWITCH TESTS

Disconnect cold start valve harness connector.

Test No. 1 Thermotime switch contact point

Tester	Leads to Pins		Notes	Should Read
	(+)	(−)		
Ohmmeter	4	Body ground	Water temperature 25°C (77°F) or above	∞Ω
			14 to 25°C (57 to 77°F)	0 or ∞Ω
			Below 14°C (57°F)	0Ω

If test is O.K., go to Test No. 2.

If test is not O.K., perform component check.

Test No. 2 Heater coil of thermotime switch bimetal

Tester	Leads to Pins		Notes	Should Read
	(+)	(−)		
Ohmmeter	26	Body ground	Disconnect starter motor "S" terminal.	40 to 70Ω

If test is O.K., thermotime switch is O.K.

If test is not O.K., perform component check.

Component check

Measure the resistance between terminal ⑮ and switch body.

● The resistance is zero when the cooling water temperature is less than 14°C (57°F). . . . . O.K.
● The resistance is infinite when the cooling water temperature is more than 25°C (77°F). . . . . O.K.

The resistance is zero or infinite when the cooling water temperature is between 14 to 25°C (57 to 77°F).

Measure the resistance between terminal ⑮ and switch body.

The ohmmeter reading is 40 to 70 ohms . . . . O.K.

If test is O.K., check harness.

If test is not O.K., replace component.

EFI DIAGNOSTIC CHART—1984 MAXIMA

AIR REGULATOR CIRCUIT TESTS

Test No. 1 Air regulator resistance

Tester	Leads to Pins		Notes	Should Read
	(+)	(−)		
Ohmmeter	21	Body ground		25 to 90Ω

If test is O.K., go to Test No. 2.

If test is not O.K., check air regulator/fuel pump.

Test No. 2 Air regulator and fuel pump power circuit

1. Connect E.F.I. harness connector to E.C.U.
2. Turn ignition switch to "ON".
3. Listen for fuel pump operating sound for a few seconds.
4. If no sound is heard, check fuel pump relay.

   If fuel pump operates, check air regulator.

CHECKING AIR REGULATOR

1. Starting engine, and pinch rubber hose between throttle chamber and air regulator.

● Engine speed decreases during warm-up. . . . . O.K.
● Engine speed remains unchanged after warm-up. . . . . . O.K.

2. Disconnect hoses from both ends of air regulator, and visually check to see if air regulator shutter opens.
3. Disconnect electric connector of air regulator, and check continuity. Continuity should exist. If not, air regulator is faulty.

4. Pry air regulator shutter to open with a flat-blade screwdriver, then close. If shutter opens and closes smoothly, it is operating properly.

If test is O.K., check harness.

If test is not O.K., replace component and retest.

EFI DIAGNOSTIC CHART—1984 MAXIMA

CONTROL UNIT GROUND CIRCUIT TESTS

Control unit ground circuit tests

Tester	Leads to Pins		Notes	Should Read
	(+)	(−)		
Ohmmeter	15 19 20 22	Body ground		Continuity

If tests are O.K., ground circuits are O.K.

If tests are not O.K., check wiring diagram and harness.

EFI DIAGNOSTIC CHART—1984 MAXIMA

COLD START VALVE TEST

Cold start valve circuit test

Tester	Leads to Pins		Notes	Should Read
	(+)	(−)		
Voltmeter	4	Body ground	1. Disconnect starter motor "S" terminal and thermotime switch harness connector. 2. Connect cold start valve harness connector and battery ground cable. 3. Ignition "START".	Battery voltage

If test is O.K., cold start valve is O.K.

If test is not O.K., perform component check.

1. Disconnect ground cable from battery.
2. Remove two screws securing cold start valve to intake manifold, and extract cold start valve.
3. Put cold start valve into a transparent glass container, plug the transparent glass container opening with a clean rag.
4. Using two jumper wires, connect each terminal to cold start valve connector.
5. Connect other terminals of jumper wire to battery positive and negative terminals.

● Fuel is injected. . . . . O.K.
● Fuel is not injected. . . . . . . N.G.

CAUTION:
Be careful to keep both terminals separate in order to avoid short circuit.

If test is O.K., check harness.

If test is not O.K., replace component and retest.

Component check

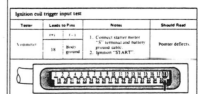

IGNITION COIL TRIGGER INPUT TEST

Ignition coil trigger input test

Tester	Leads to Pins		Notes	Should Read
	(+)	(−)		
Voltmeter	18	Body ground	1. Connect starter motor "S" terminal and battery ground cable. 2. Ignition "START".	Pointer deflects.

If test is O.K., trigger input to control unit is O.K.

If test is not O.K., check ignition coil and wire harness.

EFI DIAGNOSTIC CHART—1984 MAXIMA

INJECTOR CIRCUIT TESTS

CAUTION: Never turn the selecting switch of the tester to the "Ohmmeter" or "Ammeter" position during these tests as it may burn out the injectors and circuit.

Test No. 1 Cylinder No. 1

Tester	Leads to Pins		Notes	Should Read
	(+)	(−)		
Voltmeter	8	Body ground	Connect battery ground cable.	Battery voltage

If test is O.K., go to Test No. 2.   If test is not O.K., go to Component Check.

Test No. 2 Cylinder No. 2

Tester	Leads to Pins		Notes	Should Read
	(+)	(−)		
Voltmeter	5	Body ground		Battery voltage

If test is O.K., go to Test No. 3.   If test is not O.K., perform component check.

Test No. 3 Cylinder No. 3

Tester	Leads to Pins		Notes	Should Read
	(+)	(−)		
Voltmeter	7	Body ground		Battery voltage

If test is O.K., go to Test No. 4.   If test is not O.K., go to Component Check.

Component check

1. Disconnect ground cable from battery.
2. Disconnect electric connectors from injectors.
3. Check continuity between the two terminals. Continuity should exist. If not, injector(s) are faulty.

EFI DIAGNOSTIC CHART—1984 MAXIMA

EFI RELAY AND FUEL PUMP RELAY TESTS

Test No. 1 EFI relay test (Control unit power input circuit test)

Tester	Leads to Pins		Notes	Should Read
	(+)	(−)		
Voltmeter	27	Body ground	1. Connect battery ground cable. 2. Ignition "ON".	Battery voltage

If test is O.K., EFI relay is O.K. Go to Test No. 2.   If test is not O.K., check EFI relay.

Test No. 2 fuel pump relay

1. Connect E.F.I. harness connector to E.C.U.
2. Turn ignition switch to "IG".

3. Listen for fuel pump operating sound for a few seconds after turning ignition switch to "IG".

If no sound is heard, go to test No. 3.

Test No. 3 Fuel pump relay test

Tester	Leads to Pins		Notes	Should Read
	(+)	(−)		
Ohmmeter	13	Body ground		Except 0 and ∞Ω

If test No. 3 is O.K., check fuel pump and circuit.

If fuel pump is O.K., check component check.

If test No. 3 is not O.K., go to component check.

Check terminals	Normal condition	12V direct current is applied between terminals ① and ②
① · ②	Continuity	—
③ · ⑤	No continuity	Continuity
③ · ⑥	Continuity	No continuity

If E.F.I. relay and fuel pump relay are O.K., check harness.
If fuel pump and harness are O.K., replace control unit.

CHECKING EFI RELAY AND FUEL PUMP RELAY

E.F.I. relay and fuel pump relay to which green labels are affixed, are installed on the relay bracket. They are the same in appearance but can be distinguished by their harness color.

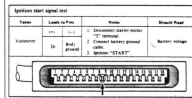

Both of the above relays are green, but can be distinguished by the color of harness.

EFI DIAGNOSTIC CHART—1984 MAXIMA

Test No. 4 Cylinder No. 4

Tester	Leads to Pins		Notes	Should Read
	(+)	(−)		
Voltmeter	6	Body ground		Battery voltage

If test is O.K., go to Test No. 5.   If test is not O.K., go to Component Check.

Test No. 5 Cylinder No. 5

Tester	Leads to Pins		Notes	Should Read
	(+)	(−)		
Voltmeter	3	Body ground		Battery voltage

If test is O.K., go to Test No. 6.   If test is not O.K., go to Component Check.

Test No. 6 Cylinder No. 6

Tester	Leads to Pins		Notes	Should Read
	(+)	(−)		
Voltmeter	2	Body ground		Battery voltage

If test is O.K., all injectors are O.K.   If test is not O.K., perform component check.

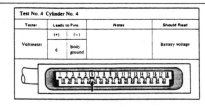

EFI DIAGNOSTIC CHART—1984 MAXIMA

IGNITION START SIGNAL TEST

Ignition start signal test

Tester	Leads to Pins		Notes	Should Read
	(+)	(−)		
Voltmeter	26	Body ground	1. Disconnect starter motor "S" terminal. 2. Connect battery ground cable. 3. Ignition "START".	Battery voltage

If test is O.K., ignition start signal is O.K.

If test is not O.K., inspect ignition coil and harness.

MIXTURE RATIO FEEDBACK INSPECTION CHART — 1984 MAXIMA

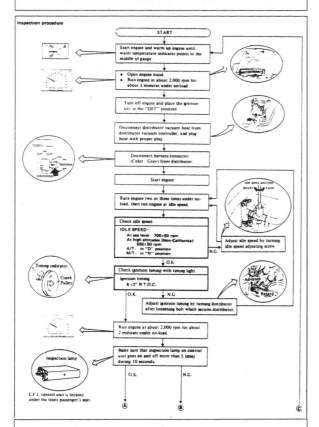

MIXTURE RATIO FEEDBACK INSPECTION CHART — 1984 MAXIMA

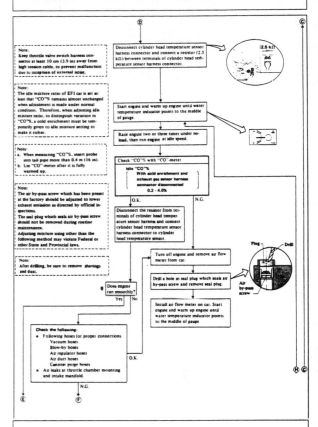

MIXTURE RATIO FEEDBACK INSPECTION CHART — 1984 MAXIMA

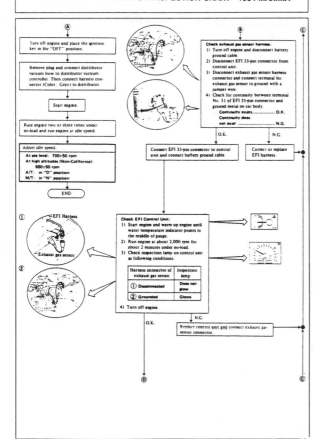

MIXTURE RATIO FEEDBACK INSPECTION CHART — 1984 MAXIMA

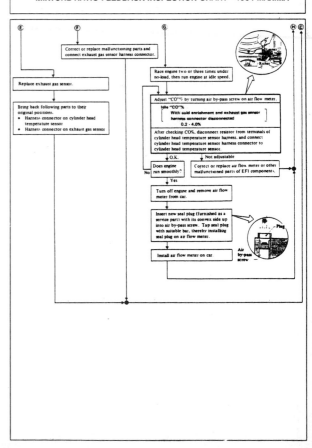

EFI SELF-DIAGNOSTIC PROCEDURE – 1984–85 STANZA

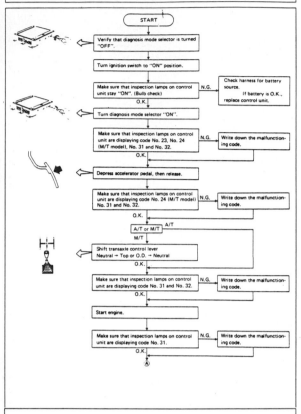

EFI SELF-DIAGNOSTIC DECODING CHART – 1984–85 STANZA

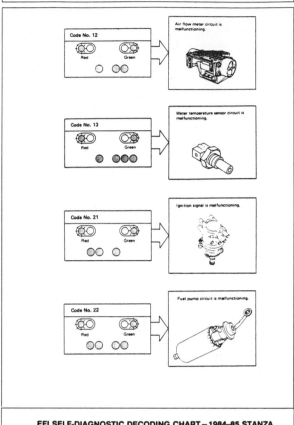

EFI SELF-DIAGNOSTIC PROCEDURE – 1984–85 STANZA

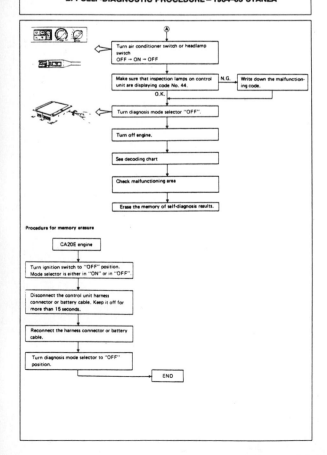

EFI SELF-DIAGNOSTIC DECODING CHART – 1984–85 STANZA

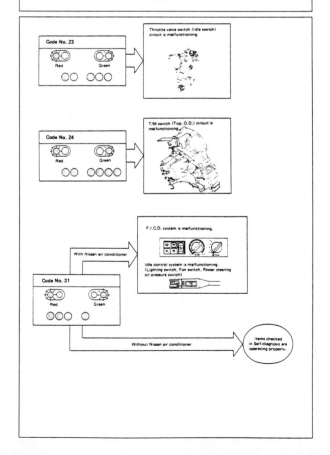

EFI SELF-DIAGNOSTIC DECODING CHART—1984–85 STANZA

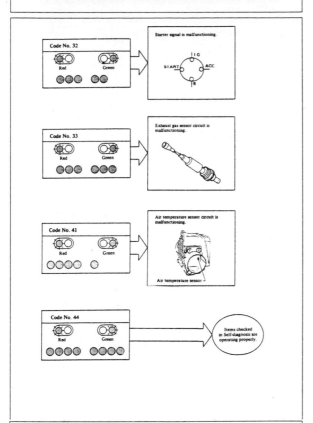

EFI SELF-DIAGNOSTIC CHART—1984–85 STANZA

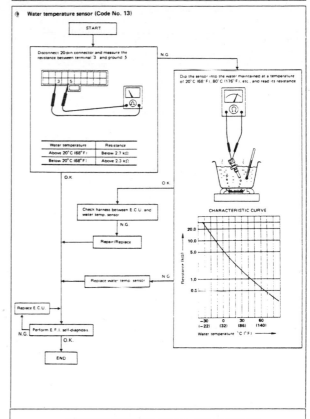

EFI SELF-DIAGNOSTIC CHART—1984–85 STANZA

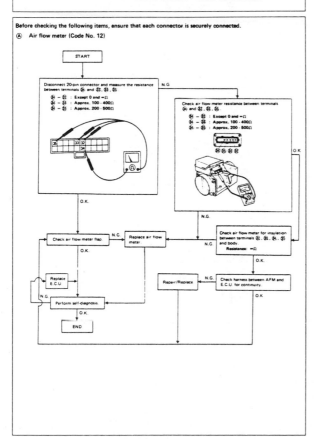

EFI SELF-DIAGNOSTIC CHART—1984–85 STANZA

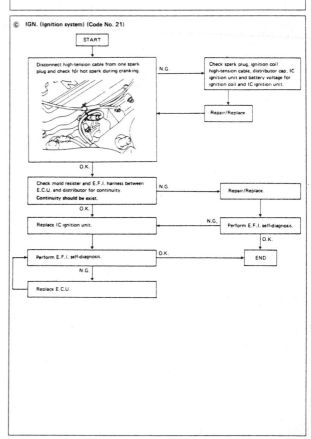

EFI SELF-DIAGNOSTIC CHART — 1984–85 STANZA

Ⓓ Fuel pump (Code No. 22)

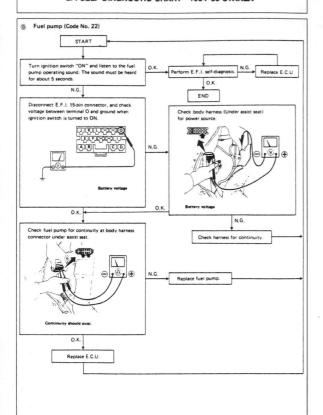

EFI SELF-DIAGNOSTIC CHART — 1984–85 STANZA

Ⓕ Manual transaxle switch (Top/O.D. switch) (Code No. 24)

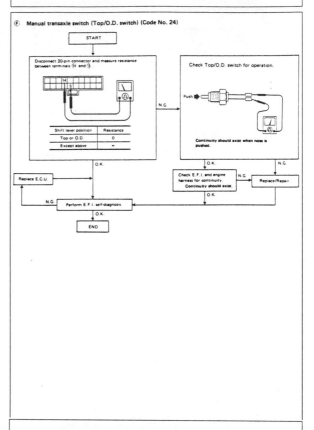

EFI SELF-DIAGNOSTIC CHART — 1984–85 STANZA

Ⓔ Throttle valve switch (Idle switch) (Code No. 23)

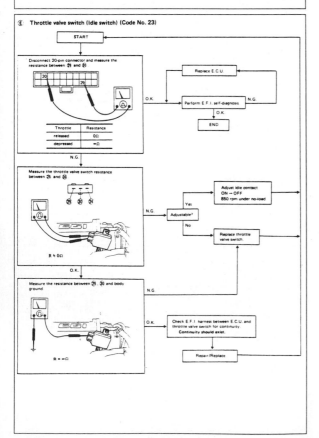

EFI SELF-DIAGNOSTIC CHART — 1984–85 STANZA

Ⓖ Air conditioner switch (Code No. 31)

Ⓗ Starter switch (Code No. 32)

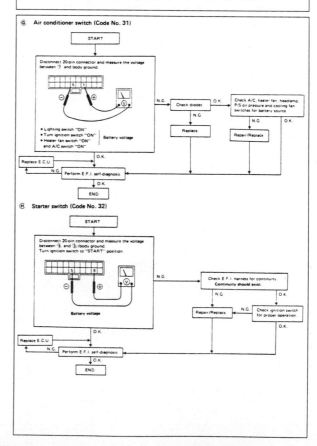

EFI SELF-DIAGNOSTIC CHART – 1984–85 STANZA

Ⓘ Exhaust gas sensor (Code No. 33)

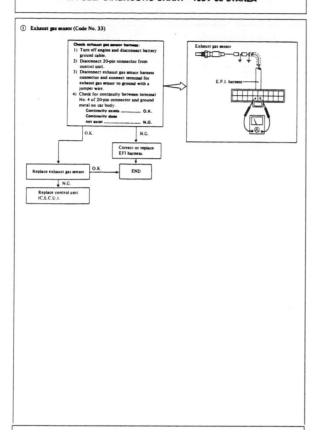

EFI SELF-DIAGNOSTIC CHART – 1984–85 STANZA

Ⓛ Air regulator

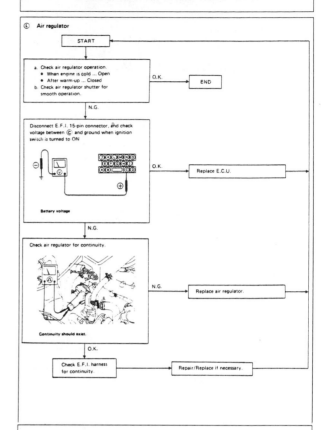

EFI SELF-DIAGNOSTIC CHART – 1984–85 STANZA

Ⓙ Air temperature sensor (Code No. 41)

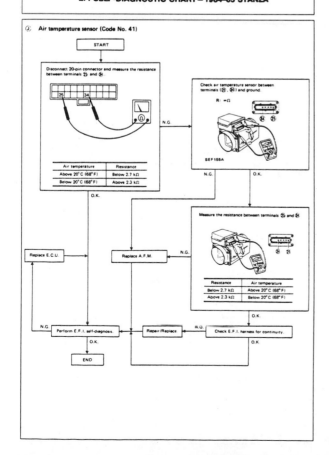

EFI SELF-DIAGNOSTIC CHART – 1984–85 STANZA

Ⓜ Injector

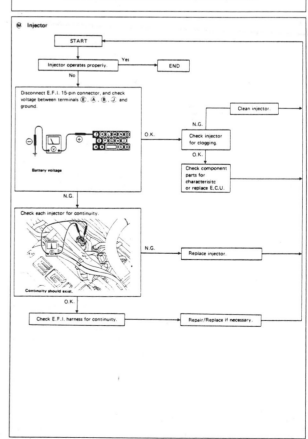

EFI SELF-DIAGNOSTIC CHART—1984–85 STANZA

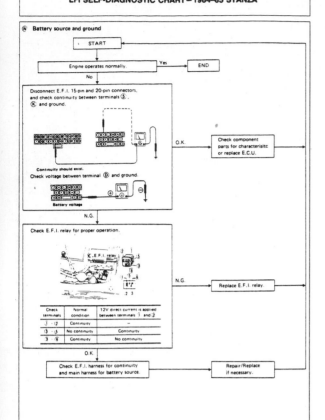

Ⓝ Battery source and ground

MIXTURE RATIO FEEDBACK INSPECTION CHART—1985–85 STANZA

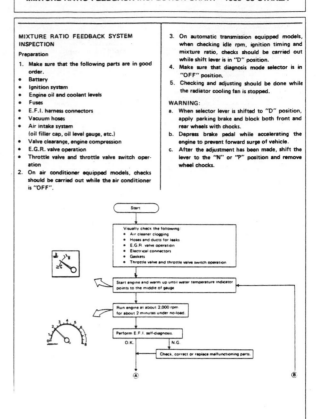

MIXTURE RATIO FEEDBACK SYSTEM INSPECTION

Preparation

1. Make sure that the following parts are in good order.
   - Battery
   - Ignition system
   - Engine oil and coolant levels
   - Fuses
   - E.F.I. harness connectors
   - Vacuum hoses
   - Air intake system
     (oil filler cap, oil level gauge, etc.)
   - Valve clearance, engine compression
   - E.G.R. valve operation
   - Throttle valve and throttle valve switch operation
2. On air conditioner equipped models, checks should be carried out while the air conditioner is "OFF".

3. On automatic transmission equipped models, when checking idle rpm, ignition timing and mixture ratio, checks should be carried out while shift lever is in "D" position.
4. Make sure that diagnosis mode selector is in "OFF" position.
5. Checking and adjusting should be done while the radiator cooling fan is stopped.

WARNING:
a. When selector lever is shifted to "D" position, apply parking brake and block both front and rear wheels with chocks.
b. Depress brake pedal while accelerating the engine to prevent forward surge of vehicle.
c. After the adjustment has been made, shift the lever to the "N" or "P" position and remove wheel chocks.

EFI SELF-DIAGNOSTIC CHART—1984–85 STANZA

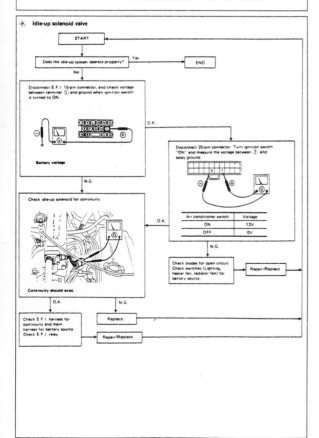

Ⓟ Idle-up solenoid valve

MIXTURE RATIO FEEDBACK INSPECTION CHART—1985–85 STANZA

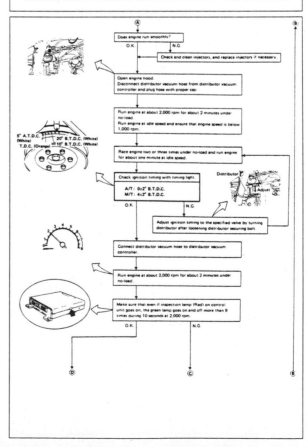

MIXTURE RATIO FEEDBACK INSPECTION CHART — 1985–85 STANZA

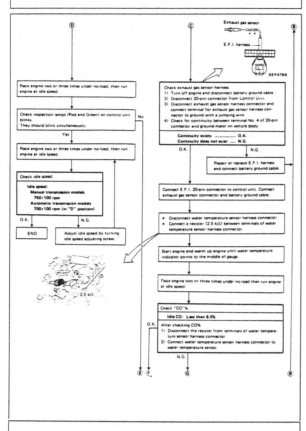

EFI SELF-DIAGNOSTIC PROCEDURE — 1984–86 200SX WITH CA20E ENGINE

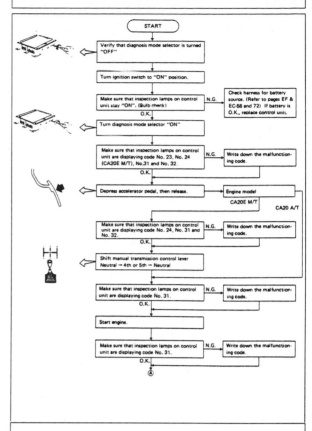

MIXTURE RATIO FEEDBACK INSPECTION CHART — 1985–85 STANZA

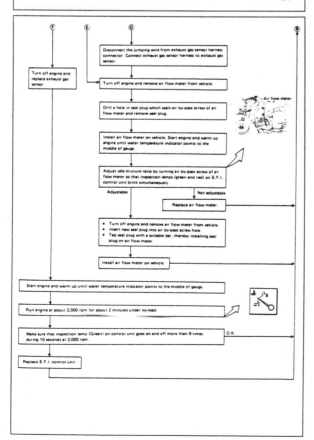

EFI SELF-DIAGNOSTIC PROCEDURE — 1984–86 200SX WITH CA20E ENGINE

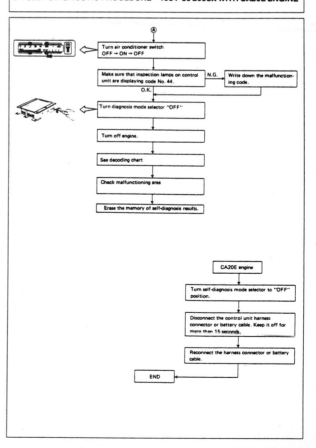

EFI SELF-DIAGNOSTIC DECODING CHART
1984–86 200SX WITH CA20E ENGINE

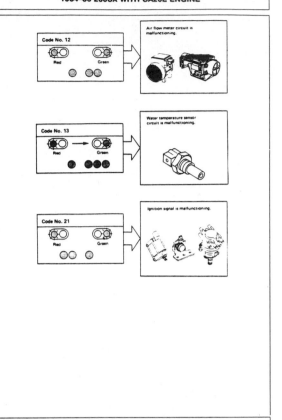

EFI SELF-DIAGNOSTIC DECODING CHART
1984–86 200SX WITH CA20E ENGINE

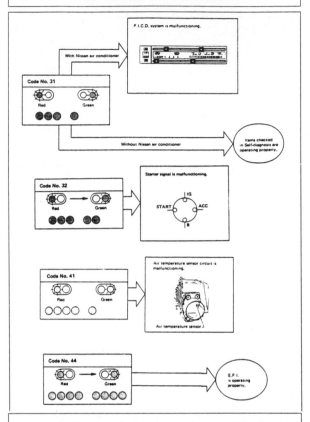

EFI SELF-DIAGNOSTIC DECODING CHART
1984–86 200SX WITH CA20E ENGINE

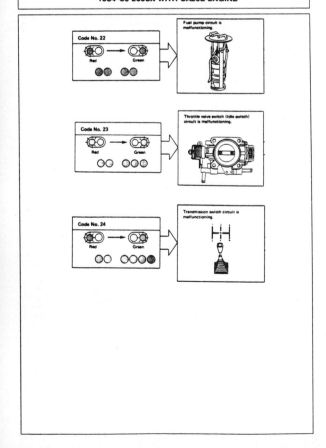

EFI SELF-DIAGNOSTIC CHART — 1984–85 200SX WITH CA20E ENGINE

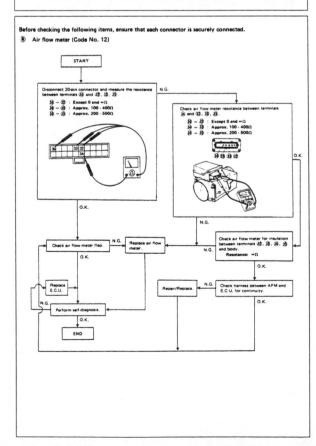

EFI SELF-DIAGNOSTIC CHART — 1986 200SX WITH CA20E ENGINE

Before checking the following items, ensure that each connector is securely connected.

Ⓑ Air flow meter (Code No. 12)

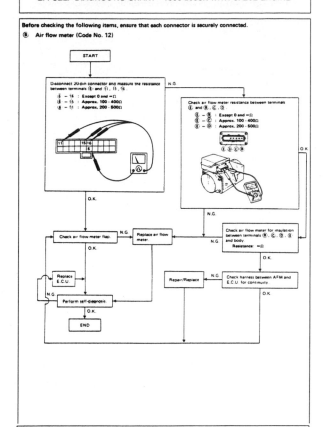

EFI SELF-DIAGNOSTIC CHART — 1984–86 200SX WITH CA20E ENGINE

Ⓓ IGN. (Ignition system) (Code No. 21)

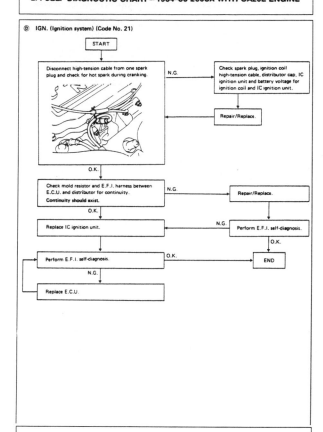

EFI SELF-DIAGNOSTIC CHART — 1984–86 200SX WITH CA20E ENGINE

Ⓒ Water temperature sensor (Code No. 13)

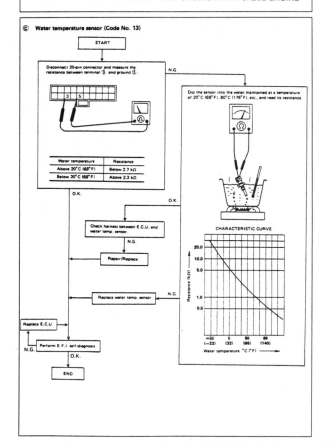

EFI SELF-DIAGNOSTIC CHART — 1984–86 200SX WITH CA20E ENGINE

Ⓔ Fuel pump (Code No. 22)

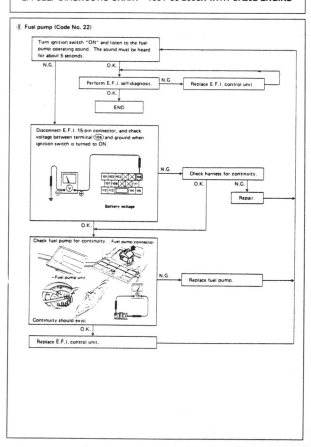

EFI SELF-DIAGNOSTIC CHART — 1984–85 200SX WITH CA20E ENGINE

(F) Throttle valve switch (Idle switch) (Code No. 23)

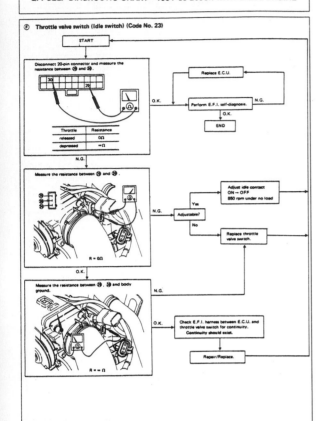

EFI SELF-DIAGNOSTIC CHART — 1986 200SX WITH CA20E ENGINE

(F) Throttle valve switch (Idle switch) (Code No. 23)

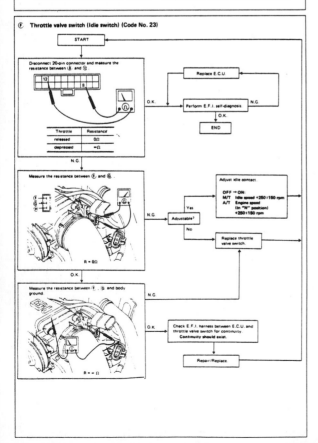

EFI SELF-DIAGNOSTIC CHART — 1984–86 200SX WITH CA20E ENGINE

(G) Transmission switch (Neutral switch) (Code No. 24)

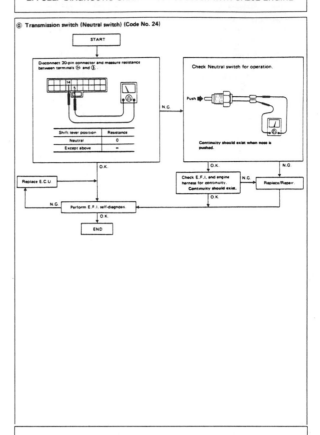

EFI SELF-DIAGNOSTIC CHART — 1984–86 200SX WITH CA20E ENGINE

(H) Air conditioner switch (Code No. 31)

(I) Starter switch (Code No. 32)

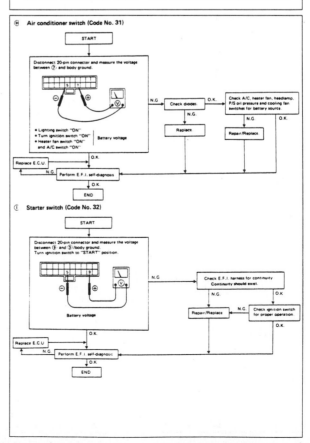

EFI SELF-DIAGNOSTIC CHART — 1984–85 200SX WITH CA20E ENGINE

Ⓚ Air temperature sensor (Code No. 41)

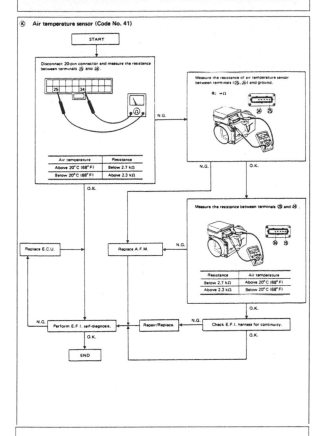

EFI SELF-DIAGNOSTIC CHART — 1984–86 200SX WITH CA20E ENGINE

Ⓛ Air regulator

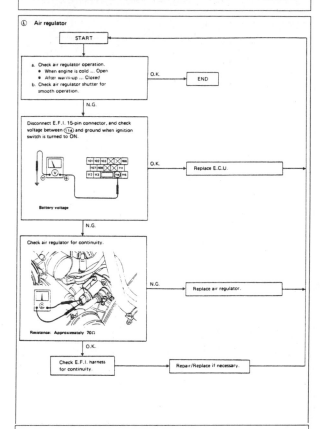

EFI SELF-DIAGNOSTIC CHART — 1986 200SX WITH CA20E ENGINE

Ⓚ Air temperature sensor (Code No. 41)

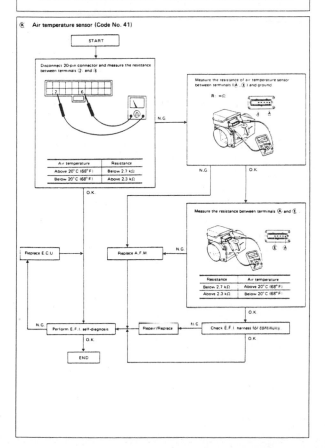

EFI SELF-DIAGNOSTIC CHART — 1984–86 200SX WITH CA20E ENGINE

Ⓜ Injector

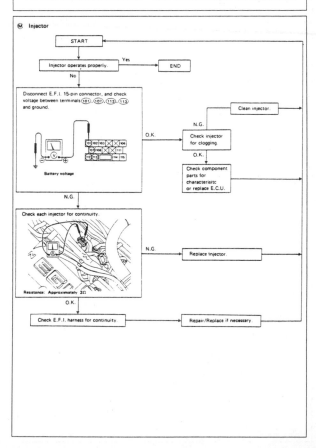

EFI SELF-DIAGNOSTIC CHART — 1984–85 200SX WITH CA20E ENGINE

Ⓝ Battery source and ground

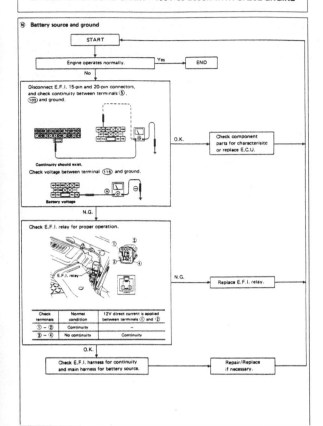

EFI SELF-DIAGNOSTIC CHART — 1984–86 200SX WITH CA20E ENGINE

Ⓞ Exhaust gas sensor
Refer to MIXTURE RATIO FEEDBACK SYSTEM INSPECTION.

Ⓠ Idle-up solenoid valve

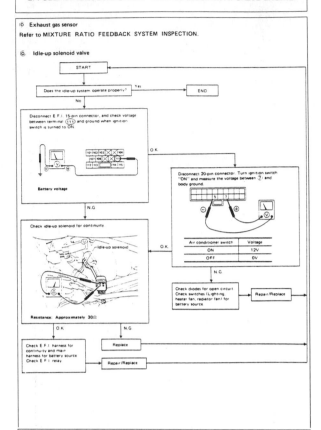

EFI SELF-DIAGNOSTIC CHART — 1986 200SX WITH CA20E ENGINE

Ⓝ Battery source and ground

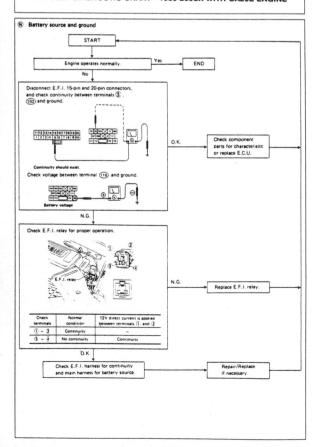

MIXTURE RATIO FEEDBACK INSPECTION CHART
1985–86 200SX WITH CA20E ENGINE

PREPARATION
1. Make sure that the following parts are in good order.
   - Battery
   - Ignition system
   - Engine oil and coolant levels
   - Fuses
   - E.F.I. harness connectors
   - Vacuum hoses
   - Air intake system
     (oil filler cap, oil level gauge, etc.)
   - Valve clearance, engine compression
   - E.G.R. valve operation
   - Throttle valve and throttle valve switch operation
2. On air conditioner equipped models, checks should be carried out while the air conditioner

is "OFF".
3. On automatic transmission equipped models, when checking idle rpm, ignition timing and mixture ratio, checks should be carried out while shift lever is in "D" position.
4. Make sure that diagnosis mode selector is in "OFF" position.

WARNING:
a. When selector lever is shifted to "D" position, apply parking brake and block both front and rear wheels with chocks.
b. Depress brake pedal while racing the engine to prevent forward surge of vehicle.
c. After the adjustment has been made, shift the lever to the "N" or "P" position and remove wheel chocks.

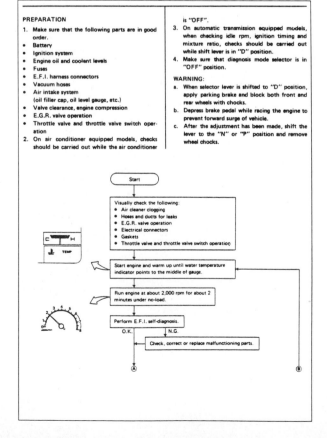

MIXTURE RATIO FEEDBACK INSPECTION CHART
1985–86 200SX WITH CA20E ENGINE

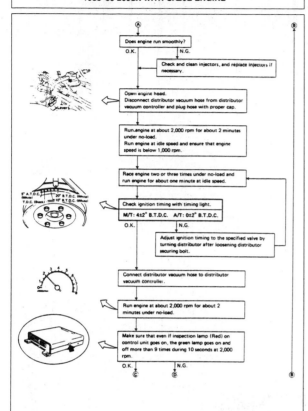

(A)

Does engine run smoothly?
→ O.K. / N.G.

N.G. → Check and clean injectors, and replace injectors if necessary.

Open engine hood.
Disconnect distributor vacuum hose from distributor vacuum controller and plug hose with proper cap.

Run engine at about 2,000 rpm for about 2 minutes under no-load.
Run engine at idle speed and ensure that engine speed is below 1,000 rpm.

Race engine two or three times under no-load and run engine for about one minute at idle speed.

Check ignition timing with timing light.
M/T: 4±2° B.T.D.C.   A/T: 0±2° B.T.D.C.
→ O.K. / N.G.

N.G. → Adjust ignition timing to the specified valve by turning distributor after loosening distributor securing bolt.

Connect distributor vacuum hose to distributor vacuum controller.

Run engine at about 2,000 rpm for about 2 minutes under no-load.

Make sure that even if inspection lamp (Red) on control unit goes on, the green lamp goes on and off more than 9 times during 10 seconds at 2,000 rpm.
→ O.K. (C) / N.G. (D)

MIXTURE RATIO FEEDBACK INSPECTION CHART
1985–86 200SX WITH CA20E ENGINE

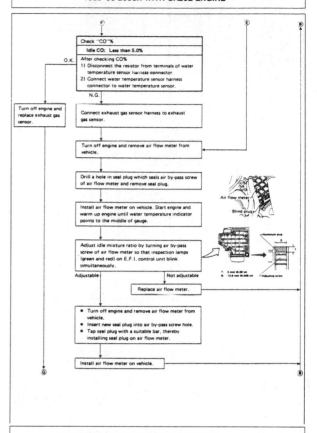

(F)

Check "CO"%
Idle CO: Less than 5.0%
→ O.K.

After checking CO%
1) Disconnect the resistor from terminals of water temperature sensor harness connector.
2) Connect water temperature sensor harness connector to water temperature sensor.
N.G.

O.K. → Turn off engine and replace exhaust gas sensor.

Connect exhaust gas sensor harness to exhaust gas sensor.

Turn off engine and remove air flow meter from vehicle.

Drill a hole in seal plug which seals air by-pass screw of air flow meter and remove seal plug.

Install air flow meter on vehicle. Start engine and warm up engine until water temperature indicator points to the middle of gauge.

Adjust idle mixture ratio by turning air by-pass screw of air flow meter so that inspection lamps (green and red) on E.F.I. control unit blink simultaneously.
Adjustable / Not adjustable

Not adjustable → Replace air flow meter.

• Turn off engine and remove air flow meter from vehicle.
• Insert new seal plug into air by-pass screw hole.
• Tap seal plug with a suitable bar, thereby installing seal plug on air flow meter.

Install air flow meter on vehicle.
(G)

MIXTURE RATIO FEEDBACK INSPECTION CHART
1985–86 200SX WITH CA20E ENGINE

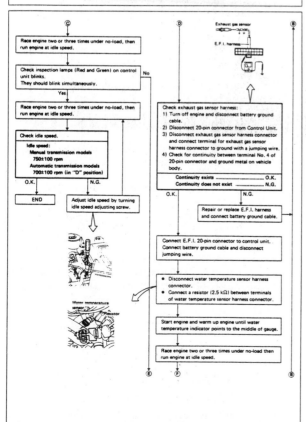

(C)

Race engine two or three times under no-load, then run engine at idle speed.

Check inspection lamps (Red and Green) on control unit blinks.
They should blink simultaneously.
→ Yes / No

Race engine two or three times under no-load, then run engine at idle speed.

Check idle speed.
Idle speed:
Manual transmission models
750±100 rpm
Automatic transmission models
700±100 rpm (in "D" position)
→ O.K. / N.G.

O.K. → END

N.G. → Adjust idle speed by turning idle speed adjusting screw.

(D) Exhaust gas sensor / E.F.I. harness

Check exhaust gas sensor harness:
1) Turn off engine and disconnect battery ground cable.
2) Disconnect 20-pin connector from Control Unit.
3) Disconnect exhaust gas sensor harness connector and connect terminal for exhaust gas sensor harness connector to ground with a jumping wire.
4) Check for continuity between terminal No. 4 of 20-pin connector and ground metal on vehicle body.
   Continuity exists .... O.K.
   Continuity does not exist .... N.G.
→ O.K. / N.G.

N.G. → Repair or replace E.F.I. harness and connect battery ground cable.

Connect E.F.I. 20-pin connector to control unit. Connect battery ground cable and disconnect jumping wire.

• Disconnect water temperature sensor harness connector.
• Connect a resistor (2.5 kΩ) between terminals of water temperature sensor harness connector.

Start engine and warm up engine until water temperature indicator points to the middle of gauge.

Race engine two or three times under no-load then run engine at idle speed.
(E) (F)

MIXTURE RATIO FEEDBACK INSPECTION CHART
1985–86 200SX WITH CA20E ENGINE

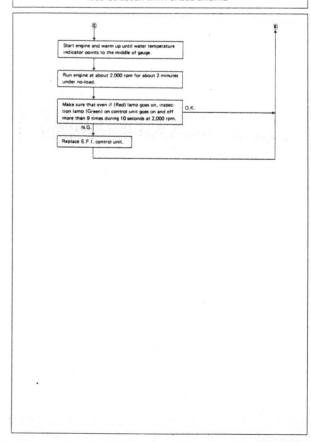

(G)

Start engine and warm up until water temperature indicator points to the middle of gauge.

Run engine at about 2,000 rpm for about 2 minutes under no-load.

Make sure that even if (Red) lamp goes on, inspection lamp (Green) on control unit goes on and off more than 9 times during 10 seconds at 2,000 rpm.
→ O.K. / N.G.

N.G. → Replace E.F.I. control unit.

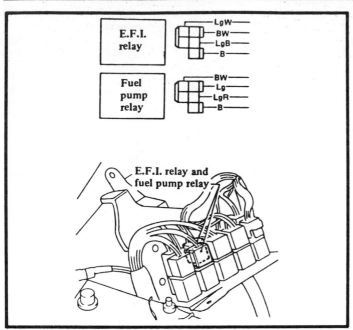

Fuel pump relay location—1984 Maximum

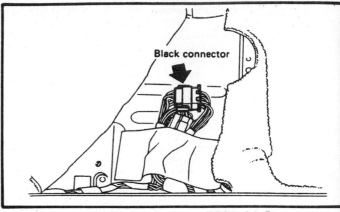

Fuel pump connector location—1984–86 Stanza

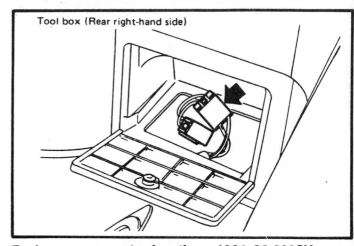

Fuel pump connector location—1984–86 200SX

COMPONENT TEST PROCEDURES

Releasing Fuel System Pressure

---------------- CAUTION ----------------

Fuel system pressure must be relieved before disconnecting any fuel lines or attempting to remove any fuel system components.

1984 MAXIMA

1. Remove relay bracket.
2. Start engine.
3. Disconnect harness connector of fuel pump relay while engine is running.
4. After engine stalls, crank engine two or three times.
5. Turn ignition switch OFF.
6. Reconnect harness connector of fuel pump relay.

1984–86 STANZA

1. Start engine.
2. Disconnect harness connector of body harness under assist seat while engine is running.
3. After engine stalls, crank engine two or three times.
4. Turn ignition switch OFF.
5. Reconnect harness connector of body harness to fuel pump.

1984–86 200SX

1. Start engine.
2. Disconnect harness connector of fuel pump (located in the tool box in right rear) with engine running.
3. After engine stalls, crank engine two or three times to make sure that pressure is released.
4. Turn ignition switch OFF and reconnect fuel pump connector.

Testing Fuel System Pressure

1. Relieve fuel system pressure as previously described.
2. Disconnect the fuel inlet hose between the fuel filter and fuel line on the engine side.
3. Install a fuel pressure gauge.
4. Start the engine and check the fuel line for leakage.

5. Read the pressure on the pressure gauge. It should be approximately 30 psi at idle and rise to 37 psi when the accelerator pedal is fully depressed.
6. Stop the engine and disconnect the fuel pressure regulator vacuum hose from the intake collector. Plug the intake collector with a rubber cap.
7. Connect a hand vacuum pump to the fuel pressure regulator.
8. Disconnect fuel pump connector and apply battery voltage to harness connector on the fuel pump side.
9. Read indication of fuel pressure gauge as vacuum is changed. Fuel pressure should decrease as vacuum increases. If results are unsatisfactory, replace fuel pressure regulator.
10 Relieve fuel system pressure again.
11 Remove the pressure gauge from the fuel line and reconnect the fuel inlet hose.

NOTE: When reconnecting a fuel line, always use a new clamp. Make sure that the screw of the clamp does not contact any adjacent parts and tighten the hose clamp to 1 ft. lb.

Component Replacement

INJECTOR AND FUEL PIPE

Removal and Installation
1984 MAXIMA L24E ENGINE

1. Relieve fuel pressure from system.

2. Disconnect electric connector from injector and cold start valve.

3. Disconnect harness from fuel pipe wire clamp.

4. Disconnect blow-by hose at rocker cover side.

5. Disconnect vacuum tube (connecting pressure regulator to intake manifold) from pressure regulator.

6. Remove air regulator pipe.

7. Disconnect fuel feed hose and fuel return from fuel pipe.

NOTE: Place a rag under fuel pipe to absorb any remaining fuel.

8. Remove bolts securing fuel pipe and cold start valve.

9. Remove screws securing fuel injectors.

10. Remove fuel pipe assembly by pulling out fuel pipe, injector, pressure regulator and cold start valve as an assembly.

11. Unfasten hose clamp on fuel injector and remove fuel injector from fuel pipe.

NOTE: Place a rag under fuel pipe to absorb any remaining fuel.

12. To install, reverse the removal procedure.

NOTE: When installing injector, check that there are no scratches or abrasion at lower rubber insulator, and securely install it, making sure it is air-tight.

1984–88 200SX CA20E ENGINE

1. Relieve fuel pressure from system.

2. Drain engine coolant.

3. Disconnect EFI harness from fuel injectors.

4. Disconnect ignition wire.

5. Remove hoses.

6. Remove collector with throttle chamber.

7. Disconnect fuel hoses and pressure regulator vacuum hose.

8. Remove injectors with fuel tube assembly.

9. Remove injector from fuel tube.

10. To install, reverse removal procedure.

1984 STANZA CA20E ENGINE

1. Relieve fuel pressure in system

2. Remove vacuum tubes and EFI harness.

3. Remove air regulator and PCV valve assembly.

4. Unfasten hose clamps.

5. Remove bolts securing fuel pipe assembly and bolts securing injectors.

6. Remove fuel pipe assembly with injectors.

7. Remove fuel hose.

8. To install, reverse removal procedure.

1985–86 STANZA CA20E ENGINE

1. Relieve fuel pressure from system.

2. Remove or disconnect the following:
- Inlet and outlet hoses
- EFI harness
- Pressure regulator vacuum hose
- Fuel pipe securing bolts
- Collector with throttle chamber
- Injector securing bolts

3. Remove injectors with fuel tube assembly.

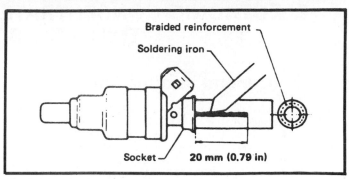

Fuel injector hose removal

4. Remove injector from fuel tube.

5. Remove fuel hose.

6. To install, reverse removal procedure.

INJECTOR RUBBER HOSE

Removal and Installation

1. On injector rubber hose, measure off a point approximately 0.79 in. (20mm) from socket end.

2. Heat soldering iron (150 watt) for 15 minutes. Cut hose into braided reinforcement from mark to socket end.

NOTE: Do not feed soldering iron until it touches injector tail piece. Be careful not to damage socket, plastic connector, etc. with solder iron. Never place injector in a vise when disconnecting rubber hose.

3. Pull rubber hose out with hand.

4. To install, clean exterior of injector tail piece.

5. Wet inside of new rubber hose with fuel.

6. Push end of rubber hose with hose socket onto injector tail piece by hand as far as it will go. Clamp is not necessary at this connection.

NOTE: After properly connecting fuel hose to injector, check connection for fuel leakage.

FUEL PRESSURE REGULATOR

Removal and Installation

1. Relieve fuel pressure from system.

2. Disengage vacuum tube connecting regulator to intake manifold from pressure regulator.

3. Remove screws securing pressure regulator.

4. Unfasten hose clamps, and disconnect pressure regulator from fuel hose.

NOTE: Place a rag under fuel pipe to absorb any remaining fuel.

5. To install, reverse the removal procedure.

ELECTRONIC CONCENTRATED CONTROL SYSTEM (ECCS) – THROTTLE BODY INJECTION

General Information

The Nissan Electro Injection System is a throttle body fuel injection system used on 1986–88 models equipped with the E16i, VG30i or Z24i engines. The electronic control unit consists of a microcomputer, inspection lamps, a diagnostic mode selector and connectors for signal input and output and for power supply. The Electronic Concentrated Control System (ECCS) computer controls the amount of fuel injected, ignition timing, mixture ratio feedback, idle speed, fuel pump operation, mixture heating, air injection valve (AIV) operation, exhaust gas recirculation (EGR) and vapor canister purge operation.

CRANK ANGLE SENSOR

The crank angle sensor is a basic component of the entire system. It monitors engine speed and piston position and sends other signals which the control unit uses to calculate ignition timing and other functions. The crank angle sensor has a rotor plate and a wave forming circuit. The rotor plate has 360 slits for 1° signals (engine speed) and 4 slits for 180° signals (crank angle). Light emitting diodes (LED's) and photo diodes are built in the wave forming circuit. When the rotor plate passes the space between the LED and the photo diode, the slits of the rotor plate continually cut the light which is sent to the photo diode from the LED, causing rough shaped pulses. These pulses are converted into on-off signals by the wave forming circuit and sent to the control unit as input signals.

AIR FLOW METER

The air flow meter measures the intake air flow rate by taking a part of the entire flow. Measurement are made in such a manner that the control unit receives electrical output signals varied by the amount of heat emitted from a hot wire placed in the stream of intake air. When intake air flows into the intake manifold through a route around the hot wire, the heat generated by the wire is taken away by the passing air. The amount of heat removed depends on the air flow, but the maximum temperature of the hot wire is automatically controlled, requiring more electrical current to maintain the controlled temperature in the wire as the amount of intake air increases. By measuring the amount of current necessary to maintain the hot wire temperature, the control unit measures the amount of intake air passing the wire and therefore knows the volume of air entering the engine.

WATER TEMPERATURE SENSOR

The water temperature sensor, located on the front side of the intake manifold, detects engine coolant temperature and sends signals to the control unit. The air temperature sensor is installed in the air cleaner and senses the temperature of the intake air. The water and air temperature sensors employs a thermistor which is sensitive to changes in temperature. The electrical resistance of a thermistor decreases as temperature rises.

EXHAUST GAS SENSOR

The exhaust gas sensor, which is placed in the exhaust pipe, monitors the amount of oxygen in the exhaust gas. The sensor is made of ceramic titania which changes electrical resistance at the ideal air/fuel ratio (14.7:1). The control unit supplies the

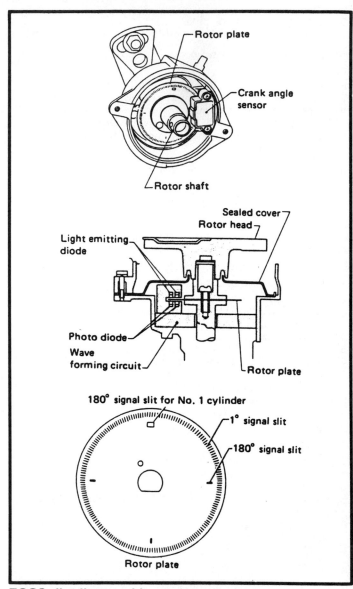

ECCS distributor with crank angle sensor

sensor with approximately 1 volt and takes the output voltage of the sensor depending on its resistance. The oxygen sensor is equipped with a heater to bring it to operating temperature quickly.

THROTTLE SENSOR/IDLE SWITCH

The throttle sensor/idle switch is attached to the throttle body and operates in response to accelerator pedal movement. This sensor has two functions; it contains an idle switch and throttle position sensor. The idle switch closes when the throttle valve is positioned at idle and opens when it is in any other position. The throttle sensor is a potentiometer which transforms the throttle valve position into output voltage and feeds the voltage signal to the control unit. In addition, the throttle sensor detects the

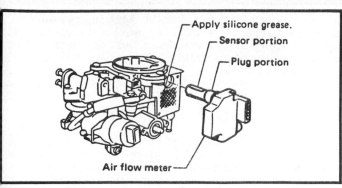

Air flow meter

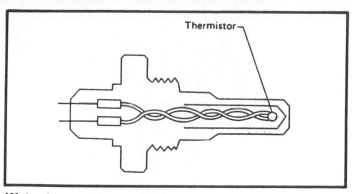

Water temperature sensor

opening or closing speed of the throttle valve and feeds the rate of voltage change to the control unit.

POWER STEERING OIL PRESSURE SWITCH

A power steering oil pressure switch is attached to the power steering high pressure line and detects the power steering load, sending a load signal to the control unit which then sends the idle-up signal to the idle speed control (ISC) valve.

FUEL PRESSURE REGULATOR

A fuel pressure regulator is built into the side of the throttle body. It maintains fuel pressure at a constant 14 psi. Since the injected fuel amount depends on injection pulse duration, it is necessary to keep the fuel pressure constant. The fuel pump with a fuel damper is located in the fuel tank. The pump is an electric, vane roller type.

FUEL INJECTOR

The fuel injector is basically a small solenoid valve. As the control unit sends injection signals to the injector, high pressure fuel, which is supplied to the coil built into the injector, pulls the ball valve back and the fuel is injected onto the throttle valve through the nozzle. The amount of injected fuel is controlled by the computer by means of longer or shorter signals (pulse duration) to the injector. A mixture heater is located between the throttle valve and the intake manifold. This is designed and operated for atomizing fuel in the cold engine start condition. The heater is also controlled by the computer.

MIXTURE HEATER

The mixture heater is located between the throttle valve and the intake manifold. This is designed and operated for atomizing fuel in the cold engine start condition. The ECU controls the heater.

IDLE SPEED CONTROL (ISC) VALVE

The idle speed control (ISC) valve is a rotary solenoid valve that receives a pulse signal from the control unit. This pulse signal determines the position of the slider, thereby varying bypass air quantity which raises or lowers the idle speed. The ISC valve has additional functions which include idle-up after cold start (fast idle), idle speed feedback control, idle-up for air conditioner and power steering (fast idle control device) and deceleration vacuum control.

POWER TRANSISTOR AND IGNITION COIL

The ignition signal from the ECU is amplified by the power

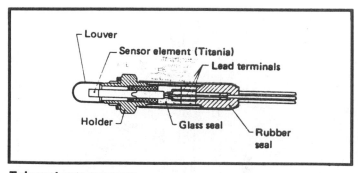

Exhaust gas sensor

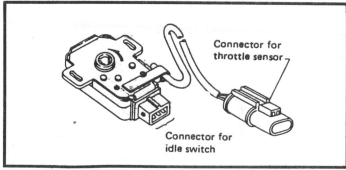

Throttle sensor and idle switch

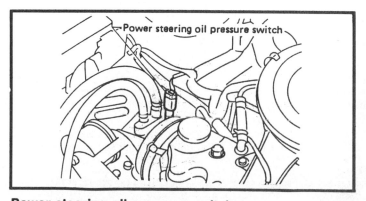

Power steering oil pressure switch

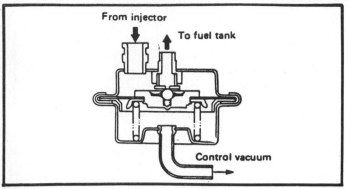

Fuel pressure regulator

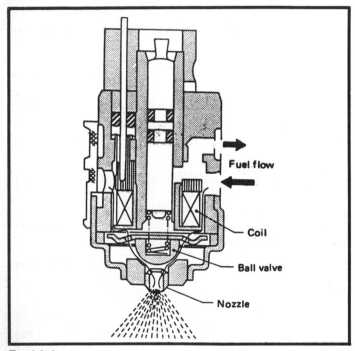

Fuel injector

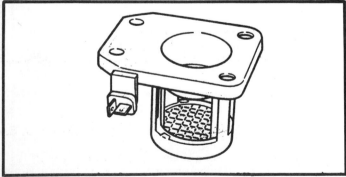

Mixture heater

transistor, which turns the ignition coil primary circuit on and off, inducing the proper high voltage in the secondary circuit. The ignition coil is a small, molded type.

ELECTRONIC CONTROL UNIT (ECU)

The ECU consists of a microcomputer, inspection lamps, a diag-nostic mode selector and connectors for signal input and output, and for power supply. The unit has control of the injected fuel amount, ignition timing, mixture ratio feedback, idle speed, fuel pump operation, mixture heating, AIV operation, and EGR and canister purge operation.

SYSTEM OPERATION

In operation, the on-board computer (control unit) calculates the basic injection pulse width by processing signals from the crank angle sensor and air flow meter. Receiving signals from each sensor which detects various engine operating conditions, the computer adds various enrichments (which are prepro-grammed) to the basic injection amount. In this manner, the op-timum amount of fuel is delivered through the injectors. The fuel is enriched when starting, during warm-up, when accelerat-ing and when operating under a heavy load. The fuel is leaned during deceleration according to the closing rate of the throttle valve.

The mixture ratio feedback system (closed loop control) is de-signed to control the air/fuel mixture precisely to the stoichio-metric or optimum point so that the three-way catalytic con-verter can minimize CO, HC and NOx emissions simultaneous-ly. The optimum air/fuel fuel mixture is 14.7:1. This system uses an exhaust gas (oxygen) sensor located in the exhaust man-ifold to give an indication of whether the fuel mixture is richer or leaner than the stoichiometric point. The control unit adjusts the injection pulse width according to the sensor voltage so the mixture ratio will be within the narrow window around the stoi-chiometric fuel ratio. The system goes into closed loop as soon as the oxygen sensor heats up enough to register. The system will operate under open loop when starting the engine, when the en-gine temperature is cold, when exhaust gas sensor temperature is cold, when driving at high speeds or under heavy load, at idle (after mixture ratio learning is completed), when the exhaust gas sensor monitors a rich condition for more than 10 seconds and during deceleration.

Ignition timing is controlled in response to engine operating conditions. The optimum ignition timing in each driving condi-tion is preprogrammed in the computer. The signal from the control unit is transmitted to the power transistor and controls ignition timing. The idle speed is also controlled according to en-gine operating conditions, temperature and gear position. On manual transmission models, if battery voltage is less than 12 volts for a few seconds, a higher idle speed will be maintained by the control unit to improve charging function.

The control unit energizes the mixture heating relay when the engine is running and the water temperature is below 122°F (50°C). The mixture heating relay will be shut off when several minutes have passed after the water temperature exceeds 122°F (50°C). In addition, the air injection valve (AIV), which supplies secondary air to the exhaust manifold, is controlled by the com-puter according to engine temperature. When the engine is cold, the AIV system operates to reduce HC and CO emissions. In ex-tremely cold conditions, the AIV control system does not oper-ate to reduce afterburning.

A signal from the control unit is also sent to the EGR and fuel vapor canister purge cut solenoid valve, which cuts the vacuum for the EGR and canister control valve. The EGR and canister purge activates when the vehicle speed is above 6 mph, the wa-ter temperature is above 140°F (60°C) and the engine is under light load at low rpm. The vacuum will be interrupted unless all of the conditions are met.

Finally, the control unit operates the air flow meter self-cleaning system. After the engine is stopped, the control unit heats up the hot wire to approximately 1832°F (1000°C) to burn off dust adhering to the hot wire. The self-cleaning function will activate if the engine speed has exceeded 2000 rpm before the key is turned off, vehicle speed has exceeded 12 mph before the

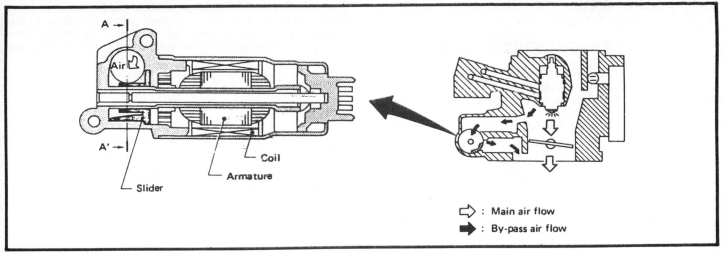

Idle speed control (ISC) valve

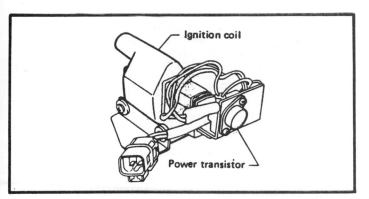

Power transistor and ignition coil

key is turned off, the water temperature is between 140–203°F (60–95°C), or the engine has been stopped by turning the ignition key OFF. Self-cleaning will be activated only if all of the above conditions are met. The hot wire will be heated for 0.3 seconds, 5 seconds after the ignition is switched OFF.

There is a fail-safe system built into the control unit should the air flow meter malfunction. If the air flow meter output voltage is higher or lower than the specified value, the control unit senses an air flow meter malfunction and substitutes the throttle sensor signal for the air flow meter input. It is possible to drive the vehicle and start the engine, but the engine speed will not rise more than 2400 rpm in order to inform the driver of fail-safe system operation while driving.

SERVICE PRECAUTIONS
- Do not operate the fuel pump when the fuel lines are empty.
- Do not reuse fuel hose clamps.
- Do not disconnect the ECCS harness connectors before the battery ground cable has been disconnected.
- Make sure all ECCS connectors are fastened securely. A poor connection can cause an extremely high surge voltage in the coil and condenser and result in damage to integrated circuits.
- Keep the ECCS harness at least 4 in. away from adjacent harnesses to prevent an ECCS system malfunction due to external electronic "noise."
- Keep all parts and harnesses dry during service.
- Before attempting to remove any parts, turn off the ignition switch and disconnect the battery ground cable.

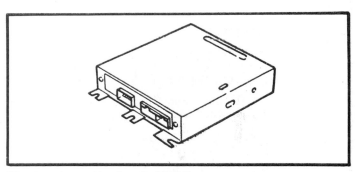

Electronic control unit (ECU)

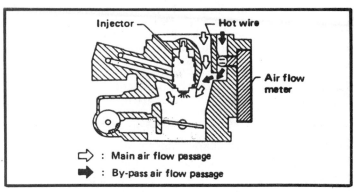

Throttle body air flow

- Always use a 12 volt battery as a power source.
- Do not attempt to disconnect the battery cables with the engine running.
- Do not depress the accelerator pedal when starting.
- Do not rev up the engine immediately after starting or just prior to shutdown.
- Do not attempt to disassemble the ECCS control unit under any circumstances.
- If a battery cable is disconnected, the memory will return to the ROM (programmed) values. Engine operation may vary slightly, but this is not an indication of a problem. Do not replace parts because of a slight variation.
- If installing a two-way or CB radio, keep the antenna as far as possible away from the electronic control unit. Keep the antenna feeder line at least 8 in. away from the ECCS harness and

do not let the two run parallel for a long distance. Be sure to ground the radio to the vehicle body.

SELF-DIAGNOSTIC SYSTEM

The self-diagnostic function is useful for diagnosing malfunctions in major sensors and actuators of the ECCS system. There are five modes in self-diagnostics:

Mode 1: Mixture Ratio Feedback Control Monitor A

During closed loop operation, the green inspection lamp turns ON when a lean condition is detected and OFF when a rich condition is detected. During open loop operation, the red inspection lamp stays OFF.

Mode 2: Mixture Ratio Feedback Control Monitor B

The green inspection lamp function is the same as in Mode 1. During closed loop operation, the red inspection lamp turns ON and OFF simultaneously with the green inspection lamp when the mixture ratio is controlled within the specified value. During open loop operation, the red inspection lamp stays OFF.

Mode 3: Self-Diagnosis

This mode is the same as the former self-diagnosis mode.

Mode 4: Switches On/Off Diagnosis

During this mode, the inspection lamps monitor the ON/OFF condition of the idle switch, starter switch and vehicle speed sensor.

In switches ON/OFF diagnosis system, ON/OFF operation of the following switches can be detected continuously:
- Idle switch
- Starter switch
- Vehicle speed sensor (if equipped)

1. Idle Switch and Starter Switch—The switches ON/OFF status at the point when mode IV is selected is stored in ECU memory. When either switch is turned from ON to OFF or OFF to ON, the red LED on ECU alternately comes on and goes off each time switching is detected.

2. Vehicle Speed Sensor—The switches ON/OFF status at the point when mode IV is selected is stored in ECU memory. When vehicle speed is 12 mph (20 km/h) or slower, the green LED on ECU is off. When vehicle speed exceeds 12 mph (20 km/h), the green LED on ECU comes ON.

Mode 5: Real Time Diagnosis

The moment a malfunction is detected, the display will be presented immediately by flashing the inspection lamps during the driving test.

In real time diagnosis, if any of the following items are judged to be faulty, a malfunction is indicated immediately:
- Crank angle sensor (180° signal and 1° signal)
- Ignition signal
- Air flow meter output signal
- Fuel pump

Consequently, this diagnosis is a very effective measure to diagnose whether the above systems cause the malfunction or not, during driving test. Compared with self-diagnosis, real time diagnosis is very sensitive, and can detect malfunctioning conditions in a moment. Further, items regarded to be malfunctions in this diagnosis are not stored in ECU memory.

To switch the modes, turn the ignition switch ON, then turn the diagnostic mode selector on the control unit fully clockwise and wait for the inspection lamps to flash. Count the number of flashes until the inspection lamps have flashed the number of the desired mode, then immediately turn the diagnostic mode selector fully counterclockwise.

NOTE: When the ignition switch is turned off during diagnosis in each mode, and then turned back on again after the power to the control unit has dropped off completely, the diagnosis will automatically return to Mode 1.

The stored memory will be lost if the battery terminal is disconnected, or Mode 4 is selected after selecting Mode 3. However, if the diagnostic mode selector is kept turned fully clockwise, it will continue to change in the order of Mode 1, 2, 3, etc., and in this case, the stored memory will not be erased.

In Mode 3, the self-diagnostic mode, the control unit constantly monitors the function of sensors and actuators regardless of ignition key position. If a malfunction occurs, the information is stored in the control unit and can be retrieved from the memory by turning on the diagnostic mode selector on the side of the control unit. When activated, the malfunction is indicated by flashing a red and green LED (also located on the control unit). Since all the self-diagnostic results are stored in the control unit memory, even intermittent malfunctions can be diagnosed. A malfunctioning part's group is indicated by the number of both red and green LED's flashing. First, the red LED flashes and the green flashes follow. The red LED refers to the number of tens, while the green refers to the number of units. If the red LED flashes twice and the green LED flashes once, a code 21 is being displayed. All malfunctions are classified by their trouble code number.

The diagnostic result is retained in the control unit memory until the starter is operated fifty times after a diagnostic item is judged to be malfunctioning. The diagnostic result will then be canceled automatically. If a diagnostic item which has been judged malfunctioning and stored in memory is again judged to be malfunctioning before the starter is operated fifty times, the second result will replace the previous one and stored in the memory until the starter is operated fifty more times.

In Mode 5 (real time diagnosis), if the crank angle sensor, ignition signal or air flow meter output signal are judged to be malfunctioning, the malfunction will be indicated immediately. This diagnosis is very effective for determining whether these systems are causing a malfunction during the driving test. Compared with self-diagnosis, real time diagnosis is very sensitive and can detect malfunctioning conditions immediately. However, malfunctioning items in this diagnosis mode are not stored in memory.

TESTING PRECAUTIONS

1. Before connecting or disconnecting control unit ECU harness connectors, make sure the ignition switch is OFF and the negative battery cable is disconnected to avoid the possibility of damage to the control unit.

2. When performing ECU input/output signal diagnosis, remove the pin terminal retainer from the 20 and 16-pin connectors to make it easier to insert tester probes into the connector.

3. When connecting or disconnecting pin connectors from the ECU, take care not to bend or break any pin terminals. Check that there are no bends or breaks on ECU pin terminals before attempting any connections.

4. Before replacing any ECU, perform the ECU input/output signal diagnosis to make sure the ECU is functioning properly or not.

5. After performing the Electronic Control System Inspection, perform the ECCS self-diagnosis and driving test.

6. When measuring supply voltage of ECU controlled components with a circuit tester, separate one tester probe from another. If the two tester probes accidentally make contact with each other during measurement, a short circuit will result and damage the power transistor in the ECU.

SELF-DIAGNOSTIC MODE III—ALL 1987 THROTTLE BODY MODEL CARS

SELF-DIAGNOSTIC PROCEDURE

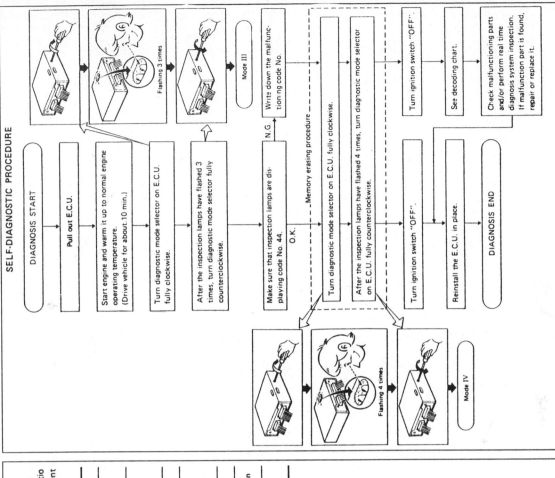

DIAGNOSIS START

Pull out E.C.U.

Start engine and warm it up to normal engine operating temperature. (Drive vehicle for about 10 min.)

Turn diagnostic mode selector on E.C.U. fully clockwise.

After the inspection lamps have flashed 3 times, turn diagnostic mode selector fully counterclockwise.

→ Mode III

Flashing 3 times

Make sure that inspection lamps are displaying code No. 44.

N.G → Write down the malfunctioning code No.

O.K. → Memory erasing procedure

Turn diagnostic mode selector on E.C.U. fully clockwise.

After the inspection lamps have flashed 4 times, turn diagnostic mode selector on E.C.U. fully counterclockwise.

→ Mode IV

Flashing 4 times

Turn ignition switch "OFF".

Reinstall the E.C.U. in place.

DIAGNOSIS END

Turn ignition switch "OFF".

See decoding chart.

Check malfunctioning parts and/or perform real time diagnosis system inspection. If malfunction part is found, repair or replace it.

CAUTION:
During displaying code No. in self-diagnosis mode (mode III), if the other diagnostic mode should be done, make sure to write down the malfunctioning code No. before turning diagnostic mode selector on E.C.U. fully clockwise, or select the diagnostic mode after turning switch "OFF". Otherwise self-diagnosis information stored in E.C.U. memory until now would be lost.

SELF-DIAGNOSTIC MODES I AND II
ALL 1987 THROTTLE BODY MODEL CARS, TRUCKS/PATHFINDERS AND VANS

Modes I & II — Mixture Ratio Feedback Control Monitors A & B

In these modes, the control unit provides the Air-fuel ratio monitor presentation and the Air-fuel ratio feedback coefficient monitor presentation.

Mode	LED	Engine stopped	Engine running	
			Open loop condition	Closed loop condition
Mode I (Monitor A)	Green	ON	OFF	• OFF: rich condition • ON: lean condition • Maintains conditions just before clamping
	Red	ON	OFF	OFF
Mode II (Monitor B)	Green	ON	OFF	• OFF: rich condition • ON: lean condition • Maintains conditions just before clamping

Compensating mixture ratio

	More than 5% rich	Between 5% lean and 5% rich	More than 5% lean
Red	OFF	Synchronized with green LED	ON

SELF-DIAGNOSTIC MODE III DISPLAY CODES
1987 THROTTLE BODY PULSAR AND SENTRA WITH E16 ENGINE

Control unit shows a malfunction signal when the following conditions are detected.

Display code	Malfunctioning circuit or parts	

CRANK ANGLE SENSOR

Code No. 11

Red → Green

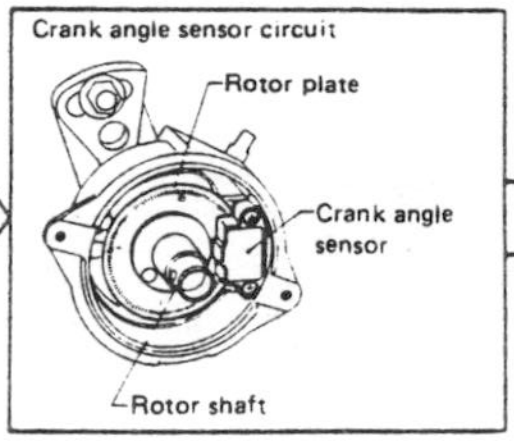

Crank angle sensor circuit

Rotor plate — Crank angle sensor
Rotor shaft

- Either 1° or 180° signal is not entered for the first few seconds during engine cranking.
- Either 1° or 180° signal is not input often enough while the engine speed is higher than the specified rpm.

AIR FLOW METER

Code No. 12

Red → Green

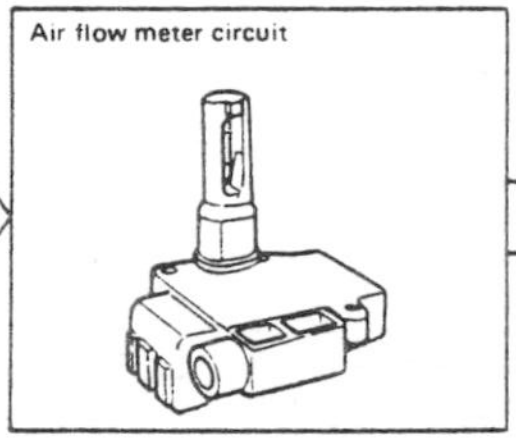

Air flow meter circuit

- The air flow meter circuit is open or shorted.
  (An abnormally high or low voltage is entered.)

WATER TEMPERATURE SENSOR

Code No. 13

Red → Green

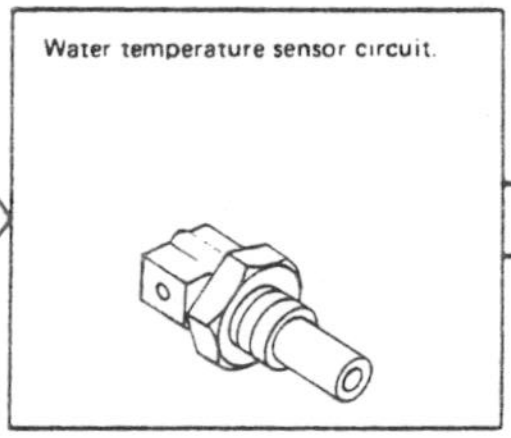

Water temperature sensor circuit.

- The water temperature sensor circuit is open or shorted.
  (An abnormally high or low output voltage is entered.)

IGNITION SIGNAL

Code No. 21

Red → Green

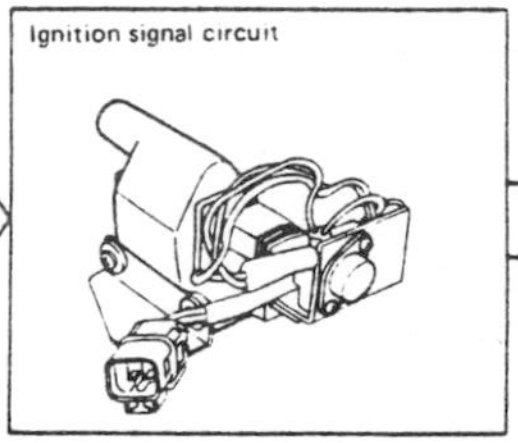

Ignition signal circuit

- The ignition signal in primary circuit is not entered during engine cranking or running.

SELF-DIAGNOSTIC MODE III
ALL 1987 THROTTLE BODY MODEL TRUCKS/PATHFINDER AND VAN

SELF-DIAGNOSTIC PROCEDURE

DIAGNOSIS START
↓
Pull out E.C.U.
↓
Start engine and warm it up to normal engine operating temperature. (Drive vehicle for about 10 min.)
↓
Turn diagnostic mode selector "ON".

ON → Flashing 3 times → OFF → Mode III

↓
After the inspection lamps have flashed 3 times, turn diagnostic mode selector "OFF".
↓
Make sure that inspection lamps are displaying code No. 44.

N.G. → Write down the malfunctioning code No.

O.K.
↓
- - - Memory erasing procedure - - -
↓
Turn diagnostic mode selector "ON".
↓
After the inspection lamps have flashed 4 times, turn diagnostic mode selector "OFF".
↓
Turn ignition switch "OFF".
↓
Reinstall the E.C.U. in place.
↓
DIAGNOSIS END

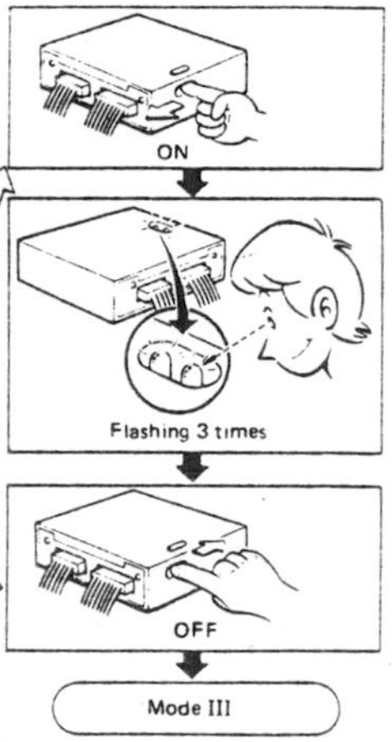

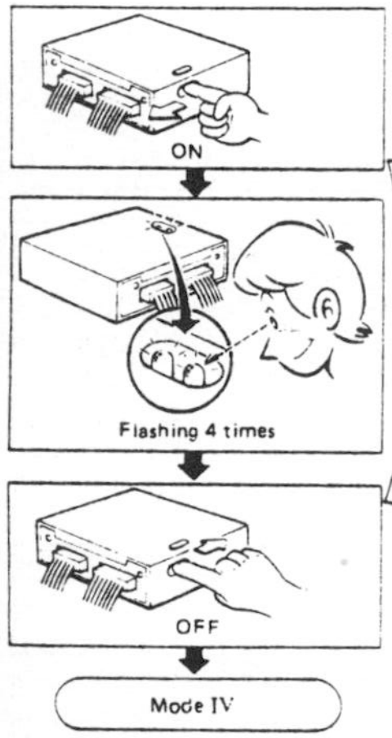

ON → Flashing 4 times → OFF → Mode IV

Write down the malfunctioning code No.
↓
Turn diagnostic mode selector "ON".
↓
After the inspection lamps have flashed 4 times, turn diagnostic mode selector "OFF".
↓
Turn ignition switch "OFF".
↓
See decoding chart.
↓
Check malfunctioning parts and/or perform real time diagnosis system inspection. If malfunction part is found, repair or replace it.

CAUTION:
During displaying code No. in self-diagnosis mode (mode III), if another diagnostic mode should be done, make sure to write down the malfunctioning code No. before turning diagnostic mode selector "ON", or select the giagnostic mode after turning ignition switch "OFF". Otherwise self-diagnosis information stored in E.C.U. memory until now would be lost.

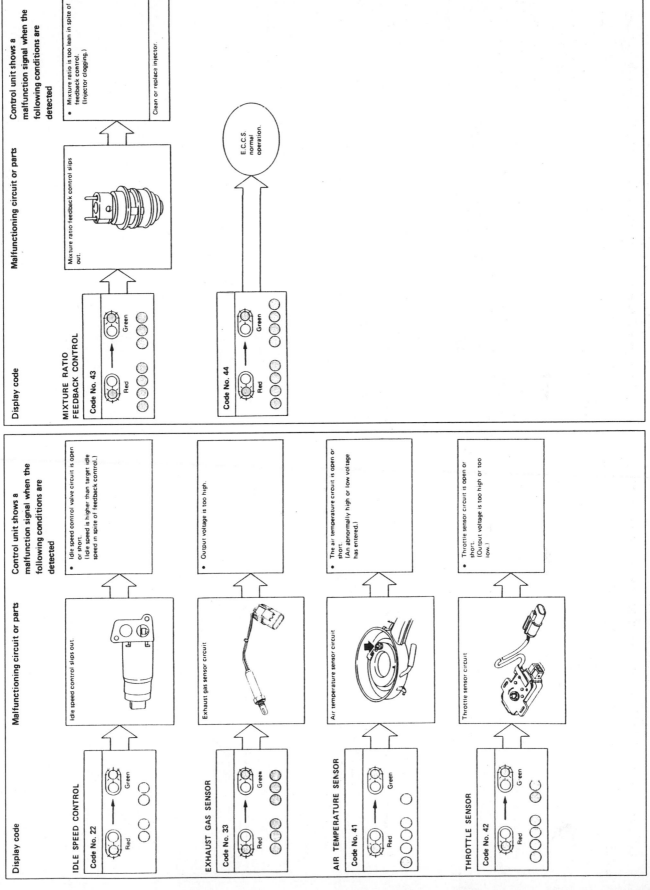

SELF-DIAGNOSTIC MODE III DISPLAY CODES
1987 THROTTLE BODY PULSAR AND SENTRA WITH E16 ENGINE

Display code	Malfunctioning circuit or parts	Control unit shows a malfunction signal when the following conditions are detected

MIXTURE RATIO FEEDBACK CONTROL

Code No. 43 — Mixture ratio feedback control slips out. — • Mixture ratio is too lean in spite of feedback control. (Injector clogging.) — Clean or replace injector.

Code No. 44 — E.C.C.S. normal operation.

SELF-DIAGNOSTIC MODE III DISPLAY CODES
1987 THROTTLE BODY PULSAR AND SENTRA WITH E16 ENGINE

Display code	Malfunctioning circuit or parts	Control unit shows a malfunction signal when the following conditions are detected

IDLE SPEED CONTROL

Code No. 22 — Idle speed control slips out. — • Idle speed control valve circuit is open or short. (Idle speed is higher than target idle speed in spite of feedback control.)

EXHAUST GAS SENSOR

Code No. 33 — Exhaust gas sensor circuit — • Output voltage is too high.

AIR TEMPERATURE SENSOR

Code No. 41 — Air temperature sensor circuit — • The air temperature circuit is open or short. (An abnormally high or low voltage has entered.)

THROTTLE SENSOR

Code No. 42 — Throttle sensor circuit — • Throttle sensor circuit is open or short. (Output voltage is too high or too low.)

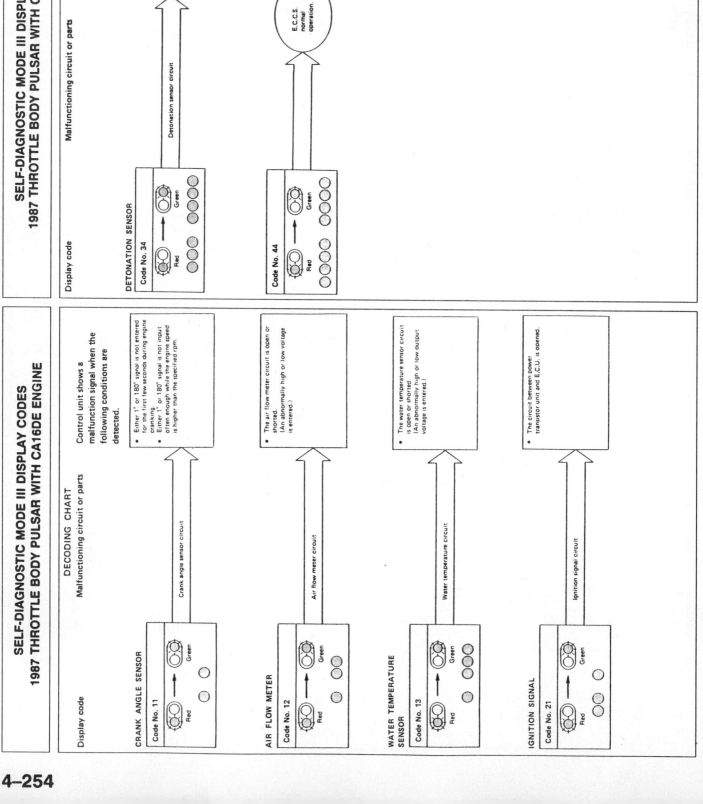

SELF-DIAGNOSTIC MODE III DISPLAY CODES
1987 THROTTLE BODY PULSAR WITH CA16DE ENGINE

DECODING CHART

Display code | Malfunctioning circuit or parts | Control unit shows a malfunction signal when the following conditions are detected.

CRANK ANGLE SENSOR

Code No. 11 — Crank angle sensor circuit
- Either 1° or 180° signal is not entered for the first few seconds during engine cranking.
- Either 1° or 180° signal is not input often enough while the engine speed is higher than the specified rpm.

AIR FLOW METER

Code No. 12 — Air flow meter circuit
- The air flow meter circuit is open or shorted. (An abnormally high or low voltage is entered.)

WATER TEMPERATURE SENSOR

Code No. 13 — Water temperature circuit
- The water temperature sensor circuit is open or shorted. (An abnormally high or low output voltage is entered.)

IGNITION SIGNAL

Code No. 21 — Ignition signal circuit
- The circuit between power transistor unit and E.C.U. is opened.

SELF-DIAGNOSTIC MODE III DISPLAY CODES
1987 THROTTLE BODY PULSAR WITH CA16DE ENGINE

Display code | Malfunctioning circuit or parts | Control unit shows a malfunction signal when the following conditions are detected

DETONATION SENSOR

Code No. 34 — Detonation sensor circuit
- The detonation sensor circuit is open or shorted.

Code No. 44 — E.C.C.S. normal operation.

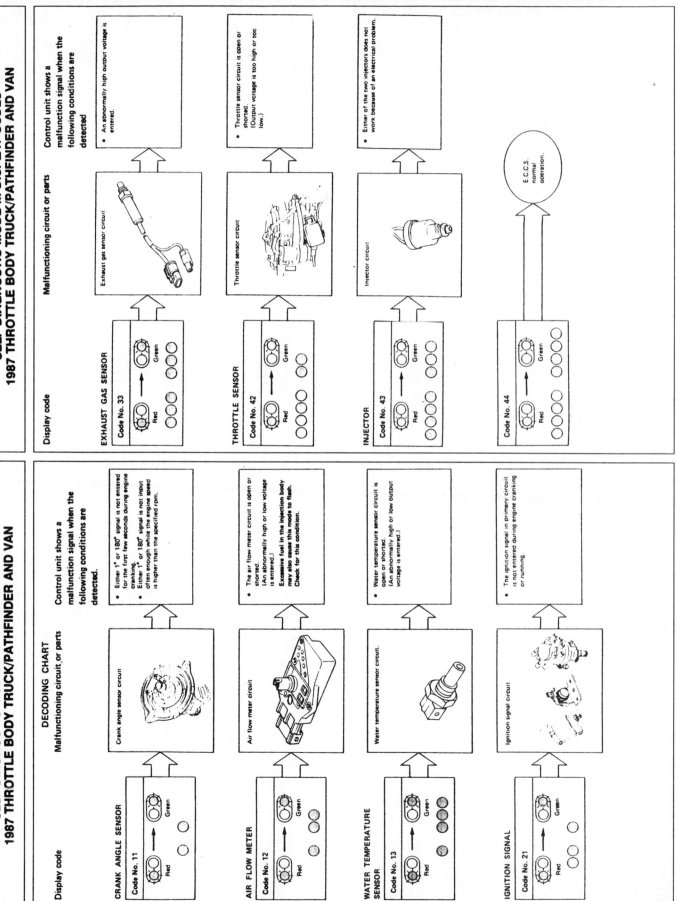

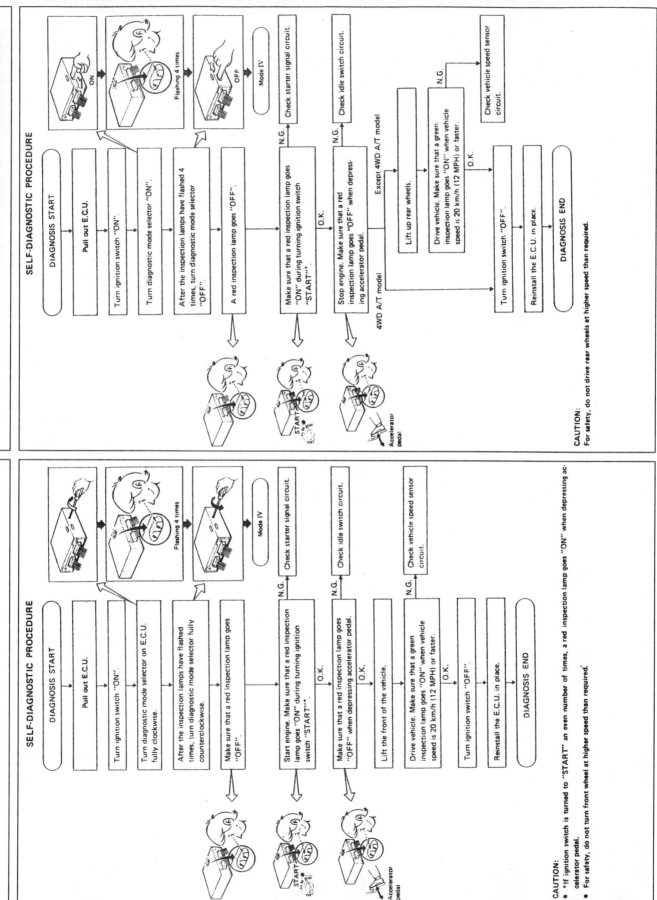

SELF-DIAGNOSTIC MODE IV
ALL 1987 THROTTLE BODY MODEL TRUCKS/PATHFINDER AND VAN

SELF-DIAGNOSTIC PROCEDURE

- DIAGNOSIS START
- Pull out E.C.U.
- Turn ignition switch "ON".
- Turn diagnostic mode selector "ON".
- After the inspection lamps have flashed 4 times, turn diagnostic mode selector "OFF".
- A red inspection lamp goes "OFF".
- Make sure that a red inspection lamp goes "ON" during turning ignition switch "START"*. → N.G. → Check starter signal circuit.
- O.K.
- Stop engine. Make sure that a red inspection lamp goes "OFF" when depressing accelerator pedal. → N.G. → Check idle switch circuit.
- 4WD A/T model / Except 4WD A/T model
- Lift up rear wheels.
- Drive vehicle. Make sure that a green inspection lamp goes "ON" when vehicle speed is 20 km/h (12 MPH) or faster. → N.G. → Check vehicle speed sensor circuit.
- O.K.
- Turn ignition switch "OFF".
- Reinstall the E.C.U. in place.
- DIAGNOSIS END

CAUTION:
For safety, do not drive rear wheels at higher speed than required.

SELF-DIAGNOSTIC MODE IV—ALL 1987 THROTTLE BODY MODEL CARS

SELF-DIAGNOSTIC PROCEDURE

- DIAGNOSIS START
- Pull out E.C.U.
- Turn ignition switch "ON".
- Turn diagnostic mode selector on E.C.U. fully clockwise.
- After the inspection lamps have flashed 4 times, turn diagnostic mode selector fully counterclockwise.
- Make sure that a red inspection lamp goes "OFF".
- Start engine. Make sure that a red inspection lamp goes "ON" during turning ignition switch "START"*. → N.G. → Check starter signal circuit.
- O.K.
- Make sure that a red inspection lamp goes "OFF" when depressing accelerator pedal. → N.G. → Check idle switch circuit.
- O.K.
- Lift the front of the vehicle.
- Drive vehicle. Make sure that a green inspection lamp goes "ON" when vehicle speed is 20 km/h (12 MPH) or faster. → N.G. → Check vehicle speed sensor circuit.
- O.K.
- Turn ignition switch "OFF".
- Reinstall the E.C.U. in place.
- DIAGNOSIS END

CAUTION:
- *If ignition switch is turned to "START" an even number of times, a red inspection lamp goes "ON" when depressing accelerator pedal.
- For safety, do not turn front wheel at higher speed than required.

SELF-DIAGNOSTIC MODE V
ALL 1987 THROTTLE BODY MODEL TRUCKS/PATHFINDER AND VAN

In real time diagnosis, if any of the following items are judged to be faulty, a malfunction is indicated immediately.

- Crank angle sensor (120° signal & 1° signal)
- Ignition signal
- Air flow meter output signal

Consequently, this diagnosis is a very effective measure to diagnose whether the above systems cause the malfunction or not, during driving test. Compared with self-diagnosis, real time diagnosis is very sensitive, and can detect malfunctioning conditions in a moment. Further, items regarded to be malfunctions in this diagnosis are not stored in E.C.U. memory.

SELF-DIAGNOSTIC PROCEDURE

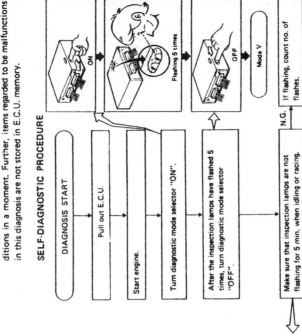

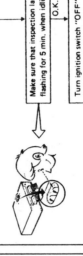

DIAGNOSIS START

Pull out E.C.U.

Start engine.

Turn diagnostic mode selector "ON".

After the inspection lamps have flashed 5 times, turn diagnostic mode selector "OFF".

Make sure that inspection lamps are not flashing for 5 min. when idling or racing.

N.G. → If flashing, count no. of flashes. → Turn ignition switch "OFF". → See decoding chart. → Perform real time-diagnosis system inspection. If malfunction part is found, repair or replace it.

O.K.

Turn ignition switch "OFF".

Reinstall the E.C.U. in place.

DIAGNOSIS END

CAUTION:
In real time diagnosis, pay attention to inspection lamp flashing. E.C.U. displays the malfunction code only once, and does not memorize the inspection.

SELF-DIAGNOSTIC MODE V – ALL 1987 THROTTLE BODY MODEL CARS

SELF-DIAGNOSITC PROCEDURE

DIAGNOSIS START

Pull out E.C.U.

Start engine.

Turn diagnostic mode selector on E.C.U. fully clockwise.

After the inspection lamps have flashed 5 times, turn diagnostic mode selector fully counterclockwise.

Make sure that inspection lamps are not flashing for 5 min. when idling or racing.

N.G. → If flashing, count no. of flashes. → Turn ignition switch "OFF". → See decoding chart. → Perform real time-diagnosis system inspection. If malfunction part is found, repair or replace it.

O.K.

Turn ignition switch "OFF".

Reinstall the E.C.U. in place.

DIAGNOSIS END

CAUTION:
In real time diagnosis, pay attention to inspection lamp flashing. E.C.U. displays the malfunction code only once, and does not memorize the inspection.

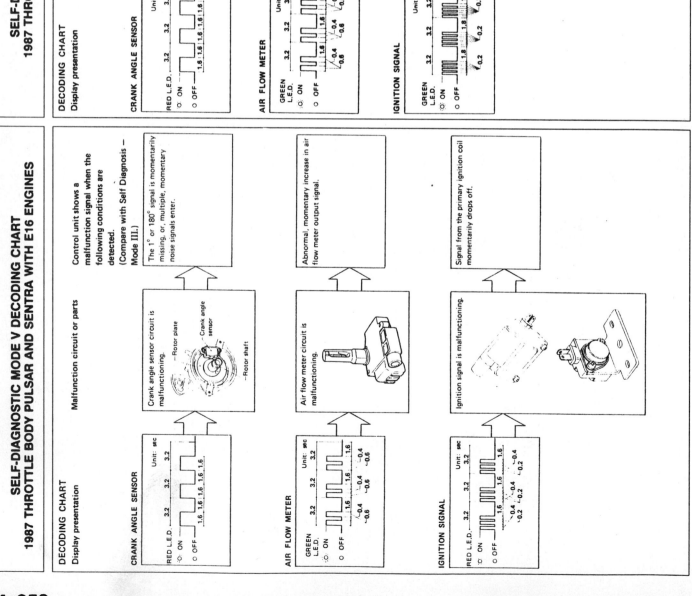

SELF-DIAGNOSTIC MODE V DECODING CHART
1987 THROTTLE BODY TRUCK/PATHFINDER AND VAN

DECODING CHART
Display presentation

Malfunction circuit or parts

Control unit shows a malfunction signal when the following conditions are detected.
(Compare with Self Diagnosis — Mode III.)

CRANK ANGLE SENSOR
Unit: sec

Crank angle sensor circuit is malfunctioning.

The 1° or 120° signal is momentarily missing, or, multiple, momentary noise signals enter.

AIR FLOW METER
Unit: sec

Air flow meter circuit is malfunctioning.

Abnormal, momentary increase in air flow meter output signal.

IGNITION SIGNAL
Unit: sec

Ignition signal is malfunctioning.

Signal from the primary ignition coil momentarily drops off.

SELF-DIAGNOSTIC MODE V DECODING CHART
1987 THROTTLE BODY PULSAR AND SENTRA WITH E16 ENGINES

DECODING CHART
Display presentation

Malfunction circuit or parts

Control unit shows a malfunction signal when the following conditions are detected.
(Compare with Self Diagnosis — Mode III.)

CRANK ANGLE SENSOR
Unit: sec

Crank angle sensor circuit is malfunctioning.

The 1° or 180° signal is momentarily missing, or, multiple, momentary noise signals enter.

AIR FLOW METER
Unit: sec

Air flow meter circuit is malfunctioning.

Abnormal, momentary increase in air flow meter output signal.

IGNITION SIGNAL
Unit: sec

Ignition signal is malfunctioning.

Signal from the primary ignition coil momentarily drops off.

MAINTENANCE REMINDER LIGHTS

Exhaust gas sensor should be checked after every 30,000 miles (48,000 km) of operation. At this time, the exhaust gas sensor warning lamp will come on to indicate that the sensor should be inspected. After inspecting and/or replacing the sensor, the sensor warning lamp should be reset. On 1984, most 1985 and Canada models, the sensor light connector is disconnected and further maintenance is not required. On 1985 Maxima and most 1986–88 models, a warning light hold relay must be located and reset at the 30,000 mile (48,000 km) and 60,000 mile (96,000 km) intervals. At 90,000 miles (144,000 km), the sensor warning light is disabled by disconnecting the sensor light connector.

SENSOR LIGHT CONNECTOR LOCATION

- 1987–88 Pulsar NX—Above fuse box
- 1987–88 Sentra—Above fuse box

SENSOR LIGHT HOLD RELAY LOCATION

- 1986 Truck (California)—Right kick panel
- 1987–88 Pulsar NX—Left kick panel
- 1987–88 Sentra—Right kick panel

Keys to symbols

 : Check after disconnecting the connector to be measured.

 : Check after connecting the connector to be measured.

When measuring voltage or resistance at connector with tester probes, there are two methods of measurement; one is done from terminal side and the other from harness side. Before measuring, confirm symbol mark again.

 : Inspection should be done from harness side.

 : Inspection should be done from terminal side.

ELECTRONIC CONTROL UNIT (ECI) LOCATION:

- 1986–87 Truck/Pathfinder—Under right (passenger) seat
- 1987 Van—Behind left (driver) trim panel behind driver's seat
- 1987 Pulsar NX—Under right (passenger) seat
- 1987 Sentra—Under right (passenger) seat

ECCS SELF-DIAGNOSTIC CHART
1987 THROTTLE BODY SENTRA AND PULSAR

CRANK ANGLE SENSOR (Code No. 11)

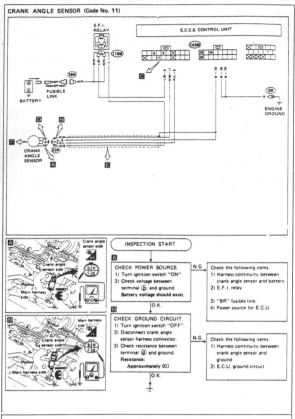

INSPECTION START

CHECK POWER SOURCE.
1) Turn ignition switch "ON".
2) Check voltage between terminal ⓑ and ground.
Battery voltage should exist.

N.G. → Check the following items.
1) Harness continuity between crank angle sensor and battery.
2) E.F.I. relay.
3) "BR" fusible link.
4) Power source for E.C.U.

O.K.

CHECK GROUND CIRCUIT.
1) Turn ignition switch "OFF".
2) Disconnect crank angle sensor connector.
3) Check resistance between terminal ⓓ and ground.
Resistance:
Approximately 0Ω

N.G. → Check the following items.
1) Harness continuity between crank angle sensor and ground
2) E.C.U. ground circuit

O.K.

ECCS SELF-DIAGNOSTIC CHART
1987 THROTTLE BODY SENTRA AND PULSAR

AIR FLOW METER (Code No. 12)

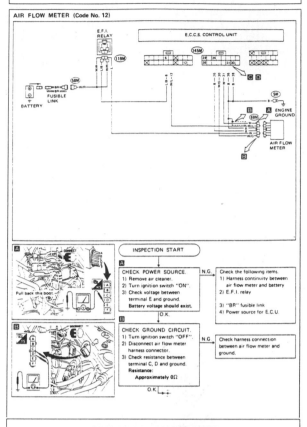

INSPECTION START

CHECK POWER SOURCE.
1) Remove air cleaner.
2) Turn ignition switch "ON".
3) Check voltage between terminal E and ground.
Battery voltage should exist.

N.G. → Check the following items.
1) Harness continuity between air flow meter and battery
2) E.F.I. relay
3) "BR" fusible link
4) Power source for E.C.U.

O.K.

CHECK GROUND CIRCUIT.
1) Turn ignition switch "OFF".
2) Disconnect air flow meter harness connector.
3) Check resistance between terminal C, D and ground.
Resistance:
Approximately 0Ω

N.G. → Check harness connection between air flow meter and ground.

O.K.

ECCS SELF-DIAGNOSTIC CHART
1987 THROTTLE BODY SENTRA AND PULSAR

CRANK ANGLE SENSOR (Code No. 11)

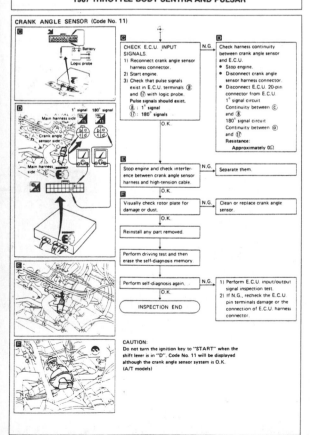

CHECK E.C.U. INPUT SIGNALS.
1) Reconnect crank angle sensor harness connector.
2) Start engine.
3) Check that pulse signals exist in E.C.U. terminals ⑧ and ⑰ with logic probe.
Pulse signals should exist.
⑧ : 1° signal
⑰ : 180° signals

N.G. → Check harness continuity between crank angle sensor and E.C.U.
• Stop engine.
• Disconnect crank angle sensor harness connector.
• Disconnect E.C.U. 20-pin connector from E.C.U.
1° signal circuit
Continuity between ⓒ and ⑧.
180° signal circuit
Continuity between ⓓ and ⑰.
Resistance:
Approximately 0Ω

O.K.

Stop engine and check interference between crank angle sensor harness and high-tension cable.

N.G. → Separate them.

O.K.

Visually check rotor plate for damage or dust.

N.G. → Clean or replace crank angle sensor.

O.K.

Reinstall any part removed.

Perform driving test and then erase the self-diagnosis memory.

Perform self-diagnosis again.

N.G. → 1) Perform E.C.U. input/output signal inspection test.
2) If N.G., recheck the E.C.U. pin terminals damage or the connection of E.C.U. harness connector.

O.K.

INSPECTION END

CAUTION:
Do not turn the ignition key to "START" when the shift lever is in "D". Code No. 11 will be displayed although the crank angle sensor system is O.K.
(A/T models)

ECCS SELF-DIAGNOSTIC CHART
1987 THROTTLE BODY SENTRA AND PULSAR

AIR FLOW METER (Code No. 12)

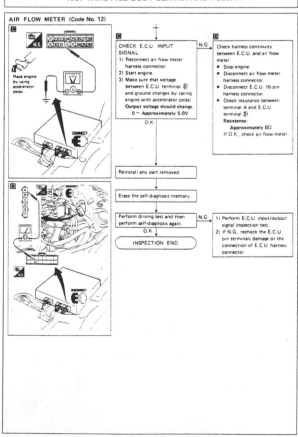

CHECK E.C.U. INPUT SIGNAL.
1) Reconnect air flow meter harness connector.
2) Start engine.
3) Make sure that voltage between E.C.U. terminal ㉛ and ground changes by racing engine with accelerator pedal.
Output voltage should change.
0 ~ Approximately 5.0V

N.G. → Check harness continuity between E.C.U. and air flow meter.
• Stop engine.
• Disconnect air flow meter harness connector.
• Disconnect E.C.U. 16-pin harness connector.
• Check resistance between terminal A and E.C.U. terminal ㉛.
Resistance:
Approximately 0Ω
If O.K., check air flow meter.

O.K.

Reinstall any part removed

Erase the self-diagnosis memory.

Perform driving test and then perform self-diagnosis again.

N.G. → 1) Perform E.C.U. input/output signal inspection test.
2) If N.G., recheck the E.C.U. pin terminals damage or the connection of E.C.U. harness connector.

O.K.

INSPECTION END

ECCS SELF-DIAGNOSTIC CHART
1987 THROTTLE BODY SENTRA AND PULSAR

WATER TEMPERATURE SENSOR (Code No. 13)

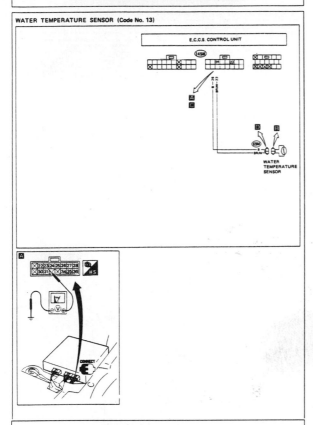

ECCS SELF-DIAGNOSTIC CHART
1987 THROTTLE BODY SENTRA AND PULSAR

IGNITION SIGNAL (Code No. 21)

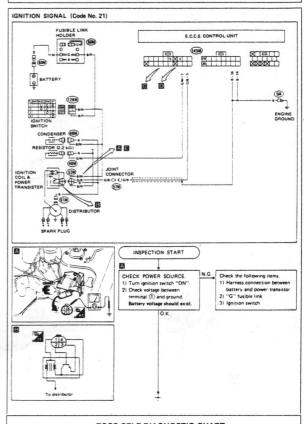

ECCS SELF-DIAGNOSTIC CHART
1987 THROTTLE BODY SENTRA AND PULSAR

WATER TEMPERATURE SENSOR (Code No. 13)

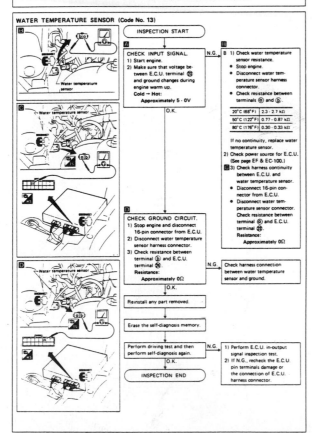

ECCS SELF-DIAGNOSTIC CHART
1987 THROTTLE BODY SENTRA AND PULSAR

IGNITION SIGNAL (Code No. 21)

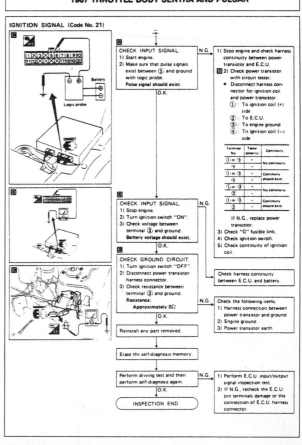

ECCS SELF-DIAGNOSTIC CHART
1987 THROTTLE BODY SENTRA AND PULSAR

IDLE SPEED CONTROL VALVE (Code No. 22)

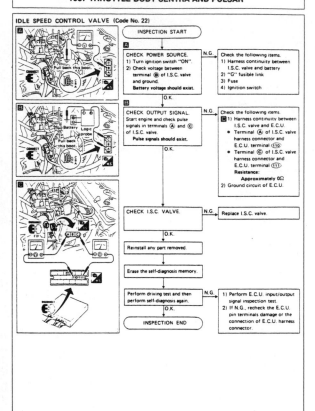

ECCS SELF-DIAGNOSTIC CHART
1987 THROTTLE BODY SENTRA AND PULSAR

EXHAUST GAS SENSOR (Code No. 33)

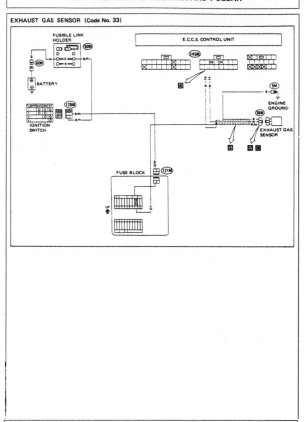

ECCS SELF-DIAGNOSTIC CHART
1987 THROTTLE BODY SENTRA AND PULSAR

IDLE SPEED CONTROL VALVE (Code No. 22)

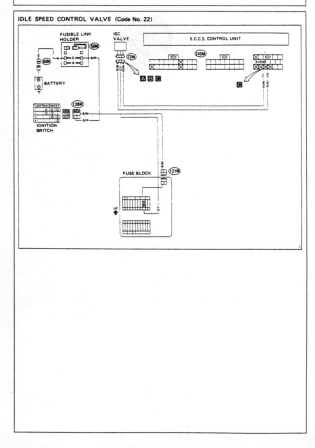

ECCS SELF-DIAGNOSTIC CHART
1987 THROTTLE BODY SENTRA AND PULSAR

EXHAUST GAS SENSOR (Code No. 33)

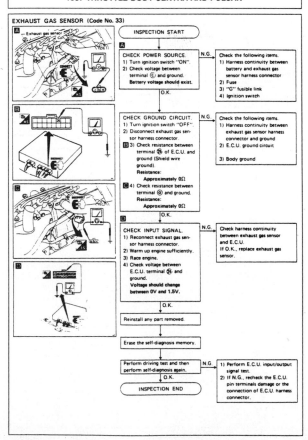

ECCS SELF-DIAGNOSTIC CHART
1987 THROTTLE BODY SENTRA AND PULSAR

AIR TEMPERATURE SENSOR (Code No. 41)

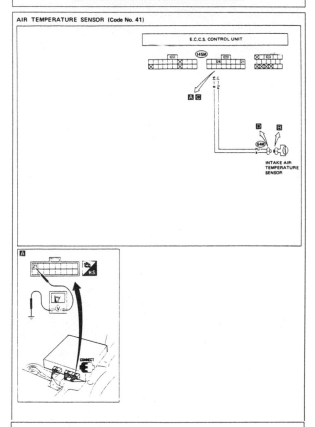

ECCS SELF-DIAGNOSTIC CHART
1987 THROTTLE BODY SENTRA AND PULSAR

THROTTLE SENSOR (Code No. 42)

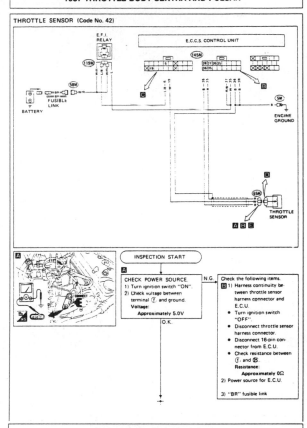

INSPECTION START

CHECK POWER SOURCE.
1) Turn ignition switch "ON".
2) Check voltage between terminal (1) and ground.
   Voltage:
   Approximately 5.0V

N.G. → Check the following items.
B 1) Harness continuity between throttle sensor harness connector and E.C.U.
- Turn ignition switch "OFF".
- Disconnect throttle sensor harness connector.
- Disconnect 16-pin connector from E.C.U.
- Check resistance between (1) and (25).
  Resistance:
  Approximately 0Ω
2) Power source for E.C.U.

3) "BR" fusible link

ECCS SELF-DIAGNOSTIC CHART
1987 THROTTLE BODY SENTRA AND PULSAR

AIR TEMPERATURE SENSOR (Code No. 41)

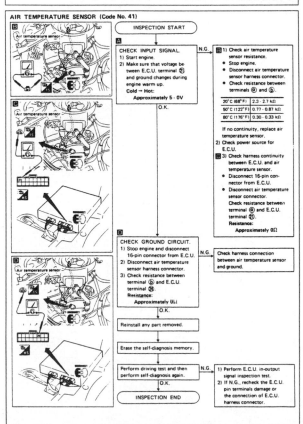

INSPECTION START

CHECK INPUT SIGNAL.
1) Start engine.
2) Make sure that voltage between E.C.U. terminal (21) and ground changes during engine warm up.
   Cold → Hot:
   Approximately 5 - 0V

N.G. → B 1) Check air temperature sensor resistance.
- Stop engine.
- Disconnect air temperature sensor harness connector.
- Check resistance between terminals (a) and (b).

20°C (68°F)	2.3 - 2.7 kΩ
50°C (122°F)	0.77 - 0.87 kΩ
80°C (176°F)	0.30 - 0.33 kΩ

If no continuity, replace air temperature sensor.
2) Check power source for E.C.U.
B 3) Check harness continuity between E.C.U. and air temperature sensor.
- Disconnect 16-pin connector from E.C.U.
- Disconnect air temperature sensor connector.
  Check resistance between terminal (a) and E.C.U. terminal (21).
  Resistance:
  Approximately 0Ω

CHECK GROUND CIRCUIT.
1) Stop engine and disconnect 16-pin connector from E.C.U.
2) Disconnect air temperature sensor harness connector.
3) Check resistance between terminal (b) and E.C.U. terminal (26).
   Resistance:
   Approximately 0Ω

N.G. → Check harness connection between air temperature sensor and ground.

Reinstall any part removed.

Erase the self-diagnosis memory.

Perform driving test and then perform self-diagnosis again.

N.G. → 1) Perform E.C.U. in-output signal inspection test.
2) If N.G., recheck the E.C.U. pin terminals damage or the connection of E.C.U. harness connector.

INSPECTION END

ECCS SELF-DIAGNOSTIC CHART
1987 THROTTLE BODY SENTRA AND PULSAR

THROTTLE SENSOR (Code No. 42)

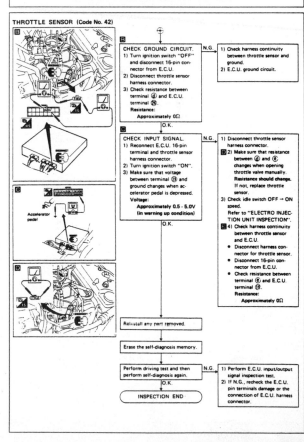

CHECK GROUND CIRCUIT.
1) Turn ignition switch "OFF" and disconnect 16-pin connector from E.C.U.
2) Disconnect throttle sensor harness connector.
3) Check resistance between terminal (d) and E.C.U. terminal (26).
   Resistance:
   Approximately 0Ω

N.G. → 1) Check harness continuity between throttle sensor and ground.
2) E.C.U. ground circuit.

CHECK INPUT SIGNAL.
1) Reconnect E.C.U. 16-pin terminal and throttle sensor harness connector.
2) Turn ignition switch "ON".
3) Make sure that voltage between terminal (19) and ground changes when accelerator pedal is depressed.
   Voltage:
   Approximately 0.5 - 5.0V
   (in warning up condition)

N.G. → 1) Disconnect throttle sensor harness connector.
B 2) Make sure that resistance between (d) and (e) changes when opening throttle valve manually. **Resistance should change.** If not, replace throttle sensor.
3) Check idle switch OFF → ON speed.
   Refer to "ELECTRO INJECTION UNIT INSPECTION".
B 4) Check harness continuity between throttle sensor and E.C.U.
- Disconnect harness connector for throttle sensor.
- Disconnect 16-pin connector from E.C.U.
- Check resistance between terminal (e) and E.C.U. terminal (19).
  Resistance:
  Approximately 0Ω

Reinstall any part removed.

Erase the self-diagnosis memory.

Perform driving test and then perform self-diagnosis again.

N.G. → 1) Perform E.C.U. input/output signal inspection test.
2) If N.G., recheck the E.C.U. pin terminals damage or the connection of E.C.U. harness connector.

INSPECTION END

ECCS SELF-DIAGNOSTIC CHART
1987 THROTTLE BODY SENTRA AND PULSAR

THROTTLE SENSOR (Code No. 42)

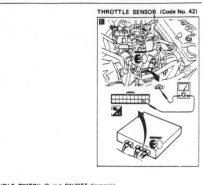

IDLE SWITCH (Switch ON/OFF diagnosis)

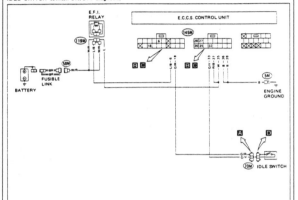

ECCS SELF-DIAGNOSTIC CHART
1987 THROTTLE BODY SENTRA AND PULSAR

START SIGNAL (Switch ON/OFF diagnosis)

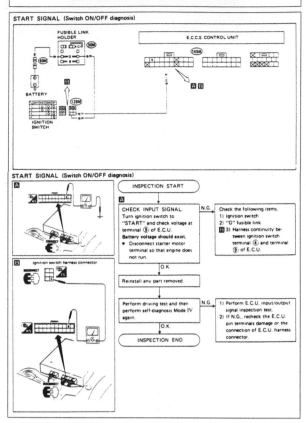

START SIGNAL (Switch ON/OFF diagnosis)

INSPECTION START

CHECK INPUT SIGNAL.
Turn ignition switch to "START" and check voltage at terminal ⑨ of E.C.U.
Battery voltage should exist.
• Disconnect starter motor terminal so that engine does not run.

N.G. → Check the following items.
1) Ignition switch
2) "G" fusible link
3) Harness continuity between ignition switch terminal ④ and terminal ⑨ of E.C.U.

O.K.

Reinstall any part removed.

Perform driving test and then perform self-diagnosis Mode IV again.

N.G. → 1) Perform E.C.U. input/output signal inspection test.
2) If N.G., recheck the E.C.U. pin terminals damage or the connection of E.C.U. harness connector.

O.K.

INSPECTION END

ECCS SELF-DIAGNOSTIC CHART
1987 THROTTLE BODY SENTRA AND PULSAR

IDLE SWITCH (Switch ON/OFF diagnosis)

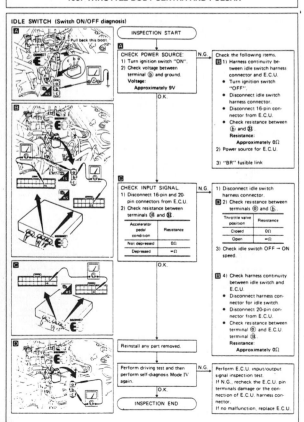

INSPECTION START

CHECK POWER SOURCE:
1) Turn ignition switch "ON".
2) Check voltage between terminal ⓑ and ground.
Voltage: Approximately 9V

N.G. → Check the following items.
1) Harness continuity between idle switch harness connector and E.C.U.
• Turn ignition switch "OFF".
• Disconnect idle switch harness connector.
• Disconnect 16-pin connector from E.C.U.
• Check resistance between ⓑ and ㉝.
Resistance: Approximately 0Ω
2) Power source for E.C.U.
3) "BR" fusible link

O.K.

CHECK INPUT SIGNAL.
1) Disconnect 16-pin and 20-pin connectors from E.C.U.
2) Check resistance between terminals ⑯ and ㉛.

Accelerator pedal condition	Resistance
Not depressed	0Ω
Depressed	∞Ω

3) Check idle switch OFF → ON speed.

N.G. → 1) Disconnect idle switch harness connector.
2) Check resistance between terminals ⓐ and ⓑ.

Throttle valve position	Resistance
Closed	0Ω
Open	∞Ω

3) Check idle switch OFF → ON speed.

4) Check harness continuity between idle switch and E.C.U.
• Disconnect harness connector for idle switch.
• Disconnect 20-pin connector from E.C.U.
• Check resistance between terminal ⓐ and E.C.U. terminal ⑯.
Resistance: Approximately 0Ω

O.K.

Reinstall any part removed.

Perform driving test and then perform self-diagnosis Mode IV again.

N.G. → Perform E.C.U. input/output signal inspection test.
If N.G., recheck the E.C.U. pin terminals damage or the connection of E.C.U. harness connector.
If no malfunction, replace E.C.U.

O.K.

INSPECTION END

ECCS SELF-DIAGNOSTIC CHART
1987 THROTTLE BODY SENTRA AND PULSAR

VEHICLE SPEED SENSOR (Switch ON/OFF diagnosis)

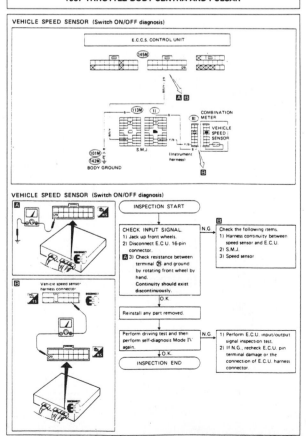

VEHICLE SPEED SENSOR (Switch ON/OFF diagnosis)

INSPECTION START

CHECK INPUT SIGNAL.
1) Jack up front wheels.
2) Disconnect E.C.U. 16-pin connector.
3) Check resistance between terminal ㉙ and ground by rotating front wheel by hand.
Continuity should exist discontinuously.

N.G. → Check the following items.
1) Harness continuity between speed sensor and E.C.U.
2) S.M.J.
3) Speed sensor

O.K.

Reinstall any part removed.

Perform driving test and then perform self-diagnosis Mode IV again.

N.G. → 1) Perform E.C.U. input/output signal inspection test.
2) If N.G., recheck the E.C.U. pin terminal damage or the connection of E.C.U. harness connector.

O.K.

INSPECTION END

ECCS SELF-DIAGNOSTIC CHART
1987 THROTTLE BODY SENTRA AND PULSAR

INJECTOR (Not self-diagnostic item)

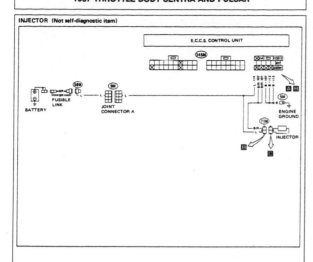

ECCS SELF-DIAGNOSTIC CHART
1987 THROTTLE BODY SENTRA AND PULSAR

AIR CONDITIONER SWITCH & POWER STEERING OIL PRESSURE SWITCH (Not self-diagnostic item)

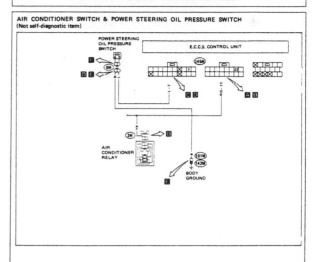

ECCS SELF-DIAGNOSTIC CHART
1987 THROTTLE BODY SENTRA AND PULSAR

INJECTOR (Not self-diagnostic item)

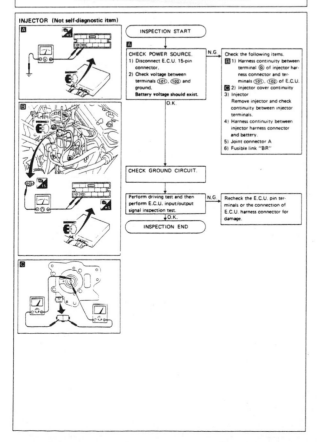

ECCS SELF-DIAGNOSTIC CHART
1987 THROTTLE BODY SENTRA AND PULSAR

AIR CONDITIONER SWITCH & POWER STEERING OIL PRESSURE SWITCH (Not self-diagnostic item)

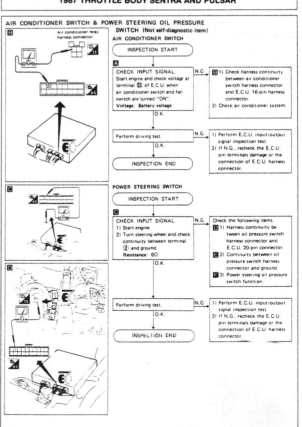
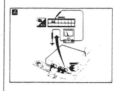

ECCS SELF-DIAGNOSTIC CHART
1987 THROTTLE BODY SENTRA AND PULSAR

AIR CONDITIONER SWITCH & POWER STEERING OIL PRESSURE SWITCH (Not self-diagnostic item)

NEUTRAL/CLUTCH/INHIBITOR SWITCH (Not self-diagnostic item)

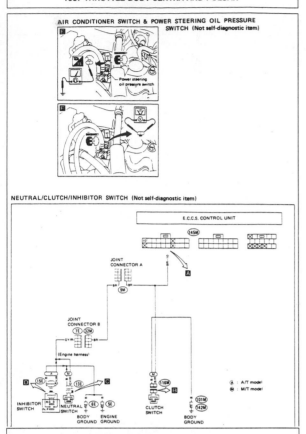

ECCS SELF-DIAGNOSTIC CHART
1987 THROTTLE BODY SENTRA AND PULSAR

MIXTURE HEATER (Not self-diagnostic item)

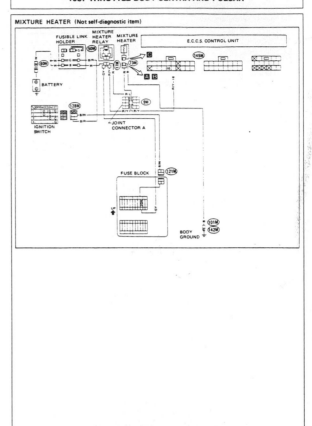

ECCS SELF-DIAGNOSTIC CHART
1987 THROTTLE BODY SENTRA AND PULSAR

NEUTRAL/CLUTCH/INHIBITOR SWITCH (Not self-diagnostic item)

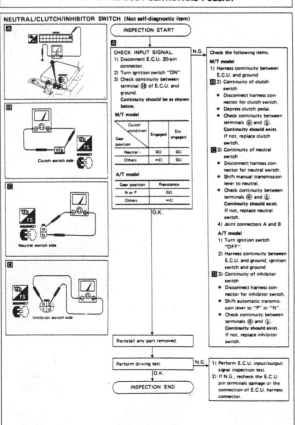

ECCS SELF-DIAGNOSTIC CHART
1987 THROTTLE BODY SENTRA AND PULSAR

MIXTURE HEATER (Not self-diagnostic item)

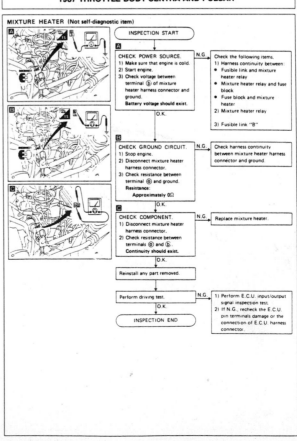

ECCS SELF-DIAGNOSTIC CHART
1987 THROTTLE BODY SENTRA AND PULSAR

MIXTURE HEATER RELAY (Not self-diagnostic item)

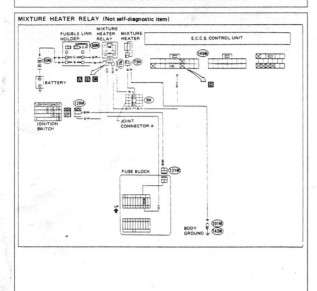

ECCS SELF-DIAGNOSTIC CHART
1987 THROTTLE BODY SENTRA AND PULSAR

FUEL PUMP (Not self-diagnostic item)

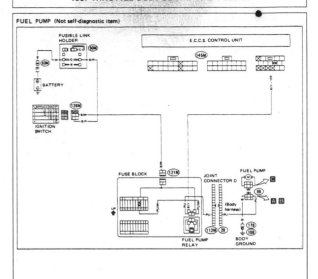

ECCS SELF-DIAGNOSTIC CHART
1987 THROTTLE BODY SENTRA AND PULSAR

MIXTURE HEATER RELAY (Not self-diagnostic item)

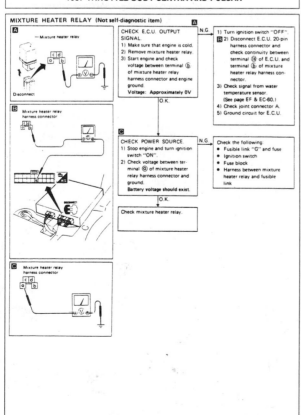

ECCS SELF-DIAGNOSTIC CHART
1987 THROTTLE BODY SENTRA AND PULSAR

FUEL PUMP (Not self-diagnostic item)

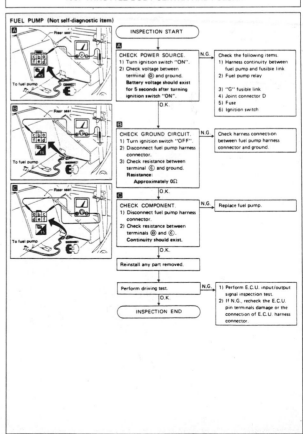

ECCS SELF-DIAGNOSTIC CHART
1987 THROTTLE BODY SENTRA AND PULSAR

FUEL PUMP RELAY (Not self-diagnostic item)

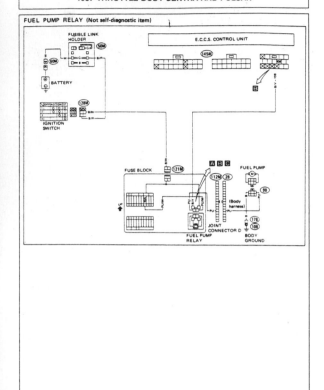

ECCS SELF-DIAGNOSTIC CHART
1987 THROTTLE BODY SENTRA AND PULSAR

E.G.R. & CANISTER PURGE CONTROL SOLENOID VALVE (Not self-diagnostic item)

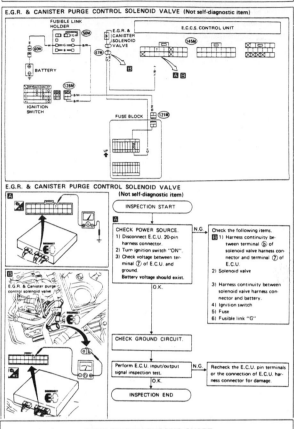

ECCS SELF-DIAGNOSTIC CHART
1987 THROTTLE BODY SENTRA AND PULSAR

FUEL PUMP RELAY (Not self-diagnostic item)

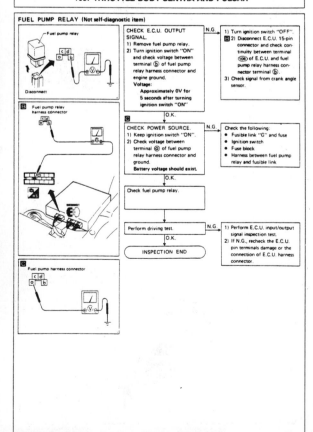

ECCS SELF-DIAGNOSTIC CHART
1987 THROTTLE BODY SENTRA AND PULSAR

A.I.V. CONTROL SOLENOID VALVE (Not self-diagnostic item)

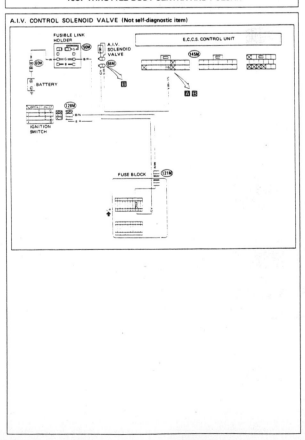

ECCS SELF-DIAGNOSTIC CHART
1987 THROTTLE BODY SENTRA AND PULSAR

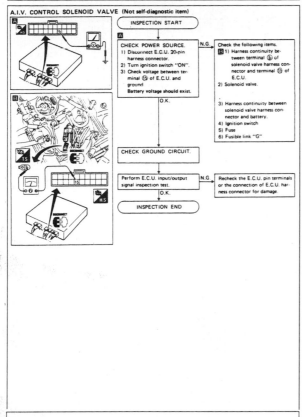

A.I.V. CONTROL SOLENOID VALVE (Not self-diagnostic item)

INSPECTION START

CHECK POWER SOURCE.
1) Disconnect E.C.U. 20-pin harness connector.
2) Turn ignition switch "ON".
3) Check voltage between terminal ⑮ of E.C.U. and ground
Battery voltage should exist.
— N.G. → Check the following items.
B 1) Harness continuity between terminal ⓑ of solenoid valve harness connector and terminal ⑮ of E.C.U.
2) Solenoid valve.

3) Harness continuity between solenoid valve harness connector and battery.
4) Ignition switch
5) Fuse
6) Fusible link "G"

O.K.

CHECK GROUND CIRCUIT.

Perform E.C.U. input/output signal inspection test. — N.G. → Recheck the E.C.U. pin terminals or the connection of E.C.U. harness connector for damage.

O.K.

INSPECTION END

ECCS SELF-DIAGNOSTIC CHART
1987 THROTTLE BODY SENTRA AND PULSAR

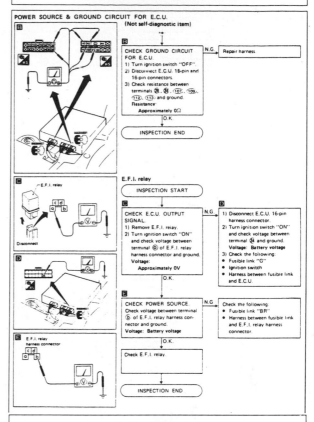

POWER SOURCE & GROUND CIRCUIT FOR E.C.U.
(Not self-diagnostic item)

CHECK GROUND CIRCUIT FOR E.C.U.
1) Turn ignition switch "OFF".
2) Disconnect E.C.U. 16-pin and 16-pin connectors.
3) Check resistance between terminals ㉑, ㉕, ⑩⑦, ⑩⑨, ⑪②, ⑪③, and ground.
Resistance:
Approximately 0Ω
— N.G. → Repair harness.

O.K.

INSPECTION END

E.F.I. relay

INSPECTION START

CHECK E.C.U. OUTPUT SIGNAL.
1) Remove E.F.I. relay.
2) Turn ignition switch "ON" and check voltage between terminal ⓒ of E.F.I. relay harness connector and ground.
Voltage:
Approximately 0V
— N.G. → 1) Disconnect E.C.U. 16-pin harness connector.
2) Turn ignition switch "ON" and check voltage between terminal ㉞ and ground.
Voltage: Battery voltage
3) Check the following:
• Fusible link "G"
• Ignition switch
• Harness between fusible link and E.C.U.

O.K.

CHECK POWER SOURCE.
Check voltage between terminal ⓑ of E.F.I. relay harness connector and ground.
Voltage: Battery voltage
— N.G → Check the following:
• Fusible link "BR"
• Harness between fusible link and E.F.I. relay harness connector.

O.K.

Check E.F.I. relay.

INSPECTION END

ECCS SELF-DIAGNOSTIC CHART
1987 THROTTLE BODY SENTRA AND PULSAR

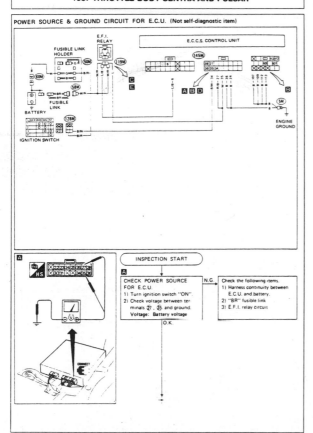

POWER SOURCE & GROUND CIRCUIT FOR E.C.U. (Not self-diagnostic item)

INSPECTION START

CHECK POWER SOURCE FOR E.C.U.
1) Turn ignition switch "ON".
2) Check voltage between terminals ㉗, ㉕, and ground.
Voltage: Battery voltage
— N.G. → Check the following items.
1) Harness continuity between E.C.U. and battery.
2) "BR" fusible link
3) E.F.I. relay circuit

O.K.

ECCS SELF-DIAGNOSTIC CHART
1987 THROTTLE BODY SENTRA AND PULSAR

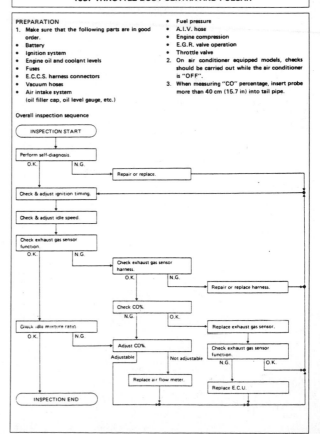

PREPARATION
1. Make sure that the following parts are in good order.
• Battery
• Ignition system
• Engine oil and coolant levels
• Fuses
• E.C.C.S. harness connectors
• Vacuum hoses
• Air intake system
(oil filler cap, oil level gauge, etc.)

• Fuel pressure
• A.I.V. hose
• Engine compression
• E.G.R. valve operation
• Throttle valve

2. On air conditioner equipped models, checks should be carried out while the air conditioner is "OFF".
3. When measuring "CO" percentage, insert probe more than 40 cm (15.7 in) into tail pipe.

Overall inspection sequence

INSPECTION START

Perform self-diagnosis.
O.K. / N.G. → Repair or replace.

Check & adjust ignition timing.

Check & adjust idle speed.

Check exhaust gas sensor function.
O.K. / N.G. → Check exhaust gas sensor harness.
O.K. / N.G. → Repair or replace harness.

Check CO%.
N.G. / O.K. → Replace exhaust gas sensor.

Check idle mixture ratio
O.K. / N.G. → Adjust CO%.
Adjustable / Not adjustable → Check exhaust gas sensor function.
N.G. / O.K.
Replace air flow meter. / Replace E.C.U.

INSPECTION END

MIXTURE RATIO FEEDBACK SYSTEM INSPECTION CHART
1987 THROTTLE BODY SENTRA AND PULSAR

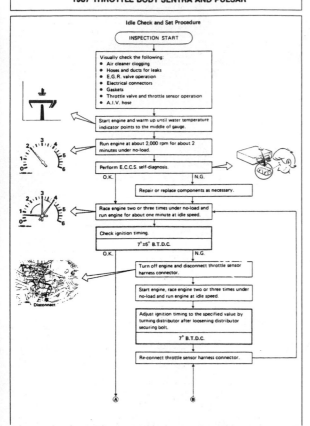

Idle Check and Set Procedure

INSPECTION START

Visually check the following:
- Air cleaner clogging
- Hoses and ducts for leaks
- E.G.R. valve operation
- Electrical connectors
- Gaskets
- Throttle valve and throttle sensor operation
- A.I.V. hose

Start engine and warm up until water temperature indicator points to the middle of gauge.

Run engine at about 2,000 rpm for about 2 minutes under no-load.

Perform E.C.C.S. self-diagnosis.
O.K. / N.G.

Repair or replace components as necessary.

Race engine two or three times under no-load and run engine for about one minute at idle speed.

Check ignition timing.

7° ±5° B.T.D.C.
O.K. / N.G.

Turn off engine and disconnect throttle sensor harness connector.

Start engine, race engine two or three times under no-load and run engine at idle speed.

Adjust ignition timing to the specified value by turning distributor after loosening distributor securing bolt.

7° B.T.D.C.

Re-connect throttle sensor harness connector.

(A) (B)

MIXTURE RATIO FEEDBACK SYSTEM INSPECTION CHART
1987 THROTTLE BODY SENTRA AND PULSAR

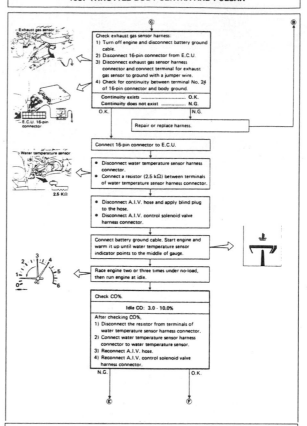

(C) (B)

Check exhaust gas sensor harness:
1) Turn off engine and disconnect battery ground cable.
2) Disconnect 16-pin connector from E.C.U.
3) Disconnect exhaust gas sensor harness connector and connect terminal for exhaust gas sensor to ground with a jumper wire.
4) Check for continuity between terminal No. 2 of 16-pin connector and body ground.

Continuity exists .... O.K.
Continuity does not exist .... N.G.
O.K. / N.G.

Repair or replace harness.

Connect 16-pin connector to E.C.U.

- Disconnect water temperature sensor harness connector.
- Connect a resistor (2.5 kΩ) between terminals of water temperature sensor harness connector.

2.5 KΩ

- Disconnect A.I.V. hose and apply blind plug to the hose.
- Disconnect A.I.V. control solenoid valve harness connector.

Connect battery ground cable. Start engine and warm it up until water temperature sensor indicator points to the middle of gauge.

Race engine two or three times under no-load, then run engine at idle.

Check CO%.

Idle CO: 3.0 - 10.0%

After checking CO%,
1) Disconnect the resistor from terminals of water temperature sensor harness connector.
2) Connect water temperature sensor harness connector to water temperature sensor.
3) Reconnect A.I.V. hose.
4) Reconnect A.I.V. control solenoid valve harness connector.

N.G. / O.K.

(E) (F)

MIXTURE RATIO FEEDBACK SYSTEM INSPECTION CHART
1987 THROTTLE BODY SENTRA AND PULSAR

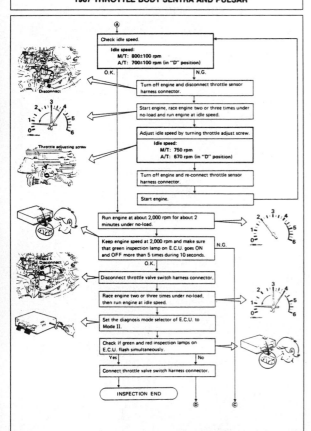

(A)

Check idle speed.

Idle speed:
M/T: 800±100 rpm
A/T: 700±100 rpm (in "D" position)
O.K. / N.G.

Turn off engine and disconnect throttle sensor harness connector.

Start engine, race engine two or three times under no-load and run engine at idle speed.

Adjust idle speed by turning throttle adjust screw.

Idle speed:
M/T: 750 rpm
A/T: 670 rpm (in "D" position)

Turn off engine and re-connect throttle sensor harness connector.

Start engine.

Run engine at about 2,000 rpm for about 2 minutes under no-load.

Keep engine speed at 2,000 rpm and make sure that green inspection lamp on E.C.U. goes ON and OFF more than 5 times during 10 seconds.
O.K. / N.G.

Disconnect throttle valve switch harness connector.

Race engine two or three times under no-load, then run engine at idle speed.

Set the diagnosis mode selector of E.C.U. to Mode II.

Check if green and red inspection lamps on E.C.U. flash simultaneously.
Yes / No

Connect throttle valve switch harness connector.

INSPECTION END

(D) (C)

MIXTURE RATIO FEEDBACK SYSTEM INSPECTION CHART
1987 THROTTLE BODY SENTRA AND PULSAR

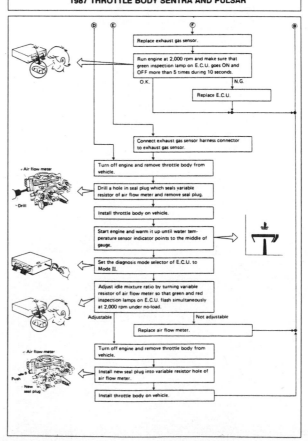

(D) (C) (F) (B)

Replace exhaust gas sensor.

Run engine at 2,000 rpm and make sure that green inspection lamp on E.C.U. goes ON and OFF more than 5 times during 10 seconds.
O.K. / N.G.

Replace E.C.U.

Connect exhaust gas sensor harness connector to exhaust gas sensor.

Turn off engine and remove throttle body from vehicle.

Drill a hole in seal plug which seals variable resistor of air flow meter and remove seal plug.

Install throttle body on vehicle.

Start engine and warm it up until water temperature sensor indicator points to the middle of gauge.

Set the diagnosis mode selector of E.C.U. to Mode II.

Adjust idle mixture ratio by turning variable resistor of air flow meter so that green and red inspection lamps on E.C.U. flash simultaneously at 2,000 rpm under no-load.
Adjustable / Not adjustable

Replace air flow meter.

Turn off engine and remove throttle body from vehicle.

Install new seal plug into variable resistor hole of air flow meter.

Install throttle body on vehicle.

ECCS SELF-DIAGNOSTIC PROCEDURE—1986 THROTTLE BODY TRUCK

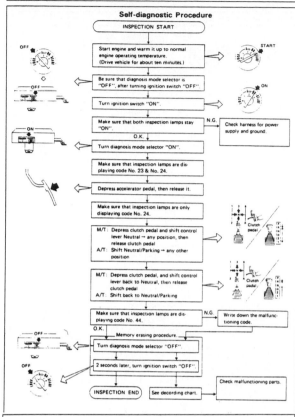

Self-diagnostic Procedure

INSPECTION START

Start engine and warm it up to normal engine operating temperature. (Drive vehicle for about ten minutes.)

Be sure that diagnosis mode selector is "OFF", after turning ignition switch "OFF".

Turn ignition switch "ON".

Make sure that both inspection lamps stay "ON". → N.G. → Check harness for power supply and ground.

O.K.

Turn diagnosis mode selector "ON".

Make sure that inspection lamps are displaying code No. 23 & No. 24.

Depress accelerator pedal, then release it.

Make sure that inspection lamps are only displaying code No. 24.

M/T: Depress clutch pedal and shift control lever Neutral → any position, then release clutch pedal
A/T: Shift Neutral/Parking → any other position

M/T: Depress clutch pedal, and shift control lever back to Neutral, then release clutch pedal
A/T: Shift back to Neutral/Parking

Make sure that inspection lamps are displaying code No. 44. → N.G. → Write down the malfunctioning code.

O.K. Memory erasing procedure.

Turn diagnosis mode selector "OFF".

2 seconds later, turn ignition switch "OFF".

INSPECTION END | See decording chart. | Check malfunctioning parts.

ECCS SELF-DIAGNOSTIC DECODING CHART
1986 THROTTLE BODY TRUCK

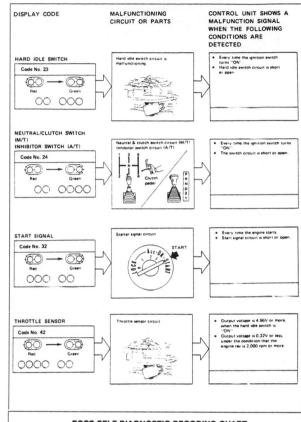

DISPLAY CODE	MALFUNCTIONING CIRCUIT OR PARTS	CONTROL UNIT SHOWS A MALFUNCTION SIGNAL WHEN THE FOLLOWING CONDITIONS ARE DETECTED
HARD IDLE SWITCH Code No. 23	Hard idle switch circuit is malfunctioning	• Every time the ignition switch turns "ON". • Hard idle switch circuit is short or open.
NEUTRAL/CLUTCH SWITCH (M/T) **INHIBITOR SWITCH (A/T)** Code No. 24	Neutral & clutch switch circuit (M/T) Inhibitor switch circuit (A/T)	• Every time the ignition switch turns "ON". • The switch circuit is short or open.
START SIGNAL Code No. 32	Starter signal circuit	• Every time the engine starts. • Start signal circuit is short or open.
THROTTLE SENSOR Code No. 42	Throttle sensor circuit	• Output voltage is 4.96V or more, when the hard idle switch is "ON". • Output voltage is 0.37V or less, under the condition that the engine rev is 2,000 rpm or more.

ECCS SELF-DIAGNOSTIC DECODING CHART
1986 THROTTLE BODY TRUCK

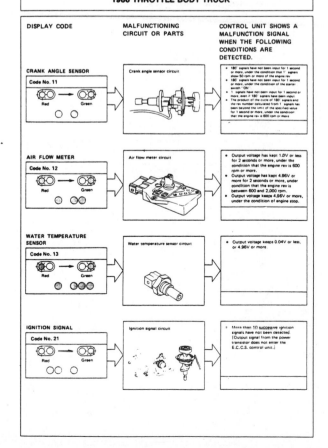

DISPLAY CODE	MALFUNCTIONING CIRCUIT OR PARTS	CONTROL UNIT SHOWS A MALFUNCTION SIGNAL WHEN THE FOLLOWING CONDITIONS ARE DETECTED
CRANK ANGLE SENSOR Code No. 11	Crank angle sensor circuit	• 180° signals have not been input for 1 second or more, under the condition that 1° signals show 50 rpm or more of the engine rev. • 180° signals have not been input for 1 second or more, under the condition of the starter switch "ON". • 1° signals have not been input for 1 second or more, even if 180° signals have been input. • The product of the cycle of 180° signals and the rev number calculated from 1° signals has been beyond the limit of the specified value for 1 second or more, under the condition that the engine rev is 600 rpm or more.
AIR FLOW METER Code No. 12	Air flow meter circuit	• Output voltage has kept 1.0V or less for 2 seconds or more, under the condition that the engine rev is 600 rpm or more. • Output voltage has kept 4.96V or more for 2 seconds or more, under condition that the engine rev is between 600 and 2,000 rpm. • Output voltage keeps 4.96V or more, under the condition of engine stop.
WATER TEMPERATURE SENSOR Code No. 13	Water temperature sensor circuit	• Output voltage keeps 0.04V or less, or 4.96V or more.
IGNITION SIGNAL Code No. 21	Ignition signal circuit	• More than 10 successive ignition signals have not been detected. (Output signal from the power transistor does not enter the E.C.C.S. control unit.)

ECCS SELF-DIAGNOSTIC DECODING CHART
1986 THROTTLE BODY TRUCK

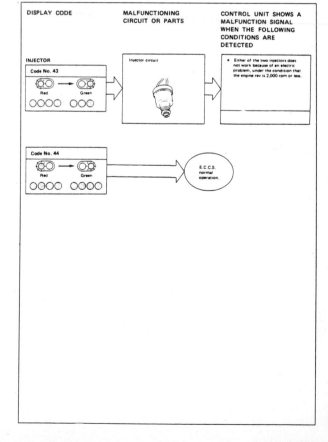

DISPLAY CODE	MALFUNCTIONING CIRCUIT OR PARTS	CONTROL UNIT SHOWS A MALFUNCTION SIGNAL WHEN THE FOLLOWING CONDITIONS ARE DETECTED
INJECTOR Code No. 43	Injector circuit	• Either of the two injectors does not work because of an electric problem, under the condition that the engine rev is 2,000 rpm or less.
Code No. 44		E.C.C.S. normal operation.

ECCS SELF-DIAGNOSTIC CHART—1986 THROTTLE BODY TRUCK

CRANK ANGLE SENSOR (Code No. 11)

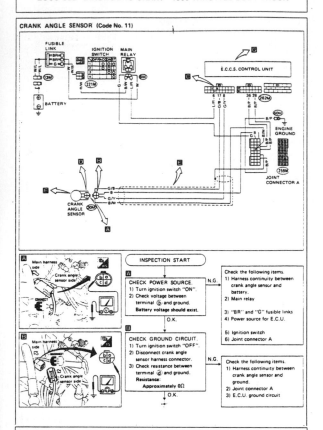

INSPECTION START

A
CHECK POWER SOURCE.
1) Turn ignition switch "ON".
2) Check voltage between terminal ⓑ and ground.
Battery voltage should exist.

N.G. → Check the following items.
1) Harness continuity between crank angle sensor and battery.
2) Main relay
3) "BR" and "G" fusible links
4) Power source for E.C.U.
5) Ignition switch
6) Joint connector A

O.K.

B
CHECK GROUND CIRCUIT.
1) Turn ignition switch "OFF".
2) Disconnect crank angle sensor harness connector.
3) Check resistance between terminal ⓓ and ground.
Resistance:
Approximately 0Ω

N.G. → Check the following items.
1) Harness continuity between crank angle sensor and ground.
2) Joint connector A
3) E.C.U. ground circuit

O.K.

ECCS SELF-DIAGNOSTIC CHART—1986 THROTTLE BODY TRUCK

AIR FLOW METER (Code No. 12)

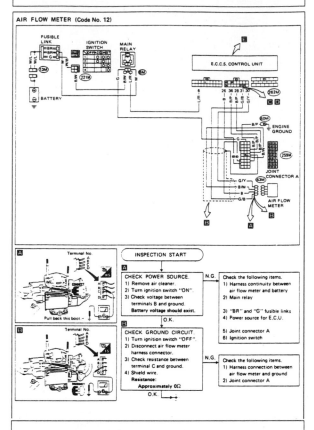

INSPECTION START

A
CHECK POWER SOURCE.
1) Remove air cleaner.
2) Turn ignition switch "ON".
3) Check voltage between terminals B and ground.
Battery voltage should exist.

N.G. → Check the following items.
1) Harness continuity between air flow meter and battery
2) Main relay
3) "BR" and "G" fusible links
4) Power source for E.C.U.
5) Joint connector A
6) Ignition switch

O.K.

B
CHECK GROUND CIRCUIT.
1) Turn ignition switch "OFF".
2) Disconnect air flow meter harness connector.
3) Check resistance between terminal C and ground.
Shield wire.
Resistance:
Approximately 0Ω

N.G. → Check the following items.
1) Harness connection between air flow meter and ground
2) Joint connector A

O.K.

ECCS SELF-DIAGNOSTIC CHART—1986 THROTTLE BODY TRUCK

CRANK ANGLE SENSOR (Code No. 11)

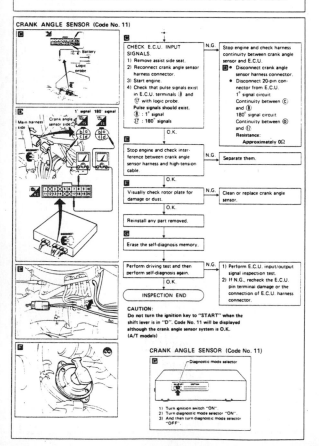

C
CHECK E.C.U. INPUT SIGNALS.
1) Remove assist side seat.
2) Reconnect crank angle sensor harness connector.
3) Start engine.
4) Check that pulse signals exist in E.C.U. terminals ⑧ and ⑰ with logic probe.
Pulse signals should exist.
⑧ : 1° signal
⑰ : 180° signals

N.G. → Stop engine and check harness continuity between crank angle sensor and E.C.U.
• Disconnect crank angle sensor harness connector.
• Disconnect 20-pin connector from E.C.U.
1° signal circuit
Continuity between ⓒ and ⑧
180° signal circuit
Continuity between ⓓ and ⑰
Resistance:
Approximately 0Ω

O.K.

Stop engine and check interference between crank angle sensor harness and high-tension cable.

N.G. → Separate them.

O.K.

Visually check rotor plate for damage or dust.

N.G. → Clean or replace crank angle sensor.

O.K.

Reinstall any part removed.

Erase the self-diagnosis memory.

Perform driving test and then perform self-diagnosis again.

N.G. → 1) Perform E.C.U. input/output signal inspection test.
2) If N.G., recheck the E.C.U. pin terminal damage or the connection of E.C.U. harness connector.

O.K.

INSPECTION END

CAUTION:
Do not turn the ignition key to "START" when the shift lever is in "D". Code No. 11 will be displayed although the crank angle sensor system is O.K. (A/T models)

CRANK ANGLE SENSOR (Code No. 11)

G Diagnostic mode selector

1) Turn ignition switch "ON".
2) Turn diagnostic mode selector "ON".
3) And then turn diagnostic mode selector "OFF".

ECCS SELF-DIAGNOSTIC CHART—1986 THROTTLE BODY TRUCK

AIR FLOW METER (Code No. 12)

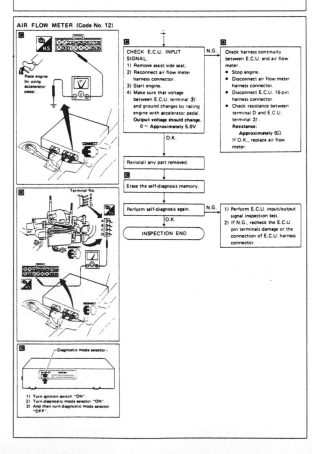

C
CHECK E.C.U. INPUT SIGNAL.
1) Remove assist side seat.
2) Reconnect air flow meter harness connector.
3) Start engine.
4) Make sure that voltage between E.C.U. terminal ㉛ and ground changes by racing engine with accelerator pedal.
Output voltage should change.
0 ~ Approximately 5.0V

N.G. → Check harness continuity between E.C.U. and air flow meter.
• Stop engine.
• Disconnect air flow meter harness connector.
• Disconnect E.C.U. 16-pin harness connector.
• Check resistance between terminal D and E.C.U. terminal ㉛.
Resistance:
Approximately 0Ω
If O.K., replace air flow meter.

O.K.

Reinstall any part removed.

E
Erase the self-diagnosis memory.

Perform self-diagnosis again.

N.G. → 1) Perform E.C.U. input/output signal inspection test.
2) If N.G., recheck the E.C.U. pin terminals damage or the connection of E.C.U. harness connector.

O.K.

INSPECTION END

AIR FLOW METER (Code No. 12)

E Diagnostic mode selector

1) Turn ignition switch "ON".
2) Turn diagnostic mode selector "ON".
3) And then turn diagnostic mode selector "OFF".

ECCS SELF-DIAGNOSTIC CHART — 1986 THROTTLE BODY TRUCK

WATER TEMPERATURE SENSOR (Code No. 13)

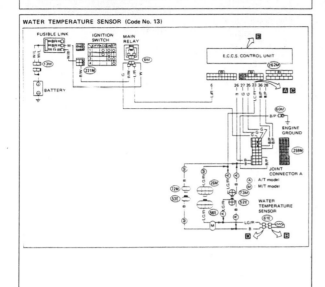

ECCS SELF-DIAGNOSTIC CHART — 1986 THROTTLE BODY TRUCK

WATER TEMPERATURE SENSOR (Code No. 13)

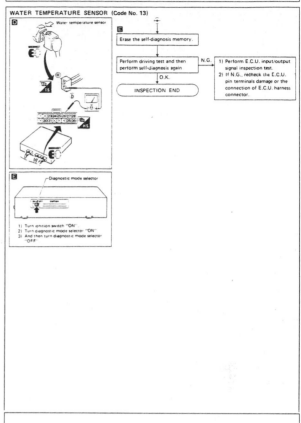

Erase the self-diagnosis memory.

Perform driving test and then perform self-diagnosis again

O.K. → INSPECTION END

N.G. →
1) Perform E.C.U. input/output signal inspection test.
2) If N.G., recheck the E.C.U. pin terminals damage or the connection of E.C.U. harness connector.

Diagnostic mode selector

1) Turn ignition switch "ON".
2) Turn diagnostic mode selector "ON".
3) And then turn diagnostic mode selector "OFF".

ECCS SELF-DIAGNOSTIC CHART — 1986 THROTTLE BODY TRUCK

WATER TEMPERATURE SENSOR (Code No. 13)

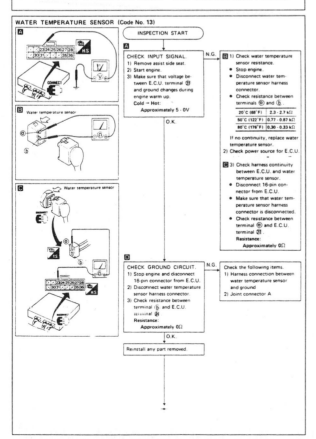

INSPECTION START

A CHECK INPUT SIGNAL.
1) Remove assist side seat.
2) Start engine.
3) Make sure that voltage between E.C.U. terminal ㉓ and ground changes during engine warm up.
Cold → Hot:
Approximately 5 - 0V

O.K. ↓

N.G. →
B 1) Check water temperature sensor resistance.
• Stop engine.
• Disconnect water temperature sensor harness connector.
• Check resistance between terminals ⓐ and ⓑ.

20°C (68°F)	2.3 - 2.7 kΩ
50°C (122°F)	0.77 - 0.87 kΩ
80°C (176°F)	0.30 - 0.33 kΩ

If no continuity, replace water temperature sensor.
2) Check power source for E.C.U.

C 3) Check harness continuity between E.C.U. and water temperature sensor.
• Disconnect 16-pin connector from E.C.U.
• Make sure that water temperature sensor harness connector is disconnected.
• Check resistance between terminal ⓐ and E.C.U. terminal ㉓.
Resistance:
Approximately 0Ω

D CHECK GROUND CIRCUIT.
1) Stop engine and disconnect 16-pin connector from E.C.U.
2) Disconnect water temperature sensor harness connector.
3) Check resistance between terminal ⓑ and E.C.U. terminal ㉘.
Resistance:
Approximately 0Ω

N.G. →
Check the following items.
1) Harness connection between water temperature sensor and ground
2) Joint connector A

O.K. ↓

Reinstall any part removed.

ECCS SELF-DIAGNOSTIC CHART — 1986 THROTTLE BODY TRUCK

IGNITION SIGNAL (Code No. 21)

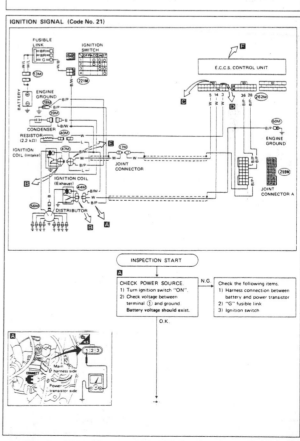

INSPECTION START

A CHECK POWER SOURCE.
1) Turn ignition switch "ON".
2) Check voltage between terminal ① and ground
Battery voltage should exist.

N.G. →
Check the following items.
1) Harness connection between battery and power transistor
2) "G" fusible link
3) Ignition switch

O.K. ↓

ECCS SELF-DIAGNOSTIC CHART—1986 THROTTLE BODY TRUCK

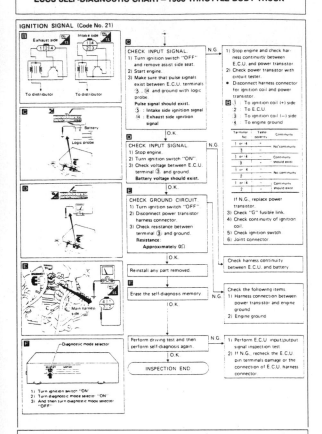

ECCS SELF-DIAGNOSTIC CHART—1986 THROTTLE BODY TRUCK

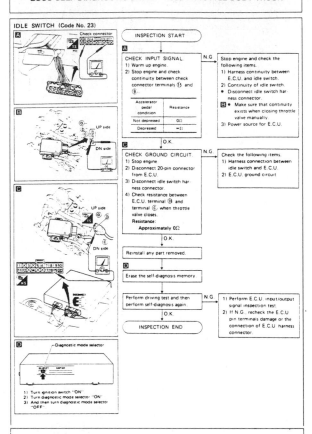

ECCS SELF-DIAGNOSTIC CHART—1986 THROTTLE BODY TRUCK

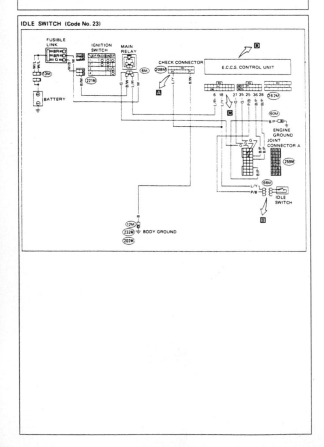

ECCS SELF-DIAGNOSTIC CHART—1986 THROTTLE BODY TRUCK

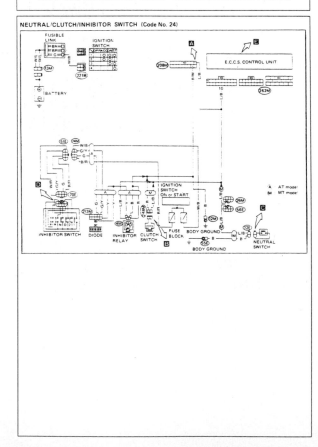

ECCS SELF-DIAGNOSTIC CHART – 1986 THROTTLE BODY TRUCK

NEUTRAL/CLUTCH/INHIBITOR SWITCH (Code No. 24)

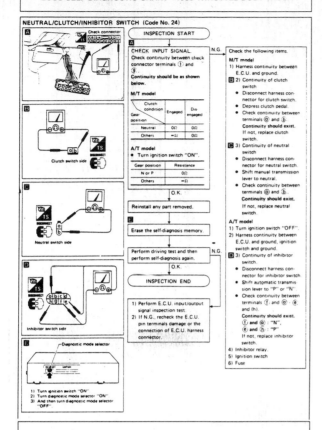

ECCS SELF-DIAGNOSTIC CHART – 1986 THROTTLE BODY TRUCK

START SIGNAL (Code No. 32)

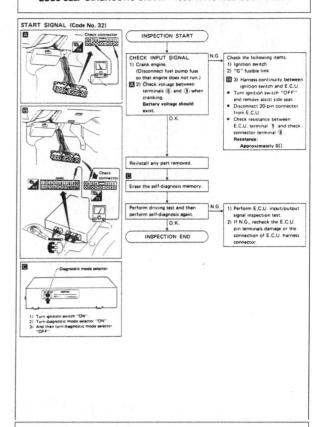

ECCS SELF-DIAGNOSTIC CHART – 1986 THROTTLE BODY TRUCK

START SIGNAL (Code No. 32)

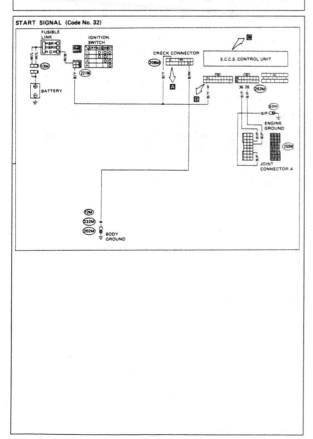

ECCS SELF-DIAGNOSTIC CHART – 1986 THROTTLE BODY TRUCK

THROTTLE SENSOR (Code No. 42)

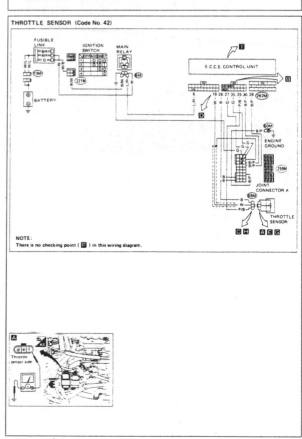

NOTE:
There is no checking point (F) in this wiring diagram.

ECCS SELF-DIAGNOSTIC CHART – 1986 THROTTLE BODY TRUCK

THROTTLE SENSOR (Code No. 42)

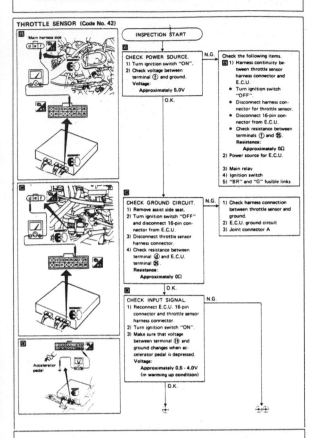

INSPECTION START

CHECK POWER SOURCE.
1) Turn ignition switch "ON".
2) Check voltage between terminal ① and ground.
Voltage: Approximately 5.0V

O.K.

N.G. → Check the following items.
1) 1) Harness continuity between throttle sensor harness connector and E.C.U.
• Turn ignition switch "OFF".
• Disconnect harness connector for throttle sensor.
• Disconnect 16-pin connector from E.C.U.
• Check resistance between terminals ① and ㉖.
Resistance: Approximately 0Ω
2) Power source for E.C.U.
3) Main relay
4) Ignition switch
5) "BR" and "G" fusible links

CHECK GROUND CIRCUIT.
1) Remove assist side seat.
2) Turn ignition switch "OFF" and disconnect 16-pin connector from E.C.U.
3) Disconnect throttle sensor harness connector.
4) Check resistance between terminal ⓓ and E.C.U. terminal ㉖.
Resistance: Approximately 0Ω

O.K.

N.G. → 1) Check harness connection between throttle sensor and ground.
2) E.C.U. ground circuit
3) Joint connector A

CHECK INPUT SIGNAL.
1) Reconnect E.C.U. 16-pin connector and throttle sensor harness connector.
2) Turn ignition switch "ON".
3) Make sure that voltage between terminal ⑲ and ground changes when accelerator pedal is depressed.
Voltage: Approximately 0.5 - 4.0V (in warming up condition)

O.K.

ECCS SELF-DIAGNOSTIC CHART – 1986 THROTTLE BODY TRUCK

THROTTLE SENSOR (Code No. 42)

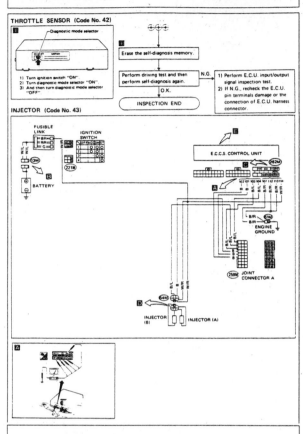

— Diagnostic mode selector

1) Turn ignition switch "ON".
2) Turn diagnostic mode selector "ON".
3) And then turn diagnostic mode selector "OFF".

Erase the self-diagnosis memory.

Perform driving test and then perform self-diagnosis again.

N.G. → 1) Perform E.C.U. input/output signal inspection test.
2) If N.G., recheck the E.C.U. pin terminals damage or the connection of E.C.U. harness connector.

O.K.

INSPECTION END

INJECTOR (Code No. 43)

FUSIBLE LINK
IGNITION SWITCH
BATTERY
E.C.C.S. CONTROL UNIT
ENGINE GROUND
JOINT CONNECTOR A
INJECTOR (B)   INJECTOR (A)

ECCS SELF-DIAGNOSTIC CHART – 1986 THROTTLE BODY TRUCK

THROTTLE SENSOR (Code No. 42)

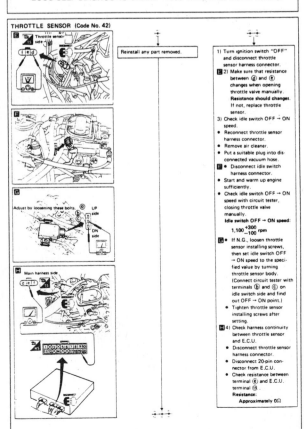

Reinstall any part removed.

1) Turn ignition switch "OFF" and disconnect throttle sensor harness connector.
2) Make sure that resistance between ⓓ and ⓔ changes when opening throttle valve manually.
Resistance should changes. If not, replace throttle sensor.
3) Check idle switch OFF → ON speed.
• Reconnect throttle sensor harness connector.
• Remove air cleaner.
• Put a suitable plug into disconnected vacuum hose.
• Disconnect idle switch harness connector.
• Start and warm up engine sufficiently.
• Check idle switch OFF → ON speed with circuit tester, closing throttle valve manually.
Idle switch OFF → ON speed: 1,100 +300 −100 rpm
• If N.G., loosen throttle sensor installing screws, then set idle switch OFF → ON speed to the specified value by turning throttle sensor body. (Connect circuit tester with terminals ⓑ and ⓒ on idle switch side and find out OFF → ON point.)
• Tighten throttle sensor installing screws after setting.
4) Check harness continuity between throttle sensor and E.C.U.
• Disconnect throttle sensor harness connector.
• Disconnect 20-pin connector from E.C.U.
• Check resistance between terminal ⓔ and E.C.U. terminal ⑲.
Resistance: Approximately 0Ω

Adjust by loosening these bolts. UP side / DN side

Main harness side

ECCS SELF-DIAGNOSTIC CHART – 1986 THROTTLE BODY TRUCK

INJECTOR (Code No. 43)

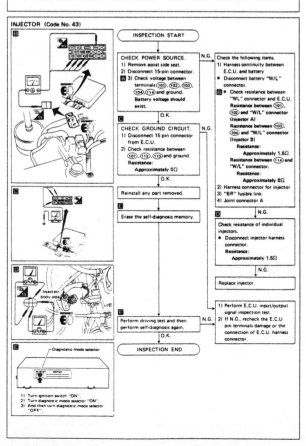

INSPECTION START

CHECK POWER SOURCE.
1) Remove assist side seat.
2) Disconnect 15-pin connector.
3) Check voltage between terminals ⑩①, ⑩②, ⑩③, ⑩④, ⑪④ and ground.
Battery voltage should exist.

O.K.

N.G. → Check the following items.
1) Harness continuity between E.C.U. and battery
• Disconnect battery "W/L" connector.
• Check resistance between "WL" connector and E.C.U.
Resistance between ⑩① ⑩② and "W/L" connector (Injector A)
Resistance between ⑩③ ⑩④ and "W/L" connector (Injector B)
Resistance: Approximately 1.5Ω
Resistance between ⑪④ and "W/L" connector.
Resistance: Approximately 0Ω
2) Harness connector for injector
3) "BR" fusible link
4) Joint connector A

CHECK GROUND CIRCUIT.
1) Disconnect 15 pin connector from E.C.U.
2) Check resistance between ⑩⑦, ⑪②, ⑪③ and ground.
Resistance: Approximately 0Ω

O.K.

N.G. →

Check resistance of individual injectors.
• Disconnect injector harness connector.
Resistance: Approximately 1.5Ω

N.G.

Reinstall any part removed.

Erase the self-diagnosis memory.

Replace injector.

Perform driving test and then perform self-diagnosis again.

N.G. → 1) Perform E.C.U. input/output signal inspection test.
2) If N.G., recheck the E.C.U. pin terminals damage or the connection of E.C.U. harness connector.

O.K.

INSPECTION END

— Diagnostic mode selector

1) Turn ignition switch "ON".
2) Turn diagnostic mode selector "ON".
3) And then turn diagnostic mode selector "OFF".

ECCS SELF-DIAGNOSTIC CHART – 1986 THROTTLE BODY TRUCK

MIXTURE HEATER (Not self-diagnostic item)

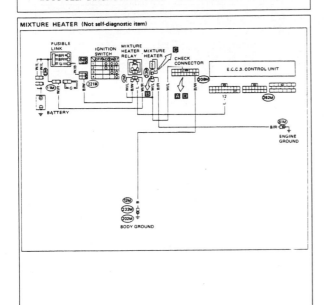

ECCS SELF-DIAGNOSTIC CHART – 1986 THROTTLE BODY TRUCK

MIXTURE HEATER RELAY (Not self-diagnostic item)

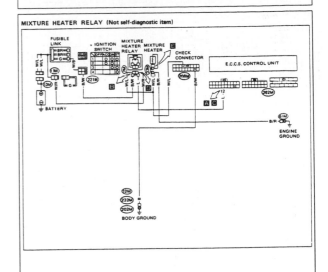

Mixture heater relay location

ECCS SELF-DIAGNOSTIC CHART – 1986 THROTTLE BODY TRUCK

MIXTURE HEATER (Not self-diagnostic item)

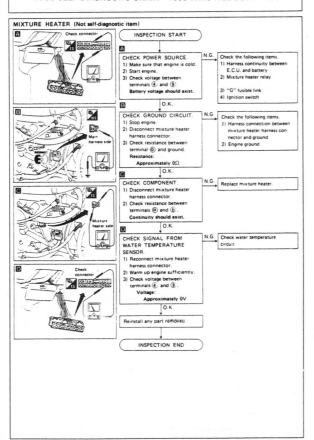

INSPECTION START

CHECK POWER SOURCE.
1) Make sure that engine is cold.
2) Start engine.
3) Check voltage between terminals ④ and ⑨.
Battery voltage should exist.

N.G. → Check the following items.
1) Harness continuity between E.C.U. and battery
2) Mixture heater relay
3) "G" fusible link
4) Ignition switch

O.K.

CHECK GROUND CIRCUIT.
1) Stop engine.
2) Disconnect mixture heater harness connector.
3) Check resistance between terminal ⓒ and ground.
Resistance: Approximately 0Ω

N.G. → Check the following items.
1) Harness connection between mixture heater harness connector and ground
2) Engine ground

O.K.

CHECK COMPONENT.
1) Disconnect mixture heater harness connector.
2) Check resistance between terminals ⓒ and ⓑ.
Continuity should exist.

N.G. → Replace mixture heater.

O.K.

CHECK SIGNAL FROM WATER TEMPERATURE SENSOR.
1) Reconnect mixture heater harness connector.
2) Warm up engine sufficiently.
3) Check voltage between terminals ④ and ⑨.
Voltage: Approximately 0V

N.G. → Check water temperature circuit

O.K.

Reinstall any part removed.

INSPECTION END

ECCS SELF-DIAGNOSTIC CHART – 1986 THROTTLE BODY TRUCK

MIXTURE HEATER RELAY (Not self-diagnostic item)

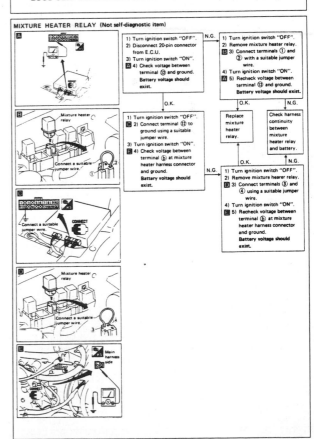

1) Turn ignition switch "OFF".
2) Disconnect 20-pin connector from E.C.U.
3) Turn ignition switch "ON".
4) Check voltage between terminal ⑫ and ground.
Battery voltage should exist.

N.G. → 1) Turn ignition switch "OFF".
2) Remove mixture heater relay.
3) Connect terminals ① and ② with a suitable jumper wire.
4) Turn ignition switch "ON".
5) Recheck voltage between terminal ⑫ and ground.
Battery voltage should exist.

O.K.

1) Turn ignition switch "OFF".
2) Connect terminal ⑫ to ground using a suitable jumper wire.
3) Turn ignition switch "ON".
4) Check voltage between terminal ⓑ at mixture heater harness connector and ground.
Battery voltage should exist.

Replace mixture heater relay.

O.K. / N.G. → Check harness continuity between mixture heater relay and battery.

O.K. / N.G.

1) Turn ignition switch "OFF".
2) Remove mixture heater relay.
3) Connect terminals ③ and ④ using a suitable jumper wire.
4) Turn ignition switch "ON".
5) Recheck voltage between terminal ⓑ at mixture heater harness connector and ground.
Battery voltage should exist.

ECCS SELF-DIAGNOSTIC CHART – 1986 THROTTLE BODY TRUCK

FUEL PUMP (Not self-diagnostic item)

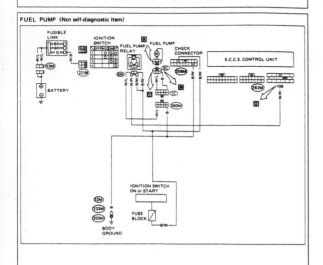

ECCS SELF-DIAGNOSTIC CHART – 1986 THROTTLE BODY TRUCK

FUEL PUMP RELAY (Not self-diagnostic item)

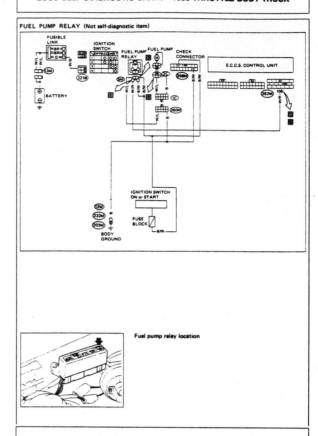

Fuel pump relay location

ECCS SELF-DIAGNOSTIC CHART – 1986 THROTTLE BODY TRUCK

FUEL PUMP (Not self-diagnostic item)

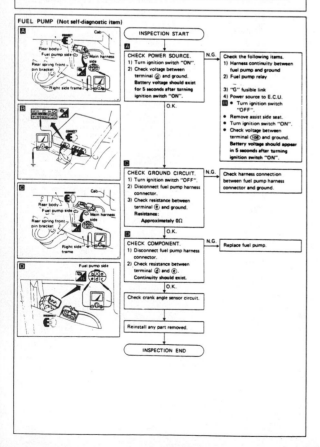

ECCS SELF-DIAGNOSTIC CHART – 1986 THROTTLE BODY TRUCK

FUEL PUMP RELAY (Not self-diagnostic item)

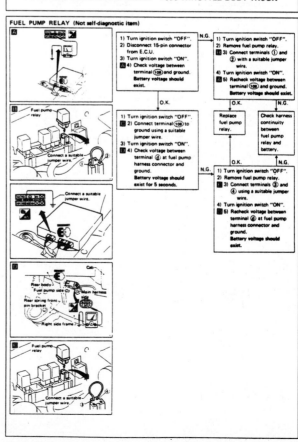

ECCS SELF-DIAGNOSTIC CHART – 1986 THROTTLE BODY TRUCK

POWER SOURCE FOR E.C.U. & GROUND CIRCUIT FOR E.C.U.
(Not self-diagnostic item)

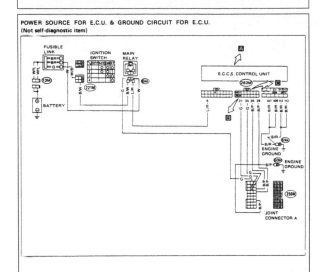

ECCS SELF-DIAGNOSTIC CHART – 1986 THROTTLE BODY TRUCK

MAIN RELAY (Not self-diagnostic item)

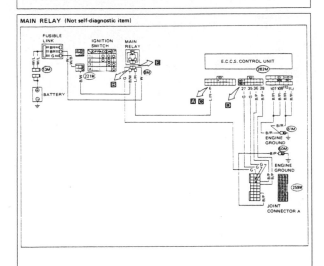

Main relay location

ECCS SELF-DIAGNOSTIC CHART – 1986 THROTTLE BODY TRUCK

POWER SOURCE FOR E.C.U. & GROUND CIRCUIT FOR E.C.U.
(Not self-diagnostic item)

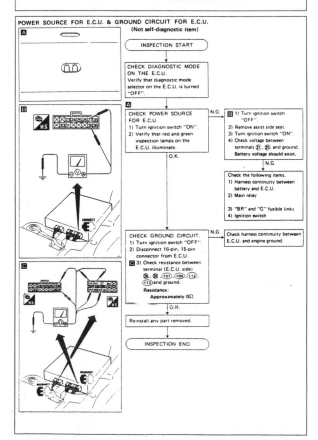

ECCS SELF-DIAGNOSTIC CHART – 1986 THROTTLE BODY TRUCK

MAIN RELAY (Not self-diagnostic item)

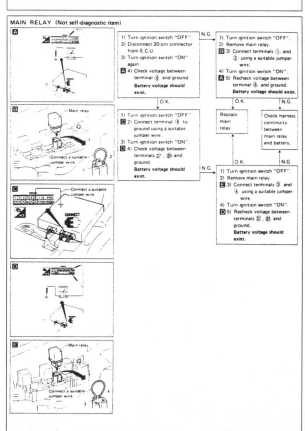

ECCS SELF-DIAGNOSTIC CHART – 1986 THROTTLE BODY TRUCK

A.I.V. (Air Injection Valve) CONTROL (Not self-diagnostic item)

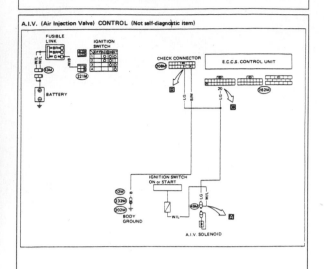

ECCS SELF-DIAGNOSTIC CHART – 1986 THROTTLE BODY TRUCK

SPARK PLUG SWITCHING CONTROL (Not self-diagnostic item)

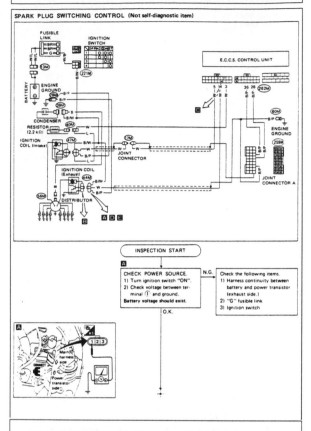

ECCS SELF-DIAGNOSTIC CHART – 1986 THROTTLE BODY TRUCK

A.I.V. (Air Injection Valve) CONTROL (Not self-diagnostic item)

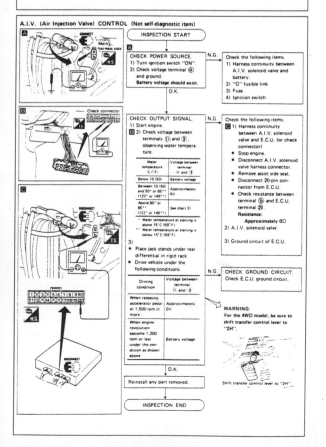

ECCS SELF-DIAGNOSTIC CHART – 1986 THROTTLE BODY TRUCK

SPARK PLUG SWITCHING CONTROL (Not self-diagnostic item)

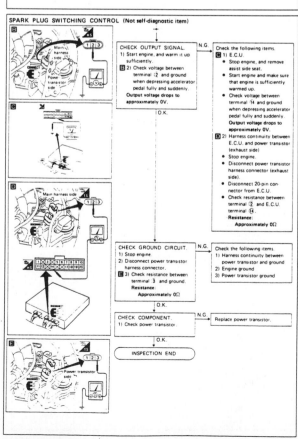

ECCS SELF-DIAGNOSTIC CHART – 1986 THROTTLE BODY TRUCK

EXHAUST GAS SENSOR (Not self-diagnostic item)

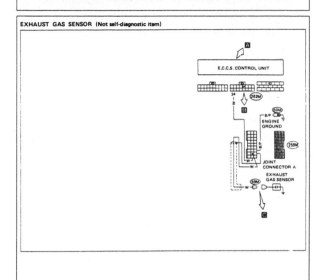

MIXTURE RATIO FEEDBACK SYSTEM INSPECTION CHART
1986 THROTTLE BODY TRUCK

PREPARATION

1. Make sure that the following parts are in good order.
   - Battery
   - Ignition system
   - Engine oil and coolant levels
   - Fuses
   - E.C.C.S. harness connectors
   - Vacuum hoses
   - Air intake system
     (oil filler cap, oil level gauge, etc.)
   - Fuel pressure
   - A.I.V. hose
   - Engine compression
   - E.G.R. valve operation
   - Throttle valve
2. On air conditioner equipped models, checks should be carried out while the air conditioner is "OFF".
3. When measuring "CO" percentage, insert probe more than 40 cm (15.7 in) into tail pipe.

Overall inspection sequence

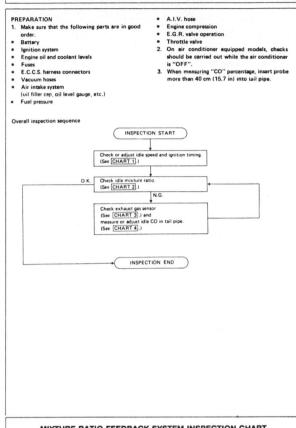

ECCS SELF-DIAGNOSTIC CHART – 1986 THROTTLE BODY TRUCK

EXHAUST GAS SENSOR (Not self-diagnostic item)

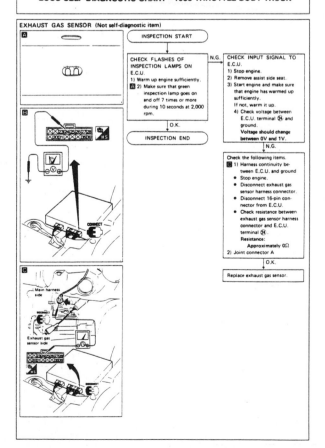

MIXTURE RATIO FEEDBACK SYSTEM INSPECTION CHART
1986 THROTTLE BODY TRUCK

CHART 1
Checking Idle Speed and Ignition Timing

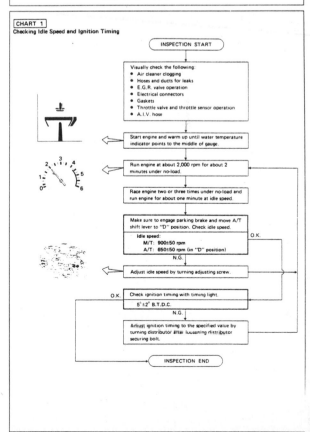

MIXTURE RATIO FEEDBACK SYSTEM INSPECTION CHART
1986 THROTTLE BODY TRUCK

CHART 2
Checking Idle Mixture Ratio

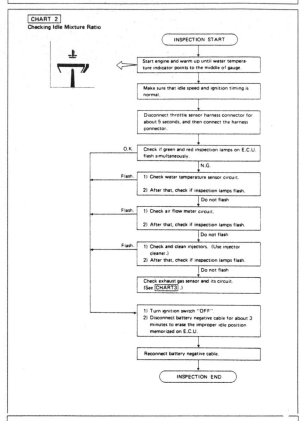

INSPECTION START

Start engine and warm up until water temperature indicator points to the middle of gauge.

Make sure that idle speed and ignition timing is normal.

Disconnect throttle sensor harness connector for about 5 seconds, and then connect the harness connector.

O.K. → Check if green and red inspection lamps on E.C.U. flash simultaneously.

N.G.

Flash. → 1) Check water temperature sensor circuit.
2) After that, check if inspection lamps flash.
Do not flash

Flash. → 1) Check air flow meter circuit.
2) After that, check if inspection lamps flash.
Do not flash

Flash. → 1) Check and clean injectors. (Use injector cleaner.)
2) After that, check if inspection lamps flash.
Do not flash

Check exhaust gas sensor and its circuit. (See CHART3 .)

1) Turn ignition switch "OFF"
2) Disconnect battery negative cable for about 3 minutes to erase the improper idle position memorized on E.C.U.

Reconnect battery negative cable.

INSPECTION END

MIXTURE RATIO FEEDBACK SYSTEM INSPECTION CHART
1986 THROTTLE BODY TRUCK

CHART 4
Measuring and Adjusting Idle CO

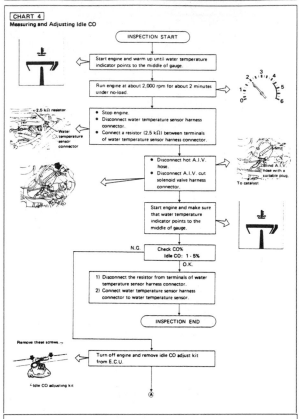

INSPECTION START

Start engine and warm until water temperature indicator points to the middle of gauge.

Run engine at about 2,000 rpm for about 2 minutes under no-load.

- Stop engine.
- Disconnect water temperature sensor harness connector.
- Connect a resistor (2.5 kΩ) between terminals of water temperature sensor harness connector.

- Disconnect hot A.I.V. hose.
- Disconnect A.I.V. cut solenoid valve harness connector.

Start engine and make sure that water temperature indicator points to the middle of gauge.

N.G. → Check CO%
Idle CO: 1 - 5%
O.K.

1) Disconnect the resistor from terminals of water temperature sensor harness connector.
2) Connect water temperature sensor harness connector to water temperature sensor.

INSPECTION END

Turn off engine and remove idle CO adjust kit from E.C.U.

Ⓐ

MIXTURE RATIO FEEDBACK SYSTEM INSPECTION CHART
1986 THROTTLE BODY TRUCK

CHART 3
Checking Exhaust Gas Sensor

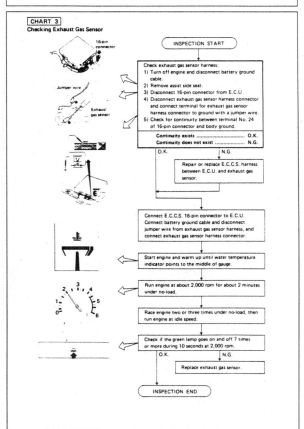

INSPECTION START

Check exhaust gas sensor harness:
1) Turn off engine and disconnect battery ground cable.
2) Remove assist side seat.
3) Disconnect 16-pin connector from E.C.U.
4) Disconnect exhaust gas sensor harness connector and connect terminal for exhaust gas sensor harness connector to ground with a jumper wire.
5) Check for continuity between terminal No. 24 of 16-pin connector and body ground.

Continuity exists .... O.K.
Continuity does not exist .... N.G.

O.K.   N.G.

Repair or replace E.C.C.S. harness between E.C.U. and exhaust gas sensor.

Connect E.C.C.S. 16-pin connector to E.C.U. Connect battery ground cable and disconnect jumper wire from exhaust gas sensor harness, and connect exhaust gas sensor harness connector.

Start engine and warm up until water temperature indicator points to the middle of gauge.

Run engine at about 2,000 rpm for about 2 minutes under no-load.

Race engine two or three times under no-load, then run engine at idle speed.

Check if the green lamp goes on and off 7 times or more during 10 seconds at 2,000 rpm.

O.K.   N.G.

Replace exhaust gas sensor.

INSPECTION END

MIXTURE RATIO FEEDBACK SYSTEM INSPECTION CHART
1986 THROTTLE BODY TRUCK

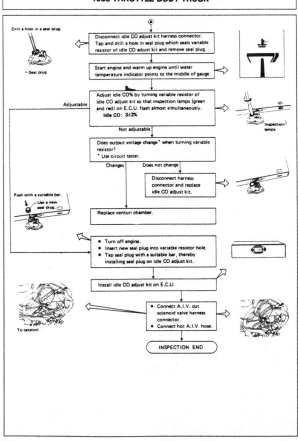

Ⓐ

Disconnect idle CO adjust kit harness connector. Tap and drill a hole in seal plug which seals variable resistor of idle CO adjust kit and remove seal plug.

Start engine and warm up engine until water temperature indicator points to the middle of gauge.

Adjust idle CO% by turning variable resistor of idle CO adjust kit so that inspection lamps (green and red) on E.C.U. flash almost simultaneously.
Idle CO: 3±2%

Not adjustable

Does output voltage change* when turning variable resistor?
* Use circuit tester.

Changes   Does not change

Disconnect harness connector and replace idle CO adjust kit.

Replace venturi chamber.

- Turn off engine.
- Insert new seal plug into variable resistor hole.
- Tap seal plug with a suitable bar, thereby installing seal plug on idle CO adjust kit.

Install idle CO adjust kit on E.C.U.

- Connect A.I.V. cut solenoid valve harness connector.
- Connect hot A.I.V. hose.

INSPECTION END

ECCS SELF-DIAGNOSTIC CHART
1987–88 THROTTLE BODY TRUCK/PATHFINDER WITH VG30i ENGINE

CRANK ANGLE SENSOR (Code No. 11)

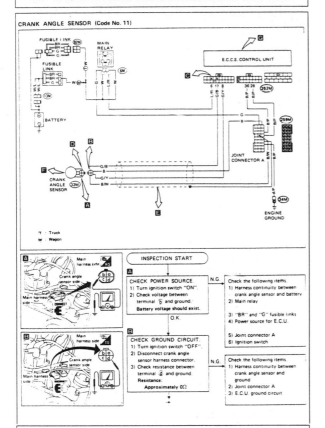

ECCS SELF-DIAGNOSTIC CHART
1987–88 THROTTLE BODY TRUCK/PATHFINDER WITH VG30i ENGINE

AIR FLOW METER (Code No. 12)

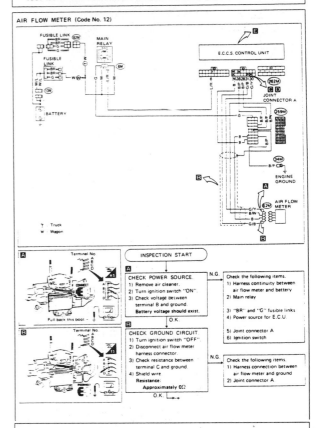

ECCS SELF-DIAGNOSTIC CHART
1987–88 THROTTLE BODY TRUCK/PATHFINDER WITH VG30i ENGINE

CRANK ANGLE SENSOR (Code No. 11)

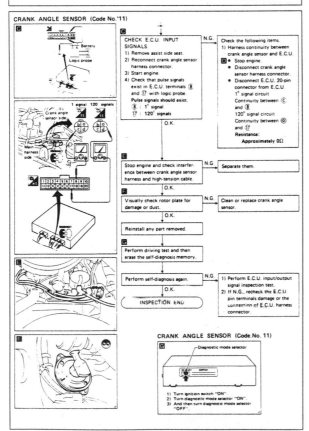

ECCS SELF-DIAGNOSTIC CHART
1987–88 THROTTLE BODY TRUCK/PATHFINDER WITH VG30i ENGINE

AIR FLOW METER (Code No. 12)

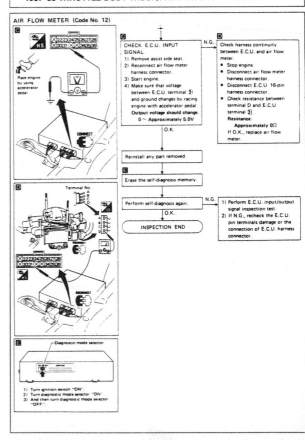

ECCS SELF-DIAGNOSTIC CHART
1987–88 THROTTLE BODY TRUCK/PATHFINDER WITH VG30I ENGINE

CYLINDER HEAD TEMPERATURE SENSOR (Code No. 13)

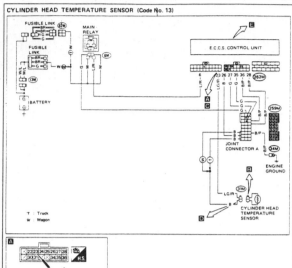

T : Truck
W : Wagon

ECCS SELF-DIAGNOSTIC CHART
1987–88 THROTTLE BODY TRUCK/PATHFINDER WITH VG30I ENGINE

CYLINDER HEAD TEMPERATURE SENSOR (Code No. 13)

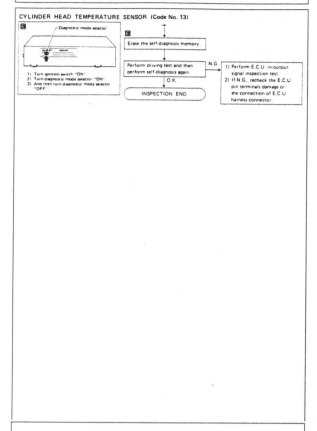

Erase the self-diagnosis memory.

Perform driving test and then perform self-diagnosis again. — N.G. →
1) Perform E.C.U. in-output signal inspection test.
2) If N.G., recheck the E.C.U. pin terminals damage or the connection of E.C.U harness connector.

O.K.

INSPECTION END

Diagnostic mode selector

1) Turn ignition switch "ON".
2) Turn diagnostic mode selector "ON".
3) And then turn diagnostic mode selector "OFF".

ECCS SELF-DIAGNOSTIC CHART
1987–88 THROTTLE BODY TRUCK/PATHFINDER WITH VG30I ENGINE

CYLINDER HEAD TEMPERATURE SENSOR (Code No. 13)

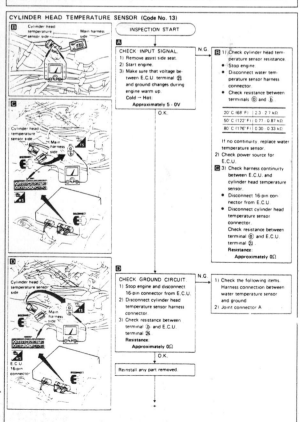

INSPECTION START

CHECK INPUT SIGNAL. — N.G. →
1) Remove assist side seat.
2) Start engine.
3) Make sure that voltage between E.C.U. terminal 23 and ground changes during engine warm up.
Cold → Hot:
Approximately 5 - 0V

O.K.

1) Check cylinder head temperature sensor resistance.
• Stop engine.
• Disconnect water temperature sensor connector.
• Check resistance between terminals 0 and b.

20°C (68°F)	2.3 - 2.7 kΩ
50°C (122°F)	0.77 - 0.87 kΩ
80°C (176°F)	0.30 - 0.33 kΩ

If no continuity, replace water temperature sensor.
2) Check power source for E.C.U.
3) Check harness continuity between E.C.U. and cylinder head temperature sensor.
• Disconnect 16-pin connector from E.C.U
• Disconnect cylinder head temperature sensor connector.
Check resistance between terminal 0 and E.C.U. terminal 23.
Resistance:
Approximately 0Ω

CHECK GROUND CIRCUIT. — N.G. →
1) Stop engine and disconnect 16-pin connector from E.C.U.
2) Disconnect cylinder head temperature sensor harness connector.
3) Check resistance between terminal b and E.C.U. terminal 26.
Resistance:
Approximately 0Ω

O.K.

1) Check the following items.
Harness connection between water temperature sensor and ground
2) Joint connector A

Reinstall any part removed.

ECCS SELF-DIAGNOSTIC CHART
1987–88 THROTTLE BODY TRUCK/PATHFINDER WITH VG30I ENGINE

IGNITION SIGNAL (Code No. 21)

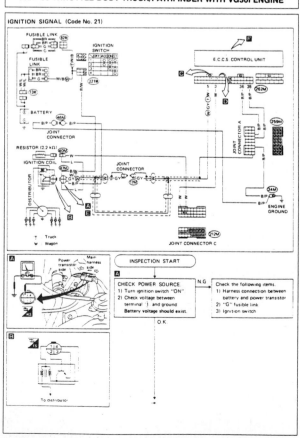

T : Truck
W : Wagon

INSPECTION START

CHECK POWER SOURCE. — N.G. →
1) Turn ignition switch "ON".
2) Check voltage between terminal 1 and ground.
Battery voltage should exist.

O.K.

Check the following items.
1) Harness connection between battery and power transistor
2) "G" fusible link
3) Ignition switch

To distributor

ECCS SELF-DIAGNOSTIC CHART
1987-88 THROTTLE BODY TRUCK/PATHFINDER WITH VG30I ENGINE

IGNITION SIGNAL (Code No. 21)

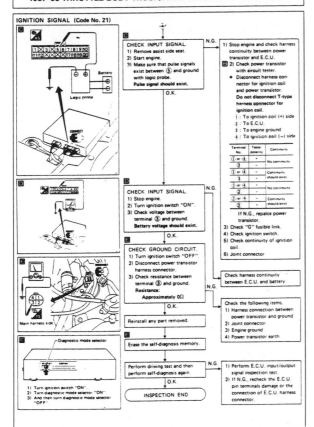

ECCS SELF-DIAGNOSTIC CHART
1987-88 THROTTLE BODY TRUCK/PATHFINDER WITH VG30I ENGINE

EXHAUST GAS SENSOR (Code No. 33)

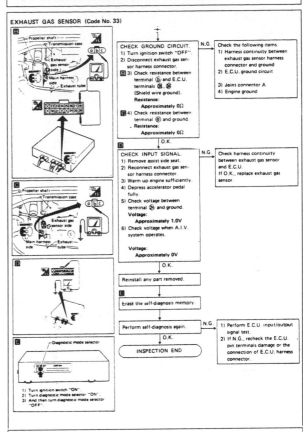

ECCS SELF-DIAGNOSTIC CHART
1987-88 THROTTLE BODY TRUCK/PATHFINDER WITH VG30I ENGINE

EXHAUST GAS SENSOR (Code No. 33)

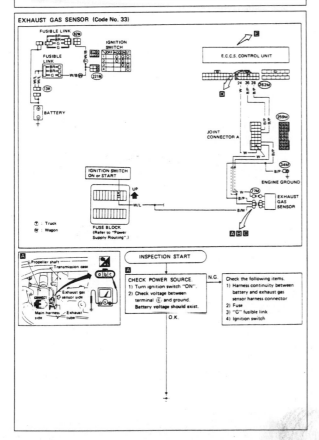

ECCS SELF-DIAGNOSTIC CHART
1987-88 THROTTLE BODY TRUCK/PATHFINDER WITH VG30I ENGINE

THROTTLE SENSOR (Code No. 42)

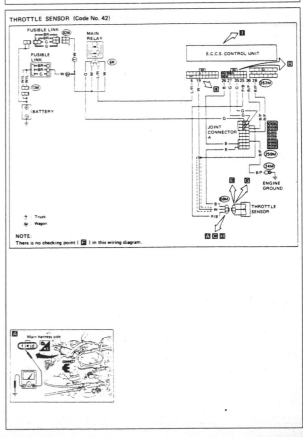

NOTE:
There is no checking point (F) in this wiring diagram.

ECCS SELF-DIAGNOSTIC CHART
1987–88 THROTTLE BODY TRUCK/PATHFINDER WITH VG30I ENGINE

Throttle. Sensor (Code No. 42)

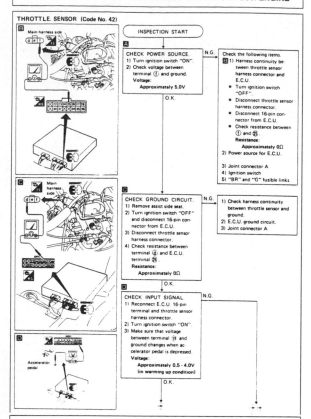

INSPECTION START

CHECK POWER SOURCE.
1) Turn ignition switch "ON".
2) Check voltage between terminal ① and ground.
Voltage:
  Approximately 5.0V

N.G. → Check the following items.
1) Harness continuity between throttle sensor harness connector and E.C.U.
  • Turn ignition switch "OFF".
  • Disconnect throttle sensor harness connector.
  • Disconnect 16-pin connector from E.C.U.
  • Check resistance between ① and ㉕.
  Resistance:
    Approximately 0Ω
2) Power source for E.C.U.
3) Joint connector A
4) Ignition switch
5) "BR" and "G" fusible links

O.K.

CHECK GROUND CIRCUIT.
1) Remove assist side seat.
2) Turn ignition switch "OFF" and disconnect 16-pin connector from E.C.U.
3) Disconnect throttle sensor harness connector.
4) Check resistance between terminal ② and E.C.U. terminal ㉖
Resistance:
  Approximately 0Ω

N.G. → 1) Check harness continuity between throttle sensor and ground.
2) E.C.U. ground circuit.
3) Joint connector A

O.K.

CHECK INPUT SIGNAL.
1) Reconnect E.C.U. 16-pin terminal and throttle sensor harness connector.
2) Turn ignition switch "ON".
3) Make sure that voltage between terminal ⑪ and ground changes when accelerator pedal is depressed.
Voltage:
  Approximately 0.5 - 4.0V
  (in warming up condition)

O.K.

ECCS SELF-DIAGNOSTIC CHART
1987–88 THROTTLE BODY TRUCK/PATHFINDER WITH VG30I ENGINE

Injector (Code No. 43)

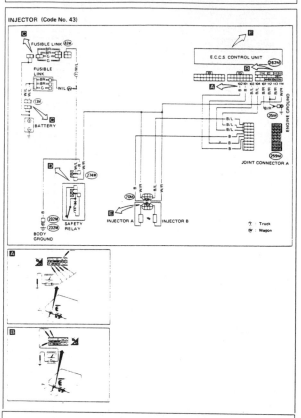

ECCS SELF-DIAGNOSTIC CHART
1987–88 THROTTLE BODY TRUCK/PATHFINDER WITH VG30I ENGINE

THROTTLE SENSOR (Code No. 42)

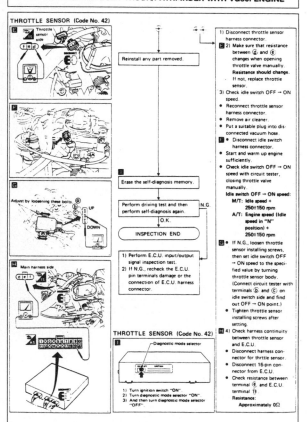

1) Disconnect throttle sensor harness connector.
2) Make sure that resistance between ② and ⓔ changes when opening throttle valve manually.
  Resistance should change.
  If not, replace throttle sensor.
3) Check idle switch OFF → ON speed.
  • Reconnect throttle sensor harness connector.
  • Remove air cleaner.
  • Put a suitable plug into disconnected vacuum hose.
  • Disconnect idle switch harness connector.
  • Start and warm up engine sufficiently.
  • Check idle switch OFF → ON speed with circuit tester, closing throttle valve manually.
  Idle switch OFF → ON speed:
  M/T: Idle speed + 250±150 rpm
  A/T: Engine speed (Idle speed in "N" position) + 250±150 rpm
  • If N.G., loosen throttle sensor installing screws, then set idle switch OFF → ON speed to the specified value by turning throttle sensor body. (Connect circuit tester with terminals ⑤ and ⓒ on idle switch side and find out OFF → ON point.)
  • Tighten throttle sensor installing screws after setting.
4) Check harness continuity between throttle sensor and E.C.U.
  • Disconnect harness connector for throttle sensor.
  • Disconnect 16-pin connector from E.C.U.
  • Check resistance between terminal ⓔ and E.C.U. terminal ⑲
  Resistance:
    Approximately 0Ω

Reinstall any part removed.

Erase the self-diagnosis memory.

Perform driving test and then perform self-diagnosis again.

N.G.

O.K.

INSPECTION END

1) Perform E.C.U. input/output signal inspection test.
2) If N.G., recheck the E.C.U. pin terminals damage or the connection of E.C.U. harness connector.

THROTTLE SENSOR (Code No. 42)

Diagnostic mode selector

1) Turn ignition switch "ON".
2) Turn diagnostic mode selector "ON".
3) And then turn diagnostic mode selector "OFF".

ECCS SELF-DIAGNOSTIC CHART
1987–88 THROTTLE BODY TRUCK/PATHFINDER WITH VG30I ENGINE

INJECTOR (Code No. 43)

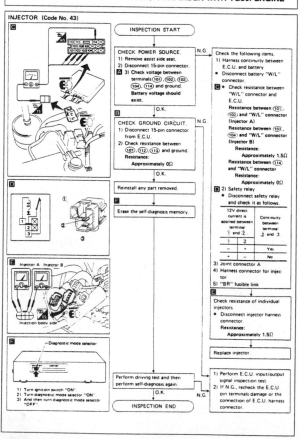

INSPECTION START

CHECK POWER SOURCE.
1) Remove assist side seat.
2) Disconnect 15-pin connector.
3) Check voltage between terminals ⑩⑪, ⑩⑫, ⑩⑬, ⑩⑭, ⑪⑭ and ground.
  Battery voltage should exist.

N.G. → Check the following items.
1) Harness continuity between E.C.U. and battery
  • Disconnect battery "W/L" connector.
2) Check resistance between "W/L" connector and E.C.U.
  Resistance between ⑩⑪, ⑩⑫ and "W/L" connector (Injector A)
  Resistance between ⑩⑬, ⑩⑭ and "W/L" connector (Injector B)
  Resistance:
    Approximately 1.5Ω
  Resistance between ⑪⑭ and "W/L" connector
  Resistance:
    Approximately 0Ω

O.K.

CHECK GROUND CIRCUIT.
1) Disconnect 15-pin connector from E.C.U.
2) Check resistance between ⑩⑦, ⑪⑫, ⑪⑬ and ground.
Resistance:
  Approximately 0Ω

N.G.

2) Safety relay
  • Disconnect safety relay and check it as follows.

12V direct current is applied between terminal		Continuity between	
①	②	② and ③	
–	+	Yes	
+	–	No	

3) Joint connector A
4) Harness connector for injector
5) "BR" fusible link

O.K.

Reinstall any part removed.

Erase the self-diagnosis memory.

Check resistance of individual injectors.
  • Disconnect injector harness connector.
  Resistance:
    Approximately 1.5Ω

Replace injector.

Perform driving test and then perform self-diagnosis again.

O.K.

INSPECTION END

N.G.

1) Perform E.C.U. input/output signal inspection test.
2) If N.G., recheck the E.C.U. pin terminals damage or the connection of E.C.U. harness connector.

Diagnostic mode selector

1) Turn ignition switch "ON".
2) Turn diagnostic mode selector "ON".
3) And then turn diagnostic mode selector "OFF".

ECCS SELF-DIAGNOSTIC CHART
1987–88 THROTTLE BODY TRUCK/PATHFINDER WITH VG30I ENGINE

IDLE SWITCH (Switch ON/OFF diagnosis)

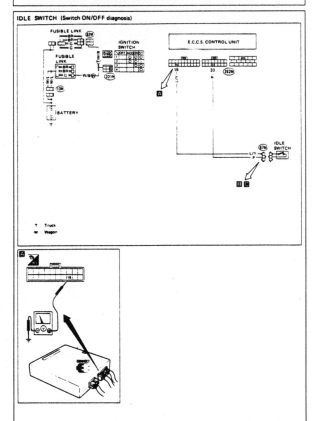

T : Truck
w : Wagon

ECCS SELF-DIAGNOSTIC CHART
1987–88 THROTTLE BODY TRUCK/PATHFINDER WITH VG30I ENGINE

STARTER SWITCH (Switch ON/OFF diagnosis)

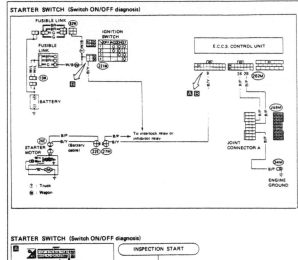

T : Truck
w : Wagon

STARTER SWITCH (Switch ON/OFF diagnosis)

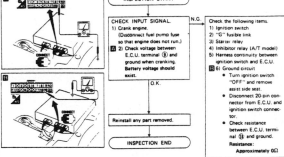

INSPECTION START

CHECK INPUT SIGNAL.
1) Crank engine.
(Disconnect fuel pump fuse so that engine does not run.)
2) Check voltage between E.C.U. terminal ⑨ and ground when cranking. Battery voltage should exist.

N.G. → Check the following items.
1) Ignition switch
2) "G" fusible link
3) Starter relay
4) Inhibitor relay (A/T model)
5) Harness continuity between ignition switch and E.C.U.
6) Ground circuit
- Turn ignition switch "OFF" and remove assist side seat.
- Disconnect 20-pin connector from E.C.U. and ignition switch connector.
- Check resistance between E.C.U. terminal ⑱ and ground.
Resistance:
Approximately 0Ω

O.K.

Reinstall any part removed.

INSPECTION END

ECCS SELF-DIAGNOSTIC CHART
1987–88 THROTTLE BODY TRUCK/PATHFINDER WITH VG30I ENGINE

IDLE SWITCH (Switch ON/OFF diagnosis)

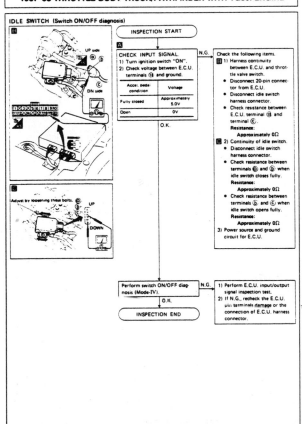

INSPECTION START

CHECK INPUT SIGNAL.
1) Turn ignition switch "ON".
2) Check voltage between E.C.U. terminals ⑱ and ground.

Accel. pedal condition	Voltage
Fully closed	Approximately 5.0V
Open	0V

N.G. → Check the following items.
1) Harness continuity between E.C.U. and throttle valve switch.
- Disconnect 20-pin connector from E.C.U.
- Disconnect idle switch harness connector.
- Check resistance between E.C.U. terminal ⑱ and terminal ⓒ.
Resistance:
Approximately 0Ω
2) Continuity of idle switch.
- Disconnect idle switch harness connector.
- Check resistance between terminals ⓐ and ⓑ when idle switch closes fully.
Resistance:
Approximately 0Ω
- Check resistance between terminals ⓑ and ⓒ when idle switch opens fully.
Resistance:
Approximately 0Ω
3) Power source and ground circuit for E.C.U.

O.K.

Perform switch ON/OFF diagnosis (Mode-IV).

N.G. → 1) Perform E.C.U. input/output signal inspection test.
2) If N.G., recheck the E.C.U. pin terminals damage or the connection of E.C.U. harness connector.

O.K.

INSPECTION END

ECCS SELF-DIAGNOSTIC CHART
1987–88 THROTTLE BODY TRUCK/PATHFINDER WITH VG30I ENGINE

VEHICLE SPEED SENSOR (Switch ON/OFF diagnosis)

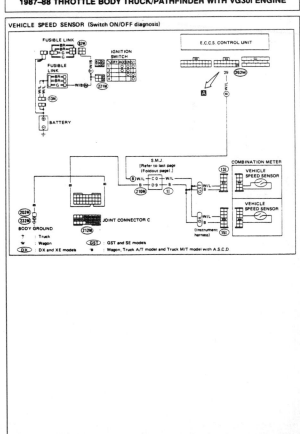

T : Truck
w : Wagon
DX : DX and XE models
GST : GST and SE models
* : Wagon, Truck A/T model and Truck M/T model with A.S.C.D

ECCS SELF-DIAGNOSTIC CHART
1987–88 THROTTLE BODY TRUCK/PATHFINDER WITH VG30I ENGINE

VEHICLE SPEED SENSOR (Switch ON/OFF diagnosis)

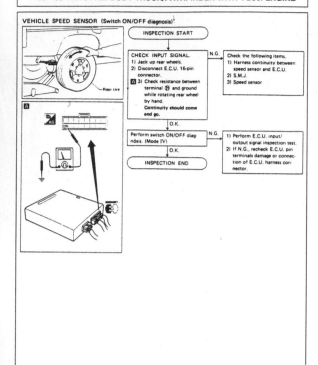

INSPECTION START

CHECK INPUT SIGNAL.
1) Jack up rear wheels.
2) Disconnect E.C.U. 16-pin connector.
3) Check resistance between terminal and ground while rotating rear wheel by hand. Continuity should come and go.

N.G. → Check the following items.
1) Harness continuity between speed sensor and E.C.U.
2) S.M.J.
3) Speed sensor

O.K.

Perform switch ON/OFF diagnosis. (Mode IV)

N.G. →
1) Perform E.C.U. input/output signal inspection test.
2) If N.G., recheck E.C.U. pin terminals damage or connection of E.C.U. harness connector.

O.K.

INSPECTION END

ECCS SELF-DIAGNOSTIC CHART
1987–88 THROTTLE BODY TRUCK/PATHFINDER WITH VG30I ENGINE

NEUTRAL/CLUTCH/INHIBITOR SWITCH (Not self-diagnostic item)

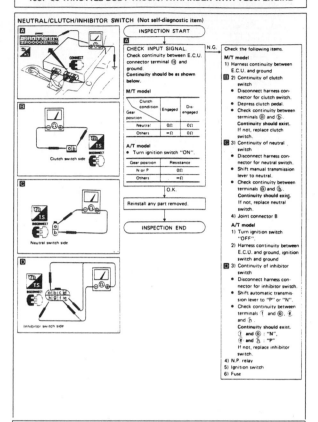

INSPECTION START

CHECK INPUT SIGNAL.
Check continuity between E.C.U. connector terminal and ground. Continuity should be as shown below.

M/T model

Gear position / Clutch condition	Engaged	Disengaged
Neutral	0Ω	0Ω
Others	∞Ω	0Ω

A/T model
• Turn ignition switch "ON".

Gear position	Resistance
N or P	0Ω
Others	∞Ω

N.G. → Check the following items.

M/T model
1) Harness continuity between E.C.U. and ground
2) Continuity of clutch switch
  • Disconnect harness connector for clutch switch.
  • Depress clutch pedal.
  • Check continuity between terminals and . Continuity should exist. If not, replace clutch switch.
3) Continuity of neutral switch
  • Disconnect harness connector for neutral switch.
  • Shift manual transmission lever to neutral.
  • Check continuity between terminals and . Continuity should exist. If not, replace neutral switch.
4) Joint connector B

A/T model
1) Turn ignition switch "OFF".
2) Harness continuity between E.C.U. and ground, ignition switch and ground
3) Continuity of inhibitor switch
  • Disconnect harness connector for inhibitor switch.
  • Shift automatic transmission lever to "P" or "N".
  • Check continuity between terminals and and . Continuity should exist.
    and : "N"
    and : "P"
  If not, replace inhibitor switch.
4) N.P. relay
5) Ignition switch
6) Fuse

O.K.

Reinstall any part removed.

INSPECTION END

ECCS SELF-DIAGNOSTIC CHART
1987–88 THROTTLE BODY TRUCK/PATHFINDER WITH VG30I ENGINE

NEUTRAL/CLUTCH/INHIBITOR SWITCH (Not self-diagnostic item)

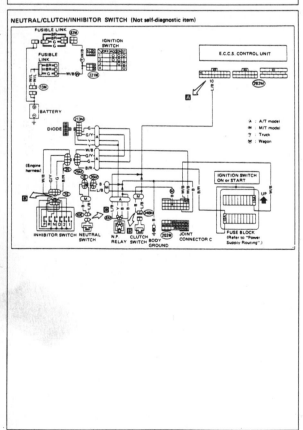

ECCS SELF-DIAGNOSTIC CHART
1987–88 THROTTLE BODY TRUCK/PATHFINDER WITH VG30I ENGINE

LOAD SIGNAL (Not self-diagnostic item)

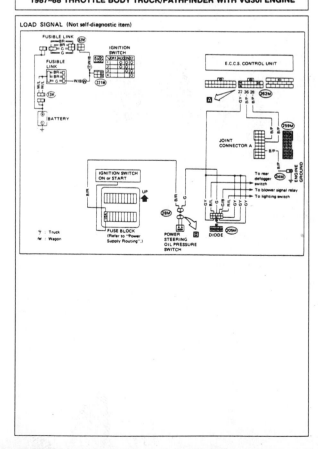

ECCS SELF-DIAGNOSTIC CHART
1987–88 THROTTLE BODY TRUCK/PATHFINDER WITH VG30I ENGINE

LOAD SIGNAL (Not self-diagnostic item)

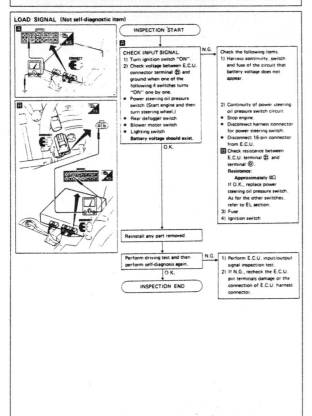

INSPECTION START

A CHECK INPUT SIGNAL.
1) Turn ignition switch "ON".
2) Check voltage between E.C.U. connector terminal 27 and ground when one of the following 4 switches turns "ON" one by one.
- Power steering oil pressure switch (Start engine and then turn steering wheel.)
- Rear defogger switch
- Blower motor switch
- Lighting switch

Battery voltage should exist.

→N.G.→ Check the following items.
1) Harness continuity, switch and fuse of the circuit that battery voltage does not appear.

2) Continuity of power steering oil pressure switch circuit
- Stop engine.
- Disconnect harness connector for power steering switch.
- Disconnect 16-pin connector from E.C.U.
B Check resistance between E.C.U. terminal 27 and terminal 2.
Resistance:
Approximately 0Ω.
If O.K., replace power steering oil pressure switch. As for the other switches, refer to EL section.
3) Fuse
4) Ignition switch

↓O.K.

Reinstall any part removed.

Perform driving test and then perform self-diagnosis again. →N.G.→
1) Perform E.C.U. input/output signal inspection test.
2) If N.G., recheck the E.C.U. pin terminals damage or the connection of E.C.U. harness connector.

↓O.K.

INSPECTION END

ECCS SELF-DIAGNOSTIC CHART
1987–88 THROTTLE BODY TRUCK/PATHFINDER WITH VG30I ENGINE

MIXTURE HEATER (Not self-diagnostic item)

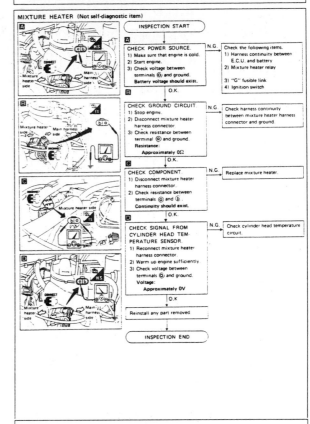

INSPECTION START

A CHECK POWER SOURCE.
1) Make sure that engine is cold.
2) Start engine.
3) Check voltage between terminals ⓐ and ground.
Battery voltage should exist.

→N.G.→ Check the following items.
1) Harness continuity between E.C.U. and battery
2) Mixture heater relay
3) "G" fusible link
4) Ignition switch

↓O.K.

B CHECK GROUND CIRCUIT.
1) Stop engine.
2) Disconnect mixture heater harness connector.
3) Check resistance between terminal ⓐ and ground.
Resistance:
Approximately 0Ω.

→N.G.→ Check harness continuity between mixture heater harness connector and ground.

↓O.K.

C CHECK COMPONENT.
1) Disconnect mixture heater harness connector.
2) Check resistance between terminals ⓐ and ⓑ.
Continuity should exist.

→N.G.→ Replace mixture heater.

↓O.K.

D CHECK SIGNAL FROM CYLINDER HEAD TEMPERATURE SENSOR.
1) Reconnect mixture heater harness connector.
2) Warm up engine sufficiently.
3) Check voltage between terminals ⓐ and ground.
Voltage:
Approximately 0V.

→N.G.→ Check cylinder head temperature circuit.

↓O.K.

Reinstall any part removed

INSPECTION END

ECCS SELF-DIAGNOSTIC CHART
1987–88 THROTTLE BODY TRUCK/PATHFINDER WITH VG30I ENGINE

MIXTURE HEATER (Not self-diagnostic item)

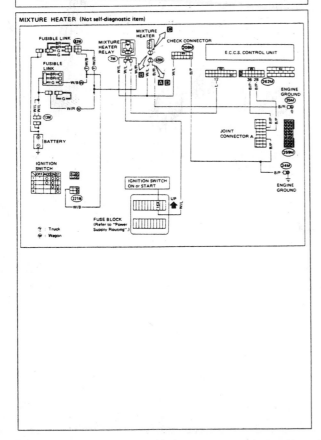

ECCS SELF-DIAGNOSTIC CHART
1987–88 THROTTLE BODY TRUCK/PATHFINDER WITH VG30I ENGINE

MIXTURE HEATER RELAY (Not self-diagnostic item)

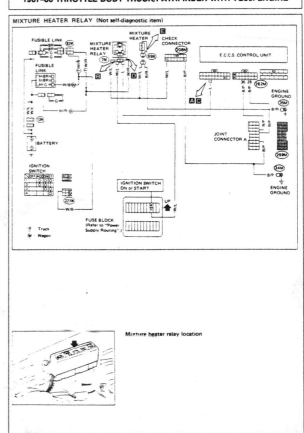

Mixture heater relay location

ECCS SELF-DIAGNOSTIC CHART
1987–88 THROTTLE BODY TRUCK/PATHFINDER WITH VG30I ENGINE

MIXTURE HEATER RELAY (Not self-diagnostic item)

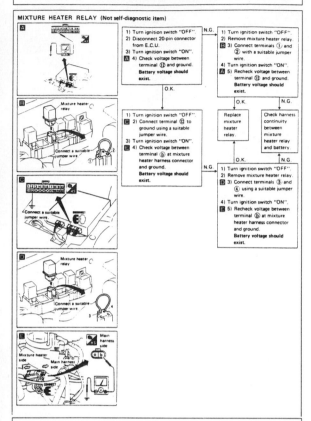

ECCS SELF-DIAGNOSTIC CHART
1987–88 THROTTLE BODY TRUCK/PATHFINDER WITH VG30I ENGINE

FUEL PUMP (Not self-diagnostic item)

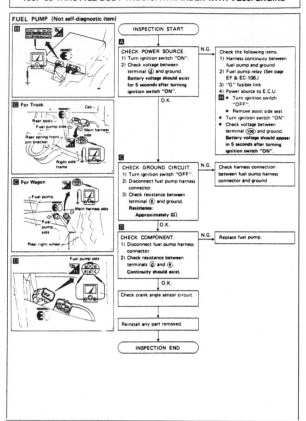

ECCS SELF-DIAGNOSTIC CHART
1987–88 THROTTLE BODY TRUCK/PATHFINDER WITH VG30I ENGINE

FUEL PUMP (Not self-diagnostic item)

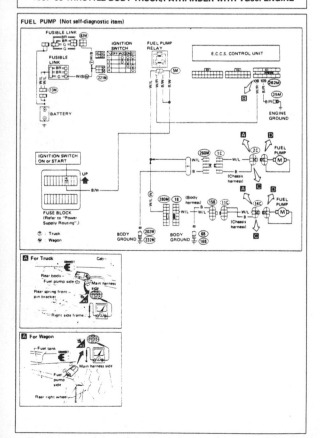

ECCS SELF-DIAGNOSTIC CHART
1987–88 THROTTLE BODY TRUCK/PATHFINDER WITH VG30I ENGINE

FUEL PUMP RELAY (Not self-diagnostic item)

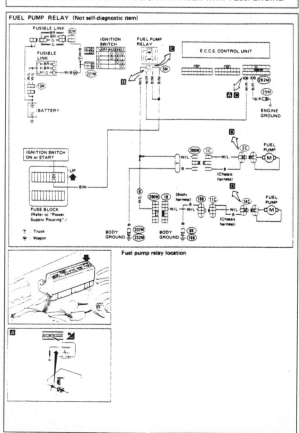

ECCS SELF-DIAGNOSTIC CHART
1987–88 THROTTLE BODY TRUCK/PATHFINDER WITH VG30I ENGINE

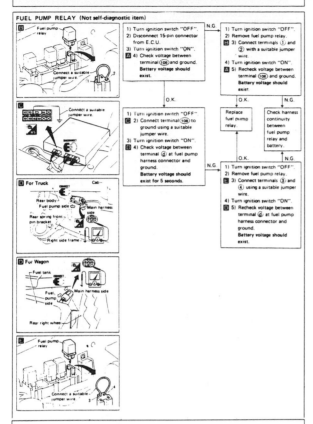

ECCS SELF-DIAGNOSTIC CHART
1987–88 THROTTLE BODY TRUCK/PATHFINDER WITH VG30I ENGINE

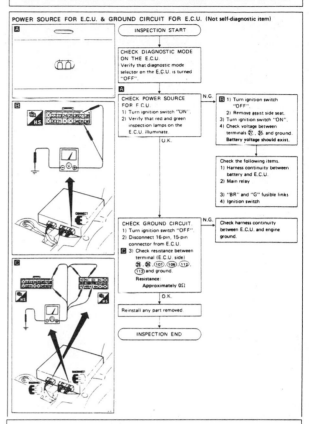

ECCS SELF-DIAGNOSTIC CHART
1987–88 THROTTLE BODY TRUCK/PATHFINDER WITH VG30I ENGINE

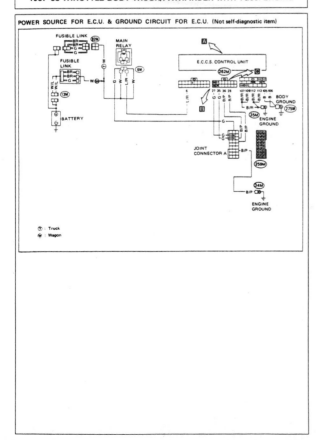

ECCS SELF-DIAGNOSTIC CHART
1987–88 THROTTLE BODY TRUCK/PATHFINDER WITH VG30I ENGINE

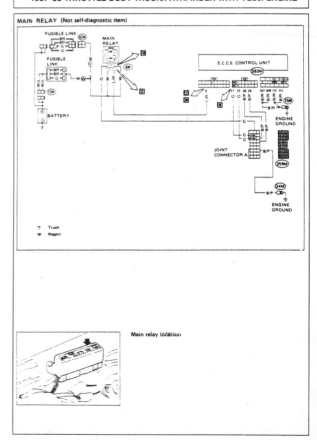

ECCS SELF-DIAGNOSTIC CHART
1987–88 THROTTLE BODY TRUCK/PATHFINDER WITH VG30i ENGINE

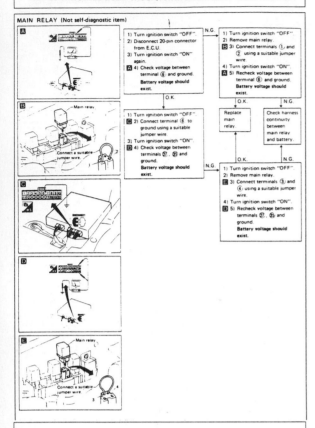

ECCS SELF-DIAGNOSTIC CHART
1987–88 THROTTLE BODY TRUCK/PATHFINDER WITH VG30i ENGINE

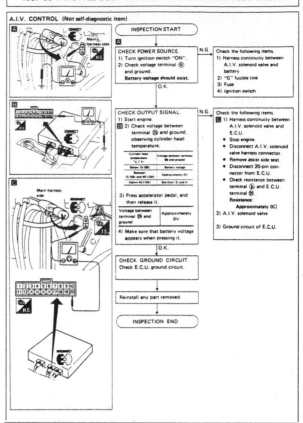

ECCS SELF-DIAGNOSTIC CHART
1987–88 THROTTLE BODY TRUCK/PATHFINDER WITH VG30i ENGINE

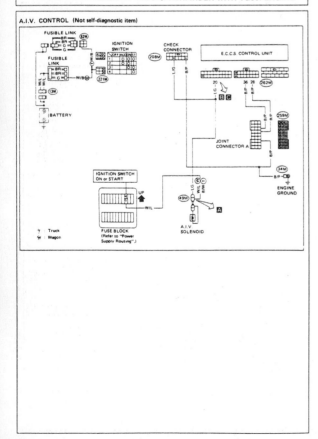

ECCS SELF-DIAGNOSTIC CHART
1987–88 THROTTLE BODY TRUCK/PATHFINDER WITH VG30i ENGINE

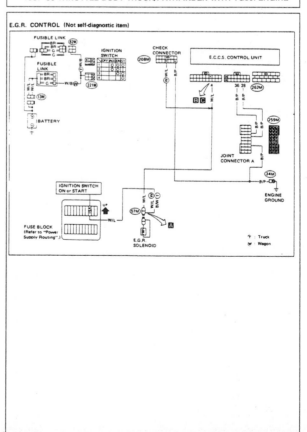

ECCS SELF-DIAGNOSTIC CHART
1987–88 THROTTLE BODY TRUCK/PATHFINDER WITH VG30I ENGINE

E.G.R. CONTROL (Not self-diagnostic item)

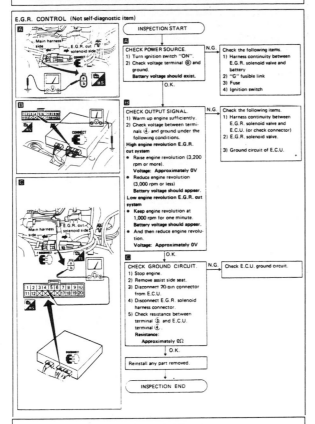

ECCS SELF-DIAGNOSTIC CHART
1987–88 THROTTLE BODY TRUCK/PATHFINDER WITH VG30I ENGINE

IDLE-UP CONTROL (Not self-diagnostic item)

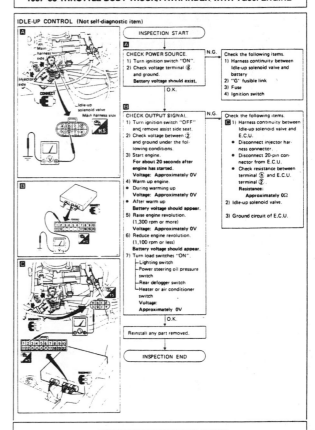

ECCS SELF-DIAGNOSTIC CHART
1987–88 THROTTLE BODY TRUCK/PATHFINDER WITH VG30I ENGINE

IDLE-UP CONTROL (Not self-diagnostic item)

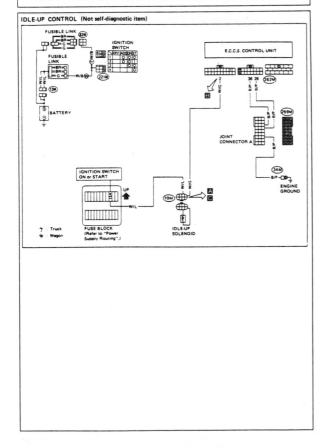

ECCS SELF-DIAGNOSTIC CHART
1987–88 THROTTLE BODY TRUCK/PATHFINDER WITH Z24I ENGINE

CRANK ANGLE SENSOR (Code No. 11)

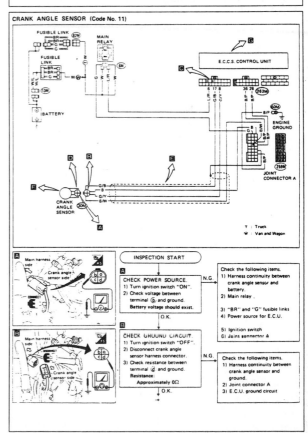

ECCS SELF-DIAGNOSTIC CHART
1987–88 THROTTLE BODY TRUCK/PATHFINDER WITH Z24I ENGINE

CRANK ANGLE SENSOR (Code No. 11)

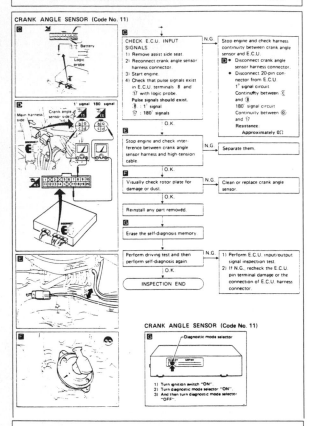

ECCS SELF-DIAGNOSTIC CHART
1987–88 THROTTLE BODY TRUCK/PATHFINDER WITH Z24I ENGINE

AIR FLOW METER (Code No. 12)

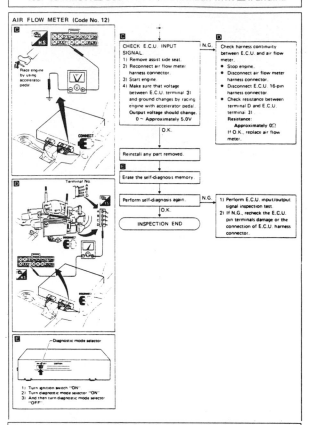

ECCS SELF-DIAGNOSTIC CHART
1987–88 THROTTLE BODY TRUCK/PATHFINDER WITH Z24I ENGINE

AIR FLOW METER (Code No. 12)

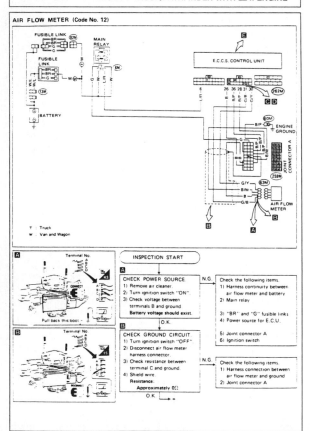

ECCS SELF-DIAGNOSTIC CHART
1987–88 THROTTLE BODY TRUCK/PATHFINDER WITH Z24I ENGINE

WATER TEMPERATURE SENSOR (Code No. 13)

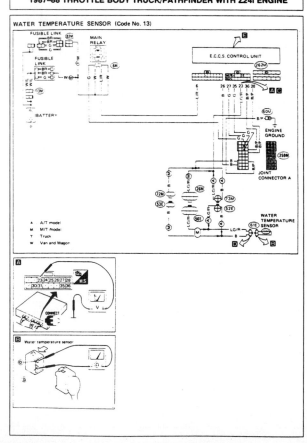

ECCS SELF-DIAGNOSTIC CHART
1987–88 THROTTLE BODY TRUCK/PATHFINDER WITH Z24i ENGINE

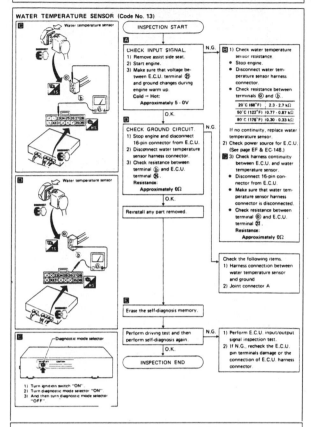

WATER TEMPERATURE SENSOR (Code No. 13)

ECCS SELF-DIAGNOSTIC CHART
1987–88 THROTTLE BODY TRUCK/PATHFINDER WITH Z24i ENGINE

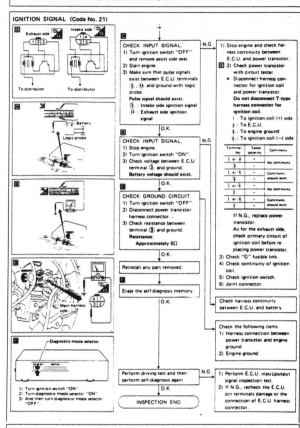

IGNITION SIGNAL (Code No. 21)

ECCS SELF-DIAGNOSTIC CHART
1987–88 THROTTLE BODY TRUCK/PATHFINDER WITH Z24i ENGINE

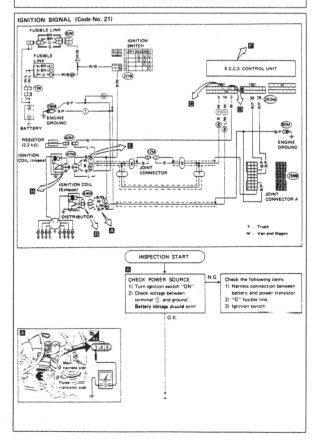

IGNITION SIGNAL (Code No. 21)

ECCS SELF-DIAGNOSTIC CHART
1987–88 THROTTLE BODY TRUCK/PATHFINDER WITH Z24i ENGINE

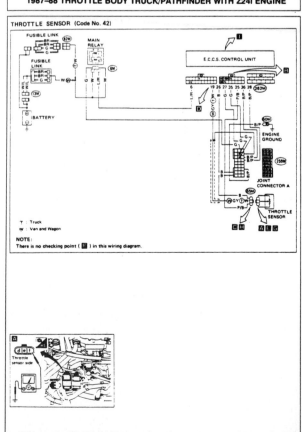

THROTTLE SENSOR (Code No. 42)

ECCS SELF-DIAGNOSTIC CHART
1987-88 THROTTLE BODY TRUCK/PATHFINDER WITH Z24I ENGINE

THROTTLE SENSOR (Code No. 42)

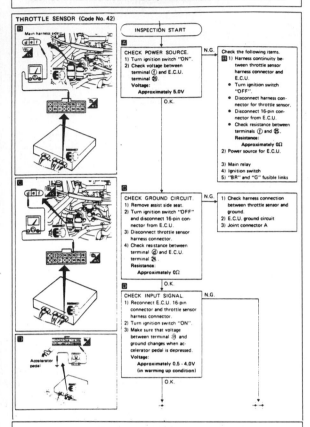

INSPECTION START

CHECK POWER SOURCE.
1) Turn ignition switch "ON".
2) Check voltage between terminal ① and E.C.U. terminal ㉕.
Voltage:
Approximately 5.0V

N.G. → Check the following items.
1) Harness continuity between throttle sensor harness connector and E.C.U.
• Turn ignition switch "OFF".
• Disconnect harness connector for throttle sensor.
• Disconnect 16-pin connector from E.C.U.
• Check resistance between terminals ① and ㉕.
Resistance:
Approximately 0Ω.
2) Power source for E.C.U.
3) Main relay
4) Ignition switch
5) "BR" and "G" fusible links

O.K.

CHECK GROUND CIRCUIT.
1) Remove assist side seat.
2) Turn ignition switch "OFF" and disconnect 16-pin connector from E.C.U.
3) Disconnect throttle sensor harness connector.
4) Check resistance between terminal ④ and E.C.U. terminal ㉖.
Resistance:
Approximately 0Ω

N.G. → Check harness connection between throttle sensor and ground.
1) Check harness connection between throttle sensor and ground.
2) E.C.U. ground circuit
3) Joint connector A

O.K.

CHECK INPUT SIGNAL.
1) Reconnect E.C.U. 16-pin connector and throttle sensor harness connector.
2) Turn ignition switch "ON".
3) Make sure that voltage between terminal ⑲ and ground changes when accelerator pedal is depressed.
Voltage:
Approximately 0.5 - 4.0V
(in warming up condition)

N.G.

O.K.

ECCS SELF-DIAGNOSTIC CHART
1987-88 THROTTLE BODY TRUCK/PATHFINDER WITH Z24I ENGINE

THROTTLE SENSOR (Code No. 42)

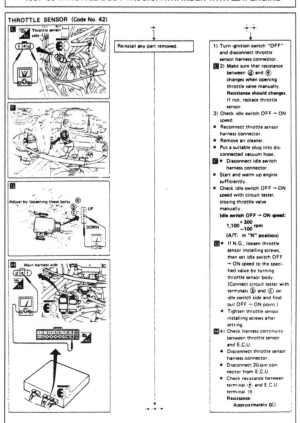

Reinstall any part removed.

1) Turn ignition switch "OFF" and disconnect throttle sensor harness connector.
2) Make sure that resistance between ④ and ⑤ changes when opening throttle valve manually. Resistance should changes. If not, replace throttle sensor.
3) Check idle switch OFF → ON speed.
• Reconnect throttle sensor harness connector.
• Remove air cleaner.
• Put a suitable plug into disconnected vacuum hose.
• Disconnect idle switch harness connector.
• Start and warm up engine sufficiently.
• Check idle switch OFF → ON speed with circuit tester, closing throttle valve manually.
Idle switch OFF → ON speed:
1,100 $^{+300}_{-100}$ rpm
(A/T: in "N" position)
• If N.G., loosen throttle sensor installing screws, then set idle switch OFF → ON speed to the specified value by turning throttle sensor body. (Connect circuit tester with terminals ⓑ and ⓒ on idle switch side and find out OFF → ON point.)
• Tighten throttle sensor installing screws after setting.
4) Check harness continuity between throttle sensor and E.C.U.
• Disconnect throttle sensor harness connector.
• Disconnect 20-pin connector from E.C.U.
• Check resistance between terminal ⓔ and E.C.U. terminal 19
Resistance:
Approximately 0Ω.

ECCS SELF-DIAGNOSTIC CHART
1987-88 THROTTLE BODY TRUCK/PATHFINDER WITH Z24I ENGINE

THROTTLE SENSOR (Code No. 42)

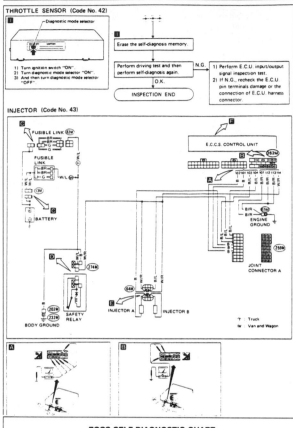

Erase the self-diagnosis memory.

Perform driving test and then perform self-diagnosis again.

N.G. → 1) Perform E.C.U. input/output signal inspection test.
2) If N.G., recheck the E.C.U. pin terminals damage or the connection of E.C.U. harness connector.

O.K.

INSPECTION END

1) Turn ignition switch "ON".
2) Turn diagnostic mode selector "ON".
3) And then turn diagnostic mode selector "OFF".

INJECTOR (Code No. 43)

ECCS SELF-DIAGNOSTIC CHART
1987-88 THROTTLE BODY TRUCK/PATHFINDER WITH Z24I ENGINE

INJECTOR (Code No. 43)

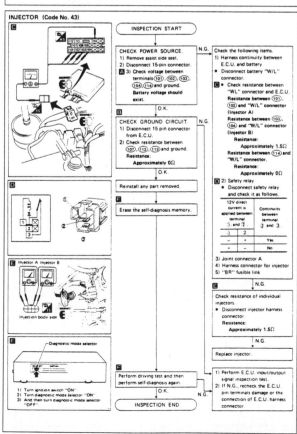

INSPECTION START

CHECK POWER SOURCE.
1) Remove assist side seat.
2) Disconnect 15-pin connector.
3) Check voltage between terminals ⑩①, ⑩②, ⑩③, ⑩④, ⑪④ and ground.
Battery voltage should exist.

N.G. → Check the following items.
1) Harness continuity between E.C.U. and battery.
• Disconnect battery "W/L" connector.
• Check resistance between "WL" connector and E.C.U.
Resistance between ⑩①, ⑩② and "W/L" connector (Injector A)
Resistance between ⑩③, ⑩④ and "W/L" connector (Injector B):
Resistance:
Approximately 1.5Ω
Resistance between ⑪④ and "W/L" connector:
Resistance:
Approximately 0Ω

O.K.

CHECK GROUND CIRCUIT.
1) Disconnect 15 pin connector from E.C.U.
2) Check resistance between ⑩⑦, ⑪②, ⑪③ and ground.
Resistance:
Approximately 0Ω.

N.G.

2) Safety relay
• Disconnect safety relay and check it as follows.

12V direct current is applied between terminal ① and ②		Continuity between terminal ② and ③
①	②	
–	+	Yes
+	–	No

3) Joint connector A
4) Harness connector for injector
5) "BR" fusible link

N.G.

O.K.

Reinstall any part removed.

Erase the self-diagnosis memory.

Check resistance of individual injectors.
• Disconnect injector harness connector.
Resistance:
Approximately 1.5Ω

N.G.

Replace injector.

Perform driving test and then perform self-diagnosis again.

O.K.

N.G. → 1) Perform E.C.U. input/output signal inspection test.
2) If N.G., recheck the E.C.U. pin terminals damage or the connection of E.C.U. harness connector.

INSPECTION END

1) Turn ignition switch "ON".
2) Turn diagnostic mode selector "ON".
3) And then turn diagnostic mode selector "OFF".

ECCS SELF-DIAGNOSTIC CHART
1987–88 THROTTLE BODY TRUCK/PATHFINDER WITH Z24i ENGINE

IDLE SWITCH (Switch ON/OFF diagnosis)

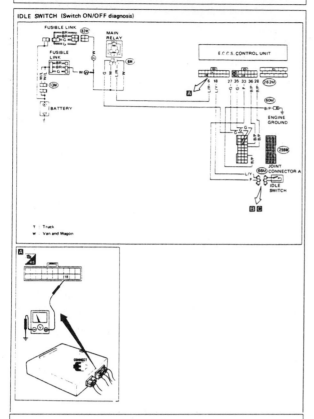

ECCS SELF-DIAGNOSTIC CHART
1987–88 THROTTLE BODY TRUCK/PATHFINDER WITH Z24i ENGINE

STARTER SWITCH (Switch ON/OFF diagnosis)

STARTER SWITCH (Switch ON/OFF diagnosis)

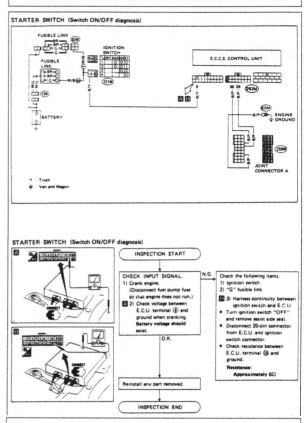

ECCS SELF-DIAGNOSTIC CHART
1987–88 THROTTLE BODY TRUCK/PATHFINDER WITH Z24i ENGINE

IDLE SWITCH (Switch ON/OFF diagnosis)

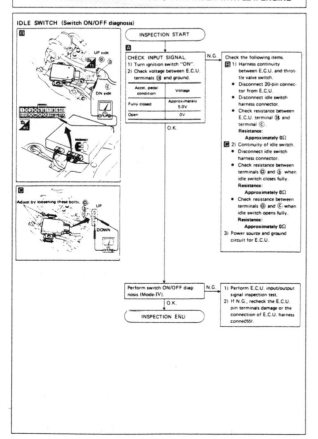

ECCS SELF-DIAGNOSTIC CHART
1987–88 THROTTLE BODY TRUCK/PATHFINDER WITH Z24i ENGINE

NEUTRAL/CLUTCH/INHIBITOR SWITCH (Not self-diagnostic item)

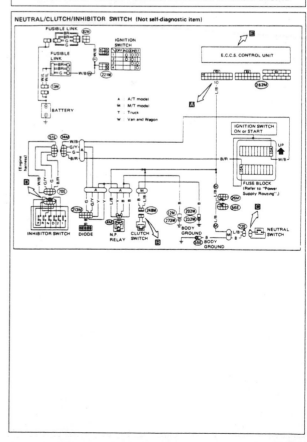

ECCS SELF-DIAGNOSTIC CHART
1987–88 THROTTLE BODY TRUCK/PATHFINDER WITH Z24I ENGINE

NEUTRAL/CLUTCH/INHIBITOR SWITCH (Not self-diagnostic item)

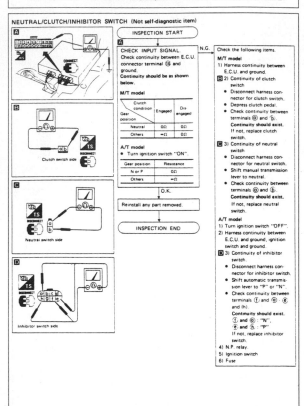

ECCS SELF-DIAGNOSTIC CHART
1987–88 THROTTLE BODY TRUCK/PATHFINDER WITH Z24I ENGINE

MIXTURE HEATER (Not self-diagnostic item)

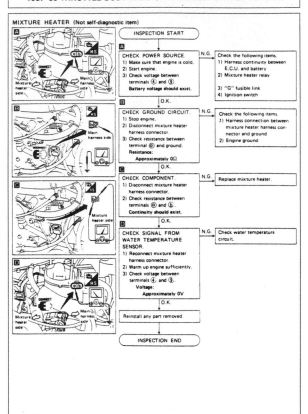

ECCS SELF-DIAGNOSTIC CHART
1987–88 THROTTLE BODY TRUCK/PATHFINDER WITH Z24I ENGINE

MIXTURE HEATER (Not self-diagnostic item)

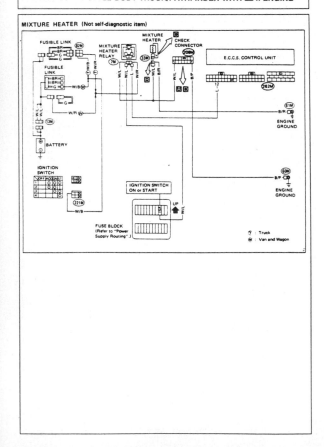

ECCS SELF-DIAGNOSTIC CHART
1987–88 THROTTLE BODY TRUCK/PATHFINDER WITH Z24I ENGINE

MIXTURE HEATER RELAY (Not self-diagnostic item)

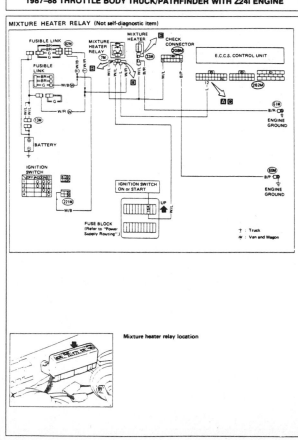

Mixture heater relay location

ECCS SELF-DIAGNOSTIC CHART
1987–88 THROTTLE BODY TRUCK/PATHFINDER WITH Z24I ENGINE

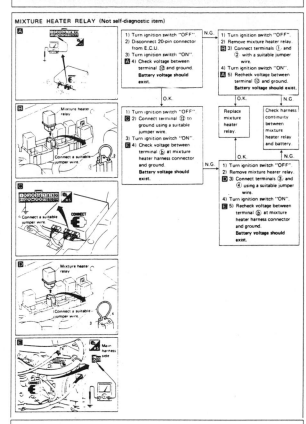

ECCS SELF-DIAGNOSTIC CHART
1987–88 THROTTLE BODY TRUCK/PATHFINDER WITH Z24I ENGINE

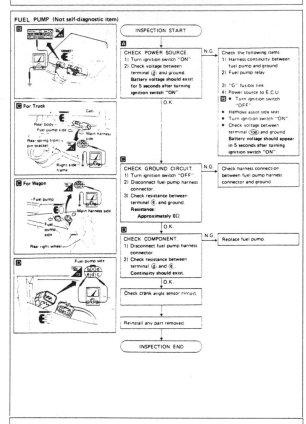

ECCS SELF-DIAGNOSTIC CHART
1987–88 THROTTLE BODY TRUCK/PATHFINDER WITH Z24I ENGINE

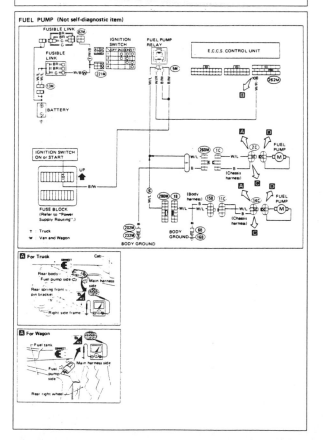

ECCS SELF-DIAGNOSTIC CHART
1987–88 THROTTLE BODY TRUCK/PATHFINDER WITH Z24I ENGINE

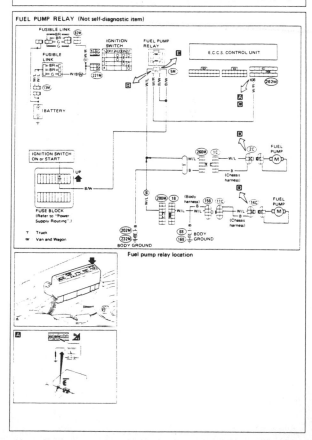

ECCS SELF-DIAGNOSTIC CHART
1987–88 THROTTLE BODY TRUCK/PATHFINDER WITH Z24I ENGINE

FUEL PUMP RELAY (Not self-diagnostic item)

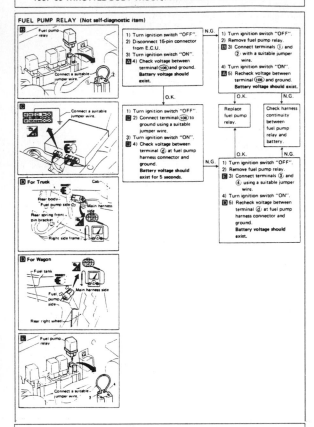

ECCS SELF-DIAGNOSTIC CHART
1987–88 THROTTLE BODY TRUCK/PATHFINDER WITH Z24I ENGINE

POWER SOURCE FOR E.C.U. & GROUND CIRCUIT FOR E.C.U. (Not self-diagnostic item)

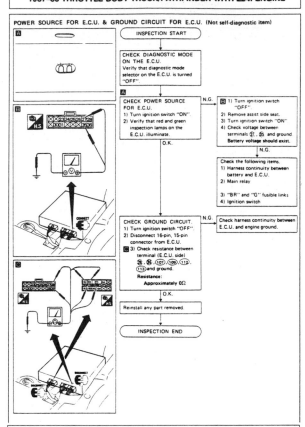

ECCS SELF-DIAGNOSTIC CHART
1987–88 THROTTLE BODY TRUCK/PATHFINDER WITH Z24I ENGINE

POWER SOURCE FOR E.C.U. & GROUND CIRCUIT FOR E.C.U. (Not self-diagnostic item)

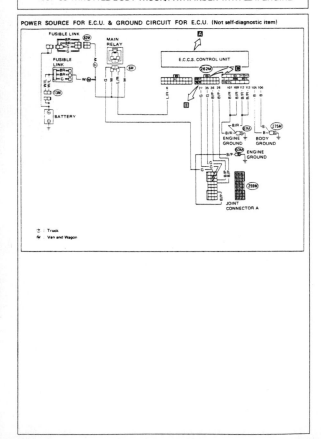

T : Truck
W : Van and Wagon

ECCS SELF-DIAGNOSTIC CHART
1987–88 THROTTLE BODY TRUCK/PATHFINDER WITH Z24I ENGINE

MAIN RELAY (Not self-diagnostic item)

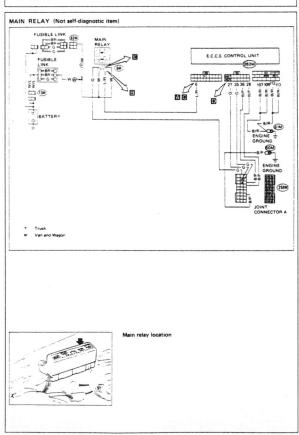

T : Truck
W : Van and Wagon

Main relay location

ECCS SELF-DIAGNOSTIC CHART
1987–88 THROTTLE BODY TRUCK/PATHFINDER WITH Z24I ENGINE

MAIN RELAY (Not self-diagnostic item)

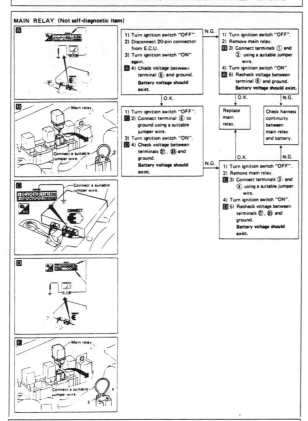

ECCS SELF-DIAGNOSTIC CHART
1987–88 THROTTLE BODY TRUCK/PATHFINDER WITH Z24I ENGINE

A.I.V. CONTROL (Not self-diagnostic item)

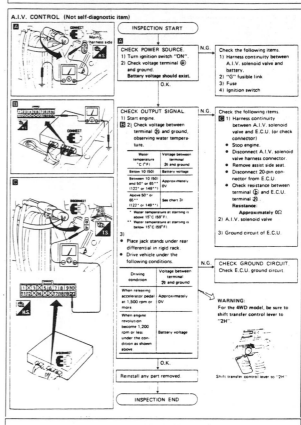

ECCS SELF-DIAGNOSTIC CHART
1987–88 THROTTLE BODY TRUCK/PATHFINDER WITH Z24I ENGINE

A.I.V. CONTROL (Not self-diagnostic item)

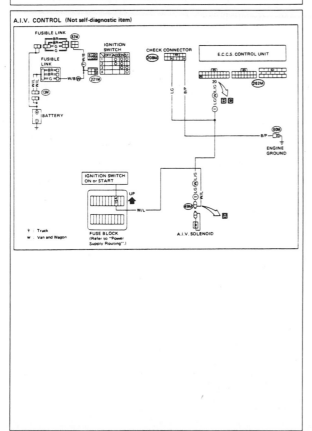

ECCS SELF-DIAGNOSTIC CHART
1987–88 THROTTLE BODY TRUCK/PATHFINDER WITH Z24I ENGINE

E.G.R. CONTROL (Not self-diagnostic item)

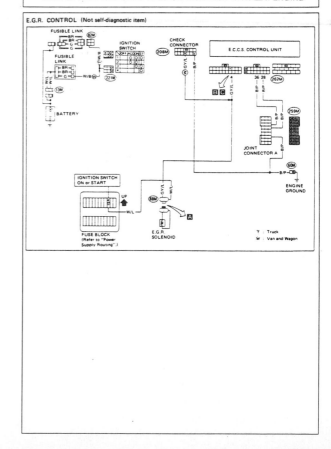

ECCS SELF-DIAGNOSTIC CHART
1987–88 THROTTLE BODY TRUCK/PATHFINDER WITH Z24I ENGINE

E.G.R. CONTROL (Not self-diagnostic item)

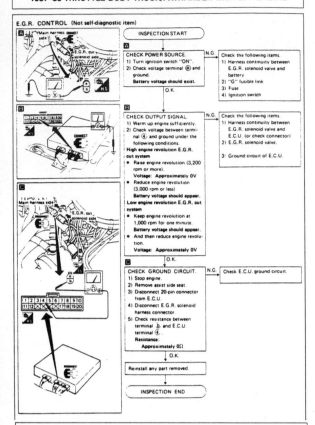

INSPECTION START

A CHECK POWER SOURCE.
1) Turn ignition switch "ON".
2) Check voltage terminal ⓐ and ground.
   Battery voltage should exist.

N.G. → Check the following items.
1) Harness continuity between E.G.R. solenoid valve and battery
2) "G" fusible link
3) Fuse
4) Ignition switch

O.K.

B CHECK OUTPUT SIGNAL.
1) Warm up engine sufficiently.
2) Check voltage between terminal ④ and ground under the following conditions.
High engine revolution E.G.R. cut system
• Raise engine revolution (3,200 rpm or more).
   Voltage: Approximately 0V
• Reduce engine revolution (3,000 rpm or less).
   Battery voltage should appear.
Low engine revolution E.G.R. cut system
• Keep engine revolution at 1,000 rpm for one minute.
   Battery voltage should appear.
• And then reduce engine revolution.
   Voltage: Approximately 0V

N.G. → Check the following items.
1) Harness continuity between E.G.R. solenoid valve and E.C.U. (or check connector)
2) E.G.R. solenoid valve.
3) Ground circuit of E.C.U.

O.K.

C CHECK GROUND CIRCUIT.
1) Stop engine.
2) Remove assist side seat.
3) Disconnect 20-pin connector from E.C.U.
4) Disconnect E.G.R. solenoid harness connector.
5) Check resistance between terminal ⓑ and E.C.U. terminal ④.
   Resistance: Approximately 0Ω

N.G. → Check E.C.U. ground circuit.

O.K.

Reinstall any part removed.

INSPECTION END

ECCS SELF-DIAGNOSTIC CHART
1987–88 THROTTLE BODY TRUCK/PATHFINDER WITH Z24I ENGINE

IDLE-UP CONTROL (Not self-diagnostic item)

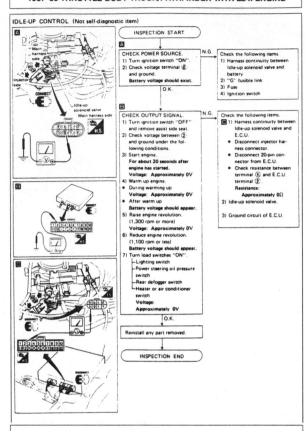

INSPECTION START

A CHECK POWER SOURCE.
1) Turn ignition switch "ON".
2) Check voltage terminal ⓔ and ground.
   Battery voltage should exist.

N.G. → Check the following items.
1) Harness continuity between Idle-up solenoid valve and battery
2) "G" fusible link
3) Fuse
4) Ignition switch

O.K.

B CHECK OUTPUT SIGNAL.
1) Turn ignition switch "OFF" and remove assist side seat.
2) Check voltage between ② and ground under the following conditions.
3) Start engine.
   For about 20 seconds after engine has started.
   Voltage: Approximately 0V
4) Warm up engine.
• During warming up
   Voltage: Approximately 0V
• After warm up
   Battery voltage should appear.
5) Raise engine revolution.
   (1,300 rpm or more)
   Voltage: Approximately 0V
6) Reduce engine revolution.
   (1,100 rpm or less)
   Battery voltage should appear.
7) Turn load switches "ON".
   ┌ Lighting switch
   │ Power steering oil pressure switch
   │ Rear defogger switch
   └ Heater or air conditioner switch
   Voltage: Approximately 0V

N.G. → Check the following items.
C 1) Harness continuity between Idle-up solenoid valve and E.C.U.
• Disconnect injector harness connector.
• Disconnect 20-pin connector from E.C.U.
• Check resistance between terminal ⓗ and E.C.U. terminal ②.
   Resistance: Approximately 0Ω
2) Idle-up solenoid valve.
3) Ground circuit of E.C.U.

O.K.

Reinstall any part removed.

INSPECTION END

ECCS SELF-DIAGNOSTIC CHART
1987–88 THROTTLE BODY TRUCK/PATHFINDER WITH Z24I ENGINE

IDLE-UP CONTROL (Not self-diagnostic item)

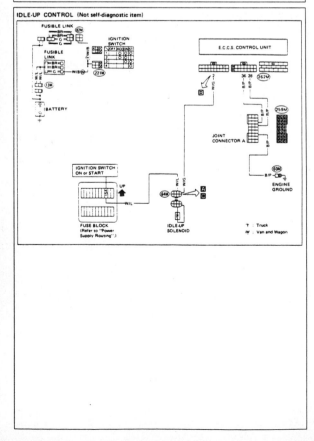

ECCS SELF-DIAGNOSTIC CHART
1987–88 THROTTLE BODY TRUCK/PATHFINDER WITH Z24I ENGINE

SPARK PLUG SWITCHING CONTROL (Not self-diagnostic item)

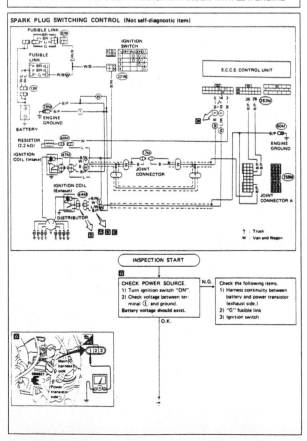

INSPECTION START

A CHECK POWER SOURCE.
1) Turn ignition switch "ON".
2) Check voltage between terminal ① and ground.
   Battery voltage should exist.

N.G. → Check the following items.
1) Harness continuity between battery and power transistor (exhaust side.)
2) "G" fusible link
3) Ignition switch

O.K.

ECCS SELF-DIAGNOSTIC CHART
1987–88 THROTTLE BODY TRUCK/PATHFINDER WITH Z24I ENGINE

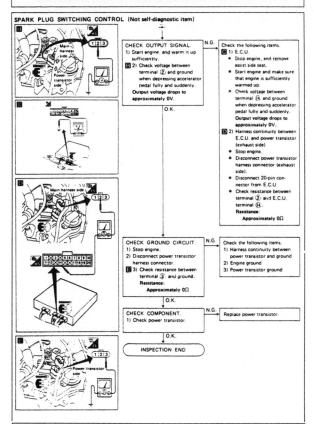

SPARK PLUG SWITCHING CONTROL (Not self-diagnostic item)

CHECK OUTPUT SIGNAL.
1) Start engine, and warm it up sufficiently.
2) Check voltage between terminal ② and ground when depressing accelerator pedal fully and suddenly.
Output voltage drops to approximately 0V.

N.G. → Check the following items.
1) E.C.U.
- Stop engine, and remove assist side seat.
- Start engine and make sure that engine is sufficiently warmed up.
- Check voltage between terminal ⑭ and ground when depressing accelerator pedal fully and suddenly.
Output voltage drops to approximately 0V.
2) Harness continuity between E.C.U. and power transistor (exhaust side)
- Stop engine.
- Disconnect power transistor harness connector (exhaust side).
- Disconnect 20-pin connector from E.C.U.
- Check resistance between terminal ② and E.C.U. terminal ⑭.
Resistance: Approximately 0Ω

O.K. ↓

CHECK GROUND CIRCUIT.
1) Stop engine.
2) Disconnect power transistor harness connector.
3) Check resistance between terminal ③ and ground.
Resistance: Approximately 0Ω

N.G. → Check the following items.
1) Harness continuity between power transistor and ground
2) Engine ground
3) Power transistor ground

O.K. ↓

CHECK COMPONENT.
1) Check power transistor.

N.G. → Replace power transistor.

O.K. ↓

INSPECTION END

ECCS SELF-DIAGNOSTIC CHART
1987–88 THROTTLE BODY TRUCK/PATHFINDER WITH Z24I ENGINE

EXHAUST GAS SENSOR (Not self-diagnostic item)

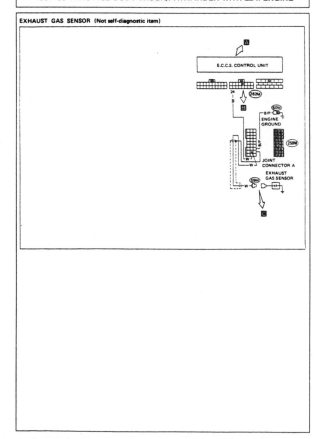

E.C.C.S. CONTROL UNIT

ENGINE GROUND

JOINT CONNECTOR A

EXHAUST GAS SENSOR

ECCS SELF-DIAGNOSTIC CHART
1987–88 THROTTLE BODY TRUCK/PATHFINDER WITH Z24I ENGINE

EXHAUST GAS SENSOR (Not self-diagnostic item)

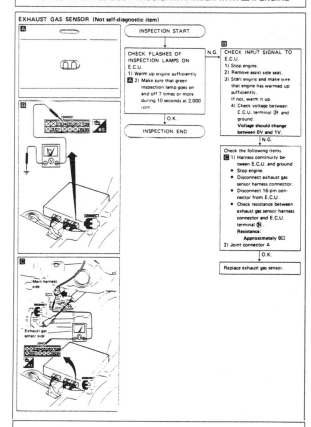

INSPECTION START

CHECK FLASHES OF INSPECTION LAMPS ON E.C.U.
1) Warm up engine sufficiently.
2) Make sure that green inspection lamp goes on and off 7 times or more during 10 seconds at 2,000 rpm.

O.K. ↓

INSPECTION END

N.G. → CHECK INPUT SIGNAL TO E.C.U.
1) Stop engine.
2) Remove assist side seat.
3) Start engine and make sure that engine has warmed up sufficiently.
If not, warm it up.
4) Check voltage between E.C.U. terminal ㉔ and ground.
Voltage should change between 0V and 1V.

N.G. ↓

Check the following items.
1) Harness continuity between E.C.U. and ground.
- Stop engine.
- Disconnect exhaust gas sensor harness connector.
- Disconnect 16-pin connector from E.C.U.
- Check resistance between exhaust gas sensor harness connector and E.C.U. terminal ㉔.
Resistance: Approximately 0Ω
2) Joint connector A

O.K. ↓

Replace exhaust gas sensor.

MIXTURE RATIO FEEDBACK SYSTEM INSPECTION CHART
1987–88 THROTTLE BODY TRUCK/PATHFINDER

PREPARATION
1. Make sure that the following parts are in good order.
- Battery
- Ignition system
- Engine oil and coolant levels
- Fuses
- E.C.C.S. harness connectors
- Vacuum hoses
- Air intake system (oil filler cap, oil level gauge, etc.)
- Fuel pressure
- A.I.V. hose
- Engine compression
- E.G.R. valve operation
- Throttle valve
2. On air conditioner equipped models, checks should be carried out while the air conditioner is "OFF".
3. When measuring "CO" percentage, insert probe more than 40 cm (15.7 in) into tail pipe.

Overall inspection sequence

INSPECTION START
↓
Perform preparation inspection outlined above.
↓
Check or adjust idle speed and ignition timing. (See CHART 1.)
↓ O.K.
Check idle mixture ratio. (See CHART 2.)
↓ N.G.
Check exhaust gas sensor circuit. (See CHART 3A.)
↓ O.K.
Adjust idle mixture ratio with E.C.U. inspection lamps. (See CHART 3B.)
↓ N.G.
Check idle CO adjust kit.
↓
Measure idle CO in tail pipe or adjust idle mixture ratio with E.C.U. inspection lamps. (See CHART 4.)
↓
INSPECTION END

MIXTURE RATIO FEEDBACK SYSTEM INSPECTION CHART
1987–88 THROTTLE BODY TRUCK/PATHFINDER WITH VG30I ENGINE

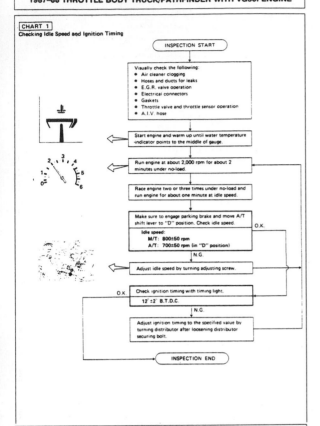

CHART 1
Checking Idle Speed and Ignition Timing

INSPECTION START

Visually check the following:
- Air cleaner clogging
- Hoses and ducts for leaks
- E.G.R. valve operation
- Electrical connectors
- Gaskets
- Throttle valve and throttle sensor operation
- A.I.V. hose

Start engine and warm up until water temperature indicator points to the middle of gauge.

Run engine at about 2,000 rpm for about 2 minutes under no-load.

Race engine two or three times under no-load and run engine for about one minute at idle speed.

Make sure to engage parking brake and move A/T shift lever to "D" position. Check idle speed.

Idle speed:
M/T: 800±50 rpm
A/T: 700±50 rpm (in "D" position)

O.K.

N.G.

Adjust idle speed by turning adjusting screw.

O.K.

Check ignition timing with timing light.
12° ±2° B.T.D.C.

N.G.

Adjust ignition timing to the specified value by turning distributor after loosening distributor securing bolt.

INSPECTION END

MIXTURE RATIO FEEDBACK SYSTEM INSPECTION CHART
1987–88 THROTTLE BODY TRUCK/PATHFINDER WITH Z24I/VG30I ENGINE

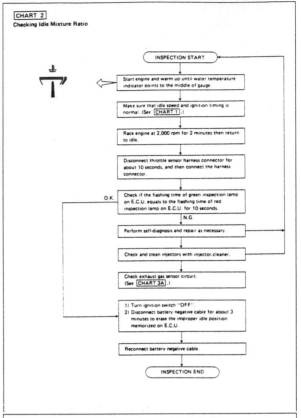

CHART 2
Checking Idle Mixture Ratio

INSPECTION START

Start engine and warm up until water temperature indicator points to the middle of gauge.

Make sure that idle speed and ignition timing is normal. (See CHART 1.)

Race engine at 2,000 rpm for 2 minutes then return to idle.

Disconnect throttle sensor harness connector for about 10 seconds, and then connect the harness connector.

Check if the flashing time of green inspection lamp on E.C.U. equals to the flashing time of red inspection lamp on E.C.U. for 10 seconds.

O.K.

N.G.

Perform self-diagnosis and repair as necessary.

Check and clean injectors with injector cleaner.

Check exhaust gas sensor circuit.
(See CHART 3A.)

1) Turn ignition switch "OFF".
2) Disconnect battery negative cable for about 3 minutes to erase the improper idle position memorized on E.C.U.

Reconnect battery negative cable.

INSPECTION END

MIXTURE RATIO FEEDBACK SYSTEM INSPECTION CHART
1987–88 THROTTLE BODY TRUCK/PATHFINDER WITH Z24I ENGINE

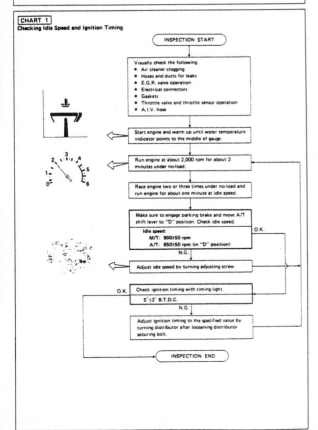

CHART 1
Checking Idle Speed and Ignition Timing

INSPECTION START

Visually check the following:
- Air cleaner clogging
- Hoses and ducts for leaks
- E.G.R. valve operation
- Electrical connectors
- Gaskets
- Throttle valve and throttle sensor operation
- A.I.V. hose

Start engine and warm up until water temperature indicator points to the middle of gauge.

Run engine at about 2,000 rpm for about 2 minutes under no-load.

Race engine two or three times under no-load and run engine for about one minute at idle speed.

Make sure to engage parking brake and move A/T shift lever to "D" position. Check idle speed.

Idle speed:
M/T: 900±50 rpm
A/T: 650±50 rpm (in "D" position)

O.K.

N.G.

Adjust idle speed by turning adjusting screw.

O.K.

Check ignition timing with timing light.
5° ±2° B.T.D.C.

N.G.

Adjust ignition timing to the specified value by turning distributor after loosening distributor securing bolt.

INSPECTION END

MIXTURE RATIO FEEDBACK SYSTEM INSPECTION CHART
1987–88 THROTTLE BODY TRUCK/PATHFINDER WITH VG30I ENGINE

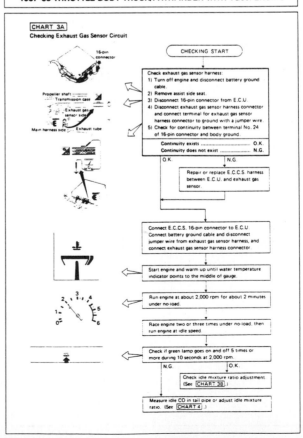

CHART 3A
Checking Exhaust Gas Sensor Circuit

16-pin connector

Propeller shaft
Transmission case
Exhaust gas sensor side
Main harness side   Exhaust tube

CHECKING START

Check exhaust gas sensor harness:
1) Turn off engine and disconnect battery ground cable.
2) Remove assist side seat.
3) Disconnect 16-pin connector from E.C.U.
4) Disconnect exhaust gas sensor harness connector and connect terminal for exhaust gas sensor harness connector to ground with a jumper wire.
5) Check for continuity between terminal No. 24 of 16-pin connector and body ground.

Continuity exists .... O.K.
Continuity does not exist .... N.G.

O.K.   N.G.

Repair or replace E.C.C.S. harness between E.C.U. and exhaust gas sensor.

Connect E.C.C.S. 16-pin connector to E.C.U. Connect battery ground cable and disconnect jumper wire from exhaust gas sensor harness, and connect exhaust gas sensor harness connector.

Start engine and warm up until water temperature indicator points to the middle of gauge.

Run engine at about 2,000 rpm for about 2 minutes under no-load.

Race engine two or three times under no-load, then run engine at idle speed.

Check if green lamp goes on and off 5 times or more during 10 seconds at 2,000 rpm.

N.G.   O.K.

Check idle mixture ratio adjustment.
(See CHART 3B.)

Measure idle CO in tail pipe or adjust idle mixture ratio. (See CHART 4.)

MIXTURE RATIO FEEDBACK SYSTEM INSPECTION CHART
1987–88 THROTTLE BODY TRUCK/PATHFINDER WITH Z24i ENGINE

CHART 3A
Checking Exhaust Gas Sensor Circuit

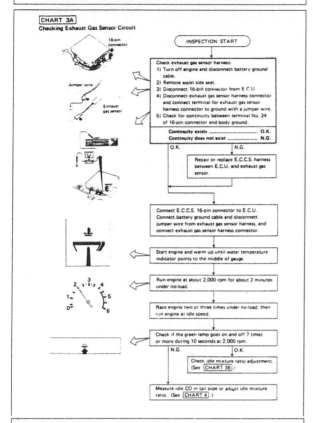

INSPECTION START

Check exhaust gas sensor harness:
1) Turn off engine and disconnect battery ground cable.
2) Remove assist side seat.
3) Disconnect 16-pin connector from E.C.U.
4) Disconnect exhaust gas sensor harness connector and connect terminal for exhaust gas sensor harness connector to ground with a jumper wire.
5) Check for continuity between terminal No. 24 of 16-pin connector and body ground.

Continuity exists .... O.K.
Continuity does not exist .... N.G.

O.K. → | N.G. →

Repair or replace E.C.C.S. harness between E.C.U. and exhaust gas sensor.

Connect E.C.C.S. 16-pin connector to E.C.U. Connect battery ground cable and disconnect jumper wire from exhaust gas sensor harness, and connect exhaust gas sensor harness connector.

Start engine and warm up until water temperature indicator points to the middle of gauge.

Run engine at about 2,000 rpm for about 2 minutes under no-load.

Race engine two or three times under no-load, then run engine at idle speed.

Check if the green lamp goes on and off 7 times or more during 10 seconds at 2,000 rpm.

N.G. | O.K.

Check idle mixture ratio adjustment. (See CHART 3B.)

Measure idle CO in tail pipe or adjust idle mixture ratio. (See CHART 4.)

MIXTURE RATIO FEEDBACK SYSTEM INSPECTION CHART
1987–88 THROTTLE BODY TRUCK/PATHFINDER WITH Z24i/VG30i ENGINE

CHART 3B < Continued >

(A)

1) Turn off engine.
2) Insert new seal plug into variable resistor hole.
3) Tap seal plug with a suitable bar, thereby installing seal plug on idle CO adjust kit.

Push with a suitable bar
Use a new seal plug

Install idle CO adjust kit on E.C.U.

Disconnect battery negative cable for about 3 minutes to erase the improper idle position memorized on E.C.U.

Reconnect battery negative cable.

INSPECTION END

MIXTURE RATIO FEEDBACK SYSTEM INSPECTION CHART
1987–88 THROTTLE BODY TRUCK/PATHFINDER WITH Z24i/VG30i ENGINE

CHART 3B
Adjusting Idle Mixture Ratio with E.C.U. Inspection Lamps

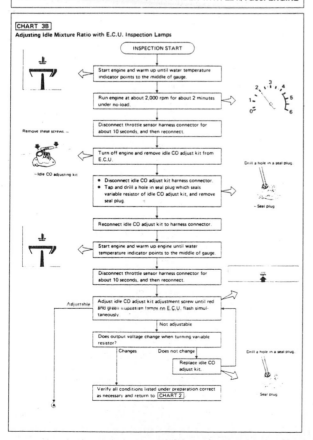

INSPECTION START

Start engine and warm up until water temperature indicator points to the middle of gauge.

Run engine at about 2,000 rpm for about 2 minutes under no-load.

Disconnect throttle sensor harness connector for about 10 seconds, and then reconnect.

Turn off engine and remove idle CO adjust kit from E.C.U.

Remove these screws —
— Idle CO adjusting kit

• Disconnect idle CO adjust kit harness connector.
• Tap and drill a hole in seal plug which seals variable resistor of idle CO adjust kit, and remove seal plug.

Drill a hole in a seal plug.
— Seal plug

Reconnect idle CO adjust kit to harness connector.

Start engine and warm up engine until water temperature indicator points to the middle of gauge.

Disconnect throttle sensor harness connector for about 10 seconds, and then reconnect.

Adjustable

Adjust idle CO adjust kit adjustment screw until red and green inspection lamps on E.C.U. flash simultaneously.

Not adjustable

Does output voltage change when turning variable resistor?

Changes | Does not change

Replace idle CO adjust kit.

Drill a hole in a seal plug.
Seal plug

Verify all conditions listed under preparation correct as necessary and return to CHART 2.

(A)

MIXTURE RATIO FEEDBACK SYSTEM INSPECTION CHART
1987–88 THROTTLE BODY TRUCK/PATHFINDER WITH VG30i ENGINE

CHART 4
Measuring Idle CO in Tail Pipe or Adjusting Idle Mixture Ratio with E.C.U. Inspection Lamps

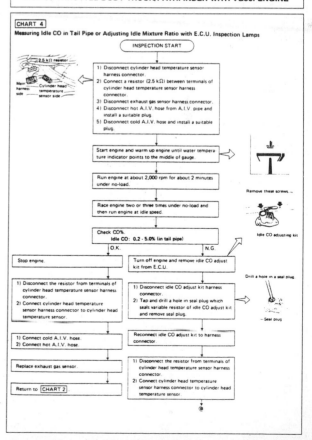

INSPECTION START

2.5 kΩ resistor
Main harness side
Cylinder head temperature sensor side

1) Disconnect cylinder head temperature sensor harness connector.
2) Connect a resistor (2.5 kΩ) between terminals of cylinder head temperature sensor harness connector.
3) Disconnect exhaust gas sensor harness connector.
4) Disconnect hot A.I.V. hose from A.I.V. pipe and install a suitable plug.
5) Disconnect cold A.I.V. hose and install a suitable plug.

Start engine and warm up engine until water temperature indicator points to the middle of gauge.

Run engine at about 2,000 rpm for about 2 minutes under no-load.

Race engine two or three times under no-load and then run engine at idle speed.

Check CO%.
Idle CO: 0.2 - 5.0% (in tail pipe)

O.K. | N.G.

Stop engine.

Turn off engine and remove idle CO adjust kit from E.C.U.

Drill a hole in a seal plug.

Remove these screws —
Idle CO adjusting kit

1) Disconnect the resistor from terminals of cylinder head temperature sensor harness connector.
2) Connect cylinder head temperature sensor harness connector to cylinder head temperature sensor.

1) Disconnect idle CO adjust kit harness connector.
2) Tap and drill a hole in seal plug which seals variable resistor of idle CO adjust kit and remove seal plug.

— Seal plug

1) Connect cold A.I.V. hose.
2) Connect hot A.I.V. hose.

Reconnect idle CO adjust kit to harness connector.

Replace exhaust gas sensor.

1) Disconnect the resistor from terminals of cylinder head temperature sensor harness connector.
2) Connect cylinder head temperature sensor harness connector to cylinder head temperature sensor.

Return to CHART 2.

(B)

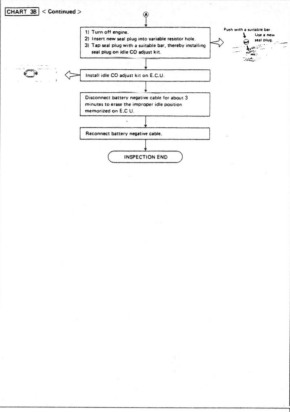

MIXTURE RATIO FEEDBACK SYSTEM INSPECTION CHART
1987–88 THROTTLE BODY TRUCK/PATHFINDER WITH VG30I ENGINE

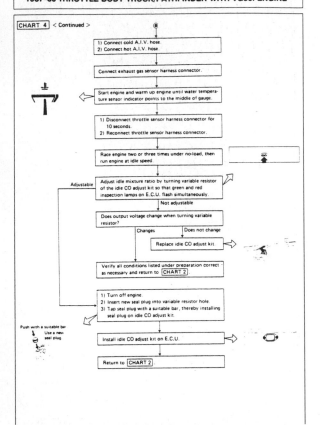

CHART 4 < Continued >

1) Connect cold A.I.V. hose.
2) Connect hot A.I.V. hose.

Connect exhaust gas sensor harness connector.

Start engine and warm up engine until water temperature sensor indicator points to the middle of gauge.

1) Disconnect throttle sensor harness connector for 10 seconds.
2) Reconnect throttle sensor harness connector.

Race engine two or three times under no-load, then run engine at idle speed.

Adjustable

Adjust idle mixture ratio by turning variable resistor of the idle CO adjust kit so that green and red inspection lamps on E.C.U. flash simultaneously.

Not adjustable

Does output voltage change when turning variable resistor?

Changes   Does not change

Replace idle CO adjust kit.

Verify all conditions listed under preparation correct as necessary and return to CHART 2.

1) Turn off engine.
2) Insert new seal plug into variable resistor hole.
3) Tap seal plug with a suitable bar, thereby installing seal plug on idle CO adjust kit.

Push with a suitable bar
Use a new seal plug

Install idle CO adjust kit on E.C.U.

Return to CHART 2.

MIXTURE RATIO FEEDBACK SYSTEM INSPECTION CHART
1987–88 THROTTLE BODY TRUCK/PATHFINDER WITH Z24I ENGINE

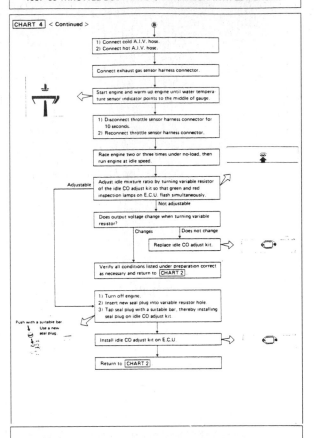

CHART 4 < Continued >

1) Connect cold A.I.V. hose.
2) Connect hot A.I.V. hose.

Connect exhaust gas sensor harness connector.

Start engine and warm up engine until water temperature sensor indicator points to the middle of gauge.

1) Disconnect throttle sensor harness connector for 10 seconds.
2) Reconnect throttle sensor harness connector.

Race engine two or three times under no-load, then run engine at idle speed.

Adjustable

Adjust idle mixture ratio by turning variable resistor of the idle CO adjust kit so that green and red inspection lamps on E.C.U. flash simultaneously.

Not adjustable

Does output voltage change when turning variable resistor?

Changes   Does not change

Replace idle CO adjust kit.

Verify all conditions listed under preparation correct as necessary and return to CHART 2.

1) Turn off engine.
2) Insert new seal plug into variable resistor hole.
3) Tap seal plug with a suitable bar, thereby installing seal plug on idle CO adjust kit.

Push with a suitable bar
Use a new seal plug.

Install idle CO adjust kit on E.C.U.

Return to CHART 2

MIXTURE RATIO FEEDBACK SYSTEM INSPECTION CHART
1987–88 THROTTLE BODY TRUCK/PATHFINDER WITH Z24I ENGINE

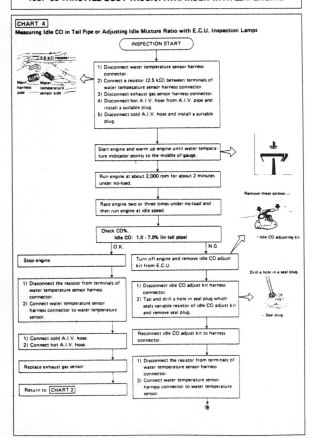

CHART 4

Measuring Idle CO in Tail Pipe or Adjusting Idle Mixture Ratio with E.C.U. Inspection Lamps

INSPECTION START

2.5 kΩ resistor

Main harness side   Water temperature sensor side

1) Disconnect water temperature sensor harness connector.
2) Connect a resistor (2.5 kΩ) between terminals of water temperature sensor harness connector.
3) Disconnect exhaust gas sensor harness connector.
4) Disconnect hot A.I.V. hose from A.I.V. pipe and install a suitable plug.
5) Disconnect cold A.I.V. hose and install a suitable plug.

Start engine and warm up engine until water temperature indicator points to the middle of gauge.

Run engine at about 2,000 rpm for about 2 minutes under no-load.

Remove these screws

Race engine two or three times under no-load and then run engine at idle speed.

Check CO%.
Idle CO: 1.0 - 7.0% (in tail pipe)

O.K.   N.G.

Idle CO adjusting kit

Drill a hole in a seal plug

Stop engine.

Turn off engine and remove idle CO adjust kit from E.C.U.

1) Disconnect the resistor from terminals of water temperature sensor harness connector.
2) Connect water temperature sensor harness connector to water temperature sensor.

1) Disconnect idle CO adjust kit harness connector.
2) Tap and drill a hole in seal plug which seals variable resistor of idle CO adjust kit and remove seal plug.

Seal plug

1) Connect cold A.I.V. hose.
2) Connect hot A.I.V. hose.

Reconnect idle CO adjust kit to harness connector.

Replace exhaust gas sensor.

1) Disconnect the resistor from terminals of water temperature sensor harness connector.
2) Connect water temperature sensor harness connector to water temperature sensor.

Return to CHART 2.

ECCS SELF-DIAGNOSTIC CHART – 1987–88 THROTTLE BODY VAN

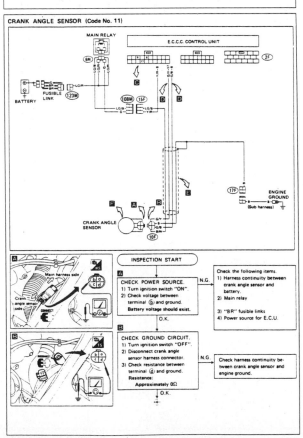

CRANK ANGLE SENSOR (Code No. 11)

MAIN RELAY

E.C.C.C. CONTROL UNIT

BATTERY   FUSIBLE LINK   (123M)

ENGINE GROUND
(Sub harness)

CRANK ANGLE SENSOR

INSPECTION START

A   CHECK POWER SOURCE.
1) Turn ignition switch "ON".
2) Check voltage between terminal (b) and ground.
Battery voltage should exist.

N.G.
Check the following items.
1) Harness continuity between crank angle sensor and battery.
2) Main relay
3) "BR" fusible links
4) Power source for E.C.U.

O.K.

B   CHECK GROUND CIRCUIT.
1) Turn ignition switch "OFF".
2) Disconnect crank angle sensor harness connector.
3) Check resistance between terminal (d) and ground.
Resistance:
Approximately 0Ω

N.G.
Check harness continuity between crank angle sensor and engine ground.

O.K.

ECCS SELF-DIAGNOSTIC CHART – 1987–88 THROTTLE BODY VAN

CRANK ANGLE SENSOR (Code No. 11)

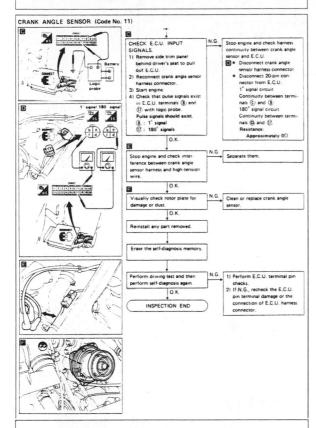

CHECK E.C.U. INPUT SIGNALS
1) Remove side trim panel behind driver's seat to pull out E.C.U.
2) Reconnect crank angle sensor harness connector.
3) Start engine.
4) Check that pulse signals exist in E.C.U. terminals ⑧ and ⑰ with logic probe.
   Pulse signals should exist.
   ⑧ : 1° signal
   ⑰ : 180° signals

N.G. → Stop engine and check harness continuity between crank angle sensor and E.C.U.
• Disconnect crank angle sensor harness connector.
• Disconnect 20-pin connector from E.C.U.
   1° signal circuit
   Continuity between terminals ⓒ and ⑧
   180° signal circuit
   Continuity between terminals ⓐ and ⑰
   Resistance:
   Approximately 0Ω

O.K. ↓

Stop engine and check interference between crank angle sensor harness and high-tension wire. **N.G.** → Separate them.

O.K. ↓

Visually check rotor plate for damage or dust. **N.G.** → Clean or replace crank angle sensor.

O.K. ↓

Reinstall any part removed.

↓

Erase the self-diagnosis memory.

↓

Perform driving test and then perform self-diagnosis again. **N.G.** → 1) Perform E.C.U. terminal pin checks.
2) If N.G., recheck the E.C.U. pin terminal damage or the connection of E.C.U. harness connector.

O.K. ↓

INSPECTION END

ECCS SELF-DIAGNOSTIC CHART – 1987–88 THROTTLE BODY VAN

AIR FLOW METER (Code No. 12)

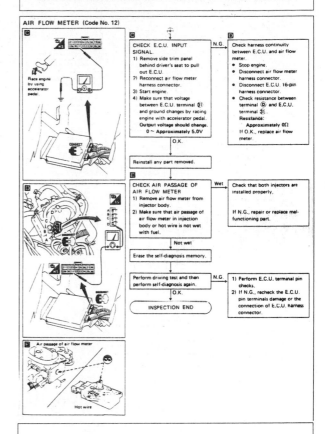

CHECK E.C.U. INPUT SIGNAL
1) Remove side trim panel behind driver's seat to pull out E.C.U.
2) Reconnect air flow meter harness connector.
3) Start engine.
4) Make sure that voltage between E.C.U. terminal ㉛ and ground changes by racing engine with accelerator pedal.
   Output voltage should change.
   0 ~ Approximately 5.0V

N.G. → Check harness continuity between E.C.U. and air flow meter.
• Stop engine.
• Disconnect air flow meter harness connector.
• Disconnect E.C.U. 16-pin harness connector.
• Check resistance between terminal ⓓ and E.C.U. terminal ㉛.
   Resistance:
   Approximately 0Ω
   If O.K., replace air flow meter.

O.K. ↓

Reinstall any part removed.

↓

CHECK AIR PASSAGE OF AIR FLOW METER
1) Remove air flow meter from injector body.
2) Make sure that air passage of air flow meter in injection body or hot wire is not wet with fuel.

Wet → Check that both injectors are installed properly,
If N.G., repair or replace malfunctioning part.

Not wet ↓

Erase the self-diagnosis memory.

↓

Perform driving test and then perform self-diagnosis again. **N.G.** → 1) Perform E.C.U. terminal pin checks.
2) If N.G., recheck the E.C.U. pin terminals damage or the connection of E.C.U. harness connector.

O.K. ↓

INSPECTION END

Air passage of air flow meter

Hot wire

ECCS SELF-DIAGNOSTIC CHART – 1987–88 THROTTLE BODY VAN

AIR FLOW METER (Code No. 12)

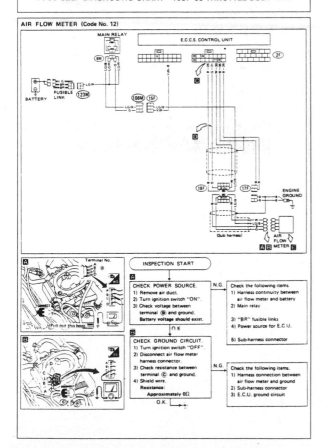

INSPECTION START

↓

CHECK POWER SOURCE.
1) Remove air duct.
2) Turn ignition switch "ON".
3) Check voltage between terminal ⓑ and ground.
   Battery voltage should exist.

N.G. → Check the following items.
1) Harness continuity between air flow meter and battery
2) Main relay
3) "BR" fusible links
4) Power source for E.C.U.
5) Sub-harness connector

O.K. ↓

CHECK GROUND CIRCUIT.
1) Turn ignition switch "OFF".
2) Disconnect air flow meter harness connector.
3) Check resistance between terminal ⓒ and ground.
4) Shield wire.
   Resistance:
   Approximately 0Ω

N.G. → Check the following items.
1) Harness connection between air flow meter and ground
2) Sub-harness connector
3) E.C.U. ground circuit

O.K. ↓

ECCS SELF-DIAGNOSTIC CHART – 1987–88 THROTTLE BODY VAN

WATER TEMPERATURE SENSOR (Code No. 13)

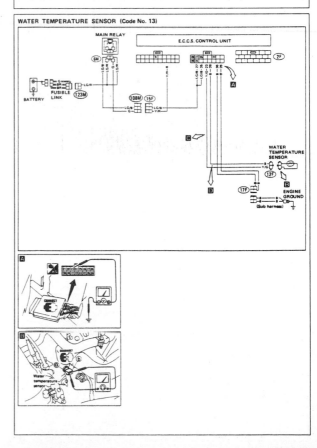

ECCS SELF-DIAGNOSTIC CHART – 1987–88 THROTTLE BODY VAN

WATER TEMPERATURE SENSOR (Code No. 13)

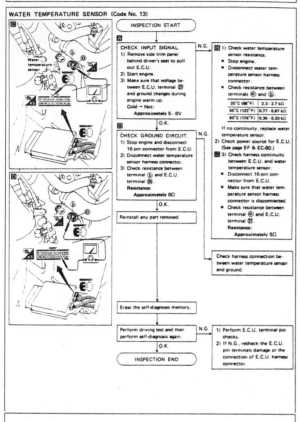

INSPECTION START

A CHECK INPUT SIGNAL.
1) Remove side trim panel behind driver's seat to pull out E.C.U.
2) Start engine.
3) Make sure that voltage between E.C.U. terminal 27 and ground changes during engine warm up.
Cold → Hot:
Approximately 5 - 0V

→ N.G. → **B** 1) Check water temperature sensor resistance.
● Stop engine.
● Disconnect water temperature sensor harness connector.
● Check resistance between terminals ⓐ and ⓑ.

20°C (68°F)	2.3 - 2.7 kΩ
50°C (122°F)	0.77 - 0.87 kΩ
80°C (176°F)	0.30 - 0.33 kΩ

If no continuity, replace water temperature sensor.
2) Check power source for E.C.U. (See page EF & EC-80.)
C 3) Check harness continuity between E.C.U. and water temperature sensor.
● Disconnect 16-pin connector from E.C.U.
● Make sure that water temperature sensor harness connector is disconnected.
● Check resistance between terminal ⓒ and E.C.U. terminal 21.
Resistance:
Approximately 0Ω

O.K.

A CHECK GROUND CIRCUIT. → N.G.
1) Stop engine and disconnect 16-pin connector from E.C.U.
2) Disconnect water temperature sensor harness connector.
3) Check resistance between terminal ⓑ and E.C.U. terminal 26.
Resistance:
Approximately 0Ω

O.K.

Reinstall any part removed.

→ Check harness connection between water temperature sensor and ground.

Erase the self-diagnosis memory.

Perform driving test and then perform self-diagnosis again. → N.G. → 1) Perform E.C.U. terminal pin checks.
2) If N.G., recheck the E.C.U. pin terminals damage or the connection of E.C.U. harness connector.

O.K.

INSPECTION END

ECCS SELF-DIAGNOSTIC CHART – 1987–88 THROTTLE BODY VAN

IGNITION SIGNAL (Code No. 21)

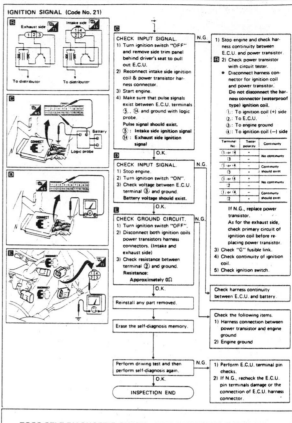

Exhaust side / Intake side
To distributor / To distributor
Battery
Logic probe

A CHECK INPUT SIGNAL. → N.G.
1) Turn ignition switch "OFF" and remove side trim panel behind driver's seat to pull out E.C.U.
2) Reconnect intake side ignition coil & power transistor harness connector.
3) Start engine.
4) Make sure that pulse signals exist between E.C.U. terminals 5 and 14 and ground with logic probe.
Pulse signal should exist.
⑤: Intake side ignition signal
⑭: Exhaust side ignition signal

→ 1) Stop engine and check harness continuity between E.C.U. and power transistor.
B 2) Check power transistor with circuit tester.
● Disconnect harness connector for ignition coil and power transistor.
Do not disconnect the harness connector (waterproof type) ignition coil.
①: To ignition coil (+) side
②: To E.C.U.
③: To engine ground
④: To ignition coil (−) side

Terminal No.	Tester polarity	Continuity
① or ④	+	No continuity
③	−	
③	+	Continuity should exist
① or ④	−	
① or ④	+	No continuity
②	−	
②	+	Continuity should exist
① or ④	−	

If N.G., replace power transistor.
As for the exhaust side, check primary circuit of ignition coil before replacing power transistor.
3) Check "G" fusible link.
4) Check continuity of ignition coil.
5) Check ignition switch.

C CHECK INPUT SIGNAL. → N.G.
1) Stop engine.
2) Turn ignition switch "ON".
3) Check voltage between E.C.U. terminal ③ and ground.
Battery voltage should exist.

O.K.

D CHECK GROUND CIRCUIT. → N.G.
1) Turn ignition switch "OFF".
2) Disconnect both ignition coils power transistors harness connectors. (Intake and exhaust side)
3) Check resistance between terminal ② and ground.
Resistance:
Approximately 0Ω

O.K.

→ Check harness continuity between E.C.U. and battery.

Reinstall any part removed.

→ Check harness connection between E.C.U. and battery.

Erase the self-diagnosis memory.

→ Check the following items.
1) Harness connection between power transistor and engine ground
2) Engine ground

Perform driving test and then perform self-diagnosis again. → N.G. → 1) Perform E.C.U. terminal pin checks.
2) If N.G., recheck the E.C.U. pin terminals damage or the connection of E.C.U. harness connector.

O.K.

INSPECTION END

ECCS SELF-DIAGNOSTIC CHART – 1987–88 THROTTLE BODY VAN

IGNITION SIGNAL (Code No. 21)

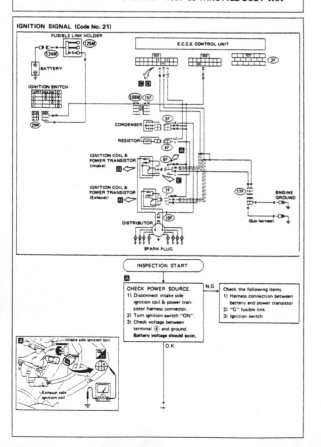

FUSIBLE LINK HOLDER
124M / 125M
BATTERY
E.C.C.S. CONTROL UNIT
2F
IGNITION SWITCH
108M / 15F
CONDENSER 9F
RESISTOR 4F
IGNITION COIL & POWER TRANSISTOR (Intake) 8F
IGNITION COIL & POWER TRANSISTOR (Exhaust) 7F
17F
ENGINE GROUND
(Sub harness)
DISTRIBUTOR 10P
SPARK PLUG

INSPECTION START

A CHECK POWER SOURCE. → N.G.
1) Disconnect intake side ignition coil & power transistor harness connector.
2) Turn ignition switch "ON".
3) Check voltage between terminal ④ and ground.
Battery voltage should exist.

→ Check the following items.
1) Harness connection between battery and power transistor
2) "G" fusible link
3) Ignition switch

O.K.

Intake side ignition coil
Exhaust side ignition coil

ECCS SELF-DIAGNOSTIC CHART – 1987–88 THROTTLE BODY VAN

EXHAUST GAS SENSOR (Code No. 33)

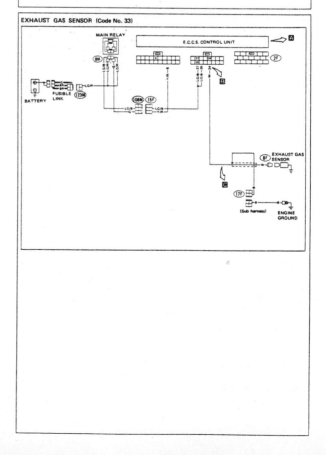

MAIN RELAY
8M
E.C.C.S. CONTROL UNIT
2F
BATTERY
FUSIBLE LINK 123M
108M / 15F
8F EXHAUST GAS SENSOR
17F
(Sub harness) ENGINE GROUND

ECCS SELF-DIAGNOSTIC CHART — 1987–88 THROTTLE BODY VAN

EXHAUST GAS SENSOR (Code No. 33)

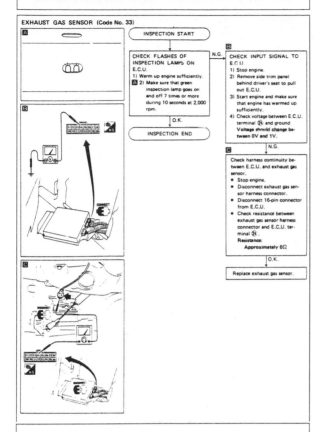

INSPECTION START

CHECK FLASHES OF INSPECTION LAMPS ON E.C.U.
1) Warm up engine sufficiently.
2) Make sure that green inspection lamp goes on and off 7 times or more during 10 seconds at 2,000 rpm.

N.G. →

CHECK INPUT SIGNAL TO E.C.U.
1) Stop engine.
2) Remove side trim panel behind driver's seat to pull out E.C.U.
3) Start engine and make sure that engine has warmed up sufficiently.
4) Check voltage between E.C.U. terminal ㉔ and ground. Voltage should change between 0V and 1V.

N.G. ↓

O.K. → **INSPECTION END**

O.K. ↓

Check harness continuity between E.C.U. and exhaust gas sensor.
• Stop engine.
• Disconnect exhaust gas sensor harness connector.
• Disconnect 16-pin connector from E.C.U.
• Check resistance between exhaust gas sensor harness connector and E.C.U. terminal ㉔.
Resistance:
  Approximately 0Ω

O.K. ↓

Replace exhaust gas sensor.

ECCS SELF-DIAGNOSTIC CHART — 1987–88 THROTTLE BODY VAN

THROTTLE SENSOR (Code No. 42)

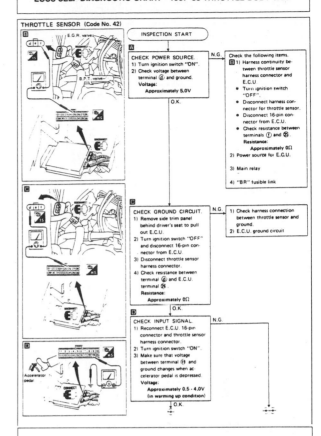

INSPECTION START

CHECK POWER SOURCE.
1) Turn ignition switch "ON".
2) Check voltage between terminal ⓓ and ground.
Voltage:
  Approximately 5.0V

N.G. →

Check the following items.
1) Harness continuity between throttle sensor harness connector and E.C.U
• Turn ignition switch "OFF".
• Disconnect harness connector for throttle sensor.
• Disconnect 16-pin connector from E.C.U.
• Check resistance between terminals ⓕ and ㉕.
Resistance:
  Approximately 0Ω
2) Power source for E.C.U.
3) Main relay
4) "BR" fusible link

O.K. ↓

CHECK GROUND CIRCUIT.
1) Remove side trim panel behind driver's seat to pull out E.C.U.
2) Turn ignition switch "OFF" and disconnect 16-pin connector from E.C.U.
3) Disconnect throttle sensor harness connector.
4) Check resistance between terminal ⓓ and E.C.U. terminal ㉖.
Resistance:
  Approximately 0Ω

N.G. →

1) Check harness connection between throttle sensor and ground.
2) E.C.U. ground circuit

O.K. ↓

CHECK INPUT SIGNAL.
1) Reconnect E.C.U. 16-pin connector and throttle sensor harness connector.
2) Turn ignition switch "ON".
3) Make sure that voltage between terminal ⑲ and ground changes when accelerator pedal is depressed.
Voltage:
  Approximately 0.5 - 4.0V
  (in warming up condition)

N.G. →

O.K. ↓

ECCS SELF-DIAGNOSTIC CHART — 1987–88 THROTTLE BODY VAN

THROTTLE SENSOR (Code No. 42)

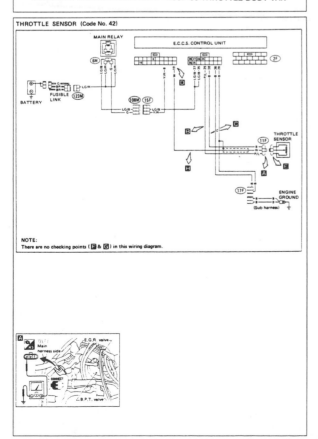

E.C.C.S. CONTROL UNIT

MAIN RELAY

BATTERY — FUSIBLE LINK

THROTTLE SENSOR

ENGINE GROUND
(Sub harness)

NOTE:
There are no checking points (F & G) in this wiring diagram.

ECCS SELF-DIAGNOSTIC CHART — 1987–88 THROTTLE BODY VAN

THROTTLE SENSOR (Code No. 42)

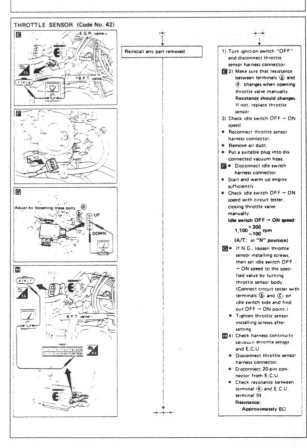

Reinstall any part removed.

1) Turn ignition switch "OFF" and disconnect throttle sensor harness connector.
2) Make sure that resistance between terminals ⓓ and ⓔ changes when opening throttle valve manually. Resistance should changes. If not, replace throttle sensor.
3) Check idle switch OFF → ON speed
• Reconnect throttle sensor harness connector.
• Remove air duct.
• Put a suitable plug into disconnected vacuum hose.
• Disconnect idle switch harness connector.
• Start and warm up engine sufficiently.
• Check idle switch OFF → ON speed with circuit tester, closing throttle valve manually.
Idle switch OFF → ON speed:
  $1,100^{+300}_{-100}$ rpm
  (A/T: in "N" position)
• If N.G., loosen throttle sensor installing screws, then set idle switch OFF → ON speed to the specified value by turning throttle sensor body. (Connect circuit tester with terminals ⓑ and ⓒ on idle switch side and find out OFF → ON point.)
• Tighten throttle sensor installing screws after setting.
4) Check harness continuity between throttle sensor and E.C.U.
• Disconnect throttle sensor harness connector.
• Disconnect 20-pin connector from E.C.U.
• Check resistance between terminal ⓔ and E.C.U. terminal ⑲.
Resistance:
  Approximately 0Ω

ECCS SELF-DIAGNOSTIC CHART – 1987–88 THROTTLE BODY VAN

THROTTLE SENSOR (Code No. 42)

INJECTOR (Code No. 43)

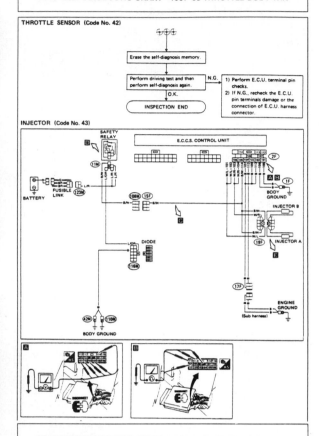

ECCS SELF-DIAGNOSTIC CHART – 1987–88 THROTTLE BODY VAN

IDLE SWITCH (Switch ON/OFF diagnosis)

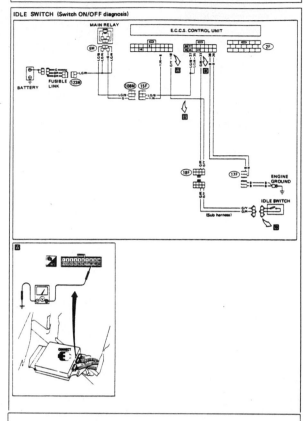

ECCS SELF-DIAGNOSTIC CHART – 1987–88 THROTTLE BODY VAN

INJECTOR (Code No. 43)

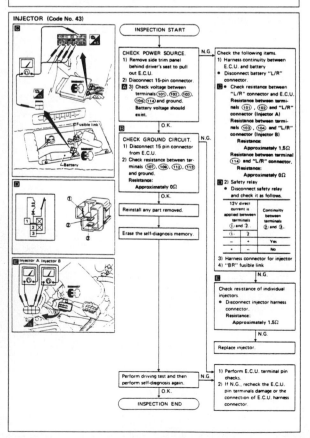

ECCS SELF-DIAGNOSTIC CHART – 1987–88 THROTTLE BODY VAN

IDLE SWITCH (Switch ON/OFF diagnosis)

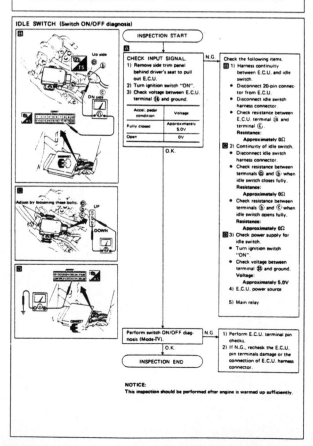

NOTICE:
This inspection should be performed after engine is warmed up sufficiently.

ECCS SELF-DIAGNOSTIC CHART – 1987–88 THROTTLE BODY VAN

STARTER SWITCH (Switch ON/OFF diagnosis)

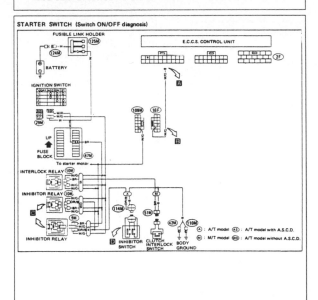

ECCS SELF-DIAGNOSTIC CHART – 1987–88 THROTTLE BODY VAN

VEHICLE SPEED SENSOR (Switch ON/OFF diagnosis)

VEHICLE SPEED SENSOR (Switch ON/OFF diagnosis)

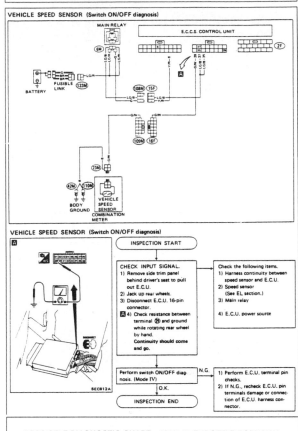

ECCS SELF-DIAGNOSTIC CHART – 1987–88 THROTTLE BODY VAN

STARTER SWITCH (Switch ON/OFF diagnosis)

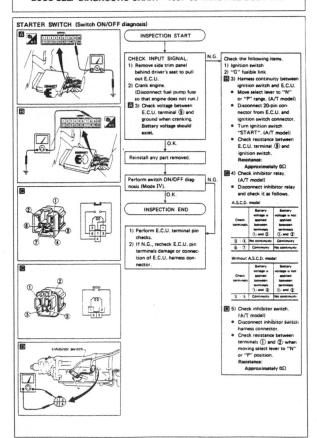

ECCS SELF-DIAGNOSTIC CHART – 1987–88 THROTTLE BODY VAN

CLUTCH SWITCH (Not self-diagnostic item)

CLUTCH SWITCH (Not self-diagnostic item)

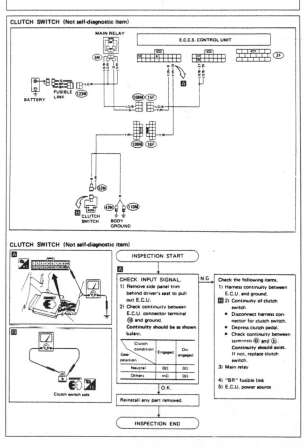

ECCS SELF-DIAGNOSTIC CHART – 1987–88 THROTTLE BODY VAN

MIXTURE HEATER (Not self-diagnostic item)

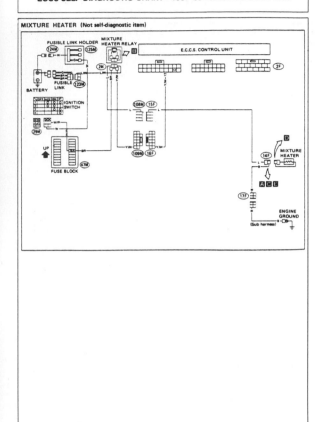

ECCS SELF-DIAGNOSTIC CHART – 1987–88 THROTTLE BODY VAN

FUEL PUMP (Not self-diagnostic item)

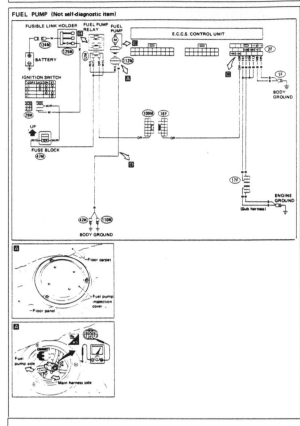

ECCS SELF-DIAGNOSTIC CHART – 1987–88 THROTTLE BODY VAN

MIXTURE HEATER (Not self-diagnostic item)

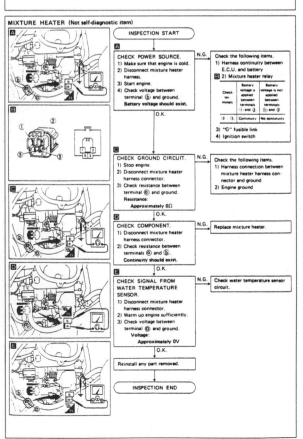

ECCS SELF-DIAGNOSTIC CHART – 1987–88 THROTTLE BODY VAN

FUEL PUMP (Not self-diagnostic item)

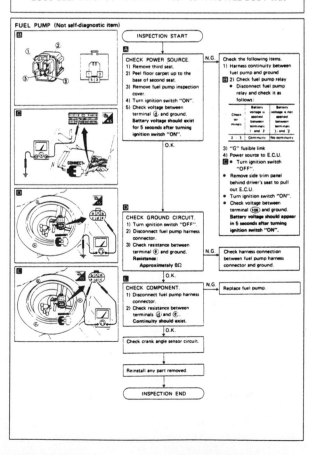

ECCS SELF-DIAGNOSTIC CHART – 1987–88 THROTTLE BODY VAN

POWER SOURCE FOR E.C.U. & GROUND CIRCUIT FOR E.C.U. (Not self-diagnostic item)

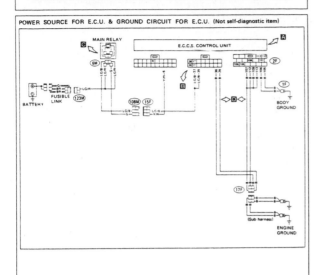

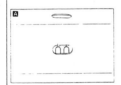

ECCS SELF-DIAGNOSTIC CHART – 1987–88 THROTTLE BODY VAN

A.I.V. CONTROL (Not self-diagnostic item)

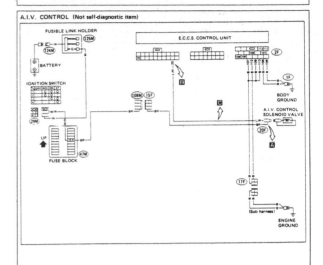

ECCS SELF-DIAGNOSTIC CHART – 1987–88 THROTTLE BODY VAN

POWER SOURCE FOR E.C.U. & GROUND CIRCUIT FOR E.C.U. (Not self-diagnostic item)

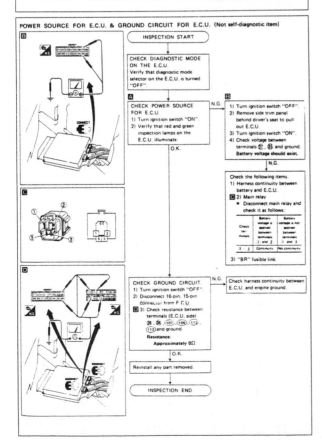

ECCS SELF-DIAGNOSTIC CHART – 1987–88 THROTTLE BODY VAN

A.I.V. CONTROL (Not self-diagnostic item)

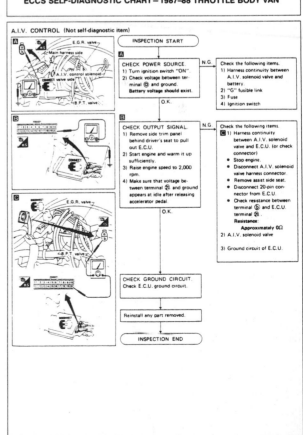

ECCS SELF-DIAGNOSTIC CHART—1987–88 THROTTLE BODY VAN

E.G.R. CONTROL (Not self-diagnostic item)

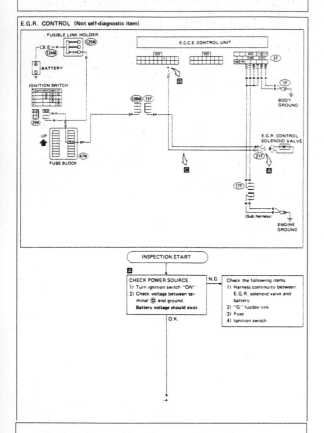

INSPECTION START

| A | CHECK POWER SOURCE | N.G | Check the following items. |

CHECK POWER SOURCE
1) Turn ignition switch "ON".
2) Check voltage between terminal ⓐ and ground.
Battery voltage should exist.

Check the following items.
1) Harness continuity between E.G.R. solenoid valve and battery
2) "G" fusible link
3) Fuse
4) Ignition switch

O.K.

ECCS SELF-DIAGNOSTIC CHART—1987–88 THROTTLE BODY VAN

IDLE-UP CONTROL (Not self-diagnostic item)

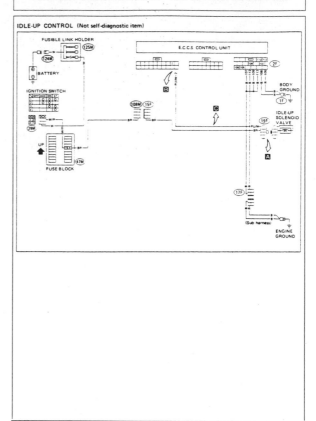

ECCS SELF-DIAGNOSTIC CHART—1987–88 THROTTLE BODY VAN

E.G.R. CONTROL (Not self-diagnostic item)

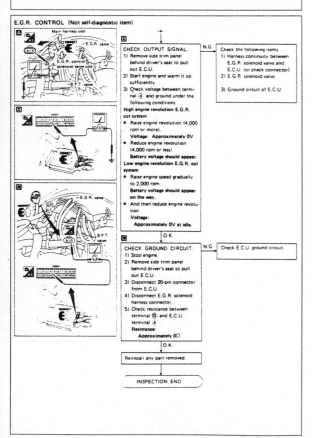

CHECK OUTPUT SIGNAL.
1) Remove side trim panel behind driver's seat to pull out E.C.U.
2) Start engine and warm it up sufficiently.
3) Check voltage between terminal ④ and ground under the following conditions.
High engine revolution E.G.R. cut system
● Raise engine revolution (4,000 rpm or more).
Voltage: Approximately 0V
● Reduce engine revolution (4,000 rpm or less).
Battery voltage should appear.
Low engine revolution E.G.R. cut system
● Raise engine speed gradually to 2,000 rpm.
Battery voltage should appear on the way.
● And then reduce engine revolution.
Voltage:
Approximately 0V at idle.

N.G → Check the following items.
1) Harness continuity between E.G.R. solenoid valve and E.C.U. (or check connector)
2) E.G.R. solenoid valve.
3) Ground circuit of E.C.U.

O.K.

CHECK GROUND CIRCUIT.
1) Stop engine.
2) Remove side trim panel behind driver's seat to pull out E.C.U.
3) Disconnect 20-pin connector from E.C.U.
4) Disconnect E.G.R. solenoid harness connector.
5) Check resistance between terminal ⓐ and E.C.U. terminal ④.
Resistance:
Approximately 0Ω

N.G → Check E.C.U. ground circuit.

O.K.

Reinstall any part removed.

INSPECTION END

ECCS SELF-DIAGNOSTIC CHART—1987–88 THROTTLE BODY VAN

IDLE-UP CONTROL (Not self-diagnostic item)

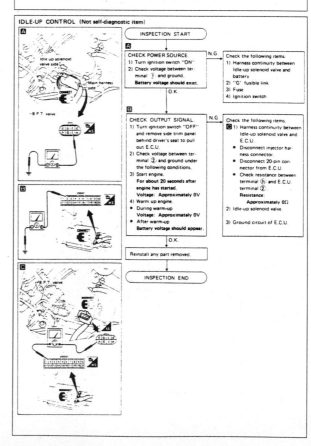

INSPECTION START

CHECK POWER SOURCE.
1) Turn ignition switch "ON".
2) Check voltage between terminal ⓕ and ground.
Battery voltage should exist.

N.G → Check the following items.
1) Harness continuity between Idle-up solenoid valve and battery
2) "G" fusible link
3) Fuse
4) Ignition switch

O.K.

CHECK OUTPUT SIGNAL.
1) Turn ignition switch "OFF" and remove side trim panel behind driver's seat to pull out E.C.U.
2) Check voltage between terminal ② and ground under the following conditions.
3) Start engine.
For about 20 seconds after engine has started.
Voltage: Approximately 0V
4) Warm up engine.
● During warm-up
Voltage: Approximately 0V
● After warm-up
Battery voltage should appear.

N.G → Check the following items.
1) Harness continuity between Idle-up solenoid valve and E.C.U.
● Disconnect injector harness connector.
● Disconnect 20-pin connector from E.C.U.
● Check resistance between terminal ⓗ and E.C.U. terminal ②.
Resistance:
Approximately 0Ω
2) Idle-up solenoid valve
3) Ground circuit of E.C.U.

O.K.

Reinstall any part removed.

INSPECTION END

ECCS SELF-DIAGNOSTIC CHART — 1987–88 THROTTLE BODY VAN

F.I.C.D. CONTROL (Not self-diagnostic item)

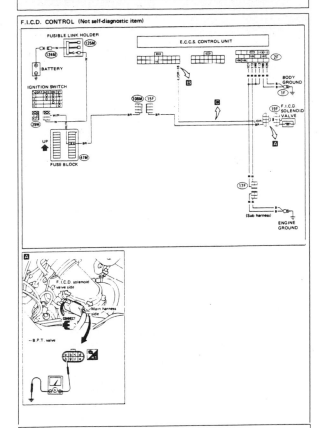

ECCS SELF-DIAGNOSTIC CHART — 1987–88 THROTTLE BODY VAN

SPARK PLUG SWITCHING CONTROL (Not self-diagnostic item)

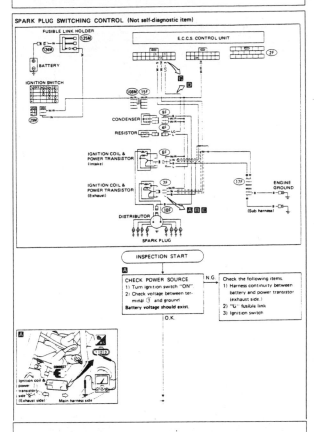

ECCS SELF-DIAGNOSTIC CHART — 1987–88 THROTTLE BODY VAN

F.I.C.D. CONTROL (Not self-diagnostic item)

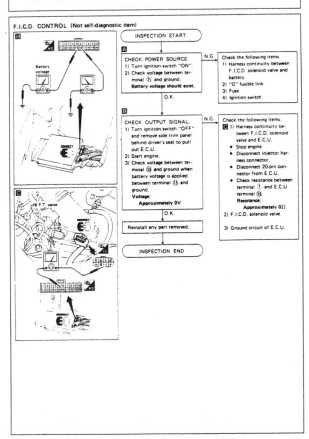

ECCS SELF-DIAGNOSTIC CHART — 1987–88 THROTTLE BODY VAN

SPARK PLUG SWITCHING CONTROL (Not self-diagnostic item)

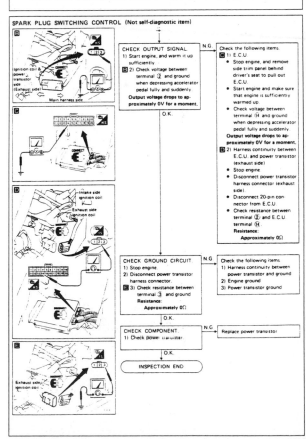

MIXTURE RATIO FEEDBACK SYSTEM INSPECTION CHART
1987–88 THROTTLE BODY VAN

PREPARATION
1. Make sure that the following parts are in good order.
   - Battery
   - Ignition system
   - Engine oil and coolant levels
   - Fuses
   - E.C.C.S. harness connectors
   - Vacuum hoses
   - Air intake system
     (oil filler cap, oil level gauge, etc.)
   - Fuel pressure
   - A.I.V. hose
   - Engine compression
   - E.G.R. valve operation
   - Throttle valve
2. On air conditioner equipped models, checks should be carried out while the air conditioner is "OFF".
3. When measuring "CO" percentage, insert probe more than 40 cm (15.7 in) into tail pipe.

Overall inspection sequence

```
INSPECTION START
        |
Perform preparation inspection outlined above.
        |
Check or adjust idle speed and ignition timing.
(See CHART 1.)
        |
Check idle mixture ratio.  ---- O.K.
(See CHART 2.)
        | N.G.
Check exhaust gas sensor circuit.  ---- N.G.
(See CHART 3A.)
        | O.K.
Adjust idle mixture ratio with E.C.U. inspection  ---- O.K.
lamps. (See CHART 3B.)
        | N.G.
Check idle CO adjust kit.
        |
Measure idle CO in tail pipe or adjust
idle mixture ratio with E.C.U. inspection
lamps. (See CHART 4.)
        |
INSPECTION END
```

MIXTURE RATIO FEEDBACK SYSTEM INSPECTION CHART
1987–88 THROTTLE BODY VAN

CHART 2
Checking Idle Mixture Ratio

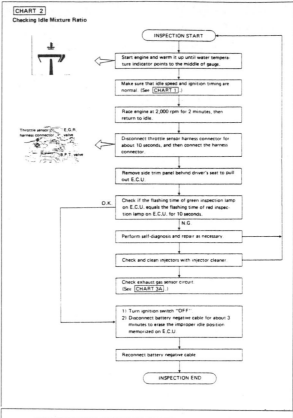

```
INSPECTION START
        |
Start engine and warm it up until water tempera-
ture indicator points to the middle of gauge.
        |
Make sure that idle speed and ignition timing are
normal. (See CHART 1.)
        |
Race engine at 2,000 rpm for 2 minutes, then
return to idle.
        |
Disconnect throttle sensor harness connector for
about 10 seconds, and then connect the harness
connector.
        |
Remove side trim panel behind driver's seat to pull
out E.C.U.
        |
Check if the flashing time of green inspection lamp   ---- O.K.
on E.C.U. equals the flashing time of red inspec-
tion lamp on E.C.U. for 10 seconds.
        | N.G.
Perform self-diagnosis and repair as necessary.
        |
Check and clean injectors with injector cleaner.
        |
Check exhaust gas sensor circuit.
(See CHART 3A.)
        |
1) Turn ignition switch "OFF"
2) Disconnect battery negative cable for about 3
   minutes to erase the improper idle position
   memorized on E.C.U.
        |
Reconnect battery negative cable
        |
INSPECTION END
```

MIXTURE RATIO FEEDBACK SYSTEM INSPECTION CHART
1987–88 THROTTLE BODY VAN

CHART 1
Checking Idle Speed and Ignition Timing

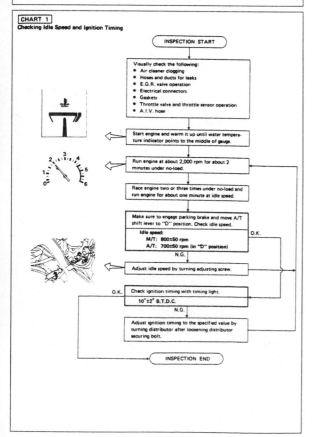

```
INSPECTION START
        |
Visually check the following:
  - Air cleaner clogging
  - Hoses and ducts for leaks
  - E.G.R. valve operation
  - Electrical connectors
  - Gaskets
  - Throttle valve and throttle sensor operation
  - A.I.V. hose
        |
Start engine and warm it up until water tempera-
ture indicator points to the middle of gauge.
        |
Run engine at about 2,000 rpm for about 2
minutes under no-load.
        |
Race engine two or three times under no-load and
run engine for about one minute at idle speed.
        |
Make sure to engage parking brake and move A/T
shift lever to "D" position. Check idle speed.   ---- O.K.
Idle speed:
  M/T:  800±50 rpm
  A/T:  700±50 rpm (in "D" position)
        | N.G.
Adjust idle speed by turning adjusting screw.
        |
Check ignition timing with timing light.   ---- O.K.
10°±2° B.T.D.C.
        | N.G.
Adjust ignition timing to the specified value by
turning distributor after loosening distributor
securing bolt.
        |
INSPECTION END
```

MIXTURE RATIO FEEDBACK SYSTEM INSPECTION CHART
1987–88 THROTTLE BODY VAN

CHART 3A
Checking Exhaust Gas Sensor Circuit

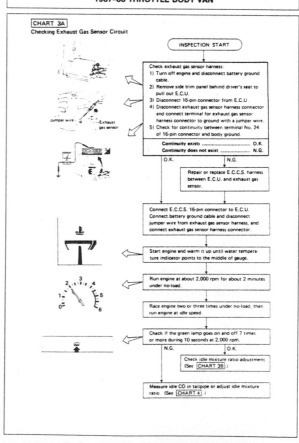

```
INSPECTION START
        |
Check exhaust gas sensor harness:
1) Turn off engine and disconnect battery ground
   cable.
2) Remove side trim panel behind driver's seat to
   pull out E.C.U.
3) Disconnect 16-pin connector from E.C.U.
4) Disconnect exhaust gas sensor harness connector
   and connect terminal for exhaust gas sensor
   harness connector to ground with a jumper wire.
5) Check for continuity between terminal No. 24
   of 16-pin connector and body ground.
   Continuity exists ................. O.K.
   Continuity does not exist ......... N.G.
        |
    O.K. / N.G.
        |
Repair or replace E.C.C.S. harness
between E.C.U. and exhaust gas
sensor.
        |
Connect E.C.C.S. 16-pin connector to E.C.U.
Connect battery ground cable and disconnect
jumper wire from exhaust gas sensor harness, and
connect exhaust gas sensor harness connector.
        |
Start engine and warm it up until water tempera-
ture indicator points to the middle of gauge.
        |
Run engine at about 2,000 rpm for about 2 minutes
under no-load.
        |
Race engine two or three times under no-load, then
run engine at idle speed.
        |
Check if the green lamp goes on and off 7 times
or more during 10 seconds at 2,000 rpm.   ---- O.K.
        | N.G.
Check idle mixture ratio adjustment.
(See CHART 3B.)
        |
Measure idle CO in tailpipe or adjust idle mixture
ratio (See CHART 4.)
```

MIXTURE RATIO FEEDBACK SYSTEM INSPECTION CHART
1987–88 THROTTLE BODY VAN

CHART 3B
Adjusting Idle Mixture Ratio with E.C.U. Inspection Lamps

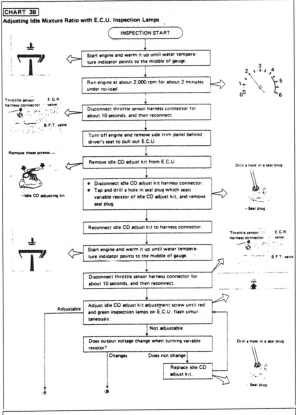

(INSPECTION START)

→ Start engine and warm it up until water temperature indicator points to the middle of gauge.

→ Run engine at about 2,000 rpm for about 2 minutes under no-load.

→ Disconnect throttle sensor harness connector for about 10 seconds, and then reconnect.

→ Turn off engine and remove side trim panel behind driver's seat to pull out E.C.U.

→ Remove idle CO adjust kit from E.C.U.

→ • Disconnect idle CO adjust kit harness connector.
• Tap and drill a hole in seal plug which seals variable resistor of idle CO adjust kit, and remove seal plug.

→ Reconnect idle CO adjust kit to harness connector.

→ Start engine and warm it up until water temperature indicator points to the middle of gauge.

→ Disconnect throttle sensor harness connector for about 10 seconds, and then reconnect.

Adjustable → Adjust idle CO adjust kit adjustment screw until red and green inspection lamps on E.C.U. flash simultaneously.

Not adjustable →

Does output voltage change when turning variable resistor?

Changes / Does not change → Replace idle CO adjust kit.

—A   —B

MIXTURE RATIO FEEDBACK SYSTEM INSPECTION CHART
1987–88 THROTTLE BODY VAN

CHART 3B < Continued >

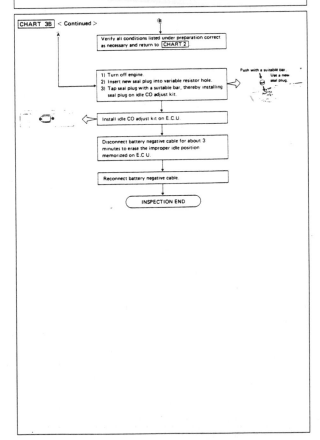

A   B

→ Verify all conditions listed under preparation correct as necessary and return to CHART 2.

→ 1) Turn off engine.
2) Insert new seal plug into variable resistor hole.
3) Tap seal plug with a suitable bar, thereby installing seal plug on idle CO adjust kit.

→ Install idle CO adjust kit on E.C.U.

→ Disconnect battery negative cable for about 3 minutes to erase the improper idle position memorized on E.C.U.

→ Reconnect battery negative cable.

(INSPECTION END)

MIXTURE RATIO FEEDBACK SYSTEM INSPECTION CHART
1987–88 THROTTLE BODY VAN

CHART 4
Measuring Idle CO in Tail Pipe or Adjusting Idle Mixture Ratio with E.C.U. Inspection Lamps

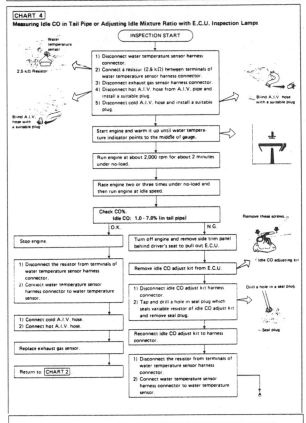

(INSPECTION START)

→ 1) Disconnect water temperature sensor harness connector.
2) Connect a resistor (2.6 kΩ) between terminals of water temperature sensor harness connector.
3) Disconnect exhaust gas sensor harness connector.
4) Disconnect hot A.I.V. hose from A.I.V. pipe and install a suitable plug.
5) Disconnect cold A.I.V. hose and install a suitable plug.

→ Start engine and warm it up until water temperature indicator points to the middle of gauge.

→ Run engine at about 2,000 rpm for about 2 minutes under no-load.

→ Race engine two or three times under no-load and then run engine at idle speed.

→ Check CO%.
Idle CO: 1.0 - 7.0% (in tail pipe)

O.K. → Stop engine.
1) Disconnect the resistor from terminals of water temperature sensor harness connector.
2) Connect water temperature sensor harness connector to water temperature sensor.

1) Connect cold A.I.V. hose.
2) Connect hot A.I.V. hose.

Replace exhaust gas sensor.

Return to CHART 2.

N.G. → Turn off engine and remove side trim panel behind driver's seat to pull out E.C.U.

→ Remove idle CO adjust kit from E.C.U.

→ 1) Disconnect idle CO adjust kit harness connector.
2) Tap and drill a hole in seal plug which seals variable resistor of idle CO adjust kit and remove seal plug.

→ Reconnect idle CO adjust kit to harness connector.

→ 1) Disconnect the resistor from terminals of water temperature sensor harness connector.
2) Connect water temperature sensor harness connector to water temperature sensor.

A

MIXTURE RATIO FEEDBACK SYSTEM INSPECTION CHART
1987–88 THROTTLE BODY VAN

CHART 4 < Continued >

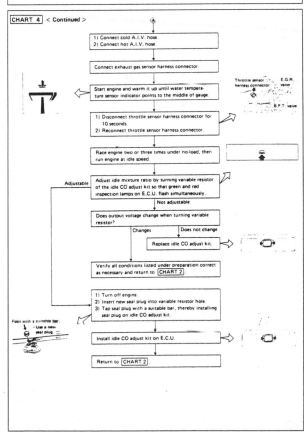

A

→ 1) Connect cold A.I.V. hose.
2) Connect hot A.I.V. hose.

→ Connect exhaust gas sensor harness connector.

→ Start engine and warm it up until water temperature sensor indicator points to the middle of gauge.

→ 1) Disconnect throttle sensor harness connector for 10 seconds.
2) Reconnect throttle sensor harness connector.

→ Race engine two or three times under no-load, then run engine at idle speed.

Adjustable → Adjust idle mixture ratio by turning variable resistor of the idle CO adjust kit so that green and red inspection lamps on E.C.U. flash simultaneously.

Not adjustable →

Does output voltage change when turning variable resistor?

Changes / Does not change → Replace idle CO adjust kit.

→ Verify all conditions listed under preparation correct as necessary and return to CHART 2.

→ 1) Turn off engine.
2) Insert new seal plug into variable resistor hole.
3) Tap seal plug with a suitable bar, thereby installing seal plug on idle CO adjust kit.

→ Install idle CO adjust kit on E.C.U.

→ Return to CHART 2.

COMPONENT TEST PROCEDURE

Releasing Fuel System Pressure

— CAUTION —

Fuel system pressure must be relieved before disconnecting any fuel lines or attempting to remove any fuel system components.

1. Remove the fuel pump fuse from the fuse box.
2. Start the engine.
3. After the engine stalls, crank it over for a few seconds to make sure all fuel is exhausted from the lines.
4. Turn the ignition switch OFF. Install the fuel pump fuse.

Testing Fuel System Pressure

1. Relieve fuel system pressure as previously described.
2. Disconnect the fuel inlet hose at the electro injection unit.
3. Install a fuel pressure gauge.
4. Start the engine and check the fuel line for leakage.
5. Read the pressure on the pressure gauge. It should be approximately 14 psi.
6. Relieve fuel system pressure again.
7. Remove the pressure gauge from the fuel line and reconnect the fuel inlet hose.

NOTE: When reconnecting a fuel line, always use a new clamp. Make sure that the screw of the clamp does not contact any adjacent parts and tighten the hose clamp to 1 ft. lb.

Air Flow Meter Testing

Before removing the air flow meter, remove the throttle valve switch. When removing the air flow meter, pull it out vertically, taking care not to bend or damage the plug portion. Never touch the sensor portion with your finger and apply silicone grease to the mating surface between the air flow meter and throttle body when installing to allow heat to escape.

NOTE: Failure to use silicone grease for heat dissipation will result in air flow meter failure.

Apply battery voltage between terminals E (+) and C (–), then measure the voltage between terminals A (+) and D (–). Voltage should be 1.5–2.0 volts without air flow at the sensor, and 2.5–4.0 volts when air is blown through the sensor. Use oral air pressure only when blowing through the sensor. If any other results are obtained during testing, replace the air flow meter.

EGR Vacuum Cut and Air Injection Control Solenoid Valve Testing

1. Check the solenoid valve for continuity after disconnecting the harness connector. Continuity should exist and resistance should be 30–40Ω. If not, replace the solenoid valve.
2. Check the solenoid valve for normal operation after disconnecting the harness connector and all vacuum hoses. Tag all hoses before removal. Supply the solenoid valve with battery voltage and check whether there is continuity between ports A, B and C. With the solenoid OFF, there should be continuity between B and C. With the solenoid ON, there should be continuity between A and

Idle Speed Control (ISC) Valve Testing

1. Use an ohmmeter to check the resistance between the terminals. Resistance between terminals A and B should be 9.5–10.5 ohms. Resistance between terminals B and C should be 8.5–9.5 ohms.
2. Check the insulation between each terminal and the ISC valve body. No continuity should exist when a probes are touched to the terminal and valve body. If continuity exists, replace the ISC valve.

3. Apply battery voltage between terminals B (+) and C (–), then check that the ISC valve is fully closed.
4. Apply battery voltage between terminals B (+) and A (–), then check that the ISC valve is fully open.
5. Check the opening clearance of the ISC valve without applying voltage to terminals. The opening clearance should be 0–0.08 in. (0–2mm).
6. If any test results are different than described, replace the ISC valve. When installing the ISC valve to the throttle body, tighten the bolts in the sequence illustrated to 3–4 ft. lbs. (4–5 Nm).

Component Replacement

INJECTOR

Removal and Installation
ALL EXCEPT 1986 TRUCK

1. Relieve fuel system pressure.
2. Remove the injector cover and pull the injector straight up to remove it from the throttle body. Be careful not to break or bend the injector terminal.
3. Remove the O-rings from the injector.
4. Coat the lower O-ring with a small amount of clean engine oil and install it on the injector.
5. Install the injector and push it into place using a suitable tool or 13mm socket. Align the direction of the injector terminals and be careful not to bend or break any terminals.
6. Install the upper O-ring by pushing it into place with a suitable tool or 19mm socket.
7. Install the upper (white) plate.
8. Install the injector cover with the rubber plug removed. Make sure that the two O-rings are installed in the injector cover.
9. Check for proper connection between the injector terminal and injector cover terminal, then install the rubber plug. After installation, make sure there is no fuel leakage and that the engine is idling properly.

1986 TRUCK

1. Relieve fuel pressure.
2. Drain approximately 1⅛ quart (1 liter) of engine coolant.
3. Remove or disconnect following parts:
- Air cleaner
- Harness connectors for throttle sensor, idle switch, injectors and air flow meter
- Accelerator wire
- Fuel hose
- Coolant hose
- ASCD wire (if equipped)
4. Remove injection body from intake manifold.
5. Remove seal rubber and injector harness grommet from injection body.
6. Remove injector cover.
7. With throttle valve kept fully open, tap bottom of fuel injector with a suitable tool.

NOTE: If nozzle tip is damaged or deformed by the tool, replace injector.

8. Disconnect harness of a malfunctioning injector from harness connector.
9. Put harness of a new injector into injector harness grommet and harness tube.

NOTE: Harness grommet should be replaced with new one every time it is removed.

 a. Fix boots and terminal in harness with terminal pliers and then put harness in connector.
 b. Put terminal retainer into connector.

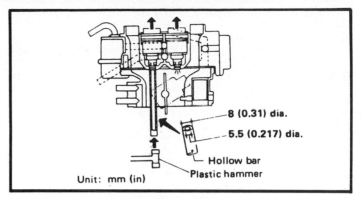

Fuel injector removal tool—1986 truck

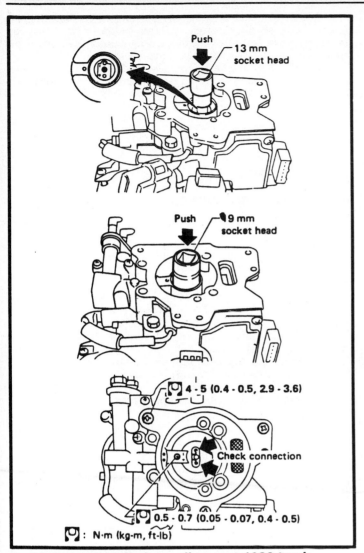

Fuel injector installation—all except 1986 truck

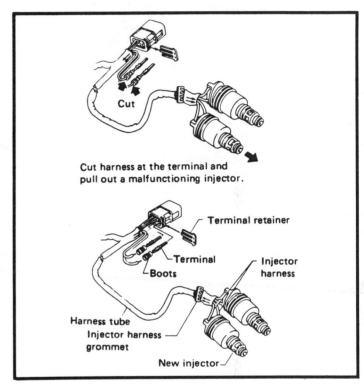

Fuel injector-from-harness removal and installation—1986 truck

10. Replace O-ring and rubber ring with new one. Lubricate O-rings before installation.
11. Put injector assembly into injection body.
12. Push injectors into injection body by hand, until O-ring are fully seated. Invert injection body and ensure that injector tips are properly seated.
13. Apply some silicone bond to injector harness grommet.

NOTE: Air-tight sealing is essential to ensures stable and proper idling condition.

14. Reinstall injector cover. Be sure to use locking sealer on screw threads. Tighten screws in a criss-cross pattern to make sure of proper seating of injector and the cover.
15. Attach seal rubber to to face of injection body with silicone bond.

NOTE: Be sure to apply some silicone bond to bottom of seal rubber, and adhere seal rubber to injection body. Do not reinstall air cleaner until silicone bond has hardened.

16. Reinstall or reconnect following parts:
● Harness connectors
● Accelerator wire
● Coolant hose
● Fuel hose
● ASCD wire (if equipped)
17. Add approximately 1⅛ quart (1 liter) of engine coolant to radiator.
18. Start engine and make sure that there is no fuel leakage from clearance between injector cover and injection body. Stop engine and make sure that fuel does not drip on throttle valve. Also, be sure that engine idling condition is stable and proper.
19. Perform mixture ratio feedback system inspection to make sure there is no fuel leakage at injector top seal.

THROTTLE VALVE SWITCH

Adjustment

1. Start the engine and allow it to reach normal operating temperature.
2. Disconnect the throttle valve switch harness connector and throttle sensor harness connector.

3. Check the idle speed. If not correct, adjust by turning the throttle adjusting screw. On automatic transmission models, shift the transaxle into Neutral and record the idle speed.

4. Manually open the throttle valve until the engine speed reaches 2000 rpm. Lower the engine speed slowly and note the rpm at which the idle contact turns from OFF to ON. It should be 900–1200 rpm on manual transmission models. On automatic transmission models, it should be approximately 300 rpm over whatever engine speed was recorded in Neutral (Step 3) ± 150 rpm. If not correct, adjust by loosening the the throttle valve switch securing screws and turning the throttle valve switch.

5. Reconnect the throttle valve switch harness connector and throttle sensor harness connector.

DASH POT

Inspection and Adjustment

1. Start the engine and allow it to reach normal operating temperature. Make sure the idle speed is adjusted properly.

2. Turn the throttle by hand and read the engine speed when the dashpot just touches the adjusting screw. It should touch at 2200–3000 rpm.

3. If out of specification, adjust it by turning the adjusting screw.

FAST IDLE

Inspection and Adjustment

1. Warm up engine sufficiently.

2. Make sure that aligning mark stamped on fast idle cam meets center of roller installed on cam follow lever. If not, correct location of fast idle cam by turning adjusting screw. If not adjustable, replace thermo element.

3. Check clearance between roller and fast idle cam. Clearance should be 0.028–0.118 in. (0.7–3.0mm). If not correct, adjust clearance by turning adjusting screw. Adjusting clearance is 0.047–0.063 in. (1.2–1.6mm).

NOTE: Make sure that the engine has sufficiently been warmed up when adjusting clearance.

F.I.C.D. SOLENOID

Inspection and Adjustment

1. Warm up engine sufficiently.
2. Check idle speeds:
   Z24i Engine With Manual Trans—900 ± 50 rpm
   VG30i Engine With Manual Trans—800 ± 50 rpm
   Z24i Engine With Auto Trans—650 ± 50 rpm in DRIVE
   VG30i Engine With Auto Trans—700 ± 50 rpm in DRIVE
3. Turn air conditioner switch ON and check idle speed. Idle speed should be 900 ± 50 rpm in NEUTRAL. If out of specification, adjust idle speed by turning adjusting screw.
4. If F.I.C.D. solenoid valve does not work, check harness and solenoid valve as follows:
   a. Disconnect 6 pin (8 pin on VG30i) and check battery voltage with ignition ON and A/C ON.
   b. Check continuity of solenoid valve.
   c. Repair and/or replace as necessary.

ELECTRONIC CONCENTRATED CONTROL SYSTEM (ECCS) – PORT FUEL INJECTION

General Information

The Nissan Electronic Concentrated Control System (ECCS) is an air flow controlled, port fuel injection and engine control system. The ECCS electronic control unit consists of a microcomputer, inspection lamps, a diagnostic mode selector and connectors for signal input and output and for power supply. The electronic control unit, or ECU, controls the following functions:

- Amount of injected fuel
- Ignition timing
- Mixture ratio feedback
- Pressure regulator control
- Exhaust gas recirculation (EGR) operation
- Idle speed control
- Fuel pump operation
- Air regulator control
- Air injection valve (AIV) operation
- Self-diagnostics
- Air flow meter self-cleaning control
- Fail safe system

CRANK ANGLE SENSOR

The crank angle sensor is a basic component of the ECCS system. It monitors engine speed and piston position, as well as sending signals which the ECU uses to control fuel injection, ignition timing and other functions. The crank angle sensor has a rotor plate and a wave forming circuit. The rotor plate has 360 slits for 1° signals (crank angle) and 6 slits for 120° signals (engine speed). Light emitting diodes (LED's) and photo diodes are built into the wave forming circuit. When the rotor plate passes the space between the LED and the photo diode, the slits of the rotor plate continually cut the light which is sent to the photo diode from the LED. This generates rough shaped pulses which are converted into ON-OFF pulses by the wave forming circuit and then sent to the ECU.

CYLINDER HEAD TEMPERATURE SENSOR

The cylinder head temperature sensor monitors changes in cylinder head temperature and transmits a signal to the ECU. The temperature sensing unit employs a thermistor which is sensitive to the change in temperature, with electrical resistance decreasing as temperature rises.

AIR FLOW METER

The air flow meter measures the mass flow rate of intake air. The volume of air entering the engine is measured by the use of a hot wire placed in the intake air stream. The control unit sends current to the wire to maintain it at a preset temperature. As the intake air moves past the wire, it removes heat and the control unit must increase the voltage to the wire to maintain it at the preset temperature. By measuring the amount of current necessary to maintain the temperature of the wire in the air stream, the ECU knows exactly how much air is entering the en-

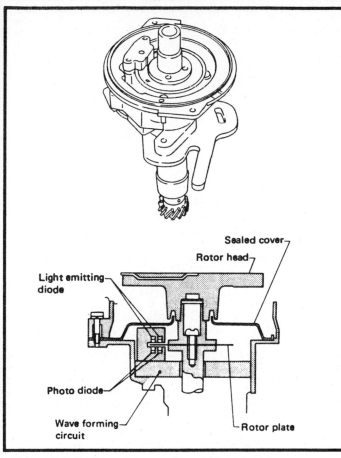

ECCS distributor with crank angle sensor

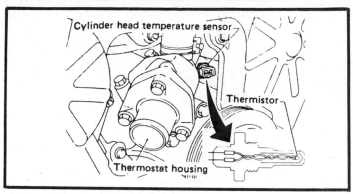

Cylinder head temperature sensor

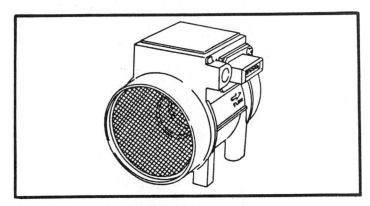

Air flow meter — CA16DE engine

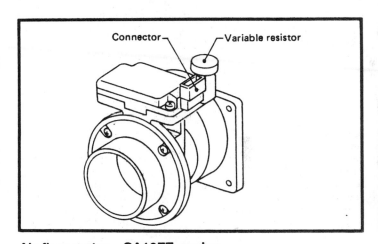

Air flow meter — CA18ET engine

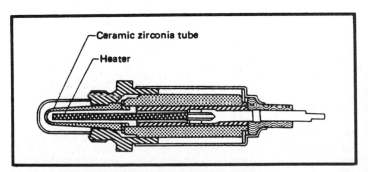

Exhaust gas sensor — zirconia tube type

gine. A self-cleaning system briefly heats the hot air wire to approximately 1832°F (1000°C) after engine shutdown to burn off any dust or contaminants on the wire.

EXHAUST GAS SENSOR

The exhaust gas sensor, which is placed in the exhaust pipe, monitors the amount of oxygen in the exhaust gas. The sensor is made of ceramic titania which changes electrical resistance at the ideal air/fuel ratio (14.7:1). The control unit supplies the sensor with approximately 1 volt and takes the output voltage of the sensor depending on its resistance. The oxygen sensor is equipped with a heater to bring it to operating temperature quickly.

THROTTLE VALVE SWITCH

A throttle valve switch is attached to the throttle chamber and operates in response to accelerator pedal movement. The switch has an idle contact and a full throttle contact. The idle contact closes when the throttle valve is positioned at idle and opens when it is in any other position.

FUEL INJECTOR

The fuel injector is a small, precision solenoid valve. As the ECU sends an injection signal to each injector, the coil built into the injector pulls the needle valve back and fuel is injected through the nozzle and into the intake manifold. The amount of fuel injected is dependent on how long the signal is (pulse duration); the longer the signal, the more fuel delivered.

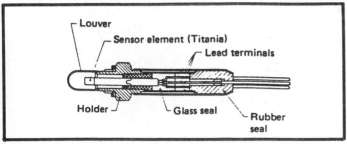

Exhaust gas sensor—titania type

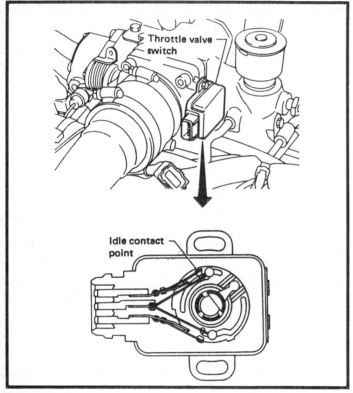

Throttle valve switch

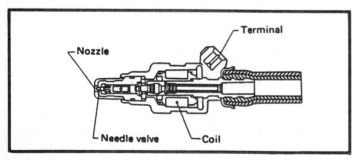

Fuel injector

DETONATION SENSOR (TURBO MODEL)

The detonation sensor is attached to the cylinder block and senses engine knocking conditions. A knocking vibration from the cylinder block is applied as pressure to the piezoelectric element. This vibrational pressure is then converted into a voltage signal which is delivered as output.

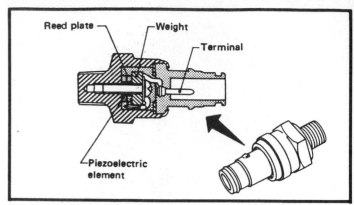

Detonation sensor (turbo model)

FUEL TEMPERATURE SENSOR

A fuel temperature sensor is built into the fuel pressure regulator. When the fuel temperature is higher than the preprogrammed level, the ECU will enrich the fuel injected to compensate for temperature expansion. The temperature sensor and pressure regulator should be replaced as an assembly if either malfunctions. The electric fuel pump with an integral damper is installed in the fuel tank. It is a vane roller type with the electric motor cooled by the fuel itself. The fuel filter is of metal construction in order to withstand the high fuel system pressure. The fuel pump develops 61–71 psi, but the pressure regulator keeps system pressure at 36 psi in operation.

POWER TRANSISTOR

The ignition signal from the ECU is amplified by the power transistor, which turns the ignition coil primary circuit on and off, inducing the necessary high voltage in the secondary circuit to fire the spark plugs. Ignition timing is controlled according to engine operating conditions, with the optimum timing advance for each driving condition preprogrammed into the ECU memory.

VEHICLE SPEED SENSOR

The vehicle speed sensor provides a vehicle speed signal to the ECU. On conventional speedometers, the speed sensor consists of a reed switch which transforms vehicle speed into a pulse signal. On digital electronic speedometers, the speed sensor consists of an LED, photo diode, shutter and wave forming circuit. It operates on the same principle as the crank angle sensor.

IDLE-UP SOLENOID VALVE

An idle-up solenoid valve is attached to the intake collector to stabilize idle speed when the engine load is heavy because of electrical load, power steering load, etc. An air regulator provides an air bypass when the engine is cold in order to increase idle speed during warmup (fast idle). A bimetal, heater and rotary shutter are built into the air regulator. When bimetal temperature is low, the air bypass port is open. As the engine starts and electric current flows through a heater, the bimetal begins to rotate the shutter to close off the air bypass port. The air passage remains closed until the engine is stopped and the bimetal temperature drops.

AIR INJECTION VALVE (AIV)

The air injection valve (AIV) sends secondary air to the exhaust

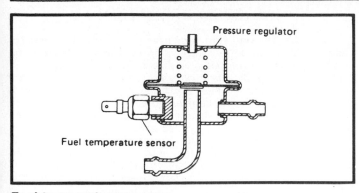

Fuel temperature sensor

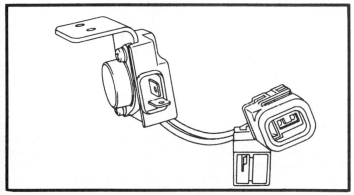

Power transistor—CA18ET engine

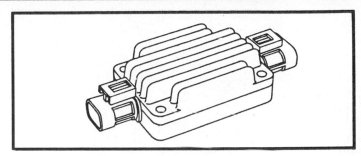

Power transistor—CA16DE engine

Power transistor and ignition coil—1987–88 300ZX

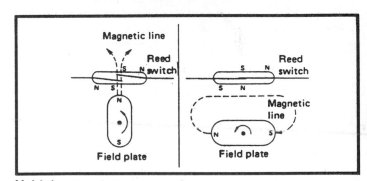

Vehicle speed sensor

manifold, utilizing a vacuum caused by exhaust pulsation in the exhaust manifold. When the exhaust pressure is below atmospheric pressure (negative pressure), secondary air is sent to the exhaust manifold. When the exhaust pressure is above atmospheric pressure, the reed valves prevent secondary air from being sent to the air cleaner. The AIV control solenoid valve cuts the intake manifold vacuum signal for AIV control. The solenoid valve actuates in response to the ON/OFF signal from the ECU. When the solenoid is off, the vacuum signal from the intake manifold is cut. As the control unit outputs an on signal, the coil pulls the plunger downward and feeds the vacuum signal to the AIV control valve.

EXHAUST GAS RECIRCULATION (EGR) VACUUM CUT SOLENOID VALVE

The EGR vacuum cut solenoid valve is the same type as that of the AIV. The EGR system is controlled by the ECU; at both low and high engine speed (rpm), the solenoid valve turns on and the EGR valve cuts the exhaust gas recirculation into the intake manifold. The pressure regulator control solenoid valve also actuates in response to the ON/OFF signal from the ECU. When it is off, a vacuum signal from the intake manifold is fed into the pressure regulator. As the control unit outputs an on signal, the coil pulls the plunger downward and cuts the vacuum signal.

ELECTRONIC CONTROL UNIT (ECU)

The ECU consists of a microcomputer, inspection lamps, a diagnostic mode selector, and connectors for signal input and output, and for power supply. The unit has control of the engine.

AIR REGULATOR

The air regulator provides an air by-pass when the engine is cold

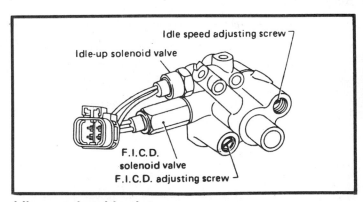

Idle-up solenoid valve

for the purpose of a fast idle during warm-up. A bimetal, heater and rotary shutter are built into the air regulator. When the bimetal temperature is low, the air by-pass port is open. As the engine starts and electric current flows through a heater, the bimetal begins to rotate the shutter to close off the by-pass port. The air passage remains closed until the engine is stopped and the bimetal temperature drops.

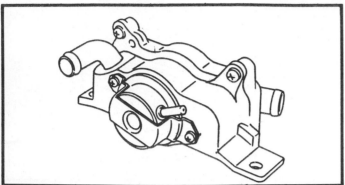

Air injection valve (AIV)

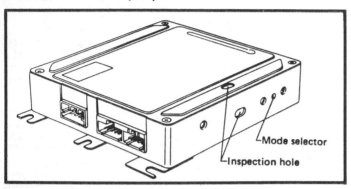

Control unit

— Mode selector
— Inspection hole

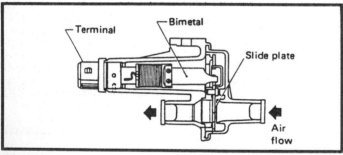

— Terminal
— Bimetal
— Slide plate

Air flow

Air regulator

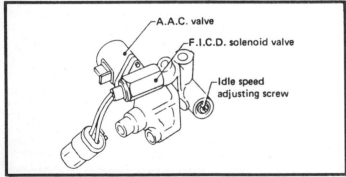

— A.A.C. valve
— F.I.C.D. solenoid valve
— Idle speed adjusting screw

Auxiliary air control (AAC) valve

AUXILIARY AIR CONTROL (AAC) VALVE

The AAC valve is attached to the intake collector. The ECU actuates the AAC valve by an ON/OFF pulse of approximately 160 Hz. The longer that ON duty is left on, the larger the amount of air that will flow through the AAC valve.

SYSTEM OPERATION

In operation, the on-board computer (control unit) calculates the basic injection pulse width by processing signals from the crank angle sensor and air flow meter. Receiving signals from each sensor which detects various engine operating conditions, the computer adds various enrichments (which are preprogrammed) to the basic injection amount. In this manner, the optimum amount of fuel is delivered through the injectors. The fuel is enriched when starting, during warm-up, when accelerating, when cylinder head temperature is high and when operating under a heavy load. The fuel is leaned during deceleration according to the closing rate of the throttle valve. Fuel shut-off is accomplished during deceleration, when vehicle speed exceeds 137 mph, or when engine speed exceeds 6400 rpm for about 500 revolutions.

The mixture ratio feedback system (closed loop control) is designed to control the air/fuel mixture precisely to the stoichiometric or optimum point so that the three-way catalytic converter can minimize CO, HC and NOx emissions simultaneously. The optimum air/fuel fuel mixture is 14.7:1. This system uses an exhaust gas (oxygen) sensor located in the exhaust manifold to give an indication of whether the fuel mixture is richer or leaner than the stoichiometric point. The control unit adjusts the injection pulse width according to the sensor voltage so the mixture ratio will be within the narrow window around the stoichiometric fuel ratio. The system goes into closed loop as soon as the oxygen sensor heats up enough to register. The system will operate under open loop when starting the engine, when the engine temperature is cold, when exhaust gas sensor temperature is cold, when driving at high speeds or under heavy load, at idle (after mixture ratio learning is completed), during deceleration, if the exhaust gas sensor malfunctions, or when the exhaust gas sensor monitors a rich condition for more than 10 seconds and during deceleration.

Ignition timing is controlled in response to engine operating conditions. The optimum ignition timing in each driving condition is preprogrammed in the computer. The signal from the control unit is transmitted to the power transistor and controls ignition timing. The idle speed is also controlled according to engine operating conditions, temperature and gear position. On manual transmission models, if battery voltage is less than 12 volts for a few seconds, a higher idle speed will be maintained by the control unit to improve charging function.

There is a fail-safe system built into the ECCS control unit. If the output voltage of the air flow meter is extremely low, the ECU will substitute a preprogrammed value for the air flow meter signal and allow the vehicle to be driven as long as the engine speed is kept below 2000 rpm. If the cylinder head temperature sensor circuit is open, the control unit clamps the warmup enrichment at a certain amount. This amount is almost the same as that when the cylinder head temperature is between 68–176°F (20–80°C). If the fuel pump circuit malfunctions, the fuel pump relay comes on until the engine stops. This allows the fuel pump to receive power from the relay.

SERVICE PRECAUTIONS

- Do not operate the fuel pump when the fuel lines are empty.
- Do not reuse fuel hose clamps.
- Do not disconnect the ECCS harness connectors before the battery ground cable has been disconnected.
- Make sure all ECCS connectors are fastened securely. A poor connection can cause an extremely high surge voltage in the coil and condenser and result in damage to integrated circuits.
- Keep the ECCS harness at least 4 in. away from adjacent harnesses to prevent an ECCS system malfunction due to external electronic "noise."
- Keep all parts and harnesses dry during service.

- Before attempting to remove any parts, turn off the ignition switch and disconnect the battery ground cable.
- Always use a 12 volt battery as a power source.
- Do not attempt to disconnect the battery cables with the engine running.
- Do not depress the accelerator pedal when starting.
- Do not rev up the engine immediately after starting or just prior to shutdown.
- Do not attempt to disassemble the ECCS control unit under any circumstances.
- If a battery cable is disconnected, the memory will return to the ROM (programmed) values. Engine operation may vary slightly, but this is not an indication of a problem. Do not replace parts because of a slight variation.
- If installing a two-way or CB radio, keep the antenna as far as possible away from the electronic control unit. Keep the antenna feeder line at least 8 in. away from the ECCS harness and do not let the two run parallel for a long distance. Be sure to ground the radio to the vehicle body.

Diagnosis and Testing

SELF-DIAGNOSTIC SYSTEM

The self-diagnostic function is useful for diagnosing malfunctions in major sensors and actuators of the ECCS system. There are five modes in self-diagnostics:

Mode 1: Mixture Ratio Feedback Control Monitor A

During closed loop operation, the green inspection lamp turns ON when a lean condition is detected and OFF when a rich condition is detected. During open loop operation, the red inspection lamp stays OFF.

Mode 2: Mixture Ratio Feedback Control Monitor B

The green inspection lamp function is the same as in Mode 1. During closed loop operation, the red inspection lamp turns ON and OFF simultaneously with the green inspection lamp when the mixture ratio is controlled within the specified value. During open loop operation, the red inspection lamp stays OFF.

Mode 3: Self-Diagnosis

This mode is the same as the former self-diagnosis mode.

Mode 4: Switches On/Off Diagnosis

During this mode, the inspection lamps monitor the ON/OFF condition of the idle switch, starter switch and vehicle speed sensor.

In switches ON/OFF diagnosis system, ON/OFF operation of the following switches can be detected continuously:

- Idle switch
- Starter switch
- Vehicle speed sensor

1. Idle Switch and Starter Switch – The switches ON/OFF status at the point when mode IV is selected is stored in ECU memory. When either switch is turned from ON to OFF or OFF to ON, the red LED on ECU alternately comes on and goes off each time switching is detected.

2. Vehicle Speed Sensor – The switches ON/OFF status at the point when mode IV is selected is stored in ECU memory. When vehicle speed is 12 mph (20 km/h) or slower, the green LED on ECU is off. When vehicle speed exceeds 12 mph (20 km/h), the green LED on ECU comes ON.

Mode 5: Real Time Diagnosis

The moment a malfunction is detected, the display will be presented immediately by flashing the inspection lamps during the driving test.

In real time diagnosis, if any of the following items are judged to be faulty, a malfunction is indicated immediately:

- Crank angle sensor (180° signal and 1° signal)
- Ignition signal
- Air flow meter output signal
- Fuel pump

Consequently, this diagnosis is a very effective measure to diagnose whether the above systems cause the malfunction or not, during driving test. Compared with self-diagnosis, real time diagnosis is very sensitive, and can detect malfunctioning conditions in a moment. Further, items regarded to be malfunctions in this diagnosis are not stored in ECU memory.

To switch the modes, turn the ignition switch ON, then turn the diagnostic mode selector on the control unit fully clockwise and wait for the inspection lamps to flash. Count the number of flashes until the inspection lamps have flashed the number of the desired mode, then immediately turn the diagnostic mode selector fully counterclockwise.

NOTE: When the ignition switch is turned off during diagnosis in each mode, and then turned back on again after the power to the control unit has dropped off completely, the diagnosis will automatically return to Mode 1.

The stored memory will be lost if the battery terminal is disconnected, or Mode 4 is selected after selecting Mode 3. However, if the diagnostic mode selector is kept turned fully clockwise, it will continue to change in the order of Mode 1, 2, 3, etc., and in this case, the stored memory will not be erased.

In Mode 3, the self-diagnostic mode, the control unit constantly monitors the function of sensors and actuators regardless of ignition key position. If a malfunction occurs, the information is stored in the control unit and can be retrieved from the memory by turning on the diagnostic mode selector on the side of the control unit. When activated, the malfunction is indicated by flashing a red and green LED (also located on the control unit). Since all the self-diagnostic results are stored in the control unit memory, even intermittent malfunctions can be diagnosed. A malfunctioning part's group is indicated by the number of both red and green LED's flashing. First, the red LED flashes and the green flashes follow. The red LED refers to the number of tens, while the green refers to the number of units. If the red LED flashes twice and the green LED flashes once, a code 21 is being displayed. All malfunctions are classified by their trouble code number.

The diagnostic result is retained in the control unit memory until the starter is operated fifty times after a diagnostic item is judged to be malfunctioning. The diagnostic result will then be canceled automatically. If a diagnostic item which has been judged malfunctioning and stored in memory is again judged to be malfunctioning before the starter is operated fifty times, the second result will replace the previous one and stored in the memory until the starter is operated fifty more times.

In Mode 5 (real time diagnosis), if the crank angle sensor, ignition signal or air flow meter output signal are judged to be malfunctioning, the malfunction will be indicated immediately. This diagnosis is very effective for determining whether these systems are causing a malfunction during the driving test. Compared with self-diagnosis, real time diagnosis is very sensitive and can detect malfunctioning conditions immediately. However, malfunctioning items in this diagnosis mode are not stored in memory.

TESTING PRECAUTIONS

1. Before connecting or disconnecting control unit ECU harness connectors, make sure the ignition switch is OFF and the negative battery cable is disconnected to avoid the possibility of damage to the control unit.

2. When performing ECU input/output signal diagnosis, re-

SELF-DIAGNOSTIC MODE III—ALL 1987 PORT INJECTED MODEL CARS

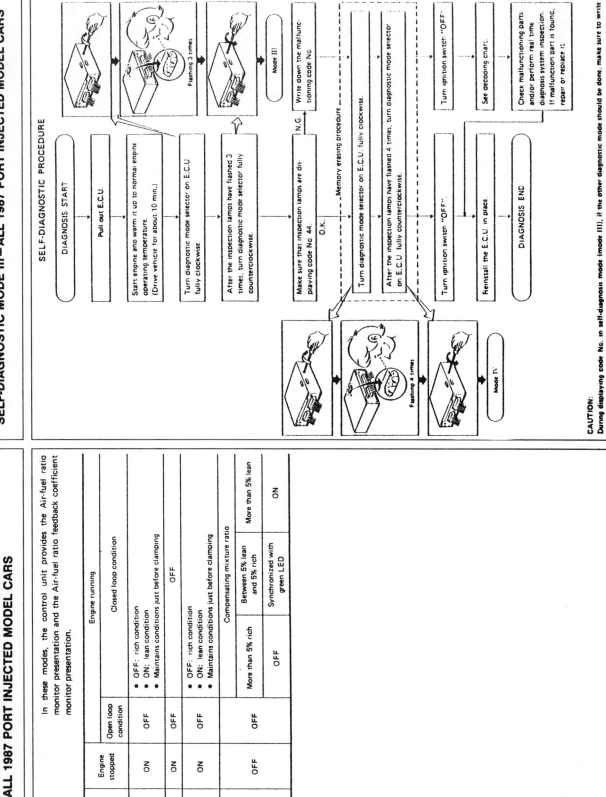

SELF-DIAGNOSTIC PROCEDURE

DIAGNOSIS START

Pull out E.C.U.

Start engine and warm it up to normal engine operating temperature. (Drive vehicle for about 10 min.)

Turn diagnostic mode selector on E.C.U fully clockwise

After the inspection lamps have flashed 3 times, turn diagnostic mode selector fully counterclockwise.

Flashing 3 times

Mode III

Write down the malfunctioning code No

Make sure that inspection lamps are displaying code No. 44.

N.G. — Memory erasing procedure

O.K.

Turn diagnostic mode selector on E.C.U. fully clockwise.

After the inspection lamps have flashed 4 times, turn diagnostic mode selector on E.C.U. fully counterclockwise.

Flashing 4 times

Mode IV

Turn ignition switch "OFF".

Turn ignition switch "OFF".

See decoding chart.

Reinstall the E.C.U. in place.

Check malfunctioning parts and/or perform real time diagnosis system inspection. If malfunction part is found, repair or replace it.

DIAGNOSIS END

CAUTION:
During displaying code No. in self-diagnosis mode (mode III), if the other diagnostic mode should be done, make sure to write down the malfunctioning code No. before turning diagnostic mode selector on E.C.U. fully clockwise, or select the diagnostic mode after turning switch "OFF". Otherwise self-diagnosis information stored in E.C.U. memory until now would be lost.

SELF-DIAGNOSTIC MODE I AND II ALL 1987 PORT INJECTED MODEL CARS

In these modes, the control unit provides the Air-fuel ratio monitor presentation and the Air-fuel ratio feedback coefficient monitor presentation.

Mode	LED	Engine stopped	Engine running		
			Open loop condition	Closed loop condition	
Mode I (Monitor A)	Green	ON	OFF	• OFF: rich condition • ON: lean condition • Maintains conditions just before clamping	
	Red	ON	OFF	OFF	
Mode II (Monitor B)	Green	ON	OFF	• OFF: rich condition • ON: lean condition • Maintains conditions just before clamping	
				Compensating mixture ratio	
	Red	OFF	OFF	More than 5% rich	Between 5% lean and 5% rich	More than 5% lean
				OFF	Synchronized with green LED	ON

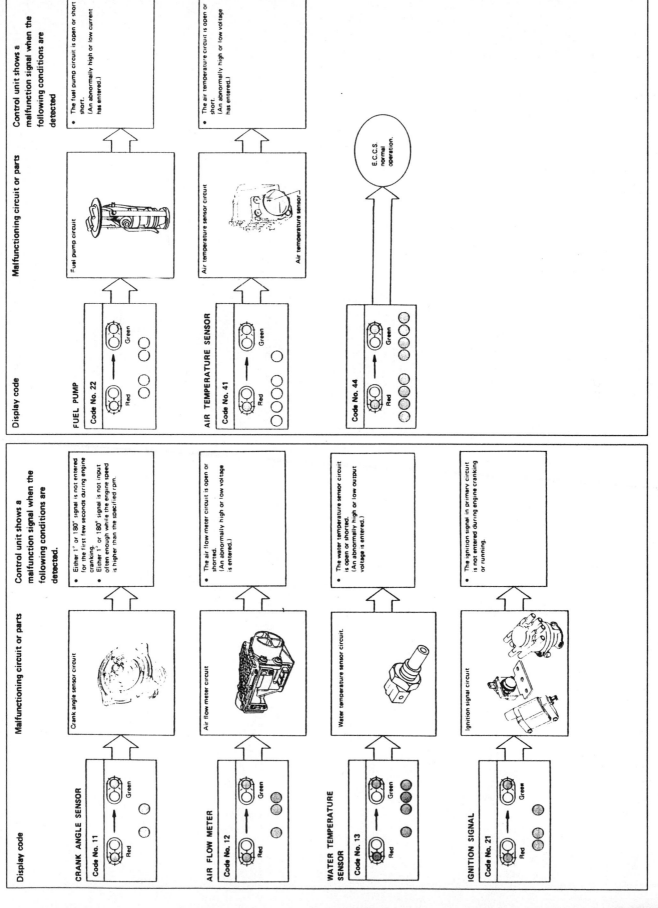

SELF-DIAGNOSTIC MODE III DECODING CHART
1987 PORT INJECTED STANZA AND 200SX WITH CA20E ENGINE

Display code — **Malfunctioning circuit or parts** — **Control unit shows a malfunction signal when the following conditions are detected**

FUEL PUMP — Code No. 22 — Fuel pump circuit
- The fuel pump circuit is open or short. (An abnormally high or low current has entered.)

AIR TEMPERATURE SENSOR — Code No. 41 — Air temperature sensor circuit
- The air temperature circuit is open or short. (An abnormally high or low voltage has entered.)

Code No. 44 — E.C.C.S. normal operation.

SELF-DIAGNOSTIC MODE III DECODING CHART
1987 PORT INJECTED STANZA AND 200SX WITH CA20E ENGINE

Display code — **Malfunctioning circuit or parts** — **Control unit shows a malfunction signal when the following conditions are detected.**

CRANK ANGLE SENSOR — Code No. 11 — Crank angle sensor circuit
- Either 1° or 180° signal is not entered for the first few seconds during engine cranking.
- Either 1° or 180° signal is not input often enough while the engine speed is higher than the specified rpm.

AIR FLOW METER — Code No. 12 — Air flow meter circuit
- The air flow meter circuit is open or shorted. (An abnormally high or low voltage is entered.)

WATER TEMPERATURE SENSOR — Code No. 13 — Water temperature sensor circuit.
- The water temperature sensor circuit is open or shorted. (An abnormally high or low output voltage is entered.)

IGNITION SIGNAL — Code No. 21 — Ignition signal circuit
- The ignition signal in primary circuit is not entered during engine cranking or running.

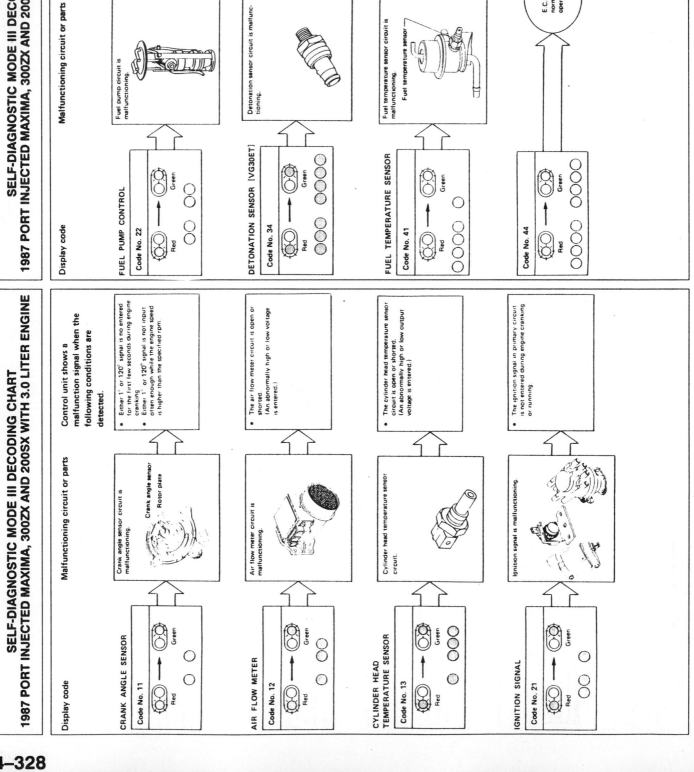

SELF-DIAGNOSTIC MODE III DECODING CHART
1987 PORT INJECTED MAXIMA, 300ZX AND 200SX WITH 3.0 LITER ENGINE

Display code — **Malfunctioning circuit or parts** — **Control unit shows a malfunction signal when the following conditions are detected**

FUEL PUMP CONTROL
Code No. 22
Red / Green

Fuel pump circuit is malfunctioning.

- Idle speed control valve circuit is open or short.
  (Idle speed is higher than target idle speed in spite of feedback control.)
- Fuel circuit is open or short.
  (An extremely high or low current is entered.)

DETONATION SENSOR [VG30ET]
Code No. 34
Red / Green

Detonation sensor circuit is malfunctioning.

- The detonation circuit is open or shorted.
  (An abnormally high or low voltage is entered.)

FUEL TEMPERATURE SENSOR
Code No. 41
Red / Green

Fuel temperature sensor circuit is malfunctioning.

- Fuel temperature circuit is open or short.
  (An abnormally high or low voltage is entered.)

Code No. 44
Red / Green

E.C.C.S. normal operation.

SELF-DIAGNOSTIC MODE III DECODING CHART
1987 PORT INJECTED MAXIMA, 300ZX AND 200SX WITH 3.0 LITER ENGINE

Display code — **Malfunctioning circuit or parts** — **Control unit shows a malfunction signal when the following conditions are detected.**

CRANK ANGLE SENSOR
Code No. 11
Red / Green

Crank angle sensor circuit is malfunctioning.

Crank angle sensor / Rotor plate

- Either 1° or 120° signal is no entered for the first few seconds during engine cranking
- Either 1° or 120° signal is not input often enough while the engine speed is higher than the specified rpm

AIR FLOW METER
Code No. 12
Red / Green

Air flow meter circuit is malfunctioning.

- The air flow meter circuit is open or shorted.
  (An abnormally high or low voltage is entered.)

CYLINDER HEAD TEMPERATURE SENSOR
Code No. 13
Red / Green

Cylinder head temperature sensor circuit.

- The cylinder head temperature sensor circuit is open or shorted.
  (An abnormally high or low output voltage is entered.)

IGNITION SIGNAL
Code No. 21
Red / Green

Ignition signal is malfunctioning.

- The ignition signal in primary circuit is not entered during engine cranking or running.

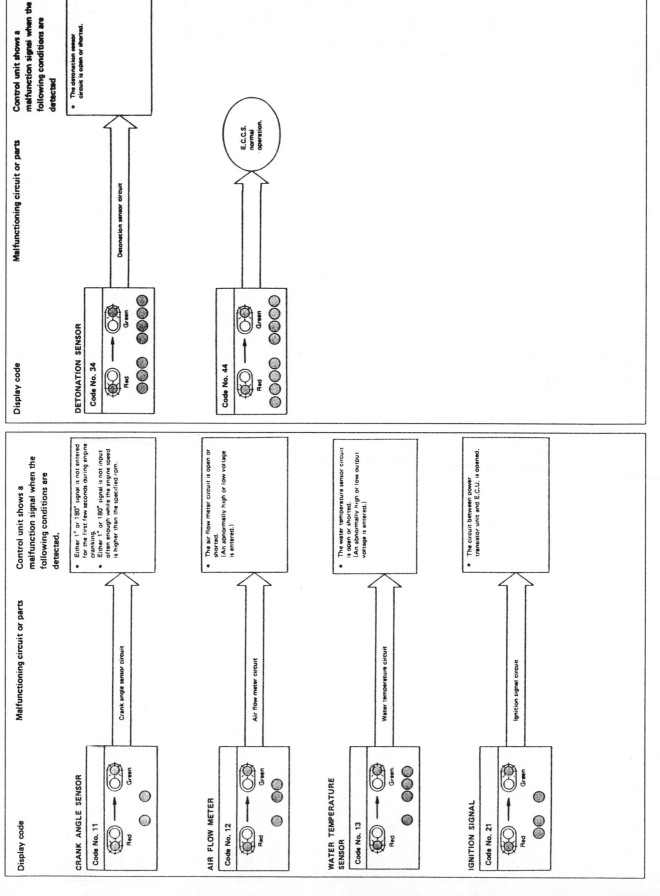

SELF-DIAGNOSTIC MODE III DECODING CHART
1987 PORT INJECTED PULSAR WITH CA16DE ENGINE

Display code — **Malfunctioning circuit or parts** — **Control unit shows a malfunction signal when the following conditions are detected**

DETONATION SENSOR

Code No. 34 — Detonation sensor circuit — • The detonation sensor circuit is open or shorted.

Code No. 44 — E.C.C.S. normal operation.

SELF-DIAGNOSTIC MODE III DECODING CHART
1987 PORT INJECTED PULSAR WITH CA16DE ENGINE

Display code — **Malfunctioning circuit or parts** — **Control unit shows a malfunction signal when the following conditions are detected.**

CRANK ANGLE SENSOR

Code No. 11 — Crank angle sensor circuit —
• Either 1° or 180° signal is not entered for the first few seconds during engine cranking.
• Either 1° or 180° signal is not input often enough while the engine speed is higher than the specified rpm.

AIR FLOW METER

Code No. 12 — Air flow meter circuit —
• The air flow meter circuit is open or shorted. (An abnormally high or low voltage is entered.)

WATER TEMPERATURE SENSOR

Code No. 13 — Water temperature circuit —
• The water temperature sensor circuit is open or shorted. (An abnormally high or low output voltage is entered.)

IGNITION SIGNAL

Code No. 21 — Ignition signal circuit —
• The circuit between power transistor unit and E.C.U. is opened.

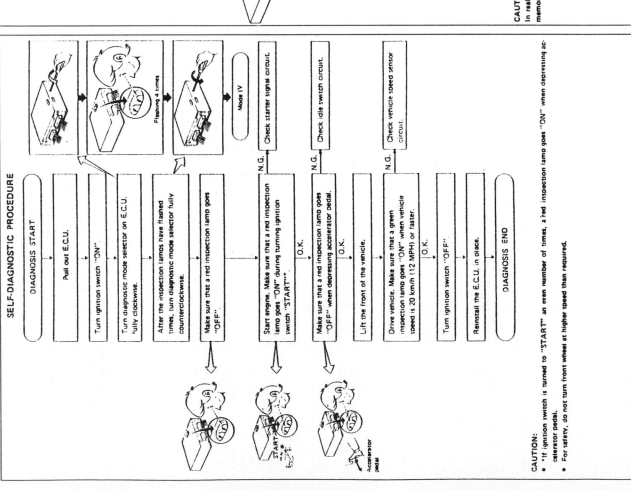

SELF-DIAGNOSTIC MODE V – ALL 1987 PORT INJECTED MODEL CARS

SELF-DIAGNOSITC PROCEDURE

DIAGNOSIS START → Pull out E.C.U. → Start engine → Turn diagnostic mode selector on E.C.U. fully clockwise. → After the inspection lamps have flashed 5 times, turn diagnostic mode selector fully counterclockwise. → Mode V

Make sure that inspection lamps are not flashing for 5 min. when idling or racing

N.G. → If flashing, count no. of flashes. → Turn ignition switch "OFF". → See decoding chart. → Perform real time diagnosis system inspection. If malfunction part is found, repair or replace it.

O.K. → Turn ignition switch "OFF".

Reinstall the E.C.U. in place. → DIAGNOSIS END

CAUTION:
In real time diagnosis, pay attention to inspection lamp flashing. E.C.U. displays the malfunction code only once, and does not memorize the inspection.

SELF-DIAGNOSTIC MODE IV – ALL 1987 PORT INJECTED MODEL CARS

SELF-DIAGNOSTIC PROCEDURE

DIAGNOSIS START → Pull out E.C.U. → Turn ignition switch "ON". → Turn diagnostic mode selector on E.C.U. fully clockwise. → After the inspection lamps have flashed 5 times, turn diagnostic mode selector fully counterclockwise. → Make sure that a red inspection lamp goes "OFF". → Mode IV

Start engine. Make sure that a red inspection lamp goes "ON" during turning ignition switch "START".
N.G. → Check starter signal circuit.
O.K. →

Make sure that a red inspection lamp goes "OFF" when depressing accelerator pedal.
N.G. → Check idle switch circuit.
O.K. →

Lift the front of the vehicle.

Drive vehicle. Make sure that a green inspection lamp goes "ON" when vehicle speed is 20 km/h (12 MPH) or faster.
N.G. → Check vehicle speed sensor circuit.
O.K. →

Turn ignition switch "OFF".

Reinstall the E.C.U. in place.

DIAGNOSIS END

CAUTION:
• "If ignition switch is turned to "START" an even number of times, a red inspection lamp goes "ON" when depressing accelerator pedal.
• For safety, do not turn front wheel at higher speed than required.

SELF-DIAGNOSTIC MODE V DECODING CHART
1987 PORT INJECTED MAXIMA, PULSAR, 300ZX, 200SX WITH 3.0 LITER ENGINE

Display presentation	Malfunction circuit or parts	Control unit shows a malfunction signal when the following conditions are detected. (Compare with Self Diagnosis — Mode III.)

CRANK ANGLE SENSOR

RED L.E.D. ON / OFF

Crank angle sensor circuit is malfunctioning.

Crank angle sensor — Rotor plate

The 1° or 120° signal is momentarily missing, or, multiple, momentary noise signals enter.

AIR FLOW METER

GREEN L.E.D. ON / OFF

Air flow meter circuit is malfunctioning.

Abnormal, momentary increase in air flow meter output signal.

IGNITION SIGNAL

GREEN L.E.D. ON / OFF

Ignition signal is malfunctioning.

Signal from the primary ignition coil momentarily drops off.

FUEL PUMP

RED L.E.D. ON / OFF

Fuel pump circuit is malfunctioning.

Fuel pump circuit is momentarily open or shorted.

SELF-DIAGNOSTIC MODE V DECODING CHART
1987 PORT INJECTED STANZA AND 200SX WITH CA20E ENGINE

Display presentation	Malfunction circuit or parts	Control unit shows a malfunction signal when the following conditions are detected. (Compare with Self Diagnosis — Mode III.)

CRANK ANGLE SENSOR

RED L.E.D. Unit: sec — 3.2 3.2 3.2 1.6 1.6 1.6 1.6 1.6 — ON / OFF

Crank angle sensor circuit is malfunctioning.

The 1° or 180° signal is momentarily missing, or, multiple, momentary noise signals enter.

AIR FLOW METER

GREEN L.E.D. Unit: sec — 3.2 3.2 1.6 1.6 0.4 0.6 — ON / OFF

Air flow meter circuit is malfunctioning.

Abnormal, momentary increase in air flow meter output signal.

IGNITION SIGNAL

GREEN L.E.D. Unit: sec — 3.2 3.2 1.8 1.8 0.4 0.2 0.2 — ON / OFF

Ignition signal is malfunctioning.

Signal from the primary ignition coil momentarily drops off.

FUEL PUMP

RED L.E.D. Unit: sec — 3.2 3.2 1.6 1.6 0.4 0.4 0.2 0.2 — ON / OFF

Fuel pump circuit is malfunctioning.

Fuel pump circuit is momentarily open or shorted.

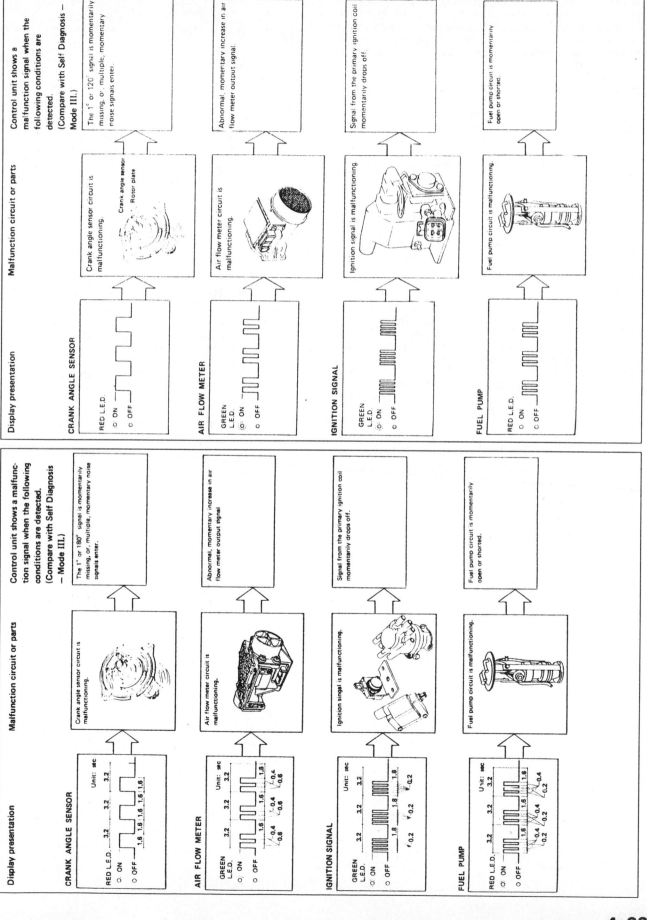

move the pin terminal retainer from the 20 and 16-pin connectors to make it easier to insert tester probes into the connector.

3. When connecting or disconnecting pin connectors from the ECU, take care not to bend or break any pin terminals. Check that there are no bends or breaks on ECU pin terminals before attempting any connections.

4. Before replacing any ECU, perform the ECU input/output signal diagnosis to make sure the ECU is functioning properly or not.

5. After performing the Electronic Control System Inspection, perform the ECCS self-diagnosis and driving test.

6. When measuring supply voltage of ECU controlled components with a circuit tester, separate one tester probe from another. If the two tester probes accidentally make contact with each other during measurement, a short circuit will result and damage the power transistor in the ECU.

MAINTENANCE REMINDER LIGHTS

Exhaust gas sensor should be checked after every 30,000 miles (48,000 km) of operation. At this time, the exhaust gas sensor warning lamp will come on to indicate that the sensor should be inspected. After inspecting and/or replacing the sensor, the sensor warning lamp should be reset. On 1984, most 1985 and Canada models, the sensor light connector is disconnected and further maintenance is not required. On 1985 Maxima and most 1986–88 models, a warning light hold relay must be located and reset at the 30,000 mile (48,000 km) and 60,000 mile (96,000 km) intervals. At 90,000 miles (144,000 km), the sensor warning light is disabled by disconnecting the sensor light connector. On 1987–88 300ZX with analog instrument panel, three sensor light connectors are located behind the right kick panel and are disconnected in order by harness color. At 30,000 miles (48,000 km) disconnect the white connector, at 60,000 miles (96,000 km) disconnect the white/yellow connector, and at 90,000 miles (144,000 km) disconnect the white/red connector.

SENSOR LIGHT CONNECTOR LOCATION

- 1984 200SX – Under right side dash
- 1985–88 200SX – Behind fuse box
- 1984–88 Maxima – Near hood release
- 1984 300ZX – Behind left kick panel
- 1985–86 300ZX – Above hood release
- 1987–88 300ZX (Digital) – Above hood release

Keys to symbols

🔌 : Check after disconnecting the connector to be measured.

🔌 : Check after connecting the connector to be measured.

When measuring voltage or resistance at connector with tester probes, there are two methods of measurement; one is done from terminal side and the other from harness side. Before measuring, confirm symbol mark again.

H.S : Inspection should be done from harness side.

T.S : Inspection should be done from terminal side.

- 1987–88 300ZX (Analog) – Behind right kick panel
- 1987–88 Stanza – Above fuse box
- 1987–88 Stanza Wagon – Above fuse box
- 1984–88 Pulsar NX – Above fuse box
- 1987–88 Sentra – Above fuse box

SENSOR LIGHT HOLD RELAY LOCATION

- 1986–88 200SX – Center console
- 1985–88 Maxima – Behind left kick panel
- 1986–88 300ZX – Near glove box
- 1987–88 Stanza – Behind right kick panel
- 1987–88 Stanza Wagon – Under right seat
- 1986 Pulsar NX – Behind right kick panel
- 1987–88 Pulsar NX – Behind left kick panel
- 1987–88 Sentra – Behind right kick panel

ELECTRONIC CONTROL UNIT (ECI) LOCATION:

- 1984–87 200SX – Behind left (driver) kick panel
- 1984–87 Maxima – Under right (passenger) seat
- 1984–87 300ZX – Behind right side dash panel
- 1987 Stanza – Under right (passenger) seat
- 1984–86 Pulsar NX – Under left (driver) seat
- 1987 Pulsar NX – Under right (passenger) seat
- 1987 Sentra – Under right (passenger) seat

ECCS SELF-DIAGNOSTIC PROCEDURE – 1984 PORT INJECTED PULSAR

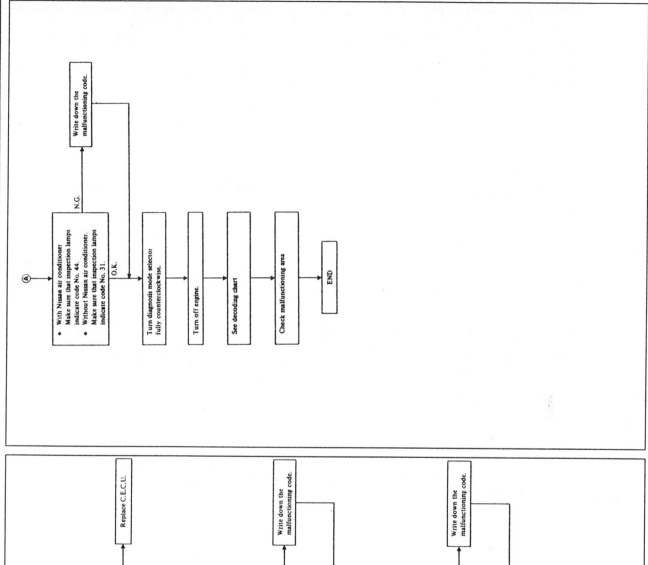

ECCS SELF-DIAGNOSTIC PROCEDURE – 1984 PORT INJECTED PULSAR

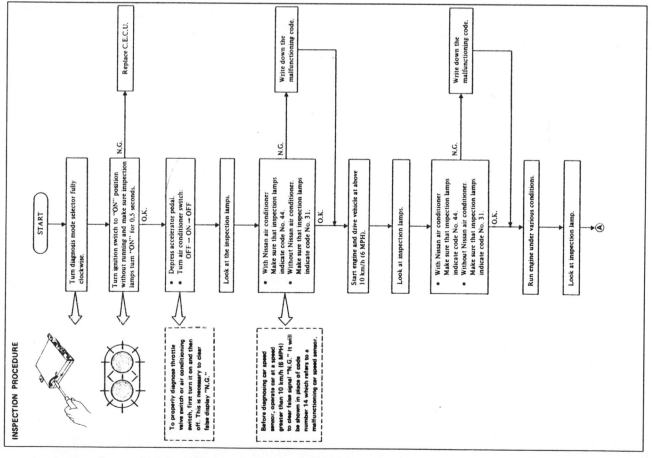

ECCS SELF-DIAGNOSTIC DECODING CHART
1984 PORT INJECTED PULSAR

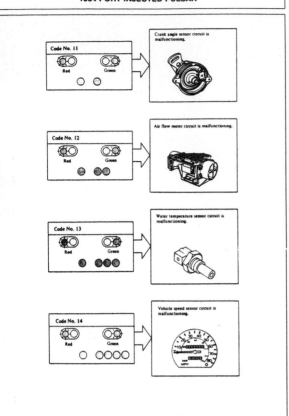

Code No. 11 — Red / Green — Crank angle sensor circuit is malfunctioning.

Code No. 12 — Red / Green — Air flow meter circuit is malfunctioning.

Code No. 13 — Red / Green — Water temperature sensor circuit is malfunctioning.

Code No. 14 — Red / Green — Vehicle speed sensor circuit is malfunctioning.

ECCS SELF-DIAGNOSTIC DECODING CHART
1984 PORT INJECTED PULSAR

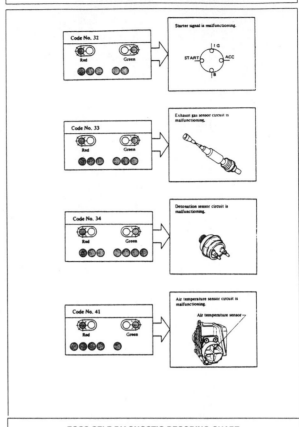

Code No. 32 — Red / Green — Starter signal is malfunctioning.

Code No. 33 — Red / Green — Exhaust gas sensor circuit is malfunctioning.

Code No. 34 — Red / Green — Detonation sensor circuit is malfunctioning.

Code No. 41 — Red / Green — Air temperature sensor circuit is malfunctioning. Air temperature sensor

ECCS SELF-DIAGNOSTIC DECODING CHART
1984 PORT INJECTED PULSAR

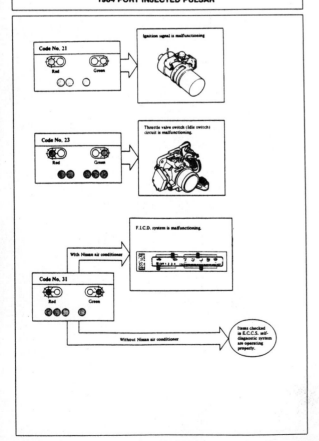

Code No. 21 — Red / Green — Ignition signal is malfunctioning

Code No. 23 — Red / Green — Throttle valve switch (idle switch) circuit is malfunctioning.

Code No. 31 — Red / Green — With Nissan air conditioner — F.I.C.D. system is malfunctioning.

Without Nissan air conditioner — Items checked in E.C.C.S. self-diagnostic system are operating properly.

ECCS SELF-DIAGNOSTIC DECODING CHART
1984 PORT INJECTED PULSAR

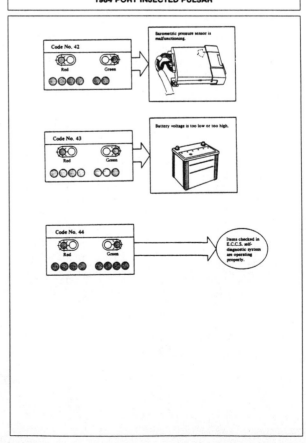

Code No. 42 — Red / Green — Barometric pressure sensor is malfunctioning.

Code No. 43 — Red / Green — Battery voltage is too low or too high.

Code No. 44 — Red / Green — Items checked in E.C.C.S. self-diagnostic system are operating properly.

ECCS SELF-DIAGNOSTIC CHART – 1984 PORT INJECTED PULSAR

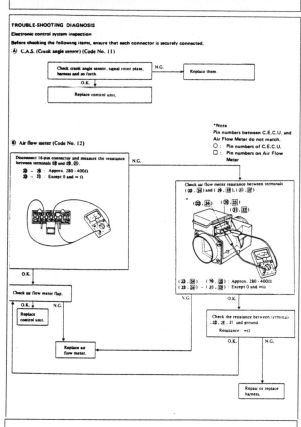

TROUBLE-SHOOTING DIAGNOSIS

Electronic control system inspection

Before checking the following items, ensure that each connector is securely connected.

Ⓐ C.A.S. (Crank angle sensor) (Code No. 11)

> Check crank angle sensor, signal rotor plate, harness and so forth. — N.G. → Replace them.
> O.K. ↓
> Replace control unit.

*Note
Pin numbers between C.E.C.U. and Air Flow Meter do not match.
○ : Pin numbers of C.E.C.U.
□ : Pin numbers on Air Flow Meter

Ⓑ Air flow meter (Code No. 12)

> Disconnect 16-pin connector and measure the resistance between terminals ㉝ and ㉖, ㉛.
> ㉝ – ㉖ : Approx. 280 - 400Ω
> ㉝ – ㉛ : Except 0 and = Ω

> Check air flow meter resistance between terminals (㉝ , ㉞) and (㉖ , ㉝), (㉛ , ㉜).
> (㉝ , ㉞) - (㉖ , ㉝) : Approx. 280 - 400Ω
> (㉝ , ㉞) - (㉛ , ㉜) : Except 0 and = Ω

> Check air flow meter flap.
> O.K. ↓ N.G.
> Replace control unit.
> Replace air flow meter.

> Check the resistance between terminals ㉝ , ㉖ , ㉛ and ground.
> Resistance : = Ω
> Repair or replace harness.

ECCS SELF-DIAGNOSTIC CHART – 1984 PORT INJECTED PULSAR

Ⓓ Vehicle speed sensor (Code No. 14)

> Check speed meter indication. — N.G. → Replace speedometer unit.
> O.K. ↓
> Check harness between 16-pin connector ㉙ and speedometer connector. — N.G. → Replace or repair it.
> O.K. ↓
> Replace control unit.

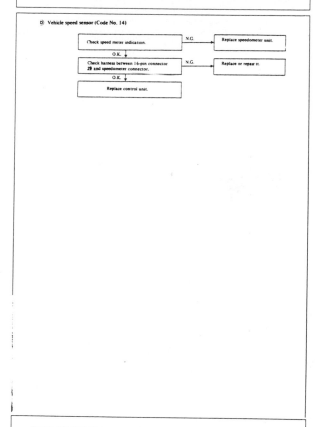

ECCS SELF-DIAGNOSTIC CHART – 1984 PORT INJECTED PULSAR

Ⓒ Water temperature sensor (Code No. 13)

> Disconnect 16-pin connector and measure the resistance between terminal ㉗ and ㉙.

Cylinder head temperature	Resistance
Above 20°C (68°F)	Below 2.9 kΩ
Below 20°C (68°F)	Above 2.1 kΩ

> Check harness. — O.K. ↓ — Replace control unit.

> Dip the sensor into water maintained at a temperature of 20°C (68°F), 80°C (176°F), etc., and read its resistance.

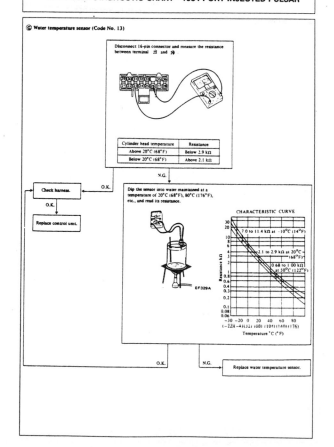

CHARACTERISTIC CURVE

7.0 to 11.4 kΩ at -10°C (14°F)
2.1 to 2.9 kΩ at 20°C (68°F)
0.68 to 1.00 kΩ at 50°C (122°F)

Resistance kΩ vs Temperature °C (°F)

EF329A

> O.K. — N.G. → Replace water temperature sensor.

ECCS SELF-DIAGNOSTIC CHART – 1984 PORT INJECTED PULSAR

Ⓔ IGN. (Ignition system) (Code No. 21)

> Disconnect high tension cable from one spark plug and check for hot spark during cranking.

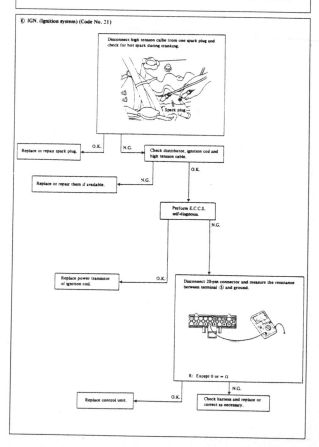

Spark plug

> Replace or repair spark plug. — O.K. — N.G. → Check distributor, ignition coil and high tension cable.
> Replace or repair them if available. — N.G.
> O.K. ↓
> Perform E.C.C.S. self-diagnosis.
> N.G.
> Replace power transistor of ignition coil. — O.K.
> Disconnect 20-pin connector and measure the resistance between terminal ⑤ and ground.
> R : Except 0 or = Ω
> Replace control unit. — O.K. — N.G. → Check harness and replace or correct as necessary.

ECCS SELF-DIAGNOSTIC CHART—1984 PORT INJECTED PULSAR

Ⓕ Idle switch (Throttle valve switch) (Code No. 23)

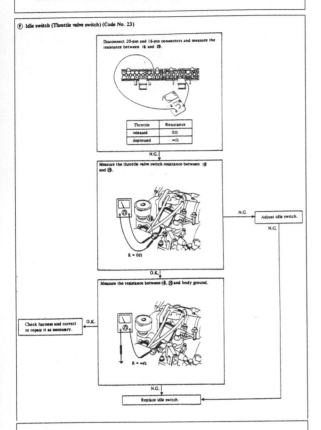

ECCS SELF-DIAGNOSTIC CHART—1984 PORT INJECTED PULSAR

Ⓘ Exhaust gas sensor (Code No. 33)

Ⓙ Detonation sensor (Code No. 34)

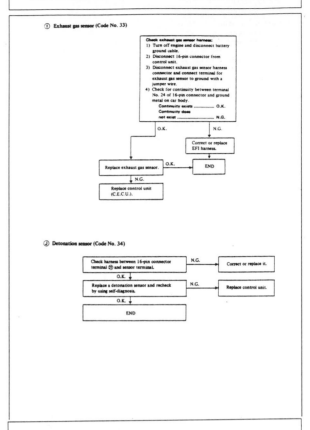

ECCS SELF-DIAGNOSTIC CHART—1984 PORT INJECTED PULSAR

Ⓖ Air conditioner switch (Code No. 31)

Ⓗ Starter switch (Code No. 32)

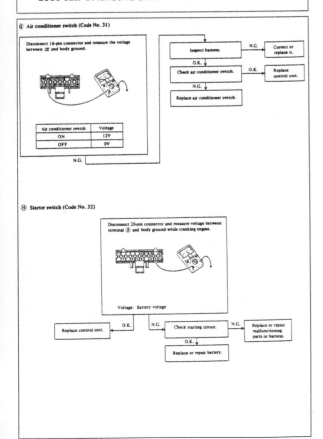

ECCS SELF-DIAGNOSTIC CHART—1984 PORT INJECTED PULSAR

Ⓚ Air temperature (Code No. 41)

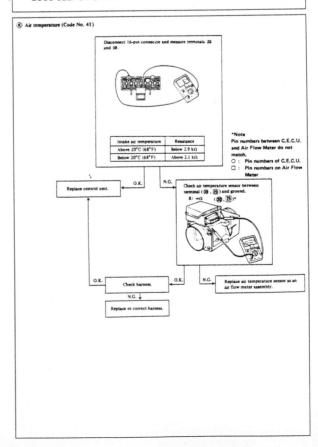

ECCS SELF-DIAGNOSTIC CHART—1984 PORT INJECTED PULSAR

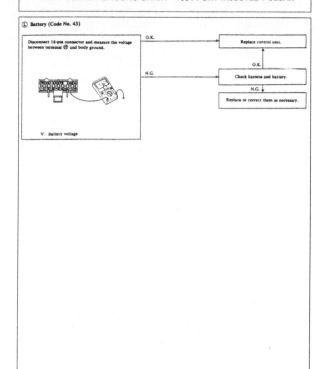

Ⓛ Battery (Code No. 43)

Disconnect 16-pin connector and measure the voltage between terminal ⑰ and body ground.
— O.K. → Replace control unit.
— N.G. → Check harness and battery.
— O.K. →
— N.G. → Replace or correct them as necessary.

V: Battery voltage

MIXTURE RATIO FEEDBACK SYSTEM INSPECTION CHART 1984 PORT INJECTED PULSAR

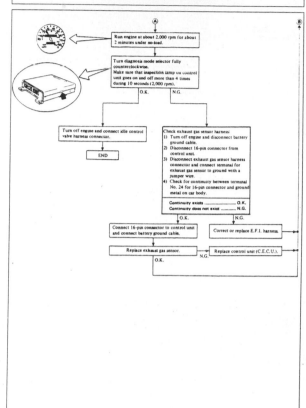

Ⓐ

Run engine at about 2,000 rpm for about 2 minutes under no-load.

Turn diagnosis mode selector fully counterclockwise. Make sure that inspection lamp on control unit goes on and off more than 4 times during 10 seconds (2,000 rpm).
— O.K. → Turn off engine and connect idle control valve harness connector. → END
— N.G. → Check exhaust gas sensor harness:
1) Turn off engine and disconnect battery ground cable.
2) Disconnect 16-pin connector from control unit.
3) Disconnect exhaust gas sensor harness connector and connect terminal for exhaust gas sensor to ground with a jumper wire.
4) Check for continuity between terminal No. 24 for 16-pin connector and ground metal on car body.

Continuity exists .... O.K.
Continuity does not exist .... N.G.

— O.K. → Connect 16-pin connector to control unit and connect battery ground cable. → Replace exhaust gas sensor. — O.K. → Replace control unit (C.E.C.U.).
— N.G. → Correct or replace E.F.I. harness. → Replace control unit (C.E.C.U.). — N.G.

Ⓑ

MIXTURE RATIO FEEDBACK SYSTEM INSPECTION CHART—1984 PORT INJECTED PULSAR

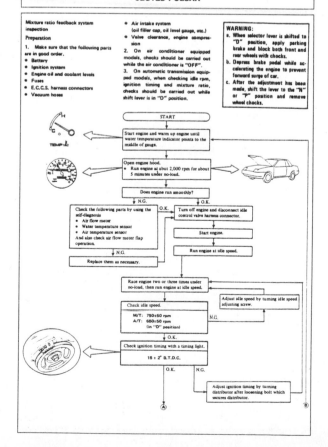

Mixture ratio feedback system inspection

Preparation

1. Make sure that the following parts are in good order.
• Battery
• Ignition system
• Engine oil and coolant levels
• Fuses
• E.C.C.S. harness connectors
• Vacuum hoses

• Air intake system (oil filler cap, oil level gauge, etc.)
• Valve clearance, engine compression

2. On air conditioner equipped models, checks should be carried out while the air conditioner is "OFF".

3. On automatic transmission equipped models, when checking idle rpm, ignition timing and mixture ratio, checks should be carried out while shift lever is in "D" position.

WARNING:
a. When selector lever is shifted to "D" position, apply parking brake and block both front and rear wheels with chocks.
b. Depress brake pedal while accelerating the engine to prevent forward surge of car.
c. After the adjustment has been made, shift the lever to the "N" or "P" position and remove wheel chocks.

START

Start engine and warm up engine until water temperature indicator points to the middle of gauge.

Open engine hood.
• Run engine at abut 2,000 rpm for about 5 minutes under no-load.

Does engine run smoothly?
— N.G. → Check the following parts by using the self-diagnosis:
• Air flow meter
• Water temperature sensor
• Air temperature sensor
And also check air flow meter flap operation.
— N.G. → Replace them as necessary.
— O.K. →

Turn off engine and disconnect idle control valve harness connector.

Start engine.

Run engine at idle speed.

Race engine two or three times under no-load, then run engine at idle speed.

Check idle speed.
M/T: 750±50 rpm
A/T: 650±50 rpm (in "D" position)
— N.G. → Adjust idle speed by turning idle speed adjusting screw.
— O.K. →

Check ignition timing with a timing light.
15 ± 2° B.T.D.C.
— O.K. →
— N.G. → Adjust ignition timing by turning distributor after loosening bolt which secures distributor.

Ⓐ   Ⓑ

ECCS SELF-DIAGNOSTIC PROCEDURE 1984–88 PORT INJECTED 200SX WITH CA18ET ENGINE

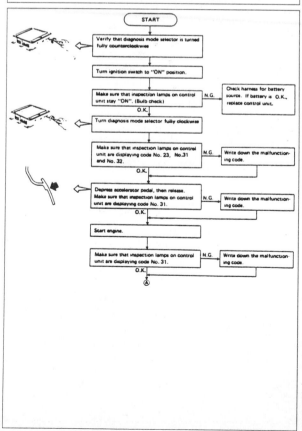

START

Verify that diagnosis mode selector is turned fully counterclockwise.

Turn ignition switch to "ON" position.

Make sure that inspection lamps on control unit stay "ON". (Bulb check)
— N.G. → Check harness for battery source. If battery is O.K., replace control unit.
— O.K. →

Turn diagnosis mode selector fully clockwise.

Make sure that inspection lamps on control unit are displaying code No. 23, No.31 and No. 32.
— N.G. → Write down the malfunctioning code.
— O.K. →

Depress accelerator pedal, then release. Make sure that inspection lamps on control unit are displaying code No. 31.
— N.G. → Write down the malfunctioning code.
— O.K. →

Start engine.

Make sure that inspection lamps on control unit are displaying code No. 31.
— N.G. → Write down the malfunctioning code.
— O.K. →

Ⓐ

ECCS SELF-DIAGNOSTIC PROCEDURE
1984–88 PORT INJECTED 200SX WITH CA18ET ENGINE

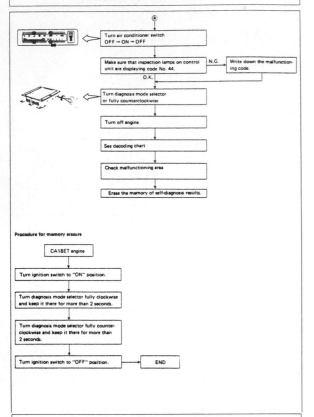

ECCS SELF-DIAGNOSTIC DECODING CHART
1984–88 PORT INJECTED 200SX WITH CA18ET ENGINE

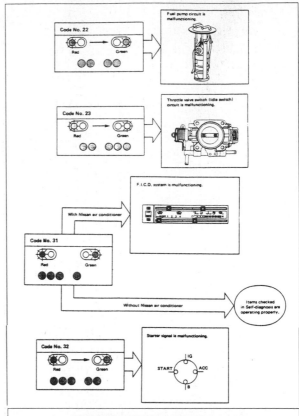

ECCS SELF-DIAGNOSTIC DECODING CHART
1984–88 PORT INJECTED 200SX WITH CA18ET ENGINE

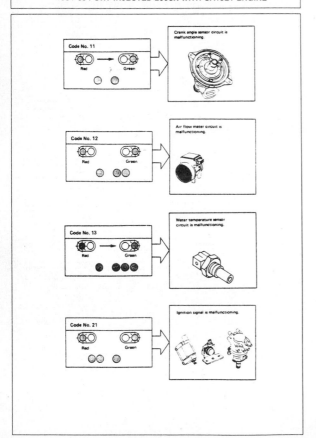

ECCS SELF-DIAGNOSTIC DECODING CHART
1984–88 PORT INJECTED 200SX WITH CA18ET ENGINE

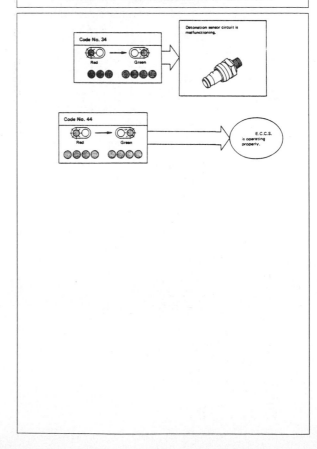

ECCS SELF-DIAGNOSTIC CHART
1984–88 PORT INJECTED 200SX WITH CA18ET ENGINE

PREPARATION

Before checking the following items, ensure that each connector is securely connected.

Ⓐ Crank angle sensor (Code No. 11)

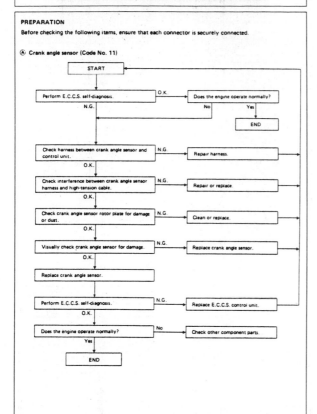

ECCS SELF-DIAGNOSTIC CHART
1984–88 PORT INJECTED 200SX WITH CA18ET ENGINE

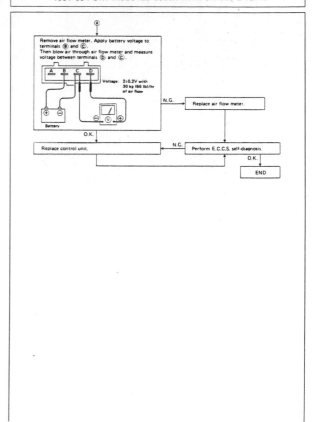

ECCS SELF-DIAGNOSTIC CHART
1984–88 PORT INJECTED 200SX WITH CA18ET ENGINE

Ⓑ Air flow meter (Code No. 12)

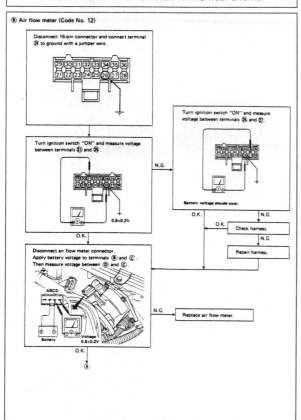

ECCS SELF-DIAGNOSTIC CHART
1984–88 PORT INJECTED 200SX WITH CA18ET ENGINE

Ⓒ Water temperature sensor (Code No. 13)

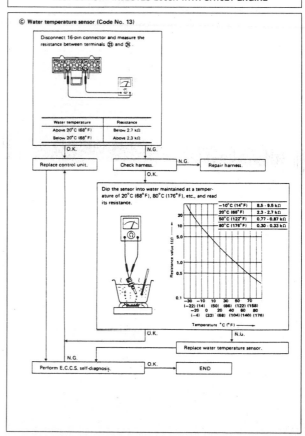

ECCS SELF-DIAGNOSTIC CHART
1984–88 PORT INJECTED 200SX WITH CA18ET ENGINE

Ⓓ Ignition signal (Code No. 21)

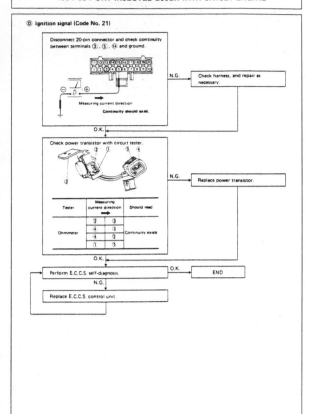

ECCS SELF-DIAGNOSTIC CHART
1984–88 PORT INJECTED 200SX WITH CA18ET ENGINE

Ⓕ Throttle valve switch (Code No. 23)

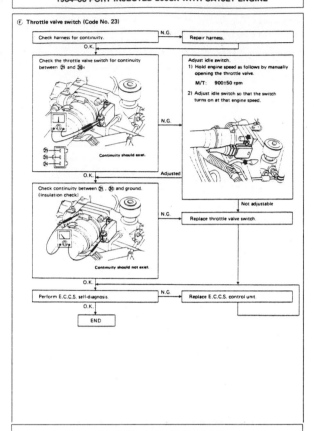

ECCS SELF-DIAGNOSTIC CHART
1984–88 PORT INJECTED 200SX WITH CA18ET ENGINE

Ⓔ Fuel pump (Code No. 22)

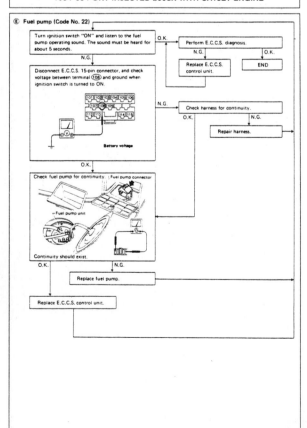

ECCS SELF-DIAGNOSTIC CHART
1984–88 PORT INJECTED 200SX WITH CA18ET ENGINE

Ⓕ Throttle valve switch (Code No. 23)

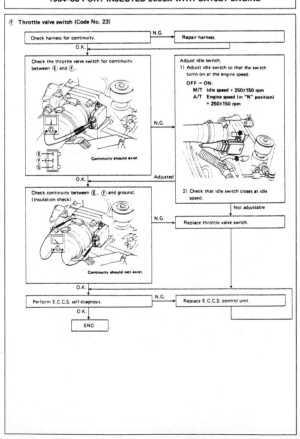

ECCS SELF-DIAGNOSTIC CHART
1984–88 PORT INJECTED 200SX WITH CA18ET ENGINE

Ⓗ Air conditioner (Code No. 31)

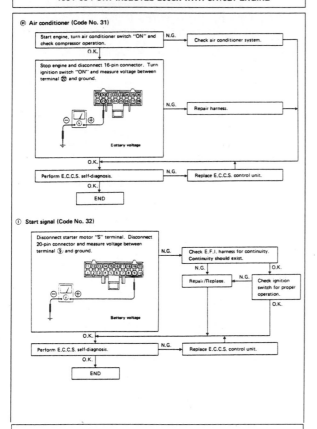

Ⓘ Start signal (Code No. 32)

ECCS SELF-DIAGNOSTIC CHART
1984–88 PORT INJECTED 200SX WITH CA18ET ENGINE

Ⓛ Air regulator

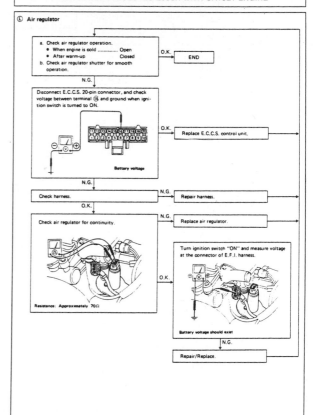

ECCS SELF-DIAGNOSTIC CHART
1984–88 PORT INJECTED 200SX WITH CA18ET ENGINE

Ⓙ Detonation sensor (Code No. 34)

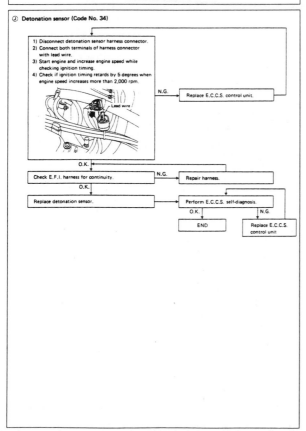

ECCS SELF-DIAGNOSTIC CHART
1984–88 PORT INJECTED 200SX WITH CA18ET ENGINE

Ⓜ Injector

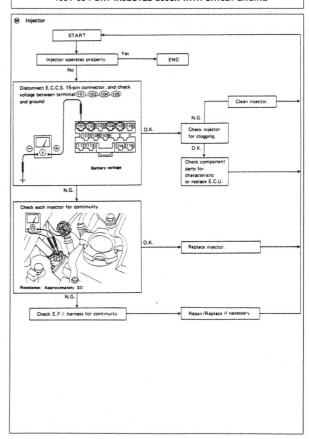

ECCS SELF-DIAGNOSTIC CHART
1984–88 PORT INJECTED 200SX WITH CA18ET ENGINE

Ⓝ Battery source and ground

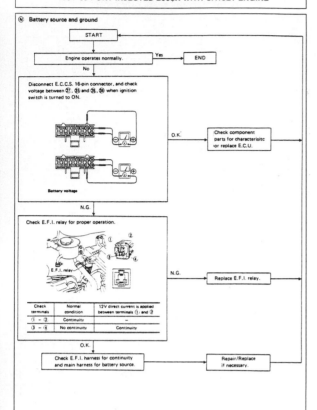

ECCS SELF-DIAGNOSTIC CHART
1984–88 PORT INJECTED 200SX WITH CA18ET ENGINE

ⓠ Idle-up solenoid valve

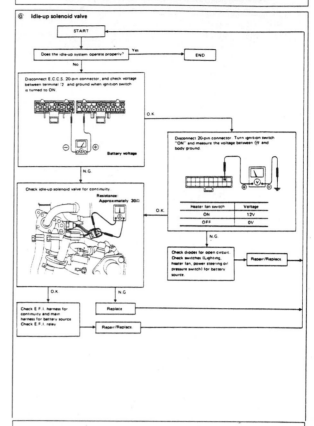

ECCS SELF-DIAGNOSTIC CHART
1984–88 PORT INJECTED 200SX WITH CA18ET ENGINE

ⓞ Exhaust gas sensor

Ⓟ Exhaust gas sensor heater

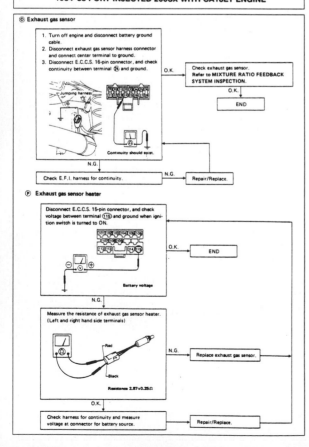

MIXTURE RATIO FEEDBACK SYSTEM INSPECTION CHART
1984–88 PORT INJECTED 200SX WITH CA18ET ENGINE

PREPARATION

1. Make sure that the following parts are in good order.
   - Battery
   - Ignition system
   - Engine oil and coolant levels
   - Fuses
   - E.F.I. harness connectors
   - Vacuum hoses
   - Air intake system
     (oil filler cap, oil level gauge, etc.)
   - Valve clearance, engine compression
   - E.G.R. valve operation
   - Throttle valve and throttle valve switch operation
2. On air conditioner equipped models, checks should be carried out while the air conditioner is "OFF".

3. On automatic transmission equipped models, when checking idle rpm, ignition timing and mixture ratio, checks should be carried out while shift lever is in "D" position.
4. Make sure that diagnosis mode selector is in "OFF" position.

WARNING:
a. When selector lever is shifted to "D" position, apply parking brake and block both front and rear wheels with chocks.
b. Depress brake pedal while racing the engine to prevent forward surge of vehicle.
c. After the adjustment has been made, shift the lever to the "N" or "P" position and remove wheel chocks.

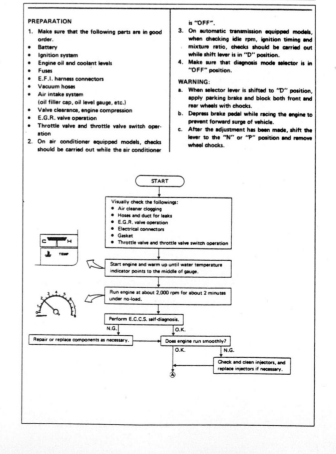

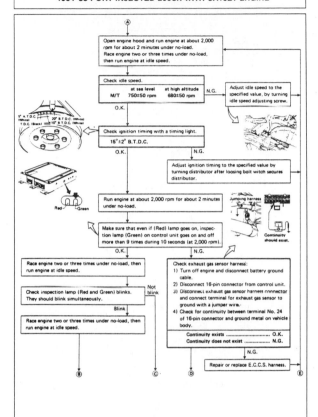

MIXTURE RATIO FEEDBACK SYSTEM INSPECTION CHART
1984–88 PORT INJECTED 200SX WITH CA18ET ENGINE

A

Open engine hood and run engine at about 2,000 rpm for about 2 minutes under no-load.
Race engine two or three times under no-load, then run engine at idle speed.

Check idle speed.

	at sea level	at high altitude
M/T	750±50 rpm	680±50 rpm

O.K. → N.G. → Adjust idle speed to the specified value, by turning idle speed adjusting screw.

Check ignition timing with a timing light.

15°±2° B.T.D.C.

O.K. → N.G. → Adjust ignition timing to the specified value by turning distributor after loosing bolt witch secures distributor.

Run engine at about 2,000 rpm for about 2 minutes under no-load.

Jumping harness

Continuity should exist.

Make sure that even if (Red) lamp goes on, inspection lamp (Green) on control unit goes on and off more than 9 times during 10 seconds (at 2,000 rpm).

O.K. → N.G. → Check exhaust gas sensor harness:
1) Turn off engine and disconnect battery ground cable.
2) Disconnect 16-pin connector from control unit.
3) Disconnect exhaust gas sensor harness connector and connect terminal for exhaust gas sensor to ground with a jumper wire.
4) Check for continuity between terminal No. 24 of 16-pin connector and ground metal on vehicle body.

Continuity exists .... O.K.
Continuity does not exist .... N.G.

Race engine two or three times under no-load, then run engine at idle speed.

Check inspection lamp (Red and Green) blinks. They should blink simultaneously. → Not blink

Blink

Race engine two or three times under no-load, then run engine at idle speed.

N.G. → Repair or replace E.C.C.S. harness. → E

B   C   D

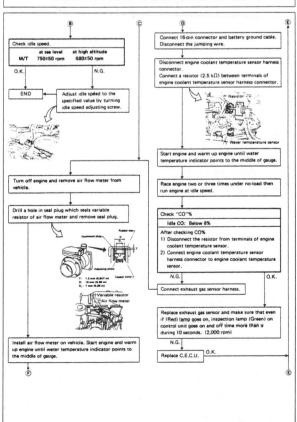

MIXTURE RATIO FEEDBACK SYSTEM INSPECTION CHART
1984–88 PORT INJECTED 200SX WITH CA18ET ENGINE

B

Check idle speed.

	at sea level	at high altitude
M/T	750±50 rpm	680±50 rpm

O.K. → END

N.G. → Adjust idle speed to the specified value by turning idle speed adjusting screw.

Turn off engine and remove air flow meter from vehicle.

Drill a hole in seal plug which seals variable resistor of air flow meter and remove seal plug.

Variable resistor
Air flow meter

Install air flow meter on vehicle. Start engine and warm up engine until water temperature indicator points to the middle of gauge.

F

C   E

Connect 16-pin connector and battery ground cable. Disconnect the jumping wire.

Disconnect engine coolant temperature sensor harness connector.
Connect a resistor (2.5 kΩ) between terminals of engine coolant temperature sensor harness connector.

Resistor

Water temperature sensor

Start engine and warm up engine until water temperature indicator points to the middle of gauge.

Race engine two or three times under no-load then run engine at idle speed.

Check "CO"%

Idle CO: Below 8%

After checking CO%
1) Disconnect the resistor from terminals of engine coolant temperature sensor.
2) Connect engine coolant temperature sensor harness connector to engine coolant temperature sensor.

N.G. → O.K. → Connect exhaust gas sensor harness.

Replace exhaust gas sensor and make sure that even if (Red) lamp goes on, inspection lamp (Green) on control unit goes on and off time more than 9 during 10 seconds. (2,000 rpm)

N.G. → O.K. → Replace C.E.C.U.

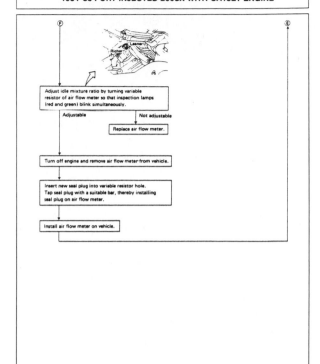

MIXTURE RATIO FEEDBACK SYSTEM INSPECTION CHART
1984–88 PORT INJECTED 200SX WITH CA18ET ENGINE

F

Richer   Leaner

Adjust idle mixture ratio by turning variable resistor of air flow meter so that inspection lamps (red and green) blink simultaneously.

Adjustable → Not adjustable → Replace air flow meter.

Turn off engine and remove air flow meter from vehicle.

Insert new seal plug into variable resistor hole.
Tap seal plug with a suitable bar, thereby installing seal plug on air flow meter.

Install air flow meter on vehicle.

E

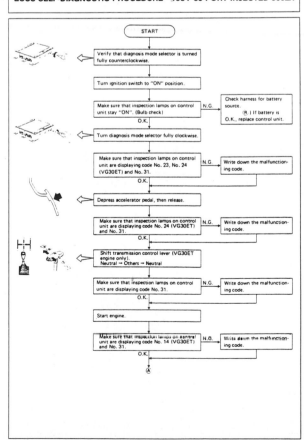

ECCS SELF-DIAGNOSTIC PROCEDURE – 1984–85 PORT INJECTED 300ZX

START

Verify that diagnosis mode selector is turned fully counterclockwise.

Turn ignition switch to "ON" position.

Make sure that inspection lamps on control unit stay "ON". (Bulb check) → N.G. → Check harness for battery source.
(R.) If battery is O.K., replace control unit.

Turn diagnosis mode selector fully clockwise.

Make sure that inspection lamps on control unit are displaying code No. 23, No. 24 (VG30ET) and No. 31. → N.G. → Write down the malfunctioning code.

O.K.

Depress accelerator pedal, then release.

Make sure that inspection lamps on control unit are displaying code No. 24 (VG30ET) and No. 31. → N.G. → Write down the malfunctioning code.

O.K.

Shift transmission control lever (VG30ET engine only).
Neutral → Others → Neutral

Make sure that inspection lamps on control unit are displaying code No. 31. → N.G. → Write down the malfunctioning code.

O.K.

Start engine.

Make sure that inspection lamps on control unit are displaying code No. 14 (VG30ET) and No. 31. → N.G. → Write down the malfunctioning code.

O.K.

A

ECCS SELF-DIAGNOSTIC PROCEDURE – 1984–85 PORT INJECTED 300ZX

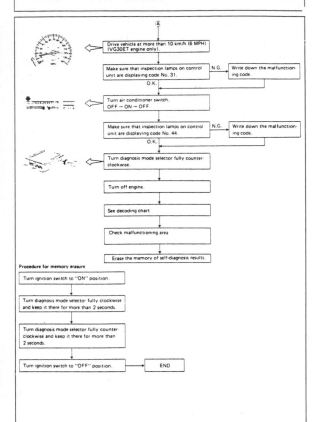

**ECCS SELF-DIAGNOSTIC DECODING CHART
1984–85 PORT INJECTED 300ZX**

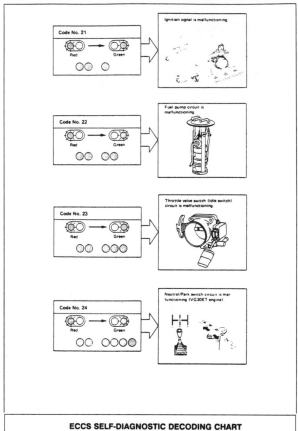

**ECCS SELF-DIAGNOSTIC DECODING CHART
1984–85 PORT INJECTED 300ZX**

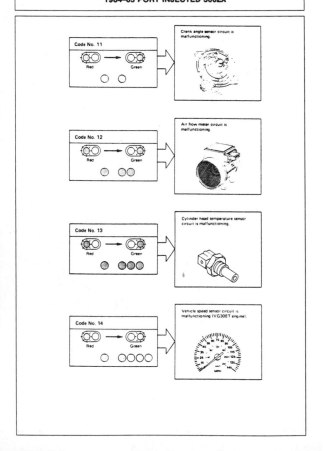

**ECCS SELF-DIAGNOSTIC DECODING CHART
1984–85 PORT INJECTED 300ZX**

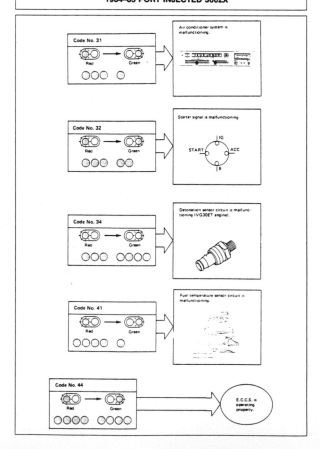

ECCS SELF-DIAGNOSTIC CHART – 1984–85 PORT INJECTED 300ZX

PREPARATION

Before checking the following items, ensure that each connector is securely connected.

Ⓐ Crank angle sensor (Code No. 11)

Check harness between crank angle sensor and control unit. → N.G. → Repair harness.

↓ O.K.

Check interference between crank angle sensor harness and high tension cable. → N.G. → Repair or replace.

↓ O.K.

Check crank angle sensor rotor plate for damage or dust. → N.G. → Clean or replace.

↓ O.K.

Visually check crank angle sensor for damage. → N.G. → Replace crank angle sensor.

↓ O.K.

Replace E.C.C.S. control unit.

ECCS SELF-DIAGNOSTIC CHART – 1984–85 PORT INJECTED 300ZX

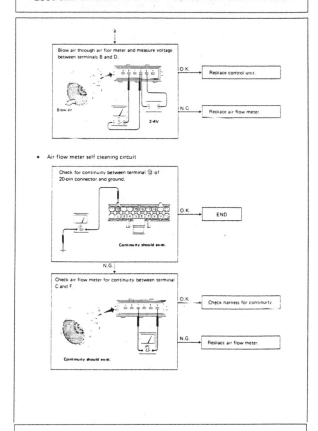

Blow air through air flow meter and measure voltage between terminals B and D. → O.K. → Replace control unit.

2-4V → N.G. → Replace air flow meter

• Air flow meter self cleaning circuit

Check for continuity between terminal 12 of 20-pin connector and ground. → O.K. → END

Continuity should exist.

↓ N.G.

Check air flow meter for continuity between terminal C and F. → O.K. → Check harness for continuity

Continuity should exist. → N.G. → Replace air flow meter.

ECCS SELF-DIAGNOSTIC CHART – 1984–85 PORT INJECTED 300ZX

Ⓑ Air flow meter (Code No. 12)

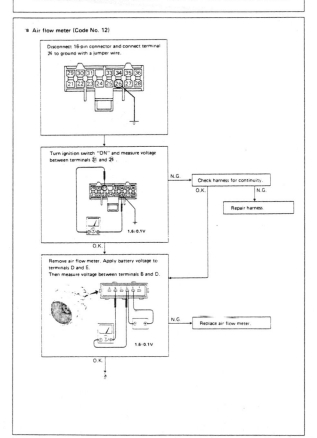

Disconnect 16-pin connector and connect terminal 26 to ground with a jumper wire.

Turn ignition switch "ON" and measure voltage between terminals 31 and 26. → N.G. → Check harness for continuity. → N.G. → Repair harness.

O.K. → 1.6-0.1V → O.K.

Remove air flow meter. Apply battery voltage to terminals D and E. Then measure voltage between terminals B and D. → N.G. → Replace air flow meter.

1.6-0.1V → O.K.

ECCS SELF-DIAGNOSTIC CHART – 1984–85 PORT INJECTED 300ZX

Ⓒ Cylinder head temperature sensor (Code No. 13)

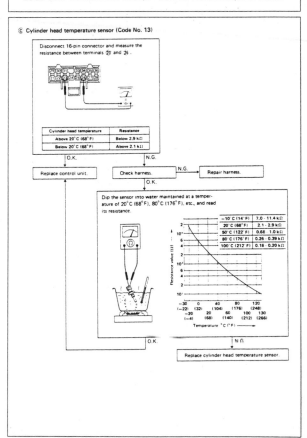

Disconnect 16-pin connector and measure the resistance between terminals 23 and 26.

Cylinder head temperature	Resistance
Above 20°C (68°F)	Below 2.9 kΩ
Below 20°C (68°F)	Above 2.1 kΩ

O.K. → Replace control unit.

N.G. → Check harness. → N.G. → Repair harness.

↓ O.K.

Dip the sensor into water maintained at a temperature of 20°C (68°F), 80°C (176°F), etc., and read its resistance.

Temperature	Resistance value
−10°C (14°F)	7.0 - 11.4 kΩ
20°C (68°F)	2.1 - 2.9 kΩ
50°C (122°F)	0.68 - 1.0 kΩ
80°C (176°F)	0.26 - 0.39 kΩ
100°C (212°F)	0.18 - 0.20 kΩ

O.K. → N.G. → Replace cylinder head temperature sensor.

ECCS SELF-DIAGNOSTIC CHART – 1984–85 PORT INJECTED 300ZX

ⓓ Vehicle speed sensor (Code No. 14)

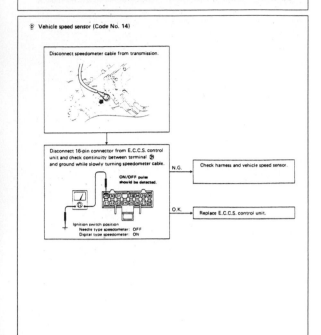

Disconnect speedometer cable from transmission.

Disconnect 16-pin connector from E.C.C.S. control unit and check continuity between terminal ㉟ and ground while slowly turning speedometer cable.

ON/OFF pulse should be detected.

→ N.G. → Check harness and vehicle speed sensor.

→ O.K. → Replace E.C.C.S. control unit.

Ignition switch position
Needle type speedometer: OFF
Digital type speedometer: ON

ECCS SELF-DIAGNOSTIC CHART – 1984–85 PORT INJECTED 300ZX

ⓕ Fuel pump (Code No. 22)

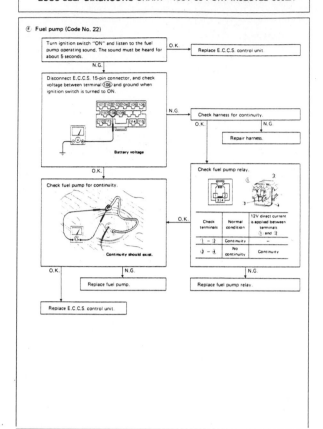

Turn ignition switch "ON" and listen to the fuel pump operating sound. The sound must be heard for about 5 seconds. → O.K. → Replace E.C.C.S. control unit.

↓ N.G.

Disconnect E.C.C.S. 15-pin connector, and check voltage between terminal ㉚ and ground when ignition switch is turned to ON.

Battery voltage

→ N.G. → Check harness for continuity. → O.K. → → N.G. → Repair harness.

↓ O.K.

Check fuel pump relay.

Check terminals	Normal condition	12V direct current is applied between terminals ① and ②
① – ②	Continuity	–
③ – ④	No continuity	Continuity

Check fuel pump for continuity.

Continuity should exist.

→ O.K. ↓   N.G. → Replace fuel pump.   → N.G. → Replace fuel pump relay.

Replace E.C.C.S. control unit.

ECCS SELF-DIAGNOSTIC CHART – 1984–85 PORT INJECTED 300ZX

ⓔ Ignition signal (Code No. 21)

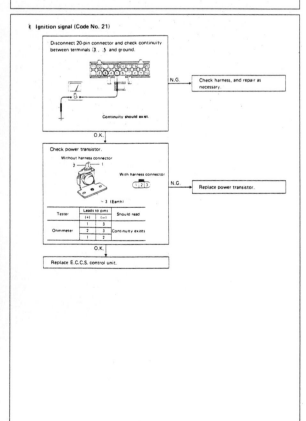

Disconnect 20-pin connector and check continuity between terminals ③, ⑤ and ground.

Continuity should exist.

→ N.G. → Check harness, and repair as necessary.

↓ O.K.

Check power transistor.

Without harness connector

With harness connector

– 3 (Earth)

Tester	Leads to pins		Should read
	(+)	(–)	
Ohmmeter	1	3	Continuity exists
	2	3	
	1	2	

→ N.G. → Replace power transistor.

↓ O.K.

Replace E.C.C.S. control unit.

ECCS SELF-DIAGNOSTIC CHART – 1984–85 PORT INJECTED 300ZX

ⓖ Throttle valve switch (Code No. 23)

Check harness for continuity. → N.G. → Repair harness.

↓ O.K.

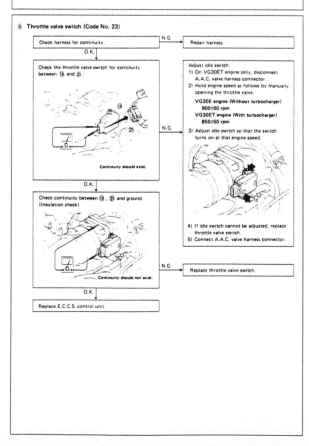

Check the throttle valve switch for continuity between ⑱ and ㉕.

Continuity should exist.

→ N.G. → Adjust idle switch.
1) On VG30ET engine only, disconnect A.A.C. valve harness connector.
2) Hold engine speed as follows by manually opening the throttle valve.

VG30E engine (Without turbocharger)
900±50 rpm
VG30ET engine (With turbocharger)
850±50 rpm

3) Adjust idle switch so that the switch turns on at that engine speed.

4) If idle switch cannot be adjusted, replace throttle valve switch.
5) Connect A.A.C. valve harness connector.

↓ O.K.

Check continuity between ⑱, ㉕ and ground. (Insulation check)

Continuity should not exist.

→ N.G. → Replace throttle valve switch.

↓ O.K.

Replace E.C.C.S. control unit.

ECCS SELF-DIAGNOSTIC CHART – 1984–85 PORT INJECTED 300ZX

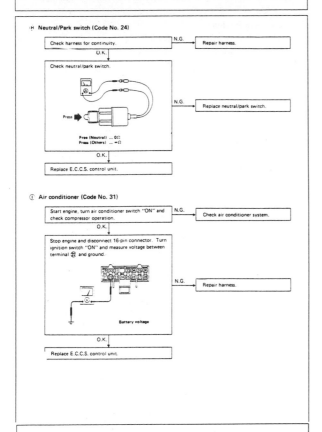

Ⓗ Neutral/Park switch (Code No. 24)

Check harness for continuity. → N.G. → Repair harness.

O.K.

Check neutral/park switch.

Press

Free (Neutral) ... 0 Ω
Press (Others) ... ∞ Ω

→ N.G. → Replace neutral/park switch.

O.K.

Replace E.C.C.S. control unit.

Ⓘ Air conditioner (Code No. 31)

Start engine, turn air conditioner switch "ON" and check compressor operation. → N.G. → Check air conditioner system.

O.K.

Stop engine and disconnect 16-pin connector. Turn ignition switch "ON" and measure voltage between terminal ㉒ and ground.

Battery voltage

→ N.G. → Repair harness.

O.K.

Replace E.C.C.S. control unit.

ECCS SELF-DIAGNOSTIC CHART – 1984–85 PORT INJECTED 300ZX

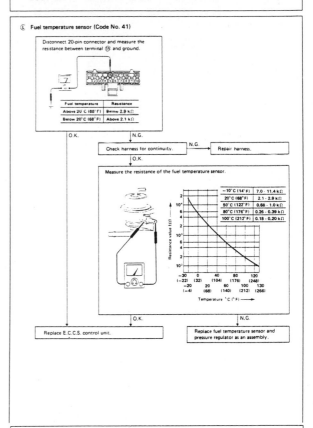

Ⓛ Fuel temperature sensor (Code No. 41)

Disconnect 20-pin connector and measure the resistance between terminal ⑮ and ground.

Fuel temperature	Resistance
Above 20°C (68°F)	Below 2.9 kΩ
Below 20°C (68°F)	Above 2.1 kΩ

O.K. | N.G.

Check harness for continuity. → N.G. → Repair harness.

O.K.

Measure the resistance of the fuel temperature sensor.

−10°C (14°F)	7.0 - 11.4 kΩ
20°C (68°F)	2.1 - 2.9 kΩ
50°C (122°F)	0.68 - 1.0 kΩ
80°C (176°F)	0.26 - 0.39 kΩ
100°C (212°F)	0.18 - 0.20 kΩ

O.K. | N.G.

Replace E.C.C.S. control unit. | Replace fuel temperature sensor and pressure regulator as an assembly.

ECCS SELF-DIAGNOSTIC CHART – 1984–85 PORT INJECTED 300ZX

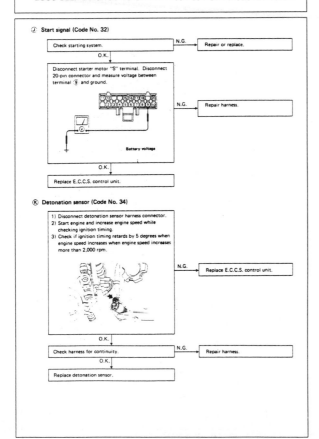

Ⓙ Start signal (Code No. 32)

Check starting system. → N.G. → Repair or replace.

O.K.

Disconnect starter motor "S" terminal. Disconnect 20-pin connector and measure voltage between terminal ⑨ and ground.

Battery voltage

→ N.G. → Repair harness.

O.K.

Replace E.C.C.S. control unit.

Ⓚ Detonation sensor (Code No. 34)

1) Disconnect detonation sensor harness connector.
2) Start engine and increase engine speed while checking ignition timing.
3) Check if ignition timing retards by 5 degrees when engine speed increases when engine speed increases more than 2,000 rpm.

→ N.G. → Replace E.C.C.S. control unit.

O.K.

Check harness for continuity. → N.G. → Repair harness.

O.K.

Replace detonation sensor.

ECCS SELF-DIAGNOSTIC CHART – 1984–85 PORT INJECTED 300ZX

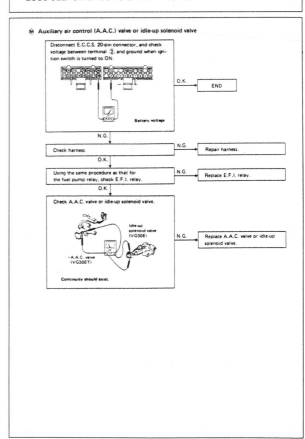

Ⓜ Auxiliary air control (A.A.C.) valve or idle-up solenoid valve

Disconnect E.C.C.S. 20-pin connector, and check voltage between terminal ② and ground when ignition switch is turned to ON.

Battery voltage

→ O.K. → END

N.G.

Check harness. → N.G. → Repair harness.

O.K.

Using the same procedure as that for the fuel pump relay, check E.F.I. relay. → N.G. → Replace E.F.I. relay.

O.K.

Check A.A.C. valve or idle-up solenoid valve.

Idle-up solenoid valve (VG30E)

A.A.C. valve (VG30ET)

Continuity should exist.

→ N.G. → Replace A.A.C. valve or idle-up solenoid valve.

ECCS SELF-DIAGNOSTIC CHART — 1984–85 PORT INJECTED 300ZX

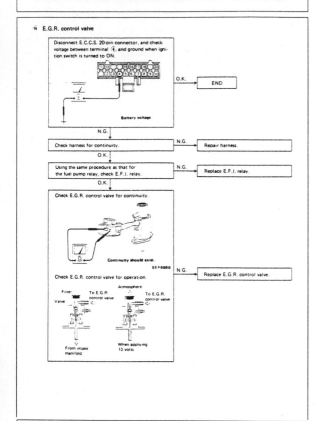

N. E.G.R. control valve

ECCS SELF-DIAGNOSTIC CHART — 1984–85 PORT INJECTED 300ZX

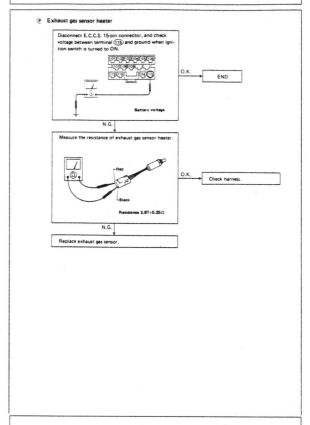

P. Exhaust gas sensor heater

ECCS SELF-DIAGNOSTIC CHART — 1984–85 PORT INJECTED 300ZX

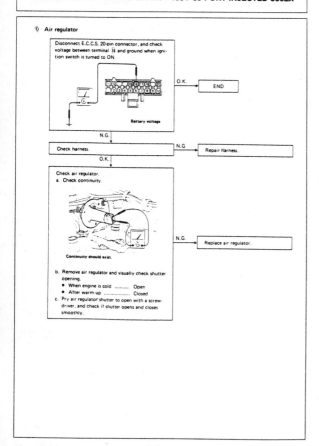

O. Air regulator

ECCS SELF-DIAGNOSTIC CHART — 1984–85 PORT INJECTED 300ZX

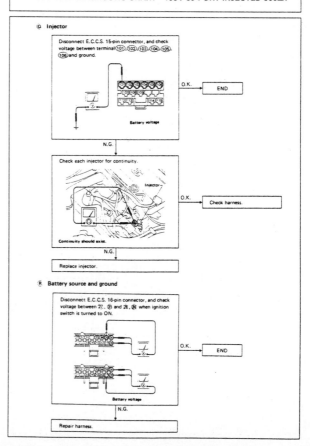

Q. Injector

R. Battery source and ground

MIXTURE RATIO FEEDBACK SYSTEM INSPECTION CHART
1984–85 PORT INJECTED 300ZX

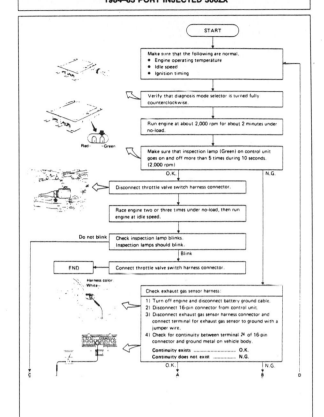

START

Make sure that the following are normal.
● Engine operating temperature
● Idle speed
● Ignition timing

Verify that diagnosis mode selector is turned fully counterclockwise.

Run engine at about 2,000 rpm for about 2 minutes under no-load.

Make sure that inspection lamp (Green) on control unit goes on and off more than 5 times during 10 seconds. (2,000 rpm)

O.K. / N.G.

Disconnect throttle valve switch harness connector.

Race engine two or three times under no-load, then run engine at idle speed.

Do not blink — Check inspection lamp blinks. Inspection lamps should blink.

Blink

END ← Connect throttle valve switch harness connector.

Check exhaust gas sensor harness:

1) Turn off engine and disconnect battery ground cable.
2) Disconnect 16-pin connector from control unit.
3) Disconnect exhaust gas sensor harness connector and connect terminal for exhaust gas sensor to ground with a jumper wire.
4) Check for continuity between terminal 24 of 16-pin connector and ground metal on vehicle body.

Continuity exists .... O.K.
Continuity does not exist .... N.G.

O.K. / N.G.
A / B / C / D

MIXTURE RATIO FEEDBACK SYSTEM INSPECTION CHART
1984–85 PORT INJECTED 300ZX

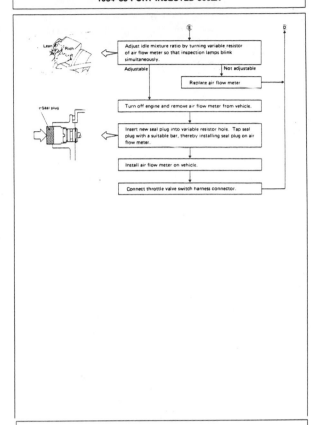

E / D

Adjust idle mixture ratio by turning variable resistor of air flow meter so that inspection lamps blink simultaneously.

Adjustable / Not adjustable

Replace air flow meter

Turn off engine and remove air flow meter from vehicle.

Insert new seal plug into variable resistor hole. Tap seal plug with a suitable bar, thereby installing seal plug on air flow meter.

Install air flow meter on vehicle.

Connect throttle valve switch harness connector.

MIXTURE RATIO FEEDBACK SYSTEM INSPECTION CHART
1984–85 PORT INJECTED 300ZX

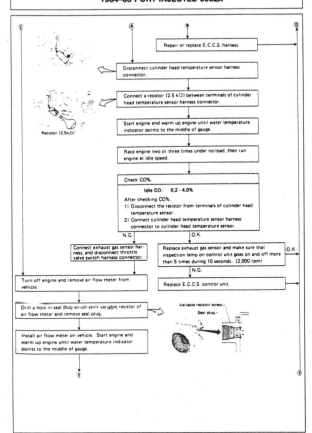

C / A / B / D

Repair or replace E.C.C.S. harness.

Disconnect cylinder head temperature sensor harness connector.

Connect a resistor (2.5 kΩ) between terminals of cylinder head temperature sensor harness connector.

Start engine and warm up engine until water temperature indicator points to the middle of gauge.

Race engine two or three times under no-load, then run engine at idle speed.

Check CO%.

Idle CO: 0.2 - 4.0%

After checking CO%,
1) Disconnect the resistor from terminals of cylinder head temperature sensor.
2) Connect cylinder head temperature sensor harness connector to cylinder head temperature sensor.

N.G. / O.K.

Connect exhaust gas sensor harness, and disconnect throttle valve switch harness connector.

Replace exhaust gas sensor and make sure that inspection lamp on control unit goes on and off more than 5 times during 10 seconds. (2,000 rpm)

O.K.

N.G.

Turn off engine and remove air flow meter from vehicle.

Replace E.C.C.S. control unit.

Drill a hole in seal plug which seals variable resistor of air flow meter and remove seal plug.

Variable resistor screw
Seal plug

Install air flow meter on vehicle. Start engine and warm up engine until water temperature indicator points to the middle of gauge.

E / D

IDLE SPEED AND IGNITION INSPECTION CHART
1985–86 PORT INJECTED MAXIMA

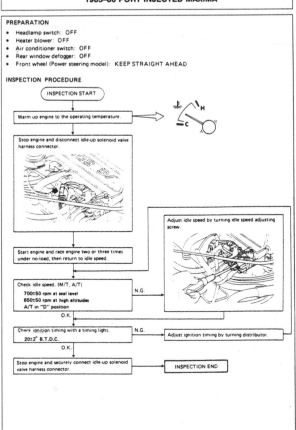

PREPARATION
● Headlamp switch: OFF
● Heater blower: OFF
● Air conditioner switch: OFF
● Rear window defogger: OFF
● Front wheel (Power steering model): KEEP STRAIGHT AHEAD

INSPECTION PROCEDURE

INSPECTION START

Warm up engine to the operating temperature.

Stop engine and disconnect idle-up solenoid valve harness connector.

Start engine and race engine two or three times under no-load, then return to idle speed.

Adjust idle speed by turning idle speed adjusting screw.

Check idle speed. (M/T, A/T)

700±50 rpm at seal level
650±50 rpm at high altitudes
A/T in "D" position

N.G.

O.K.

Check ignition timing with a timing light.
20±2° B.T.D.C.

N.G. → Adjust ignition timing by turning distributor.

O.K.

Stop engine and securely connect idle-up solenoid valve harness connector.

INSPECTION END

IDLE MIXTURE RATIO INSPECTION CHART
1985–86 PORT INJECTED MAXIMA

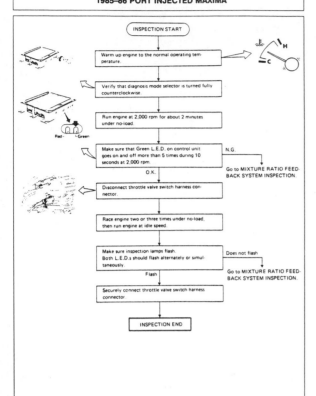

INSPECTION START

Warm up engine to the normal operating temperature.

Verify that diagnosis mode selector is turned fully counterclockwise.

Run engine at 2,000 rpm for about 2 minutes under no-load.

Make sure that Green L.E.D. on control unit goes on and off more than 5 times during 10 seconds at 2,000 rpm. — N.G. → Go to MIXTURE RATIO FEEDBACK SYSTEM INSPECTION.

O.K.

Disconnect throttle valve switch harness connector.

Race engine two or three times under no-load, then run engine at idle speed.

Make sure inspection lamps flash. Both L.E.D.s should flash alternately or simultaneously. — Does not flash → Go to MIXTURE RATIO FEEDBACK SYSTEM INSPECTION.

Flash

Securely connect throttle valve switch harness connector.

INSPECTION END

ECCS SELF-DIAGNOSTIC PROCEDURE
1985–86 PORT INJECTED MAXIMA

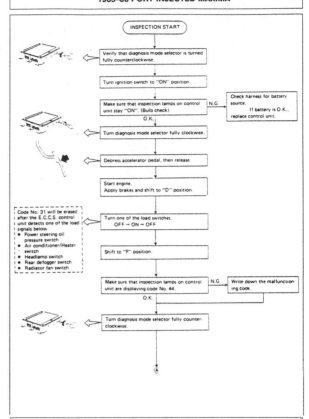

INSPECTION START

Verify that diagnosis mode selector is turned fully counterclockwise.

Turn ignition switch to "ON" position.

Make sure that inspection lamps on control unit stay "ON". (Bulb check) — N.G. → Check harness for battery source. If battery is O.K., replace control unit.

Turn diagnosis mode selector fully clockwise.

Depress accelerator pedal, then release.

Start engine. Apply brakes and shift to "D" position.

[Code No. 31 will be erased after the E.C.C.S. control unit detects one of the load signals below.
● Power steering oil pressure switch
● Air conditioner/Heater switch
● Headlamp switch
● Rear defogger switch
● Radiator fan switch]

Turn one of the load switches. OFF → ON → OFF

Shift to "P" position.

Make sure that inspection lamps on control unit are displaying code No. 44. — N.G → Write down the malfunctioning code.

O.K.

Turn diagnosis mode selector fully counterclockwise.

Ⓐ

ECCS SELF-DIAGNOSTIC CODES — 1985–86 PORT INJECTED MAXIMA

DISPLAYED CODE

CODE	L.E.D. display Red	L.E.D. display Green	Malfunctioning area	Items retained in memory
11	○	○	Crank angle sensor circuit	X
12	○	○○	Air flow meter circuit	X
13	○	○○○	Cylinder head temperature circuit	X
21	○○	○	Ignition signal missing in primary coil	X
22	○○	○○	Fuel pump circuit	X
23	○○	○○○	Throttle valve switch (Idle switch) circuit	–
31	○○○	○	Load signal circuit (Power steering oil pressure switch, Headlamp switch, Radiator fan switch, Rear defogger switch, Heater/air conditioner switch)	–
32	○○○	○○	Starter signal circuit	–
41	○○○○	○	Fuel temperature sensor circuit	X
44	○○○○	○○○○	No malfunctioning in the above circuit (Check other electrical systems.)	–

X: Yes –: No

ECCS SELF-DIAGNOSTIC PROCEDURE
1985–86 PORT INJECTED MAXIMA

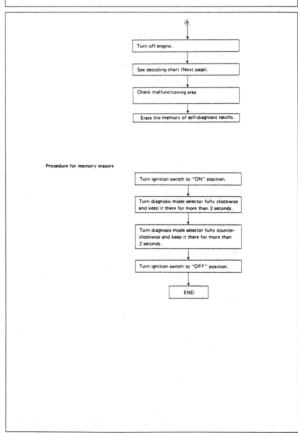

Ⓐ

Turn off engine.

See decoding chart (Next page).

Check malfunctioning area

Erase the memory of self-diagnosis results.

Procedure for memory erasure

Turn ignition switch to "ON" position.

Turn diagnosis mode selector fully clockwise and keep it there for more than 2 seconds.

Turn diagnosis mode selector fully counterclockwise and keep it there for more than 2 seconds.

Turn ignition switch to "OFF" position.

END

ECCS SELF-DIAGNOSTIC DECODING CHART
1985–86 PORT INJECTED MAXIMA

Code No.	Diagnosis	Inspection
11	• 1° or 120° signal is not entered for one second while engine is running. • 120° signal is not entered for one second during engine cranking. • Either 1° or 120° signal is not entered often enough while the engine speed is higher than 600 rpm.	• Crank angle sensor harness and connectors • Starting system • Crank angle sensor • E.C.U.
12	• An abnormally high output voltage is entered while engine is off. • An abnormally low output voltage is entered while the engine speed is higher than 600 rpm.	• Air flow meter harness and connectors • Air flow meter • Air flow meter self-cleaning system • E.C.U.
13	• The cylinder head temperature circuit is open or shorted. (An abnormally high or low output is entered)	• Cylinder head temperature sensor harness and connectors • Cylinder head temperature sensor
21	• The ignition signal in the primary coil is not entered more than 10 times.	• Harness between E.C.U. and ignition coil. • Power transistor • Ignition coil • High tension cables • Spark plugs • Distributor • E.C.U.
22	• The electric current for fuel pump is extremely low or high.	• Fuel pump harness and connectors • Fuel pump • Fuel pump relay • E.C.U.
23	• The ON-OFF signal from idle switch is not entered after ignition switch is turned to "ON".	• Throttle valve switch harness and connectors • Throttle valve switch • Idle switch improper adjustment
31	• An ON-OFF signal from the switches is not entered after ignition switch is turned to "ON".	• Power steering oil pressure switch harness and connectors • Power steering oil pressure switch • Lighting system • Air conditioner system • Rear defogger system • Radiator fan control system • Heater system
32	• The start signal from the ignition switch is not entered after the engine has started.	• Ignition switch • Ignition system harness and connectors
41	• The fuel temperature sensor circuit is open or shorted. (An abnormally high or low output is entered.)	• Fuel temperature sensor harness and connectors • Fuel temperature sensor
44	• The systems which are diagnosed by E.C.U. are working normally.	• Inspect other electric control systems.

ECCS SELF-DIAGNOSTIC CHART — 1985–86 PORT INJECTED MAXIMA

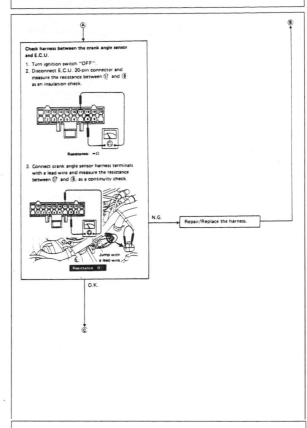

ECCS SELF-DIAGNOSTIC CHART — 1985–86 PORT INJECTED MAXIMA

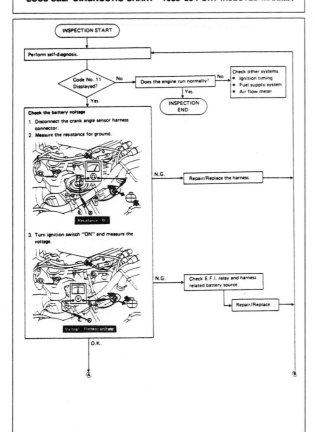

ECCS SELF-DIAGNOSTIC CHART — 1985–86 PORT INJECTED MAXIMA

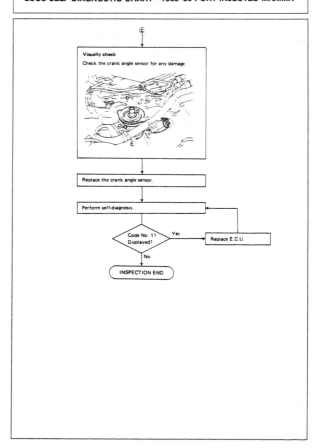

ECCS SELF-DIAGNOSTIC CHART—1985–86 PORT INJECTED MAXIMA

Air Flow Meter

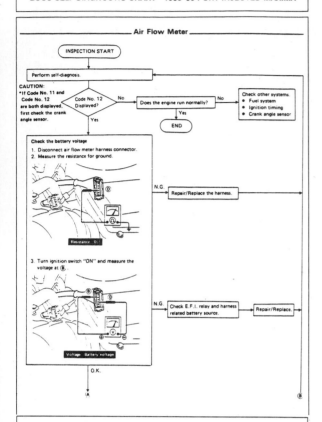

INSPECTION START

Perform self-diagnosis.

CAUTION:
*If Code No. 11 and Code No. 12 are both displayed, first check the crank angle sensor.

Code No. 12 Displayed? — No → Does the engine run normally? — No → Check other systems.
• Fuel system
• Ignition timing
• Crank angle sensor

Yes ↓ / Yes → END

Check the battery voltage
1. Disconnect air flow meter harness connector.
2. Measure the resistance for ground.

Resistance : 0Ω

N.G. → Repair/Replace the harness.

3. Turn ignition switch "ON" and measure the voltage at (B).

Voltage : Battery voltage

N.G. → Check E.F.I. relay and harness related battery source. → Repair/Replace.

O.K. ↓

(A)

(B)

ECCS SELF-DIAGNOSTIC CHART—1985–86 PORT INJECTED MAXIMA

Air Flow Meter (Cont'd)

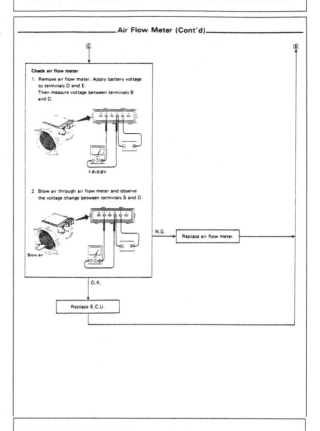

(C)

(D)

Check air flow meter
1. Remove air flow meter. Apply battery voltage to terminals D and E.
   Then measure voltage between terminals B and D.

1.6±0.5V

2. Blow air through air flow meter and observe the voltage change between terminals B and D.

Blow air

N.G. → Replace air flow meter.

O.K. ↓

Replace E.C.U.

ECCS SELF-DIAGNOSTIC CHART—1985–86 PORT INJECTED MAXIMA

Air Flow Meter (Cont'd)

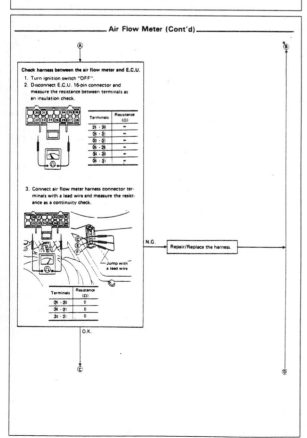

(A)

(B)

Check harness between the air flow meter and E.C.U.
1. Turn ignition switch "OFF".
2. Disconnect E.C.U. 16-pin connector and measure the resistance between terminals as an insulation check.

Terminals	Resistance (Ω)
25 - 30	∞
25 - 31	∞
30 - 31	∞
30 - 25	∞
34 - 30	∞
35 - 30	∞

3. Connect air flow meter harness connector terminals with a lead wire and measure the resistance as a continuity check.

Jump with a lead wire

N.G. → Repair/Replace the harness.

Terminals	Resistance (Ω)
25 - 30	0
25 - 31	0
30 - 31	0

O.K. ↓

(C)

(D)

ECCS SELF-DIAGNOSTIC CHART—1985–86 PORT INJECTED MAXIMA

Cylinder Head Temperature Sensor

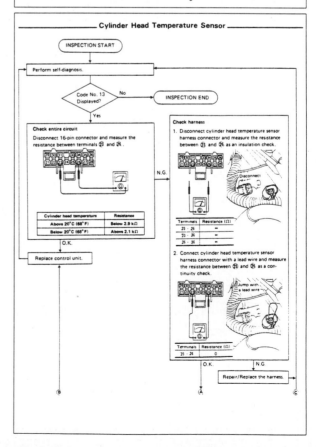

INSPECTION START

Perform self-diagnosis.

Code No. 13 Displayed? — No → INSPECTION END

Yes ↓

Check entire circuit
Disconnect 16-pin connector and measure the resistance between terminals 23 and 26.

Cylinder head temperature	Resistance
Above 20°C (68°F)	Below 2.9 kΩ
Below 20°C (68°F)	Above 2.1 kΩ

O.K. ↓

Replace control unit.

Check harness
1. Disconnect cylinder head temperature sensor harness connector and measure the resistance between 23 and 26 as an insulation check.

Disconnect

Terminals	Resistance (Ω)
23 - 26	∞
23 - 36	∞
26 - 36	∞

2. Connect cylinder head temperature sensor harness connector with a lead wire and measure the resistance between 23 and 26 as a continuity check.

Jump with a lead wire

Terminals	Resistance (Ω)
23 - 26	0

O.K. ↓ / N.G. → Repair/Replace the harness.

(B)

(A)

(C)

ECCS SELF-DIAGNOSTIC CHART — 1985–86 PORT INJECTED MAXIMA

--- Cylinder Head Temperature Sensor (Cont'd) ---

Ⓑ   Ⓐ   Ⓒ

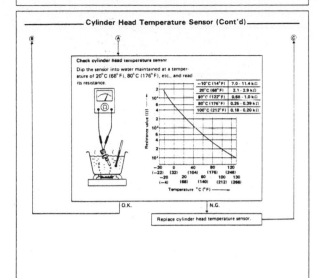

Check cylinder head temperature sensor

Dip the sensor into water maintained at a temperature of 20°C (68°F), 80°C (176°F), etc., and read its resistance.

Temperature	Resistance
−10°C (14°F)	7.0 - 11.4 kΩ
20°C (68°F)	2.1 - 2.9 kΩ
50°C (122°F)	0.68 - 1.0 kΩ
80°C (176°F)	0.26 - 0.39 kΩ
100°C (212°F)	0.18 - 0.20 kΩ

O.K.   N.G.

Replace cylinder head temperature sensor.

ECCS SELF-DIAGNOSTIC CHART — 1985–86 PORT INJECTED MAXIMA

--- Ignition Signal ---

INSPECTION START

Perform self-diagnosis.

Code No. 21 Displayed? — No → Does the engine run normally? — No → Check other systems.
• Fuel supply system
• Air flow meter
• Crank angle sensor

Yes → INSPECTION END

↓ Yes

Check spark plugs, ignition wires, distributor cap and distributor rotor.

If abnormality is found, repair or replace.

Check battery voltage at power transistor

1. Disconnect the harness connector at power transistor.
2. Turn ignition switch "ON" and measure the voltage.

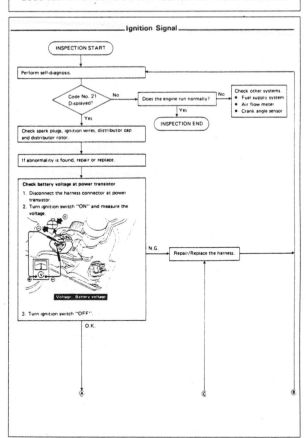

Voltage: Battery voltage

3. Turn ignition switch "OFF".

N.G. → Repair/Replace the harness.

O.K.

Ⓐ   Ⓒ   Ⓑ

ECCS SELF-DIAGNOSTIC CHART — 1985–86 PORT INJECTED MAXIMA

--- Ignition Signal (Cont'd) ---

Ⓐ   Ⓒ   Ⓑ

Check harness between E.C.U. and power transistor

1. Disconnect E.C.U. 20-pin connector and check for insulation at ③ and ⑤.

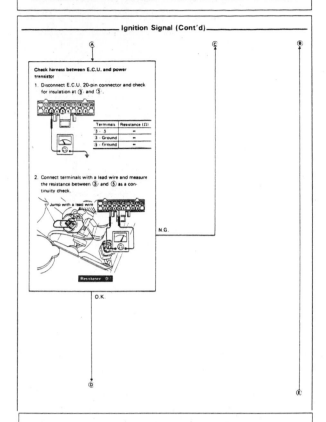

Terminals	Resistance (Ω)
③ - ⑤	∞
③ - Ground	∞
⑤ - Ground	∞

2. Connect terminals with a lead wire and measure the resistance between ③ and ⑤ as a continuity check.

Jump with a lead wire

Resistance: 0Ω

O.K.

Ⓓ   Ⓔ

ECCS SELF-DIAGNOSTIC CHART — 1985–86 PORT INJECTED MAXIMA

--- Ignition Signal (Cont'd) ---

Ⓓ   Ⓔ

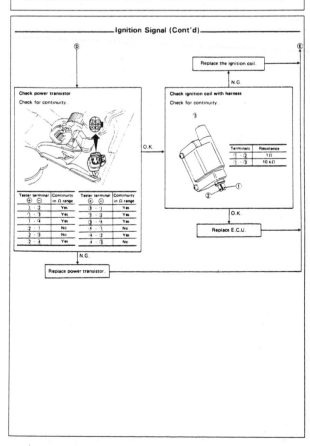

Check power transistor
Check for continuity.

Tester terminal ⊕ ⊖	Continuity in Ω range
3 - 2	Yes
1 - 3	Yes
1 - 4	Yes
2 - 1	No
2 - 3	No
2 - 4	Yes

O.K. →

Replace the ignition coil.

N.G.

Check ignition coil with harness
Check for continuity.

Terminals	Resistance
① - ②	1 Ω
① - ③	10 kΩ

Tester terminal ⊕ ⊖	Continuity in Ω range
3 - 2	Yes
3 - 1	Yes
4 - 1	Yes
4 - 2	No
1 - 2	Yes
4 - 3	No

O.K. → Replace E.C.U.

N.G.

Replace power transistor.

ECCS SELF-DIAGNOSTIC CHART — 1985–86 PORT INJECTED MAXIMA

Fuel Pump

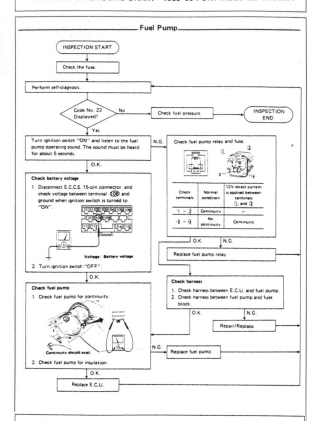

ECCS SELF-DIAGNOSTIC CHART — 1985–86 PORT INJECTED MAXIMA

Throttle Valve Switch (Cont'd)

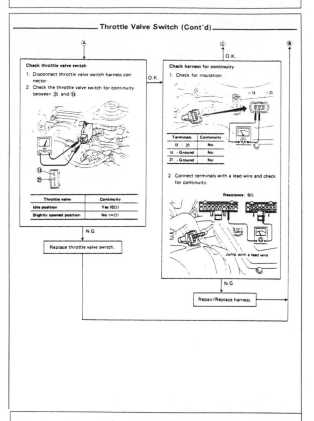

ECCS SELF-DIAGNOSTIC CHART — 1985–86 PORT INJECTED MAXIMA

Throttle Valve Switch

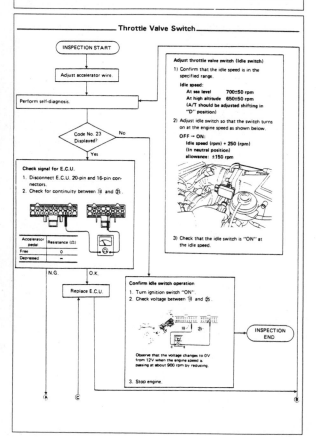

ECCS SELF-DIAGNOSTIC CHART — 1985–86 PORT INJECTED MAXIMA

Load Signal

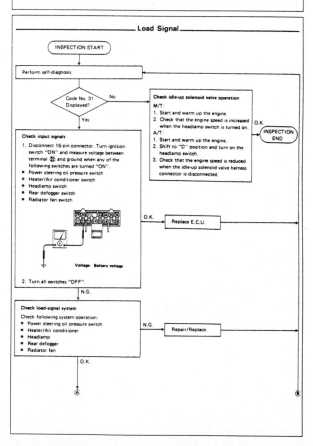

ECCS SELF-DIAGNOSTIC CHART – 1985–86 PORT INJECTED MAXIMA

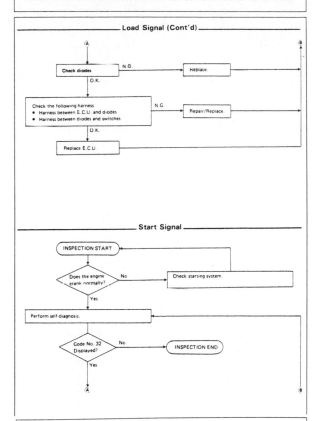

Load Signal (Cont'd)

Ⓐ   Ⓑ

Check diodes → N.G. → Replace.

O.K.

Check the following harness:
• Harness between E.C.U. and diodes
• Harness between diodes and switches → N.G. → Repair/Replace.

O.K.

Replace E.C.U.

Start Signal

INSPECTION START

Does the engine crank normally? — No → Check starting system.

Yes

Perform self-diagnosis.

Code No. 32 Displayed? — No → INSPECTION END

Yes

Ⓐ   :B

ECCS SELF-DIAGNOSTIC CHART – 1985–86 PORT INJECTED MAXIMA

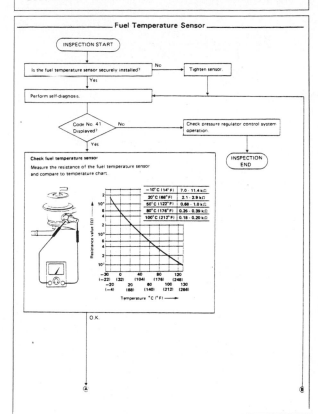

Fuel Temperature Sensor

INSPECTION START

Is the fuel temperature sensor securely installed? — No → Tighten sensor.

Yes

Perform self-diagnosis.

Code No. 41 Displayed? — No → Check pressure regulator control system operation. → INSPECTION END

Yes

Check fuel temperature sensor
Measure the resistance of the fuel temperature sensor and compare to temperature chart.

–10°C (14°F)	7.0 - 11.4 kΩ
20°C (68°F)	2.1 - 2.9 kΩ
50°C (122°F)	0.68 - 1.0 kΩ
80°C (176°F)	0.26 - 0.39 kΩ
100°C (212°F)	0.18 - 0.20 kΩ

O.K.

Ⓐ   Ⓑ

ECCS SELF-DIAGNOSTIC CHART – 1985–86 PORT INJECTED MAXIMA

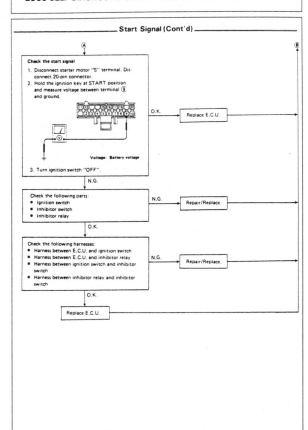

Start Signal (Cont'd)

Ⓐ   Ⓑ

Check the start signal
1. Disconnect starter motor "S" terminal. Disconnect 20-pin connector.
2. Hold the ignition key at START position and measure voltage between terminal ⑨ and ground.

Voltage: Battery voltage

3. Turn ignition switch "OFF". → O.K. → Replace E.C.U.

N.G.

Check the following parts:
• Ignition switch
• Inhibitor switch
• Inhibitor relay → N.G. → Repair/Replace.

O.K.

Check the following harnesses:
• Harness between E.C.U. and ignition switch
• Harness between E.C.U. and inhibitor relay
• Harness between ignition switch and inhibitor switch
• Harness between inhibitor relay and inhibitor switch → N.G. → Repair/Replace.

O.K.

Replace E.C.U.

ECCS SELF-DIAGNOSTIC CHART – 1985–86 PORT INJECTED MAXIMA

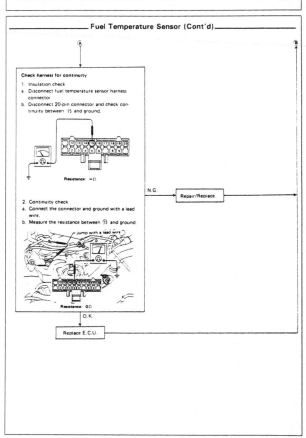

Fuel Temperature Sensor (Cont'd)

Ⓐ   Ⓑ

Check harness for continuity

1. Insulation check
a. Disconnect fuel temperature sensor harness connector.
b. Disconnect 20-pin connector and check continuity between 15 and ground.

Resistance: ∞Ω

2. Continuity check
a. Connect the connector and ground with a lead wire.
b. Measure the resistance between ⑮ and ground.

Jump with a lead wire

Resistance: 0Ω → O.K. → Replace E.C.U. → N.G. → Repair/Replace.

ECCS SELF-DIAGNOSTIC CHART — 1985–86 PORT INJECTED MAXIMA

Injector

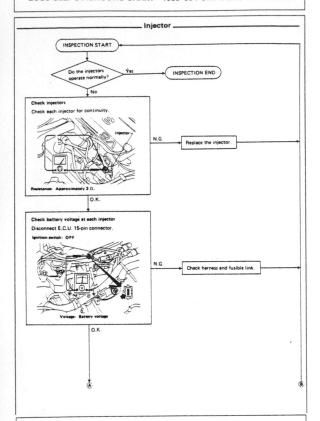

ECCS SELF-DIAGNOSTIC CHART — 1985–86 PORT INJECTED MAXIMA

Battery Voltage and Ground Test

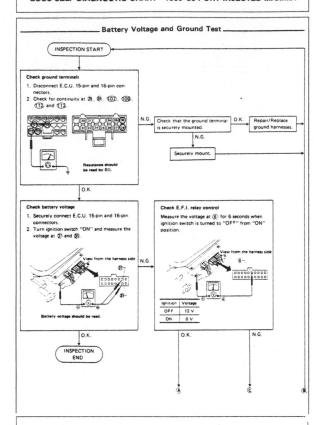

ECCS SELF-DIAGNOSTIC CHART — 1985–86 PORT INJECTED MAXIMA

Injector (Cont'd)

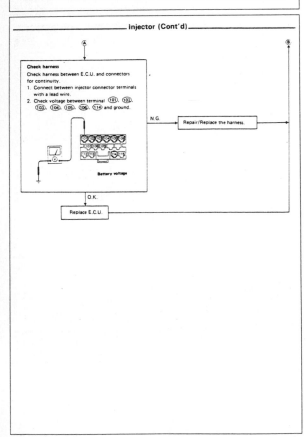

ECCS SELF-DIAGNOSTIC CHART — 1985–86 PORT INJECTED MAXIMA

Battery Voltage and Ground Test (Cont'd)

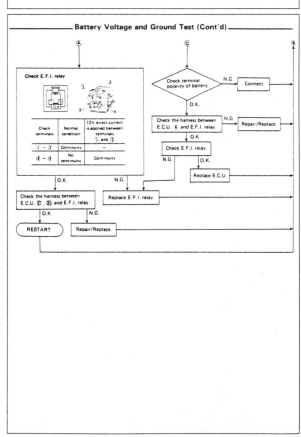

ECCS SELF-DIAGNOSTIC CHART—1985–86 PORT INJECTED MAXIMA

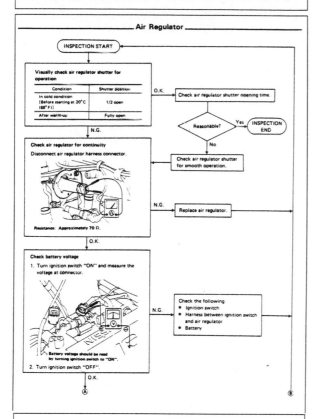

— Air Regulator —

INSPECTION START

Visually check air regulator shutter for operation

Condition	Shutter position
In cold condition (Before starting at 20°C (68°F))	1/2 open
After warm-up	Fully open

O.K. → Check air regulator shutter opening time.

Reasonable? — Yes → INSPECTION END

No → Check air regulator shutter for smooth operation.

N.G.

Check air regulator for continuity
Disconnect air regulator harness connector.

Resistance: Approximately 70 Ω.

N.G. → Replace air regulator.

O.K.

Check battery voltage
1. Turn ignition switch "ON" and measure the voltage at connector.

Battery voltage should be read by turning ignition switch to "ON".

2. Turn ignition switch "OFF".

N.G. → Check the following:
- Ignition switch
- Harness between ignition switch and air regulator
- Battery

O.K. → (A)

(B)

ECCS SELF-DIAGNOSTIC CHART—1985–86 PORT INJECTED MAXIMA

— Air Regulator (Cont'd) —

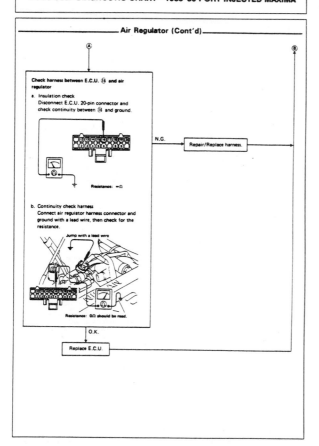

(A)

(B)

Check harness between E.C.U. and air regulator

a. Insulation check
Disconnect E.C.U. 20-pin connector and check continuity between 16 and ground.

Resistance: ∞ Ω.

N.G. → Repair/Replace harness.

b. Continuity check harness
Connect air regulator harness connector and ground with a lead wire, then check for the resistance.

Jump with a lead wire

Resistance: 0Ω should be read.

O.K.

Replace E.C.U.

ECCS SELF-DIAGNOSTIC CHART—1985–86 PORT INJECTED MAXIMA

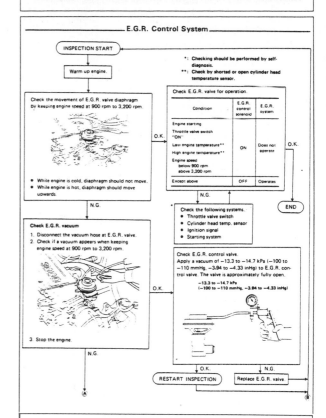

— E.G.R. Control System —

INSPECTION START

Warm up engine.

*: Checking should be performed by self-diagnosis.
**: Check by shorted or open cylinder head temperature sensor.

Check the movement of E.G.R. valve diaphragm by keeping engine speed at 900 rpm to 3,200 rpm.

- While engine is cold, diaphragm should not move.
- While engine is hot, diaphragm should move upwards.

O.K. →

Check E.G.R. valve for operation.

Condition	E.G.R. control solenoid	E.G.R. system
Engine starting		
Throttle valve switch "ON"		
Low engine temperature**	ON	Does not operate
High engine temperature**		
Engine speed below 900 rpm above 3,200 rpm		
Except above	OFF	Operates

O.K. → END

N.G.

N.G.

Check E.G.R. vacuum
1. Disconnect the vacuum hose at E.G.R. valve.
2. Check if a vacuum appears when keeping engine speed at 900 rpm to 3,200 rpm.

O.K. →

Check the following systems:
- Throttle valve switch
- Cylinder head temp. sensor
- Ignition signal
- Starting system

Check E.G.R. control valve.
Apply a vacuum of −13.3 to −14.7 kPa (−100 to −110 mmHg, −3.94 to −4.33 inHg) to E.G.R. control valve. The valve is approximately fully open.

−13.3 to −14.7 kPa (−100 to −110 mmHg, −3.94 to −4.33 inHg)

3. Stop the engine.

N.G.

O.K. → RESTART INSPECTION

N.G. → Replace E.G.R. valve.

(A)

(B)

ECCS SELF-DIAGNOSTIC CHART—1985–86 PORT INJECTED MAXIMA

— E.G.R. Control System (Cont'd) —

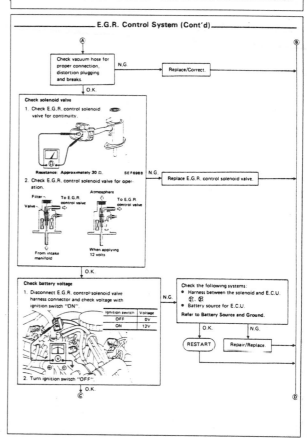

(A)

(B)

Check vacuum hose for proper connection, distortion plugging and breaks.

N.G. → Replace/Correct.

O.K.

Check solenoid valve
1. Check E.G.R. control solenoid valve for continuity.

Resistance: Approximately 30 Ω.   SEF698B

N.G. → Replace E.G.R. control solenoid valve.

2. Check E.G.R. control solenoid valve for operation.

Filter   To E.G.R. control valve   Atmosphere   To E.G.R. control valve

Valve

From intake manifold

When applying 12 volts

O.K.

Check battery voltage
1. Disconnect E.G.R. control solenoid valve harness connector and check voltage with ignition switch "ON".

Ignition switch	Voltage
OFF	0V
ON	12V

N.G. → Check the following systems:
- Harness between the solenoid and E.C.U.
- Battery source for E.C.U.

Refer to Battery Source and Ground.

O.K. → RESTART

N.G. → Repair/Replace.

2. Turn ignition switch "OFF".

O.K.

(D)

ECCS SELF-DIAGNOSTIC CHART – 1985–86 PORT INJECTED MAXIMA

E.G.R. Control System (Cont'd)

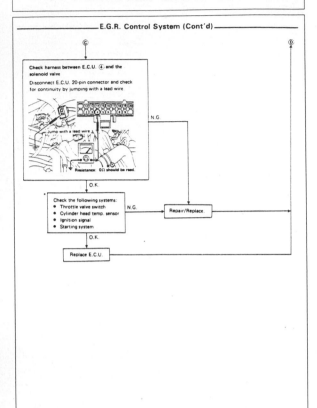

Check harness between E.C.U. ④ and the solenoid valve

Disconnect E.C.U. 20-pin connector and check for continuity by jumping with a lead wire.

Jump with a lead wire

Resistance: 0Ω should be read.

N.G. →

O.K. ↓

Check the following systems:
- Throttle valve switch
- Cylinder head temp. sensor
- Ignition signal
- Starting system

N.G. → Repair/Replace.

O.K. ↓

Replace E.C.U.

ECCS SELF-DIAGNOSTIC CHART – 1985–86 PORT INJECTED MAXIMA

Exhaust Gas Sensor (Cont'd)

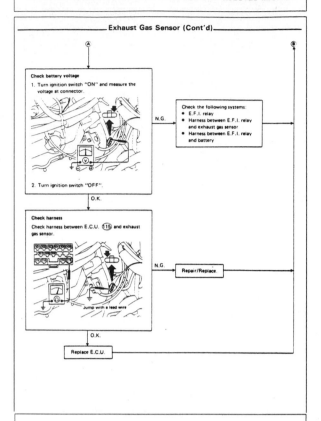

Check battery voltage
1. Turn ignition switch "ON" and measure the voltage at connector.

2. Turn ignition switch "OFF".

N.G. → Check the following systems:
- E.F.I. relay
- Harness between E.F.I. relay and exhaust gas sensor
- Harness between E.F.I. relay and battery

O.K. ↓

Check harness
Check harness between E.C.U. ⑪⑤ and exhaust gas sensor.

Jump with a lead wire

N.G. → Repair/Replace.

O.K. ↓

Replace E.C.U.

ECCS SELF-DIAGNOSTIC CHART – 1985–86 PORT INJECTED MAXIMA

Exhaust Gas Sensor

MAIN CIRCUIT
Refer to MIXTURE RATIO FEEDBACK SYSTEM INSPECTION.

HEATER CIRCUIT

INSPECTION START

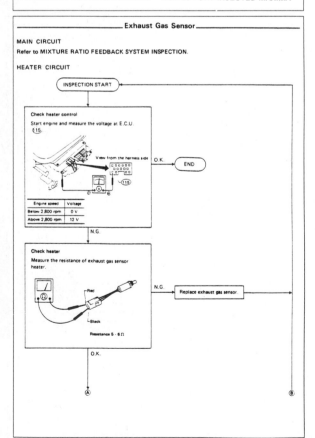

Check heater control
Start engine and measure the voltage at E.C.U. ⑪⑤.

View from the harness side

O.K. → END

Engine speed	Voltage
Below 2,800 rpm	0 V
Above 2,800 rpm	12 V

N.G. ↓

Check heater
Measure the resistance of exhaust gas sensor heater.

Red

Black

Resistance 5 - 6 Ω

N.G. → Replace exhaust gas sensor.

O.K. ↓

Ⓐ   Ⓑ

ECCS SELF-DIAGNOSTIC CHART – 1985–86 PORT INJECTED MAXIMA

Idle-up System

INSPECTION START

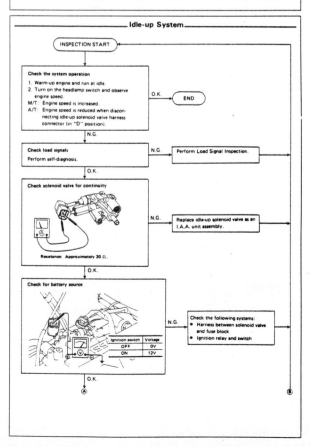

Check the system operation
1. Warm-up engine and run at idle.
2. Turn on the headlamp switch and observe engine speed.
M/T: Engine speed is increased.
A/T: Engine speed is reduced when disconnecting idle-up solenoid valve harness connector (in "D" position).

O.K. → END

N.G. ↓

Check load signals
Perform self-diagnosis.

N.G. → Perform Load Signal Inspection.

O.K. ↓

Check solenoid valve for continuity

Resistance: Approximately 30 Ω.

N.G. → Replace idle-up solenoid valve as an I.A.A. unit assembly.

O.K. ↓

Check for battery source

Ignition switch	Voltage
OFF	0V
ON	12V

N.G. → Check the following systems:
- Harness between solenoid valve and fuse block
- Ignition relay and switch

O.K. ↓

Ⓐ   Ⓑ

ECCS SELF-DIAGNOSTIC CHART – 1985–86 PORT INJECTED MAXIMA

ECCS SELF-DIAGNOSTIC CHART – 1985–86 PORT INJECTED MAXIMA

Idle-up System (Cont'd)

Self-cleaning Hot Wire (Cont'd)

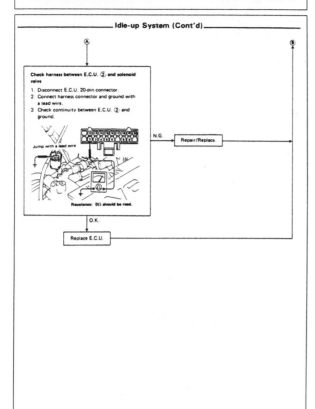

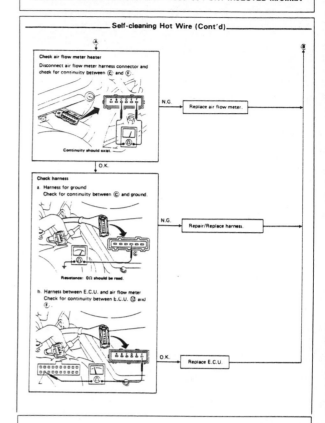

ECCS SELF-DIAGNOSTIC CHART – 1985–86 PORT INJECTED MAXIMA

ECCS SELF-DIAGNOSTIC CHART – 1985–86 PORT INJECTED MAXIMA

Self-cleaning Hot Wire

Pressure Regulator Control Solenoid Valve

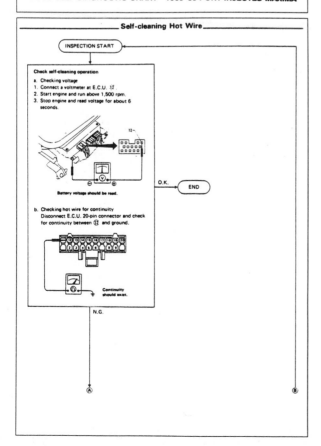

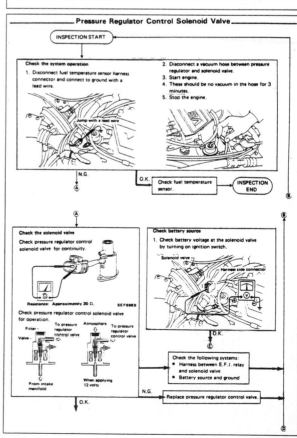

ECCS SELF-DIAGNOSTIC CHART – 1985–86 PORT INJECTED MAXIMA

Pressure Regulator Control Solenoid Valve (Cont'd)

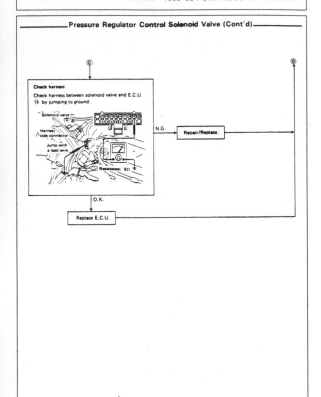

Check harness

Check harness between solenoid valve and E.C.U. ⑲ by jumping to ground.

N.G. → Repair/Replace.

O.K.

Replace E.C.U.

ECCS SELF-DIAGNOSTIC CHART – 1985–86 PORT INJECTED MAXIMA

Air Injection Valve (A.I.V.) Control System (Cont'd)

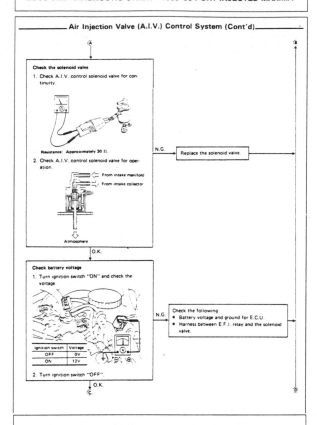

Check the solenoid valve

1. Check A.I.V. control solenoid valve for continuity.

Resistance: Approximately 30 Ω.

2. Check A.I.V. control solenoid valve for operation.

From intake manifold
From intake collector

Atmosphere

N.G. → Replace the solenoid valve.

O.K.

Check battery voltage

1. Turn ignition switch "ON" and check the voltage.

Ignition switch	Voltage
OFF	0V
ON	12V

N.G. → Check the following:
- Battery voltage and ground for E.C.U.
- Harness between E.F.I. relay and the solenoid valve.

2. Turn ignition switch "OFF".

O.K.

ECCS SELF-DIAGNOSTIC CHART – 1985–86 PORT INJECTED MAXIMA

Air Injection Valve (A.I.V.) Control System

INSPECTION START

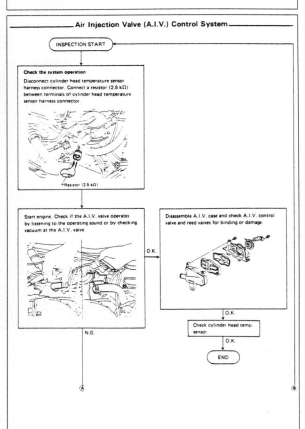

Check the system operation

Disconnect cylinder head temperature sensor harness connector. Connect a resistor (2.5 kΩ) between terminals of cylinder head temperature sensor harness connector.

Resistor (2.5 kΩ)

Start engine. Check if the A.I.V. valve operates by listening to the operating sound or by checking vacuum at the A.I.V. valve.

O.K. → Disassemble A.I.V. case and check A.I.V. control valve and reed valves for binding or damage.

O.K. → Check cylinder head temp. sensor.

O.K. → END

N.G.

ECCS SELF-DIAGNOSTIC CHART – 1985–86 PORT INJECTED MAXIMA

Air Injection Valve (A.I.V.) Control System (Cont'd)

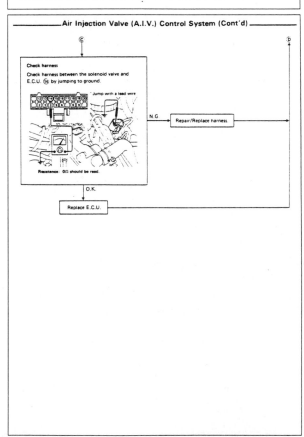

Check harness

Check harness between the solenoid valve and E.C.U. ⑭ by jumping to ground.

Jump with a lead wire

Resistance: 0Ω should be read.

N.G. → Repair/Replace harness.

O.K.

Replace E.C.U.

MIXTURE RATIO FEEDBACK SYSTEM INSPECTION CHART
1985–86 PORT INJECTED MAXIMA

PREPARATION

1. Make sure that the following parts are in good order.
   - Battery charge
   - Ignition system
   - Engine oil and coolant levels
   - Fuses
   - E.C.C.S. harness connectors
   - Vacuum hoses
   - Air intake system (oil filler cap, oil level gauge, etc.)
   - Engine compression
   - E.G.R. valve operation
   - Throttle valve and throttle valve switch operation

- B.C.D.D. operation
2. On air conditioner equipped models, checks should be carried out while the air conditioner is "OFF".
3. Make sure that diagnosis mode selector on E.C.C.S. control unit is turned fully counterclockwise.

WARNING:

a. When selector lever is shifted to "D" position, apply parking brake and block both front and rear wheels with chocks.

b. Depress brake pedal while racing the engine to prevent forward surge of vehicle.

INSPECTION START

Make sure that the following are normal.
- Engine operating temperature
- Idle speed
- Ignition timing

Verify that diagnosis mode selector is turned fully counterclockwise.

Run engine at about 2,000 rpm for about 2 minutes under no-load.

Make sure that the green L.E.D. on control unit goes on and off more than 5 times during 10 seconds at 2,000 rpm.

O.K. → Disconnect throttle valve switch harness connector.

Race engine two or three times under no-load, then run engine at idle speed.

Ⓐ Ⓑ Ⓒ

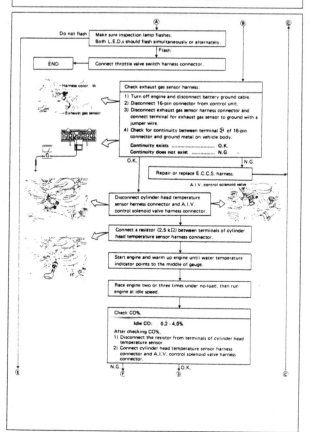

MIXTURE RATIO FEEDBACK SYSTEM INSPECTION CHART
1985–86 PORT INJECTED MAXIMA

Ⓐ Ⓑ Ⓒ

Do not flash → Make sure inspection lamp flashes. Both L.E.D.s should flash simultaneously or alternately.

Flash → Connect throttle valve switch harness connector.

END

Check exhaust gas sensor harness:
1) Turn off engine and disconnect battery ground cable.
2) Disconnect 16-pin connector from control unit.
3) Disconnect exhaust gas sensor harness connector and connect terminal for exhaust gas sensor to ground with a jumper wire.
4) Check for continuity between terminal 24 of 16-pin connector and ground metal on vehicle body.
   Continuity exists .... O.K.
   Continuity does not exist .... N.G.

O.K. N.G. → Repair or replace E.C.C.S. harness.

Disconnect cylinder head temperature sensor harness connector and A.I.V. control solenoid valve harness connector.

Connect a resistor (2.5 kΩ) between terminals of cylinder head temperature sensor harness connector.

Start engine and warm up engine until water temperature indicator points to the middle of gauge.

Race engine two or three times under no-load, then run engine at idle speed.

Check CO%.
Idle CO: 0.2 - 4.6%
After checking CO%,
1) Disconnect the resistor from terminals of cylinder head temperature sensor.
2) Connect cylinder head temperature sensor harness connector and A.I.V. control solenoid valve harness connector.

Ⓔ N.G. Ⓕ O.K. Ⓓ Ⓒ

MIXTURE RATIO FEEDBACK SYSTEM INSPECTION CHART
1985–86 PORT INJECTED MAXIMA

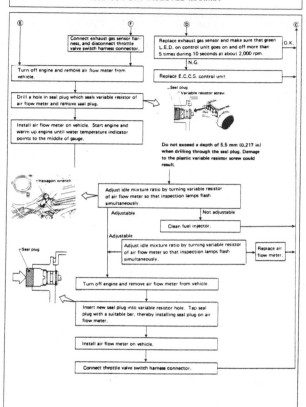

Ⓔ Ⓕ Ⓓ Ⓒ

Ⓔ → Connect exhaust gas sensor harness, and disconnect throttle valve switch harness connector.

Ⓕ → Turn off engine and remove air flow meter from vehicle.

Drill a hole in seal plug which seals variable resistor of air flow meter and remove seal plug.

Install air flow meter on vehicle. Start engine and warm up engine until water temperature indicator points to the middle of gauge.

Ⓓ → Replace exhaust gas sensor and make sure that green L.E.D. on control unit goes on and off more than 5 times during 10 seconds at about 2,000 rpm.

O.K. Ⓒ N.G. → Replace E.C.C.S. control unit

Do not exceed a depth of 5.5 mm (0.217 in) when drilling through the seal plug. Damage to the plastic variable resistor screw could result.

Adjust idle mixture ratio by turning variable resistor of air flow meter so that inspection lamps flash simultaneously.

Adjustable Not adjustable → Clean fuel injector.

Adjustable

Adjust idle mixture ratio by turning variable resistor of air flow meter so that inspection lamps flash simultaneously. → Replace air flow meter.

Turn off engine and remove air flow meter from vehicle.

Insert new seal plug into variable resistor hole. Tap seal plug with a suitable bar, thereby installing seal plug on air flow meter.

Install air flow meter on vehicle.

Connect throttle valve switch harness connector.

IDLE SPEED AND IGNITION TIMING INSPECTION CHART
1986 PORT INJECTED 300ZX

PREPARATION
- Headlamp switch: OFF
- Heater blower: OFF
- Air conditioner switch: OFF
- Rear window defogger: OFF
- Front wheel (Power steering model): KEEP STRAIGHT AHEAD

INSPECTION PROCEDURE (VG30E engine)

INSPECTION START

Warm up engine to the operating temperature.

Stop engine and disconnect idle-up solenoid valve harness connector.

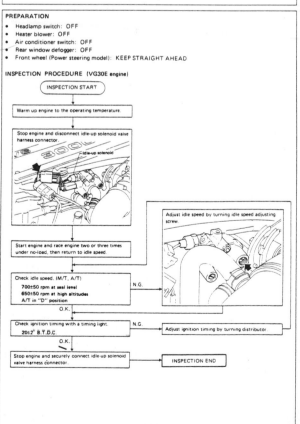

Start engine and race engine two or three times under no-load, then return to idle speed.

Check idle speed. (M/T, A/T)
700±50 rpm at sea level
650±50 rpm at high altitudes
A/T in "D" position

N.G. → Adjust idle speed by turning idle speed adjusting screw.

O.K.

Check ignition timing with a timing light.
20±2° B.T.D.C.

N.G. → Adjust ignition timing by turning distributor.

O.K.

Stop engine and securely connect idle-up solenoid valve harness connector. → INSPECTION END

IDLE SPEED AND IGNITION TIMING INSPECTION CHART 1986 PORT INJECTED 300ZX

INSPECTION PROCEDURE (VG30ET engine)

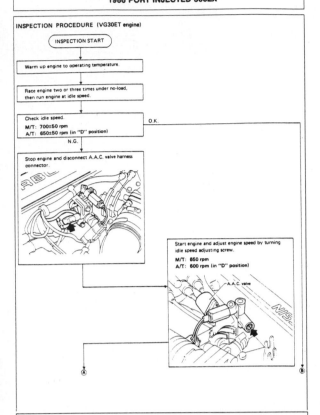

(INSPECTION START)

Warm up engine to operating temperature.

Race engine two or three times under no-load, then run engine at idle speed.

Check idle speed.
M/T: 700±50 rpm
A/T: 650±50 rpm (in "D" position)

O.K. →

N.G.

Stop engine and disconnect A.A.C. valve harness connector.

Start engine and adjust engine speed by turning idle speed adjusting screw.
M/T: 850 rpm
A/T: 600 rpm (in "D" position)

A.A.C. valve

(A)   (B)

IDLE SPEED AND IGNITION TIMING INSPECTION CHART 1986 PORT INJECTED 300ZX

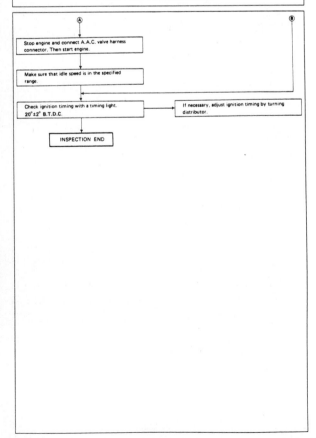

(A)   (B)

Stop engine and connect A.A.C. valve harness connector. Then start engine.

Make sure that idle speed is in the specified range.

Check ignition timing with a timing light.
20°±2° B.T.D.C.

If necessary, adjust ignition timing by turning distributor.

(INSPECTION END)

IDLE MIXTURE RATIO INSPECTION CHART – 1986 PORT INJECTED 300ZX

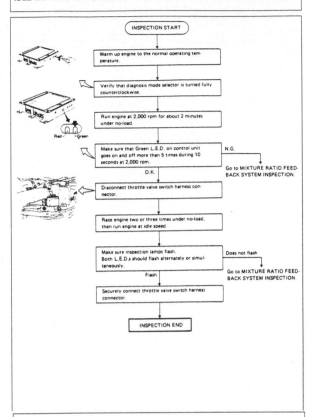

(INSPECTION START)

Warm up engine to the normal operating temperature.

Verify that diagnosis mode selector is turned fully counterclockwise.

Run engine at 2,000 rpm for about 2 minutes under no-load.

Make sure that Green L.E.D. on control unit goes on and off more than 5 times during 10 seconds at 2,000 rpm.

N.G. → Go to MIXTURE RATIO FEED-BACK SYSTEM INSPECTION.

O.K.

Disconnect throttle valve switch harness connector.

Race engine two or three times under no-load, then run engine at idle speed.

Make sure inspection lamps flash. Both L.E.D.s should flash alternately or simultaneously.

Does not flash → Go to MIXTURE RATIO FEED-BACK SYSTEM INSPECTION.

Flash

Securely connect throttle valve switch harness connector.

(INSPECTION END)

Red ── Green

ECCS SELF-DIAGNOSTIC CODES – 1986 PORT INJECTED 300ZX

DISPLAYED CODE

CODE	L.E.D. display Red → Green		Malfunctioning area	Items retained in memory
11	○	○	Crank angle sensor circuit	X
12	○	○○	Air flow meter circuit	X
13	○	○○○	Cylinder head temperature circuit	X
14	○	○○○○	Vehicle speed sensor (VG30ET engine)	–
21	○○	○	Ignition signal missing in primary coil	X
22	○○	○○	Fuel pump circuit	X
23	○○	○○○	Throttle valve switch (Idle switch) circuit	–
24	○○	○○○○	Neutral/Park switch (VG30ET engine)	–
31	○○○	○	Load signal circuit (Power steering oil pressure switch, Headlamp switch, Radiator fan switch, Rear defogger switch, Heater/air conditioner switch)	–
32	○○○	○○	Starter signal circuit	–
34	○○○	○○○○	Detonation sensor (VG30ET engine)	X
41	○○○○	○	Fuel temperature sensor circuit	X
44	○○○○	○○○○	No malfunctioning in the above circuit (Check other electrical systems.)	–

X: Yes   –: No

ECCS SELF-DIAGNOSTIC PROCEDURE—1986 PORT INJECTED 300ZX

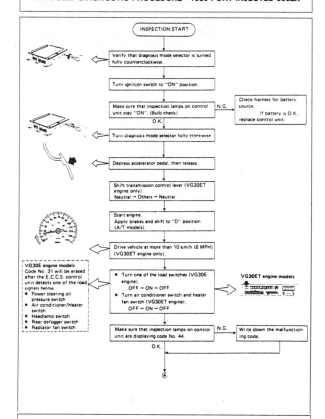

VG30E engine models
Code No. 31 will be erased after the E.C.C.S. control unit detects one of the load signals below.
- Power steering oil pressure switch
- Air conditioner/Heater switch
- Headlamp switch
- Rear defogger switch
- Radiator fan switch

ECCS SELF-DIAGNOSTIC PROCEDURE—1986 PORT INJECTED 300ZX

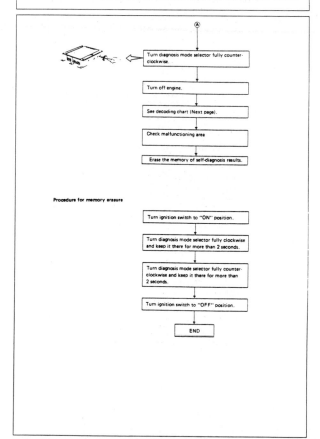

ECCS SELF-DIAGNOSTIC DECODING CHART
1986 PORT INJECTED 300ZX

Code No.	Diagnosis	Inspection
11	• 1° or 120° signal is not entered for one second while engine is running. • 120° signal is not entered for one second during engine cranking. • Either 1° or 120° signal is not entered often enough while the engine speed is higher than 600 rpm.	• Crank angle sensor harness and connectors • Starting system • Crank angle sensor • E.C.U.
12	• An abnormally high output voltage is entered while engine is off. • An abnormally low output voltage is entered while the engine speed is higher than 600 rpm.	• Air flow meter harness and connectors • Air flow meter • Air flow meter self-cleaning system • E.C.U.
13	• The cylinder head temperature circuit is open or shorted. (An abnormally high or low output is entered)	• Cylinder head temperature sensor harness and connectors • Cylinder head temperature sensor
14	• The vehicle speed signal is not entered while the vehicle is running.	• Vehicle speed sensor harness and connectors • Vehicle speed sensor
21	• The ignition signal in the primary coil is not entered more than 10 times.	• Harness between E.C.U. and ignition coil • Power transistor • Ignition coil • High tension cables • Spark plugs • Distributor • E.C.U.
22	• The electric current for fuel pump is extremely low or high.	• Fuel pump harness and connectors • Fuel pump • Fuel pump relay • E.C.U.
23	• The ON-OFF signal from idle switch is not entered after ignition switch is turned to "ON".	• Throttle valve switch harness and connectors • Throttle valve switch • Idle switch improper adjustment
24	• The ON-OFF signal from neutral/park switch is not entered after ignition switch is turned to "ON".	• Neutral/Park switch harness and connectors • Neutral/Park switch

ECCS SELF-DIAGNOSTIC DECODING CHART
1986 PORT INJECTED 300ZX

Code No.	Diagnosis	Inspection
31	VG30E engine models • An ON-OFF signal from the switches is not entered after ignition switch is turned to "ON". VG30ET engine models • An ON-OFF signal from the air conditioner system is not entered after the ignition switch is turned to "ON".	• Power steering oil pressure switch harness and connectors • Power steering oil pressure switch • Lighting system • Air conditioner system • Rear defogger system • Radiator fan control system • Heater system • Air conditioner system
32	• The start signal from the ignition switch is not entered after the engine has started.	• Ignition switch • Ignition system harness and connectors
34	• The detonation sensor circuit is shorted with the engine operating at a speed of above 2,000 rpm.	• Detonation sensor harness and connectors • Detonation sensor
41	• The fuel temperature sensor circuit is open or shorted. (An abnormally high or low output is entered.)	• Fuel temperature sensor harness and connectors • Fuel temperature sensor
44	• The systems which are diagnosed by E.C.U. are working normally.	• Inspect other electric control systems.

ECCS SELF-DIAGNOSTIC CHART—1986 PORT INJECTED 300ZX

Crank Angle Sensor

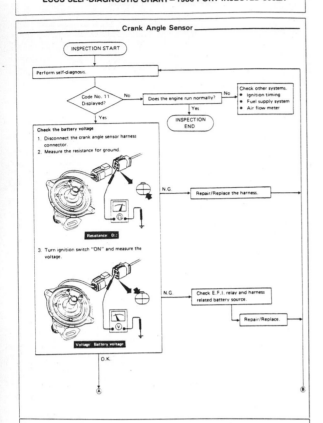

ECCS SELF-DIAGNOSTIC CHART—1986 PORT INJECTED 300ZX

Crank Angle Sensor (Cont'd)

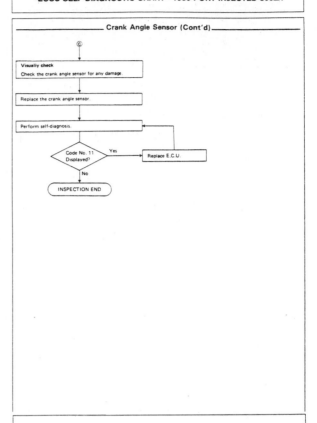

ECCS SELF-DIAGNOSTIC CHART—1986 PORT INJECTED 300ZX

Crank Angle Sensor (Cont'd)

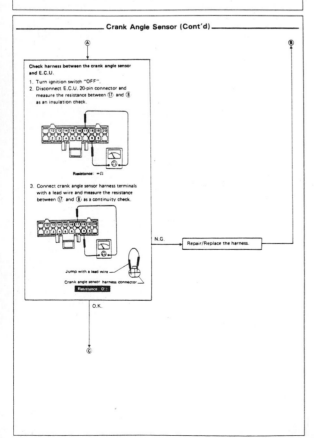

ECCS SELF-DIAGNOSTIC CHART—1986 PORT INJECTED 300ZX

Air Flow Meter

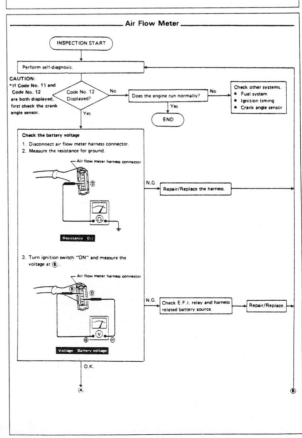

ECCS SELF-DIAGNOSTIC CHART – 1986 PORT INJECTED 300ZX

Air Flow Meter (Cont'd)

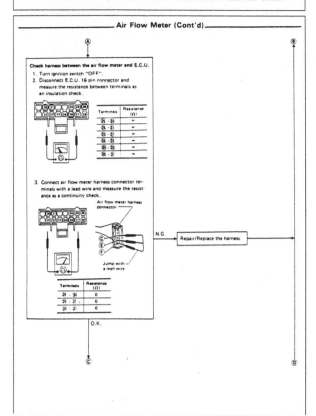

Check harness between the air flow meter and E.C.U.

1. Turn ignition switch "OFF".
2. Disconnect E.C.U. 16-pin connector and measure the resistance between terminals as an insulation check.

Terminals	Resistance (Ω)
26 - 30	∞
26 - 31	∞
30 - 31	∞
36 - 26	∞
36 - 30	∞
36 - 31	∞

3. Connect air flow meter harness connector terminals with a lead wire and measure the resistance as a continuity check.

Terminals	Resistance (Ω)
26 - 30	0
26 - 31	0
30 - 31	0

N.G. → Repair/Replace the harness.

O.K.

ECCS SELF-DIAGNOSTIC CHART – 1986 PORT INJECTED 300ZX

Air Flow Meter (Cont'd)

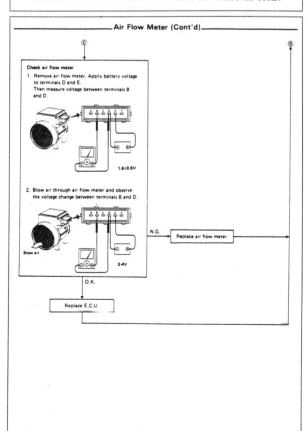

Check air flow meter

1. Remove air flow meter. Apply battery voltage to terminals D and E.
   Then measure voltage between terminals B and D.

   1.6±0.5V

2. Blow air through air flow meter and observe the voltage change between terminals B and D.

   Blow air

   2-4V

N.G. → Replace air flow meter.

O.K.

Replace E.C.U.

ECCS SELF-DIAGNOSTIC CHART – 1986 PORT INJECTED 300ZX

Cylinder Head Temperature Sensor

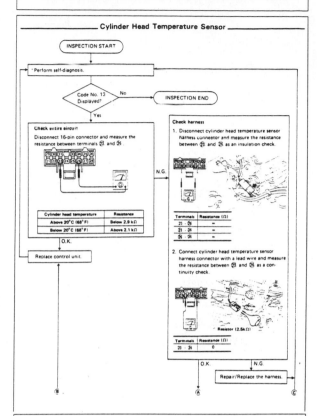

INSPECTION START

Perform self-diagnosis.

Code No. 13 Displayed? — No → INSPECTION END

Yes

Check entire circuit

Disconnect 16-pin connector and measure the resistance between terminals 23 and 26.

Cylinder head temperature	Resistance
Above 20°C (68°F)	Below 2.9 kΩ
Below 20°C (68°F)	Above 2.1 kΩ

O.K.

Replace control unit.

N.G. →

Check harness

1. Disconnect cylinder head temperature sensor harness connector and measure the resistance between 23 and 26 as an insulation check.

Terminals	Resistance (Ω)
23 - 26	∞
23 - 36	∞
26 - 36	∞

2. Connect cylinder head temperature sensor harness connector with a lead wire and measure the resistance between 23 and 26 as a continuity check.

Resistor (2.5kΩ)

Terminals	Resistance (Ω)
23 - 26	0

O.K.   N.G. → Repair/Replace the harness.

ECCS SELF-DIAGNOSTIC CHART – 1986 PORT INJECTED 300ZX

Cylinder Head Temperature Sensor (Cont'd)

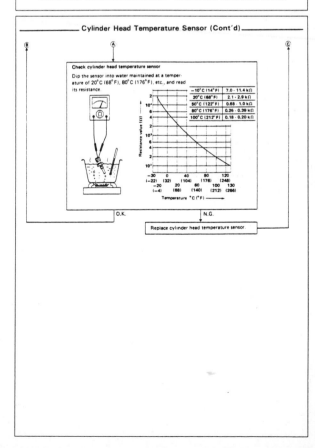

Check cylinder head temperature sensor

Dip the sensor into water maintained at a temperature of 20°C (68°F), 80°C (176°F), etc., and read its resistance.

−10°C (14°F)	7.0 - 11.4 kΩ
20°C (68°F)	2.1 - 2.9 kΩ
50°C (122°F)	0.68 - 1.0 kΩ
80°C (176°F)	0.26 - 0.39 kΩ
100°C (212°F)	0.18 - 0.20 kΩ

O.K.   N.G. →

Replace cylinder head temperature sensor.

ECCS SELF-DIAGNOSTIC CHART — 1986 PORT INJECTED 300ZX

Vehicle Speed Sensor

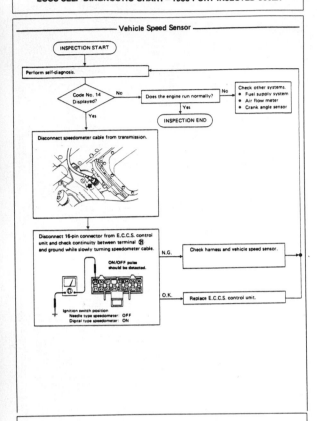

ECCS SELF-DIAGNOSTIC CHART — 1986 PORT INJECTED 300ZX

Ignition Signal (Cont'd)

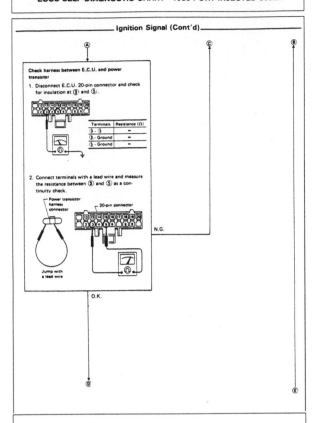

ECCS SELF-DIAGNOSTIC CHART — 1986 PORT INJECTED 300ZX

Ignition Signal

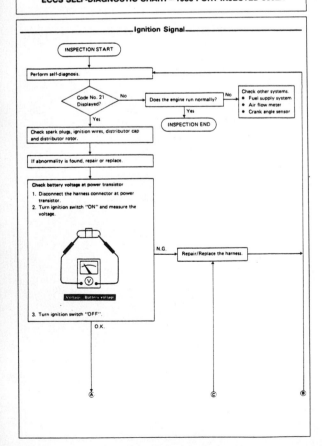

ECCS SELF-DIAGNOSTIC CHART — 1986 PORT INJECTED 300ZX

Ignition Signal (Cont'd)

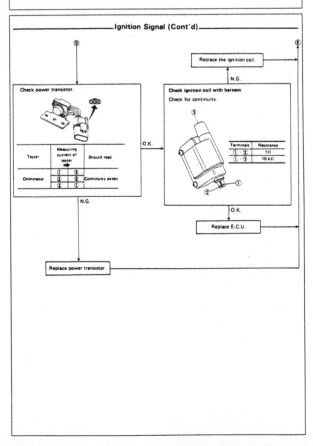

ECCS SELF-DIAGNOSTIC CHART – 1986 PORT INJECTED 300ZX

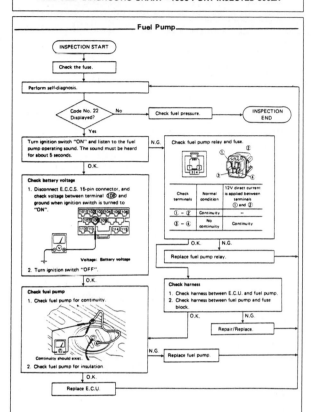

Fuel Pump

ECCS SELF-DIAGNOSTIC CHART – 1986 PORT INJECTED 300ZX

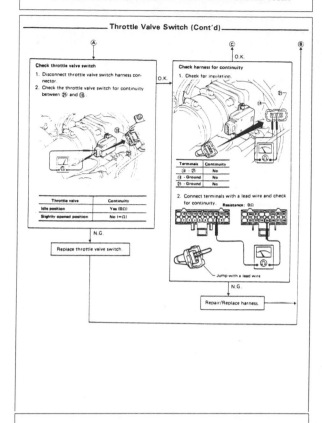

Throttle Valve Switch (Cont'd)

ECCS SELF-DIAGNOSTIC CHART – 1986 PORT INJECTED 300ZX

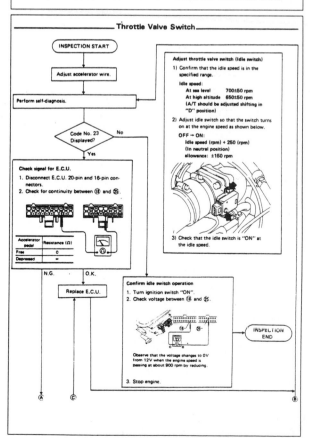

Throttle Valve Switch

ECCS SELF-DIAGNOSTIC CHART – 1986 PORT INJECTED 300ZX

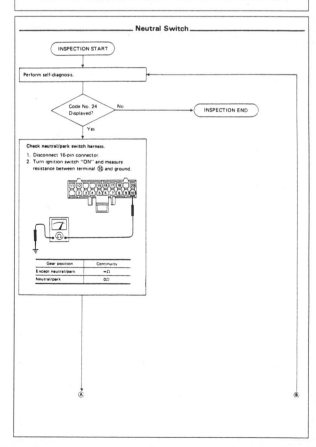

Neutral Switch

ECCS SELF-DIAGNOSTIC CHART — 1986 PORT INJECTED 300ZX

Neutral Switch (Cont'd)

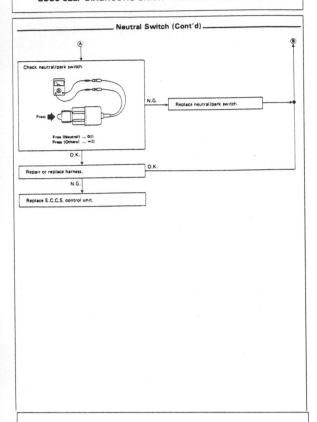

ECCS SELF-DIAGNOSTIC CHART — 1986 PORT INJECTED 300ZX

Load Signal (Cont'd)

Air Conditioner Signal

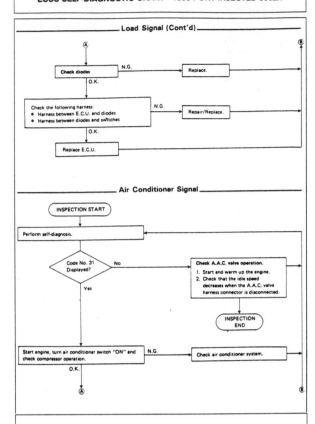

ECCS SELF-DIAGNOSTIC CHART — 1986 PORT INJECTED 300ZX

Load Signal

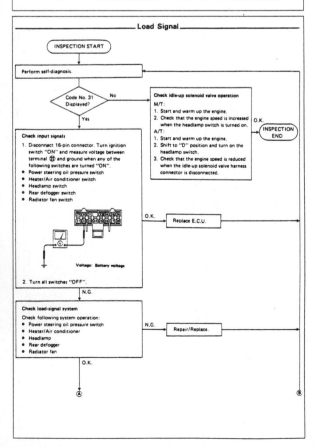

ECCS SELF-DIAGNOSTIC CHART — 1986 PORT INJECTED 300ZX

Air Conditioner Signal (Cont'd)

Start Signal

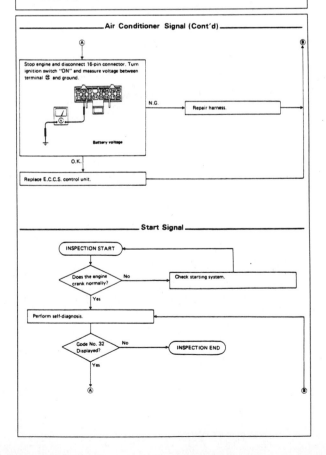

ECCS SELF-DIAGNOSTIC CHART — 1986 PORT INJECTED 300ZX

Start Signal (Cont'd)

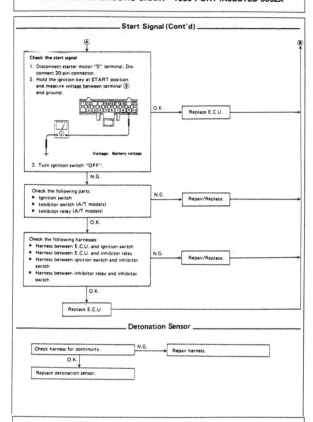

Ⓐ

Check the start signal
1. Disconnect starter motor "S" terminal. Disconnect 20-pin connector.
2. Hold the ignition key at START position and measure voltage between terminal ⑨ and ground.

Voltage: Battery voltage

O.K. → Replace E.C.U.

3. Turn ignition switch "OFF".

N.G.

Check the following parts:
• Ignition switch
• Inhibitor switch (A/T models)
• Inhibitor relay (A/T models)

N.G. → Repair/Replace.

O.K.

Check the following harnesses:
• Harness between E.C.U. and ignition switch
• Harness between E.C.U. and inhibitor relay
• Harness between ignition switch and inhibitor switch
• Harness between inhibitor relay and inhibitor switch

N.G. → Repair/Replace.

O.K.

Replace E.C.U.

Ⓑ

Detonation Sensor

Check harness for continuity. → N.G. → Repair harness.

O.K.

Replace detonation sensor.

ECCS SELF-DIAGNOSTIC CHART — 1986 PORT INJECTED 300ZX

Fuel Temperature Sensor (Cont'd)

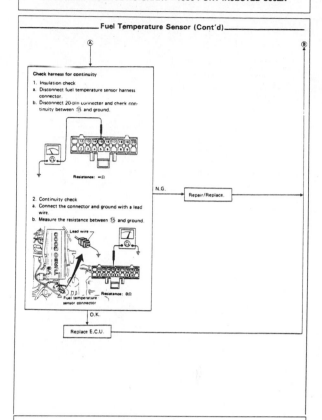

Ⓐ

Check harness for continuity
1. Insulation check
a. Disconnect fuel temperature sensor harness connector.
b. Disconnect 20-pin connector and check continuity between ⑮ and ground.

Resistance: ∞ Ω

2. Continuity check
a. Connect the connector and ground with a lead wire.
b. Measure the resistance between ⑮ and ground.

Lead wire

Resistance: 0 Ω

Fuel temperature sensor connector

N.G. → Repair/Replace.

O.K.

Replace E.C.U.

Ⓑ

ECCS SELF-DIAGNOSTIC CHART — 1986 PORT INJECTED 300ZX

Fuel Temperature Sensor

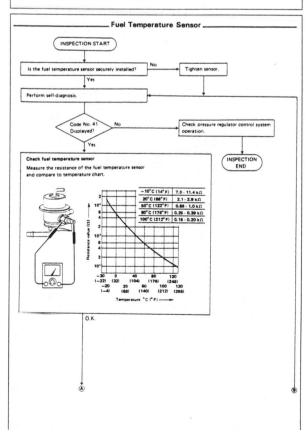

INSPECTION START

Is the fuel temperature sensor securely installed? — No → Tighten sensor.

Yes

Perform self-diagnosis.

Code No. 41 Displayed? — No → Check pressure regulator control system operation.

Yes

INSPECTION END

Check fuel temperature sensor
Measure the resistance of the fuel temperature sensor and compare to temperature chart.

−10°C (14°F)	7.0 - 11.4 kΩ
20°C (68°F)	2.1 - 2.9 kΩ
50°C (122°F)	0.68 - 1.0 kΩ
80°C (176°F)	0.26 - 0.39 kΩ
100°C (212°F)	0.18 - 0.20 kΩ

Temperature °C (°F)

O.K.

Ⓐ

Ⓑ

ECCS SELF-DIAGNOSTIC CHART — 1986 PORT INJECTED 300ZX

Injector

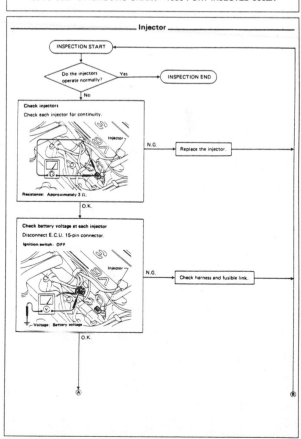

INSPECTION START

Do the injectors operate normally? — Yes → INSPECTION END

No

Check injectors
Check each injector for continuity.

Injector

Resistance: Approximately 3 Ω

N.G. → Replace the injector.

O.K.

Check battery voltage at each injector
Disconnect E.C.U. 15-pin connector.
Ignition switch: OFF

Injector

Voltage: Battery voltage

N.G. → Check harness and fusible link.

O.K.

Ⓐ

Ⓑ

ECCS SELF-DIAGNOSTIC CHART — 1986 PORT INJECTED 300ZX

Injector (Cont'd)

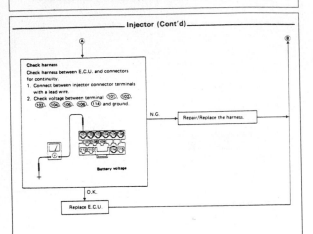

Check harness

Check harness between E.C.U. and connectors for continuity.

1. Connect between injector connector terminals with a lead wire.
2. Check voltage between terminal (101), (102), (103), (104), (105), (106), (114) and ground.

N.G. → Repair/Replace the harness.

O.K. → Replace E.C.U.

ECCS SELF-DIAGNOSTIC CHART — 1986 PORT INJECTED 300ZX

Battery Voltage and Ground Test (Cont'd)

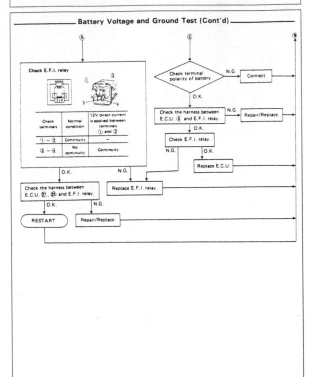

Check E.F.I. relay

12V direct current is applied between terminals ① and ②

Check terminals	Normal condition	12V direct current is applied between terminals ① and ②
① – ②	Continuity	—
③ – ④	No continuity	Continuity

O.K. → Check the harness between E.C.U. ② , ③ and E.F.I. relay.

O.K. → RESTART

N.G. → Repair/Replace.

Check terminal polarity of battery

N.G. → Connect.

O.K. → Check the harness between E.C.U. ⑥ and E.F.I. relay.

O.K. → Check E.F.I. relay.

N.G. → Repair/Replace.

N.G. → Replace E.F.I. relay.

O.K. → Replace E.C.U.

Replace E.F.I. relay.

ECCS SELF-DIAGNOSTIC CHART — 1986 PORT INJECTED 300ZX

Battery Voltage and Ground Test

INSPECTION START

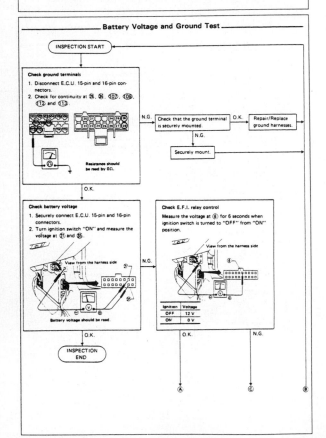

Check ground terminals

1. Disconnect E.C.U. 15-pin and 16-pin connectors.
2. Check for continuity at ㉘, ㉞, (107), (109), (112) and (113).

Resistance should be read by 0 Ω.

N.G. → Check that the ground terminal is securely mounted.

O.K. → Repair/Replace ground harnesses.

N.G. → Securely mount.

O.K. →

Check battery voltage

1. Securely connect E.C.U. 15-pin and 16-pin connectors.
2. Turn ignition switch "ON" and measure the voltage at ㉗ and ㉟.

Battery voltage should be read.

Check E.F.I. relay control

Measure the voltage at ⑥ for 6 seconds when ignition switch is turned to "OFF" from "ON" position.

View from the harness side

Ignition	Voltage
OFF	12 V
ON	0 V

O.K. → INSPECTION END

N.G. →

A   C   B

ECCS SELF-DIAGNOSTIC CHART — 1986 PORT INJECTED 300ZX

Air Regulator

INSPECTION START

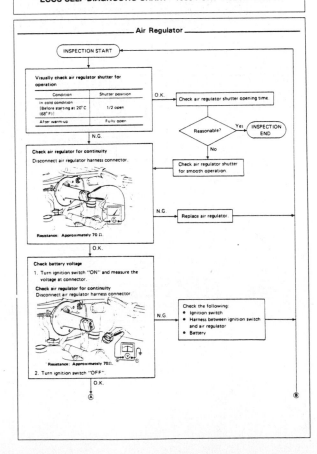

Visually check air regulator shutter for operation

Condition	Shutter position
In cold condition (Before starting at 20°C (68°F))	1/2 open
After warm-up	Fully open

O.K. → Check air regulator shutter opening time.

Reasonable? — Yes → INSPECTION END

No → Check air regulator shutter for smooth operation.

N.G. →

Check air regulator for continuity

Disconnect air regulator harness connector.

Resistance: Approximately 70 Ω.

N.G. → Replace air regulator.

O.K. →

Check battery voltage

1. Turn ignition switch "ON" and measure the voltage at connector.

Check air regulator for continuity

Disconnect air regulator harness connector.

Resistance: Approximately 70 Ω.

2. Turn ignition switch "OFF".

N.G. → Check the following:
- Ignition switch
- Harness between ignition switch and air regulator
- Battery

A   B

ECCS SELF-DIAGNOSTIC CHART – 1986 PORT INJECTED 300ZX

Air Regulator (Cont'd)

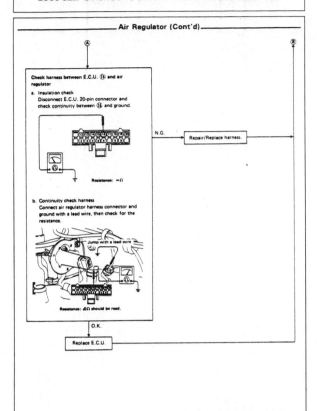

Check harness between E.C.U. ⑯ and air regulator

a. Insulation check
Disconnect E.C.U. 20-pin connector and check continuity between ⑯ and ground.

Resistance: ∞Ω

N.G. → Repair/Replace harness.

b. Continuity check harness
Connect air regulator harness connector and ground with a lead wire, then check for the resistance.

Jump with a lead wire

Resistance: 0Ω should be read.

O.K.

Replace E.C.U.

ECCS SELF-DIAGNOSTIC CHART – 1986 PORT INJECTED 300ZX

E.G.R. Control System (Cont'd)

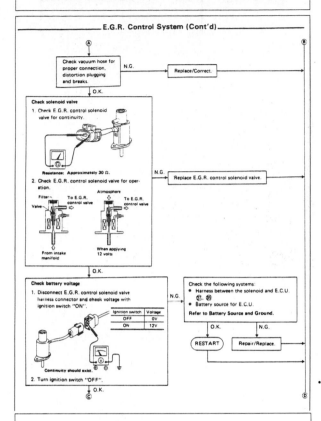

Check vacuum hose for proper connection, distortion plugging and breaks. → N.G. → Replace/Correct.

O.K.

Check solenoid valve

1. Check E.G.R. control solenoid valve for continuity.

Resistance: Approximately 30 Ω.

2. Check E.G.R. control solenoid valve for operation.

Filter — To E.G.R. control valve
Valve — Atmosphere — To E.G.R. control valve

From intake manifold — When applying 12 volts

N.G. → Replace E.G.R. control solenoid valve.

O.K.

Check battery voltage

1. Disconnect E.G.R. control solenoid valve harness connector and check voltage with ignition switch "ON".

Ignition switch	Voltage
OFF	0V
ON	12V

Continuity should exist.

2. Turn ignition switch "OFF".

N.G. → Check the following systems:
• Harness between the solenoid and E.C.U. ㉗, ㊽
• Battery source for E.C.U.
Refer to Battery Source and Ground.

O.K. → RESTART

N.G. → Repair/Replace.

O.K.

ECCS SELF-DIAGNOSTIC CHART – 1986 PORT INJECTED 300ZX

E.G.R. Control System

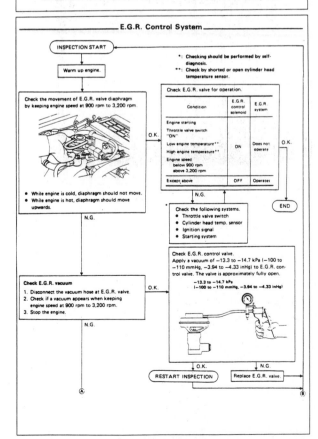

INSPECTION START

Warm up engine.

*: Checking should be performed by self-diagnosis.
**: Check by shorted or open cylinder head temperature sensor.

Check the movement of E.G.R. valve diaphragm by keeping engine speed at 900 rpm to 3,200 rpm.

• While engine is cold, diaphragm should not move.
• While engine is hot, diaphragm should move upwards.

O.K. → Check E.G.R. valve for operation.

Condition	E.G.R. control solenoid	E.G.R. system
Engine starting		
Throttle valve switch "ON"	ON	Does not operate
Low engine temperature**		
High engine temperature**		
Engine speed below 900 rpm above 3,200 rpm		
Except above	OFF	Operates

N.G. → Check the following systems.
• Throttle valve switch
• Cylinder head temp. sensor
• Ignition signal
• Starting system

O.K. → END

N.G.

Check E.G.R. vacuum

1. Disconnect the vacuum hose at E.G.R. valve.
2. Check if a vacuum appears when keeping engine speed at 900 rpm to 3,200 rpm.
3. Stop the engine.

O.K. → Check E.G.R. control valve.
Apply a vacuum of −13.3 to −14.7 kPa (−100 to −110 mmHg, −3.94 to −4.33 inHg) to E.G.R. control valve. The valve is approximately fully open.

−13.3 to −14.7 kPa
(−100 to −110 mmHg, −3.94 to −4.33 inHg)

O.K. → RESTART INSPECTION

N.G. → Replace E.G.R. valve.

ECCS SELF-DIAGNOSTIC CHART – 1986 PORT INJECTED 300ZX

E.G.R. Control System (Cont'd)

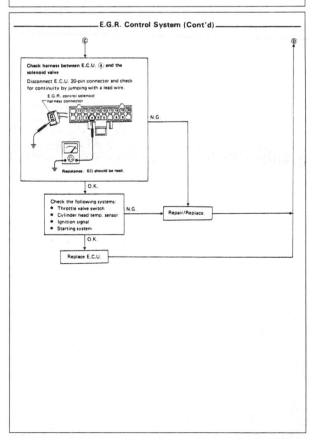

Check harness between E.C.U. ④ and the solenoid valve

Disconnect E.C.U. 20-pin connector and check for continuity by jumping with a lead wire.

E.G.R. control solenoid harness connector

Resistance: 0Ω should be read.

N.G.

O.K.

Check the following systems:
• Throttle valve switch
• Cylinder head temp. sensor
• Ignition signal
• Starting system

N.G. → Repair/Replace.

O.K.

Replace E.C.U.

ECCS SELF-DIAGNOSTIC CHART—1986 PORT INJECTED 300ZX

— Exhaust Gas Sensor —

MAIN CIRCUIT
Refer to MIXTURE RATIO FEEDBACK SYSTEM INSPECTION.

HEATER CIRCUIT

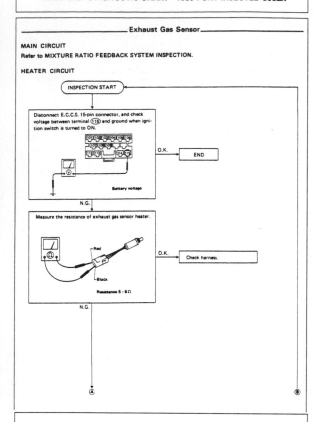

ECCS SELF-DIAGNOSTIC CHART—1986 PORT INJECTED 300ZX

— Auxiliary air Control (A.A.C.) Valve or Idle-up Solenoid Valve —

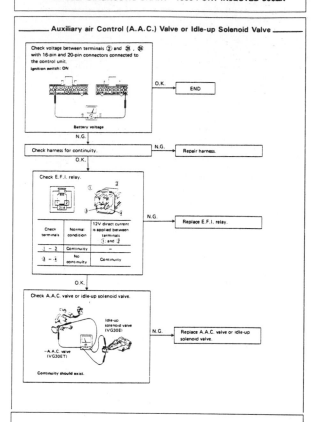

ECCS SELF-DIAGNOSTIC CHART—1986 PORT INJECTED 300ZX

— Exhaust Gas Sensor (Cont'd) —

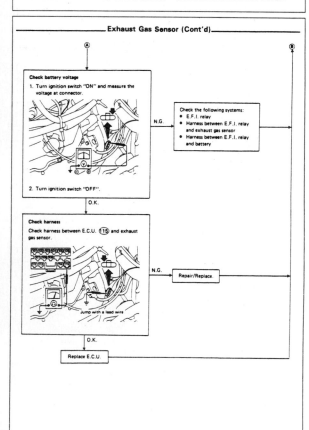

ECCS SELF-DIAGNOSTIC CHART—1986 PORT INJECTED 300ZX

— Self-cleaning Hot Wire —

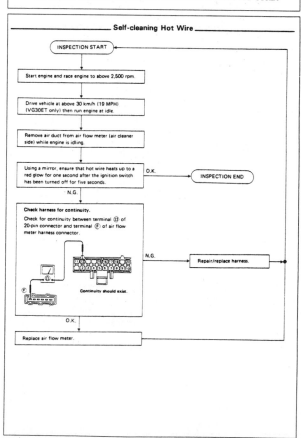

ECCS SELF-DIAGNOSTIC CHART – 1986 PORT INJECTED 300ZX

Pressure Regulator Control Solenoid Valve

INSPECTION START

Check the system operation
1. Disconnect fuel temperature sensor harness connector and connect to ground with a lead wire.

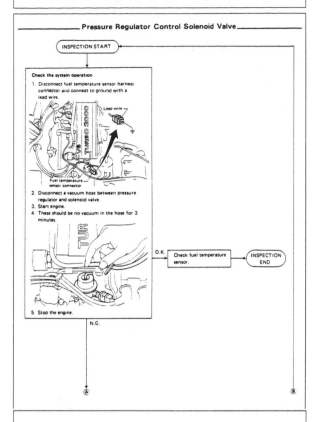

2. Disconnect a vacuum hose between pressure regulator and solenoid valve.
3. Start engine.
4. These should be no vacuum in the hose for 3 minutes.

O.K. → Check fuel temperature sensor. → INSPECTION END

5. Stop the engine.

N.G.

(A)   (B)

ECCS SELF-DIAGNOSTIC CHART – 1986 PORT INJECTED 300ZX

Pressure Regulator Control Solenoid Valve (Cont'd)

(C)   (D)

Check harness
Check harness between solenoid valve and E.C.U. (19) by jumping to ground.

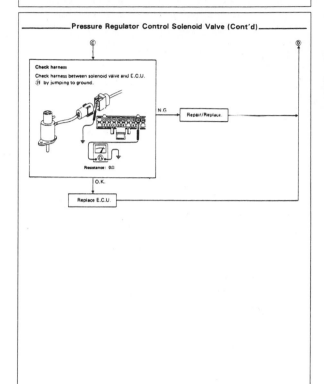

N.G → Repair/Replace.

Resistance: 0 Ω

O.K.

Replace E.C.U.

ECCS SELF-DIAGNOSTIC CHART – 1986 PORT INJECTED 300ZX

Pressure Regulator Control Solenoid Valve (Cont'd)

(A)   (B)

Check the solenoid valve
Check pressure regulator control solenoid valve for continuity.

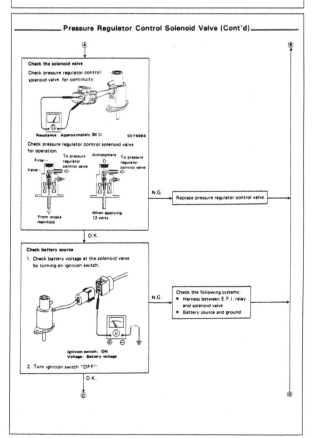

Resistance: Approximately 30 Ω.   SEF698B

Check pressure regulator control solenoid valve for operation.

N.G. → Replace pressure regulator control valve.

O.K.

Check battery source
1. Check battery voltage at the solenoid valve by turning on ignition switch.

N.G. → Check the following systems:
• Harness between E.F.I. relay and solenoid valve
• Battery source and ground

Ignition switch: ON
Voltage: Battery voltage

2. Turn ignition switch "OFF".

O.K.

(C)   (D)

ECCS SELF-DIAGNOSTIC CHART – 1986 PORT INJECTED 300ZX

Air Injection Valve (A.I.V.) Control System

INSPECTION START

Check the system operation
Disconnect cylinder head temperature sensor harness connector. Connect a resistor (2.5 kΩ) between terminals of cylinder head temperature sensor harness connector.

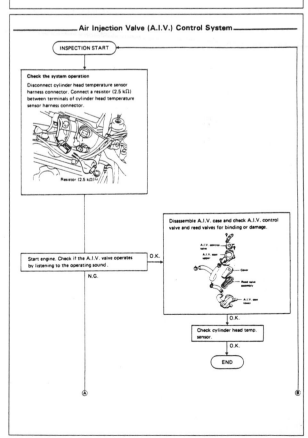

Resistor (2.5 kΩ)

Disassemble A.I.V. case and check A.I.V. control valve and reed valves for binding or damage.

Start engine. Check if the A.I.V. valve operates by listening to the operating sound.

O.K.

N.G.

O.K.

Check cylinder head temp. sensor.

O.K.

END

(A)   (B)

ECCS SELF-DIAGNOSTIC CHART – 1986 PORT INJECTED 300ZX

Air Injection Valve (A.I.V.) Control System (Cont'd)

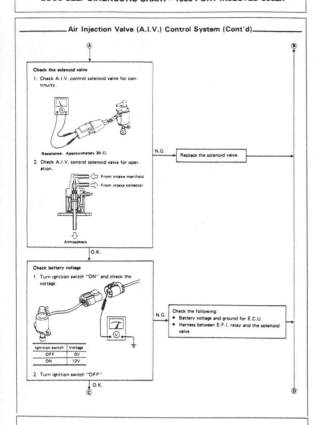

Ⓐ

Ⓑ

Check the solenoid valve

1. Check A.I.V. control solenoid valve for continuity.

Resistance: Approximately 30 Ω.

N.G. → Replace the solenoid valve.

2. Check A.I.V. control solenoid valve for operation.

From intake manifold
From intake collector

Atmosphere

O.K.

Check battery voltage

1. Turn ignition switch "ON" and check the voltage.

N.G. → Check the following:
• Battery voltage and ground for E.C.U.
• Harness between E.F.I. relay and the solenoid valve.

Ignition switch	Voltage
OFF	0V
ON	12V

2. Turn ignition switch "OFF".

O.K.
Ⓒ

Ⓓ

ECCS SELF-DIAGNOSTIC CHART – 1986 PORT INJECTED 300ZX

Air Injection Valve (A.I.V.) Control System (Cont'd)

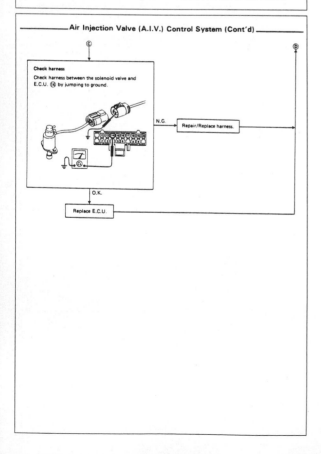

Ⓒ

Ⓓ

Check harness

Check harness between the solenoid valve and E.C.U. ⑭ by jumping to ground.

N.G. → Repair/Replace harness.

O.K.

Replace E.C.U.

MIXTURE RATIO FEEDBACK SYSTEM INSPECTION CHART
1986 PORT INJECTED 300ZX

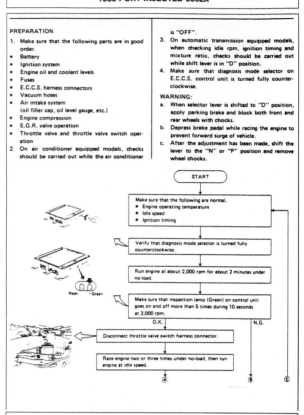

PREPARATION

1. Make sure that the following parts are in good order.
• Battery
• Ignition system
• Engine oil and coolant levels
• Fuses
• E.C.C.S. harness connectors
• Vacuum hoses
• Air intake system
  (oil filler cap, oil level gauge, etc.)
• Engine compression
• E.G.R. valve operation
• Throttle valve and throttle valve switch operation
2. On air conditioner equipped models, checks should be carried out while the air conditioner

is "OFF".
3. On automatic transmission equipped models, when checking idle rpm, ignition timing and mixture ratio, checks should be carried out while shift lever is in "D" position.
4. Make sure that diagnosis mode selector on E.C.C.S. control unit is turned fully counterclockwise.

WARNING:

a. When selector lever is shifted to "D" position, apply parking brake and block both front and rear wheels with chocks.
b. Depress brake pedal while racing the engine to prevent forward surge of vehicle.
c. After the adjustment has been made, shift the lever to the "N" or "P" position and remove wheel chocks.

START

Make sure that the following are normal.
• Engine operating temperature
• Idle speed
• Ignition timing

Verify that diagnosis mode selector is turned fully counterclockwise.

Run engine at about 2,000 rpm for about 2 minutes under no-load.

Make sure that inspection lamp (Green) on control unit goes on and off more than 5 times during 10 seconds at 2,000 rpm.

Red– –Green

O.K. / N.G.

Disconnect throttle valve switch harness connector.

Race engine two or three times under no-load, then run engine at idle speed.

Ⓐ   Ⓑ   Ⓒ

MIXTURE RATIO FEEDBACK SYSTEM INSPECTION CHART
1986 PORT INJECTED 300ZX

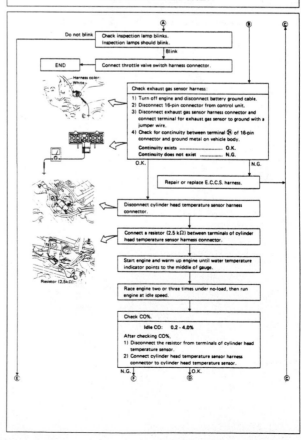

Ⓐ   Ⓑ   Ⓒ

Do not blink → Check inspection lamp blinks.
Inspection lamps should blink.

Blink

END ← Connect throttle valve switch harness connector.

Harness color:
White

Check exhaust gas sensor harness:

1) Turn off engine and disconnect battery ground cable.
2) Disconnect 16-pin connector from control unit.
3) Disconnect exhaust gas sensor harness connector and connect terminal for exhaust gas sensor to ground with a jumper wire.
4) Check for continuity between terminal Ⓡ of 16-pin connector and ground metal on vehicle body.

Continuity exists .... O.K.
Continuity does not exist .... N.G.

O.K. / N.G.

Repair or replace E.C.C.S. harness.

Disconnect cylinder head temperature sensor harness connector.

Connect a resistor (2.5 kΩ) between terminals of cylinder head temperature sensor harness connector.

Start engine and warm up engine until water temperature indicator points to the middle of gauge.

Resistor (2.5kΩ)

Race engine two or three times under no-load, then run engine at idle speed.

Check CO%.

Idle CO:	0.2 - 4.0%

After checking CO%,
1) Disconnect the resistor from terminals of cylinder head temperature sensor.
2) Connect cylinder head temperature sensor harness connector to cylinder head temperature sensor.

Ⓔ   N.G. Ⓕ   Ⓓ O.K.   Ⓒ

MIXTURE RATIO FEEDBACK SYSTEM INSPECTION CHART
1986 PORT INJECTED 300ZX

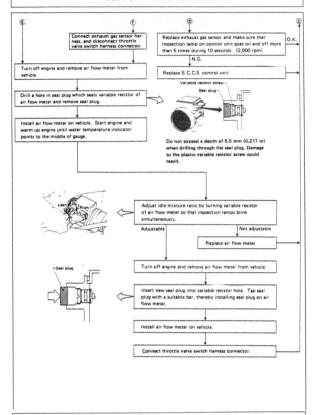

ECCS SELF-DIAGNOSTIC CHART — 1987–88 PORT INJECTED MAXIMA

CRANK ANGLE SENSOR (Code No. 11)

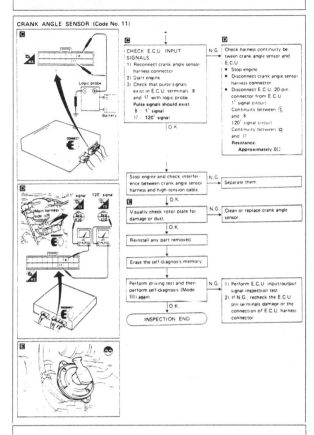

ECCS SELF-DIAGNOSTIC CHART — 1987–88 PORT INJECTED MAXIMA

CRANK ANGLE SENSOR (Code No. 11)

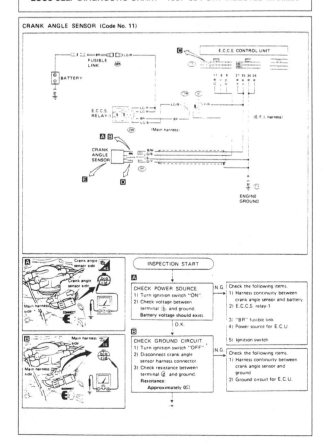

ECCS SELF-DIAGNOSTIC CHART — 1987–88 PORT INJECTED MAXIMA

AIR FLOW METER (Code No. 12)

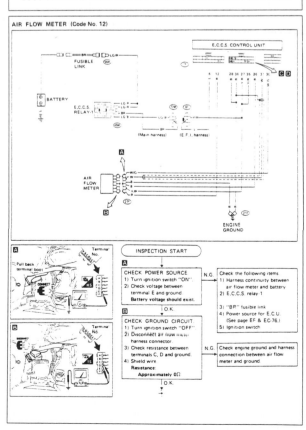

ECCS SELF-DIAGNOSTIC CHART — 1987–88 PORT INJECTED MAXIMA

AIR FLOW METER (Code No. 12)

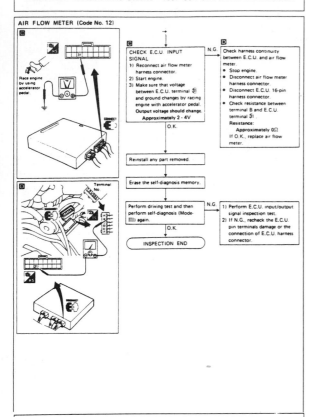

CHECK E.C.U. INPUT SIGNAL
1) Reconnect air flow meter harness connector.
2) Start engine.
3) Make sure that voltage between E.C.U. terminal 31 and ground changes by racing engine with accelerator pedal. Output voltage should change.
Approximately 2 - 4V.

O.K.

Reinstall any part removed.

Erase the self-diagnosis memory.

Perform driving test and then perform self-diagnosis (Mode-III) again.

O.K.

INSPECTION END

N.G. → Check harness continuity between E.C.U. and air flow meter.
- Stop engine.
- Disconnect air flow meter connector.
- Disconnect E.C.U. 16-pin harness connector.
- Check resistance between terminal B and E.C.U. terminal 31.
Resistance:
Approximately 0Ω
If O.K., replace air flow meter.

N.G. → 1) Perform E.C.U. input/output signal inspection test.
2) If N.G., recheck the E.C.U. pin terminals damage or the connection of E.C.U. harness connector.

ECCS SELF-DIAGNOSTIC CHART — 1987–88 PORT INJECTED MAXIMA

CYLINDER HEAD TEMPERATURE SENSOR (Code No. 13)

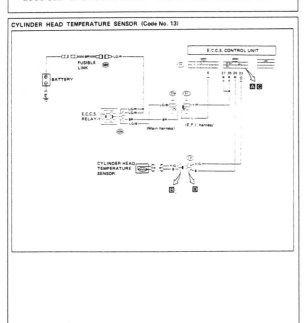

ECCS SELF-DIAGNOSTIC CHART — 1987–88 PORT INJECTED MAXIMA

CYLINDER HEAD TEMPERATURE SENSOR (Code No. 13)

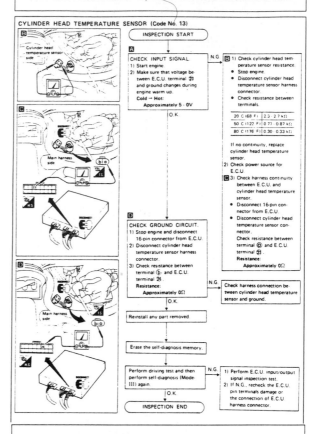

INSPECTION START

CHECK INPUT SIGNAL
1) Start engine.
2) Make sure that voltage between E.C.U. terminal 23 and ground changes during engine warm up.
Cold → Hot:
Approximately 5 - 0V

O.K.

CHECK GROUND CIRCUIT.
1) Stop engine and disconnect 16-pin connector from E.C.U.
2) Disconnect cylinder head temperature sensor harness connector.
3) Check resistance between terminal b and E.C.U. terminal 26.
Resistance:
Approximately 0Ω

O.K.

Reinstall any part removed.

Erase the self-diagnosis memory.

Perform driving test and then perform self-diagnosis (Mode-III) again.

O.K.

INSPECTION END

N.G. → 1) Check cylinder head temperature sensor resistance.
- Stop engine.
- Disconnect cylinder head temperature sensor harness connector.
- Check resistance between terminals.

20 C (68 F)	2.3 - 2.7 kΩ
50 C (122 F)	0.77 - 0.87 kΩ
80 C (176 F)	0.30 - 0.33 kΩ

If no continuity, replace cylinder head temperature sensor.
2) Check power source for E.C.U.
3) Check harness continuity between E.C.U. and cylinder head temperature sensor.
- Disconnect 16-pin connector from E.C.U.
- Disconnect cylinder head temperature sensor connector.
Check resistance between terminal a and E.C.U. terminal 23.
Resistance:
Approximately 0Ω

N.G. → Check harness connection between cylinder head temperature sensor and ground.

N.G. → 1) Perform E.C.U. input/output signal inspection test.
2) If N.G., recheck the E.C.U. pin terminals damage or the connection of E.C.U. harness connector.

ECCS SELF-DIAGNOSTIC CHART — 1987–88 PORT INJECTED MAXIMA

IGNITION SIGNAL (Code No. 21)

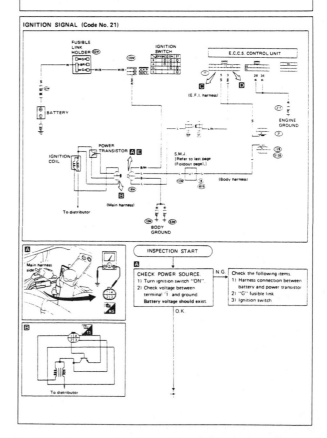

INSPECTION START

CHECK POWER SOURCE.
1) Turn ignition switch "ON".
2) Check voltage between terminal 1 and ground.
Battery voltage should exist.

O.K.

N.G. → Check the following items.
1) Harness connection between battery and power transistor.
2) "G" fusible link
3) Ignition switch

ECCS SELF-DIAGNOSTIC CHART – 1987–88 PORT INJECTED MAXIMA

IGNITION SIGNAL (Code No. 21)

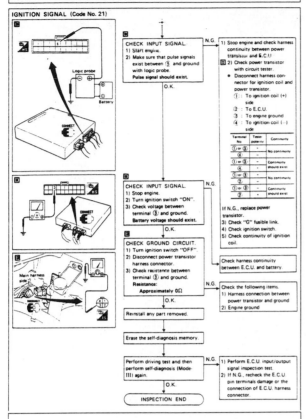

C CHECK INPUT SIGNAL.
1) Start engine.
2) Make sure that pulse signals exist between ⑤ and ground with logic probe.
Pulse signal should exist.

O.K.

D CHECK INPUT SIGNAL.
1) Stop engine.
2) Turn ignition switch "ON".
3) Check voltage between terminal ③ and ground.
Battery voltage should exist.

O.K.

E CHECK GROUND CIRCUIT.
1) Turn ignition switch "OFF".
2) Disconnect power transistor harness connector.
3) Check resistance between terminal ③ and ground.
Resistance: Approximately 0Ω

O.K.

Reinstall any part removed.

Erase the self-diagnosis memory.

Perform driving test and then perform self-diagnosis (Mode-III) again.

O.K.

(INSPECTION END)

N.G. →
1) Stop engine and check harness continuity between power transistor and E.C.U.
B 2) Check power transistor with circuit tester.
• Disconnect harness connector for ignition coil and power transistor.
① : To ignition coil (+) side
② : To E.C.U.
③ : To engine ground
④ : To ignition coil (−) side

Terminal No.	Tester polarity	Continuity
① or ③		No continuity
④		
① or ③		Continuity should exist
④		
① or ③		No continuity
②		
① or ③		Continuity should exist
②		

If N.G., replace power transistor.
3) Check "G" fusible link.
4) Check ignition switch.
5) Check continuity of ignition coil.

N.G. → Check harness continuity between E.C.U. and battery.

N.G. → Check the following items.
1) Harness connection between power transistor and ground
2) Engine ground

N.G. →
1) Perform E.C.U. input/output signal inspection test.
2) If N.G., recheck the E.C.U. pin terminals damage or the connection of E.C.U. harness connector.

ECCS SELF-DIAGNOSTIC CHART – 1987–88 PORT INJECTED MAXIMA

FUEL PUMP (Code No. 22)

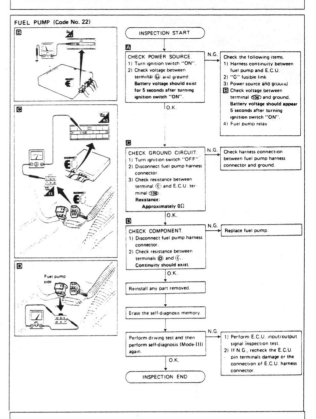

(INSPECTION START)

A CHECK POWER SOURCE.
1) Turn ignition switch "ON".
2) Check voltage between terminal ⑩ and ground.
Battery voltage should exist for 5 seconds after turning ignition switch "ON".

O.K.

C CHECK GROUND CIRCUIT.
1) Turn ignition switch "OFF".
2) Disconnect fuel pump harness connector.
3) Check resistance between terminal ⓒ and E.C.U. terminal ⑩.
Resistance: Approximately 0Ω

O.K.

CHECK COMPONENT.
1) Disconnect fuel pump harness connector.
2) Check resistance between terminals ⓐ and ⓒ.
Continuity should exist.

O.K.

Reinstall any part removed.

Erase the self-diagnosis memory

Perform driving test and then perform self-diagnosis (Mode-III) again.

O.K.

(INSPECTION END)

N.G. → Check the following items.
1) Harness continuity between fuel pump and E.C.U.
2) "G" fusible link
3) Power source and ground
B Check voltage between terminal ⑩ and ground.
Battery voltage should appear 5 seconds after turning ignition switch "ON".
4) Fuel pump relay

N.G. → Check harness connection between fuel pump harness connector and ground.

N.G. → Replace fuel pump.

N.G. →
1) Perform E.C.U. input/output signal inspection test.
2) If N.G., recheck the E.C.U. pin terminals damage or the connection of E.C.U. harness connector.

ECCS SELF-DIAGNOSTIC CHART – 1987–88 PORT INJECTED MAXIMA

FUEL PUMP (Code No. 22)

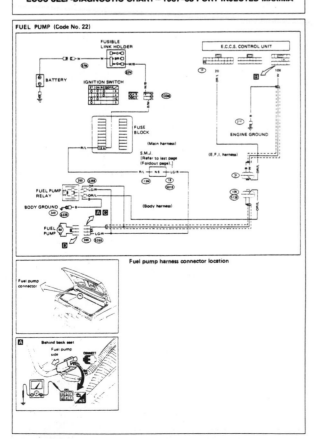

Fuel pump harness connector location

ECCS SELF-DIAGNOSTIC CHART – 1987–88 PORT INJECTED MAXIMA

FUEL TEMPERATURE SENSOR (Code No. 41)

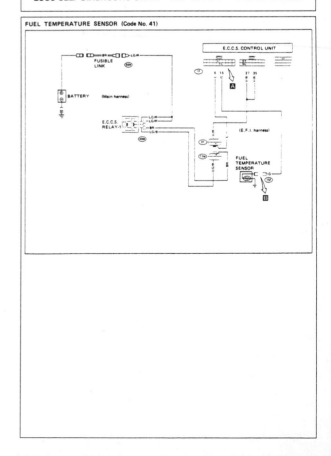

ECCS SELF-DIAGNOSTIC CHART – 1987–88 PORT INJECTED MAXIMA

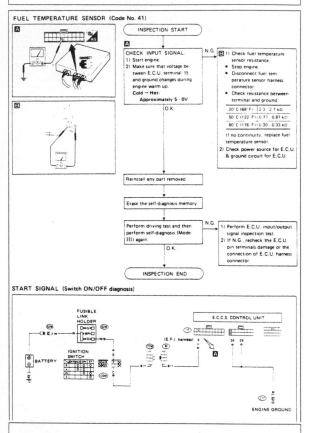

FUEL TEMPERATURE SENSOR (Code No. 41)

INSPECTION START

A CHECK INPUT SIGNAL.
1) Start engine.
2) Make sure that voltage between E.C.U. terminal 15 and ground changes during engine warm up.
Cold → Hot:
Approximately 5 - 0V

N.G. → B 1) Check fuel temperature sensor resistance.
• Stop engine.
• Disconnect fuel temperature sensor harness connector.
• Check resistance between terminal and ground.

20°C (68°F)	2.3 – 2.7 kΩ
50°C (122°F)	0.77 – 0.87 kΩ
80°C (176°F)	0.30 – 0.33 kΩ

If no continuity, replace fuel temperature sensor.

2) Check power source for E.C.U. & ground circuit for E.C.U.

O.K.

Reinstall any part removed.

Erase the self-diagnosis memory.

Perform driving test and then perform self-diagnosis (Mode-III) again.

N.G. → 1) Perform E.C.U. input/output signal inspection test.
2) If N.G., recheck the E.C.U. pin terminals damage or the connection of E.C.U. harness connector.

O.K.

INSPECTION END

START SIGNAL (Switch ON/OFF diagnosis)

ECCS SELF-DIAGNOSTIC CHART – 1987–88 PORT INJECTED MAXIMA

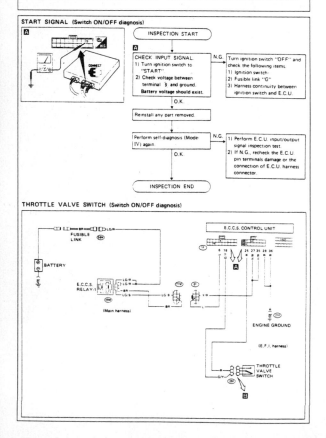

START SIGNAL (Switch ON/OFF diagnosis)

INSPECTION START

A CHECK INPUT SIGNAL.
1) Turn ignition switch to "START".
2) Check voltage between terminal 9 and ground.
Battery voltage should exist.

N.G. → Turn ignition switch "OFF" and check the following items.
1) Ignition switch
2) Fusible link "G"
3) Harness continuity between ignition switch and E.C.U.

O.K.

Reinstall any part removed.

Perform self-diagnosis (Mode-IV) again.

N.G. → 1) Perform E.C.U. input/output signal inspection test.
2) If N.G., recheck the E.C.U. pin terminals damage or the connection of E.C.U. harness connector.

O.K.

INSPECTION END

THROTTLE VALVE SWITCH (Switch ON/OFF diagnosis)

ECCS SELF-DIAGNOSTIC CHART – 1987–88 PORT INJECTED MAXIMA

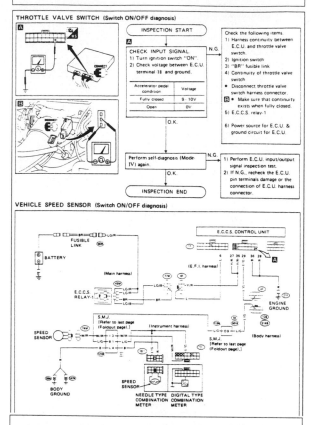

THROTTLE VALVE SWITCH (Switch ON/OFF diagnosis)

INSPECTION START

A CHECK INPUT SIGNAL.
1) Turn ignition switch "ON".
2) Check voltage between E.C.U. terminal 18 and ground.

Accelerator pedal condition	Voltage
Fully closed	9 - 10V
Open	0V

N.G. → Check the following items.
1) Harness continuity between E.C.U. and throttle valve switch.
2) Ignition switch
3) "BR" fusible link
4) Continuity of throttle valve switch
• Disconnect throttle valve switch harness connector.
B • Make sure that continuity exists when fully closed.
5) E.C.C.S. relay-1
6) Power source for E.C.U. & ground circuit for E.C.U.

O.K.

Perform self-diagnosis (Mode-IV) again.

N.G. → 1) Perform E.C.U. input/output signal inspection test.
2) If N.G., recheck the E.C.U. pin terminals damage or the connection of E.C.U. harness connector.

O.K.

INSPECTION END

VEHICLE SPEED SENSOR (Switch ON/OFF diagnosis)

ECCS SELF-DIAGNOSTIC CHART – 1987–88 PORT INJECTED MAXIMA

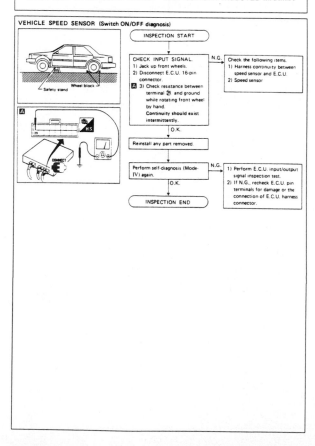

VEHICLE SPEED SENSOR (Switch ON/OFF diagnosis)

INSPECTION START

A CHECK INPUT SIGNAL.
1) Jack up front wheels.
2) Disconnect E.C.U. 16-pin connector.
A 3) Check resistance between terminal 25 and ground while rotating front wheel by hand.
Continuity should exist intermittently.

N.G. → Check the following items.
1) Harness continuity between speed sensor and E.C.U.
2) Speed sensor

O.K.

Reinstall any part removed.

Perform self-diagnosis (Mode-IV) again.

N.G. → 1) Perform E.C.U. input/output signal inspection test.
2) If N.G., recheck E.C.U. pin terminals for damage or the connection of E.C.U. harness connector.

O.K.

INSPECTION END

ECCS SELF-DIAGNOSTIC CHART – 1987–88 PORT INJECTED MAXIMA

EXHAUST GAS SENSOR (Not self-diagnostic item)

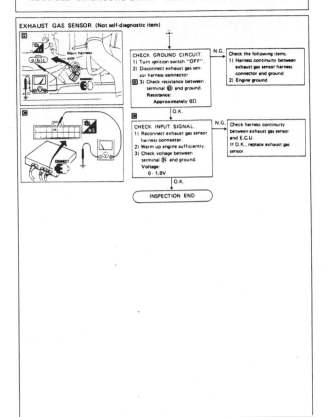

CHECK GROUND CIRCUIT.
1) Turn ignition switch "OFF".
2) Disconnect exhaust gas sensor harness connector.
3) Check resistance between terminal ⓒ and ground.
   Resistance:
   Approximately 0Ω

N.G. → Check the following items.
1) Harness continuity between exhaust gas sensor harness connector and ground
2) Engine ground

O.K.

CHECK INPUT SIGNAL.
1) Reconnect exhaust gas sensor harness connector.
2) Warm up engine sufficiently.
3) Check voltage between terminal ㉔ and ground.
   Voltage:
   0 - 1.0V

N.G. → Check harness continuity between exhaust gas sensor and E.C.U.
If O.K., replace exhaust gas sensor.

O.K.

→ **INSPECTION END**

ECCS SELF-DIAGNOSTIC CHART – 1987–88 PORT INJECTED MAXIMA

INJECTOR (Not self-diagnostic item)

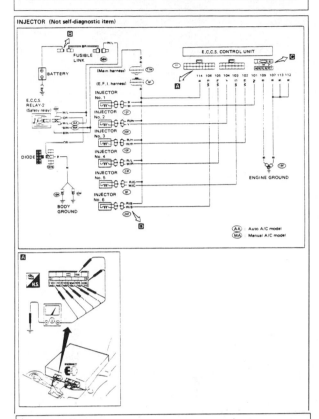

Ⓐ Ⓐ : Auto A/C model
Ⓜ Ⓐ : Manual A/C model

ECCS SELF-DIAGNOSTIC CHART – 1987–88 PORT INJECTED MAXIMA

EXHAUST GAS SENSOR (Not self-diagnostic item)

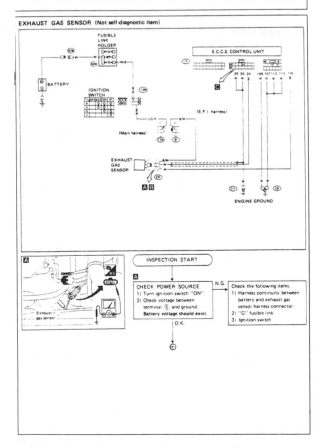

→ **INSPECTION START**

CHECK POWER SOURCE.
1) Turn ignition switch "ON".
2) Check voltage between terminal ⓒ and ground.
   Battery voltage should exist.

N.G. → Check the following items.
1) Harness continuity between battery and exhaust gas sensor harness connector
2) "G" fusible link
3) Ignition switch

O.K.

ECCS SELF-DIAGNOSTIC CHART – 1987–88 PORT INJECTED MAXIMA

INJECTOR (Not self-diagnostic item)

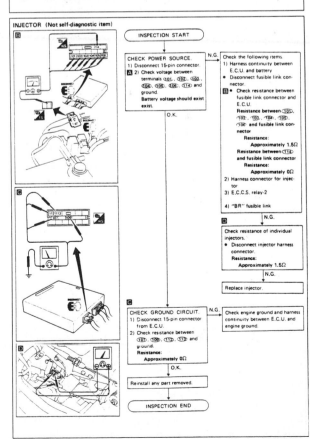

→ **INSPECTION START**

CHECK POWER SOURCE.
1) Disconnect 15-pin connector.
2) Check voltage between terminals ⑩①, ⑩②, ⑩③, ⑩④, ⑩⑤, ⑩⑥, ⑪④ and ground.
   Battery voltage should exist.

N.G. → Check the following items.
1) Harness continuity between E.C.U. and battery
   • Disconnect fusible link connector.
   Check resistance between fusible link connector and E.C.U.
   Resistance between ⑩①, ⑩②, ⑩③, ⑩④, ⑩⑥ and fusible link connector
   Resistance:
   Approximately 1.5Ω
   Resistance between ⑪④ and fusible link connector
   Resistance:
   Approximately 0Ω
2) Harness connector for injector
3) E.C.C.S. relay-2
4) "BR" fusible link

N.G.

Check resistance of individual injectors.
• Disconnect injector harness connector.
   Resistance:
   Approximately 1.5Ω

N.G.

Replace injector.

O.K.

CHECK GROUND CIRCUIT.
1) Disconnect 15-pin connector from E.C.U.
2) Check resistance between ⑩⑦, ⑩⑨, ⑪②, ⑪③ and ground.
   Resistance:
   Approximately 0Ω

N.G. → Check engine ground and harness continuity between E.C.U. and engine ground.

O.K.

Reinstall any part removed.

→ **INSPECTION END**

ECCS SELF-DIAGNOSTIC CHART – 1987–88 PORT INJECTED MAXIMA

POWER SOURCE FOR E.C.U. & GROUND CIRCUIT FOR E.C.U. (Not self-diagnostic item)

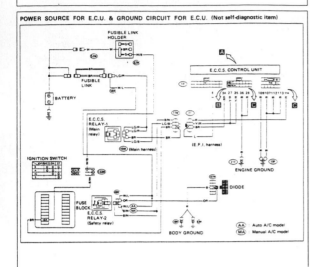

ECCS SELF-DIAGNOSTIC CHART – 1987–88 PORT INJECTED MAXIMA

MAIN RELAY (Not self-diagnostic item)

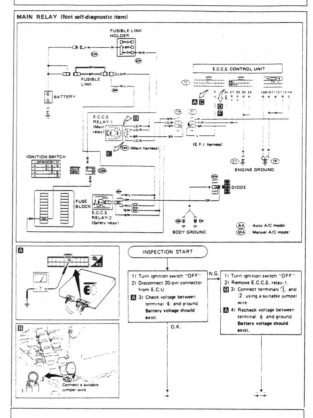

ECCS SELF-DIAGNOSTIC CHART – 1987–88 PORT INJECTED MAXIMA

POWER SOURCE FOR E.C.U. & GROUND CIRCUIT FOR E.C.U. (Not self-diagnostic item)

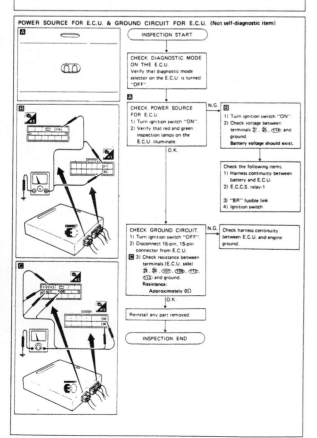

ECCS SELF-DIAGNOSTIC CHART – 1987–88 PORT INJECTED MAXIMA

MAIN RELAY (Not self-diagnostic item)

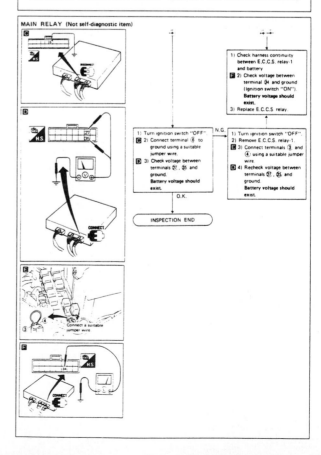

ECCS SELF-DIAGNOSTIC CHART—1987–88 PORT INJECTED MAXIMA

A.I.V. CONTROL (Not self-diagnostic item)

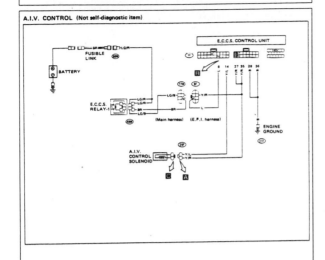

ECCS SELF-DIAGNOSTIC CHART—1987–88 PORT INJECTED MAXIMA

E.G.R. CONTROL (Not self-diagnostic item)

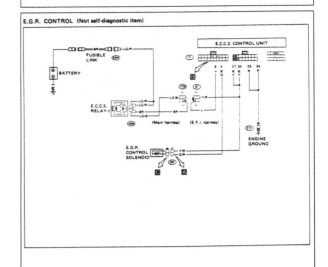

ECCS SELF-DIAGNOSTIC CHART—1987–88 PORT INJECTED MAXIMA

A.I.V. CONTROL (Not self-diagnostic item)

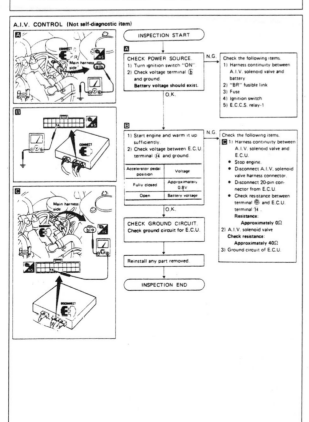

ECCS SELF-DIAGNOSTIC CHART—1987–88 PORT INJECTED MAXIMA

E.G.R. CONTROL (Not self-diagnostic item)

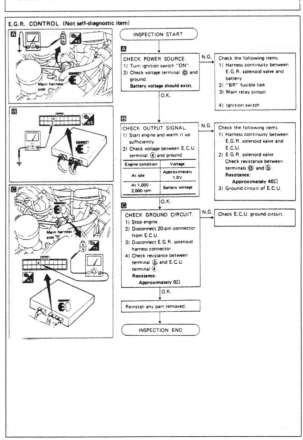

ECCS SELF-DIAGNOSTIC CHART – 1987–88 PORT INJECTED MAXIMA

IDLE-UP CONTROL (Not self-diagnostic item)

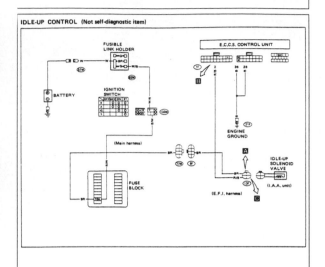

ECCS SELF-DIAGNOSTIC CHART – 1987–88 PORT INJECTED MAXIMA

FUEL PUMP RELAY (Not self-diagnostic item)

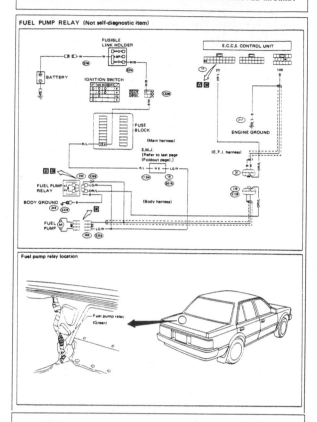

Fuel pump relay location

ECCS SELF-DIAGNOSTIC CHART – 1987–88 PORT INJECTED MAXIMA

IDLE-UP CONTROL (Not self-diagnostic item)

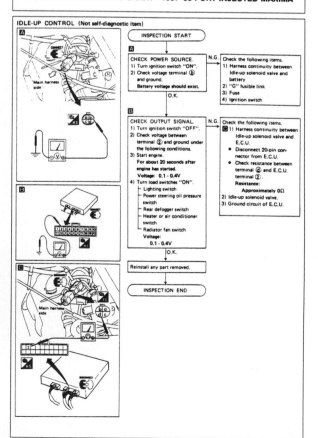

ECCS SELF-DIAGNOSTIC CHART – 1987–88 PORT INJECTED MAXIMA

FUEL PUMP RELAY (Not self-diagnostic item)

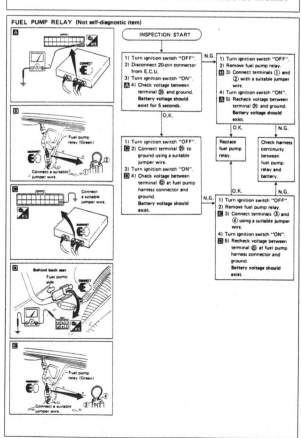

ECCS SELF-DIAGNOSTIC CHART – 1987–88 PORT INJECTED MAXIMA

NEUTRAL/INHIBITOR SWITCH (Not self-diagnostic item)

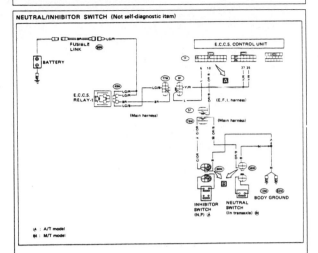

(A): A/T model
(M): M/T model

NEUTRAL/INHIBITOR SWITCH (Not self-diagnostic item)

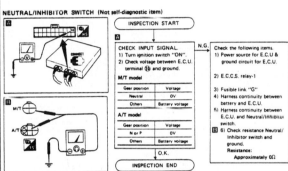

CHECK INPUT SIGNAL.
1) Turn ignition switch "ON".
2) Check voltage between E.C.U. terminal (15) and ground.

M/T model

Gear position	Voltage
Neutral	0V
Others	Battery voltage

A/T model

Gear position	Voltage
N or P	0V
Others	Battery voltage

N.G. Check the following items.
1) Power source for E.C.U & ground circuit for E.C.U.
2) E.C.C.S. relay-1
3) Fusible link "G"
4) Harness continuity between battery and E.C.U.
5) Harness continuity between E.C.U. and Neutral/Inhibitor switch.
6) Check resistance Neutral/Inhibitor switch and ground.
Resistance:
Approximately 0Ω

O.K.

INSPECTION END

ECCS SELF-DIAGNOSTIC CHART – 1987–88 PORT INJECTED MAXIMA

PRESSURE REGULATOR CONTROL SOLENOID (Not self-diagnostic item)

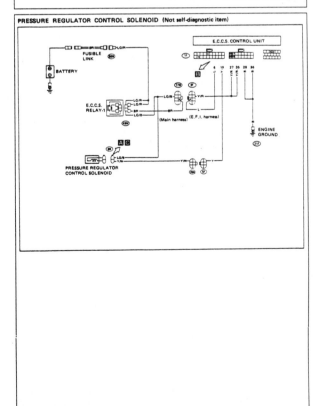

PRESSURE REGULATOR CONTROL SOLENOID

ECCS SELF-DIAGNOSTIC CHART – 1987–88 PORT INJECTED MAXIMA

PRESSURE REGULATOR CONTROL SOLENOID (Not self-diagnostic item)

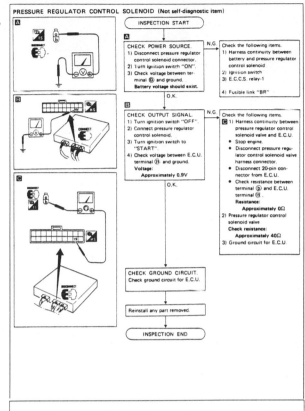

INSPECTION START

CHECK POWER SOURCE.
1) Disconnect pressure regulator control solenoid connector.
2) Turn ignition switch "ON".
3) Check voltage between terminal (C) and ground.
Battery voltage should exist.

N.G. Check the following items.
1) Harness continuity between battery and pressure regulator control solenoid
2) Ignition switch
3) E.C.C.S. relay-1
4) Fusible link "BR"

O.K.

CHECK OUTPUT SIGNAL.
1) Turn ignition switch "OFF".
2) Connect pressure regulator control solenoid.
3) Turn ignition switch to "START".
4) Check voltage between E.C.U. terminal (19) and ground.
Voltage:
Approximately 0.9V

N.G. Check the following items.
1) Harness continuity between pressure regulator control solenoid valve and E.C.U.
   • Stop engine.
   • Disconnect pressure regulator control solenoid valve harness connector.
   • Disconnect 20-pin connector from E.C.U.
   • Check resistance between terminal (b) and E.C.U. terminal (19)
   Resistance:
   Approximately 0Ω
2) Pressure regulator control solenoid valve
   Check resistance:
   Approximately 40Ω
3) Ground circuit for E.C.U.

O.K.

CHECK GROUND CIRCUIT.
Check ground circuit for E.C.U.

Reinstall any part removed.

INSPECTION END

ECCS SELF-DIAGNOSTIC CHART – 1987–88 PORT INJECTED MAXIMA

AIR REGULATOR (Not self-diagnostic item)

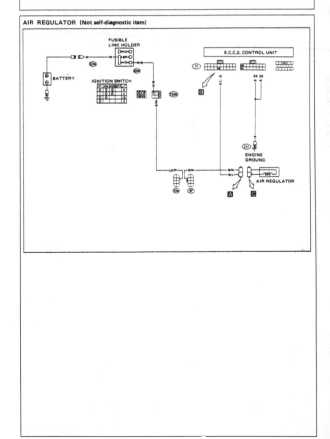

ECCS SELF-DIAGNOSTIC CHART – 1987-88 PORT INJECTED MAXIMA

AIR REGULATOR (Not self-diagnostic item)

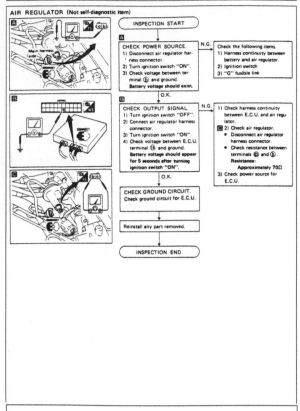

INSPECTION START

A CHECK POWER SOURCE.
1) Disconnect air regulator harness connector.
2) Turn ignition switch "ON".
3) Check voltage between terminal ⓑ and ground.
Battery voltage should exist.
O.K.

N.G. → Check the following items.
1) Harness continuity between battery and air regulator.
2) Ignition switch
3) "G" fusible link

CHECK OUTPUT SIGNAL.
1) Turn ignition switch "OFF".
2) Connect air regulator harness connector.
3) Turn ignition switch "ON".
4) Check voltage between E.C.U. terminal ⑯ and ground.
Battery voltage should appear for 5 seconds after turning ignition switch "ON".
O.K.

N.G. →
1) Check harness continuity between E.C.U. and air regulator.
2) Check air regulator.
  • Disconnect air regulator harness connector.
  • Check resistance between terminals ⓒ and ⓑ.
    Resistance:
    Approximately 70Ω.
3) Check power source for E.C.U.

CHECK GROUND CIRCUIT.
Check ground circuit for E.C.U.

Reinstall any part removed.

INSPECTION END

MIXTURE RATIO FEEDBACK SYSTEM INSPECTION CHART 1987-88 PORT INJECTED MAXIMA

PREPARATION
1. Make sure that the following parts are in good order.
   • Battery
   • Ignition system
   • Engine oil and coolant levels
   • Fuses
   • E.C.C.S. harness connectors
   • Vacuum hoses
   • Air intake system
     (oil filler cap, oil level gauge, etc.)
   • Fuel pressure

   • A.I.V. hose
   • Engine compression
   • E.G.R. valve operation
   • Throttle valve
2. On air conditioner equipped models, checks should be carried out while the air conditioner is "OFF".
3. When measuring "CO" percentage, insert probe more than 40 cm (15.7 in) into tail pipe.

Overall inspection sequence

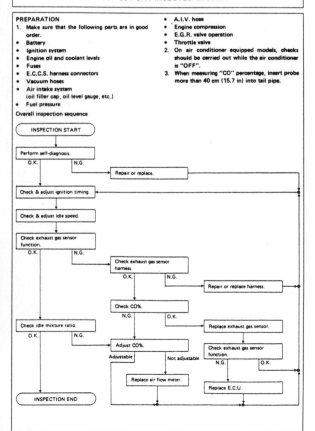

INSPECTION START

Perform self-diagnosis.
O.K. / **N.G.** → Repair or replace.

Check & adjust ignition timing.

Check & adjust idle speed.

Check exhaust gas sensor function.
O.K. / **N.G.** → Check exhaust gas sensor harness.
O.K. / **N.G.** → Repair or replace harness.

Check idle mixture ratio.
O.K. / **N.G.** → Check CO%.
N.G. / **O.K.** → Replace exhaust gas sensor.

Adjust CO%.
Adjustable / **Not adjustable** → Check exhaust gas sensor function.
N.G. / **O.K.**

Replace air flow meter.

Replace E.C.U.

INSPECTION END

MIXTURE RATIO FEEDBACK SYSTEM INSPECTION CHART 1987-88 PORT INJECTED MAXIMA

Idle Check and Set Procedure

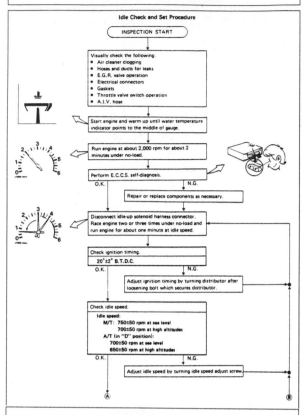

INSPECTION START

Visually check the following:
  • Air cleaner clogging
  • Hoses and ducts for leaks
  • E.G.R. valve operation
  • Electrical connectors
  • Gaskets
  • Throttle valve switch operation
  • A.I.V. hose

Start engine and warm up until water temperature indicator points to the middle of gauge.

Run engine at about 2,000 rpm for about 2 minutes under no-load.

Perform E.C.C.S. self-diagnosis.
O.K. / **N.G.** → Repair or replace components as necessary.

Disconnect idle-up solenoid harness connector. Race engine two or three times under no-load and run engine for about one minute at idle speed.

Check ignition timing.
20°±2° B.T.D.C.
O.K. / **N.G.** → Adjust ignition timing by turning distributor after loosening bolt which secures distributor.

Check idle speed.
Idle speed:
  M/T: 750±50 rpm at sea level
       700±50 rpm at high altitudes
  A/T (in "D" position):
       700±50 rpm at sea level
       650±50 rpm at high altitudes
O.K. / **N.G.** → Adjust idle speed by turning idle speed adjust screw.

Ⓐ   Ⓑ

MIXTURE RATIO FEEDBACK SYSTEM INSPECTION CHART 1987-88 PORT INJECTED MAXIMA

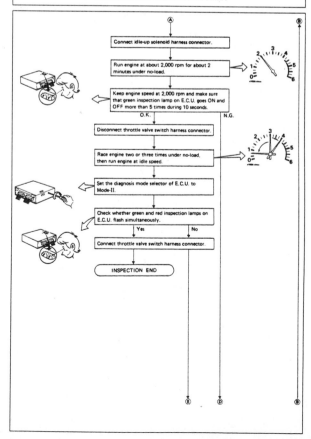

Ⓐ   Ⓑ

Connect idle-up solenoid harness connector.

Run engine at about 2,000 rpm for about 2 minutes under no-load.

Keep engine speed at 2,000 rpm and make sure that green inspection lamp on E.C.U. goes ON and OFF more than 5 times during 10 seconds.
O.K. / **N.G.**

Disconnect throttle valve switch harness connector.

Race engine two or three times under no-load, then run engine at idle speed.

Set the diagnosis mode selector of E.C.U. to Mode-II.

Check whether green and red inspection lamps on E.C.U. flash simultaneously.
Yes / **No**

Connect throttle valve switch harness connector.

INSPECTION END

Ⓔ   Ⓓ   Ⓑ

MIXTURE RATIO FEEDBACK SYSTEM INSPECTION CHART
1987–88 PORT INJECTED MAXIMA

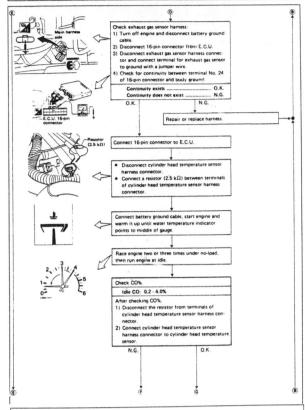

Check exhaust gas sensor harness:
1) Turn off engine and disconnect battery ground cable.
2) Disconnect 16-pin connector from E.C.U.
3) Disconnect exhaust gas sensor harness connector and connect terminal for exhaust gas sensor to ground with a jumper wire.
4) Check for continuity between terminal No. 24 of 16-pin connector and body ground!

Continuity exists .... O.K.
Continuity does not exist .... N.G.

O.K. / N.G.

Repair or replace harness.

Connect 16-pin connector to E.C.U.

• Disconnect cylinder head temperature sensor harness connector.
• Connect a resistor (2.5 kΩ) between terminals of cylinder head temperature sensor harness connector.

Connect battery ground cable, start engine and warm it up until water temperature indicator points to middle of gauge.

Race engine two or three times under no-load, then run engine at idle.

Check CO%.

Idle CO: 0.2 - 4.0%

After checking CO%.
1) Disconnect the resistor from terminals of cylinder head temperature sensor harness connector.
2) Connect cylinder head temperature sensor harness connector to cylinder head temperature sensor.

N.G. / O.K.

MIXTURE RATIO FEEDBACK SYSTEM INSPECTION CHART
1987–88 PORT INJECTED MAXIMA

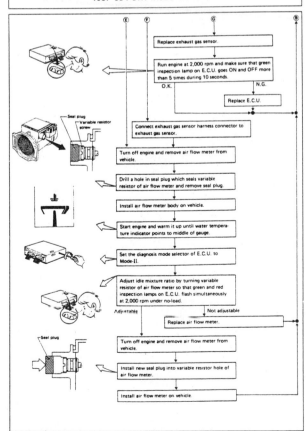

Replace exhaust gas sensor.

Run engine at 2,000 rpm and make sure that green inspection lamp on E.C.U. goes ON and OFF more than 5 times during 10 seconds.

O.K. / N.G.

Replace E.C.U.

Connect exhaust gas sensor harness connector to exhaust gas sensor.

Turn off engine and remove air flow meter from vehicle.

Drill a hole in seal plug which seals variable resistor of air flow meter and remove seal plug.

Install air flow meter body on vehicle.

Start engine and warm it up until water temperature indicator points to middle of gauge.

Set the diagnosis mode selector of E.C.U. to Mode-II.

Adjust idle mixture ratio by turning variable resistor of air flow meter so that green and red inspection lamps on E.C.U. flash simultaneously at 2,000 rpm under no-load.

Adjustable / Not adjustable

Replace air flow meter.

Turn off engine and remove air flow meter from vehicle.

Install new seal plug into variable resistor hole of air flow meter.

Install air flow meter on vehicle.

ECCS SELF-DIAGNOSTIC CHART – 1987–88 PORT INJECTED PULSAR

POWER SOURCE & GROUND CIRCUIT FOR E.C.U. (Not self-diagnostic item)

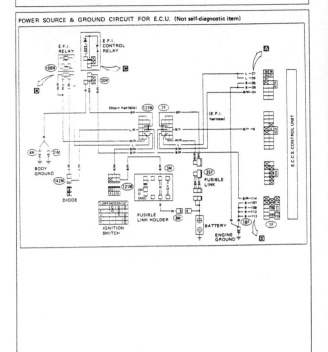

ECCS SELF-DIAGNOSTIC CHART – 1987–88 PORT INJECTED PULSAR

POWER SOURCE & GROUND CIRCUIT FOR E.C.U. (Not self-diagnostic item)

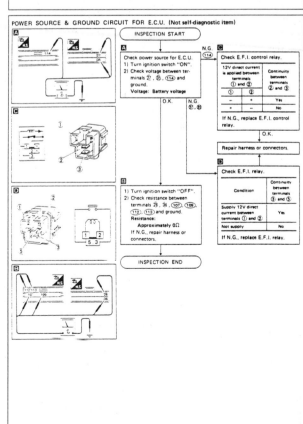

INSPECTION START

Check power source for E.C.U.
1) Turn ignition switch "ON".
2) Check voltage between terminals 27, 35, 114 and ground.
Voltage: Battery voltage

O.K. / N.G.

Check E.F.I. control relay.

12V direct current is applied between terminals ① and ②	Continuity between terminals ② and ③
①	②	
–	+	Yes
+	–	No

If N.G., replace E.F.I. control relay.

O.K.

Repair harness or connectors.

Check E.F.I. relay.

Condition	Continuity between terminals ③ and ⑤
Supply 12V direct current between terminals ① and ②	Yes
Not supply	No

If N.G., replace E.F.I. relay.

1) Turn ignition switch "OFF".
2) Check resistance between terminals 28, 36, 107, 108, 112, 113 and ground.
Resistance: Approximately 0Ω
If N.G., repair harness or connectors.

INSPECTION END

ECCS SELF-DIAGNOSTIC CHART – 1987–88 PORT INJECTED PULSAR

ECCS SELF-DIAGNOSTIC CHART – 1987–88 PORT INJECTED PULSAR

CRANK ANGLE SENSOR (Code No. 11)

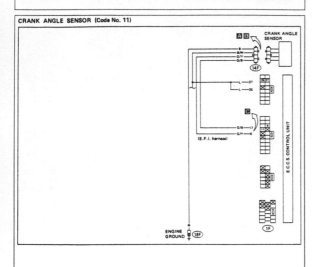

AIR FLOW METER (Code No. 12)

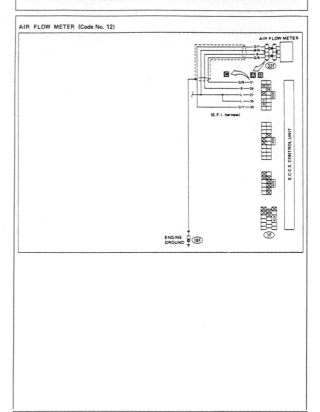

ECCS SELF-DIAGNOSTIC CHART – 1987–88 PORT INJECTED PULSAR

ECCS SELF-DIAGNOSTIC CHART – 1987–88 PORT INJECTED PULSAR

CRANK ANGLE SENSOR (Code No. 11)

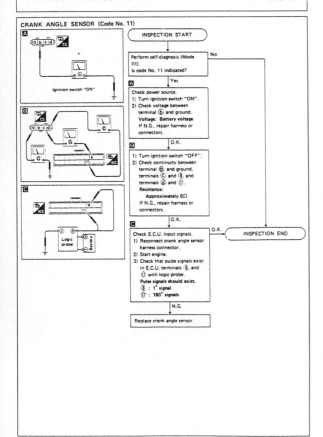

AIR FLOW METER (Code No. 12)

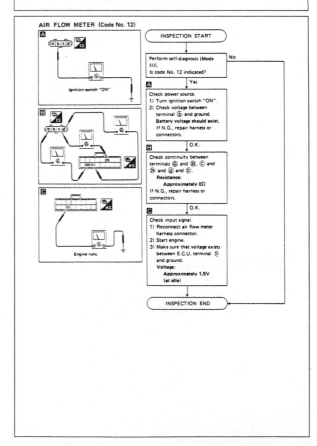

ECCS SELF-DIAGNOSTIC CHART—1987–88 PORT INJECTED PULSAR

WATER TEMPERATURE SENSOR (Code No. 13)

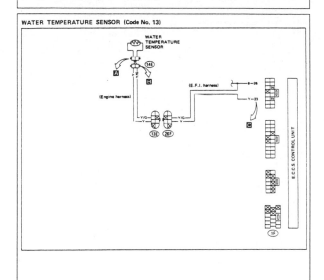

ECCS SELF-DIAGNOSTIC CHART—1987–88 PORT INJECTED PULSAR

IGNITION SIGNAL (Code No. 21)

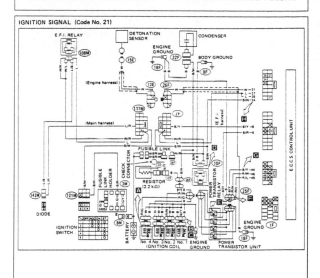

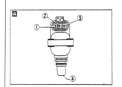

ECCS SELF-DIAGNOSTIC CHART—1987–88 PORT INJECTED PULSAR

WATER TEMPERATURE SENSOR (Code No. 13)

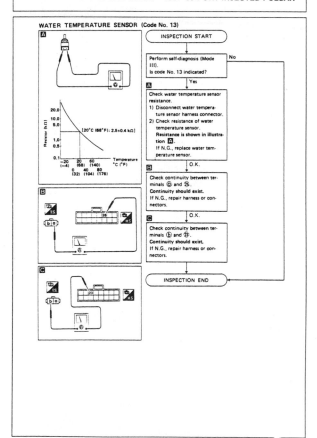

ECCS SELF-DIAGNOSTIC CHART—1987–88 PORT INJECTED PULSAR

IGNITION SIGNAL (Code No. 21)

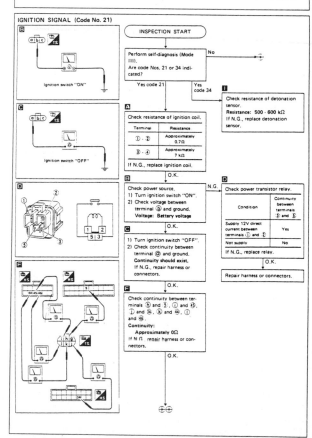

ECCS SELF-DIAGNOSTIC CHART – 1987–88 PORT INJECTED PULSAR

IGNITION SIGNAL (Code No. 21)

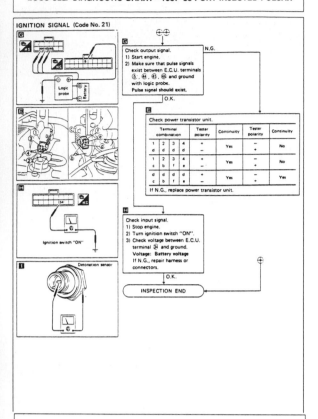

G Check output signal.
1) Start engine.
2) Make sure that pulse signals exist between E.C.U. terminals ⑤, 44, 45, 46 and ground with logic probe. Pulse signal should exist.

N.G. →

O.K. ↓

E Check power transistor unit.

Terminal combination				Tester polarity	Continuity	Tester polarity	Continuity
1	2	3	4	+	Yes	–	No
d	d	d	d	–		+	
1	2	3	4	+	Yes	–	No
c	b	f	e	–		+	
d	d	d	d	+	Yes	–	Yes
c	b	f	e	–		+	

If N.G., replace power transistor unit.

↓

H Check input signal.
1) Stop engine.
2) Turn ignition switch "ON".
3) Check voltage between E.C.U. terminal 34 and ground.
Voltage: Battery voltage
If N.G., repair harness or connectors.

O.K. ↓

(INSPECTION END)

ECCS SELF-DIAGNOSTIC CHART – 1987–88 PORT INJECTED PULSAR

FUEL PUMP (Not self-diagnosis item)

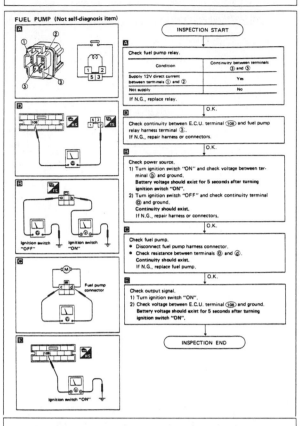

(INSPECTION START)

A Check fuel pump relay.

Condition	Continuity between terminals ③ and ⑤
Supply 12V direct current between terminals ① and ②	Yes
Not supply	No

If N.G., replace relay.

O.K. ↓

D Check continuity between E.C.U. terminal ⑩⑥ and fuel pump relay harness terminal ③.
If N.G., repair harness or connectors.

O.K. ↓

B Check power source.
1) Turn ignition switch "ON" and check voltage between terminal ⓑ and ground.
Battery voltage should exist for 5 seconds after turning ignition switch "ON".
2) Turn ignition switch "OFF" and check continuity terminal ⓓ and ground.
Continuity should exist.
If N.G., repair harness or connectors.

O.K. ↓

C Check fuel pump.
• Disconnect fuel pump harness connector.
• Check resistance between terminals ⓒ and ⓓ.
Continuity should exist.
If N.G., replace fuel pump.

O.K. ↓

E Check output signal.
1) Turn ignition switch "ON".
2) Check voltage between E.C.U. terminal ⑩⑥ and ground.
Battery voltage should exist for 5 seconds after turning ignition switch "ON".

(INSPECTION END)

ECCS SELF-DIAGNOSTIC CHART – 1987–88 PORT INJECTED PULSAR

FUEL PUMP (Not self-diagnosis item)

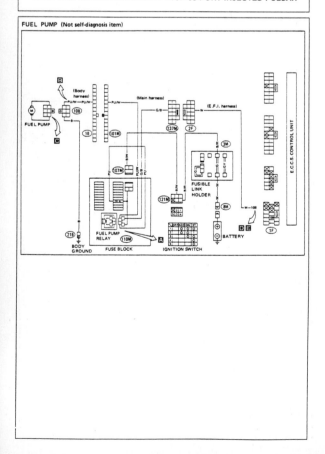

ECCS SELF-DIAGNOSTIC CHART – 1987–88 PORT INJECTED PULSAR

START SIGNAL (Switch ON/OFF diagnosis)

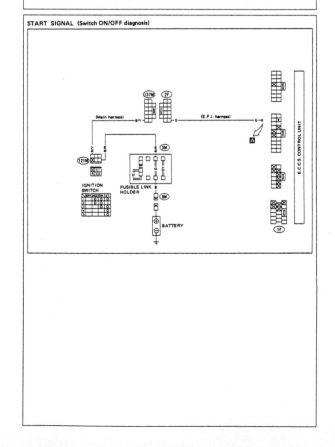

ECCS SELF-DIAGNOSTIC CHART – 1987–88 PORT INJECTED PULSAR

START SIGNAL (Switch ON/OFF diagnosis)

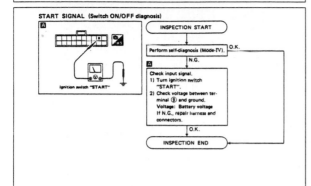

INSPECTION START

Perform self-diagnosis (Mode-IV).   O.K.

N.G.

Check input signal.
1) Turn ignition switch "START".
2) Check voltage between terminal ⑨ and ground.
   Voltage: Battery voltage
   If N.G., repair harness and connectors.

O.K.

INSPECTION END

ECCS SELF-DIAGNOSTIC CHART – 1987–88 PORT INJECTED PULSAR

THROTTLE VALVE SWITCH (Switch ON/OFF diagnosis)

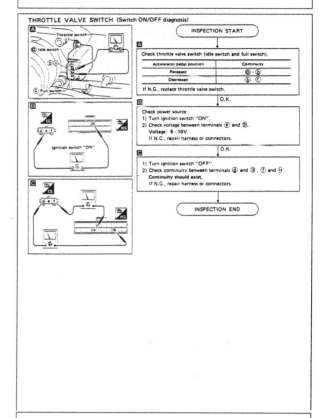

INSPECTION START

Check throttle valve switch (idle switch and full switch).

Accelerator pedal position	Continuity
Released	ⓒ - ⓑ
Depressed	ⓑ - ⓒ

If N.G., replace throttle valve switch.

O.K.

Check power source.
1) Turn ignition switch "ON".
2) Check voltage between terminals ⓔ and ㉕.
   Voltage: 9 - 10V
   If N.G., repair harness or connectors.

O.K.

1) Turn ignition switch "OFF".
2) Check continuity between terminals ⓓ and ⑱, ⓕ and ⑭.
   Continuity should exist.
   If N.G., repair harness or connectors.

INSPECTION END

ECCS SELF-DIAGNOSTIC CHART – 1987–88 PORT INJECTED PULSAR

THROTTLE VALVE SWITCH (Switch ON/OFF diagnosis)

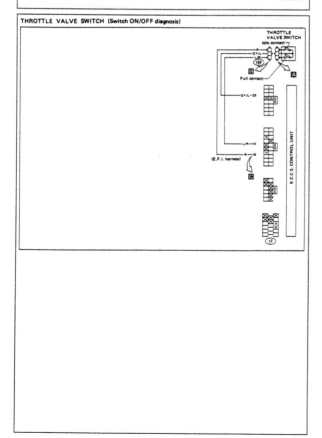

ECCS SELF-DIAGNOSTIC CHART – 1987–88 PORT INJECTED PULSAR

VEHICLE SPEED SENSOR (Switch ON/OFF diagnosis)

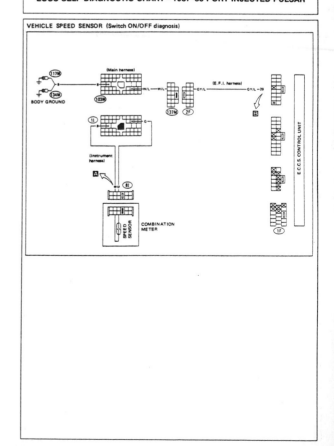

ECCS SELF-DIAGNOSTIC CHART – 1987–88 PORT INJECTED PULSAR

VEHICLE SPEED SENSOR (Switch ON/OFF diagnosis)

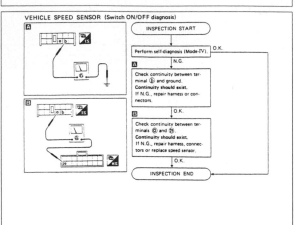

ECCS SELF-DIAGNOSTIC CHART – 1987–88 PORT INJECTED PULSAR

AUXILIARY AIR CONTROL (A.A.C.) VALVE (Not self-diagnostic item)

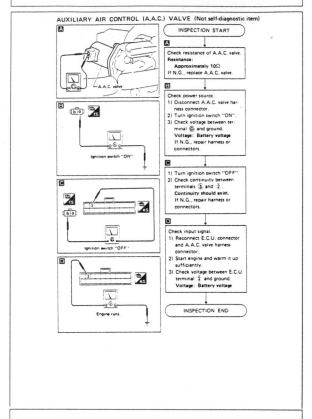

ECCS SELF-DIAGNOSTIC CHART – 1987–88 PORT INJECTED PULSAR

AUXILIARY AIR CONTROL (A.A.C.) VALVE (Not self-diagnostic item)

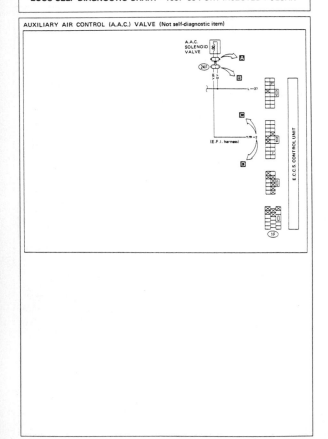

ECCS SELF-DIAGNOSTIC CHART – 1987–88 PORT INJECTED PULSAR

I.A.A. CONTROL (F.I.C.D. CONTROL) (Not self-diagnosis item)

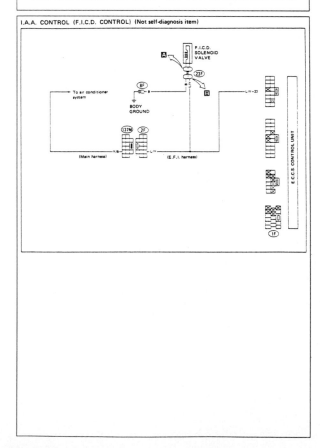

ECCS SELF-DIAGNOSTIC CHART — 1987–88 PORT INJECTED PULSAR

I.A.A. CONTROL (F.I.C.D. CONTROL) (Not self-diagnosis item)

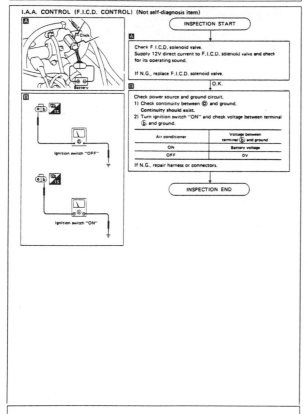

INSPECTION START

A Check F.I.C.D. solenoid valve.
Supply 12V direct current to F.I.C.D. solenoid valve and check for its operating sound.
If N.G., replace F.I.C.D. solenoid valve.

O.K.

B Check power source and ground circuit.
1) Check continuity between ⓒ and ground.
Continuity should exist.
2) Turn ignition switch "ON" and check voltage between terminal ⓑ and ground.

Air conditioner	Voltage between terminal ⓑ and ground
ON	Battery voltage
OFF	0V

If N.G., repair harness or connectors.

INSPECTION END

ECCS SELF-DIAGNOSTIC CHART — 1987–88 PORT INJECTED PULSAR

AIR REGULATOR (Not self-diagnostic item)

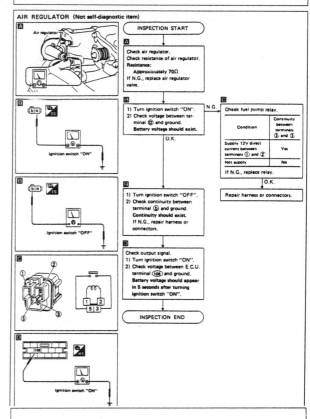

INSPECTION START

A Check air regulator.
Check resistance of air regulator.
Resistance:
Approximately 70Ω
If N.G., replace air regulator valve.

B 1) Turn ignition switch "ON".
2) Check voltage between terminal ⓓ and ground.
Battery voltage should exist.

N.G. → **C** Check fuel pump relay.

Condition	Continuity between terminals ③ and ⑤
Supply 12V direct current between terminals ① and ②	Yes
Not supply	No

If N.G., replace relay.

Repair harness or connectors.

O.K.

H 1) Turn ignition switch "OFF".
2) Check continuity between terminal ⓑ and ground.
Continuity should exist.
If N.G., repair harness or connectors.

G Check output signal.
1) Turn ignition switch "ON".
2) Check voltage between E.C.U. terminal (108) and ground.
Battery voltage should appear in 5 seconds after turning ignition switch "ON".

INSPECTION END

ECCS SELF-DIAGNOSTIC CHART — 1987–88 PORT INJECTED PULSAR

AIR REGULATOR (Not self-diagnostic item)

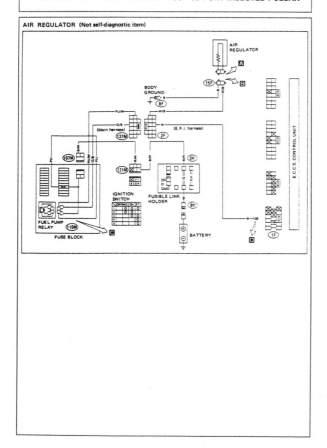

ECCS SELF-DIAGNOSTIC CHART — 1987–88 PORT INJECTED PULSAR

INJECTOR (Not self-diagnosis item)

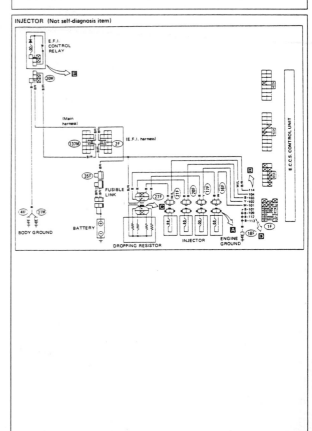

ECCS SELF-DIAGNOSTIC CHART—1987–88 PORT INJECTED PULSAR

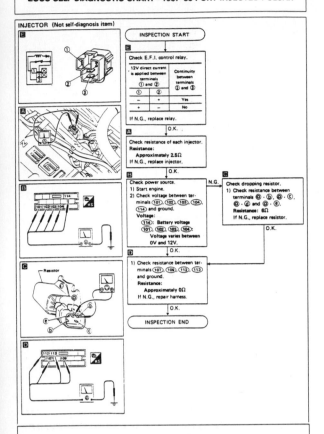

ECCS SELF-DIAGNOSTIC CHART—1987–88 PORT INJECTED PULSAR

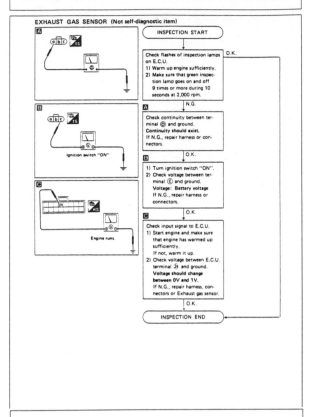

ECCS SELF-DIAGNOSTIC CHART—1987–88 PORT INJECTED PULSAR

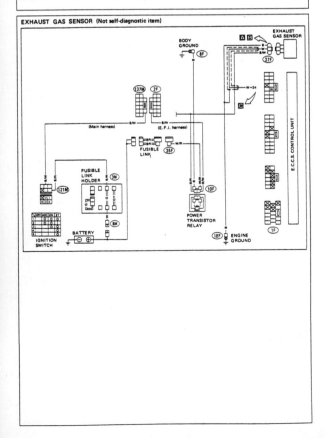

ECCS SELF-DIAGNOSTIC CHART—1987–88 PORT INJECTED PULSAR

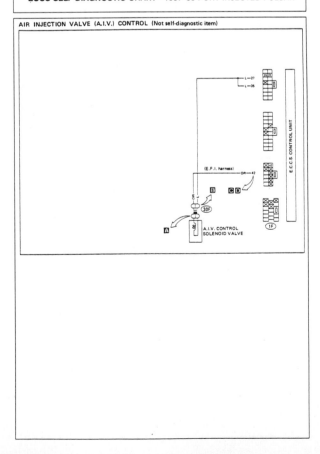

ECCS SELF-DIAGNOSTIC CHART — 1987–88 PORT INJECTED PULSAR

AIR INJECTION VALVE (A.I.V.) CONTROL (Not self-diagnostic item)

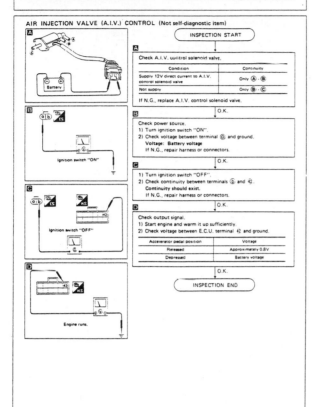

INSPECTION START

A Check A.I.V. control solenoid valve.

Condition	Continuity
Supply 12V direct current to A.I.V. control solenoid valve	Only (A) - (B)
Not supply	Only (B) - (C)

If N.G., replace A.I.V. control solenoid valve.

O.K.

B Check power source.
1) Turn ignition switch "ON".
2) Check voltage between terminal (a) and ground.
   Voltage: Battery voltage
   If N.G., repair harness or connectors.

O.K.

C 1) Turn ignition switch "OFF".
2) Check continuity between terminals (b) and 42.
   Continuity should exist.
   If N.G., repair harness or connectors.

O.K.

D Check output signal.
1) Start engine and warm it up sufficiently.
2) Check voltage between E.C.U. terminal 42 and ground.

Accelerator pedal position	Voltage
Released	Approximately 0.8V
Depressed	Battery voltage

O.K.

INSPECTION END

ECCS SELF-DIAGNOSTIC CHART — 1987–88 PORT INJECTED PULSAR

E.G.R. CONTROL (Not self-diagnosis item)

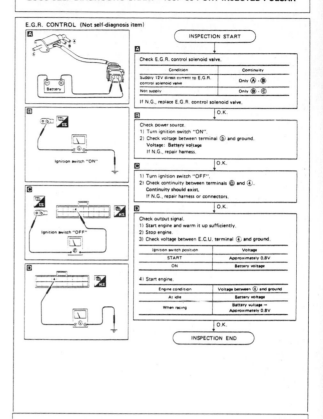

INSPECTION START

A Check E.G.R. control solenoid valve.

Condition	Continuity
Supply 12V direct current to E.G.R. control solenoid valve	Only (A) - (B)
Not supply	Only (B) - (C)

If N.G., replace E.G.R. control solenoid valve.

O.K.

B Check power source.
1) Turn ignition switch "ON".
2) Check voltage between terminal (b) and ground.
   Voltage: Battery voltage
   If N.G., repair harness.

O.K.

C 1) Turn ignition switch "OFF".
2) Check continuity between terminals (c) and ④.
   Continuity should exist.
   If N.G., repair harness or connectors.

O.K.

D Check output signal.
1) Start engine and warm it up sufficiently.
2) Stop engine.
3) Check voltage between E.C.U. terminal ④ and ground.

Ignition switch position	Voltage
START	Approximately 0.8V
ON	Battery voltage

4) Start engine.

Engine condition	Voltage between ④ and ground
At idle	Battery voltage
When racing	Battery voltage — Approximately 0.8V

O.K.

INSPECTION END

ECCS SELF-DIAGNOSTIC CHART — 1987–88 PORT INJECTED PULSAR

E.G.R. CONTROL (Not self-diagnosis item)

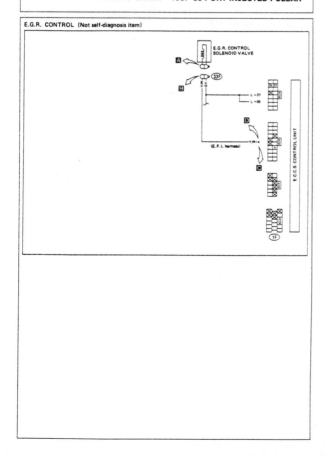

ECCS SELF-DIAGNOSTIC CHART — 1987–88 PORT INJECTED PULSAR

PRESSURE REGULATOR VACUUM RELEASE (P.R.V.R.) CONTROL SOLENOID VALVE
(Not self-diagnostic item)

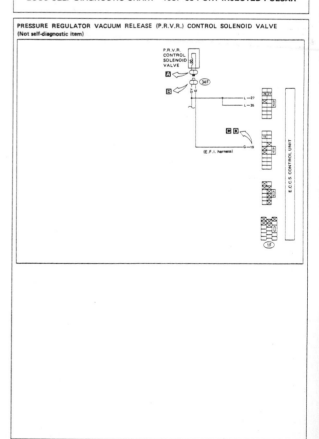

ECCS SELF-DIAGNOSTIC CHART—1987–88 PORT INJECTED PULSAR

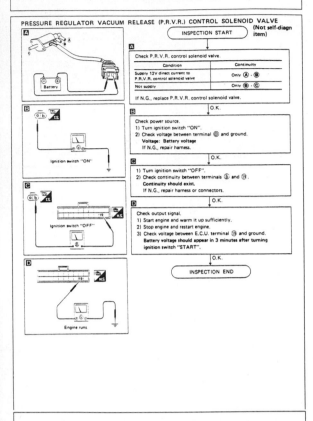

ECCS SELF-DIAGNOSTIC CHART—1987–88 PORT INJECTED PULSAR

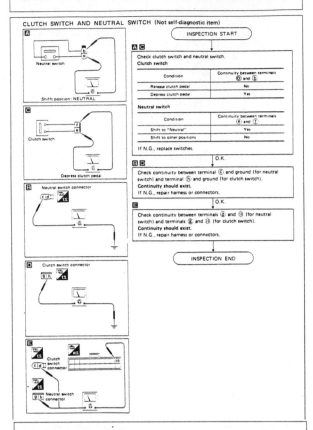

ECCS SELF-DIAGNOSTIC CHART—1987–88 PORT INJECTED PULSAR

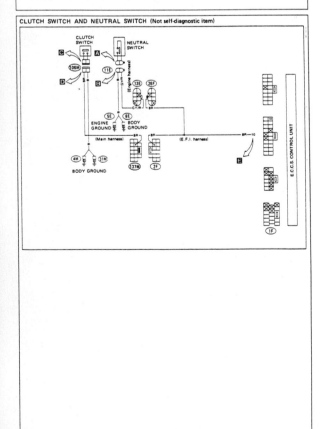

ECCS SELF-DIAGNOSTIC CHART—1987–88 PORT INJECTED PULSAR

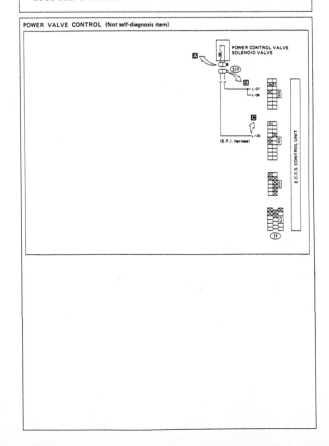

ECCS SELF-DIAGNOSTIC CHART – 1987–88 PORT INJECTED PULSAR

POWER VALVE CONTROL (Not self-diagnosis item)

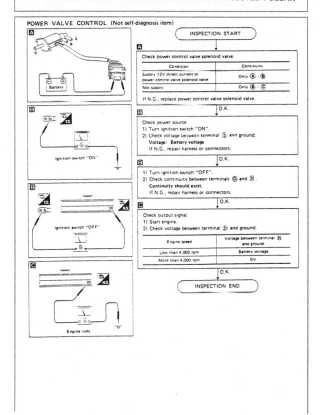

ECCS SELF-DIAGNOSTIC CHART – 1987–88 PORT INJECTED PULSAR

ALTITUDE SWITCH (Not self-diagnosis item)

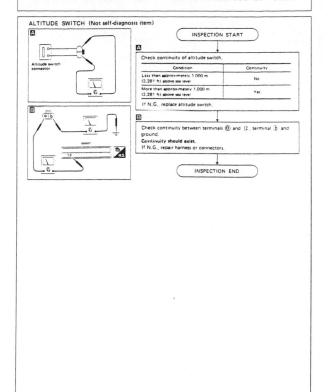

ECCS SELF-DIAGNOSTIC CHART – 1987–88 PORT INJECTED PULSAR

ALTITUDE SWITCH (Not self-diagnosis item)

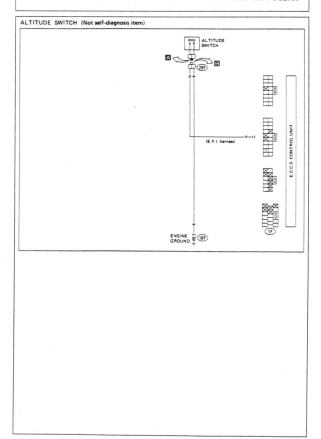

ECCS SELF-DIAGNOSTIC CHART – 1987–88 PORT INJECTED PULSAR

ACCELERATION CUT CONTROL (Not self-diagnostic item)

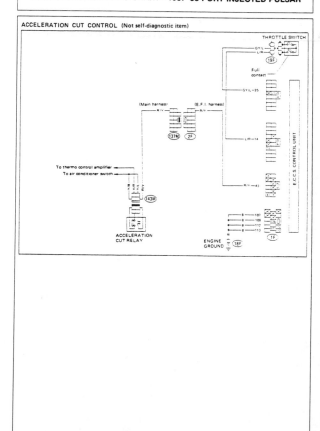

MIXTURE RATIO FEEDBACK SYSTEM INSPECTION CHART
1987–88 PORT INJECTED PULSAR

MIXTURE RATIO FEEDBACK SYSTEM INSPECTION

Preparation

1. Make sure that the following parts are in good order.
- Battery
- Ignition system
- Engine oil and coolant levels
- Fuses
- E.C.C.S. harness connectors
- Vacuum hoses
- Air intake system (oil filler cap, oil level gauge, etc.)

- Valve clearance, engine compression
- E.G.R. valve operation
- Throttle valve and throttle valve switch operation
2. On air conditioner equipped models, checks should be carried out while the air conditioner is "OFF".
3. When measuring "CO" percentage, insert probe more than 40 cm (15.7 in) into tail pipe.
4. Checking and adjusting should be done while the radiator cooling fan is stopped.

Overall inspection sequence

INSPECTION START

↓

Perform E.C.C.S. self-diagnosis.

↓

Check or adjust idle speed and ignition timing.

↓

Check idle mixture ratio by using E.C.U. inspection lamp (Green). → N.G. → Check exhaust gas sensor harness.

↓ O.K.

Check idle mixture ratio by using E.C.U. inspection lamps (Red and Green) (in diagnostic mode III). → Check base idle CO in tail pipe under the following conditions.
- Throttle valve switch harness connector disconnected (No A.I.V. controlled condition)
- Water temperature sensor harness connector disconnected and then 2.5 kΩ resistor connected
- Exhaust gas sensor harness connector disconnected

↓ O.K.

INSPECTION END

N.G. → Replace exhaust gas sensor. ← O.K. ← N.G.

↓

Adjust idle mixture ratio by using air flow meter by-pass screw.

MIXTURE RATIO FEEDBACK SYSTEM INSPECTION CHART
1987–88 PORT INJECTED PULSAR

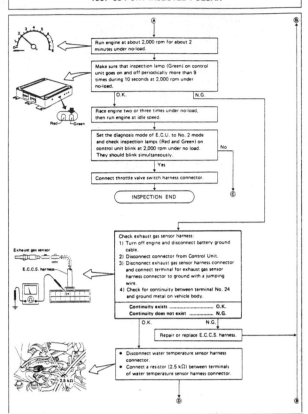

(A)

Run engine at about 2,000 rpm for about 2 minutes under no-load.

↓

Make sure that inspection lamp (Green) on control unit goes on and off periodically more than 9 times during 10 seconds at 2,000 rpm under no-load.

O.K. ↓   N.G. →

Race engine two or three times under no-load, then run engine at idle speed.

↓

Set the diagnosis mode of E.C.U. to No. 2 mode and check inspection lamps (Red and Green) on control unit blink at 2,000 rpm under no load. They should blink simultaneously. → No

↓ Yes

Connect throttle valve switch harness connector.

↓

INSPECTION END

Check exhaust gas sensor harness:
1) Turn off engine and disconnect battery ground cable.
2) Disconnect connector from Control Unit.
3) Disconnect exhaust gas sensor harness connector and connect terminal for exhaust gas sensor harness connector to ground with a jumping wire.
4) Check for continuity between terminal No. 24 and ground metal on vehicle body.

Continuity exists .... O.K.
Continuity does not exist .... N.G.

O.K. ↓   N.G. →

Repair or replace E.C.C.S. harness.

↓

- Disconnect water temperature sensor harness connector.
- Connect a resistor (2.5 kΩ) between terminals of water temperature sensor harness connector.

↓

(D)

(B)

MIXTURE RATIO FEEDBACK SYSTEM INSPECTION CHART
1987–88 PORT INJECTED PULSAR

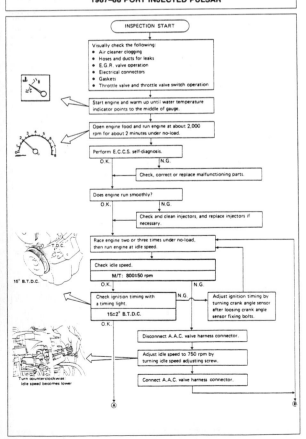

INSPECTION START

↓

Visually check the following:
- Air cleaner clogging
- Hoses and ducts for leaks
- E.G.R. valve operation
- Electrical connectors
- Gaskets
- Throttle valve and throttle valve switch operation

↓

Start engine and warm up until water temperature indicator points to the middle of gauge.

↓

Open engine hood and run engine at about 2,000 rpm for about 2 minutes under no-load.

↓

Perform E.C.C.S. self-diagnosis.

O.K. ↓   N.G. →

Check, correct or replace malfunctioning parts.

↓

Does engine run smoothly?

O.K. ↓   N.G. →

Check and clean injectors, and replace injectors if necessary.

↓

Race engine two or three times under no-load, then run engine at idle speed.

↓

Check idle speed.

M/T: 800±50 rpm

O.K. ↓   N.G. →

Check ignition timing with a timing light.

15±2° B.T.D.C. → N.G. → Adjust ignition timing by turning crank angle sensor after loosing crank angle sensor fixing bolts.

↓ O.K.

Disconnect A.A.C. valve harness connector.

↓

Adjust idle speed to 750 rpm by turning idle speed adjusting screw.

↓

Connect A.A.C. valve harness connector.

↓

(A)   (B)

Turn counterclockwise: Idle speed becomes lower

MIXTURE RATIO FEEDBACK SYSTEM INSPECTION CHART
1987–88 PORT INJECTED PULSAR

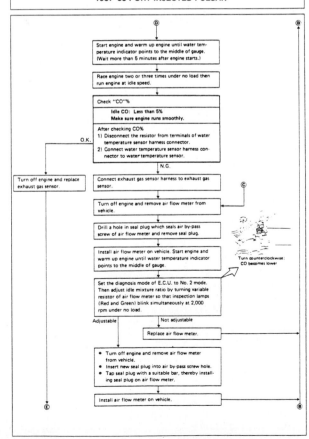

(D)   (B)

Start engine and warm up until water temperature indicator points to the middle of gauge. (Wait more than 5 minutes after engine starts.)

↓

Race engine two or three times under no load then run engine at idle speed.

↓

Check "CO"%

Idle CO: Less than 5%
Make sure engine runs smoothly.

After checking CO%
1) Disconnect the resistor from terminals of water temperature sensor harness connector.
2) Connect water temperature sensor harness connector to water temperature sensor.

O.K. ←   ↓ N.G.

Turn off engine and replace exhaust gas sensor.   Connect exhaust gas sensor harness to exhaust gas sensor.

↓

Turn off engine and remove air flow meter from vehicle.

↓

Drill a hole in seal plug which seals air by-pass screw of air flow meter and remove seal plug.

↓

Install air flow meter on vehicle. Start engine and warm up engine until water temperature indicator points to the middle of gauge.

↓

Set the diagnosis mode of E.C.U. to No. 2 mode. Then adjust idle mixture ratio by turning variable resistor of air flow meter so that inspection lamps (Red and Green) blink simultaneously at 2,000 rpm under no load.

Adjustable ↓   Not adjustable →

Replace air flow meter.

↓

- Turn off engine and remove air flow meter from vehicle.
- Insert new seal plug into air by-pass screw hole.
- Tap seal plug with a suitable bar, thereby installing seal plug on air flow meter.

↓

Install air flow meter on vehicle.

(E)   (B)

Turn counterclockwise: CO becomes lower

MIXTURE RATIO FEEDBACK SYSTEM INSPECTION CHART
1987–88 PORT INJECTED PULSAR

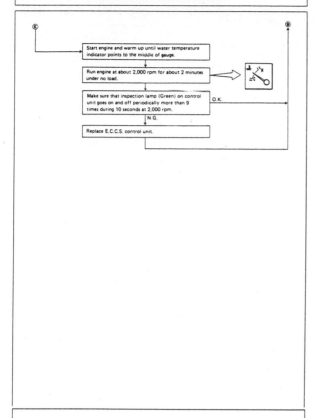

ECCS SELF-DIAGNOSTIC CHART – 1987–88 PORT INJECTED STANZA

CRANK ANGLE SENSOR (Code No. 11)

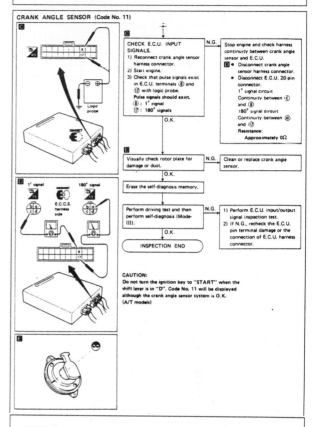

CAUTION:
Do not turn the ignition key to "START" when the shift lever is in "D". Code No. 11 will be displayed although the crank angle sensor system is O.K. (A/T models)

ECCS SELF-DIAGNOSTIC CHART – 1987–88 PORT INJECTED STANZA

CRANK ANGLE SENSOR (Code No. 11)

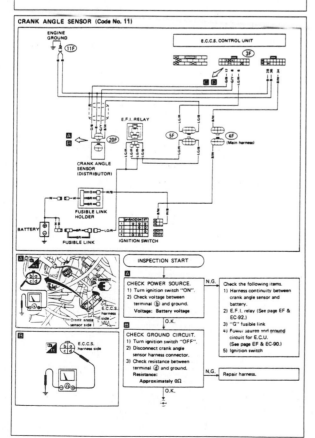

ECCS SELF-DIAGNOSTIC CHART – 1987–88 PORT INJECTED STANZA

AIR FLOW METER (Code No. 12)

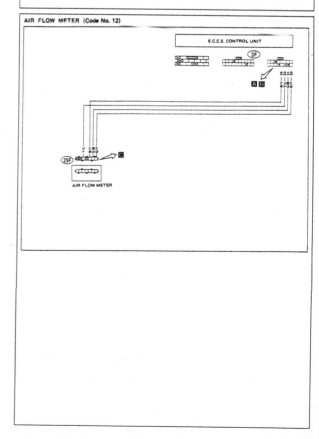

ECCS SELF-DIAGNOSTIC CHART—1987–88 PORT INJECTED STANZA

AIR FLOW METER (Code No. 12)

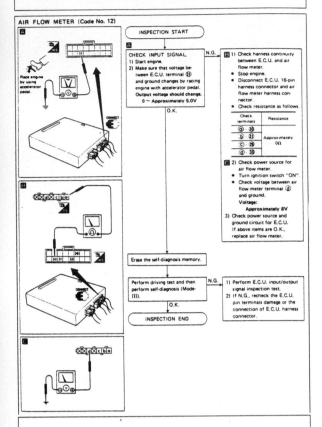

ECCS SELF-DIAGNOSTIC CHART—1987–88 PORT INJECTED STANZA

WATER TEMPERATURE SENSOR (Code No. 13)

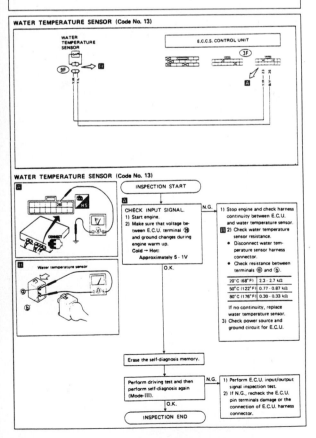

ECCS SELF-DIAGNOSTIC CHART—1987–88 PORT INJECTED STANZA

IGNITION SIGNAL (Code No. 21)

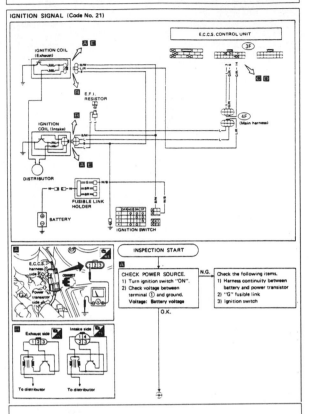

ECCS SELF-DIAGNOSTIC CHART—1987–88 PORT INJECTED STANZA

IGNITION SIGNAL (Code No. 21)

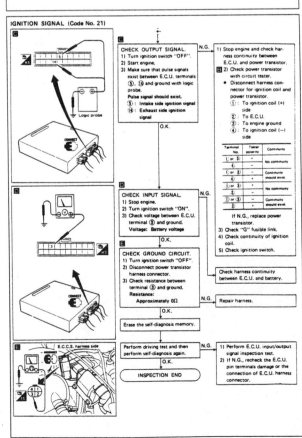

ECCS SELF-DIAGNOSTIC CHART—1987–88 PORT INJECTED STANZA

FUEL PUMP (Code No. 22)

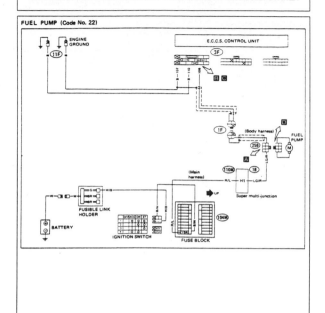

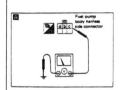

ECCS SELF-DIAGNOSTIC CHART—1987–88 PORT INJECTED STANZA

FUEL PUMP (Code No. 22)

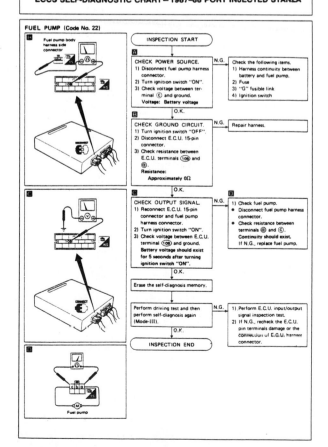

ECCS SELF-DIAGNOSTIC CHART—1987–88 PORT INJECTED STANZA

START SIGNAL (Switch ON/OFF diagnosis)

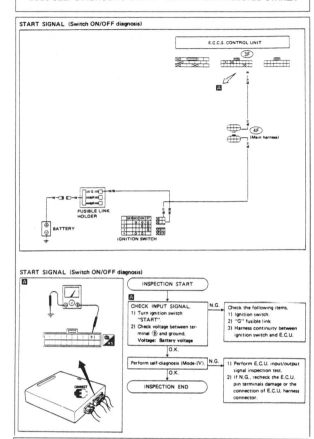

START SIGNAL (Switch ON/OFF diagnosis)

INSPECTION START

A CHECK INPUT SIGNAL.
1) Turn ignition switch "START".
2) Check voltage between terminal ⑨ and ground.
Voltage: Battery voltage

→ N.G. → Check the following items.
1) Ignition switch.
2) "G" fusible link
3) Harness continuity between ignition switch and E.C.U.

O.K.

Perform self-diagnosis (Mode-[V]).

→ N.G. → 1) Perform E.C.U. input/output signal inspection test.
2) If N.G., recheck the E.C.U. pin terminals damage or the connection of E.C.U. harness connector.

O.K.

INSPECTION END

ECCS SELF-DIAGNOSTIC CHART—1987–88 PORT INJECTED STANZA

THROTTLE VALVE SWITCH (Switch ON/OFF diagnosis)

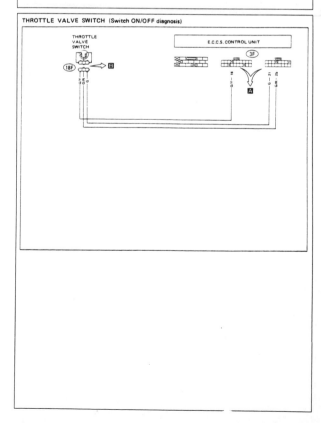

ECCS SELF-DIAGNOSTIC CHART – 1987–88 PORT INJECTED STANZA

THROTTLE VALVE SWITCH (Switch ON/OFF diagnosis)

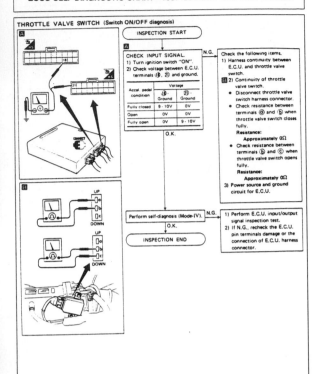

INSPECTION START

A
CHECK INPUT SIGNAL.
1) Turn ignition switch "ON".
2) Check voltage between E.C.U. terminals ⑲, ㉑ and ground.

Accel. pedal condition	Voltage	
	⑲ · Ground	㉑ · Ground
Fully closed	9 · 10V	0V
Open	0V	0V
Fully open	0V	9 · 10V

N.G. → Check the following items.
1) Harness continuity between E.C.U. and throttle valve switch.
B 2) Continuity of throttle valve switch.
• Disconnect throttle valve switch harness connector.
• Check resistance between terminals ⓐ and ⓑ when throttle valve switch closes fully.
Resistance:
Approximately 0Ω
• Check resistance between terminals ⓑ and ⓒ when throttle valve switch opens fully.
Resistance:
Approximately 0Ω
3) Power source and ground circuit for E.C.U.

O.K.

B
Perform self-diagnosis (Mode-IV).
N.G. → 1) Perform E.C.U. input/output signal inspection test.
2) If N.G., recheck the E.C.U. pin terminals damage or the connection of E.C.U. harness connector.

O.K.

INSPECTION END

ECCS SELF-DIAGNOSTIC CHART – 1987–88 PORT INJECTED STANZA

VEHICLE SPEED SENSOR (Switch ON/OFF diagnosis)

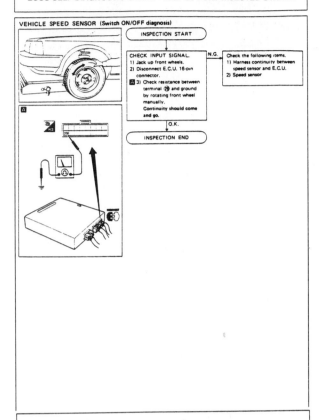

INSPECTION START

CHECK INPUT SIGNAL.
1) Jack up front wheels.
2) Disconnect E.C.U. 16-pin connector.
A 3) Check resistance between terminal ㉙ and ground by rotating front wheel manually. Continuity should come and go.

N.G. → Check the following items.
1) Harness continuity between speed sensor and E.C.U.
2) Speed sensor

O.K.

INSPECTION END

ECCS SELF-DIAGNOSTIC CHART – 1987–88 PORT INJECTED STANZA

VEHICLE SPEED SENSOR (Switch ON/OFF diagnosis)

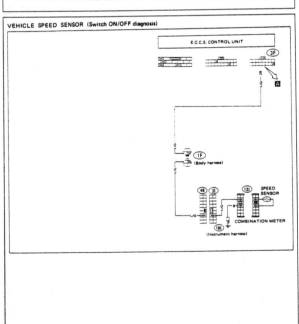

ECCS SELF-DIAGNOSTIC CHART – 1987–88 PORT INJECTED STANZA

AUXILIARY AIR CONTROL (A.A.C.) VALVE (Not self-diagnostic item)

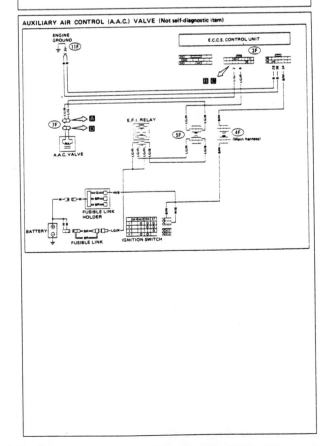

ECCS SELF-DIAGNOSTIC CHART—1987-88 PORT INJECTED STANZA

AUXILIARY AIR CONTROL (A.A.C.) VALVE (Not self-diagnostic item)

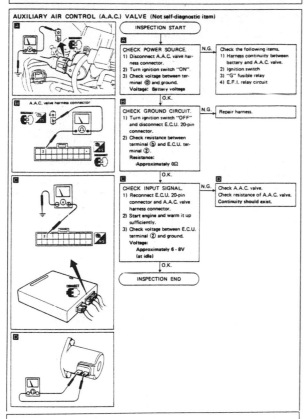

ECCS SELF-DIAGNOSTIC CHART—1987-88 PORT INJECTED STANZA

AIR REGULATOR (Not self-diagnostic item)

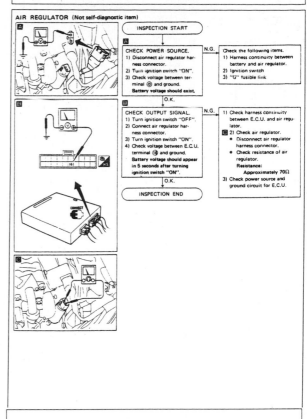

ECCS SELF-DIAGNOSTIC CHART—1987-88 PORT INJECTED STANZA

AIR REGULATOR (Not self-diagnostic item)

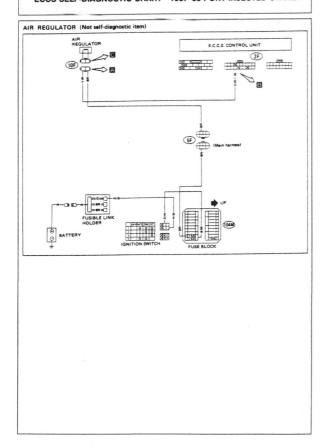

ECCS SELF-DIAGNOSTIC CHART—1987-88 PORT INJECTED STANZA

INJECTOR (Not self-diagnostic item)

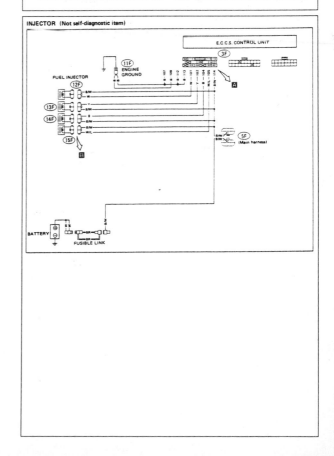

ECCS SELF-DIAGNOSTIC CHART — 1987–88 PORT INJECTED STANZA

INJECTOR (Not self-diagnostic item)

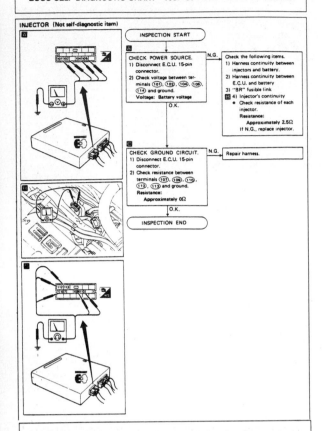

INSPECTION START

CHECK POWER SOURCE.
1) Disconnect E.C.U. 15-pin connector.
2) Check voltage between terminals (101), (102), (104), (105), (114) and ground.
   Voltage: Battery voltage

O.K.

N.G. → Check the following items.
1) Harness continuity between injectors and battery.
2) Harness continuity between E.C.U. and battery.
3) "BR" fusible link.
4) Injector's continuity
   • Check resistance of each injector.
   Resistance:
     Approximately 2.5Ω
   If N.G., replace injector.

CHECK GROUND CIRCUIT.
1) Disconnect E.C.U. 15-pin connector.
2) Check resistance between terminals (107), (109), (110), (112), (113) and ground.
   Resistance:
     Approximately 0Ω

O.K.

N.G. → Repair harness.

INSPECTION END

ECCS SELF-DIAGNOSTIC CHART — 1987–88 PORT INJECTED STANZA

EXHAUST GAS SENSOR (Not self-diagnostic item)

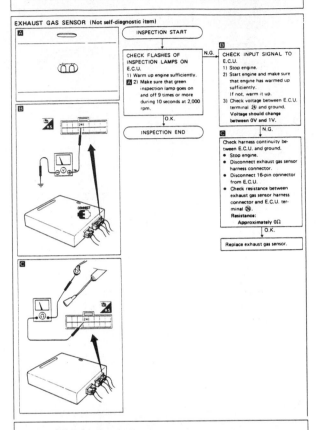

INSPECTION START

CHECK FLASHES OF INSPECTION LAMPS ON E.C.U.
1) Warm up engine sufficiently.
2) Make sure that green inspection lamp goes on and off 9 times or more during 10 seconds at 2,000 rpm.

O.K.

INSPECTION END

N.G. → CHECK INPUT SIGNAL TO E.C.U.
1) Stop engine.
2) Start engine and make sure that engine has warmed up sufficiently.
   If not, warm it up.
3) Check voltage between E.C.U. terminal 24 and ground.
   Voltage should change between 0V and 1V.

O.K. / N.G.

Check harness continuity between E.C.U. and ground.
• Stop engine.
• Disconnect exhaust gas sensor harness connector.
• Disconnect 16-pin connector from E.C.U.
• Check resistance between exhaust gas sensor connector and E.C.U. terminal 24.
   Resistance:
     Approximately 0Ω

O.K.

Replace exhaust gas sensor.

ECCS SELF-DIAGNOSTIC CHART — 1987–88 PORT INJECTED STANZA

EXHAUST GAS SENSOR (Not self-diagnostic item)

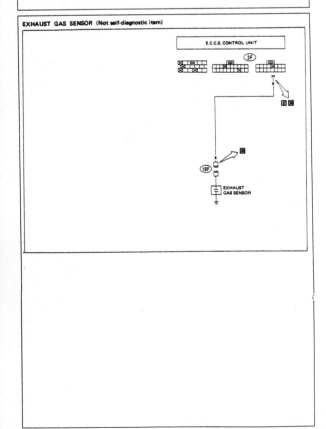

ECCS SELF-DIAGNOSTIC CHART — 1987–88 PORT INJECTED STANZA

SPARK PLUG SWITCHING CONTROL (Not self-diagnostic item)

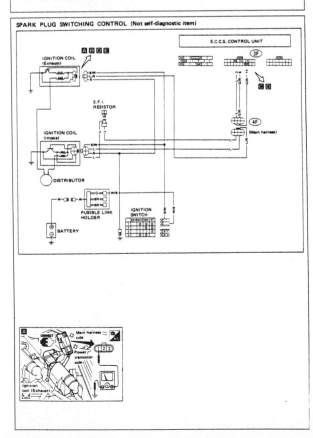

ECCS SELF-DIAGNOSTIC CHART – 1987–88 PORT INJECTED STANZA

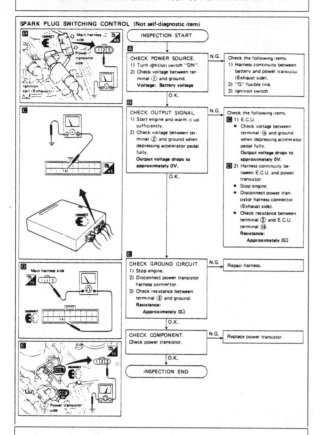

SPARK PLUG SWITCHING CONTROL (Not self-diagnostic item)

ECCS SELF-DIAGNOSTIC CHART – 1987–88 PORT INJECTED STANZA

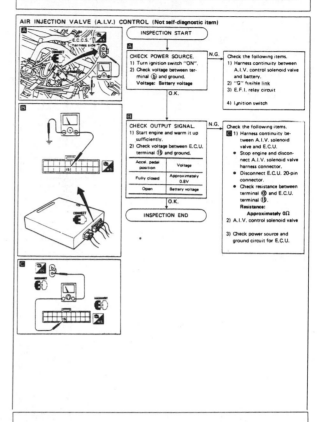

AIR INJECTION VALVE (A.I.V.) CONTROL (Not self-diagnostic item)

ECCS SELF-DIAGNOSTIC CHART – 1987–88 PORT INJECTED STANZA

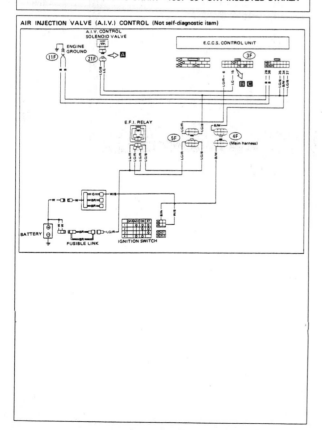

AIR INJECTION VALVE (A.I.V.) CONTROL (Not self-diagnostic item)

ECCS SELF-DIAGNOSTIC CHART – 1987–88 PORT INJECTED STANZA

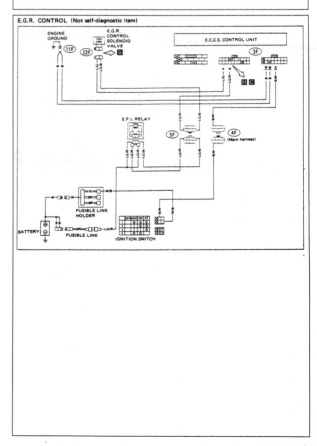

E.G.R. CONTROL (Not self-diagnostic item)

ECCS SELF-DIAGNOSTIC CHART—1987–88 PORT INJECTED STANZA

E.G.R. CONTROL (Not self-diagnostic item)

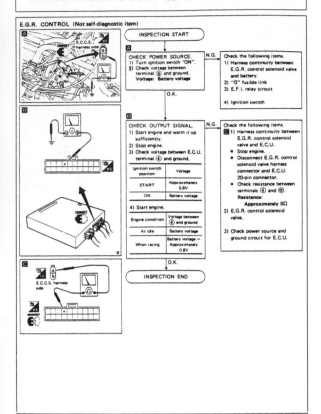

INSPECTION START

A CHECK POWER SOURCE.
1) Turn ignition switch "ON".
2) Check voltage between terminal ⓑ and ground.
  Voltage: Battery voltage

O.K.

N.G. → Check the following items.
1) Harness continuity between E.G.R. control solenoid valve and battery.
2) "G" fusible link
3) E.F.I. relay circuit
4) Ignition switch

B CHECK OUTPUT SIGNAL.
1) Start engine and warm it up sufficiently.
2) Stop engine.
3) Check voltage between E.C.U. terminal ④ and ground.

Ignition switch position	Voltage
START	Approximately 0.8V
ON	Battery voltage

4) Start engine.

Engine condition	Voltage between ④ and ground
At idle	Battery voltage
When racing	Battery voltage — Approximately 0.8V

N.G. → Check the following items.
C 1) Harness continuity between E.G.R. control solenoid valve and E.C.U.
● Stop engine.
● Disconnect E.G.R. control solenoid valve harness connector and E.C.U. 20-pin connector.
● Check resistance between terminals ④ and ⓐ.
  Resistance: Approximately 0Ω
2) E.G.R. control solenoid valve.

3) Check power source and ground circuit for E.C.U.

O.K.

INSPECTION END

C E.C.C.S. harness side

ECCS SELF-DIAGNOSTIC CHART—1987–88 PORT INJECTED STANZA

PRESSURE REGULATOR (P.R.) CONTROL SOLENOID VALVE (Not self-diagnostic item)

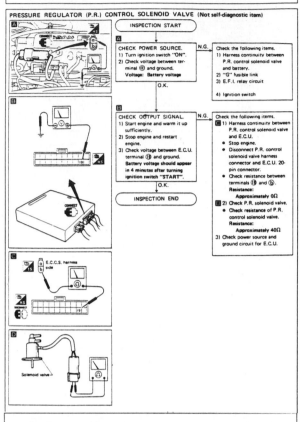

INSPECTION START

A CHECK POWER SOURCE.
1) Turn ignition switch "ON".
2) Check voltage between terminal ⓐ and ground.
  Voltage: Battery voltage

O.K.

N.G. → Check the following items.
1) Harness continuity between P.R. control solenoid valve and battery.
2) "G" fusible link
3) E.F.I. relay circuit
4) Ignition switch

B CHECK OUTPUT SIGNAL.
1) Start engine and warm it up sufficiently.
2) Stop engine and restart engine.
3) Check voltage between E.C.U. terminal ⑲ and ground. Battery voltage should appear in 4 minutes after turning ignition switch "START".

O.K.

INSPECTION END

N.G. → Check the following items.
C 1) Harness continuity between P.R. control solenoid valve and E.C.U.
● Stop engine.
● Disconnect P.R. control solenoid valve harness connector and E.C.U. 20-pin connector.
● Check resistance between terminals ⑲ and ⓑ.
  Resistance: Approximately 0Ω
D 2) Check P.R. solenoid valve.
● Check resistance of P.R. control solenoid valve.
  Resistance: Approximately 40Ω
3) Check power source and ground circuit for E.C.U.

C E.C.C.S. harness side
a
b

D Solenoid valve

ECCS SELF-DIAGNOSTIC CHART—1987–88 PORT INJECTED STANZA

PRESSURE REGULATOR (P.R.) CONTROL SOLENOID VALVE (Not self-diagnostic item)

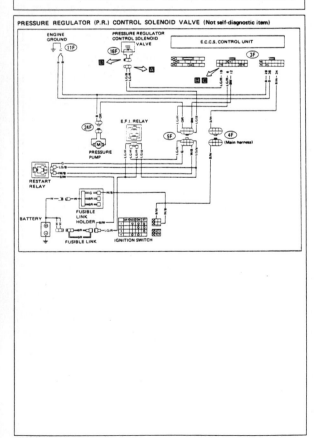

ECCS SELF-DIAGNOSTIC CHART—1987–88 PORT INJECTED STANZA

PRESSURE PUMP (Not self-diagnostic item)

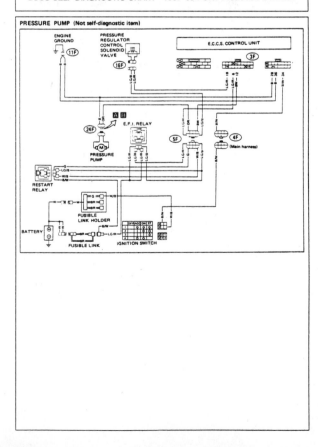

ECCS SELF-DIAGNOSTIC CHART—1987-88 PORT INJECTED STANZA

PRESSURE PUMP (Not self-diagnostic item)

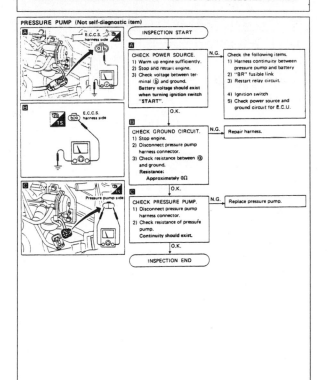

INSPECTION START

A CHECK POWER SOURCE.
1) Warm up engine sufficiently.
2) Stop and restart engine.
3) Check voltage between terminal ⓑ and ground.
   Battery voltage should exist when turning ignition switch "START".

N.G. → Check the following items.
1) Harness continuity between pressure pump and battery
2) "BR" fusible link
3) Restart relay circuit.
4) Ignition switch
5) Check power source and ground circuit for E.C.U.

O.K.

B CHECK GROUND CIRCUIT.
1) Stop engine.
2) Disconnect pressure pump harness connector.
3) Check resistance between ⓐ and ground.
   Resistance: Approximately 0Ω

N.G. → Repair harness.

O.K.

C CHECK PRESSURE PUMP.
1) Disconnect pressure pump harness connector.
2) Check resistance of pressure pump.
   Continuity should exist.

N.G. → Replace pressure pump.

O.K.

INSPECTION END

ECCS SELF-DIAGNOSTIC CHART—1987-88 PORT INJECTED STANZA

RESTART RELAY (For pressure pump) (Not self-diagnostic item)

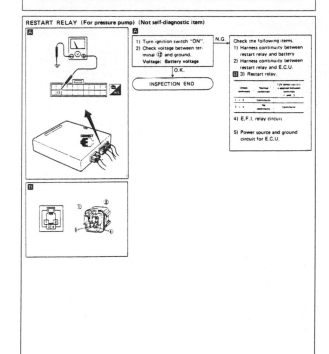

A
1) Turn ignition switch "ON".
2) Check voltage between terminal ⑫ and ground.
   Voltage: Battery voltage

N.G. → Check the following items.
1) Harness continuity between restart relay and battery
2) Harness continuity between restart relay and E.C.U.
3) Restart relay.

O.K.

INSPECTION END

4) E.F.I. relay circuit
5) Power source and ground circuit for E.C.U.

ECCS SELF-DIAGNOSTIC CHART—1987-88 PORT INJECTED STANZA

RESTART RELAY (For pressure pump) (Not self-diagnostic item)

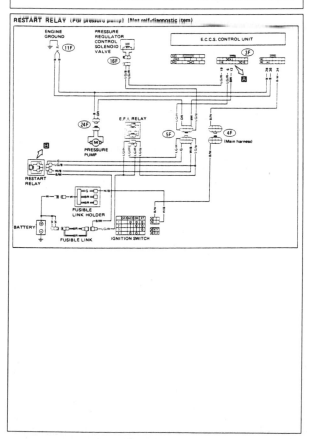

ECCS SELF-DIAGNOSTIC CHART—1987-88 PORT INJECTED STANZA

NEUTRAL SWITCH (Not self-diagnostic item)

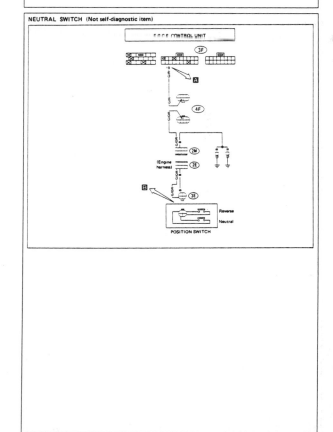

ECCS SELF-DIAGNOSTIC CHART – 1987–88 PORT INJECTED STANZA

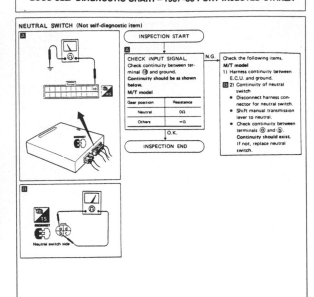

ECCS SELF-DIAGNOSTIC CHART – 1987–88 PORT INJECTED STANZA

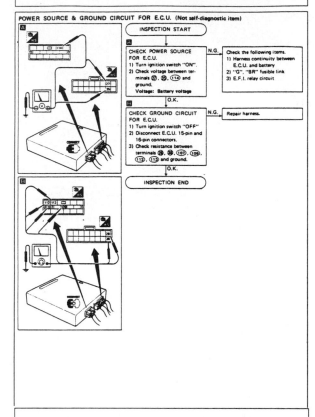

ECCS SELF-DIAGNOSTIC CHART – 1987–88 PORT INJECTED STANZA

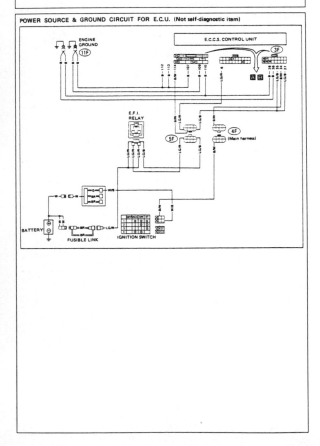

ECCS SELF-DIAGNOSTIC CHART – 1987–88 PORT INJECTED STANZA

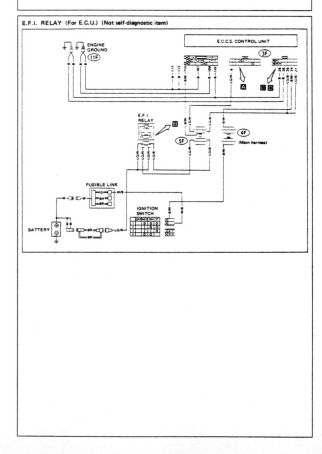

ECCS SELF-DIAGNOSTIC CHART – 1987–88 PORT INJECTED STANZA

E.F.I. RELAY (For E.C.U.) (Not self-diagnostic item)

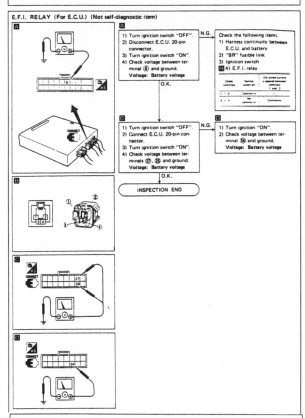

A
1) Turn ignition switch "OFF".
2) Disconnect E.C.U. 20-pin connector.
3) Turn ignition switch "ON".
4) Check voltage between terminal ⑥ and ground.
   Voltage: Battery voltage

N.G. → Check the following items:
1) Harness continuity between E.C.U. and battery
2) "BR" fusible link
3) Ignition switch
4) E.F.I. relay

O.K. ↓

C
1) Turn ignition switch "OFF".
2) Connect E.C.U. 20-pin connector.
3) Turn ignition switch "ON".
4) Check voltage between terminals ㉗, ㉟ and ground.
   Voltage: Battery voltage

N.G. → **D**
1) Turn ignition switch "ON".
2) Check voltage between terminal ㉞ and ground.
   Voltage: Battery voltage

O.K. ↓

INSPECTION END

MIXTURE RATIO FEEDBACK SYSTEM INSPECTION CHART
1987–88 PORT INJECTED STANZA

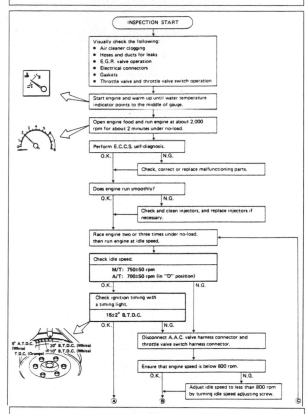

INSPECTION START

Visually check the following:
- Air cleaner clogging
- Hoses and ducts for leaks
- E.G.R. valve operation
- Electrical connectors
- Gaskets
- Throttle valve and throttle valve switch operation

↓

Start engine and warm up until water temperature indicator points to the middle of gauge.

↓

Open engine hood and run engine at about 2,000 rpm for about 2 minutes under no-load.

↓

Perform E.C.C.S. self-diagnosis.

O.K. ↓ / N.G. → Check, correct or replace malfunctioning parts.

↓

Does engine run smoothly?

O.K. ↓ / N.G. → Check and clean injectors, and replace injectors if necessary.

↓

Race engine two or three times under no-load, then run engine at idle speed.

↓

Check idle speed.
M/T: 750±50 rpm
A/T: 700±50 rpm (in "D" position)

O.K. ↓ / N.G. →

Check ignition timing with a timing light.
15±2° B.T.D.C.

O.K. ↓ (A) / N.G. →

Disconnect A.A.C. valve harness connector and throttle valve switch harness connector.

↓

Ensure that engine speed is below 800 rpm.

O.K. ↓ (B) / N.G. → Adjust idle speed to less than 800 rpm by turning idle speed adjusting screw. (C)

MIXTURE RATIO FEEDBACK SYSTEM INSPECTION CHART
1987–88 PORT INJECTED STANZA

MIXTURE RATIO FEEDBACK SYSTEM INSPECTION

Preparation

1. Make sure that the following parts are in good order.
   - Battery
   - Ignition system
   - Engine oil and coolant levels
   - Fuses
   - E.C.C.S. harness connectors
   - Vacuum hoses
   - Air intake system (oil filler cap, oil level gauge, etc.)
   - Valve clearance, engine compression
   - E.G.R. valve operation
   - Throttle valve and throttle valve switch operation

2. On air conditioner equipped models, checks should be carried out while the air conditioner is "OFF".

3. On automatic transaxle equipped models, when checking idle rpm, ignition timing and mixture ratio, checks should be carried out while shift lever is in "D" position.

4. When measuring "CO" percentage, insert probe more than 40 cm (15.7 in) into tail pipe.

5. Checking and adjusting should be done while the radiator cooling fan is stopped.

WARNING:

a. When selector lever is shifted to "D" position, apply parking brake and block both front and rear wheels with chocks.

b. Depress brake pedal while accelerating the engine to prevent forward surge of vehicle.

c. After the adjustment has been made, shift the lever to the "N" or "P" position and remove wheel chocks.

Overall inspection sequence

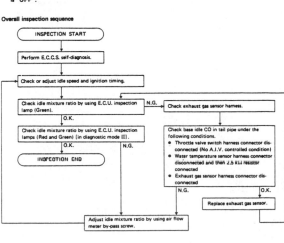

INSPECTION START

↓

Perform E.C.C.S. self-diagnosis.

↓

Check or adjust idle speed and ignition timing.

↓

Check idle mixture ratio by using E.C.U. inspection lamp (Green). **N.G.** → Check exhaust gas sensor harness.

O.K. ↓

Check idle mixture ratio by using E.C.U. inspection lamps (Red and Green) (in diagnostic mode II).

O.K. ↓ / N.G. →

INSPECTION END

Check base idle CO in tail pipe under the following conditions.
- Throttle valve switch harness connector disconnected (No A.I.V. controlled condition)
- Water temperature sensor harness connector disconnected and then 2.5 kΩ resistor connected
- Exhaust gas sensor harness connector disconnected

N.G. ↓ / O.K. → Replace exhaust gas sensor.

↓

Adjust idle mixture ratio by using air flow meter by-pass screw.

MIXTURE RATIO FEEDBACK SYSTEM INSPECTION CHART
1987–88 PORT INJECTED STANZA

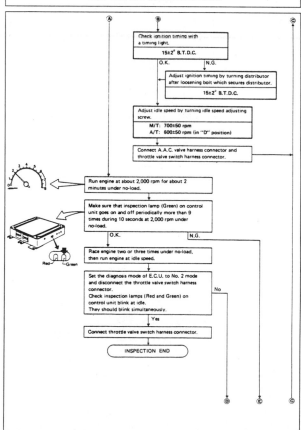

(A) (B)

Check ignition timing with a timing light.
15±2° B.T.D.C.

O.K. ↓ / N.G. →

Adjust ignition timing by turning distributor after loosening bolt which secures distributor.
15±2° B.T.D.C.

↓

Adjust idle speed by turning idle speed adjusting screw.
M/T: 700±50 rpm
A/T: 600±50 rpm (in "D" position)

↓

Connect A.A.C. valve harness connector and throttle valve switch harness connector.

↓

Run engine at about 2,000 rpm for about 2 minutes under no-load.

↓

Make sure that inspection lamp (Green) on control unit goes on and off periodically more than 9 times during 10 seconds at 2,000 rpm under no-load.

O.K. ↓ / N.G. →

Race engine two or three times under no-load, then run engine at idle speed.

↓

Set the diagnosis mode of E.C.U. to No. 2 mode and disconnect the throttle valve switch harness connector.
Check inspection lamps (Red and Green) on control unit blink at idle.
They should blink simultaneously.

No →

Yes ↓

Connect throttle valve switch harness connector.

↓

INSPECTION END

(D) (E) (d)

MIXTURE RATIO FEEDBACK SYSTEM INSPECTION CHART
1987–88 PORT INJECTED STANZA

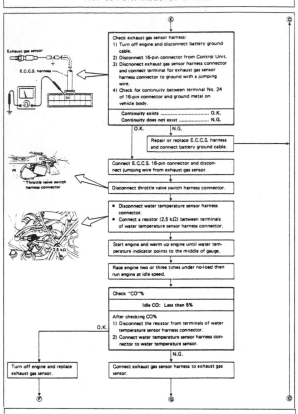

Check exhaust gas sensor harness:
1) Turn off engine and disconnect battery ground cable.
2) Disconnect 16-pin connector from Control Unit.
3) Disconnect exhaust gas sensor harness connector and connect terminal for exhaust gas sensor harness connector to ground with a jumping wire.
4) Check for continuity between terminal No. 24 of 16-pin connector and ground metal on vehicle body.

Continuity exists .... O.K.
Continuity does not exist .... N.G.

Repair or replace E.C.C.S. harness and connect battery ground cable.

Connect E.C.C.S. 16-pin connector and disconnect jumping wire from exhaust gas sensor.

Disconnect throttle valve switch harness connector.

• Disconnect water temperature sensor harness connector.
• Connect a resistor (2.5 kΩ) between terminals of water temperature sensor harness connector.

Start engine and warm up engine until water temperature indicator points to the middle of gauge.

Race engine two or three times under no-load then run engine at idle speed.

Check "CO"%

Idle CO: Less than 5%

After checking CO%
1) Disconnect the resistor from terminals of water temperature sensor harness connector.
2) Connect water temperature sensor harness connector to water temperature sensor.

Turn off engine and replace exhaust gas sensor.

Connect exhaust gas sensor harness to exhaust gas sensor.

MIXTURE RATIO FEEDBACK SYSTEM INSPECTION CHART
1987–88 PORT INJECTED STANZA

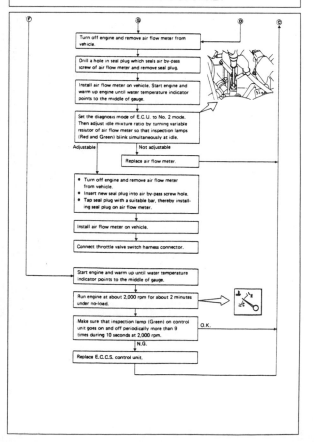

Turn off engine and remove air flow meter from vehicle.

Drill a hole in seal plug which seals air by-pass screw of air flow meter and remove seal plug.

Install air flow meter on vehicle. Start engine and warm up engine until water temperature indicator points to the middle of gauge.

Set the diagnosis mode of E.C.U. to No. 2 mode. Then adjust idle mixture ratio by turning variable resistor of air flow meter so that inspection lamps (Red and Green) blink simultaneously at idle.

Adjustable / Not adjustable

Replace air flow meter.

• Turn off engine and remove air flow meter from vehicle.
• Insert new seal plug into air by-pass screw hole.
• Tap seal plug with a suitable bar, thereby installing seal plug on air flow meter.

Install air flow meter on vehicle.

Connect throttle valve switch harness connector.

Start engine and warm up engine until water temperature indicator points to the middle of gauge.

Run engine at about 2,000 rpm for about 2 minutes under no-load.

Make sure that inspection lamp (Green) on control unit goes on and off periodically more than 9 times during 10 seconds at 2,000 rpm.

Replace E.C.C.S. control unit.

ECCS SELF-DIAGNOSTIC CHART
1987–88 PORT INJECTED 200SX WITH CA20E ENGINE

CRANK ANGLE SENSOR (Code No. 11)

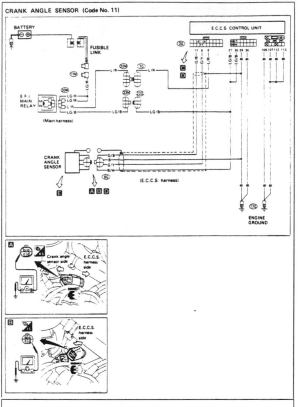

ECCS SELF-DIAGNOSTIC CHART
1987–88 PORT INJECTED 200SX WITH CA20E ENGINE

CRANK ANGLE SENSOR (Code No. 11)

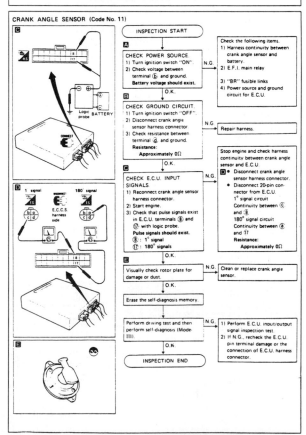

INSPECTION START

A CHECK POWER SOURCE.
1) Turn ignition switch "ON".
2) Check voltage between terminal ⓑ and ground.
Battery voltage should exist.

Check the following items.
1) Harness continuity between crank angle sensor and battery.
2) E.F.I. main relay
3) "BR" fusible links
4) Power source and ground circuit for E.C.U.

B CHECK GROUND CIRCUIT.
1) Turn ignition switch "OFF".
2) Disconnect crank angle sensor harness connector
3) Check resistance between terminal ⓓ and ground.
Resistance:
Approximately 0Ω

Repair harness.

CHECK E.C.U. INPUT SIGNALS
1) Reconnect crank angle sensor harness connector.
2) Start engine.
3) Check that pulse signals exist in E.C.U. terminals ⑧ and ⑰ with logic probe.
Pulse signals should exist.
⑧ : 1° signal
⑰ : 180° signals

Stop engine and check harness continuity between crank angle sensor and E.C.U.
D • Disconnect crank angle sensor harness connector.
• Disconnect 20-pin connector from E.C.U.
1° signal circuit
Continuity between ⓒ and ⑧
180° signal circuit
Continuity between ⑧ and ⑰
Resistance:
Approximately 0Ω

E Visually check rotor plate for damage or dust.

Clean or replace crank angle sensor.

Erase the self-diagnosis memory.

Perform driving test and then perform self-diagnosis (Mode-III).

1) Perform E.C.U. input/output signal inspection test.
2) If N.G., recheck the E.C.U. pin terminal damage or the connection of E.C.U. harness connector.

INSPECTION END

ECCS SELF-DIAGNOSTIC CHART
1987–88 PORT INJECTED 200SX WITH CA20E ENGINE

AIR FLOW METER (Code No. 12)

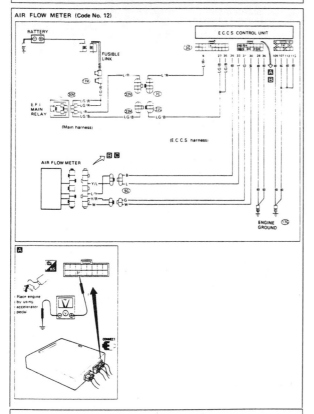

ECCS SELF-DIAGNOSTIC CHART
1987–88 PORT INJECTED 200SX WITH CA20E ENGINE

WATER TEMPERATURE SENSOR (Code No. 13)

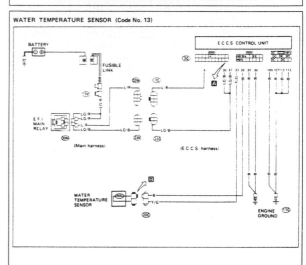

ECCS SELF-DIAGNOSTIC CHART
1987–88 PORT INJECTED 200SX WITH CA20E ENGINE

AIR FLOW METER (Code No. 12)

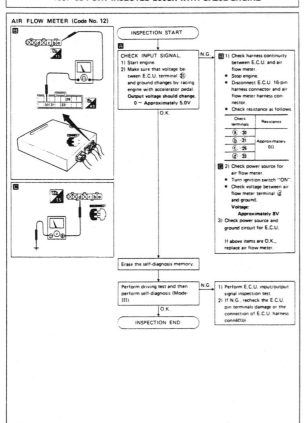

ECCS SELF-DIAGNOSTIC CHART
1987–88 PORT INJECTED 200SX WITH CA20E ENGINE

WATER TEMPERATURE SENSOR (Code No. 13)

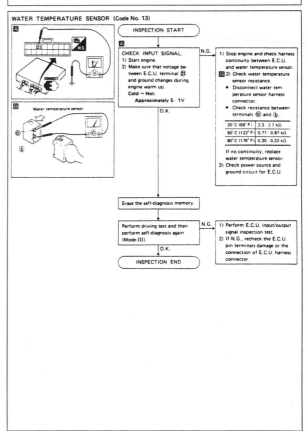

ECCS SELF-DIAGNOSTIC CHART
1987–88 PORT INJECTED 200SX WITH CA20E ENGINE

IGNITION SIGNAL (Code No. 21)

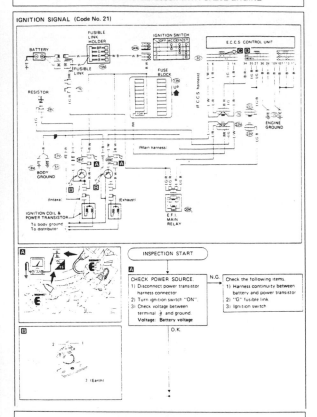

ECCS SELF-DIAGNOSTIC CHART
1987–88 PORT INJECTED 200SX WITH CA20E ENGINE

FUEL PUMP (Code No. 22)

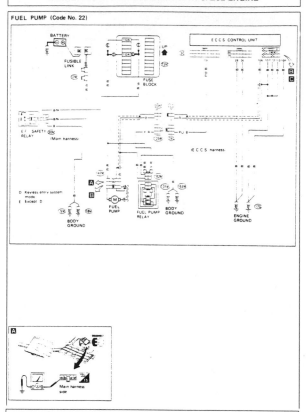

ECCS SELF-DIAGNOSTIC CHART
1987–88 PORT INJECTED 200SX WITH CA20E ENGINE

IGNITION SIGNAL (Code No. 21)

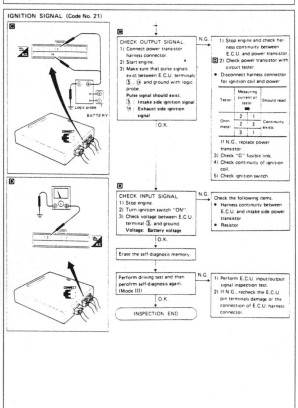

ECCS SELF-DIAGNOSTIC CHART
1987–88 PORT INJECTED 200SX WITH CA20E ENGINE

FUEL PUMP (Code No. 22)

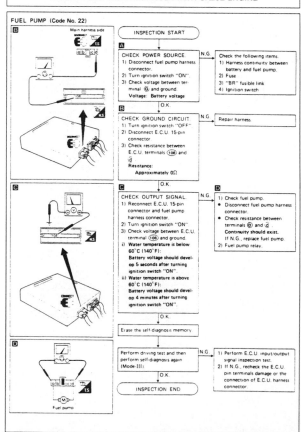

ECCS SELF-DIAGNOSTIC CHART
1987–88 PORT INJECTED 200SX WITH CA20E ENGINE

START SIGNAL (Switch ON/OFF diagnosis)

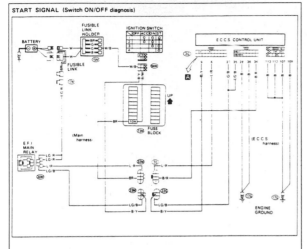

START SIGNAL (Switch ON/OFF diagnosis)

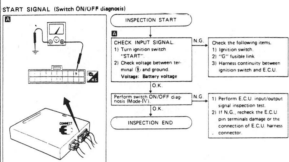

ECCS SELF-DIAGNOSTIC CHART
1987–88 PORT INJECTED 200SX WITH CA20E ENGINE

THROTTLE VALVE SWITCH (Switch ON/OFF diagnosis)

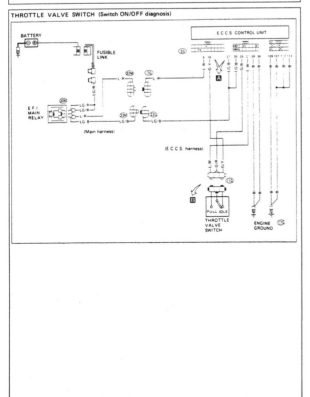

ECCS SELF-DIAGNOSTIC CHART
1987–88 PORT INJECTED 200SX WITH CA20E ENGINE

THROTTLE VALVE SWITCH (Switch ON/OFF diagnosis)

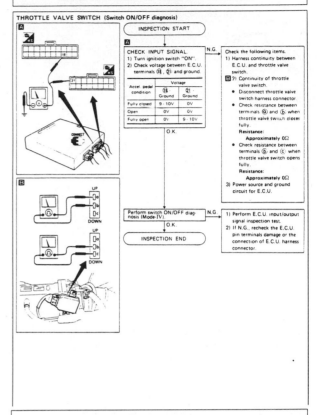

ECCS SELF-DIAGNOSTIC CHART
1987–88 PORT INJECTED 200SX WITH CA20E ENGINE

VEHICLE SPEED SENSOR (Switch ON/OFF diagnosis)

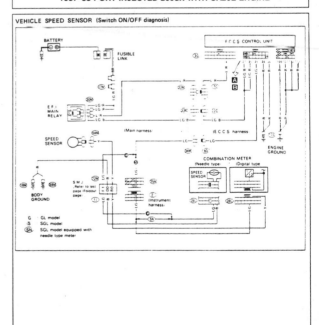

ECCS SELF-DIAGNOSTIC CHART
1987–88 PORT INJECTED 200SX WITH CA20E ENGINE

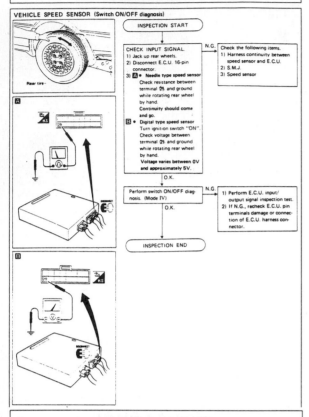

VEHICLE SPEED SENSOR (Switch ON/OFF diagnosis)

ECCS SELF-DIAGNOSTIC CHART
1987–88 PORT INJECTED 200SX WITH CA20E ENGINE

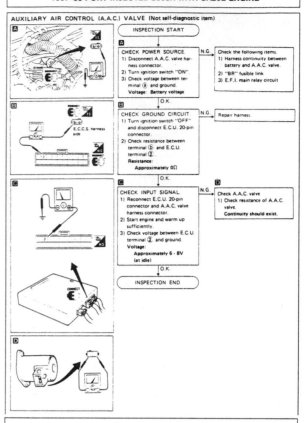

AUXILIARY AIR CONTROL (A.A.C.) VALVE (Not self-diagnostic item)

ECCS SELF-DIAGNOSTIC CHART
1987–88 PORT INJECTED 200SX WITH CA20E ENGINE

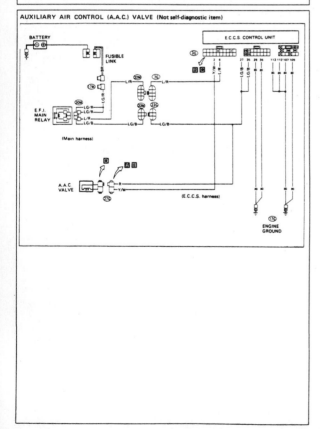

AUXILIARY AIR CONTROL (A.A.C.) VALVE (Not self-diagnostic item)

ECCS SELF-DIAGNOSTIC CHART
1987–88 PORT INJECTED 200SX WITH CA20E ENGINE

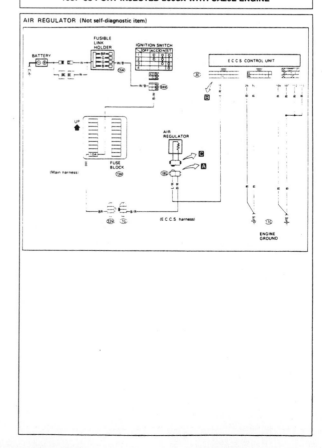

AIR REGULATOR (Not self-diagnostic item)

ECCS SELF-DIAGNOSTIC CHART
1987-88 PORT INJECTED 200SX WITH CA20E ENGINE

AIR REGULATOR (Not self-diagnostic item)

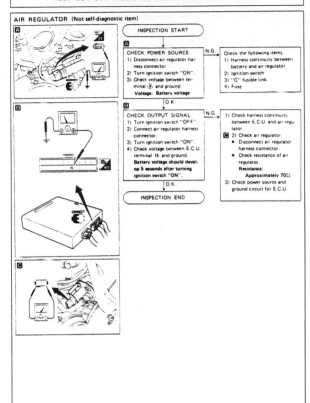

INSPECTION START

A CHECK POWER SOURCE.
1) Disconnect air regulator harness connector.
2) Turn ignition switch "ON".
3) Check voltage between terminal (a) and ground.
Voltage: Battery voltage

N.G. → Check the following items.
1) Harness continuity between battery and air regulator.
2) Ignition switch
3) "G" fusible link
4) Fuse

O.K. ↓

B CHECK OUTPUT SIGNAL.
1) Turn ignition switch "OFF".
2) Connect air regulator harness connector.
3) Turn ignition switch "ON".
4) Check voltage between E.C.U. terminal 16 and ground.
Battery voltage should develop 5 seconds after turning ignition switch "ON".

N.G. → 1) Check harness continuity between E.C.U. and air regulator.
2) Check air regulator.
C • Disconnect air regulator harness connector.
• Check resistance of air regulator.
Resistance: Approximately 70Ω
3) Check power source and ground circuit for E.C.U.

O.K. ↓

INSPECTION END

ECCS SELF-DIAGNOSTIC CHART
1987-88 PORT INJECTED 200SX WITH CA20E ENGINE

INJECTOR (Not self-diagnostic item)

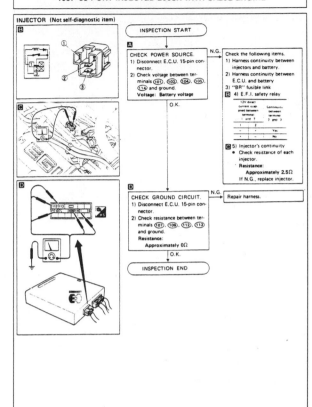

INSPECTION START

A CHECK POWER SOURCE.
1) Disconnect E.C.U. 15-pin connector.
2) Check voltage between terminals (101), (104), (105), (114) and ground.
Voltage: Battery voltage

N.G. → Check the following items.
1) Harness continuity between injectors and battery.
2) Harness continuity between E.C.U. and battery.
3) "BR" fusible link
B 4) E.F.I. safety relay

12v direct current is applied between terminal	Continuity between terminal
1 and 2	3 and 3
1	2	Yes
1	2	No

C 5) Injector's continuity
• Check resistance of each injector.
Resistance: Approximately 2.5Ω
If N.G., replace injector.

O.K. ↓

D CHECK GROUND CIRCUIT.
1) Disconnect E.C.U. 15-pin connector.
2) Check resistance between terminals (107), (108), (112), (113) and ground.
Resistance: Approximately 0Ω

N.G. → Repair harness.

O.K. ↓

INSPECTION END

ECCS SELF-DIAGNOSTIC CHART
1987-88 PORT INJECTED 200SX WITH CA20E ENGINE

INJECTOR (Not self-diagnostic item)

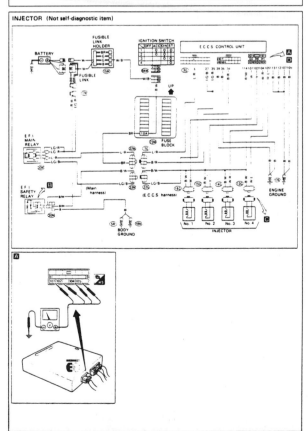

ECCS SELF-DIAGNOSTIC CHART
1987-88 PORT INJECTED 200SX WITH CA20E ENGINE

EXHAUST GAS SENSOR (Not self-diagnostic item)

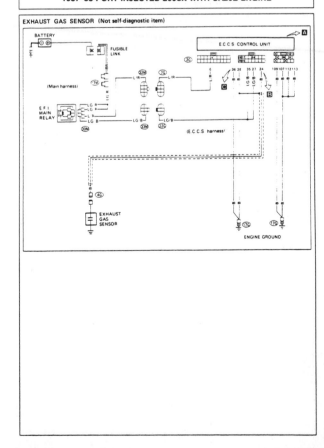

ECCS SELF-DIAGNOSTIC CHART
1987–88 PORT INJECTED 200SX WITH CA20E ENGINE

EXHAUST GAS SENSOR (Not self-diagnostic item)

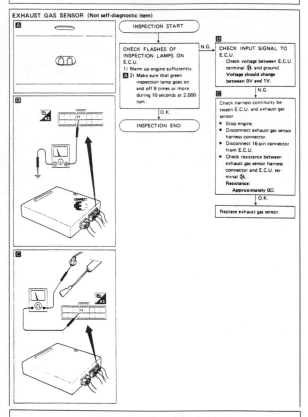

ECCS SELF-DIAGNOSTIC CHART
1987–88 PORT INJECTED 200SX WITH CA20E ENGINE

SPARK PLUG SWITCHING CONTROL (Not self-diagnostic item)

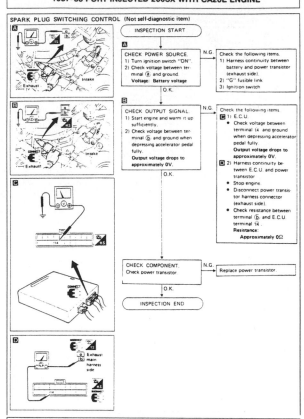

ECCS SELF-DIAGNOSTIC CHART
1987–88 PORT INJECTED 200SX WITH CA20E ENGINE

SPARK PLUG SWITCHING CONTROL (Not self-diagnostic item)

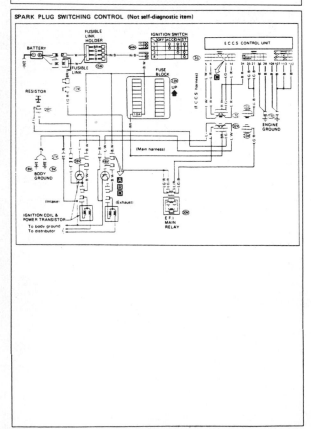

ECCS SELF-DIAGNOSTIC CHART
1987–88 PORT INJECTED 200SX WITH CA20E ENGINE

AIR INJECTION VALVE (A.I.V.) CONTROL (Not self-diagnostic item)

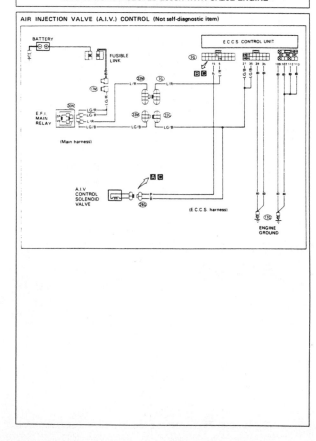

ECCS SELF-DIAGNOSTIC CHART
1987–88 PORT INJECTED 200SX WITH CA20E ENGINE

AIR INJECTION VALVE (A.I.V.) CONTROL (Not self-diagnostic item)

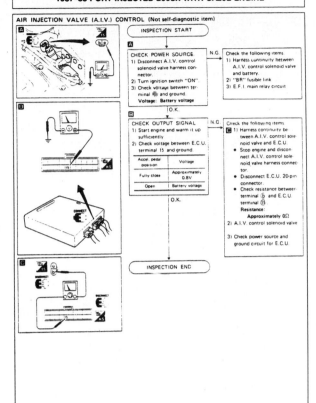

INSPECTION START

A CHECK POWER SOURCE
1) Disconnect A.I.V. control solenoid valve harness connector.
2) Turn ignition switch "ON".
3) Check voltage between terminal ⓐ and ground.
Voltage: Battery voltage

N.G. → Check the following items.
1) Harness continuity between A.I.V. control solenoid valve and battery.
2) "BR" fusible link
3) E.F.I. main relay circuit

O.K.

B CHECK OUTPUT SIGNAL
1) Start engine and warm it up sufficiently.
2) Check voltage between E.C.U. terminal 15 and ground.

Accel. pedal position	Voltage
Fully close	Approximately 0.8V
Open	Battery voltage

N.G. → Check the following items.
C 1) Harness continuity between A.I.V. control solenoid valve and E.C.U.
● Stop engine and disconnect A.I.V. control solenoid valve connector.
● Disconnect E.C.U. 20-pin connector.
● Check resistance between terminal ⓑ and E.C.U. terminal 15.
Resistance: Approximately 0Ω
2) A.I.V. control solenoid valve
3) Check power source and ground circuit for E.C.U.

O.K.

INSPECTION END

ECCS SELF-DIAGNOSTIC CHART
1987–88 PORT INJECTED 200SX WITH CA20E ENGINE

E.G.R. CONTROL (Not self-diagnostic item)

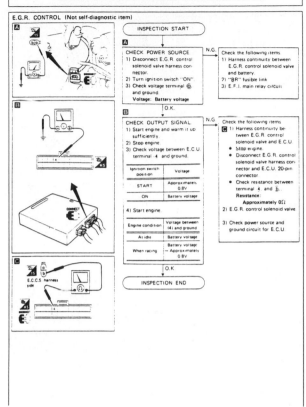

INSPECTION START

A CHECK POWER SOURCE
1) Disconnect E.G.R. control solenoid valve harness connector.
2) Turn ignition switch "ON".
3) Check voltage terminal ⓐ and ground.
Voltage: Battery voltage

N.G. → Check the following items.
1) Harness continuity between E.G.R. control solenoid valve and battery.
2) "BR" fusible link
3) E.F.I. main relay circuit

O.K.

B CHECK OUTPUT SIGNAL
1) Start engine and warm it up sufficiently.
2) Stop engine.
3) Check voltage between E.C.U. terminal 4 and ground.

Ignition switch position	Voltage
START	Approximately 0.8V
ON	Battery voltage

4) Start engine.

Engine condition	Voltage between (4) and ground
At idle	Battery voltage
When racing	Battery voltage − Approximately 0.8V

N.G. → Check the following items.
C 1) Harness continuity between E.G.R. control solenoid valve and E.C.U.
● Stop engine.
● Disconnect E.G.R. control solenoid valve harness connector and E.C.U. 20-pin connector.
● Check resistance between terminal 4 and ⓑ.
Resistance: Approximately 0Ω
2) E.G.R. control solenoid valve.
3) Check power source and ground circuit for E.C.U.

O.K.

INSPECTION END

E.C.C.S. harness side

ECCS SELF-DIAGNOSTIC CHART
1987–88 PORT INJECTED 200SX WITH CA20E ENGINE

E.G.R. CONTROL (Not self-diagnostic item)

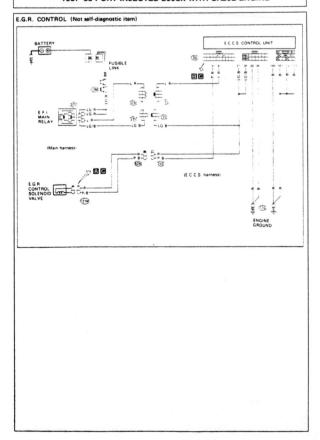

ECCS SELF-DIAGNOSTIC CHART
1987–88 PORT INJECTED 200SX WITH CA20E ENGINE

PRESSURE REGULATOR (P.R.) CONTROL SOLENOID VALVE (Not self-diagnostic item)

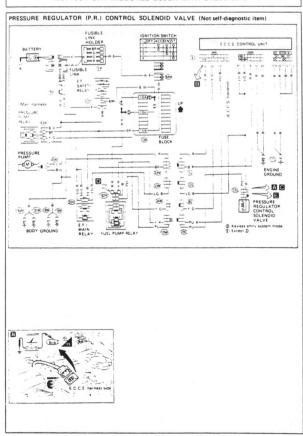

ECCS SELF-DIAGNOSTIC CHART
1987–88 PORT INJECTED 200SX WITH CA20E ENGINE

PRESSURE REGULATOR (P.R.) CONTROL SOLENOID VALVE (Not self-diagnostic item)

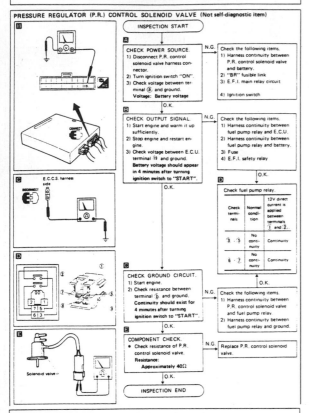

INSPECTION START

CHECK POWER SOURCE.
1) Disconnect P.R. control solenoid valve harness connector.
2) Turn ignition switch "ON".
3) Check voltage between terminal ⓐ and ground.
Voltage: Battery voltage

N.G. → Check the following items.
1) Harness continuity between P.R. control solenoid valve and battery.
2) "BR" fusible link
3) E.F.I. main relay circuit
4) Ignition switch

↓ O.K.

CHECK OUTPUT SIGNAL.
1) Start engine and warm it up sufficiently.
2) Stop engine and restart engine.
3) Check voltage between E.C.U. terminal 19 and ground.
Battery voltage should appear in 4 minutes after turning ignition switch to "START".

N.G. → Check the following items.
1) Harness continuity between fuel pump relay and E.C.U.
2) Harness continuity between fuel pump relay and battery.
3) Fuse
4) E.F.I. safety relay

↓ O.K.

Check fuel pump relay.		
Check terminals	Normal condition	12V direct current is applied between terminals ① and ②.
③ · ⑤	No continuity	Continuity
⑥ · ⑦	No continuity	Continuity

↓ O.K.

CHECK GROUND CIRCUIT.
1) Start engine.
2) Check resistance between terminal ⓑ and ground.
Continuity should exist for 4 minutes after turning ignition switch to "START".

N.G. → Check the following items.
1) Harness continuity between P.R. control solenoid valve and fuel pump relay.
2) Harness continuity between fuel pump relay and ground.

↓ O.K.

COMPONENT CHECK.
● Check resistance of P.R. control solenoid valve.
Resistance:
Approximately 40Ω

N.G. → Replace P.R. control solenoid valve.

↓ O.K.

INSPECTION END

ECCS SELF-DIAGNOSTIC CHART
1987–88 PORT INJECTED 200SX WITH CA20E ENGINE

PRESSURE PUMP (Not self-diagnostic item)

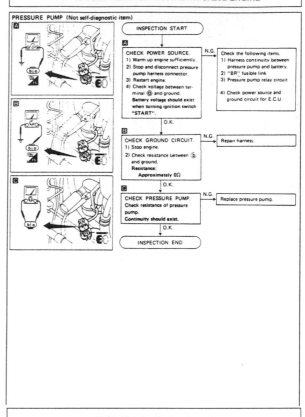

INSPECTION START

CHECK POWER SOURCE.
1) Warm up engine sufficiently.
2) Stop and disconnect pressure pump harness connector.
3) Restart engine.
4) Check voltage between terminal ⓒ and ground.
Battery voltage should exist when turning ignition switch "START".

N.G. → Check the following items.
1) Harness continuity between pressure pump and battery.
2) "BR" fusible link
3) Pressure pump relay circuit
4) Check power source and ground circuit for E.C.U.

↓ O.K.

CHECK GROUND CIRCUIT.
1) Stop engine.
2) Check resistance between ⓑ and ground.
Resistance:
Approximately 0Ω

N.G. → Repair harness.

↓ O.K.

CHECK PRESSURE PUMP.
Check resistance of pressure pump.
Continuity should exist.

N.G. → Replace pressure pump.

↓ O.K.

INSPECTION END

ECCS SELF-DIAGNOSTIC CHART
1987–88 PORT INJECTED 200SX WITH CA20E ENGINE

PRESSURE PUMP (Not self-diagnostic item)

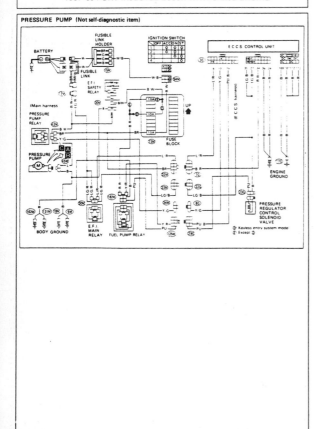

ECCS SELF-DIAGNOSTIC CHART
1987–88 PORT INJECTED 200SX WITH CA20E ENGINE

PRESSURE PUMP RELAY (Not self-diagnostic item)

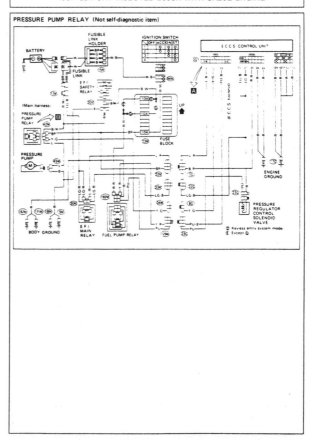

ECCS SELF-DIAGNOSTIC CHART
1987–88 PORT INJECTED 200SX WITH CA20E ENGINE

PRESSURE PUMP RELAY (Not self-diagnostic item)

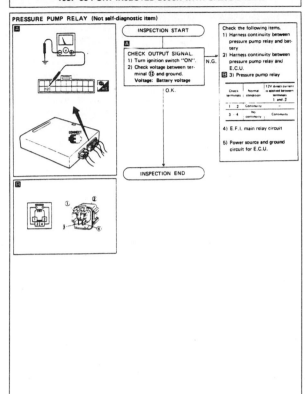

INSPECTION START

A CHECK OUTPUT SIGNAL.
1) Turn ignition switch "ON".
2) Check voltage between terminal ⑫ and ground.
Voltage: Battery voltage

N.G.

O.K.

INSPECTION END

Check the following items.
1) Harness continuity between pressure pump relay and battery
2) Harness continuity between pressure pump relay and E.C.U.
B 3) Pressure pump relay

Check terminals	Normal condition	12V direct current is applied between terminals 1 and 2
1 · 2	Continuity	—
3 · 4	No continuity	Continuity

4) E.F.I. main relay circuit
5) Power source and ground circuit for E.C.U.

ECCS SELF-DIAGNOSTIC CHART
1987–88 PORT INJECTED 200SX WITH CA20E ENGINE

NEUTRAL/INHIBITOR SWITCH (Not self-diagnostic item)

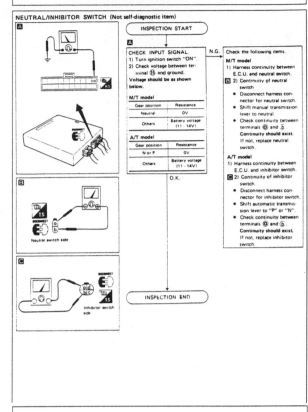

INSPECTION START

A CHECK INPUT SIGNAL.
1) Turn ignition switch "ON".
2) Check voltage between terminal ⑯ and ground.
Voltage should be as shown below.

M/T model

Gear position	Resistance
Neutral	0V
Others	Battery voltage (11 - 14V)

A/T model

Gear position	Resistance
N or P	0V
Others	Battery voltage (11 - 14V)

O.K.

INSPECTION END

N.G. Check the following items.

M/T model
1) Harness continuity between E.C.U. and neutral switch.
B 2) Continuity of neutral switch
  - Disconnect harness connector for neutral switch.
  - Shift manual transmission lever to neutral.
  - Check continuity between terminals ⓐ and ⓑ. Continuity should exist. If not, replace neutral switch.

A/T model
1) Harness continuity between E.C.U. and inhibitor switch.
C 2) Continuity of inhibitor switch.
  - Disconnect harness connector for inhibitor switch.
  - Shift automatic transmission lever to "P" or "N".
  - Check continuity between terminals ⓐ and ⓑ. Continuity should exist. If not, replace inhibitor switch.

Neutral switch side

Inhibitor switch side

ECCS SELF-DIAGNOSTIC CHART
1987–88 PORT INJECTED 200SX WITH CA20E ENGINE

NEUTRAL/INHIBITOR SWITCH (Not self-diagnostic item)

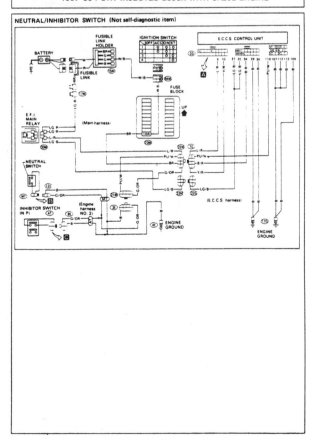

ECCS SELF-DIAGNOSTIC CHART
1987–88 PORT INJECTED 200SX WITH CA20E ENGINE

POWER SOURCE & GROUND CIRCUIT FOR E.C.U. (Not self-diagnostic item)

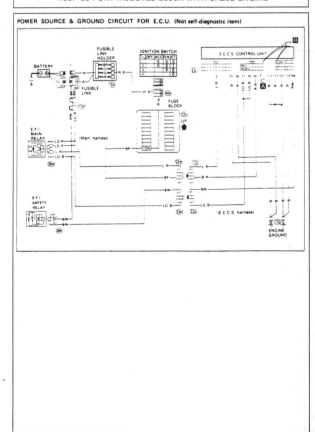

ECCS SELF-DIAGNOSTIC CHART
1987–88 PORT INJECTED 200SX WITH CA20E ENGINE

POWER SOURCE & GROUND CIRCUIT FOR E.C.U. (Not self-diagnostic item)

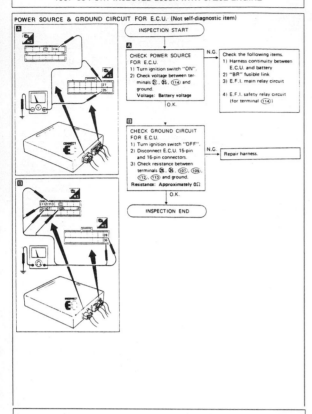

ECCS SELF-DIAGNOSTIC CHART
1987–88 PORT INJECTED 200SX WITH CA20E ENGINE

E.F.I. MAIN RELAY (For E.C.U.) (Not self-diagnostic item)

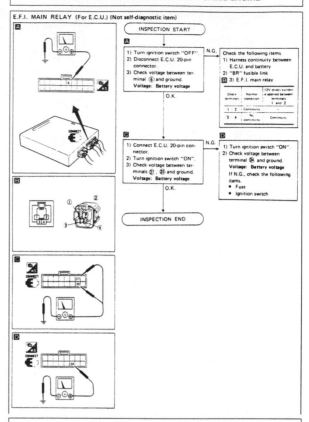

ECCS SELF-DIAGNOSTIC CHART
1987–88 PORT INJECTED 200SX WITH CA20E ENGINE

E.F.I. MAIN RELAY (For E.C.U.) (Not self-diagnostic item)

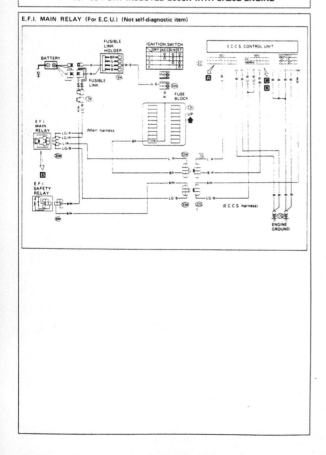

MIXTURE RATIO FEEDBACK SYSTEM INSPECTION CHART
1987–88 PORT INJECTED 200SX WITH CA20E ENGINE

MIXTURE RATIO FEEDBACK SYSTEM INSPECTION
Preparation
1. Make sure that the following parts are in good order.
   - Battery
   - Ignition system
   - Engine oil and coolant levels
   - Fuses
   - E.C.C.S. harness connectors
   - Vacuum hoses
   - Air intake system
     (oil filler cap, oil level gauge, etc.)
   - Valve clearance, engine compression
   - E.G.R. valve operation
   - Throttle valve and throttle valve switch operation
2. On air conditioner equipped models, checks should be carried out while the air conditioner is "OFF".

3. On automatic transmission equipped models, when checking idle rpm, ignition timing and mixture ratio, checks should be carried out while shift lever is in "D" position.
4. When measuring "CO" percentage, insert probe more 40 cm (15.7 in) into tail pipe.
5. Checking and adjusting should be done while the radiator cooling fan is stopped.
WARNING:
a. When selector lever is shifted to "D" position, apply parking brake and block both front and rear wheels with chocks.
b. Depress brake pedal while accelerating the engine to prevent forward surge of vehicle.
c. After the adjustment has been made, shift the lever to the "N" or "P" position and remove wheel chocks.

Overall inspection sequence

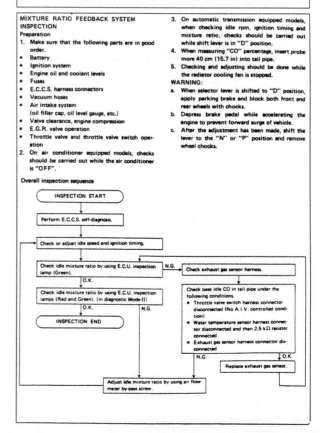

MIXTURE RATIO FEEDBACK SYSTEM INSPECTION CHART
1987–88 PORT INJECTED 200SX WITH CA20E ENGINE

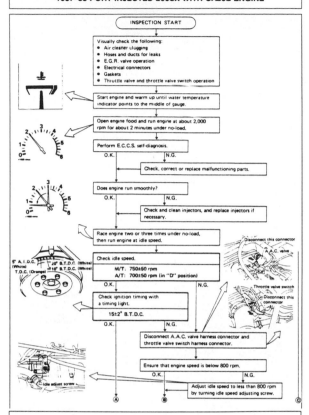

INSPECTION START

Visually check the following:
- Air cleaner clogging
- Hoses and ducts for leaks
- E.G.R. valve operation
- Electrical connectors
- Gaskets
- Throttle valve and throttle valve switch operation

Start engine and warm up until water temperature indicator points to the middle of gauge.

Open engine hood and run engine at about 2,000 rpm for about 2 minutes under no-load.

Perform E.C.C.S. self-diagnosis.
O.K. / N.G.

Check, correct or replace malfunctioning parts.

Does engine run smoothly?
O.K. / N.G.

Check and clean injectors, and replace injectors if necessary.

Race engine two or three times under no-load, then run engine at idle speed.

Check idle speed.
M/T: 750±50 rpm
A/T: 700±50 rpm (in "D" position)
O.K. / N.G.

Check ignition timing with a timing light.
15±2° B.T.D.C.
O.K. / N.G.

Disconnect A.A.C. valve harness connector and throttle valve switch harness connector.

Ensure that engine speed is below 800 rpm.
O.K. / N.G.

Adjust idle speed to less than 800 rpm by turning idle speed adjusting screw.

(A) (B) (C)

MIXTURE RATIO FEEDBACK SYSTEM INSPECTION CHART
1987–88 PORT INJECTED 200SX WITH CA20E ENGINE

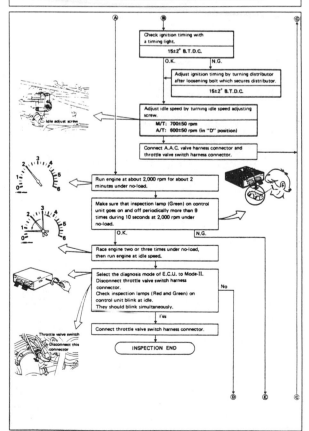

(A) (B) (C)

Check ignition timing with a timing light.
15±2° B.T.D.C.
O.K. / N.G.

Adjust ignition timing by turning distributor after loosening bolt which secures distributor.
15±2° B.T.D.C.

Adjust idle speed by turning idle speed adjusting screw.
M/T: 700±50 rpm
A/T: 800±50 rpm (in "D" position)

Connect A.A.C. valve harness connector and throttle valve switch harness connector.

Run engine at about 2,000 rpm for about 2 minutes under no-load.

Make sure that inspection lamp (Green) on control unit goes on and off periodically more than 9 times during 10 seconds at 2,000 rpm under no-load.
O.K. / N.G.

Race engine two or three times under no-load, then run engine at idle speed.

Select the diagnosis mode of E.C.U. to Mode-II. Disconnect throttle valve switch harness connector. Check inspection lamps (Red and Green) on control unit blink at idle. They should blink simultaneously.
No / Yes

Connect throttle valve switch harness connector.

INSPECTION END

(D) (E) (C)

MIXTURE RATIO FEEDBACK SYSTEM INSPECTION CHART
1987–88 PORT INJECTED 200SX WITH CA20E ENGINE

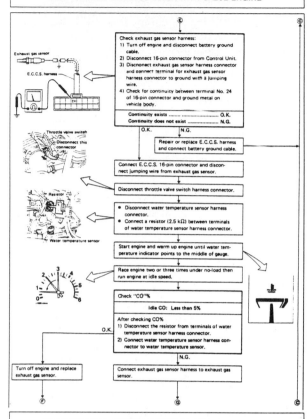

(E) (C)

Check exhaust gas sensor harness:
1) Turn off engine and disconnect battery ground cable.
2) Disconnect 16-pin connector from Control Unit.
3) Disconnect exhaust gas sensor harness connector and connect terminal for exhaust gas sensor harness connector to ground with a jumping wire.
4) Check for continuity between terminal No. 24 of 16-pin connector and ground metal on vehicle body.

Continuity exists .... O.K.
Continuity does not exist .... N.G.
O.K. / N.G.

Repair or replace E.C.C.S. harness and connect battery ground cable.

Connect E.C.C.S. 16-pin connector and disconnect jumping wire from exhaust gas sensor.

Disconnect throttle valve switch harness connector.

- Disconnect water temperature sensor harness connector.
- Connect a resistor (2.5 kΩ) between terminals of water temperature sensor harness connector.

Start engine and warm up engine until water temperature indicator points to the middle of gauge.

Race engine two or three times under no-load then run engine at idle speed.

Check "CO"%
Idle CO: Less than 5%

After checking CO%
1) Disconnect the resistor from terminals of water temperature sensor harness connector.
2) Connect water temperature sensor harness connector to water temperature sensor.
O.K. / N.G.

Turn off engine and replace exhaust gas sensor.

Connect exhaust gas sensor harness to exhaust gas sensor.

(F) (G) (C)

MIXTURE RATIO FEEDBACK SYSTEM INSPECTION CHART
1987–88 PORT INJECTED 200SX WITH CA20E ENGINE

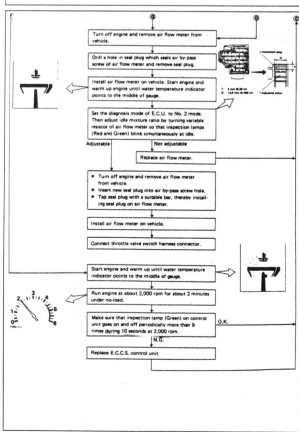

(F) (G) (D) (C)

Turn off engine and remove air flow meter from vehicle.

Drill a hole in seal plug which seals air by-pass screw of air flow meter and remove seal plug.

Install air flow meter on vehicle. Start engine and warm up engine until water temperature indicator points to the middle of gauge.

Set the diagnosis mode of E.C.U. to No. 2 mode. Then adjust idle mixture ratio by turning variable resistor of air flow meter so that inspection lamps (Red and Green) blink simultaneously at idle.
Adjustable / Not adjustable

Replace air flow meter.

- Turn off engine and remove air flow meter from vehicle.
- Insert new seal plug into air by-pass screw hole.
- Tap seal plug with a suitable bar, thereby installing seal plug on air flow meter.

Install air flow meter on vehicle.

Connect throttle valve switch harness connector.

Start engine and warm up until water temperature indicator points to the middle of gauge.

Run engine at about 2,000 rpm for about 2 minutes under no-load.

Make sure that inspection lamp (Green) on control unit goes on and off periodically more than 9 times during 10 seconds at 2,000 rpm.
O.K. / N.G.

Replace E.C.C.S. control unit.

ECCS SELF-DIAGNOSTIC CHART
1987–88 PORT INJECTED 200SX WITH VG30E ENGINE

CRANK ANGLE SENSOR (Code No. 11)

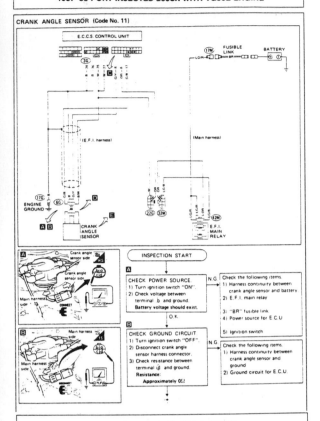

CHECK POWER SOURCE
1) Turn ignition switch "ON".
2) Check voltage between terminal b and ground.
Battery voltage should exist.
O.K.

N.G. → Check the following items.
1) Harness continuity between crank angle sensor and battery
2) E.F.I. main relay
3) "BR" fusible link
4) Power source for E.C.U
5) Ignition switch

CHECK GROUND CIRCUIT
1) Turn ignition switch "OFF".
2) Disconnect crank angle sensor harness connector.
3) Check resistance between terminal d and ground.
Resistance:
Approximately 0Ω

N.G. → Check the following items.
1) Harness continuity between crank angle sensor and ground
2) Ground circuit for E.C.U

ECCS SELF-DIAGNOSTIC CHART
1987–88 PORT INJECTED 200SX WITH VG30E ENGINE

CRANK ANGLE SENSOR (Code No. 11)

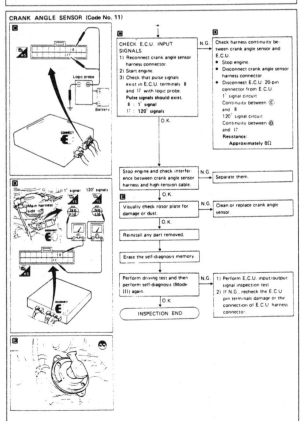

CHECK E.C.U. INPUT SIGNALS
1) Reconnect crank angle sensor harness connector.
2) Start engine.
3) Check that pulse signals exist in E.C.U. terminals 8 and 17 with logic probe.
Pulse signals should exist.
8 : 1° signal
17 : 120° signals
O.K.

N.G. → Check harness continuity between crank angle sensor and E.C.U.
• Stop engine.
• Disconnect crank angle sensor harness connector
• Disconnect E.C.U. 20-pin connector from E.C.U.
1° signal circuit
Continuity between C and 8
120° signal circuit
Continuity between D and 17
Resistance:
Approximately 0Ω

Stop engine and check interference between crank angle sensor harness and high-tension cable.
O.K.

N.G. → Separate them.

Visually check rotor plate for damage or dust.
O.K.

N.G. → Clean or replace crank angle sensor.

Reinstall any part removed.

Erase the self-diagnosis memory.

Perform driving test and then perform self-diagnosis (Mode III) again.
O.K.

N.G. → 1) Perform E.C.U. input/output signal inspection test.
2) If N.G., recheck the E.C.U. pin terminals damage or the connection of E.C.U. harness connector.

INSPECTION END

ECCS SELF-DIAGNOSTIC CHART
1987–88 PORT INJECTED 200SX WITH VG30E ENGINE

AIR FLOW METER (Code No. 12)

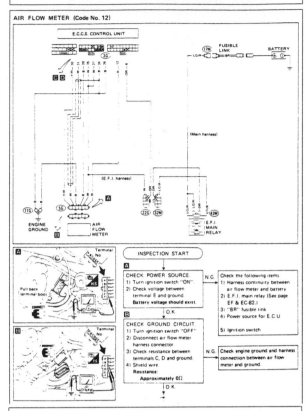

INSPECTION START

CHECK POWER SOURCE
1) Turn ignition switch "ON".
2) Check voltage between terminal E and ground.
Battery voltage should exist.
O.K.

N.G. → Check the following items
1) Harness continuity between air flow meter and battery
2) E.F.I. main relay (See page EF & EC-82.)
3) "BR" fusible link
4) Power source for E.C.U
5) Ignition switch

CHECK GROUND CIRCUIT
1) Turn ignition switch "OFF".
2) Disconnect air flow meter harness connector.
3) Check resistance between terminals C, D and ground.
4) Shield wire.
Resistance:
Approximately 0Ω

N.G. → Check engine ground and harness connection between air flow meter and ground.
O.K.

ECCS SELF-DIAGNOSTIC CHART
1987–88 PORT INJECTED 200SX WITH VG30E ENGINE

AIR FLOW METER (Code No. 12)

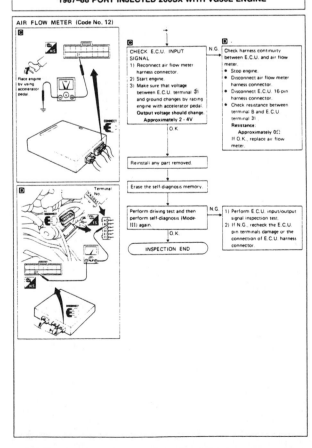

CHECK E.C.U. INPUT SIGNAL
1) Reconnect air flow meter harness connector.
2) Start engine.
3) Make sure that voltage between E.C.U. terminal 31 and ground changes by racing engine with accelerator pedal.
Output voltage should change.
Approximately 2 - 4V
O.K.

N.G. → Check harness continuity between E.C.U. and air flow meter.
• Stop engine.
• Disconnect air flow meter harness connector.
• Disconnect E.C.U. 16-pin harness connector.
• Check resistance between terminal B and E.C.U. terminal 31.
Resistance:
Approximately 0Ω
If O.K., replace air flow meter.

Reinstall any part removed.

Erase the self-diagnosis memory.

Perform driving test and then perform self-diagnosis (Mode III) again.
O.K.

N.G. → 1) Perform E.C.U. input/output signal inspection test.
2) If N.G., recheck the E.C.U. pin terminals damage or the connection of E.C.U. harness connector.

INSPECTION END

ECCS SELF-DIAGNOSTIC CHART
1987–88 PORT INJECTED 200SX WITH VG30E ENGINE

CYLINDER HEAD TEMPERATURE SENSOR (Code No. 13)

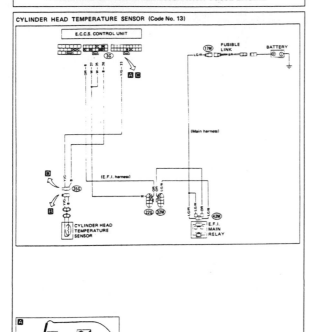

ECCS SELF-DIAGNOSTIC CHART
1987–88 PORT INJECTED 200SX WITH VG30E ENGINE

IGNITION SIGNAL (Code No. 21)

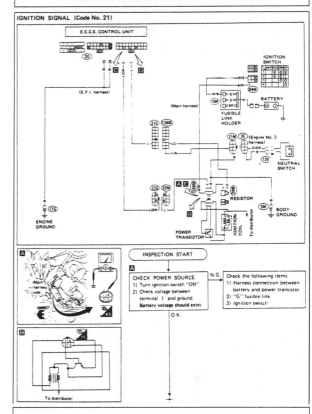

ECCS SELF-DIAGNOSTIC CHART
1987–88 PORT INJECTED 200SX WITH VG30E ENGINE

CYLINDER HEAD TEMPERATURE SENSOR (Code No. 13)

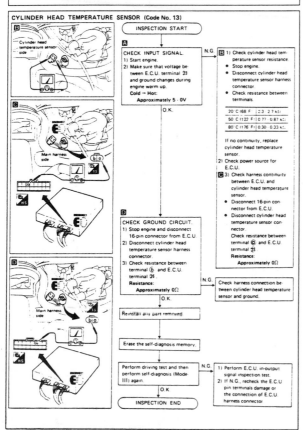

INSPECTION START

A CHECK INPUT SIGNAL.
1) Start engine.
2) Make sure that voltage between E.C.U. terminal 23 and ground changes during engine warm up.
Cold → Hot:
Approximately 5 - 0V

N.G. → **B** 1) Check cylinder head temperature sensor resistance.
- Stop engine.
- Disconnect cylinder head temperature sensor harness connector.
- Check resistance between terminals.

20 C (68 F)	2.3 - 2.7 kΩ
50 C (122 F)	0.77 - 0.87 kΩ
80 C (176 F)	0.30 - 0.33 kΩ

If no continuity, replace cylinder head temperature sensor.
2) Check power source for E.C.U.
C 3) Check harness continuity between E.C.U. and cylinder head temperature sensor.
- Disconnect 16-pin connector from E.C.U.
- Disconnect cylinder head temperature sensor connector.
Check resistance between terminal ⓒ and E.C.U. terminal 23.
Resistance:
Approximately 0Ω

O.K.

D CHECK GROUND CIRCUIT.
1) Stop engine and disconnect 16-pin connector from E.C.U.
2) Disconnect cylinder head temperature sensor harness connector.
3) Check resistance between terminal ⓑ and E.C.U. terminal 26.
Resistance:
Approximately 0Ω

N.G. → Check harness connection between cylinder head temperature sensor and ground.

O.K.

Reinstall any part removed.

Erase the self-diagnosis memory.

Perform driving test and then perform self-diagnosis (Mode-III) again.

N.G. → 1) Perform E.C.U. in-output signal inspection test.
2) If N.G., recheck the E.C.U. pin terminals damage or the connection of E.C.U. harness connector.

O.K.

INSPECTION END

IGNITION SIGNAL (Code No. 21)

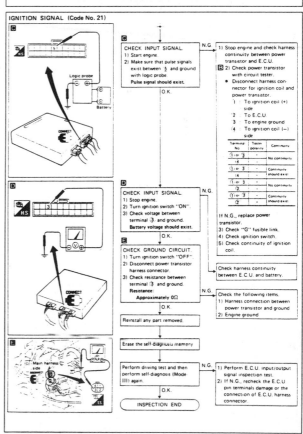

INSPECTION START

A CHECK POWER SOURCE.
1) Turn ignition switch "ON".
2) Check voltage between terminal 1 and ground.
Battery voltage should exist.

N.G. → Check the following items.
1) Harness connection between battery and power transistor and E.C.U.
2) "G" fusible link
3) Ignition switch

O.K.

C CHECK INPUT SIGNAL.
1) Start engine.
2) Make sure that pulse signals exist between 5 and ground with logic probe.
Pulse signal should exist.

N.G. → **C** 1) Stop engine and check harness continuity between power transistor and E.C.U.
B 2) Check power transistor with circuit tester.
- Disconnect harness connector for ignition coil and power transistor.
  1 To ignition coil (+) side
  2 To E.C.U.
  3 To engine ground
  4 To ignition coil (−) side

Terminal No	Tester polarity	Continuity
1 or 3	—	No continuity
4	—	
1 or 3	—	Continuity should exist
4	—	
1 or 3	—	No continuity
2	—	
1 or 3	—	Continuity should exist
2	—	

If N.G., replace power transistor.
3) Check "G" fusible link.
4) Check ignition switch.
5) Check continuity of ignition coil.

O.K.

D CHECK INPUT SIGNAL.
1) Stop engine.
2) Turn ignition switch "ON".
3) Check voltage between terminal 3 and ground.
Battery voltage should exist.

N.G. → Check harness continuity between E.C.U. and battery.

O.K.

E CHECK GROUND CIRCUIT.
1) Turn ignition switch "OFF".
2) Disconnect power transistor harness connector.
3) Check resistance between terminal 3 and ground.
Resistance:
Approximately 0Ω

N.G. → Check the following items.
1) Harness connection between power transistor and ground
2) Engine ground

O.K.

Reinstall any part removed.

Erase the self-diagnosis memory.

Perform driving test and then perform self-diagnosis (Mode-III) again.

N.G. → 1) Perform E.C.U. input/output signal inspection test.
2) If N.G., recheck the E.C.U. pin terminals damage or the connection of E.C.U. harness connector.

O.K.

INSPECTION END

ECCS SELF-DIAGNOSTIC CHART
1987–88 PORT INJECTED 200SX WITH VG30E ENGINE

FUEL PUMP (Code No. 22)

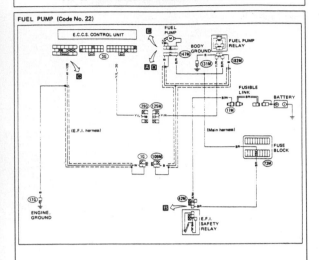

ECCS SELF-DIAGNOSTIC CHART
1987–88 PORT INJECTED 200SX WITH VG30E ENGINE

FUEL TEMPERATURE SENSOR (Code No. 41)

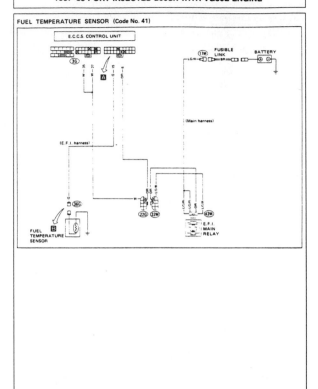

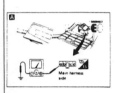

ECCS SELF-DIAGNOSTIC CHART
1987–88 PORT INJECTED 200SX WITH VG30E ENGINE

FUEL PUMP (Code No. 22)

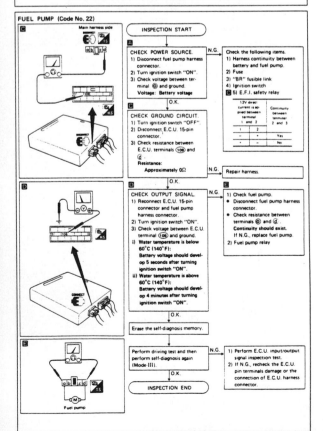

ECCS SELF-DIAGNOSTIC CHART
1987–88 PORT INJECTED 200SX WITH VG30E ENGINE

FUEL TEMPERATURE SENSOR (Code No. 41)

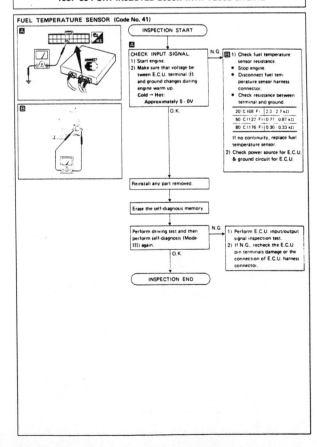

ECCS SELF-DIAGNOSTIC CHART
1987–88 PORT INJECTED 200SX WITH VG30E ENGINE

START SIGNAL (Switch ON/OFF diagnosis)

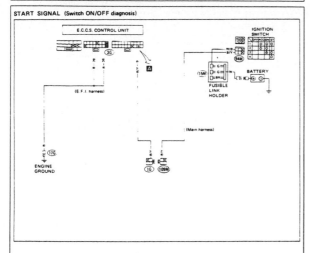

START SIGNAL (Switch ON/OFF diagnosis)

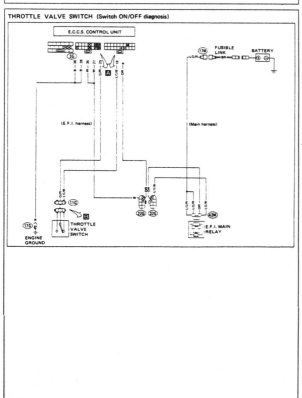

ECCS SELF-DIAGNOSTIC CHART
1987–88 PORT INJECTED 200SX WITH VG30E ENGINE

THROTTLE VALVE SWITCH (Switch ON/OFF diagnosis)

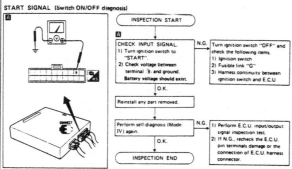

ECCS SELF-DIAGNOSTIC CHART
1987–88 PORT INJECTED 200SX WITH VG30E ENGINE

THROTTLE VALVE SWITCH (Switch ON/OFF diagnosis)

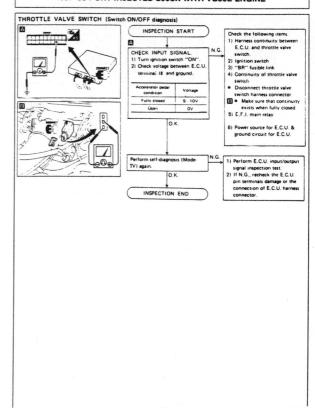

Accelerator pedal condition	Voltage
Fully closed	9 - 10V
Open	0V

Check the following items:
1) Harness continuity between E.C.U. and throttle valve switch.
2) Ignition switch
3) "BR" fusible link
4) Continuity of throttle valve switch.
- Disconnect throttle valve switch harness connector
- Make sure that continuity exists when fully closed.
5) E.F.I. main relay
6) Power source for E.C.U. & ground circuit for E.C.U.

ECCS SELF-DIAGNOSTIC CHART
1987–88 PORT INJECTED 200SX WITH VG30E ENGINE

VEHICLE SPEED SENSOR (Switch ON/OFF diagnosis)

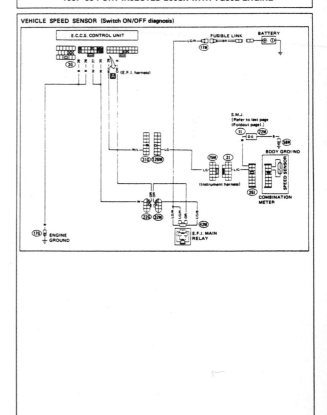

ECCS SELF-DIAGNOSTIC CHART
1987–88 PORT INJECTED 200SX WITH VG30E ENGINE

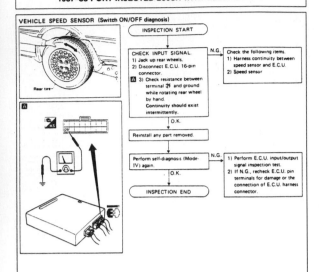

VEHICLE SPEED SENSOR (Switch ON/OFF diagnosis)

ECCS SELF-DIAGNOSTIC CHART
1987–88 PORT INJECTED 200SX WITH VG30E ENGINE

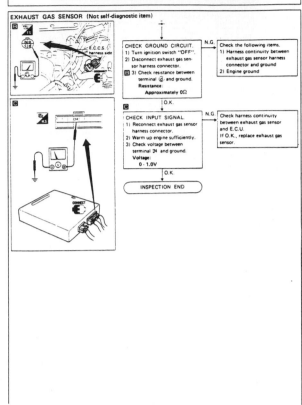

EXHAUST GAS SENSOR (Not self-diagnostic item)

ECCS SELF-DIAGNOSTIC CHART
1987–88 PORT INJECTED 200SX WITH VG30E ENGINE

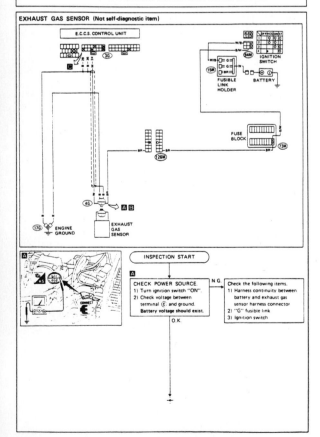

EXHAUST GAS SENSOR (Not self-diagnostic item)

ECCS SELF-DIAGNOSTIC CHART
1987–88 PORT INJECTED 200SX WITH VG30E ENGINE

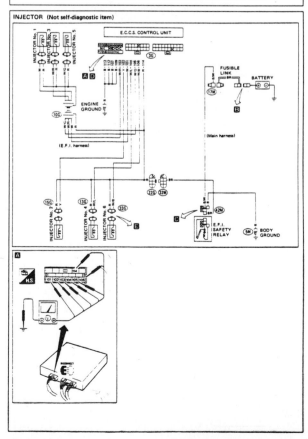

INJECTOR (Not self-diagnostic item)

ECCS SELF-DIAGNOSTIC CHART
1987–88 PORT INJECTED 200SX WITH VG30E ENGINE

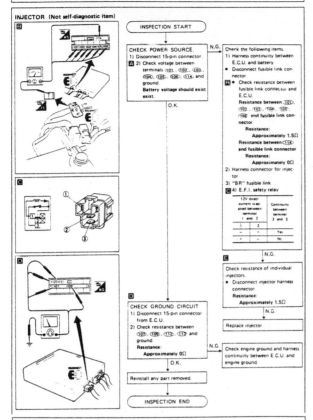

INJECTOR (Not self-diagnostic item)

ECCS SELF-DIAGNOSTIC CHART
1987–88 PORT INJECTED 200SX WITH VG30E ENGINE

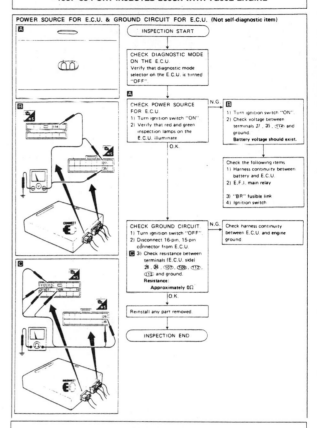

POWER SOURCE FOR E.C.U. & GROUND CIRCUIT FOR E.C.U. (Not self-diagnostic item)

ECCS SELF-DIAGNOSTIC CHART
1987–88 PORT INJECTED 200SX WITH VG30E ENGINE

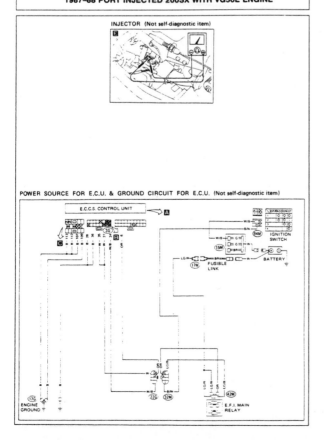

INJECTOR (Not self-diagnostic item)

POWER SOURCE FOR E.C.U. & GROUND CIRCUIT FOR E.C.U. (Not self-diagnostic item)

ECCS SELF-DIAGNOSTIC CHART
1987–88 PORT INJECTED 200SX WITH VG30E ENGINE

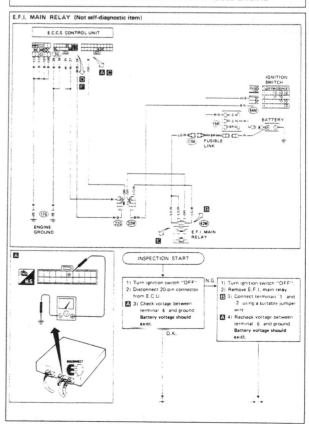

E.F.I. MAIN RELAY (Not self-diagnostic item)

ECCS SELF-DIAGNOSTIC CHART
1987–88 PORT INJECTED 200SX WITH VG30E ENGINE

E.F.I. MAIN RELAY (Not self-diagnostic item)

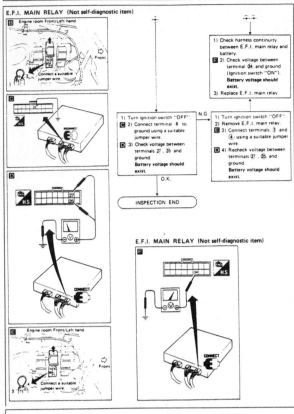

1) Check harness continuity between E.F.I. main relay and battery.
2) Check voltage between terminal ③4 and ground (Ignition switch "ON"). **Battery voltage should exist.**
3) Replace E.F.I. main relay.

---

1) Turn ignition switch "OFF".
2) Connect terminal 6 to ground using a suitable jumper wire.
3) Check voltage between terminals 27 , 35 and ground. **Battery voltage should exist.**

N.G. →

1) Turn ignition switch "OFF".
2) Remove E.F.I. main relay.
3) Connect terminals ③ and ④ using a suitable jumper wire.
4) Recheck voltage between terminals 27 , 35 and ground. **Battery voltage should exist.**

O.K. → INSPECTION END

E.F.I. MAIN RELAY (Not self-diagnostic item)

ECCS SELF-DIAGNOSTIC CHART
1987–88 PORT INJECTED 200SX WITH VG30E ENGINE

A.I.V. (Air Injection Valve) CONTROL (Not self-diagnostic item)

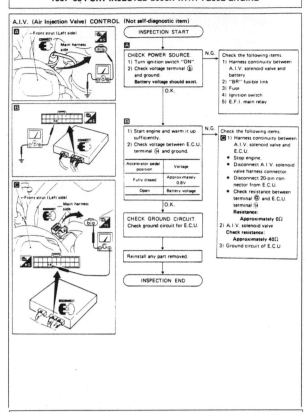

INSPECTION START

CHECK POWER SOURCE.
1) Turn ignition switch "ON".
2) Check voltage terminal ⓑ and ground. **Battery voltage should exist.**

N.G. → Check the following items.
1) Harness continuity between A.I.V. solenoid valve and battery
2) "BR" fusible link
3) Fuse
4) Ignition switch
5) E.F.I. main relay

O.K.

1) Start engine and warm it up sufficiently.
2) Check voltage between E.C.U. terminal ⑭ and ground.

Accelerator pedal position	Voltage
Fully closed	Approximately 0.8V
Open	Battery voltage

N.G. → Check the following items.
1) Harness continuity between A.I.V. solenoid valve and E.C.U.
 • Stop engine.
 • Disconnect A.I.V. solenoid valve harness connector.
 • Disconnect 20-pin connector from E.C.U.
 • Check resistance between terminal ⓒ and E.C.U. terminal ⑭. **Resistance: Approximately 0Ω**
2) A.I.V. solenoid valve **Check resistance: Approximately 40Ω**
3) Ground circuit of E.C.U.

O.K.

CHECK GROUND CIRCUIT.
Check ground circuit for E.C.U.

Reinstall any part removed.

INSPECTION END

ECCS SELF-DIAGNOSTIC CHART
1987–88 PORT INJECTED 200SX WITH VG30E ENGINE

A.I.V. (Air Injection Valve) CONTROL (Not self-diagnostic item)

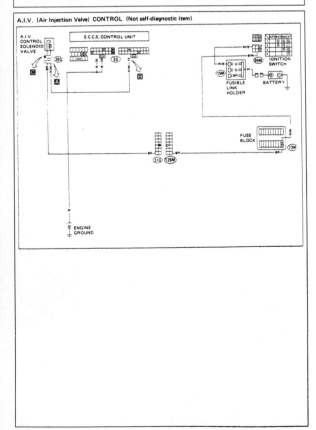

ECCS SELF-DIAGNOSTIC CHART
1987–88 PORT INJECTED 200SX WITH VG30E ENGINE

E.G.R. CONTROL (Not self-diagnostic item)

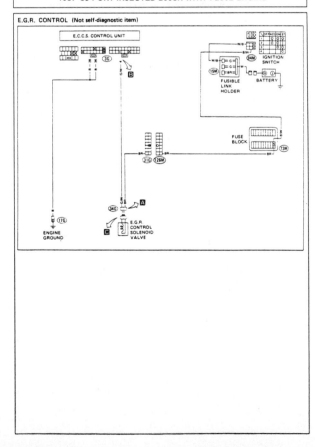

ECCS SELF-DIAGNOSTIC CHART
1987–88 PORT INJECTED 200SX WITH VG30E ENGINE

E.G.R. CONTROL (Not self-diagnostic item)

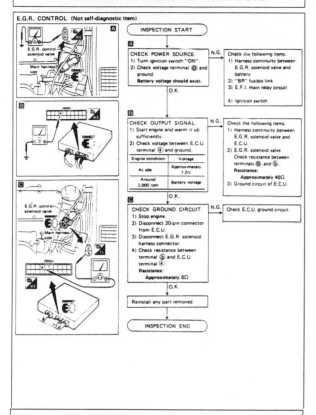

INSPECTION START

A

CHECK POWER SOURCE.
1) Turn ignition switch "ON".
2) Check voltage terminal ⓐ and ground.
   Battery voltage should exist.

N.G. → Check the following items.
1) Harness continuity between E.G.R. solenoid valve and battery
2) "BR" fusible link
3) E.F.I. main relay circuit
4) Ignition switch

O.K.

B

CHECK OUTPUT SIGNAL.
1) Start engine and warm it up sufficiently.
2) Check voltage between E.C.U. terminal ④ and ground.

Engine condition	Voltage
At idle	Approximately 1.0V
Around 2,000 rpm	Battery voltage

N.G. → Check the following items.
1) Harness continuity between E.G.R. solenoid valve and E.C.U.
2) E.G.R. solenoid valve
   Check resistance between terminals ⓐ and ⓑ.
   Resistance:
   Approximately 40Ω
3) Ground circuit of E.C.U.

O.K.

C

CHECK GROUND CIRCUIT.
1) Stop engine.
2) Disconnect 20-pin connector from E.C.U.
3) Disconnect E.G.R. solenoid harness connector.
4) Check resistance between terminal ⓑ and E.C.U. terminal ④.
   Resistance:
   Approximately 0Ω

N.G. → Check E.C.U. ground circuit.

O.K.

Reinstall any part removed.

INSPECTION END

ECCS SELF-DIAGNOSTIC CHART
1987–88 PORT INJECTED 200SX WITH VG30E ENGINE

IDLE-UP CONTROL (Not self-diagnostic item)

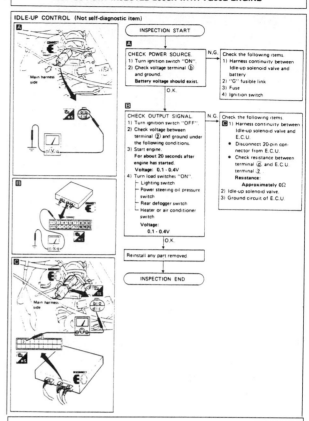

INSPECTION START

A

CHECK POWER SOURCE.
1) Turn ignition switch "ON".
2) Check voltage terminal ⓑ and ground.
   Battery voltage should exist.

N.G. → Check the following items.
1) Harness continuity between Idle-up solenoid valve and battery
2) "G" fusible link
3) Fuse
4) Ignition switch

O.K.

B

CHECK OUTPUT SIGNAL.
1) Turn ignition switch "OFF".
2) Check voltage between terminal ② and ground under the following conditions.
3) Start engine.
   For about 20 seconds after engine has started.
   Voltage: 0.1 - 0.4V
4) Turn load switches "ON".
   — Lighting switch
   — Power steering oil pressure switch
   — Rear defogger switch
   — Heater or air conditioner switch
   Voltage:
   0.1 - 0.4V

N.G. → Check the following items.
C 1) Harness continuity between Idle-up solenoid valve and E.C.U.
   • Disconnect 20-pin connector from E.C.U.
   • Check resistance between terminal ⓓ and E.C.U. terminal ②.
   Resistance:
   Approximately 0Ω
2) Idle-up solenoid valve.
3) Ground circuit of E.C.U.

O.K.

Reinstall any part removed.

INSPECTION END

ECCS SELF-DIAGNOSTIC CHART
1987–88 PORT INJECTED 200SX WITH VG30E ENGINE

IDLE-UP CONTROL (Not self-diagnostic item)

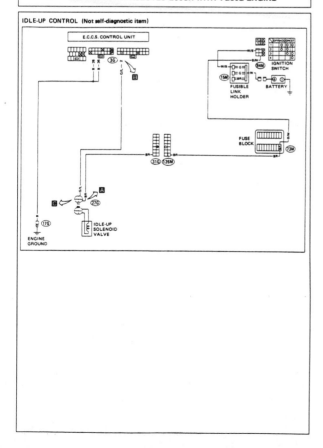

ECCS SELF-DIAGNOSTIC CHART
1987–88 PORT INJECTED 200SX WITH VG30E ENGINE

FUEL PUMP RELAY (Not self-diagnostic item)

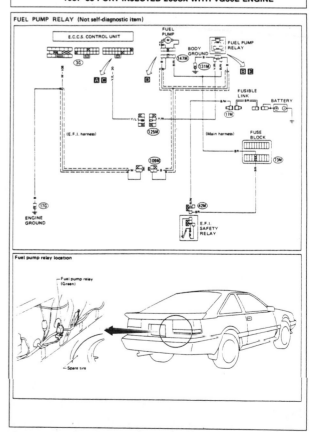

Fuel pump relay location

ECCS SELF-DIAGNOSTIC CHART
1987–88 PORT INJECTED 200SX WITH VG30E ENGINE

FUEL PUMP RELAY (Not self-diagnostic item)

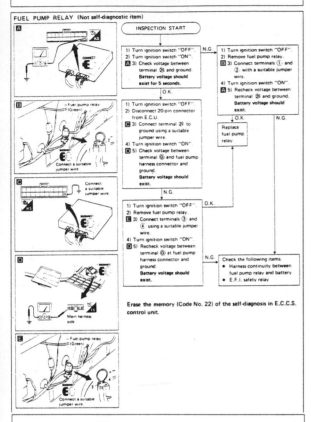

INSPECTION START

1) Turn ignition switch "OFF".
2) Turn ignition switch "ON".
A 3) Check voltage between terminal ⑳ and ground. Battery voltage should exist for 5 seconds.

O.K.

1) Turn ignition switch "OFF".
2) Disconnect 20-pin connector from E.C.U.
C 3) Connect terminal ⑳ to ground using a suitable jumper wire.
4) Turn ignition switch "ON".
D 5) Check voltage between terminal ⓒ and fuel pump harness connector and ground. Battery voltage should exist.

N.G.

1) Turn ignition switch "OFF".
2) Remove fuel pump relay.
B 3) Connect terminals ③ and ④ using a suitable jumper wire.
4) Turn ignition switch "ON".
D 5) Recheck voltage between terminal ⓒ at fuel pump harness connector and ground. Battery voltage should exist.

N.G. → Check the following items.
- Harness continuity between fuel pump relay and battery
- E.F.I. safety relay

---

1) Turn ignition switch "OFF".
2) Remove fuel pump relay.
B 3) Connect terminals ① and ② with a suitable jumper wire.
4) Turn ignition switch "ON".
A 5) Recheck voltage between terminal ⑳ and ground. Battery voltage should exist.

O.K. / N.G.

Replace fuel pump relay.

Erase the memory (Code No. 22) of the self-diagnosis in E.C.C.S. control unit.

ECCS SELF-DIAGNOSTIC CHART
1987–88 PORT INJECTED 200SX WITH VG30E ENGINE

NEUTRAL SWITCH (Not self-diagnostic item) (Only for M/T model)

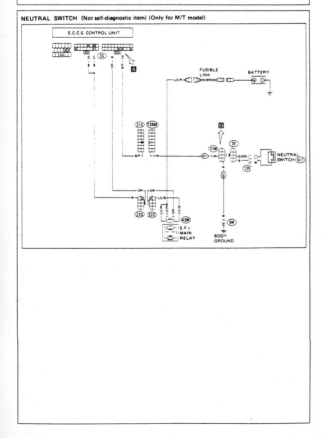

ECCS SELF-DIAGNOSTIC CHART
1987–88 PORT INJECTED 200SX WITH VG30E ENGINE

NEUTRAL SWITCH (Not self-diagnostic item) (Only for M/T model)

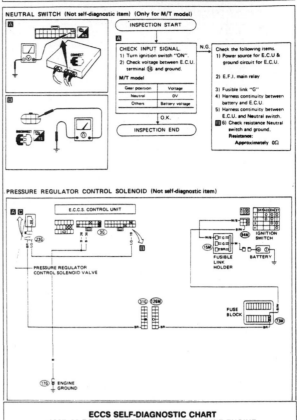

INSPECTION START

A CHECK INPUT SIGNAL.
1) Turn ignition switch "ON".
2) Check voltage between E.C.U. terminal ⑩ and ground.

M/T model

Gear position	Voltage
Neutral	0V
Others	Battery voltage

N.G. → Check the following items.
1) Power source for E.C.U & ground circuit for E.C.U.
2) E.F.I. main relay
3) Fusible link "G"
4) Harness continuity between battery and E.C.U.
5) Harness continuity between E.C.U. and Neutral switch.
B 6) Check resistance Neutral switch and ground. Resistance: Approximately 0Ω

O.K.

INSPECTION END

PRESSURE REGULATOR CONTROL SOLENOID (Not self-diagnostic item)

ECCS SELF-DIAGNOSTIC CHART
1987–88 PORT INJECTED 200SX WITH VG30E ENGINE

PRESSURE REGULATOR CONTROL SOLENOID (Not self-diagnostic item)

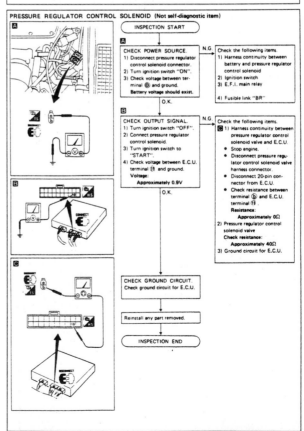

INSPECTION START

A CHECK POWER SOURCE.
1) Disconnect pressure regulator control solenoid connector.
2) Turn ignition switch "ON".
3) Check voltage between terminal ⓒ and ground. Battery voltage should exist.

N.G. → Check the following items.
1) Harness continuity between battery and pressure regulator control solenoid
2) Ignition switch
3) E.F.I. main relay
4) Fusible link "BR"

O.K.

B CHECK OUTPUT SIGNAL.
1) Turn ignition switch "OFF".
2) Connect pressure regulator control solenoid.
3) Turn ignition switch to "START".
4) Check voltage between E.C.U. terminal ⑪ and ground. Voltage: Approximately 0.9V

N.G. → Check the following items.
C 1) Harness continuity between pressure regulator control solenoid valve and E.C.U.
- Stop engine.
- Disconnect pressure regulator control solenoid valve harness connector.
- Disconnect 20-pin connector from E.C.U.
- Check resistance between terminal ⓑ and E.C.U. terminal ⑪. Resistance: Approximately 0Ω
2) Pressure regulator control solenoid valve Check resistance: Approximately 40Ω
3) Ground circuit for E.C.U.

O.K.

C CHECK GROUND CIRCUIT. Check ground circuit for E.C.U.

Reinstall any part removed.

INSPECTION END

SELF-DIAGNOSTIC CHART
1987–88 PORT INJECTED 200SX WITH VG30E ENGINE

AIR REGULATOR (Not self-diagnostic item)

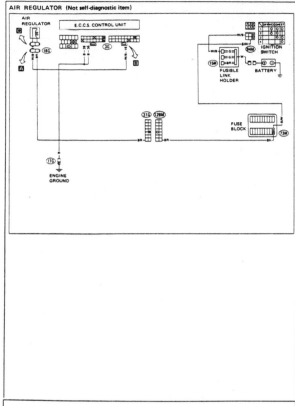

ECCS SELF-DIAGNOSTIC CHART
1987–88 PORT INJECTED 200SX WITH VG30E ENGINE

AIR REGULATOR (Not self-diagnostic item)

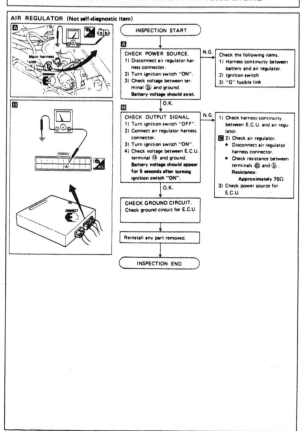

MIXTURE RATIO FEEDBACK SYSTEM INSPECTION CHART
1987–88 PORT INJECTED 200SX WITH VG30E ENGINE

PREPARATION

1. Make sure that the following parts are in good order.
   - Battery
   - Ignition system
   - Engine oil and coolant levels
   - Fuses
   - E.C.C.S. harness connectors
   - Vacuum hoses
   - Air intake system (oil filler cap, oil level gauge, etc.)
   - Fuel pressure
   - A.I.V. hose
   - Engine compression
   - E.G.R. valve operation
   - Throttle valve
2. On air conditioner equipped models, checks should be carried out while the air conditioner is "OFF".
3. When measuring "CO" percentage, insert probe more than 40 cm (15.7 in) into tail pipe.

Overall inspection sequence

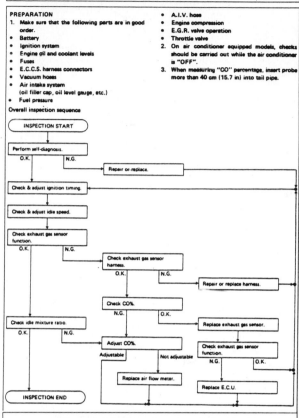

MIXTURE RATIO FEEDBACK SYSTEM INSPECTION CHART
1987–88 PORT INJECTED 200SX WITH VG30E ENGINE

Idle Check and Set Procedure

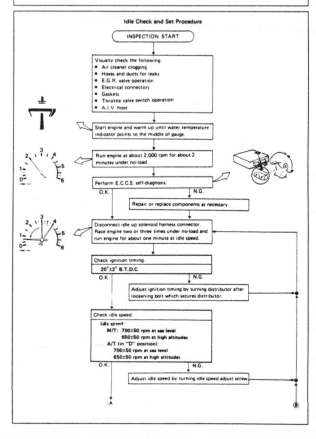

MIXTURE RATIO FEEDBACK SYSTEM INSPECTION CHART
1987–88 PORT INJECTED 200SX WITH VG30E ENGINE

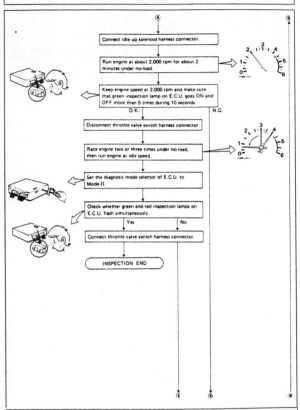

MIXTURE RATIO FEEDBACK SYSTEM INSPECTION CHART
1987–88 PORT INJECTED 200SX WITH VG30E ENGINE

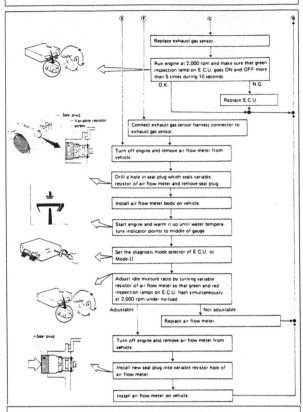

MIXTURE RATIO FEEDBACK SYSTEM INSPECTION CHART
1987–88 PORT INJECTED 200SX WITH VG30E ENGINE

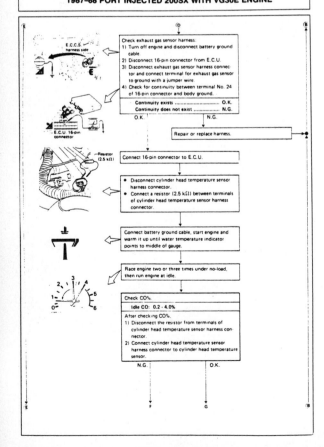

ECCS SELF-DIAGNOSTIC CHART
1987–88 PORT INJECTED 300ZX

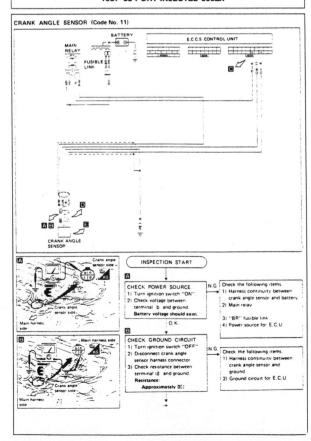

CRANK ANGLE SENSOR (Code No. 11)

ECCS SELF-DIAGNOSTIC CHART – 1987–88 PORT INJECTED 300ZX

CRANK ANGLE SENSOR (Code No. 11)

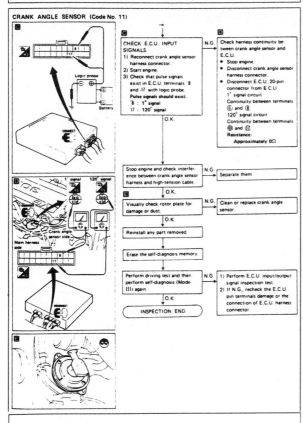

CHECK E.C.U. INPUT SIGNALS.
1) Reconnect crank angle sensor harness connector.
2) Start engine.
3) Check that pulse signals exist in E.C.U. terminals 8 and 17 with logic probe.
   Pulse signals should exist.
   8 : 1° signal
   17 : 120° signal

N.G. → Check harness continuity between crank angle sensor and E.C.U.
- Stop engine.
- Disconnect crank angle sensor harness connector.
- Disconnect E.C.U. 20-pin connector from the E.C.U.
  1° signal circuit
  Continuity between terminals C and 8
  120° signal circuit
  Continuity between terminals D and 17
  Resistance:
  Approximately 0Ω

O.K. ↓

Stop engine and check interference between crank angle sensor harness and high-tension cable.

N.G. → Separate them.

O.K. ↓

Visually check rotor plate for damage or dust.

N.G. → Clean or replace crank angle sensor.

O.K. ↓

Reinstall any part removed.

↓

Erase the self-diagnosis memory.

↓

Perform driving test and then perform self-diagnosis (Mode-III) again.

N.G. → 1) Perform E.C.U. input/output signal inspection test.
2) If N.G., recheck the E.C.U. pin terminals damage or the connection of E.C.U. harness connector.

O.K. ↓

INSPECTION END

ECCS SELF-DIAGNOSTIC CHART – 1987–88 PORT INJECTED 300ZX

AIR FLOW METER (Code No. 12)

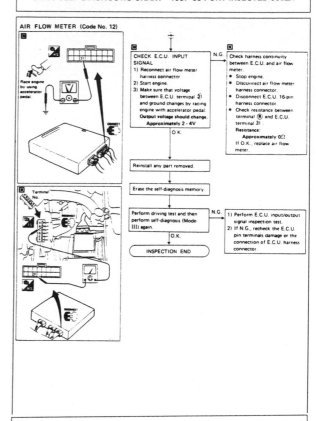

CHECK E.C.U. INPUT SIGNAL
1) Reconnect air flow meter harness connector.
2) Start engine.
3) Make sure that voltage between E.C.U. terminal 31 and ground changes by racing engine with accelerator pedal.
   Output voltage should change.
   Approximately 2 - 4V

N.G. → Check harness continuity between E.C.U. and air flow meter.
- Stop engine.
- Disconnect air flow meter harness connector.
- Disconnect E.C.U. 16-pin connector.
- Check resistance between terminal B and E.C.U. terminal 31:
  Resistance:
  Approximately 0Ω
  If O.K., replace air flow meter.

O.K. ↓

Reinstall any part removed.

↓

Erase the self-diagnosis memory.

↓

Perform driving test and then perform self-diagnosis (Mode-III) again.

N.G. → 1) Perform E.C.U. input/output signal inspection test.
2) If N.G., recheck the E.C.U. pin terminals damage or the connection of E.C.U. harness connector.

O.K. ↓

INSPECTION END

ECCS SELF-DIAGNOSTIC CHART – 1987–88 PORT INJECTED 300ZX

AIR FLOW METER (Code No. 12)

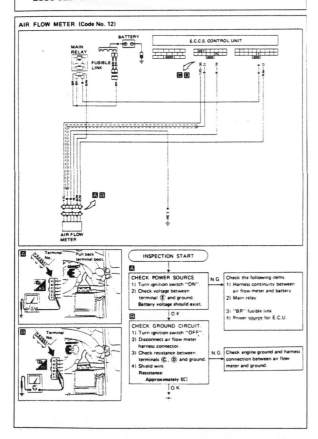

INSPECTION START

↓

CHECK POWER SOURCE
1) Turn ignition switch "ON".
2) Check voltage between terminal E and ground.
   Battery voltage should exist.

N.G. → Check the following items:
1) Harness continuity between air flow meter and battery
2) Main relay
3) "BR" fusible link
4) Power source for E.C.U.

O.K. ↓

CHECK GROUND CIRCUIT.
1) Turn ignition switch "OFF".
2) Disconnect air flow meter harness connector.
3) Check resistance between terminals C, D and ground.
4) Shield wire.
   Resistance:
   Approximately 0Ω

N.G. → Check engine ground and harness connection between air flow meter and ground.

O.K. ↓

ECCS SELF-DIAGNOSTIC CHART – 1987–88 PORT INJECTED 300ZX

CYLINDER HEAD TEMPERATURE SENSOR (Code No. 13)

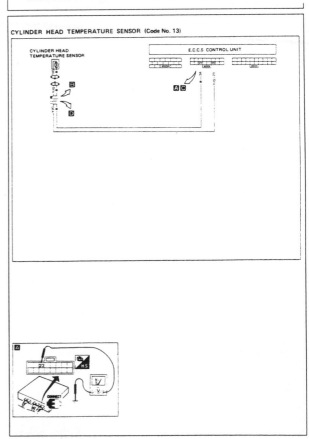

ECCS SELF-DIAGNOSTIC CHART—1987–88 PORT INJECTED 300ZX

CYLINDER HEAD TEMPERATURE SENSOR (Code No. 13)

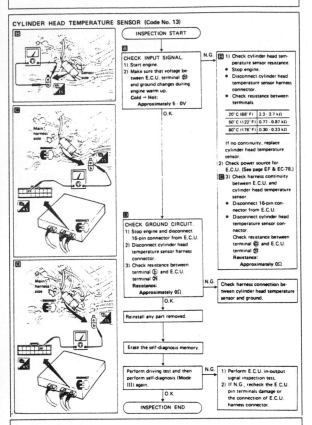

INSPECTION START

A CHECK INPUT SIGNAL.
1) Start engine.
2) Make sure that voltage between E.C.U. terminal ㉒ and ground changes during engine warm up.
Cold → Hot:
Approximately 5 - 0V

N.G. → **B** 1) Check cylinder head temperature sensor resistance.
• Stop engine.
• Disconnect cylinder head temperature sensor harness connector.
• Check resistance between terminals.

20°C (68°F)	2.3 - 2.7 kΩ
50°C (122°F)	0.77 - 0.87 kΩ
80°C (176°F)	0.30 - 0.33 kΩ

If no continuity, replace cylinder head temperature sensor.
2) Check power source for E.C.U. (See page EF & EC-78.)
C 3) Check harness continuity between E.C.U. and cylinder head temperature sensor.
• Disconnect 16-pin connector from E.C.U.
• Disconnect cylinder head temperature sensor connector.
Check resistance between terminal ㉒ and E.C.U. terminal ㉒.
Resistance:
Approximately 0Ω

O.K.

D CHECK GROUND CIRCUIT.
1) Stop engine and disconnect 16-pin connector from E.C.U.
2) Disconnect cylinder head temperature sensor harness connector.
3) Check resistance between terminal ㉖ and E.C.U. terminal ㉖.
Resistance:
Approximately 0Ω

N.G. → Check harness connection between cylinder head temperature sensor and ground.

O.K.

Reinstall any part removed.

Erase the self-diagnosis memory.

Perform driving test and then perform self-diagnosis (Mode III) again.

N.G. → 1) Perform E.C.U. in-output signal inspection test.
2) If N.G., recheck the E.C.U. pin terminals damage or the connection of E.C.U. harness connector.

O.K.

INSPECTION END

ECCS SELF-DIAGNOSTIC CHART—1987–88 PORT INJECTED 300ZX

IGNITION SIGNAL (Code No. 21)

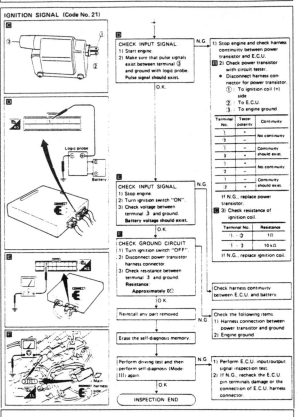

C (illustration)

D CHECK INPUT SIGNAL.
1) Start engine.
2) Make sure that pulse signals exist between terminal ⑤ and ground with logic probe.
Pulse signal should exist.

O.K.

N.G. → 1) Stop engine and check harness continuity between power transistor and E.C.U.
B 2) Check power transistor with circuit tester.
• Disconnect harness connector for power transistor.
①: To ignition coil (+) side
②: To E.C.U.
③: To engine ground

Terminal No.	Tester polarity	Continuity
①	+	No continuity
③	–	
①	–	Continuity should exist.
③	+	
①	+	No continuity
②	–	
①	–	Continuity should exist.
②	+	

If N.G., replace power transistor.
C 3) Check resistance of ignition coil.

Terminal No.	Resistance
① - ②	1Ω
① - ③	10 kΩ

If N.G., replace ignition coil.

E CHECK INPUT SIGNAL.
1) Stop engine.
2) Turn ignition switch "ON".
3) Check voltage between terminal ③ and ground.
Battery voltage should exist.

O.K.

N.G. → Check harness continuity between E.C.U. and battery.

E CHECK GROUND CIRCUIT
1) Turn ignition switch "OFF".
2) Disconnect power transistor harness connector.
3) Check resistance between terminal ③ and ground.
Resistance:
Approximately 0Ω

O.K.

N.G. → Check the following items
1) Harness connection between power transistor and ground
2) Engine ground

Reinstall any part removed.

Erase the self-diagnosis memory.

Perform driving test and then perform self-diagnosis (Mode III) again.

N.G. → 1) Perform E.C.U. input/output signal inspection test.
2) If N.G., recheck the E.C.U. pin terminals damage or the connection of E.C.U. harness connector.

O.K.

INSPECTION END

ECCS SELF-DIAGNOSTIC CHART—1987–88 PORT INJECTED 300ZX

IGNITION SIGNAL (Code No. 21)

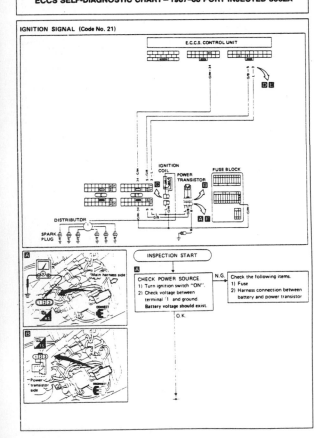

E.C.C.S. CONTROL UNIT

IGNITION COIL
POWER TRANSISTOR
FUSE BLOCK
DISTRIBUTOR
SPARK PLUG

INSPECTION START

A CHECK POWER SOURCE.
1) Turn ignition switch "ON".
2) Check voltage between terminal ① and ground.
Battery voltage should exist.

N.G. → Check the following items.
1) Fuse
2) Harness connection between battery and power transistor

O.K.

ECCS SELF-DIAGNOSTIC CHART—1987–88 PORT INJECTED 300ZX

FUEL PUMP (Code No. 22)

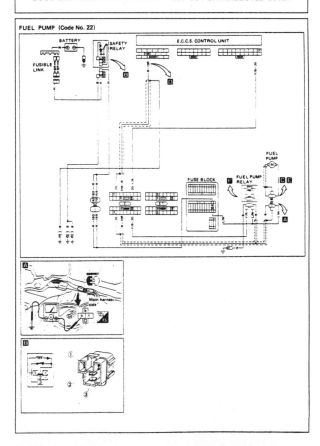

BATTERY
SAFETY RELAY
FUSIBLE LINK
E.C.C.S. CONTROL UNIT
FUSE BLOCK
FUEL PUMP RELAY
FUEL PUMP

ECCS SELF-DIAGNOSTIC CHART — 1987–88 PORT INJECTED 300ZX

FUEL PUMP (Code No. 22)

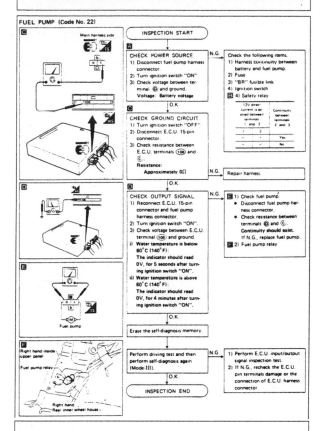

C Main harness side

INSPECTION START

A CHECK POWER SOURCE
1) Disconnect fuel pump harness connector.
2) Turn ignition switch "ON".
3) Check voltage between terminal © and ground.
Voltage: Battery voltage

O.K.

N.G. → Check the following items.
1) Harness continuity between battery and fuel pump.
2) Fuse
3) "BR" fusible link
4) Ignition switch
B 4) Safety relay

	12v direct current is applied between terminal 1 and 2	Continuity between terminals 2 and 3
	1 and 2	2 and 3
–	–	Yes
–	–	No

C CHECK GROUND CIRCUIT
1) Turn ignition switch "OFF".
2) Disconnect E.C.U. 15-pin connector.
3) Check resistance between E.C.U. terminals ⑩⑥ and ©.
Resistance:
Approximately 0Ω

N.G. → Repair harness.

O.K.

D

D CHECK OUTPUT SIGNAL.
1) Reconnect E.C.U. 15-pin connector and fuel pump harness connector.
2) Turn ignition switch "ON".
3) Check voltage between E.C.U. terminal ⑩⑥ and ground.
i) Water temperature is below 60°C (140°F):
The indicator should read 0V, for 5 seconds after turning ignition switch "ON".
ii) Water temperature is above 60°C (140°F):
The indicator should read 0V, for 4 minutes after turning ignition switch "ON".

N.G. → **E** 1) Check fuel pump.
- Disconnect fuel pump harness connector.
- Check resistance between terminals © and ©.
Continuity should exist. If N.G., replace fuel pump.
F 2) Fuel pump relay

E

Fuel pump

O.K.

Erase the self-diagnosis memory.

F Right hand inside upper panel

Fuel pump relay

Perform driving test and then perform self-diagnosis again (Mode-III).

N.G. → 1) Perform E.C.U. input/output signal inspection test.
2) If N.G., recheck the E.C.U. pin terminals damage or the connection of E.C.U. harness connector.

O.K.

INSPECTION END

Right hand Rear inner wheel house

ECCS SELF-DIAGNOSTIC CHART — 1987–88 PORT INJECTED 300ZX

DETONATION SENSOR (Code No. 34)

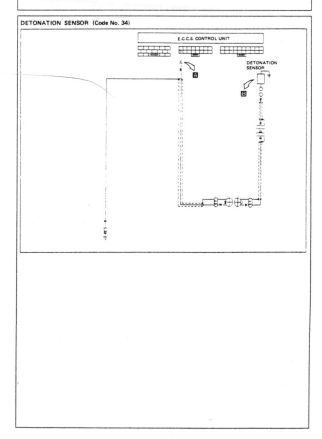

E.C.C.S. CONTROL UNIT

DETONATION SENSOR

ECCS SELF-DIAGNOSTIC CHART — 1987–88 PORT INJECTED 300ZX

DETONATION SENSOR (Code No. 34)

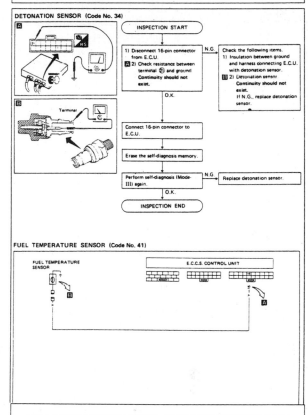

INSPECTION START

1) Disconnect 16-pin connector from E.C.U.
A 2) Check resistance between terminal ⑪ and ground. Continuity should not exist.

N.G. → Check the following items.
1) Insulation between ground and harness connecting E.C.U. with detonation sensor.
B 2) Detonation sensor. Continuity should not exist. If N.G., replace detonation sensor.

O.K.

B Terminal

Connect 16-pin connector to E.C.U.

Erase the self-diagnosis memory.

Perform self-diagnosis (Mode-III) again.

N.G. → Replace detonation sensor.

O.K.

INSPECTION END

FUEL TEMPERATURE SENSOR (Code No. 41)

FUEL TEMPERATURE SENSOR

E.C.C.S. CONTROL UNIT

ECCS SELF-DIAGNOSTIC CHART — 1987–88 PORT INJECTED 300ZX

FUEL TEMPERATURE SENSOR (Code No. 41)

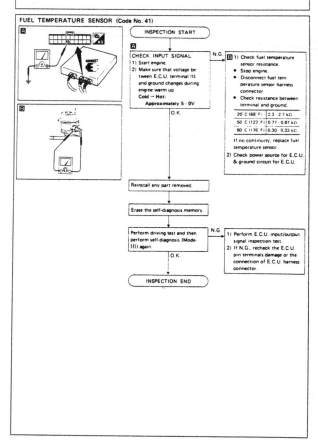

A

INSPECTION START

A CHECK INPUT SIGNAL.
1) Start engine.
2) Make sure that voltage between E.C.U. terminal 15 and ground changes during engine warm up.
Cold → Hot:
Approximately 5 - 0V

N.G. → **B** 1) Check fuel temperature sensor resistance.
- Stop engine.
- Disconnect fuel temperature sensor harness connector.
- Check resistance between terminal and ground.

20°C (68°F)	2.3 - 2.7 kΩ
50°C (122°F)	0.77 - 0.87 kΩ
80°C (176°F)	0.30 - 0.33 kΩ

If no continuity, replace fuel temperature sensor.
2) Check power source for E.C.U. & ground circuit for E.C.U.

O.K.

B

Reinstall any part removed.

Erase the self-diagnosis memory.

Perform driving test and then perform self-diagnosis (Mode-III) again.

N.G. → 1) Perform E.C.U. input/output signal inspection test.
2) If N.G., recheck the E.C.U. pin terminals damage or the connection of E.C.U. harness connector.

O.K.

INSPECTION END

ECCS SELF-DIAGNOSTIC CHART – 1987–88 PORT INJECTED 300ZX

START SIGNAL (Switch ON/OFF diagnosis)

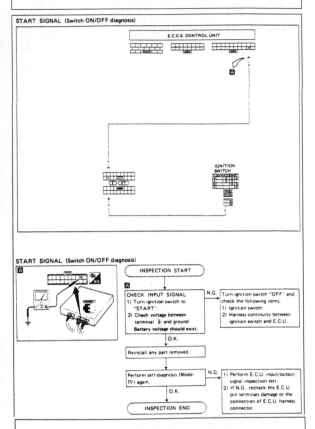

START SIGNAL (Switch ON/OFF diagnosis)

INSPECTION START

CHECK INPUT SIGNAL.
1) Turn ignition switch to "START".
2) Check voltage between terminal ⑨ and ground. Battery voltage should exist.

N.G. → Turn ignition switch "OFF" and check the following items.
1) Ignition switch
2) Harness continuity between ignition switch and E.C.U.

O.K.

Reinstall any part removed.

Perform self-diagnosis (Mode-IV) again.

N.G. → 1) Perform E.C.U. input/output signal inspection test.
2) If N.G., recheck the E.C.U. pin terminals damage or the connection of E.C.U. harness connector.

O.K.

INSPECTION END

ECCS SELF-DIAGNOSTIC CHART – 1987–88 PORT INJECTED 300ZX

THROTTLE VALVE SWITCH (Switch ON/OFF diagnosis)

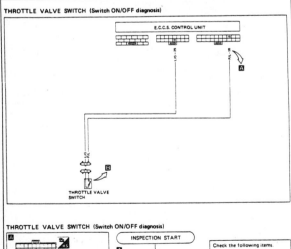

THROTTLE VALVE SWITCH (Switch ON/OFF diagnosis)

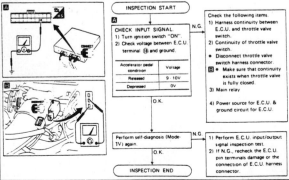

INSPECTION START

CHECK INPUT SIGNAL.
1) Turn ignition switch "ON".
2) Check voltage between E.C.U. terminal ⑱ and ground.

Accelerator pedal condition	Voltage
Released	9 - 10V
Depressed	0V

N.G. → Check the following items.
1) Harness continuity between E.C.U. and throttle valve switch.
2) Continuity of throttle valve switch.
● Disconnect throttle valve switch harness connector.
● Make sure that continuity exists when throttle valve is fully closed.
3) Main relay.
4) Power source for E.C.U. & ground circuit for E.C.U.

O.K.

Perform self-diagnosis (Mode-IV) again.

N.G. → 1) Perform E.C.U. input/output signal inspection test.
2) If N.G., recheck the E.C.U. pin terminals damage or the connection of E.C.U. harness connector.

O.K.

INSPECTION END

ECCS SELF-DIAGNOSTIC CHART – 1987–88 PORT INJECTED 300ZX

VEHICLE SPEED SENSOR (Switch ON/OFF diagnosis)

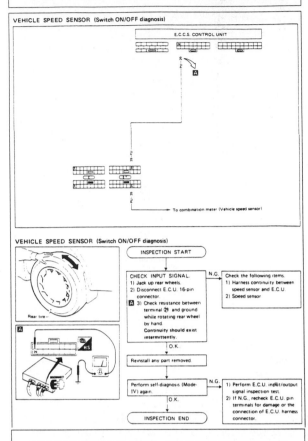

To combination meter (Vehicle speed sensor)

VEHICLE SPEED SENSOR (Switch ON/OFF diagnosis)

Rear tire

INSPECTION START

CHECK INPUT SIGNAL.
1) Jack up rear wheels.
2) Disconnect E.C.U. 16-pin connector.
3) Check resistance between terminal ㉙ and ground while rotating rear wheel by hand. Continuity should exist intermittently.

N.G. → Check the following items.
1) Harness continuity between speed sensor and E.C.U.
2) Speed sensor

O.K.

Reinstall any part removed.

Perform self-diagnosis (Mode-IV) again.

N.G. → 1) Perform E.C.U. input/output signal inspection test.
2) If N.G., recheck E.C.U. pin terminals for damage or the connection of E.C.U. harness connector.

O.K.

INSPECTION END

ECCS SELF-DIAGNOSTIC CHART – 1987–88 PORT INJECTED 300ZX

EXHAUST GAS SENSOR (Not self-diagnostic item)

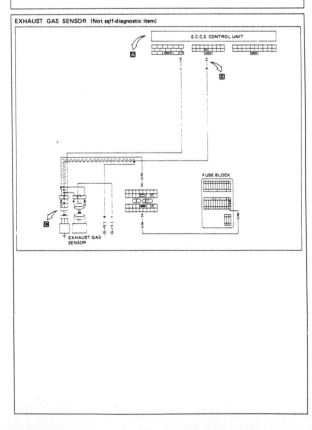

FUSE BLOCK

EXHAUST GAS SENSOR

ECCS SELF-DIAGNOSTIC CHART — 1987–88 PORT INJECTED 300ZX

EXHAUST GAS SENSOR (Not self-diagnostic item)

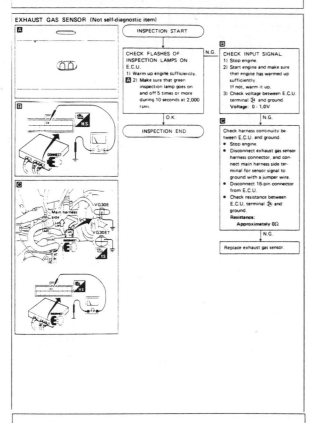

INSPECTION START

CHECK FLASHES OF INSPECTION LAMPS ON E.C.U.
1) Warm up engine sufficiently.
2) Make sure that green inspection lamp goes on and off 5 times or more during 10 seconds at 2,000 rpm.

O.K. → **INSPECTION END**

N.G. → **B**

B CHECK INPUT SIGNAL.
1) Stop engine.
2) Start engine and make sure that engine has warmed up sufficiently.
   If not, warm it up.
3) Check voltage between E.C.U. terminal 24 and ground.
   Voltage: 0 - 1.0V

O.K. ↓   N.G. → **C**

C Check harness continuity between E.C.U. and ground.
- Stop engine.
- Disconnect exhaust gas sensor harness connector, and connect main harness side terminal for sensor signal to ground with a jumper wire.
- Disconnect 16-pin connector from E.C.U.
- Check resistance between E.C.U. terminal 24 and ground.
  Resistance: Approximately 0Ω

N.G. ↓

Replace exhaust gas sensor.

ECCS SELF-DIAGNOSTIC CHART — 1987–88 PORT INJECTED 300ZX

INJECTOR (Not self-diagnostic item)

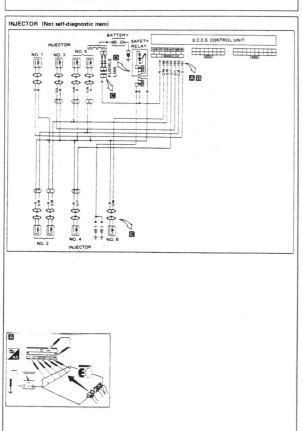

ECCS SELF-DIAGNOSTIC CHART — 1987–88 PORT INJECTED 300ZX

INJECTOR (Not self-diagnostic item)

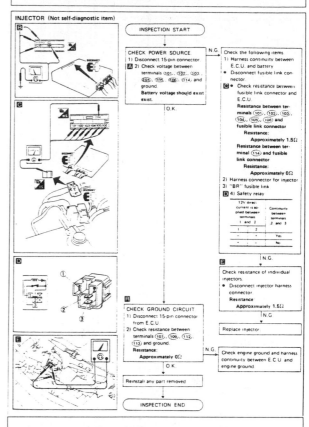

INSPECTION START

CHECK POWER SOURCE
1) Disconnect 15-pin connector
2) Check voltage between terminals 101, 102, 103, 105, 106, 114, and ground.
   Battery voltage should exist.

N.G. → Check the following items
1) Harness continuity between E.C.U. and battery
   - Disconnect fusible link connector.
   - Check resistance between fusible link connector and E.C.U.
     Resistance between terminals 101, 102, 103, 104, 105, 106 and fusible link connector
     Resistance: Approximately 1.5Ω
     Resistance between terminal 114 and fusible link connector
     Resistance: Approximately 0Ω
2) Harness connector for injector
3) "BR" fusible link
4) Safety relay

12v direct current is applied between terminals		Continuity between terminals
1	2	3 and 3
		Yes
		No

N.G. ↓

E Check resistance of individual injectors.
- Disconnect injector harness connector
  Resistance: Approximately 1.5Ω

N.G. ↓

Replace injector

CHECK GROUND CIRCUIT
1) Disconnect 15-pin connector from E.C.U.
2) Check resistance between terminals 107, 109, 112, 113 and ground.
   Resistance: Approximately 0Ω

N.G. → Check engine ground and harness continuity between E.C.U. and engine ground.

O.K. ↓

Reinstall any part removed

INSPECTION END

ECCS SELF-DIAGNOSTIC CHART — 1987–88 PORT INJECTED 300ZX

POWER SOURCE & GROUND CIRCUIT FOR E.C.U. (Not self-diagnostic item)

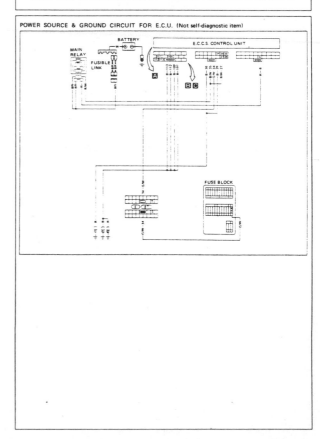

ECCS SELF-DIAGNOSTIC CHART – 1987–88 PORT INJECTED 300ZX

POWER SOURCE & GROUND CIRCUIT FOR E.C.U. (Not self-diagnostic item)

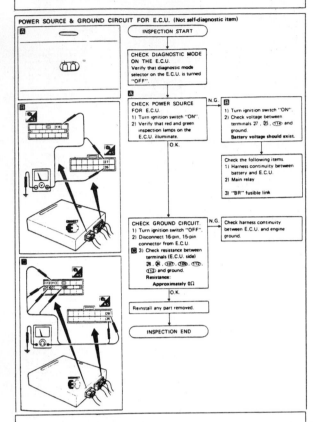

INSPECTION START

CHECK DIAGNOSTIC MODE ON THE E.C.U.
Verify that diagnostic mode selector on the E.C.U. is turned "OFF".

CHECK POWER SOURCE FOR E.C.U.
1) Turn ignition switch "ON".
2) Verify that red and green inspection lamps on the E.C.U. illuminate.

N.G. →
1) Turn ignition switch "ON".
2) Check voltage between terminals 27, 35, (114) and ground.
Battery voltage should exist.

Check the following items.
1) Harness continuity between battery and E.C.U.
2) Main relay
3) "BR" fusible link

O.K. ↓

CHECK GROUND CIRCUIT.
1) Turn ignition switch "OFF".
2) Disconnect 16-pin, 15-pin connector from E.C.U.
3) Check resistance between terminals (E.C.U. side) 21, 24, (107), (109), (112), (113) and ground.
Resistance: Approximately 0Ω

N.G. →
Check harness continuity between E.C.U. and engine ground.

O.K. ↓

Reinstall any part removed.

INSPECTION END

ECCS SELF-DIAGNOSTIC CHART – 1987–88 PORT INJECTED 300ZX

A.I.V. CONTROL SOLENOID VALVE (Not self-diagnostic item)

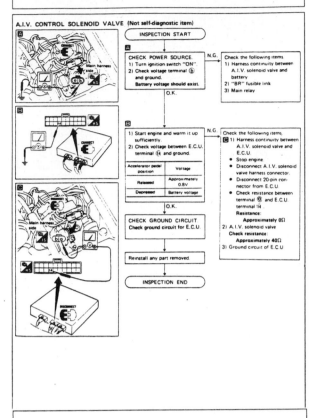

INSPECTION START

CHECK POWER SOURCE.
1) Turn ignition switch "ON".
2) Check voltage terminal ⓑ and ground.
Battery voltage should exist.

N.G. →
Check the following items.
1) Harness continuity between A.I.V. solenoid valve and battery
2) "BR" fusible link
3) Main relay

O.K. ↓

1) Start engine and warm it up sufficiently.
2) Check voltage between E.C.U. terminal (14) and ground.

Accelerator pedal position	Voltage
Released	Approximately 0.8V
Depressed	Battery voltage

N.G. →
Check the following items.
1) Harness continuity between A.I.V. solenoid valve and E.C.U.
  ● Stop engine
  ● Disconnect A.I.V. solenoid valve harness connector.
  ● Disconnect 20-pin connector from E.C.U.
  ● Check resistance between terminal ⓒ and E.C.U. terminal (14).
  Resistance: Approximately 0Ω
2) A.I.V. solenoid valve
  Check resistance: Approximately 40Ω
3) Ground circuit of E.C.U.

O.K. ↓

CHECK GROUND CIRCUIT.
Check ground circuit for E.C.U.

Reinstall any part removed.

INSPECTION END

ECCS SELF-DIAGNOSTIC CHART – 1987–88 PORT INJECTED 300ZX

A.I.V. CONTROL SOLENOID VALVE (Not self-diagnostic item)

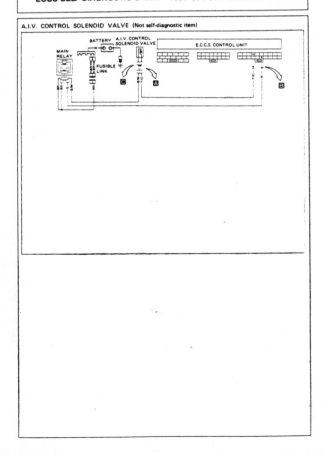

ECCS SELF-DIAGNOSTIC CHART – 1987–88 PORT INJECTED 300ZX

E.G.R. CONTROL SOLENOID VALVE (Not self-diagnostic item)

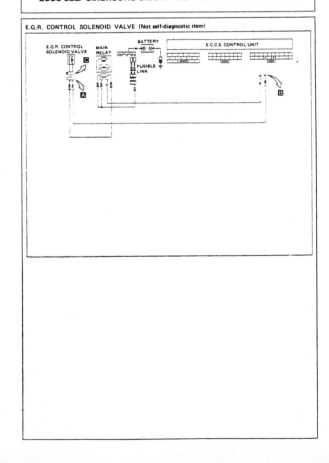

ECCS SELF-DIAGNOSTIC CHART—1987–88 PORT INJECTED 300ZX

E.G.R. CONTROL SOLENOID VALVE (Not self-diagnostic item)

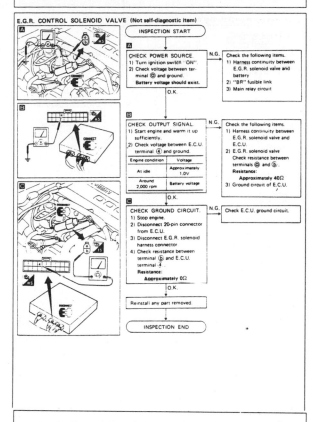

INSPECTION START

A CHECK POWER SOURCE.
1) Turn ignition switch "ON".
2) Check voltage between terminal ⓒ and ground.
Battery voltage should exist.

N.G. → Check the following items.
1) Harness continuity between E.G.R. solenoid valve and battery
2) "BR" fusible link
3) Main relay circuit

O.K.

B CHECK OUTPUT SIGNAL.
1) Start engine and warm it up sufficiently.
2) Check voltage between E.C.U. terminal ⓒ and ground.

Engine condition	Voltage
At idle	Approximately 1.0V
Around 2,000 rpm	Battery voltage

N.G. → Check the following items.
1) Harness continuity between E.G.R. solenoid valve and E.C.U.
2) E.G.R. solenoid valve Check resistance between terminals ⓐ and ⓑ.
Resistance: Approximately 40Ω
3) Ground circuit of E.C.U.

O.K.

C CHECK GROUND CIRCUIT.
1) Stop engine.
2) Disconnect 20-pin connector from E.C.U.
3) Disconnect E.G.R. solenoid harness connector
4) Check resistance between terminal ⓑ and E.C.U. terminal ④.
Resistance: Approximately 0Ω

N.G. → Check E.C.U. ground circuit.

O.K.

Reinstall any part removed.

INSPECTION END

ECCS SELF-DIAGNOSTIC CHART—1987–88 PORT INJECTED 300ZX

IDLE-UP SOLENOID VALVE (Not self-diagnostic item)

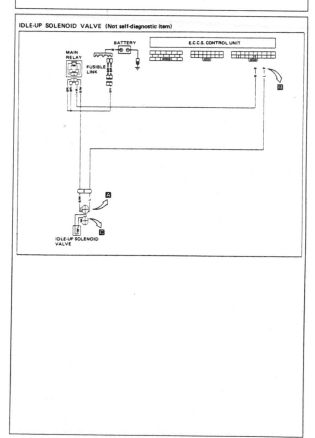

IDLE-UP SOLENOID VALVE

ECCS SELF-DIAGNOSTIC CHART—1987–88 PORT INJECTED 300ZX

IDLE-UP SOLENOID VALVE (Not self-diagnostic item)

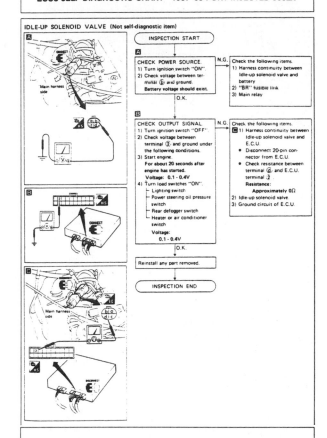

INSPECTION START

A CHECK POWER SOURCE.
1) Turn ignition switch "ON".
2) Check voltage between terminal ⓑ and ground.
Battery voltage should exist.

N.G. → Check the following items.
1) Harness continuity between Idle-up solenoid valve and battery
2) "BR" fusible link
3) Main relay

O.K.

B CHECK OUTPUT SIGNAL.
1) Turn ignition switch "OFF".
2) Check voltage between terminal ② and ground under the following conditions.
3) Start engine.
For about 20 seconds after engine has started.
Voltage: 0.1 - 0.4V
4) Turn load switches "ON".
 – Lighting switch
 – Power steering oil pressure switch
 – Rear defogger switch
 – Heater or air conditioner switch
Voltage: 0.1 - 0.4V

N.G. → Check the following items.
C 1) Harness continuity between Idle-up solenoid valve and E.C.U.
 • Disconnect 20-pin connector from E.C.U.
 • Check resistance between terminal ⓓ and E.C.U. terminal ②
Resistance: Approximately 0Ω
2) Idle-up solenoid valve.
3) Ground circuit of E.C.U.

O.K.

Reinstall any part removed.

INSPECTION END

ECCS SELF-DIAGNOSTIC CHART—1987–88 PORT INJECTED 300ZX

A.A.C. VALVE (Not self-diagnostic item)

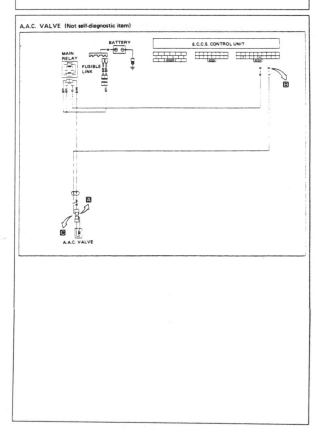

A.A.C. VALVE

ECCS SELF-DIAGNOSTIC CHART — 1987–88 PORT INJECTED 300ZX

A.A.C. VALVE (Not self-diagnostic item)

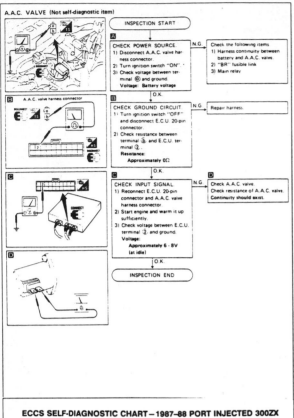

INSPECTION START

A CHECK POWER SOURCE.
1) Disconnect A.A.C. valve harness connector.
2) Turn ignition switch "ON".
3) Check voltage between terminal ⓐ and ground.
Voltage: Battery voltage

N.G. → Check the following items.
1) Harness continuity between battery and A.A.C. valve.
2) "BR" fusible link
3) Main relay

O.K.

B CHECK GROUND CIRCUIT.
1) Turn ignition switch "OFF" and disconnect E.C.U. 20-pin connector.
2) Check resistance between terminal ⓑ and E.C.U. terminal ②.
Resistance: Approximately 0Ω

N.G. → Repair harness.

O.K.

C CHECK INPUT SIGNAL.
1) Reconnect E.C.U. 20-pin connector and A.A.C. valve harness connector.
2) Start engine and warm it up sufficiently.
3) Check voltage between E.C.U. terminal ② and ground.
Voltage: Approximately 6 - 8V (at idle)

N.G. → Check A.A.C. valve.
Check resistance of A.A.C. valve.
Continuity should exist.

O.K.

INSPECTION END

ECCS SELF-DIAGNOSTIC CHART — 1987–88 PORT INJECTED 300ZX

NEUTRAL/INHIBITOR SWITCH (Not self-diagnostic item)

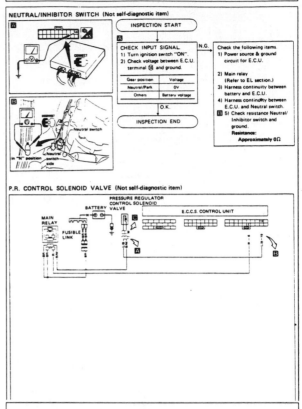

INSPECTION START

A CHECK INPUT SIGNAL.
1) Turn ignition switch "ON".
2) Check voltage between E.C.U. terminal ⑯ and ground.

Gear position	Voltage
Neutral/Park	0V
Others	Battery voltage

N.G. → Check the following items.
1) Power source & ground circuit for E.C.U.
2) Main relay (Refer to EL section.)
3) Harness continuity between battery and E.C.U.
4) Harness continuity between E.C.U. and Neutral switch.
B 5) Check resistance Neutral/Inhibitor switch and ground.
Resistance: Approximately 0Ω

O.K.

INSPECTION END

P.R. CONTROL SOLENOID VALVE (Not self-diagnostic item)

ECCS SELF-DIAGNOSTIC CHART — 1987–88 PORT INJECTED 300ZX

NEUTRAL/INHIBITOR SWITCH (Not self-diagnostic item)

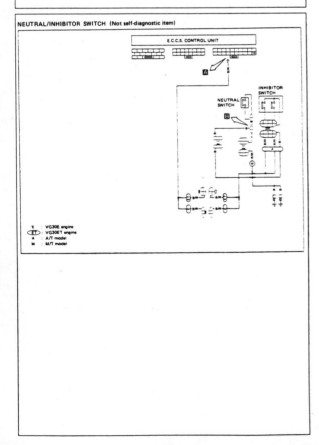

VG30E engine
VG30ET engine
A : A/T model
M : M/T model

ECCS SELF-DIAGNOSTIC CHART — 1987–88 PORT INJECTED 300ZX

P.R. CONTROL SOLENOID VALVE (Not self-diagnostic item)

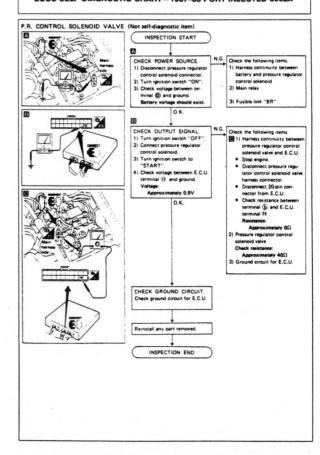

INSPECTION START

A CHECK POWER SOURCE.
1) Disconnect pressure regulator control solenoid connector.
2) Turn ignition switch "ON".
3) Check voltage between terminal ⓐ and ground.
Battery voltage should exist.

N.G. → Check the following items.
1) Harness continuity between battery and pressure regulator control solenoid
2) Main relay
3) Fusible link "BR"

O.K.

B CHECK OUTPUT SIGNAL.
1) Turn ignition switch "OFF".
2) Connect pressure regulator control solenoid.
3) Turn ignition switch to "START".
4) Check voltage between E.C.U. terminal ⑲ and ground.
Voltage: Approximately 0.9V

N.G. → Check the following items.
C 1) Harness continuity between pressure regulator control solenoid valve and E.C.U.
• Stop engine.
• Disconnect pressure regulator control solenoid valve harness connector.
• Disconnect 20-pin connector from E.C.U.
• Check resistance between terminal ⓑ and E.C.U. terminal ⑲.
Resistance: Approximately 0Ω
2) Pressure regulator control solenoid valve
Check resistance: Approximately 40Ω
3) Ground circuit for E.C.U.

O.K.

CHECK GROUND CIRCUIT.
Check ground circuit for E.C.U.

Reinstall any part removed.

INSPECTION END

ECCS SELF-DIAGNOSTIC CHART – 1987–88 PORT INJECTED 300ZX

AIR REGULATOR (Not self-diagnostic item)

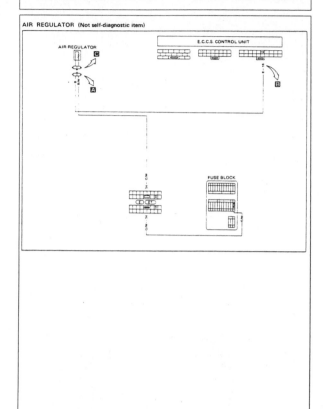

MIXTURE RATIO FEEDBACK SYSTEM INSPECTION CHART
1987–88 PORT INJECTED 300ZX

PREPARATION

1. Make sure that the following parts are in good order.
   - Battery
   - Ignition system
   - Engine oil and coolant levels
   - Fuses
   - E.C.C.S. harness connectors
   - Vacuum hoses
   - Air intake system (oil filler cap, oil level gauge, etc.)
   - Fuel pressure
   - A.I.V. hose
   - Engine compression
   - E.G.R. valve operation
   - Throttle valve

2. On air conditioner equipped models, checks should be carried out while the air conditioner is "OFF".
3. On automatic transmission equipped models, when checking idle rpm, ignition timing and mixture ratio, checks should be carried out while shift lever is in "D" position.
4. When measuring "CO" percentage, insert probe more than 40 cm (15.7 in) into tail pipe.

WARNING:
a. When selector lever is shifted to "D" position, apply parking brake and block both front and rear wheels with chocks.
b. Depress brake pedal while racing the engine to prevent forward surge of vehicle.
c. After the adjustment has been made, shift the lever to the "N" or "P" position and remove wheel chocks.

Overall inspection sequence

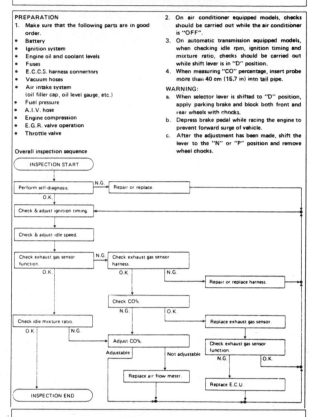

ECCS SELF-DIAGNOSTIC CHART – 1987–88 PORT INJECTED 300ZX

AIR REGULATOR (Not self-diagnostic item)

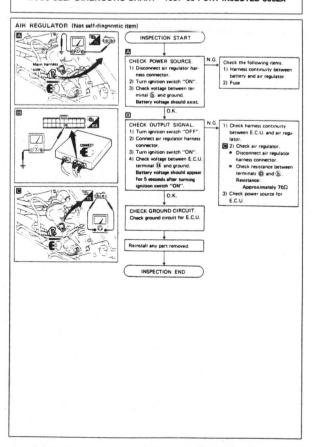

MIXTURE RATIO FEEDBACK SYSTEM INSPECTION CHART
1987–88 PORT INJECTED 300ZX

Idle Check and Set Procedure

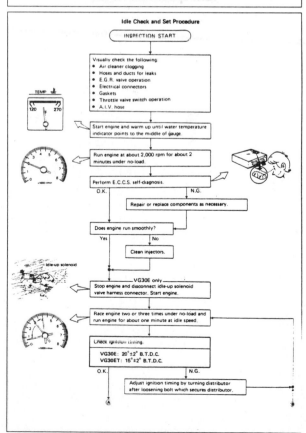

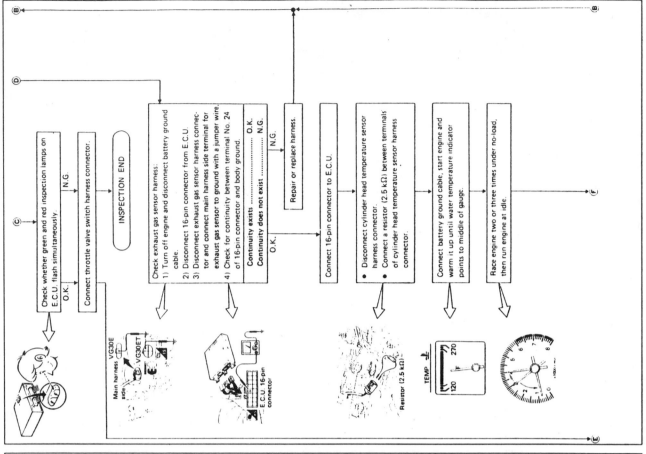

MIXTURE RATIO FEEDBACK SYSTEM INSPECTION CHART
1987–88 PORT INJECTED 300ZX

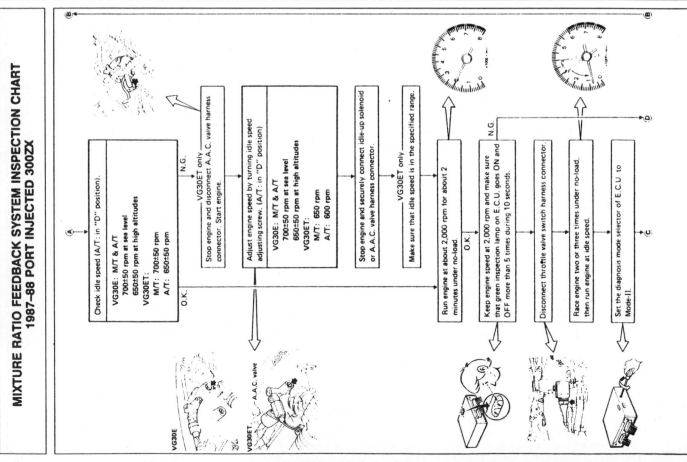

MIXTURE RATIO FEEDBACK SYSTEM INSPECTION CHART
1987–88 PORT INJECTED 300ZX

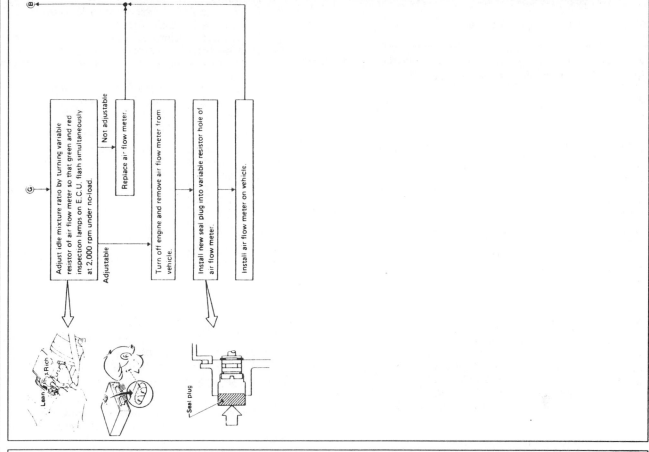

MIXTURE RATIO FEEDBACK SYSTEM INSPECTION CHART
1987–88 PORT INJECTED 300ZX

Ⓖ → Adjust idle mixture ratio by turning variable resistor of air flow meter so that green and red inspection lamps on E.C.U. flash simultaneously at 2,000 rpm under no-load.

- Not adjustable → Replace air flow meter. → Ⓑ
- Adjustable → Turn off engine and remove air flow meter from vehicle. → Install new seal plug into variable resistor hole of air flow meter. → Install air flow meter on vehicle. → Ⓑ

Seal plug

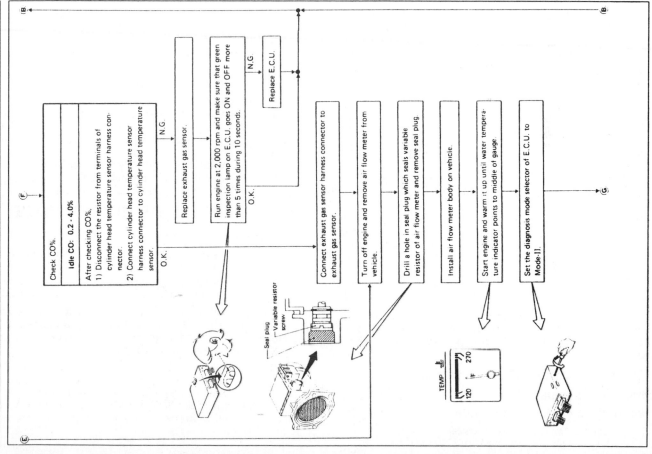

MIXTURE RATIO FEEDBACK SYSTEM INSPECTION CHART
1987–88 PORT INJECTED 300ZX

Ⓕ → Check CO%.

Idle CO: 0.2 - 4.0%

After checking CO%,
1) Disconnect the resistor from terminals of cylinder head temperature sensor harness connector.
2) Connect cylinder head temperature sensor harness connector to cylinder head temperature sensor.

- N.G. → Replace exhaust gas sensor.
- O.K. → Run engine at 2,000 rpm and make sure that green inspection lamp on E.C.U. goes ON and OFF more than 5 times during 10 seconds.
  - N.G. → Replace E.C.U. → Ⓑ
  - O.K. → Connect exhaust gas sensor harness connector to exhaust gas sensor. → Turn off engine and remove air flow meter from vehicle. → Drill a hole in seal plug which seals variable resistor of air flow meter and remove seal plug. → Install air flow meter body on vehicle. → Start engine and warm it up until water temperature indicator points to middle of gauge. → Set the diagnosis mode selector of E.C.U. to Mode-II. → Ⓖ

Ⓑ

Seal plug
Variable resistor screw

TEMP
120 270

Ⓔ

COMPONENT TEST PROCEDURE

Releasing Fuel System Pressure

—————————— CAUTION ——————————

Fuel system pressure must be relieved before disconnecting any fuel lines or attempting to remove any fuel system components.

1985 MAXIMA

1. Remove luggage floor mat.
2. Start engine.
3. Disconnect fuel pump connector with engine running.
4. After engine stalls, crank engine two or three times to make sure that pressure is released.
5. Turn ignition switch OFF and connect fuel pump connector.

1984–85 300ZX

1. Start engine.
2. Remove luggage floor mat.
3. Disconnect fuel pump connector with engine running.
4. After engine stalls, crank engine two or three times to make sure that pressure is released.
5. Turn ignition switch OFF and connect fuel pump connector.

1986–88 MAXIMA, 300ZX AND 1987–88 STANZA, 200SX

1. Remove the fuel pump fuse from the fuse box.
2. Start the engine.
3. After the engine stalls, crank it over for a few seconds to make sure all fuel is exhausted from the lines.
4. Turn the ignition switch OFF and install the fuel pump fuse. Erase the trouble code memory of the ECCS control unit to eliminate false Code 22.

TESTING FUEL SYSTEM PRESSURE

1. Relieve fuel system pressure as previously described.
2. Disconnect the fuel inlet hose between the fuel filter and fuel line on the engine side.
3. Install a fuel pressure gauge.
4. Start the engine and check the fuel line for leakage.
5. Read the pressure on the pressure gauge. It should be approximately 30 psi at idle and rise to 37 psi when the accelerator pedal is fully depressed.
6. Stop the engine and disconnect the fuel pressure regulator vacuum hose from the intake collector. Plug the intake collector with a rubber cap.
7. Connect a hand vacuum pump to the fuel pressure regulator.
8. Disconnect the ECCS harness connectors at the ECU.
9. Install a jumper wire to connect terminal No. 108 of the ECU to a body ground.
10. Turn the ignition switch ON and read the fuel pressure gauge as the vacuum is changed with the hand vacuum pump. Fuel pressure should decrease as vacuum increases. If not, replace the fuel pressure regulator.
11. Relieve fuel system pressure again.
12. Remove the pressure gauge from the fuel line and reconnect the fuel inlet hose.

NOTE: When reconnecting a fuel line, always use a new clamp. Make sure that the screw of the clamp does not contact any adjacent parts and tighten the hose clamp to 1 ft. lb.

INJECTOR AND FUEL PIPE

Removal and Installation

1984–88 200SX CA18ET ENGINE

1. Relieve fuel pressure from system.

2. Disconnect air intake pipe.
3. Disconnect ECCS harness from injectors.
4. Disconnect ignition wire.
5. Disconnect accelerator wire.
6. Remove throttle chamber.
7. Disconnect fuel hoses and pressure regulator vacuum hose.
8. Remove injectors with fuel tube assembly.
9. Remove injector from fuel tube.
10. To install, reverse removal procedure.

1984–88 VG30E AND VG30ET ENGINE

1. Relieve fuel pressure from system.
2. Disconnect the following from intake collector:
● Air duct
● Accelerator wire
● Blow-by hoses
● Air regulator hose
● BCDD hose (Maxima)
● EGR tube
● Harness clamps
● Harness connectors
● Intake collector cover
● Water hoses (when necessary)
3. Disconnect fuel hoses.
4. Remove intake collector. ·
5. Remove bolts securing fuel tube.
6. Remove bolts securing injectors and remove injectors, fuel tubes and pressure regulator as an assembly.
7. To install, reverse removal procedure.

1987–88 STANZA CA20E ENGINE

1. Relieve fuel pressure from system.
2. Disconnect ECCS harness and ignition wires.
3. Disconnect fuel hoses and pressure regulator vacuum hose.
4. Remove bolts securing fuel tube.
5. Remove bolts securing injectors; then take out fuel tube and injector as an assembly.
6. Remove injector from fuel tube.
7. Remove fuel hose.
8. To install, reverse removal procedure.

1987–88 PULSAR CA16DE ENGINE

1. Relieve fuel pressure from system.
2. Remove throttle chamber, intake manifold stay, IAA unit and intake side rocker cover.
3. Disconnect fuel hoses and pressure regulator vacuum hose.
4. Remove injector assembly fixing bolts.
5. Remove injectors from fuel tube.
6. To install, reverse removal procedure.

INJECTOR RUBBER HOSE

Removal and Installation

1. On injector rubber hose, measure off a point approximately 0.79 in. (20mm) from socket end.
2. Heat soldering iron (150 watt) for 15 minutes. Cut hose into braided reinforcement from mark to socket end.

NOTE: Do not feed soldering iron until it touches injector tail piece. Be careful not to damage socket, plastic connector, etc. with solder iron. Never place injector in a vise when disconnecting rubber hose.

3. Pull rubber hose out with hand.
4. To install, clean exterior of injector tail piece.
5. Wet inside of new rubber hose with fuel.
6. Push end of rubber hose with hose socket onto injector tail piece by hand as far as it will go. Clamp is not necessary at this connection.

NOTE: After properly connecting fuel hose to injector, check connection for fuel leakage.

FUEL PRESSURE REGULATOR

Removal and Installation

1. Relieve fuel pressure from system.
2. Disengage vacuum tube connecting regulator to intake manifold from pressure regulator.
3. Remove screws securing pressure regulator.
4. Unfasten hose clamps, and disconnect pressure regulator from fuel hose.

NOTE: Place a rag under fuel pipe to absorb any remaining fuel.

5. To install, reverse the removal procedure.

EGR VACUUM CUT AND AIR INJECTION CONTROL SOLENOID VALVE TESTING

1. Check the solenoid valve for continuity after disconnecting the harness connector. Continuity should exist and resistance should be 30–40Ω. If not, replace the solenoid valve.
2. Check the solenoid valve for normal operation after disconnecting the harness connector and all vacuum hoses. Tag all hoses before removal. Supply the solenoid valve with battery voltage and check whether there is continuity between ports A, B and C. With the solenoid OFF, there should be continuity between B and C. With the solenoid ON, there should be continuity between A and B.

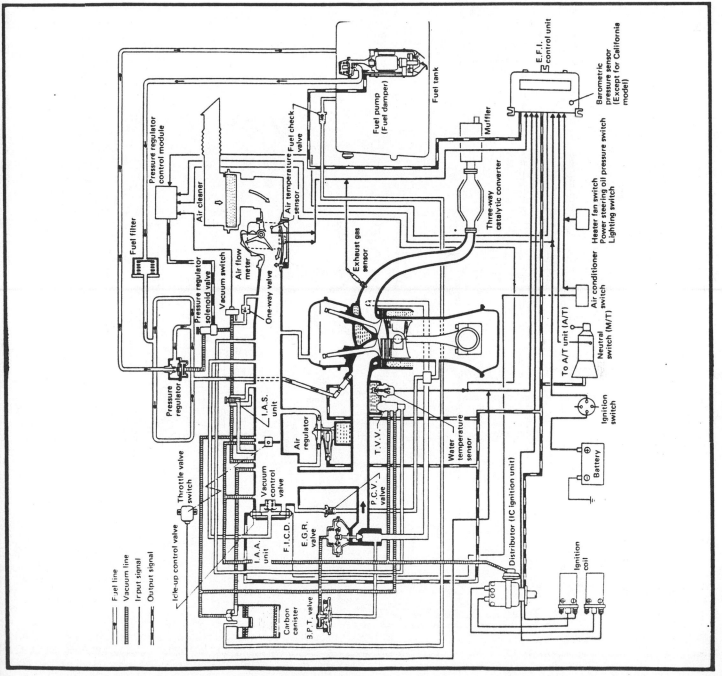

Electronic Fuel Injection (EFI) System schematic

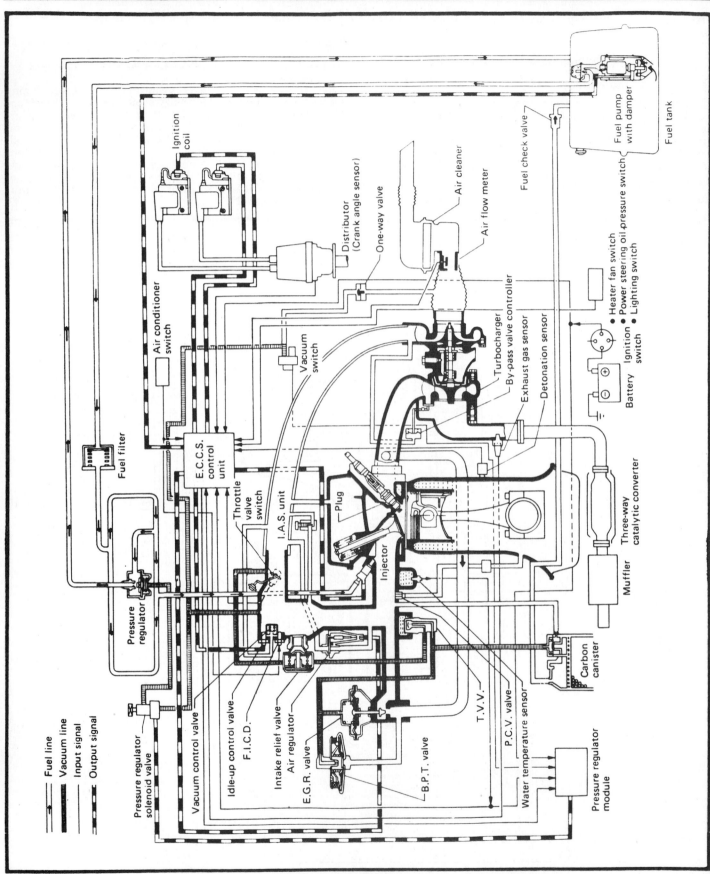

Electronic Concentrated Control System (ECCS) schematic

TOYOTA

ENGINE CONTROL SYSTEM APPLICATION CHART

Year	Model	Engine cc (liter)	Engine VIN	Fuel System	Ignition System
1984	Camry	1995 (2.0)	2S-E	EFI	IIA
	Celica	2367 (2.4)	22R	EFI	Electronic
	Celica	2367 (2.4)	22R-E	EFI	Electronic
	Corolla	1587 (1.6)	4A-C	2-BBL	IIA
	Corolla	1587 (1.6)	4A-LC	2-BBL	IIA
	Cressida	2759 (2.8)	5M-GE	EFI	ESA
	Starlet	1290 (1.3)	4K-E	EFI	Electronic
	Supra	2759 (2.8)	5M-GE	EFI	ESA
	Tercel	1452 (1.4)	3A	2-BBL	IIA
	Tercel	1452 (1.4)	3A-C	2-BBL	IIA
	Van	1998 (2.0)	3Y-EC	EFI	IIA
	Truck & 4-Runner	2367 (2.4)	22R	2-BBL	Electronic
	Truck & 4-Runner	2367 (2.4)	22R-E	EFI	ESA
1985	Camry	1995 (2.0)	2S-E	EFI	IIA
	Celica	2367 (2.4)	22R	EFI	ESA
	Celica	2367 (2.4)	22R-E	EFI	ESA
	Corolla	1587 (1.6)	4A-C	EFI	IIA
	Corolla	1587 (1.6)	4A-LC	2-BBL	IIA
	Corolla	1587 (1.6)	4A-GE	EFI	IIA
	Cressida	2759 (2.8)	5M-GE	EFI	ESA
	Supra	2759 (2.8)	5M-GE	EFI	ESA
	Tercel	1452 (1.4)	3A	2-BBL	IIA
	Tercel	1452 (1.4)	3A-C	2-BBL	IIA
	Van	1998 (2.0)	3Y-EC	EFI	IIA
	Truck & 4-Runner	2367 (2.4)	22R	2-BBL	Electronic
	Truck & 4-Runner	2367 (2.4)	22R-E	EFI	ESA
	Truck & 4-Runner	2367 (2.4)	22R-TE	EFI	ESA
1986	Camry	1995 (2.0)	2S-EL	EFI	IIA
	Celica	1995 (2.0)	2S-E	EFI	IIA
	Celica	1998 (2.0)	3S-GE	EFI	Electronic
	Corolla	1587 (1.6)	4A-C	EFI	IIA
	Corolla	1587 (1.6)	4A-LC	2-BBL	IIA
	Corolla	1587 (1.6)	4A-GE	EFI	IIA
	Cressida	2759 (2.8)	5M-GE	EFI	ESA
	MR2	1587 (1.6)	4A-GE	EFI	ESA
	Supra	2759 (2.8)	5M-GE	EFI	ESA
	Supra	2954 (3.0)	7M-GE	EFI	ESA
	Tercel	1452 (1.4)	3A	2-BBL	IIA
	Tercel	1452 (1.4)	3A-C	2-BBL	IIA
	Van	2237 (2.2)	4Y-EC	EFI	IIA/ESA

ENGINE CONTROL SYSTEM APPLICATION CHART

Year	Model	Engine cc (liter)	Engine VIN	Fuel System	Ignition System
	Truck & 4-Runner	2367 (2.4)	22R	2-BBL	ESA
	Truck & 4-Runner	2367 (2.4)	22R-E	EFI	ESA
	Truck & 4-Runner	2367 (2.4)	22R-TE	EFI	ESA
1987-88	Camry	1998 (2.0)	3S-FE	EFI	IIA
	Celica	1998 (2.0)	3S-GE	EFI	Electronic
	Celica	1998 (2.0)	3S-FE	EFI	Electronic
	Corolla	1587 (1.6)	4A-LC	EFI	IIA
	Corolla	1587 (1.6)	4A-GEC	EFI	ESA
	Corolla	1587 (1.60	4A-GELC	EFI	ESA
	Cressida	2759 (.8)	5M-GE	EFI	ESA
	MR2	1587 (1.6)	4A-GELC	EFI	ESA
	Supra	2954 (3.0)	7M-GE	EFI	ESA
	Supra	2954 (3.0)	7M-GTE	EFI	ESA
	Tercel	1456 (1.4)	3E	2-BBL	IIA
	Tercel	1452 (1.4)	3A-C	2-BBL	IIA
	Van	2237 (2.2)	4Y-EC	EFI	IIA/ESA
	Truck & 4-Runner	2367 (2.4)	22R	2-BBL	ESA
	Truck & 4-Runner	2367 (2.4)	22R-E	EFI	ESA
	Truck & 4-Runner	2367 (2.4)	22R-TE	EFI	ESA

IIA — Integrated Ignition Assembly
ESA — Electronic Spark Advance Ignition System

Electronic — Electronic Ignition Toyota Computer Controlled Emission System (TCCC)

ELECTRONIC FUEL INJECTION (EFI) SYSTEM

This system is broken down into three major systems. The Fuel System, Air Induction System and Electronic Control System.

FUEL SYSTEM

An electric fuel pump supplies sufficient fuel, under a constant pressure, to the EFI injectors. These injectors inject a metered quantity of fuel into the intake manifold in accordance with signals from the EFI computer. Each injector injects at the same time, one half of the fuel required for ideal combustion with each engine revolution.

AIR INDUCTION SYSTEM

The air induction system provides sufficient air for the engine operation.

ELECTRONIC CONTROL SYSTEM

The most engines are equipped with a Toyota Computer Control System (TCCS) which centrally controls the electronic fuel injection, electronic spark advance and the exhaust gas recirculation valve. The systems can be diagnosed by means of an Electronic Control Unit (ECU) which employs a microcomputer. The ECU and the TCCS control the following functions:

Electronic Fuel Injection (EFI)

The ECU receives signals from the various sensors indicating changing engine operations conditions such as:

1. Intake air volume.
2. Intake air temperature.
3. Coolant temperature sensor.
4. Engine rpm.
5. Acceleration/deceleration.
6. Exhaust oxygen content.

These signals are utilized by the ECU to determine the injection duration necessary for an optimum air-fuel ratio.

The Electronic Spark Advance (ESA)

The ECU is programmed with data for optimum ignition timing during any and all operating conditions. Using the data provided by sensors which monitor various engine functions (rpm, intake air volume, coolant temperature, etc.), the microcomputer (ECU) triggers the spark at precisely the right moment.

Idle Speed Control (ISC)

The ECU is programmed with specific engine speed values to respond to different engine conditions (coolant temperature, air conditioner on/off, etc.). Sensors transmit signals to the ECU which controls the flow of air through the by-pass of the throttle valve and adjusts the idle speed to the specified value.

Exhaust Gas Recirculation (EGR)

The ECU detects the coolant temperature and controls the EGR operations accordingly.

Electronic Controlled Transmission (ECT—Automatic Transmission Only)

A serial signal is transmitted to the ECT computer to prevent shift up to third or overdrive during cold engine operation. Diagnostics, which are outlined below.

Fail-Safe Function

In the event of a computer malfunction, a backup circuit will take over to provide minimal driveability. Simultaneously, the "Check Engine" warning light is activated.

Turbo Indicator

The ECU detects turbocharger pressure, which is determined by the intake volume and the engine rpm, and lights a green colored turbocharger indicator light located in the combination meter. Moreover, if the turbocharger pressure increases abnormally, the ECU will light the "Check Engine" warning light on the instrument panel.

Partial Lean Burn System

Some earlier Toyota models may be equipped with a lean burn system which provides a leaner than theroretical air-fuel mixture when there is only a partial load on the engine (except constant speed cruising) to improve the fuel economy. Also an Mechatro Spark Control (MS) is used to control the ignition timing for improved drivability.

SERVICE PRECAUTIONS

- Do not operate the fuel pump when the fuel lines are empty.
- Do not reuse fuel hose clamps.
- Make sure all EFI harness connectors are fastened securely. A poor connection can cause an extremely high surge voltage in the coil and condenser and result in damage to integrated circuits.
- Keep the EFI harness at least 4 in. away from adjacent harnesses to prevent an EFI system malfunction due to external electronic "noise."
- Keep EFI all parts and harnesses dry during service.
- Before attempting to remove any parts, turn off the ignition switch and disconnect the battery ground cable.
- Always use a 12 volt battery as a power source.
- Do not attempt to disconnect the battery cables with the engine running.
- Do not depress the accelerator pedal when starting.
- Do not rev up the engine immediately after starting or just prior to shutdown.
- Do not attempt to disassemble the EFI control unit under any circumstances.
- If installing a two-way or CB radio, keep the antenna as far as possible away from the electronic control unit. Keep the antenna feeder line at least 8 in. away from the EFI harness and do not let the two run parallel for a long distance. Be sure to ground the radio to the vehicle body.
- Do not apply battery power directly to injectors.
- Handle air flow meter carefully to avoid damage.
- Do not disassemble air flow meter or clean meter with any type of detergent.

TESTING PRECAUTIONS

1. Before connecting or disconnecting control unit ECU harness connectors, make sure the ignition switch is OFF and the negative battery cable is disconnected to avoid the possibility of damage to the control unit.

2. When performing ECU input/output signal diagnosis, remove the pin terminal retainer from the connectors to make it easier to insert tester probes into the connector.

3. When connecting or disconnecting pin connectors from the ECU, take care not to bend or break any pin terminals. Check that there are no bends or breaks on ECU pin terminals before attempting any connections.

4. Before replacing any ECU, perform the ECU input/output signal diagnosis to make sure the ECU is functioning properly or not.

5. After checking throught EFI troubleshooting, perform the EFI self-diagnosis and driving test.

6. When measuring supply voltage of ECU controlled components with a circuit tester, separate one tester probe from another. If the two tester probes accidentally make contact with each other during measurement, a short circuit will result and damage the power transistor in the ECU.

ON-VEHICLE INSPECTION

Fuel Pump Operation

1. Turn on the ignition switch, but do not start the engine.
2. Short both terminals of the fuel pump connector. Check that there is pressure in the hose to the cold start injector.

NOTE: At this point, you will hear fuel return noise from the pressure regulator.

3. Remove the service wire and install the rubber cap on the fuel pump check connector. Turn off the ignition switch.
4. If there is no pressure check the following components:
   a. Fusible link.
   b. EFI and Ignition fuses.
   c. Circuit opening relay.
   d. Fuel pump.
   e. Wiring connector.

Fuel Pressure Check

1. Disconnect the negative battery cable. Disconnect the wiring connector from the cold start injector.
2. Place a suitable container or shop towel under the rear end of the delivery pipe.
3. Slowly loosen the union bolt of the cold start injector (on some models it may be necessary to remove the cold start valve in order to connect the pressure gauge) hose and remove the bolt and two gaskets from the delivery pipe.
4. Drain the fuel from the delivery pipe. Install a gasket, a pressure gauge (tool SST-09268-45011 or equivalent), another gasket and the union bolt to the delivery pipe.
5. Wipe up any excess gasoline, reconnect the negative battery cable and start the engine.

NOTE: On the later models short the terminals on the fuel pump check connector (Fp and +B) and turn the ignition switch to the on position, then take a fuel pressure reading.

6. Disconnect the vacuum sensing hose from the pressure regulator and pinch it off. Measure the fuel pressure at idle. The fuel pressure should be as follows:
   a. Camry—33–38 psi.
   b. Celica—33–38 psi except for the 3S-FE engine 38–44 psi.
   c. Corolla—33–40 psi.
   d. Cressida—33–38 psi.
   e. MR2—33–40 psi.
   f. Starlet—36–38 psi.
   g. Supra—33–38 psi. except for the 1987 Supra 33–40 psi.
   h. Van—33–38 psi.
   i. Truck and 4-Runner—33–38 psi.

7. If the fuel pressure is too high, replace the pressure regulator.

8. If the fuel pressure is low, check the following components:
   a. Fuel hoses and fuel connections.
   b. Fuel pump.
   c. Fuel filter.
   d. Pressure regulator.

9. Remove the service wire from the check connector (if still installed). Start the engine.

10. Disconnect the vacuum sensing hose from the pressure regulator and pinch it off. Measure the fuel pressure at idle. The fuel pressure should be as follows:
   a. Camry—33–38 psi.
   b. Celica—33–38 psi except for the 3S-FE engine 38–44 psi.
   c. Corolla—33–40 psi.
   d. Cressida—33–38 psi.
   e. MR2—33–40 psi.
   f. Starlet—36–38 psi.
   g. Supra—33–38 psi. except for the 1987 Supra 33–40 psi.
   h. Van—33-38 psi.
   i. Truck and 4-Runner—33–38 psi.

11. Reconnect the vacuum sensing hose to the pressure regulator. Measure the fuel pressure at idling:
   a. Camry—27–31 psi.
   b. Celica—27–31 psi except for the 3S-FE engine 33–37 psi.
   c. Corolla—24–31 psi.
   d. Cressida—27-31 psi.
   e. MR2—24–31 psi.
   f. Starlet—28 psi.
   g. Supra—27–31 psi. except for the 1987 Supra 23–30 psi.
   h. Van—28 psi.
   i. Truck and 4-Runner—27–31 psi.

12. If there is no fuel pressure, check the vacuum sensing hose and pressure regulator. Stop the engine. Check that the fuel pressure remains above 21 psi. for five minutes after the engine has been shut off.

13. If not within specifications, check the fuel pump, pressure regulator and or the injectors.

14. After checking the fuel pressure, disconnect the battery ground cable and carefully remove the pressure gauge to prevent gasoline from splashing.

15. Using new gaskets, reconnect the cold start injector hose to the delivery pipe (install the cold start injector valve if it was removed). Connect the wiring connector to the cold start injector. Check for fuel leakage.

FUEL INJECTION PUMP

Removal and Installation

On all models the electric fuel pump is located in the fuel tank usually attached to the fuel sending unit. On some earlier fuel injected models, the fuel pump is mounted at the rear of the vehicle (usually located on the frame rail) outside of the gas tank.

1. Disconnect the negative battery cable.

2. Remove the fuel tank, if necessary (fuel tank removal is necessary on most models).

3. On sedans and hardtops, remove the trim panel from inside the trunk.

4. On station wagons, raise the rear of the vehicle in order to gain access to the pump.

5. Remove the retaining screws which secure the pump access plate to the fuel tank. Withdraw the plate, gasket and pump assembly.

6. Disconnect the leads and hoses from the fuel pump.

7. Installation is the reverse order of the removal procedure.

NOTE: On any models that may be using the in-line fuel pump, the pump is simply removed by disconnecting the fuel lines and electrical connectors from the fuel pump and dismounting the pump from the vehicle.

INJECTOR NOZZLE

Removal and Installation

CAMRY, CELICA (3S-FE), COROLLA AND 1984-86 SUPRA

1. Disconnect the negative battery cable. Remove the cold start injector pipe.

2. Disconnect the vacuum sensing hose from the fuel pressure regulator.

3. Disconnect the injector connectors. Disconnect the hose from the fuel return pipe.

4. Remove the fuel pressure pulsation damper and two gaskets, if so equipped.

5. Remove the two delivery (fuel rail) pipe bolts together with the four injectors. Be careful not to drop the injectors, when removing the delivery (fuel rail) pipe.

6. Remove the four insulators and two spacers from the cylinder head. Pull out the four injectors and the delivery (fuel rail) pipe.

7. installation is the reverse order of the removal procedure. Be sure to use new gaskets and O-rings were needed. Torque the two delivery (fuel rail) pipe bolts to 9 ft. lbs.

CELICA 3S-GE

1. Disconnect the negative battery cable. Drain the engine coolant into a suitable container.

2. On models equipped with a automatic transmission, disconnect the throttle cable from the throttle linkage.

3. Disconnect the accelerator cable from the throttle linkage.

4. Remove the suspension brace. Disconnect the air cleaner.

5. Remove the igniter assembly.

6. Remove the suspension lower crossmemeber. Remove the throttle body assembly.

7. Remove the intake manifold assembly.

8. Remove the three delivery (fuel rail) pipe bolts and remove the delivery (fuel rail) pipe together with the four injectors. Be careful not to drop the injectors, when removing the delivery (fuel rail) pipe.

9. Remove the three spacers and four insulators from the cylinder head. Pull out the four injectors from the delivery (fuel rail) pipe.

10. Installation is the reverse order of the removal procedure. Be sure to use new gaskets and O-rings were needed. Torque the delivery (fuel rail) pipe bolts to 14 ft. lbs.

CRESSIDA

1. Disconnect the negative battery cable.

2. Remove the air intake chamber. Remove the distributor.

3. Remove the number one fuel pipe. Disconnect and remove the wiring harness.

4. Remove the four delivery (fuel rail) pipe bolts and remove the delivery (fuel rail) pipe together with the injectors. Be careful not to drop the injectors, when removing the delivery (fuel rail) pipe.

5. Remove the six insulators from the intake manifold.

6. Installation is the reverse order of the removal procedure. Be sure to use new gaskets and O-rings were needed. Torque the delivery (fuel rail) pipe bolts to 10 ft. lbs.

MR2

1. Disconnect the negative battery cable.

2. Disconnect the PCV hose from the cylinder head cover. Disconnect the vacuum sensing hose from the fuel pressure regulator.

3. Remove the pressure regulator. Remove the cold start injector pipe.

4. Disconnect the fuel inlet hose. Disconnect the injector connectors.

5. Remove the three delivery (fuel rail) pipe bolts and remove the delivery (fuel rail) pipe together with the injectors. Be careful not to drop the injectors, when removing the delivery (fuel rail) pipe. Do not remove the injector cover.

6. Remove the four insulators and three collars from the cylinder head.

7. installation is the reverse order of the removal procedure. Be sure to use new gaskets and O-rings were needed. Torque the delivery (fuel rail) pipe bolts to 13 ft. lbs.

STARLET

1. Disconnect the negative battery cable. Remove the cold start injector pipe.

2. Remove the air intake pipe by, removing the nut and four bolts from the air chamber side. remove the five bolts from the manifold side.

3. Remove the fuel inlet pipe, fuel return hose, vacuum sensing hose, EFI solenoid wire harness clamp and injector wires.

4. Remove the three delivery (fuel rail) pipe nuts and remove the delivery (fuel rail) pipe together with the injectors. Be careful not to drop the injectors, when removing the delivery (fuel rail) pipe. Do not remove the cover.

5. Remove the four insulators from the intake manifold.

6. installation is the reverse order of the removal procedure. Be sure to use new gaskets and O-rings were needed. Torque the delivery (fuel rail) pipe bolts to 11–15 ft. lbs.

1987-88 SUPRA

1. Disconnect the negative battery cable. Drain the engine coolant into a suitable container.

2. Disconnect the following hoses:
   a. The water hoses from the throttle body (7M-GE) or water bypass hose (7M-GTE).
   b. Vacuum hoses from the throttle body.
   c. Idle speed control hoses from the throttle body.
   d. Vacuum hose from the pressure regulator.

3. Disconnect the throttle position sensor connector, Idle Speed Control valve connector and the cold start injector (7M-GE).

4. Disconnect the accelerator connecting rod. Remove the air intake connector (7M-GE) by, disconnecting the air cleaner hose from the throttle body and remove the throttle body with air intake connector brackets. Remove the four bolts and two nuts, intake connector and gasket.

5. Remove the throttle body assembly (7M-GTE).

6. Disconnect the number two water bypass hose from the idle speed control valve. Remove the two bolts and the idle speed control valve with gaskets.

7. Disconnect the injector connectors. Disconnect the cold start injector tube from the delivery pipe.

8. Remove the pulsation damper and two gaskets. Remove the union bolts and two gaskets from the fuel return pipe support. Remove the clamp bolts, the number one fuel pipe and the vacuum switching valve.

9. Remove the union bolt and two gaskets from the pressure regulator. Disconnect the fuel hose from the number two fuel pipe. Remove the clamp bolt and the fuel return pipe.

10. Loosen the pressure regulator lock nut and remove the pressure regulator with the two gaskets.

11. Remove the three delivery (fuel rail) pipe bolts and remove the delivery (fuel rail) pipe together with the injectors. Be careful not to drop the injectors, when removing the delivery (fuel rail) pipe.

12. Remove the six insulators and three spacers from the cylinder head. Pull the injectors from the delivery pipe.

13. Installation is the reverse order of the removal procedure. Be sure to use new gaskets and O-rings were needed. Torque the delivery (fuel rail) pipe bolts to 13 ft. lbs.

VAN

1. Disconnect the negative battery cable. Drain the engine coolant into a suitable container.

2. Disconnect the accelerator cable with bracket from the throttle body. Remove the air cleaner hose.

3. Disconnect the throttle position sensor connector. Remove the two bypass hoses. Disconnect the vacuum hoses from the throttle body. Remove the throttle body from the air intake chamber.

4. Remove the EGR valve. Remove the two nuts from the air intake chamber. Remove the union nut from the exhaust manifold.

5. Disconnect the PCV hoses and vacuum hoses from the air intake chamber.

6. Disconnect the cold start injector valve connector. Disconnect the clod start injector pipe, water bypass hoses and pressure regulator hose.

7. Remove the air intake chamber brackets and remove the air intake chamber with the air valve.

8. Disconnect the fuel inlet and outlet pipe from the fuel delivery pipe. Remove the bolt and nut and then remove the fuel delivery pipe with injectors. Be careful not to drop the injectors, when removing the delivery (fuel rail) pipe. Do not remove the cover.

9. Remove the four insulators from the intake manifold.

10. installation is the reverse order of the removal procedure. Be sure to use new gaskets and O-rings were needed. Torque the delivery (fuel rail) pipe bolts to 14 ft. lbs.

TRUCK AND 4-RUNNER

1. Disconnect the negative battery cable.
2. Remove the air chamber with the throttle body.
3. Disconnect the injector wire connectors.
4. Disconnect the fuel hose from the delivery pipe.
5. Remove the two delivery pipe bolts and remove the delivery pipe with the injectors. Be careful not to drop the injectors, when removing the delivery (fuel rail) pipe. Do not remove the cover.
6. installation is the reverse order of the removal procedure. Be sure to use new gaskets and O-rings were needed. Torque the delivery (fuel rail) pipe bolts to 14 ft. lbs.

Injector Resistance Inspection

ALL MODELS

1. Unplug the wiring conector on the fuel injector.
2. Using a suitable ohmmeter, check the continuity of both terminals.
3. The ohmmeter reading should be as follows:
   a. Camry—1.5–3.0 ohms.
   b. Celica—1.5–3.0 ohms except for the 3S-GE engine—14 ohms and the 3S-FE engine—2 ohms.
   c. Corolla—1.5–3.0 ohms.
   d. Cressida—1.5–3.0 ohms.
   e. MR2—1.5–3.0 ohms.
   f. Starlet—1.5–3.0 ohms.
   g. Supra—1.5–3.0 ohms except for the 1987 Supra 1.8–3.4 ohms.
   h. Van—1.5–3.0 ohms.
   i. Truck and 4-Runner—1.5–3.0 ohms.
4. If the resistance is not as specified, replace the injector.

COLD START INJECTOR

Removal and Installation

CAMRY, CELICA, COROLLA, MR2, STARLET, VAN AND 1984-86 SUPRA

1. Disconnect the negative battery cable. Disconnect the cold start valve connector.

2. Place a suitable container or shop towel under the cold start injector pipe. Remove the two union bolts, four gaskets and the injector pipe.

3. Remove the two bolts, cold start injector and gasket.

4. Installation is the reverse order of the removal procedure. Use new gaskets and O-rings as needed. Torque the injector

bolts to 82 inch lbs. (52 inch lbs on the 3S-GE engine and the Van) and the two injector pipe union bolts to 13 ft. lbs.

CRESSIDA

1. Disconnect the negative battery cable. Drain the coolant into a suitable drain pan.
2. Remove the air intake connector.
3. Disconnect the following hoses:
   a. The number one bypass hose from the idle speed control valve body.
   b. The number two bypass hose from the throttle body.
   c. The air valve hose from the idle speed control valve body.
   d. The PCV hose from the throttle body.
   e. Brake booster vacuum hose from the air intake chamber.
   f. Actuator vacuum hose from the air intake chamber.
   g. Disconnect and tag all necessary emission hoses from the throttle body and air intake chamber that allow the removal of the vacuum pipe subassembly.
4. Disconnect the accelerator linkage and cable from the throttle body.
5. Disconnect the cold start injector wire, throttle position sensor wire, the two idle speed control valve connectors and the vacuum switching valve connector.
6. Remove the air intake chamber stay. Remove the vacuum pipe subassembly.
7. Loosen the EGR pipe connecting nut. Disconnect the cold start fuel hose from the delivery pipe.
8. Remove the air intake chamber. Remove the cold start injector from the air intake chamber.
9. Installation is the reverse order of the removal procedure. Use new gaskets and O-rings as needed.

1987–88 SUPRA

1. Disconnect the negative battery cable. Disconnect the cold start valve connector.
2. Place a suitable container or shop towel under the cold start injector pipe.Remove the two union bolts, cold start injector tube and gaskets.
3. Remove the two bolts, cold start injector and gasket. On the 7M-GTE engine remove the two bolts and disconnect the connector, remove the cold start injector with gaskets.
4. Installation is the reverse order of the removal procedure. Use new gaskets and O-rings as needed. Torque the injector bolts to 48 inch lbs. and the two injector pipe union bolts to 22 ft. lbs. on the delivery pipe side and cold start injector side 13 ft. lbs.

TRUCK AND 4-RUNNER

1. Disconnect the negative battery cable. Disconnect the cold start valve connector.
2. Remove the fuel pipe between the cold start injector and the fuel delivery pipe.
3. Remove the cold start injector wire gasket.
4. Remove the cold start injector and place a suitable container or shop towel under the rear end of the delivery pipe.
5. Installation is the reverse order of the removal procedure. Be sure to install a new wire gasket.

Cold Start Injector Resistance Inspection

ALL MODELS

1. Unplug the wiring connector on the cold start injector.
2. Using a suitable ohmmeter, check the continuity of both terminals.
3. The ohmmeter reading should be as follows:
   a. Camry – 2–4 ohms.
   b. Celica – 2–4 ohms except for the 3S-GE .engine – 3–5 ohms.
   c. Corolla – 3–5 ohms.
   d. Cressida – 3–5 ohms.
   e. MR2 – 3–5 ohms.
   f. Starlet – 3–5 ohms.
   g. Supra – 3–5 ohms except for the 1987 Supra 2–4 ohms.
   h. Van – 3–5 ohms.
   i. Truck and 4-Runner – 2–4 ohms.
4. If the resistance is not as specified, replace the injector.

PRESSURE REGULATOR

Removal and Installation

CAMRY, CELICA, COROLLA, VAN AND 1984-86 SUPRA

1. Disconnect the negative battery cable. Disconnect the vacuum sensing vacuum hose.
2. Place a suitable container or shop towel under the pressure regulator. Remove the two union bolts, gaskets and disconnect the fuel return pipe.
3. Remove the two bolts and pull out the pressure regulator. On the 3S-GE engine, remove the regulator lock nut and remove the regulator.
4. Installation is the reverse order of the removal procedure. Use new gaskets and O-rings as needed. Torque the regulator bolts to 48 inch lbs., 82 inch lbs. on the Corolla models (torque the lock nut to 22 ft. lbs.) and the two union bolts to 13 ft. lbs.

CRESSIDA

1. Disconnect the negative battery cable. Disconnect the vacuum sensing vacuum hose.
2. Place a suitable container or shop towel under the pressure regulator. Disconnect the fuel line from the pressure regulator.
3. Disconnect the number two fuel line from the pressure regulator. Remove the regulator lock nut and remove the pressure regulator.
4. Installation is the reverse order of the removal procedure. Use new gaskets and O-rings as needed. Torque the regulator lock nut 29 ft. lbs. and the union bolt to 22 ft. lbs.

MR2

1. Disconnect the negative battery cable. Disconnect the vacuum sensing vacuum hose.
2. Place a suitable container or shop towel under the pressure regulator. Remove the flare nut and the fuel fuel pipe from the regulator.
3. Remove the two bolts and pull out the pressure regulator.
4. Installation is the reverse order of the removal procedure. Use new gaskets and O-rings as needed. Torque the regulator bolts to 82 inch lbs. and the two union bolts to 22 ft. lbs.

STARLET

1. Disconnect the negative battery cable. Disconnect the vacuum sensing vacuum hose.
2. Place a suitable container or shop towel under the pressure regulator. Disconect the fuel hose from the regulator.
3. Unscrew the pressure regulator from the fuel rail.
4. Installation is the reverse order of the removal procedure. Use new gaskets and O-rings as needed. Torque the pressure regulator to 19–25 ft. lbs.

1987–88 SUPRA

1. Disconnect the negative battery cable. Disconnect the PCV hose and the vacuum sensing vacuum hose.
2. Place a suitable container or shop towel under the pressure regulator. Disconnect the fuel line from the pressure regulator.
3. Remove the clamp bolt of the fuel return pipe. Remove the regulator lock nut and remove the pressure regulator.
4. Installation is the reverse order of the removal procedure. Use new gaskets and O-rings as needed. Torque the regulator lock nut 18 ft. lbs. and the union bolt to 18 ft. lbs.

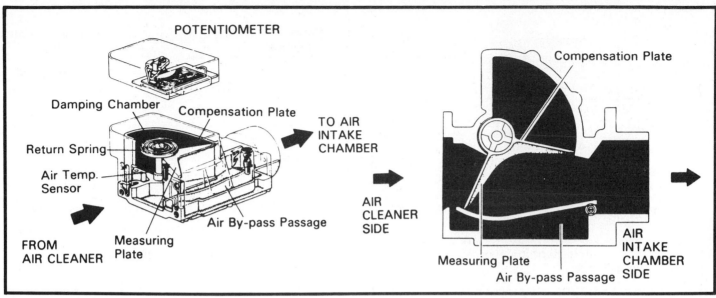

Exploded view of a typical air flow meter

TRUCK AND 4-RUNNER

1. Disconnect the negative battery cable. Disconnect the vacuum sensing hose from the pressure regulator.
2. Remove the number one EGR pipe. Place a suitable container or shop towel under the pressure regulator. Disconnect the fuel line from the pressure regulator.
3. Loosen the lock nut and remove the pressure regulator.
4. Installation is the reverse order of the removal procedure. Use new gaskets and O-rings as needed. Torque the regulator lock nut 22 ft. lbs.

Air Induction System

AIR FLOW METER

Removal and Installion

ALL MODELS

1. Disconnect the negative battery cable and the air flow meter connector.
2. Disconnect the vacuum hoses and air cleaner hose. On the MR2 and 1987-88 Supra models, remove the air cleaner cap. Disconnect the air flow meter wire, if so equipped.
3. Remove the air flow meter retaining bolts and nuts (on some models it may be necessary to pry off the lock plate in order to gain access to the retaining bolts) and remove the air flow meter.
4. On the 7M-GTE engine, remove the air flow meter with the air cleaner case and remove the air flow meter from the air cleaner assembly.
4. Installation is the reverse of the removal procedure.

Air Flow Connector Resistance Inspection

ALL MODELS

1. Disconnect the air flow meter connector.
2. Using a suitable ohmmeter, measure the resistance between each terminal.
3. If the resistance is not as specified, replace the air flow meter.

Between terminals	Resistance	Temperature
$V_s - E_2$	20 − 3,000 Ω	—
$V_c - E_2$	100 − 300 Ω	—
$V_B - E_2$	200 − 400 Ω	—
$THA - E_2$	10 − 20 kΩ	− 20°C (−4°F)
	4 − 7 kΩ	0°C (32°F)
	2 − 3 kΩ	20°C (68°F)
	0.9 − 1.3 kΩ	40°C (104°F)
	0.4 − 0.7 kΩ	60°C (140°F)
$F_c - E_1$	Infinity	—

Air flow meter connector terminal identification—Camry, Celica, Cressida and 1984-86 Supra

Between terminals	Resistance	Temperature
$V_s - E_2$	20 − 3,000 Ω	—
$V_c - E_2$	100 − 300 Ω	—
$V_B - E_2$	200 − 400 Ω	—
$THA - E_2$	10 − 20 kΩ	− 20°C (−4°F)
	4 − 7 kΩ	0°C (32°F)
	2 − 3 kΩ	20°C (68°F)
	0.9 − 1.3 kΩ	40°C (104°F)
	0.4 − 0.7 kΩ	60°C (204°F)
$F_c - E_1$	Infinity	—

Air flow meter connector terminal identification—Corolla, MR2 and Van

Between terminals	Resistance	Temperature
$E_2 - V_S$	20 – 400 Ω	–
$E_2 - V_C$	100 – 300 Ω	–
$E_2 - V_B$	200 – 400 Ω	–
$E_2 - THA$	10 – 20 KΩ	−20°C (−4°F)
	4 – 7 KΩ	0°C (32°F)
	2 – 3 KΩ	20°C (68°F)
	0.9 – 1.3 KΩ	40°C (104°F)
	0.4 – 0.7 KΩ	60°C (140°F)
$E_1 - F_C$	Infinity	–

Air flow meter connector terminal identification — Starlet, Truck and 4-Runner

Terminals	Resistance	Temperature
$V_S - E_2$	20 – 600 Ω	–
$V_C - E_2$	200 – 400 Ω	–
$THA - E_2$	10 – 20 KΩ	−20°C (4°F)
	4 – 7 KΩ	0°C (32°F)
	2 – 3 KΩ	20°C (68°F)
	0.9 – 1.3 KΩ	40°C (104°F)
	0.4 – 0.7 KΩ	60°C (140°F)
$F_C - E_1$	Infinity	–

Air flow meter connector terminal identification — 1987-88 Supra

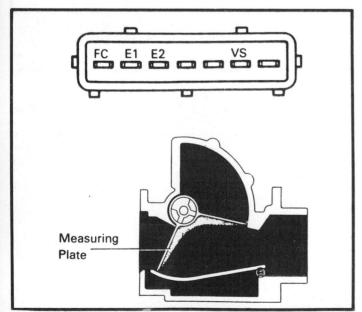

Air flow meter terminal location — Camry, Celica and 1984-86 Supra

Between Terminals	Resistance Ω	Measuring plate opening
E1 — FC	Infinity	Fully closed
	Zero	Other than closed
E2 — VS	200 — 600	Fully closed
	200 — 1,200	Fully closed to fully open

Air flow meter terminal identification — Camry, Celica and Supra

Air Flow Meter Resistance Inspection
ALL MODELS

1. Using a suitable ohmmeter, measure the resistance between each terminal of the air flow meter, at different measuring plate positions.
2. Resistance between Vs and E_2 will change in accordance with the measuring plate opening.
3. If the resistance is not as specified, replace the air flow meter.

THROTTLE BODY

Removal and Installation
ALL MODELS

1. Disconnect the negative battery cable. Drain the engine coolant into a suitable drain pan.
2. On models equipped with automatic transmissions, disconnect the throttle cable from the throttle linkage.
3. Disconnect the accelerator cable from the throttle linkage. Disconnect the throttle return spring, if so equipped. Remove the air intake connector , if so equipped.
4. Disconnect the air cleaner hose. Disconnect the throttle position sensor connector. Remove the vacuum transmitting pipe, if so equipped.
5. Disconnect the PCV hose, water hoses, all vacuum and air hoses. Remove the vacuum transmitting valve , if so equipped.
6. Remove the throttle body retaining bolts and remove the throttle body and the gaskets.
7. Installation is the reverse order of the removal procedure, be sure to use new gaskets as needed.

AIR VALVE

Removal and Installation
CAMRY, CELICA (EXCEPT FOR THE 3S-GE ENGINE) AND VAN

1. Disconnect the negative battery cable. Disconnect the air valve connector.
2. Disconnect the two air valve hoses. On the Van models, the air intake chamber must be removed.
3. Remove the air valve retaining bolts or nuts and remove the air valve from the engine.
4. Installation is the reverse order of the removal procedure.

NOTE: To remove the air valve on the 3S-GE engine, remove the throttle body as previously outlined and remove the air valve assembly.

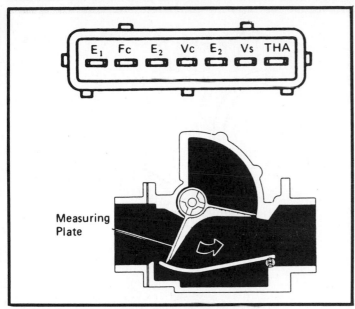

Air flow meter terminal location — Cressida

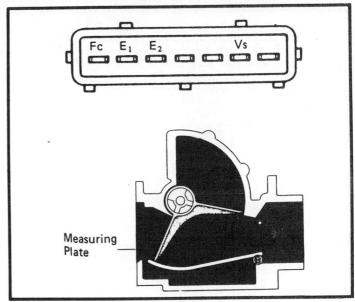

Air flow meter terminal location — Corolla, MR2 and Van

Between terminals	Resistance Ω	Measuring plate Opening
$E_1 - F_c$	Infinity	Fully closed
	Zero	Other than closed position
$E_2 - V_s$	20 — 400	Fully closed
	20 — 1000	Fully closed to fully open position

Air flow meter terminal identification — Cressida

Between terminals	Resistance Ω	Measuring plate Opening
$F_c - E_1$	Infinity	Fully closed
	Zero	Other than closed position
$V_s - E_2$	20 — 400	Fully closed
	20 — 3,000	Fully closed to fully open position

Air flow meter terminal identification — Corlla, MR2 and Van

STARLET

1. Disconnect the negative battery cable. Drain the coolant into a suitable drain pan.
2. Remove the cold start injector pipe. Remove the air intake pipe.
3. Disconnect the air valve inlet water hose, air valve outlet water hose, air valve inlet air hose and the air valve oulet air hose.
4. Remove the two air valve retaining bolts and remove the air valve from the air intake chamber.
5. Installation is the reverse order of the removal procedure.

Air Valve Inspection

ALL MODELS

1. Connect a suitable tachometer to the engine.
2. With the coolant temperature below 140°F, pinch the air valve hose the engine rpm should drop.
3. When the coolant temperature is over 140°F., pinch the air valve hose and make sure that the engine rpm does not drop more than 50 rpm (100 rpm on the 3S-GE engine).
4. Using a suitable ohmmeter, measure the heat coil resistance of the air valve. The resistance should be checked with the coolant temperature below 176°F and the air valve closed. The resistance should be 40–60 ohms.
5. The final inspection should be to see that the air valve slightly opens, when the temperature is 68°F.

AUXILIARY AIR VALVE

Some models are equipped with an auxiliary air valve. This air valve operates in the same manner as the main air valve. To remove the auxiliary air valve the throttle body must first be removed and then the auxiliary air valve can be removed. This valve can be tested in the same manner as the main air valve.

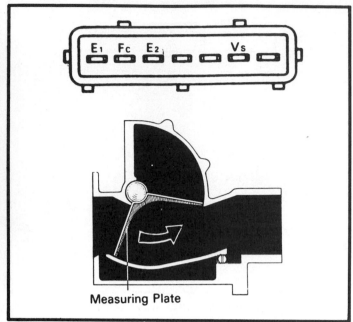

Air flow meter terminal location — Starlet, Truck and 4-Runner

Between Terminals	Resistance Ω	Measuring plate Opening
$E_1 - Fc$	Infinity	Fully closed
	Zero	Other than closed position
$E_2 - Vs$	20 – 400	Fully closed
	20 – 1000	Fully closed to fully open position

Air flow meter terminal identification — Starlet, Truck and 4-Runner

IDLE SPEED CONTROL (ISC) VALVE

Removal and Installation

CAMRY, CRESSIDA AND 1987-88 SUPRA

On the Camry models equipped with the idle speed control valve, the throttle body must be removed and the idle speed control valve removed from the throttle body.

1. Disconnect the negative battery cable. Disconnect the two idle speed control valve connectors.
2. Disconnect the two water bypass hoses and vacuum hoses.
3. Remove the idle speed control valve retaining bolts and remove the valve with gaskets from the engine. On the 7M-GTE engine, remove the steel washer and check ball from the intake chamber.
4. Installation is the reverse order of the removal procedure.

ISC Valve Resistance Test

1. Disconnect the idle speed control valve connector.
2. Using a suitable ohmmeter, measure the resistance between the center terminal(s) and the other two terminals in the connector of the ISC valve.

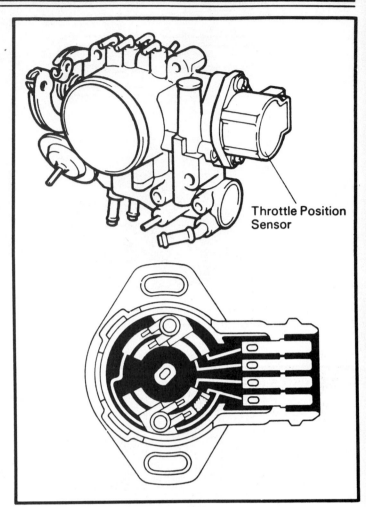

Throttle Position Sensor

Typical throttle body assembly

3. The resistance should be as follows:
   a. Camry — 16.0–17.0 ohms.
   b. Cressida — 10–30 ohms.
   c. 1987-88 Supra — 10–30 ohms.

ISC Valve Inspection

CRESSIDA AND 1987-88 SUPRA

1. Using an ohmmeter. Measure the resistance between terminals B1 – S1 or S3 and B2 – S2 or S4. The resistance should be as follows:
   a. B1 – S1 or S3 – 10–30 ohms.
   b. B2 – S2 04 S4 – 10–30 ohms.
2. After making the resistance test, apply battery voltage to terminals B1 and B2 and while repeatedly grounding S1, S2, S3, S4 and S1 in sequence, check that the valve moves toward the closed position.
3. Apply battery voltage to terminals B1 and B2 and while repeatedly grounding S4 – S3 – S2 – S1- and in sequence, check that the valve moves toward the open position.
4. If the idle speed control valve fails any of this inspection, replace it with a new one.

START INJECTOR TIME SWITCH

Inspection

1. Disconnect the start injector time switch electrical connector.

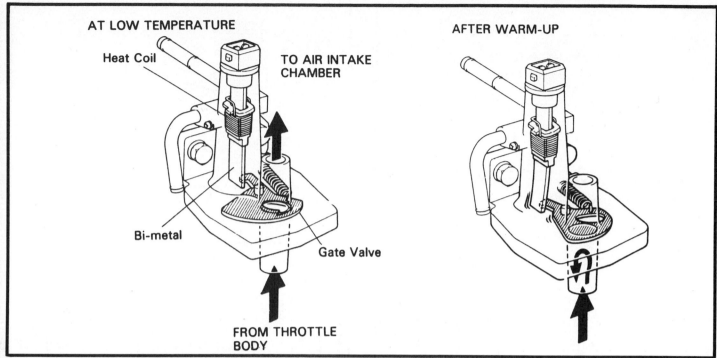

Exploded view of a typical air valve

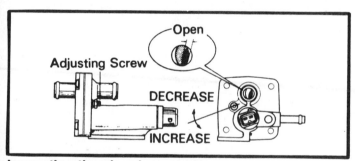

Inspecting the air valve opening

2. Using a suitable ohmmeter, measure the resistance between each terminal. The ohmmeter reading should read as follows:

a. Between STA—STJ terminals—20–40 ohms with the coolant temperature below 86°F. 40–60 ohms with the coolant temperature above 104°F.

b. STA—Ground terminals—20–80.

NOTE:The resistance reading may vary from model to model, the above specifications are the standard resistance readings.

WATER THERMO SENSOR

Inspection

1. Disconnect the electrical connector to the water thermo sensor.

2. Using a suitable ohmmeter, measure the resistance between both charts. Refer to the water thermo sensor resistance chart.

FUEL CUT RPM

Inspection

1. Start the engine and let it run until it reaches normal operating temperature.

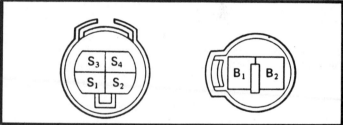

ISC valve connector terminal identification—Cressida and 1987-88 Supra

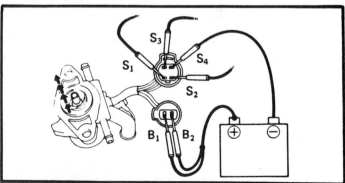

ISC inspection valve terminal identification—Cressida and 1987-88 Supra

2. Disconnect the throttle position sensor connector from the throttle position sensor.

3. Short circuit terminals E_1 (or E_2) and IDL on the wire connector side. Gradually raise the engine rpm and check that there is fluctuation between the fuel cut and fuel return points. The fuel cut rpm should be 1,800 rpm and the fuel return points 1,200.

NOTE: The vehicle should be stopped.

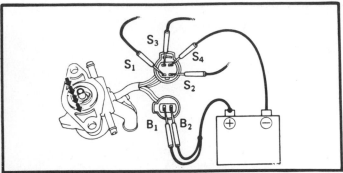

ISC inspection valve terminal identification—Cressida and 1987-88 Supra (cont.)

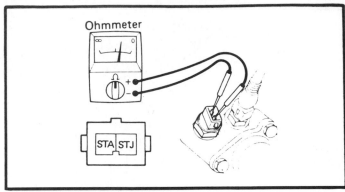

Making a resistance test on the start injection time switch

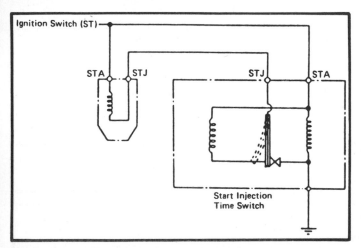

Typical start injection time switch wiring schematic

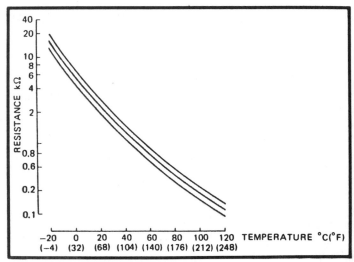

Water thermo sensor resistance chart

EFI MAIN RELAY

Inspection

1. When the ignition switch is turn to the on position, there should be a noise heard from the EFI main relay.

2. Locate the EFI main relay and remove it from the relay block. Using a suitable ohmmeter, check that there is continuity between terminals 1 and 3 (1 and 2 on the Cressida, Truck and 4-Runner).

3. Check that there is no continuity between terminals 2 and 4 ((3 and 4 on the Cressida, Truck and 4-Runner).

4. If the continuity is not a specified, replace the relay.

PARTIAL LEAN BURN SYSTEM

Road Test Inspection

1984 STARLET

Perform this inspection only in the event of excess fuel consumption. Check that all other systems are normal before performing this inspection.

1. Connect a suitable pair of jumper wire (or SST-09842-14010) to the EFI service connector and then connect a suitable voltmeter to the jumper wires.

NOTE: When performing the road test inspection, connect an extension the jumper wires and place the voltmeter on the front passenger seat.

2. Start the engine and let run until it reaches normal operating temperature.

3. Inspect the Vf voltage (Vf=Vb which is battery voltage) 2=7 ± 2 volts.

4. While driving on a level surface, with the transmission in top gear and the vehicle speed at 25 mph, confirm that there is standard Vf voltage 220 seconds after the engine has started. Standard voltage: 7±2 volts to 1–5 volts.

5. Disconnect the voltmeter and jumper wires. Install the rubber cap to the EFI service connector.

Vehicle Stopped Inspection

1984 STARLET

1. Connect a timing light and tachometer. Connect a suitable pair of jumper wire (or SST-09842-14010) to the EFI service connector and then connect a suitable voltmeter to the jumper wires.

2. Set the idle speed at 800 rpm and the ignition timing to 0° before top dead center.

3. Race the engie at 2000 rpm for approximately 90 seconds. Recheck and make sure the idle is at 800 rpm.

4. Inspect the Vf voltage (Vf=Vb which is battery voltage) 2=7 ± 2 volts.

5. Inspect the ignition timing and Vf voltage with the throttle position sensor connector disconnected.

6. Ignition timing 0–7° before top dead center The Vf voltage: 7±2 volts to 1–5 volts.

7. Reconnect the throttle position sensor connector. Recheck the Vf battery voltage.

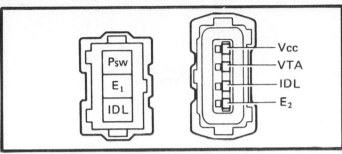

Typical terminal(s) location on the wire connector

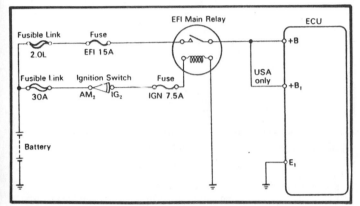

Typical EFI main relay wiring schematic

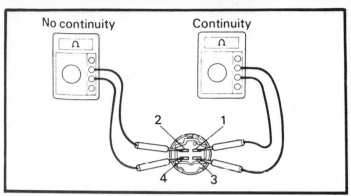

Testing the EFI main relay

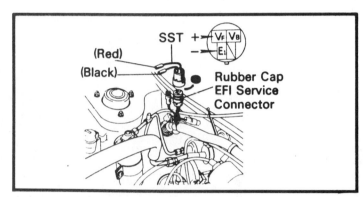

Connect the voltmeter to the EFI service connector

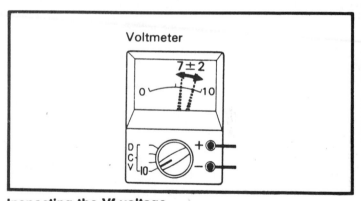

Inspecting the Vf voltage.

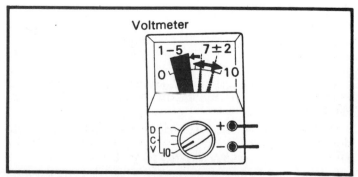

Inspecting the standard Vf voltage

8. Adjust the idle speed to 700 rpm (with the engine cooling fan off) and the ignition timing to 5° before top dead center (with the vacuum advancer disconnected).

9. Disconnect all the test equipment, the voltmeter and jumper wires. Install the rubber cap to the EFI service connector.

Electronic Control Unit (ECU)
DIAGNOSIS

The ECU contains a built in self diagnosis system by which troubles with the engine signal the engine signal network are detected and a "Check Engine" warning light on the instrument panel flashes code numbers 12, 13, 14, 21, 22, 31, 32, 42, 52 and 53 (these code numbers vary from model to model). The "Check Engine" light on the instrument panel informs the driver that a malfunction has been detected. The light goes out automatically when the malfunction has been cleared.

The diagnostic code can be read by the number of blinks of the "Check Engine" warning light when the proper terminals of the check connector are short-circuited. If the vehicle is equipped with a supper monitor display, the diagnostic code is indicated on the display screen.

Check Engine Warning Light

1. The "Check Engine" warning light will come on when the ignition switch is placed On and the engine is not running.

2. When the engine is started, the "Check Engine" warning light should go out.

3. If the light remains on, the diagnosis system has detected a malfunction in the system.

Output Of Diagnostic Codes

1. The battery voltage should be above 11 volts. Throttle

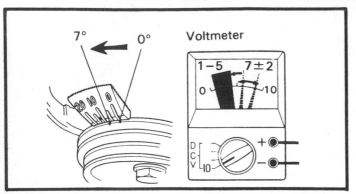

Inspecting the partial lean burn system and Vf voltage

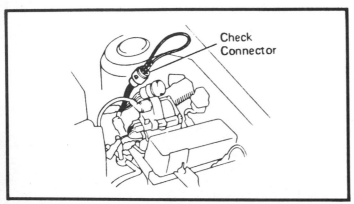

Short circuiting the check connector

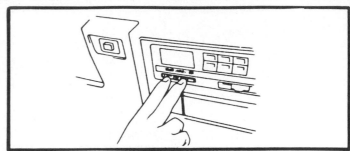

Holding in the SELECT and INPUT buttons

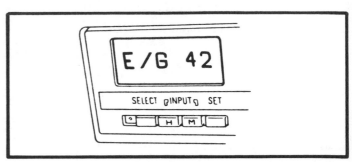

Typical super monitor display of trouble codes

valve fully closed (throttle position sensor IDL points closed).

2. Place the transmission in "P" or "N" range. Turn the A/C switch Off. Start the engine and let it run to reach its normal operating temperature.

WITHOUT SUPER MONITOR DISPLAY

1. Turn the ignition switch to the On position. Do not start the engine. Use a suitable jumper wire and short the terminals of the check connector.

2. Read the diagnostic code as indicated by the number of flashes of the "Check Engine" warning light.

3. If the system is operating normally (no malfunction), the light will blink once every 0.25 seconds.

4. In the event of a malfunction, the light will blink once every 0.5 seconds (some models it may 1 to 2 or 3 seconds). The first number of blinks will equal the first digit of a two digit diagnostic code. After a 1.5 second pause, the second number of blinks will equal the second number of a 2 digit diagnostic code. If there are two or more codes, there will be a 2.5 second pause between each.

5. After all the codes have been output, there will be a 4.5 second pause and they will be repeated as long as the terminals of the check connector are shorted.

NOTE: In event of a number of trouble codes, indication will begin from the smaller value and continue to the larger in order.

6. After the diagnosis check, remove the jumper wire from the check connector.

WITH SUPER MONITOR DISPLAY

1. Turn the ignition switch to the On position. Do not start the engine.

2. Simultaneously push and hold in the SELECT and INPUT M keys for at least three seconds. The letters DIAG will appear on the screen.

3. After a short pause, hold the SET key in for at least three seconds. If the system is normal (no malfunctions), ENG-OK will appear on the screen.

4. If there is a malfunction, the code number for it will appear on the screen. In the event of two or more numbers, there will be a three second pause between each (Example ENG-42).

5. After confirmation of the diagnostic code, either turn off the ignition switch or push the super monitor display key on so the time appears.

Cancelling Out The Diagnostic Code

1. After repairing the trouble area, the diagnostic code that is retained in the ECU memory must be cancelled out by removing the EFI (15A) fuse for thirty seconds or more, depending on the ambient temperature (the lower temperature, the longer the fuse must be left out with the ignition switch off).

NOTE: Cancellation can also be done by removing the battery negative terminal, but keep in mind when removing the negative battery cable, the other memory systems (radio, ETR, clock, etc.) will also be cancelled out.

If the diagnostic code is not cancelled out, it will be retained by the ECU and appear along with a new code in event of future trouble. If it is necessary to work on engine components requiring removal of the battery terminal, a check must first be made to see if a diagnostic code is detected.

2. After cancellation, perform a road test, if necessary, confirm that a normal code is now read on the "Check Engine" warning light or super monitor display.

3. If the same diagnostic code is still indicated, it indicates that the trouble area has not been repaired throughly.

Diagnosis Indication

1. Including "Normal", the ECU is programmed with sixteen diagnostic codes.

Code No.	Light Pattern	Code No.	Light Pattern
–	ON / OFF ⨆⨆⨆⨆⨆⨆	31	⨆⨆⨆ ⨆
11	⨆ ⨆	32	⨆⨆⨆ ⨆⨆
12	⨆ ⨆⨆	41	⨆⨆⨆⨆ ⨆
13	⨆ ⨆⨆⨆	42	⨆⨆⨆⨆ ⨆⨆
14	⨆ ⨆⨆⨆⨆	43	⨆⨆⨆⨆ ⨆⨆⨆
21	⨆⨆ ⨆	51	⨆⨆⨆⨆⨆ ⨆
22	⨆⨆ ⨆⨆	52	⨆⨆⨆⨆⨆ ⨆⨆
23	⨆⨆ ⨆⨆⨆	53	⨆⨆⨆⨆⨆ ⨆⨆⨆

Typical trouble code (flashes) light pattern

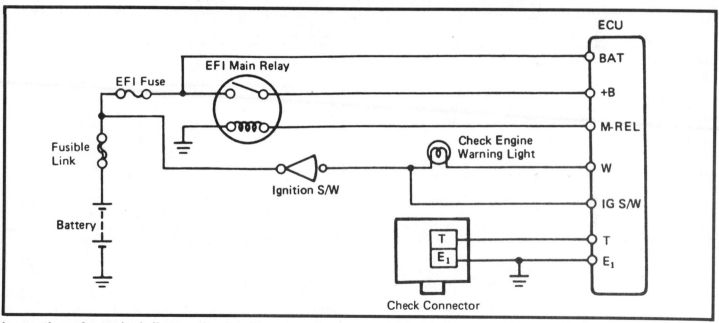

Inspection of a typical diagnostic circuit

2. When two or more codes are indicated, the lowest number code will appear first. However, no other code will appear along with code nuber eleven.

3. All dectected diagnostic codes, except fifty one and fifty three, will be retained in memory by the ECU from the time of detection until cancelled out.

4. Once the malfunction is cleared, the "Check Engine" warning light on the instrument panel will go out but the diagnostic code(s) remain stored in the ECU memory (except for code fifty one).

ECU Connectors Voltage Inspection

The EFI circuit can be checked by measuring the resistance and the voltage at the wiring connectors of the ECU. The following list should be followed before making the ECU inspection:

1. Perform all voltage measurements with the connectors connected.

2. Verify that the battery voltage is 11 volts or more when the ignition switch is turned off.

3. The testing probes must not make contact with the ECU Ox and Vf terminals.

Symbol	Terminal Name	Symbol	Terminal Name	Symbol	Terminal Name
E$_{01}$	ENGINE GROUND	G$\ominus$	ENGINE REVOLUTION SENSOR	A/C	A/C MAGNET SWITCH
E$_{02}$	ENGINE GROUND	V$_F$	CHECK CONNECTOR	SPD	SPEEDOMETER
No. 10	INJECTOR	G	ENGINE REVOLUTION SENSOR	W	WARNING LIGHT
No. 20	INJECTOR	T	CHECK CONNECTOR	THA	AIR TEMP. SENSOR
STA	STARTER SWITCH	VTA	THROTTLE SWITCH	Vs	AIR FLOW METER
IGt	IGNITER	Ne	ENGINE REVOLUTION SENSOR	Vc	AIR FLOW METER
EGR	EGR VSV	IDL	THROTTLE SWITCH	BAT	BATTERY +B
E$_1$	ENGINE GROUND	KNK	KNOCK SENSOR	IG S/W	IGNITION SWITCH
N/C	NEUTRAL START SWITCH (A/T)	IGf	IGNITER	+B	MAIN RELAY
	CLUTCH SWITCH (M/T)	Ox	Ox SENSOR	TCD	ECT COMPUTER
ISC$_1$	ISC MOTOR NO. 1 COIL	THW	WATER TEMP. SENSOR	L$_1$	ECT COMPUTER
ISC$_2$	ISC MOTOR NO. 2 COIL	E$_2$	SENSOR EARTH	L$_2$	ECT COMPUTER
ISC$_3$	ISC MOTOR NO. 3 COIL	E$_1$	ENGINE GROUND	L$_3$	ECT COMPUTER
ISC$_4$	ISC MOTOR NO. 4 COIL	M-REL	MAIN RELAY COIL	OIL	OIL PRESSURE SWITCH

| E$_{01}$ | No. 10 | STA | EGR | N/C | ISC 1 | ISC 2 | G$\ominus$ | | G | Ne | | IGf | THW | L$_1$ | L$_2$ | L$_3$ | M-REL | | SPD | | THA | Vs | Vc | BAT | IG S/W |
| E$_{02}$ | No. 20 | IGt | E$_1$ | | ISC 3 | ISC 4 | V$_F$ | | T | VTA | IDL | KNK | Ox | E$_2$ | E$_2$ | E$_1$ | TCD | | A/C | W | OIL | | | +B | +B |

Exploded view of a typical ECU connector with terminal identification

4. Remove the glove box turn the ignition switch to the on position and using a suitable volt/ohmmeter with a high impedance (10 Kilo ohms) measure the voltage at each terminal.

ECU Connectors Resistance Inspection

Be sure not to touch the ECU terminals. The tester probe should be inserted into the wiring connector from the wiring side.

1. Remove the glove box. Unplug the wiring connectors from the ECU.

2. Using a suitable volt/ohmmeter with a high impedance (10 Kilo ohms) measure the resistance at each terminal of the wiring connector.

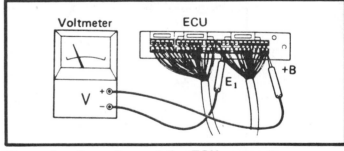

Measuring the voltage at the ECU connectors

OXYGEN SENSOR

The following oxygen sensor test are general diagnostic procedures, for a more detailed version of these test, refer to the diagnostic charts at the end of this section.

Testing With a Voltmeter

1. With the engine at normal operating temperature, connect a voltmeter to the service connector usually located on the right fender apron below the wiper motor or the EBCV. Connect the positive (+) probe to the oxygen sensor terminal and the negative (–) probe to terminal E. If using the service connector test wire lead (SST 09842 - 14010 or equivalent), connect the positive (+) testing probe to the red wire of the service connector test wire lead and the negative (–) probe to the black wire.

2. Raise the engine speed to 2500 rpm for about 90 seconds.

3. Maintain the engine speed at 2500 rpm and check that the needle of the voltmeter fluctuates 8 times or more in 10 seconds within 0–7 volts.

NOTE: If this test is positive, the oxygen sensor is functioning properly. If not, inspect the other parts, hose connections and wiring of the air bleed system. If no problem is found, replace the oxygen sensor.

Testing With a EFI Tester

1. Install EFI tester SST 09991-00100 or equivalent to the EFI service connector and oxygen sensor check connector EFI.

2. Start the engine and let it run until it reaches normal operating temperature. Connect a tachometer to the engine. On models with electronic ignition, attach the tachometer to the negative (–) side of the ignition coil, not to the distributor primary lead. Damage to the ignition control unit will result from improper connections.

NOTE: A-series engines require a special type of tachometer which hooks up to the service connector wire coming out of the distributor. As many tachometers are not compatible with this hookup, consult with the tachometer manufacturer's instructions to make sure the unit will work on this type of system. Never allow the tachometer terminal; to touch the ground as it could result in damage to the ignition igniter and/or the ignition coil.

3. Race the engine at 2,500 rpm for approximately 90 seconds. Then maintain a steady engine speed at 2,500 rpm.

4. Check that the oxygen sensor indicator light blinks 8 times or more in 10 seconds. If it does not, inspect the EFI system and replace the oxygen sensor if necessary.

5. Stop the engine and remove all test equipment. Install the rubber caps to the EFI service connector and the oxygen sensor check connector.

OXYGEN SENSOR MAINTENANCE REMINDER LIGHT

Reset Procedure

ALL GASOLINE ENGINES

There are some Toyota models with gasoline engines, equipped with an oxygen sensor reset light. At 30,000 mile intervals, a mileage counter activates a warning light in the dash panel. At this time the oxygen sensor must be inspected and/or replaced. After the oxygen sensor is replaced it will be necessary to reset the oxygen sensor reminder light. Use the procedure above to test the oxygen sensor. Reset the oxygen sensor reminder light as follows:

1. Remove the cancel switch from the top of the left kick panel, except on the Cressida.

NOTE: The cancel switch can be difficult to find sometimes. It may be located behind the left kick panel, on top of the left kick panel or in the wiring harness under the left side of the instrument panel.

2. On the Cressida models, remove the small panel next to the steering column and remove the cancel switch.

3. Pry open the tab on the cancel switch and move the switch to the opposite position, this will reset the cancel switch and should turn out the reminder light. Reinstall the cancel switch once it has been reset.

TIMING BELT WARNING LIGHT

On the Toyota diesel pick-up trucks, an instrument panel maintenance reminder light will come on at 50,000 miles. The engine timing belt should be replaced at this time. After the belt is replaced, reset the timing belt warning switch, by removing the rubber grommet on the speedometer and push the reset knob in with a thin rod or equivalent. The reset switch operates only when the warning light is on.

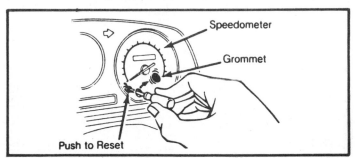

Resetting the speedometer counter on the Toyota diesel pickup

DIAGNOSIS CODES—1984-85 CAMRY

Code No.	Number of "CHECK ENGINE" blinks	System	Diagnosis	Trouble area
1		Normal	This appears when none of the other codes (2 thru 7) are identified	—
2		Air flow meter signal (Vc)	• Open circuit in Vc or Vc – Vs short circuited. • Open circuit in Vs	1. Air flow meter circuit (Vc, Vs) 2. Air flow meter 3. ECU
3		Air flow meter signal (Vs)	• Open circuit in Vs, or Vs – Es short circuited. • Open circuit in Vs	1. Air flow meter circuit (Vs, Vc, Vs, Es) 2. Air flow meter 3. ECU
4		Water thermo sensor signal (THW)	• Open circuit in coolant temperature sensor signal.	1. Coolant temperature sensor circuit 2. Coolant temperature sensor 3. ECU
5 *		Oxygen sensor signal	• Open or short circuit in Oxygen sensor signal (only lean or rich indication)	1. Oxygen sensor circuit 2. Oxygen sensor 3. ECU
6		Ignition signal	• No ignition signal	1. Ignition system circuit 2. IIA 3. ECU
7		Throttle position sensor signal	• IDL-Psw short circuited	1. Throttle position sensor circuit 2. Throttle position sensor 3. ECU

* NOTE Code No.5 is applicable to USA only.

INSPECTION OF THE DIAGNOSIS CIRCUIT – 1984-85 CAMRY

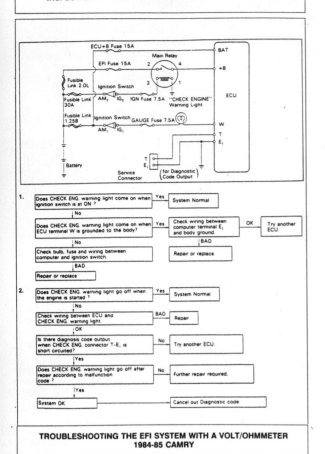

1. Does CHECK ENG. warning light come on when ignition switch is at ON ?
   - Yes → System Normal
   - No ↓
   Does CHECK ENG. warning light come on when ECU terminal W is grounded to the body?
   - Yes → Check wiring between computer terminal E₁ and body ground. → OK → Try another ECU.
   - No ↓ / BAD → Repair or replace
   Check bulb, fuse and wiring between computer and ignition switch.
   - BAD ↓
   Repair or replace

2. Does CHECK ENG. warning light go off when the engine is started ?
   - Yes → System Normal
   - No ↓
   Check wiring between ECU and CHECK ENG. warning light.
   - BAD → Repair
   - OK ↓
   Is there diagnosis code output when CHECK ENG. connector T-E₁ is short circuited?
   - No → Try another ECU.
   - Yes ↓
   Does CHECK ENG. warning light go off after repair according to malfunction code ?
   - No → Further repair required.
   - Yes ↓
   System OK → Cancel out Diagnostic code

TROUBLESHOOTING THE NO. 1 TERMINAL ON THE EFI CONNECTOR 1984-85 CAMRY

No.	Terminals	Trouble	Condition	STD Voltage
1	+B – E₁	No voltage	IG S/W ON	10 – 14 V

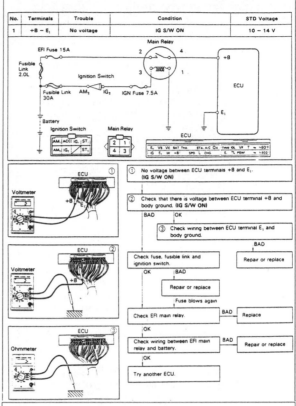

① No voltage between ECU terminals +B and E₁. (IG S/W ON)

② Check that there is voltage between ECU terminal +B and body ground. (IG S/W ON)
   - BAD ↓ / OK →
   ③ Check wiring between ECU terminal E₁ and body ground.
   - BAD → Repair or replace
   Check fuse, fusible link and ignition switch.
   - OK ↓ / BAD → Repair or replace
   Fuse blows again
   Check EFI main relay.
   - BAD → Replace
   - OK ↓
   Check wiring between EFI main relay and battery.
   - BAD → Repair or replace
   - OK ↓
   Try another ECU.

TROUBLESHOOTING THE EFI SYSTEM WITH A VOLT/OHMMETER 1984-85 CAMRY

PREPARATION

Remove the ECU wiring cover.

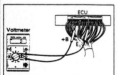

EFI SYSTEM CHECK PROCEDURE

NOTE:
- The EFI circuit can be checked by measuring the resistance and voltage at the wiring connectors of the ECU.
- Perform all voltage measurements with the connectors connected.
- Verify that the battery voltage is 11V or above when the ignition switch is ON.

Using a voltmeter with high impedance (10 kΩ/V minimum), measure the voltage at each terminal of the wiring connector.

NOTE: If there is any problem, see TROUBLESHOOTING EFI ELECTRONIC CIRCUIT WITH VOLT/OHMMETER.

No.	Terminals	Voltage (V)	Condition
1	+B – E₁	10 – 14	Ignition switch ON
2	BAT – E₁	10 – 14	–
3	IDL – E₁	8 – 14	Throttle valve fully closed (IG S/W ON)
	Psw – E₁	8 – 14	Throttle valve fully open (IG S/W ON)
	TL – E₁	8 – 14	
4	IG – E₁	6 – 12	Cranking or engine running
5	STA – E₁	6 – 12	Cranking
6	No.10 – E₁	9 – 14	Ignition switch ON
	No.20 – E₁	9 – 14	Ignition switch ON
7	W – E₁	8 – 14	No trouble ("CHECK ENGINE" warning light off and engine running
8	Vc – E₂	4 – 9	
	Vs – E₂	0.5 – 2.5	Measuring plate fully closed (IG S/W ON)
		5 – 8	Measuring plate fully open (IG S/W ON)
		2.5 – 5.5	Idling
9	THA – E₂	2 – 6	Intake air temperature 20°C or 68°F
10	THW – E₂	0.5 – 2.5	Coolant temperature 80°C or 176°F
11	A/C – E₁	8 – 14	Air conditioning ON

ECU connectors

E₂	Vs	Vc	BAT	THA		STA	A/C	Ox		THW	IDL	Vₚ	T	No.10	EO1
IG	E₁	W	+B			SPD	L	CHG			E₁	TL	Psw	No.20	EO2

TROUBLESHOOTING THE NO. 2 TERMINAL ON THE EFI CONNECTOR 1984-85 CAMRY

No.	Terminals	Trouble	Condition	STD Voltage
2	BAT – E₁	No voltage	–	10 – 14 V

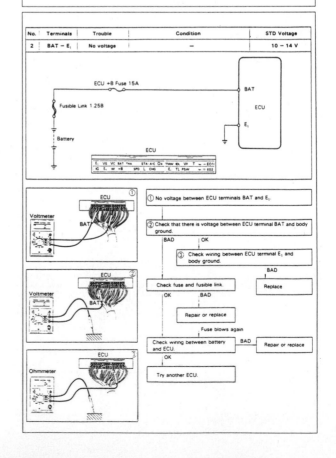

① No voltage between ECU terminals BAT and E₁.

② Check that there is voltage between ECU terminal BAT and body ground.
   - BAD ↓ / OK →
   ③ Check wiring between ECU terminal E₁ and body ground.
   - BAD → Replace
   Check fuse and fusible link.
   - OK ↓ / BAD
   Repair or replace
   Fuse blows again
   Check wiring between battery and ECU.
   - BAD → Repair or replace
   - OK ↓
   Try another ECU.

TROUBLESHOOTING THE NO. 3 TERMINAL ON THE EFI CONNECTOR
1984-85 CAMRY

No.	Terminals	Trouble		Condition	STD Voltage
3	TL − E_1	No voltage	IG S/W ON	−	8 − 14 V
	IDL − E_1			Throttle valve fully closed	8 − 14 V
	Psw − E_1			Throttle valve fully open	8 − 14 V

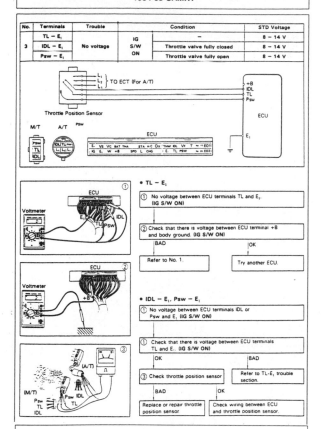

• TL − E_1

① No voltage between ECU terminals TL and E_1. (IG S/W ON)

② Check that there is voltage between ECU terminal +B and body ground. (IG S/W ON)

BAD	OK
Refer to No. 1.	Try another ECU.

• IDL − E_1, Psw − E_1

① No voltage between ECU terminals IDL or Psw and E_1 (IG S/W ON)

① Check that there is voltage between ECU terminals TL and E_1. (IG S/W ON)

OK	BAD
③ Check throttle position sensor	Refer to TL-E_1 trouble section.

BAD	
Replace or repair throttle position sensor.	Check wiring between ECU and throttle position sensor.

TROUBLESHOOTING THE NO. 4 TERMINAL ON THE EFI CONNECTOR
1984-85 CAMRY

No.	Terminals	Trouble	Condition	STD Voltage
4	IG − E_1	No voltage	Cranking or engine running	6 − 12 V

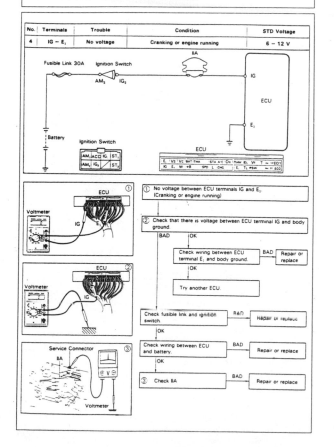

① No voltage between ECU terminals IG and E_1. (Cranking or engine running)

② Check that there is voltage between ECU terminal IG and body ground.

BAD	OK

Check wiring between ECU terminal E_1 and body ground.	BAD → Repair or replace
OK	
Try another ECU.	

Check fusible link and ignition switch.	BAD → Repair or replace
OK	

Check wiring between ECU and battery.	BAD → Repair or replace
OK	

③ Check IIA	BAD → Repair or replace

TROUBLESHOOTING THE NO. 5 TERMINAL ON THE EFI CONNECTOR
1984-85 CAMRY

No.	Terminals	Trouble	Condition	STD Voltage
5	STA − E_1	No voltage	Cranking	6 − 12 V

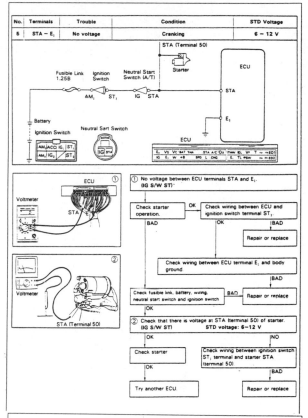

① No voltage between ECU terminals STA and E_1. (IG S/W ST)

Check starter operation.	OK → Check wiring between ECU and ignition switch terminal ST_1
BAD	OK	BAD → Repair or replace

Check wiring between ECU terminal E_1 and body ground.
BAD → Repair or replace

Check fusible link, battery, wiring, neutral start switch and ignition switch.	BAD → Repair or replace
OK	

② Check that there is voltage at STA (terminal 50) of starter. (IG S/W ST)   STD voltage: 6−12 V

OK	NO
Check starter	Check wiring between ignition switch ST_1 terminal and starter STA (terminal 50)
OK	BAD → Repair or replace
Try another ECU.	

TROUBLESHOOTING THE NO. 6 TERMINAL ON THE EFI CONNECTOR
1984-85 CAMRY

No.	Terminals	Trouble	Condition	STD Voltage
6	No.10 − E_1	No voltage	IG S/W ON	9 − 14 V
	No.20 − E_1			

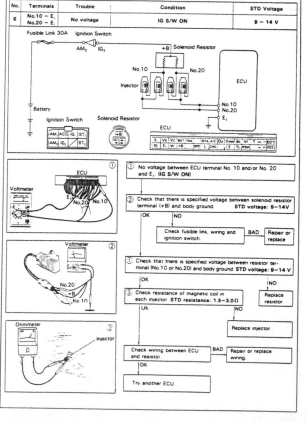

① No voltage between ECU terminal No. 10 and/or No. 20 and E_1. (IG S/W ON)

② Check that there is specified voltage between solenoid resistor terminal (+B) and body ground.   STD voltage: 9−14V

OK	NO
	Check fusible link, wiring and ignition switch.	BAD → Repair or replace

① Check that there is specified voltage between resistor terminal (No.10 or No.20) and body ground. STD voltage: 9−14 V

OK	NO
	Replace resistor

③ Check resistance of magnetic coil in each injector STD resistance: 1.5−3.0 Ω

OK	NO
	Replace injector

Check wiring between ECU and resistor.	BAD → Repair or replace wiring
OK	
Try another ECU.	

TROUBLESHOOTING THE NO. 7 TERMINAL ON THE EFI CONNECTOR
1984-85 CAMRY

No.	Terminals	Trouble	Condition	STD Voltage
7	W – E₁	No voltage	No trouble (CHECK ENGINE warning light off) and Engine running	8 – 14 V

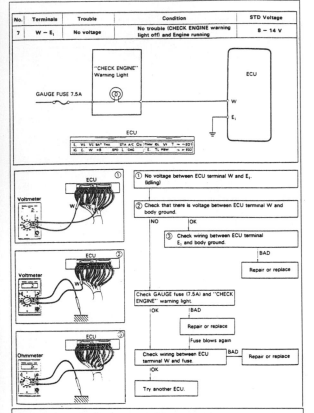

TROUBLESHOOTING THE NO. 8 TERMINAL ON THE EFI CONNECTOR
1984-85 CAMRY

No.	Terminals	Trouble	Condition	STD Voltage
8	Vc – E₂	No voltage	IG S/W ON —	4 – 9 V
	Vs – E₂		Measuring plate fully closed	0.5 – 2.5 V
	Vs – E₂		Measuring plate fully open	5 – 8 V
	Vs – E₂		Idling	2.5 – 5.5 V

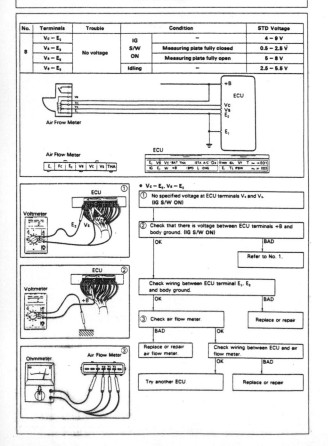

TROUBLESHOOTING THE NO. 9 TERMINAL ON THE EFI CONNECTOR
1984-85 CAMRY

No.	Terminals	Trouble	Condition	STD Voltage
9	THA – E₂	No voltage	IG S/W ON — Intake air temperature 20°C (68°F)	2 – 6 V

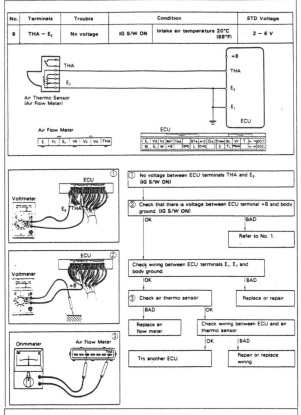

TROUBLESHOOTING THE NO. 10 TERMINAL ON THE EFI CONNECTOR
1984-85 CAMRY

No.	Terminals	Trouble	Condition	STD Voltage
10	THW – E₂	No voltage	IG S/W ON Coolant temperature 80°C (176°F)	0.5 – 2.5 V

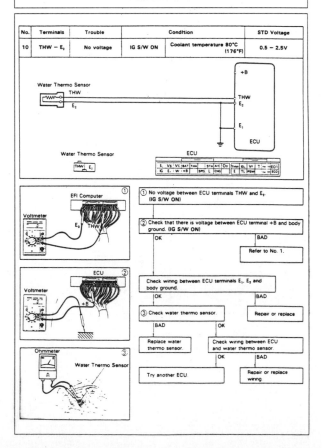

TROUBLESHOOTING THE NO. 11 TERMINAL ON THE EFI CONNECTOR 1984-85 CAMRY

No.	Terminals	Trouble	Condition	STD Voltage
11	A/C – E_1	No voltage	Air conditioning ON	8 – 14 V

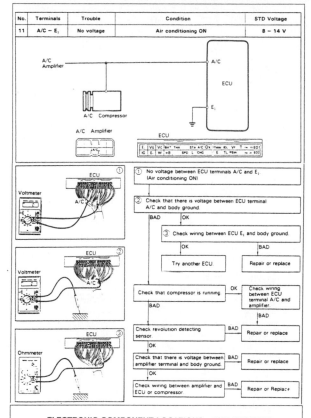

ELECTRONIC COMPONENT LOCATIONS – 1984-85 CAMRY

Location of Electronic Control Parts

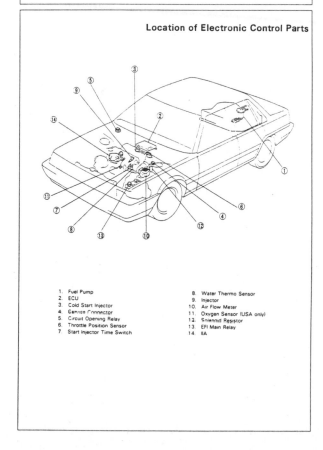

1. Fuel Pump
2. ECU
3. Cold Start Injector
4. Service Connector
5. Circuit Opening Relay
6. Throttle Position Sensor
7. Start Injector Time Switch
8. Water Thermo Sensor
9. Injector
10. Air Flow Meter
11. Oxygen Sensor (USA only)
12. Solenoid Resistor
13. EFI Main Relay
14. IIA

TESTING THE OXYGEN SENSOR – 1984-85 CAMRY

INSPECTION OF OXYGEN SENSOR

1. Warm up the engine.
2. Using a voltmeter, connect the positive (+) probe to terminal V_f of the service connector and negative (–) prove to terminal E_1.
3. Warm up the oxygen sensor with the engine at 2,500 rpm for about 120 seconds.

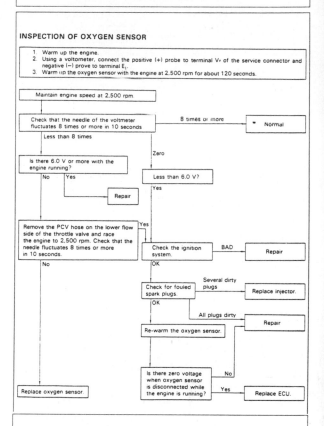

TESTING THE OXYGEN SENSOR (CONT.) – 1984-85 CAMRY

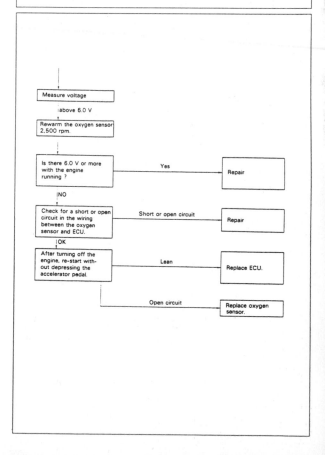

INSPECTING THE EFI COMPUTER—1984-85 CAMRY

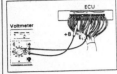

1. **MEASURE VOLTAGE OF ECU**

   NOTE:
   - The ECU, itself, cannot be checked independently.
   - The EFI circuit can be checked by measuring the resistance and voltage at the wiring connectors of the ECU.

   Check the voltages at the wiring connectors.
   - Turn the ignition switch on.
   - Measure the voltage at each terminal.

NOTE: 1. Perform all voltage measurements with the connectors connected.
2. Verify that the battery voltage is 11V or above when the ignition switch is ON.

Voltages at ECU Wiring Connectors

Terminals	Voltage	
+B – E$_1$	10 – 14 V	(Ignition switch ON)
BAT – E$_1$	10 – 14 V	
IDL – E$_1$	8 – 14 V	(Throttle valve fully closed)
Psw – E$_1$	8 – 14 V	(Throttle valve fully open)
TL – E$_1$	8 – 14 V	
IG – E$_1$	6 – 12 V	(Cranking and engine running)
STA – E$_1$	6 – 12 V	(Cranking)
No.10 – E$_1$	9 – 14 V	(Ignition ON)
No.20 – E$_1$	9 – 14 V	(Ignition ON)
W – E$_1$	8 – 14 V	(No trouble and engine running)
L, CHG – E$_1$	9 – 14 V	(Idling)
Vc – E$_2$	4 – 9 V	
Vs – E$_2$	0.5 – 2.5 V	(Measuring plate fully closed)
	5 – 8 V	(Measuring plate fully open)
	2.5 – 5.5 V	(Idling)
THA – E$_2$	2 – 6 V	(Intake air temperature 20°C or 68°F)
THW – E$_2$	0.5 – 2.5 V	(Coolant temperature 80°C or 176°F)
A/C – E$_1$	8 – 14 V	(Air conditioning ON)

ECU connectors

E$_2$	Vs	Vc	BAT	THA		STA	A/C	O$_X$	THW	IDL	V$_f$	T	No.10	EO1
IG	E$_1$	W	+B		SPD	L	CHG		E$_1$	TL	PSW		No.20	EO2

INSPECTING THE CHARGE WARNING SYSTEM—1984-85 CAMRY

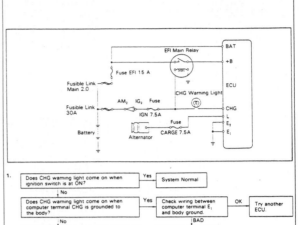

1.
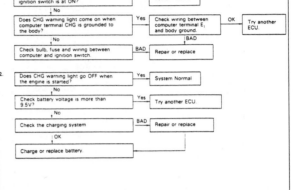

2.

INSPECTING THE EFI COMPUTER (CONT.)—1984-85 CAMRY

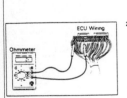

2. **MEASURE RESISTANCE AT ECU**

   CAUTION:
   - Do not touch the ECU terminals.
   - The tester probe should be inserted into the wiring connector from the wiring side.

   Check the resistance between each terminal of the wiring connector.
   - Disconnect the wiring connectors from the ECU.
   - Measure the resistance between each terminal of the wiring connectors.

Resistances at ECU Wiring Connectors

Terminals	Resistance	
TL – IDL	0	(Throttle valve fully closed)
TL – IDL	∞	(Throttle valve fully open)
TL – Psw	∞	(Throttle valve fully closed)
TL – Psw	0	(Throttle valve fully open)
IDL, TL, P$_{sw}$ – Ground	∞	
THW – E$_2$	200 – 400 Ω	(Coolant temp. 80°C or 176°F)
THA – E$_2$	2 – 3 kΩ	(Intake air temp. 20°C or 68°F)
+B – E$_2$	200 – 400 Ω	
Vc – E$_2$	100 – 300 Ω	
Vs – E$_2$	20 – 400 Ω	(Measuring plate fully closed)
Vs – E$_2$	20 – 1,000 Ω	(Measuring plate fully open)
E$_1$, E$_{01}$, E$_{02}$ – Ground	0	

ECU connectors

E$_2$	Vs	Vc	BAT	THA		STA	A/C	O$_X$	THW	IDL	V$_f$	T	No.10	EO1
IG	E$_1$	W	+B		SPD	L	CHG		E$_1$	TL	PSW		No.20	EO2

EFI WIRING SCHEMATIC—1984-85 CAMRY

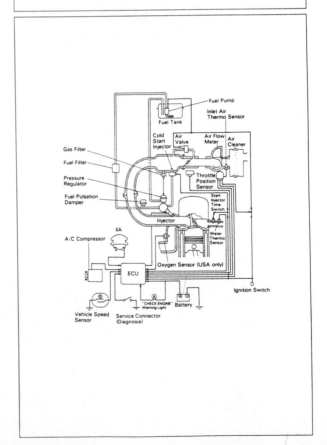

EFI WIRING SCHEMATIC – 1986 CAMRY

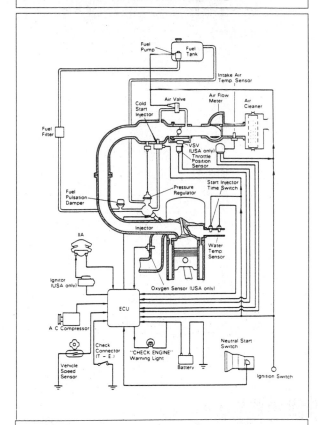

DIAGNOSIS CODES – 1986 CAMRY

(Canada)

Code No.	Number of "CHECK ENGINE" blinks	System	Diagnosis	Trouble area
1	ON ON ON ON ON / OFF OFF OFF OFF	Normal	This appears when none of the other codes (2 thru 7) are identified	–
2		Air flow meter signal (Vc)	• Vc circuit open or Vc – Vs short circuited. • Open circuit in Vs	1 Air flow meter circuit (Vc, Vs) 2 Air flow meter 3 ECU
3		Air flow meter signal (Vs)	• Vs circuit open or Vs – E, short circuited. • Open circuit in Vs	1 Air flow meter circuit (Vs, Vc, Vs) 2 Air flow meter 3 ECU
4		Water temp sensor signal (THW)	Open circuit in water temp sensor signal	1 Water temp sensor circuit 2 Water temp sensor 3 ECU
6		Ignition signal	No ignition signal	1 Ignition system circuit 2 Distributor 3 Ignition coil 4 Igniter 5 ECU
7		Throttle position sensor signal	IDL – Psw short circuited	1 Throttle position sensor circuit 2 Throttle position sensor 3 ECU

INSPECTION OF THE DIAGNOSIS CIRCUIT (USA) 1986 CAMRY

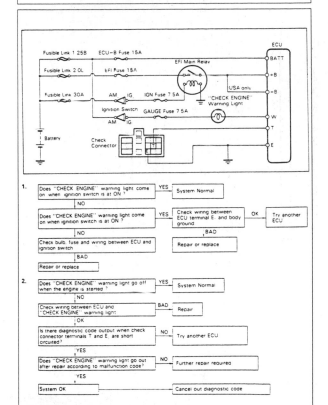

1. Does "CHECK ENGINE" warning light come on when ignition switch is at ON ? — YES → System Normal

   NO

   Does "CHECK ENGINE" warning light come on when ignition switch is at ON ? — YES → Check wiring between ECU terminal E. and body ground — OK → Try another ECU

   NO / BAD

   Check bulb, fuse and wiring between ECU and ignition switch — BAD → Repair or replace

   BAD

   Repair or replace

2. Does "CHECK ENGINE" warning light go off when the engine is started ? — YES → System Normal

   NO

   Check wiring between ECU and "CHECK ENGINE" warning light — BAD → Repair

   OK

   Is there diagnostic code output when check connector terminals T and E. are short circuited? — NO → Try another ECU

   YES

   Does "CHECK ENGINE" warning light go out after repair according to malfunction code? — NO → Further repair required

   YES

   System OK — Cancel out diagnostic code

TROUBLESHOOTING THE EFI SYSTEM WITH A VOLT/OHMMETER (USA) 1986 CAMRY

NOTE The following troubleshooting procedures are designed for inspection of each separate system, and therefore the actual procedure may vary somewhat However. troubleshooting should be performed refering to the inspection methods described in this manual.

Before beginning inspection, it is best to first make a simple check of the fuses, fusible links and the condition of the connectors

The following troubleshooting procedures are based on the supposition that the trouble lies in either a short or open circuit in a component outside the computer or a short circuit within the computer

If engine trouble occurs even though proper operating voltage is detected in the computer connector, then the ECU is faulty and should be replaced.

LOCATION OF FUSES AND FUSIBLE LINKS

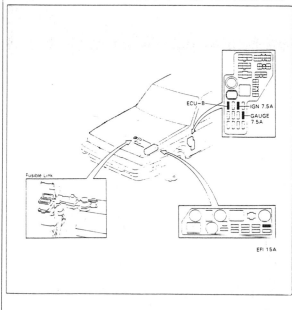

TROUBLESHOOTING THE EFI SYSTEM WITH A VOLT/OHMMETER (CONT.) – 1986 CAMRY

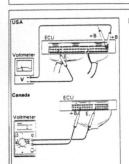

USA

Canada

EFI SYSTEM CHECK PROCEDURE

NOTE:
- Perform all voltage measurements with the connectors connected.
- Verify that the battery voltage is 11V or above when the ignition switch is at ON.

Using a voltmeter with high impedance (10 kΩ/V minimum), measure the voltage at each terminal of the wiring connector.

Connectors of ECU

[USA]

Symbol	Terminal Name	Symbol	Terminal Name
E_{01}	ENGINE GROUND	IGf	IGNITER
E_{02}	ENGINE GROUND	E_2	SENSOR GROUND
No. 10	INJECTOR	OX	OXYGEN SENSOR
No. 20	INJECTOR	Psw	THROTTLE POSITION SENSOR
STA	STARTER SWITCH	Ne	ENGINE REVOLUTION SENSOR
IGt	IGNITER	THW	WATER TEMP SENSOR
VF	CHECK CONNECTOR	Vc	AIR FLOW METER
E_1	ENGINE GROUND	E	SENSOR GROUND
NSW	NEUTRAL START SWITCH	Vs	AIR FLOW METER
V–ISC	ISC VSV	THA	AIR TEMP SENSOR
W	WARNING LIGHT	SPD	SPEED SENSOR
T	CHECK CONNECTOR	BATT	BATTERY
IDL	THROTTLE POSITION SENSOR	+B	MAIN RELAY
A/C	A/C MAGNET SWITCH	+B	MAIN RELAY

ECU connectors

E	No 10	STA	VF	NSW		V-ISC	W		T	IDL	IGf			Ne			Vc	Vs	THA	BATT	+B
E	No 20	IGt	E						A C	E	OX		Psw	THW			E		SPD		+B

VOLTAGE SUPPLIED AT THE ECU WIRING CONNECTOR (USA) 1986 CAMRY

[USA]

No.	Terminals	STD voltage	Condition	
1	+B +B – E	10 – 14	Ignition S/W ON	
2	BATT – E	10 – 14	–	
3	IDL – E	8 – 14	Ignition S/W ON	Throttle valve open
	Psw – E	8 – 14		Throttle valve fully closed
4	IGt – E	0.7 – 1.0	Idling	
5	STA – E	6 – 12	Cranking	
6	No. 10 – E_{01} No. 20 – E_{02}	9 – 14	Ignition S/W ON	
7	W – E	8 – 14	No trouble ("CHECK ENGINE" warning light off) and engine running	
8	Vc – E_2	6 – 10		–
	Vs – E	0.5 – 2.5	Ignition S/W ON	Measuring plate fully closed
		5 – 10		Measuring plate fully open
		2 – 8		Idling
9	THA – E	1 – 3	Ignition S/W ON	Intake air temperature 20°C (68°F)
10	THW – E	0.5 – 2.5	Ignition S/W ON	Coolant temperature 80°C (176°F)
11	A/C – E	8 – 14	Ignition S/W ON	Air conditioning ON

ECU connectors

E	No 10	STA	VF	NSW		V-ISC	W		T	IDL	IGf			Ne			Vc	Vs	THA	BATT	+B
E	No 20	IGt	E						A C	E	OX		Psw	THW			E		SPD		+B

TROUBLESHOOTING THE NO. 1 TERMINAL ON THE EFI CONNECTOR USA) 1986 CAMRY

No.	Terminals	Trouble	Condition	STD Voltage
1	+B – E_1 +B – E_1	No voltage	Ignition S/W ON	10 – 14 V

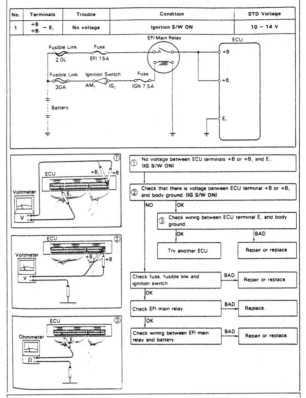

① No voltage between ECU terminals +B or B_1 and E_1. (IG S/W ON)

② Check that there is voltage between ECU terminal +B or B_1 and body ground. (IG S/W ON)

NO — ③ Check wiring between ECU terminal E_1 and body ground.
OK — Try another ECU.
BAD — Repair or replace.

OK — Check fuse, fusible link and ignition switch.
BAD — Repair or replace.
OK — Check EFI main relay.
BAD — Replace.
OK — Check wiring between EFI main relay and battery.
BAD — Repair or replace.

TROUBLESHOOTING THE NO. 2 TERMINAL ON THE EFI CONNECTOR (USA) 1986 CAMRY

No.	Terminals	Trouble	Condition	STD Voltage
2	BATT – E	No voltage	—	10 – 14 V

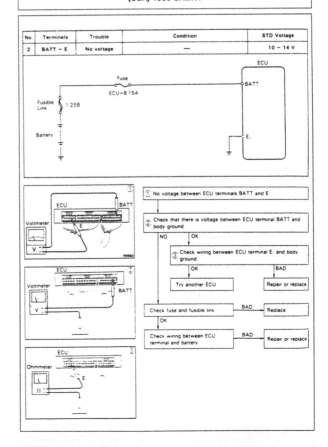

① No voltage between ECU terminals BATT and E.

② Check that there is voltage between ECU terminal BATT and body ground.

NO — ③ Check wiring between ECU terminal E and body ground.
OK — Try another ECU.
BAD — Repair or replace.

OK — Check fuse and fusible link.
BAD — Replace.
OK — Check wiring between ECU terminal and battery.
BAD — Repair or replace.

TROUBLESHOOTING THE NO. 3 TERMINAL ON THE EFI CONNECTOR (USA) 1986 CAMRY

No.	Terminals	Trouble	Condition		STD Voltage
3	IDL – E,	No voltage	IG S/W ON	Throttle valve open	8 – 14 V
	Psw – E,			Throttle valve fully closed	8 – 14 V

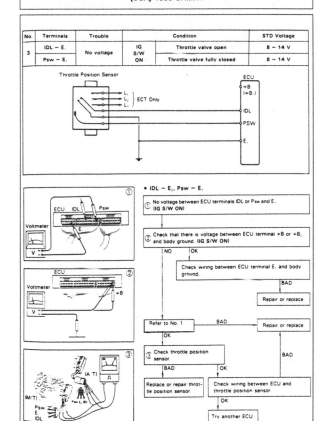

• IDL – E,, Psw – E,

① No voltage between ECU terminals IDL or Psw and E. (IG S/W ON)

② Check that there is voltage between ECU terminal +B or +B, and body ground. (IG S/W ON)

NO → Check wiring between ECU terminal E. and body ground. → BAD → Repair or replace

OK

Refer to No. 1 → BAD → Repair or replace

OK

③ Check throttle position sensor. → BAD → Replace or repair throttle position sensor → OK → Check wiring between ECU and throttle position sensor. → OK → Try another ECU

TROUBLESHOOTING THE NO. 4 TERMINAL ON THE EFI CONNECTOR (USA) 1986 CAMRY

No.	Terminals	Trouble	Condition	STD Voltage
4	IGt – E,	No voltage	Idling	0.7 – 1.0 V

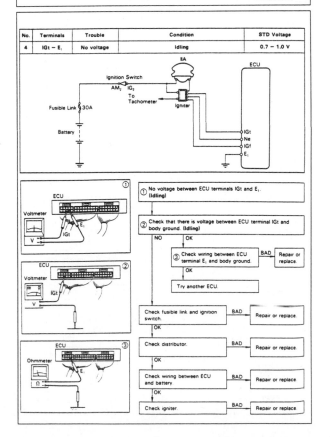

① No voltage between ECU terminals IGt and E,. (Idling)

② Check that there is voltage between ECU terminal IGt and body ground. (Idling)

NO → ③ Check wiring between ECU terminal E, and body ground. → BAD → Repair or replace. → OK → Try another ECU.

OK

Check fusible link and ignition switch. → BAD → Repair or replace.

OK

Check distributor. → BAD → Repair or replace.

OK

Check wiring between ECU and battery. → BAD → Repair or replace.

OK

Check igniter. → BAD → Repair or replace.

TROUBLESHOOTING THE NO. 5 TERMINAL ON THE EFI CONNECTOR (USA) – 1986 CAMRY

No.	Terminals	Trouble	Condition	STD Voltage
5	STA – E,	No voltage	Cranking	6 – 12 V

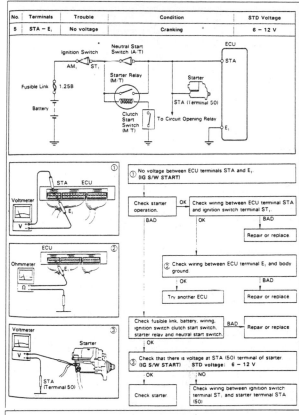

① No voltage between ECU terminals STA and E,. (IG S/W START)

Check starter operation. → OK → Check wiring between ECU terminal STA and ignition switch terminal ST,.

BAD | OK | BAD → Repair or replace.

② Check wiring between ECU terminal E, and body ground.

OK → Try another ECU → BAD → Repair or replace.

Check fusible link, battery, wiring, ignition switch clutch start switch, starter relay and neutral start switch. → BAD → Repair or replace

OK

③ Check that there is voltage at STA (50) terminal of starter. (IG S/W START) STD voltage: 6 – 12 V

OK → Check starter | NO → Check wiring between ignition switch terminal ST, and starter terminal STA (50)

TROUBLESHOOTING THE NO. 6 TERMINAL ON THE EFI CONNECTOR (USA) – 1986 CAMRY

No.	Terminals	Trouble	Condition	STD Voltage
6	No.10 – E...	No voltage	IG S/W ON	9 – 14 V
	No.20 – E...			

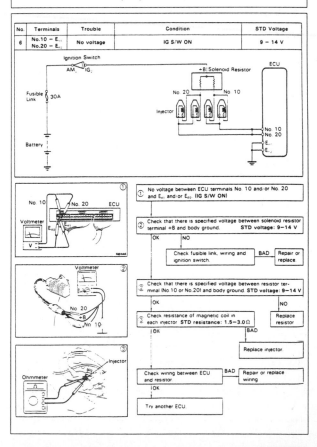

① No voltage between ECU terminals No. 10 and/or No. 20 and E,, and/or E,,. (IG S/W ON)

② Check that there is specified voltage between solenoid resistor terminal +B and body ground. STD voltage: 9–14 V

OK | NO → Check fusible link, wiring and ignition switch. → BAD → Repair or replace.

③ Check that there is specified voltage between resistor terminal (No 10 or No.20) and body ground. STD voltage: 9–14 V

OK | NO → Replace resistor

④ Check resistance of magnetic coil in each injector. STD resistance: 1.5–3.0 Ω → BAD → Replace injector.

OK

Check wiring between ECU and resistor. → BAD → Repair or replace wiring.

OK

Try another ECU.

TROUBLESHOOTING THE NO. 7 TERMINAL ON THE EFI CONNECTOR (USA) — 1986 CAMRY

No.	Terminals	Trouble	Condition	STD Voltage
7	W – E.	No voltage	No trouble ("CHECK ENGINE" warning light off) and engine running	8 – 14 V

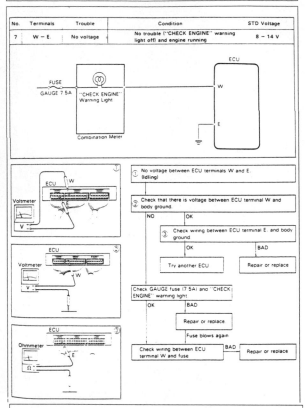

TROUBLESHOOTING THE NO. 8 TERMINAL ON THE EFI CONNECTOR (USA) — 1986 CAMRY

No.	Terminals	Trouble	Condition	STD Voltage
8	Vc – E.	No voltage	–	6 – 10 V
	Vs – E.		Measuring plate fully closed	0.5 – 2.5 V
	Vs – E.		Measuring plate fully open	5 – 10 V
	Vs – E.		Idling	2 – 8 V

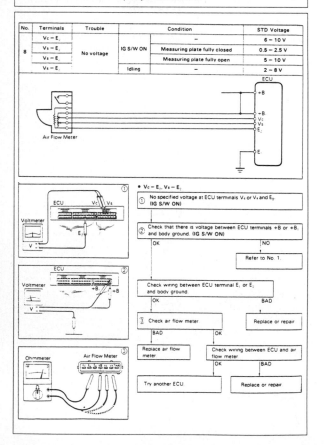

TROUBLESHOOTING THE NO. 9 TERMINAL ON THE EFI CONNECTOR (USA) — 1986 CAMRY

No.	Terminals	Trouble	Condition		STD Voltage
9	THA – E.	No voltage	IG S/W ON	Intake air temperature 20°C (68°F)	1 – 3 V

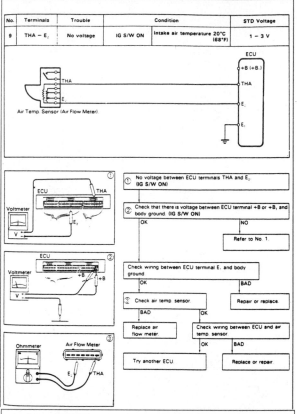

TROUBLESHOOTING THE NO. 10 TERMINAL ON THE EFI CONNECTOR (USA) — 1986 CAMRY

No.	Terminals	Trouble	Condition		STD Voltage
10	THW – E.	No voltage	IG S/W ON	Coolant temperature 80°C (176°F)	0.5 – 2.5 V

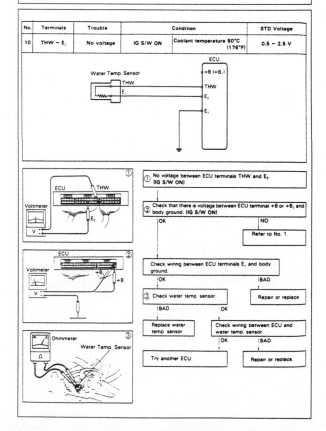

TROUBLESHOOTING THE NO. 11 TERMINAL ON THE EFI CONNECTOR (USA) — 1986 CAMRY

No.	Terminals	Trouble	Condition	STD Voltage
11	A/C – E₁	No voltage	Air conditioning ON	8 – 14 V

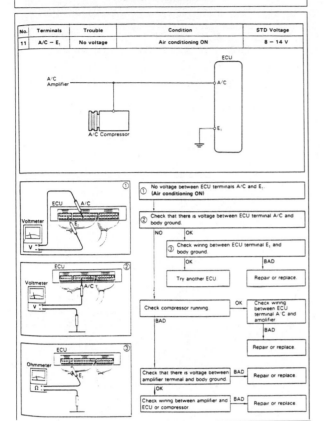

VOLTAGE SUPPLIED AT THE ECU WIRING CONNECTOR (CANADA) — 1986 CAMRY

[Canada]

No.	Terminals	STD voltage	Condition	
1	+B – E₁	10 – 14	Ignition S/W ON	
2	BATT – E₁	10 – 14	—	
3	TL – E₁			—
	IDL – E₁	8 – 14	Ignition S/W ON	Throttle valve fully closed
	Psw – E₁			Throttle valve fully open
4	Ig – E	6 – 12	Cranking or engine running	
5	STA – E₁	6 – 12	Cranking	
6	No. 10 – E₁	9 – 14	Ignition S/W ON	
	No. 20 – E₁			
7	W – E₁	8 – 14	No trouble ("CHECK ENGINE" warning light off) and engine running	
8	Vc – E₂	4 – 9		—
	Vs – E₂	0.5 – 2.5	Ignition S/W ON	Measuring plate fully closed
		5 – 8		Measuring plate fully open
		2.5 – 5.5		Idling
9	THA – E₂	2 – 6	Ignition switch ON	Intake air temperature 20°C (68°F)
10	THW – E₂	0.5 – 2.5	Ignition switch ON	Coolant temperature 80°C (176°F)
11	A/C – E₁	8 – 14	Ignition switch ON	Air conditioning ON

ECU connector

E₂	Vs	Vc	BATT	THA		STA	A/C	NSW	THW	IDL	VF	T	No. 10	E₁
Ig	E	W	+B		SPD	L	CHG		E	TL	Psw		No. 20	E₁

ECU CONNECTORS (CANADA) — 1986 CAMRY

[Canada]

Symbol	Terminal Name	Symbol	Terminal Name
E₂	SENSOR GROUND	CHG	GARGE LIGHT
Ig	IGNITION COIL	NSW	NEUTRAL START SWITCH
Vs	AIR FLOW METER	THW	WATER TEMP. SENSOR
E₁	SENSOR GROUND	E₁	ENGINE GROUND
Vc	AIR FLOW METER	IDL	THROTTLE POSITION SENSOR
W	WARNING LIGHT	TL	THROTTLE POSITION SENSOR
BATT	BATTERY +B	VF	CHECK CONNECTOR
+B	MAIN RELAY	Psw	THROTTLE POSITION SENSOR
THA	AIR TEMP. SENSOR	T	CHECK CONNECTOR
SPD	SPEED SENSOR	No. 10	INJECTOR
STA	STARTER SWITCH	No. 20	INJECTOR
L	ALTERNATOR	E₀₁	ENGINE GROUND
A/C	A/C MAGNET SWITCH	E₀₂	ENGINE GROUND

ECU Connectors

E₂	Vs	Vc	BATT	THA		STA	A/C	NSW	THW	IDL	VF	T	No. 10	E₁
Ig	E₁	W	+B		SPD	L	CHG		E	TL	Psw		No. 20	E₀₂

TROUBLESHOOTING THE NO. 2 TERMINAL ON THE EFI CONNECTOR (CANADA) — 1986 CAMRY

No.	Terminals	Trouble	Condition	STD Voltage
2	BATT – E₁	No voltage	—	10 – 14 V

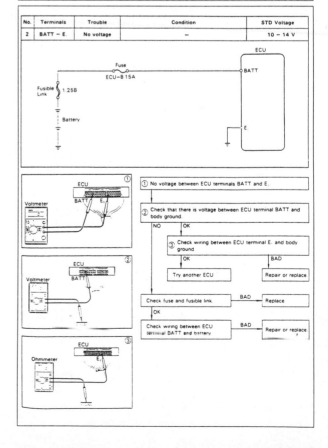

TROUBLESHOOTING THE NO. 3 TERMINAL ON THE EFI CONNECTOR (CANADA) – 1986 CAMRY

No.	Terminals	Trouble		Condition	STD Voltage
3	TL – E,	No voltage	IG S/W ON	–	8 – 14 V
	IDL – E,			Throttle valve fully closed	8 – 14 V
	Psw – E,			Throttle valve fully open	8 – 14 V

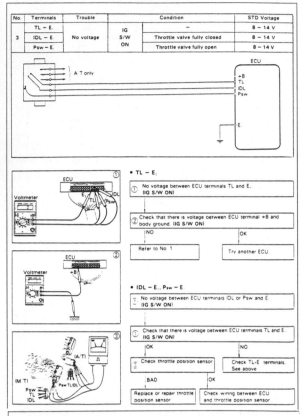

TROUBLESHOOTING THE NO. 4 TERMINAL ON THE EFI CONNECTOR (CANADA) – 1986 CAMRY

No.	Terminals	Trouble	Condition	STD Voltage
4	Ig – E,	No voltage	Cranking or engine running	6 – 12 V

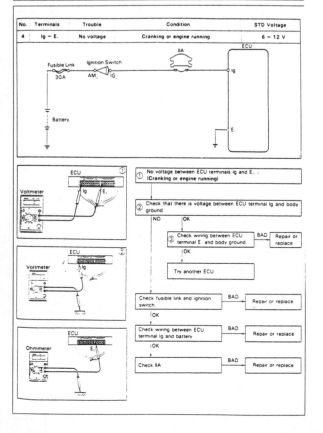

TROUBLESHOOTING THE NO. 5 TERMINAL ON THE EFI CONNECTOR (CANADA) – 1986 CAMRY

No.	Terminals	Trouble	Condition	STD Voltage
5	STA – E,	No voltage	Cranking	6 – 12 V

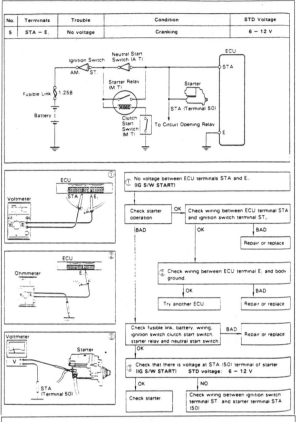

TROUBLESHOOTING THE NO. 6 TERMINAL ON THE EFI CONNECTOR (CANADA) – 1986 CAMRY

No.	Terminals	Trouble	Condition	STD Voltage
6	No.10 – E	No voltage	IG S/W ON	9 – 14 V
	No.20			

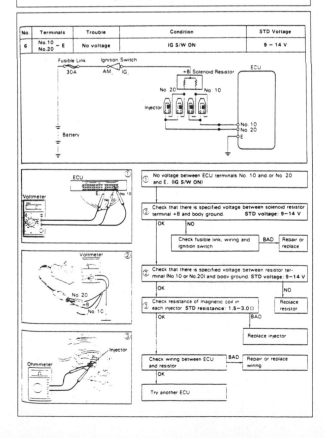

TROUBLESHOOTING THE NO. 7 TERMINAL ON THE EFI CONNECTOR
(CANADA) — 1986 CAMRY

No.	Terminals	Trouble	Condition	STD Voltage
7	W – E₁	No voltage	No trouble ("CHECK ENGINE" warning light off) and engine running	8 – 14 V

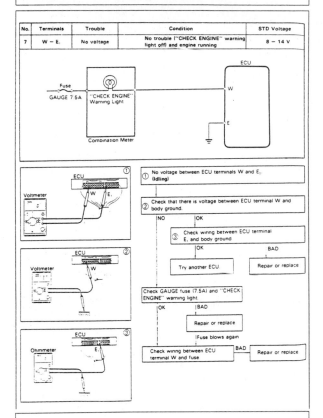

TROUBLESHOOTING THE NO. 8 TERMINAL ON THE EFI CONNECTOR
(CANADA) — 1986 CAMRY

No.	Terminals	Trouble		Condition	STD Voltage
8	Vc – E₂	No voltage	IG S/W ON	—	4 – 9 V
	Vs – E₂			Measuring plate fully closed	0.5 – 2.5 V
	Vs – E₂			Measuring plate fully open	5 – 8 V
	Vs – E₂		Idling	—	2.5 – 5.5 V

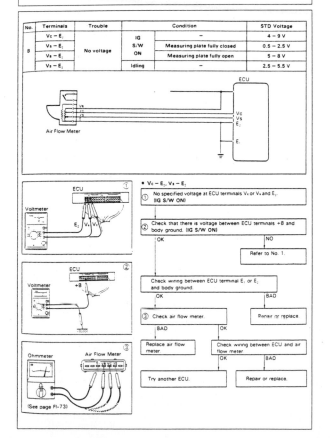

TROUBLESHOOTING THE NO. 9 TERMINAL ON THE EFI CONNECTOR
(CANADA) — 1986 CAMRY

No.	Terminals	Trouble	Condition		STD Voltage
9	THA – E₂	No voltage	IG S/W ON	Intake air temperature 20°C (68°F)	2 – 6 V

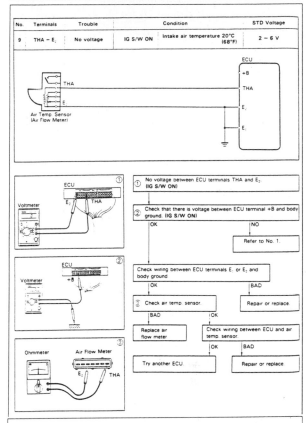

TROUBLESHOOTING THE NO. 10 TERMINAL ON THE EFI CONNECTOR
(CANADA) — 1986 CAMRY

No.	Terminals	Trouble	Condition		STD Voltage
10	THW – E₂	No voltage	IG S/W ON	Coolant temperature 80°C (176°F)	0.5 – 2.5 V

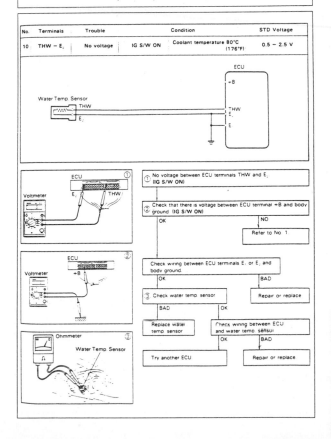

TROUBLESHOOTING THE NO. 11 TERMINAL ON THE EFI CONNECTOR (CANADA) — 1986 CAMRY

No.	Terminals	Trouble	Condition	STD Voltage
11	A/C – E₁	No voltage	Air conditioning ON	8 – 14 V

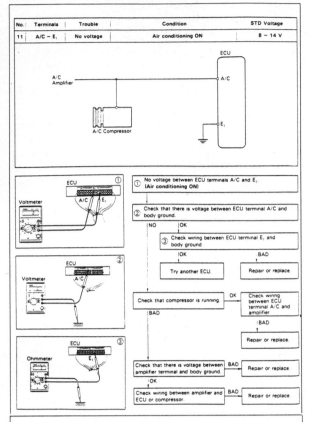

ELECTRONIC COMPONENT LOCATIONS — 1986 CAMRY

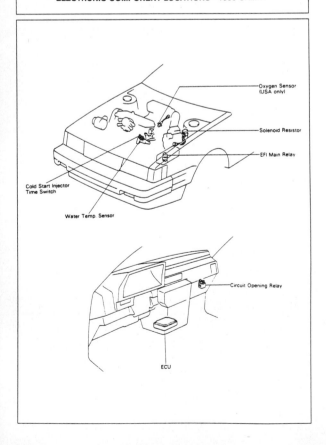

TESTING THE OXYGEN SENSOR (USA) — 1986 CAMRY

Oxygen Sensor (USA only)
INSPECTION OF FEEDBACK VOLTAGE (Vf)

1. Warm up the engine.
2. Connect the positive (+) lead of a voltmeter to terminal Vf of the check connector and negative (–) lead to terminal E₁.

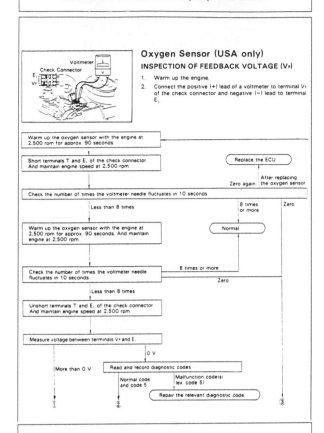

TESTING THE OXYGEN SENSOR (CONT.) — 1986 CAMRY

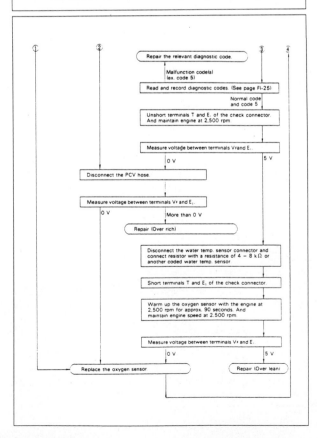

INSPECTING THE EFI COMPUTER – 1986 CAMRY

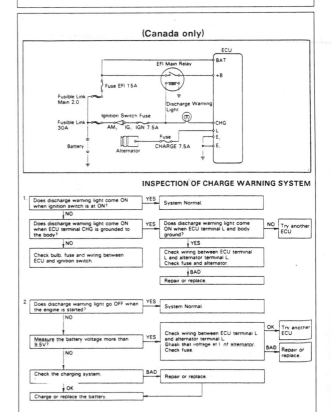

USA

ECU

Voltmeter

Canada

ECU

Voltmeter

Electronic Controlled Unit (ECU)

INSPECTION OF ECU

1. MEASURE VOLTAGE OF ECU

   NOTE: The EFI circuit can be checked by measuring the resistance and voltage at the wiring connectors of the ECU.

   Check the voltage at the wiring connectors.
   - Turn the ignition switch.
   - Measure the voltage at each terminal.

NOTE: 1. Perform all voltage measurements with the connectors connected.
2. Verify that the battery voltage is 11 V or more when the ignition switch is ON.

INSPECTING THE VOLTAGE AT THE ECU WIRING CONNECTOR (CANADA) 1986 CAMRY

[Canada]

Terminals	Conditions	Resistance (Ω)
IDL – TL	Throttle valve open	∞
	Throttle valve fully closed	0
Psw – TL	Throttle valve fully open	0
	Throttle valve fully closed	∞
+B – E₂	—	200 – 400
Vc – E₂	—	100 – 300
Vs – E₂	Measuring plate fully closed	20 – 400
	Measuring plate fully open	20 – 1,000
THA – E₂	Intake air temperature 20° (68°F)	2,000 – 3,000
THW – E₂	Coolant temperature 80°C (176°F)	200 – 400

ECU Connectors

E₂	Vs	Vc	BATT	THA		STA	A/C	NSW	THW	IDL	VF	T	No. 10	E₀₁
Ig	E₃	W	+B		SPD	L	CHG		E₁	TL	Psw		No. 20	E₀₂

INSPECTING THE VOLTAGE AT THE ECU WIRING CONNECTOR (USA) 1986 CAMRY

[USA]

Terminals	Condition		STD voltage
+B +B₁ – E₁	Ignition S/W ON		10 – 14
BATT – E₁	—		10 – 14
IDL – E₁	Ignition S/W ON	Throttle valve open	8 – 14
Psw – E₁		Throttle valve fully closed	8 – 14
IGt – E₁	Idling		0.7 – 1.0
STA – E₁	Cranking		6 – 12
No. 10 – E₀₁ No. 20 – E₀₂	Ignition S/W ON		9 – 14
W – E₁	No trouble ("CHECK ENGINE" warning light off) and engine running		8 – 14
Vc – E₂		—	6 – 10
Vs – E₂	Ignition S/W ON	Measuring plate fully closed	0.5 – 2.5
		Measuring plate fully open	5 – 10
		Idling	2 – 8
THA – E₂	Ignition S/W ON	Intake air temperature 20°C (68°F)	1 – 3
THW – E₂	Ignition S/W ON	Coolant temperature 80°C (176°F)	0.5 – 2.5
A/C – E₁	Ignition S/W ON	Air conditioning ON	8 – 14
T – E₁	Ignition S/W ON	Check connector T-E₁ not short	10 – 14
		Check connector T-E₁ short	0

ECU Connectors

E₀₁ No. 10	STA	VF	NSW		V-ISC	W	T	IDL	IGf			Ne		Vc	Vs	THA	BATT	+B₁
E₀₂ No. 20	IGt	E₁				A/C	E₂	OX		Psw	THW			E₂₁		SPD		+B

INSPECTING THE CHARGE WARNING SYSTEM – 1986 CAMRY

(Canada only)

ECU

EFI Main Relay — BAT — +B

Fuse EFI 15A

Fusible Link Main 2.0

Ignition Switch Fuse

Fusible Link 30A — AM₂ IG₂ IGN 7.5A

Battery

Alternator

Discharge Warning Light — CHG — L — E₂ — E₁

Fuse CHARGE 7.5A

INSPECTION OF CHARGE WARNING SYSTEM

1. Does discharge warning light come ON when ignition switch is at ON? — **YES** → System Normal.
   - **NO**
   Does discharge warning light come ON when ECU terminal CHG is grounded to the body? — **YES** → Does discharge warning light come ON when ECU terminal L and body ground? — **NO** → Try another ECU
   - **NO**
   Check bulb, fuse and wiring between ECU and ignition switch.
   - **YES** → Check wiring between ECU terminal L and alternator terminal L. Check fuse and alternator.
   - **BAD** → Repair or replace.

2. Does discharge warning light go OFF when the engine is started? — **YES** → System Normal.
   - **NO**
   Measure the battery voltage more than 9.5V? — **YES** → Check wiring between ECU terminal L and alternator terminal L. Check that voltage at L of alternator. Check fuse.
     - **OK** → Try another ECU
     - **BAD** → Repair or replace.
   - **NO**
   Check the charging system. — **BAD** → Repair or replace.
   - **OK**
   Charge or replace the battery.

EFI WIRING SCHEMATIC – 1987-88 CAMRY

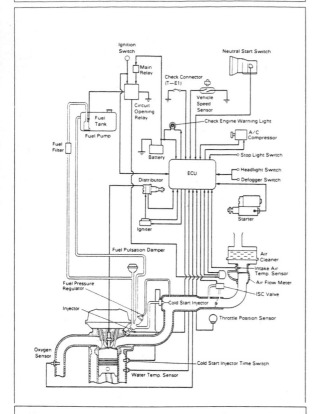

INSPECTION OF THE DIAGNOSIS CIRCUIT – 1987-88 CAMRY

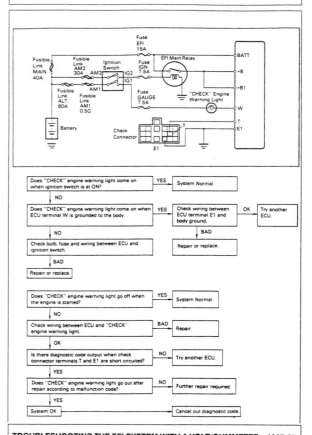

DIAGNOSIS CODES – 1987-88 CAMRY

Code No.	Number of CHECK ENGINE blinks	System	Diagnosis	Trouble area
—	ON/OFF	Normal	This appears when none of the other codes (11 thru 51) are identified.	—
11		ECU (+B)	Wire severance, however slight, in +B (ECU).	1. Main relay circuit 2. Main relay 3. ECU
12		RPM signal	No NE, G signal to ECU within several seconds after engine is cranked.	1. Distributor circuit 2. Distributor 3. Starter signal circuit 4. ECU
13		RPM signal	No NE signal to ECU within several seconds after engine reaches 1,000 rpm.	Same as 12, above.
14		Ignition signal	No signal from igniter 4 — 5 times in succession.	1. Igniter circuit (+B, IGT, IGF) 2. Igniter 3. ECU
21		Oxygen sensor signal	Open circuit in oxygen sensor signal (only lean indication).	1. Oxygen sensor circuit 2. Oxygen sensor 3. ECU
22		Water temp. sensor signal	Open or short circuit in water temp. sensor signal (THW).	1. Water temp. sensor circuit 2. Water temp. sensor 3. ECU
24		Intake air temp. sensor signal	Open or short circuit in intake air temp. sensor (THA).	1. Intake air temp. sensor circuit 2. Intake air temp. sensor 3. ECU
31		Air flow meter signal	VC circuit open or VC—E2 short circuit.	1. Air flow meter circuit 2. Air flow meter 3. ECU
32		Air flow meter signal	E2 circuit open or VC—VS short circuited.	Same as 31, above.
41		Throttle position sensor signal	Open or short circuit in throttle position sensor signal (VTA).	1. Throttle position sensor circuit 2. Throttle position sensor 3. ECU
42		Vehicle speed sensor signal	Signal informing ECU that vehicle stopped has been input to ECU for 5 seconds with engine running between 2,500 — 5,500 rpm.	1. Vehicle speed sensor circuit 2. Vehicle speed sensor 3. ECU
43		Starter signal	No STA signal to ECU when vehicle stopped and engine running over 800 rpm.	1. Main relay circuit 2. IG switch circuit (starter) 3. IG switch 4. ECU
51		Switch signal	Air conditioner switch ON, idle switch OFF or shift position other than P or N range during diagnosis check.	1. Air con. switch 2. Throttle position sensor circuit 3. Throttle position sensor 4. Neutral start switch 5. ECU

TROUBLESHOOTING THE EFI SYSTEM WITH A VOLT/OHMMETER – 1987-88 CAMRY

NOTE: The following troubleshooting procedures are designed for inspection of each separate system, and therefore the actual procedure may vary somewhat. However, troubleshooting should be performed refering to the inspection methods described in this manual.

Before beginning inspection, it is best to first make a simple check of the fuses, fusible links and the codition of the connectors.

The following troubleshooting procedures are based on the supposition that the trouble lies in either a short or open circuit in a component outside the computer or a short circuit within the computer.

If engine trouble occurs even though proper operating voltage is detected in the computer connector, then that the ECU is faulty and should be replaced.

LOCATION OF FUSES AND FUSIBLE LINKS

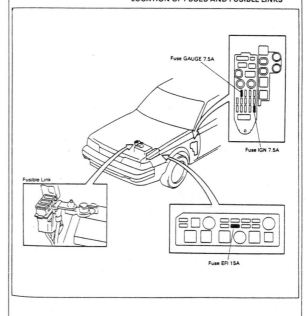

TROUBLESHOOTING THE EFI SYSTEM WITH A VOLT/OHMMETER (CONT.) – 1987-88 CAMRY

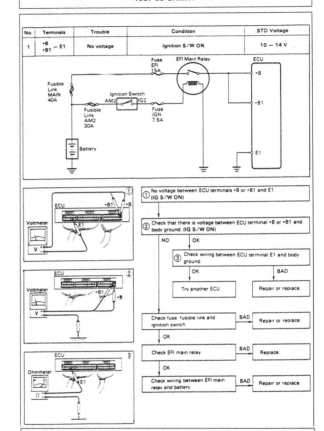

NOTE:
- Perform all voltage measurements with the connectors connected.
- Verify that the battery voltage is 11 V or more when the ignition switch is at "ON".

Using a voltmeter with high impedance (10 kΩ/V minimum), measure the voltage at each terminal of the wiring connectors.

Terminals of ECU

Symbol	Terminal Name	Symbol	Terminal Name	Symbol	Terminal Name
E01	ENGINE GROUND	IDL	THROTTLE POSITION SENSOR	L1	ECU ECT
E02	ENGINE GROUND	A/C	A/C MAGNET SWITCH	L2	ECU ECT
No.10	INJECTOR	ACT	A/C AMPLIFIER	VC	AIR FLOW METER
No.20	INJECTOR	IGF	IGNITER	E21	SENSOR GROUND
STA	STARTER SWITCH	E2	SENSOR GROUND	VS	AIR FLOW METER
IGT	IGNITER	G⊖	ENGINE REVOLUTION SENSOR	STP	STOP LIGHT SWITCH
VF	CHECK CONNECTOR	OX	OXYGEN SENSOR	THA	AIR TEMP. SENSOR
E1	ENGINE GROUND	G	ENGINE REVOLUTION SENSOR	SPD	SPEED SENSOR
NSW	NEUTRAL START SWITCH	VTA	THROTTLE POSITION SENSOR	BATT	BATTERY
ISC1	ISC VALVE	NE	ENGINE REVOLUTION SENSOR	ELS	HEADLIGHT and DEFOGGER
ISC2	ISC VALVE	THW	WATER TEMP. SENSOR	+B1	MAIN RELAY
W	WARNING LIGHT	L3	ECU ECT	+B	MAIN RELAY
T	CHECK CONNECTOR	ECT	ECU ECT		

ECU Terminals

E01	No.10	STA	VF	NSW		ISC1	W	T		IDL	IGF	G⊖	G		NE	L1	VC	VS	THA	BATT	+B1
E02	No.20	IGT	E1			ISC2			ACT	A/C	E2	OX		VTA	THW		ECT	L2	E21	STP	SPD	ELS	+B

VOLTAGE SUPPLIED AT THE ECU WIRING CONNECTOR 1987-88 CAMRY

No.	Terminals	STD Voltage	Condition	
1	+B — E1 +B1	10 — 14	Ignition S/W ON	
2	BATT — E1	10 — 14	—	
3	IDL — E2	10 — 14	Ignition S/W ON	Throttle valve open
	VTA — E2	0.1 — 1.0		Throttle valve fully closed
		4 — 5		Throttle valve fully open
	VC — E2	4 — 6		—
4	IGT — E1	0.7 — 1.0	Cranking or Idling	
5	STA — E1	6 — 12	Cranking	
6	No.10 E01 — No.20 E02	9 — 14	Ignition S/W ON	
7	W — E1	8 — 14	No troble ("CHECK" engine warning light off) and engine running	
8	VC — E2	4 — 6	—	
	VS — E2	4 — 5	Ignition S/W ON	Measuring plate fully closed
		0.02 — 0.5		Measuring plate fully open
		2 — 4	Idling	
9	THA — E2	1 — 2	Ignition S/W ON	Intake air temperature 20°C (68°F)
10	THW — E2	0.1 — 1.0	Ignition S/W ON	Coolant temperature 80°C (176°F)
11	ISC1 — E1 ISC2	9 — 14	Ignition S/W ON	
12	A/C — E1	8 — 14	Air conditionin ON	

ECU Terminals

E01	No.10	STA	VF	NSW		ISC1	W	T		IDL	IGF	G⊖	G		NE	L1	VC	VS	THA	BATT	+B1
E02	No.20	IGT	E1			ISC2			ACT	A/C	E2	OX		VTA	THW		ECT	L2	E21	STP	SPD	ELS	+B

TROUBLESHOOTING THE NO. 1 TERMINAL ON THE EFI CONNECTOR 1987-88 CAMRY

No.	Terminals	Trouble	Condition	STD Voltage
1	+B — E1 +B1	No voltage	Ignition S/W ON	10 — 14 V

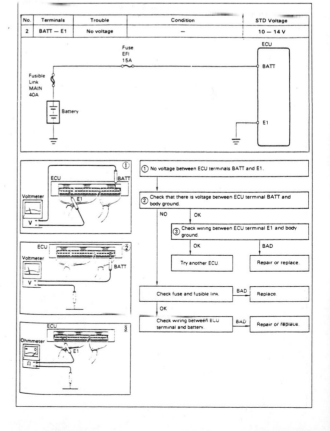

TROUBLESHOOTING THE NO. 2 TERMINAL ON THE EFI CONNECTOR 1987-88 CAMRY

No.	Terminals	Trouble	Condition	STD Voltage
2	BATT — E1	No voltage	—	10 — 14 V

TROUBLESHOOTING THE NO. 3 TERMINAL ON THE EFI CONNECTOR
1987-88 CAMRY

No.	Terminals	Trouble		Condition	STD Voltage
3	IDL — E2	No voltage	IG S/W ON	Throttle valve open	4 — 6 V
	VTA — E2			Throttle valve fully closed	0.1 — 1.0 V
				Throttle valve fully open	4 — 5 V
	VC — E2			—	4 — 6 V

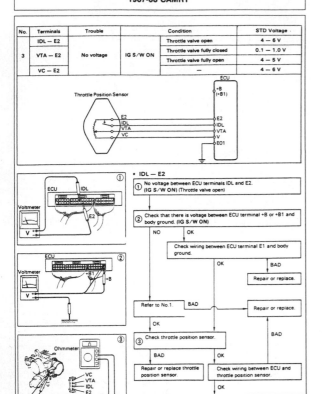

TROUBLESHOOTING THE NO. 3 TERMINAL ON THE EFI CONNECTOR
1987-88 CAMRY

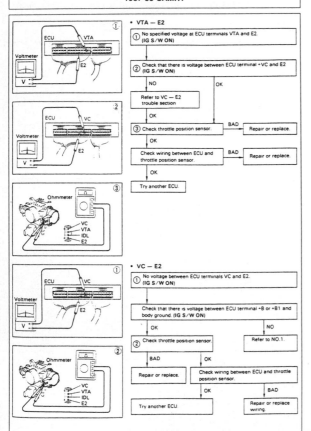

TROUBLESHOOTING THE NO. 4 TERMINAL ON THE EFI CONNECTOR
1987-88 CAMRY

No.	Terminals	Trouble	Condition	STD Voltage
4	IGT — E1	No voltage	Idling	0.7 — 1.0 V

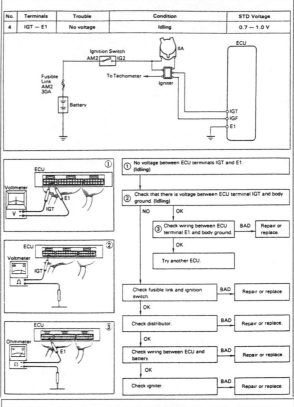

TROUBLESHOOTING THE NO. 5 TERMINAL ON THE EFI CONNECTOR
1987-88 CAMRY

No.	Terminals	Trouble	Condition	STD Voltage
5	STA — E1	No voltage	Cranking	6 — 12 V

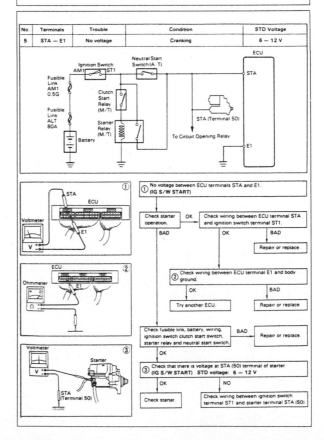

TROUBLESHOOTING THE NO. 6 TERMINAL ON THE EFI CONNECTOR
1987-88 CAMRY

No.	Terminals	Trouble	Condition	STD Voltage
6	No. 10 — E01 No. 20 — E02	No voltage	IG S/W ON	9 — 14 V

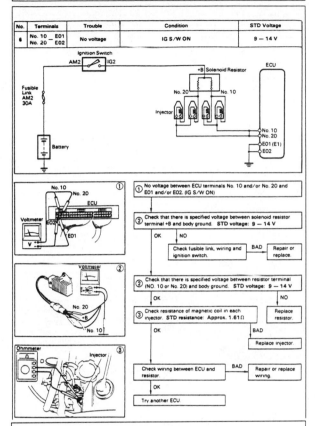

TROUBLESHOOTING THE NO. 7 TERMINAL ON THE EFI CONNECTOR
1987-88 CAMRY

No.	Terminals	Trouble	Condition	STD Voltage
7	W — E1	No voltage	No trouble ("CHECK" engine warning light off) and engine running	8 — 14 V

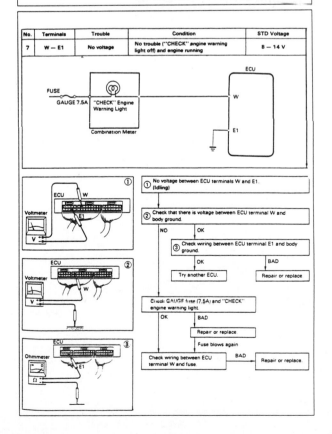

TROUBLESHOOTING THE NO. 8 TERMINAL ON THE EFI CONNECTOR
1987-88 CAMRY

No.	Terminals	Trouble	Condition		STD Voltage
8	VC — E2	No voltage	IG S/W ON	—	4 — 6 V
	VS — E2			Measuring plate fully closed	4 — 5 V
	VS — E2			Measuring plate fully open	0.02 — 0.5 V
	VS — E2		Idling	—	2 — 4 V

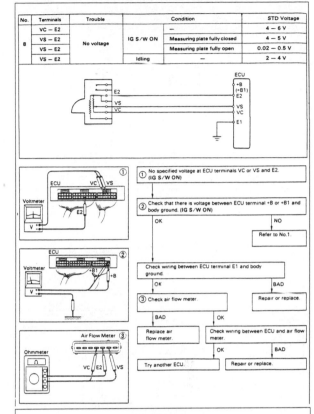

TROUBLESHOOTING THE NO. 9 TERMINAL ON THE EFI CONNECTOR
1987-88 CAMRY

No.	Terminals	Trouble	Condition		STD Voltage
9	THA — E2	No voltage	IG S/W ON	Intake air temperature 20°C (68°F)	1 — 2 V

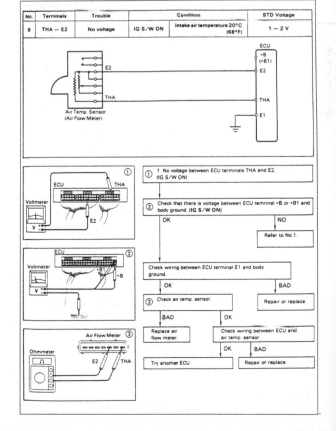

TROUBLESHOOTING THE NO. 10 TERMINAL ON THE EFI CONNECTOR 1987-88 CAMRY

No.	Terminals	Trouble	Condition		STD Voltage
10	THW — E2	No voltage	IG S/W ON	Coolant temperature 80° (176°F)	0.5 — 2.5 V

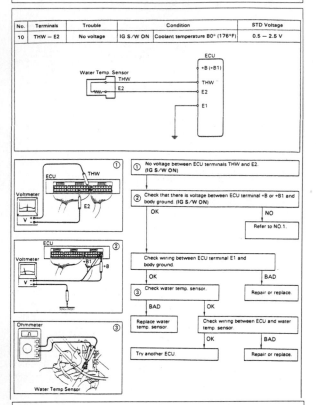

TROUBLESHOOTING THE NO. 11 TERMINAL ON THE EFI CONNECTOR 1987-88 CAMRY

No.	Terminals	Trouble	Condition	STD Voltage
11	ISC1 ISC2 — E1	No voltage	IG S/W ON	9 — 14 V

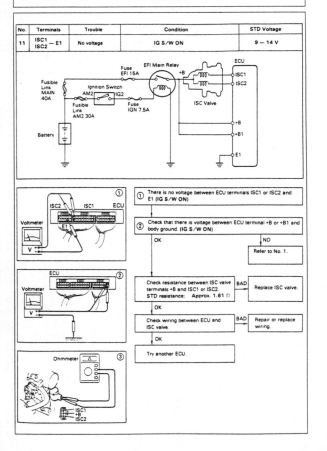

TROUBLESHOOTING THE NO. 12 TERMINAL ON THE EFI CONNECTOR 1987-88 CAMRY

No.	Terminals	Trouble	Condition	STD Voltage
12	A/C — E1	No voltage	Air conditioning ON	8 — 14 V

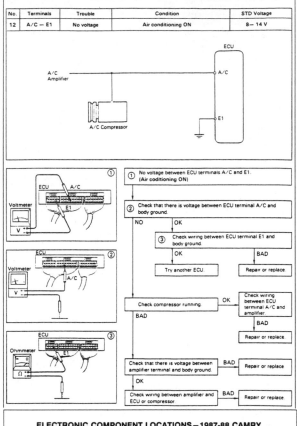

ELECTRONIC COMPONENT LOCATIONS—1987-88 CAMRY

Location of Electronic Control Parts

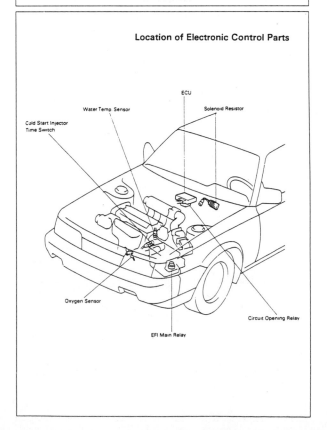

TESTING THE OXYGEN SENSOR – 1987-88 CAMRY

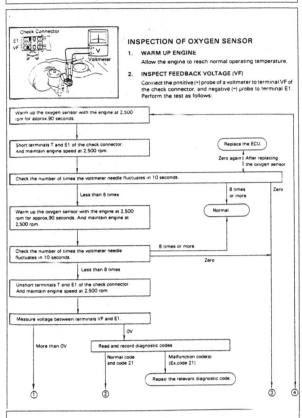

INSPECTION OF OXYGEN SENSOR

1. **WARM UP ENGINE**

   Allow the engine to reach normal operating temperature.

2. **INSPECT FEEDBACK VOLTAGE (VF)**

   Connect the positive (+) probe of a voltmeter to terminal VF of the check connector, and negative (–) probe to terminal E1. Perform the test as follows:

Warm up the oxygen sensor with the engine at 2,500 rpm for approx. 90 seconds.

↓

Short terminals T and E1 of the check connector. And maintain engine speed at 2,500 rpm.

→ Replace the ECU.
Zero again | After replacing the oxygen sensor

↓

Check the number of times the voltmeter needle fluctuates in 10 seconds.

— Less than 8 times → Warm up the oxygen sensor with the engine at 2,500 rpm for approx. 90 seconds. And maintain engine at 2,500 rpm.
— 8 times or more → Normal
— Zero

↓

Check the number of times the voltmeter needle fluctuates in 10 seconds.

— Less than 8 times
— 8 times or more
— Zero

↓

Unshort terminals T and E1 of the check connector. And maintain engine speed at 2,500 rpm.

↓

Measure voltage between terminals VF and E1.

— More than 0V
— 0V → Read and record diagnostic codes.
   — Normal code and code 21
   — Malfunction code(s) (Ex.code 21) → Repair the relevant diagnostic code.

① ② ③ ④

TESTING THE OXYGEN SENSOR (CONT.) – 1987-88 CAMRY

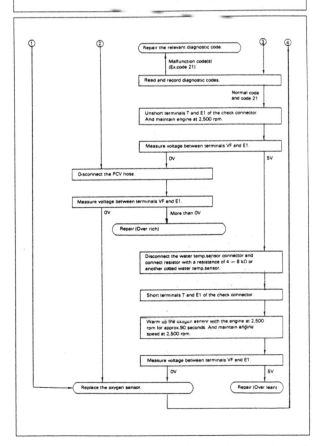

① ②

Repair the relevant diagnostic code.
Malfunction code(s) (Ex.code 21)

↓

Read and record diagnostic codes.
Normal code and code 21

↓

Unshort terminals T and E1 of the check connector. And maintain engine at 2,500 rpm.

↓

Measure voltage between terminals VF and E1.

— 0V
— 5V

③ ④

Disconnect the PCV hose.

↓

Measure voltage between terminals VF and E1.

— 0V
— More than 0V → Repair (Over rich)

↓

Disconnect the water temp. sensor connector and connect resistor with a resistance of 4 — 8 kΩ or another coded water temp. sensor.

↓

Short terminals T and E1 of the check connector.

↓

Warm up the oxygen sensor with the engine at 2,500 rpm for approx. 90 seconds. And maintain engine speed at 2,500 rpm.

↓

Measure voltage between terminals VF and E1.

— 0V → Replace the oxygen sensor.
— 5V → Repair (Over lean)

TESTING THE OXYGEN SENSOR (CONT.) – 1987-88 CAMRY

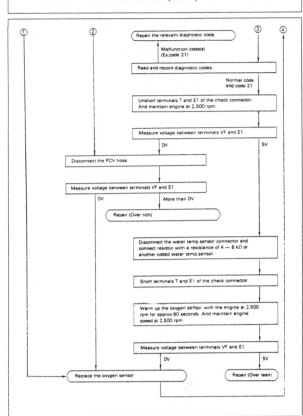

① ②

Repair the relevant diagnostic code.
Malfunction code(s) (Ex.code 21)

↓

Read and record diagnostic codes.
Normal code and code 21

↓

Unshort terminals T and E1 of the check connector. And maintain engine at 2,500 rpm.

↓

Measure voltage between terminals VF and E1.

— 0V
— 5V

③ ④

Disconnect the PCV hose.

↓

Measure voltage between terminals VF and E1.

— 0V
— More than 0V → Repair (Over rich)

↓

Disconnect the water temp. sensor connector and connect resistor with a resistance of 4 — 8 kΩ or another coded water temp. sensor.

↓

Short terminals T and E1 of the check connector.

↓

Warm up the oxygen sensor with the engine at 2,500 rpm for approx. 90 seconds. And maintain engine speed at 2,500 rpm.

↓

Measure voltage between terminals VF and E1.

— 0V → Replace the oxygen sensor.
— 5V → Repair (Over lean)

INSPECTING THE VOLTAGE AT THE ECU WIRING CONNECTOR 1987-88 CAMRY

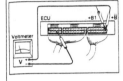

INSPECTION OF ECU

1. **INSPECT VOLTAGE OF ECU**

   NOTE: The EFI circuit can be checked by measuring the voltage at the wiring connectors of the ECU.

   Check the voltage between each terminal of the wiring connectors.

   • Turn the ignition switch.
   • Measure the voltage at each terminal.

   NOTE:
   • Perform all voltage measurements with the connectors connected.
   • Verify that the battery voltage is 11V or more when the ignition switch is ON.

Voltage at ECU Wiring Connectors

Terminals	Condition		STD voltage
+B +B1 — E1	Ignition S/W ON		10 — 14
BATT — E1	—		10 — 14
IDL — E2		Throttle valve open	4 — 6
VTA — E2	Ignition S/W ON	Throttle valve fully closed	0.1 — 1.0
		Throttle valve fully open	4 — 5
VC — E2		—	4 — 6
IGT — E1		Cranking or idling	0.7 — 1.0
STA — E1		Cranking	6 — 12
No. 10 EO1 No. 20 EO2		Ignition S/W ON	9 — 14
W — E1	No trouble ("CHECK" engine warning light off) and engine running		8 — 14
VC — E1		—	4 — 6
VS — E2	Ignition S/W ON	Measuring plate fully closed	4 — 5
		Measuring plate fully open	0.02 — 0.5
		Idling	2 — 4
THA — E2	Ignition S/W ON	Intake air temperature 20°C (68°F)	1 — 2
THW — E2		Coolant temperature 80°C (176°F)	0.1 — 1.0
ISC1 ISC2 — E1		Ignition S/W ON	9 — 14
A/C — E1	Ignition S/W ON	Air conditioning ON	8 — 14
ACT — E1		Throttle valve fully closed	4 — 5

ECU Terminals

ED1	NO. 10	STA	VF	NSW		ISC1	W.	T.	IDL	IGF	GO	G		NE		L3	L1	VC	VS	THA	BATT	+B1
EO2	NO. 20	IGT	E1		ISC2		ACT	A/C	E2	OX		VTA	THW		ECT	L2	E21	STP	SPD	ELS		+B

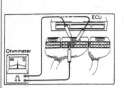

INSPECTING THE RESISTANCE AT THE ECU WIRING CONNECTOR 1987-88 CAMRY

2. INSPECT RESISTANCE OF ECU
CAUTION:
- Do not touch the ECU terminals.
- The tester probe should be inserted into the wiring connector from the wiring side.

Check the resistance between each terminal of the wiring connectors.
- Disconnect the connectors from the ECU.
- Measure the resistance at each terminal.

Resistance of ECU Wiring Connectors

Terminals	Condition	Resistance (Ω)
IDL — E2	Throttle valve open	∞
	Throttle valve fully closed	Less than 2,300
VTA — E2	Throttle valve fully open	3,000 — 10,000
	Throttle valve fully closed	200 — 800
VS — E2	Measuring plate fully closed	200 — 600
	Measuring plate fully open	
THA — E2	Intake air temperature 20°C (68°F)	2,000 — 3,000
THW — E2	Coolant temperature 80°C (176°F)	200 — 400
G — G⊖	—	140 — 180
NE — G⊖	—	140 — 180

ECU Terminals

E01	NE 10	STA	VF	NSW		ISC1	W	T	IDL	IGF	GO	G		NE	J3		VC	VS	THA	BATT	B1
E02	NE 20	IGT	E1		ISC2		ACT	A-C	E2	OX		VTA	THW		ECT	L2	E21	STP	SPD	ELS	-B

DIAGNOSIS CODES — 1984 CELICA

Code	Number of blinks "CHECK ENGINE"	System	Diagnosis	Trouble area
1	1/3 seconds / 3 seconds	Normal	This appears when none of the other codes (2 thru 7) are identified	
2	1 second	Air flow meter signal (Vc)	• Open circuit in Vc, or Vc — Vs short circuited • Open circuit in Vs	1. Air flow meter circuit (Vc, Vs) 2. Air flow meter 3. EFI computer
3		Air flow meter signal (Vs)	• Open circuit in Vs, or Vs — E2 short circuited • Open circuit in Vs	1. Air flow meter circuit (Vs, Vc, Vs) 2. Air flow meter 3. EFI computer
4		Water thermo signal (THW)	• Open circuit in water thermo sensor signal	1. Water thermo sensor circuit 2. Water thermo sensor 3. EFI computer
5		Ox sensor signal	• Open circuit in Ox sensor signal (only lean indication)	1. Ox sensor circuit 2. Ox sensor 3. EFI computer
6		Ignition signal	• No ignition signal	1. Ignition system circuit 2. Distributor 3. Ignition coil and igniter 4. EFI computer
7		Throttle position sensor signal	• IDL-Psw short circuited	1. Throttle position sensor circuit 2. Throttle position sensor 3. EFI computer

EFI WIRING SCHEMATIC — 1984 CELICA

SYSTEM DESCRIPTION

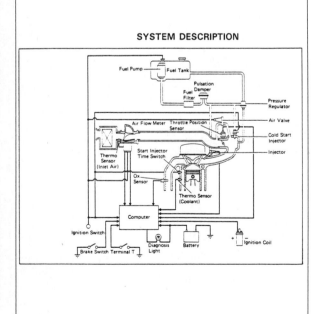

INSPECTION OF THE DIAGNOSIS CIRCUIT — 1984 CELICA

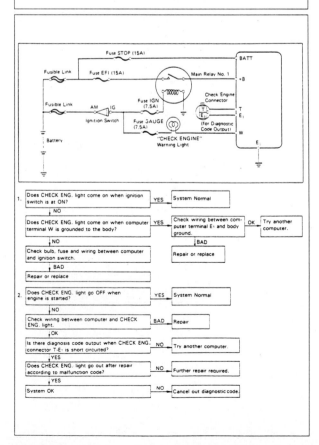

TROUBLESHOOTING THE EFI SYSTEM WITH A VOLT/OHMMETER
1984 CELICA

PREPARATION FOR TROUBLESHOOTING

1. Remove the glove box.
2. Remove the EFI computer with the wire harness.

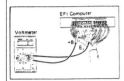

EFI SYSTEM CHECK PROCEDURE

NOTE:

1. The EFI circuit can be checked by measuring the resistance and voltage at the wiring connectors of the computer.
2. Perform all voltage measurement with the connectors connected.
3. Verify that the battery voltage is 11 V or above when the ignition switch is ON.

Using a voltmeter with high impedance (10 kΩ/V minimum) measure the voltage at each terminal of the wiring connector.

NOTE: If there is any problem, see TROUBLESHOOTING FOR EFI ELECTRONIC CIRCUIT WITH VOLT/OHMMETER.

No.	Terminals	Voltage (V)	Condition
1	+B — E₁	10 — 14	Ignition switch ON
2	BATT — E₁	10 — 14	—
3	IDL — E₁	8 — 14	Throttle valve fully closed
	Psw — E₁	8 — 14	Throttle valve fully open
	TL — E₁	8 — 14	
4	IG — E₁	above 3	Cranking and engine running
5	STA — E₁	6 — 12	Cranking
6	#10 — E₁	9 — 14	Ignition switch ON
	#20 — E₁	9 — 14	Ignition switch ON
7	W — E₁	8 — 14	No trouble (CHECK ENGINE light go off) and engine running
8	Vs — E₂	8 — 14	
	Vc — E₂	4 — 9	
	Vs — E₂	0.5 — 2.5	Measuring plate fully closed
		5 — 8	Measuring plate fully open
		2.5 — 5.5	Idling
9	THA — E₂	2 — 6	Intake air temperature 20°C or 68°F
10	THW — E₂	0.5 — 2.5	Coolant temperature 80°C or 176°F
11	B/K — E₂	8 — 14	Stop light switch ON

E₁	Vs	Vc	BATT	THA	B/K	STA		Ox	THW	IDL	VF	T	#10	E₂₁
IG	E₁	W	+B		SPD				E₁	TL	Psw		#20	E₂

TROUBLESHOOTING THE EFI SYSTEM WITH A VOLT/OHMMETER
(CONT.) – 1984 CELICA

NOTE: Because the following troubleshooting procedure are designed for inspection of each separate system, the actual troubleshooting procedure may vary somewhat. However, please refer to these procedures and perform actual troubleshooting, conforming to the inspection methods described.

For example, it is better to first make a simple check of the fuses, fusible links and connecting condition of the connectors before making your inspection according to the procedures listed.

LOCATION OF FUSE AND FUSIBLE LINK

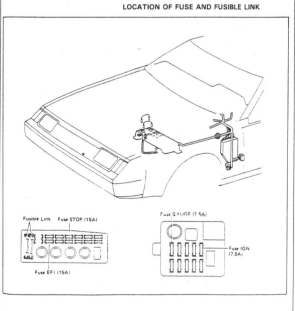

TROUBLESHOOTING THE NO. 1 TERMINAL ON THE EFI CONNECTOR
1984 CELICA

No.	Terminals	Trouble	Condition	STD Voltage
1	+B — E₁	No voltage	IG S/W ON	10 — 14 V

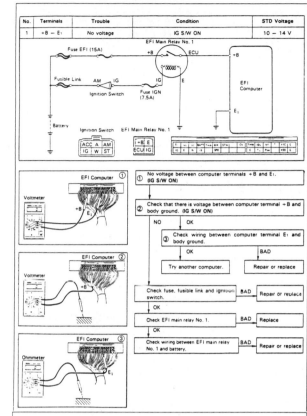

TROUBLESHOOTING THE NO. 2 TERMINAL ON THE EFI CONNECTOR
1984 CELICA

No.	Terminals	Trouble	Condition	STD Voltage
2	BATT — E₁	No voltage	IG S/W ON	10 — 14 V

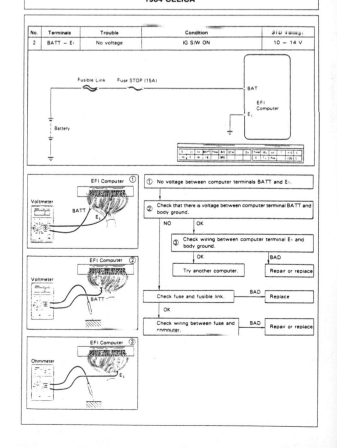

TROUBLESHOOTING THE NO. 3 TERMINAL ON THE EFI CONNECTOR
1984 CELICA

No.	Terminals	Trouble	Condition		STD Voltage
3	TL − E₁	No voltage	IG S/W ON	−	8 − 14 V
	IDL − E₁			Throttle valve fully closed	8 − 14 V
	Psw − E₁			Throttle valve fully open	8 − 14 V

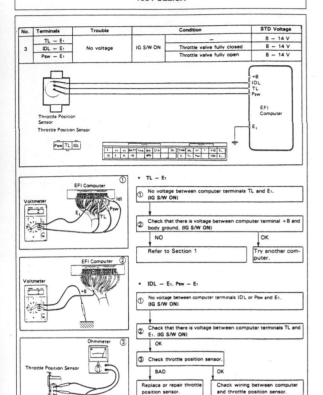

• TL − E₁

① No voltage between computer terminals TL and E₁. (IG S/W ON)

② Check that there is voltage between computer terminal +B and body ground. (IG S/W ON)

- NO → Refer to Section 1
- OK → Try another computer.

• IDL − E₁, Psw − E₁

① No voltage between computer terminals IDL and Psw and E₁. (IG S/W ON)

② Check that there is voltage between computer terminals TL and E₁. (IG S/W ON)

- OK → ③ Check throttle position sensor.
  - BAD → Replace or repair throttle position sensor.
  - OK → Check wiring between computer and throttle position sensor.

TROUBLESHOOTING THE NO. 4 TERMINAL ON THE EFI CONNECTOR
1984 CELICA

No.	Terminals	Trouble	Condition	STD Voltage
4	IG − E₁	No voltage	Engine cranking and running	Above 3 V

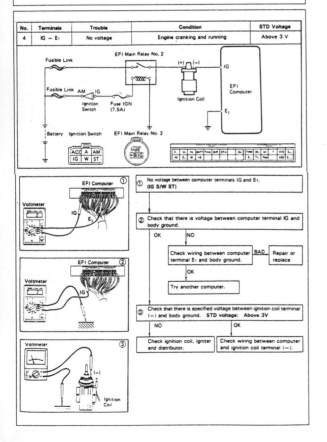

① No voltage between computer terminals IG and E₁. (IG S/W ST)

② Check that there is voltage between computer terminal IG and body ground.

- OK
- NO → Check wiring between computer terminal E₁ and body ground. → BAD → Repair or replace
  - OK → Try another computer.

③ Check that there is specified voltage between ignition coil terminal (−) and body ground. STD voltage: Above 3V

- NO → Check ignition coil, igniter and distributor.
- OK → Check wiring between computer and ignition coil terminal (−).

TROUBLESHOOTING THE NO. 5 TERMINAL ON THE EFI CONNECTOR
1984 CELICA

No.	Terminals	Trouble	Condition	STD Voltage
5	STA − E₁	No voltage	Engine cranking	6 − 12 V

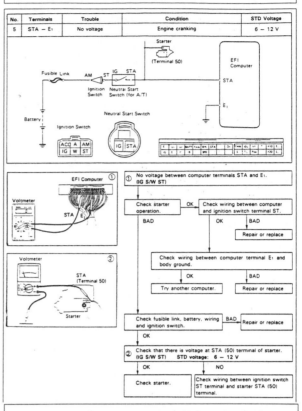

① No voltage between computer terminals STA and E₁. (IG S/W ST)

Check starter operation.

- OK → Check wiring between computer and ignition switch terminal ST.
  - BAD → Repair or replace
- BAD

② Check wiring between computer terminal E₁ and body ground.

- OK → Try another computer.
- BAD → Repair or replace

Check fusible link, battery, wiring and ignition switch.

- BAD → Repair or replace
- OK

② Check that there is voltage at STA (50) terminal of starter. (IG S/W ST) STD voltage: 6 − 12 V

- OK → Check starter.
- NO → Check wiring between ignition switch ST terminal and starter STA (50) terminal.

TROUBLESHOOTING THE NO. 6 TERMINAL ON THE EFI CONNECTOR
1984 CELICA

No.	Terminals	Trouble	Condition	STD Voltage
6	No. 10 − E₁	No voltage	IG S/W ON	9 − 14 V
	No. 20 − E₁			

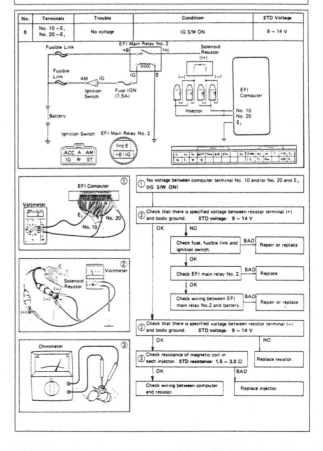

① No voltage between computer terminal No. 10 and/or No. 20 and E₁. (IG S/W ON)

② Check that there is specified voltage between resistor terminal (+) and body ground. STD voltage: 9 − 14 V

- OK
- NO → Check fuse, fusible link and ignition switch.
  - BAD → Repair or replace
  - OK → Check EFI main relay No. 2.
    - BAD → Replace
    - OK → Check wiring between EFI main relay No.2 and battery.
      - BAD → Repair or replace

② Check that there is specified voltage between resistor terminal (−) and body ground. STD voltage: 9 − 14 V

- OK
- NO → Replace resistor.

③ Check resistance of magnetic coil in each injector. STD resistance: 1.5 − 3.0 Ω

- OK → Check wiring between computer and resistor.
- BAD → Replace injector.

TROUBLESHOOTING THE NO. 7 TERMINAL ON THE EFI CONNECTOR
1984 CELICA

No.	Terminals	Trouble	Condition	STD Voltage
7	W – E₁	No voltage	No trouble (CHECK ENGINE light off) and engine running	8 – 14 V

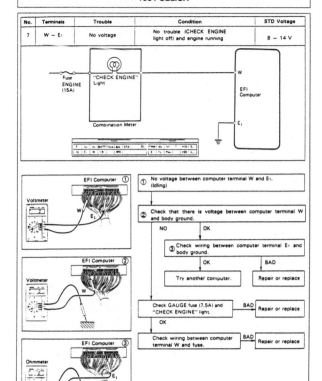

TROUBLESHOOTING THE NO. 8 TERMINAL ON THE EFI CONNECTOR
1984 CELICA

No.	Terminals	Trouble	Condition		STD Voltage
8	Vc – E₂	No voltage	IG S/W ON	–	4 – 9 V
	Vs – E₂			Measuring plate fully closed	0.5 – 2.5 V
	Vs – E₂			Measuring plate fully open	5 – 8 V
	Vs – E₂		Idling	–	2.5 – 5.5 V

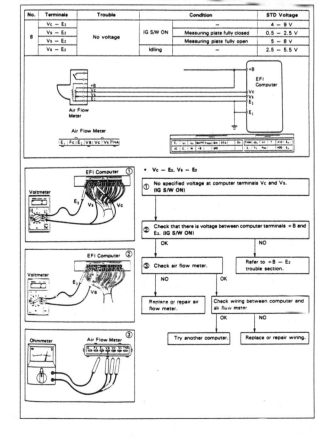

TROUBLESHOOTING THE NO. 9 TERMINAL ON THE EFI CONNECTOR
1984 CELICA

No.	Terminals	Trouble	Condition		STD Voltage
9	THA – E₂	No voltage	IG S/W ON	Intake air temperature 20°C (68°F)	2 – 6 V

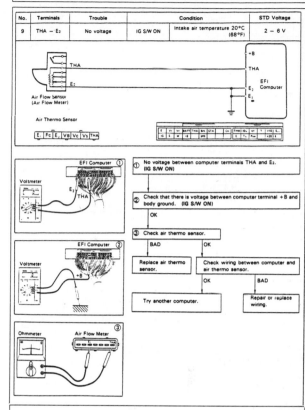

TROUBLESHOOTING THE NO. 10 TERMINAL ON THE EFI CONNECTOR
1984 CELICA

No.	Terminals	Trouble	Condition		STD Voltage
10	THW – E₁	No voltage	IG S/W ON	Coolant temperature 80°C (176°F)	0.5 – 2.5 V

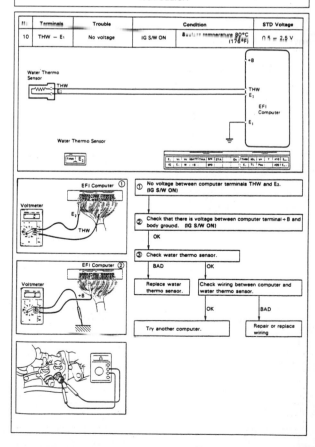

TROUBLESHOOTING THE NO. 11 TERMINAL ON THE EFI CONNECTOR 1984 CELICA

No.	Terminals	Trouble	Condition	STD Voltage
11	B/K – E₁	No voltage	Stop light switch ON	8 – 14 V

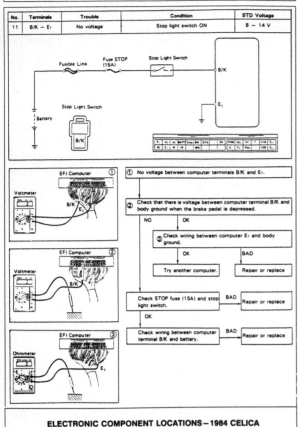

① No voltage between computer terminals B/K and E₁.

② Check that there is voltage between computer terminal B/K and body ground when the brake pedal is depressed.

NO ↓ YES →

③ Check wiring between computer E₁ and body ground.

OK → Try another computer.
BAD → Repair or replace

Check STOP fuse (15A) and stop light switch.
BAD → Repair or replace
OK ↓

Check wiring between computer terminal B/K and battery.
BAD → Repair or replace

ELECTRONIC COMPONENT LOCATIONS – 1984 CELICA

Location of Electronic Control Parts

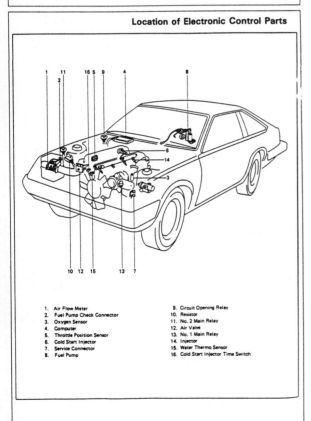

1. Air Flow Meter
2. Fuel Pump Check Connector
3. Oxygen Sensor
4. Computer
5. Throttle Position Sensor
6. Cold Start Injector
7. Service Connector
8. Fuel Pump
9. Circuit Opening Relay
10. Resistor
11. No. 2 Main Relay
12. Air Valve
13. No. 1 Main Relay
14. Injector
15. Water Thermo Sensor
16. Cold Start Injector Time Switch

TESTING THE OXYGEN SENSOR WITH EFI CHECKER – 1984 CELICA

WITH EFI CHECKER

1. Warm up the engine.
2. Connect a SST to the EFI service connector SST 09991-00100
3. Warm up the Ox sensor with the engine at 2,500 rpm for about 90 seconds.

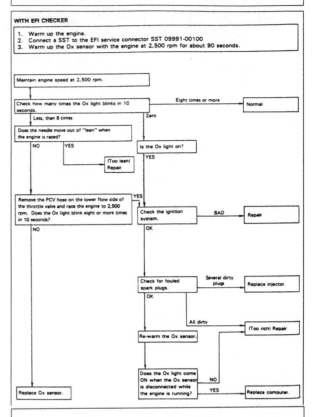

TESTING THE OXYGEN SENSOR WITH EFI CHECKER – 1984 CELICA

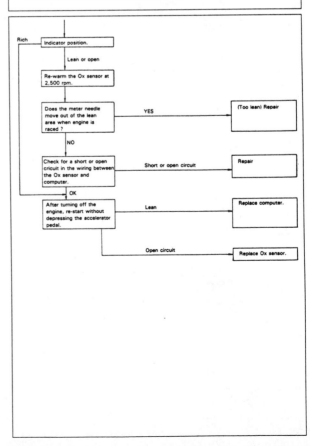

TESTING THE OXYGEN SENSOR WITH A VOLT/OHMMETER – 1984 CELICA

WITH VOLTMETER

1. Warm up the engine.
2. Connect a SST to the 4-terminal connector. SST 09842-14010
3. Using a voltmeter connect the positive probe to the red wire of the SST and negative testing probe to the block wire.
4. Warm up the Ox sensor with the engine at 2,500 rpm for about 90 seconds.

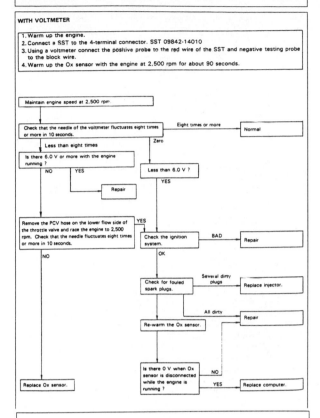

TESTING THE OXYGEN SENSOR WITH A VOLT/OHMMETER – 1984 CELICA

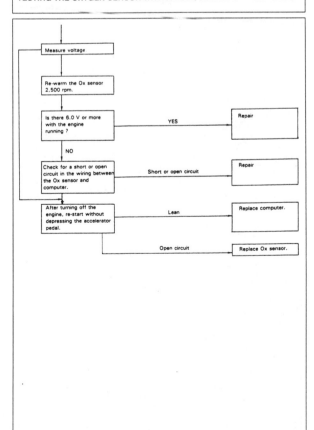

INSPECTING THE VOLTAGE AT THE ECU WIRING CONNECTOR 1984 CELICA

INSPECTION OF COMPUTER

1. **MEASURE VOLTAGE OF COMPUTER**

   NOTE:
   1. The computer itself cannot be checked directly.
   2. The EFI circuit can be checked by measuring the resistance and voltage at the wiring connectors of the computer.

   Check the voltages at the wiring connectors.
   * Remove the right kick panel.
   * Turn the ignition switch ON.
   * Measure the voltage at each terminal.

NOTE: 1. Perform all voltage measurements with the connectors connected.
2. Verify that the battery voltage is 11V or above when the ignition switch is ON.

Voltages at Computer Wiring Connectors

Terminals	Voltage	
+B — E_1	10 – 14 V	(Ignition switch ON)
BATT — E_1	10 – 14 V	
IDL — E_1	8 – 14 V	(Throttle valve fully closed)
Psw — E_1	8 – 14 V	(Throttle valve fully open)
TL — E_1	8 – 14 V	
IG — E_1	Above 3 V	(Cranking and engine running)
STA — E_1	6 – 12 V	(Cranking)
No.10 — E_1	9 – 14 V	(Ignition switch ON)
No.20 — E_1	9 – 14 V	(Ignition switch ON)
+B — E_2	8 – 14 V	
Vc — E_2	4 – 9 V	
Vs — E_2	0.5 – 2.5 V	(Measuring plate fully closed)
	5 – 8V	(Measuring plate fully open)
	2.5 – 5.5 V	(Idling)
THA — E_2	2 – 6 V	(Intake air temperature 20°C or 68°F)
THW — E_2	0.5 – 2.5 V	(Coolant temperature 80°C or 176°F)
B/K — E_1	8 – 14 V	(Stop light switch ON)

Computer Connectors

E_2	V_s	Vc	BATT	THA	B/K	STA		Ox	THW	IDL	Vf	T	#10	E_{o1}
IG	E_1	W	+B			SPD			E_1	TL	Psw		#20	E_{o2}

INSPECTING THE RESISTANCE AT THE ECU WIRING CONNECTOR 1984 CELICA

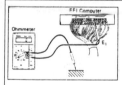

2. **MEASURE RESISTANCE OF COMPUTER**

   CAUTION:
   1. Do not touch the computer terminals.
   2. The tester probe should be inserted into wiring connector from the wiring side.

   Check the resistance between each terminal of the wiring connector.
   * Remove the right kick panel.
   * Unplug the wiring connectors from the EFI computer.
   * Measure the resistance between each terminal of the wiring connectors.

Resistance at Computer Wiring Connectors

Terminals	Resistance	
TL — IDL	0	(Throttle valve fully closed)
TL — IDL	∞	(Throttle valve fully open)
TL — Psw	∞	(Throttle valve fully closed)
TL — Psw	0	(Throttle valve fully open)
IDL, TL, Psw — Ground	∞	
THW — E_2	200 – 400 Ω	(Coolant temp. 80°C or 176°F)
THA — E_2	2 – 3 kΩ	(Intake air temp. 20°C or 68°F)
THW, THA — Ground	∞	
+B — E_2	200 – 400 Ω	
Vc — E_2	100 – 300 Ω	
Vs — E_2	20 – 100 Ω	(Measuring plate fully closed)
Vs — E_2	20 – 1,000 Ω	(Measuring plate fully open)
+B, Vc, Vs — Ground	∞	
E_1, E_2, E_{o1}, E_{o2} — Ground	0	

Computer Connectors

E_2	V_s	Vc	BATT	THA	B/K	STA		Ox	THW	IDL	Vf	T	#10	E_{o1}
IG	E_1	W	+B			SPD			E_1	TL	Psw		#20	E_{o2}

EFI WIRING SCHEMATIC – 1985 CELICA

SYSTEM DESCRIPTION

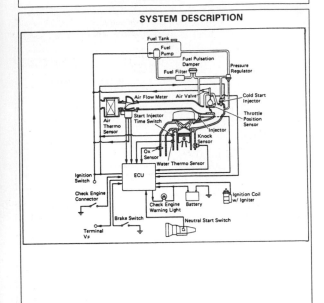

DIAGNOSIS CODES – 1985 CELICA

Code	Number of blinks "CHECK ENGINE"	System	Diagnosis	Trouble area
1		Normal	This appears when none of other codes (2 thru 13) are identified.	
2		Air flow meter signal	Air flow meter signal open or short circuited.	1. Air flow meter circuit 2. Air flow meter 3. ECU
3		Ignition signal	No signal from IGf four times in succession	1. Igniter circuit (+B, IGt, IGf) 2. Igniter 3. ECU
4		Water thermo sensor signal	Open or short circuit in water thermo sensor signal	1. Water thermo sensor circuit 2. Water thermo sensor 3. ECU
5		Ox sensor signal	Sufficiented feed back condition but not changed Ox sensor signal	1. Ox sensor circuit 2. Ox sensor 3. ECU
6		RPM signal (crank angle pulse)	No Ne signal to ECU within cranking, or Ne value being over 1,000 rpm in spite of no Ne signal to ECU	1. Ignitor circuit 2. Ignitor 3. Distributor 4. ECU
7		Throttle position sensor signal	Open or short circuit in throttle position sensor signal	1. Throttle position sensor circuit 2. Throttle position sensor 3. ECU
8		Intake air thermo sensor signal	Open or short circuit in intake air thermo sensor signal	1. Intake air thermo sensor circuit 2. Intake air thermo sensor 3. ECU
10		Starter signal	No STA signal to ECU when vehicle speed 0 km/h and engine is running over 800 rpm	1. Speed sensor circuit 2. Main relay circuit 3. IG switch circuit (Starter) 4. IG switch 5. ECU
11		Switch signal	Short circuit in terminal T when air conditioner switch ON or IDL point OFF	1. Air conditioner switch 2. Throttle position sensor circuit 3. Throttle position sensor 4. ECU
12		Knock control sensor signal	Knock control sensor signal is not reached judgement level in succession	1. Knock control sensor circuit 2. Knock control sensor 3. ECU
13		Knock control CPU (ECU)	Knock CPU faulty	Knock control CPU (ECU)

INSPECTION OF THE DIAGNOSIS CIRCUIT – 1985 CELICA

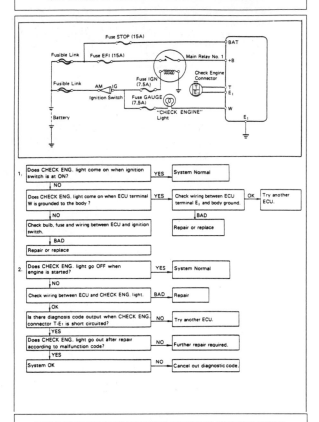

TROUBLESHOOTING THE EFI SYSTEM WITH A VOLT/OHMMETER 1985 CELICA

PREPARATION FOR TROUBLESHOOTING

1. Remove the glove box.

2. Remove the ECU with the wire harness.

EFI SYSTEM CHECK PROCEDURE

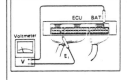

NOTE:
1. The EFI circuit can be checked by measuring the resistance and voltage at the wiring connectors of the ECU.

2. Perform all voltage measurement with the connectors connected.

3. Verify that the battery voltage is 11 V or above when the ignition switch is ON.

Using a voltmeter with high impedance (10 kΩ/V minimum) measure the voltage at each terminal of the wiring connector.

NOTE: If there is any problems, see TROUBLESHOOTING FOR EFI ELECTRONIC CIRCUIT WITH VOLT/OHMMETER.

Connectors of ECU

Symbol	Terminal Name	Symbol	Terminal Name
+B₁	MAIN RELAY	E_{01}	ENGINE GROUND
BAT	BATTERY +B	+B	MAIN RELAY
THA	AIR THERMO SENSOR	B/K	BRAKE SWITCH
Vs	AIR FLOW METER	SPD	SPEED SENSOR
Vc	AIR FLOW METER	E_{21}	SENSOR EARTH
Ne	ENGINE REVOLUTION SENSOR	THW	WATER THERMO SENSOR
KNK	KNOCK SENSOR	VTA	THROTTLE
IGf	IGNITER	Vcc	THROTTLE SWITCH +B
IDL	THROTTLE SWITCH	Ox	Ox SENSOR
T	CHECK CONNECTOR	E_2	SENSOR EARTH
W	WARNING LIGHT	E_1	ENGINE EARTH
NSW	NEUTRAL START SWITCH	IGt	IGNITER
VF	CHECK CONNECTOR	No. 20	INJECTOR
STA	STARTER SWITCH	E_{02}	ENGINE GROUND
No. 10	INJECTOR		

TROUBLESHOOTING THE EFI SYSTEM WITH A VOLT/OHMMETER (CONT.) – 1985 CELICA

NOTE: Because the following troubleshooting procedures are designed for inspection of each separate system, the actual troubleshooting procedure may vary somewhat. However, please refer to these procedures and perform actual troubleshooting, conforming to the inspection methods described.

For example, it is better to first make a simple check of the fuses, fusible links and connecting condition of the connectors before making your inspection according to the procedures listed.

LOCATION OF FUSE AND FUSIBLE LINK

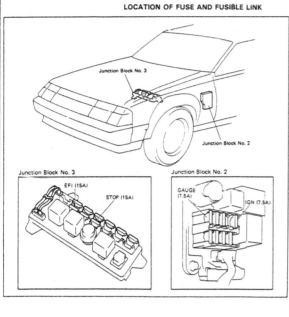

VOLTAGE SUPPLIED AT THE ECU WIRING CONNECTOR 1985 CELICA

No.	Terminals		Condition		STD Voltage
1	+B – E₁		Ignition switch ON		10 – 14
2	BAT – E₁		—		10 – 14
3	IDL – E₂	Ignition switch ON	Throttle valve open		4 – 10
	VTA – E₂		Throttle valve fully closed		0.1 – 1.0
			Throttle valve fully open		4 – 6
	Vcc – E₂		—		4 – 6
4	IGt – E₁		Idling		0.7 – 1.0
5	STA – E₁		Ignition switch ST position		6 – 12
6	No. 10 – E₁ No. 20 – E₁		Ignition switch ON		9 – 14
7	W – E₁		No trouble (CHECK ENGINE light off) and engine running		8 – 14
8	Vc – E₂	Ignition switch ON	—		4 – 10
	Vs – E₂		Measuring plate fully closed		0.5 – 2.5
			Measuring plate fully open		4 – 10
			Idling		2.5 – 7.5
9	THA – E₂	Ignition switch ON	Intake air temperature	20°C (68°F)	2 – 4.5
10	THW – E₂	Ignition switch ON	Coolant temperature	80°C (176°F)	0.3 – 2.5
11	B/K – E₁		Stop light switch ON		8 – 14

TROUBLESHOOTING THE NO. 1 TERMINAL ON THE EFI CONNECTOR 1985 CELICA

No.	Terminals	Trouble	Condition	STD Voltage
1	+B – E₁	No voltage	IG S/W ON	10 – 14 V

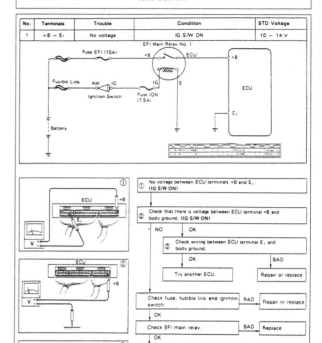

TROUBLESHOOTING THE NO. 2 TERMINAL ON THE EFI CONNECTOR 1985 CELICA

No.	Terminals	Trouble	Condition	STD Voltage
2	BAT – E₁	No voltage	———	10 – 14 V

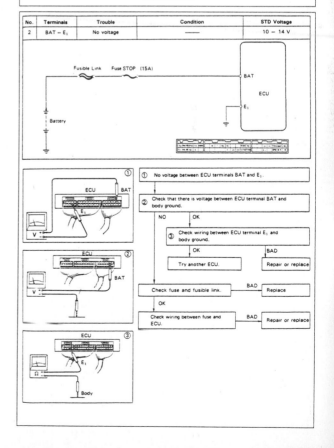

TROUBLESHOOTING THE NO. 3 TERMINAL ON THE EFI CONNECTOR
1985 CELICA

No.	Terminals	Trouble		Condition	STD Voltage
3	IDL – E$_2$	No voltage	Ignition switch ON	Throttle valve open	4 – 10 V
	VTA – E$_2$			Throttle valve fully closed	0.1 – 1.0 V
				Throttle valve fully open	4 – 6 V
	Vcc – E$_2$				4 – 6 V

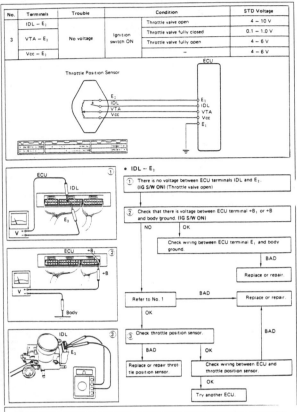

TROUBLESHOOTING THE NO. 3 TERMINAL ON THE EFI CONNECTOR (CONT.) – 1985 CELICA

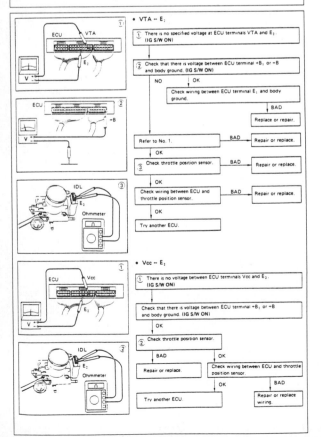

TROUBLESHOOTING THE NO. 4 TERMINAL ON THE EFI CONNECTOR
1985 CELICA

No.	Terminals	Trouble	Condition	STD Voltage
4	IGt – E$_1$	No voltage	Idling	0.7 – 1.0 V

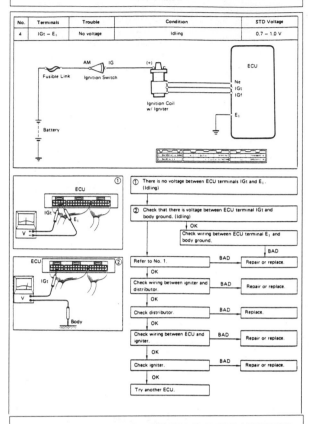

TROUBLESHOOTING THE NO. 5 TERMINAL ON THE EFI CONNECTOR
1985 CELICA

No.	Terminals	Trouble	Condition	STD Voltage
5	STA – E$_1$	No voltage	Ignition switch ST position	6 – 12 V

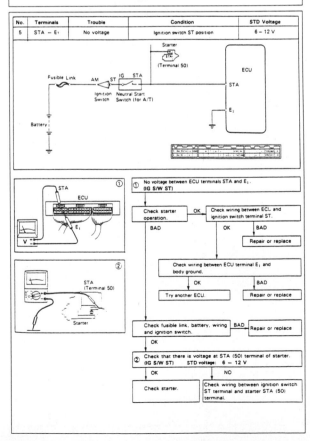

TROUBLESHOOTING THE NO. 6 TERMINAL ON THE EFI CONNECTOR
1985 CELICA

No.	Terminals	Trouble	Condition	STD Voltage
6	No. 10 – E_1 No. 20 – E_1	No voltage	Ignition switch ON	9 – 14 V

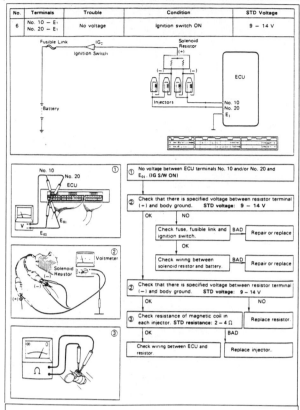

① No voltage between ECU terminals No. 10 and/or No. 20 and E_{01}. (IG S/W ON)

② Check that there is specified voltage between resistor terminal (+) and body ground. **STD voltage: 9 – 14 V**

— OK / NO →
NO → Check fuse, fusible link and ignition switch. — OK → [BAD] Repair or replace
OK → Check wiring between solenoid resistor and battery. [BAD] Repair or replace

② Check that there is specified voltage between resistor terminal (−) and body ground. **STD voltage: 9 – 14 V**
OK / NO →

③ Check resistance of magnetic coil in each injector. STD resistance: 2 – 4 Ω
OK / BAD → Replace resistor.

③ Check wiring between ECU and resistor. [BAD] Replace injector.

TROUBLESHOOTING THE NO. 7 TERMINAL ON THE EFI CONNECTOR
1985 CELICA

No.	Terminals	Trouble	Condition	STD Voltage
7	W – E_1	No voltage	No trouble (CHECK ENGINE light off) and engine running	8 – 14 V

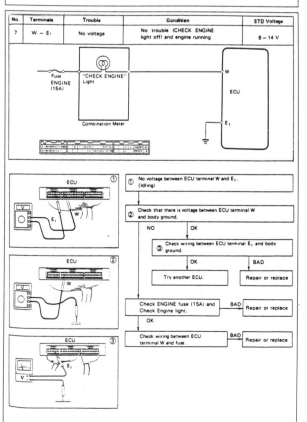

① No voltage between ECU terminal W and E_1. (Idling)

② Check that there is voltage between ECU terminal W and body ground.
NO / OK →
OK → ③ Check wiring between ECU terminal E_1 and body ground.
OK → Try another ECU. / BAD → Repair or replace

② Check ENGINE fuse (15A) and Check Engine light.
OK / BAD → Repair or replace

③ Check wiring between ECU terminal W and fuse.
BAD → Repair or replace

TROUBLESHOOTING THE NO. 8 TERMINAL ON THE EFI CONNECTOR
1985 CELICA

No.	Terminals	Trouble	Condition		STD Voltage
8	V_c – E_2	No voltage	Ignition switch ON	–	4 – 10 V
	V_s – E_2			Measuring plate fully closed	0.5 – 2.5 V
	V_s – E_2			Measuring plate fully open	4 – 10 V
	V_s – E_2		Idling	–	2.5 – 7.5 V

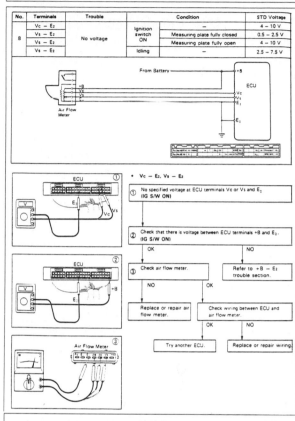

• V_c – E_2, V_s – E_2

① No specified voltage at ECU terminals V_c or V_s and E_2. (IG S/W ON)

② Check that there is voltage between ECU terminals +B and E_2. (IG S/W ON)
OK / NO →
NO → Refer to +B – E_2 trouble section.

③ Check air flow meter.
NO / OK →
NO → Replace or repair air flow meter.
OK → Check wiring between ECU and air flow meter.
OK → Try another ECU. / NO → Replace or repair wiring.

TROUBLESHOOTING THE NO. 9 TERMINAL ON THE EFI CONNECTOR
1985 CELICA

No.	Terminals	Trouble	Condition		STD Voltage
9	THA – E_2	No voltage	Ignition switch ON	Intake air temperature 20°C (68°F)	2 – 4.5 V

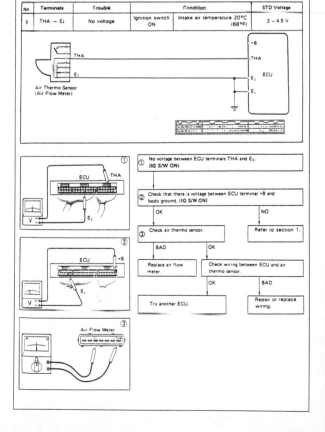

① No voltage between ECU terminals THA and E_2. (IG S/W ON)

② Check that there is voltage between ECU terminal +B and body ground. (IG S/W ON)
OK / NO →
NO → Refer to section 1.

③ Check air thermo sensor.
BAD / OK →
BAD → Replace air flow meter.
OK → Check wiring between ECU and air thermo sensor.
OK → Try another ECU. / BAD → Repair or replace wiring.

TROUBLESHOOTING THE NO. 10 TERMINAL ON THE EFI CONNECTOR 1985 CELICA

No.	Terminals	Trouble	Condition		STD Voltage
10	THW – E_2	No voltage	Ignition switch ON	Coolant temperature 80°C (176°F)	0.3 – 2.5 V

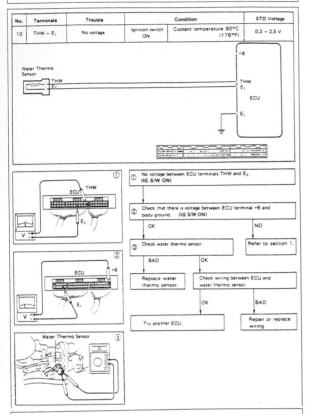

① No voltage between ECU terminals THW and E_2. (IG S/W ON)

② Check that there is voltage between ECU terminal +B and body ground. (IG S/W ON)

OK → ③ Check water thermo sensor.

NO → Refer to section 1.

BAD → Replace water thermo sensor.

OK → Check wiring between ECU and water thermo sensor.

OK → Try another ECU.

BAD → Repair or replace wiring

TROUBLESHOOTING THE NO. 11 TERMINAL ON THE EFI CONNECTOR 1985 CELICA

No.	Terminals	Trouble	Condition	STD Voltage
11	B/K – E_1	No voltage	Stop light switch ON	8 – 14 V

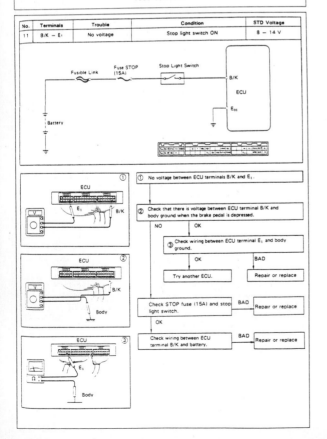

① No voltage between ECU terminals B/K and E_1.

② Check that there is voltage between ECU terminal B/K and body ground when the brake pedal is depressed.

NO → ③ Check wiring between ECU terminal E_1 and body ground.

OK → Try another ECU.

BAD → Repair or replace

Check STOP fuse (15A) and stop light switch.

BAD → Repair or replace

Check wiring between ECU terminal B/K and battery.

BAD → Repair or replace

ELECTRONIC COMPONENT LOCATIONS – 1985 CELICA

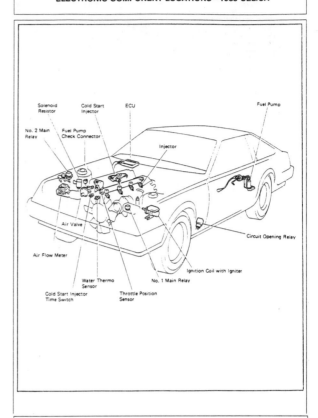

TESTING THE OXYGEN SENSOR – 1985 CELICA

1. Warm-up the engine.
2. Connect a SST to the 4-terminal connector. SST 09842-14010
3. Using a voltmeter connect the positive probe to the red wire of the SST and negative testing probe to the block wire.
4. Warm up the Ox sensor with the engine at 2,500 rpm for about 90 seconds.

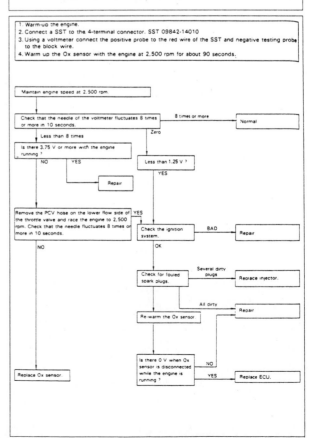

TESTING THE OXYGEN SENSOR (CONT.) – 1985 CELICA

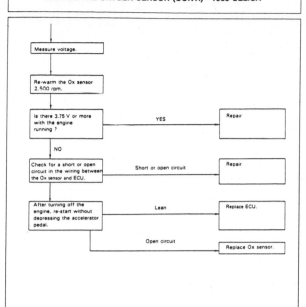

Measure voltage.
↓
Re-warm the Ox sensor 2,500 rpm.
↓
Is there 3.75 V or more with the engine running? — YES → Repair
↓ NO
Check for a short or open circuit in the wiring between the Ox sensor and ECU. — Short or open circuit → Repair
↓
After turning off the engine, re-start without depressing the accelerator pedal. — Lean → Replace ECU.

Open circuit → Replace Ox sensor.

INSPECTING THE RESISTANCE AT THE ECU WIRING CONNECTOR 1985 CELICA

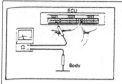

2. MEASURE RESISTANCE OF ECU
   CAUTION:
   1. Do not touch the ECU terminals.
   2. The tester probe should be inserted into wiring connector from the wiring side.

   Check the resistance between each terminal of the wiring connector.
   • Remove the glove box.
   • Unplug wiring connectors from the ECU.
   • Measure the resistance between each terminal of the wiring connectors.

Resistance at ECU Wiring Connectors

Terminals	Condition	Resistance (kΩ)
E_1 – Body	–	0
E_1 – E_2	–	0
IDL – E_2	Throttle valve open	Infinity
	Throttle valve fully closed	0 – 0.1
VTA – E_2	Throttle valve fully open	3.3 – 10
	Throttle valve fully closed	0.2 – 0.8
V_{cc} – E_2	–	3 – 7
THA – E_2	Intake air temperature 20°C (68°F)	2 – 3
THW – E_2	Coolant temperature 80°C (176°F)	0.2 – 0.4
+B – E_2	–	0.2 – 0.4
V_c – E_2	–	0.1 – 0.3
V_s – E_2	Measuring plate fully closed	0.02 – 0.4
	Measuring plate fully open	0.02 – 1
Ne – E_1	–	0.14 – 0.18

INSPECTING THE VOLTAGE AT THE ECU WIRING CONNECTOR 1985 CELICA

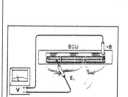

1. MEASURE VOLTAGE OF ECU
   NOTE:
   1. The ECU itself cannot be checked directly.
   2. The EFI circuit can be checked by measuring the resistance and voltage at the wiring connectors of the ECU.

   Check the voltages at the wiring connectors.
   • Remove the glove box.
   • Turn the ignition switch ON.
   • Measure the voltage at each terminal.

NOTE: 1. Perform all voltage measurements with the connectors connected.
2. Verify that the battery voltage is 11V or above when the ignition switch is ON.

Voltage at ECU Wiring Connectors

Terminals	Condition		STD voltage
+B – E_1	Ignition switch ON		10 – 14
BATT – E_1	–		10 – 14
IDL – E_2	Ignition switch ON	Throttle valve open	4 – 10
VTA – E_2		Throttle valve fully closed	0.1 – 1.0
		Throttle valve fully open	4 – 6
V_{cc} – E_2		–	4 – 6
IGt – E_1	Idling		0.7 – 1.0
STA – E_1	Ignition switch ST position		6 – 12
No. 10 – E_1 No. 20 – E_1	Ignition switch ON		9 – 14
W – E_1	No trouble (CHECK ENGINE light off) and engine running		8 – 14
V_c – E_2	Ignition switch ON	–	4 – 10
V_s – E_2		Measuring plate fully closed	0.5 – 2.5
		Measuring plate fully open	4 – 10
	Idling		2.5 – 7.5
THA – E_2	Ignition switch ON	Intake air temperature 20°C (68°F)	2 – 4.5
THW – E_2	Ignition switch ON	Coolant temperature 80°C (176°F)	0.3 – 2.5
B/K – E_1	Stop light switch ON		8 – 14

ECU Connectors

| E_{01} | No.10 | STA | V_s | NSW | | W | T | IDL | IGt | | KNK | Ne | | V_c | V_s | THA | BAT | +B₁ |
| E_{02} | No.20 | IGt | E_1 | | | E_2 | Ox | V_{cc} | VTA | | | THW | | E_{21} | SPD | B/K | +B |

EFI WIRING SCHEMATIC (2S-E) – 1986 CELICA

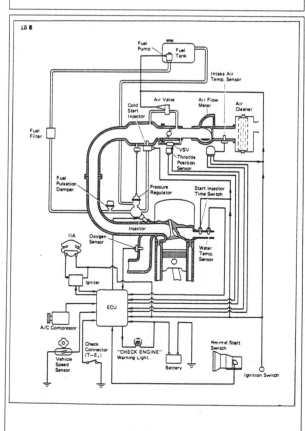

EFI WIRING SCHEMATIC (3S-GE) — 1986 CELICA

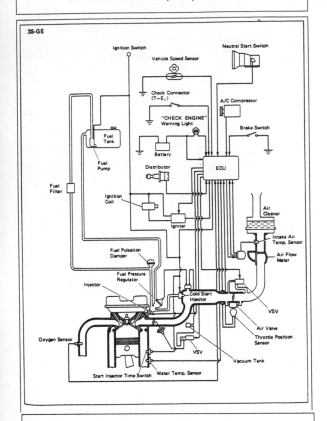

3S-GE

DIAGNOSIS CODES (3S-GE) — 1986 CELICA

[3S-GE]

Code No.	Number of "CHECK ENGINE" blinks	System	Diagnosis	Trouble area
—	ON / OFF	Normal	This appears when none of the other codes (11 thru 51) are identified.	—
11		ECU (+B)	Wire severance, however slight, in +B (ECU).	1. Main relay circuit 2. Main relay 3. ECU
12		RPM signal	No Ne, G signal to ECU within several seconds after engine is cranked.	1. Distributor circuit 2. Distributor 3. Starter signal circuit 4. ECU
13		RPM signal	No Ne signal to ECU within several seconds after engine reaches 1,000 rpm.	Same as 12, above.
14		Ignition signal	No signal from igniter 8 ~ 11 times in succession.	1. Igniter circuit (+B, IGt, IGf) 2. Igniter 3. ECU
21		Oxygen sensor signal	Open circuit in oxygen sensor signal (only lean indication).	1. Oxygen sensor circuit 2. Oxygen sensor 3. ECU
22		Water temp. sensor signal	Open or short circuit in water temp. sensor signal.	1. Water temp. sensor circuit 2. Water temp. sensor 3. ECU
23		Intake air temp. sensor signal	Open or short circuit in intake air temp. sensor signal.	1. Intake air temp. sensor circuit 2. Intake air temp. sensor 3. ECU
31		Air flow meter signal	Vc circuit open or Vs — E₁ short circuit.	1. Air flow meter circuit 2. Air flow meter 3. ECU
32		Air flow meter signal	E₁ circuit open or Vc — Vs short circuited.	Same as 31, above.
41		Throttle position sensor signal	Simultaneous IDL and Psw signal to ECU.	1. Throttle position sensor circuit 2. Throttle position sensor 3. ECU
42		Vehicle speed sensor signal	Signal informing ECU that vehicle stopped has been input to ECU for 5 seconds with engine running between 1,500 — 6,000 rpm.	1. Vehicle speed sensor circuit 2. Vehicle speed sensor 3. ECU
43		Starter signal	No STA signal to ECU when vehicle stopped and engine running over 800 rpm.	1. Main relay circuit 2. IG switch circuit (starter) 3. IG switch 4. ECU
51		Switch signal	Air conditioner switch ON, idle switch OFF or shift position other than P or N range during diagnosis check.	1. Air con. S/W 2. Throttle position sensor circuit 3. Throttle position sensor 4. Neutral start switch 5. ECU

DIAGNOSIS CODES (2S-E) — 1986 CELICA

[2S-E]

Code No.	Number of "CHECK ENGINE" blinks	System	Diagnosis	Trouble area
1	ON ON ON ON / OFF OFF OFF OFF	Normal	This appears when none of the other codes (2 thru 11) are identified.	—
2		Air flow meter signal	• Vc circuit open or Vs — E₂ short circuited. • E₁ circuit open or Vc — Vs short circuited.	1. Air flow meter circuit 2. Air flow meter 3. ECU
3		Ignition signal	No signal from igniter four times in succession.	1. Ignition circuit (+B, IGf, IGt) 2. Igniter 3. ECU
4		Water temp. sensor signal	Open or short circuit in water temp. sensor signal.	1. Water temp. sensor circuit 2. Water temp. sensor 3. ECU
5		Oxygen sensor signal	Open or short circuit in oxygen sensor signal (only lean indication)	1. Oxygen sensor circuit 2. Oxygen sensor 3. ECU
6		RPM signal	No Ne signal to ECU while cranking, or Ne value over 1,000 rpm in spite of no Ne signal to ECU	1. Distributor circuit 2. Distributor 3. Igniter 4. Starter signal circuit 5. ECU
7		Throttle position sensor signal	Open or short circuit in throttle position sensor signal.	1. Throttle position sensor circuit 2. Throttle position sensor 3. ECU
8		Intake air temp. sensor signal	Open or short circuit in intake air temperature sensor.	1. Air temp. sensor circuit 2. ECU
9		Vehicle speed sensor signal	Signal informing ECU that vehicle stopped has been input to ECU for 8 seconds with engine running between 2,400 — 5,000 rpm.	1. Vehicle speed sensor circuit 2. Vehicle sensor 3. ECU
10		Starter signal	No STA signal to ECU when vehicle stopped and engine running over 800 rpm	1. Starter relay circuit 2. IG switch circuit (starter) 3. IG Switch 4. ECU
11		Switch signal	Air conditioner switch ON, idle switch OFF or shift position in any position other than P or N range during diagnosis check.	1. Air con. S/W 2. Throttle position sensor circuit 3. Throttle position sensor 4. Neutral start switch 5. ECU

INSPECTION OF THE DIAGNOSIS CIRCUIT — 1986 CELICA

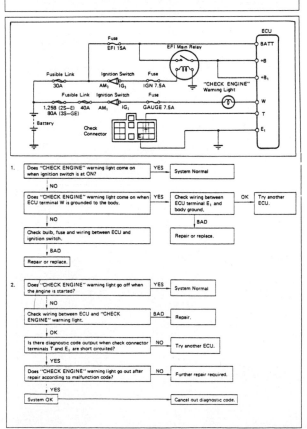

TROUBLESHOOTING THE EFI SYSTEM WITH A VOLT/OHMMETER – 1986 CELICA

NOTE: The following troubleshooting procedures are designed for inspection of each separate system, and therefore the actual procedure may vary somewhat. However, troubleshooting should be performed refering to the inspection methods described in this manual.

Before beginning inspection, it is best to first make a simple check of the fuses, fusible links and the condition of the connectors.

The following troubleshooting procedures are based on the supposition that the trouble lies in either a short or open circuit in a component outside the computer or a short circuit within the computer.

If engine trouble occurs even though proper operating voltage is detected in the computer connector, then that the ECU is faulty and should be replaced.

LOCATION OF FUSES AND FUSIBLE LINKS

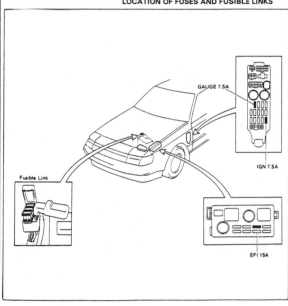

CONNECTORS OF THE ECU (2S-E) – 1986 CELICA

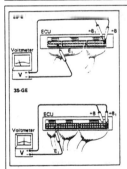

NOTE:
- Perform all voltage measurements with the connectors connected.
- Verify that the battery voltage is 11V or above when the ignition switch is at ON.

Using a voltmeter with high impedance (10 kΩ/V minimum), measure the voltage at each terminal of the wiring connector.

Connectors of ECU

[2S-E]

Symbol	Terminal Name	Symbol	Terminal Name
E_{01}	ENGINE GROUND	IGf	IGNITER
E_{02}	ENGINE GROUND	E_1	SENSOR GROUND
No. 10	INJECTOR	OX	OXYGEN SENSOR
No. 20	INJECTOR	Psw	THROTTLE POSITION SENSOR
STA	STARTER SWITCH	Ne	ENGINE REVOLUTION SENSOR
IGt	IGNITER	THW	WATER TEMP. SENSOR
VF	CHECK CONNECTOR	Vc	AIR FLOW METER
E_1	ENGINE GROUND	E_{21}	SENSOR GROUND
NSW	NEUTRAL START SWITCH	Vs	AIR FLOW METER
V-ISC	ISC VSV	THA	AIR TEMP. SENSOR
W	WARNING LIGHT	SPD	SPEED SENSOR
T	CHECK CONNECTOR	BATT	BATTERY
IDL	THROTTLE POSITION SENSOR	$+B_1$	MAIN RELAY
A/C	A/C MAGNET SWITCH	$+B$	MAIN RELAY

ECU Connectors

E_{01}	No. 10	STA	VF	NSW		V-ISC	W	T	IDL	IGf			Ne		Vc	Vs	THA	BATT	$+B_1$
E_{02}	No. 20	IGt	E_1					A/C	E_1	OX		Psw	THW			E_{21}		SPD	$-B$

VOLTAGE SUPPLIED AT THE ECU WIRING CONNECTOR (2S-E) – 1986 CELICA

[2S-E]

No.	Terminals	STD Voltage	Condition	
1	$+B$ – E_1 $+B_1$	10 – 14	Ignition S/W ON	
2	BATT – E_1	10 – 14	–	
3	IDL – E_1	8 – 14	Ignition S/W ON	Throttle valve open
	Psw – E_1	8 – 14		Throttle valve fully closed
4	IGt – E_1	0.7 – 1.0	Idling	
5	STA – E_1	6 – 12	Cranking	
6	No. 10 E_{01} – No. 20 E_{02}	9 – 14	Ignition S/W ON	
7	W – E_1	8 – 14	No troble ("CHECK ENGINE" warning light off) and engine running	
8	Vc – E_2	6 – 10	–	
	Vs – E_2	0.5 – 2.5	Ignition S/W ON	Measuring plate fully closed
		5 – 10		Measuring plate fully open
		2 – 8	Idling	
9	THA – E_2	1 – 3	Ignition S/W ON	Intake air temperature 20°C (68°F)
10	THW – E_2	0.5 – 2.5	Ignition S/W ON	Coolant temperature 80°C (176°F)
11	A/C – E_1	8 – 14	Ignition S/W ON	Air conditioning ON

ECU Connectors

E_{01}	No. 10	STA	VF	NSW		V-ISC	W	T	IDL	IGt			Ne		Vc	Vs	THA	BATT	$+B_1$
E_{02}	No. 20	IGt	E_1					A/C	E_1	OX		Psw	THW			E_{21}		SPD	$-B$

TROUBLESHOOTING THE NO. 1 TERMINAL ON THE EFI CONNECTOR (2S-E) – 1986 CELICA

No.	Terminals	Trouble	Condition	STD Voltage
1	$+B$ $+B_1$ – E_1	No voltage	Ignition S/W ON	10 – 14 V

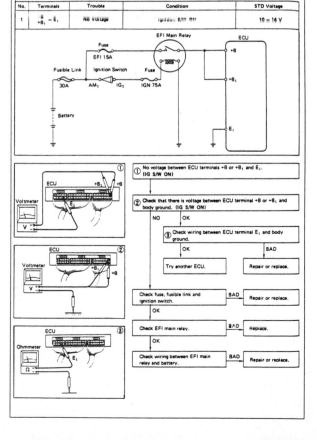

TROUBLESHOOTING THE NO. 2 TERMINAL ON THE EFI CONNECTOR (2S-E) — 1986 CELICA

No.	Terminals	Trouble	Condition	STD Voltage
2	BATT – E_1	No voltage	–	10 – 14 V

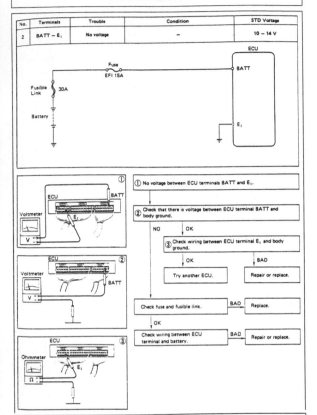

TROUBLESHOOTING THE NO. 4 TERMINAL ON THE EFI CONNECTOR (2S-E) — 1986 CELICA

No.	Terminals	Trouble	Condition	STD Voltage
4	IGt – E_1	No voltage	Idling	0.7 – 1.0 V

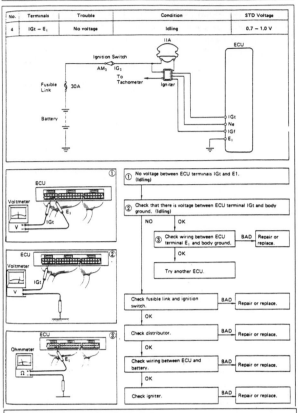

TROUBLESHOOTING THE NO. 3 TERMINAL ON THE EFI CONNECTOR (2S-E) — 1986 CELICA

No.	Terminals	Trouble	Condition	STD Voltage
3	IDL – E_1	No voltage	IG S/W ON	Throttle valve open	8 – 14 V
	Psw – E_1			Throttle valve fully closed	8 – 14 V

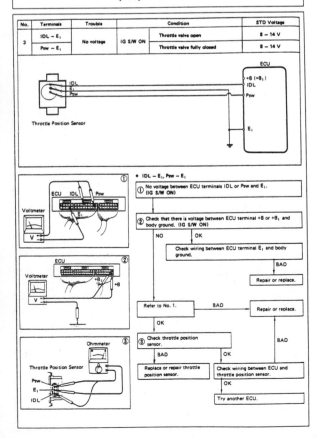

TROUBLESHOOTING THE NO. 5 TERMINAL ON THE EFI CONNECTOR (2S-E) — 1986 CELICA

No.	Terminal	Trouble	Condition	STD Voltage
5	STA – E_1	No voltage	Cranking	6 – 12 V

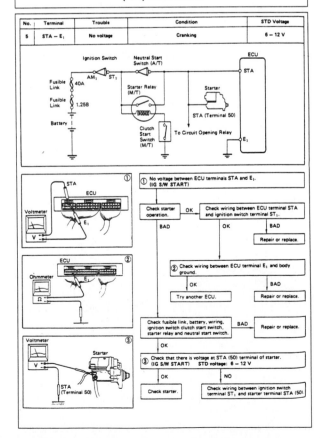

TROUBLESHOOTING THE NO. 6 TERMINAL ON THE EFI CONNECTOR
(2S-E) — 1986 CELICA

No.	Terminals	Trouble	Condition	STD Voltage
6	No. 10 E_{01} No. 20 E_{02}	No voltage	IG S/W ON	9 – 14 V

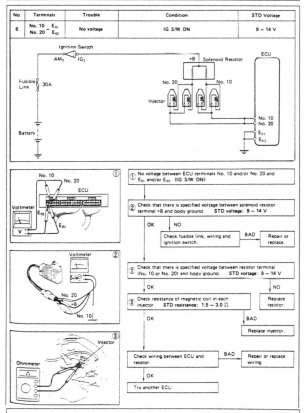

TROUBLESHOOTING THE NO. 7 TERMINAL ON THE EFI CONNECTOR
(2S-E) — 1986 CELICA

No.	Terminals	Trouble	Condition	STD Voltage
7	W – E_1	No voltage	No trouble ("CHECK ENGINE" warning light off) and engine running	8 – 14 V

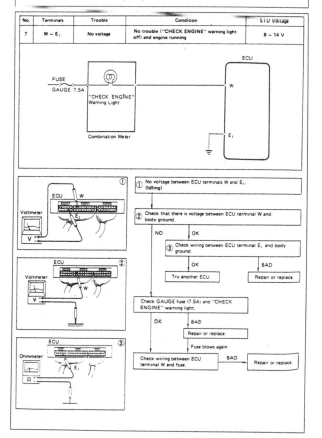

TROUBLESHOOTING THE NO. 8 TERMINAL ON THE EFI CONNECTOR
(2S-E) — 1986 CELICA

No.	Terminals	Trouble		Condition	STD Voltage
8	Vc – E_2	No voltage	IS S/W ON	–	6 – 10 V
	Vs – E_2			Measuring plate fully closed	0.5 – 2.5 V
	Vs – E_2			Measuring plate fully open	5 – 10 V
	Vs – E_2		Idling	–	2 – 8 V

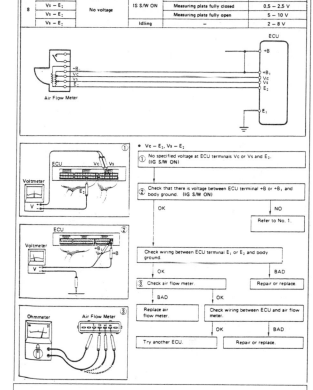

TROUBLESHOOTING THE NO. 9 TERMINAL ON THE EFI CONNECTOR
(2S-E) — 1986 CELICA

No.	Terminals	Trouble	Condition		STD Voltage
9	THA – E_2	No voltage	IG S/W ON	Intake air temperature 20°C (68°F)	1 – 9 V

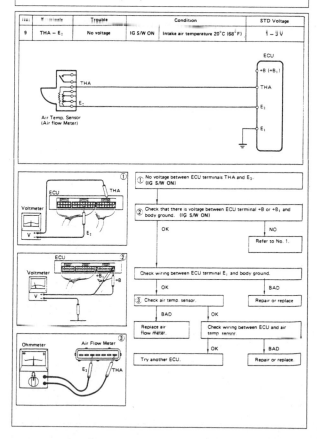

TROUBLESHOOTING THE NO. 10 TERMINAL ON THE EFI CONNECTOR (2S-E) — 1986 CELICA

No.	Terminals	Trouble	Condition		STD Voltage
10	THW – E_2	No voltage	IG S/W ON	Coolant temperature 80°C (176°F)	0.5 – 2.5 V

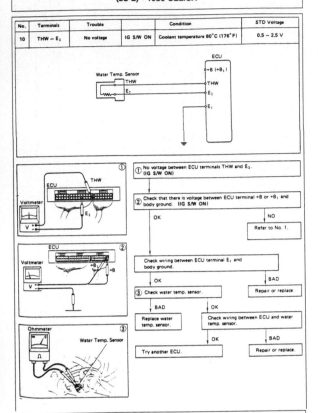

CONNECTORS OF THE ECU (3S-GE) — 1986 CELICA

[3S-GE]

Symbol	Terminal Name	Symbol	Terminal Name	Symbol	Terminal Name
E_{01}	ENGINE GROUND	G_1	ENGINE REVOLUTION SENSOR	L_1	ECU ECT
E_{02}	ENGINE GROUND	T	CHECK CONNECTOR	L_3	ECU ECT
STA	STARTER SWITCH	G_2	ENGINE REVOLUTION SENSOR	L_2	ECU ECT
IGt	IGNITER	VTA	THROTTLE POSITION SENSOR	OD_1	ECU ECT
STJ	COLD START INJECTOR	Ne	ENGINE REVOLUTION SENSOR	A/C	A/C MAGNET SWITCH
E_1	ENGINE GROUND	IDL	THOTTLE POSITION SENSOR	SPD	SPEED SENSOR
NSW	NEUTRAL START SWITCH	V–ISC	ISC–VSV	W	WARNING LIGHT
T–VIS	T–VIS VSV	IGf	IGNITER	STP	STOP LIGHT SWITCH
No. 1	INJECTOR	Ox	OXYGEN SENSOR	THA	AIR FLOW METER
No. 2	INJECTOR	THW	WATER TEMP. SENSOR	Vs	AIR FLOW METER
No. 3	INJECTOR	E_2	SENSOR GROUND	Vc	AIR FLOW METER
No. 4	INJECTOR	Ox_1	OXYGEN SENSOR	BATT	BATTERY
$G\ominus$	ENGINE REVOLUTION SENSOR	E_{22}	SENSOR GROUND	+B	MAIN RELAY
VF	CHECK CONNECTOR	E_{11}	ENGINE GROUND	$+B_1$	MAIN RELAY

ECU Connectors

TROUBLESHOOTING THE NO. 11 TERMINAL ON THE EFI CONNECTOR (2S-E) — 1986 CELICA

No.	Terminals	Trouble	Condition	STD Voltage
11	A/C – E_1	No voltage	Air conditioning ON	8 – 14 V

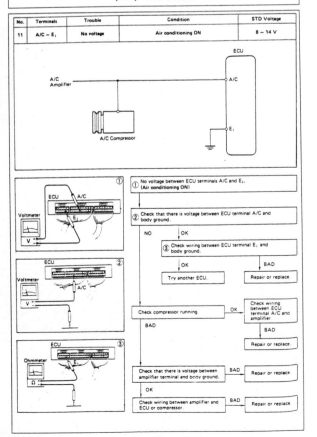

VOLTAGE SUPPLIED AT THE ECU WIRING CONNECTOR (3S-GE) — 1986 CELICA

[3S-GE]

No.	Terminals	STD Voltage	Condition	
1	+B – E_1 $+B_1$	10 – 14	Ignition S/W ON	
2	BATT – E_1	10 – 14	—	
3	IDL – E_2	4 – 6		Throttle valve open
	VTA – E_1	0.1 – 1.0	Ignition S/W ON	Throttle valve fully closed
		4 – 5		Throttle valve fully open
	Vcc – E_2	4 – 6		—
4	IGt – E_1	0.7 – 1.0	Cranking or Idling	
5	STA – E_1	6 – 12	Cranking	
6	No. 1 No. 2 E_{01} No. 3 E_{02} No. 4	9 – 14	Ignition S/W ON	
7	W – E_1	8 – 14	No trouble ("CHECK ENGINE" warning light off) and engine running	
8	Vc – E_2	4 – 6	—	
	Vs – V_2	4 – 5	Ignition S/W ON	Measuring plate fully closed
		0.02 – 0.5		Measuring plate fully open
		2 – 4	Idling	
9	THA – E_2	1 – 2	Ignition S/W ON	Intake air temperature 20°C (68°F)
10	THW – E_2	0.1 – 1.0	Ignition S/W ON	Coolant temperature 80°C (176°F)
11	A/C – E_1	8 – 14	Air conditioning ON	

ECU Connectors

TROUBLESHOOTING THE NO. 1 TERMINAL ON THE EFI CONNECTOR (3S-GE) – 1986 CELICA

No.	Terminals	Trouble	Condition	STD Voltage
1	+B +B₁ – E₁	No voltage	Ignition S/W ON	10 – 14 V

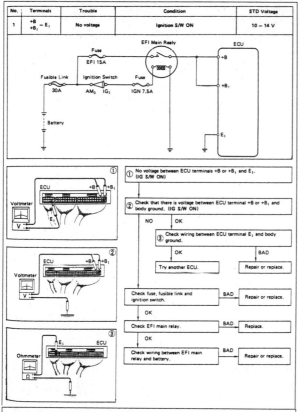

TROUBLESHOOTING THE NO. 2 TERMINAL ON THE EFI CONNECTOR (3S-GE) – 1986 CELICA

No.	Terminals	Trouble	Condition	STD Voltage
2	BATT – E₁	No voltage	–	10 – 14 V

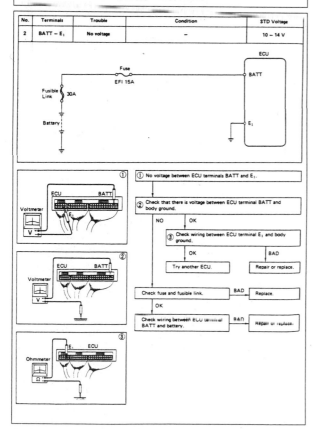

TROUBLESHOOTING THE NO. 3 TERMINAL ON THE EFI CONNECTOR (3S-GE) – 1986 CELICA

No.	Terminals	Trouble	Condition	STD Voltage
3	IDL – E₂	No voltage	Throttle valve open	4 – 6 V
	VTA – E₂		Throttle valve fully closed	0.1 – 1.0 V
		IG S/W ON	Throttle valve fully open	4 – 5 V
	Vc – E₂		–	4 – 6 V

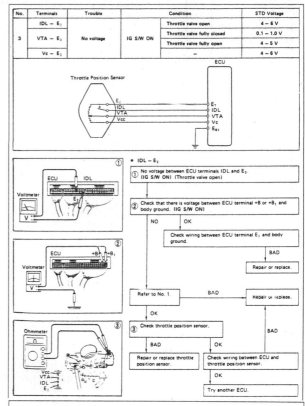

TROUBLESHOOTING THE NO. 3 TERMINAL ON THE EFI CONNECTOR (3S-GE) – 1986 CELICA

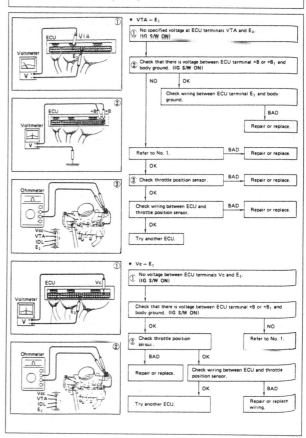

TROUBLESHOOTING THE NO. 4 TERMINAL ON THE EFI CONNECTOR (3S-GE) — 1986 CELICA

No.	Terminals	Trouble	Condition	STD Voltage
4	IGt – E_1	No voltage	Cranking or Idling	0.7 – 1.0 V

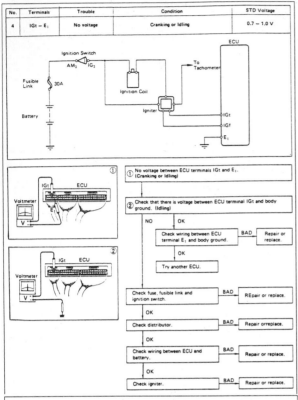

① No voltage between ECU terminals IGt and E_1. (Cranking or Idling)

② Check that there is voltage between ECU terminal IGt and body ground. (Idling)

NO → Check wiring between ECU terminal E_1 and body ground. → BAD → Repair or replace.
→ OK → Try another ECU.

OK → Check fuse, fusible link and ignition switch. → BAD → REpair or replace.
→ OK → Check distributor. → BAD → Repair or replace.
→ OK → Check wiring between ECU and battery. → BAD → Repair or replace.
→ OK → Check igniter. → BAD → Repair or replace.

TROUBLESHOOTING THE NO. 5 TERMINAL ON THE EFI CONNECTOR (3S-GE) — 1986 CELICA

No.	Terminals	Trouble	Condition	STD Voltage
5	STA – E_1	No voltage	Cranking	6 – 12 V

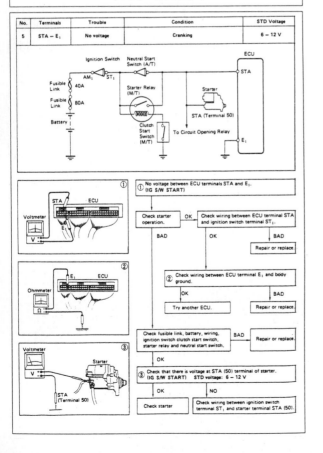

① No voltage between ECU terminals STA and E_1. (IG S/W START)

Check starter operation. → OK → Check wiring between ECU terminal STA and ignition switch terminal ST_1. → OK → Repair or replace. → BAD

BAD → ② Check wiring between ECU terminal E_1 and body ground. → OK → Try another ECU. → BAD → Repair or replace.

OK → Check fusible link, battery, wiring, ignition switch clutch start switch, starter relay and neutral start switch. → BAD → Repair or replace.

OK → ③ Check that there is voltage at STA (50) terminal of starter. (IG S/W START) STD voltage: 6 – 12 V → OK → Check starter. → NO → Check wiring between ignition switch terminal ST_1 and starter terminal STA (50).

TROUBLESHOOTING THE NO. 6 TERMINAL ON THE EFI CONNECTOR (3S-GE) — 1986 CELICA

No.	Terminals	Trouble	Condition	STD Voltage
6	No.1 No.2 No.3 No.4 – E_{01} E_{02}	No voltage	IG S/W ON	9 – 14 V

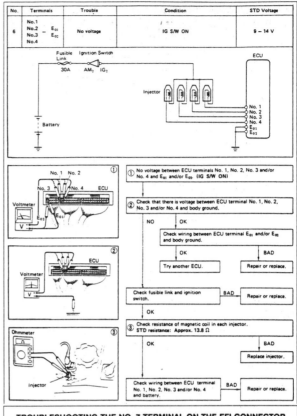

① No voltage between ECU terminals No. 1, No. 2, No. 3 and/or No. 4 and E_{01} and/or E_{02}. (IG S/W ON)

② Check that there is voltage between ECU terminal No. 1, No. 2, No. 3 and/or No. 4 and body ground.

NO → Check wiring between ECU terminal E_{01} and/or E_{02} and body ground. → BAD → Repair or replace.
→ OK → Try another ECU.

OK → Check fusible link and ignition switch. → BAD → Repair or replace.

OK → ③ Check resistance of magnetic coil in each injector. STD resistance: Approx. 13.8 Ω → BAD → Replace injector.

OK → Check wiring between ECU terminal No. 1, No. 2, No. 3 and/or No. 4 and battery. → BAD → Repair or replace.

TROUBLESHOOTING THE NO. 7 TERMINAL ON THE EFI CONNECTOR (3S-GE) — 1986 CELICA

No.	Terminals	Trouble	Condition	STD Voltage
7	W – E_1	No voltage	No trouble ("CHECK ENGINE" warning light off) and engine running	8 – 14 V

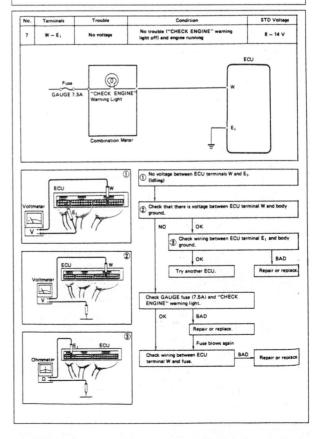

① No voltage between ECU terminals W and E_1. (Idling)

② Check that there is voltage between ECU terminal W and body ground.

NO → ③ Check wiring between ECU terminal E_1 and body ground. → OK → Try another ECU. → BAD → Repair or replace.

OK → Check GAUGE fuse (7.5A) and "CHECK ENGINE" warning light. → OK → → BAD → Repair or replace. → Fuse blows again → Check wiring between ECU terminal W and fuse. → BAD → Repair or replace.

TROUBLESHOOTING THE NO. 8 TERMINAL ON THE EFI CONNECTOR (3S-GE) — 1986 CELICA

No.	Terminals	Trouble	Condition		STD Voltage
8	Vc – E₂	No voltage	IG S/W ON	–	4 – 6 V
	Vs – E₂			Measuring plate fully closed	4 – 5 V
	Vs – E₂			Measuring plate fully open	0.02 – 0.5 V
	Vs – E₂		Idling	–	7 – 4 V

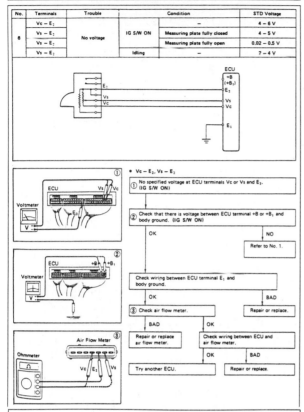

TROUBLESHOOTING THE NO. 9 TERMINAL ON THE EFI CONNECTOR (3S-GE) — 1986 CELICA

No.	Terminals	Trouble	Condition		STD Voltage
9	THA – E₂	No voltage	IG S/W ON	Intake air temperature 20°C (68°F)	1 – 2 V

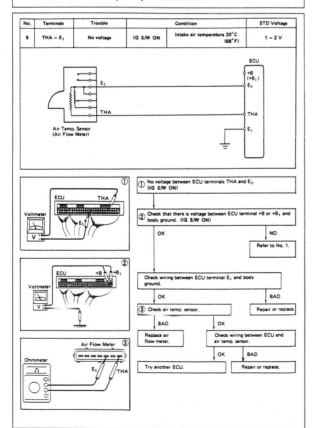

TROUBLESHOOTING THE NO. 10 TERMINAL ON THE EFI CONNECTOR (3S-GE) — 1986 CELICA

No.	Terminals	Trouble	Condition		STD Voltage
10	THW – E₂	No voltage	IG S/W ON	Coolant temperature 80°C (176°F)	0.1 – 1.0 V

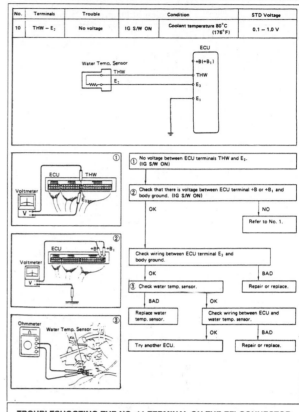

TROUBLESHOOTING THE NO. 11 TERMINAL ON THE EFI CONNECTOR (3S-GE) — 1986 CELICA

No	Terminal	Trouble	Condition	STD Voltage
11	A/C – E₁	No voltage	Air conditioning ON	8 – 14 V

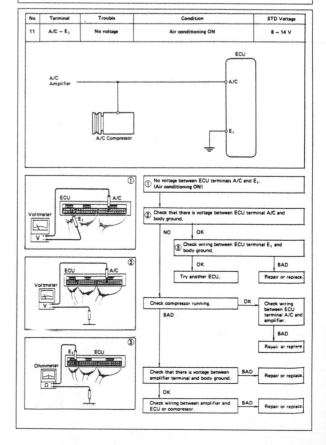

ELECTRONIC COMPONENT LOCATIONS – 1986 CELICA

Location of Electronic Control Parts

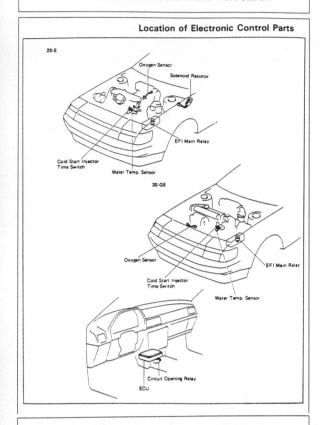

TESTING THE OXYGEN SENSOR (CONT.) – 1986 CELICA

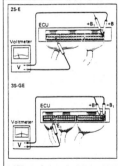

TESTING THE OXYGEN SENSOR – 1986 CELICA

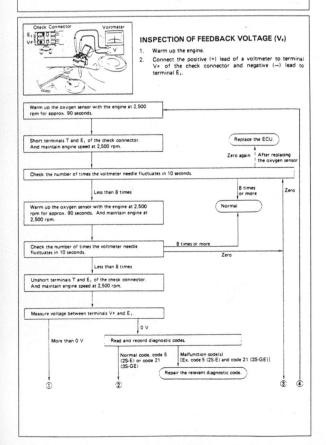

INSPECTION OF FEEDBACK VOLTAGE (V$_F$)

1. Warm up the engine.
2. Connect the positive (+) lead of a voltmeter to terminal V$_F$ of the check connector and negative (−) lead to terminal E$_1$.

INSPECTING THE VOLTAGE AT THE ECU WIRING CONNECTOR
1986 CELICA

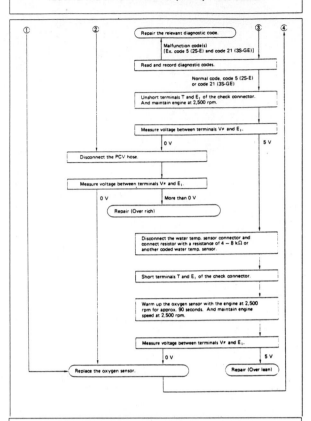

INSPECTION OF ECU

1. MEASURE VOLTAGE OF ECU

   NOTE: The EFI circuit can be checked by measuring the resistance and voltage at the wiring connectors of the ECU.

   Check the voltage at the wiring connectors.

   • Turn the ignition switch
   • Measure the voltage at each terminal.

NOTE: 1. Perform all voltage measurements with the connectors connected.
2. Verify that the battery voltage is 11V or more when the ignition switch is ON.

INSPECTING THE VOLTAGE AT THE ECU WIRING CONNECTOR (2S-E) — 1986 CELICA

[2S-E]

Terminals	Condition		STD voltage
+B +B$_1$ — E$_1$	Ignition S/W ON		10 – 14
BATT — E$_1$			10 – 14
IDL — E$_1$	Ignition S/W ON	Throttle valve open	8 – 14
Psw — E$_1$		Throttle valve fully closed	8 – 14
IGt — E$_1$		Idling	0.7 – 1.0
STA — E$_1$		Cranking	6 – 12
No. 10 No. 20 — E$_{01}$ E$_{02}$	Ignition S/W ON		9 – 14
W — E$_1$	No trouble ("CHECK ENGINE" warning light off) and engine running		8 – 14
Vc — E$_2$		–	6 – 10
Vs — E$_2$	Ignition S/W ON	Measuring plate fully closed	0.5 – 2.5
		Measuring plate fully open	5 – 10
		Idling	2 – 8
THA — E$_2$	Ignition S/W ON	Intake air temperature 20°C (68°F)	1 – 3
THW — E$_2$	Ignition S/W ON	Coolant temperature 80°C (176°F)	0.5 – 2.5
A/C — E$_1$	Ignition S/W ON	Air conditioning ON	8 – 14
T — E$_1$	Ignition S/W ON	Check connector T–E$_1$ not short	10 – 14
	Ignition S/W ON	Check connector T–E$_1$ short	0

ECU Connectors

E$_{01}$	No. 10	STA	VF	NSW		V-ISC	W	T	IDL	IGt			Ne			Vc	Vs	THA	BATT	+B$_1$
E$_{02}$	No. 20	IGt	E$_1$					A/C	E$_2$	OX		Psw	THW			E$_{21}$		SPD		+B

INSPECTING THE RESISTANCE AT THE ECU WIRING CONNECTOR (2S-E) — 1986 CELICA

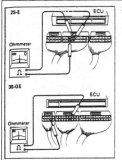

2. MEASURE RESISTANCE OF ECU

CAUTION:
- Do not touch the computer terminals.
- The tester probe should be inserted into the wiring connector from the wiring side.

Check the resistance between each terminal of the wiring connector.
- Disconnect the ECU wiring connectors.
- Measure the resistance between each terminal of the wiring connectors.

[2S-E]

Terminals	Condition	Resistance (Ω)
IDL — E$_1$	Throttle valve open	∞
	Throttle valve fully closed	0
Psw — E$_1$	Throttle valve fully open	0
	Throttle valve fully closed	∞
+B — E$_2$	–	200 – 400
Vc — E$_2$	–	100 – 300
Vs — E$_2$	Measuring plate fully closed	20 – 400
	Measuring plate full open	20 – 1,000
THA — E$_2$	Intake air temperature 20°C (68°F)	2,000 – 3,000
THW — E$_2$	Coolant temperature 80°C (176°F)	200 – 400

ECU Connectors

E$_{01}$	No. 10	STA	VF	NSW		V-ISC	W	T	IDL	IGt			Ne			Vc	Vs	THA	BATT	+B$_1$
E$_{02}$	No. 20	IGt	E$_1$					A/C	E$_2$	OX		Psw	THW			E$_{21}$		SPD		+B

INSPECTING THE VOLTAGE AT THE ECU WIRING CONNECTOR (3S-GE) — 1986 CELICA

[3S-GE]

Terminals	Condition		STD voltage
+B +B$_1$ — E$_1$	Ignition S/W ON		10 – 14
BATT — E$_1$	–		10 – 14
IDL — E$_2$		Throttle valve open	4 – 6
VTA — E$_2$	Ignition S/W ON	Throttle valve fully closed	0.1 – 1.0
		Throttle valve fully open	4 – 5
Vcc — E$_2$		–	4 – 6
IGt — E$_1$		Cranking or Idling	0.7 – 1.0
STA — E$_1$		Cranking	6 – 12
No. 1 No. 2 No. 3 No. 4 — E$_{01}$ E$_{02}$	Ignition S/W ON		9 – 14
W — E$_1$	No trouble ("CHECK ENGINE" warning light off) and engine running		8 – 14
Vc — E$_2$		–	4 – 6
Vs — E$_2$	Ignition S/W ON	Measuring plate fully closed	4 – 5
Vs — E$_2$		Measuring plate fully open	0.02 – 0.5
		Idling	2 – 4
THA — E$_2$	Ignition S/W ON	Intake air temperature 20°C (68°F)	1 – 2
THW — E$_2$	Ignition S/W ON	Coolant temperature 80°C (176°F)	0.1 – 1.0
A/C — E$_1$	Ignition S/W ON	Air conditioning ON	8 – 14
T-VIS — E$_1$		Idling	0 – 2
		More than 4,400 rpm	10 – 14
T — E$_1$	Ignition S/W ON	Check connector T–E$_1$ not short	4 – 6
	Ignition S/W ON	Check connector T–E$_1$ short	0

ECU Connectors

E$_{01}$		STA	STJ	NSW	No. 2	G⊝	G$_1$	G$_2$	Ne	V-ISC	IGt	THW	OX$_1$		L$_1$	L$_2$		SPD	STP	THA	Vs	Vc	BATT	
E$_{02}$		IGt	E$_1$	T-VIS	No. 4	VF	T	VTA	IDL		OX$_2$	E$_{22}$	E$_{11}$	L$_3$	OD$_1$	A/C	W					+B	+B$_1$	

INSPECTING THE RESISTANCE AT THE ECU WIRING CONNECTOR (3S-GE) — 1986 CELICA

[3S-GE]

Terminals	Condition	Resistance (Ω)
IDL — E$_2$	Throttle valve open	∞
	Throttle valve fully closed	Less than 2,300
VTA — E$_1$	Throttle valve fully open	3,000 – 10,000
	Throttle valve fully closed	200 – 800
Vs — E$_2$	Measuring plate fully closed	200 – 600
	Measuring plate fully open	200 – 1,200
THA — E$_2$	Intake air temperature 20°C (68°F)	2,000 – 3,000
THW — E$_2$	Coolant temperature 80°C (176°F)	200 – 400
G$_1$, G$_2$ — G⊝	–	140 – 180
Ne — G⊝	–	140 – 180

ECU Connectors

E$_{01}$		STA	STJ	NSW	No. 1 No. 2	G⊝	G$_1$	G$_2$	Ne	V-ISC	IGt	THW	OX$_1$		L$_1$	L$_2$		SPD	STP	THA	Vs	Vc	BATT	
E$_{02}$		IGt	E$_1$	T-VIS	No. 3 No. 4	VF	T	VTA	IDL		OX$_2$	E$_{22}$	E$_{11}$	L$_3$	OD$_1$	A/C	W					+B	+B$_1$	

EFI WIRING SCHEMATIC (3S-FE) – 1987-88 CELICA

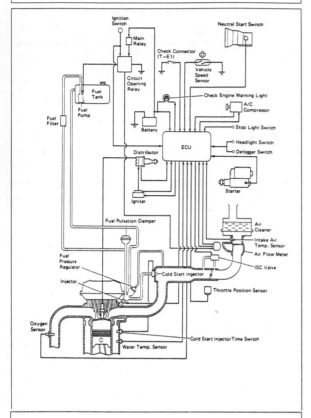

EFI WIRING SCHEMATIC (3S-GE) – 1987-88 CELICA

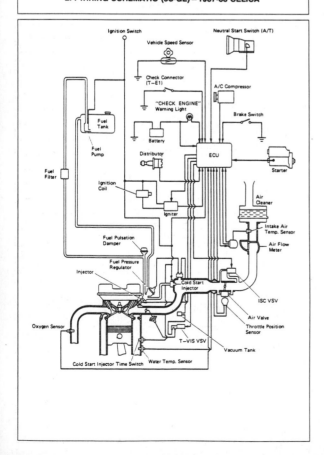

DIAGNOSIS CODES – 1987-88 CELICA

Code No.	Number of "CHECK ENGINE" blinks	System	Diagnosis	Trouble area
–	ON OFF	Normal	This appears when none of the other codes (11 thru 51) are identified.	–
11		ECU (+B)	Wire severence, however slight, in +B (ECU).	1. Main relay circuit 2. Main relay 3. ECU
12		RPM signal	No. NE, G signal to ECU within several seconds after engine is cranked.	1. Distributor circuit 2. Distributor 3. Starter signal circuit 4. ECU
13		RPM signal	No Ne signal to ECU within several seconds after engine reaches 1,000 rpm.	Same as 12, above.
14		Ignition signal	No signal from igniter 4 – 11 times (3S-FE) or 8 – 11 times (3S-GE) times in succession.	1. Igniter circuit (+B, IGT, IGF) 2. Igniter 3. ECU
21		Oxygen sensor signal	Open circuit in oxygen sensor signal (only lean indication).	1. Oxygen sensor circuit 2. Oxygen sensor 3. ECU
22		Water temp. sensor signal	Open or short circuit in water temp. sensor signal.	1. Water temp. sensor circuit 2. Water temp. sensor 3. ECU
24		Intake air temp. sensor signal	Open or short circuit in intake air temp. sensor.	1. Intake air temp. sensor circuit 2. Intake air temp. sensor 3. ECU
31		Air flow meter signal	VC circuit open or VC – E2 short circuit.	1. Air flow meter circuit 2. Air flow meter 3. ECU
32		Air flow meter signal	E2 circuit open or VC – VS short circuited.	Same as 31, above.
41		Throttle position sensor signal	Open or short circuit in throttle position sensor signal.	1. Throttle position sensor circuit 2. Throttle position sensor 3. ECU
42		Vehicle speed sensor signal	Signal informing ECU that vehicle stopped has been input to ECU for 5 seconds with engine running between 2,500 – 5,900 rpm (3S-FE) or 2,500 – 6,000 rpm (3S-GE).	1. Vehicle speed sensor circuit 2. Vehicle speed sensor 3. ECU
43		Starter signal	No STA signal to ECU when over 2 km/h and engine running over 800 rpm.	1. Main relay circuit 2. IG switch circuit (starter) 3. IG switch 4. ECU
51		Switch signal	Air conditioner switch ON, idle switch OFF or shift position other than P or N range during diagnosis check.	1. Air con. S/W 2. Throttle position sensor circuit 3. Throttle position sensor 4. Neutral start switch 5. ECU

INSPECTION OF THE DIAGNOSIS CIRCUIT – 1987-88 CELICA

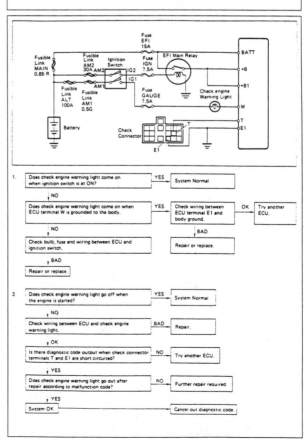

TROUBLESHOOTING THE EFI SYSTEM WITH A VOLT/OHMMETER – 1987-88 CELICA

NOTE: The following troubleshooting procedures are designed for inspection of each separate system, and therefore the actual procedure may vary somewhat. However, troubleshooting should be performed refering to the inspection methods described in this manual.

Before beginning inspection, it is best to first make a simple check of the fuses, fusible links and the condition of the connectors.

The following troubleshooting procedures are based on the supposition that the trouble lies in either a short or open circuit in a component outside the computer or a short circuit within the computer.

If engine trouble occurs even though proper operating voltage is detected in the computer connector, then the ECU is faulty and should be replaced.

LOCATION OF FUSES AND FUSIBLE LINKS

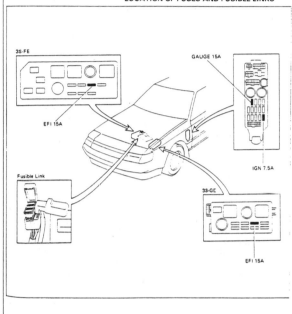

3S-FE

GAUGE 15A

EFI 15A

Fusible Link

IGN 7.5A

3S-GE

EFI 15A

TROUBLESHOOTING THE EFI SYSTEM WITH A VOLT/OHMMETER (CONT.) – 1987-88 CELICA

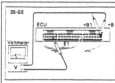

3S-GE

ECU   +B1   +B

Voltmeter   E1

V

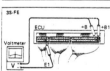

3S-FE

ECU   +B   +B1

Voltmeter   E1

V

NOTE:
* Perform all voltage measurements with the connectors connected.
* Verify that the battery voltage is 11 V or more when the ignition switch is at "ON".

Using a voltmeter with high impedance (10 kΩ/V minimum), measure the voltage at each terminal of the wiring connectors.

CONNECTORS OF THE ECU (3S-FE) – 1987-88 CELICA

Symbol	Terminal Name	Symbol	Terminal Name
E01	ENGINE GROUND	G⊖	DISTRIBUTOR
E02	ENGINE GROUND	OX	OXYGEN SENSOR
No. 10	INJECTOR	G	DISTRIBUTOR
No. 20	INJECTOR	PSW	THROTTLE POSITION SENSOR
STA	STARTER SWITCH	NE	DISTRIBUTOR
IGT	IGNITER	THW	WATER TEMP. SENSOR
VF	CHECK CONNECTOR	VC	AIR FLOW METER
E1	SENSOR GROUND	E21	SENSOR GROUND
NSW	NEUTRAL START SWITCH	VS	AIR FLOW METER
ISC1	ISC VALVE	STP	STP LIGHT SWITCH
ISC2	ISC VALVE	THA	AIR TEMP. SENSOR
W	WARNING LIGHT	SPD	SPEED SENSOR
T	CHECK CONNECTOR	BATT	BATTERY
IDL	THROTTLE POSITION SENSOR	ELS	HEADLIGHT and DEFOGGER
A/C	A/C MAGNET SWITCH	+B1	MAIN RELAY
IGF	IGNITER	+B	MAIN RELAY
E2	SENSOR GROUND		

ECU Terminals

E01	No.10	STA	VF	NSW		ISC1	W	T	IDL	IGF	G⊖	G		NE			VC	VS	THA	BATT	+B1
E02	No.20	IGT	E1			ISC2			A/C	E2	OX			PSW	THW			E21	STP	SPD	ELS	+B

VOLTAGE SUPPLIED AT THE ECU WIRING CONNECTOR (3S-FE) – 1987-88 CELICA

No.	Terminals	STD Voltage	Condition	
1	+B +B1 – E1	10 – 14	Ignition S/W ON	
2	BATT – E1	10 – 14	—	
3	IDL – E1	8 – 14	Ignition S/W ON	Throttle valve open
	PSW – E1	8 – 14		Throttle valve fully closed
4	IGT – E1	0.7 – 1.0	Idling	
5	STA – E1	6 – 12	Cranking	
6	No. 10 – E01 No. 20 – E02	9 – 14	Ignition S/W ON	
7	W – E1	8 – 14	No trouble (check engine warning light off) and engine running	
8	VC – E2	4 – 6	—	
	VS – E2	4 – 5	Ignition S/W ON	Measuring plate fully closed
		0.02 – 0.5		Measuring plate fully open
		2 – 4	Idling	
9	THA – E2	1 – 3	Ignition S/W ON	Intake air temperature 20°C (68°F)
10	THW – E2	0.5 – 2.5	Ignition S/W ON	Coolant temperature 80°C (176°F)
11	ISC1 ISC2 – E1	9 – 14	Ignition S/W ON	
12	A/C – E1	8 – 14	Ignition S/W ON	Air conditioning ON

ECU Terminals

E01	No.10	STA	VF	NSW		ISC1	W	T	IDL	IGF	G⊖	G		NE			L3	L1	VC	VS	THA	BATT	+B1
E02	No.20	IGT	E1			ISC2			A/C	E2	OX			PSW	THW		ECT	L2	E21	STP	SPD	ELS	+B

TROUBLESHOOTING THE NO. 1 TERMINAL ON THE EFI CONNECTOR (3S-FE) — 1987-88 CELICA

No.	Terminals	Trouble	Condition	STD Voltage
1	+B +B1 – E1	No Voltage	Ignition S/W ON	10 – 14 V

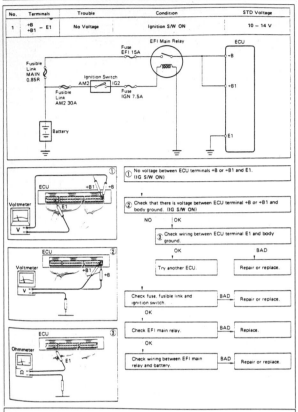

① No voltage between ECU terminals +B or +B1 and E1. (IG S/W ON)

② Check that there is voltage between ECU terminal +B or +B1 and body ground. (IG S/W ON)

NO → ③ Check wiring between ECU terminal E1 and body ground.
   OK → Try another ECU.   BAD → Repair or replace.

OK → Check fuse, fusible link and ignition switch.
   OK → Check EFI main relay.   BAD → Repair or replace.
   OK → Check wiring between EFI main relay and battery.   BAD → Replace.
   BAD → Repair or replace.

TROUBLESHOOTING THE NO. 3 TERMINAL ON THE EFI CONNECTOR (3S-FE) — 1987-88 CELICA

No.	Terminals	Trouble	Condition	STD Voltage
3	IDL – E1	No voltage	IG S/W ON — Throttle valve open	8 – 14 V
	PSW – E1		Throttle valve fully closed	8 – 14 V

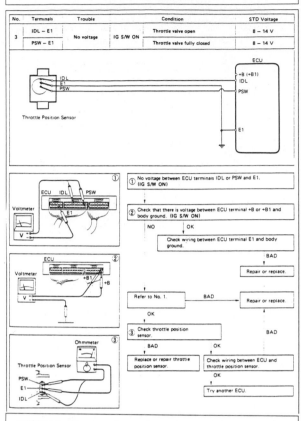

① No voltage between ECU terminals IDL or PSW and E1. (IG S/W ON)

② Check that there is voltage between ECU terminal +B or +B1 and body ground. (IG S/W ON)

NO → Check wiring between ECU terminal E1 and body ground.
   BAD → Repair or replace.

OK → Refer to No. 1.   BAD → Repair or replace.

OK → ③ Check throttle position sensor.
   BAD → Replace or repair throttle position sensor.
   OK → Check wiring between ECU and throttle position sensor.
   OK → Try another ECU.

TROUBLESHOOTING THE NO. 2 TERMINAL ON THE EFI CONNECTOR (3S-FE) — 1987-88 CELICA

No.	Terminals	Trouble	Condition	STD Voltage
2	BATT – E1	No voltage	–	10 – 14 V

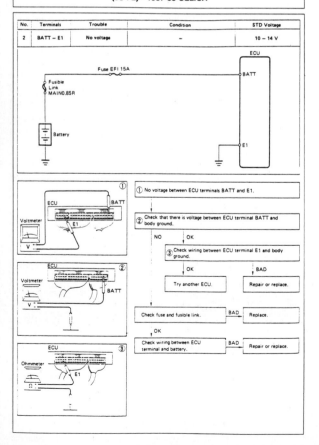

① No voltage between ECU terminals BATT and E1.

② Check that there is voltage between ECU terminal BATT and body ground.

NO → ③ Check wiring between ECU terminal E1 and body ground.
   OK → Try another ECU.   BAD → Repair or replace.

OK → Check fuse and fusible link.   BAD → Replace.

Check wiring between ECU terminal and battery.   BAD → Repair or replace.

TROUBLESHOOTING THE NO. 4 TERMINAL ON THE EFI CONNECTOR (3S-FE) — 1987-88 CELICA

No.	Terminals	Trouble	Condition	STD Voltage
4	IGT – E1	No voltage	Idling	0.7 – 1.0 V

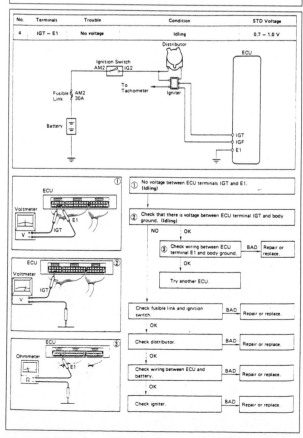

① No voltage between ECU terminals IGT and E1. (Idling)

② Check that there is voltage between ECU terminal IGT and body ground. (Idling)

NO → ③ Check wiring between ECU terminal E1 and body ground.   BAD → Repair or replace.
   OK → Try another ECU.

OK → Check fusible link and ignition switch.   BAD → Repair or replace.
   OK → Check distributor.   BAD → Repair or replace.
   OK → Check wiring between ECU and battery.   BAD → Repair or replace.
   OK → Check igniter.   BAD → Repair or replace.

TROUBLESHOOTING THE NO. 5 TERMINAL ON THE EFI CONNECTOR (3S-FE) — 1987-88 CELICA

No.	Terminal	Trouble	Condition	STD Voltage
5	STA – E1	No voltage	Cranking	6 – 12 V

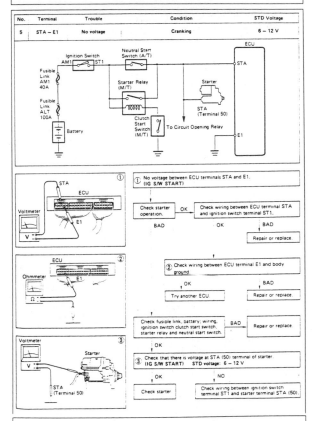

TROUBLESHOOTING THE NO. 6 TERMINAL ON THE EFI CONNECTOR (3S-FE) — 1987-88 CELICA

No.	Terminals	Trouble	Condition	STD Voltage
6	No. 10 – E01 No. 20 – E02	No voltage	IG S/W ON	9 – 14 V

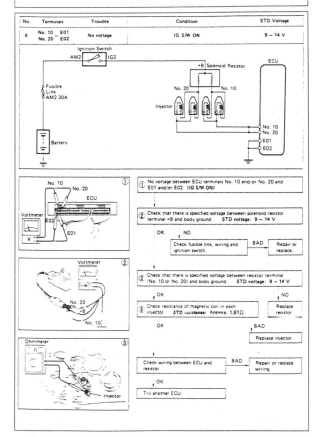

TROUBLESHOOTING THE NO. 7 TERMINAL ON THE EFI CONNECTOR (3S-FE) — 1987-88 CELICA

No.	Terminals	Trouble	Condition	STD Voltage
7	W – E1	No voltage	No trouble ("CHECK ENGINE" warning light off) and engine running	8 – 14 V

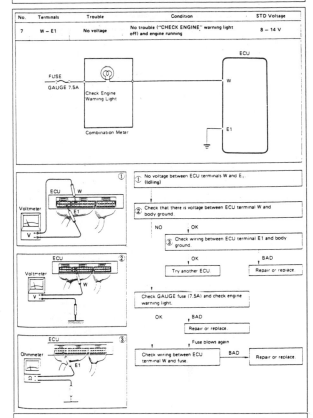

TROUBLESHOOTING THE NO. 8 TERMINAL ON THE EFI CONNECTOR (3S-FE) — 1987-88 CELICA

No.	Terminals	Trouble		Condition	STD Voltage
8	VC – E2			–	4 – 6 V
	VS – E2	No voltage	IG S/W ON	Measuring plate fully closed	4 – 5 V
	VS – E2			Measuring plate fully open	0.02 – 0.5 V
	VS – E2		Idling	–	2 – 4 V

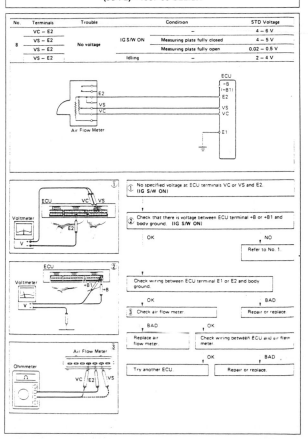

TROUBLESHOOTING THE NO. 9 TERMINAL ON THE EFI CONNECTOR (3S-FE) — 1987-88 CELICA

No.	Terminals	Trouble	Condition		STD Voltage
9	THA – E2	No voltage	IG S/W ON	Intake air temperature 20°C (68°F)	1 – 2 V

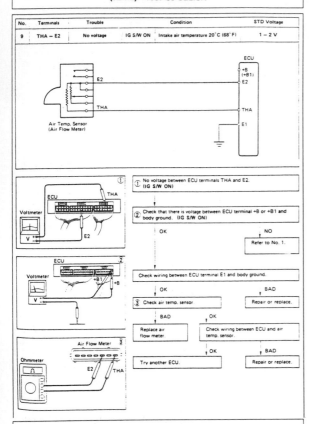

TROUBLESHOOTING THE NO. 11 TERMINAL ON THE EFI CONNECTOR (3S-FE) — 1987-88 CELICA

No.	Terminals	Trouble	Condition	STD Voltage
11	ISC1 ISC2 – E1	No voltage	IG S/W ON	9 – 14 V

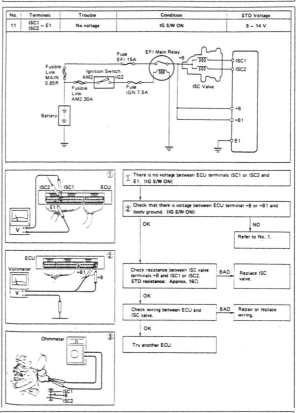

TROUBLESHOOTING THE NO. 10 TERMINAL ON THE EFI CONNECTOR (3S-FE) — 1987-88 CELICA

No.	Terminals	Trouble	Condition		STD Voltage
10	THW – E2	No voltage	IG S/W ON	Coolant temperature 80°C (176°F)	0.5 – 2.5 V

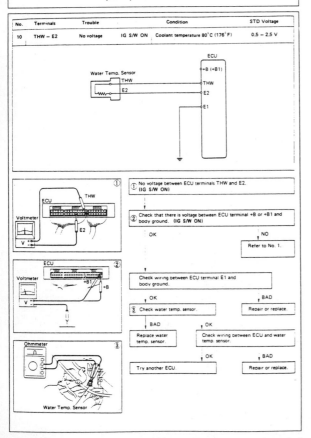

TROUBLESHOOTING THE NO. 12 TERMINAL ON THE EFI CONNECTOR (3S-FE) — 1987-88 CELICA

No.	Terminals	Trouble	Condition	STD Voltage
12	A/C – E1	No voltage	Air conditioning ON	8 – 14 V

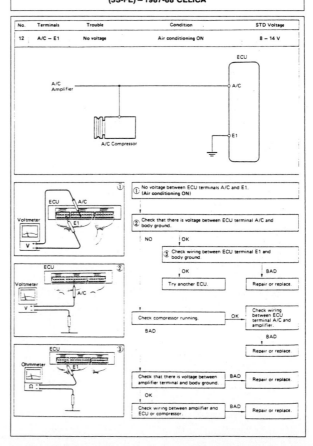

CONNECTORS OF THE ECU (3S-GE) – 1987-88 CELICA

Terminals of ECU (3S-GE)

Symbol	Terminal Name	Symbol	Terminal Name	Symbol	Terminal Name
E01	ENGINE GROUND	G1	ENGINE REVOLUTION SENSOR	L1	ECU ECT
E02	ENGINE GROUND	T	CHECK CONNECTOR	L3	ECU ECT
STA	STARTER SWITCH	G2	ENGINE REVOLUTION SENSOR	L2	ECU ECT
IGT	IGNITER	VTA	THROTTLE POSITION SENSOR	OD1	ECU ECT
STJ	COLD START INJECTOR	NE	ENGINE REVOLUTION SENSOR	A/C	A/C MAGNET SWITCH
E1	ENGINE GROUND	IDL	THROTTLE POSITION SENSOR	SPD	SPEED SENSOR
NSW	NEUTRAL START SWITCH	V-ISC	ISC-VSV	W	WARNING LIGHT
T-VIS	T-VIS VSV	IGf	IGNITER	STP	STOP LIGHT SWITCH
No. 1	INJECTOR	OX	OXYGEN SENSOR	THA	AIR TEMP. SENSOR
No. 2	INJECTOR	THW	WATER TEMP. SENSOR	VS	AIR FLOW METER
No. 3	INJECTOR	E2	SENSOR GROUND	VC	AIR FLOW METER
No. 4	INJECTOR	OX1	OXYGEN SENSOR	BATT	BATTERY
G⊖	ENGINE REVOLUTION SENSOR	E22	SENSOR GROUND	+B	MAIN RELAY
VF	CHECK CONNECTOR	E11	ENGINE GROUND	+B1	MAIN RELAY

ECU Terminals

E01		STA	STJ	NSW	No. 1	G⊖	IG	G1	G2	NE	V-ISC	IGF	THW	OX1		L1	L2		SPD	STP	THA	VS	VC	BATT	
E02		IGT	E1	T-VIS	No. 3 / No. 4	VF	T	VTA	IDL		OX	E2	E22	E11	L3	OD1	A/C	W				+B	+B1		

VOLTAGE SUPPLIED AT THE ECU WIRING CONNECTOR (3S-GE) – 1987-88 CELICA

Voltage at ECU Wiring Connectors (3S-GE)

No.	Terminals	STD Voltage	Condition	
1	+B – E1 / +B1	10 – 14	Ignition S/W ON	
2	BATT – E1	10 – 14	–	
3	IDL – E2	4 – 6	Ignition S/W ON	Throttle valve open
	VTA – E2	0.1 – 1.0		Throttle valve fully closed
		4 – 5		Throttle valve fully open
	VC – E2	4 – 6		–
4	IGT – E1	0.7 – 1.0	Cranking or Idling	
5	STA – E1	6 – 12	Cranking	
6	No. 1 / No. 2 E01 / No. 3 E02 / No. 4	9 – 14	Ignition S/W ON	
7	W – E1	8 – 14	No trouble (check engine warning light off) and engine running	
8	VC – E2	4 – 6		–
	VS – E2	4 – 5	Ignition S/W ON	Measuring plate fully closed
		0.02 – 0.5		Measuring plate fully open
		2 – 4	Idling	
9	THA – E2	1 – 2	Ignition S/W ON	Intake air temperature 20°C (68°F)
10	THW – E2	0.1 – 1.0	Ignition S/W ON	Coolant temperature 80°C (176°F)
11	A/C – E1	8 – 14	Air conditioning ON	

ECU Terminals

E01		STA	STJ	NSW	No. 1 / No. 2	G⊖	IG	G1	G2	NE	V-ISC	IG	THW	OX1		L1	L2		SPD	STP	THA	VS	VC	BATT	
E0		IGT	E2	T-VIS	No. 3 / No. 4	VF	T	VTA	IDL		OX	E2	E22	E11	L3	OD1	A/C	W				+B	+B1		

TROUBLESHOOTING THE NO. 1 TERMINAL ON THE EFI CONNECTOR (3S-GE) – 1987-88 CELICA

No.	Terminals	Trouble	Condition	STD Voltage
1	+B – E1 / +B1	No voltage	Ignition S/W ON	10 – 14 V

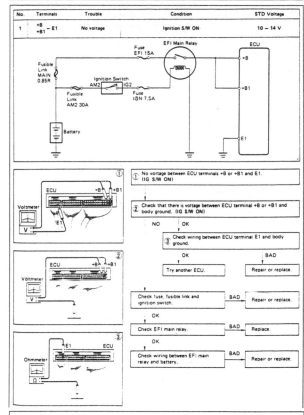

TROUBLESHOOTING THE NO. 2 TERMINAL ON THE EFI CONNECTOR (3S-GE) – 1987-88 CELICA

No.	Terminals	Trouble	Condition	STD Voltage
2	BATT – E1	No voltage	–	10 – 14 V

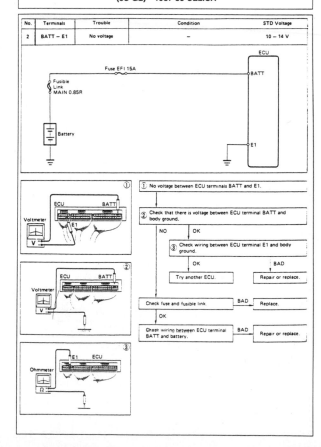

TROUBLESHOOTING THE NO. 3 TERMINAL ON THE EFI CONNECTOR (3S-GE) — 1987-88 CELICA

No.	Terminals	Trouble	Condition	STD Voltage
3	IDL – E2	No voltage	Throttle valve open	4 – 6 V
	VTA – E2	IG S/W ON	Throttle valve fully closed	0.1 – 1.0 V
			Throttle valve fully open	4 – 5 V
	VC – E2		–	4 – 6 V

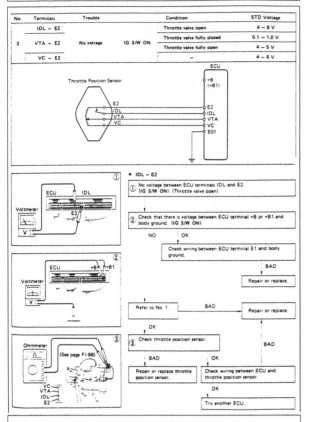

TROUBLESHOOTING THE NO. 3 TERMINAL ON THE EFI CONNECTOR (3S-GE) — 1987-88 CELICA

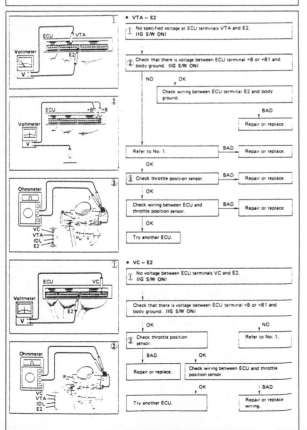

TROUBLESHOOTING THE NO. 4 TERMINAL ON THE EFI CONNECTOR (3S-GE) — 1987-88 CELICA

No.	Terminals	Trouble	Condition	STD Voltage
4	IGT – E1	No voltage	Cranking or Idling	0.7 – 1.0 V

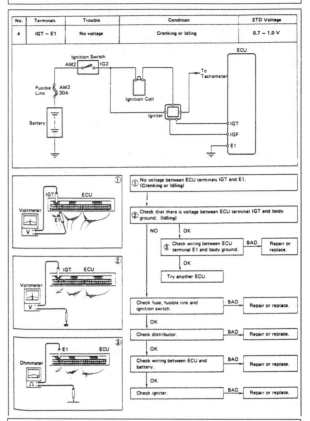

TROUBLESHOOTING THE NO. 5 TERMINAL ON THE EFI CONNECTOR (3S-GE) — 1987-88 CELICA

No.	Terminals	Trouble	Condition	STD Voltage
5	STA – E1	No voltage	Cranking	6 – 12 V

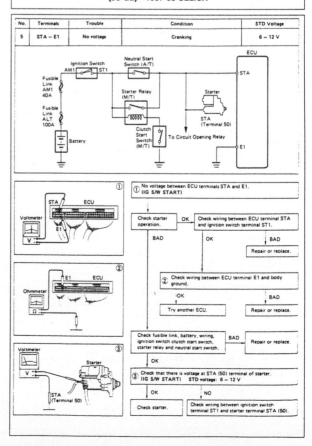

TROUBLESHOOTING THE NO. 6 TERMINAL ON THE EFI CONNECTOR (3S-GE) — 1987-88 CELICA

No.	Terminals	Trouble	Condition	STD Voltage
6	No.1 No.2 — E01 No.3 — E02 No.4	No voltage	IG S/W ON	9 – 14 V

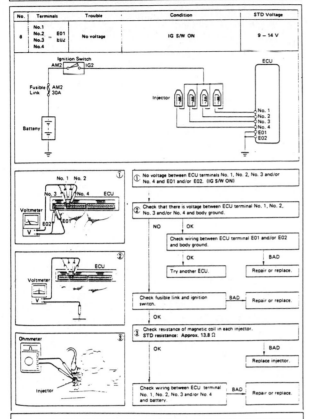

① No voltage between ECU terminals No. 1, No. 2, No. 3 and/or No. 4 and E01 and/or E02. (IG S/W ON)

② Check that there is voltage between ECU terminal No. 1, No. 2, No. 3 and/or No. 4 and body ground.

   NO / OK

Check wiring between ECU terminal E01 and/or E02 and body ground.

   OK / BAD

Try another ECU. | Repair or replace.

Check fusible link and ignition switch. — BAD — Repair or replace.

   OK

③ Check resistance of magnetic coil in each injector.
STD resistance: Approx. 13.8 Ω

   OK / BAD

Replace injector.

Check wiring between ECU terminal No. 1, No. 2, No. 3 and/or No. 4 and battery. — BAD — Repair or replace.

TROUBLESHOOTING THE NO. 7 TERMINAL ON THE EFI CONNECTOR (3S-GE) — 1987-88 CELICA

No.	Terminals	Trouble	Condition	STD Voltage
7	W – E1	No voltage	No trouble ("CHECK ENGINE" warning light off) and engine running	8 – 14 V

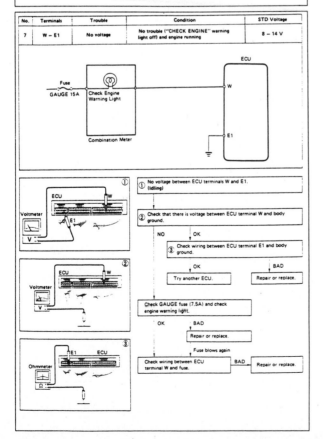

① No voltage between ECU terminals W and E1. (Idling)

② Check that there is voltage between ECU terminal W and body ground.

   NO / OK

Check wiring between ECU terminal E1 and body ground.

   OK / BAD

Try another ECU. | Repair or replace.

Check GAUGE fuse (7.5A) and check engine warning light.

   OK / BAD

Repair or replace.

   Fuse blows again

③ Check wiring between ECU terminal W and fuse. — BAD — Repair or replace.

TROUBLESHOOTING THE NO. 8 TERMINAL ON THE EFI CONNECTOR (3S-GE) — 1987-88 CELICA

No.	Terminals	Trouble	Condition	STD Voltage
8	VC – E2	No voltage	–	4 – 6 V
	VS – E2		Measuring plate fully closed	4 – 5 V
	VS – E2		Measuring plate fully open	0.02 – 0.5 V
	VS – E2		Idling	2 – 4 V

With "IG S/W ON" for the first three rows.

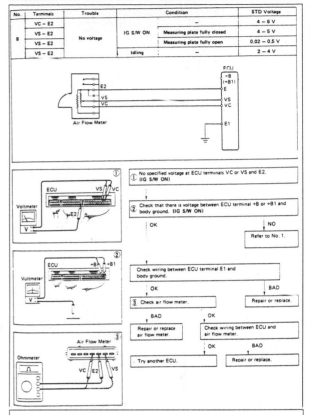

① No specified voltage at ECU terminals VC or VS and E2. (IG S/W ON)

② Check that there is voltage between ECU terminal +B or +B1 and body ground. (IG S/W ON)

   OK / NO

Refer to No. 1.

Check wiring between ECU terminal E1 and body ground.

   OK / BAD

Repair or replace.

③ Check air flow meter.

   BAD / OK

Repair or replace air flow meter. | Check wiring between ECU and air flow meter.

   OK / BAD

Try another ECU. | Repair or replace.

TROUBLESHOOTING THE NO. 9 TERMINAL ON THE EFI CONNECTOR (3S-GE) — 1987-88 CELICA

No.	Terminals	Trouble	Condition	STD Voltage
9	THA – E2	No voltage	IG S/W ON	Intake air temperature 20°C (68°F)	1 – 2 V

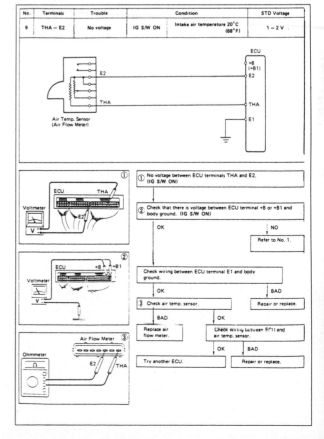

① No voltage between ECU terminals THA and E2. (IG S/W ON)

② Check that there is voltage between ECU terminal +B or +B1 and body ground. (IG S/W ON)

   OK / NO

Refer to No. 1.

Check wiring between ECU terminal E1 and body ground.

   OK / BAD

Repair or replace.

③ Check air temp. sensor.

   BAD / OK

Replace air flow meter. | Check wiring between ECU and air temp. sensor.

   OK / BAD

Try another ECU. | Repair or replace.

TROUBLESHOOTING THE NO. 10 TERMINAL ON THE EFI CONNECTOR (3S-GE) — 1987-88 CELICA

No.	Terminals	Trouble	Condition	STD Voltage
10	THW – E2	No voltage	IG S/W ON · Coolant temperature 80°C (176°F)	0.1 – 1.0 V

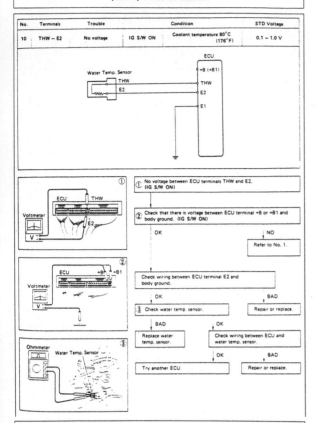

① No voltage between ECU terminals THW and E2. (IG S/W ON)

② Check that there is voltage between ECU terminal +B or +B1 and body ground. (IG S/W ON)

OK — NO → Refer to No. 1.

Check wiring between ECU terminal E2 and body ground.

OK — BAD → Repair or replace.

③ Check water temp. sensor.

BAD → Replace water temp. sensor.

OK → Check wiring between ECU and water temp. sensor.

OK — BAD → Try another ECU. / Repair or replace.

ELECTRONIC COMPONENT LOCATIONS — 1987-88 CELICA

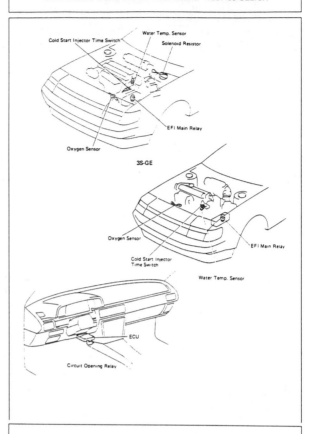

3S-GE

TROUBLESHOOTING THE NO. 11 TERMINAL ON THE EFI CONNECTOR (3S-GE) — 1987-88 CELICA

No	Terminal	Trouble	Condition	STD Voltage
11	A/C – E1	No voltage	Air conditioning ON	8 – 14 V

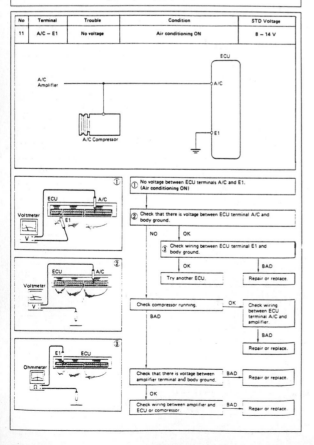

① No voltage between ECU terminals A/C and E1. (Air conditioning ON)

② Check that there is voltage between ECU terminal A/C and body ground.

NO — OK

③ Check wiring between ECU terminal E1 and body ground.

OK — BAD → Try another ECU. / Repair or replace.

Check compressor running.

OK → Check wiring between ECU terminal A/C and amplifier.

BAD

BAD → Repair or replace.

③ Check that there is voltage between amplifier terminal and body ground.

BAD → Repair or replace.

OK

Check wiring between amplifier and ECU or compressor.

BAD → Repair or replace.

TESTING THE OXYGEN SENSOR — 1987-88 CELICA

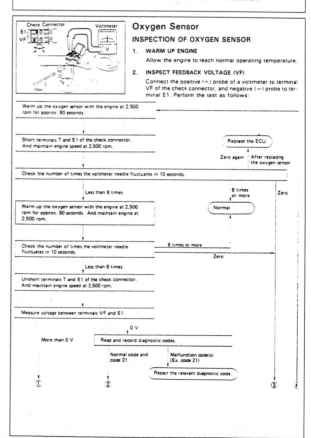

Oxygen Sensor
INSPECTION OF OXYGEN SENSOR

1. **WARM UP ENGINE**
   Allow the engine to reach normal operating temperature.

2. **INSPECT FEEDBACK VOLTAGE (VF)**
   Connect the positive (+) probe of a voltmeter to terminal VF of the check connector, and negative (–) probe to terminal E1. Perform the test as follows:

Warm up the oxygen sensor with the engine at 2,500 rpm for approx. 90 seconds.

Short terminals T and E1 of the check connector. And maintain engine speed at 2,500 rpm.

Replace the ECU.

Zero again | After replacing the oxygen sensor

Check the number of times the voltmeter needle fluctuates in 10 seconds.

Less than 8 times | 8 times or more | Zero

Warm up the oxygen sensor with the engine at 2,500 rpm for approx. 90 seconds. And maintain engine at 2,500 rpm.

Normal

Check the number of times the voltmeter needle fluctuates in 10 seconds.

8 times or more

Less than 8 times | Zero

Unshort terminals T and E1 of the check connector. And maintain engine speed at 2,500 rpm.

Measure voltage between terminals VF and E1.

0 V

More than 0 V | Read and record diagnostic codes.

Normal code and code 21 | Malfunction code(s) (Ex. code 21)

Repair the relevant diagnostic code.

① ② ③ ④

TESTING THE OXYGEN SENSOR (CONT.) – 1987-88 CELICA

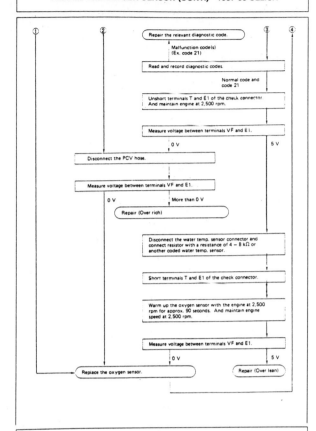

```
①        ②              Repair the relevant diagnostic code.        ③        ④
                                    │
                        Malfunction code(s)
                        (Ex. code 21)
                        Read and record diagnostic codes.
                                    │
                        Normal code and
                        code 21
                        Unshort terminals T and E1 of the check connector.
                        And maintain engine at 2,500 rpm.
                                    │
                        Measure voltage between terminals VF and E1.
                       0 V │              │ 5 V
    Disconnect the PCV hose.
                                    │
                        Measure voltage between terminals VF and E1.
            0 V │          │ More than 0 V
                        ( Repair (Over rich) )
                                    │
                        Disconnect the water temp. sensor connector and
                        connect resistor with a resistance of 4 – 8 kΩ or
                        another coded water temp. sensor.
                                    │
                        Short terminals T and E1 of the check connector.
                                    │
                        Warm up the oxygen sensor with the engine at 2,500
                        rpm for approx. 90 seconds.  And maintain engine
                        speed at 2,500 rpm.
                                    │
                        Measure voltage between terminals VF and E1.
                       0 V │              │ 5 V
    ( Replace the oxygen sensor. )                     ( Repair (Over lean) )
```

INSPECTING THE VOLTAGE AT THE ECU WIRING CONNECTOR 1987-88 CELICA

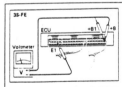

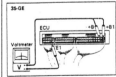

Electronic Controlled Unit (ECU)

INSPECTION OF ECU

1. **INSPECT VOLTAGE OF ECU**

   NOTE: The EFI circuit can be checked by measuring the and voltage at the wiring connectors of the ECU.

   Check the voltage between each terminal of the wiring connectors.

   - Turn the ignition switch.
   - Measure the voltage at each terminal.

   NOTE:
   - Perform all voltage measurements with the connectors connected.
   - Verify that the battery voltage is 11V or more when the ignition switch is ON.

INSPECTING THE VOLTAGE AT THE ECU WIRING CONNECTOR (3S-FE) – 1987-88 CELICA

Voltage at ECU Wiring Connectors (3S-FE)

Terminals		Condition	STD voltage
+B +B1 – E1		Ignition S/W ON	10 – 14
BATT – E1		–	10 – 14
IDL – E1		Throttle valve open	8 – 14
Psw – E1	Ignition S/W ON	Throttle valve fully closed	8 – 14
IGT – E1		Idling	0.7 – 1.0
STA – E1		Cranking	6 – 12
No 10 E01 No. 20 E02		Ignition S/W ON	9 – 14
W – E1		No trouble (check engine warning light off) and engine running	8 – 14
VC – E2		–	4 – 6
VS – E2		Measuring plate fully closed	4 – 5
VS – E2	Ignition S/W ON	Measuring plate fully open	0.02 – 0.5
		Idling	2 – 4
THA – E2	Ignition S/W ON	Intake air temperatur 20°C (68°F)	1 – 3
THW – E2	Ignition S/W ON	Coolant temperature 80°C (176°F)	0.5 – 2.5
ISC1 ISC2 – E1		Ignition S/W ON	9 – 14
A/C – E1	Ignition S/W ON	Air conditioning ON	8 – 14
T – E1	Ignition S/W ON	Check connector T – E1 not short	10 – 14
	Ignition S/W ON	Check connector T – E1 short	0

ECU Terminals

E01	No. 10	STA	VF	NSW		ISC1	W	T	IDL	IGF	G⊖	G		NE		VC	VS	THA	BATT	+B
E02	No. 20	IGT	E1			ISC2		A/C	E2	OX						E21	STP	SPD	ELS	+B

INSPECTING THE VOLTAGE AT THE ECU WIRING CONNECTOR (3S-GE) – 1987-88 CELICA

Voltage at ECU Wiring Connectors (3S-GE)

Terminals		Condition	STD voltage
+B +B1 – E1		Ignition S/W ON	10 – 14
BATT – E1		–	10 – 14
IDL – E2		Throttle valve open	4 – 6
VTA – E2		Throttle valve fully closed	0.1 – 1.0
	Ignition S/W ON	Throttle valve fully open	4 – 5
VC – E2		–	4 – 6
IGT – E1		Cranking or Idling	0.7 – 1.0
STA – E1		Cranking	6 – 12
No. 1 No. 2 E01 No. 3 E02 No. 4		Ignition S/W ON	9 – 14
W – E1		No trouble (check engine warning light off) and engine running	8 – 14
VC – E2		–	4 – 6
VS – E2		Measuring plate fylly closed	4 – 5
VS – E2	Ignition S/W ON	Measuring plate fully open	0.02 – 0.5
		Idling	2 – 4
THA – E2	Ignition S/W ON	Intake air temperature 20°C (68°F)	1 – 2
THW – E2	Ignition S/W ON	Coolant temperature 80°C (176°F)	0.1 – 1.0
A/C – E1	Ignition S/W ON	Air conditioning ON	8 – 14
T-VIS – E1		Idling	0 – 2
		More than 4,400 rpm	10 – 14
T – E1	Ignition S/W ON	Check connector T – E1 not short	4 – 6
		Check connector T – E1 short	0

ECU Terminals

E01	STA	STJ	NSW		No. 1	No. 2	G1	G2	NE	V- ISC	IGF	THW	OX1		L1	L2		SPD	STP	THA	VS	VC	BATT
E02	IGT	E1	T- VIS		No. 3	No. 4		VF	T	IVTA	IDL		OX2	E22	E11	L3	OD1	A/C	W			+B	+B1

INSPECTING THE RESISTANCE AT THE ECU WIRING CONNECTOR (3S-FE) – 1987-88 CELICA

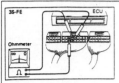

2. **INSPECT RESISTANCE OF ECU**
   CAUTION:
   - Do not touch the ECU terminals.
   - The tester probe should be inserted into the wiring connector from the wiring side.

   Check the resistance between each terminal of the wiring connectors.
   - Disconnect the connectors from the ECU.
   - Measure the resistance at each terminal.

Resistance of ECU Wiring Connectors (3S-FE)

Terminals	Condition	Resistance (Ω)
IDL – E1	Throttle valve open	∞
	Throttle valve fully closed	0
PSW – E1	Throttle valve fully open	0
	Throttle valve fully closed	∞
VS – E2	Measuring plate fully closed	200 – 600
	Measuring plate fully open	200 – 1,200
THA – E2	Intake air temperature 20°C (68°F)	2,000 – 3,000
THW – E2	Coolant temperature 80°C (176°F)	200 – 400
G – G⊖	–	140 – 180
NE – G⊖	–	140 – 180

ECU Terminals

E01 No.10	STA	VF	NSW	ISC1	W	T		IDL	IGF	G⊖	G		NE			VC	VS	THA	BATT
E02 No.20	IGT	E1		ISC2		A/C	E2	OX		PSW	THW					E21	STP	SPD	ELS	+B

INSPECTING THE RESISTANCE AT THE ECU WIRING CONNECTOR (3S-GE) – 1987-88 CELICA

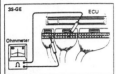

Resistance of ECU Wiring Connectors (3S-GE)

Terminals	Condition	Resistance (Ω)
IDL – E2	Throttle valve open	∞
	Throttle valve fully closed	Less than 2,300
VTA – E2	Throttle valve fully open	3,000 – 10,000
	Throttle valve fully closed	200 – 800
VS – E2	Measuring plate fully closed	200 – 600
	Measuring plate fully open	200 – 1,200
THA – E2	Intake air temperature 20°C (68°F)	2,000 – 3,000
THW – E2	Coolant temperature 80°C (176°F)	200 – 400
G1, G2 – G⊖	–	140 – 180
NE – G⊖	–	140 – 180

ECU Terminals

E01	STA	STJ	NSW	No.1	No.2	G⊖	G1	G2	NE	V-ISC	IGF	THW	OX1			L1	L2		SPD	STP	THA	VS	VC	BATT
E02	IGT	E1	V-IS	No.3	No.4	VF	T	VTA	IDL		OX	E2	E22	E11	L3	OD1	A/C	W					+B	+B1

EFI WIRING SCHEMATIC – 1985 COROLLA (RWD)

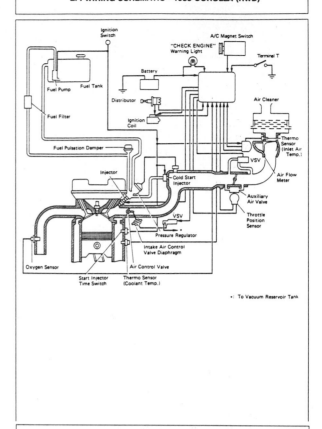

*: To Vacuum Reservoir Tank

DIAGNOSIS CODES – 1985 COROLLA (RWD)

Code No.	Number of blinks "CHECK ENGINE"	System	Diagnosis	Trouble area
1	ON 0.5 ON ON ON OFF OFF OFF OFF 4.5 (Seconds)	Normal	This appears when none of the other codes (2 thru 11) are identified	–
2	0.5 (Seconds)	Air flow meter signal	• Open circuit in Vc, or Vs – E2 short circuit • Open circuit in E2 or Vc – Vs short circuit.	1. Air flow meter circuit 2. Air flow meter 3. ECU
3		Ignition signal	No signal from igniter four times in succession.	1. Ignition circuit (+B, IGt, IGf) 2. Igniter 3. ECU
4		Water thermo sensor signal	Open or short circuit in coolant temperature sensor signal.	1. Coolant Temp. sensor circuit 2. Coolant Temp. sensor 3. ECU
5		Ox sensor signal	Open circuit in Ox Sensor signal (only lean indication)	1. Ox sensor circuit 2. Ox sensor 3. ECU
6		RPM signal	• No Ne, G signal to ECU within several seconds after engine is cranked. • No Ne, signal to ECU within several seconds after engine reaches 1,000 rpm.	1. Distributor circuit 2. Distributor 3. Igniter 4. Starter signal circuit 5. ECU
7		Throttle position sensor signal	Open or short circuit in throttle position sensor signal.	1. Throttle position sensor circuit 2. Throttle position sensor 3. ECU
8		Intake air thermo sensor signal	Open or short circuit in intake air temperature sensor.	1. Air thermo sensor circuit 2. ECU
10		Starter signal	No STA signal to ECU when engine is running over 800 rpm.	1. Starter relay circuit 2. IG switch circuit (starter) 3. IG Switch 4. ECU
11		Switch signal	Air conditioner switch ON during diagnosis check.	1. Air con. S/W 2. ECU

NOTE:
- There is no diagnosis code No. 9.
- Diagnosis code No. 10 will be indicated if the vehicle is push started.

INSPECTION OF THE DIAGNOSIS CIRCUIT—1985 COROLLA (RWD)

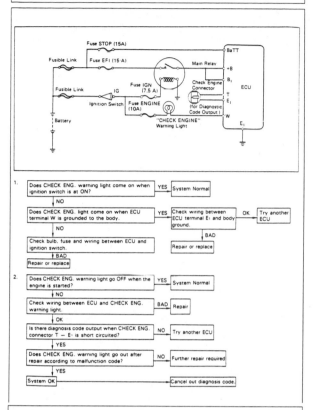

1.
| Does CHECK ENG. warning light come on when ignition switch is at ON? | YES → System Normal |

↓ NO

| Does CHECK ENG. light come on when ECU terminal W is grounded to the body. | YES → Check wiring between ECU terminal E₁ and body ground. | OK → Try another ECU |

↓ NO   ↓ BAD

| Check bulb, fuse and wiring between ECU and ignition switch. | | Repair or replace |

↓ BAD

| Repair or replace |

2.
| Does CHECK ENG. warning light go OFF when the engine is started? | YES → System Normal |

↓ NO

| Check wiring between ECU and CHECK ENG. warning light. | BAD → Repair |

↓ OK

| Is there diagnosis code output when CHECK ENG. connector T — E₁ is short circuited? | NO → Try another ECU |

↓ YES

| Does CHECK ENG. warning light go out after repair according to malfunction code? | NO → Further repair required |

↓ YES

| System OK | ————→ | Cancel out diagnosis code. |

TROUBLESHOOTING THE EFI SYSTEM WITH A VOLT/OHMMETER—1985 COROLLA (RWD)

PREPARATION OF TROUBLESHOOTING

1. Remove the kick panel on the front passenger's side.
2. Remove the ECU with the wire harness.

EFI SYSTEM CHECK PROCEDURE

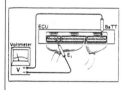

NOTE:
1. The EFI circuit can be checked by measuring the resistance and voltage at the wiring connectors of the ECU.
2. Perform all voltage measurement with the connectors connected.
3. Verify that the battery voltage is 11 V or above when the ignition switch is at ON.

Using a voltmeter with high impedance (10 kΩ/V minimum), measure the voltage at each terminal of the wiring connector.

NOTE: If there is any problem, see TROUBLESHOOTING FOR EFI ELECTRONIC CIRCUIT WITH VOLT/OHMMETER.

Voltage at ECU wiring connectors

No.	Terminals	STD voltage	Condition	
1	BaTT-E₁	—		
	+B₁ — E₁	10 — 14	Ignition S/W ON	
	+B — E₁			
2	IDL — E₂₁	10 — 14	Ignition S/W ON	Throttle valve open
	VTA — E₂₁	0.1 — 1.0		Throttle valve fully closed
		4 — 5		Throttle valve fully open
	Vcc — E₂₁	4 — 6		—
3	+B₁ — E₂	10 — 14	Ignition S/W ON	—
	Vc — E₂	6 — 10		—
	Vs — E₂	0.5 — 2.5		Measuring plate fully closed
		5 — 10	Engine running	Measuring plate fully open
		2 — 8	Idling	
4	No. 10 — E₁ No. 20 — E₁	10 — 14	Ignition S/W ON	
5	THA — E₂	1 — 3	Ignition S/W ON	Intake air temperature 20°C (68°F)
6	THW — E₂	0.1 — 1.0	Ignition S/W ON	Coolant temperature 80°C (176°F)
7	STA — E₁	6 — 14	Ignition S/W ST position	
8	IGt — E₁	0.7 — 1.0	Idling	

ECU Connectors

| E₀₁ | No.10 | STA | Vf | | W | T | IDL | IGf | G | ⊕G | ⊕ | Ne | | Vc | Vs | THA | BaTT | +B₁ |
| E₀₂ | No.20 | IGt | E₁ | S/TH | | VISC | | A/C | E₂ | Ox | Vcc | VTA | THW | | E₂₁ | | SPD | +B |

TROUBLESHOOTING THE EFI SYSTEM WITH A VOLT/OHMMETER (CONT.)—1985 COROLLA (RWD)

NOTE: The following troubleshooting procedures are designed for inspection of each separate system and, therefore, the actual procedure may vary somewhat. However, troubleshooting should be performed by refering to the inspection methods described.

Before beginning inspection, it is best to first make a simple check of the fuses, fusible links and the condition of the connectors.

The following troubleshooting procedures are based on the supposition that the trouble lies in either a short or open circuit in a component outside the computer or a short circuit within the computer.

If engine trouble occurs eventhough proper operating voltage is detected in the computer connector, it can be assumed that the computer is at fault and should be replaced.

LOCATION OF FUSE AND FUSIBLE LINK

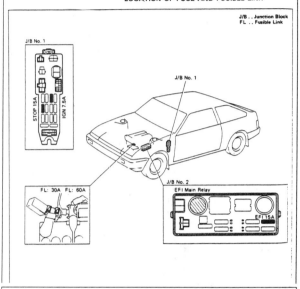

J/B .. Junction Block
FL .. Fusible Link

TROUBLESHOOTING THE NO. 1 TERMINAL ON THE EFI CONNECTOR 1985 COROLLA (RWD)

No.	Terminals	Trouble	Condition	STD voltage
1	BaTT — E₁	No voltage	—	10 — 14
	+B₁ — E₁	No voltage	Ignition switch ON	10 — 14
	+B			

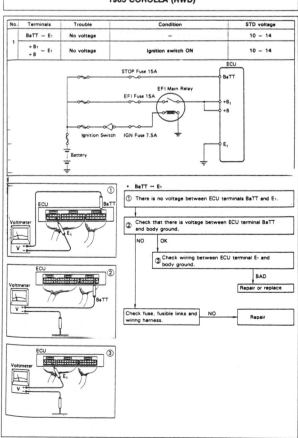

• BaTT — E₁

① There is no voltage between ECU terminals BaTT and E₁.

↓

② Check that there is voltage between ECU terminal BaTT and body ground.

NO ↓   ↓ OK

③ Check wiring between ECU terminal E₁ and body ground.

↓ BAD

Repair or replace.

Check fuse, fusible links and wiring harness. | NO → Repair |

TROUBLESHOOTING THE NO. 1 TERMINAL ON THE EFI CONNECTOR
1985 COROLLA (RWD)

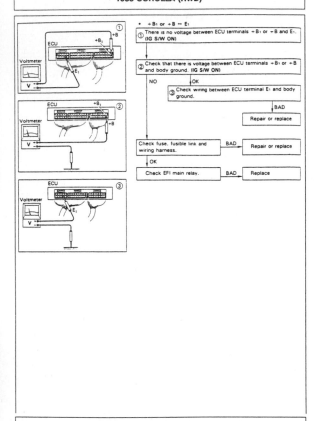

TROUBLESHOOTING THE NO. 2 TERMINAL ON THE EFI CONNECTOR
1985 COROLLA (RWD)

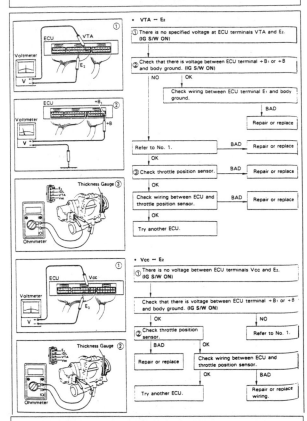

TROUBLESHOOTING THE NO. 2 TERMINAL ON THE EFI CONNECTOR
1985 COROLLA (RWD)

No.	Terminals	Trouble		Condition	STD voltage
	IDL — E21			Throttle valve open	10 — 14
2	VTA — E21	No voltage	Ignition switch ON	Throttle valve fully closed	0.1 — 1.0
				Throttle valve fully open	4 — 5
	Vcc — E21			—	4 — 6

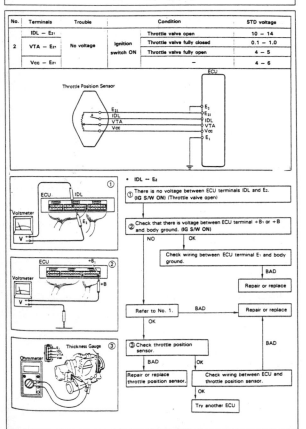

TROUBLESHOOTING THE NO. 3 TERMINAL ON THE EFI CONNECTOR
1985 COROLLA (RWD)

No.	Terminal	Trouble	Condition		STD Voltage
	+B1 — E2		Ignition switch ON	—	10 — 14V
	Vc — E2			—	6 — 10V
3	Vs — E2	No voltage		Measuring plate fully closed	0.5 — 2.5V
	Vs — E2		Engine running	Measuring plate fully open	5 — 10V
	Vs — E2		Iding	—	2 — 8V

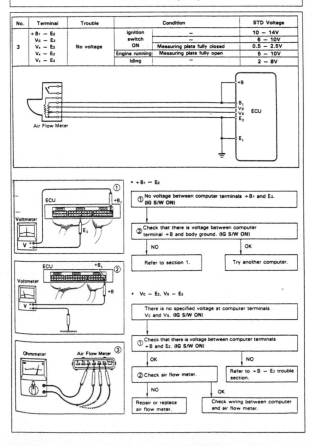

TROUBLESHOOTING THE NO. 4 TERMINAL ON THE EFI CONNECTOR
1985 COROLLA (RWD)

No.	Terminals	Trouble	Condition		STD Voltage
4	No. 10 — E₁ / No. 20 — E₁	No voltage	Ignition switch ON		10 — 14V

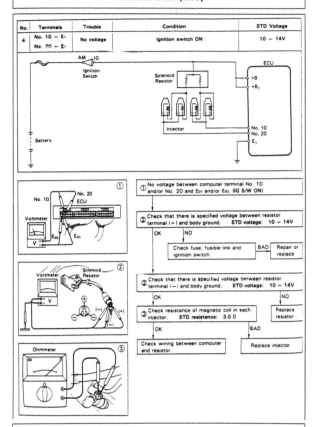

TROUBLESHOOTING THE NO. 6 TERMINAL ON THE EFI CONNECTOR
1985 COROLLA (RWD)

No.	Terminals	Trouble	Condition		STD voltage
6	THW — E₂	No voltage	Ignition switch ON	Coolant temperature 80°C (176°F)	0.1 — 1.0 V

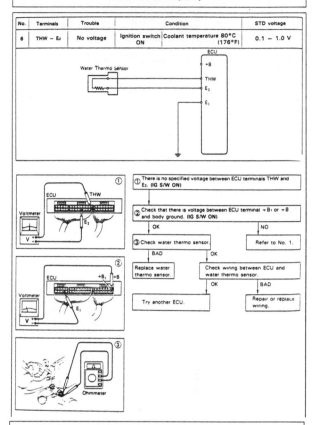

TROUBLESHOOTING THE NO. 5 TERMINAL ON THE EFI CONNECTOR
1985 COROLLA (RWD)

No.	Terminals	Trouble	Condition		STD voltage
5	THA — E₂	No voltage	Ignition switch ON	Intake air temperature 20 °C (68 °F)	1 — 3 V

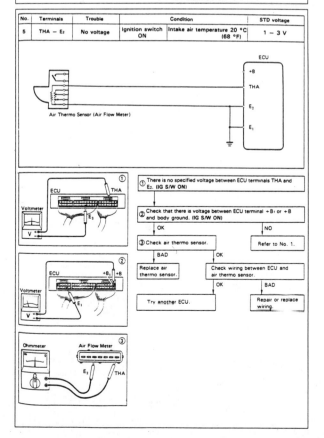

TROUBLESHOOTING THE NO. 7 TERMINAL ON THE EFI CONNECTOR
1985 COROLLA (RWD)

No.	Terminals	Trouble	Condition	STD voltage
7	STA — E₁	No voltage	Ignition switch ST position	6 — 14 V

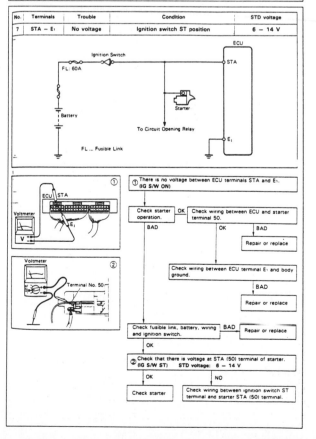

TROUBLESHOOTING THE NO. 8 TERMINAL ON THE EFI CONNECTOR 1985 COROLLA (RWD)

No.	Terminals	Trouble	Condition	STD voltage
8	IGt – E₁	No voltage	Idling	0.7 – 1.0 V

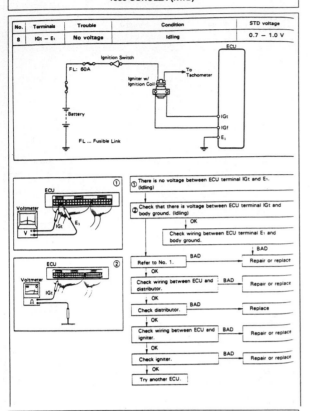

ELECTRONIC COMPONENT LOCATIONS – 1985 COROLLA (RWD)

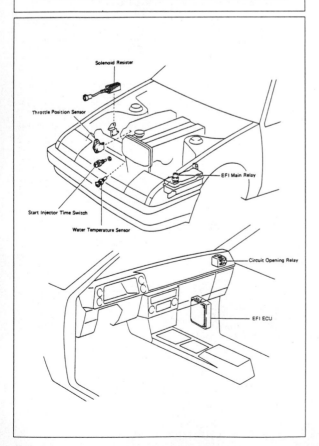

INSPECTION OF THE ELECTRONIC CONTROL UNIT – 1985 COROLLA (RWD)

INSPECTION OF ECU
Connectors of ECU

Symbol	Terminal	Symbol	Terminal	Symbol	Terminal
E₀₁	Engine ground (Power)	T	Check connector		—
E₀₂	Engine ground (Power)		—		—
No. 10	No.3, 4 injector	IDL	Throttle sensor		—
No. 20	No.1, 2 injector	A/C	A/C Magnet clutch		—
STA	Starter switch	IGf	Igniter	VC	Air flow meter
IGt	Igniter	E₂₁	Sensor earth	E₂	Sensor earth
VF	Check connector	G–	Engine revolution sensor	VS	Air flow meter
E₁	Engine ground	Ox	Oxygen sensor		—
	—	G+	Engine revolution sensor	THA	Inlet air temp. sensor
S/TH	Vacuum switching valve	Vcc	Throttle sensor	SPD	Speedometer
				BaTT	Bettey
VISC	Vacuum switching valve	VTA	Throttle sensor		—
W	Warning light	NE	Engine revolution sensor	+B1	Main relay
		THW	Water temp. sensor	+B	Main relay

ECU Connectors

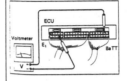

1. **MEASURE VOLTAGE OF ECU**
   (a) Remove the kick panel on the front passenger's side.
   (b) Turn the ignition switch ON.
   (c) Using a voltmeter, measure the voltage at each terminal of the wiring connector.
   CAUTION:
   - Perform all voltage measurements with the connectors connected.
   - Verify that the battery voltage is 11 V or above when the ignition switch is ON.
   - The testing probes MUST NOT make contact with the ECU Vᵣ terminal.

INSPECTING THE VOLTAGE AT THE ECU WIRING CONNECTOR 1985 COROLLA (RWD)

Terminals	STD voltage	Condition	
BaTT – E₁		—	
+B – E₁	10 – 14	IG S/W ON	
+B₁ – E₁			
IDL – E₁	10 – 14	IG S/W ON	Throttle valve open
Vc – E₂	6 – 10	IG S/W ON	—
	0.5 – 2.5		Measuring plate fully closed
Vs – E₂	5 – 10	Engine running	Measuring plate fully open
	2 – 8	Idling	
THA – E₂	1 – 3	IG S/W ON	Intake air temperature 20°C (68°F)
THW – E₂	0.1 – 1.0	IG S/W ON	Coolant temperature 80°C (176°F)
STA – E₁	6 – 14	IG S/W ST position	
No. 10 – E₁ / No. 20 – E₁	10 – 14	IG S/W ON	
IGt – E₁	0.7 – 1.0	Idling	
T – E₁	10 – 14	IG S/W ON	Check connector T ↔ E₁ not short
	0		Check connector T ↔ E₂ short
A/C – E₁	10 – 13	IG S/W ON	A/C switch ON
	0		A/C switch OFF
W – E₁	0	IG S/W ON	
	10 – 13	Engine start	
S/TH – E₁	0 – 2	Idling	
	10 – 14	More than 4,350 rpm	
VTA – E₂	0.1 – 1.0	IG S/W ON	Throttle valve fully closed
	4 – 5		Throttle valve fully open
Vcc – E₂	4 – 6	IG S/W ON	

2. **MEASURE RESISTANCE OF ECU**
   (a) Remove the kick panel on the front passenger's side.
   (b) Disconnect the wiring connectors from the ECU.
   (c) Using an ohmmeter, measure the resistance between each terminal of the wiring connectors.
   CAUTION: Do not touch the ECU terminals. The tester probe should be inserted into the wiring connector from the wiring side.

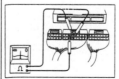

Resistances at ECU Wiring Connectors

Terminals	Condition	Resistance
IDL – E₂	Throttle valve open	Infinity
	Throttle valve fully closed	Less than 2.3 kΩ
VTA – E₂	Throttle valve fully open	3.3 – 10 kΩ
	Throttle valve fully closed	0.2 – 0.8 kΩ
Vcc – E₂	—	3 – 7 kΩ
THA – E₂	Intake air temperature 20°C (68°F)	2 – 3 kΩ
THW – E₂	Coolant temperature 80°C (176°F)	0.2 – 0.4 kΩ
G₁ – G ⊝	—	140 – 180 Ω

EFI WIRING SCHEMATIC—1986 COROLLA (RWD)

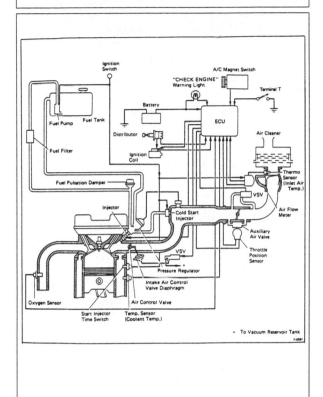

INSPECTION OF THE DIAGNOSIS CIRCUIT—1986 COROLLA (RWD)

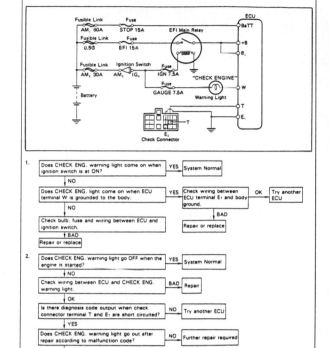

1.

Does CHECK ENG. warning light come on when ignition switch is at ON?	YES → System Normal
↓ NO	
Does CHECK ENG. light come on when ECU terminal W is grounded to the body.	YES → Check wiring between ECU terminal E₁ and body ground.	OK → Try another ECU
↓ NO	↓ BAD
Check bulb, fuse and wiring between ECU and ignition switch.	Repair or replace
↓ BAD	
Repair or replace	

2.

Does CHECK ENG. warning light go OFF when the engine is started?	YES → System Normal
↓ NO	
Check wiring between ECU and CHECK ENG. warning light.	BAD → Repair
↓ OK	
Is there diagnosis code output when check connector terminal T and E₁ are short circuited?	NO → Try another ECU
↓ YES	
Does CHECK ENG. warning light go out after repair according to malfunction code?	NO → Further repair required
↓ YES	
System OK	→ Cancel out diagnosis code.

DIAGNOSIS CODES—1986 COROLLA (RWD)

Code No.	Number of blinks "CHECK ENGINE"	System	Diagnosis	Trouble area
1	ON OFF... (Seconds)	Normal	This appears when none of the other codes (2 thru 11) are identified	
2		Air flow meter signal	• Open circuit in Vc, Vs, Vb or Es • Short circuit in Vc.	1. Air flow meter circuit 2. Air flow meter 3. ECU
3		Ignition signal	No signal from igniter four times in succession.	1. Ignition circuit (+B, IGf) 2. Igniter 3. ECU
4		Water temp. sensor signal	Open or short circuit in coolant temperature sensor signal.	1. Coolant Temp. sensor circuit 2. Coolant Temp. sensor 3. ECU
5		Oxygen sensor signal	Open circuit in Oxygen Sensor signal (only lean indication)	1. Oxgen sensor circuit 2. Oxygen sensor 3. ECU
6		RPM signal	No Ne, G signal to ECU within several seconds after engine is cranked.	1. Distributor circuit 2. Distributor 3. Igniter 4. Starter signal circuit 5. ECU
7		Throttle position sensor signal	Open or short circuit in throttle position sensor signal.	1. Throttle position sensor circuit 2. Throttle position sensor 3. ECU
8		Intake air temp. sensor signal	Open or short circuit in intake air temperature sensor.	1. Air temp. sensor circuit 2. ECU
10		Starter signal	No STA signal to ECU when vehicle is stopped and engine is running over 800 rpm.	1. Starter relay circuit 2. IG switch circuit (starter) 3. IG Switch 4. ECU
11		Switch signal	Air conditioner switch ON or idle switch OFF during diagnosis check.	1. Air con. S/W 2. ECU 3. Idle S/W

NOTE: • There is no diagnosis code No. 9.
• Diagnosis code No. 10 will be indicated if the vehicle is push started.

TROUBLE SHOOTING THE EFI SYSTEM WITH A VOLT/OHMMETER 1986 COROLLA (RWD)

1. Remove the kick panel on the front passenger's side.
2. Remove the ECU with the wire harness.

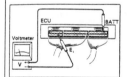

EFI SYSTEM CHECK PROCEDURE

NOTE:
1. The EFI circuit can be checked by measuring the resistance and voltage at the wiring connectors of the ECU.
2. Perform all voltage measurements with the connectors connected.
3. Verify that the battery voltage is 11V or above when the ignition switch is ON.

Using a voltmeter with high impedance (10 kΩ/V minimum), measure the voltage at each terminal of the wiring connector.

NOTE: If there is any problem, see TROUBLESHOOTING FOR EFI ELECTRONIC CIRCUIT WITH VOLT/OHMMETER.

Connectors of ECU

Symbol	Terminal	Symbol	Terminal	Symbol	Terminal
E₀₁	Engine ground (Power)	T	Check connector	—	—
E₀₂	Engine ground (Power)	—	—	—	—
No. 10	No. 3, 4 injector	IDL	Throttle position sensor	—	—
No. 20	No. 1, 2 injector	A/C	A/C Magnet clutch	Vc	Air flow meter
STA	Starter switch	IGf	Igniter	E₂₁	Sensor ground
IGt	Igniter	E₂	Sensor ground	Vs	Air flow meter
Vf	Check connector	G ⊖	Engine revolution sensor	THA	Inlet air temp. sensor
E₁	Engine ground	Ox	Oxygen sensor	SPD	Speedometer sensor
—	—	G ⊕	Engine revolution sensor	BaTT	Battery
S/TH	VSV (T-VIS)	Vcc	Throttle position sensor	—	—
V-ISC	VSV (Idle-up)	VTA	Throttle position sensor	+B₁	EFI main relay
W	Warning light	Ne	Engine revolution sensor	+B	EFI main relay
—	—	THW	Water temp. sensor		

ECU Connectors

E₀₁	No. 10	STA	Vf		W	T	IDL	IGf	G⊖ G⊕		Ne		Vc	Vs	THA BaTT	+B₁
E₀₂	No. 20	IGt	E₁	S/TH	V-ISC	A/C	E₂	Ox	Vcc	VTA THW			E₂₁		SPD	+B

TROUBLESHOOTING THE EFI SYSTEM WITH A VOLT/OHMMETER—1986 COROLLA (RWD)

Voltage at ECU wiring connectors

No.	Terminals	STD voltage	Condition	
1	BaTT – E₁	10 – 14	–	
	+B₁		Ignition S/W ON	
	+B – E₁			
2	IDL – E₂	10 – 14	Throttle valve open	
	VTA – E₂	0.1 – 1.0	Ignition S/W ON	Throttle valve fully closed
		4 – 5		Throttle valve fully open
	Vcc – E₂	4 – 6	–	
	+B₁ – E₂	10 – 14	–	
3	Vc – E₂	6 – 10	Ignition S/W ON	
	Vs – E₂	0.5 – 2.5		Measuring plate fully closed
		5 – 10	Engine running	Measuring plate fully open
		2 – 8	Idling	–
4	No.10 – E₁ No.20	10 – 14	Ignition S/W ON	
5	THA – E₂	1 – 3	Ignition S/W ON	Intake air temperature 20°C (68°F)
6	THW – E₂	0.1 – 1.0	Ignition S/W ON	Coolant temperature 80°C (176°F)
7	STA – E₁	6 – 14	Ignition S/W ST position	
8	IGt – E₁	0.7 – 1.0	Idling	
9	A/C – E₁	10 – 14	Air conditioning ON	

ECU Connectors

E₀₁	No. 10	STA	Vf		W	T	IDL	IGt	G⊖	G⊕		Ne		Vc	Vs	THA	+B₁	
E₀₂	No. 20	IGt	E₁	S/TH	V-ISC		A/C	E₂	Ox	Vcc	VTA	THW		E₁₁		SPD	+B	

TROUBLESHOOTING THE EFI SYSTEM WITH A VOLT/OHMMETER (CONT.)—1986 COROLLA (RWD)

NOTE: The following troubleshooting procedures are designed for inspection of each separate system and, therefore, the actual procedure may vary somewhat. However, troubleshooting should be performed refering to the inspection methods described in this manual.

Before beginning inspection, it is best to first make a simple check of the fuses, fusible links and the condition of the connectors.

The following troubleshooting procedures are based on the supposition that the trouble lies in either a short or open circuit in a component outside the computer or a short circuit within the computer.

If engine trouble occurs even though proper operating voltage is detected in the computer connector, it can be assumed that the computer is faulty and should be replaced.

LOCATION OF FUSES AND FUSIBLE LINKS

J/B .. Junction Block
FL .. Fusible Link

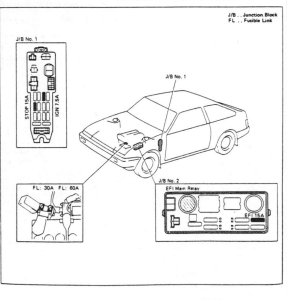

TROUBLESHOOTING THE NO. 1 TERMINAL ON THE EFI CONNECTOR 1986 COROLLA (RWD)

No.	Terminals	Trouble	Condition	STD voltage
1	BaTT – E₁	No voltage	–	10 – 14
	+B₁ – E₁ +B	No voltage	Ignition switch ON	10 – 14

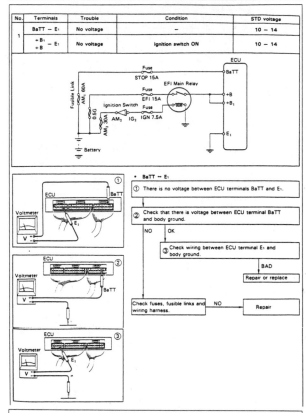

• BaTT – E₁

① There is no voltage between ECU terminals BaTT and E₁.

② Check that there is voltage between ECU terminal BaTT and body ground.

NO — OK

③ Check wiring between ECU terminal E₁ and body ground.

— BAD → Repair or replace

Check fuses, fusible links and wiring harness. — NO → Repair

TROUBLESHOOTING THE NO. 1 TERMINAL ON THE EFI CONNECTOR 1986 COROLLA (RWD)

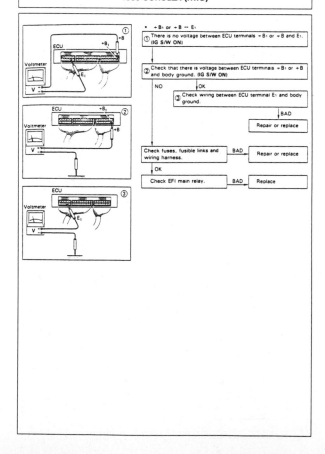

• +B₁ or +B – E₁

① There is no voltage between ECU terminals +B₁ or +B and E₁. (IG S/W ON)

② Check that there is voltage between ECU terminals +B₁ or +B and body ground. (IG S/W ON)

NO — OK

③ Check wiring between ECU terminal E₁ and body ground.

— BAD → Repair or replace

Check fuses, fusible links and wiring harness. — BAD → Repair or replace

OK

Check EFI main relay. — BAD → Replace

TROUBLESHOOTING THE NO. 2 TERMINAL ON THE EFI CONNECTOR
1986 COROLLA (RWD)

No.	Terminals	Trouble	Condition		STD voltage
2	IDL — E₂	No voltage	Ignition switch ON	Throttle valve open	10 — 14
	VTA — E₂			Throttle valve fully closed	0.1 — 1.0
				Throttle valve fully open	4 — 5
	Vcc — E₂			—	4 — 6

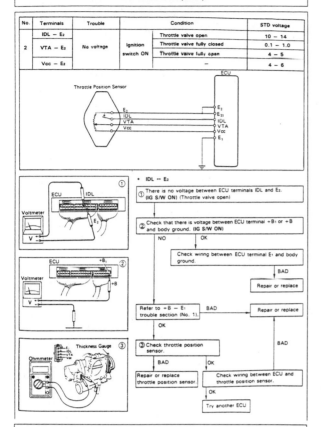

TROUBLESHOOTING THE NO. 2 TERMINAL ON THE EFI CONNECTOR
1986 COROLLA (RWD)

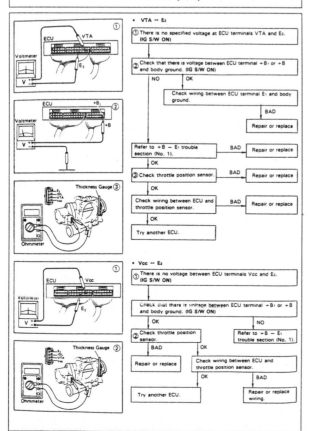

TROUBLESHOOTING THE NO. 3 TERMINAL ON THE EFI CONNECTOR
1986 COROLLA (RWD)

No.	Terminal	Trouble	Condition		STD Voltage
3	+ B₁ — E₂	No voltage	Ignition switch ON	—	10 — 14V
	Vc — E₂			—	6 — 10V
	Vs — E₂		Engine running	Measuring plate fully closed	0.5 — 2.5V
	Vs — E₂			Measuring plate fully open	5 — 10V
	Vs — E₂		Idling		2 — 8V

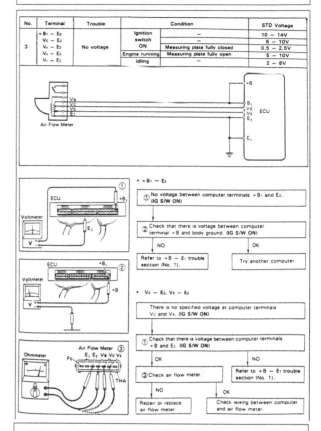

TROUBLESHOOTING THE NO. 4 TERMINAL ON THE EFI CONNECTOR
1986 COROLLA (RWD)

No.	Terminals	Trouble	Condition	STD Voltage
4	No. 10 — E₁	No voltage	Ignition switch ON	10 — 14V
	No. 20 — E₁			

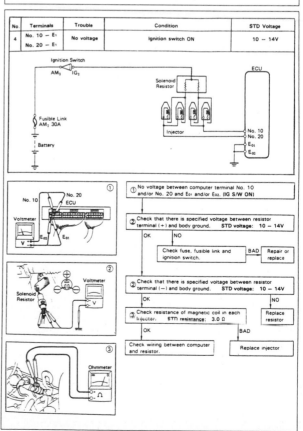

TROUBLESHOOTING THE NO. 5 TERMINAL ON THE EFI CONNECTOR
1986 COROLLA (RWD)

No.	Terminals	Trouble	Condition		STD voltage
5	THA — E₂	No voltage	Ignition switch ON	Intake air temperature 20 °C (68 °F)	1 – 3 V

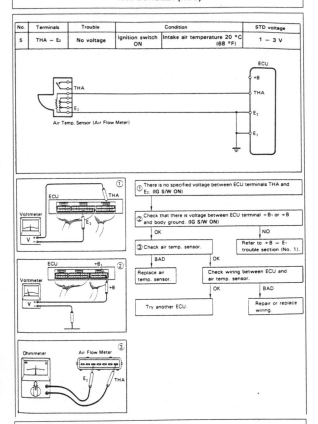

TROUBLESHOOTING THE NO. 6 TERMINAL ON THE EFI CONNECTOR
1986 COROLLA (RWD)

No.	Terminals	Trouble	Condition		STD voltage
6	THW — E₂	No voltage	Ignition switch ON	Coolant temperature 80°C (176°F)	0.1 – 1.0 V

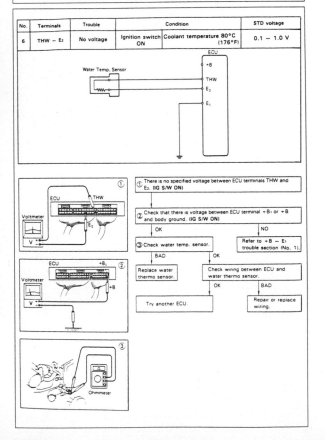

TROUBLESHOOTING THE NO. 7 TERMINAL ON THE EFI CONNECTOR
1986 COROLLA (RWD)

No.	Terminals	Trouble	Condition	STD voltage
7	STA — E₁	No voltage	Ignition switch ST position	6 – 14 V

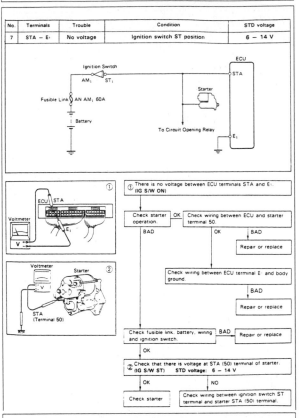

TROUBLESHOOTING THE NO. 8 TERMINAL ON THE EFI CONNECTOR
1986 COROLLA (RWD)

No.	Terminals	Trouble	Condition	STD voltage
8	IGt — E₁	No voltage	Idling	0.7 – 1.0 V

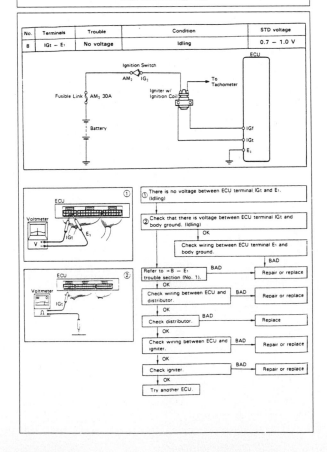

TROUBLESHOOTING THE NO. 9 TERMINAL ON THE EFI CONNECTOR 1986 COROLLA (RWD)

No.	Terminals	Trouble	Condition	STD Voltage
9	A/C – E₁	No voltage	Air conditioning ON	10 – 14 V

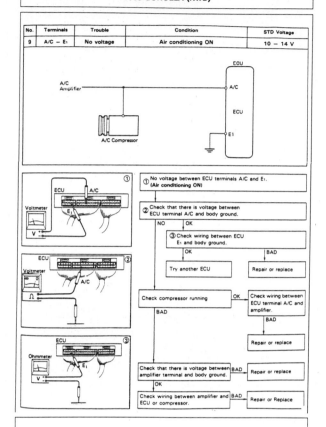

ELECTRONIC COMPONENT LOCATIONS – 1986 COROLLA (RWD)

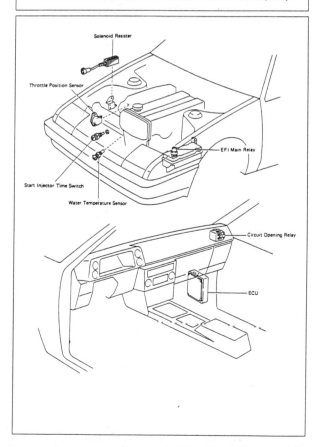

TESTING THE OXYGEN SENSOR – 1986 COROLLA (RWD)

Oxygen Sensor
INSPECTION OF FEEDBACK VOLTAGE (V_F)

1. Warm up the engine.
2. Connect the voltmeter to the check connector terminals V₁ and E₁.

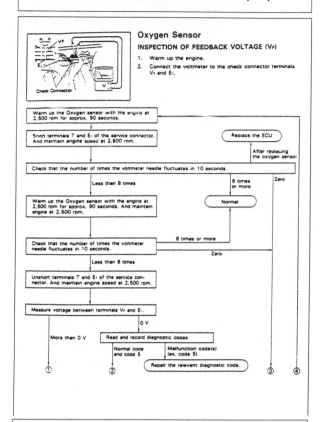

TESTING THE OXYGEN SENSOR (CONT.) – 1986 COROLLA (RWD)

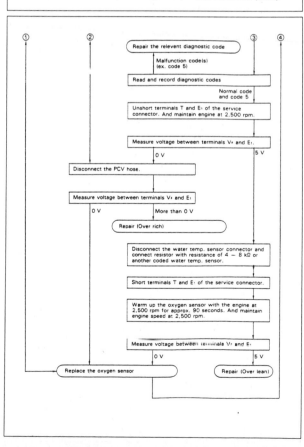

INSPECTION OF THE ELECTRONIC CONTROL UNIT – 1986 COROLLA (RWD)

1. **MEASURE ECU VOLTAGE**

   NOTE: The EFI circuit can be checked by measuring the resistance and voltage at the wiring connectors of the ECU. Check the voltage at the wiring connectors.

   - Remove the kick panel on the front passenger's side.
   - Turn the ignition switch to ON.
   - Measure the voltage at each terminal.

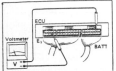

NOTE: 1. Perform all voltage measurements with the connectors connected.
2. Verify that the battery voltage is 11 V or above when the ignition switch is on.

Connectors of ECU

Symbol	Terminal	Symbol	Terminal	Symbol	Terminal
E_{01}	Engine ground (Power)	T	Service connector		–
E_{02}	Engine ground (Power)				–
No. 10	No. 3, 4 injector	IDL	Throttle position sensor		–
No. 20	No. 1, 2 injector	A/C	A/C Magnet clutch		–
STA	Starter switch	IGf	Igniter	Vc	Air flow meter
IGt	Igniter	E_2	Sensor ground		–
VF	Check connector	G ⊖	Engine revolution sensor	Vs	Air flow meter
E_1	Engine ground	Ox	Oxygen sensor		–
–		G ⊕	Engine revolution sensor	THA	Inlet air temp. sensor
S/TH	VSV (T-VIS)	Vcc	Throttle position sensor	SPD	Speedometer sensor
				BaTT	Battery
V-ISC	VSV (Idle-up)	VTA	Throttle position sensor	$+B_1$	EFI main relay
W	Warming light	Ne	Engine revolution sensor	$+B$	EFI main relay
–		THW	Water temp. sensor		

ECU Connectors

E_{01}	NO. 10	STA	VF		W	T	IDL	IGf	G⊖	G⊕		Ne		Vc	Vs	THA	BaTT	$+B_1$
E_{02}	NO. 20	IGt	E_1	S/TH	V-ISC	A/C	E_2	Ox		Vcc	VTA	THW		E_{21}		SPD		$+B$

INSPECTING THE VOLTAGE AT THE ECU WIRING CONNECTOR 1986 COROLLA (RWD)

Terminals	STD Voltage		Condition
BaTT – E_1			–
+B – E_1	10 – 14		IG S/W ON
$+B_1$ – E_1			
IDL – E_2	10 – 14	IG S/W ON	Throttle valve open
Vc – E_2	6 – 10	IG S/W ON	
	0.5 – 2.5		Measuring plate fully closed
Vs – E_2	5 – 10	Engine running	Measuring plate fully open
	2 – 8		Idling
THA – E_2	1 – 3	IG S/W ON	Intake air temperature 20°C (68°F)
THW – E_2	0.1 – 1.0	IG S/W ON	Coolant temperature 80°C (176°F)
STA – E_1	6 – 14		IG S/W ST position
No.10 No.20	10 – 14		IG S/W ON
IGt – E_1	0.7 – 1.0		Idling
T – E_1	10 – 14	IG S/W ON	Check connector T ↔ E_1 not short
	0		Check connector T ↔ E_1 short
A/C – E_1	10 – 14	IG S/W ON	A/C switch ON
	0		A/C switch OFF
W – E_1	0		IG S/W ON
	10 – 14		Engine start
S/TH – E_1	0 – 2		Idling
	10 – 14		More than 4,350 rpm
VTA – E_2	0.1 – 1.0	IG S/W ON	Throttle valve fully closed
	4 – 5		Throttle valve fully open
Vcc – E_2	4 – 6		IG S/W ON

TROUBLESHOOTING THE NO. 1 TERMINAL ON THE EFI CONNECTOR 1987-88 COROLLA (FWD)

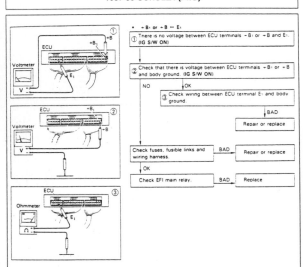

• $+B_1$ or $+B$ ↔ E_1

① There is no voltage between ECU terminals $+B_1$ or $+B$ and E_1. (IG S/W ON)

② Check that there is voltage between ECU terminals $+B_1$ or $+B$ and body ground. (IG S/W ON)

NO | OK

③ Check wiring between ECU terminal E_1 and body ground.

BAD → Repair or replace

Check fuses, fusible links and wiring harness. → BAD → Repair or replace

OK

Check EFI main relay. → BAD → Replace

INSPECTING THE RESISTANCE AT THE ECU WIRING CONNECTOR 1986 COROLLA (RWD)

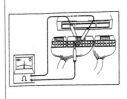

2. **MEASURE RESISTANCE OF ECU**

   CAUTION:
   1. Do not touch the ECU terminals.
   2. The tester probe should be inserted into the wiring connector from the wiring side.

   Check the resistance between each terminal of the wiring connector.

   - Remove the kick panel on the front passenger's side.
   - Unplug the wiring connectors from the ECU.
   - Measure the resistance between each terminal of the wiring connectors.

Resistances at ECU Wiring Connectors

Terminals	Condition	Resistance
IDL – E_2	Throttle valve open	Infinity
	Throttle valve fully closed	Less than 2.3 kΩ
VTA – E_2	Throttle valve fully open	3.3 – 10 kΩ
	Throttle valve fully closed	0.2 – 0.8 kΩ
Vc – E_2	–	100 – 300 Ω
Vs – E_2	Measuring plate fully closed	20 – 400 Ω
	Measuring plate fully open	20 – 3,000 Ω
Vcc – E_2	–	3 – 7 kΩ
THA – E_2	Intake air temperature 20°C (68°F)	2 – 3 kΩ
THW – E_2	Coolant temperature 80°C (176°F)	0.2 – 0.4 kΩ
G ⊕ – G ⊖	–	140 – 180 Ω

EFI WIRING SCHEMATIC – 1987-88 COROLLA (RWD)

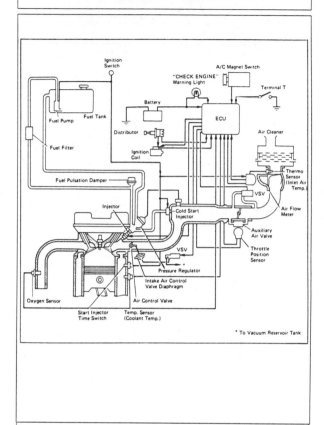

* To Vacuum Reservoir Tank

INSPECTION OF THE DIAGNOSIS CIRCUIT – 1987-88 COROLLA (RWD)

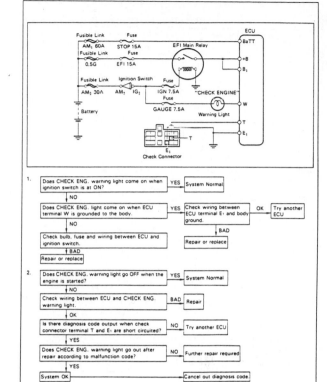

1.
   - Does CHECK ENG. warning light come on when ignition switch is at ON? **YES** → System Normal
   - **NO** ↓
   - Does CHECK ENG. light come on when ECU terminal W is grounded to the body. **YES** → Check wiring between ECU terminal E₁ and body ground. **OK** → Try another ECU
   - **NO** ↓ / **BAD** → Repair or replace
   - Check bulb, fuse and wiring between ECU and ignition switch. **BAD** → Repair or replace

2.
   - Does CHECK ENG. warning light go OFF when the engine is started? **YES** → System Normal
   - **NO** ↓
   - Check wiring between ECU and CHECK ENG. warning light. **BAD** → Repair
   - **OK** ↓
   - Is there diagnosis code output when check connector terminal T and E₁ are short circuited? **NO** → Try another ECU
   - **YES** ↓
   - Does CHECK ENG. warning light go out after repair according to malfunction code? **NO** → Further repair required
   - **YES** ↓
   - System OK → Cancel out diagnosis code.

DIAGNOSIS CODES – 1987-88 COROLLA (RWD)

Code No.	Number of blinks "CHECK ENGINE"	System	Diagnosis	Trouble area
1	ON 0.5 ON ON ON / OFF OFF OFF OFF / 4.5 (Seconds)	Normal	This appears when none of the other codes (2 thru 11) are identified	—
2	0.5 / T (Seconds)	Air flow meter signal	• Open circuit in Vc, Vs, Vs or E₂. • Short circuit in Vc.	1. Air flow meter circuit 2. Air flow meter 3. ECU
3		Ignition signal	No signal from igniter four times in succession.	1. Ignition circuit (+B, IGf) 2. Igniter 3. ECU
4		Water temp. sensor signal	Open or short circuit in coolant temperature sensor signal.	1. Coolant Temp. sensor circuit 2. Coolant Temp. sensor 3. ECU
5		Oxygen sensor signal	Open circuit in oxygen sensor circuit (only lean indication)	1. Oxgen sensor circuit 2. Oxygen sensor 3. ECU
6		RPM signal	No Ne, G signal to ECU within several seconds after engine is cranked	1. Distributor circuit 2. Distributor 3. Igniter 4. Starter signal circuit 5. ECU
7		Throttle position sensor signal	Open or short circuit in throttle position sensor signal.	1. Throttle position sensor circuit 2. Throttle position sensor 3. ECU
8		Intake air temp. sensor signal	Open or short circuit in intake air temperature sensor.	1. Air temp. sensor circuit 2. ECU
10		Starter signal	No STA signal to ECU when vehicle is stopped and engine is running over 800 rpm.	1. Starter relay circuit 2. IG switch circuit (starter) 3. IG Switch 4. ECU
11		Switch signal	Air conditioner switch ON or idle switch OFF during diagnosis check.	1. Air con. S/W 2. ECU 3. Idle S/W

NOTE:
- There is no diagnosis code No. 9.
- Diagnosis code No. 10 will be indicated if the vehicle is push started.

TROUBLESHOOTING THE EFI SYSTEM WITH A VOLT/OHMMETER – 1987-88 COROLLA (RWD)

1. Remove the kick panel on the front passenger's side.
2. Remove the ECU with the wire harness.

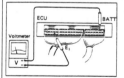

EFI SYSTEM CHECK PROCEDURE

NOTE:
1. The EFI circuit can be checked by measuring the resistance and voltage at the wiring connectors of the ECU.
2. Perform all voltage measurements with the connectors connected.
3. Verify that the battery voltage is 11V or above when the ignition switch is ON.

Using a voltmeter with high impedance (10 kΩ/V minimum), measure the voltage at each terminal of the wiring connector.

NOTE: If there is any problem, see TROUBLESHOOTING FOR EFI ELECTRONIC CIRCUIT WITH VOLT/OHMMETER.

Connectors of ECU

Symbol	Terminal	Symbol	Terminal	Symbol	Terminal
E₀₁	Engine ground (Power)	T	Check connector		
E₀₂	Engine ground (Power)		—		—
No. 10	No. 3, 4 injector	IDL	Throttle position sensor		—
No. 20	No. 1, 2 injector	A/C	A/C Magnet clutch		—
STA	Starter switch	IGf	Igniter	Vc	Air flow meter
IGt	Igniter	E₂	Sensor ground	E₂₁	Sensor ground
V₌	Check connector	G ⊖	Engine revolution sensor	Vs	Air flow meter
E₁	Engine ground	Ox	Oxygen sensor		—
		G ⊕	Engine revolution sensor	THA	Inlet air temp. sensor
S/TH	VSV (T-VIS)	Vcc	Throttle position sensor	SPD	Speedometer sensor
				BaTT	Battery
V-ISC	VSV (Idle-up)	VTA	Throttle position sensor	+B₁	EFI main relay
W	Warning light	Ne	Engine revolution sensor	+B	EFI main relay
		THW	Water temp. sensor		

ECU Connectors

| E₀₁ No.10 | STA | V₌ | | W | T | IDL | IGf | G⊖ G⊕ | | Ne | | Vc | Vs | THA BaTT | +B₁ |
| E₀₂ No.20 | IGt | E₁ | S/TH | V-ISC | A/C | E₂ | Ox | VTA THW | | | | E₂₁ | | SPD | +B |

VOLTAGE SUPPLIED AT THE ECU WIRING CONNECTOR

Voltage at ECU wiring connectors

No.	Terminals	STD voltage	Condition	
1	BaTT – E₁		–	
	+B₁ – E₁	10 – 14	Ignition S/W ON	
	+B – E₁			
2	IDL – E₂	10 – 14	Ignition S/W ON	Throttle valve open
	VTA – E₂	0.1 – 1.0		Throttle valve fully closed
		4 – 5		Throttle valve fully open
	Vcc – E₂	4 – 6		–
	+B₁ – E₂	10 – 14		–
3	Vc – E₂	6 – 10	Ignition S/W ON	–
	Vs – E₂	0.5 – 2.5		Measuring plate fully closed
		5 – 10	Engine running	Measuring plate fully open
		2 – 8	Idling	–
4	No.10 / No.20 – E₁	10 – 14	Ignition S/W ON	
5	THA – E₂	1 – 3	Ignition S/W ON	Intake air temperature 20°C (68°F)
6	THW – E₂	0.1 – 1.0	Ignition S/W ON	Coolant temperature 80°C (176°F)
7	STA – E₁	6 – 14	Ignition S/W ST position	
8	IGt – E₁	0.7 – 1.0	Idling	
9	A/C – E₁	10 – 14	Air conditioning ON	

ECU Connectors

E₀₁	No.10	STA	V₁			W	T	IDL	IGt	G⊖	G⊕		N₈				Vc	Vs	THA	BaTT	+B₁
E₀₂	No.20	IGt	E₁	S/TH	V-ISC		A/C	E₂	Ox	Vcc	VTA	THW					E₁₁		SPD		+B

TROUBLESHOOTING THE EFI SYSTEM WITH A VOLT/OHMMETER (CONT.) – 1987-88 COROLLA (RWD)

NOTE: The following troubleshooting procedures are designed for inspection of each separate system and, therefore, the actual procedure may vary somewhat. However, troubleshooting should be performed refering to the inspection methods described in this manual.

Before beginning inspection, it is best to first make a simple check of the fuses, fusible links and the condition of the connectors.

The following troubleshooting procedures are based on the supposition that the trouble lies in either a short or open circuit in a component outside the computer or a short circuit within the computer.

If engine trouble occurs even though proper operating voltage is detected in the computer connector, then the computer is faulty and should be replaced.

LOCATION OF FUSES AND FUSIBLE LINKS

J/B .. Junction Block
FL .. Fusible Link

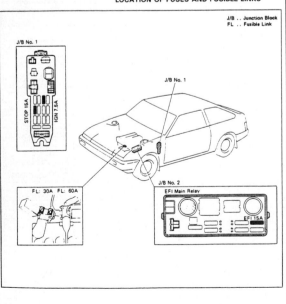

TROUBLESHOOTING THE NO. 1 TERMINAL ON THE EFI CONNECTOR 1987-88 COROLLA (RWD)

No.	Terminals	Trouble	Condition	STD voltage
1	BaTT – E₁	No voltage	–	10 – 14
	+B₁ – E₁	No voltage	Ignition switch ON	10 – 14
	+B – E₁			

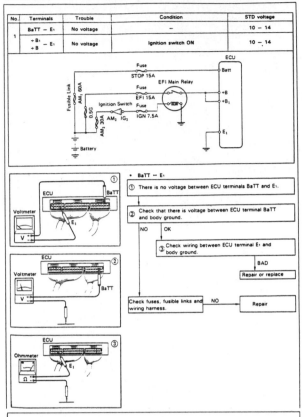

TROUBLESHOOTING THE NO. 1 TERMINAL ON THE EFI CONNECTOR 1987-88 COROLLA (RWD)

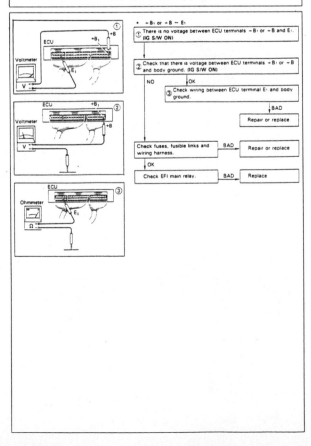

TROUBLESHOOTING THE NO. 2 TERMINAL ON THE EFI CONNECTOR
1987-88 COROLLA (RWD)

No.	Terminals	Trouble	Condition		STD voltage
2	IDL — E2	No voltage	Ignition switch ON	Throttle valve open	10 — 14
	VTA — E2			Throttle valve fully closed	0.1 — 1.0
				Throttle valve fully open	4 — 5
	Vcc — E2			—	4 — 6

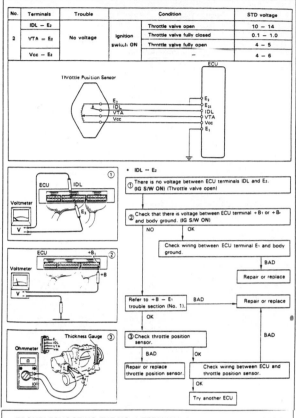

TROUBLESHOOTING THE NO. 2 TERMINAL ON THE EFI CONNECTOR
1987-88 COROLLA (RWD)

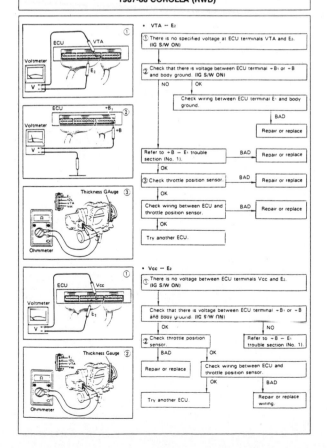

TROUBLESHOOTING THE NO. 3 TERMINAL ON THE EFI CONNECTOR
1987-88 COROLLA (RWD)

No.	Terminal	Trouble	Condition		STD Voltage
3	+B1 — E2	No voltage	Ignition switch ON		10 — 14V
	Vc — E2				6 — 10V
	Vs — E2		Engine running	Measuring plate fully closed	0.5 — 2.5V
	Vs — E2			Measuring plate fully open	5 — 10V
	Vs — E2		Idling	—	2 — 8V

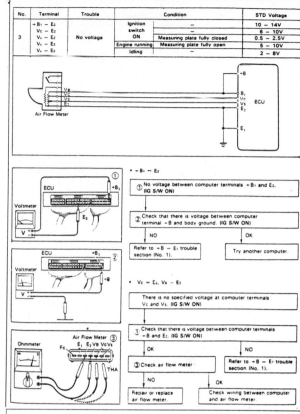

TROUBLESHOOTING THE NO. 4 TERMINAL ON THE EFI CONNECTOR
1987-88 COROLLA (RWD)

No.	Terminals	Trouble	Condition	STD Voltage
4	No. 10 — E1	No voltage	Ignition switch ON	10 — 14V
	No. 20 — E1			

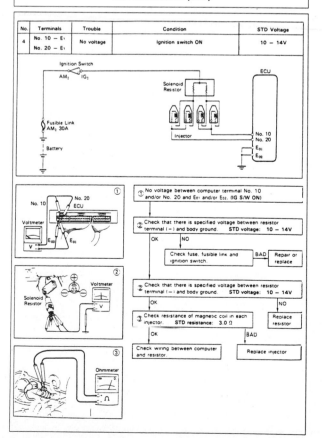

TROUBLESHOOTING THE NO. 5 TERMINAL ON THE EFI CONNECTOR
1987-88 COROLLA (RWD)

No.	Terminals	Trouble	Condition		STD voltage
5	THA – E$_2$	No voltage	Ignition switch ON	Intake air temperature 20 °C (68 °F)	1 – 3 V

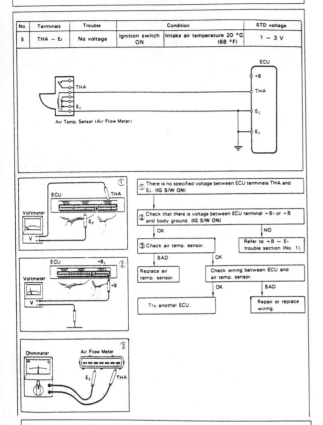

TROUBLESHOOTING THE NO. 6 TERMINAL ON THE EFI CONNECTOR
1987-88 COROLLA (RWD)

No.	Terminals	Trouble	Condition		STD voltage
6	THW – E$_2$	No voltage	Ignition switch ON	Coolant temperature 80°C (176°F)	0.1 – 1.0 V

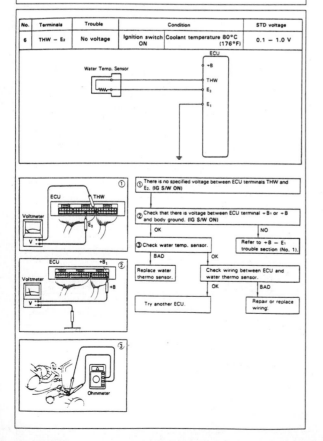

TROUBLESHOOTING THE NO. 7 TERMINAL ON THE EFI CONNECTOR
1987-88 COROLLA (RWD)

No.	Terminals	Trouble	Condition	STD voltage
7	STA – E$_1$	No voltage	Ignition switch ST position	6 – 14 V

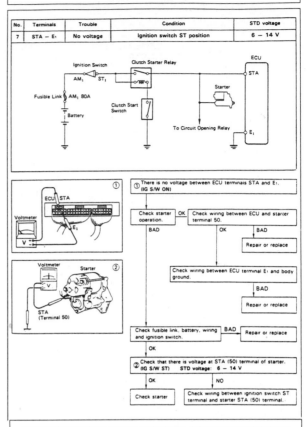

TROUBLESHOOTING THE NO. 8 TERMINAL ON THE EFI CONNECTOR
1987-88 COROLLA (RWD)

No.	Terminals	Trouble	Condition	STD voltage
8	IGt – E$_1$	No voltage	Idling	0.7 – 1.0 V

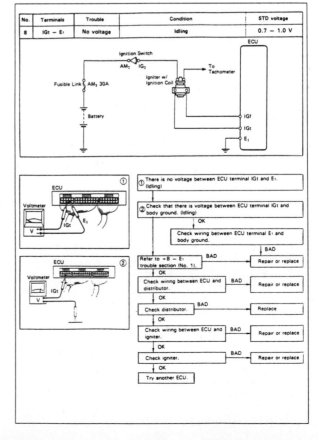

TROUBLESHOOTING THE NO. 9 TERMINAL ON THE EFI CONNECTOR 1987-88 COROLLA (RWD)

No.	Terminals	Trouble	Condition	STD Voltage
9	A/C — E₁	No voltage	Air conditioning ON	10 — 14 V

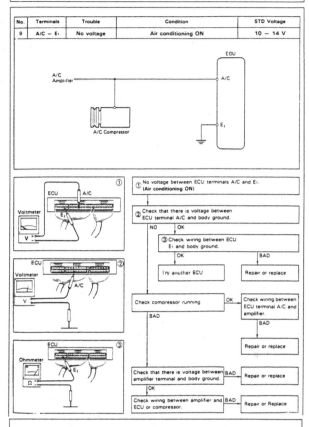

ELECTRONIC COMPONENT LOCATIONS — 1987-88 COROLLA (RWD)

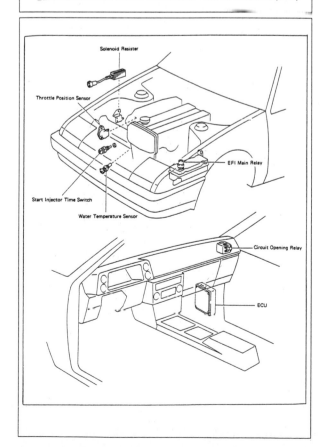

- Solenoid Resister
- Throttle Position Sensor
- EFI Main Relay
- Start Injector Time Switch
- Water Temperature Sensor
- Circuit Opening Relay
- ECU

TESTING THE OXYGEN SENSOR — 1987-88 COROLLA (RWD)

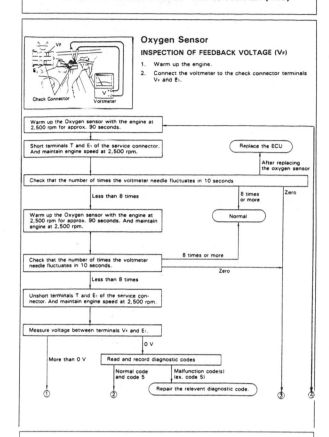

Oxygen Sensor
INSPECTION OF FEEDBACK VOLTAGE (VF)

1. Warm up the engine.
2. Connect the voltmeter to the check connector terminals VF and E₁.

TESTING THE OXYGEN SENSOR (CONT.) — 1987-88 COROLLA (RWD)

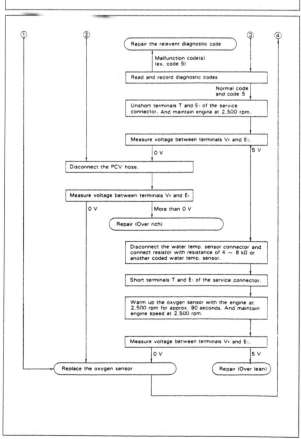

INSPECTION OF THE ELECTRONIC CONTROL UNIT—1987-88 COROLLA (RWD)

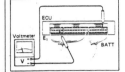

1. MEASURE ECU VOLTAGE

   NOTE: The EFI circuit can be checked by measuring the resistance and voltage at the wiring connectors of the ECU. Check the voltage at the wiring connectors.

   - Remove the kick panel on the front passenger's side.
   - Turn the ignition switch to ON.
   - Measure the voltage at each terminal.

NOTE: 1. Perform all voltage measurements with the connectors connected.
2. Verify that the battery voltage is 11 V or above when the ignition switch is on.

Connectors of ECU

Symbol	Terminal	Symbol	Terminal	Symbol	Terminal
E_{01}	Engine ground (Power)	T	Service connector	–	–
E_{02}	Engine ground (Power)	–	–	–	–
No. 10	No. 3, 4 injector	IDL	Throttle position sensor	–	–
No. 20	No. 1, 2 injector	A/C	A/C Magnet clutch	–	–
STA	Starter switch	IGf	Igniter	Vc	Air flow meter
IGt	Igniter	E_2	Sensor ground	E_{21}	Sensor ground
V#	Check connector	G ⊖	Engine revolution sensor	Vs	Air flow meter
E_1	Engine ground	Ox	Oxygen sensor		
–	–	G ⊕	Engine revolution sensor	THA	Inlet air temp. sensor
S'TH	VSV (T-VIS)	Vcc	Throttle position sensor	SPD	Speedometer sensor
–	–			BaTT	Battery
V-ISC	VSV (Idle-up)	VTA	Throttle position sensor	+B_1	EFI main relay
W	Warning light	Ne	Engine revolution sensor	+B	EFI main relay
–	–	THW	Water temp. sensor		

ECU Connectors

E_{01}	NO 10	STA	VF		W	T	IDL	IGf	G⊖	G⊕		Ne		Vc	Vs	THA	BaTT	+B_1
E_{02}	NO 20	IGt	E_1	S/TH		A/C	E_2	Ox	Vcc	VTA	THW		E_{21}		SPD		+B

INSPECTING THE VOLTAGE AT THE ECU WIRING CONNECTOR 1987-88 COROLLA (RWD)

Voltage at ECU Wiring Connectors

Terminals	STD Voltage	Condition	
BaTT – E_1		–	
+B – E_1	10 – 14		IG S/W ON
+B_1 – E_1			
IDL – E_2	10 – 14	IG S/W ON	Throttle valve open
Vc – E_2	6 – 10	IG S/W ON	–
Vs – E_2	0.5 – 2.5		Measuring plate fully closed
	5 – 10	Engine running	Measuring plate fully open
	2 – 8		Idling
THA – E_2	1 – 3	IG S/W ON	Intake air temperature 20°C (68°F)
THW – E_2	0.1 – 1.0	IG S/W ON	Coolant temperature 80°C (176°F)
STA – E_1	6 – 14		IG S/W ST position
No. 10 No. 20 – E_1	10 – 14		IG S/W ON
IGt – E_1	0.7 – 1.0		Idling
T – E_1	10 – 14	IG S/W ON	Check connector T — E_1 not short
	0		Check connector T — E_1 short
A/C – E_1	10 – 14	IG S/W ON	A/C switch ON
	0		A/C switch OFF
W – E_1	0		IG S/W ON
	10 – 14		Engine start
S/TH – E_1	0 – 2		Idling
	10 – 14		More than 4,350 rpm
VTA – E_2	0.1 – 1.0	IG S/W ON	Throttle valve fully closed
	4 – 5		Throttle valve fully open
Vcc – E_2	4 – 6		IG S/W ON

INSPECTING THE RESISTANCE AT THE ECU WIRING CONNECTOR 1987-88 COROLLA (RWD)

2. MEASURE RESISTANCE OF ECU

   CAUTION:
   1. Do not touch the ECU terminals.
   2. The tester probe should be inserted into the wiring connector from the wiring side.

   Check the resistance between each terminal of the wiring connector.

   - Remove the kick panel on the front passenger's side.
   - Unplug the wiring connectors from the ECU.
   - Measure the resistance between each terminal of the wiring connectors.

Resistances at ECU Wiring Connectors

Terminals	Condition	Resistance
IDL – E_2	Throttle valve open	Infinity
	Throttle valve fully closed	Less than 2.3 kΩ
VTA – E_2	Throttle valve fully open	3.3 – 10 kΩ
	Throttle valve fully closed	0.2 – 0.8 kΩ
Vc – E_2	–	100 – 300 Ω
Vs – E_2	Measuring plate fully closed	20 – 400 Ω
	Measuring plate fully open	20 – 3,000 Ω
Vcc – E_2	–	3 – 7 kΩ
THA – E_2	Intake air temperature 20°C (68°F)	2 – 3 kΩ
THW – E_2	Coolant temperature 80°C (176°F)	0.2 – 0.4 kΩ
G ⊕ – G ⊖	–	140 – 180 Ω

EFI WIRING SCHEMATIC—1987-88 COROLLA (FWD)

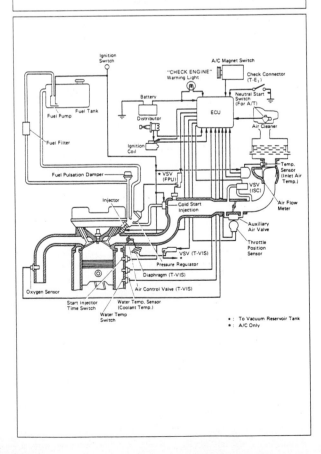

- * : To Vacuum Reservoir Tank
- • : A/C Only

DIAGNOSIS CODES – 1987-88 COROLLA (FWD)

Code No.	Number of blinks "CHECK ENGINE"	System	Diagnosis	Trouble area
1	ON 0.5 ON ON ON OFF OFF OFF OFF 4.5 (Seconds)	Normal	This appears when none of the other codes (2 thru 11) are identified	—
2	0.5 T (Seconds)	Air flow meter signal	• Open circuit in Vc, Vs, Vs or E2. • Short circuit in Vc.	1. Air flow meter circuit 2. Air flow meter 3. ECU
3		Ignition signal	No signal from igniter four times in succession.	1. Ignition circuit (−B, IGf) 2. Igniter 3. ECU
4		Water temp. sensor signal	Open or short circuit in coolant temperature sensor signal.	1. Coolant Temp. sensor circuit 2. Coolant Temp. sensor 3. ECU
5		Oxygen sensor signal	Open circuit in oxygen sensor signal (only lean indication)	1. Oxgen sensor circuit 2. Oxgen sensor 3. ECU
6		RPM signal	No Ne, G signal to ECU within several seconds after engine is cranked.	1. Distributor circuit 2. Distributor 3. Igniter 4. Starter signal circuit 5. ECU
7		Throttle position sensor signal	Open or short circuit in throttle position sensor signal.	1. Throttle position sensor circuit 2. Throttle position sensor 3. ECU
8		Intake air temp. sensor signal	Open or short circuit in intake air sensor.	1. Air temp. sensor circuit 2. ECU
10		Starter signal	No STA signal to ECU when vehicle is stopped and engine is running over 800 rpm.	1. Starter relay circuit 2. IG switch circuit (starter) 3. IG Switch 4. ECU
11		Switch signal	Air conditioner switch ON idle switch OFF or shift position D range (A/T only) during diagnosis check.	1. Air con. S/W 2. ECU 3. Idle S/W 4. Neutral S/W (A/T only)

NOTE: • There is no diagnosis code No. 9.
• Diagnosis code No. 10 will be indicated if the vehicle is push started.

INSPECTION OF THE DIAGNOSIS CIRCUIT – 1987-88 COROLLA (FWD)

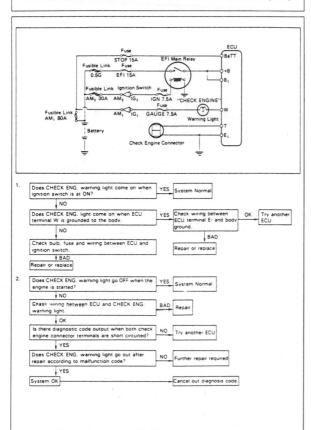

1.
- Does CHECK ENG. warning light come on when ignition switch is at ON? — YES → System Normal
  - NO ↓
- Does CHECK ENG. light come on when ECU terminal W is grounded to the body. — YES → Check wiring between ECU terminal E1 and body ground. — OK → Try another ECU
  - NO ↓ / BAD ↓
- Check bulb, fuse and wiring between ECU and ignition switch. — Repair or replace
  - BAD ↓
- Repair or replace

2.
- Does CHECK ENG. warning light go OFF when the engine is started? — YES → System Normal
  - NO ↓
- Check wiring between ECU and CHECK ENG. warning light. — BAD → Repair
  - OK ↓
- Is there diagnostic code output when both check engine connector terminals are short circuited? — NO → Try another ECU
  - YES ↓
- Does CHECK ENG. warning light go out after repair according to malfunction code? — NO → Further repair required
  - YES ↓
- System OK — Cancel out diagnosis code.

TROUBLESHOOTING THE EFI SYSTEM WITH A VOLT/OHMMETER – 1987-88 COROLLA (FWD)

TROUBLESHOOTING WITH VOLT/OHMMETER

PREPARATION OF TROUBLESHOOTING

1. Remove the ECU cover under the center console.
2. Remove the ECU with the wire harness.

EFI SYSTEM CHECK PROCEDURE

NOTE:
1. The EFI circuit can be checked by measuring the resistance and the voltage at the wiring connectors of the ECU.
2. Perform all voltage measurements with the connectors connected.
3. Verify that the battery voltage is 11V or above when the ignition switch is ON.

Using a voltmeter with high impedance (10 kΩ/V minimum), measure the voltage at each terminal of the wiring connector.

NOTE: If there is any problem, see TROUBLESHOOTING FOR EFI ELECTRONIC CIRCUIT WITH VOLT/OHMMETER.

Connectors of ECU

Symbol	Terminal	Symbol	Terminal	Symbol	Terminal
E01	Engine ground (Power)	T	Check connector	*L3	ECT computer
E02	Engine ground (Power)	TSW	Water temperature switch	*ECT	ECT computer
No. 10	No. 3, 4 injector	IDL	Throttle position sensor	*L1	ECT computer
No. 20	No. 1, 2 injector	A/C	A/C Magnet clutch	*L2	ECT computer
STA	Starter switch	IGf	Igniter	Vc	Air flow meter
IGt	Igniter	E2	Sensor ground	E21	Sensor ground
Vf	Check connector	G ⊖	Engine revolution sensor	Vs	Air flow meter
E1	Engine ground	Ox	Oxygen sensor	—	—
*NSW	Neutral start switch	G ⊕	Engine revolution sensor	THA	Inlet air temp. sensor
S/TH	VSV (T-VIS)	Vcc	Throttle position sensor	SPD	Speedometer sensor
*FPU	VSV (FPU)	—	—	BaTT	Battery
V-ISC	VSV (Idle-up)	VTA	Throttle position sensor	+B1	EFI main relay
W	Warning light	Ne	Engine revolution sensor	+B1	EFI main relay
		THW	Water temperature sensor	+B	EFI main relay

*: A/T only

ECU Connectors

E1	No.10	STA	Vf	NSW	FPU	W	T	IDL	IGf	G⊖	G⊕		Ne	*L3	*L1	Vc	Vs	THA	BaTT	+B1
E01	No.20	IGt	E1	S/TH	V-ISC		TSW	A/C	E2	Ox	Vcc	VTA	THW	*ECT	*L2	E21		SPD		+B

VOLTAGE SUPPLIED AT THE ECU WIRING CONNECTOR

Voltage at ECU wiring connectors

No.	Terminals	STD voltage	Condition
1	BaTT – E1		—
	+B1 – E1 +B	10 – 14	Ignition S/W ON
2	IDL – E2	10 – 14	Throttle valve open
	VTA – E2	0.1 – 1.0	Throttle valve fully closed
		4 – 5	Throttle valve fully open
	Vcc – E2	4 – 6	—
	+B1 – E2	10 – 14	Ignition S/W ON
3	Vc – E2	6 – 10	Ignition S/W ON
	Vs – E2	0.5 – 2.5	Measuring plate fully closed
		5 – 10	Engine running Measuring plate fully open
		2 – 8	Idling —
4	No.10 No.20 – E1	10 – 14	Ignition S/W ON
5	THA – E2	1 – 3	Ignition S/W ON Intake air temperature 20°C (68°F)
6	THW – E2	0.1 – 1.0	Ignition S/W ON Coolant temperature 80°C (176°F)
7	STA – E1	6 – 14	Ignition S/W ST position
8	IGt – E1	0.7 – 1.0	Idling
9	A/C – E1	10 – 14	Air conditioning ON

*: A/T only

ECU Connectors

E01	No.10	STA	Vf	NSW	FPU	W	T	IDL	IGf	G⊖	G⊕		Ne	*L1	*L3	Vc	Vs	THA	BaTT	+B1
E02	No.20	IGt	E1	S/TH	V-ISC		TSW	A/C	E2	Ox	Vcc	VTA	THW	*ECT	*L2	E1		SPD		+B

TROUBLESHOOTING THE EFI SYSTEM WITH A VOLT/OHMMETER (CONT.) – 1987-88 COROLLA (FWD)

NOTE: The following troubleshooting procedures are designed for inspection of each separate system and, therefore, the actual procedure may vary somewhat. However, troubleshooting should be performed refering to the inspection methods described in this manual.

Before beginning inspection, it is best to first make a simple check of the fuses, fusible links and the condition of the connectors.

The following troubleshooting procedures are based on the supposition that the trouble lies in either a short or open circuit in a component outside the computer or a short circuit within the computer.

If engine trouble occurs even though proper operating voltage is detected in the computer connector, then the computer is faulty and should be replaced.

LOCATION OF FUSES AND FUSIBLE LINKS

J/B .. Junction Block
FL .. Fusible Link

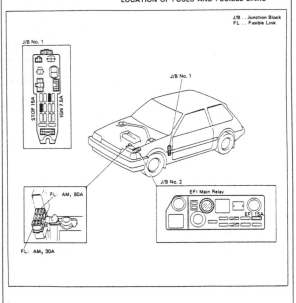

TROUBLESHOOTING THE NO. 1 TERMINAL ON THE EFI CONNECTOR
1987-88 COROLLA (FWD)

No.	Terminals	Trouble	Condition	STD voltage
1	BaTT – E₁	No voltage	–	10 – 14
	+B₁ – E₁ +B – E₁	No voltage	Ignition switch ON	10 – 14

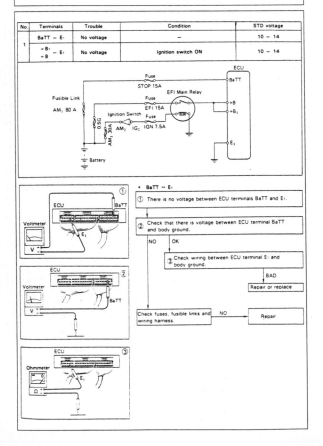

TROUBLESHOOTING THE NO. 2 TERMINAL ON THE EFI CONNECTOR
1987-88 COROLLA (FWD)

No.	Terminals	Trouble	Condition	STD voltage
2	IDL – E₂	No voltage	Ignition switch ON	Throttle valve open	10 – 14
	VTA – E₂			Throttle valve fully closed	0.1 – 1.0
				Throttle valve fully open	4 – 5
	Vcc – E₂			–	4 – 6

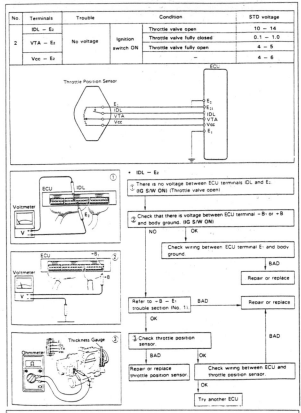

TROUBLESHOOTING THE NO. 2 TERMINAL ON THE EFI CONNECTOR
1987-88 COROLLA (FWD)

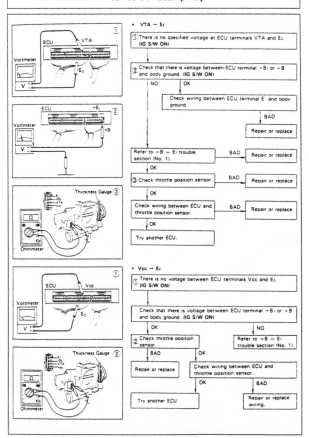

TROUBLESHOOTING THE NO. 3 TERMINAL ON THE EFI CONNECTOR
1987-88 COROLLA (FWD)

No.	Terminal	Trouble	Condition		STD Voltage
3	+B₁ — E₂	No voltage	Ignition switch ON	—	10 — 14V
	Vc — E₂			—	6 — 10V
	Vₛ — E₂			Measuring plate fully closed	0.5 — 2.5V
	Vₛ — E₂		Engine running	Measuring plate fully open	5 — 10V
	Vₛ — E₂			Idling	2 — 8V

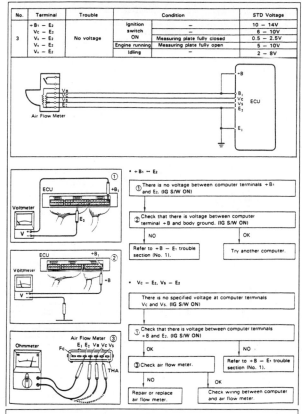

TROUBLESHOOTING THE NO. 4 TERMINAL ON THE EFI CONNECTOR
1987-88 COROLLA (FWD)

No.	Terminals	Trouble	Condition	STD Voltage
4	No. 10 — E₁	No voltage	Ignition switch ON	10 — 14V
	No. 20 — E₁			

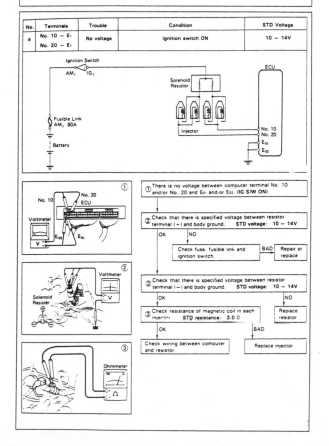

TROUBLESHOOTING THE NO. 5 TERMINAL ON THE EFI CONNECTOR
1987-88 COROLLA (FWD)

No.	Terminals	Trouble	Condition		STD voltage
5	THA — E₂	No voltage	Ignition switch ON	Intake air temperature 20 °C (68 °F)	1 — 3 V

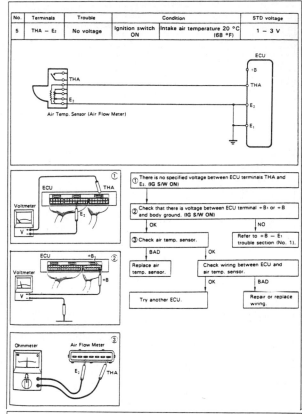

TROUBLESHOOTING THE NO. 6 TERMINAL ON THE EFI CONNECTOR
1987-88 COROLLA (FWD)

No.	Terminals	Trouble	Condition		STD voltage
6	THW — E₂	No voltage	Ignition switch ON	Coolant temperature 80 °C (176 °F)	0.1 — 1.0 V

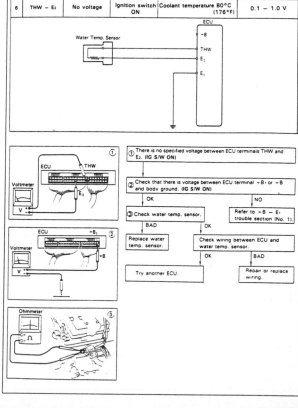

TROUBLESHOOTING THE NO. 7 TERMINAL ON THE EFI CONNECTOR
1987-88 COROLLA (FWD)

No.	Terminals	Trouble	Condition	STD voltage
7	STA – E₁	No voltage	Ignition switch ST position	6 – 14 V

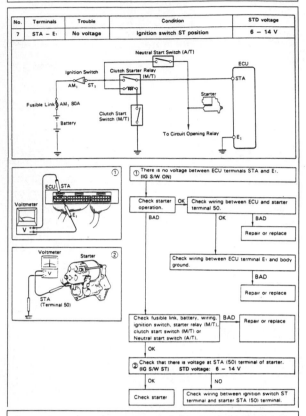

TROUBLESHOOTING THE NO. 8 TERMINAL ON THE EFI CONNECTOR
1987-88 COROLLA (FWD)

No.	Terminals	Trouble	Condition	STD voltage
8	IGt – E₁	No voltage	Idling	0.7 – 1.0 V

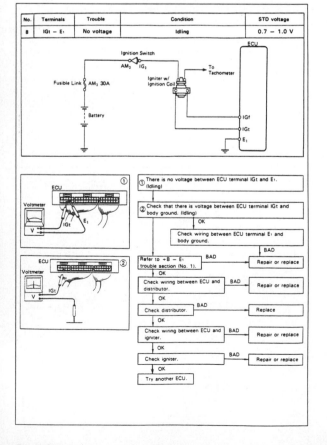

TROUBLESHOOTING THE NO. 9 TERMINAL ON THE EFI CONNECTOR
1987-88 COROLLA (FWD)

No.	Terminals	Trouble	Condition	STD Voltage
9	A/C – E₁	No voltage	Air conditioning ON	10 – 14 V

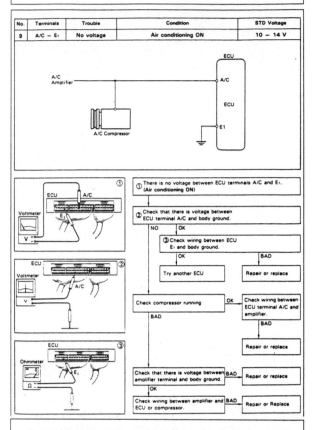

ELECTRONIC COMPONENT LOCATIONS – 1987-88 COROLLA (FWD)

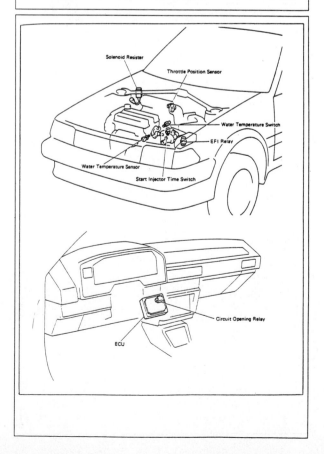

TESTING THE OXYGEN SENSOR – 1987-88 COROLLA (FWD)

Oxygen Sensor
INSPECTION OF FEEDBACK VOLTAGE (Vf)

1. Warm up the engine.
2. Connect the voltmeter to the check connector terminals Vf and E₁.

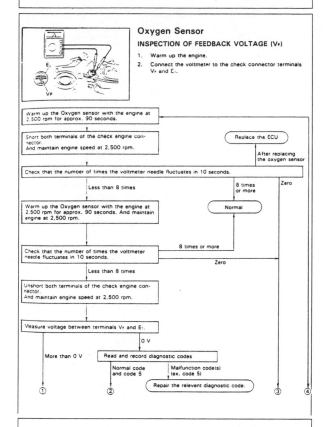

```
┌─────────────────────────────────────┐
│ Warm up the Oxygen sensor with the   │
│ engine at 2,500 rpm for approx. 90   │
│ seconds.                             │
└─────────────────────────────────────┘
              │
┌─────────────────────────────────────┐        ┌──────────────────┐
│ Short both terminals of the check    │        │ Replace the ECU  │
│ engine connector.                    │        └──────────────────┘
│ And maintain engine speed at 2,500   │              ▲
│ rpm.                                 │         After replacing
└─────────────────────────────────────┘         the oxygen sensor
              │
┌─────────────────────────────────────┐    8 times      Zero
│ Check that the number of times the   │    or more
│ voltmeter needle fluctuates in 10    │────────┐
│ seconds.                             │    ┌────────┐
└─────────────────────────────────────┘    │ Normal │
    │ Less than 8 times                     └────────┘
┌─────────────────────────────────────┐
│ Warm up the Oxygen sensor with the   │      8 times or more
│ engine at 2,500 rpm for approx. 90   │─────────────────────┐
│ seconds. And maintain engine at      │                     │
│ 2,500 rpm.                           │                     │
└─────────────────────────────────────┘                     │
              │                            Zero              │
┌─────────────────────────────────────┐                     │
│ Check that the number of times the   │                     │
│ voltmeter needle fluctuates in 10    │                     │
│ seconds.                             │                     │
└─────────────────────────────────────┘                     │
    │ Less than 8 times                                      │
┌─────────────────────────────────────┐                     │
│ Unshort both terminals of the check  │                     │
│ engine connector.                    │                     │
│ And maintain engine speed at 2,500   │                     │
│ rpm.                                 │                     │
└─────────────────────────────────────┘                     │
              │                                               │
┌─────────────────────────────────────┐                     │
│ Measure voltage between terminals Vf │                     │
│ and E₁.                              │                     │
└─────────────────────────────────────┘                     │
      │ 0 V                                                   │
  More than 0 V  ┌──────────────────────────┐                │
  ───────────────│ Read and record          │                │
                 │ diagnostic codes         │                │
                 └──────────────────────────┘                │
                  Normal code │  Malfunction code(s)          │
                  and code 5  │  (ex. code 5)                 │
                     │     ┌──────────────────────────┐       │
                     │     │ Repair the relevent      │       │
                     │     │ diagnostic code.         │       │
                     │     └──────────────────────────┘       │
      ①          ②                              ③          ④
```

TESTING THE OXYGEN SENSOR (CONT.) – 1987-88 COROLLA (FWD)

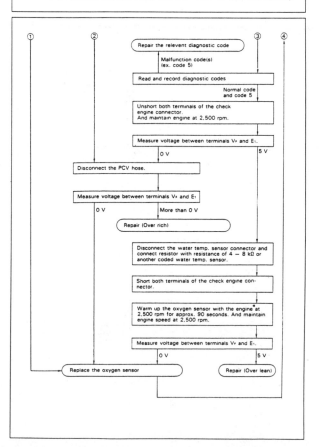

```
   ①        ②                        ③      ④
                ┌──────────────────────────┐
                │ Repair the relevent      │
                │ diagnostic code.         │
                └──────────────────────────┘
                 Malfunction code(s)
                 (ex. code 5)
                ┌──────────────────────────┐
                │ Read and record          │
                │ diagnostic codes         │
                └──────────────────────────┘
                      Normal code
                      and code 5
                ┌──────────────────────────┐
                │ Unshort both terminals of the check
                │ engine connector.
                │ And maintain engine at 2,500 rpm.
                └──────────────────────────┘
                ┌──────────────────────────┐
                │ Measure voltage between terminals Vf
                │ and E₁.
                └──────────────────────────┘
                  0 V │        │ 5 V
        ┌──────────────────────┐
        │ Disconnect the PCV hose. │
        └──────────────────────┘
        ┌──────────────────────────────┐
        │ Measure voltage between terminals Vf and E₁
        └──────────────────────────────┘
          0 V │        More than 0 V
              │    ┌──────────────────┐
              │    │ Repair (Over rich) │
              │    └──────────────────┘
        ┌────────────────────────────────────────┐
        │ Disconnect the water temp. sensor connector and │
        │ connect resistor with resistance of 4 – 8 kΩ or │
        │ another coded water temp. sensor.      │
        └────────────────────────────────────────┘
        ┌────────────────────────────────────────┐
        │ Short both terminals of the check engine con- │
        │ nector.                                │
        └────────────────────────────────────────┘
        ┌────────────────────────────────────────┐
        │ Warm up the oxygen sensor with the engine at │
        │ 2,500 rpm for approx. 90 seconds. And maintain │
        │ engine speed at 2,500 rpm.             │
        └────────────────────────────────────────┘
        ┌────────────────────────────────────────┐
        │ Measure voltage between terminals Vf and E₁. │
        └────────────────────────────────────────┘
          0 V │                │ 5 V
   ┌──────────────────────────┐   ┌──────────────────┐
   │ Replace the oxygen sensor │   │ Repair (Over lean) │
   └──────────────────────────┘   └──────────────────┘
```

INSPECTION OF THE ELECTRONIC CONTROL UNIT – 1987-88 COROLLA (FWD)

Electronic Controlled Unit (ECU)
INSPECTION OF ECU

1. **MEASURE ECU VOLTAGE**

   NOTE: The EFI circuit can be checked by measuring the resistance and voltage at the wiring connectors of the ECU.

   Check the voltage at the wiring connectors.
   - Remove the ECU cover.
   - Turn the ignition switch to ON.
   - Measure the voltage at each terminal.

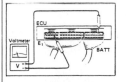

NOTE: 1. Perform all voltage measurements with the connectors connected.
2. Verify that the battery voltage is 11 V or above when the ignition switch is on.

Connectors of ECU

Symbol	Terminal	Symbol	Terminal	Symbol	Terminal
E₀₁	Engine ground (Power)	T	Service connector	*L₃	ECT computer
E₀₂	Engine ground (Power)	TSW	Water temperature switch	*ECT	ECT computer
No. 10	No. 3, 4 injector	IDL	Throttle position sensor	*L₁	ECT computer
No. 20	No. 1, 2 injector	A/C	A/C Magnet clutch	*L₂	ECT computer
STA	Starter switch	IGf	Igniter	Vc	Air flow meter
IGt	Igniter	E₂	Sensor ground	E₁₂	Sensor ground
Vf	Check connector	G ⊖	Engine revolution sensor	Vs	Air flow meter
E₁	Engine ground	Ox	Oxygen sensor	—	—
*NSW	Neutral start switch	G ⊕	Engine revolution sensor	THA	Inlet air temp. sensor
S/TH	VSV (T-VIS)	Vcc	Throttle position sensor	SPD	Speedometer sensor
FPU	VSV (FPU)	—	—	BaTT	Battery
V-ISC	VSV (Idle-up)	VTA	Throttle position sensor	+B₁	EFI main relay
W	Warming light	Ne	Engine revolution sensor	+B	EFI main relay
—	—	THW	Water temp. sensor		

*: A/T only

ECU Connectors

E₀₁	No. 10	STA	Vf	NSW	FPU	W	T	IDL	IGf	G⊖ G⊕		Ne	*L₃	*L₁	Vc	Vs	THA BaTT	+B₁
E₀₂	No. 20	IGt	E₁	S/TH	V-ISC		TSW	A/C	E₂	Ox	Vcc	VTA THW	*ECT	*L₁	E₂₁		SPD	+B

INSPECTING THE VOLTAGE AT THE ECU WIRING CONNECTOR 1987-88 COROLLA (FWD)

Terminals	STD Voltage		Condition
BaTT – E₁			—
+B – E₁	10 – 14		IG S/W ON
+B₁ – E₁			
IDL – E₂	10 – 14	IG S/W ON	Throttle valve open
Vc – E₂	6 – 10	IG S/W ON	—
Vs – E₂	0.5 – 2.5	IG S/W ON	Measuring plate fully closed
	5 – 10	Engine running	Measuring plate fully open
	2 – 8		Idling
THA – E₂	1 – 3	IG S/W ON	Intake air temperature 20°C (68°F)
THW – E₂	0.1 – 1.0	IG S/W ON	Coolant temperature 80°C (176°F)
STA – E₁	6 – 14		IG S/W ST position
No.10 / No.20 – E₁	10 – 14		IG S/W ON
IGt – E₁	0.7 – 1.0		Idling
T – E₁	10 – 14	IG S/W ON	Check connector T – E₁ not short
	0		Check connector T – E₁ short
A/C – E₁	10 – 14	IG S/W ON	A/C switch ON
	0		A/C switch OFF
W – E₁	0	IG S/W ON	
	10 – 14		Engine start
S/TH – E₁	0 – 2		Idling
	10 – 14		More than 4,350 rpm
VTA – E₂	0.1 – 1.0	IG S/W ON	Throttle valve fully closed
	4 – 5		Throttle valve fully open
Vcc – E₃	4 – 6	IG S/W ON	
*NSW – E₁	0	IG S/W ON	Shift position P or N range
	10 – 14		Ex. P or N range
	9 – 11	Cranking	

*: A/T only

INSPECTING THE RESISTANCE AT THE ECU WIRING CONNECTOR 1987-88 COROLLA (FWD)

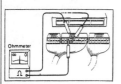

2. **MEASURE RESISTANCE OF ECU**
CAUTION:
1. Do not touch the ECU terminals.
2. The tester probe should be inserted into the wiring connector from the wiring side.

Check the resistance between each terminal of the wiring connector.
- Remove the ECU cover.
- Unplug the wiring connectors from the ECU.
- Measure the resistance between each terminal of the wiring connectors.

Resistances at ECU Wiring Connectors

Terminals	Condition	Resistance
IDL – E$_2$	Throttle valve fully open	Infinity
	Throttle valve fully closed	Less than 2.3 kΩ
VTA – E$_2$	Throttle valve fully open	3.3 – 10 kΩ
	Throttle valve fully closed	0.2 – 0.8 kΩ
Vc – E$_2$	—	100 – 300 Ω
Vs – E$_2$	Measuring plate fully closed	20 – 400 Ω
	Measuring plate fully open	20 – 3,000 Ω
Vcc – E$_2$	—	3 – 7 kΩ
THA – E$_2$	Intake air temperature 20°C (68°F)	2 – 3 kΩ
THW – E$_2$	Coolant temperature 80°C (176°F)	0.2 – 0.4 kΩ
G ⊕ – G ⊖	—	140 – 180 Ω

DIAGNOSIS CODES – 1984 CRESSIDA

Code No.	System	Diagnosis	Trouble Area
	Normal	This appears when none of the other codes (11 thru 51) are identified.	
11	ECU (+ B)	Wire severence, however slight, in + B (ECU).	1. Main relay circuit 2. Main relay 3. ECU
12	RPM Signal	No Ne, G signal to ECU within several seconds after engine is cranked.	1. Distributor circuit 2. Distributor 3. Starter signal circuit 4. ECU
13	RPM Signal	No Ne signal to ECU within several seconds after engine reaches 1,000 rpm.	Same as 12, above.
14	Ignition Signal	No signal from igniter six times in succession	1. Igniter circuit (+B, IGt, IGf) 2. Igniter 3. ECU
21	Ox Sensor Signal	Ox sensor gives a lean signal for several seconds even when coolant temperature is above 50°C and engine is running under high load conditions above 1,500 rpm.	1. Ox sensor circuit 2. Ox sensor 3. ECU
22	Water Thermo Sensor Signal	Open or short circuit in coolant temperature sensor signal.	1. Coolant Temp. sensor circuit 2. Coolant Temp. sensor 3. ECU
23	Intake Air Thermo Sensor Signal	Open or short circuit in intake air temperature sensor.	1. Intake air temp. sensor circuit 2. Intake air temp. sensor 3. ECU
31	Air Flow Meter Signal	Open circuit in Vc signal or Vs and E$_2$ short circuited when idle points are closed.	1. Air flow meter circuit 2. Air flow meter 3. ECU
32	Air Flow Meter Signal	Open circuit in E$_2$ or Vc and Vs short-circuited.	Same as 31, above.
41	Throttle Position Sensor Signal	Simultaneous IDL and PSW signal to ECU.	1. Throttle position sensor circuit 2. Throttle position sensor 3. ECU
42	Vehicle Speed Sensor Signal	(A/T): No signal for over 5 seconds when vehicle is travelling under 1.7 km/h and engine running over 2,500 rpm and shift lever is in other than N or P range. (M/T): No signal for over 5 seconds when vehicle is travelling under 1.7 km/h and engine running over 2,500 rpm.	1. Vehicle speed sensor circuit 2. Vehicle speed sensor 3. Torque converter slipping 4. ECU
43	Starter Signal (+ B)	No STA signal to ECU when engine is running over 800 rpm.	1. Main relay circuit 2. IG switch circuit (starter) 3. IG switch 4. ECU
51	Switch Signal	Neutral start switch OFF or air conditioner switch ON during diagnostic check.	1. Neutral start S/W 2. Air con. S/W 3. ECU

EFI WIRING SCHEMATIC – 1984 CRESSIDA

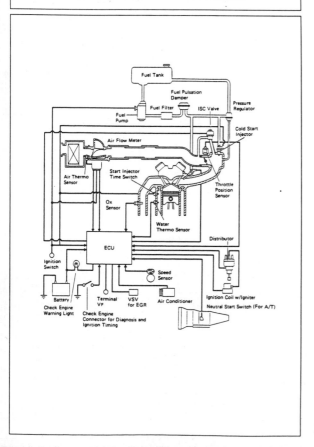

INSPECTION OF THE DIAGNOSIS CIRCUIT – 1984 CRESSIDA

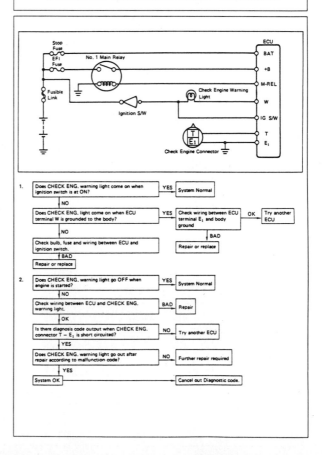

TROUBLESHOOTING THE EFI SYSTEM WITH A VOLT/OHMMETER—1984 CRESSIDA

PREPARATION FOR TROUBLESHOOTING

1. Remove the glove box door and glove box.
2. Remove the ECU with wire harness.

EFI SYSTEM CHECK PROCEDURE

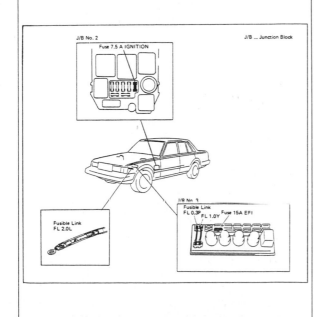

NOTE:
1. The EFI circuit can be checked by measuring the resistance and voltage at the wiring connectors of the ECU.
2. Perform all voltage measurement with the connectors connected.
3. Verify that the battery voltage is 11V or above when the ignition switch is ON.

Using a voltmeter, measure the voltage at each terminal of the wiring connector.

NOTE: If there is any problem, see TROUBLESHOOTING FOR EFI ELECTRONIC CIRCUIT WITH VOLT/OHMMETER.

Connectors of ECU

Symbol	Terminal Name	Symbol	Terminal Name	Symbol	Terminal Name
E_{01}	ENGINE GROUND	G⊖	ENGINE REVOLUTION SENSOR	SPD	SPEEDOMETER
E_{02}	ENGINE GROUND	VF	CHECK CONNECTOR	W	WARNING LAMP
No. 10	INJECTOR	G	ENGINE REVOLUTION SENSOR	THA	AIR TEMP SENSOR
No. 20	INJECTOR	T	CHECK CONNECTOR	Vs	AIR FLOW METER
STA	STARTER SWITCH	PSW	THROTTLE SWITCH	Vc	AIR FLOW METER
IGt	IGNITER	Ne	ENGINE REVOLUTION SENSOR	BAT	BATTERY +B
EGR	EGR VSV	IDL	THROTTLE SWITCH	IG S/W	IGNITION SWITCH
E_1	ENGINE GROUND	IGf	IGNITER	+B	MAIN RELAY
N/C	NEUTRAL START SWITCH (A/T)	Ox	Ox SENSOR	ECT	ECT COMPUTER
N/C	CLUTCH SWITCH (M/T)	THW	WATER TEMP SENSOR	S_1	ECT COMPUTER
ISC_1	ISC MOTOR NO. 1 COIL	E_2	SENSOR EARTH	S_2	ECT COMPUTER
ISC_2	ISC MOTOR NO. 2 COIL	E_1	ENGINE GROUND	OIL	OIL PRESSURE SWITCH
ISC_3	ISC MOTOR NO. 3 COIL	M-REL	MAIN RELAY COIL		
ISC_4	ISC MOTOR NO. 4 COIL	A/C	A/C MAGNET SWITCH		

E_{01}	No. 10	STA	EGR	N/C		ISC_1	ISC_2	G⊖		G	Ne		IGf	THW	Ox		M-REL		SPD	S_1	THA	Vs	Vc	BAT	IG S/W
E_{02}	No. 20	IGt	E_1			ISC_3	ISC_4	VF		T	PSW	IDL		Ox	E_2	E_2	E_1	ECT	A/C	W	OIL	S_2		+B	+B

TROUBLESHOOTING THE EFI SYSTEM WITH A VOLT/OHMMETER (CONT.)—1984 CRESSIDA

NOTE: Because the following troubleshooting procedure are designed for inspection of each separate system, the actual troubleshooting procedure may vary somewhat. However, please refer to these procedures and perform actual troubleshooting, conforming to the inspection methods described.

For example, it is better to first make a simple check of the fuses, fusible links and connecting condition of the connectors before making your inspection according to the procedures listed.

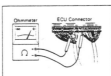

J/B No. 2

Fuse 7.5 A IGNITION

J/B ... Junction Block

J/B No. 3

Fusible Link
FL 0.3P FL 1.0Y   Fuse 15A EFI

Fusible Link
FL 2.0L

VOLTAGE SUPPLIED AT THE ECU WIRING CONNECTOR 1984 CRESSIDA

No.	Terminals	Condition		STD Voltage
1	BAT – E_1	—		
	+B – E_1	Ignition S/W ON		10 – 14
	IG S/W – E_1			
	M-REL – E_1			
2	IDL – E_1	Ignition S/W ON	Throttle valve open	4 – 6
	PSW – E_1		Throttle valve fully closed	4 – 6
3	Vc – E_2	Ignition S/W ON	—	4 – 6
	Vs – E_2		Measuring plate fully closed	4 – 5
			Measuring plate fully open	0.02 – 0.08
			Idling	2 – 4
			3,000 rpm	0.3 – 1.0
	THA – E_2	IG S/W ON	Intake air temperature 20°C (68°F)	1 – 2
4	THW – E_2	IG S/W ON	Coolant temperature 80°C (176°F)	0.1 – 0.5
5	STA – E_1	Ignition switch ST position		6 – 12
6	No.10 / No.20 – E_1	Ignition switch ON		9 – 14
7	IGt – E_1	Idling		0.7 – 1.0
8	ISC_1 – E_1	Ignition switch ON		9 – 14
	ISC_4	2–3 secs. after engine off		9 – 14

RESISTANCE SUPPLIED AT THE ECU WIRING CONNECTOR 1984 CRESSIDA

MEASURE RESISTANCE OF ECU

CAUTION:
1. Do not touch the ECU terminals.
2. The tester probe should be inserted into the wiring connector from the wiring side.

Using a ohmmeter, check the resistance between each terminal of the wiring connector.

- Remove the glove box.
- Disconnect the wiring connectors from the ECU.
- Measure the resistance between each terminal of the wiring connectors.

Resistances at ECU Wiring Connectors

Terminals	Condition	Resistance (Ω)
IDL – E_1	Throttle valve open	∞
	Throttle valve fully closed	0
PSW – E_1	Throttle valve open	0
	Throttle valve fully closed	∞
Vc – E_2	—	200 – 400
Vs – E_2	Measuring plate fully closed	20 – 400
	Measuring plate fully open	20 – 1000
THA – E_2	Intake air temperature 20°C (68°F)	2000 – 3000
G – G⊖	—	140 – 180
Ne – G⊖	—	
ISC_1, ISC_2 / ISC_3, ISC_4 – +B	—	10 – 30

TROUBLESHOOTING THE NO. 1 TERMINAL ON THE EFI CONNECTOR
1984 CRESSIDA

No.	Terminals	Trouble	Condition	STD Voltage
1	BAT – E_1	No voltage		10 – 14
	+B – E_1	No voltage	Ignition switch ON	10 – 14
	IG S/W – E_1	No voltage	Ignition switch ON	10 – 14
	M-REL – E_1	No voltage	Ignition switch ON	10 – 14

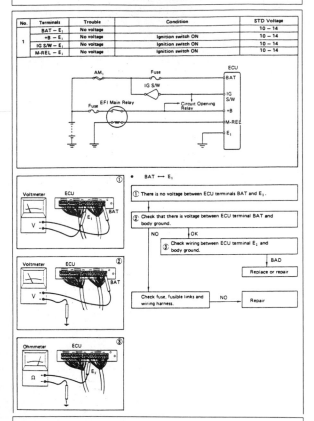

TROUBLESHOOTING THE NO. 1 TERMINAL ON THE EFI CONNECTOR
1984 CRESSIDA

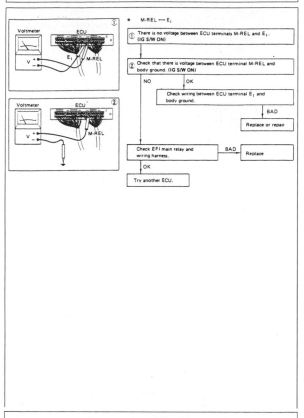

TROUBLESHOOTING THE NO. 1 TERMINAL ON THE EFI CONNECTOR
1984 CRESSIDA

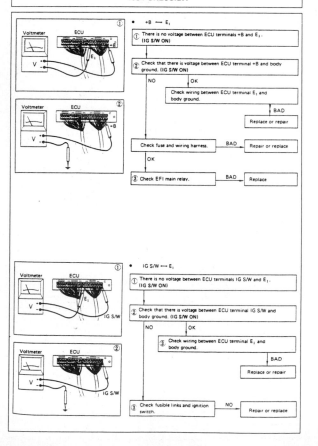

TROUBLESHOOTING THE NO. 2 TERMINAL ON THE EFI CONNECTOR
1984 CRESSIDA

No.	Terminal	Trouble	Condition		STD Voltage
2	IDL – E_1	No voltage	Ignition S/W ON	Throttle valve open	4 – 6 V
	Psw – E_1			Throttle valve fully closed	4 – 6 V

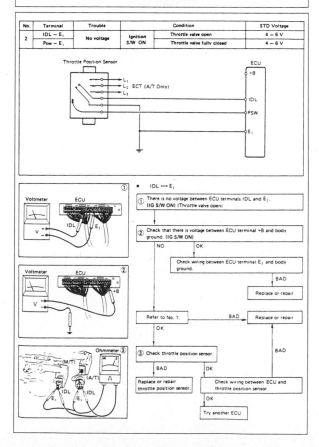

TROUBLESHOOTING THE NO. 2 TERMINAL ON THE EFI CONNECTOR
1984 CRESSIDA

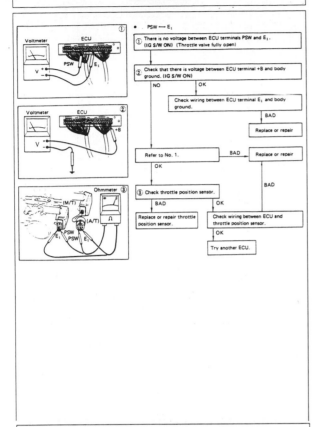

● PSW ⟷ E₁

① There is no voltage between ECU terminals PSW and E₁. (IG S/W ON) (Throttle valve fully open)

② Check that there is voltage between ECU terminal +B and body ground. (IG S/W ON)

NO / OK

→ Check wiring between ECU terminal E₁ and body ground.

→ BAD → Replace or repair

Refer to No. 1. — BAD → Replace or repair

OK / BAD

③ Check throttle position sensor.

BAD → Replace or repair throttle position sensor.

OK → Check wiring between ECU and throttle position sensor.

OK → Try another ECU.

TROUBLESHOOTING THE NO. 3 TERMINAL ON THE EFI CONNECTOR
1984 CRESSIDA

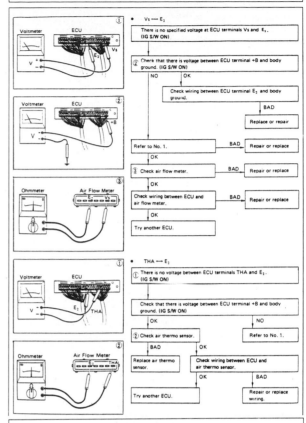

● Vs ⟷ E₂

① There is no specified voltage at ECU terminals Vs and E₁. (IG S/W ON)

② Check that there is voltage between ECU terminal +B and body ground. (IG S/W ON)

NO / OK

→ Check wiring between ECU terminal E₂ and body ground.

→ BAD → Replace or repair

Refer to No. 1. — BAD → Repair or replace

OK

③ Check air flow meter. — BAD → Repair or replace

Check wiring between ECU and air flow meter. — BAD → Repair or replace

OK

Try another ECU.

● THA ⟷ E₂

① There is no voltage between ECU terminals THA and E₂. (IG S/W ON)

Check that there is voltage between ECU terminal +B and body ground. (IG S/W ON)

OK / NO

② Check air thermo sensor. / Refer to No. 1.

BAD / OK

Replace air thermo sensor. / Check wiring between ECU and air thermo sensor.

OK / BAD

Try another ECU. / Repair or replace wiring.

TROUBLESHOOTING THE NO. 3 TERMINAL ON THE EFI CONNECTOR
1984 CRESSIDA

No.	Terminal	Trouble	Condition		STD Voltage
3	Vc – E₂	No voltage	Ignition S/W ON	–	4 – 6 V
	Vs – E₂			Measuring plate fully closed	4 – 5 V
	Vs – E₂			Measuring plate fully open	0.02 – 0.08 V
	Vs – E₂		Idling	–	2 – 4 V
	Vs – E₂		3,000 rpm	–	0.3 – 1.0 V
	THA – E₂		IG S/W ON	Intake air temperature 20°C (68°F)	1 – 2 V

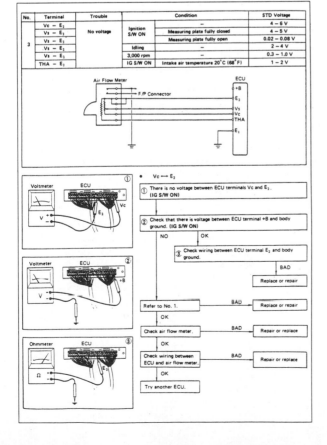

● Vc ⟷ E₂

① There is no voltage between ECU terminals Vc and E₂. (IG S/W ON)

② Check that there is voltage between ECU terminal +B and body ground. (IG S/W ON)

NO / OK

③ Check wiring between ECU terminal E₂ and body ground.

→ BAD → Replace or repair

Refer to No. 1. — BAD → Replace or repair

OK

Check air flow meter. — BAD → Repair or replace

Check wiring between ECU and air flow meter. — BAD → Repair or replace

Try another ECU.

TROUBLESHOOTING THE NO. 4 TERMINAL ON THE EFI CONNECTOR
1984 CRESSIDA

No.	Terminals	Trouble	Condition			STD Voltage
4	THW – E₂	No voltage	Ignition switch ON	Coolant temperature 80°C (176°F)		0.1 – 0.5 V

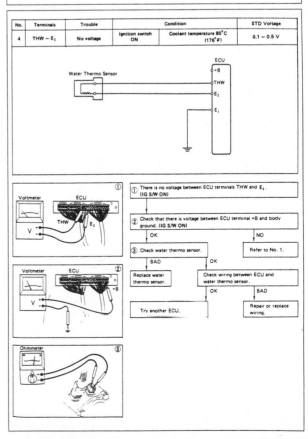

Water Thermo Sensor

① There is no voltage between ECU terminals THW and E₂. (IG S/W ON)

② Check that there is voltage between ECU terminal +B and body ground. (IG S/W ON)

OK / NO

③ Check water thermo sensor. / Refer to No. 1.

BAD / OK

Replace water thermo sensor. / Check wiring between ECU and water thermo sensor.

OK / BAD

Try another ECU. / Repair or replace wiring.

TROUBLESHOOTING THE NO. 5 TERMINAL ON THE EFI CONNECTOR
1984 CRESSIDA

No.	Terminals	Trouble	Condition	STD Voltage
5	STA – E_1	No voltage	Ignition switch ST position	6 – 12 V

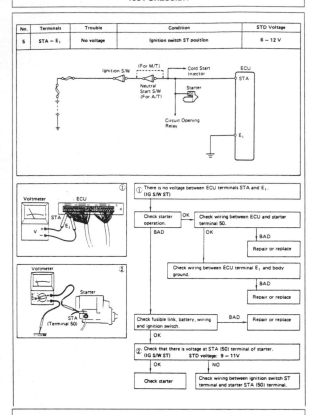

TROUBLESHOOTING THE NO. 6 TERMINAL ON THE EFI CONNECTOR
1984 CRESSIDA

No.	Terminals	Trouble	Condition	STD Voltage
6	No. 10 – E_1 No. 20 – E_1	No voltage	Ignition switch ON	9 – 14 V

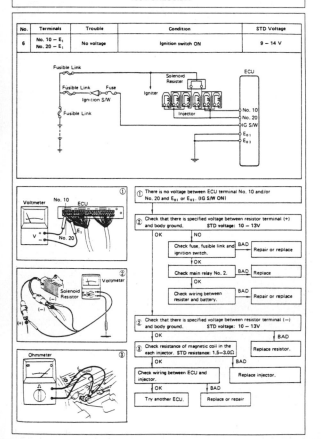

TROUBLESHOOTING THE NO. 7 TERMINAL ON THE EFI CONNECTOR
1984 CRESSIDA

No.	Terminals	Trouble	Condition	STD Voltage
7	IGt – E_1	No voltage	Idling	0.7 – 1.0 V

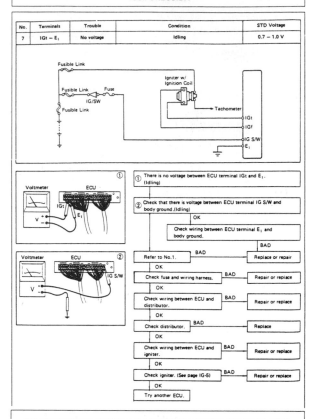

TROUBLESHOOTING THE NO. 8 TERMINAL ON THE EFI CONNECTOR
1984 CRESSIDA

No.	Terminal	Trouble	Condition	STD Voltage
8	$ISC_1 - ISC_4 - E_1$	No voltage	Ignition S/W ON	9 – 14 V

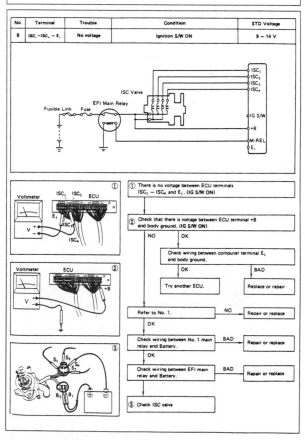

ELECTRONIC COMPONENT LOCATIONS — 1984 CRESSIDA

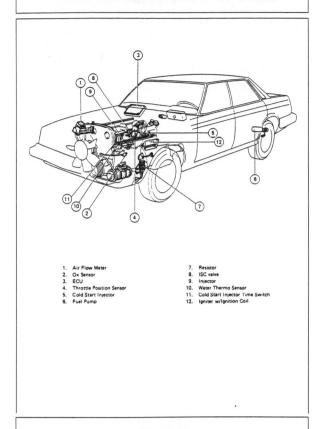

1. Air Flow Meter
2. Ox Sensor
3. ECU
4. Throttle Position Sensor
5. Cold Start Injector
6. Fuel Pump
7. Resistor
8. ISC valve
9. Injector
10. Water Thermo Sensor
11. Cold Start Injector Time Switch
12. Igniter w/Ignition Coil

TESTING THE OXYGEN SENSOR (CONT.) — 1984 CRESSIDA

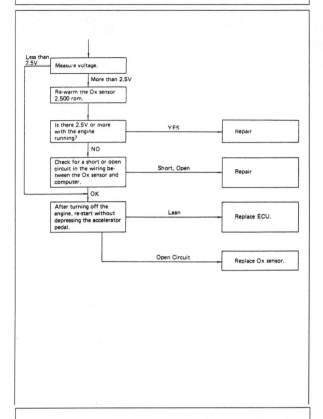

TESTING THE OXYGEN SENSOR — 1984 CRESSIDA

1. Warm up the engine.
2. Connect SST to the 4-terminal connector. SST 09842-14010
3. Using a voltmeter connect the positive probe to the red wire of the SST and negative testing probe to the block wire.
4. Warm up the Ox sensor with the engine at 2,500 rpm for about 2 minutes.

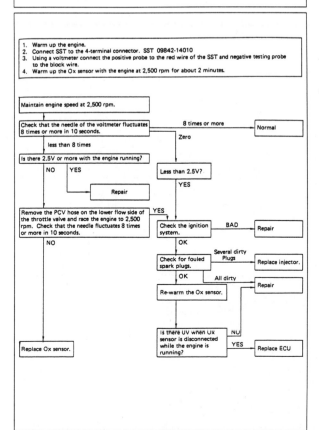

INSPECTION OF THE ELECTRONIC CONTROL UNIT — 1984 CRESSIDA

1. **MEASURE VOLTAGE OF ECU**

   NOTE: The EFI circuit can be checked by measuring the resistance and voltage at the wiring connectors of the ECU.

   Check the voltages at the wiring connectors.
   - Remove the glove box
   - Turn on the ignition switch.
   - Measure the voltage at each terminal.

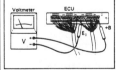

NOTE: 1. Perform all voltage measurements with the connectors connected.
2. Verify that the battery voltage is 11V or above when the ignition switch is ON.
3. The testing probes MUST NOT make contact with the ECU Ox and Vf terminals.

Connectors of ECU

Symbol	Terminal Name	Symbol	Terminal Name	Symbol	Terminal Name
E$_{01}$	ENGINE GROUND	G$\ominus$	ENGINE REVOLUTION SENSOR	SPD	SPEEDOMETER
E$_{02}$	ENGINE GROUND	VF	CHECK CONNECTOR	W	WARNING LAMP
No. 10	INJECTOR	G	ENGINE REVOLUTION SENSOR	THA	AIR TEMP SENSOR
No. 20	INJECTOR	T	CHECK CONNECTOR	V$_s$	AIR FLOW METER
STA	STARTER SWITCH	PSW	THROTTLE SWITCH	Vc	AIR FLOW METER
IGt	IGNITER	Ne	ENGINE REVOLUTION SENSOR	BAT	BATTERY +B
EGR	EGR VSV	IDL	THROTTLE SWITCH	IG S/W	IGNITION SWITCH
E$_1$	ENGINE GROUND	IG†	IGNITER	+B	MAIN RELAY
N/C	NEUTRAL START SWITCH (A/T)	Ox	Ox SENSOR	ECT	ECT COMPUTER
	CLUTCH SWITCH (M/T)	THW	WATER TEMP SENSOR	S$_1$	ECT COMPUTER
ISC$_1$	ISC MOTOR NO. 1 COIL	E$_2$	SENSOR EARTH	S$_2$	ECT COMPUTER
ISC$_2$	ISC MOTOR NO. 2 COIL	E$_1$	ENGINE GROUND	OIL	OIL PRESSURE SWITCH
ISC$_3$	ISC MOTOR NO. 3 COIL	M-REL	MAIN RELAY COIL		
ISC$_4$	ISC MOTOR NO. 4 COIL	A/C	A/C MAGNET SWITCH		

E$_{01}$	No. 10	STA	EGR	N/C		ISC$_1$	ISC$_2$	G$\ominus$		G	Ne		IGt	THW	Ox		M-REL		SPD	S$_1$	THA	V$_s$	Vc	BAT	IG S/W
E$_{02}$	No. 20	IGt	E$_1$		ISC$_3$	ISC$_4$	V$_F$		T	PSW	IDL		Ox	E$_2$	E$_1$	ECT		A/C	W	OIL	S$_2$			+B	+B

INSPECTING THE VOLTAGE AT THE ECU WIRING CONNECTOR
1984 CRESSIDA

Terminals	STD Voltage		Condition
BAT − E_1			−
+B − E_1	10 − 14		
IG S/W − E_1			IG S/W ON
M-REL − E_1			
IDL − E_1	4 − 6	IG S/W ON	Throttle valve open
PSW − E_1	4 − 6		Throttle valve fully closed
Vc − E_2	4 − 6		−
	4 − 5	IG S/W ON	Measuring plate fully closed
	0.02 − 0.08		Measuring plate fully open
Vs − E_2	2 − 4		Idling
	0.3 − 1.0		3,000 rpm
THA − E_2	1 − 2	IG S/W ON	Intake air temperature 20°C (68°F)
THW − E_1	0.1 − 0.5	IG S/W ON	Coolant temperature 80°C (176°F)
STA − E_1	6 − 12		IG S/W ST position
No. 10 No. 20 − E_1	9 − 14		IG S/W ON
IGt − E_1	0.7 − 1.0		Idling
ISC_1 / ISC_4 − E_1	9 − 14		IG S/W ON
	9 − 14		2−3 secs, after engine off
+B − EGR	10 − 13		IG S/W ON
	0		Start engine and warm up Ox sensor
N/C − E_1	0	IG S/W ON	Shift position P or N range (for A/T)
	4 − 6		Ex. P or N range (for A/T)
	0		Clutch pedal not depressed (for M/T)
	4 − 6		Clutch pedal depressed (for M/T)
	9 − 11		Cranking
T − E_1	4 − 6	IG S/W ON	Check connector T ↔ E_1 not short
	0		Check connector T ↔ E_1 short

INSPECTING THE VOLTAGE AT THE ECU WIRING CONNECTOR
1984 CRESSIDA

OIL − E_1	4 − 6		IG S/W ON (Warning light on)
	0		Start engine (Warning light out)
A/C − E_1	10 − 13	IG S/W ON	A/C S/W ON
	0		A/C S/W OFF
VF − E_1	0 ↔ 5		Start engine (Throttle valve open)
W − E_1	0	IG S/W ON	
	10 − 13		Start engine
ECT − E_1	2 − 3	IG S/W ON	Coolant Temp. Less than 35°C (95°F)
	0		Coolant Temp. 35 − 60°C (95 − 140°F)
	4 − 6		Coolant Temp. More than 60°C (140°F)

INSPECTING THE RESISTANCE AT THE ECU WIRING CONNECTOR
1984 CRESSIDA

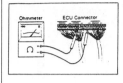

2. MEASURE RESISTANCE OF ECU
CAUTION:
1. Do not touch the ECU terminals.
2. The tester probe should be inserted into wiring connector from wiring side.

Check the resistance between each terminal of the wiring connector.
• Remove the glove box.
• Unplug the wiring connectors from the ECU.
• Measure the resistance between each terminal of the wiring connectors.

Resistances at ECU Wiring Connectors

Terminals	Condition	Resistance (Ω)
IDL − E_1	Throttle valve open	∞
	Throttle valve fully closed	0
PSW − E_1	Throttle valve open	0
	Throttle valve fully closed	∞
Vc − E_2	−	200 − 400
Vs − E_2	Measuring plate fully closed	20 − 400
	Measuring plate fully open	20 − 1000
THA − E_2	Intake air temperature 20°C (68°F)	2,000 − 3,000
G − G⊖	−	140 − 180
Ne − G⊖	−	
ISC_1, ISC_3 ISC_2, ISC_4 − +B	−	10 − 30

EFI WIRING SCHEMATIC − 1985-88 CRESSIDA

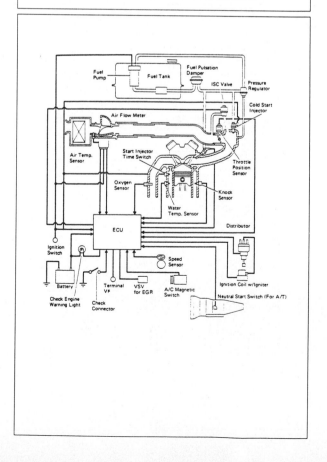

DIAGNOSIS CODES—1985-88 CRESSIDA

Code No.	System	Diagnosis	Trouble Area
	Normal	This appears when none of the other codes (11 thru 53) are identified.	
11	ECU (+ B)	Wire severence, however slight, in + B (ECU).	1. Main relay circuit 2. Main relay 3. ECU
12	RPM Signal	No Ne, G signal to ECU within several seconds after engine is cranked.	1. Distributor circuit 2. Distributor 3. Starter signal circuit 4. ECU
13	RPM Signal	No Ne signal to ECU within several seconds after engine reaches 1,000 rpm.	Same as 12, above.
14	Ignition Signal	No signal from igniter six times in succession.	1. Igniter circuit (+B, IGt, IGf) 2. Igniter 3. ECU
21	Oxygen Sensor Signal	Oxygen sensor gives a lean signal for several seconds even when coolant temperature is above 50°C (122°F) and engine is running under high load conditions above 1,500 rpm.	1. Oxygen sensor circuit 2. Oxygen sensor 3. ECU

INSPECTION OF THE DIAGNOSIS CIRCUIT—1985-88 CRESSIDA

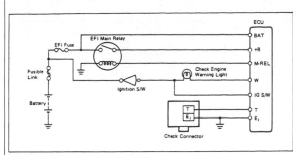

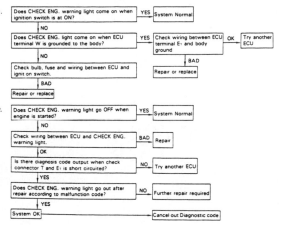

1. Does CHECK ENG. warning light come on when ignition switch is at ON? — YES → System Normal
   NO ↓
   Does CHECK ENG. light come on when ECU terminal W is grounded to the body? — YES → Check wiring between ECU terminal E₁ and body ground — OK → Try another ECU
   NO ↓ | BAD → Repair or replace
   Check bulb, fuse and wiring between ECU and ignit on switch.
   BAD ↓
   Repair or replace

2. Does CHECK ENG. warning light go OFF when engine is started? — YES → System Normal
   NO ↓
   Check wiring between ECU and CHECK ENG. warning light. — BAD → Repair
   OK ↓
   Is there diagnosis code output when check connector T and E₁ is short circuited? — NO → Try another ECU
   YES ↓
   Does CHECK ENG. warning light go out after repair according to malfunction code? — NO → Further repair required
   YES ↓
   System OK ————————————→ Cancel out Diagnostic code

DIAGNOSIS CODES—1985-88 CRESSIDA

Code No.	System	Diagnosis	Trouble Area
22	Water Temp. Sensor Signal	Open or short circuit in coolant temp. sensor signal.	1. Water temp. sensor circuit 2. Water temp. sensor 3. ECU
23	Intake Air Temp. Sensor Signal	Open or short circuit in intake air temp. sensor.	1. Intake air temp. sensor circuit 2. Intake air temp. sensor 3. ECU
31	Air Flow Meter Signal	Open circuit in Vc signal or Vs and E₂ short circuited when idle points are closed.	1. Air flow meter circuit 2. Air flow meter 3. ECU
32	Air Flow Meter Signal	Open circuit in E₂ or Vc and Vs short circuited.	Same as 31, above.
41	Throttle Position Sensor Signal	Open or short circuit in throttle position sensor signal.	1. Throttle position sensor circuit 2. Throttle position sensor 3. ECU
42	Vehile Speed Sensor Signal	(A/T): Signal informing ECU that vehicle speed has been 2.0 km/h or less has been input ECU for 5 seconds with engine running at 2,500 rpm or more and shift lever in other than N or P range. (M/T): Signal informing ECU that vehicle speed has been 2.0 km/h or less has been input ECU for 5 seconds with engine running at 2,500 rpm or more.	1. Vehicle speed sensor circuit 2. Vehicle speed sensor 3. Torque converter slipping 4. ECU
43	Starter Signal (+ B)	No STA signal to ECU when engine is running over 800 rpm.	1. Main relay circuit 2. IG switch circuit (starter) 3. IG switch 4. ECU
51	Switch Signal	Neutral start switch OFF or air conditioner switch ON during diagnostic check.	1. Neutral start S/W 2. Air con. S/W 3. ECU
52	Knock Sensor Signal	Open or short circuit in knock sensor.	1. Knock sensor circuit 2. Knock sensor 3. ECU
53	Knock Control Part (ECU)	Faulty ECU.	ECU

TROUBLESHOOTING THE EFI SYSTEM WITH A VOLT/OHMMETER—1985-88 CRESSIDA

1. Remove the glove box door and glove box.
2. Remove the ECU with wire harness.

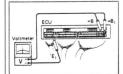

EFI SYSTEM CHECK PROCEDURE

NOTE:
1. The EFI circuit can be checked by measuring the resistance and voltage at the wiring connectors of the ECU.
2. Perform all voltage measurement with the connectors connected.
3. Verify that the battery voltage is 11V or above when the ignition switch is ON.

Using a voltmeter, measure the voltage at each terminal of the wiring connector.

NOTE: If there is any problem, see TROUBLESHOOTING FOR EFI ELECTRONIC CIRCUIT WITH VOLT/OHMMETER.

Connectors of ECU

Symbol	Terminal Name	Symbol	Terminal Name	Symbol	Terminal Name
E₀₁	ENGINE GROUND	G⊖	ENGINE REVOLUTION SENSOR	L₃	ECT COMPUTER
E₀₂	ENGINE GROUND	V₊	CHECK CONNECTOR	E₂₂	SENSOR EARTH
No.10	INJECTOR	T	CHECK CONNECTOR	TCD	ECT COMPUTER
No.20	INJECTOR	G	ENGINE REVOLUTION SENSOR	M-REL	MAIN RELAY COIL
STA	STARTER SWITCH	VTA	THROTTLE POSITION SENSOR	A/C	A/C MAGNETIC SWITCH
IGt	IGNITER	Ne	ENGINE REVOLUTION SENSOR	SPD	SPEEDOMETER
EGR	EGR VSV	IDL	THROTTLE POSITION SENSOR	W	WARNING LIGHT
E₁	ENGINE GROUND	KNK	KNOCK SENSOR	OIL	OIL PRESSURE SWITCH
N/C	NEUTRAL START SWITCH (A/T)	IGf	IGNITER	THA	AIR TEMP. SENSOR
	CLUTCH SWITCH (M/T)	Ox	OXYGEN SENSOR	V₊	AIR FLOW METER
ISC₁	ISC MOTOR NO.1 COIL	THW	WATER TEMP. SENSOR	Vc	AIR FLOW METER
ISC₂	ISC MOTOR NO.2 COIL	E₂	SENSOR EARTH	BAT	BATTERY – B
ISC₃	ISC MOTOR NO.3 COIL	L₁	ECT COMPUTER	+B	MAIN RELAY
ISC₄	ISC MOTOR NO.4 COIL	L₂	ECT COMPUTER	IG S/W	IGNITION SWITCH
				+B₁	BATTERY

E₀₁	No.10	STA	EGR	E₁	ISC₁	ISC₃	G⊖		G	Ne	IGf	THW	L₁	L₃	M-REL		SPD		THA	V₊	Vc	BAT	IG S/W
E₀₂	No.20	IGt	E₁	STJ	ISC₂	ISC₄	V₊		VTA	IDL	KNK	Ox	E₂	E₂₂		TCD		A/C	W	OIL		+B	+B₁

TROUBLESHOOTING THE EFI SYSTEM WITH A VOLT/OHMMETER (CONT.) – 1985-88 CRESSIDA

NOTE: Because the following troubleshooting procedures are designed for inspection of each separate system, the actual troubleshooting procedure may vary somewhat.
However, please refer to these procedures and perform actual troubleshooting, conforming to the inspection methods described in this manual.
For example, it is better to first make a simple check of the fuses, fusible links and connecting condition of the connectors before making your inspection according to the procedures listed.
The following troubleshooting procedures are based on the supposition that the trouble lies in either a short or open circuit in a component outside the computer or a short circuit within the computer.
If engine trouble occurs even though proper operating voltage is detected in the computer connector, then the ECU is faulty and should be replaced.

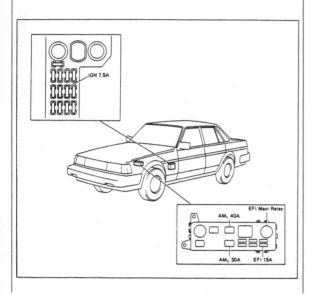

RESISTANCE SUPPLIED AT THE ECU WIRING CONNECTOR
1985-88 CRESSIDA

CAUTION:
1. Do not touch the ECU terminals.
2. The tester probe should be inserted into the wiring connector from the wiring side.

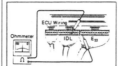

Using an ohmmeter, check the resistance between each terminal of the wiring connector.
- Remove the glove box.
- Disconnect the wiring connectors from the ECU.
- Measure the resistance between each terminal of the wiring connectors.

Resistances at ECU Wiring Connectors

Terminals	Condition	Resistance (Ω)
IDL – E22	Throttle valve open	∞
	Throttle valve fully closed	0 – 100Ω
VTA – E22	Throttle valve fully opened	3,300 – 10,000
	Throttle valve fully closed	200 – 800
Vc – E22	Disconnect air flow meter connector	3,000 – 7,000
	Disconnect throttle position sensor connector	200 – 400
Vs – E2	Measuring plate fully closed	20 – 400
	Measuring plate fully opened	20 – 1,000
THA – E2	Intake air temperature 20°C (68°F)	2,000 – 3,000
G – G⊖	—	140 – 180
Ne – G⊖	—	140 – 180
ISC1, ISC2 ISC3, ISC4 – B		10 – 30

VOLTAGE SUPPLIED AT THE ECU WIRING CONNECTOR
1985-88 CRESSIDA

No.	Terminals	Condition		STD Voltage
1	BAT – E1	—		10 – 14
	+B – E1	Ignition S/W ON		
	IG S/W – E1			
	M-REL – E1			
2	IDL – E22	Ignition S/W ON	Throttle valve open	4 – 6
	Vc – E22		—	4 – 6
	VTA – E22		Throttle valve fully closed	0.1 – 1.0
			Throttle valve fully opened	4 – 5
3	Vc – E2	Ignition S/W ON	—	4 – 6
			Measuring plate fully closed	4 – 5
	Vs – E2		Measuring plate fully open	0.02 – 0.08
			Idling	2 – 4
			3,000 rpm	0.3 – 1.0
	THA – E2	IG S/W ON	Intake air temperature 20°C (68°F)	1 – 2
4	THW – E2	IG S/W ON	Coolant temperature 80°C (176°F)	0.1 – 0.5
5	STA – E1	Ignition S/W ST position		6 – 12
6	No. 10 – E1 No. 20	Ignition S/W ON		9 – 14
7	IGt – E1	Cranking or idling		0.7 – 1.0
8	ISC1 ? – E1 ISC4	Ignition S/W ON		9 – 14
		2 – 3 secs. after engine off		9 – 14

TROUBLESHOOTING THE NO. 1 TERMINAL ON THE EFI CONNECTOR
1985-88 CRESSIDA

No.	Terminals	Trouble	Condition	STD Voltage
1	BAT – E1	No voltage	—	10 – 14
	+B – E1	No voltage	Ignition switch ON	10 – 14
	IG S/W – E1	No voltage	Ignition switch ON	10 – 14
	M-REL – E1	No voltage	Ignition switch ON	10 – 14

TROUBLESHOOTING THE NO. 1 TERMINAL ON THE EFI CONNECTOR
1985-88 CRESSIDA

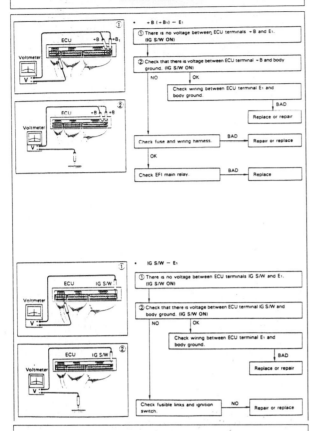

• +B (+B₁) — E₁:

① There is no voltage between ECU terminals +B and E₁. (IG S/W ON)

② Check that there is voltage between ECU terminal +B and body ground. (IG S/W ON)

NO / OK

OK → Check wiring between ECU terminal E₁ and body ground.
↓ BAD
Replace or repair

Check fuse and wiring harness. → BAD → Repair or replace
↓ OK
Check EFI main relay. → BAD → Replace

• IG S/W — E₁

① There is no voltage between ECU terminals IG S/W and E₁. (IG S/W ON)

② Check that there is voltage between ECU terminal IG S/W and body ground. (IG S/W ON)

NO / OK

OK → Check wiring between ECU terminal E₁ and body ground.
↓ BAD
Replace or repair

Check fusible links and ignition switch. → NO → Repair or replace

TROUBLESHOOTING THE NO. 1 TERMINAL ON THE EFI CONNECTOR
1985-88 CRESSIDA

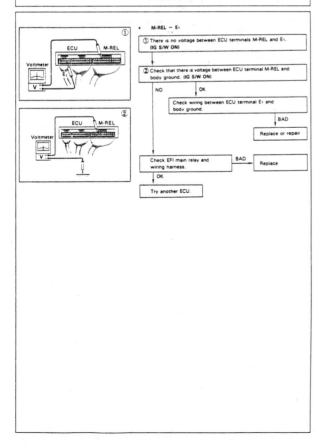

• M-REL — E₁

① There is no voltage between ECU terminals M-REL and E₁. (IG S/W ON)

② Check that there is voltage between ECU terminal M-REL and body ground. (IG S/W ON)

NO / OK

OK → Check wiring between ECU terminal E₁ and body ground.
↓ BAD
Replace or repair

Check EFI main relay and wiring harness. → BAD → Replace
↓ OK
Try another ECU.

TROUBLESHOOTING THE NO. 2 TERMINAL ON THE EFI CONNECTOR
1985-88 CRESSIDA

No.	Terminals	Trouble	Condition		STD voltage
2	IDL — E₂₂	No voltage	Ignition switch ON	Throttle valve open	4 — 6
	VTA — E₂₂			Throttle valve fully closed	0.1 — 1.0
				Throttle valve fully open	4 — 5
	Vc — E₂₂			—	4 — 6

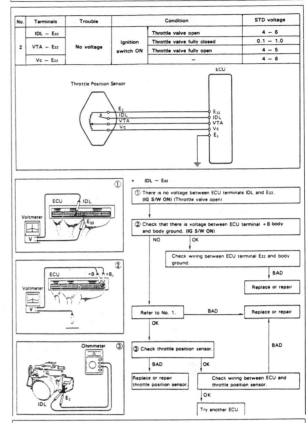

Throttle Position Sensor

• IDL — E₂₂

① There is no voltage between ECU terminals IDL and E₂₂. (IG S/W ON) (Throttle valve open)

② Check that there is voltage between ECU terminal +B body and body ground. (IG S/W ON)

NO / OK

OK → Check wiring between ECU terminal E₂₂ and body ground.
↓ BAD
Replace or repair

Refer to No. 1. → BAD → Replace or repair
↓ OK
③ Check throttle position sensor.
BAD / OK
BAD → Replace or repair throttle position sensor.
OK → Check wiring between ECU and throttle position sensor.
↓ OK
Try another ECU.

TROUBLESHOOTING THE NO. 2 TERMINAL ON THE EFI CONNECTOR
1985-88 CRESSIDA

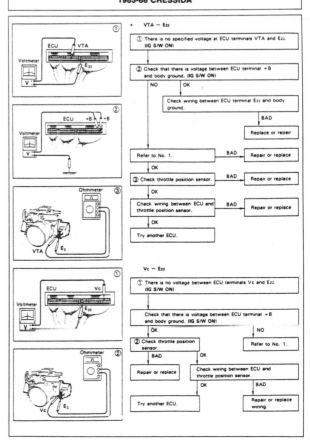

• VTA — E₂₂

① There is no specified voltage at ECU terminals VTA and E₂₂. (IG S/W ON)

② Check that there is voltage between ECU terminal +B and body ground. (IG S/W ON)

NO / OK

OK → Check wiring between ECU terminal E₂₂ and body ground.
↓ BAD
Replace or repair

Refer to No. 1. → BAD → Repair or replace
↓ OK
③ Check throttle position sensor. → BAD → Repair or replace
↓ OK
Check wiring between ECU and throttle position sensor. → BAD → Repair or replace
↓ OK
Try another ECU.

• Vc — E₂₂

① There is no voltage between ECU terminals Vc and E₂₂. (IG S/W ON)

Check that there is voltage between ECU terminal +B and body ground. (IG S/W ON)

OK / NO

NO → Refer to No. 1.

② Check throttle position sensor.
BAD / OK
BAD → Repair or replace
OK → Check wiring between ECU and throttle position sensor.
OK → Try another ECU.
BAD → Repair or replace wiring.

TROUBLESHOOTING THE NO. 3 TERMINAL ON THE EFI CONNECTOR
1985-88 CRESSIDA

No.	Terminal	Trouble		Condition	STD Voltage
3	Vc – E₂	No voltage	Ignition S/W ON	—	4 – 6 V
	Vs – E₂			Measuring plate fully closed	4 – 5 V
	Vs – E₂			Measuring plate fully open	0.02 – 0.08 V
	Vs – E₂		Idling		2 – 4 V
	Vs – E₂		3,000 rpm		0.3 – 1.0 V
	THA – E₂		IG S/W ON	Intake air temperature 20°C (68°F)	1 – 2 V

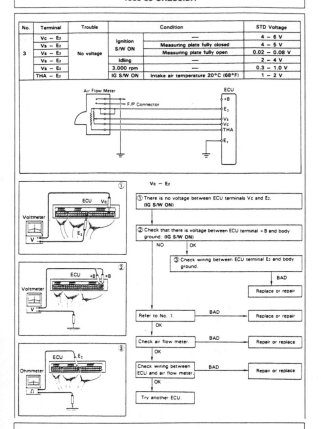

TROUBLESHOOTING THE NO. 3 TERMINAL ON THE EFI CONNECTOR
1985-88 CRESSIDA

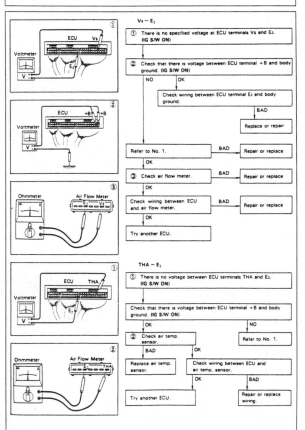

TROUBLESHOOTING THE NO. 4 TERMINAL ON THE EFI CONNECTOR
1985-88 CRESSIDA

No.	Terminals	Trouble	Condition		STD Voltage
4	THW – E₂	No voltage	Ignition switch ON	Coolant temperature 80°C (176°F)	0.1 – 0.5 V

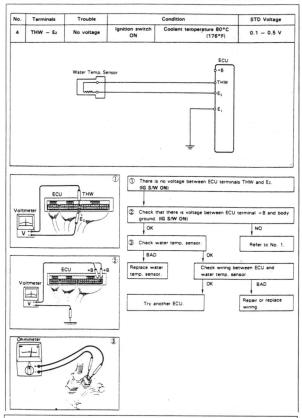

TROUBLESHOOTING THE NO. 5 TERMINAL ON THE EFI CONNECTOR
1985-88 CRESSIDA

No.	Terminals	Trouble	Condition	STD Voltage
5	STA – E₁	No voltage	Ignition switch ST position	6 – 12 V

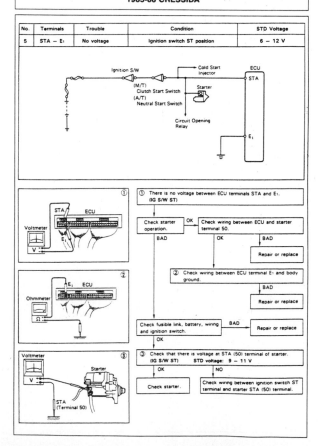

TROUBLESHOOTING THE NO. 6 TERMINAL ON THE EFI CONNECTOR
1985-88 CRESSIDA

No.	Terminals	Trouble	Condition	STD Voltage
6	No. 10 — E_{01} No. 20 — E_{01}	No voltage	Ignition switch ON	9 – 14V

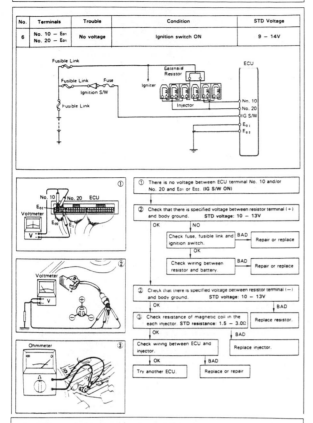

① There is no voltage between ECU terminal No. 10 and/or No. 20 and E_{01} or E_{02}. (IG S/W ON)

② Check that there is specified voltage between resistor terminal (+) and body ground.   STD voltage: 10 – 13V

- OK / NO
  - NO → Check fuse, fusible link and ignition switch. → BAD → Repair or replace
    - OK → Check wiring between resistor and battery. → BAD → Repair or replace

② Check that there is specified voltage between resistor terminal (−) and body ground.   STD voltage: 10 – 13V

- OK / BAD
  - BAD → Replace resistor.

③ Check resistance of magnetic coil in the each injector. STD resistance: 1.5 – 3.0Ω → BAD → Replace resistor.

- OK
  - Check wiring between ECU and injector. → BAD → Replace injector.
    - OK / BAD
      - OK → Try another ECU.
      - BAD → Replace or repair

TROUBLESHOOTING THE NO. 7 TERMINAL ON THE EFI CONNECTOR
1985-88 CRESSIDA

No.	Terminals	Trouble	Condition	STD Voltage
7	IGt — E_1	No voltage	Cranking or Idling	0.7 – 1.0V

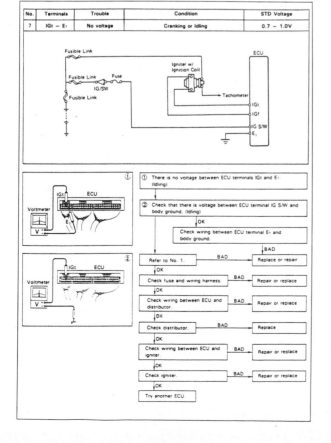

① There is no voltage between ECU terminals IGt and E_1. (Idling)

② Check that there is voltage between ECU terminal IG S/W and body ground. (Idling)

- OK
  - Check wiring between ECU terminal E_1 and body ground.

- BAD
  - Refer to No. 1. → BAD → Replace or repair
    - OK → Check fuse and wiring harness. → BAD → Repair or replace
      - OK → Check wiring between ECU and distributor. → BAD → Repair or replace
        - OK → Check distributor. → BAD → Replace
          - OK → Check wiring between ECU and igniter. → BAD → Repair or replace
            - OK → Check igniter. → BAD → Repair or replace
              - OK → Try another ECU.

TROUBLESHOOTING THE NO. 8 TERMINAL ON THE EFI CONNECTOR
1985-88 CRESSIDA

No.	Terminal	Trouble	Condition	STD Voltage
8	ISC_1–ISC_4 — E_1	No voltage	Ignition switch ON	9 – 14V

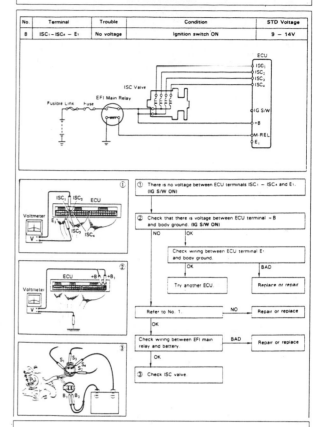

① There is no voltage between ECU terminals ISC_1 – ISC_4 and E_1. (IG S/W ON)

② Check that there is voltage between ECU terminal –B and body ground. (IG S/W ON)

- NO / OK
  - OK → Check wiring between ECU terminal E_1 and body ground. → BAD → Replace or repair
    - OK → Try another ECU.

- Refer to No. 1. → NO → Repair or replace
  - OK → Check wiring between EFI main relay and battery. → BAD → Repair or replace
    - OK

③ Check ISC valve.

ELECTRONIC COMPONENT LOCATIONS – 1985-88 CRESSIDA

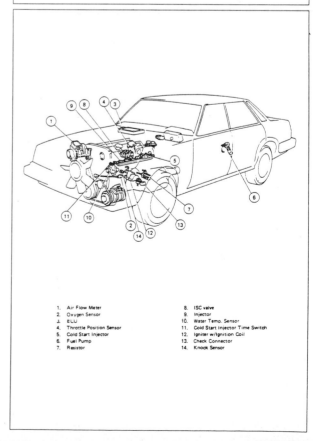

1. Air Flow Meter
2. Oxygen Sensor
3. ECU
4. Throttle Position Sensor
5. Cold Start Injector
6. Fuel Pump
7. Resistor
8. ISC valve
9. Injector
10. Water Temp. Sensor
11. Cold Start Injector Time Switch
12. Igniter w/Ignition Coil
13. Check Connector
14. Knock Sensor

TESTING THE OXYGEN SENSOR – 1985-88 CRESSIDA

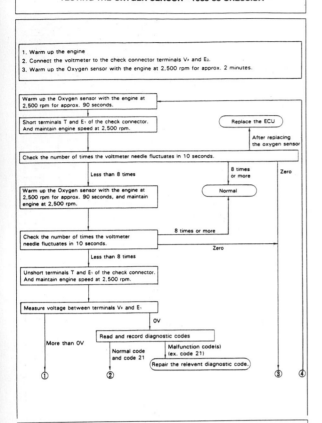

1. Warm up the engine
2. Connect the voltmeter to the check connector terminals V$_f$ and E$_2$.
3. Warm up the Oxygen sensor with the engine at 2,500 rpm for approx. 2 minutes.

Warm up the Oxygen sensor with the engine at 2,500 rpm for approx. 90 seconds.

Short terminals T and E$_1$ of the check connector. And maintain engine speed at 2,500 rpm.

Replace the ECU

After replacing the oxygen sensor

Check the number of times the voltmeter needle fluctuates in 10 seconds.

Less than 8 times

8 times or more — Zero

Normal

Warm up the Oxygen sensor with the engine at 2,500 rpm for approx. 90 seconds, and maintain engine at 2,500 rpm.

8 times or more

Check the number of times the voltmeter needle fluctuates in 10 seconds.

Zero

Less than 8 times

Unshort terminals T and E$_1$ of the check connector. And maintain engine speed at 2,500 rpm.

Measure voltage between terminals V$_f$ and E$_1$.

0V

More than 0V

Read and record diagnostic codes

Normal code and code 21

Malfunction code(s) (ex. code 21)

Repair the relevent diagnostic code.

① ② ③ ④

TESTING THE OXYGEN SENSOR (CONT.) – 1985-88 CRESSIDA

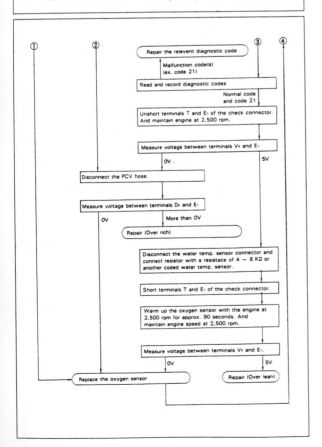

① ② ③ ④

Repair the relevent diagnostic code

Malfunction code(s) (ex. code 21)

Read and record diagnostic codes

Normal code and code 21

Unshort terminals T and E$_1$ of the check connector. And maintain engine at 2,500 rpm.

Measure voltage between terminals V$_f$ and E$_1$.

0V — 5V

Disconnect the PCV hose.

Measure voltage between terminals D$_f$ and E$_1$.

0V — More than 0V

Repair (Over rich)

Disconnect the water temp. sensor connector and connect resistor with a resistance of 4 — 8 KΩ or another coded water temp. sensor.

Short terminals T and E$_1$ of the check connector.

Warm up the oxygen sensor with the engine at 2,500 rpm for approx. 90 seconds. And maintain engine speed at 2,500 rpm.

Measure voltage between terminals V$_f$ and E$_1$.

0V — 5V

Replace the oxygen sensor — Repair (Over lean)

INSPECTION OF THE ELECTRONIC CONTROL UNIT – 1985-88 CRESSIDA

1. MEASURE VOLTAGE OF ECU
    NOTE: The EFI circuit can be checked by measuring the resistance and voltage at the wiring connectors of the ECU.
    Check the voltages at the wiring connectors.
    • Remove the glove box.
    • Turn on the ignition switch.
    • Measure the voltage at each terminal.

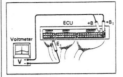

NOTE: 1. Perform all voltage measurements with the connectors connected.
       2. Verify that the battery voltage is 11V or above when the ignition switch is ON.

Connectors of ECU

Symbol	Terminal Name	Symbol	Terminal Name	Symbol	Terminal Name
E$_{01}$	ENGINE GROUND	G⊖	ENGINE REVOLUTION SENSOR	L$_3$	ECT COMPUTER
E$_{02}$	ENGINE GROUND	V$_f$	CHECK CONNECTOR	E$_{22}$	SENSOR EARTH
No.10	INJECTOR	T	CHECK CONNECTOR	TCD	ECT COMPUTER
No.20	INJECTOR	G	ENGINE REVOLUTION SENSOR	M-REL	MAIN RELAY COIL
STA	STARTER SWITCH	Ne	ENGINE REVOLUTION SENSOR	A/C	A/C MAGNETIC SWITCH
IGt	IGNITER	VTA	THROTTLE POSITION SENSOR	SPD	SPEEDOMETER
EGR	EGR VSV	IDL	THROTTLE POSITION SENSOR	W	WARNING LIGHT
E$_1$	ENGINE GROUND	KNK	KNOCK SENSOR	OIL	OIL PRESSURE SWITCH
N/C	NEUTRAL START SWITCH (A/T)	IGf	IGNITER	THA	AIR TEMP. SENSOR
	CLUTCH SWITCH (M/T)	Ox	OXYGEN SENSOR	V$_s$	AIR FLOW METER
ISC$_1$	ISC MOTOR NO.1 COIL	THW	WATER TEMP. SENSOR	V$_c$	AIR FLOW METER
ISC$_2$	ISC MOTOR NO.2 COIL	E$_2$	SENSOR EARTH	BAT	BATTERY +B
ISC$_3$	ISC MOTOR NO.3 COIL	L$_1$	ECT COMPUTER	–B	MAIN RELAY
ISC$_4$	ISC MOTOR NO.4 COIL	L$_2$	ECT COMPUTER	IG S/W	IGNITION SWITCH
				+B$_1$	BATTERY

E$_{01}$	No.10	STA	EGR	N/C	ISC$_1$	ISC$_3$	G⊖		G	Ne		IGf	THW	L$_1$	L$_3$	M-REL		SPD		THA	V$_s$	V$_c$	BAT	IG S/W
E$_{02}$	No.20	IGt	E$_1$		ISC$_2$	ISC$_4$	V$_f$	T	VTA	IDL	KNK	Ox	E$_2$	E$_{22}$		TCD	A/C	W	OIL			+B	+B$_1$

INSPECTING THE VOLTAGE AT THE ECU WIRING CONNECTOR 1985-88 CRESSIDA

Terminals	STD Voltage		Condition
BAT — E$_1$		—	—
+B — E$_1$	10 — 14		—
IG S/W — E$_1$			
M-REL — E$_1$			
IDL — E$_2$	4 — 6	IG S/W ON	Throttle valve open
VTA — E$_2$	0.1 — 1.0		Throttle valve fully closed
	4 — 5		Throttle valve fully opened
Vc — E$_2$	4 —		—
Vs — E$_2$	4 — 5		Measuring plate fully closed
	0.02 — 0.08		Measuring plate fully open
	2 — 4		Idling
	0.3 — 1.0		3,000 rpm
THA — E$_2$	1 — 2	IG S/W ON	Intake air temperature 20°C (68°F)
THW — E$_1$	0.1 — 0.5		Coolant temperature 80°C (176°F)
STA — E$_1$	6 — 12		IG S/W ST position
No. 10 No. 20 — E$_1$	9 — 14	IG S/W ON	—
IGt — E$_1$	0.7 — 1.0		Cranking or idling
ISC$_1$ ⌇ ISC$_4$ — E$_1$	9 — 14	IG S/W ON	—
	9 — 14		2 — 3 secs. after engine off
+B — EGR	10 — 13	IG S/W ON	—
	0		Start engine and warm up oxygen sensor
N/C — E$_1$	0		Shift position P or N range (for A/T)
	10 — 14	IG S/W ON	Ex. P or N range (for A/T)
	0		Clutch pedal not depressed (for M/T)
	10 — 14		Clutch pedal depressed (for M/T)
	9 — 11		Cranking
T — E$_1$	4 — 6	IG S/W ON	Check connector T and E$_1$ not short
	0		Check connector T and E$_1$ short

INSPECTING THE VOLTAGE AT THE ECU WIRING CONNECTOR 1985-88 CRESSIDA

OIL – E₁	4 – 6		IG S/W ON (Warning light on)
	0		Start engine (Warning light out)
A/C – E₁	10 – 13	IG S/W ON	Air con S/W ON
	0		Air con S/W OFF
Vₑ – E₁	0 – 5		Start engine (Throttle valve open)
W – E₁	0	IG S/W ON	
	10 – 13		Start engine
TCD – E₁	2 – 3	IG S/W ON	Coolant temperature Less than 35°C (95°F)
	0		Coolant temperature 35 – 60°C (95 – 140°F)
	4 – 6		Coolant temperature More than 60°C (140°F)

INSPECTING THE RESISTANCE AT THE ECU WIRING CONNECTOR 1985-88 CRESSIDA

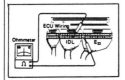

2. **MEASURE RESISTANCE OF ECU**

CAUTION:
1. Do not touch the ECU terminals.
2. The tester probe should be inserted into wiring connector from wiring side.

Check the resistance between each terminal of the wiring connector.
- Remove the glove box.
- Unplug the wiring connectors from the ECU.
- Measure the resistance between each terminal of the wiring connectors.

Resistances at ECU Wiring Connectors

Terminals	Condition	Resistance (Ω)
IDL – E₂₂	Throttle valve open	∞
	Throttle valve fully closed	0
VTA – E₂₂	Throttle valve fully opened	3,300 – 10,000
	Throttle valve fully closed	200 – 800
Vc – E₂₂	Disconnect air flow meter connector	3,000 – 7,000
	Disconnect throttle position sensor connector	200 – 400
Vs – E₂	Measuring plate fully closed	20 – 400
	Measuring plate fully open	20 – 1000
THA – E₂	Intake air temperature 20°C (68°F)	2,000 – 3,000
G – G ⊖	—	140 – 180
Ne – G ⊖	—	
ISC₁, ISC₂ ISC₃, ISC₄ – +B		10 – 30

EFI WIRING SCHEMATIC – 1986-88 MR2

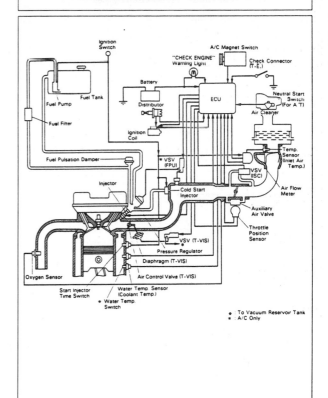

DIAGNOSIS CODES – 1986-88 MR2

Code No.	Number of blinks "CHECK ENGINE"	System	Diagnosis	Trouble area
1		Normal	This appears when none of the other codes (2 thru 11) are identified	
2		Air flow meter signal	• Open circuit in VC, VS, VB or E2 • Short circuit in VC	1. Air flow meter circuit 2. Air flow meter 3. ECU
3		Ignition signal	No signal from igniter four times in succession	1. Ignition circuit (+B, IGF) 2. Igniter 3. ECU
4		Water temp. sensor signal	Open or short circuit in coolant temperature sensor signal.	1. Coolant Temp. sensor circuit 2. Coolant Temp. sensor 3. ECU
5		Oxygen sensor signal	Open circuit in Oxygen Sensor signal (only lean indication)	1. Oxygen sensor circuit 2. Oxygen sensor 3. ECU
6		RPM signal	No "Ne", "G" signal to ECU within several seconds after engine is cranked.	1. Distributor circuit 2. Distributor 3. Igniter 4. Starter signal circuit 5. ECU
7		Throttle position sensor signal	Open or short circuit in throttle position sensor signal.	1. Throttle position sensor circuit 2. Throttle position sensor 3. ECU
8		Intake air temp. sensor signal	Open or short circuit in intake air temperature sensor.	1. Air temp. sensor circuit 2. ECU
10		Starter signal	No STA signal to ECU when engine is running over 800 rpm.	1. Starter relay circuit 2. IG switch circuit (starter) 3. IG switch 4. ECU
11		Switch signal	Air conditioner switch ON, idle switch OFF or shift position D range (A/T only) during diagnosis check.	1. Air con. S/W 2. ECU 3. Idle S/W 4. Neutral S/W (A/T only)

NOTE:
- There is no diagnosis code No. 9.
- Diagnosis code No. 10 will be indicated if the vehicle is push started.

INSPECTION OF THE DIAGNOSIS CIRCUIT – 1986-88 MR2

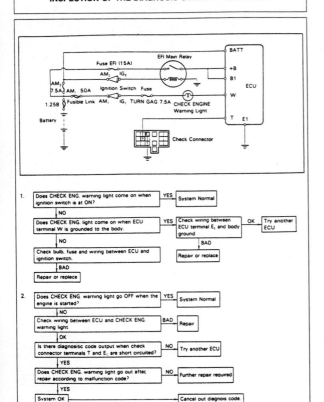

1.

| Does CHECK ENG. warning light come on when ignition switch is at ON? | YES → | System Normal |

NO ↓

| Does CHECK ENG. light come on when ECU terminal W is grounded to the body. | YES → | Check wiring between ECU terminal E₁ and body ground. | OK → | Try another ECU |

NO ↓

BAD → Repair or replace

| Check bulb, fuse and wiring between ECU and ignition switch. |

BAD ↓

Repair or replace

2.

| Does CHECK ENG. warning light go OFF when the engine is started? | YES → | System Normal |

NO ↓

| Check wiring between ECU and CHECK ENG. warning light. | BAD → | Repair |

OK ↓

| Is there diagnostic code output when check connector terminals T and E₁ are short circuited? | NO → | Try another ECU |

YES ↓

| Does CHECK ENG. warning light go out after repair according to malfunction code? | NO → | Further repair required |

YES ↓

| System OK | → | Cancel out diagnosis code. |

TROUBLESHOOTING THE EFI SYSTEM WITH A VOLT/OHMMETER – 1986-88 MR2

1. Remove the rear luggage compartment trim.
2. Remove the ECU with the wire harness.

EFI SYSTEM CHECK PROCEDURE

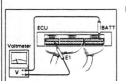

NOTE:
1. The EFI circuit can be checked by measuring the resistance and voltage at the wiring connectors of the ECU.

2. Perform all voltage measurements with the connectors connected.

3. Verify that the battery voltage is 11V or above when the ignition switch is at ON.

Using a voltmeter with high impedance (10 kΩ/V minimum), measure the voltage at each terminal of the wiring connector.

NOTE: If there is any problem, see TROUBLESHOOTING FOR EFI ELECTRONIC CIRCUIT WITH VOLT/OHMMETER.

Connectors of ECU

Symbol	Terminal	Symbol	Terminal	symbol	Terminal
EO1	Engine ground (Power)	T	Service connector	* L3	ECT Computer
EO2	Engine ground (Power)	TSW	Water temperature switch	* ECT	ECT Computer
No. 10	No. 3, 4 injector	IDL	Throttle position sensor	* L1	ECT Computer
No. 20	No. 1, 2 injector	A/C	A/C Magnet clutch	* L2	ECT Computer
STA	Starter switch	IGF	Igniter	VC	Air flow meter
IGT	Igniter	E2	Sensor ground	E21	Sensor ground
VF	Service connector	OX	Oxygen sensor	—	—
E1	Engine ground	G ⊝	Engine revolution sensor	VS	Air flow meter
* NSW	Neutral start switch	G ⊝	Engine revolution sensor	THA	Inlet air temp. sensor
S/TH	VSV (T-VIS)	VCC	Throttle position sensor	SPD	Speedometer sensor
FPU	VSV (FPU)	—	—	BATT	Battery
V-ISC	VSV (ISC)	VTA	Throttle position sensor	+ B1	EFI main relay
W	Warning light	NE	Engine revolution sensor	+ B	EFI main relay
		THW	Water temperature sensor		

* : A/T only

ECU Connectors

EO1	No. 10	STA	VF	*NSW	FPU	W	T	IDL	IGF	G–	G÷		NE		*L3	*L1	VC	VS	THA	BATT	+B1
EO2	No. 20	IGT	E1	S/TH	V-ISC		TSW	A/C	E2	OX	VCC	VTA	THW		*ECT	*L2	E21		SPD		+B

VOLTAGE SUPPLIED AT THE ECU WIRING CONNECTOR 1986-88 MR2

Voltage at ECU wiring connectors

No.	Terminals	STD voltage		Condition
1	BATT – E1	—		—
	+ B1 – E1	10 – 14		Ignition S/W ON
	+ B			
2	IDL – E2	10 – 14		Throttle valve open
	VTA – E2	0.1 – 1.0	Ignition S/W ON	Throttle valve fully closed
		4 – 5		Throttle valve fully open
	VCC – E2	4 – 6		—
3	+B1 – E2	10 – 14	Ignition S/W ON	—
	VC – E2	6 – 10		—
	VS – E2	0.5 – 2.5	Engine running	Measuring plate fully closed
		5 – 10		Measuring plate fully open
		2 – 8	Idling	—
4	No. 10 – E1 No. 20	10 – 14		Ignition S/W ON
5	THA – E2	1 – 3	Ignition S/W ON	Intake air temperature 20°C (68°F)
6	THW – E2	0.1 – 1.0	Ignition S/W ON	Coolant temperature 80°C (176°F)
7	STA – E1	6 – 14		Ignition S/W ST position and press on the clutch pedal (M/T)
8	IGT – E1	0.7 – 1.0		Idling
9	A/C – E1	10 – 14		Air conditioning ON

* : A/T only

ECU Connectors

EO1	No. 10	STA	VF	*NSW	FPU	W	T	IDL	IGF	G⊝	G⊕		NE		*L3	*L1	VC	VS		THA	BATT	+B1
EO2	No. 20	IGT	E1	S/TH	V-ISC		TSW	A/C	E2	OX	VCC	VTA	THW		*ECT	*L2	E21			SPD		+B

TROUBLESHOOTING THE EFI SYSTEM WITH A VOLT/OHMMETER (CONT.) – 1986-88 MR2

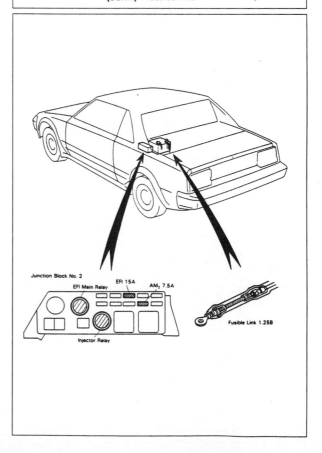

Junction Block No. 2

EFI Main Relay

EFI 15A

AM₂ 7.5A

Injector Relay

Fusible Link 1.25B

TROUBLESHOOTING THE NO. 1 TERMINAL ON THE EFI CONNECTOR
1986-88 MR2

No.	Terminals	Trouble	Condition	STD Voltage
1	BATT — E1	No voltage	—	10 – 14
	+B1 — E1 +B — E1	No voltage	Ignition switch ON	10 – 14

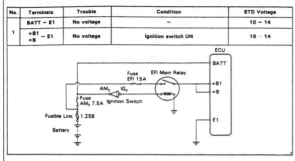

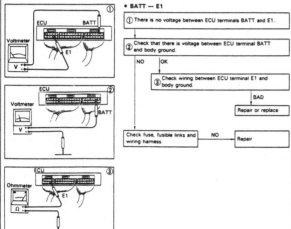

• BATT — E1

① There is no voltage between ECU terminals BATT and E1.

↓

② Check that there is voltage between ECU terminal BATT and body ground.

NO / OK

③ Check wiring between ECU terminal E1 and body ground.

↓ BAD

Repair or replace

Check fuse, fusible links and wiring harness. — NO → Repair

TROUBLESHOOTING THE NO. 1 TERMINAL ON THE EFI CONNECTOR
1986-88 MR2

• +B1 or +B — E1

① There is no voltage between ECU terminals +B1 or +B and E1. (IG S/W ON)

↓

② Check that there is voltage between ECU terminals +B1 or +B and body ground. (IG S/W ON)

NO / OK

③ Check wiring between ECU terminal E1 and body ground.

↓ BAD

Repair or replace

Check fuse, fusible link and wiring harness. — BAD → Repair or replace

↓ OK

Check EFI main relay. — BAD → Replace

TROUBLESHOOTING THE NO. 2 TERMINAL ON THE EFI CONNECTOR
1986-88 MR2

No.	Terminals	Trouble	Condition	STD Voltage
2	IDL — E2	No voltage	Ignition switch ON	Throttle valve open	10 – 14
	VTA — E2			Throttle valve fully closed	0.1 – 1.0
				Throttle valve fully open	4 – 5
	VCC — E2		—	4 – 6

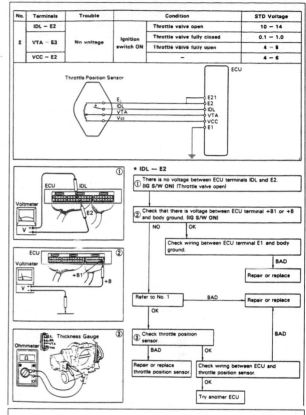

• IDL — E2

① There is no voltage between ECU terminals IDL and E2. (IG S/W ON) (Throttle valve open)

↓

② Check that there is voltage between ECU terminal +B1 or +B and body ground. (IG S/W ON)

NO / OK

Check wiring between ECU terminal E1 and body ground.

↓ BAD

Repair or replace

Refer to No. 1 — BAD → Repair or replace

↓ OK

③ Check throttle position sensor.

BAD / OK

Repair or replace throttle position sensor. / Check wiring between ECU and throttle position sensor.

↓ OK

Try another ECU

TROUBLESHOOTING THE NO. 2 TERMINAL ON THE EFI CONNECTOR
1986-88 MR2

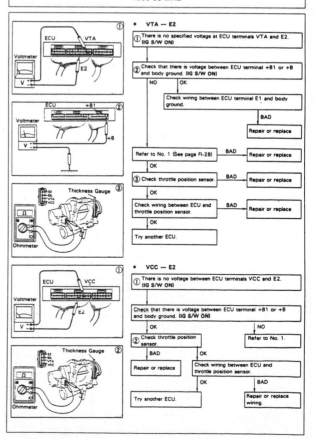

• VTA — E2

① There is no specified voltage at ECU terminals VTA and E2. (IG S/W ON)

↓

② Check that there is voltage between ECU terminal +B1 or +B and body ground. (IG S/W ON)

NO / OK

Check wiring between ECU terminal E1 and body ground.

↓ BAD

Repair or replace

Refer to No. 1 (See page FI-28) — BAD → Repair or replace

↓ OK

③ Check throttle position sensor. — BAD → Repair or replace

↓ OK

Check wiring between ECU and throttle position sensor. — BAD → Repair or replace

↓ OK

Try another ECU.

• VCC — E2

① There is no voltage between ECU terminals VCC and E2. (IG S/W ON)

↓

② Check that there is voltage between ECU terminal +B1 or +B and body ground. (IG S/W ON)

OK / NO

Refer to No. 1.

Check throttle position sensor.

BAD / OK

Repair or replace / Check wiring between ECU and throttle position sensor.

OK / BAD

Try another ECU. / Repair or replace wiring.

TROUBLESHOOTING THE NO. 3 TERMINAL ON THE EFI CONNECTOR
1986-88 MR2

No.	Terminals	Trouble	Condition		STD Voltage
3	+B1 — E2	No voltage	Ignition switch ON	—	10 — 14V
	VC — E2			—	6 — 10V
	VS — E2		Measuring plate fully closed	0.5 — 2.5V
	VS — E2		Engine running Measuring plate fully open	5 — 10V
	VS — E2		Idling	—	2 — 8V

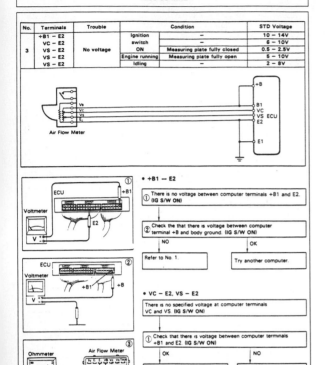

Air Flow Meter

① • +B1 — E2

① There is no voltage between computer terminals +B1 and E2. (IG S/W ON)

② Check the that there is voltage between computer terminal +B and body ground. (IG S/W ON)

NO — Refer to No. 1.
OK — Try another computer.

② • VC — E2, VS — E2

There is no specified voltage at computer terminals VC and VS. (IG S/W ON)

① Check that there is voltage between computer terminals +B1 and E2. (IG S/W ON)

OK ↓   NO →

③ Check air flow meter.   Refer to No. 1

NO ↓   OK →

Repair or replace air flow meter.   Check wiring between computer and air flow meter.

TROUBLESHOOTING THE NO. 4 TERMINAL ON THE EFI CONNECTOR
1986-88 MR2

No.	Terminals	Trouble	Condition	STD Voltage
4	No. 10 — E1 No. 20 — E1	No voltage	Ignition switch ON	10 — 14V

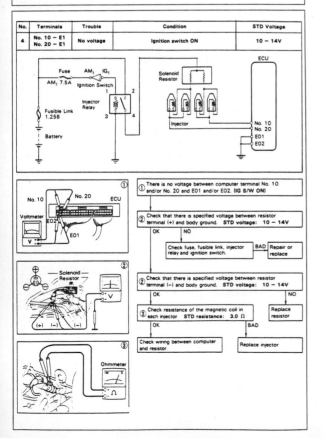

① There is no voltage between computer terminal No. 10 and/or No. 20 and E01 and/or E02. (IG S/W ON)

② Check that there is specified voltage between resistor terminal (+) and body ground. STD voltage: 10 — 14V

OK   NO

Check fuse, fusible link, injector relay and ignition switch. BAD → Repair or replace

② Check that there is specified voltage between resistor terminal (−) and body ground. STD voltage: 10 — 14V

OK   NO

③ Check resistance of the magnetic coil in each injector. STD resistance: 3.0 Ω   Replace resistor

OK   BAD

Check wiring between computer and resistor.   Replace injector

TROUBLESHOOTING THE NO. 5 TERMINAL ON THE EFI CONNECTOR
1986-88 MR2

No.	Terminals	Trouble	Condition		STD voltage
5	THA — E2	No voltage	Ignition switch ON	Intake air temperature 20°C (68°F)	1 — 3 V

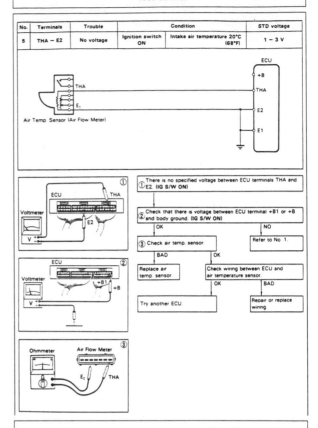

Air Temp. Sensor (Air Flow Meter)

① There is no specified voltage between ECU terminals THA and E2. (IG S/W ON)

② Check that there is voltage between ECU terminal +B1 or +B and body ground. (IG S/W ON)

OK   NO → Refer to No. 1.

③ Check air temp. sensor.

BAD   OK

Replace air temp. sensor.   Check wiring between ECU and air temperature sensor.

OK   BAD

Try another ECU.   Repair or replace wiring.

TROUBLESHOOTING THE NO. 6 TERMINAL ON THE EFI CONNECTOR
1986-88 MR2

No.	Terminals	Trouble	Condition		STD Voltage
6	THW — E2	No voltage	Ignition switch ON	Coolant temperature 80°C (176°F)	0.1 — 1.0 V

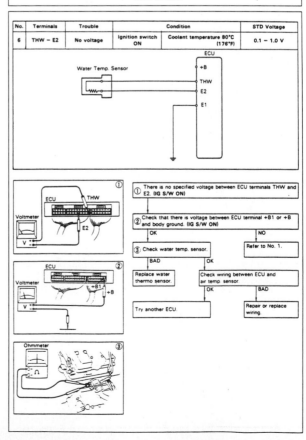

Water Temp. Sensor

① There is no specified voltage between ECU terminals THW and E2. (IG S/W ON)

② Check that there is voltage between ECU terminal +B1 or +B and body ground. (IG S/W ON)

OK   NO → Refer to No. 1.

③ Check water temp. sensor.

BAD   OK

Replace water thermo sensor.   Check wiring between ECU and air temp. sensor.

OK   BAD

Try another ECU.   Repair or replace wiring.

TROUBLESHOOTING THE NO. 7 TERMINAL ON THE EFI CONNECTOR
1986-88 MR2

No.	Terminals	Trouble	Condition	STD Voltage
7	STA – E1	No voltage	Ignition switch ST position	6 – 14 V

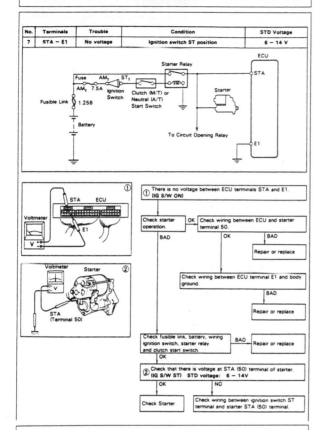

TROUBLESHOOTING THE NO. 9 TERMINAL ON THE EFI CONNECTOR
1986-88 MR2

No.	Terminals	Trouble	Condition.	STD Voltage
9	A/C – E1	No voltage	Air conditioning ON	10 – 14 V

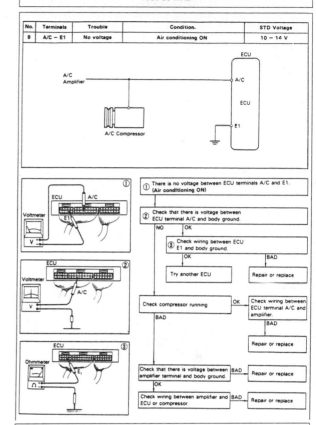

TROUBLESHOOTING THE NO. 8 TERMINAL ON THE EFI CONNECTOR
1986-88 MR2

No.	Terminals	Trouble	Condition	STD Voltage
8	IGT – E₁	No voltage	Idling	0.7 – 1.0 V

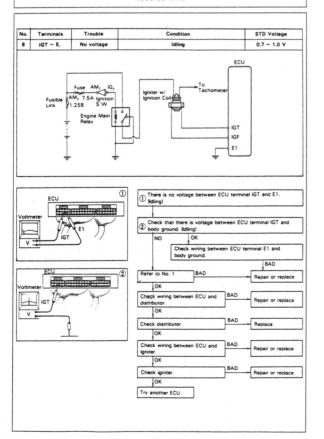

ELECTRONIC COMPONENT LOCATIONS – 1986-88 MR2

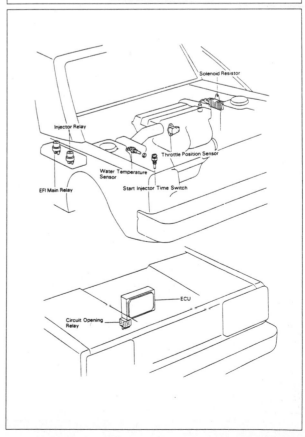

TESTING THE OXYGEN SENSOR – 1986-88 MR2

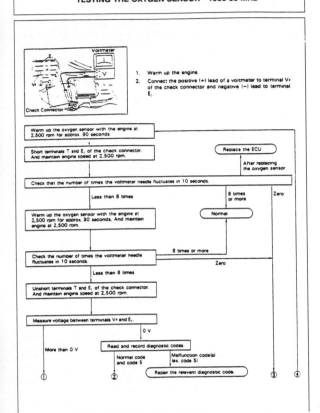

1. Warm up the engine.
2. Connect the positive (+) lead of a voltmeter to terminal V_F of the check connector and negative (−) lead to terminal E_1.

Warm up the oxygen sensor with the engine at 2,500 rpm for approx. 90 seconds.

Short terminals T and E_1 of the check connector. And maintain engine speed at 2,500 rpm.

→ Replace the ECU → After replacing the oxygen sensor

Check that the number of times the voltmeter needle fluctuates in 10 seconds.

Less than 8 times | 8 times or more | Zero

→ Normal

Warm up the oxygen sensor with the engine at 2,500 rpm for approx. 90 seconds. And maintain engine at 2,500 rpm.

8 times or more

Check the number of times the voltmeter needle fluctuates in 10 seconds.

Less than 8 times | Zero

Unshort terminals T and E_1 of the check connector. And maintain engine speed at 2,500 rpm.

Measure voltage between terminals V_F and E_1.

More than 0 V | 0 V

Read and record diagnostic codes.

Normal code and code 5 | Malfunction code(s) (ex. code 5)

Repair the relevent diagnostic code.

① ② ③ ④

INSPECTION OF THE ELECTRONIC CONTROL UNIT – 1986-88 MR2

1. **MEASURE VOLTAGE OF ECU**

   NOTE: The EFI circuit can be checked by measuring the resistance and voltage at the wiring connectors of the ECU.

   Check the voltages at the wiring connectors.
   - Remove the rear luggage compartment trim.
   - Turn the ignition switch ON.
   - Measure the voltage at each terminal.

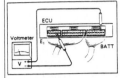

NOTE: 1. Perform all voltage measurements with the connectors connected.
2. Verify that the battery voltage is 11 V or above when the ignition switch is ON.

Connectors of ECU

Symbol	Terminal	Symbol	Terminal	Symbol	Terminal
EO1	Engine ground (Power)	T	Service connector	*L3	ECT Computor
EO2	Engine ground (Power)	TSW	Water temperature switch	*ECT	ECT Computor
No. 10	No.3, 4 injector	IDL	Throttle position sensor	*L1	ECT Computor
No. 20	No.1, 2 injector	A/C	A/C Magnet clutch	*L2	ECT Computor
STA	Starter switch	IGF	Igniter	VC	Air flow meter
IG	Igniter	E2	Sensor ground	E21	Sensor ground
VF	Service connector	G ⊖	Engine revolution sensor	VS	Air flow meter
E1	Engine ground	OX	Oxygen sensor		
*NSW	Neutral Start Switch	G ⊕	Engine revolution sensor	THA	Inlet air temp. sensor
S/TH	VSV (T-VIS)	VCC	Throttle position sensor	SPD	Speedometer sensor
FPU	VSV (FPU)	—		BATT	Battery
V-ISC	VSV (ISC)	VTA	Throttle position sensor	—	
W	Warning light	NE	Engine revolution sensor	+B1	EFI main relay
—		THW	Water temp. sensor	+B	EFI main relay

* A/T only

ECU Connectors

EO1	NO. 10	STA	VF	*NSW	FPU	W	T	IDL	IGF	G⊖	G⊕		NE	*L3	*L1		VS	THA	BATT	+B1
EO2	NO. 20	IGT	E1	S/TH	V-ISC		TSW	A/C	E2	OX	VCC	VTA	THW	*ECT	*L2	E21		SPD		+B

TESTING THE OXYGEN SENSOR (CONT.) – 1986-88 MR2

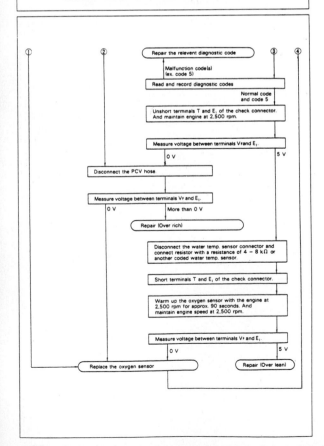

① ② ③ ④

Repair the relevent diagnostic code.

Malfunction code(s) (ex. code 5)

Read and record diagnostic codes.

Normal code and code 5

Unshort terminals T and E_1 of the check connector. And maintain engine at 2,500 rpm.

Measure voltage between terminals V_F and E_1.

0 V | 5 V

Disconnect the PCV hose.

Measure voltage between terminals V_F and E_1.

0 V | More than 0 V

Repair (Over rich)

Disconnect the water temp. sensor connector and connect resistor with a resistance of 4 – 8 kΩ or another coded water temp. sensor.

Short terminals T and E_1 of the check connector.

Warm up the oxygen sensor with the engine at 2,500 rpm for approx. 90 seconds. And maintain engine speed at 2,500 rpm.

Measure voltage between terminals V_F and E_1.

0 V | 5 V

Replace the oxygen sensor | Repair (Over lean)

INSPECTING THE VOLTAGE AT THE ECU WIRING CONNECTOR 1986-88 MR2

Voltage at ECU Wiring Connectors

Terminals	STD voltage		Condition
BATT – E1			—
+B – E1	10 – 14	IG S/W ON	
+B1 – E1			
IDL – E1	10 – 14	IG S/W ON	Throttle valve open
VC – E2	6 – 10	IG S/W ON	—
VS – E2	0.5 – 2.5		Measuring plate fully closed
	5 – 10	Engine running	Measuring plate fully open
	2 – 8	Idling	
THA – E2	1 – 3	IG S/W ON	Intake air temperature 20°C (68°F)
THW – E2	0.1 – 1.0	IG S/W ON	Coolant temperature 80°C (176°F)
STA – E1	6 – 14		IG S/W ST position
No. 10 No. 20 – E1	10 – 14		IG S/W ON
IGT – E1	0.7 – 1.0		Idling
T – E1	10 – 14	IG S/W ON	Service connector T ↔ E_1 not short
	0		Service connector T ↔ E_1 short
A/C – E1	10 – 14	IG S/W ON	A/C switch ON
	0		A/C switch OFF
W – E1	0		IG S/W ON
	10 – 14		Engine start
S/TH – E1	0 – 2		Idling
	10 – 14		More than 4,350 rpm
VTA – E2	0.1 – 1.0	IG S/W ON	Throttle valve fully closed
	4 – 5		Throttle valve fully open
VCC – E2	4 – 6	IG S/W ON	
*NSW – E1	0	IG S/W ON	Shift position P or N range
	10 – 14		Ex. P or N range
	9 – 11		Cranking

* : A/T only

INSPECTING THE RESISTANCE AT THE ECU WIRING CONNECTOR 1986-88 MR2

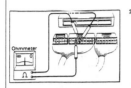

2. MEASURE RESISTANCE OF ECU
CAUTION:
1. Do not touch the ECU terminals.
2. The tester probe should be inserted into the wiring connector from the wiring side.

Check the resistance between each terminal of the wiring connector.

- Remove the rear luggage compartment trim.
- Unplug the wiring connectors from the ECU.
- Measure the resistance between each terminal of the wiring connectors.

Resistances at ECU Wiring Connectors

Terminals	Condition	Resistance
IDL – E2	Throttle valve open	Infinity
	Throttle valve fully closed	Less than 2.3 kΩ
VTA – E2	Throttle valve fully open	3.3 – 10 kΩ
	Throttle valve fully closed	0.2 – 0.8 kΩ
VC – E2	—	100 – 300 Ω
VS – E2	Measuring plate fully closed	20 – 400 Ω
	Measuring plate fully open	20 – 3,000 Ω
VCC – E2	—	3 – 7 kΩ
THA – E2	Intake air temperature 20°C (68°F)	2 – 3 kΩ
THW – E2	Coolant temperature 80°C (176°F)	0.2 – 0.4 kΩ
G⊖ – G⊖	—	140 – 180 Ω

EFI WIRING SCHEMATIC – 1984 STARLET

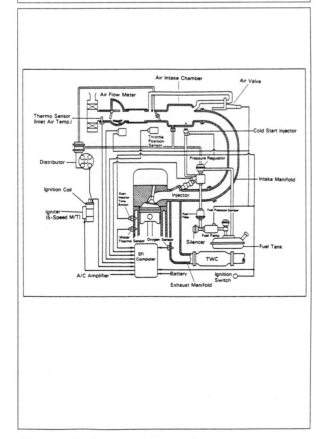

DIAGNOSIS CODES – 1984 STARLET

DIAGNOSIS CODES

Code No.	Number of blinks "CHECK ENGINE"	System	Diagnosis	Trouble area
1	Normal	This appears when none of the other codes (2 thru 7) are identified	—
2	Air flow meter signal (V$_s$)	Open circuit in V$_c$ or V$_c$–V$_s$ short circuited	1. Air flow meter circuit 2. Air flow meter 3. EFI computer
3	Air flow meter signal (V$_s$)	Open circuit in V$_s$ short circuited	1. Air flow meter circuit (V$_c$, V$_s$, V$_s$) 2. Air flow meter 3. EFI computer
4	Water thermo sensor signal (THW)	Open circuit in coolant temperature sensor signal.	1. Coolant temperature sensor circuit 2. Coolant temperature sensor 3. EFI computer
5	O$_2$ sensor signal	Open or short circuit in O$_2$ sensor signal (only lean or rich indication)	1. O$_2$ sensor circuit 2. O$_2$ sensor 3. EFI computer
6	Ignition signal	No ignition signal	1. Ignition system circuit 2. Distributor 3. Ignition coil and igniter 4. EFI computer
7*	Throttle position sensor signal	IDL–Psw short circuited	1. Throttle position sensor circuit 2. Throttle position sensor 3. EFI computer

Note: Code No. 7 : Note applicable for 5 speed M/T

INSPECTION OF THE DIAGNOSIS CIRCUIT – 1984 STARLET

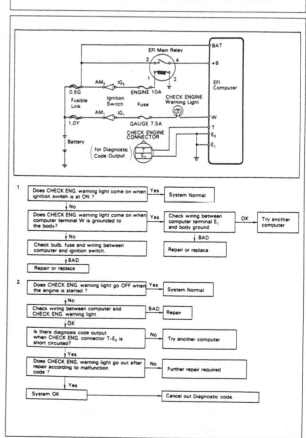

1. Does CHECK ENG. warning light come on when ignition switch is at ON ?
   - Yes → System Normal
   - No ↓

   Does CHECK ENG. warning light come on when computer terminal W is grounded to the body?
   - Yes → Check wiring between computer terminal E$_1$ and body ground → OK → Try another computer
   - No ↓
   - BAD → Repair or replace

   Check bulb, fuse and wiring between computer and ignition switch.
   - BAD → Repair or replace

2. Does CHECK ENG. warning light go OFF when the engine is started ?
   - Yes → System Normal
   - No ↓

   Check wiring between computer and CHECK ENG. warning light
   - BAD → Repair
   - OK ↓

   Is there diagnosis code output when CHECK ENG. connector T-E$_1$ is short circuited?
   - No → Try another computer
   - Yes ↓

   Does CHECK ENG. warning light go out after repair according to malfunction code ?
   - No → Further repair required
   - Yes ↓

   System OK → Cancel out Diagnostic code.

TROUBLESHOOTING THE EFI SYSTEM WITH A VOLT/OHMMETER—1984 STARLET

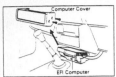

Remove the computer cover.

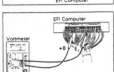

EFI SYSTEM CHECK PROCEDURE

NOTE:
1. The EFI circuit can be checked by measuring the resistance and voltage at the wiring connectors of the computer.
2. Perform all voltage measurements with the connectors connected.
3. Verify that the battery voltage is 11V or above when the ignition switch is ON.

Using a voltmeter with high impedance (10 kΩ/V minimum), measure the voltage at each terminal of the wiring connector.

NOTE: If there is any problem, see TROUBLESHOOTING FOR EFI ELECTRONIC CIRCUIT WITH VOLT/OHMMETER.

No.	Terminals	Voltage (V)	Condition
1	+B – E₁	10 – 14	Ignition switch ON
2	BAT – E₁	10 – 14	—
3	IDL – E₁	8 – 14	Throttle valve fully closed (IG s/w ON)
	Psw – E₁	8 – 14	Throttle valve fully open (IG s/w ON)
	TL – E₁	8 – 14	
4	IG – E₁	above 3	Cranking and engine running
5	STA – E₁	6 – 12	Cranking
6	#10 – E₁	9 – 14	Ignition switch ON
	#20 – E₁	9 – 14	Ignition switch ON
7	W – B	8 – 14	No trouble (CHECK ENGINE light off) and engine running
8	MS – E₁	8 – 14	Idling
9	Vₛ – E₂	4 – 9	Measuring plate fully closed (IG s/w ON)
	Vₛ – E₂	0.5 – 2.5	Measuring plate fully open (IG s/w ON)
		5 – 8	
		2.5 – 5.5	Idling
10	THA – E₂	2 – 6	Intake air temperature 20°C or 68°F
11	THW – E₂	0.5 – 2.5	Coolant temperature 80°C or 176°F
12	A/C – E₁	8 – 14	Air conditioning ON

Connectors of computer

E₂	Vₛ	Vc	BAT	THA		STA	A/C	Oₓ		THW	IDL	V₁		T	#10	E01
IG	E₁	W	+B	MS						E₁		TL	Psw		#20	E02

TROUBLESHOOTING THE EFI SYSTEM WITH A VOLT/OHMMETER (CONT.)—1984 STARLET

NOTE: The following troubleshooting procedures are designed for inspection of each separate system and, therefore, the actual procedure may vary somewhat. However, troubleshooting should be performed by referring to the inspection methods described.

Before beginning inspection, it is best to first make a simple check of the fuses, fusible links and the condition of the connectors.

LOCATION OF FUSE AND FUSIBLE LINK

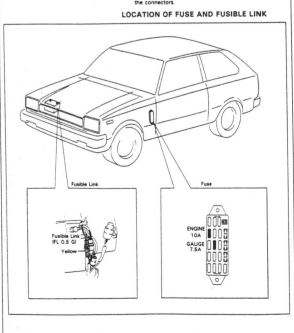

TROUBLESHOOTING THE NO. 1 TERMINAL ON THE EFI CONNECTOR 1984 STARLET

No.	Terminal	Trouble	Condition	STD Voltage
1	+B – E₁	NO voltage	IG S/W ON	10 – 14V

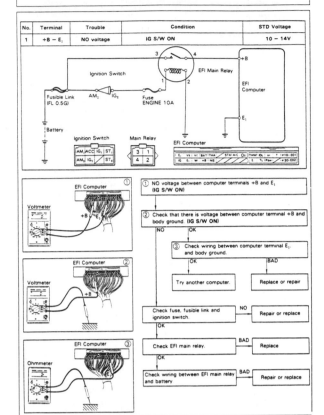

① NO voltage between computer terminals +B and E₁ (IG S/W ON)

② Check that there is voltage between computer terminal +B and body ground. (IG S/W ON)

③ Check wiring between computer terminal E₁ and body ground.

OK	BAD
Try another computer.	Replace or repair

Check fuse, fusible link and ignition switch. → NO → Repair or replace
OK

Check EFI main relay. → BAD → Replace
OK

Check wiring between EFI main relay and battery. → BAD → Repair or replace

TROUBLESHOOTING THE NO. 2 TERMINAL ON THE EFI CONNECTOR 1984 STARLET

No.	Terminals	Trouble	Condition	STD Voltage
2	BAT – E₁	No voltage	—	10 – 14V

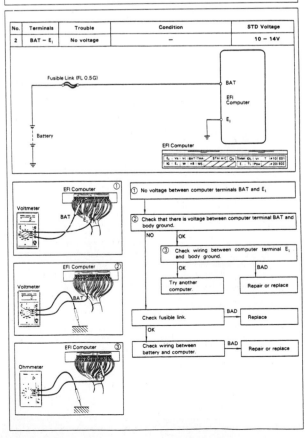

① No voltage between computer terminals BAT and E₁

② Check that there is voltage between computer terminal BAT and body ground.

③ Check wiring between computer terminal E₁ and body ground.

OK	BAD
Try another computer.	Repair or replace

Check fusible link. → BAD → Replace
OK

Check wiring between battery and computer. → BAD → Repair or replace

TROUBLESHOOTING THE NO. 3 TERMINAL ON THE EFI CONNECTOR
1984 STARLET

No.	Terminal	Trouble	Condition		STD Voltage
3	TL – E_1	No voltage	Ignition switch ON	–	8 – 14V
	IDL – E_1			Throttle valve fully closed	8 – 14V
	Psw – E_1			Throttle valve fully open	8 – 14V

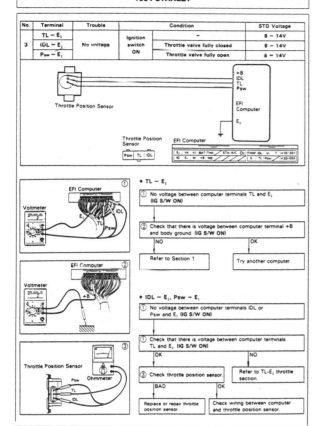

TROUBLESHOOTING THE NO. 4 TERMINAL ON THE EFI CONNECTOR
1984 STARLET

No.	Terminal	Trouble	Condition	STD Voltage
4	IG – E_1	No voltage	Cranking and engine running	Above 3 V

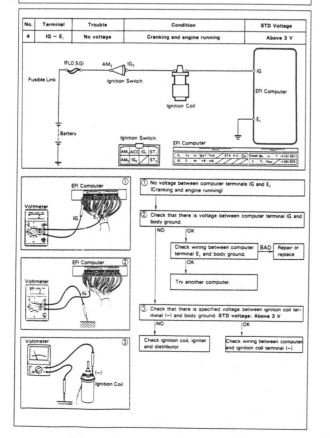

TROUBLESHOOTING THE NO. 5 TERMINAL ON THE EFI CONNECTOR
1984 STARLET

No.	Terminal	Trouble	Condition	STD Voltage
5	STA – E_1	No voltage	Cranking	6 – 12 V

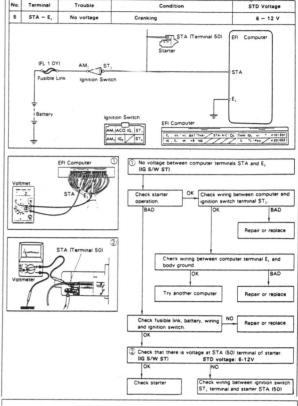

TROUBLESHOOTING THE NO. 6 TERMINAL ON THE EFI CONNECTOR
1984 STARLET

No.	Terminal	Trouble	Condition	STD Voltage
6	No.10 – E_1	No voltage	IG S/W ON	9 – 14 V
	No.20 – E_1			

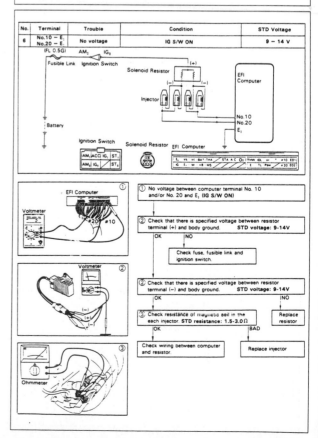

TROUBLESHOOTING THE NO. 7 TERMINAL ON THE EFI CONNECTOR
1984 STARLET

No.	Terminal	Trouble	Condition	STD Voltage
7	W – E₁	No voltage	No trouble (CHECK ENGINE warning light off) and Engine running	8 – 14 V

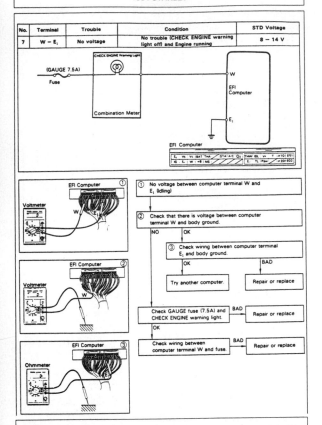

TROUBLESHOOTING THE NO. 9 TERMINAL ON THE EFI CONNECTOR
1984 STARLET

No.	Terminal	Trouble		Condition	STD Voltage
9	Vc – E₂	No voltage	Ignition switch ON	–	4 – 9V
	Vs – E₂			Measuring plate fully closed	0.5 – 2.5V
	Vs – E₂			Measuring plate fully open	5 – 8V
	Vs – E₂		Idling	–	2.5 – 5.5V

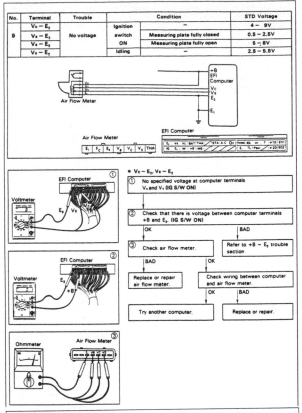

TROUBLESHOOTING THE NO. 8 TERMINAL ON THE EFI CONNECTOR
1984 STARLET

No.	Terminal	Trouble	Condition	STD Voltage
8	MS – E₁	No voltage	Idling	8 – 14V

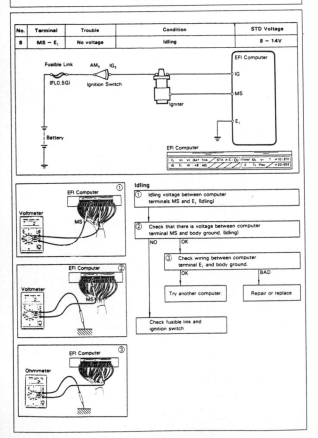

TROUBLESHOOTING THE NO. 10 TERMINAL ON THE EFI CONNECTOR
1984 STARLET

No.	Terminals	Trouble	Condition		STD Voltage
10	THA – E₂	NO voltage	IG S/W ON	Intake air temperature 20°C (68°F)	2 – 6 V

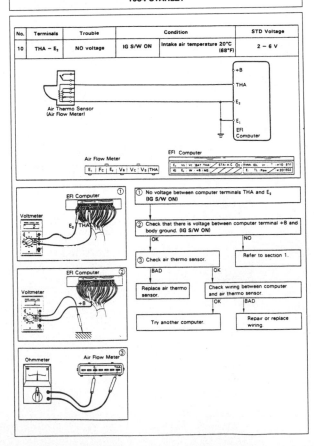

TROUBLESHOOTING THE NO. 11 TERMINAL ON THE EFI CONNECTOR 1984 STARLET

No.	Terminals	Trouble	Condition	STD Voltage
11	THW − E_2	NO voltage	IG S/W ON	Coolant temperature 80°C (176°F)	0.5 − 2.5V

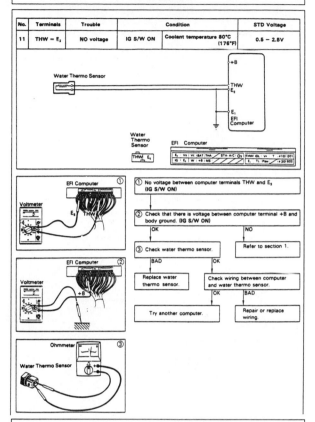

① No voltage between computer terminals THW and E_2 (IG S/W ON)

② Check that there is voltage between computer terminal +B and body ground. (IG S/W ON)
- OK → ③
- NO → Refer to section 1.

③ Check water thermo sensor.
- BAD → Replace water thermo sensor.
- OK → Check wiring between computer and water thermo sensor.
  - OK → Try another computer.
  - BAD → Repair or replace wiring.

TROUBLESHOOTING THE NO. 12 TERMINAL ON THE EFI CONNECTOR 1984 STARLET

No.	Terminal	Trouble	Condition	STD Voltage
12	A/C	No voltage	Air conditioning ON	8 − 14 V

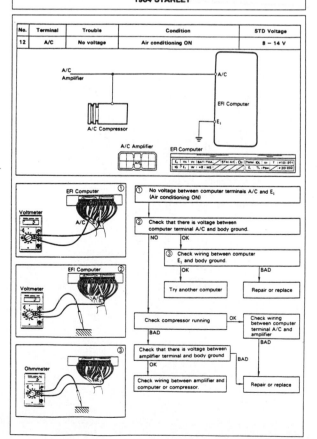

① No voltage between computer terminals A/C and E_1 (Air conditioning ON)

② Check that there is voltage between computer terminal A/C and body ground.
- NO → ③ Check wiring between computer E_1 and body ground.
  - OK → Try another computer.
  - BAD → Repair or replace
- OK →

Check compressor running.
- OK → Check wiring between computer terminal A/C and amplifier.
  - BAD →
- BAD → Check that there is voltage between amplifier terminal and body ground.
  - OK → Check wiring between amplifier and computer or compressor.
  - BAD → Repair or replace

ELECTRONIC COMPONENT LOCATIONS – 1984 STARLET

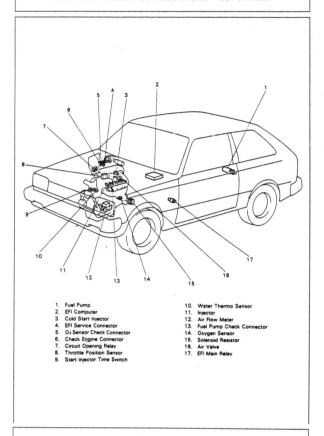

1. Fuel Pump
2. EFI Computer
3. Cold Start Injector
4. EFI Service Connector
5. O_2 Sensor Check Connector
6. Check Engine Connector
7. Circuit Opening Relay
8. Throttle Position Sensor
9. Start Injector Time Switch
10. Water Thermo Sensor
11. Injector
12. Air Flow Meter
13. Fuel Pump Check Connector
14. Oxygen Sensor
15. Solenoid Resistor
16. Air Valve
17. EFI Main Relay

TESTING THE OXYGEN SENSOR – 1984 STARLET

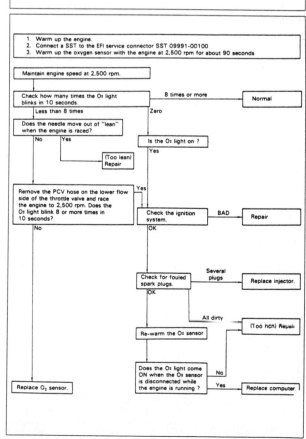

1. Warm up the engine.
2. Connect a SST to the EFI service connector SST 09991-00100
3. Warm up the oxygen sensor with the engine at 2,500 rpm for about 90 seconds

Maintain engine speed at 2,500 rpm.

Check how many times the O_2 light blinks in 10 seconds.
- 8 times or more → Normal
- Less than 8 times
- Zero → Is the O_2 light on?
  - Yes →

Does the needle move out of "lean" when the engine is raced?
- No
- Yes → (Too lean) Repair

Remove the PCV hose on the lower flow side of the throttle valve and race the engine to 2,500 rpm. Does the O_2 light blink 8 or more times in 10 seconds?
- Yes → Check the ignition system.
  - BAD → Repair
  - OK →
- No →

Check for fouled spark plugs.
- Several plugs → Replace injector.
- OK →

Re-warm the O_2 sensor.
- All dirty → (Too rich) Repair

Does the O_2 light come ON when the O_2 sensor is disconnected while the engine is running?
- No → Replace O_2 sensor.
- Yes → Replace computer.

TESTING THE OXYGEN SENSOR (CONT.) – 1984 STARLET

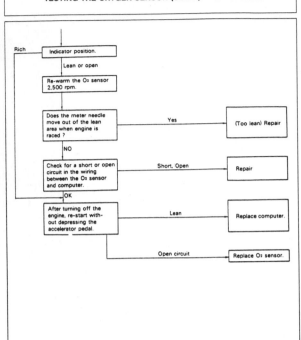

Rich
Lean or open

Indicator position.

Re-warm the O₂ sensor 2,500 rpm.

Does the meter needle move out of the lean area when engine is raced? → Yes → (Too lean) Repair

NO

Check for a short or open circuit in the wiring between the O₂ sensor and computer. → Short, Open → Repair

OK

After turning off the engine, re-start without depressing the accelerator pedal. → Lean → Replace computer.

Open circuit → Replace O₂ sensor.

INSPECTING THE RESISTANCE AT THE ECU WIRING CONNECTOR 1984 STARLET

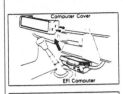
Computer Cover
EFI Computer

EFI Computer Wiring
Voltmeter

2. **MEASURE RESISTANCE OF COMPUTER**
   CAUTION:
   1. Do not touch the computer terminals.
   2. The tester probe should be inserted into the wiring connector from the wiring side.

   Check the resistance between each terminal of the wiring connector.
   ● Remove the computer cover.
   ● Unplug the wiring connectors from the EFI computer.
   ● Measure the resistance between each terminal of the wiring connectors.

Resistances at Computer Wiring Connectors

Terminals	Resistance	
TL – IDL	0	(Throttle valve fully closed)
TL – IDL	∞	(Throttle valve fully open)
TL – Psw	∞	(Throttle valve fully closed)
TL – Psw	0	(Throttle valve fully open)
IDL, TL, Psw – Ground	∞	
THW – E₂	200 – 400 Ω	(Coolant temp. 80°C or 176°F)
THA – E₂	2 – 3 kΩ	(Intake air temp. 20°C or 68°F)
THW, THA – Ground	∞	
Vв – E₂	200 – 400 Ω	
Vc – E₂	100 – 300 Ω	
Vs – E₂	20 – 400 Ω	(Measuring plate fully closed)
Vs – E₂	20 – 1,000 Ω	(Measuring plate fully open)
Vв, Vc, Vs – Ground	∞	
E₁, E₀₁, E₀₂ – Ground	0	

Connectors of computer

E₁	Vs	Vc	BAT	THA			STA	A/C	O₂	THW	IDL	Vғ	T	#10	E01
IG	E₂	W	+B	MS						E₁	TL	Psw		#20	E02

INSPECTING THE VOLTAGE AT THE ECU WIRING CONNECTOR 1984 STARLET

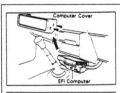
Computer Cover
EFI Computer

EFI Computer
Voltmeter
+B E₁

Computer

INSPECTION OF COMPUTER

1. **MEASURE VOLTAGE OF COMPUTER**
   NOTE:
   1. The computer cannot be checked directly.
   2. The EFI circuit can be checked by measuring the resistance and voltage at the wiring connectors of the computer.

   Check the voltages at the wiring connectors.
   ● Remove the computer cover.
   ● Turn the ignition switch on.
   ● Measure the voltage at each terminal.

NOTE: 1. Perform all voltage measurements with the connectors connected.
2. Verify that the battery voltage is 11V or above when the ignition switch is ON.

Voltages At Computer Wiring Connectors

Terminals	Voltage	
+B – E₁	10 – 14 V	(Ignition switch ON)
BAT – E₁	10 – 14 V	
IDL – E₁	8 – 14 V	(Throttle valve fully closed)
Psw – E₁	8 – 14 V	(Throttle valve fully open)
TL – E₁	8 – 14 V	
IG – E₁	Above 3 V	(Cranking and engine running)
STA – E₁	6 – 12 V	(Cranking)
No.10 – E₁	9 – 14 V	(Ignition ON)
No.20 – E₁	9 – 14 V	(Ignition ON)
W – E₁	8 – 14 V	(No trouble and engine runing)
MS – E₁	8 – 14 V	(Idling)
Vc – E₂	4 – 9 V	
Vs – E₂	0.5 – 2.5 V	(Measuring plate fully closed)
	5 – 8 V	(Measuring plate fully open)
	2.5 – 5.5 V	(Idling)
THA – E₂	2 – 6 V	(Intake air temperature 20°C or 68°F)
THW – E₂	0.5 – 2.5 V	(Coolant temperature 80°C or 176°F)
A/C – E₁	8 – 14 V	(Air conditioning ON)

Connectors of computer

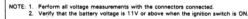

E₁	Vs	Vc	BAT	THA			STA	A/C	O₂	THW	IDL	Vғ	T	#10	E01
IG	E₂	W	+B	MS						E₁	TL	Psw		#20	E02

EFI WIRING SCHEMATIC – 1984 SUPRA

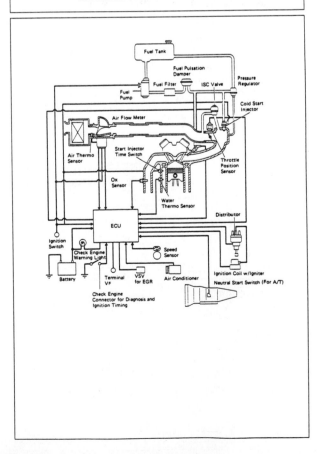

DIAGNOSIS CODES – 1984 SUPRA

Code No.	System	Diagnosis	Trouble Area
	Normal	This appears when none of the other codes (11 thru 51) are identified.	
11	ECU (+ B)	Wire severance, however slight, in + B (ECU).	1. Main relay circuit 2. Main relay 3. ECU
12	RPM Signal	No Ne, G signal to ECU within several seconds after engine is cranked.	1. Distributor circuit 2. Distributor 3. Starter signal circuit 4. ECU
13	RPM Signal	No Ne signal to ECU within several seconds after engine reaches 1,000 rpm.	Same as 12, above.
14	Ignition Signal	No signal from igniter six times in succession	1. Igniter circuit (+B, IGt, IGf) 2. Igniter 3. ECU
21	Ox Sensor Signal	Ox sensor gives a lean signal for several seconds even when coolant temperature is above 50°C and engine is running under high load conditions above 1,500 rpm.	1. Ox sensor circuit 2. Ox sensor 3. ECU
22	Water Thermo Sensor Signal	Open or short circuit in coolant temperature sensor signal.	1. Coolant Temp. sensor circuit 2. Coolant Temp. sensor 3. ECU
23	Intake Air Thermo Sensor Signal	Open or short circuit in intake air temperature sensor.	1. Intake air temp. sensor circuit 2. Intake air temp. sensor 3. ECU
31	Air Flow Meter Signal	Open circuit in Vc signal or Vs and E₂ short circuited when idle points are closed.	1. Air flow meter circuit 2. Air flow meter 3. ECU
32	Air Flow Meter Signal	Open circuit in E₂ or Vc and Vs short-circuited.	Same as 31, above.
41	Throttle Position Sensor Signal	Simultaneous IDL and PSW signal to ECU.	1. Throttle position sensor circuit 2. Throttle position sensor 3. ECU
42	Vehicle Speed Sensor Signal	(A/T): No signal for over 5 seconds when vehicle is travelling under 1.7 km/h and engine running over 2,500 rpm and shift lever is in other than N or P range. (M/T): No signal for over 5 seconds when vehicle is travelling under 1.7 km/h and engine running over 2,500 rpm.	1. Vehicle speed sensor circuit 2. Vehicle speed sensor 3. Torque converter slipping 4. ECU
43	Starter Signal (+ B)	No STA signal to ECU when engine is running over 800 rpm.	1. Main relay circuit 2. IG switch circuit (starter) 3. IG switch 4. ECU
51	Switch Signal	Neutral start switch OFF or air conditioner switch ON during diagnostic check.	1. Neutral start S/W 2. Air con. S/W 3. ECU

INSPECTION OF THE DIAGNOSIS CIRCUIT – 1984 SUPRA

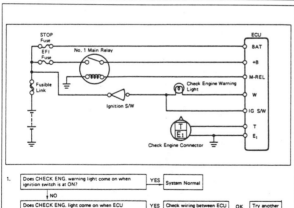

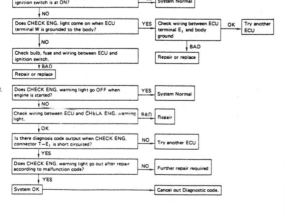

VOLTAGE SUPPLIED AT THE ECU WIRING CONNECTOR
1984 SUPRA

No.	Terminals	Condition		STD Voltage
1	BAT – E₁		—	
	+B – E₁		Ignition S/W ON	10 – 14
	IG S/W – E₁			
	M-REL – E₁			
2	IDL – E₁	Ignition S/W ON	Throttle valve open	4 – 6
	PSW – E₁		Throttle valve fully closed	4 – 6
3	Vc – E₂	Ignition S/W ON	—	4 – 6
	Vs – E₂		Measuring plate fully closed	4 – 5
			Measuring plate fully open	0.02 – 0.08
			Idling	2 – 4
			3,000 rpm	0.3 – 1.0
4	THA – E₂	IG S/W ON	Intake air temperature 20°C (68°F)	1 – 2
	THW – E₂	IG S/W ON	Coolant temperature 80°C (176°F)	0.1 – 0.5
5	STA – E₁		Ignition switch ST position	6 – 12
6	No.10 / No.20 – E₁		Ignition switch ON	9 – 14
7	IGt – E₁		Idling	0.7 – 1.0
8	ISC₁ / ISC₄ – E₁		Ignition switch ON	9 – 14
			2–3 secs. after engine off	9 – 14

RESISTANCE SUPPLIED AT THE ECU WIRING CONNECTOR
1984 SUPRA

MEASURE RESISTANCE OF ECU

CAUTION:
1. Do not touch the ECU terminals.
2. The tester probe should be inserted into the wiring connector from the wiring side.

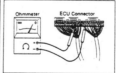

Using a ohmmeter, check the resistance between each terminal of the wiring connector.
- Remove the glove box.
- Disconnect the wiring connectors from the ECU.
- Measure the resistance between each terminal of the wiring connectors.

Resistances at ECU Wiring Connectors

Terminals	Condition	Resistance (Ω)
IDL – E₁	Throttle valve open	∞
	Throttle valve fully closed	0
PSW – E₁	Throttle valve open	0
	Throttle valve fully closed	∞
Vc – E₂	—	200 – 400
Vs – E₂	Measuring plate fully closed	20 – 400
	Measuring plate fully open	20 – 1000
THA – E₂	Intake air temperature 20°C (68°F)	2000 – 3000
G – G ⊖	—	140 – 180
Ne – G ⊖	—	140 – 180
ISC₁, ISC₃ / ISC₂, ISC₄ – +B	—	10 – 30

TROUBLESHOOTING THE NO. 1 TERMINAL ON THE EFI CONNECTOR
1984 SUPRA

No.	Terminals	Trouble	Condition	STD Voltage
1	BAT – E_1	No voltage		10 – 14
	+B – E_1		Ignition switch ON	10 – 14
	IG S/W – E_1	No voltage	Ignition switch ON	10 – 14
	M-REL – E_1	No voltage	Ignition switch ON	10 – 14

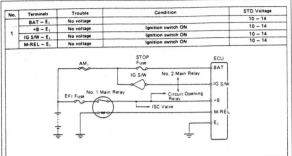

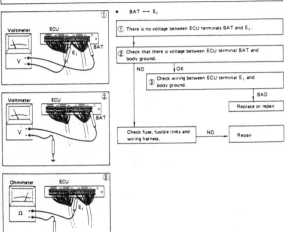

TROUBLESHOOTING THE NO. 1 TERMINAL ON THE EFI CONNECTOR
1984 SUPRA

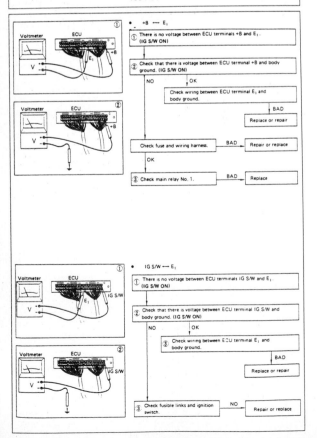

TROUBLESHOOTING THE NO. 1 TERMINAL ON THE EFI CONNECTOR
1984 SUPRA

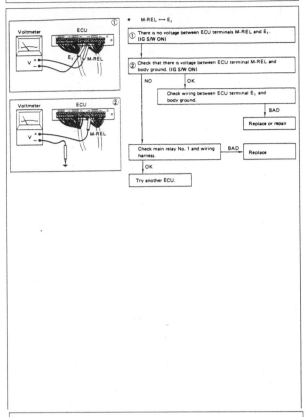

TROUBLESHOOTING THE NO. 2 TERMINAL ON THE EFI CONNECTOR
1984 SUPRA

No.	Terminal	Trouble		Condition	STD Voltage
2	IDL – E_1	No voltage	Ignition S/W ON	Throttle valve open	4 – 6 V
	Psw – E_1			Throttle valve fully closed	4 – 6 V

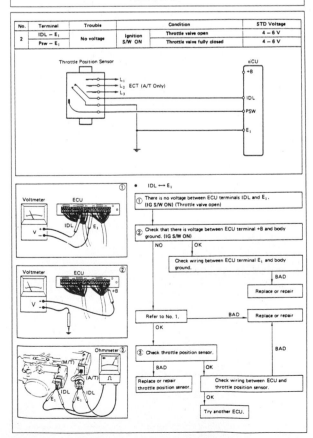

TROUBLESHOOTING THE NO. 2 TERMINAL ON THE EFI CONNECTOR
1984 SUPRA

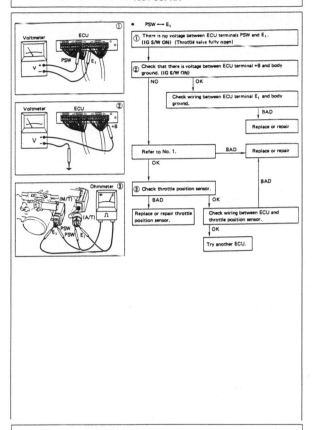

- PSW ⟷ E_1

① There is no voltage between ECU terminals PSW and E_1. (IG S/W ON) (Throttle valve fully open)

② Check that there is voltage between ECU terminal +B and body ground. (IG S/W ON)

NO — OK — Check wiring between ECU terminal E_1 and body ground. — BAD — Replace or repair

Refer to No. 1. — BAD — Replace or repair
OK

③ Check throttle position sensor.

BAD — Replace or repair throttle position sensor.
OK — Check wiring between ECU and throttle position sensor. — BAD — Replace or repair
OK — Try another ECU.

TROUBLESHOOTING THE NO. 3 TERMINAL ON THE EFI CONNECTOR
1984 SUPRA

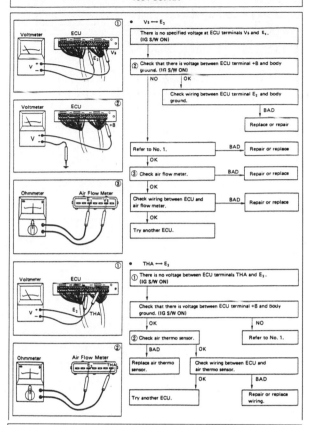

- Vs ⟷ E_2

① There is no specified voltage at ECU terminals Vs and E_2. (IG S/W ON)

② Check that there is voltage between ECU terminal +B and body ground. (IG S/W ON)

NO — OK — Check wiring between ECU terminal E_2 and body ground. — BAD — Replace or repair

Refer to No. 1. — BAD — Repair or replace
OK

③ Check air flow meter. — BAD — Repair or replace
OK

Check wiring between ECU and air flow meter. — BAD — Repair or replace
OK

Try another ECU.

- THA ⟷ E_2

① There is no voltage between ECU terminals THA and E_2. (IG S/W ON)

Check that there is voltage between ECU terminal +B and body ground. (IG S/W ON)

OK — NO — Refer to No. 1.

② Check air thermo sensor.

BAD — Replace air thermo sensor.
OK — Check wiring between ECU and air thermo sensor.
OK — BAD — Repair or replace wiring.
Try another ECU.

TROUBLESHOOTING THE NO. 3 TERMINAL ON THE EFI CONNECTOR
1984 SUPRA

No.	Terminal	Trouble	Condition		STD Voltage
3	Vc — E_2	No voltage	Ignition S/W ON	—	4 – 6 V
	Vs — E_2			—	4 – 5 V
	Vs — E_2		Measuring plate fully closed	0.02 – 0.08 V
	Vs — E_2		Measuring plate fully open	2 – 4 V
	Vs — E_2		Idling	
	Vs — E_2		3,000 rpm	0.3 – 1.0 V
	THA — E_2		IG S/W ON	Intake air temperature 20°C (68°F)	1 – 2 V

Air Flow Meter — F/P Connector — ECU: +B, E_2, Vs, Vc, THA, E_1

- Vc ⟷ E_2

① There is no voltage between ECU terminals Vc and E_2. (IG S/W ON)

② Check that there is voltage between ECU terminal +B and body ground. (IG S/W ON)

NO — OK — ③ Check wiring between ECU terminal E_2 and body ground. — BAD — Replace or repair

Refer to No. 1. — BAD — Replace or repair
OK

Check air flow meter — BAD — Repair or replace
OK

Check wiring between ECU and air flow meter. — BAD — Repair or replace
OK

Try another ECU.

TROUBLESHOOTING THE NO. 4 TERMINAL ON THE EFI CONNECTOR
1984 SUPRA

No.	Terminals	Trouble	Condition		STD Voltage
4	THW — E_2	No voltage	Ignition switch ON	Coolant temperature 80°C (176°F)	0.1 – 0.5 V

Water Thermo Sensor — ECU: +B, THW, E_2, E_1

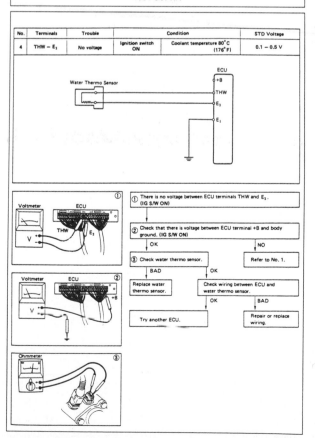

① There is no voltage between ECU terminals THW and E_2. (IG S/W ON)

② Check that there is voltage between ECU terminal +B and body ground. (IG S/W ON)

OK — NO — Refer to No. 1.

③ Check water thermo sensor.

BAD — Replace water thermo sensor.
OK — Check wiring between ECU and water thermo sensor.
OK — BAD — Repair or replace wiring.
Try another ECU.

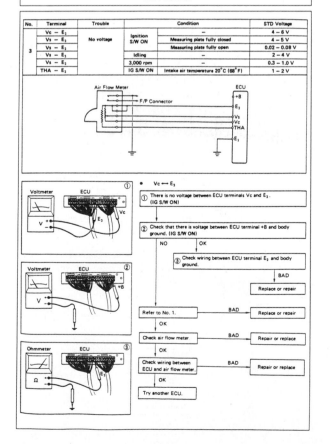

TROUBLESHOOTING THE NO. 5 TERMINAL ON THE EFI CONNECTOR
1984 SUPRA

No.	Terminals	Trouble	Condition	STD Voltage
5	STA – E₁	No voltage	Ignition switch ST position	6 – 12 V

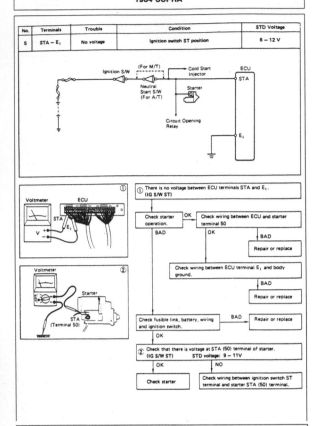

TROUBLESHOOTING THE NO. 6 TERMINAL ON THE EFI CONNECTOR
1984 SUPRA

No.	Terminals	Trouble	Condition	STD Voltage
6	No. 10 – E₁ \ No. 20 – E₁	No voltage	Ignition switch ON	9 – 14 V

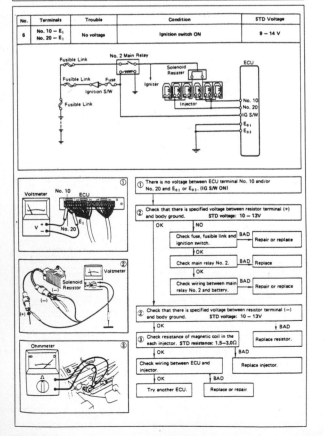

TROUBLESHOOTING THE NO. 7 TERMINAL ON THE EFI CONNECTOR
1984 SUPRA

No.	Terminals	Trouble	Condition	STD Voltage
7	IGt – E₁	No voltage	Idling	0.7 – 1.0 V

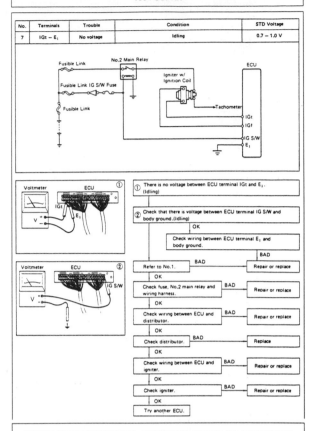

TROUBLESHOOTING THE NO. 8 TERMINAL ON THE EFI CONNECTOR
1984 SUPRA

No.	Terminal	Trouble	Condition	STD Voltage
8	ISC₁ ~ISC₄ – E₁	No voltage	Ignition S/W ON	9 – 14 V

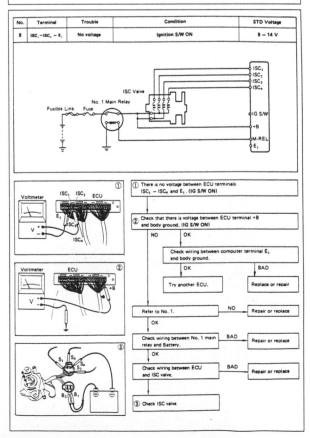

ELECTRONIC COMPONENT LOCATIONS – 1984 SUPRA

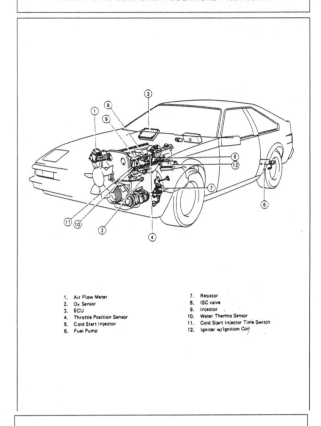

1. Air Flow Meter
2. O_x Sensor
3. ECU
4. Throttle Position Sensor
5. Cold Start Injector
6. Fuel Pump
7. Resistor
8. ISC valve
9. Injector
10. Water Thermo Sensor
11. Cold Start Injector Time Switch
12. Igniter w/Ignition Coil

TESTING THE OXYGEN SENSOR (CONT.) – 1984 SUPRA

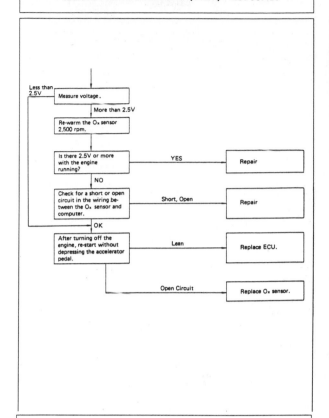

TESTING THE OXYGEN SENSOR – 1984 SUPRA

1. Warm up the engine.
2. Connect SST to the 4-terminal connector. SST 09842-14010
3. Using a voltmeter connect the positive probe to the red wire of the SST and negative testing probe to the block wire.
4. Warm up the O_x sensor with the engine at 2,500 rpm for about 2 minutes.

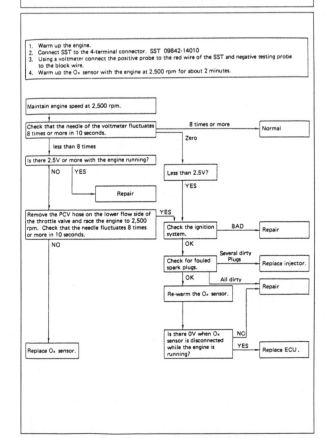

INSPECTING THE ECU WIRING CONNECTOR
1984 SUPRA

1. MEASURE VOLTAGE OF ECU

   NOTE: The EFI circuit can be checked by measuring the resistance and voltage at the wiring connectors of the ECU.

   Check the voltages at the wiring connectors.
   - Remove the glove box
   - Turn on the ignition switch.
   - Measure the voltage at each terminal.

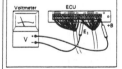

NOTE: 1. Perform all voltage measurements with the connectors connected.
2. Verify that the battery voltage is 11V or above when the ignition switch is ON.
3. The testing probes MUST NOT make contact with the ECU O_x and V_F terminals.

Connectors of ECU

Symbol	Terminal Name	Symbol	Terminal Name	Symbol	Terminal Name
E_{01}	ENGINE GROUND	G⊖	ENGINE REVOLUTION SENSOR	SPD	SPEEDOMETER
E_{02}	ENGINE GROUND	VF	CHECK CONNECTOR	W	WARNING LAMP
No. 10	INJECTOR	G	ENGINE REVOLUTION SENSOR	THA	AIR TEMP SENSOR
No. 20	INJECTOR	T	CHECK CONNECTOR	V_s	AIR FLOW METER
STA	STARTER SWITCH	PSW	THROTTLE SWITCH	Vc	AIR FLOW METER
IG1	IGNITER	Ne	ENGINE REVOLUTION SENSOR	BAT	BATTERY +B
EGR	EGR VSV	IDL	THROTTLE SWITCH	IG S/W	IGNITION SWITCH
E_1	ENGINE GROUND	IGf	IGNITER	+B	MAIN RELAY
N/C	NEUTRAL START SWITCH (A/T)	O_x	O_x SENSOR	ECT	ECT COMPUTER
	CLUTCH SWITCH (M/T)	THW	WATER TEMP SENSOR	S_1	ECT COMPUTER
ISC_1	ISC MOTOR NO. 1 COIL	E_2	SENSOR EARTH	S_2	ECT COMPUTER
ISC_2	ISC MOTOR NO. 2 COIL	E_1	ENGINE GROUND	OIL	OIL PRESSURE SWITCH
ISC_3	ISC MOTOR NO. 3 COIL	M-REL	MAIN RELAY COIL		
ISC_4	ISC MOTOR NO. 4 COIL	A/C	A/C MAGNET SWITCH		

INSPECTING THE VOLTAGE AT THE ECU WIRING CONNECTOR
1984 SUPRA

Terminals			
OIL – E_1	4 – 6		IG S/W ON (Warning light on)
	0		Start engine (Warning light out)
A/C – E_1	10 – 13	IG S/W ON	A/C S/W ON
	0		A/C S/W OFF
VF – E_1	0 ↔ 5		Start engine (Throttle valve open)
W – E_1	0		IG S/W ON
	10 – 13		Start engine
ECT – E_1	2 – 3	IG S/W ON	Coolant Temp. Less than 35°C (95°F)
	0		Coolant Temp. 35 – 60°C (95 – 140°F)
	4 – 6		Coolant Temp. More than 60°C (140°F)

INSPECTING THE RESISTANCE AT THE ECU WIRING CONNECTOR
1984 SUPRA

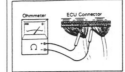

Ohmmeter   ECU Connector

2. MEASURE RESISTANCE OF ECU
   CAUTION:
   1. Do not touch the ECU terminals.
   2. The tester probe should be inserted into wiring connector from wiring side.

Check the resistance between each terminal of the wiring connector.
- Remove the glove box.
- Unplug the wiring connectors from the ECU.
- Measure the resistance between each terminal of the wiring connectors.

Resistances at ECU Wiring Connectors

Terminals	Condition	Resistance (Ω)
IDL – E_1	Throttle valve open	∞
	Throttle valve fully closed	0
PSW – E_1	Throttle valve open	0
	Throttle valve fully closed	∞
Vc – E_2	—	200 – 400
Vs – E_2	Measuring plate fully closed	20 – 400
	Measuring plate fully open	20 – 1000
THA – E_2	Intake air temperature 20°C (68°F)	2000 – 3000
G – G⊖	—	140 – 180
Ne – G⊖	—	
ISC_1, ISC_2 ISC_3, ISC_4 – +B	—	10 – 30

INSPECTING THE VOLTAGE AT THE ECU WIRING CONNECTOR
1984 SUPRA

Terminals	STD Voltage		Condition
BAT – E_1			–
+B – E_1	10 – 14		IG S/W ON
IG S/W – E_1			
M-REL – E_1			
IDL – E_1	4 – 6	IG S/W ON	Throttle valve open
PSW – E_1	4 – 6		Throttle valve fully closed
Vc – E_2	4 – 6		–
Vs – E_2	4 – 5	IG S/W ON	Measuring plate fully closed
	0.02 – 0.08		Measuring plate fully open
	2 – 4		Idling
	0.3 – 1.0		3,000 rpm
THA – E_2	1 – 2	IG S/W ON	Intake air temperature 20°C (68°F)
THW – E_2	0.1 – 0.5	IG S/W ON	Coolant temperature 80°C (176°F)
STA – E_1	6 – 12		IG S/W ST position
No. 10 No. 20 – E_1	9 – 14		IG S/W ON
IGt – E_1	0.7 – 1.0		Idling
ISC_1 ISC_4 – E_1	9 – 14		IG S/W ON
	9 – 14		2–3 secs after engine off
+B – EGR	10 – 13		IG S/W ON
	0		Start engine and warm up Ox sensor
N/C – E_1	0	IG S/W ON	Shift position P or N range (for A/T)
	4 – 6		Ex. P or N range (for A/T)
	0		Clutch pedal not depressed (for M/T)
	4 – 6		Clutch pedal depressed (for M/T)
	9 – 11		Cranking
T – E_1	4 – 6	IG S/W ON	Check connector T ↔ E_1 not short
	0		Check connector T ↔ E_2 short

EFI WIRING SCHEMATIC – 1985-86 SUPRA

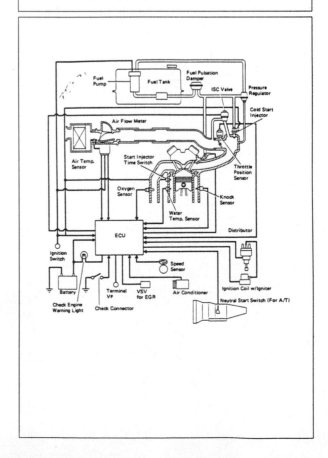

DIAGNOSIS CODES—1985-86 SUPRA

Code No.	System	Diagnosis	Trouble Area
	Normal	This appears when none of the other codes (11 thru 51) are identified.	
11	ECU (+ B)	Wire severence, however slight, in + B (ECU).	1. Main relay circuit 2. Main relay 3. ECU
12	RPM Signal	No Ne, G signal to ECU within several seconds after engine is cranked.	1. Distributor circuit 2. Distributor 3. Starter signal circuit 4. ECU
13	RPM Signal	No Ne signal to ECU within several seconds after engine reaches 1,000 rpm.	Same as 12, above.
14	Ignition Signal	No signal from igniter six times in succession	1. Igniter circuit (+ B, IGt, IGf) 2. Igniter 3. ECU
21	Oxygen Sensor Signal	Oxygen sensor gives a lean signal for several seconds even when coolant temperature is above 50°C (122°F) and engine is running under high load conditions above 1,500 rpm.	1. Oxygen sensor circuit 2. Oxygen sensor 3. ECU

INSPECTION OF THE DIAGNOSIS CIRCUIT—1985-86 SUPRA

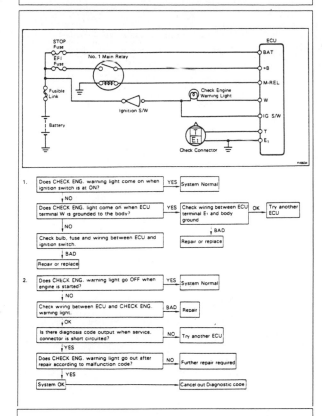

1.
   - Does CHECK ENG. warning light come on when ignition switch is at ON? → YES → System Normal
   - NO ↓
   - Does CHECK ENG. light come on when ECU terminal W is grounded to the body? → YES → Check wiring between ECU terminal E₁ and body ground → OK → Try another ECU
   - NO ↓ ... → BAD → Repair or replace
   - Check bulb, fuse and wiring between ECU and ignition switch. → BAD → Repair or replace

2.
   - Does CHECK ENG. warning light go OFF when engine is started? → YES → System Normal
   - NO ↓
   - Check wiring between ECU and CHECK ENG. warning light. → BAD → Repair
   - OK ↓
   - Is there diagnosis code output when service. connector is short circuited? → NO → Try another ECU
   - YES ↓
   - Does CHECK ENG. warning light go out after repair according to malfunction code? → NO → Further repair required
   - YES ↓
   - System OK ───── → Cancel out Diagnostic code

DIAGNOSIS CODES—1985-86 SUPRA

Code No.	System	Diagnosis	Trouble Area
22	Water Temp. Sensor Signal	Open or short circuit in coolant temp. sensor signal.	1. Water temp. sensor circuit 2. Water temp. sensor 3. ECU
23	Intake Air Temp. Sensor Signal	Open or short circuit in intake air temp. sensor.	1. Intake air temp. sensor circuit 2. Intake air temp. sensor 3. ECU
31	Air Flow Meter Signal	Open circuit in Vc signal or Vs and E₂ short circuited when idle points are closed.	1. Air flow meter circuit 2. Air flow meter 3. ECU
32	Air Flow Meter Signal	Open circuit in E₂ or Vc and Vs short circuited.	Same as 31, above.
41	Throttle Position Sensor Signal	Open or short circuit in throttle position sensor signal.	1. Throttle position sensor circuit 2. Throttle position sensor 3. ECU
42	Vehicle Speed Sensor Signal	(A/T): Signal informing ECU that vehicle speed is 2.0 km/h or less has been input ECU for 5 seconds with engine running at 2,500 rpm or more and shift lever is in other than N or P range. (M/T): Signal informing ECU that vehicle speed is 2.0 km/h or less has been input ECU for 5 seconds with engine running at 2,500 rpm or more.	1. Vehicle speed sensor circuit 2. Vehicle speed sensor 3. Torque converter slipping 4. ECU
43	Starter Signal (+ B)	No STA signal to ECU when engine is running over 800 rpm.	1. Main relay circuit 2. IG switch circuit (starter) 3. IG switch 4. ECU
51	Switch Signal	Neutral start switch OFF or air conditioner switch ON during diagnostic check.	1. Neutral start S/W 2. Air con. S/W 3. ECU
52	Knock Sensor Signal	Open or short circuit in knock sensor.	1. Knock sensor circuit 2. Knock sensor 3. ECU
53	Knock Sensor Signal	Faulty ECU. (KNOCK CPU)	ECU

TROUBLESHOOTING THE EFI SYSTEM WITH A VOLT/OHMMETER—1985-86 SUPRA

1. Remove the glove box door and glove box.

2. Remove the ECU with wire harness.

EFI SYSTEM CHECK PROCEDURE

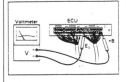

NOTE:

1. The EFI circuit can be checked by measuring the resistance and voltage at the wiring connectors of the ECU.

2. Perform all voltage measurement with the connectors connected.

3. Verify that the battery voltage is 11V or above when the ignition switch is ON.

Using a voltmeter, measure the voltage at each terminal of the wiring connector.

NOTE: If there is any problem, see TROUBLESHOOTING FOR EFI ELECTRONIC CIRCUIT WITH VOLT/ OHMMETER.

Connectors of ECU

Symbol	Terminal Name	Symbol	Terminal Name	Symbol	Terminal Name
E₀₁	ENGINE GROUND	G⊖	ENGINE REVOLUTION SENSOR	A/C	A/C MAGNET SWITCH
E₀₂	ENGINE GROUND	V₁	CHECK CONNECTOR	SPD	SPEEDOMETER
No.10	INJECTOR	G	ENGINE REVOLUTION SENSOR	W	WARNING LIGHT
No.20	INJECTOR	T	CHECK CONNECTOR	THA	AIR TEMP. SENSOR
STA	STARTER SWITCH	VTA	THROTTLE SWITCH	Vs	AIR FLOW METER
IGt	IGNITER	Ne	ENGINE REVOLUTION SENSOR	Vc	AIR FLOW METER
EGR	EGR VSV	IDL	THROTTLE SWITCH	BAT	BATTERY +B
E₁	ENGINE GROUND	KNK	KNOCK SENSOR	IG S/W	IGNITION SWITCH
N/C	NEUTRAL START SWITCH (A/T)	IGf	IGNITER	+B	MAIN RELAY
	CLUTCH SWITCH (M/T)	Ox	OXYGEN SENSOR	TCD	ECT COMPUTER
ISC₁	ISC MOTOR NO.1 COIL	THW	WATER TEMP. SENSOR	OIL	OIL PRESSURE SWITCH
ISC₂	ISC MOTOR NO.2 COIL	E₂	SENSOR EARTH	L₁	ECT COMPUTER
ISC₃	ISC MOTOR NO.3 COIL	E₁	ENGINE GROUND	L₂	ECT COMPUTER
ISC₄	ISC MOTOR NO.4 COIL	M-REL	MAIN RELAY COIL	L₃	ECT COMPUTER

E₁	No.10	STA	EGR	N/C	ISC₃	ISC₁	G⊖		G	Ne	IGt	THW		L₁	L₂	M-REL		SPD		THA	V₁	Vc	BAT	IG S/W
E₂	No.20	IGt	E₁		ISC₄	ISC₂	V₁	T	VTA	IDL	KNK	Ox	E₂	E₁	TCD		A/C	W	OIL			+B	+B	

TROUBLESHOOTING THE EFI SYSTEM WITH A VOLT/OHMMETER (CONT.) – 1985-86 SUPRA

NOTE: Because the following troubleshooting procedures are designed for inspection of each separate system, the actual troubleshooting procedure may vary somewhat. However, please refer to these procedures and perform actual troubleshooting, conforming to the inspection methods described in this manual.
For example, it is better to first make a simple check of the fuses, fusible links and connecting condition of the connectors before making your inspection according to the procedures listed.

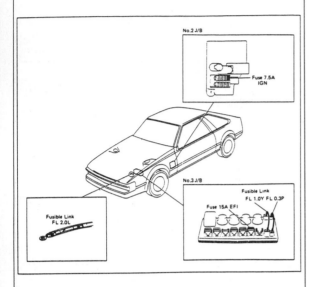

RESISTANCE SUPPLIED AT THE ECU WIRING CONNECTOR
1985-86 SUPRA

CAUTION:
1. Do not touch the ECU terminals.
2. The tester probe should be inserted into the wiring connector from the wiring side.

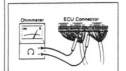

Using an ohmmeter, check the resistance between each terminal of the wiring connector.
- Remove the glove box.
- Disconnect the wiring connectors from the ECU.
- Measure the resistance between each terminal of the wiring connectors.

Resistances at ECU Wiring Connectors

Terminals	Condition	Resistance (Ω)
IDL — E₂	Throttle valve open	∞
	Throttle valve fully closed	0 – 100 Ω
VTA — E₂	Throttle valve fully opened	3,300 – 10,000
	Throttle valve fully closed	200 – 800
Vc — E₂	Disconnect air flow meter connector	3,000 – 7,000
	Disconnect throttle position sensor connector	200 – 400
Vs — E₂	Measuring plate fully closed	20 – 400
	Measuring plate fully opened	20 – 1,000
THA — E₂	Intake air temperature 20°C (68°F)	2,000 – 3,000
G — G⊖	—	140 – 180
Ne — G⊖	—	140 – 180
ISC₁, ISC₂ ISC₃, ISC₄ — +B	—	10 – 30

VOLTAGE SUPPLIED AT THE ECU WIRING CONNECTOR
1985-86 SUPRA

No.	Terminals	Condition	STD Voltage
1	BAT — E₁	—	10 – 14
	+B — E₁	—	
	IG S/W — E₁	—	
	M-REL — E₁	—	
2	IDL — E₂	Throttle valve open	4 – 6
	Vc — E₂		4 – 6
	VTA — E₂	Throttle valve fully closed	0.1 – 1.0
		Throttle valve fully opened	4 – 5
3	Vc — E₂		4 – 6
	Vs — E₂	Measuring plate fully closed	4 – 5
		Measuring plate fully open	0.02 – 0.08
		Idling	2 – 4
		3,000 rpm	0.3 – 1.0
4	THA — E₂	Intake air temperature 20°C (68°F)	1 – 2
	THW — E₂	Coolant temperature 80°C (176°F)	0.1 – 0.5
5	STA — E₁	IG S/W ST position	6 – 12
6	No. 10 No. 20 — E₁	IG S/W ON	9 – 14
7	IGt — E₁	Cranking or Idling	0.7 – 1.0
8	ISC₁ l — E₁ ISC₄	IG S/W ON	9 – 14
		2 – 3 secs, after engine off	9 – 14

(IG S/W ON applies to rows 2–4, 6, 8)

TROUBLESHOOTING THE NO. 1 TERMINAL ON THE EFI CONNECTOR
1985-86 SUPRA

No.	Terminals	Trouble	Condition	STD Voltage
1	BAT — E₁	No voltage	—	10 – 14
	+B — E₁	No voltage	Ignition switch ON	10 – 14
	IG S/W — E₁	No voltage	Ignition switch ON	10 – 14
	M-REL — E₁	No voltage	Ignition switch ON	10 – 14

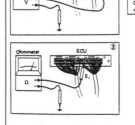

- BAT — E₁

① There is no voltage between ECU terminals BAT and E₁.

② Check that there is voltage between ECU terminal BAT and body ground.
 NO → ③ Check wiring between ECU terminal E₁ and body ground. → BAD → Repair or replace
 OK →

Check fuse, fusible links and wiring harness. → NO → Repair

TROUBLESHOOTING THE NO. 1 TERMINAL ON THE EFI CONNECTOR 1985-86 SUPRA

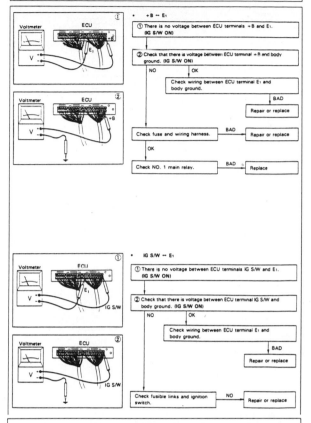

* +B — E₁

① There is no voltage between ECU terminals +B and E₁. (IG S/W ON)

② Check that there is voltage between ECU terminal +B and body ground. (IG S/W ON)

→ NO / OK

OK → Check wiring between ECU terminal E₁ and body ground. → BAD → Repair or replace

NO → Check fuse and wiring harness. → BAD → Repair or replace

OK → Check NO. 1 main relay. → BAD → Replace

* IG S/W — E₁

① There is no voltage between ECU terminals IG S/W and E₁. (IG S/W ON)

② Check that there is voltage between ECU terminal IG S/W and body ground. (IG S/W ON)

NO / OK

OK → Check wiring between ECU terminal E₁ and body ground. → BAD → Repair or replace

NO → Check fusible links and ignition switch. → NO → Repair or replace

TROUBLESHOOTING THE NO. 1 TERMINAL ON THE EFI CONNECTOR 1985-86 SUPRA

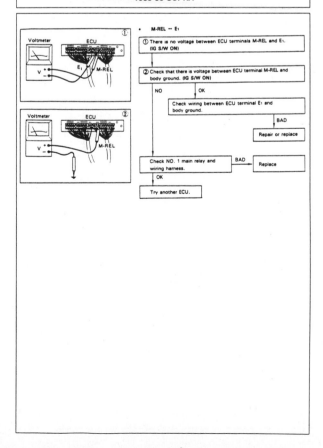

* M-REL — E₁

① There is no voltage between ECU terminals M-REL and E₁. (IG S/W ON)

② Check that there is voltage between ECU terminal M-REL and body ground. (IG S/W ON)

NO / OK

OK → Check wiring between ECU terminal E₁ and body ground. → BAD → Repair or replace

OK → Check NO. 1 main relay and wiring harness. → BAD → Replace

OK → Try another ECU.

TROUBLESHOOTING THE NO. 2 TERMINAL ON THE EFI CONNECTOR 1985-86 SUPRA

No.	Terminals	Trouble	Condition		STD voltage
2	IDL — E₂	No voltage	Ignition switch ON	Throttle valve open	4 — 6
	VTA — E₂			Throttle valve fully closed	0.1 — 1.0
				Throttle valve fully open	4 — 5
	Vc — E₂			—	4 — 6

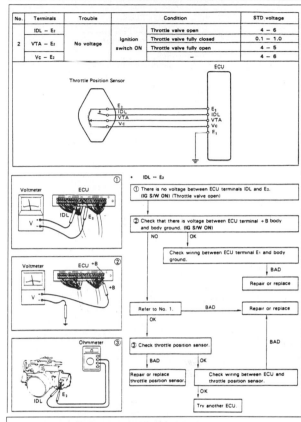

Throttle Position Sensor

* IDL — E₂

① There is no voltage between ECU terminals IDL and E₂. (IG S/W ON) (Throttle valve open)

② Check that there is voltage between ECU terminal +B body and body ground. (IG S/W ON)

NO / OK

OK → Check wiring between ECU terminal E₁ and body ground. → BAD → Repair or replace

NO → Refer to No. 1. → BAD → Repair or replace

OK → ③ Check throttle position sensor. → BAD → Repair or replace throttle position sensor / OK → Check wiring between ECU and throttle position sensor. → BAD

OK → Try another ECU.

TROUBLESHOOTING THE NO. 2 TERMINAL ON THE EFI CONNECTOR 1985-86 SUPRA

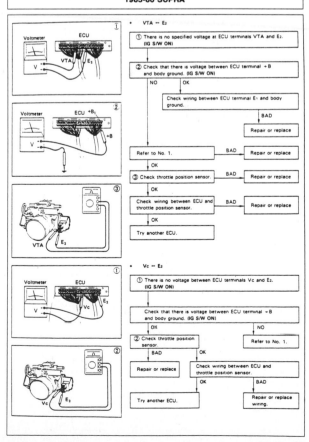

* VTA — E₂

① There is no specified voltage at ECU terminals VTA and E₂. (IG S/W ON)

② Check that there is voltage between ECU terminal +B and body ground. (IG S/W ON)

NO / OK

OK → Check wiring between ECU terminal E₁ and body ground. → BAD → Repair or replace

Refer to No. 1. → BAD → Repair or replace

OK → ③ Check throttle position sensor. → BAD → Repair or replace

OK → Check wiring between ECU and throttle position sensor. → BAD → Repair or replace

OK → Try another ECU.

* Vc — E₂

① There is no voltage between ECU terminals Vc and E₂. (IG S/W ON)

Check that there is voltage between ECU terminal +B and body ground. (IG S/W ON)

OK / NO

NO → Refer to No. 1.

OK → ② Check throttle position sensor. → BAD → Repair or replace / OK → Check wiring between ECU and throttle position sensor. → BAD → Repair or replace wiring.

OK → Try another ECU.

TROUBLESHOOTING THE NO. 3 TERMINAL ON THE EFI CONNECTOR
1985-86 SUPRA

No.	Terminal	Trouble	Condition		STD Voltage
3	Vc – E2	No voltage	Ignition S/W ON	—	4 – 6 V
	Vs – E2			Measuring plate fully closed	4 – 5 V
	Vs – E2			Measuring plate fully open	0.02 – 0.08 V
	Vs – E2		Idling	—	2 – 4 V
	Vs – E2		3,000 rpm	—	0.3 – 1.0 V
	THA – E2		IG S/W ON	Intake air temperature 20°C (68°F)	1 – 2 V

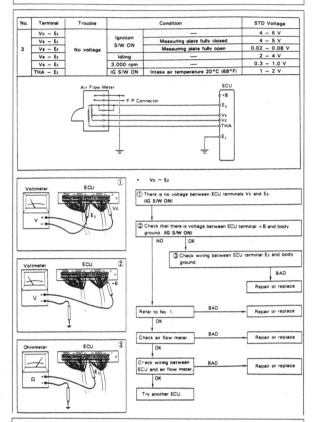

TROUBLESHOOTING THE NO. 3 TERMINAL ON THE EFI CONNECTOR
1985-86 SUPRA

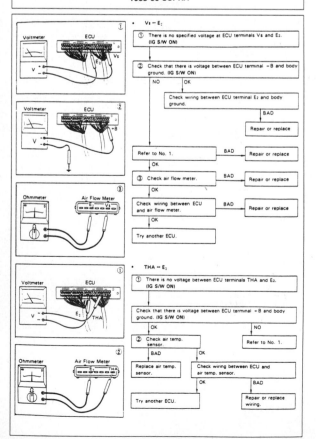

TROUBLESHOOTING THE NO. 4 TERMINAL ON THE EFI CONNECTOR
1985-86 SUPRA

No.	Terminals	Trouble	Condition		STD Voltage
4	THW – E2	No voltage	Ignition switch ON	Coolant temperature 80°C (176°F)	0.1 – 0.5 V

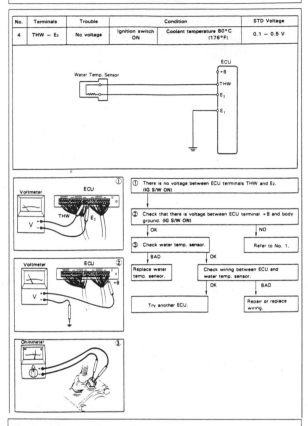

TROUBLESHOOTING THE NO. 5 TERMINAL ON THE EFI CONNECTOR
1985-86 SUPRA

No.	Terminals	Trouble	Condition	STD Voltage
5	STA – E1	No voltage	Ignition switch ST position	6 – 12 V

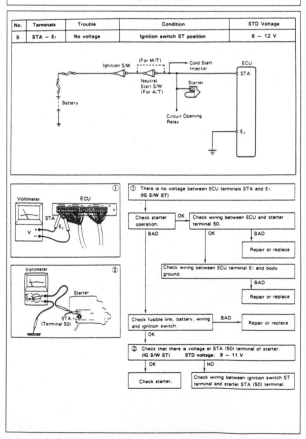

TROUBLESHOOTING THE NO. 6 TERMINAL ON THE EFI CONNECTOR 1985-86 SUPRA

No.	Terminals	Trouble	Condition	STD Voltage
6	No. 10 — E_1 No. 20 — E_1	No voltage	Ignition switch ON	9 — 14V

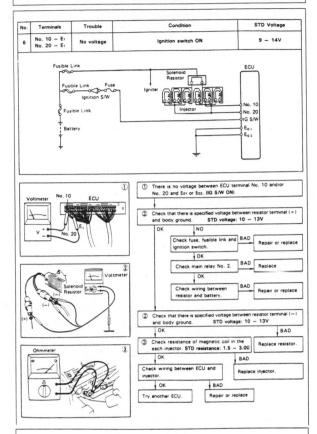

TROUBLESHOOTING THE NO. 7 TERMINAL ON THE EFI CONNECTOR 1985-86 SUPRA

No.	Terminals	Trouble	Condition	STD Voltage
7	IGt — E_1	No voltage	Cranking or Idling	0.7 — 1.0V

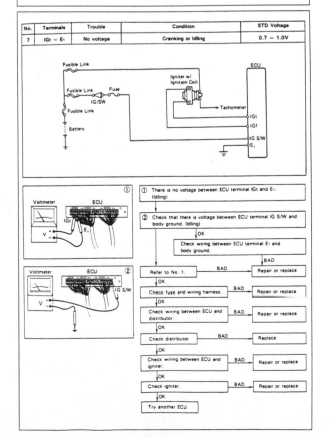

TROUBLESHOOTING THE NO. 8 TERMINAL ON THE EFI CONNECTOR 1985-86 SUPRA

No.	Terminal	Trouble	Condition	STD Voltage
8	$ISC_1 - ISC_4 - E_1$	No voltage	Ignition switch ON	9 — 14V

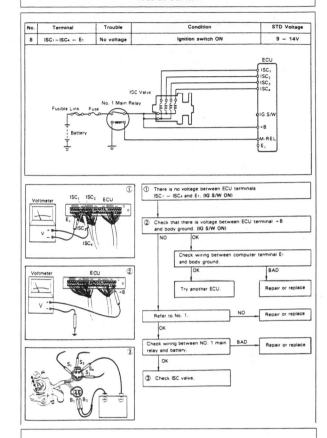

ELECTRONIC COMPONENT LOCATIONS — 1985-86 SUPRA

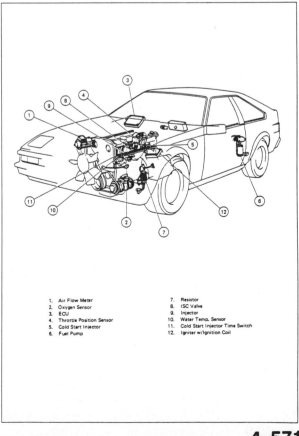

1. Air Flow Meter
2. Oxygen Sensor
3. ECU
4. Throttle Position Sensor
5. Cold Start Injector
6. Fuel Pump
7. Resistor
8. ISC Valve
9. Injector
10. Water Temp. Sensor
11. Cold Start Injector Time Switch
12. Igniter w/Ignition Coil

TESTING THE OXYGEN SENSOR — 1985-86 SUPRA

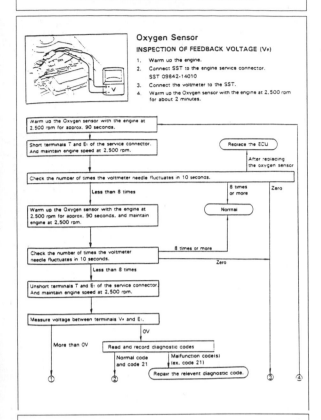

Oxygen Sensor
INSPECTION OF FEEDBACK VOLTAGE (V+)

1. Warm up the engine.
2. Connect SST to the engine service connector.
   SST 09842-14010
3. Connect the voltmeter to the SST.
4. Warm up the Oxygen sensor with the engine at 2,500 rpm for about 2 minutes.

TESTING THE OXYGEN SENSOR (CONT.) — 1985-86 SUPRA

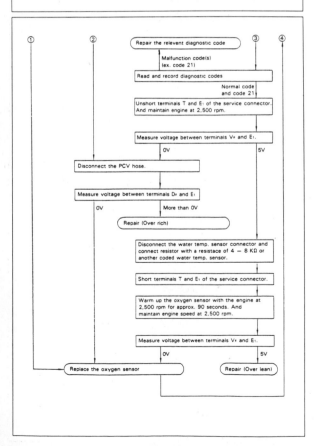

INSPECTING THE ECU WIRING CONNECTOR 1985-86 SUPRA

1. MEASURE VOLTAGE OF ECU
   NOTE: The EFI circuit can be checked by measuring the resistance and voltage at the wiring connectors of the ECU.
   Check the voltages at the wiring connectors.
   • Remove the glove box.
   • Turn on the ignition switch.
   • Measure the voltage at each terminal.

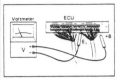

NOTE: 1. Perform all voltage measurements with the connectors connected.
      2. Verify that the battery voltage is 11V or above when the ignition switch is ON.

Connectors of ECU

Symbol	Terminal Name	Symbol	Terminal Name	Symbol	Terminal Name
E01	ENGINE GROUND	G⊖	ENGINE REVOLUTION SENSOR	A/C	A/C MAGNET SWITCH
E02	ENGINE GROUND	V+	CHECK CONNECTOR	SPD	SPEEDOMETER
No. 10	INJECTOR	G	ENGINE REVOLUTION SENSOR	W	WARNING LIGHT
No. 20	INJECTOR	T	CHECK CONNECTOR	THA	AIR TEMP. SENSOR
STA	STARTER SWITCH	VTA	THROTTLE SWITCH	Vs	AIR FLOW METER
IGt	IGNITER	Ne	ENGINE REVOLUTION SENSOR	Vc	AIR FLOW METER
EGR	EGR VSV	IDL	THROTTLE SWITCH	BAT	BATTERY - B
E1	ENGINE GROUND	KNK	KNOCK SENSOR	IG S/W	IGNITION SWITCH
N/C	NEUTRAL START SWITCH (A/T)	IGf	IGNITER	+B	MAIN RELAY
	CLUTCH SWITCH (M/T)	Ox	OXYGEN SENSOR	TCD	ECT COMPUTER
ISC1	ISC MOTOR NO. 1 COIL	THW	WATER TEMP. SENSOR	OIL	OIL PRESSURE SWITCH
ISC2	ISC MOTOR NO. 2 COIL	E2	SENSOR EARTH	L1	ECT COMPUTER
ISC3	ISC MOTOR NO. 3 COIL	E1	ENGINE GROUND	L2	ECT COMPUTER
ISC4	ISC MOTOR NO. 4 COIL	M-REL	MAIN RELAY COIL	L3	ECT COMPUTER

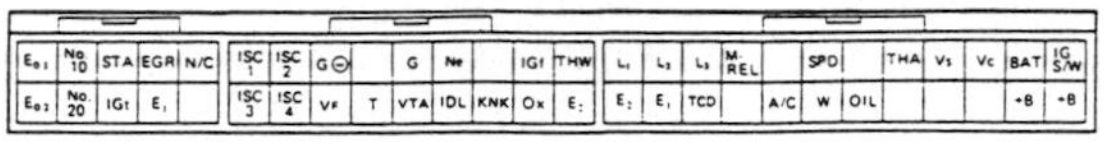

INSPECTING THE VOLTAGE AT THE ECU WIRING CONNECTOR 1985-86 SUPRA

Terminals	STD Voltage	Condition
BAT — E1		—
+B — E1	10 – 14	—
IG S/W — E1		—
M-REL — E1		—
IDL — E2	4 – 6	Throttle valve open
VTA — E2	0.1 – 1.0	Throttle valve fully closed
VTA — E2	4 – 5	Throttle valve fully opened
Vc — E2	4 – 6	
Vs — E2	4 – 5	Measuring plate fully closed
Vs — E2	0.02 – 0.08	Measuring plate fully open
Vs — E2	2 – 4	Idling
Vs — E2	0.3 – 1.0	3,000 rpm
THA — E2	1 – 2	Intake air temperature 20°C (68°F)
THW — E1	0.1 – 0.5	Coolant temperature 80°C (176°F)
STA — E1	6 – 12	IG S/W ST position
No. 10 / No. 20 — E1	9 – 14	IG S/W ON
IGt — E1	0.7 – 1.0	Cranking or Idling
ISC1 / ISC4 — E1	9 – 14	IG S/W ON
ISC1 / ISC4 — E1	9 – 14	2 – 3 secs. after engine off
+B — EGR	10 – 13	IG S/W ON
N/C — E1	0	Start engine and warm up oxygen sensor
N/C — E1	0	Shift position P or N range (for A/T)
N/C — E1	10 – 14	Ex. P or N range (for A/T)
N/C — E1	0	Clutch pedal not depressed (for M/T)
N/C — E1	10 – 14	Clutch pedal depressed (for M/T)
N/C — E1	9 – 11	Cranking
T — E1	4 – 6	Check connector not short
T — E1	0	Check connector short

Note: The "IG S/W ON" and "IG S/W ST position" conditions are grouped spanning several terminal rows in the original.

INSPECTING THE VOLTAGE AT THE ECU WIRING CONNECTOR 1985-86 SUPRA

OIL – E₁	4 – 6		IG S/W ON (Warning light on)
	0		Start engine (Warning light out)
A/C – E₁	10 – 13	IG S/W ON	A/C S/W ON
	0		A/C S/W OFF
Vr – E₁	0 – 5		Start engine (Throttle valve open)
W – E₁	0	IG S/W ON	
	10 – 13		Start engine
TCD – E₁	2 – 3	IG S/W ON	Coolant temperature Less than 35°C (95°F)
	0		Coolant temperature 35 – 60°C (95 – 140°F)
	4 – 6		Coolant temperature More than 60°C (140°F)

INSPECTING THE RESISTANCE AT THE ECU WIRING CONNECTOR 1985-86 SUPRA

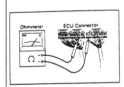

2. MEASURE RESISTANCE OF ECU

CAUTION:
1. Do not touch the ECU terminals.
2. The tester probe should be inserted into wiring connector from wiring side.

Check the resistance between each terminal of the wiring connector.
- Remove the glove box.
- Unplug the wiring connectors from the ECU.
- Measure the resistance between each terminal of the wiring connectors.

Resistances at ECU Wiring Connectors

Terminals	Condition	Resistance (Ω)
IDL – E₂	Throttle valve open	∞
	Throttle valve fully closed	0
VTA – E₂	Throttle valve fully opened	3,300 – 10,000
	Throttle valve fully closed	200 – 800
Vc – E₂	Disconnect air flow meter connector	3,000 – 7,000
	Disconnect throttle position sensor connector	200 – 400
Vs – E₂	Measuring plate fully closed	20 – 400
	Measuring plate fully open	20 – 1000
THA – E₂	Intake air temperature 20°C (68°F)	2,000 – 3,000
G – G⊖	—	140 – 180
Ne – G⊖	—	
ISC₁, ISC₂ – B ISC₃, ISC₄	—	18 30

EFI WIRING SCHEMATIC – 7M-GE – 1987-88 SUPRA

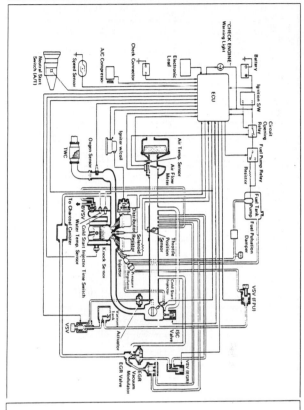

EFI WIRING SCHEMATIC – 7M-GTE – 1987-88 SUPRA

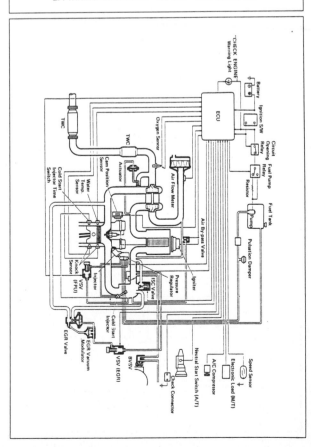

DIAGNOSIS CODES – 1987-88 SUPRA

Code No.	System	Diagnosis	Trouble Area
—	Normal	This appears when none of the other codes are identified.	
11	ECU (+B)	Wire severance, however slight, in +B (ECU).	1. Main relay circuit 2. Main relay 3. ECU
12	RPM Signal	No Ne or G signal to ECU within several seconds after engine is cranked.	1. Distributor circuit 2. Distributor 3. Starter signal circuit 4. ECU
13	RPM Signal	No Ne signal to ECU within several seconds after engine reaches 1,000 rpm.	Same as 12, above.
14	Ignition Signal	No IGf signal from igniter approx. six times in succession.	1. Igniter circuit (IGf) 2. Igniter 3. ECU
21	Oxygen Sensor Signal	Open or short circuit in oxygen sensor signal.	1. Oxygen sensor circuit 2. Oxygen sensor 3. ECU
22	Water Temp. Sensor Signal	Open or short circuit in coolant temperature sensor signal.	1. Coolant Temp. sensor circuit 2. Coolant Temp. sensor 3. ECU
24	Intake Air Temp. Sensor Signal	Open or short circuit in intake air temperature sensor.	1. Intake air temp. sensor circuit 2. Intake air temp. sensor 3. ECU
31	(7M-GE) Air Flow Meter Signal	(7M-GE) Open circuit in Vc signal or Vs and E₂ short circuited when idle points are closed. (7M-GTE) Open or short circuit in air flow meter signal.	(7M-GE) 1. Air flow meter circuit 2. Air flow meter 3. ECU
32	(7M-GE) Air Flow Meter Signal (7M-GTE) HAC Sensor Signal	(7M-GE) Open circuit in E₂ Vc and Vs short-circuited. (7M-GTE) Open or short circuit in HAC sensor signal.	(7M-GE) Same as 31, above. (7M-GTE) 1. HAC sensor circuit 2. HAC sensor 3. ECU
*¹ 34	Turbocharger pressure	*¹ The turbocharger pressure is abnormal.	1. Turbocharger 2. Air flow meter 3. ECU
41	Throttle Position Sensor Signal	Open or short circuit in throttle position sensor signal.	1. Throttle position sensor circuit 2. Throttle position sensor 3. ECU
42	Vehicle Speed Sensor Signal	Open or short circuit in vehicle speed sensor signal.	1. Vehicle speed sensor circuit 2. Vehicle speed sensor 3. ECU
43	Starter Signal (+B)	No STA signal to ECU when engine is running over 800 rpm.	1. Main relay circuit 2. IG switch circuit (starter) 3. IG switch 4. ECU
51	Switch Signal	Air conditioner switch ON or idle switch OFF or shift position other than P or N range during diagnostic check.	1. Air con. S/W 2. Throttle position sensor circuit 3. Throttle position sensor 4. Neutral start switch 5. ECU
52	Knock Sensor Signal	Open or short knock control sensor signal.	1. Knock control circuit 2. Knock control sensor 3. ECU
53	Knock Control Part (ECU)	Faulty ECU	ECU

*¹ : 7M-GTE only
*² : Abnormalities in the air flow meter may also be detected.
NOTE: Diagnosis code No. 43 will be indicated if the vehicle is push started.

INSPECTION OF THE DIAGNOSIS CIRCUIT – 1987-88 SUPRA

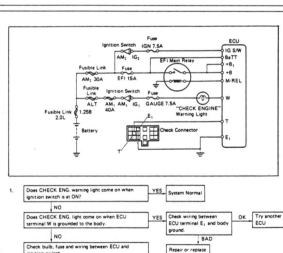

1.
- Does CHECK ENG. warning light come on when ignition switch is at ON? — YES → System Normal
  - NO
- Does CHECK ENG. light come on when ECU terminal W is grounded to the body. — YES → Check wiring between ECU terminal E₁ and body ground. — OK → Try another ECU
  - NO
  - BAD → Repair or replace
- Check bulb, fuse and wiring between ECU and ignition switch.
  - BAD
- Repair or replace

2.
- Does CHECK ENG. warning light go off when the engine is started? — YES → System Normal
  - NO
- Check wiring between ECU and CHECK ENG. warning light. — BAD → Repair
  - OK
- Is there diagnostic code output when check connector terminals T and E₁ are short circuited? — NO → Try another ECU
  - YES
- Does CHECK ENG. warning light go out after repair according to malfunction code? — NO → Further repair required
  - YES
- System OK → Cancel out diagnosis code.

TROUBLESHOOTING THE EFI SYSTEM WITH A VOLT/OHMMETER – 1987-88 SUPRA

NOTE: The following troubleshooting procedures are designed for inspection of each separate system and therefore, the actual procedure may vary somewhat. However, troubleshooting should be performed by refering to the inspection methods described.

Before beginning inspection, it is best to first make a simple check of the fuses, fusible links and the condition of the connectors.

The following troubleshooting procedures are based on the supposition that the trouble lies in either a short or open circuit in a component outside the computer or a short circuit within the computer.

If engine trouble occurs even though proper operating voltage is detected in the computer connector, then the computer is faulty and should be replaced.

LOCATION OF FUSE AND FUSIBLE LINK

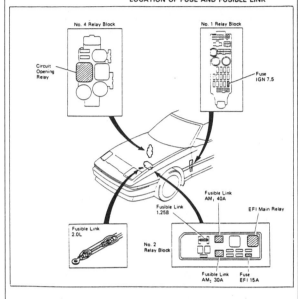

ECU CONNECTOR IDENTIFICATION – 7M-GE – 1987-88 SUPRA

PREPARATION
1. Remove the glove box door and glove box.
2. Remove the ECU with wire harness.

EFI SYSTEM CHECK PROCEDURE
NOTE:
1. The EFI circuit can be checked by measuring the voltage at the wiring connectors of the ECU.
2. Perform all voltage measurements with the connectors connected.
3. Verify that the battery voltage is 11V or above when the ignition switch is ON.

Using a voltmeter with high-impedance (10 k Λ/ minimum), measure the voltage at each terminal of the wiring connector.

NOTE: If there is any problem, see TROUBLESHOOTING EFI ELECTRONIC CIRCUIT WITH VOLT/OHMMETER.

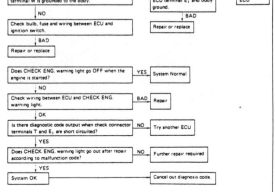

ECU Connectors (7M-GE)

Symbol	Terminal Name	Symbol	Terminal Name	Symbol	Terminal Name
E₀₁	POWER GROUND	T	CHECK CONNECTOR	L₃	ECT COMPUTER
E₀₂	POWER GROUND	G₂	DISTRIBUTOR	EGR	VSV (EGR)
No. 10	INJECTOR (No. 1 and 4)	VTA	THROTTLE POSITION SENSOR	A/C	A/C MAGNETIC SWITCH
No. 20	INJECTOR (No. 2 and 6)	Ne	DISTRIBUTOR	SPD	SPEEDOMETER
STA	STARTER SWITCH	IDL	THROTTLE POSITION SENSOR	W	WARNING LIGHT
No. 30	INJECTOR (No. 3 and 5)	IGt	IGNITER	Fp	FUEL PUMP RELAY
STJ	COLD START INJECTOR			DFG	DEFOGGER RELAY
E₁	COMPUTER GROUND	IGf	IGNITER	THA	AIR TEMP. SENSOR
NSW	NEUTRAL START SWITCH (A/T)			ECT	ECT COMPUTER
N/C	CLUTCH SWITCH (M/T)	THW	WATER TEMP. SENSOR	Vs	AIR FLOW METER
		KNK	KNOCK SENSOR	LP	HEADLIGHT RELAY
ISC1	ISC MOTOR NO. 1 COIL	Ox	OXYGEN SENSOR	Vc	AIR FLOW METER
ISC3	ISC MOTOR NO. 3 COIL	E₂	SENSOR GROUND	Batt	BATTERY
ISC2	ISC MOTOR NO. 2 COIL	VSV1	VSV (AIR CONTROL)	+B	EFI MAIN RELAY
ISC4	ISC MOTOR NO. 4 COIL	L₁	ECT COMPUTER	+B₁	EFI MAIN RELAY
G⊖	DISTRIBUTOR	VSV2	VSV (FPU)	IG S/W	IGNITION SWITCH
VF	CHECK CONNECTOR	L₂	ECT COMPUTER	+B₁	EFI MAIN RELAY
G₁	DISTRIBUTOR	M-REL	EFI MAIN RELAY (COIL)		

No. 10	STA	STJ	NSW N/C	ISC 1	ISC 3	G⊖	G₁	G₂	Ne	IGt	IGf	THW		Ox	VSV1 VSV2 VSVM-1	EGR	Fp	THA		Vs	Batt	IG S/W
E₀₁	No. 20	No. 30	E₁		ISC 2	ISC 4	VF	VTA IDL				KNK	E₂	L₁	L₂ L₃	A/C	DFG ECT	LP	+B	+B₁			

*For cruise control

VOLTAGE SUPPLIED AT THE ECU WIRING CONNECTOR 7M-GE—1987-88 SUPRA

Symbol	Terminal Name	Symbol	Terminal Name	Symbol	Terminal Name
E01	POWER GROUND	G2	CAM POSITION SENSOR	A/C	A/C MAGNETIC SWITCH
E02	POWER GROUND	VTA	THROTTLE POSITION SENSOR	SPD	SPEEDOMETER
No. 10	INJECTOR (No. 1 and 4)	Ne	CAM POSITION SENSOR	W	WARNING LIGHT
No. 20	INJECTOR (No. 2 and 6)	IDL	THROTTLE POSITION SENSOR	Fp	FUEL PUMP RELAY
STA	STARTER SWITCH	IGt	IGNITER	OIL	OIL PRESSURE SWITCH
No. 30	INJECTOR (No. 3 and 5)	IGdA	IGNITER	THA	AIR TEMP. SENSOR
STJ	COLD START INJECTOR	IGf	IGNITER	ECT	ECT COMPUTER
E1	COMPUTER GROUND	KNK1	KNOCK SENSOR	HAC	ALTITUDE COMPENSATION SENSOR
NSW	NEUTRAL START SWITCH (A/T)	THW	WATER TEMP. SENSOR	Fc	CIRCUIT OPENING RELAY
N/C	CLUTCH SWITCH (M/T)	KNK2	KNOCK SENSOR	Vc	AIR FLOW METER
IGdB	IGNITER	Ox	OXYGEN SENSOR	Ks	AIR FLOW METER
ISC1	ISC MOTOR NO. 1 COIL	E2	SENSOR GROUND	Batt	BATTERY
ISC3	ISC MOTOR NO. 3 COIL	VSV	VSV (FPU)	+B	EFI MAIN RELAY
ISC2	ISC MOTOR NO. 2 COIL	L1	ECT COMPUTER	IG S/W	IGNITION SWITCH
ISC4	ISC MOTOR NO. 4 COIL	HT	OXGEN SENSOR	+B1	EFI MAIN RELAY
G⊖	CAM POSITION SENSOR	L2	ECT COMPUTER	TIL	TURBO INDICATOR
VF	CHECK CONNECTOR	M-REL	EFI MAIN RELAY (COIL)	DFG	DEFOGGER RELAY
G1	CAM POSITION SENSOR	L3	ECT COMPUTER	LP	HEADLIGHT RELAY
T	CHECK CONNECTOR	EGR	VSV (EGR)		

*For cruise control

VOLTAGE SUPPLIED AT THE ECU WIRING CONNECTOR 7M-GT 1987-88 SUPRA

No.	Terminals	Condition		STD Voltage
1	Batt – E1	–		
	+B (+B1) – E1	Ignition S/W ON		10 – 14
	IG S/W – E1			
	M-REL – E1			
2	IDL – E2	Ignition S/W ON	Throttle valve open	10 – 14
	VTA – E2		Throttle valve closed	0.1 – 1.0
			Throttle valve fully open	4 – 5
	Vc – E2		–	4 – 6
3	Vc – E2	Ignition S/W ON	–	4 – 6
	Ks – E2	Cranking or running		2 – 4
4	No. 10 / No. 20 – E01 / No. 30	Ignition switch ON		9 – 14
5	THA – E2	Ignition S/W ON	Intake air temperature 20°C (68°F)	1 – 3
6	THW – E2		Coolant temperature 80°C (176°F)	0.1 – 1.0
7	STA – E1	Ignition switch ST position		6 – 14
8	IGf, IGt – E1	Idling		0.7 – 1.0
9	IGdA, IGdB – E1	Idling		1 – 3
10	ISC1 / ISC4 – E1	Ignition switch ON		9 – 14
		2-3 secs. after engine off		9 – 14
11	A/C – E1	Air conditioning ON		10 – 14
12	HAC – E2	Ignition S/W ON	540 mmHg (21.26 in.Hg, 72.0 kPa)	Approx. 2.8
			750 mmHg (29.53 in.Hg, 100.0 kPa)	Approx. 3.6

VOLTAGE SUPPLIED AT THE ECU WIRING CONNECTOR 7M-GTE—1987-88 SUPRA

No.	Terminals	Condition		STD Voltage
1	Batt – E1	–		
	+B (+B1) – E1	Ignition S/W ON		10 – 14
	IG S/W – E1			
	M-REL – E1			
2	IDL – E2	Ignition S/W ON	Throttle valve open	10 – 14
	VTA – E2		Throttle valve closed	0.1 – 1.0
			Throttle valve fully open	4 – 5
	Vc – E2		–	4 – 6
3	Vc – E2		–	4 – 6
	Vs – E2	Ignition S/W ON	Measuring plate fully closed	4 – 5
			Measuring plate fully open	0.02 – 0.08
		Idling		2 – 4
		3,000 rpm		0.3 – 1.0
4	No. 10 / No. 20 – E01 / No. 30	Ignition switch ON		9 – 14
5	THA – E2	Ignition S/W ON	Intake air temperature 20°C (68°F)	1 – 3
6	THW – E2		Coolant temperature 80°C (176°F)	0.1 – 1.0
7	STA – E1	Ignition switch ST position		6 – 14
8	IGf, IGt – E1	Idling		0.7 – 1.0
10	ISC1 / ISC4 – E1	Ignition switch ON		9 – 14
		2-3 secs. after engine off		9 – 14
11	A/C – E1	Air conditioning ON		10 – 14

TROUBLESHOOTING THE NO. 1 TERMINAL ON THE EFI CONNECTOR 1987-88 SUPRA

No.	Terminals	Trouble	Condition	STD Voltage
1	Batt – E1 / +B (+B1) – E1 / IG S/W – E1 / M-REL – E1	No voltage	Ignition switch ON	10 – 14 V

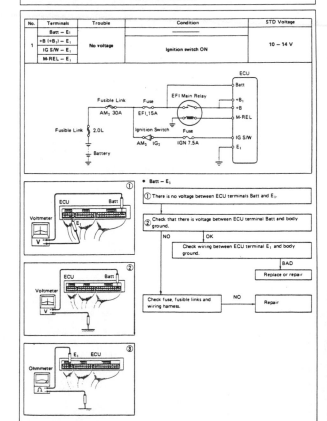

① There is no voltage between ECU terminals Batt and E1.

② Check that there is voltage between ECU terminal Batt and body ground.

- NO → Check fuse, fusible links and wiring harness. → NO → Repair
- OK → Check wiring between ECU terminal E1 and body ground. → BAD → Replace or repair

TROUBLESHOOTING THE NO. 1 TERMINAL ON THE EFI CONNECTOR
1987-88 SUPRA

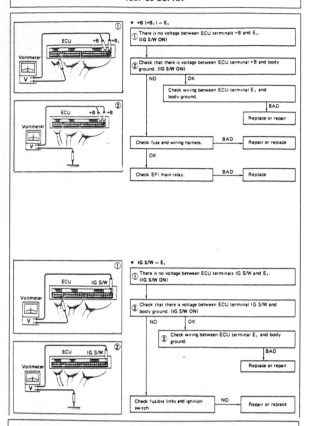

- +B (+B₁) − E₁

① There is no voltage between ECU terminals +B and E₁.
(IG S/W ON)

② Check that there is voltage between ECU terminal +B and body ground. (IG S/W ON)

NO | OK

OK → Check wiring between ECU terminal E₁ and body ground.

BAD → Replace or repair

Check fuse and wiring harness. — BAD → Repair or replace

OK

Check EFI main relay. — BAD → Replace

- IG S/W − E₁

① There is no voltage between ECU terminals IG S/W and E₁.
(IG S/W ON)

② Check that there is voltage between ECU terminal IG S/W and body ground. (IG S/W ON)

NO | OK

③ Check wiring between ECU terminal E₁ and body ground.

BAD → Replace or repair

Check fusible links and ignition switch. — NO → Repair or replace

TROUBLESHOOTING THE NO. 1 TERMINAL ON THE EFI CONNECTOR
1987-88 SUPRA

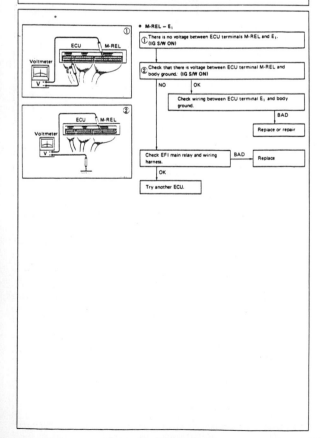

- M-REL − E₁

① There is no voltage between ECU terminals M-REL and E₁.
(IG S/W ON)

② Check that there is voltage between ECU terminal M-REL and body ground. (IG S/W ON)

NO | OK

OK → Check wiring between ECU terminal E₁ and body ground.

BAD → Replace or repair

Check EFI main relay and wiring harness. — BAD → Replace

OK

Try another ECU.

TROUBLESHOOTING THE NO. 2 TERMINAL ON THE EFI CONNECTOR
1987-88 SUPRA

No.	Terminals	Trouble	Condition		STD voltage
2	IDL − E₂	No voltage	Ignition switch ON	Throttle valve open	10 − 14 V
	VTA − E₂			Throttle valve fully closed	0.1 − 1.0 V
				Throttle valve fully open	4 − 5 V
	Vc − E₂			−	4 − 6 V

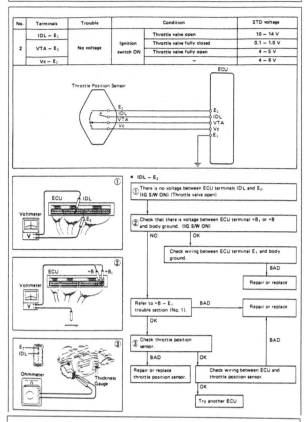

- IDL − E₂

① There is no voltage between ECU terminals IDL and E₂.
(IG S/W ON) (Throttle valve open)

② Check that there is voltage between ECU terminal +B₁ or +B and body ground. (IG S/W ON)

NO | OK

OK → Check wiring between ECU terminal E₁ and body ground.

BAD → Repair or replace

Refer to +B − E₁ trouble section (No. 1). — BAD → Repair or replace

③ Check throttle position sensor.

BAD | OK

BAD → Repair or replace throttle position sensor.

OK → Check wiring between ECU and throttle position sensor.

OK

Try another ECU

TROUBLESHOOTING THE NO. 2 TERMINAL ON THE EFI CONNECTOR
1987-88 SUPRA

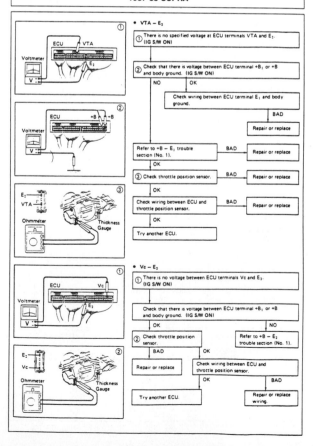

- VTA − E₂

① There is no specified voltage at ECU terminals VTA and E₂.
(IG S/W ON)

② Check that there is voltage between ECU terminal +B₁ or +B and body ground. (IG S/W ON)

NO | OK

OK → Check wiring between ECU terminal E₁ and body ground.

BAD → Repair or replace

Refer to +B − E₁ trouble section (No. 1). — BAD → Repair or replace

OK

③ Check throttle position sensor. — BAD → Repair or replace

OK

Check wiring between ECU and throttle position sensor. — BAD → Repair or replace

OK

Try another ECU.

- Vc − E₂

① There is no voltage between ECU terminals Vc and E₂.
(IG S/W ON)

Check that there is voltage between ECU terminal +B₁ or +B and body ground. (IG S/W ON)

OK | NO

NO → Refer to +B − E₁ trouble section (No. 1).

② Check throttle position sensor.

BAD | OK

BAD → Repair or replace

OK → Check wiring between ECU and throttle position sensor.

OK | BAD

Try another ECU. | Repair or replace wiring.

TROUBLESHOOTING THE NO. 3 TERMINAL ON THE EFI CONNECTOR
1987-88 SUPRA

No.	Terminals	Trouble		Condition	STD Voltage
3	$Vc - E_2$	No voltage	Ignition S/W ON	–	4 – 6 V
	(7M-GE)			Measuring plate fully closed	4 – 5 V
	$Vs - E_2$			Measuring plate fully open	0.02 – 0.08 V
				Idling	2 – 4 V
				3,000 rpm	0.3 – 1.0 V
	(7M-GTE)			Ignition S/W ON	4 – 6 V
	$Ks - E_2$	4 – 6 V		Cranking or running	2 – 4 V

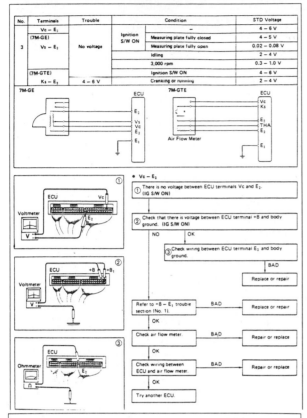

TROUBLESHOOTING THE NO. 3 TERMINAL ON THE EFI CONNECTOR
1987-88 SUPRA

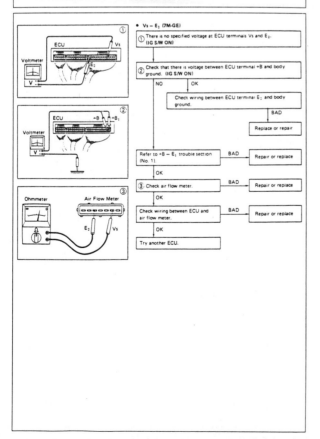

TROUBLESHOOTING THE NO. 3 TERMINAL ON THE EFI CONNECTOR
1987-88 SUPRA

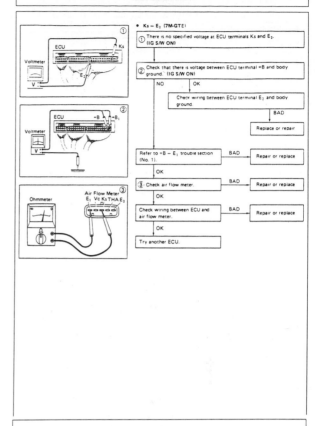

TROUBLESHOOTING THE NO. 4 TERMINAL ON THE EFI CONNECTOR
1987-88 SUPRA

No.	Terminals	Trouble	Condition	STD Voltage
4	No. 10 – E_{01}	No voltage	Ignition switch ON	9 – 14 V
	No. 20 – E_{01}			
	No. 30 – E_{01}			

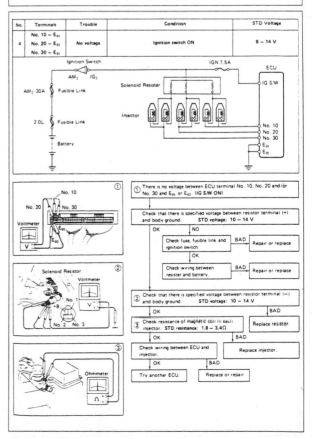

TROUBLESHOOTING THE NO. 5 TERMINAL ON THE EFI CONNECTOR
1987-88 SUPRA

No.	Terminals	Trouble	Condition		STD Voltage
5	THA – E₂	No voltage	IG S/W ON	Intake air temperature 20°C (68°F)	1 – 3 V

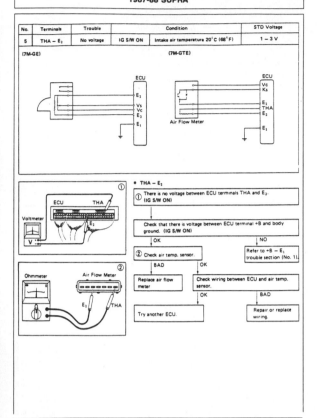

TROUBLESHOOTING THE NO. 6 TERMINAL ON THE EFI CONNECTOR
1987-88 SUPRA

No.	Terminals	Trouble	Condition		STD Voltage
6	THW – E₂	No voltage	Ignition switch ON	Coolant temperature 80°C (176°F)	0.1 – 1.0 V

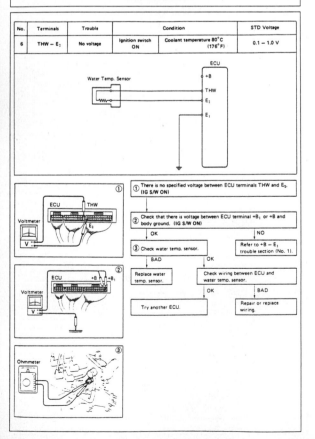

TROUBLESHOOTING THE NO. 7 TERMINAL ON THE EFI CONNECTOR
1987-88 SUPRA

No.	Terminals	Trouble	Condition	STD Voltage
7	STA – E₁	No voltage	Ignition switch ST position	6 – 14 V

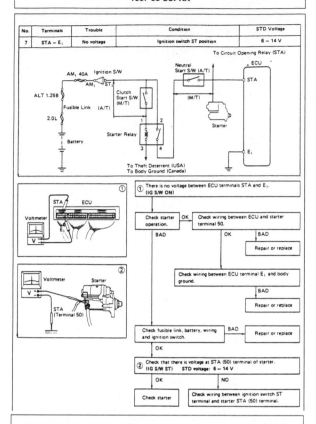

TROUBLESHOOTING THE NO. 8 TERMINAL ON THE EFI CONNECTOR
1987-88 SUPRA

7M-GE

No.	Terminals	Trouble	Condition	STD Voltage
8	IGf, IGt – E₁	No voltage	Idling	0.7 – 1.0 V

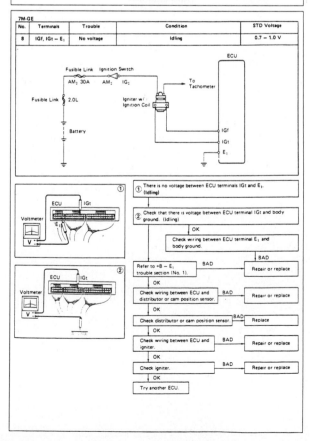

TROUBLESHOOTING THE NO. 9 TERMINAL ON THE EFI CONNECTOR
1987-88 SUPRA

7M-GTE

No.	Terminals	Trouble	Condition	STD Voltage
9	IGdA / IGdB − E$_1$	No voltage	Idling	1 − 3 V

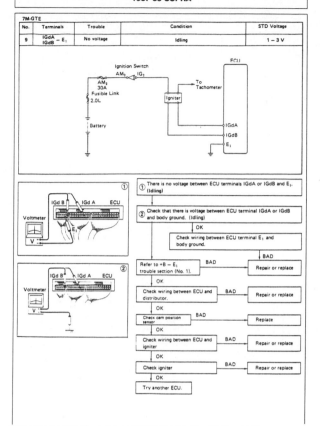

① There is no voltage between ECU terminals IGdA or IGdB and E$_1$. (Idling)

② Check that there is voltage between ECU terminal IGdA or IGdB and body ground. (Idling)

— OK → Check wiring between ECU terminal E$_1$ and body ground.

Refer to +B − E$_1$ trouble section (No. 1). — BAD → Repair or replace

— OK —

Check wiring between ECU and distributor. — BAD → Repair or replace

— OK —

Check cam position sensor — BAD → Replace

— OK —

Check wiring between ECU and igniter — BAD → Repair or replace

— OK —

Check igniter — BAD → Repair or replace

— OK —

Try another ECU.

TROUBLESHOOTING THE NO. 10 TERMINAL ON THE EFI CONNECTOR
1987-88 SUPRA

No.	Terminals	Trouble	Condition	STD Voltage
10	ISC$_1$ ~ ISC$_4$ − E$_1$	No voltage	Ignition switch ON	9 − 14 V

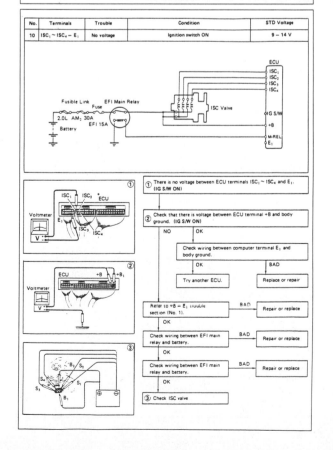

① There is no voltage between ECU terminals ISC$_1$ ~ ISC$_4$ and E$_1$. (IG S/W ON)

② Check that there is voltage between ECU terminal +B and body ground. (IG S/W ON)

NO / OK

— OK → Check wiring between computer terminal E$_1$ and body ground.

— OK → Try another ECU.
— BAD → Replace or repair

Refer to +B − E$_1$ trouble section (No. 1). — BAD → Repair or replace

— OK —

Check wiring between EFI main relay and battery. — BAD → Repair or replace

— OK —

Check wiring between EFI main relay and battery. — BAD → Repair or replace

— OK —

③ Check ISC valve

TROUBLESHOOTING THE NO. 11 TERMINAL ON THE EFI CONNECTOR
1987-88 SUPRA

No.	Terminals	Trouble	Condition	STD Voltage
11	A/C − E$_1$	No voltage	Air conditioning ON	10 − 14 V

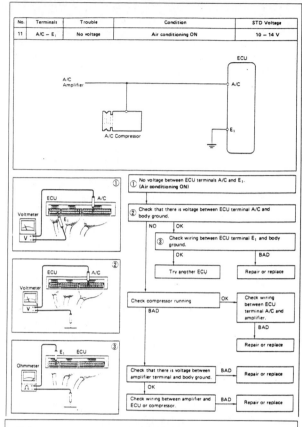

① No voltage between ECU terminals A/C and E$_1$. (Air conditioning ON)

② Check that there is voltage between ECU terminal A/C and body ground.

NO / OK

③ Check wiring between ECU terminal E$_1$ and body ground.

— OK → Try another ECU.
— BAD → Repair or replace

Check compressor running — OK → Check wiring between ECU terminal A/C and amplifier.
— BAD —

— BAD → Repair or replace

Check that there is voltage between amplifier terminal and body ground. — BAD → Repair or replace

— OK —

Check wiring between amplifier and ECU or compressor. — BAD → Repair or replace

TROUBLESHOOTING THE NO. 12 TERMINAL ON THE EFI CONNECTOR
1987-88 SUPRA

(7M-GTE)

No.	Terminals	Trouble	Condition		STD Voltage
12	HAC − E$_2$	No voltage	Ignition S/W ON	540 mmHg (21.26 in.Hg, 72.0 kPa)	Approx. 2.8 V
				750 mmHg (29.53 in.Hg, 100.0 kPa)	Approx. 3.6 V

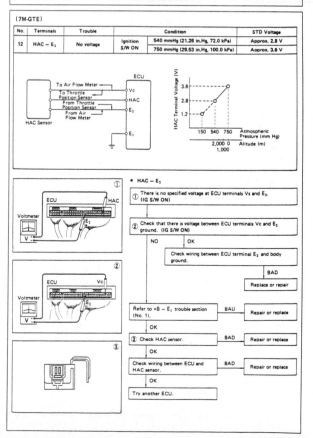

• HAC − E$_2$

① There is no specified voltage at ECU terminals Vs and E$_2$. (IG S/W ON)

② Check that there is voltage between ECU terminals Vc and E$_2$ ground. (IG S/W ON)

NO / OK

— OK → Check wiring between ECU terminal E$_2$ and body ground.

— BAD → Replace or repair

Refer to +B − E$_1$ trouble section (No. 1). — BAD → Repair or replace

— OK —

③ Check HAC sensor. — BAD → Repair or replace

— OK —

Check wiring between ECU and HAC sensor. — BAD → Repair or replace

— OK —

Try another ECU.

ELECTRONIC COMPONENT LOCATIONS – 1987-88 SUPRA

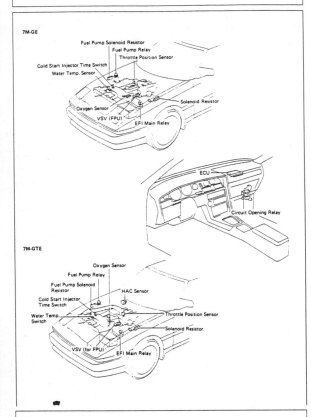

7M-GE

Fuel Pump Solenoid Resistor
Fuel Pump Relay
Throttle Position Sensor
Cold Start Injector Time Switch
Water Temp. Sensor
Oxygen Sensor
VSV (FPU)
Solenoid Resistor
EFI Main Relay
ECU
Circuit Opening Relay

7M-GTE

Oxygen Sensor
Fuel Pump Relay
Fuel Pump Solenoid Resistor
HAC Sensor
Cold Start Injector Time Switch
Water Temp. Switch
Throttle Position Sensor
Solenoid Resistor
VSV (for FPU)
EFI Main Relay

TESTING THE OXYGEN SENSOR – 1987-88 SUPRA

Oxygen Sensor
INSPECTION OF FEEDBACK VOLTAGE (VF)

1. Warm up the engine.
2. Connect the voltmeter to the check connector terminals V_F and E_1.

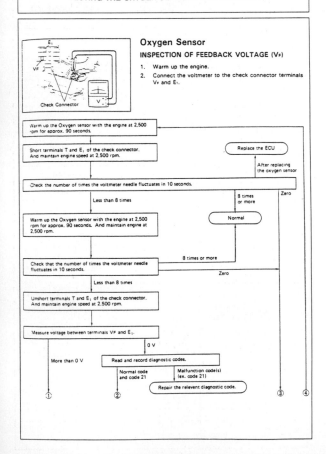

Check Connector

Warm up the Oxygen sensor with the engine at 2,500 rpm for approx. 90 seconds.

Short terminals T and E_1 of the check connector. And maintain engine speed at 2,500 rpm.

Check the number of times the voltmeter needle fluctuates in 10 seconds.

Less than 8 times → 8 times or more | Zero

Replace the ECU

After replacing the oxygen sensor

Warm up the Oxygen sensor with the engine at 2,500 rpm for approx. 90 seconds. And maintain engine at 2,500 rpm.

Check that the number of times the voltmeter needle fluctuates in 10 seconds.

8 times or more → Normal

Less than 8 times | Zero

Unshort terminals T and E_1 of the check connector. And maintain engine speed at 2,500 rpm.

Measure voltage between terminals V_F and E_1.

0 V

More than 0 V

Read and record diagnostic codes.

Normal code and code 21 | Malfunction code(s) (ex. code 21)

Repair the relevent diagnostic code.

① ② ③ ④

TESTING THE OXYGEN SENSOR (CONT.) – 1987-88 SUPRA

① ② ③ ④

Repair the relevent diagnostic code

Malfunction code(s) (ex. code 21)

Read and record diagnostic codes

Normal code and code 21

Unshort terminals T and E_1 of the check connector, and maintain engine at 2,500 rpm.

Measure voltage between terminals VF and E_1.

0 V | 5 V

Disconnect the PCV hose.

Measure voltage between terminals VF and E_1.

0 V | More than 0 V

Repair (Over rich)

Disconnect the water temp. sensor connector and connect resistor with resistance of 4 – 8 KΩ or another coded water temp. sensor.

Short terminals T and E_1 of the check connector.

Warm up the oxygen sensor with the engine at 2,500 rpm for approx. 90 seconds. And maintain engine speed at 2,500 rpm.

Measure voltage between terminals VF and E_1.

0 V | 5 V

Replace the oxygen sensor | Repair (Over lean)

INSPECTING THE ECU WIRING CONNECTOR
7M-GE – 1987-88 SUPRA

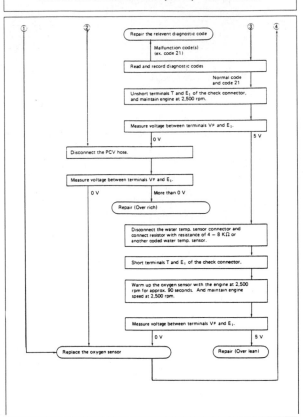

Electronic Controlled Unit (ECU)
INSPECTION OF ECU

1. MEASURE VOLTAGE OF ECU
   NOTE: The EFI circuit can be checked by measuring the resistance and voltage at the wiring connectors of the ECU.

   Check the voltage at the wiring connectors.
   • Remove the glove box.
   • Turn the ignition switch ON.
   • Measure the voltage at each terminal.

NOTE:
1. Perform all voltage measurements with the connectors connected.
2. Verify that battery voltage is 11V or above when the ignition switch is ON.

Connectors of ECU (7M-GE)

Symbol	Terminal Name	Symbol	Terminal Name	Symbol	Terminal Name
E_{01}	POWER GROUND	T	CHECK CONNECTOR	L_3	ECT COMPUTER
E_{02}	POWER GROUND	G_2	DISTRIBUTOR	EGR	VSV (EGR)
No. 10	INJECTOR (No. 1 and 4)	VTA	THROTTLE POSITION SENSOR	A/C	A/C MAGNETIC SWITCH
No. 20	INJECTOR (No. 2 and 6)	Ne	DISTRIBUTOR	SPD	SPEEDOMETER
STA	STARTER SWITCH	IDL	THROTTLE POSITION SENSOR	W	WARNING LIGHT
No. 30	INJECTOR (No. 3 and 5)	IGt	IGNITER	Fp	FUEL PUMP RELAY
STJ	COLD START INJECTOR			DFG	DEFOGGER RELAY
E_1	COMPUTER GROUND	IGf	IGNITER	THA	AIR TEMP. SENSOR
NSW	NEUTRAL START SWITCH (A/T)			ECT	ECT COMPUTER
N/C	*CLUTCH SWITCH (M/T)	THW	WATER TEMP. SENSOR	Vs	AIR FLOW METER
		KNK	KNOCK SENSOR	LP	HEADLIGHT RELAY
ISC1	ISC MOTOR NO. 1 COIL	Ox	OXYGEN SENSOR	Vc	AIR FLOW METER
ISC3	ISC MOTOR NO. 3 COIL	E_2	SENSOR GROUND		
ISC2	ISC MOTOR NO. 2 COIL	VSV1	VSV (AIR CONTROL)	Batt	BATTERY
ISC4	ISC MOTOR NO. 4 COIL	L_1	ECT COMPUTER	+B	EFI MAIN RELAY
G⊖	DISTRIBUTOR	VSV2	VSV (FPU)	IG S/W	IGNITION SWITCH
V_F	CHECK CONNECTOR	L_2	ECT COMPUTER	+B	EFI MAIN RELAY
G_1	DISTRIBUTOR	M-REL	EFI MAIN RELAY (COIL)		

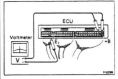

E_{01}	No. 10	STA	STJ	NSW N/C	ISC 1	ISC 3	G⊖	G_1	G_2	Ne	IGt	IGf	THW		Ox	VSV 1	VSV M-2 REL	EGR	SPD	Fp	THA	Vs	Vc	Batt	IG S/W
E_{02}	No. 20	No. 30	E_1		ISC 2	ISC 4	VF		VTA	IDL		KNK		E_2	L_1	L_2	L_3	A/C	DFG	ECT	LP			+B	+B

T

*For cruise control

INSPECTING THE ECU WIRING CONNECTOR
7M-GTE – 1987-88 SUPRA

Connectors of ECU (7M-GTE)

Symbol	Terminal Name	Symbol	Terminal Name	Symbol	Terminal Name
E$_{01}$	POWER GROUND	G$_2$	CAM POSITION SENSOR	A/C	A/C MAGNETIC SWITCH
E$_{02}$	POWER GROUND	VTA	THROTTLE POSITION SENSOR	SPD	SPEEDOMETER
No. 10	INJECTOR (No. 1 and 4)	Ne	CAM POSITION SENSOR	W	WARNING LIGHT
No. 20	INJECTOR (No. 2 and 6)	IDL	THROTTLE POSITION SENSOR	Fp	FUEL PUMP RELAY
STA	STARTER SWITCH	IGt	IGNITER	OIL	OIL PRESSURE SWITCH
No. 30	INJECTOR (No. 3 and 5)	IGdA	IGNITER	THA	AIR TEMP. SENSOR
STJ	COLD START INJECTOR	IGf	IGNITER	ECT	ECT COMPUTER
E$_1$	COMPUTER GROUND	KNK1	KNOCK SENSOR	HAC	ALTITUDE COMPENSATION SENSOR
NSW	NEUTRAL START SWITCH (A/T)	THW	WATER TEMP. SENSOR	Fc	CIRCUIT OPENING RELAY
N/C	*CLUTCH SWITCH (M/T)	KNK2	KNOCK SENSOR	Vc	AIR FLOW METER
IGdB	IGNITER	Ox	OXYGEN SENSOR	KS	AIR FLOW METER
ISC1	ISC MOTOR NO. 1 COIL	E$_2$	SENSOR GROUND	Batt	BATTERY
ISC3	ISC MOTOR NO. 3 COIL	VSV	VSV (FPU)	+B	EFI MAIN RELAY
ISC2	ISC MOTOR NO. 2 COIL	L$_1$	ECT COMPUTER	IG S/W	IGNITION SWITCH
ISC4	ISC MOTOR NO. 4 COIL	HT	OXYGEN SENSOR	+B$_1$	EFI MAIN RELAY
G ⊖	CAM POSITION SENSOR	L$_2$	ECT COMPUTER	TIL	TURBO INDICATOR
VF	CHECK CONNECTOR	M-REL	EFI MAIN RELAY (COIL)	DFG	DEFOGGER RELAY
G$_1$	CAM POSITION SENSOR	L$_3$	ECT COMPUTER	LP	HEADLIGHT RELAY
T	CHECK CONNECTOR	EGR	VSV (EGR)		

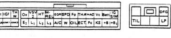

*For cruise control

INSPECTING THE VOLTAGE AT THE ECU WIRING CONNECTOR
7M-GTE – 1987-88 SUPRA

(7M-GTE)

Terminals	STD Voltage		Condition
Batt – E$_1$			–
+B (+B$_1$) – E$_1$	10 – 14		IG S/W ON
IS S/W – E$_1$			
M-REL – E$_1$			
IDL – E$_2$	10 – 14	IG S/W ON	Throttle valve open
VTA – E$_2$	0.1 – 1.0	IG S/W ON	Throttle valve fully closed
	4 – 5		Throttle valve fully open
Vc – E$_2$	4 – 6		IG S/W ON
Vc – E$_2$	4 – 6	IG S/W ON	–
	4 – 5	IG S/W ON	Measuring plate fully closed
*1 Vs – E$_2$	0.02 – 0.08		Measuring plate fully open
	2 – 4		Idling
	0.3 – 1.0		3,000 rpm
*2 Ks – E$_2$	2 – 4		Cranking or running
THA – E$_2$	1 – 3	IG S/W ON	Intake air temperature 20°C (68°F)
THW – E$_2$	0.1 – 1.0	IG S/W ON	Coolant temperature 80°C (176°F)
STA – E$_1$	6 – 14		IG S/W ST position
No. 10 No. 20 – E$_1$ No. 30	9 – 14		IG S/W ON
IGf, IGt – E$_1$	0.7 – 1.0		Idling
*2 IGdA, IGdB – E$_1$	1 – 3		Idling
ISC$_1$ ⌇ – E$_1$ ISC$_4$	9 – 14		IG S/W ON
	9 – 14		2-3 secs. after engine off
HAC – E$_2$	Approx. 2.8	IG S/W ON	540 mmHg (21.26 in.Hg, 72.0 kPa)
	Approx. 3.6		750 mmHg (29.53 in.Hg, 100.0 kPa)

*1 7M-GE only
*2 7M-GTE only

INSPECTING THE VOLTAGE AT THE ECU WIRING CONNECTOR
1987-88 SUPRA

NSW (A/T) – E$_1$	0	IG S/W ON	Shift position P or N range
	10 – 14		Ex. P or N range
N/C (M/T) – E$_1$	0	IG S/W ON	Clutch pedal not depressed
	10 – 14		Clutch pedal depressed
	9 – 11		Cranking
T – E$_1$	4 – 6	IG S/W ON	Check connector T and E$_1$ not short
	0		Check connector T and E$_1$ short
A/C – E$_1$	10 – 14	IG S/W ON	Air con S/W ON
	0		Air con S/W OFF
VF – E$_1$	0 ↔ 5		Start engine (Throttle valve open)
W – E$_1$	0		IG S/W ON
	10 – 13		Start engine
DFG – E$_1$	10 – 14	IG S/W ON	Defogger S/W OFF
	0		Defogger S/W ON
LP – E$_1$	10 – 14		Headlight S/W OFF
	0		Headlight S/W ON

INSPECTING THE RESISTANCE AT THE ECU WIRING CONNECTOR
1987-88 SUPRA

2. MEASURE RESISTANCE OF ECU

CAUTION:
1. Do not touch the ECU terminals.
2. The tester probe should be inserted into the wiring connector from the wiring side.

Check the resistance between each terminal of the wiring connector.
- Remove the glove box.
- Unplug the wiring connectors from the ECU.
- Measure the resistance between each terminal of the wiring connectors.

Resistances at ECU Wiring Connectors

Terminals	Condition	Resistance (Ω)
IDL – E$_2$	Throttle valve open	∞
	Throttle valve fully closed	Less than 2.3 kΩ
VTA – E$_2$	Throttle valve fully open	3.5 – 10.3 kΩ
	Throttle valve fully closed	0.3 – 6.3 kΩ
Vc – E$_2$	–	200 – 400
*1 Vs – E$_2$	Measuring plate fully closed	20 – 600
	Measuring plate fully open	20 – 3,000
*2 Ks – E$_2$	–	∞
*2 E$_2$ → Ks	–	5,000 – 10,000
*2 Vc – E$_2$	–	10,000 – 15,000
*2 E$_2$ – Vc	–	5,000 – 10,000
THA – E$_2$	Intake air temperature 20°C (68°F)	2,000 – 3,000
THW – E$_2$	Coolant temperature 80°C (176°F)	200 – 400
G$_1$, G$_2$ – G⊖	–	140 – 180
Ne – G⊖	–	
ISC$_1$, ISC$_2$ ISC$_3$, ISC$_4$ – +B	–	10 – 30
*2 HAC – E$_2$	–	2,900 – 4,200

*1 7M-GE only
*2 7M-GTE only

EFI WIRING SCHEMATIC – 1984-85 VAN

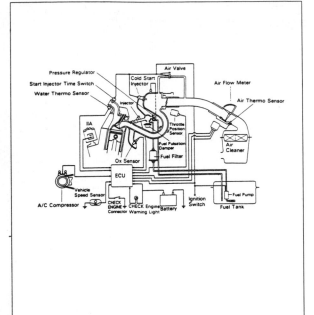

Pressure Regulator
Start Injector Time Switch
Water Thermo Sensor
Air Valve
Cold Start Injector
Air Flow Meter
Air Thermo Sensor
Injector
Throttle Position Sensor
Air Cleaner
IIA
Fuel Pulsation Damper
Fuel Filter
Ox Sensor
ECU
Vehicle Speed Sensor
CHECK ENGINE Connector
CHECK Engine Warning Light
Battery
Ignition Switch
Fuel Pump
Fuel Tank
A/C Compressor

INSPECTION OF THE DIAGNOSIS CIRCUIT – 1984-85 VAN

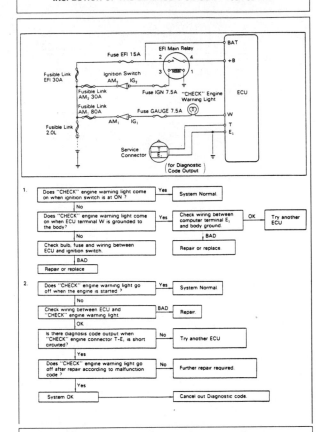

1.
Does "CHECK" engine warning light come on when ignition switch is at ON ? — Yes → System Normal.
No ↓
Does "CHECK" engine warning light come on when ECU terminal W is grounded to the body? — Yes → Check wiring between computer terminal E₁ and body ground. — OK → Try another ECU / BAD → Repair or replace.
No ↓
Check bulb, fuse and wiring between ECU and ignition switch. — BAD → Repair or replace.
Repair or replace

2.
Does "CHECK" engine warning light go off when the engine is started ? — Yes → System Normal.
No ↓
Check wiring between ECU and "CHECK" engine warning light — BAD → Repair.
OK ↓
Is there diagnosis code output when "CHECK" engine connector T-E₁ is short circuited? — No → Try another ECU
Yes ↓
Does "CHECK" engine warning light go off after repair according to malfunction code ? — No → Further repair required.
Yes ↓
System OK → Cancel out Diagnostic code.

DIAGNOSIS CODES – 1984-85 VAN

Code No.	Number of blinks "CHECK ENGINE"	System	Diagnosis	Trouble area
1		Normal	This appears when none of the other codes (2 thru 7) are identified	—
2		Air flow meter signal (V₅)	• Open circuit in V₅ or V₅–V₅ • Open circuit in V₅	1. Air flow meter circuit 2. Air flow meter 3. ECU
3		Air flow meter signal (V₅)	• Open circuit in V₅, or V₅–E₅ short circuited • Open circuit in V₅	1. Air flow meter circuit 2. Air flow meter 3. ECU
4		Water thermo sensor signal (THW)	• Open circuit in coolant temperature sensor signal	1. Coolant circuit 2. Coolant sensor 3. ECU
5		Ox sensor signal	• Open or short circuit in Oxygen sensor signal (only lean or rich indication)	1. Oxygen sensor circuit 2. Oxygen sensor 3. ECU
6		Ignition signal	• No ignition signal	1. Ignition system circuit 2. IIA 3. ECU
7		Throttle position sensor signal	• IDL-Psw short circuited	1. Throttle position sensor circuit 2. Throttle position sensor 3. ECU

TROUBLESHOOTING THE EFI SYSTEM WITH A VOLT/OHMMETER – 1984-85 VAN

PREPARATION

(a) Remove the center pillar garnish.
(b) Remove the seat belt retractor.

EFI SYSTEM CHECK PROCEDURE

NOTE:
1. The EFI circuit can be checked by measuring the resistance and voltage at the wiring connectors of the ECU.
2. Perform all voltage measurements with the connectors connected.
3. Verify that the battery voltage is 11V or more when the ignition switch is ON.

Using a voltmeter with high impedance (10 kΩ/V minimum), measure the voltage at each terminal of the wiring connector.

NOTE: If there is any problem, see TROUBLESHOOTING EFI ELECTRONIC CIRCUIT WITH VOLT/OHMMETER.

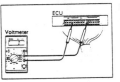

No.	Terminals	Voltage (V)	Condition
1	+B – E₁	10 – 14	Ignition switch ON
2	BAT – E₁	10 – 14	—
3	IDL – E₁	8 – 14	Throttle valve fully closed (IG s/w ON)
	Psw – E₁	8 – 14	Throttle valve fully open (IG s/w ON)
	TL – E₁	8 – 14	
4	IG – E₁	above 3	Cranking or engine running
5	STA – E₁	6 – 12	Cranking
6	No.10 – E₁	9 – 14	Ignition switch ON
	No.20 – E₁	9 – 14	Ignition switch ON
7	W – E₁	8 – 14	No trouble ("CHECK" engine warning light off) and engine runn
8	V₅ – E₂	4 – 9	Measuring plate fully closed (IG s/w ON)
	V₅ – E₂	0.5 – 2.5	Measuring plate fully open (IG s/w ON)
		5 – 8	Idling
		2.5 – 5.5	
9	THA – E₂	2 – 6	Intake air temperature 20°C (68°F)
10	THW – E₂	0.5 – 2.5	Coolant temperature 80°C (176°F)
11	A/C – E₁	8 – 14	Air conditioning ON

ECU Connectors

E₂	V₅	Vc	BAT	THA	TWS	STA	A/C	OX	THW	IDL	V₅	T	No.10	E₀₁
IG	E₁	W	+B	VSV₁	SPD	L	CHG	VSV	E₁	TL	Psw		No.20	E₀₂

TROUBLESHOOTING THE EFI SYSTEM WITH A VOLT/OHMMETER (CONT.) – 1984-85 VAN

NOTE: The following troubleshooting procedures are designed for inspection of each separate system, so the actual procedure may vary somewhat. However, troubleshooting should be performed by refering to the inspection methods described.

Before beginning inspection, it is best to first make a simple check of the fuses, fusible links and the condition of the connectors.

The following troubleshooting procedures are based on the supposition that the trouble lies in either a short or open circuit in a component outside the ECU or a short circuit within the ECU.

If engine trouble occurs eventhough proper operating voltage is detected in the ECU connector, then the ECU is at fault and should be replaced.

LOCATION OF FUSE AND FUSIBLE LINK

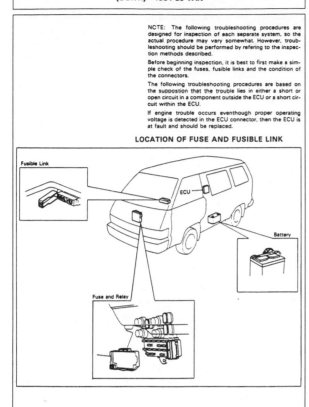

TROUBLESHOOTING THE NO. 1 TERMINAL ON THE EFI CONNECTOR 1984-85 VAN

No.	Terminals	Trouble	Condition	STD Voltage
1	$+B - E_1$	No voltage	IG S/W ON	10 – 14V

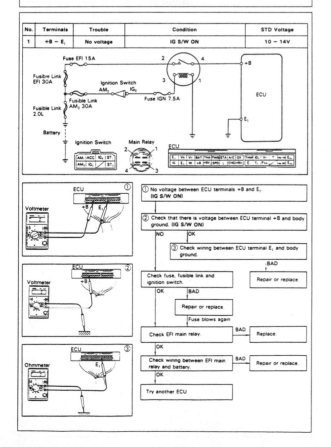

TROUBLESHOOTING THE NO. 2 TERMINAL ON THE EFI CONNECTOR 1984-85 VAN

No.	Terminals	Trouble	Condition	STD Voltage
2	$BAT - E_1$	No voltage	–	10 – 14V

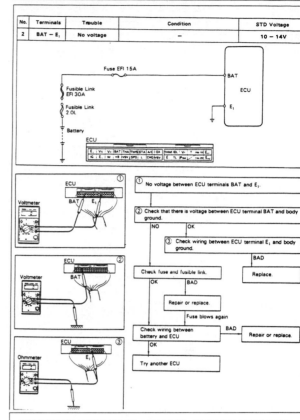

TROUBLESHOOTING THE NO. 3 TERMINAL ON THE EFI CONNECTOR 1984-85 VAN

No.	Terminal	Trouble		Condition	STD Voltage
3	$TL - E_1$	No voltage	Ignition switch ON	–	8 – 14V
	$IDL - E_1$			Throttle valve fully closed	8 – 14V
	$Psw - E_1$			Throttle valve fully open	8 – 14V

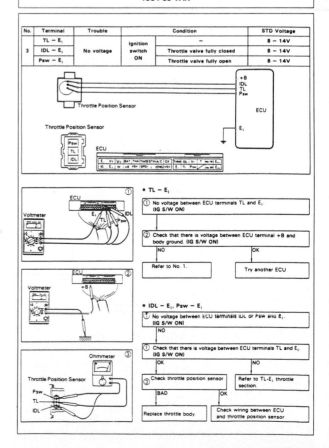

TROUBLESHOOTING THE NO. 4 TERMINAL ON THE EFI CONNECTOR
1984-85 VAN

No.	Terminal	Trouble	Condition	STD Voltage
4	IG – E₁	No voltage	Cranking or engine running	Above 3V

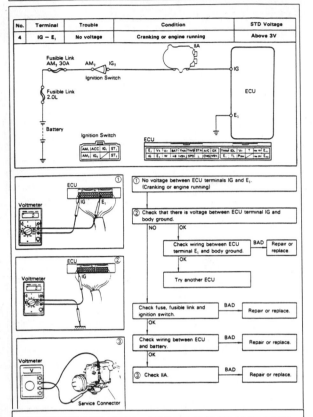

TROUBLESHOOTING THE NO. 5 TERMINAL ON THE EFI CONNECTOR
1984-85 VAN

No.	Terminal	Trouble	Condition	STD Voltage
5	STA – E₁	No voltage	Cranking	6 – 12 V

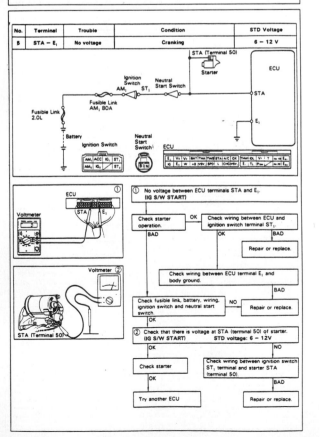

TROUBLESHOOTING THE NO. 6 TERMINAL ON THE EFI CONNECTOR
1984-85 VAN

No.	Terminal	Trouble	Condition	STD Voltage
6	No.10 – E₁ / No.20 – E₁	No voltage	IG S/W ON	9 – 14 V

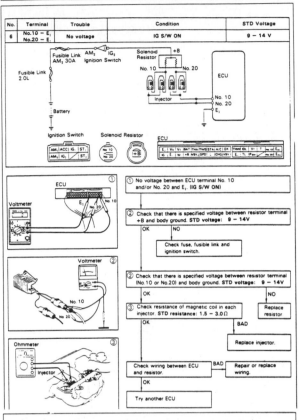

TROUBLESHOOTING THE NO. 7 TERMINAL ON THE EFI CONNECTOR
1984-85 VAN

No.	Terminal	Trouble	Condition	STD Voltage
7	W – E₁	No voltage	No trouble ("CHECK" engine warning light off) and engine running	8 – 14 V

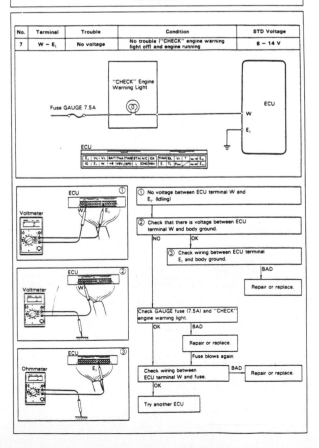

TROUBLESHOOTING THE NO. 8 TERMINAL ON THE EFI CONNECTOR
1984-85 VAN

No.	Terminals	Trouble	Condition		STD Voltage
8	$V_c - E_2$	No voltage	Ignition switch ON	—	4 — 9V
	$V_s - E_2$			Measuring plate fully closed	0.5 — 2.5V
	$V_s - E_2$			Measuring plate fully open	5 — 8V
	$V_s - E_2$		Idling	—	2.5 — 5.5V

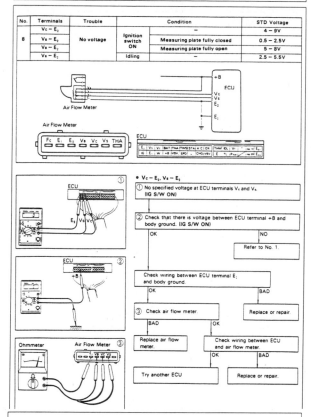

TROUBLESHOOTING THE NO. 9 TERMINAL ON THE EFI CONNECTOR
1984-85 VAN

No.	Terminals	Trouble	Condition		STD Voltage
9	$THA - E_2$	No voltage	IG S/W ON	Intake air temperature 20°C (68°F)	2 — 6 V

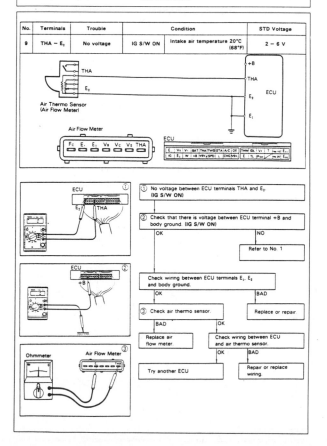

TROUBLESHOOTING THE NO. 10 TERMINAL ON THE EFI CONNECTOR
1984-85 VAN

No.	Terminals	Trouble	Condition		STD Voltage
10	$THW - E_2$	No voltage	IG S/W ON	Coolant temperature 80°C (176°F)	0.5 — 2.5V

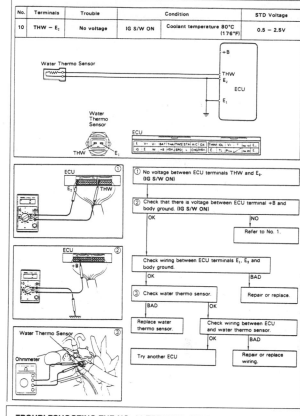

TROUBLESHOOTING THE NO. 11 TERMINAL ON THE EFI CONNECTOR
1984-85 VAN

No.	Terminals	Trouble	Condition	STD Voltage
11	$A/C-E_1$	No voltage	Air conditioning ON	8 — 14 V

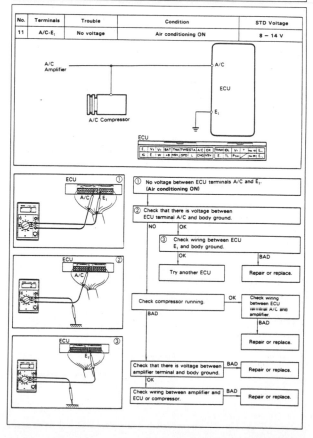

ELECTRONIC COMPONENT LOCATIONS – 1984-85 VAN

Location of Electronic Control Parts

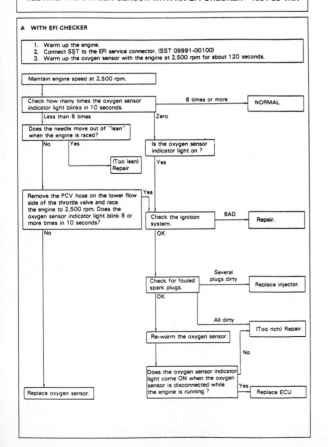

1. Fuel Pump
2. ECU
3. Cold Start Injector
4. ENGINE Service Connector
5. Circuit Opening Relay
6. Throttle Position Sensor
7. Start Injector Time Switch
8. Water Thermo Sensor
9. Injector
10. Air Flow Meter
11. Oxygen Sensor
12. Solenoid Resistor
13. EFI Main Relay
14. IIA

TESTING THE OXYGEN SENSOR WITH AN EFI CHECKER (CONT.) – 1984-85 VAN

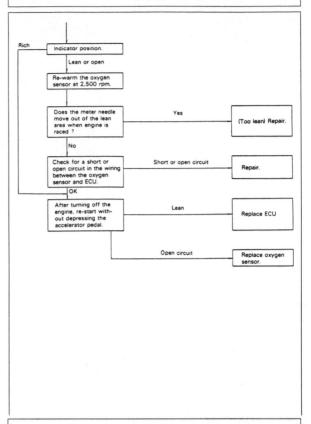

TESTING THE OXYGEN SENSOR WITH AN EFI CHECKER – 1984-85 VAN

A WITH EFI CHECKER

1. Warm up the engine.
2. Connect S$T to the EFI service connector. (SST 09991-00100)
3. Warm up the oxygen sensor with the engine at 2,500 rpm for about 120 seconds.

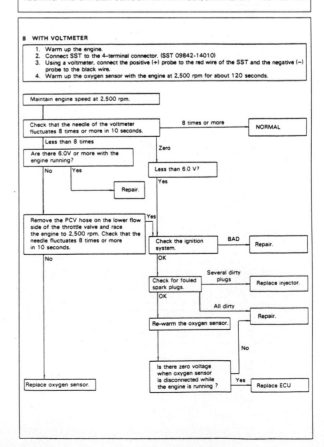

TESTING THE OXYGEN SENSOR WITH A VOLT/OHMMETER – 1984-85 VAN

B WITH VOLTMETER

1. Warm up the engine.
2. Connect SST to the 4-terminal connector. (SST 09842-14010)
3. Using a voltmeter, connect the positive (+) probe to the red wire of the SST and the negative (−) probe to the black wire.
4. Warm up the oxygen sensor with the engine at 2,500 rpm for about 120 seconds.

TESTING THE OXYGEN SENSOR WITH A VOLT OHMMETER (CONT.) – 1984-85 VAN

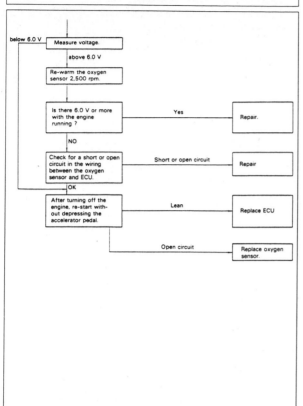

```
below 6.0 V ──┐   ┌─────────────────┐
              │   │ Measure voltage.│
              │   └─────────────────┘
        above 6.0 V
              ┌──────────────────────┐
              │ Re-warm the oxygen   │
              │ sensor 2,500 rpm.    │
              └──────────────────────┘

              ┌──────────────────────┐                  ┌─────────┐
              │ Is there 6.0 V or more│  ── Yes ──       │ Repair. │
              │ with the engine      │                  └─────────┘
              │ running ?            │
              └──────────────────────┘
                    │ NO
              ┌──────────────────────┐                  ┌─────────┐
              │ Check for a short or │  Short or open   │ Repair  │
              │ open circuit in the  │  circuit         └─────────┘
              │ wiring between the   │
              │ oxygen sensor and ECU.│
              └──────────────────────┘
                    │ OK
              ┌──────────────────────┐                  ┌─────────────┐
              │ After turning off the│  ── Lean ──       │ Replace ECU │
              │ engine, re-start     │                  └─────────────┘
              │ with-out depressing  │
              │ the accelerator pedal.│
              └──────────────────────┘
                                        Open circuit    ┌──────────────┐
                                                        │ Replace oxygen│
                                                        │ sensor.      │
                                                        └──────────────┘
```

INSPECTING THE ECU WIRING CONNECTOR 1984-85 VAN

INSPECTION OF ECU

1. **MEASURE VOLTAGE OF ECU**

   NOTE:
   1. The ECU, itself, cannot be checked directly.
   2. The EFI circuit can be checked by measuring the resistance and voltage at the wiring connectors of the ECU.

   Check the voltages at the wiring connectors.
   - Turn the ignition switch ON.
   - Measure the voltage at each terminal.

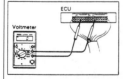

NOTE: 1. Perform all voltage measurements with the connectors connected.
2. Verify that the battery voltage is 11V or more when the ignition switch is ON.

Voltages at ECU Wiring Connectors

Terminals	Condition	Voltage
+B – E₁	10 – 14 V	(Ignition switch ON)
BAT – E₁	10 – 14 V	
IDL – E₁	8 – 14 V	(Throttle valve fully closed)
Psw – E₁	8 – 14 V	(Throttle valve fully open)
TL – E₁	8 – 14 V	
IG – E₁	Above 3 V	(Cranking and engine running)
STA – E₁	6 – 12 V	(Cranking)
No.10 – E₁	9 – 14 V	(Ignition ON)
No.20 – E₁	9 – 14 V	(Ignition ON)
W – E₁	8 – 14 V	(No trouble and engine running)
L. CHG – E₁	9 – 14 V	(Idling)
Vc – E₂	4 – 9 V	
Vs – E₂	0.5 – 2.5 V	(Measuring plate fully closed)
	5 – 8 V	(Measuring plate fully open)
	2.5 – 5.5 V	(Idling)
THA – E₂	2 – 0 V	(Intake air temperature 20°C or 68°F)
THW – E₂	0.5 – 2.5 V	(Coolant temperature 80°C or 176°F)
A/C – E₁	8 – 14 V	(Air conditioning ON)
TWS – Ground	10 – 14 V	
VSV₂ – E₁	10 – 14 V	

ECU Connectors

E₂	Vs	Vc		BAT	THA	TWS	STA	A/C	OX		THW	IDL	V₁		T	No. 10	E₀₁
IG	E₃	W		+B	VSV₂	SPD		L	CHG	VSV₁		E₁	TL	Psw		No. 20	E₀₂

EFI WIRING SCHEMATIC – 1986-88 VAN

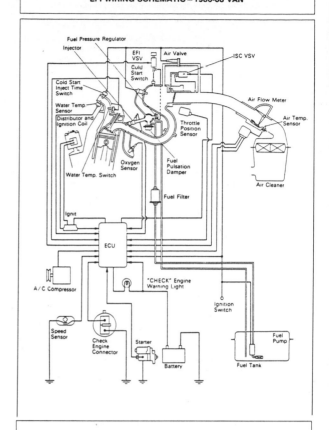

DIAGNOSIS CODES – 1986-88 VAN

Code No.	Number of CHECK ENGINE blinks	System	Diagnosis	Trouble area
1	ON ON ON ON ON / OFF OFF OFF	Normal	This appears when none of the other codes (2 thru 11) are identified.	—
2		Air flow meter signal	• VC circuit open or VS–E2 short circuited • E2 circuit open or VC–VS short circuited	1. Air flow meter circuit 2. Air flow meter 3. ECU
3		Ignition signal	No signal from igniter four times in succession.	1. Ignition circuit (+B, IGF, IGT) 2. Igniter 3. ECU
4		Water temp. sensor signal	Open or short circuit in water temp. sensor signal.	1. Water temp. sensor circuit 2. Water temp. sensor 3. ECU
5		Oxygen sensor signal	Open circuit in oxygen sensor signal (only lean indication).	1. Oxygen sensor circuit 2. Oxygen sensor 3. ECU
6		RPM signal	No Ne signal to ECU while cranking, or Ne value over 1,500 rpm in spite of no Ne signal to ECU.	1. Distributor circuit 2. Distributor 3. Igniter 4. Starter signal circuit 5. ECU
7		Throttle position sensor signal	Open or short circuit in throttle position sensor signal.	1. Throttle position sensor circuit 2. Throttle position sensor 3. ECU
8		Intake air temp. sensor signal	Open or short circuit in intake air temperature sensor.	1. Air temp. sensor circuit 2. ECU
9		Vehicle speed sensor signal	No signal for over 8 seconds when vehicle is travelling 0 km/h in spite of engine running between 2,800 – 4,500 rpm	1. Vehicle speed sensor circuit 2. Vehicle sensor 3. ECU
10		Starter signal	No STA signal to ECU when vehicle stopped and engine running over.	1. Starter relay circuit 2. IG switch circuit (starter) 3. IG Switch 4. ECU
11		Switch signal	Air conditioner switch ON, idle switch OFF.	1. Air conditioner switch 2. Throttle position sensor circuit 3. Throttle position sensor 4. Neutral start switch 5. ECU

INSPECTION OF THE DIAGNOSIS CIRCUIT – 1986-88 VAN

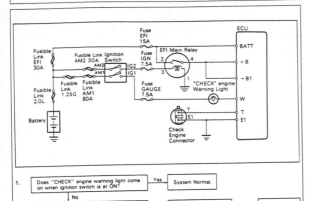

1. Does "CHECK" engine warning light come on when ignition switch is at ON? **Yes** → System Normal.

No

Does "CHECK" engine warning light come on when ECU terminal W is grounded to the body? **Yes** → Check wiring between computer terminal E1 and body ground. **OK** → Try another ECU.

No   **BAD**

Check bulb, fuse and wiring between ECU and ignition switch. → Repair or replace.

BAD

Repair or replace.

2. Does "CHECK" engine warning light go off when the engine is started? **Yes** → System Normal.

No

Check wiring between ECU and "CHECK" engine warning light. **BAD** → Repair.

OK

Is there diagnosis code output when check engine connector terminals (T – E1) are short circuited? **No** → Try another ECU.

Yes

Does "CHECK" engine warning light go off after repair according to malfunction code? **No** → Further repair required.

Yes

System OK → Cancel out Diagnostic code.

TROUBLESHOOTING THE EFI SYSTEM WITH A VOLT/OHMMETER – 1986-88 VAN

NOTE: The following troubleshooting procedures are designed for inspection of each separate system, and therefore the actual procedure may vary somewhat. However, troubleshooting should be performed referring to the inspection methods described in this manual.

Before beginning inspection, it is best to first make a simple check of the fuses, fusible links and the condition of the connectors.

The following troubleshooting procedures are based on the supposition that the trouble lies in either a short or open circuit in a component outside the computer or a short circuit within the computer.

If engine trouble occurs even though proper operating voltage is detected in the computer connector, then that the ECU is faulty and should be replaced.

LOCATION OF FUSES AND FUSIBLE LINKS

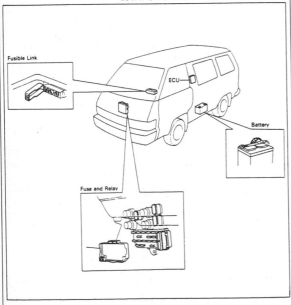

ECU CONNECTOR IDENTIFICATION – 1986-88 VAN

PREPARATION

(a) Remove the center pillar garnish.
(b) Remove the seat belt retractor.

EFI SYSTEM CHECK PROCEDURE

NOTE:
• Perform all voltage measurements with the connectors connected.
• Verify that the battery voltage is 11V or above when the ignition switch is at ON.

Using a voltmeter with high impedance (10kΩ/V minimum), measure the voltage at each terminal of the wiring connector.

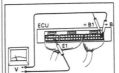

Terminals of ECU

Symbol	Terminal Name	Symbol	Terminal Name
EO1	ENGINE GROUND	A/C	A/C MAGNET CLUTCH
EO2	ENGINE GROUND	IGF	IGNITER
No. 10	INJECTOR	E2	SENSOR GROUND
No. 20	INJECTOR	OX	OXYGEN SENSOR
STA	STARTER SWITCH	PSW	THROTTLE POSITION SENSOR
IGT	IGNITER	NE	ENGINE REVOLUTION SENSOR
VF	EFI CHECK CONNECTOR	THW	WATER TEMP. SENSOR
E1	ENGINE GROUND	VC	AIR FLOW METER
FPU	EFI VSV	E21	SENSOR GROUND
V-ISC	ISC VSV	VS	AIR FLOW METER
ACV	A/C VSV	THA	AIR TEMP. SENSOR
W	CHECK ENGINE WARNING LIGHT	SPD	SPEED SENSOR
TSW	WATER TEMP. SWITCH	BATT	BATTERY
T	CHECK ENGINE CONNECTOR	+B1	MAIN RELAY
IDL	THROTTLE POSITION SENSOR	+B	MAIN RELAY

ECU Terminals:

EO1	No 10	STA	VF		V ISC	W	T	IDL	IGF			NE			VC	VS	THA BATT	+B1
EO2	No 20	IGT	E1	FPU	ACV TSW		A/C	E2	OX		PSW THW				E21		SPD	+B

VOLTAGE SUPPLIED AT THE ECU WIRING CONNECTOR 1986-88 VAN

[USA]

No.	Terminals	STD voltage	Condition	
1	+B – E1 / +B1 – E1	10 – 14	Ignition switch ON	
2	BATT – E1	10 – 14	—	
3	IDL – E1	8 – 14	Ignition switch ON	Throttle valve open
	PSW – E1	8 – 14		Throttle valve fully closed
4	IGT – E1	0.7 – 1.0	Idling	
5	STA – E1	6 – 12	Cranking	
6	No. 10 – EO1 / No. 20 – EO2	9 – 14	Ignition switch ON	
7	W – E1	8 – 14	No trouble ("CHECK" engine warning light off) and engine running	
8	VC – E2	6 – 10	—	
	VS – E2	0.5 – 2.5	Ignition switch ON	Measuring plate fully closed
		5 – 10		Measuring plate fully open
		2 – 8		
9	THA – E2	1 – 3	Ignition switch ON	Intake air temperature 20°C (68°F)
10	THW – E2	0.5 – 2.5	Ignition switch ON	Coolant temperature 80°C (176°F)
11	A/C – E1	8 – 14	Ignition switch ON	A/C ON

ECU Terminals:

EO1	No 10	STA	VF		V ISC	W	T	IDL	IGF			NE			VC	VS	THA BATT	+B1
EO2	No 20	IGT	E1	FPU	ACV TSW		A/C	E2	OX		PSW THW				E21		SPD	+B

TROUBLESHOOTING THE NO. 1 TERMINAL ON THE EFI CONNECTOR
1986-88 VAN

No.	Terminals	Trouble	Condition	STD Voltage
1	+B +B1 – E1	No voltage	Ignition S/W ON	19 – 14 V

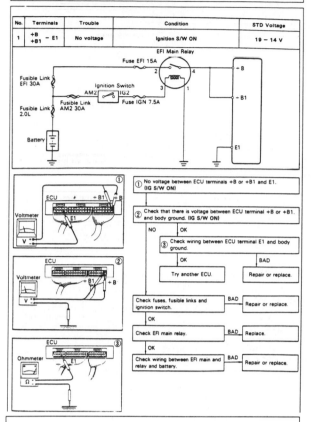

TROUBLESHOOTING THE NO. 3 TERMINAL ON THE EFI CONNECTOR
1986-88 VAN

No.	Terminals	Trouble		Condition	STD Voltage
3	IDL – E1	No voltage	IG S/W ON	Throttle valve open	8 – 14 V
	PSW – E1			Throttle valve fully closed	8 – 14 V

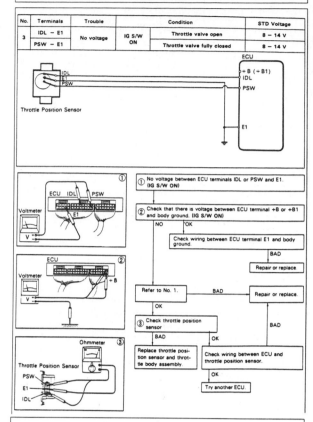

TROUBLESHOOTING THE NO. 2 TERMINAL ON THE EFI CONNECTOR
1986-88 VAN

No.	Terminals	Trouble	Condition	STD Voltage
2	BATT – E1	No voltage	—	10 – 14 V

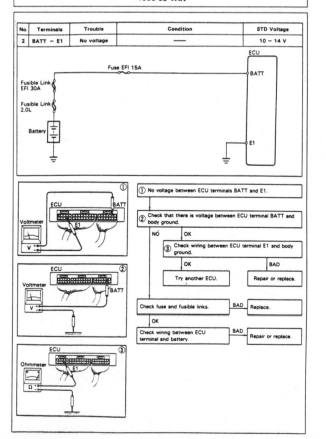

TROUBLESHOOTING THE NO. 4 TERMINAL ON THE EFI CONNECTOR
1986-88 VAN

No.	Terminals	Trouble	Condition	STD Voltage
4	IGT – E1	No voltage	Idling	0.7 – 1.0 V

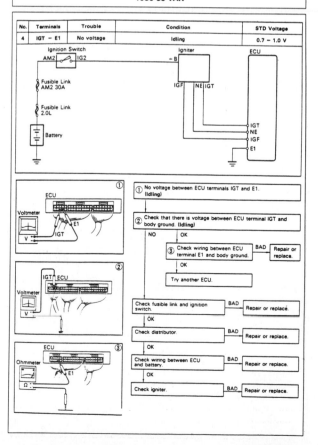

TROUBLESHOOTING THE NO. 5 TERMINAL ON THE EFI CONNECTOR
1986-88 VAN

No.	Terminals	Trouble	Condition	STD Voltage
5	STA – E1	No voltage	Cranking	6 – 12 V

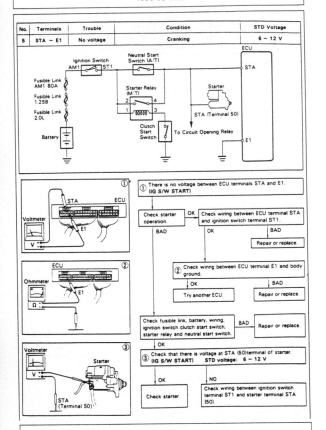

TROUBLESHOOTING THE NO. 7 TERMINAL ON THE EFI CONNECTOR
1986-88 VAN

No.	Terminals	Trouble	Condition	STD Voltage
7	W – E1	No voltage	No trouble ("CHECK" engine warning light off) and Engine running	8 – 14 V

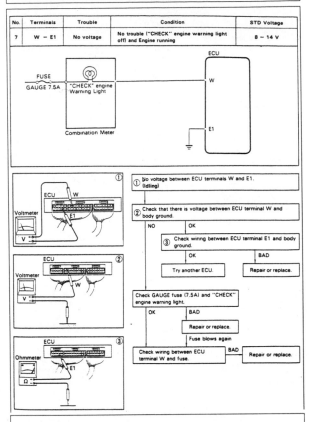

TROUBLESHOOTING THE NO. 6 TERMINAL ON THE EFI CONNECTOR
1986-88 VAN

No.	Terminals	Trouble	Condition	STD Voltage
6	No.10 – E01 No.20 – E02	No voltage	IG S/W ON	9 – 14 V

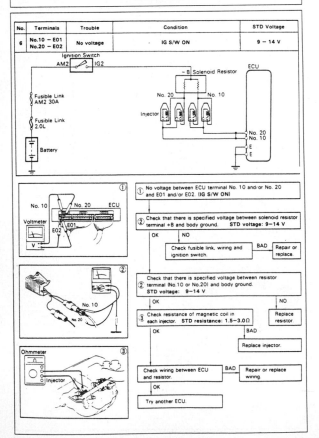

TROUBLESHOOTING THE NO. 8 TERMINAL ON THE EFI CONNECTOR
1986-88 VAN

No.	Terminals	Trouble		Condition	STD Voltage
8	VC – E2	No voltage		—	6 – 10 V
	VS – E2		IG S/W ON	Measuring plate fully closed	0.5 – 2.5 V
	VS – E2			Measuring plate fully open	5 – 10 V
	VS – E2		Idling	—	2 – 8 V

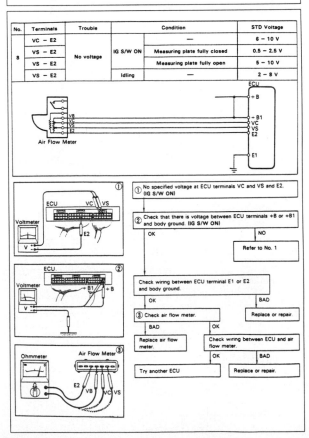

TROUBLESHOOTING THE NO. 9 TERMINAL ON THE EFI CONNECTOR
1986-88 VAN

No.	Terminals	Trouble	Condition		STD Voltage
9	THA — E2	No voltage	IG S/W ON	Intake air temp. 20°C (68°F)	1 — 3 V

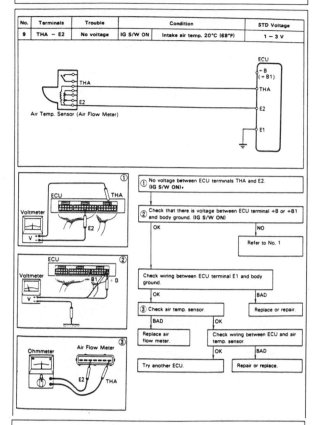

TROUBLESHOOTING THE NO. 10 TERMINAL ON THE EFI CONNECTOR
1986-88 VAN

No.	Terminals	Trouble	Condition		STD Voltage
10	THW — E2	No voltage	IG S/W ON	Coolant temp. 80°C (176°F)	0.5 — 2.5 V

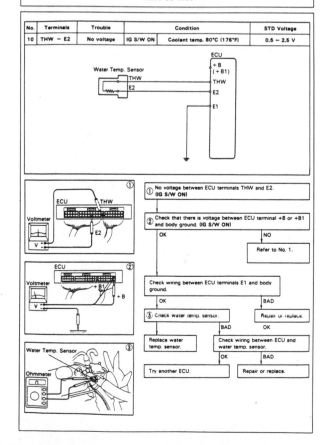

TROUBLESHOOTING THE NO. 11 TERMINAL ON THE EFI CONNECTOR
1986-88 VAN

No.	Terminals	Trouble	Condition	STD Voltage
11	A/C — E1	No voltage	Air conditioning ON	8 — 14 V

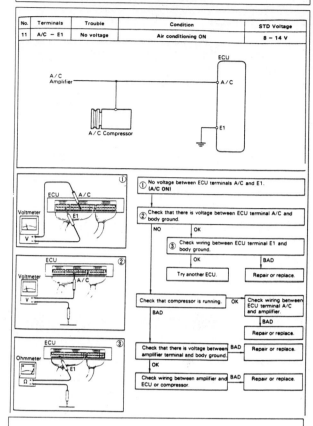

ELECTRONIC COMPONENT LOCATIONS — 1986-88 VAN

Location of Electronic Control Parts

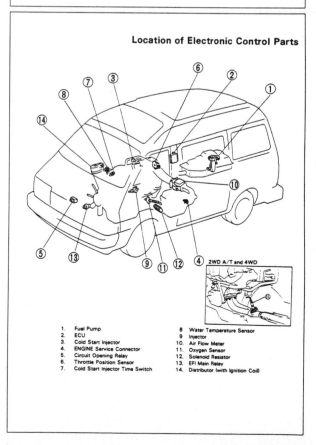

1. Fuel Pump
2. ECU
3. Cold Start Injector
4. ENGINE Service Connector
5. Circuit Opening Relay
6. Throttle Position Sensor
7. Cold Start Injector Time Switch
8. Water Temperature Sensor
9. Injector
10. Air Flow Meter
11. Oxygen Sensor
12. Solenoid Resistor
13. EFI Main Relay
14. Distributor (with Ignition Coil)

TESTING THE OXYGEN SENSOR – 1986-88 VAN

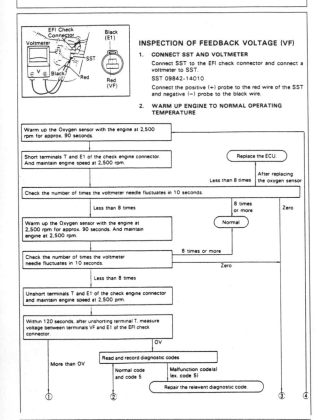

INSPECTION OF FEEDBACK VOLTAGE (VF)

1. **CONNECT SST AND VOLTMETER**

   Connect SST to the EFI check connector and connect a voltmeter to SST.

   SST 09842-14010

   Connect the positive (+) probe to the red wire of the SST and negative (−) probe to the black wire.

2. **WARM UP ENGINE TO NORMAL OPERATING TEMPERATURE**

Warm up the Oxygen sensor with the engine at 2,500 rpm for approx. 90 seconds.

Short terminals T and E1 of the check engine connector. And maintain engine speed at 2,500 rpm.

→ Replace the ECU. → After replacing the oxygen sensor → Less than 8 times

Check the number of times the voltmeter needle fluctuates in 10 seconds.

Less than 8 times / 8 times or more / Zero

→ Normal

Warm up the Oxygen sensor with the engine at 2,500 rpm for approx. 90 seconds. And maintain engine at 2,500 rpm.

8 times or more

Check the number of times the voltmeter needle fluctuates in 10 seconds.

Less than 8 times / Zero

Unshort terminals T and E1 of the check engine connector and maintain engine speed at 2,500 prm.

Within 120 seconds, after unshorting terminal T, measure voltage between terminals VF and E1 of the EFI check connector.

0V

More than 0V

Read and record diagnostic codes

Normal code and code 5 / Malfunction code(s) (ex. code 5)

Repair the relevent diagnostic code.

① ② ③ ④

TESTING THE OXYGEN SENSOR (CONT.) – 1986-88 VAN

① ② ③ ④

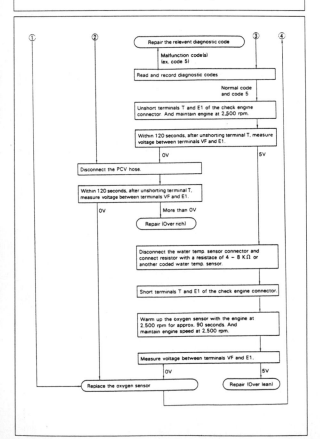

Repair the relevent diagnostic code

Malfunction code(s) (ex. code 5)

Read and record diagnostic codes

Normal code and code 5

Unshort terminals T and E1 of the check engine connector. And maintain engine at 2,500 rpm.

Within 120 seconds, after unshorting terminal T, measure voltage between terminals VF and E1.

0V / 5V

Disconnect the PCV hose.

Within 120 seconds, after unshorting terminal T, measure voltage between terminals VF and E1.

0V / More than 0V

Repair (Over rich)

Disconnect the water temp. sensor connector and connect resistor with a resistance of 4 – 8 KΩ or another coded water temp. sensor.

Short terminals T and E1 of the check engine connector.

Warm up the oxygen sensor with the engine at 2,500 rpm for approx. 90 seconds. And maintain engine at 2,500 rpm.

Measure voltage between terminals VF and E1.

0V / 5V

Replace the oxygen sensor / Repair (Over lean)

INSPECTING THE VOLTAGE AT THE ECU WIRING CONNECTOR 1986-88 VAN

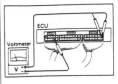

INSPECTION OF ECU

1. **INSPECT VOLTAGE OF ECU**

   NOTE:
   1. The ECU, itself, cannot be checked directly.
   2. The EFI circuit can be checked by measuring the resistance and voltage at the wiring connectors of the ECU.

   Check the voltage at the wiring connectors.
   - Turn the ignition switch ON.
   - Measure the voltage at each terminal.

NOTE:
1. Perform all voltage measurements with the connectors connected.
2. Verify that the battery voltage is 11V or more when the ignition switch is ON.

Voltages at ECU Wiring Connectors

Terminals	Condition		Voltage (V)
+B / +B1	Ignition switch ON		10 – 14
BATT – E1	—		10 – 14
IDL – E1	Ignition switch ON	Throttle valve open	8 – 14
PSW – E1	Ignition switch ON	Throttle valve closed	8 – 14
IGT – E1	Idling		0.7 – 1.0
STA – E1	Cranking		6 – 12
No. 10 / No. 20	Ignition switch ON		9 – 14
W – E1	No trouble ("CHECK" engine warning light off) and engine running		8 – 12
VC – E2	Ignition switch ON		6 – 10
VS – E2 / E21	Ignition switch ON	Measuring plate fully closed	0.5 – 2.5
		Measuring plate fully open	5 – 10
	Idling		2 – 8
THA – E2	Ignition switch ON	Intake temperature 20°C (68°F)	1 – 3
THW – E2	Ignition switch ON	Coolant temperature 80°C (176°F)	0.5 – 2.5
A/C – E1	Ignition switch ON	Air conditioning ON	10 – 14
T – E1	Ignition switch ON	Check engine connector (T – E1) not short	10 – 14
		Check connector (T – E1) short	0

ECU Terminals

E01	No 10	STA	VF		V ISC	W	T	IDL	IGF			NE			VC	VS	THA	BATT	– B1
E02	No 20	IGT	E1	FPU	ACV	TSW		A/C	E2	OX		PSW	THW			E21		SPD	– B

INSPECTING THE RESISTANCE AT THE ECU WIRING CONNECTOR 1986-88 VAN

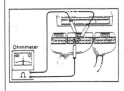

2. **INSPECT RESISTANCE OF ECU**

   CAUTION:
   1. Do not touch the ECU terminals.
   2. The tester probe should be inserted into the wiring connector from the wiring side.

   Check the resistance between each terminal of the wiring connectors.
   - Disconnect the ECU wiring connectors.
   - Measure the resistance between each terminal of the wiring connectors.

Resistance at ECU Wiring Connectors

Terminals	Condition	Resistance (Ω)
IDL – E1	Throttle valve open	∞
	Throttle valve fully closed	0
PSW – E1	Throttle valve open	0
	Throttle valve fully closed	∞
+B – E2	—	200 – 400
VC – E2	—	100 – 300
VS – E2	Measuring plate fully closed	20 – 400
	Measuring plate fully open	20 – 1,000
THA – E2	Intake air temperature 20°C (68°F)	2,000 – 3,000
THW – E2	Coolant temperature 80°C (176°F)	200 – 400

ECU Terminals

E01	No 10	STA	VF		V ISC	W	T	IDL	IGF			NE			VC	VS	THA	BATT	– B1
E02	No 20	IGT	E1	FPU	ACV	TSW		A/C	E2	OX		PSW	THW			E21		SPD	– B

EFI WIRING SCHEMATIC – 1984 TRUCK & 4-RUNNER

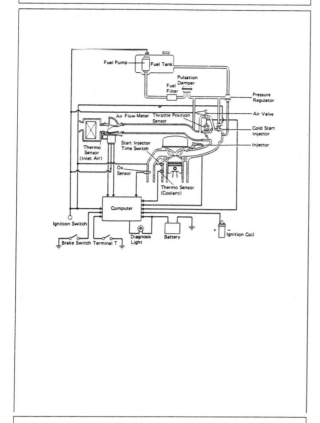

INSPECTION OF THE DIAGNOSIS CIRCUIT – 1984 TRUCK & 4-RUNNER

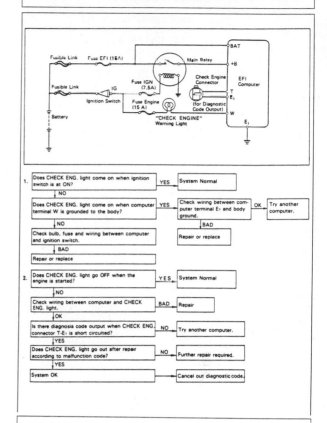

1. Does CHECK ENG. light come on when ignition switch is at ON? — YES → System Normal
   - NO
   Does CHECK ENG. light come on when computer terminal W is grounded to the body? — YES → Check wiring between computer terminal E₁ and body ground. — OK → Try another computer.
   - NO / BAD
   Check bulb, fuse and wiring between computer and ignition switch. — BAD → Repair or replace
   - BAD
   Repair or replace

2. Does CHECK ENG. light go OFF when the engine is started? — YES → System Normal
   - NO
   Check wiring between computer and CHECK ENG. light. — BAD → Repair
   - OK
   Is there diagnosis code output when CHECK ENG. connector T-E₁ is short circuited? — NO → Try another computer.
   - YES
   Does CHECK ENG. light go out after repair according to malfunction code? — NO → Further repair required.
   - YES
   System OK → Cancel out diagnostic code.

DIAGNOSIS CODES – 1984 TRUCK & 4-RUNNER

Code	Number of blinks "CHECK ENGINE"	System	Diagnosis	Trouble area
1	1/3 seconds / 3 seconds	Normal	This appears when none of the other codes (2 thru 7) are identified	
2	1 second	Air flow meter signal (Vc)	• Open circuit in Vc, or Vc – Vs short circuited. • Open circuit in Vs	1. Air flow meter circuit (Vc, Vs) 2. Air flow meter 3. EFI computer
3		Air flow meter signal (Vs)	• Open circuit in Vs, or Vs – E₂ short circuited. • Open circuit in Vs	1. Air flow meter circuit (Vs, Vc, Vs) 2. Air flow meter 3. EFI computer
4		Water thermo signal (THW)	• Open circuit in water thermo sensor signal.	1. Water thermo sensor circuit 2. Water thermo sensor 3. EFI computer
5		Ox sensor signal	• Open circuit in Ox sensor signal (only lean indication)	1. Ox sensor circuit 2. Ox sensor 3. EFI computer
6		Ignition signal	• No ignition signal	1. Ignition system circuit 2. Distributor 3. Ignition coil and igniter 4. EFI computer
7		Throttle position sensor signal	• IDL-PSW short circuited	1. Throttle position sensor circuit 2. Throttle position sensor 3. EFI computer

TROUBLESHOOTING THE EFI SYSTEM WITH A VOLT/OHMMETER – 1984 RUCK & 4-RUNNER

PREPARATION OF TROUBLESHOOTING

1. Remove the glove box.
2. Remove the EFI computer with the wire harness.

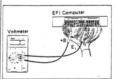

EFI SYSTEM CHECK PROCEDURE

NOTE:
1. The EFI circuit can be checked by measuring the resistance and voltage at the wiring connectors of the computer.
2. Perform all voltage measurement with the connectors connected.
3. Verify that the battery voltage is 11 V or above when the ignition switch is ON.

Using a voltmeter with high impedance (10 kΩ/V minimum) measure the voltage at each terminal of the wiring connector.

NOTE: If there is any problem, see TROUBLESHOOTING FOR EFI ELECTRONIC CIRCUIT WITH VOLT/OHMMETER.

No.	Terminals	Voltage (V)	Condition
1	+B – E₁	10 – 14	Ignition switch ON
2	BAT – E₁	10 – 14	—
3	IDL – E₁	8 – 14	Throttle valve fully closed
	PSW – E₁	8 – 14	Throttle valve fully open
	TL – E₁	8 – 14	
4	IG – E₁	above 3	Cranking and engine running
5	STA – E₁	6 – 12	Cranking
6	#10 – E₁	9 – 14	Ignition switch ON
	#20 – E₁	9 – 14	Ignition switch ON
7	W – E₁	8 – 14	No trouble(CHECK ENGINE light go off)and engine running
8	Vs – E₂	8 – 14	
	Vc – E₂	4 – 9	
	Vs – E₂	0.5 – 2.5	Measuring plate fully closed
		5 – 0	Measuring plate fully open
		2.5 – 5.5	Idling
9	THA – E₂	2 – 6	Intake air temperature 20°C or 68°F
10	THW – E₂	0.5 – 2.5	Coolant temperature 80°C or 176°F
11	B/K – E₂	8 – 14	Stop light switch ON

E₁	Vs	Vc	BATT	THA	B/K	STA		Ox	THW	Idl	V⁺	T	#10	E₀₁
IG	E₂	W	+B		SPD				E₁	TL	Psw		#20	E₀₂

TROUBLESHOOTING THE NO. 2 TERMINAL
ON THE EFI CONNECTOR
1984 TRUCK & 4-RUNNER

TROUBLESHOOTING FOR
EFI ELECTRONIC CIRCUIT WITH
VOLT/OHMMETER

NOTE: Because the following troubleshooting procedure are designed for inspection of each separate system, the actual troubleshooting procedure may vary somewhat. However, please refer to these procedures and perform actual troubleshooting, conforming to the inspection methods described.

For example, it is better to first make a simple check of the fuses, fusible links and connecting condition of the connectors before making your inspection according to the procedures listed.

LOCATION OF FUSE AND FUSIBLE LINK

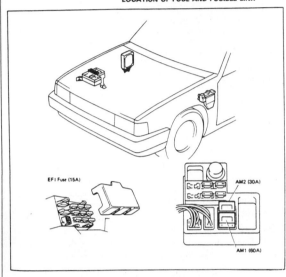

EFI Fuse (15A)

AM2 (30A)

AM1 (60A)

TROUBLESHOOTING THE NO. 1 TERMINAL
ON THE EFI CONNECTOR
1984 TRUCK & 4-RUNNER

No.	Terminals	Trouble	Condition	STD Voltage
1	+B — E₁	No voltage	IG S/W ON	10 — 14 V

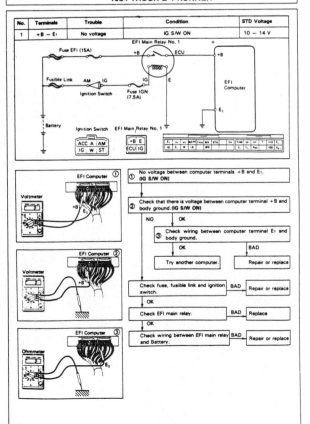

TROUBLESHOOTING THE NO. 2 TERMINAL
ON THE EFI CONNECTOR
1984 TRUCK & 4-RUNNER

No.	Terminals	Trouble	Condition	STD Voltage
2	BATT — E₁	No voltage	IG S/W ON	10 — 14 V

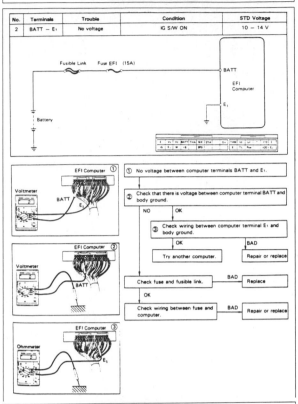

TROUBLESHOOTING THE NO. 3 TERMINAL
ON THE EFI CONNECTOR
1984 TRUCK & 4-RUNNER

No.	Terminals	Trouble	Condition	STD Voltage
3	TL — E₁	No voltage	Ignition switch ON	Throttle valve fully closed	8 — 14 V
	IDL — E₁			—	8 — 14 V
	Psw — E₁			Throttle valve fully open	8 — 14 V

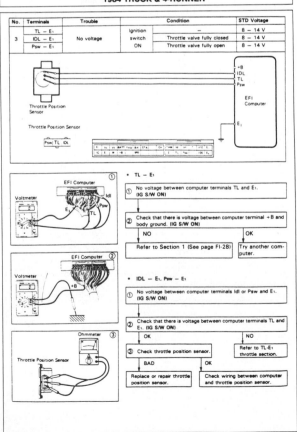

TROUBLESHOOTING THE NO. 4 TERMINAL ON THE EFI CONNECTOR
1984 TRUCK & 4-RUNNER

No.	Terminals	Trouble	Condition	STD Voltage
4	IG — E₁	No voltage	Engine cranking and running	Above 3 V

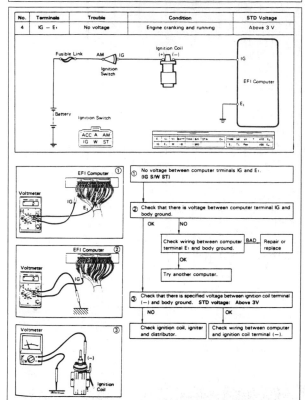

TROUBLESHOOTING THE NO. 6 TERMINAL ON THE EFI CONNECTOR
1984 TRUCK & 4-RUNNER

No.	Terminals	Trouble	Condition	STD Voltage
6	No. 10 — E₁ No. 20 — E₁	No voltage	Ignition switch ON	9 — 14 V

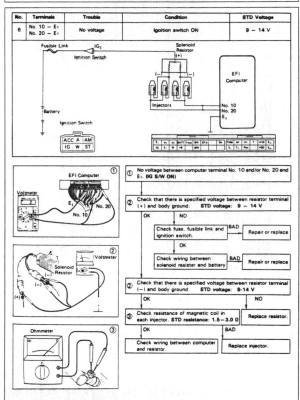

TROUBLESHOOTING THE NO. 5 TERMINAL ON THE EFI CONNECTOR
1984 TRUCK & 4-RUNNER

No.	Terminals	Trouble	Condition	STD Voltage
5	STA — E₁	No voltage	Engine cranking	6 — 12 V

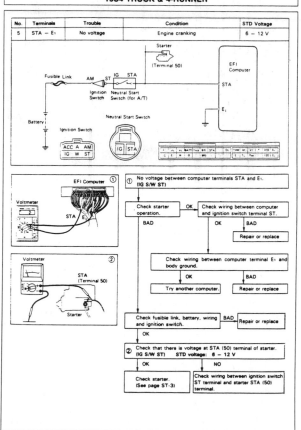

TROUBLESHOOTING THE NO. 7 TERMINAL ON THE EFI CONNECTOR
1984 TRUCK & 4-RUNNER

No.	Terminals	Trouble	Condition	STD Voltage
7	W — E₁	No voltage	No trouble (CHECK ENGINE light off) and engine running	8 — 14 V

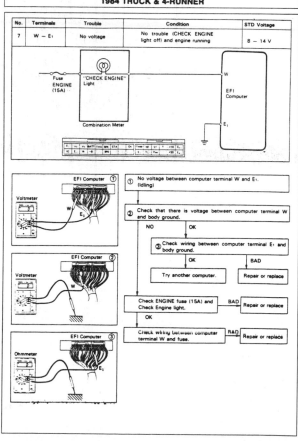

TROUBLESHOOTING THE NO. 8 TERMINAL ON THE EFI CONNECTOR
1984 TRUCK & 4-RUNNER

No.	Terminals	Trouble	Condition		STD Voltage
8	$V_c - E_2$	No voltage	Ignition switch ON	—	4 – 9 V
	$V_s - E_2$			Measuring plate fully closed	0.5 – 2.5 V
	$V_s - E_2$			Measuring plate fully open	5 – 8 V
	$V_s - E_2$		Idling	—	2.5 – 5.5 V

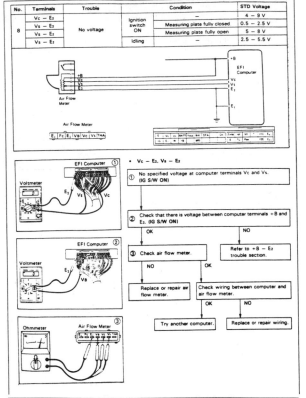

- $V_c - E_2$, $V_s - E_2$

① No specified voltage at computer terminals Vc and Vs. (IG S/W ON)

② Check that there is voltage between computer terminals +B and E₂. (IG S/W ON)

OK → ③ Check air flow meter.

NO → Refer to +B – E₂ trouble section.

③ Check air flow meter.

NO → Replace or repair air flow meter.

OK → Check wiring between computer and air flow meter.

OK → Try another computer.

NO → Replace or repair wiring.

TROUBLESHOOTING THE NO. 9 TERMINAL ON THE EFI CONNECTOR
1984 TRUCK & 4-RUNNER

No.	Terminals	Trouble	Condition	STD Voltage
9	$THA - E_2$	No voltage	Ignition switch ON, Intake air temperature 20°C (68°F)	2 – 6 V

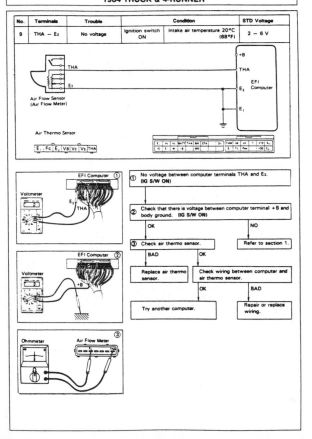

① No voltage between computer terminals THA and E₂. (IG S/W ON)

② Check that there is voltage between computer terminal +B and body ground. (IG S/W ON)

OK → ③ Check air thermo sensor.

NO → Refer to section 1.

③ Check air thermo sensor.

BAD → Replace air thermo sensor.

OK → Check wiring between computer and air thermo sensor.

OK → Try another computer.

BAD → Repair or replace wiring.

TROUBLESHOOTING THE NO. 10 TERMINAL ON THE EFI CONNECTOR
1984 TRUCK & 4-RUNNER

No.	Terminals	Trouble	Condition		STD Voltage
10	$THW - E_1$	No voltage	Ignition switch ON	Coolant temperature 80°C (176°F)	0.5 – 2.5 V

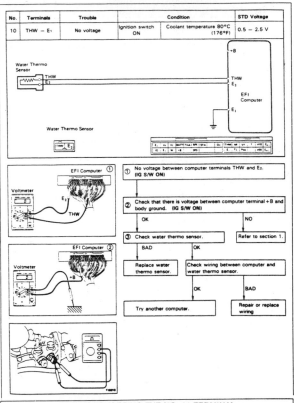

① No voltage between computer terminals THW and E₂. (IG S/W ON)

② Check that there is voltage between computer terminal +B and body ground. (IG S/W ON)

OK → ③ Check water thermo sensor.

NO → Refer to section 1.

③ Check water thermo sensor.

BAD → Replace water thermo sensor.

OK → Check wiring between computer and water thermo sensor.

OK → Try another computer.

BAD → Repair or replace wiring.

TROUBLESHOOTING THE NO. 11 TERMINAL ON THE EFI CONNECTOR
1984 TRUCK & 4-RUNNER

No.	Terminals	Trouble	Condition	STD Voltage
11	$B/K - E_1$	No voltage	Stop light switch ON	8 – 14 V

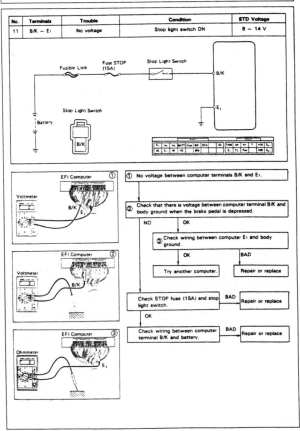

① No voltage between computer terminals B/K and E₁.

② Check that there is voltage between computer terminal B/K and body ground when the brake pedal is depressed.

NO ← → OK

③ Check wiring between computer E₁ and body ground.

OK → Try another computer.

BAD → Repair or replace

Check STOP fuse (15A) and stop light switch.

BAD → Repair or replace

OK → Check wiring between computer terminal B/K and battery.

BAD → Repair or replace

ELECTRONIC COMPONENT LOCATIONS
1984 TRUCK & 4-RUNNER

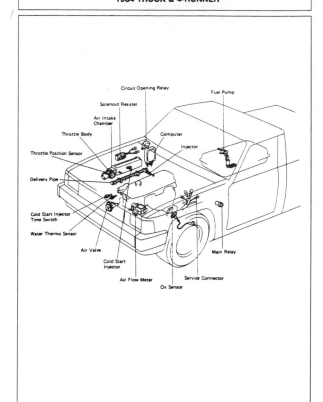

TESTING THE OXYGEN SENSOR WITH AN EFI CHECKER (CONT.)
1984 RUCK & 4-RUNNER

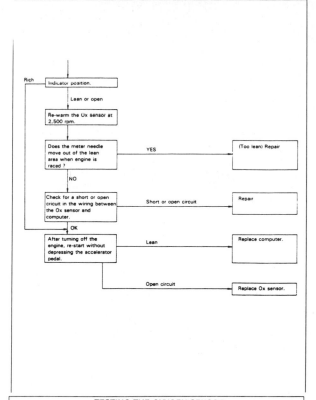

TESTING THE OXYGEN SENSOR WITH AN EFI CHECKER
1984 TRUCK & 4-RUNNER

WITH EFI CHECKER

1. Warm up the engine.
2. Connect a SST to the EFI service connector SST 09991-00100
3. Warm up the Ox sensor with the engine at 2,500 rpm for about 90 seconds.

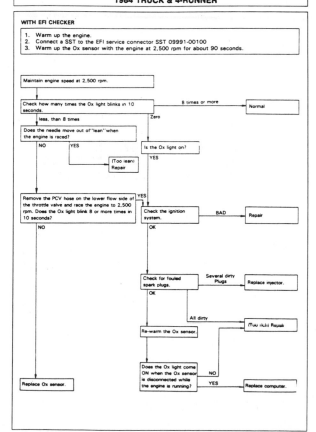

TESTING THE OXYGEN SENSOR WITH A VOLT/OHMMETER
1984 TRUCK & 4-RUNNER

WITH VOLTMETER

1. Warm up the engine.
2. Connect a SST to the 4-terminal connector. SST 09842-14010
3. Using a voltmeter connect the positive probe to the red wire of the SST and negative testing probe to the block wire.
4. Warm up the Ox sensor with the engine at 2,500 rpm for about 90 seconds.

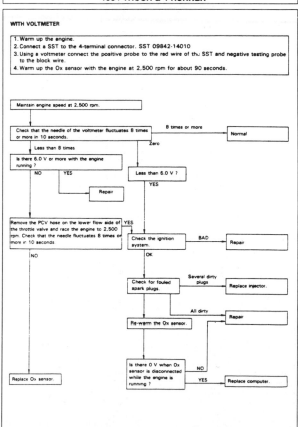

TESTING THE OXYGEN SENSOR
WITH A VOLT OHMMETER (CONT.)
1984 RUCK & 4-RUNNER

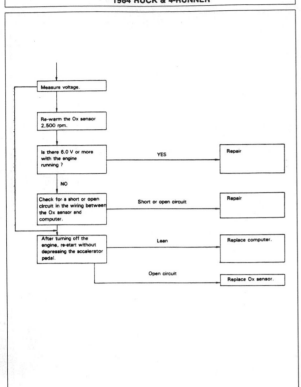

```
Measure voltage.
        │
Re-warm the Ox sensor
2,500 rpm.
        │
Is there 6.0 V or more
with the engine          ──YES──►  Repair
running ?
        │ NO
Check for a short or open
circuit in the wiring between ──Short or open circuit──► Repair
the Ox sensor and
computer.
        │
After turning off the       ──Lean──► Replace computer.
engine, re-start without
depressing the accelerator  ──Open circuit──► Replace Ox sensor.
pedal.
```

INSPECTING THE VOLTAGE
AT THE ECU WIRING CONNECTOR
1984 RUCK & 4-RUNNER

INSPECTION OF COMPUTER

1. **MEASURE VOLTAGE OF COMPUTER**
   NOTE:
   1. The computer itself cannot be checked directly.
   2. The EFI circuit can be checked by measuring the resistance and voltage at the wiring connectors of the computer.

   Check the voltages at the wiring connectors.
   • Remove the right kick panel.
   • Turn the ignition switch ON.
   • Measure the voltage at each terminal.

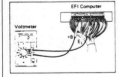

NOTE: 1. Perform all voltage measurements with the connectors connected.
2. Verify that the battery voltage is 11V or above when the ignition switch is ON.

Voltages at Computer Wiring Connectors

Terminals	Voltage	
+B − E₁	10 − 14 V	(Ignition switch ON)
BATT − E₁	10 − 14 V	
IDL − E₁	8 − 14 V	(Throttle valve fully closed)
Psw − E₁	8 − 14 V	(Throttle valve fully open)
TL − E₁	8 − 14 V	
IG − E₁	Above 3 V	(Cranking and engine running)
STA − E₁	6 − 12 V	(Cranking)
No.10 − E₁	9 − 14 V	(Ignition switch ON)
No.20 − E₁	9 − 14 V	(″ ″ ″)
+B − E₂	8 − 14 V	
Vc − E₂	4 − 9 V	
Vs − E₂	0.5 − 2.5 V	(Measuring plate fully closed)
	5 − 8V	(Measuring plate fully open)
	2.5 − 5.5 V	(Idling)
THA − E₂	2 − 6 V	(Intake air temperature 20°C or 68°F)
THW − E₂	0.5 − 2.5 V	(Coolant temperature 80°C or 176°F)
B/K − E₁	8 − 14 V	(Stop light switch ON)

Computer Connectors

E₂	Vs	Vc	BATT	THA	B/K	STA		Ox	THW	Idl	VF	T	#10	E₂₁
IG	E₁	W	+B		SPD				E₁	TL	Psw		#20	E₂₂

INSPECTING THE RESISTANCE
AT THE ECU WIRING CONNECTOR
1984 RUCK & 4-RUNNER

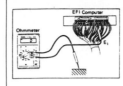

2. **MEASURE RESISTANCE OF COMPUTER**
   CAUTION:
   1. Do not touch the computer terminals.
   2. The tester probe should be inserted into wiring connector from the wiring side.

   Check the resistance between each terminal of the wiring connector.
   • Remove the right kick panel.
   • Unplug the wiring connectors from the EFI computer.
   • Measure the resistance between each terminal of the wiring connectors.

Resistance at Computer Wiring Connectors

Terminals	Resistance	
TL − IDL	0	(Throttle valve fully closed)
TL − IDL	∞	(Throttle valve fully open)
TL − Psw	∞	(Throttle valve fully closed)
TL − Psw	0	(Throttle valve fully open)
IDL, TL, Psw − Ground	∞	
THW − E₂	200 − 400Ω	(Coolant temp. 80°C or 176°F)
THA − E₂	2 − 3kΩ	(Intake air temp. 20°C or 68°F)
THW, THA − Ground	∞	
+B − E₃	200 − 400Ω	
Vc − E₂	100 − 300Ω	
Vs − E₂	20 − 100Ω	(Measuring plate fully closed)
Vs − E³	20 − 1,000Ω	(Measuring plate fully open)
+B, Vc, Vs − Ground	∞	
E₁, E₂, Eo₁, Eo₂ − Ground	0	

Computer Connectors

E₂	Vs	Vc	BATT	THA	B/K	STA		Ox	THW	Idl	VF	T	#10	E₂₁
IG	E₁	W	+B		SPD				E₁	TL	Psw		#20	E₂₂

EFI WIRING SCHEMATIC
1985 TRUCK & 4-RUNNER

SYSTEM DESCRIPTION

DIAGNOSIS CODES
1985 TRUCK & 4-RUNNER

DIAGNOSIS CODES

Code	Number of blinks "CHECK ENGINE"	System	Diagnosis	Trouble area	Page
1	⎍_⎍_⎍_⎍	Normal	This appears when none of other codes (2 thru 13) are identified.		
2	⎍⎍___⎍⎍___⎍⎍	Air flow meter signal	• Open circuit in V_C, or $V_S - E_2$ short circuited. • Open circuit in E_2, or $V_C - V_S$ short circuited.	1. Air flow meter circuit 2. Air flow meter 3. ECU	FI-56 FI-56 FI-73
3	⎍⎍⎍___⎍⎍⎍___⎍⎍⎍	Ignition signal	No signal from IGF four times in succession	1. Igniter circuit (+B, IGT, IGF) 2. Igniter 3. ECU	FI-73
4	⎍⎍⎍⎍___⎍⎍⎍⎍	Water thermo sensor signal	Open or short circuit in water thermo sensor signal	1. Water thermo sensor circuit 2. Water thermo sensor 3. ECU	FI-68 FI-68 FI-73
5	⎍⎍⎍⎍⎍___⎍⎍⎍⎍⎍	Ox sensor signal	Sufficiented feed back condition but not changed Ox sensor signal	1. Ox sensor circuit 2. Ox sensor 3. ECU	FI-69 FI-69 FI-73
6	⎍⎍⎍⎍⎍⎍___⎍⎍⎍⎍⎍⎍	RPM signal (crank angle pulse)	No Ne signal to ECU within cranking, or Ne value being over 1,000 rpm in spite of no Ne signal to ECU	1. Igniter circuit 2. Igniter 3. Distributor 4. ECU	FI-73
7	⎍⎍⎍⎍⎍⎍⎍___⎍⎍⎍⎍⎍⎍⎍	Throttle position sensor signal	Open or short circuit in throttle position sensor signal	1. Throttle position sensor circuit 2. Throttle position sensor 3. ECU	FI-59 FI-59 FI-73
8	⎍⎍⎍⎍⎍⎍⎍⎍___⎍⎍⎍⎍⎍⎍⎍⎍	Intake air thermo sensor signal	Open or short circuit in intake air thermo sensor signal	1. Intake air thermo sensor circuit 2. Intake air thermo sensor 3. ECU	FI-73
10	⎍⎍⎍⎍⎍⎍⎍⎍⎍⎍___⎍⎍⎍⎍⎍⎍⎍⎍⎍⎍	Starter signal	No STA signal to ECU when vehicle speed 0 km/h and engine is running over 800 rpm	1. Speed sensor circuit 2. Main relay circuit 3. IG switch circuit (Starter) 4. IG switch 5. ECU	FI-64 FI-73
11	⎍⎍⎍⎍⎍⎍⎍⎍⎍⎍⎍	Switch signal	Short circuit in terminal T when air conditioner switch ON or IDL point OFF	1. Air conditioner switch 2. Throttle position sensor circuit 3. Throttle position sensor 4. ECU	FI-59 FI-59 FI-73
12	⎍⎍⎍⎍⎍⎍⎍⎍⎍⎍⎍⎍	Knock control sensor signal	Knock control sensor signal is not reached judgement level in succession	1. Knock control sensor circuit 2. Knock control sensor 3. ECU	
13	⎍⎍⎍⎍⎍⎍⎍⎍⎍⎍⎍⎍⎍	Knock control CPU (ECU)	Knock CPU faulty	Knock control CPU (ECU)	

INSPECTION OF THE DIAGNOSIS CIRCUIT
1985 TRUCK & 4-RUNNER

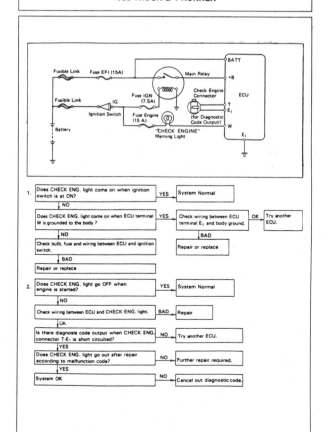

1.
Does CHECK ENG. light come on when ignition switch is at ON? — **YES** → System Normal
— **NO** ↓
Does CHECK ENG. light come on when ECU terminal W is grounded to the body? — **YES** → Check wiring between ECU terminal E_1 and body ground. — **OK** → Try another ECU.
— **NO** ↓ | — **BAD** ↓
Check bulb, fuse and wiring between ECU and ignition switch. | Repair or replace
— **BAD** ↓
Repair or replace

2.
Does CHECK ENG. light go OFF when engine is started? — **YES** → System Normal
— **NO** ↓
Check wiring between ECU and CHECK ENG. light. — **BAD** → Repair
— **OK** ↓
Is there diagnosis code output when CHECK ENG. connector T-E₁ is short circuited? — **NO** → Try another ECU.
— **YES** ↓
Does CHECK ENG. light go out after repair according to malfunction code? — **NO** → Further repair required.
— **YES** ↓
System OK — **NO** → Cancel out diagnostic code.

TROUBLESHOOTING THE EFI SYSTEM WITH A VOLT/OHMMETER
1985 RUCK & 4-RUNNER

PREPARATION FOR TROUBLESHOOTING

1. Remove the glove box.
2. Remove the ECU with the wire harness.

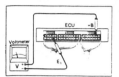

EFI SYSTEM CHECK PROCEDURE

NOTE:
1. The EFI circuit can be checked by measuring the resistance and voltage at the wiring connectors of the ECU.
2. Perform all voltage measurement with the connectors connected.
3. Verify that the battery voltage is 11 V or above when the ignition switch is ON.

Using a voltmeter with high impedance (10 kΩ/V minimum) measure the voltage at each terminal of the wiring connector.

NOTE: If there is any problems, see TROUBLESHOOTING FOR EFI ELECTRONIC CIRCUIT WITH VOLT/OHMMETER.

Connectors of ECU

Symbol	Terminal Name	Symbol	Terminal Name
+B₁	MAIN RELAY	+B	MAIN RELAY
BATT	BATTERY +B	B/K	BRAKE SWITCH
THA	AIR THERMO SENSOR	SPD	SPEED SENSOR
Vs	AIR FLOW METER	4WD	4WD SWITCH
Vc	AIR FLOW METER	E₂₁	SENSOR EARTH
Ne	ENGINE REVOLUTION SENSOR	THW	WATER THERMO SENSOR
KNK	KNOCK SENSOR	VTA	THROTTLE
IGf	IGNITER	Vcc	THROTTLE SWITCH +B
IDL	THROTTLE SWITCH	Ox	OX SENSOR
T	CHECK CONNECTOR	E₂	SENSOR EARTH
W	WARNING LIGHT	TSW	WATER THERMO SWITCH
Fpu	FUEL PRESSURE UP SWITCH	ACV	A/C IDLE UP
NSW	NEUTRAL START SWITCH	E₁	ENGINE EARTH
VF	CHECK CONNECTOR	IGt	IGNITER
STA	STARTER SWITCH	No. 20	INJECTOR
No. 10	INJECTOR	E₀₂	ENGINE GROUND
E₀₁	ENGINE GROUND		

| E₀₁ | No.10 | STA | VF | NSW | | Fpu | W | T | IDL | IGf | | | KNK | Ne | | | Vc | Vs | THA | BATT | +B₁ |
| E₀₂ | No.20 | IGt | E₁ | | | ACV | | TSW | | E₂ | Ox | Vcc | VTA | THW | | | E₂₁ | 4WD | SPD | B/K | +B |

TROUBLESHOOTING THE EFI SYSTEM WITH A VOLT/OHMMETER (CONT.)
1985 TRUCK & 4-RUNNER

NOTE: Because the following troubleshooting procedures are designed for inspection of each separate system, the actual troubleshooting procedure may vary somewhat. However, please refer to these procedures and perform actual troubleshooting, conforming to the inspection methods described.

For example, it is better to first make a simple check of the fuses, fusible links and connecting condition of the connectors before making your inspection according to the procedures listed.

LOCATION OF FUSE AND FUSIBLE LINK

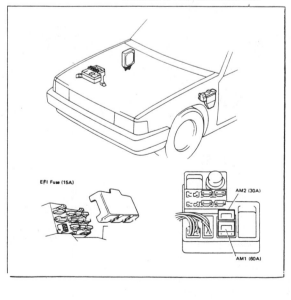

EFI Fuse (15A)

AM2 (30A)

AM1 (60A)

VOLTAGE SUPPLIED AT THE ECU WIRING CONNECTORS
1986-88 TRUCK & 4-RUNNER

VOLTAGE AT ECU WIRING CONNECTORS

No.	Terminals	Condition		STD Voltage
1	+B – E_1	Ignition switch ON		10 – 14
2	BATT – E_1	–		10 – 14
3	IDL – E_2		Throttle valve open	4 – 10
	VTA – E_2	Ignition switch ON	Throttle valve fully closed	0.1 – 1.0
			Throttle valve fully open	4 – 5
	Vcc – E_2		–	4 – 6
4	IGt – E_1	Idling		0.7 – 1.0
5	STA – E_1	Ignition switch ST position		6 – 12
6	No. 10 – E_1 No. 20 – E_1	Ignition switch ON		9 – 14
7	W – E_1	No trouble (CHECK ENGINE light off) and engine running		8 – 14
8	Vc – E_2		–	4 – 9
		Ignition switch ON	Measuring plate fully closed	0.5 – 2.5
	Vs – E_2		Measuring plate fully open	5 – 8
			Idling	2.5 – 5.5
9	THA – E_2	Ignition switch ON	Intake air temperature 20°C (68°F)	2 – 6
10	THW – E_2	Ignition switch ON	Coolant temperature 80°C (176°F)	0.5 – 2.5
11	B/K – E_1	Stop light switch ON		8 – 14

TROUBLESHOOTING THE NO. 2 TERMINAL ON THE EFI CONNECTOR
1985 TRUCK & 4-RUNNER

No.	Terminals	Trouble	Condition	STD Voltage
2	BATT – E_1	No voltage	—	10 – 14 V

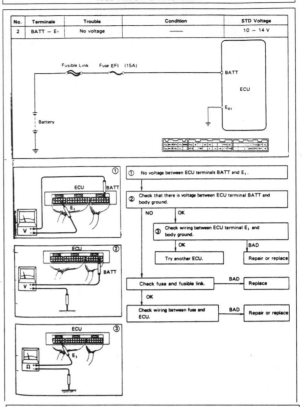

TROUBLESHOOTING THE NO. 1 TERMINAL ON THE EFI CONNECTOR
1985 TRUCK & 4-RUNNER

No.	Terminals	Trouble	Condition	STD Voltage
1	+B – E_1	No voltage	IG S/W ON	10 – 14 V

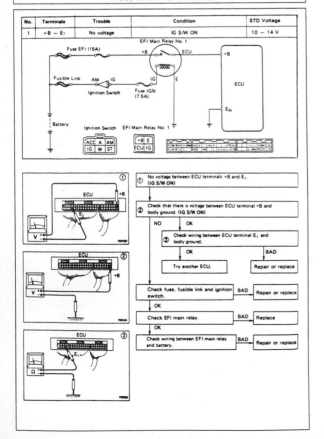

TROUBLESHOOTING THE NO. 3 TERMINAL ON THE EFI CONNECTOR
1985 TRUCK & 4-RUNNER

No.	Terminals	Trouble		Condition	STD Voltage
3	IDL – E_2			Throttle valve open	4 – 10 V
	VTA – E_2	No voltage	Ignition switch ON	Throttle valve fully closed	0.1 – 1.0 V
				Throttle valve fully open	4 – 5 V
	Vcc – E_2			—	4 – 6 V

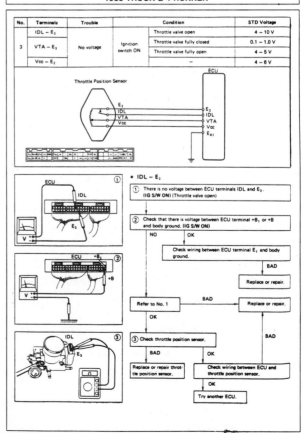

TROUBLESHOOTING THE NO. 3 TERMINAL ON THE EFI CONNECTOR
1985 TRUCK & 4-RUNNER

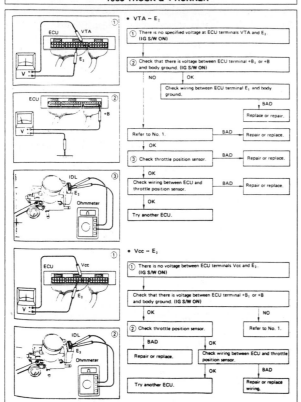

• VTA – E₂

① There is no specified voltage at ECU terminals VTA and E₂. (IG S/W ON)

② Check that there is voltage between ECU terminal +B₁ or +B and body ground. (IG S/W ON)

NO / OK

OK → Check wiring between ECU terminal E₁ and body ground.

BAD → Replace or repair.

Refer to No. 1. — BAD → Repair or replace.

OK

③ Check throttle position sensor. — BAD → Repair or replace.

OK

Check wiring between ECU and throttle position sensor. — BAD → Repair or replace.

OK

Try another ECU.

• Vcc – E₂

① There is no voltage between ECU terminals Vcc and E₂. (IG S/W ON)

② Check that there is voltage between ECU terminal +B₁ or +B and body ground. (IG S/W ON)

OK / NO

② Check throttle position sensor. — Refer to No. 1.

BAD / OK

Repair or replace. — Check wiring between ECU and throttle position sensor.

OK / BAD

Try another ECU. — Repair or replace wiring.

TROUBLESHOOTING THE NO. 4 TERMINAL ON THE EFI CONNECTOR
1985 TRUCK & 4-RUNNER

No.	Terminals	Trouble	Condition	STD Voltage
5	STA – E₁	No voltage	Ignition switch ST position	6 – 12 V

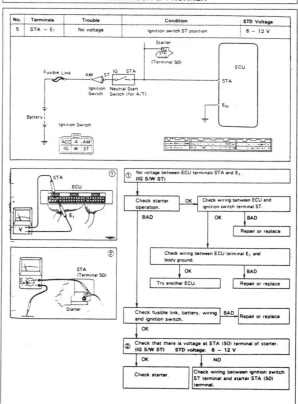

① No voltage between ECU terminals STA and E₁. (IG S/W ST)

Check starter operation. — OK → Check wiring between ECU and ignition switch terminal ST.

BAD / OK / BAD

Repair or replace

Check wiring between ECU terminal E₁ and body ground.

OK / BAD

Try another ECU. — Repair or replace

Check fusible link, battery, wiring and ignition switch. — BAD → Repair or replace

OK

② Check that there is voltage at STA (50) terminal of starter. (IG S/W ST) STD voltage: 6 – 12 V

OK / NO

Check starter. — Check wiring between ignition switch ST terminal and starter STA (50) terminal.

TROUBLESHOOTING THE NO. 5 TERMINAL ON THE EFI CONNECTOR
1985 TRUCK & 4-RUNNER

No.	Terminals	Trouble	Condition	STD Voltage
4	IGt – E₁	No voltage	Idling	0.7 – 1.0 V

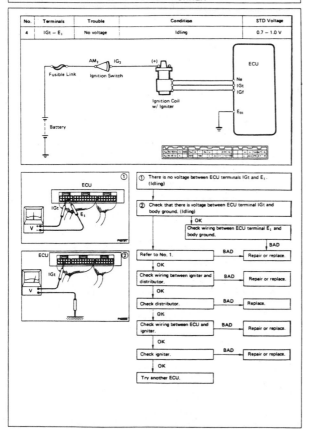

① There is no voltage between ECU terminals IGt and E₁. (Idling)

② Check that there is voltage between ECU terminal IGt and body ground. (Idling)

OK

Check wiring between ECU terminal E₁ and body ground.

BAD

Refer to No. 1. — BAD → Repair or replace.

OK

Check wiring between igniter and distributor. — BAD → Repair or replace.

OK

Check distributor. — BAD → Replace.

OK

Check wiring between ECU and igniter. — BAD → Repair or replace.

OK

Check igniter. — BAD → Repair or replace.

OK

Try another ECU.

TROUBLESHOOTING THE NO. 6 TERMINAL ON THE EFI CONNECTOR
1985 TRUCK & 4-RUNNER

No.	Terminals	Trouble	Condition	STD Voltage
6	No. 10 – E₁ No. 20 – E₁	No voltage	Ignition switch ON	9 – 14 V

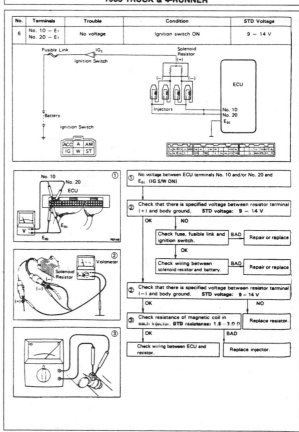

① No voltage between ECU terminals No. 10 and/or No. 20 and E₀₁. (IG S/W ON)

② Check that there is specified voltage between resistor terminal (+) and body ground. STD voltage: 9 – 14 V

OK / NO

Check fuse, fusible link and ignition switch. — BAD → Repair or replace

OK

Check wiring between solenoid resistor and battery. — BAD → Repair or replace

② Check that there is specified voltage between resistor terminal (–) and body ground. STD voltage: 9 – 14 V

OK / NO

Check resistance of magnetic coil in each injector. STD resistance: 1.5 – 3.0 Ω — Replace resistor.

OK / BAD

Check wiring between ECU and resistor. — Replace injector.

TROUBLESHOOTING THE NO. 7 TERMINAL ON THE EFI CONNECTOR
1985 TRUCK & 4-RUNNER

No.	Terminals	Trouble	Condition	STD Voltage
7	W – E₁	No voltage	No trouble (CHECK ENGINE light off) and engine running	8 – 14 V

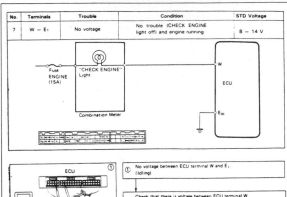

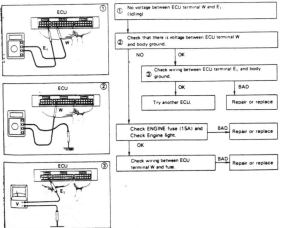

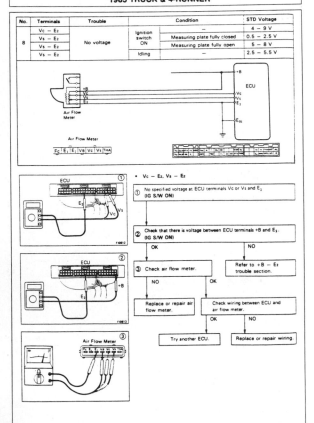

TROUBLESHOOTING THE NO. 8 TERMINAL ON THE EFI CONNECTOR
1985 TRUCK & 4-RUNNER

No.	Terminals	Trouble	Condition		STD Voltage
8	Vc – E₂	No voltage	Ignition switch ON	–	4 – 9 V
	Vs – E₂			Measuring plate fully closed	0.5 – 2.5 V
	Vs – E₂			Measuring plate fully open	5 – 8 V
	Vs – E₂		Idling	–	2.5 – 5.5 V

TROUBLESHOOTING THE NO. 9 TERMINAL ON THE EFI CONNECTOR
1985 TRUCK & 4-RUNNER

No.	Terminals	Trouble	Condition		STD Voltage
9	THA – E₂	No voltage	Ignition switch ON	Intake air temperature 20°C (68°F)	2 – 6 V

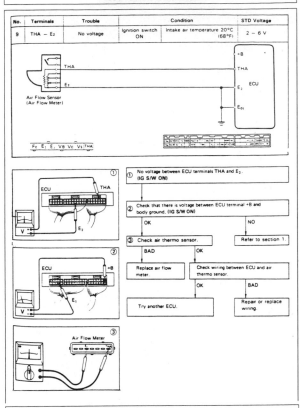

TROUBLESHOOTING THE NO. 10 TERMINAL ON THE EFI CONNECTOR
1985 TRUCK & 4-RUNNER

No.	Terminals	Trouble	Condition		STD Voltage
10	THW – E₁	No voltage	Ignition switch ON	Coolant temperature 80°C (176°F)	0.5 – 2.5 V

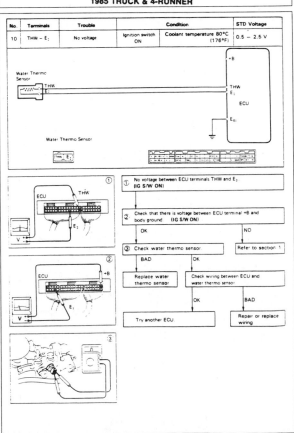

TROUBLESHOOTING THE NO. 11 TERMINAL ON THE EFI CONNECTOR
1985 TRUCK & 4-RUNNER

No.	Terminals	Trouble	Condition	STD Voltage
11	B/K – E₁	No voltage	Stop light switch ON	8 – 14 V

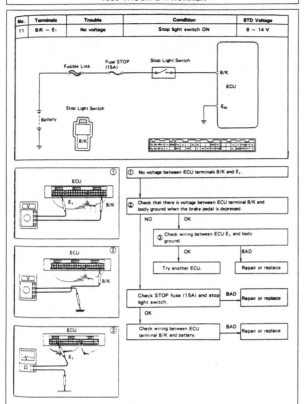

ELECTRONIC COMPONENT LOCATIONS
1985 TRUCK & 4-RUNNER

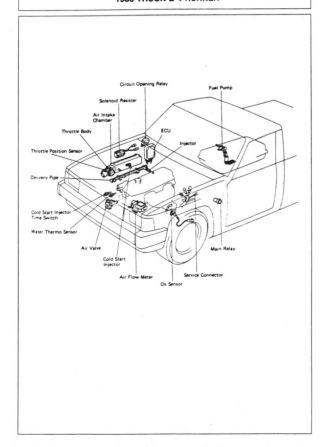

TESTING THE OXYGEN SENSOR
1985 TRUCK & 4-RUNNER

INSPECTION OF OX SENSOR

1. Warm-up the engine.
2. Connect a SST to the 4-terminal connector. SST 09842-14010
3. Using a voltmeter connect the positive probe to the red wire of the SST and negative testing probe to the block wire.
4. Warm up the Ox sensor with the engine at 2,500 rpm for about 90 seconds.

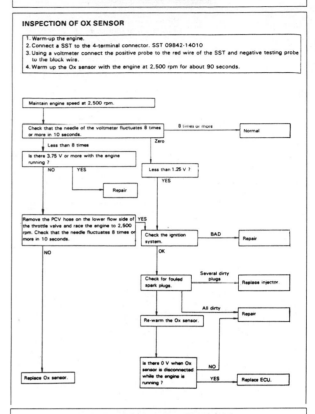

TESTING THE OXYGEN SENSOR (CONT.)
1985 TRUCK & 4-RUNNER

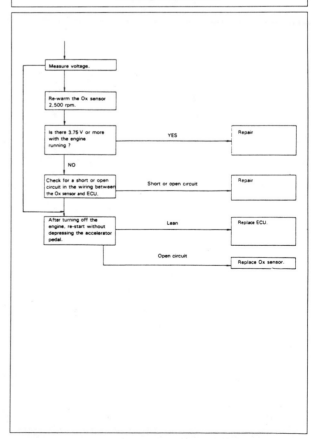

INSPECTING THE VOLTAGE AT THE ECU WIRING CONNECTOR
1985 RUCK & 4-RUNNER

ECU
INSPECTION OF ECU

1. MEASURE VOLTAGE OF ECU

NOTE:
1. The ECU itself cannot be checked directly.
2. The EFI circuit can be checked by measuring the resistance and voltage at the wiring connectors of the ECU.

Check the voltages at the wiring connectors.
- Remove the right kick panel.
- Turn the igniton switch ON.
- Measure the voltage at each terminal.

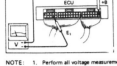

NOTE:
1. Perform all voltage measurements with the connectors connected.
2. Verify that the battery voltage is 11V or above when the ignition switch is ON.

Voltage at ECU Wiring Connectors

Terminals	Condition		STD voltage
+B – E₁	Ignition switch ON		10 – 14
BATT – E₁			10 – 14
IDL – E₂	Ignition switch ON	Throttle valve open	4 – 10
VTA – E₂		Throttle valve fully closed	0.1 – 1.0
		Throttle valve fully open	4 – 5
Vcc – E₂		–	4 – 6
IGt – E₁		Idling	0.7 – 1.0
STA – E₁	Ignition switch ST position		6 – 12
No. 10 – E₁	Ignition switch ON		9 – 14
No. 20 – E₁			
W – E₁	No trouble (CHECK ENGINE light off) and engine running		8 – 14
Vc – E₂	Ignition switch ON	–	4 – 9
Vs – E₂		Measuring plate fully closed	0.5 – 2.5
		Measuring plate fully open	5 – 8
		Idling	2.5 – 7.5
THA – E₂	Ignition switch ON	Intake air temperature 20°C (68°F)	2 – 6
THW – E₂	Ignition switch ON	Coolant temperature 80°C (176°F)	0.5 – 2.5
B/K – E₁	Stop light switch ON		8 – 14

ECU Connectors

E₀₁	No.10	STA	Vᶠ	NSW		Fᵖᵤ	W	T	IDL	IGt			KNK	Nₑ			Vc	Vₛ	THA	BATT	+B₁
E₀₂	No.20	IGt	E₁			ACV		TSW		E₂	Oₓ	Vcc	VTA	THW			E₂₁	4WD	SPD	B/K	+B

INSPECTING THE RESISTANCE AT THE ECU WIRING CONNECTOR
1985 RUCK & 4-RUNNER

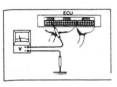

2. MEASURE RESISTANCE OF ECU
CAUTION:
1. Do not touch the ECU terminals.
2. The tester probe should be inserted into wiring connector from the wiring side.

Check the resistance between each terminal of the wiring connector.
- Remove the right kick panel.
- Unplug the wiring connectors from the ECU.
- Measure the resistance between each terminal of the wiring connectors.

Resistance at ECU Wiring Connectors

Terminals	Condition	Resistance (kΩ)
IDL – E₂	Throttle valve open	Infinity
	Throttle valve fully closed	0 – 0.1
VTA – E₂	Throttle valve fully open	3.3 – 10
	Throttle valve fully closed	0.2 – 0.8
Vcc – E₂	–	3 – 7
THA – E₂	Intake air temperature 20°C (68°F)	2 – 3
THW – E₂	Coolant temperature 80°C (176°F)	0.2 – 0.4
+B – E₁	–	0.2 – 0.4
Vc – E₂	–	0.1 – 0.3
Vs – E₂	Measuring plate fully closed	0.02 – 0.1
	Measuring plate fully open	0.02 – 1
Ne – E₁	–	0.14 – 0.18

EFI WIRING SCHEMATIC
1986-88 TRUCK & 4-RUNNER

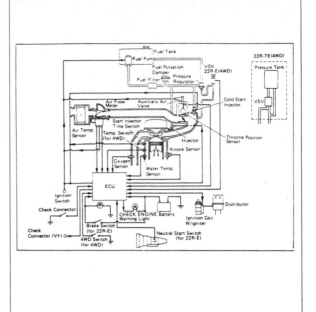

DIAGNOSIS CODES
1986-88 TRUCK & 4-RUNNER

DIAGNOSTIC CODES

Code	Number of blinks "CHECK ENGINE"	System	Diagnosis	Trouble area
1		Normal	This appears when none of the other codes (2 thru 13) are identified.	
2		Air flow meter signal	• Vc circuit open or Vs – E₂ short circuited. • E₂ circuit open or Vc – Vs short circuited.	1. Air flow meter circuit 2. Air flow meter 3. ECU
3		Ignition signal	No signal from IGf four times in succession.	1. Igniter circuit (+B, IGt, IGF) 2. Igniter 3. ECU
4		Water temp. sensor signal	Open or short circuit in coolant temp. sensor signal.	1. Water temp. sensor circuit 2. Water temp. sensor 3. ECU
5		Oxygen sensor signal	Sufficient feed back but oxygen sensor signal unchanged.	1. Oxygen sensor circuit 2. Oxygen sensor 3. ECU
6		RPM signal (crank angle pulse)	No "Ne" signal to ECU while cranking, or "Ne" value over 1,000 rpm in spite of no "Ne" signal to ECU.	1. Igniter circuit 2. Igniter 3. Distributor 4. ECU
7		Throttle position sensor signal	Open or short circuit in throttle position sensor signal.	1. Throttle position sensor circuit 2. Throttle position sensor 3. ECU
8		Intake air temp. sensor signal	Open or short circuit in intake air temp. sensor signal.	1. Intake air temp. sensor circuit 2. Intake air temp. sensor 3. ECU
10		Starter signal	No STA signal to ECU when vehicle stopped and engine running over 800 rpm.	1. Speed sensor circuit 2. Main relay circuit 3. IG switch circuit (Starter) 4. IG switch 5. ECU
11		Switch signal	Neutral start switch ON (22R-E) or IDL point in the throttle position sensor is OFF during diagnostic check.	1. Throttle position sensor circuit 2. Throttle position sensor 3. Neutral start switch (22R-E only) 4. ECU
12		Knock sensor signal	Knock sensor signal is not reached judgement level in succession.	1. Knock sensor circuit 2. Knock sensor 3. ECU
13		Knock control Part (ECU)	Faulty ECU.	ECU
*1 14		Turbocharger pressure	*2 The turbocharger pressure is abnormal.	1. Turbocharger 2. Air flow meter 3. ECU

*1 22R-TE only.
*2 Abnormalities in the air flow meter may also be detected.

INSPECTION OF THE DIAGNOSIS CIRCUIT
1986-88 TRUCK & 4-RUNNER

INSPECTION OF DIAGNOSIS CIRCUIT

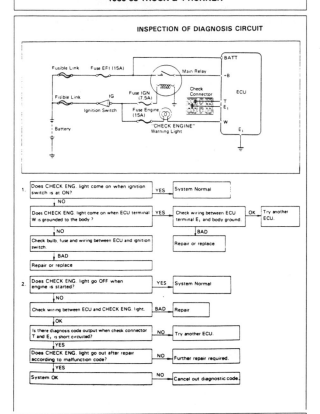

1.
| Does CHECK ENG. light come on when ignition switch is at ON? | YES → | System Normal |

↓ NO

| Does CHECK ENG. light come on when ECU terminal W is grounded to the body? | YES → | Check wiring between ECU terminal E₁ and body ground. | OK → | Try another ECU. |

↓ NO

| Check bulb, fuse and wiring between ECU and ignition switch. | BAD → | Repair or replace |

↓ BAD

| Repair or replace |

2.
| Does CHECK ENG. light go OFF when engine is started? | YES → | System Normal |

↓ NO

| Check wiring between ECU and CHECK ENG. light. | BAD → | Repair |

↓ OK

| Is there diagnosis code output when check connector T and E₁ is short circuited? | NO → | Try another ECU. |

↓ YES

| Does CHECK ENG. light go out after repair according to malfunction code? | NO → | Further repair required. |

↓ YES

| System OK | NO → | Cancel out diagnostic code. |

TROUBLESHOOTING THE EFI SYSTEM WITH A VOLT/OHMMETER
1986-88 TRUCK & 4-RUNNER

PREPARATION FOR TROUBLESHOOTING

1. Remove the right kick panel.
2. Remove the ECU with the wire harness.

EFI SYSTEM CHECK PROCEDURE

NOTE:
1. The EFI circuit can be checked by measuring the resistance and voltage at the wiring connectors of the ECU.
2. Perform all voltage measurement with the connectors connected.
3. Verify that the battery voltage is 11 V or above when the ignition switch is ON.

Using a voltmeter with high impedance (10 kΩ/V minimum) measure the voltage at each terminal of the wiring connector.

NOTE: If there is any problems, see TROUBLESHOOTING FOR EFI ELECTRONIC CIRCUIT WITH VOLT/OHMMETER.

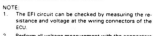
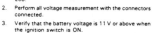

Connectors of ECU

Symbol	Terminal Name	Symbol	Terminal Name
+B₁	MAIN RELAY	*¹B/K	BRAKE SWITCH
BATT	BATTERY +B	SPD	SPEED SENSOR
THA	AIR TEMP. SENSOR	*¹4WD	4WD SWITCH
Vs	AIR FLOW METER	*¹HAC	ALTITUDE COMPENSATION SWITCH
Vc	AIR FLOW METER	E₂₁	SENSOR GROUND
*⁴L₁	ECT COMPUTER	*⁴L₂	ECT COMPUTER
*⁴L₃	ECT COMPUTER	*⁴ECT	ECT COMPUTER
Ne	ENGINE REVOLUTION SENSOR	THW	WATER TEMP. SENSOR
KNK	KNOCK SENSOR	VTA	THROTTLE SENSOR
IGf	IGNITER	Vcc	THROTTLE SENSOR +B
IDL	THROTTLE SENSOR	Ox	OXYGEN SENSOR
T	CHECK CONNECTOR	E₂	SENSOR GROUND
W	WARNING LIGHT	*¹TSW	WATER TEMP. SWITCH
*¹Fpu	FUEL PRESSURE UP SWITCH	*¹ACV	A/C IDLE UP
*³NSW	NEUTRAL START SWITCH	E₁	ENGINE GROUND
VF	CHECK CONNECTOR	IGt	IGNITER
STA	STARTER SWITCH	No. 20	INJECTOR
No. 10	INJECTOR	E₀₂	ENGINE GROUND
E₀₁	ENGINE GROUND	*²TIL	TURBO INDICATOR LAMP
+B	MAIN RELAY		

*¹ 4WD only   *³ 22R-E only   *⁵ C & C (2WD) only
*² 22R-TE only   *⁴ ECT only

TROUBLESHOOTING THE EFI SYSTEM WITH A VOLT/OHMMETER (CONT.)
1986-88 TRUCK & 4-RUNNER

NOTE: Because the following troubleshooting procedures are designed for inspection of each separate system, the actual troubleshooting procedure may vary somewhat.

However, please refer to these procedures and perform actual troubleshooting conforming to the inspection methods described.

For example, it is better to first make a simple check of the fuses, fusible links and connecting condition of the connectors before making your inspection according to the procedures listed.

The following troubleshooting procedures are based on the supposition that the trouble lies in either a short or open circuit in a component outside the computer or a short circuit within the computer. If engine trouble occurs even though proper operating voltage is detected in the computer connector, then the ECU is faulty and should be replaced.

LOCATION OF FUSES AND FUSIBLE LINKS

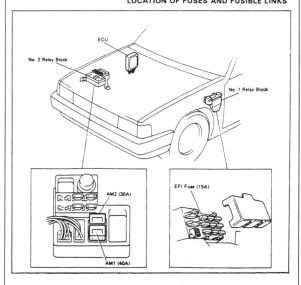

VOLTAGE SUPPLIED AT THE ECU WIRING CONNECTORS
1986-88 TRUCK & 4-RUNNER

VOLTAGE AT ECU WIRING CONNECTORS

No.	Terminals	Condition		STD Voltage	See page
1	+B – E₁	Ignition switch ON		10 – 14	FI-30
2	BATT – E₁	–		10 – 14	FI-31
3	IDL – E₂	Ignition switch ON	Throttle valve open	4 – 10	FI-32
	Vcc – E₂			4 – 6	
	VTA – E₂		Throttle valve fully closed	0.1 – 1.0	FI-33
			Throttle valve fully open	4 – 5	
4	IGt – E₁	Idling		0.7 – 1.0	FI-34
5	STA – E₁	Ignition switch ST position		6 – 12	FI-35
6	No. 10 – E₀₁ No. 20 – E₀₂	Ignition switch ON		9 – 14	FI-36
7	W – E₁	No trouble (CHECK ENGINE light off) and engine running		8 – 14	FI-37
8	Vc – E₂	Ignition switch ON		4 – 9	FI-38
	Vs – E₂		Measuring plate fully closed	0.5 – 2.5	
			Measuring plate fully open	5 – 8	
			Idling	2.5 – 7.5	
9	THA – E₂	Ignition switch ON	Intake air temperature 20°C (68°F)	2 – 6	FI-39
10	THW – E₂	Ignition switch ON	Coolant temperature 80°C (176°F)	0.5 – 2.5	FI-40
11	*B/K – E₁	Stop light switch ON		8 – 14	FI-41

* 22R-E only

TROUBLESHOOTING THE NO. 1 TERMINAL ON THE EFI CONNECTOR
1986-88 TRUCK & 4-RUNNER

No.	Terminals	Trouble	Condition	STD Voltage
1	+B — E₁	No voltage	IG S/W ON	10 – 14 V

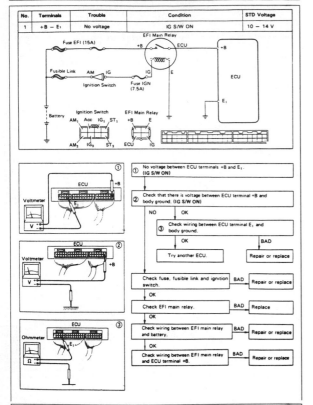

TROUBLESHOOTING THE NO. 2 TERMINAL ON THE EFI CONNECTOR
1986-88 TRUCK & 4-RUNNER

No.	Terminals	Trouble	Condition	STD Voltage
2	BATT — E₁	No voltage	—	10 – 14 V

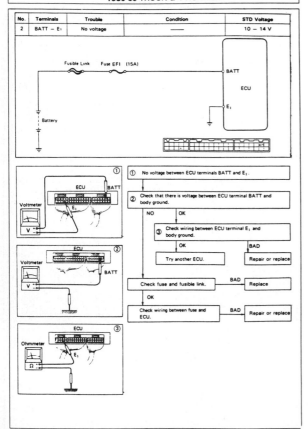

TROUBLESHOOTING THE NO. 3 TERMINAL ON THE EFI CONNECTOR
1986-88 TRUCK & 4-RUNNER

No.	Terminals	Trouble	Condition		STD Voltage
3	IDL — E₂	No voltage	Ignition switch ON	Throttle valve open	4 – 10 V
	Vcc — E₂			—	4 – 6 V
	VTA — E₂			Throttle valve fully closed	0.1 – 1.0 V
				Throttle valve fully open	4 – 5 V

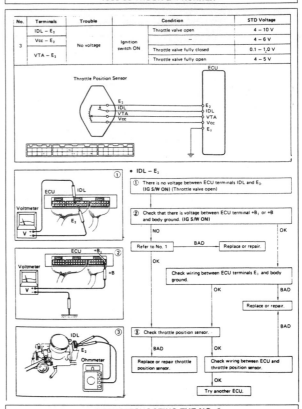

TROUBLESHOOTING THE NO. 3 TERMINAL ON THE EFI CONNECTOR
1986-88 TRUCK & 4-RUNNER

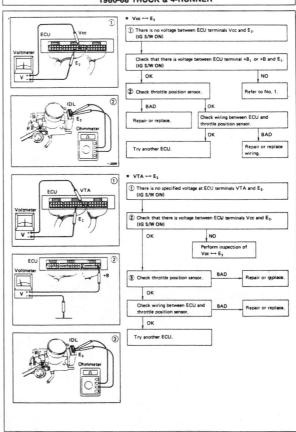

TROUBLESHOOTING THE NO. 4 TERMINAL ON THE EFI CONNECTOR
1986-88 TRUCK & 4-RUNNER

No.	Terminals	Trouble	Condition	STD Voltage
4	IGt – E₁	No voltage	Idling	0.7 – 1.0 V

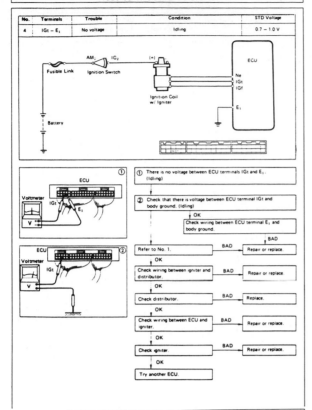

① There is no voltage between ECU terminals IGt and E₁. (Idling)

② Check that there is voltage between ECU terminal IGt and body ground. (Idling)
- OK → Check wiring between ECU terminal E₁ and body ground.

② Refer to No. 1. — BAD → Repair or replace.
- OK
- Check wiring between igniter and distributor. — BAD → Repair or replace.
- OK
- Check distributor. — BAD → Replace.
- OK
- Check wiring between ECU and igniter. — BAD → Repair or replace.
- OK
- Check igniter. — BAD → Repair or replace.
- OK
- Try another ECU.

TROUBLESHOOTING THE NO. 5 TERMINAL ON THE EFI CONNECTOR
1986-88 TRUCK & 4-RUNNER

No.	Terminals	Trouble	Condition	STD Voltage
5	STA – E₁	No voltage	Ignition switch ST position	6 – 12 V

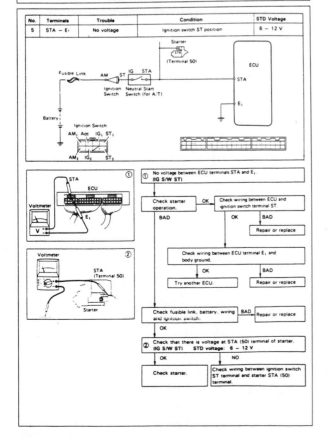

① No voltage between ECU terminals STA and E₁. (IG S/W ST)

- Check starter operation. — OK → Check wiring between ECU and ignition switch terminal ST.
- BAD — OK / BAD → Repair or replace.
- Check wiring between ECU terminal E₁ and body ground.
- OK — Try another ECU.
- BAD → Repair or replace.

- Check fusible link, battery, wiring and ignition switch. — BAD → Repair or replace.
- OK
② Check that there is voltage at STA (50) terminal of starter. (IG S/W ST) STD voltage: 6 – 12 V
- OK — NO
- Check starter. — Check wiring between ignition switch ST terminal and starter STA (50) terminal.

TROUBLESHOOTING THE NO. 6 TERMINAL ON THE EFI CONNECTOR
1986-88 TRUCK & 4-RUNNER

No.	Terminals	Trouble	Condition	STD Voltage
6	No. 10 – E₀₁ No. 20 – E₀₂	No voltage	Ignition switch ON	9 – 14 V

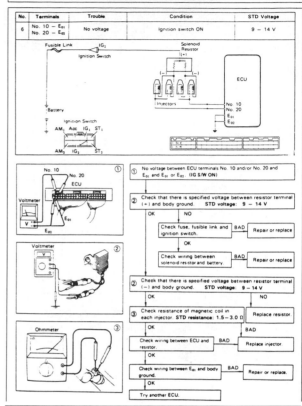

① No voltage between ECU terminals No. 10 and/or No. 20 and E₀₁ and E₀₁ or E₀₂. (IG S/W ON)

② Check that there is specified voltage between resistor terminal (+) and body ground. STD voltage: 9 – 14 V
- OK — NO → Check fuse, fusible link and ignition switch. — OK / BAD → Repair or replace.
- OK → Check wiring between solenoid resistor and battery. — BAD → Repair or replace.

② Check that there is specified voltage between resistor terminal (–) and body ground. STD voltage: 9 – 14 V
- OK — NO
③ Check resistance of magnetic coil in each injector. STD resistance: 1.5 – 3.0 Ω — Replace resistor.
- OK — BAD
- Check wiring between ECU and resistor. — BAD → Replace injector.
- OK
- Check wiring between E₀₁ and body ground. — BAD → Repair or replace.
- OK
- Try another ECU.

TROUBLESHOOTING THE NO. 7 TERMINAL ON THE EFI CONNECTOR
1986-88 TRUCK & 4-RUNNER

No.	Terminals	Trouble	Condition	STD Voltage
7	W – E₁	No voltage	No trouble (CHECK ENGINE light off) and engine running	8 – 14 V

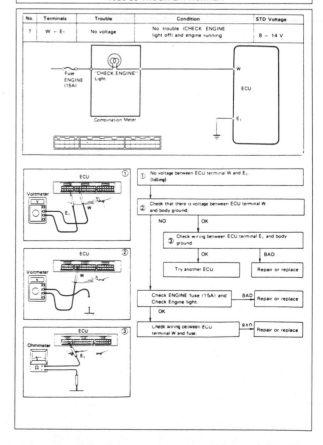

① No voltage between ECU terminal W and E₁. (Idling)

② Check that there is voltage between ECU terminal W and body ground.
- NO — OK
③ Check wiring between ECU terminal E₁ and body ground.
- OK — BAD
- Try another ECU. — Repair or replace.

- Check ENGINE fuse (15A) and Check Engine light. — BAD → Repair or replace.
- OK
- Check wiring between ECU terminal W and fuse. — BAD → Repair or replace.

TROUBLESHOOTING THE NO. 8 TERMINAL ON THE EFI CONNECTOR
1986-88 TRUCK & 4-RUNNER

No.	Terminals	Trouble		Condition	STD Voltage
8	$V_C - E_2$	No voltage	Ignition switch ON	—	4 – 9 V
	$V_S - E_2$			Measuring plate fully closed	0.5 – 2.5 V
	$V_S - E_2$			Measuring plate fully open	5 – 8 V
	$V_S - E_2$			Idling	2.5 – 7.5 V

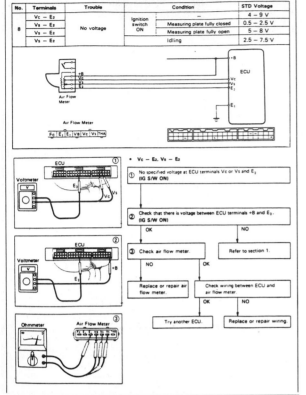

TROUBLESHOOTING THE NO. 9 TERMINAL ON THE EFI CONNECTOR
1986-88 TRUCK & 4-RUNNER

No.	Terminals	Trouble	Condition		STD Voltage
9	$THA - E_2$	No voltage	Ignition switch ON	Intake air temperature 20°C (68°F)	2 – 6 V

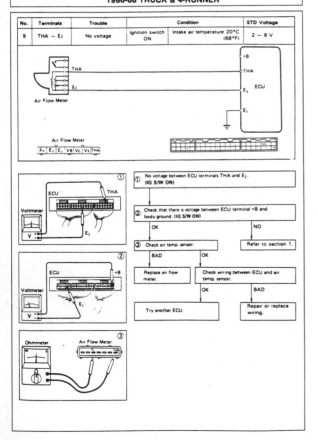

TROUBLESHOOTING THE NO. 10 TERMINAL ON THE EFI CONNECTOR
1986-88 TRUCK & 4-RUNNER

No.	Terminals	Trouble	Condition		STD Voltage
10	$THW - E_2$	No voltage	Ignition switch ON	Coolant temperature 80°C (176°F)	0.5 – 2.5 V

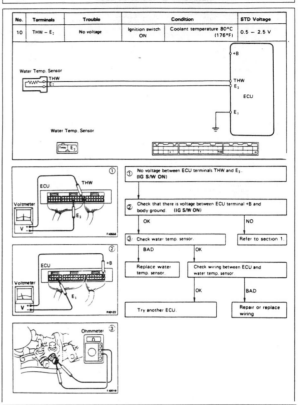

TROUBLESHOOTING THE NO. 11 TERMINAL ON THE EFI CONNECTOR
1986-88 TRUCK & 4-RUNNER

No.	Terminals	Trouble	Condition	STD Voltage
11	$B/K - E_1$ (22R-E only)	No voltage	Stop light switch ON	8 – 14 V

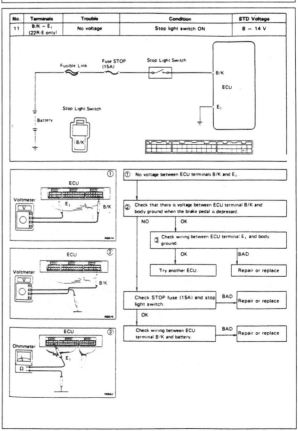

OXYGEN SENSOR INSPECTION
1986-88 TRUCK & 4-RUNNER

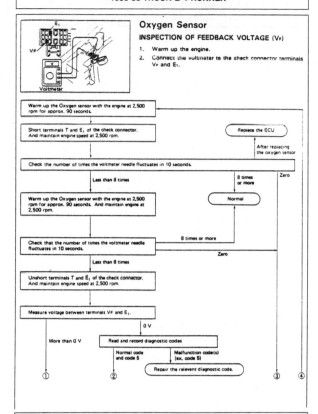

Oxygen Sensor
INSPECTION OF FEEDBACK VOLTAGE (VF)
1. Warm up the engine.
2. Connect the voltmeter to the check connector terminals VF and E₁.

```
Warm up the Oxygen sensor with the engine at 2,500
rpm for approx. 90 seconds.
          │
Short terminals T and E₁ of the check connector.      ──────►  Replace the ECU
And maintain engine speed at 2,500 rpm.                              │
          │                                                  After replacing
          │                                                  the oxygen sensor
Check the number of times the voltmeter needle fluctuates in 10 seconds.
     │              │                         │
Less than 8 times   8 times or more          Zero
     │              │
     │           Normal ◄──────────
Warm up the Oxygen sensor with the engine at 2,500       │
rpm for approx. 90 seconds.  And maintain engine at      │
2,500 rpm.                                               │
     │                                                   │
          │              8 times or more  ──────────────►
Check that the number of times the voltmeter needle
fluctuates in 10 seconds.                        Zero
     │
Less than 8 times
     │
Unshort terminals T and E₁ of the check connector.
And maintain engine speed at 2,500 rpm.
     │
Measure voltage between terminals VF and E₁.
  │                    │
More than 0 V         0 V
  │            Read and record diagnostic codes
  │              │                    │
  │          Normal code        Malfunction code(s)
  │          and code 5         (ex. code 5)
  │                             Repair the relevent diagnostic code.
  ①              ②                         ③        ④
```

① ② ③ ④

OXYGEN SENSOR INSPECTION (CONT'D)
1986-88 TRUCK & 4-RUNNER

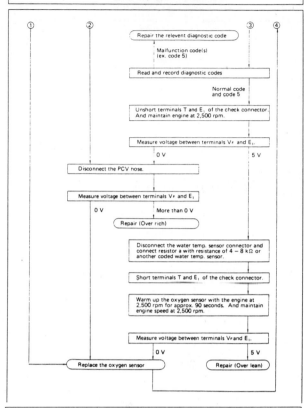

```
①        ②                                      ③        ④
                Repair the relevent diagnostic code
                        │
                   Malfunction code(s)
                   (ex. code 5)
          Read and record diagnostic codes
                        │
                   Normal code
                   and code 5
          Unshort terminals T and E₁ of the check connector.
          And maintain engine at 2,500 rpm.
                        │
          Measure voltage between terminals VF and E₁.
                  │                    │
                 0 V                  5 V
          Disconnect the PCV nose.
                        │
          Measure voltage between terminals VF and E₁
            │                    │
           0 V              More than 0 V
                        Repair (Over rich)
          Disconnect the water temp. sensor connector and
          connect resistor a with resistance of 4 – 8 kΩ or
          another coded water temp. sensor.
                        │
          Short terminals T and E₁ of the check connector.
                        │
          Warm up the oxygen sensor with the engine at
          2,500 rpm for approx. 90 seconds.  And maintain
          engine speed at 2,500 rpm.
                        │
          Measure voltage between terminals VF and E₁.
                  │                    │
                 0 V                  5 V
   Replace the oxygen sensor          Repair (Over lean)
```

COMPONENT LOCATION
1986-88 TRUCK & 4-RUNNER

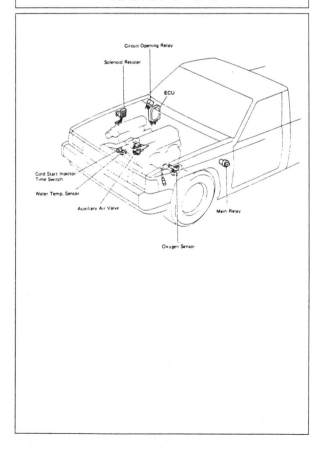

Circuit Opening Relay
Solenoid Resister
ECU
Cold Start Injector
Time Switch
Water Temp. Sensor
Auxiliary Air Valve
Main Relay
Oxygen Sensor

INSPECTING THE RESISTANCE
AT THE ECU WIRING CONNECTOR
1986-88 TRUCK & 4-RUNNER

INSPECTION OF ECU
1. MEASURE VOLTAGE OF ECU

NOTE:
1. The ECU itself cannot be checked directly.
2. The EFI circuit can be checked by measuring the resistance and voltage at the wiring connectors of the ECU.

Check the voltage at the wiring connectors.
- Remove the right kick panel.
- Turn the igniton switch ON.
- Measure the voltage at each terminal.

NOTE: 1. Perform all voltage measurements with the connectors connected.
2. Verify that the battery voltage is 11V or above when the ignition switch is ON.

Voltage at ECU Wiring Connectors

Terminals	Condition		STD voltage
+B – E₁	Ignition switch ON		10 – 14
BATT – E₁	–		10 – 14
IDL – E₂		Throttle valve open	4 – 10
VTA – E₂		Throttle valve fully closed	0.1 – 1.0
	Ignition switch ON	Throttle valve fully open	4 – 5
Vcc – E₂		–	4 – 6
IGt – E₁		Idling	0.7 – 1.0
STA – E₁		Ignition switch ST position	6 – 12
No. 10 – E₀₁ No. 20 – E₀₂		Ignition switch ON	9 – 14
W – E₁	No trouble (CHECK ENGINE light off) and engine running		8 – 14
Vc – E₂		–	4 – 9
Vs – E₂	Ignition switch ON	Measuring plate fully closed	0.5 – 2.5
		Measuring plate fully open	5 – 8
		Idling	2.5 – 7.5
THA – E₂	Ignition switch ON	Intake air temperature 20°C (68°F)	2 – 6
THW – E₂		Coolant temperature 80°C (176°F)	0.75 – 2.5
*³ B/K – E₁		Stop light switch ON	8 – 14

ECU Connectors

E₀₁	No.10	STA	VF	NSW		Fpu	W	T	IDL	IGt			KNK	No		L₁	L₂		Vc	Vs	THA	BATT	+B₁
E₀₂	No.20	IGf	E₁			ACV	TIL	TSW		E₂	Ox	Vcc	VTA	THW		ECT	L₃	E₂₁			SPD	B/K	+B

*³ 22R-E only

INSPECTING THE RESISTANCE AT THE ECU WIRING CONNECTOR
1986-88 TRUCK & 4-RUNNER

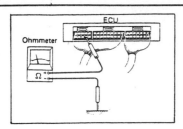

Ohmmeter

2. **MEASURE RESISTANCE OF ECU**

CAUTION:

1. Do not touch the ECU terminals.
2. The tester probe should be inserted into wiring connector from the wiring side.

Check the resistance between each terminal of the wiring connector.

- Remove the right kick panel.
- Unplug the wiring connectors from the ECU.
- Measure the resistance between each terminal of the wiring connectors.

Resistance at ECU Wiring Connectors

Terminals	Condition	Resistance (kΩ)
IDL − E_2	Throttle valve open	Infinity
	Throttle valve fully closed	0 − 0.1
VTA − E_2	Throttle valve fully open	3.3 − 10
	Throttle valve fully closed	0.2 − 0.8
Vcc − E_2	−	3 − 7
THA − E_2	Intake air temperature 20°C (68°F)	2 − 3
THW − E_2	Coolant temperature 80°C (176°F)	0.2 − 0.4
+B − E_2	−	0.2 − 0.4
Vc − E_2	−	0.1 − 0.3
Vs − E_2	Measuring plate fully closed	0.02 − 0.1
	Measuring plate fully open	0.02 − 1
Ne − E_1	−	0.14 − 0.18

VOLKSWAGEN CIS-E SYSTEM
ENGINE CONTROL SYSTEM APPLICATION CHART

Year	Model	Engine cc (liter)	Engine VIN	Fuel System	Ignition System
1984	Cabriolet	1780 (1.8)	GX	CIS	Hall
	Golf GTI	1780 (1.8)	HT	CIS	Hall
	Jetta	1715 (1.7)	EN	CIS	Hall
	Jetta GLI	1780 (1.8)	GX	CIS	Hall
	Quantum	2144 (2.1)	WE	CIS	Hall
	Rabbit	1715 (1.7)	FX	FBC	Hall
	Rabbit (Calif.)	1715 (1.7)	EN	CIS	Hall
	Scirocco	1780 (1.8)	EN	CIS	Hall
	Vanagon	1915 (1.9)	DH	Digijet	Hall
1985	Cabriolet	1780 (1.8)	GX	CIS	Hall
	Golf	1780 (1.8)	HT	CIS-E	Hall
	GTI	1780 (1.8)	RD	CIS-E	Hall
	Jetta	1780 (1.8)	HT	CIS-E	Hall
	Quantum	2144 (2.1)	KX	CIS-E	Hall
	Scirocco	1780 (1.8)	EN	CIS	Hall
	Vanagon	2109 (2.1)	MV	Digijet	Hall
1986	Cabriolet	1780 (1.8)	GX	CIS	Hall
	Golf	1780 (1.8)	HT	CIS	Hall
	GTI	1780 (1.8)	RD	CIS-E①	Hall
	Jetta	1780 (1.8)	GX	CIS	Hall
	Jetta GLI	1780 (1.8)	RD	CIS-E①	Hall
	Quantum	2226 (2.2)	KX	CIS-E	Hall
	Scirocco	1780 (1.8)	HT	CIS	Hall
	Vanagon	2109 (2.1)	MV	Digijet	Hall②
	Vanagon Synchro	2109 (2.1)	MV	Digijet	Hall②
1987	Cabriolet	1780 (1.8)	GX	CIS	Hall
	Fox	1780 (1.8)	UM	CIS-E①	Hall
	Golf GL	1780 (1.8)	HT	CIS	Hall
	Golf GT	1780 (1.8)	PL	CIS-E①	Hall
	GTI	1780 (1.8)③	PL	CIS-E①	Hall
	Jetta	1780 (1.8)	JN	CIS	Hall
	Jetta GLI	1780 (1.8)	PL	CIS-E①	Hall
	Quantum	2226 (2.2)	KX	CIS-E①	Hall
	Quantum Synchro	2226 (2.2)	JT	CIS-E①	Hall
	Scirocco	1780 (1.8)	JN	CIS	Hall
	Scirocco	1780 (1.8)③	PL	CIS-E①	Hall
	Vanagon	2109 (2.1)	MV	Digifant	Hall②
	Vanagon Synchro	2109 (2.1)	MV	Digifant	Hall②

ENGINE CONTROL SYSTEM APPLICATION CHART

Year	Model	Engine cc (liter)	Engine VIN	Fuel System	Ignition System
1988	Cabriolet	1780 (1.8)	GX	CIS	Hall
	Fox	1780 (1.8)	UM	CIS-E①	Hall
	Golf GL	1780 (1.8)	Digifant II	Hall④	
	Golf GLI	1780 (1.8)	PL	CIS-E①	Hall⑤
	Golf GT	1780 (1.8)	Digifant II		Hall④
	GTI	1780 (1.8)③ PL	CIS-E①	Hall⑤	
	Jetta	1780 (1.8)	Digifant II		Hall④
	Jetta GL	1780 (1.8)	Digifant II		Hall④
	Jetta GT	1780 (1.8)	Digifant II		Hall④
	Quantum	2226 (2.2)	KX	CIS-E①	Hall
	Quantum Synchro	2226 (2.2)	JT	CIS-E①	Hall
	Scirocco	1780 (1.8)③	PL	CIS-E①	Hall⑤
	Vanagon	2109 (2.1)	MV	Digifant	Hall②
	Vanagon Synchro	2109 (2.1)	MV	Digifant	Hall②

NOTE: All fuel injection and ignition systems are manufactured by Bosch
Digifant—Air Flow Controlled (AFC) fuel injection system
Digifant II—AFC fuel injection system with knock sensor and integral idle stabilizer
CIS—Constant Injection System
CIS-E—Electronically controlled constant injection system using an electro-hydraulic actuator to regulate fuel mixture
FBC—Feedback Carburetor System
Hall—Bosch Hall Effect electronic ignition system

① With idle stabilizer
② Digifant systems use either a Fairchild or an AEG Hall control unit. The idle stabilizer uses a separate control unit mounted under the hood
③ 6-valve engine
④ Digifant II uses a knock sensor and has idle stabilizer circuitry built into the control unit (ECU)
⑤ With knock sensor

General Information

The CIS-E is an electronically controlled continuous fuel injection system. This system uses the basic CIS mechanical system for injection, with electronically controlled correction functions. The electronic portion of the system consists of an air flow sensor position indicator, electro-hydraulic actuator, thermo time switch, coolant temperature sensor, electronic control unit (ECU), transistorized ignition switching unit, microswitch, throttle valve switch, altitude correction indicator, lambda control and oxygen sensor. The mechanical portion of the CIS-E system consists of a mixture control unit, control pressure regulator, auxiliary air valve, cold start valve, injector nozzles, fuel pump and fuel filter.

Component Inspection and Testing

ELECTRO-HYDRAULIC ACTUATOR DEVICE (EHA)

This actuator is flanged onto the fuel distributor and acts as a pressure regulator which operates as a plate valve. The position of the plate valve can be varied causing a differential pressure change in the actuator and lower chamber, and this will cause a mixture correction. When the engine is running a constant system pressure of 78 psi is applied to the fuel inlet. The plate valve is adjusted depending on current intensity and there by determines the flow rate, in combination with the fixed orifice. The corresponding pressure change in the lower chamber cause movement of the diaphragm and influences the volume of fuel flowing to the fuel injector valve.

COLD START DEVICE

Electrical current at the actuator is 120–8mA or less. The plate valve is positioned in the direction of the intake port. Differential pressure drop in the lower chamber, is 5.8–22 psi. As the coolant temperature increases, the current at the actuator drops to 8 mA and at the same rate, the differential pressure drops down to 5.8 psi.

ACCELERATION ENRICHMENT DEVICE

Electrical current to the actuator depends on the coolant temperature and on the speed at which the air flow meter plate is deflected. When the plate valve is moved closer to the intake, the differential pressure will decrease by 22 psi. When the coolant temperature reaches 168°F., the acceleration enrichment is cancelled and the ECU will provide acceleration enrichment as an impulse, which will increase the instantaneous current value. During acceleration enrichment, the lambda control is influenced by the ECU.

VOLTAGE PROTECTION RELAY

This relay is located in the engine compartment on the right side at the electrical center. The function of this relay is to protect the electronic components of the CIS-E system. There is a ten (10) amp fuse located on top of the relay. When the ignition

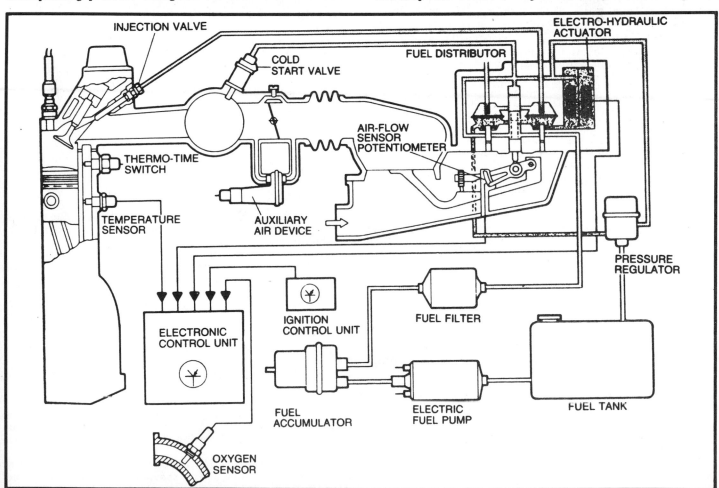

Typical schematic of Bosch KE-Jetronic fuel system

switch is turned to the ON position, the relay closes and directs battery voltage to the ECU.

The locations of the various components in this system may differ from model to model.

ELECTRONIC CONTROL UNIT (ECU)

This unit is located on the main firewall in the engine compartment on the right side. There is a vent system installed for dissipating heat. The ECU acts as the brain of the system and is supplied with a voltage correction circuit (operating voltage – 8 volts) to prevent voltage fluctuations when different vehicle components are switched on. The ECU uses various input signals for control of fuel delivery and exhaust emissions. The input signals are then converted into corresponding current values and sent to the electro-hydraulic actuator and to the idle speed air valve. During cranking, an enrichment signal is provided through terminal #50 and the amount of enrichment depends on the coolant temperature. A timing element regulates the enrichment after one second to the warm-up and after starting value. The value will remain constant, as long as the enrichment is cranked. After-start enrichment is used to provide a smooth running engine after starting and the amount and duration of the after start enrichment depends on the coolant temperature. Warm-up enrichment again depends on the coolant temperature, the lower the coolant temperature, the higher the current at the actuator and the greater the fuel enrichment.

The maximum engine speed is limited by the ECU by sending the necessary current to the electro-hydraulic actuator. The lower chamber pressure is increased to the system pressure and the fuel supply to the injection valves is interrupted. Depending on the altitude, the amount of fuel is changed based on a signal from the altitude correction capsule. Once the ignition switch is turned on, the altitude correction indicator will receive a constant voltage signal of 8 volts from the ECU.

The lambda (oxygen sensor) control monitors the input signals from the sensors and amplifies them and calculates the output signals for the electro-hydraulic actuator. The electronic idle speed control is also incorporated into the ECU and the signals are received by the idle speed air valve, which is located in a hose which by-passes the throttle valve. When the ignition switch is turned on, the ECU is energized and the electronic control system will generate a basic frequency of 100 Hz. The idle speed air valve is opened to the maximum position by a set of return springs, when the ignition switch is in the off position. Once the ignition switch is turned on the valve is activated by a specific voltage, providing an air valve opening (dependent on the coolant temperature). The nominal speed is controlled, depending on the coolant temperature, 1000 rpm at 0°F to 720 rpm at 68°F.

The microswitch is energized by the ECU with a constant voltage signal of 8 volts. During decel operation, the circuit to the ECU is closed by the microswitch. The setting-in rate of speed of decel shutoff depends on the coolant temperature.

FUEL SYSTEM

The CIS-E fuel system is continuous fuel injection system. This system uses the basic CIS mechanical system for injection, with electronically controlled correction functions. The mechanical portion of the CIS-E system consists of a mixture control unit, control pressure regulator, auxiliary air valve, cold start valve, injector nozzles, fuel pump and fuel filter.

Testing and Adjustments

1. Remove the air cleaner and may a visible check for any fuel leaks. Pull off the fuel pump relay and place a jumper wire between terminals 7 and 8 for a minute or two, so as to establish fuel pressure.

2. Push the air flow sensor plate down by hand, take note that a equal resistance should be felt across the entire path and there should be no resistance felt during the fast upward movement. If upward movement is slow, check the control piston.

3. Check the control piston in the fuel distributor for any fuel leaks.

4. Push the air flow sensor plate as far down as it can go for a minute or less, if a small amount of fuel leaks it is in proper order, and if there is no signs of large fuel leaks go on to the next test.

Fuel Pressure Check

1. Using fuel pressure gauge No. 100-589-13-21-00 or equivalent, connect the gauge to the fuel line on fuel distributor lower chamber and connect the other hose to the upper chamber of the fuel distributor.

2. Disconnect the fuel pump relay and with a jumper wire connect the number 7 and 8 terminals and check the lower chamber fuel pressure with the engine off.

3. Start the engine and bring up to operating temperature, pull off the electrical connection on the electro-hydraulic controlling element. Be sure to note the position of the pressure gauge control valve.

4. Take the pressure reading on the lower chamber, the pressure at normal operating temperature should be 6 psi below system pressure. When plugging in the electrical connections, there should be no changes in the fuel pressure.

5. Disconnect the plug from the coolant temperature sensor and using a multi-meter or equivalent connect the leads to the mA scale. Turn the ignition switch to the ON position and bypass the fuel pump relay, by inserting a jumper wire into the relay terminals 7 and 8. Read The lower chamber pressure and amperage.

NOTE: Whenever switching from amps to volts, pull off connecting lines from the meter.

6. The pressure reading in the lower chamber should be 78 psi or 5.8 psi below system pressure. Amperage should be 75 mA.

7. If the pressure is not within specifications, check the coolant temperature sensor, the coolant level, the ECU and the electro-hydraulic controlling element.

8. If the pressure in the lower chamber is higher than specifications, check the throttle orifice in the fuel distributor for a blocked passage.

Decel Shut-Off Test

1. With the fuel pump relay installed and the engine running at normal operating temperature, be sure that the control valve on the fuel gauge is open.

2. Increase the engine speed for a minute or two to 2500 rpm, when the engine speed drops, the fuel pressure should increase by 6.0 psi. Combustion should start again at around 900 rpm.

3. If the pressure can not be attained, check the microswitch, control current on the controlling element, the TDC signal and The ECU.

Full-Load Enrichment Test

1. Seperate the coupling between the throttle valve switch and the ECU. Check the resistance from the throttle valve switch with a ohmmeter.

2. In the idle speed position the resistance from the throttle valve switch should read to the maximum resistance of the scale, and under a full load the resistance should read 0 ohms.

3. If the throttle valve switch does not pass the test, remove and replace it.

4. Connect test cable No. 102-589-04-63-00 or equivalent to the controlling element and set the multi-meter to the mA scale. Use a jumper wire to connect the throttle valve switch to the ECU.

5. Turn the ignition switch ON, the reading on the meter should be 7–9 mA. Check the circuit between the ECU and controlling element for passage, there should be 0 ohms there. If the readings check out all right, replace the ECU. If the readings do not check out all right, repair the short in the circuit.

Electronic Idle Speed Test

l. Connect the test cable of the Bosch tester No. KDJE-P-600 or equivalent to the idle speed air valve. Push the IR 100% button, with the engine idling and at operating temperature the reading should be 27–29% at 750 rpm. If the reading is within specifications the test is over, if the reading is out of specifications go on to the next step.

2. If the reading is higher or lower than specifications, adjust the nominal value or test the microswitch. If the reading is 0, test the voltage on the plug for the idle speed air valve.

3. Use pin socket number 2 to ground, the reading should be l2 volts, if the reading checks out, go on to the next step. If the reading does not check out, repair the short in the circuit.

4. Test the resistance on the idle speed air valve terminals 2 and 3, it should be l2 ohms. Terminal 2 and 1 should be 12 ohms, if the reading are out of range replace the idle speed air valve.

Throttle Valve Switch (TVS) Test

1. Using a multimeter, set the ohm scale to zero and check the full throttle stop.

2. Push the TVS against the full throttle stop, the reading should be 0, turn the TVS slightly in the direction of the idle, reading should go to the maximum resistance of the scale.

3. If the readings do not meet the specifications, replace the throttle valve switch.

OXYGEN SENSOR

Removal and Installation

The oxygen sensor must be replaced every 30000 miles. A service reminder light located on the dash board will illuminate at 30000 mile intervals to indicate the need for oxygen sensor service. Once the sensor is replaced, the service reminder must be reset to extinguish the dash indicator light.

The oxygen sensor is located in the exhaust manifold. The exhaust system should be slightly warm to make removal easier. When installing a new oxygen sensor, coat the threads with an anti-seize compound but do not allow any anti-seize to contaminate the sensor body or it will ruin the probe.

Resetting the Maintenance Reminder Light

1. On all models except the Vanagon, locate the mileage counter (usually on the firewall, in-line with the speedometer) and push the white reset button. Be sure the maintenance light is out.

2. On Vanagon models, locate the mileage counter (usually under the spare tire or under the driver's side floorboard, in-line with the speedometer cable). Using a pointed instrument, depress the raised area on the reset box. Be sure the maintenence light is out.

MIXTURE CONTROL UNIT

The air -flow sensor contains a plate, mounted on a hinged lever, which moves in a cone shaped venturi. All engine air is drawn past this sensor. The plate moves as air is drawn into the engine, moving the hinged lever up or down.

Movement of the sensor plate raises or lowers a fuel control plunger in the fuel distributor, which meteres the amount of fuel injected into each cylinder. The movement of the plate is controlled by the air flow, cone shape of the venturi, a balanced weight and fuel pressure.

The fuel distribution can be equal only if the pressure to each injector is equal. Pressure regulating valves located in the fuel distributor equalize system pressure. These valves are adjusted during assembly of the fuel distributor and cannot be be adjusted when the distributor is in service.

AUXILIARY AIR VALVE

The auxiliary air valve, or regulator, provides additional air to the engine to increase idle speed when the engine is cold. It allows air to by-pass the throttle valves which are closed at idle. A heating coil in the valve is connected to the fuel pump circuit. As the coil warms up , it gradually closes the air passage. The valve is calibrated to maintain a smooth idle without a large engine speed change as the engine is warming up.

CONTROL PRESSURE REGULATOR

The control pressure regulator (or warm-up regulator) controls the fuel pressure to the top of the plunger in the fuel distributor. During cold start operation, reduced pressure allows the plate to open further with the same air flow. This supplies more fuel to the cylinders to improve the engine warm-up, until normal operating temperature (or a pretermined time passes), the control pressure regulator increases control pressure, leaning the air/fuel ratio.

A bi-metallic strip in the control pressure regulator is heated by an electric coil. As it heats up, it gradually increases the control pressure. Poor electrical connections will cause warm-up functions of the regulator to cease operation. Some regulators have an altitude sensitive function that compensates for changes in barometric pressure.

FUEL INJECTOR NOZZLES

The injectors in the CIs system open at a predetermined pressure. The fuel is always present in the lines between the fuel distributor and the injectors to ensure good starting. As the pressure in the fuel distributor increases (when the engine is started), the valves open and spray constantly. The amount of fuel injected will be determined by control pressure and the position of the control plunger.

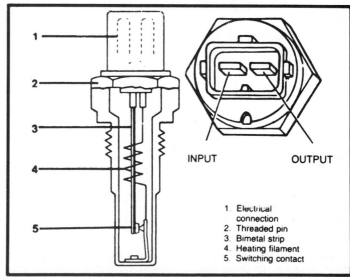

Typical thermo-time switch showing construction and terminal location

THERMO-TIME SWITCH AND HOT START RELAY

The thermo-time switch controls the opening time of the cold start valve. It is affected by the engine temperature and the starter current. Depending the coolant temperature (or the engine temperature on the air-cooled engine), the switch will take from three to ten seconds to pen. The fuel injection through the cold start valve will then stop.

Some models may use a hot start pulse relay to improve hot starting. While the starter is being operated, the relay allows the cold start valve to spray small amounts of fuel at regular intervals, until the engine is started.

FUEL PUMP

An electric fuel pump is used to provide a fuel pressure 60–80 psi. There is a check valve located in the pump that will aid in the starting process, This check valve will work in conjunction with the accumulator and the piston seal in the fuel distributor, to maintain a constant pressure in the system when the engine is not running.

The fuel pump is controlled by a relay to prevent it from operating if the engine stalls. It can be wired in several ways, the most common way is through a switch on the air flow sensor or through a coil energized by the ignition system. When testing this system, the safety relay must by-passed.

ELECTRONIC CONTROL UNIT AND FREQUENCY VALVE

The electronic control unit is designed to continually correct air/fuel ratio, based on signals from the oxygen sensor. It sends a series of pulses to a frequency valve. The frequency valve is located in a fuel line that connects the upper and lower halves of the fuel distributor.

When the frequency valve is closed, fuel pressure to the injectors is determined by a spring in each pressure regulating valve. When the frequency valve is open, the fuel pressure deceases in the lower half of the fuel distributor, the tension on the spring is relieved and more fuel is directed to the cylinders.

The electronic control unit opens and closes the frequency valve many times a second to ensure a smooth regulation of fuel pressure and mixture. When the engine is cold, the ratio of the valve open to the valve closed is approximately 50%.

After the engine warms up, the voltage produced by the oxygen sensor determines the amount of the time the frequency valve must be open or closed. This ratio can be read on a dwell meter (on most models). A dwell meter reading of 45° indicates a ratio of 50% open and 50% closed.

Preliminary Checks

NOTE: Before doing any injection system testing, first check the three basics; ignition, compression and fuel gauge.

Always make a complete ignition check first and then perform all the injection pressure test in sequence. The cause of many CIS complaints is a minor vacuum leak. Vacuum leaks fool the metering system and affect the mixture. This gives poor gas economy and poor performance. Look for leaks at the following components. The EGR valve, the intake manifold, the cold start injector, the air sensor boot, the brake booster vacuum lines and the air ducts.

Also check the vacuum limiter, evaporative canister and A/C door actuator. To quick test the system for leaks, disconnect the auxiliary air valve hose, block open the throttle and apply pressure to the hose. Use a spray bottle of soapy water to hit all the fittings where leaks could occur.

Relieving Fuel System Pressure

The fuel pressure must be relieved before attempting to disconnect any fuel lines.
1. Carefully loosen the fuel line on the control pressure regulator (large connection).
2. Wrap a clean shop rag around the connection while loosening to catch any fuel.

ALTERNATE METHOD FOR RELIEVING FUEL PRESSURE

1. Disconnect the electrical plug from the cold start valve. Using a jumper wire, apply 12 volts to the cold start valve terminal for 10 seconds.
2. Remove the jumper wire and reconnect the cold start valve.

Fuel Pump Test

The electric fuel pump is a roller cell type with the electric motor permanently surrounded by fuel. An eccentrically mounted roller disc is fitted with rollers resting in notches around the circumference. These rollers are pressured against the thrust ring of the pump housing by centrifugal force.

The fuel is carried in the cavities between the rollers and the pump delivers more than the maximum requirement to the engine so that the fuel pressure is maintained under all operating conditions. During starting, the pump runs as long as the ignition key is turned. The pump continues to run as long as the ignition key is turned on. The pump continues to run once the engine is starts, but has a safety device that will stop the pump if the ignition is turned on but the engine stops moving.

NOTE: Some models utilize a priming fuel pump, mounted in the tank, in addition to the main fuel pump.

FUEL PUMP POWER CHECK

Remove the round cover plate from the top of the fuel pump and measure the voltage between the positive and negative terminals when the pump is operating. The lowest permissible voltage is 11.5 volts. Disconnect the terminals connecting the pump to the air flow sensor and the warm-up regulator if these are to be checked later. If the pump is dead, check the fuse, the ground and try bridging the relay with a jumper wire.

FUEL PUMP SAFETY CIRCUIT CHECK

The pump will only run if the starter motor is actuated or if the engine is running.
1. Remove the air filter, turn on the ignition switch and briefly depress the sensor plate.
2. Remove the coil wire from the distributor. Connect a voltmeter to the positive terminal on the fuel pump and the ground.
3. Actuate the starter. The voltmeter should indicate 11 volts. If the fuel pump runs only when the sensor plate is depressed or only when the engine is cranked, replace the fuel pump relay. If the pump is already running when the ignition switch is turned "ON", replace the safety switch.

FUEL VOLUME TEST

The test point for the fuel pump operation depends on the type of fuel distributor. Fuel distributors with push valves have two fuel lines connecting with the warm-up regulator, the other line connects to the "T" and returns to the gas tank. Determine whether the vehicle to be tested is fitted with or without a push valve before proceeding any further.
1. Remove the gas cap to vent the tank pressure. Disconnect the return line leading to the gas tank at the appropriate test point.
2. Hold the line coming from the fuel distributor in a large container. Inflexible metal fuel lines may require a rubber hose to reach the container.

3. Remove the electric plug from the warm-up regulator and then auxiliary air valve. Jump the electric safety circuit for 30 seconds. The delivery rate should be approximately one quart in thirty seconds.

4. If the fuel quantity is not within specifications, check for sufficient voltage supply to the fuel pump (minimum 11.5 volts) or a dirty fuel filter. If all the above are satisfactory, replace the electric fuel pump.

NOTE: Use a bridging adapter to energize the fuel pump through the relay connector on early models without push valves.

Pressure Test

Diagnose the fuel system in this order, check the cold control pressure first, hot control pressure, primary pressure and the rest pressure. Use a pressure gauge that ties into the line running between the fuel distributor and the warm-up compensator. With the 3-way valve open, the gauge remains teed-in and therfore read control pressure. Remember that control pressure is derived or fed from the primary circuit pressure so a pressure change in one circuit means a change in the other circuit.

Closing the valve shut off fuel flow to the warm-up compensator and forces the gauge to read only one circuit that one being the primary circuit. When you shut the engine off and leave the 3-way valve open, the teed in gauge should show the system's holding pressure. This residual pressure is called rest pressure. The valve functions are, valve open – control pressure; valve closed – primary pressure; valve open and engine off – rest pressure.

CONTROL PRESSURE TEST-ENGINE COLD

1. Connect a pressure gauge between the fuel distributor and the control pressure regualtor. Remove the electrical connector from the regulator.

2. Idle the engine for no more than one minute. The control pressure should be 49–55 psi.

3. If the control pressure is not within specifications, check the control pressure (warm-up) regulator for proper operation.

CONTROL PRESSURE TEST-ENGINE WARM

1. Carry out this test when poor performance has been experienced when the engine is warm. Connect a gauge and a three-way valve.

2. Open the valve. Connect the warm-up regulator plug. Leave the ignition switch on until the rest pressure (23–35 psi) is present. If the control pressure (49–55 psi) and or the rest pressure (23–35 psi) is not within specifications, replace the warm-up regulator.

NOTE: Perform the primary and rest pressure tests before disconnecting the quage and three-way valve.

PRIMARY PRESSURE TEST

1. Close the three-way valve. Turn the ignition switch on. If the line pressure (49–55 psi) should not meet specifications the problem could be :
   a. Insufficient pressure from the fuel pump.
   b. Blockage of the strainer in the tank.
   c. Leakage in the fuel line.

2. When you close the three-way valve with the engine idling and the primary pressure reads low, there could be a fuel pump problem or a primary regulator problem. To isolate on from the other, locate the return line from the fuel distributor back to the gas tank.

3. Plug the return line securely at some convenient point. Have an assistant switch on the pump just long enough to get a pressure reading.

4. If the pump is good, the pressure will jump almost instantly 100 psi or higher. Should the primary pressure exceed 116 psi

during this momentary test, the check valve in the intake side of the fuel pump will vent the pressure back into the gas tank.

5. If the fuel pump produces good pressure with the return line plugged, then the primary pressure is causing a low primary pressure reading.

REST PRESSURE AND LEAK TEST

1. After a correct warm engine control pressure has been obtained, stop the fuel pump and take note of the pressure drop.

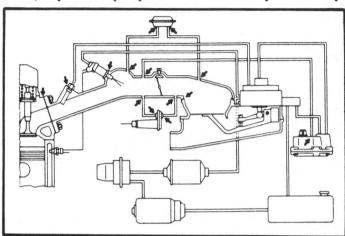

Checking the CIS-E system for vacuum leaks at the arrows

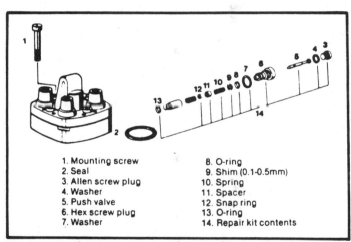

1. Mounting screw	8. O-ring
2. Seal	9. Shim (0.1-0.5mm)
3. Allen screw plug	10. Spring
4. Washer	11. Spacer
5. Push valve	12. Snap ring
6. Hex screw plug	13. O-ring
7. Washer	14. Repair kit contents

Fuel control pressure regulator with push valve

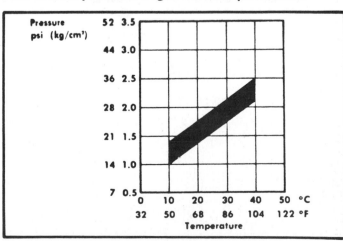

Test graph for cold engine control pressure

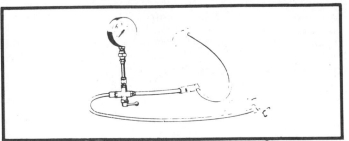

Typical fuel pressure test connection

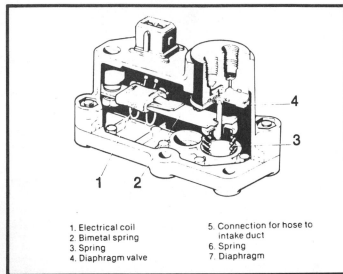

1. Electrical coil
2. Bimetal spring
3. Spring
4. Diaphragm valve

5. Connection for hose to intake duct
6. Spring
7. Diaphragm

Warm up regulator typical of federal (49 states) models

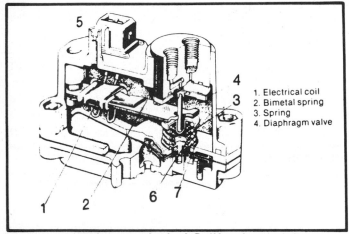

1. Electrical coil
2. Bimetal spring
3. Spring
4. Diaphragm valve

Warm up regulator typical of California models

2. The pressure gauge should be in the correct position. The minimum pressure after 20 minutes should be 35 psi.

3. If the fuel pressure drop to quickly, run the fuel pump again and close the valve. Stop the pump and take note of the pressure.

4. If the pressures are now correct, the control pressure regulator is not working properly and should be replaced.

5. If the pressure still drops, check all connections, the fuel pump check valve, cold start valve and fuel injectors.

6. The pressure test specifications are as follows:
   a. System Pressure: 68–78 psi.
   b. Warm Control Pressure: 49–55 psi.
   c. Rest Pressure: 35 psi.
   d. Injector Opening Pressure: 46–55 psi.

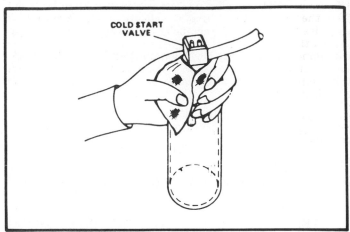

Testing the cold start valve

Cold Start Valve Test

1. If the engine coolant is below 85°F. disconnect the plug on the cold start valve and connect a test lamp across the terminals.

2. Remove the coil wire to prevent starting and operate the starter.

3. The test lamp will light for several seconds. If the test lamp does not light, test the thermo time switch for continuity below operating temperature.

4. If the thermo time switch is good, check the wiring to the starter terminal.

5. Remove the cold start valve from the manifold and leave the fuel line attached. Place the valve in a container. Connect a jumper wire from one terminal to a ground and from the other terminal of the cold start valve to a (toggle) switch. The other side of the (toggle) switch should be connected to the a source of battery voltage.

NOTE: Do not connect the wire directly to the battery . Extreme fire danger is probable due to atomized fuel. Sparks could result if the wire is touched directly to the battery.

6. Operate the fuel pump. Turn on the (toggle) switch, the cold start injector should spray. Turn the switch off, but leave the fuel pump running.

7. The cold start injector should not spray. Wipe off the injector nozzle and check for leakage. With the pump running, no drops should form within one minutes time.

8. If the cold start valve fails any part of this test, replace it. If it passes this test replace the O-ring and install it back in the manifold.

Fuel Injectors Test

1. Remove the injectors but leave the fuel lines connected. Place the injectors in individual measuring containers.

2. With the sensor plate in the idle position, connect a jumper wire in place of the fuel pump relay.

3. Disconnect the fuel pump when the measuring container with the highest level of fuel reaches specified capacity 0.58–0.78 ounces at idle, 2.43–2.98 ounces at full throttle.

4. Compare amounts of fuel in measuring containers. The fuel should not vary by more than then the specified amount.

5. Repeat this test with the sensor plate in the full throttle position.

Auxiliary Air Valve Test

1. Disconnect the hoses from the auxiliary air valve. Use a small mirror and a suitable flashlight to inspect the air valve.

2. At room temperature, the valve should be slightly open.

Disconnect the wires from the air flow sensor, if so equipped. With the ignition switch in the "ON" position the the auxiliary air valve should cover the opening within five minutes.

3. If the valve does not operate properly, check for power at the connector with the engine running.

4. Connect a test lamp across the connector terminals. If the test lamp does nor light, check the fuse and wiring.

5. If the test lamp does light, check the resistance of the auxiliary air valve. If there is no resistance measured at the valve, the valve is defective and should be replaced. Be sure the electrical connections are tight and the terminals are clean, before checking the air auxiliary valve for resistance.

LAMBDA CONTROL SYSTEM

Test

NOTE: The frequency valve is operated by a pulsating voltage from the electronic control unit (ECU). By measuring this signal, certain operations of the Lambda system can be tested. A special tester (Bosch KDJE-7453 or equivalent) should be used for this test, but a high quality dwell meter may be used instead.

1. Connect a dwell meter to the testing connector. The testing connector is located behind the throttle valve housing (black/white).

2. Set the dwell meter to the 4-cylinder scale. Start the engine and let it run until it reaches normal operating temperature and then shut the engine off.

3. Disconnect the oxygen sensor connector and observe the dwell meter needle, the needle should not fluctuate. Place a piece of tape on the dwell meter face to indicate the 50% position.

OPERATIONAL TEST

1. Remove the fuel pump relay and connect a jumper wire across the sockets in relationship to terminals 30 and 87. Remove the plug at the air flow sensor and turn the ignition switch to the "ON" position.

2. The frequency valve should operate (if it is operating it will make a buzzing noise). The dwell meter reading should indicate 45–60 degrees.

3. Disconnect the wire connector from the oxygen sensor and touch the connector to a suitable engine ground. The reading on the dwell meter should start to rise.

4. Ground the end of one 1.5 volt dry cell battery. Touch the positive end to the oxygen sensor wire. The dwell meter reading should drop to less than 15 degrees.

5. If the vehicle is equipped with a throttle enrichment switch, the dwell meter reading should be higher at idle or at wide open throttle.

6. If the engine is cold, the enrichment switch will be closed. Disconnect the lead wire at the temperature sender. The dwell meter reading should drop slightly.

7. If the engine is hot, connect the temperature sender lead wire to a suitable engine ground, the dwell meter reading should rise.

8. If the starter enrichment relay is used, disconnect the high tension lead wire at the coil and crank the engine. The dwell meter reading should rise above the normal reading. If vacuum switched are used, apply vacuum to the vacuum switch and note the readings. The dwell meter reading should be higher with the vacuum switch closed and lower with the vacuum switch open.

9. Reconnect the oxygen sensor wire connector and start the engine. With a cold engine, the dwell meter reading should be stable.

10. When the engine warms up, the dwell meter needle should fluctuate 10–20 degrees. It may be necessary to run the engine at a higher rpm than idle to heat the oxygen sensor and cause the dwell meter needle fluctuation.

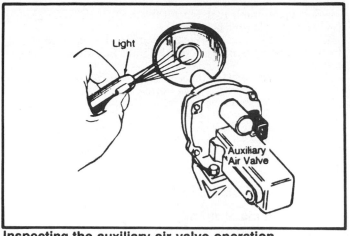

Inspecting the auxiliary air valve operation

11. Connect a CO meter to the exhaust test point. With the oxygen sensor disconnected, the dwell meter reading should be stable. Be sure to take note of the CO percentage reading.

12. With the oxygen sensor lead grounded, the dwell meter reading should rise and the CO percentage should increase. With the oxygen sensor lead connected to a 1.5 volt dry cell battery, the CO percentage should decrease.

13. If the dwell meter reading does not rise with the sensor grounded, check the oxygen sensor wiring. If the wiring is good, replace the electronic control unit.

14. If the dwell meter reading rises and the CO percentage does not, check the frequency valve and wiring. Replace and repair as necessary.

15. If the dwell meter reading does not decrease with the battery connected to the oxygen sensor lead, check the oxygen sensor wiring. If the wiring is good, replace the electronic control unit.

16. If the dwell meter reading does decrease and the CO percentage does not, check the frequency valve and wiring. Replace and repair as necessary.

17. Adjust the CO percentage to the rich level (3%) with the oxygen sensor still disconnected. Reconnect the oxygen sensor. The CO percentage reading should drop at least 1%. If the CO percentage does not drop, replace the oxygen sensor.

Component Replacement

NOTE: On all models, before removing any of the CIS components, disconnect the negative battery cable and relieve the fuel pressure from the fuel system.

CONTROL PRESSURE REGULATOR

Removal and Installation

1. Disconnect the electrical connections. Remove and plug all vacuum lines , if so equipped.

2. Remove and cap the fuel lines, wipe up any spilled fuel. Remove the control pressure regulator retaining bolts and remove the regulator from the engine.

3. Installation is the reverse order of the removal procedure. Once the installation is complete, start the engine and check for vacuum and or fuel leaks.

MIXTURE CONTROL UNIT

Removal and Installation

1. Remove the top of the mixture control unit so as to be able to extract the mixture screw plug or steel ball which blocks the access opening.

2. Using a suitable tool, tap out the mixture screw plug or ball from the control unit housing.

3. Clean all around the fuel line connections. Remove and cap the fuel lines to the mixture control unit. Be sure to wipe up all spilled fuel.

4. Disconnect and tag all necessary electrical connections and remove the rubber boot to the intake manifold.

5. Remove the mixture control unit retaining screws and lift the mixture control unit off of the engine.

6. Installation is the reverse order of the removal procedure. Replace all gaskets and seal. Once the installation is complete, start the engine and check for vacuum and or fuel leaks.

FUEL DISTRIBUTOR

Removal and Installation

1. Remove the mixture control unit.

2. Remove the retaining screws from the top of the fuel distributor. Carefully lift off the fuel distributor, make sure that the control plunger does not fall out of the fuel distributor.

3. Installation is the reverse order of the removal procedure. If the control plunger has been removed from the fuel distributor, moisten it with clean gasoline before installing it into the fuel distributor. Be sure to insert the small shoulder on the control plunger first.

4. Only pressure regulator shims may be replaced. If the plunger or piston is scored, replace the fuel distributor. Always use new gaskets and O-rings when removing and installing the fuel distributor. Lock all retaining screws with Loctite® or its equivalent.

FREQUENCY VALVE

Removal and Installation

1. Disconnect the electrical connection to the valve. Hold the small nut at the fuel line and loosen the larger nut.

2. Do not spill gasoline on the rubber mounting insulator as it will cause the rubber to swell.

3. Remove the fuel return lines at the fuel distributor and/or the pressure regulator.

4. Installation is the reverse order of the removal procedure. Always use new gaskets and O-rings when removing and installing the frequency valve. Once the installation is complete, start the engine and check for vacuum and or fuel leaks.

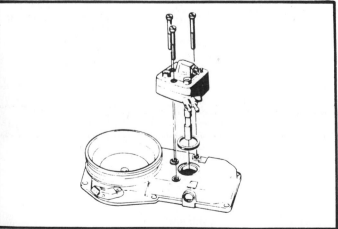

Typical location of the fuel distributor mounting screws

AUXILIARY AIR VALVE

Removal and Installation

1. Remove and plug all vacuum lines to the valve. Disconnect the electrical connectors at the valve.

2. Remove the auxiliary air valve mounting bolts and remove the valve from the engine.

3. Installation is the reverse order of the removal procedure. Once the installation is complete, start the engine and check for vacuum and or fuel leaks.

THERMAL SWITCH

Removal and Installation

1. Drain the coolant below the level switch. Be careful not to damage the connectors on the switch while removing it from the engine.

2. Installation is the reverse order of the removal procedure. Coat the threads of the switch with a suitable sealant.

COLD START VALVE

Removal and Installation

1. Remove the electrical connector and fuel line from the cold start valve.

2. Loosen the cold start valve mounting bolt and remove the cold start valve.

3. Installation is the reverse order of the removal procedure. Once the installation is complete, start the engine and check for fuel leaks.

FUEL INJECTORS

Removal and Installation

1. Clean the area around the fuel injectors. Hold the injector securely and remove the fuel line from the injector, do not allow the injector to turn.

2. Remove the retaining plate (if so equipped) and pull the injectors out carefully. Do not remove the insulator sleeve from the injector.

3. Installation is the reverse order of the removal procedure. Replace all O-rings and lubricate then with a drop of clean oil. Place the injectors into the sleeves and press down on them until they are seated. Tighten the fuel lines.

4. Once the installation is complete, start the engine and check for fuel leaks.

AIR FLOW SENSOR

This device measures the amount of air drawn in by the engine. It operates according to the suspended body principle, using a counterbalanced sensor plate that is connected to the fuel distributor control plunger by a lever system. A small leaf spring assures that the sensor plate assumes the correct zero position when the engine is stationary.

The air flow sensor consists of an air venturi tube in which an air flow sensor plate moves. The air flowing into the venturi from the air cleaner lifts the air flow sensor plate, allowing the air to flow through. The greater the amount of air, the higher the sensor plate will be raised.

The air flow sensor plate is fitted to a lever which is compensated by a counterweight. The lever acts on the control plunger in the fuel distributor which is pressed down by the control pressure, thus counteracting the lifting force of the air flow sensor plate. The height to which the air flow sensor plate is raised is governed by the magnitude of the air flow.

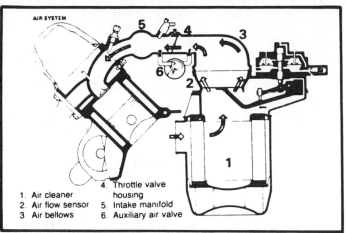

1. Air cleaner
2. Air flow sensor
3. Air bellows
4. Throttle valve housing
5. Intake manifold
6. Auxiliary air valve

Air flow through a typical CIS-E induction system

The air/fuel mixture varies with the engine load. The inclination of the venturi walls therefore varies in stages in order to provide a correct air/fuel mixture at all loads. Thus, the mixture is enriched at full load and leaned at idle.

The lever acts on the control plunger in the fuel distributor by means of an adjustable link with a needle bearing at the contact point. The basic fuel setting, and thus the CO setting, is adjusted by means of the adjustment screw on the link. This adjustment is made with a special tool and access to the screw can be gained through a hole in the air flow sensor between the air venturi and the fuel distributor. The CO adjustment is sealed on later models. A rubber bellows connects the air flow sensor to the throttle valve housing.

Testing

The air flow sensor plate in the fuel distributor must operate smoothly in order to do a good job of measuring air. Remove the air boot and check the sensor plate movement. When released, the plate should fall freely with one or two bounces. If the plate sticks, loosen the mounting screws and retighten them uniformly. Clean the funnel and sensor plate too, as these can get dirty from PCV fumes.

Check for leakage in the inlet system between the air flow sensor and the engine Air leaking into the system may result in poor engine performance, owing to the fact that it bypasses the air flow sensor, causing a lean mixture.
Leakage can occur in the following places:

a. At the rubber bellows between the air flow sensor and the throttle valve housing.

b. At the gasket on the flange of the cold start valve.

c. At the gasket between the throttle valve housing and the inlet manifold.

d. At the gasket between the inlet manifold and the cylinder head.

e. At the hose connections on the throttle valve housing, auxiliary air valve or inlet manifold.

f. Via the crankcase ventilation hose from the oil filler cap, dip stick or valve cover gasket.

NOTE: Move the sensor plate gently with a small magnet.

The plate should not bind, and although the plate will offer some resistance when depressed (due to the control pressure), it should return to its rest position when released. Be careful not to scratch the plate or venturi.

To check the air flow sensor contact switch, depress or lift the sensor plate by hand. The fuel injectors should buzz, and the fuel pump should activate. If the pump operates, but the injectors do not buzz, check the fuel pressure. If the pump does not operate, check for a short in the air flow sensor connector.

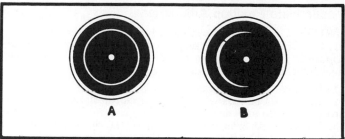

Sensor plate showing the correct (A) and incorrect (B) centering in the venturi

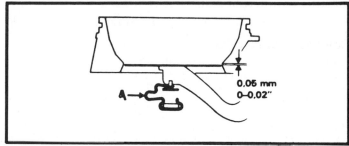

0.05 mm
0–0.02"

Correct sensor plate height in the venturi. Adjust it by bending the spring (A)

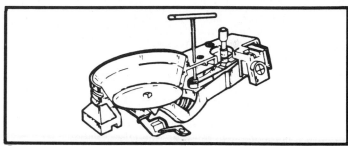

Cutaway of the air flow sensor assembly ahowing the direction of the air flow and proper placement of the mixture (CO) adjusting tool. Never accelerate the engine with this tool in place

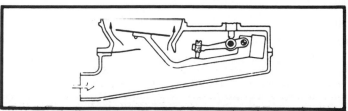

1. Air funnel
2. Sensor plate
3. Relief cross section
4. Idle mixture adjusting screw
5. Counterweight
6. Fulcrum
7. Main lever
8. Leaf spring

Updraft air flow sensor in the zero position

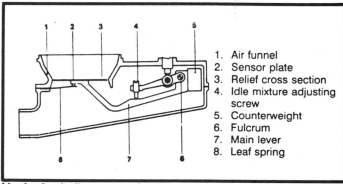

Updraft air flow sensor plate movement

Sensor Plate Position Adjustment

NOTE: The air flow sensor plate adjustment is critical. The distance between the sensor plate and the plate stop must be 0-0.2 in. The plate must also be centered in the venturi, and must not contact the venturi walls.

1. Remove the air cleaner assembly.
2. Using a 0.004 in. feeler gauge, check the clearance around the sensor plate at four opposite points around the plate.
3. If necessary, loosen the bolt in the center of the sensor plate and center the plate. Torque the bolt to 3.6 ft. lbs. Do not scratch the venturi or the plate.

Sensor Plate Height Adjustment

NOTE: The sensor plate height adjustment must be checked under fuel pressure.

1. Install a pressure gauge in the line between the fuel distributor and the control pressure regulator as previously described.
2. Remove the rubber elbow from the air flow sensor assembly.
3. Check that the fuel pressure is within specifications as previously described.
4. The sensor plate should be flush or 0.02 in. below the beginning of the venturi taper. If necessary to adjust, remove the mixture control from the intermediate housing and bend the spring accordingly.

NOTE: With the sensor plate too high, the engine will run on and with the sensor plate too low, poor cold and warm engine start-up will result. If the sensor plate movement is erratic, the control piston can be sticking.

5. Recheck the pressure reading after any adjustments.
6. Remove the pressure gauge, reconnect the fuel lines and install the fuel pump relay, if removed.
7. Reset the idle speed if necessary. See the individual car sections for details. Anytime an adjustment is made on the fuel system, or if a component is replaced, the idle CO should be reset with a CO meter.

Removal and Installation

1. Relieve the fuel system pressure as previously described. Wrap a cloth around the connection to catch any escaping fuel.
2. Thoroughly clean all fuel lines on the fuel distributor and then remove them.
3. Remove the rubber air intake duct.
4. Remove the air flow sensor/fuel distributor as a unit.
5. Remove the three retaining screws and remove the fuel distributor.
6. Installation is in the reverse order of removal. When installing the air flow sensor, always replace the O-ring and gaskets. Use Loctite® on all retaining bolts.

IDLE SPEED AND MIXTURE ADJUSTMENTS

NOTE: The following information is being published from the latest information available at the time of publication. If the information differs from the values given on the underhood emission control label, use the data on the label.

Adjustment

1984 ALL MODELS

NOTE: Certain 1.8 Liter engines are equipped with a manual pre-heat valve located on the air cleaner housing. The valve is marked"S" (summer) and "W" (winter). When servicing, position the valve to S (unless work area is below freezing). After servicing, return the valve to the position that matches climate conditions.

1. The engine must be at normal operating temperature.
2. Leave the crankcase breather hose open with the exception of the 5 cylinder models. Plug the hose on the 5 cylinder models.
3. Disconnect the two plugs on the idle stabilizer at the control unit and plug them together.
4. Make sure that all the electrical accessories are "OFF".
5. Connect a suitable CO meter to the CO fitting on the exhaust manifold in the front or on the catayltic converter. Connect a timing light according to manufacturers instructions. Check the timing and adjust in the conventional manner, if necessary.
6. Connect the dwell meter to the oxygen sensor system test receptacle (blue and white wire) and the negative lead goes to a suitable ground. Set the dwell meter on the four cylinder scale. Briefly accelerate, the dwell meter reading should range between 23–59° with the oxygen sensor still connected. If the dwell does not fluctuate, check the oxygen sensor system.
7. Check the idle speed. Adjust the idle speed by turning the idle adjustment screw located on the throttle chamber.

NOTE: Only adjust the idle when the radiator fan is off.

8. The CO percentage should range between 0.3–3.0% with the oxygen sensor disconnected. The dwell meter reading should be steady between 43–47° with the oxygen sensor disconnected.
9. If it is not, an adjustment will be necessary. Remove the plug from the air sensor housing. Adjust the dwell with the mixture adjusting screw. The CO reading should read between 0.8–1.2%.
10. Stop the engine. Reconnect all vacuum hoses and wires. Install a new tamper-proof plug in the air sensor housing. Reconnect the idle stabilizer. Remove all test equipment.

1985-88 4 CYLINDER MODELS

On all models, the idle speed, mixture adjustment and ignition timing must be checked together. Exhaust gas mixture must be

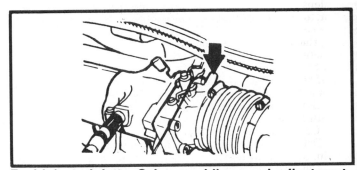

Fuel injected Jetta, Scirrocco idle speed adjustment screw

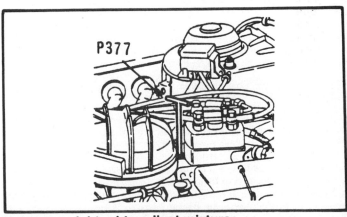

Using special tool to adjust mixture

checked and adjusted by measuring milliamps (mA), with a special meter and with the oxygen sensor connected. Refer to the underhood vacuum diagram for all hose locations.

1. On all models except the Golf, GTI and Jetta GLI, pinch close the vacuum line from the idle boost valve to the throttle intake chamber. Start the engine and allow it to reach normal operating temperature. The radiator fan must come on at least once.

2. Switch OFF all accessories. The radiator fan and air conditioner must not be running during the test.

3. Pull the crankcase breather hose off the valve cover and allow it to vent to the atmosphere.

4. Remove the cap from the T-piece in the charcoal canister vent hose near the right fender well. Turn the T-piece 90° and reinsert the blank side with restrictor into the vent hose.

6. Connect SIEMENS 451 tester (or equivalent) according to the manufacturer's instructions.

7. Remove the cap from the CO probe receptacle and insert the CO probe. The hose must fit tightly so there is no exhaust leak. Check the idle speed and adjust to specifications if necessary. Check the ignition timing and adjust to specifications if necessary.

8. On the Golf, GTI and Jetta GLI (to measure milliamps (mA)), connect a digital multimeter to the differential pressure regulator. Remove the connector from the differential pressure regulator and install adaptor VW 1315 A/1 or equivalent. Connect a dwell meter and the multimeter to the adaptor and the oxygen sensor test connection. Set the selector switch to DCA 200 mA. Breifly accelerate the engine, the dwell meter reading should range between 26–30° or 4–16mA on the multimeter with the oxygen sensor connected.

NOTE: If the engine does not run after the adaptor is connected, the connections may be improper. Reverse the plug and try again.

9. On all other models, connect adapter VW1315 A/1 or equivalent to the differential pressure regulator. Connect a multimeter to the adaptor and the oxygen sensor test connection. Set the selector switch to DCA 200 mA. Breifly accelerate the engine, the meter reading should range between 4–16mA on the multimeter with the oxygen sensor connected. The CO value should be 0.3–1.2%.

12. If the current reading is less than 4 mA or more than 16 mA, remove the CO adjustment plug as follows:

   a. Stop the engine and remove the boot on the mixture control unit.

   b. Centerpunch the plug in the CO adjusting hole.

   c. Drill a $\frac{3}{32}$ in. (2.5mm) hole in the center of the plug $\frac{9}{64}$–$\frac{5}{32}$ in. (3.5–4mm) deep.

   d. Carefully clean up any metal shavings and insert a $\frac{1}{8}$ in. sheet metal screw into the drilled hole, then remove the screw and plug with pliers.

13. Start the engine and allow it to idle.

14. Adjust the current reading on the multimeter by turning the CO adjusting screw with tool P377 or equivalent to obtain 10–12 mA or 27–29° (reading fluctuates). Turn the adjusting screw clockwise to lower the current reading (CO higher) and counterclockwise to raise the current reading (CO lower).

— CAUTION —

Do not push adjustment tool down when making CO adjustment and do not accelerate the engine with the tool in place. Remove the tool after each adjustment and accelerate the engine briefly before reading multimeter. Always adjust in direction from high to low.

15. Run the engine at 3000 rpm for approximately 3 minutes and recheck the meter readings. After CO adjustment is complete, recheck the idle speed and adjust if necessary. Reconnect the crankcase breather hose. If, after reconnecting the breather hose, the current reading drops below specifications, an oil change may be necessary.

16. Turn the ignition OFF and drive in a new mixture plug, flush with the mixture control unit.

17. Remove all test equipment, attach CO probe cap and remove the device used to pinch the idle speed boost valve hose.

1985-88 CYLINDER MODELS

NOTE: Idle speed, ignition timing and oxygen sensor duty cycle (mixture) must be checked and adjusted together.

1. Check that there are no leaks in the exhaust system and connect Siemens 451 tester or equivalent according to the manufacturer's instructions. Make sure the TDC sending unit is installed snugly into the transmission housing.

2. Remove the cap from the CO probe receptacle and install CO test probe. Make sure the hose fits snugly so there is no exhaust leak.

3. Disconnect the crankcase breather hose at the cylinder head cover and plug the hose.

4. Disconnect both plugs at the idle stabilizer and plug the connectors together to bypass the unit. Make sure the connectors are tight.

5. Turn OFF all accessories. If any fuel lines were disconnected or replaced, start the engine and run it to 3000 rpm several times, then let idle for at least two minutes.

6. Start the engine and allow it to reach normal operating temperature. The radiator fan must come on at least once.

NOTE: The radiator fan must not be running during all tests and adjustments.

7. Check and adjust the idle speed if necessary.

8. Check and adjust the ignition timing if necessary. Turn ignition OFF.

9. Connect the dwell lead on the tester to the oxygen sensor blue/white test connection. Remove the cap from the charcoal canister purge line.

10. Remove the test lead from No. 1 ignition wire and TDC sending unit. Make sure the tester is on the 4 cylinder scale and press "%" button. Start the engine and check the oxygen sensor duty cycle (dwell) and CO at idle speed.

11. The OXS duty cycle should be 25–65% (reading should fluctuate) and the CO should be between 0.3–1.2%. If the CO is more than 1.2%, but the dwell range is correct, check for leaks in the intake or exhaust system, malfunctioning fuel distributor, or a faulty injector spray pattern.

12. If the OXS duty cycle is less than 25% or more than 65%, remove the tamper-proof plug as described in Step 12 of the 4 cylinder procedure, above.

13. Using adjusting tool P377 or equivalent, adjust the OXS duty cycle (mixture) by turning the adjusting screw clockwise to lower the meter reading, or counterclockwise to increase the reading. Adjust to 44–56% (reading should fluctuate). The radiator fan must not be running during adjustment.

— CAUTION —

Do not push adjustment tool down while adjusting CO level. Never accelerate the engine with the tool in place and remove the tool and accelerate the engine briefly after each adjustment.

14. Readjust the idle speed, if necessary, then turn ignition OFF and remove the test equipment. Be sure to replace the CO probe cap to prevent exhaust leaks. Reconnect the crankcase breather hose and idle stabilizer. Install the cap to the charcoal canister purge line and replace the tamper-proof adjustment plug.

1984–88 VANAGON

1. Start the engine and let it run to reach normal operating temperature. Connect a suitable CO meter to the CO fitting on the exhaust manifold in the front or on the catayltic converter.

2. Connect a suitable tachometer and check the idle speed, adjust if necessary.

3. Leave the idle stabilzer plugs connected to the ECU and disconnect the oxygen sensor connector. Check the CO reading. The CO should be 0.3–1.1% (0.3–1.2% on 1985–87 models).

4. If the CO reading is above 1.1%, pinch the crankcase breather hose. If the CO reading drops below 1.1% engine oil dilution is indicated. If the CO reading does not drop, adjustment is necessary.

5. Shut down the engine and remove the intake air sensor. Center punch the plug in the CO adjusting hole. Using a $^3/_{32}$ in. drill bit and drill a hole through the center of the plug about ⅛ in.

6. Remove any metal shavings. Screw a sheet metal screw into the hole in the plug and pull the plug out. Use a suitable pair of pliers to pull on the sheet metal screw.

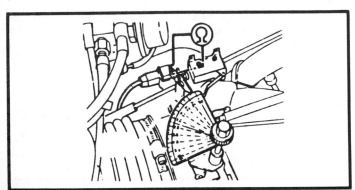

Tool 3084 mounted on the first stage throttle valve

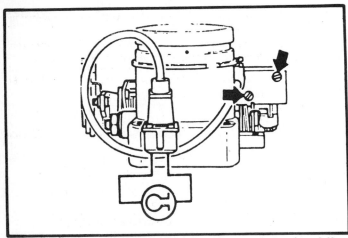

Ohmeter connection and adjusting points for idle switch adjustment

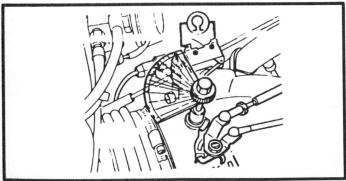

Tool 3084 mounting and ohmeter connections for the full throttle switch adjustment

7. Reinstall the intake air sensor. Start the engine and and adjust the CO percentage to the proper specifications.

8. Stop the engine. Reconnect all vacuum hoses and wires. Install a new tamper-proof plug in the air sensor housing. Remove all test equipment.

THROTTLE VALVE SWITCHES

NOTE: To check and adjust the idle and full throttle switch on various 1984 and later models, Special Tool No. 3084 and an ohmmeter are necessary.

Idle Switch Adjustment

ALL MODELS EXCEPT THE VANAGON

1. Loosen the upper left bolt from the throttle valve housing and install the pointer for tool 3084 or equivalent. Tighten the bolt.

2. Attach the protractor (tool 3084 or equivalent) to first stage throttle valve shaft (remove the nut if necessary).

3. Disconnect the switch wire and plug and connect the ohmmeter. Adjust the protractor to "ZERO". Open the throttle approximately 20° then close the throttle slowly.

4. The ohmmeter should show continuity (0 ohms) when the pointer indicates the throttle position is at 1–2.5°. If it is not within specifications, remove the housing cover and adjust the idle switch position. The ohmmeter must indicate continuity (0 ohms) before the throttle reaches the idle position.

Full Throttle Switch Adjustment

ALL MODELS EXCEPT THE VANAGON

1. Mount the pointer as in the Idle Switch procedure Step 1.

2. Attach the protractor (Tool 3084 or equivalent) to the second stage throttle valve shaft (remove the nut if necessary).

3. Remove the full throttle switch connectors and connect the ohmmeter. Open the second stage throttle fully and "ZERO" the protractor.

4. Close the throttle to approximately 30°. Open the throttle valve slowly and watch the protractor and ohmmeter. The ohmmeter should read continuity (0 ohms) when the protractor is at 12° or 8° before full throttle.

5. Adjust the throttle switch position as necessary. The ohmmeter must indicate zero ohms at full throttle.

Throttle Valve Adjustment

VANAGON

The throttle stop screw is preset at the factory and therefore no adjustments should be attempted. Basic adjustment should only be checked if the screw position has been altered.

1. Turn the throttle valve adjustment screw out until a gap

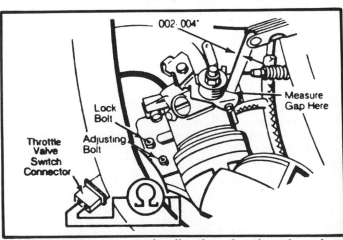

Measuring the gap and adjusting the throttle valve switch

can be seen between the end of the screw and the throttle stop.

2. Place a thin piece of paper between the throttle screw and throttle stop. Slide the paper back and forth while turning the throttle screw.

3. When the throttle screw touches the paper, remove the paper and turn the screw clockwise a half of a turn further.

4. Secure the screw with a suitable thread sealant. Check the idle speed and CO reading, adjust as necessary.

5. Loosen the throttle switch retaining screw and using a suitable ohmmeter, move the switch until the switch on point is reached and a gap of .002–.004 in. is present between the idle stop and the idle adjusting screw.

BOSH AIRFLOW CONTROLLED (AFC) DIGIJET INJECTION SYSTEM

General Information

This Bosch AFC Digijet system is a modified AFC system. The main difference in the two systems is that Digijet does not use a cold start system (this includes the cold start injector and the thermo-time switch). The entire system can be checked at the multipin connector of the electronic control unit (ECU). Using a suitable ohmmeter and voltmeter and the chart provided below, check the system at each terminal noted. Be sure the ignition system is on while testing and to prevent any damage to the ohmmeter while testing, connect the ohmmeter leads only to the terminals specified in the charts.

Component Inspection and Testing

DIGIJET FUEL PUMP

Testing

1. Disconnect the fuel return line at the pressure regulator and plug the line.

2. Attach a hose to the return line fitting and place the other end of hose in a measuring container.

3. Remove the fuel pump relay. Place a jumper wire across terminals 30 and 87 for 30 seconds. The minimum delivery rate should be 17 ounces (500cc).

FUEL PRESSURE REGULATOR

Testing

Using a T-fitting, connect the fuel pressure gauge in the fuel delivery line. Run the engine at idle speed. The pressure should be 29 psi with the pressure regulator vacuum line connected. The pressure should be 36 psi with the vacuum hose disconnected.

Removal and Installation

1. Relieve fuel system pressure.

2. Disengage the vacuum line connecting the regulator to the intake manifold from the pressure regulator.

3. Remove the bolt and washers securing the pressure regulator mounting bracket and carefully pull the regulator and bracket upward. Note the position of the regulator.

4. Unfasten the hose clamps and disconnect the pressure regulator from the fuel hose. Inspect the hose for signs of wear, cracks or fuel leaks.

NOTE: Place a clean rag under the pressure regulator to catch any spilled fuel.

5. Remove the lock nut and remove the pressure regulator.
6. Installation is the reverse of removal.

NOTE: Torque the fuel delivery union bolt to 18–25 ft. lbs. Do not overtighten.

AFC DIGIJET OHMMETER RESISTANCE TEST CHART

Terminals To Be Tested	Components Tested	Test Specifications
Terminals 2 and 7	Coolant Temperature Sensor	2300–2700 ohms at 68° F.
Terminals 4 and 7 ①	Throttle Valve Switch (Idle & Full)	0 ohms at idle and full throttle
Terminals 5 and 7	Oxygen Sensor	②
Terminals 6 and 19	Airflow Meter	Approximately 560 ohms
Terminals 7 and 25	ECU Ground Connection	0 ohms
Terminals 11 and 7 plus 12 and 7	Cylinders 3 and 4 Injectors and Wiring	Approximately 16–16.4 ohms
Terminals 14 and 6	Intake Air Temperature	2300–2700 ohms at 68° F.
Terminals 15 and 19	Airflow Meter	③
Terminals 23 and 7 plus 24 and 7	Cylinders 1 and 2 Injectors and Wiring	Approximately 16–16.4 ohms
Terminals 25 and 7	ECU Ground Connection	0 ohms

① Do not connect the test light to this terminal if the multi-pin plug is connected to the ECU.
② 0 ohms with the oxygen sensor disconnected and grounded. Infinity with the sensor connected.
③ The resistance changes as the sensor plate is moved.

AFC DIGIJET VOLTMETER VOLTAGE TEST CHART

Terminals To Be Tested	Components Tested	Test Specifications
Terminals 1 and 7	AEG Hall Control Unit	①
Terminals 1 and Ignition coil terminal 15	Fairchild Hall Control Unit	①
Terminals 13 and 7	Power Supply (Left) Relay	Battery Voltage
Terminals 21 and 7	Starting Enrichment and Circuit Wiring	②
Terminals 20 and 25 ③	Fuel Pump (Right) Relay	④
Terminals 20 and 25 ③	Auxiliary Air Regulator	⑤

① Battery voltage or slightly less. 1.5 volts or slightly less when the center wire of the ignition distributor connector is grounded.
② Unplug all four injectors. Cranking voltage (starter terminal number 50) present when cranking the engine.
③ Do not connect the test light to this terminal if the multi-pin plug is connected to the ECU.
④ Connect a jumper wire between the terminals. Fuel pump must run.
⑤ There should be battery voltage present at the auxiliary air regulator connector.

FUEL INJECTORS

Fuel in the L-Jetronic system is not injected directly into the cylinder. Fuel is injected into the intake port, where the air/fuel mixture is drawn into the cylinder when the intake valve opens to start the intake stroke. An electrical signal from each engine sensor is introduced into the control unit for computation. The open valve time period of the injector is controlled by the duration of the pulse computed in the control unit.

The injector operates on the solenoid valve principle. When an electric signal is applied to the coil built into the injector, the plunger is pulled into the solenoid, thereby opening the needle valve for fuel injection. The quantity of injected fuel is in proportion to the duration of the pulse applied from the control unit. The longer the pulse, the more fuel is delivered.

The fuel injectors are electrically connected, in parallel, in the control unit. All injectors receive the injection signal form the control unit at the same time. Therefore, injection is made independently of the engine stroke cycle (intake, combustion and exhaust).

A bad injection valve can cause a number of problems:

1. Hot restart troubles
2. Rough idle
3. Hesitation
4. Poor power

Hot starting complaints can come from an injector or injectors that are leaking fuel droplets when they're supposed to be completely shut. The next three problems can be caused by a bad spray pattern from one or more of the injectors. Dribble patterns, fire hose shots, and uneven sprays will produce hesitation, stumbling and general lack of power. Replace any injector with a bad spray pattern.

DIGIJET FUEL INJECTOR

Testing

NOTE: Do not disconnect terminal number one at the ignition coil when operating the starter.

SPRAY PATTERN

1. Remove a pair of injectors from one side of the engine. Leave the electrical plugs and the fuel lines connected. Unplug the connector from the fuel injectors which are still installed.

2. Hold the injectors over a suitable drain pan. Operate the starter briefly. The spray pattern must be an even, cone-shaped spray. Repeat the test for the remaining injectors.

LEAK TEST

Remove the injectors from the engine. Leave the fuel lines connected but unplug the electrical connectors. Turn the ignition ON for about 5 seconds. No more than two drops should leak form each injector in one minute. Replace the sealing rings when installing the injectors.

NOTE: To prevent unit damage when checking the injector voltage supply, do not short circuit the connector contacts.

VOLTAGE SUPPLY

Unplug the electrical connectors from the injectors. Connect the test lamp across harness plug connector. The test lamp should flicker when operating the starter. If not, check the relays and the ground connections at the cylinder head and the Hall control unit.

AIR FLOW OR AIR MASS SENSOR

On L and LU injection systems, the air flow sensor measures the quantity of intake air, and sends a signal to the control unit so that the base pulse width (voltage signal) can be determined for correct fuel injection by the injector. The air flow sensor is provided with a flap in the air passage. As the air flows through the passage, the flap rotates and its angle of rotation electronically signals the control unit by means of a potentiometer. The engine will draw in a certain volume of fresh air depending on the throttle valve position and engine speed.

This air stream will cause the sensor plate inside the air flow sensor to move against the force of its return spring. The sensor plate is connected to the potentiometer, which sends a voltage signal to the control unit. The temperature sensor in the air flow sensor influences this signal. The control unit then sends out and opening signal to the fuel injectors to make sure that the volume of injected fuel is exactly right for the volume of intake air. A damping flap in the air flow sensor eliminates unwanted movement of the sensor plate. As the sensor plate moves into its damping chamber, acting like a shock absorber for the sensor plate.

A small amount of intake air volume moves around the sensor plate via a bypass port. The air/fuel mixture of idling can be adjusted by changing the amount of air flowing through the bypass port with the adjusting screw.

If the sensor plate or its attached damper should become stuck inside the air flow sensor, excessive fuel consumption, marginal performance or a no-start condition could result. LH,

LH II and Motronic injection systems incorporate an air mass sensor into the air box. On these systems, the flap valve is replaced with a heated platinum wire that is used to measure air mass without altitude influences.

NOTE: Because of the sensitivity of the air flow (or air mass) meter, there cannot be any air leaks in the ducts. Even the smallest leak could unbalance the system and affect the performance of the engine. During every check, pay attention to hose connections, dipstick and oil filler cap for evidence of air leaks. Should you encounter any, take steps to correct the problem before proceeding with testing.

Removal and Installation

1. Disconnect the air duct hoses form both sides of the air box.
2. Disconnect the electrical connector from the wire harness.
3. Remove all bolts, lockwashers, washers and bushings holding the air flow sensor to the bracket. Remove the unit assembly.
4. Reinstall in reverse order.

Testing Air Flow Sensor

1. Connect an ohmmeter to any terminal on the flow meter. Touch the flow meter body with the other connector. If any continuity is indicated, the unit is defective and must be replaced.
2. Reach into the air flow meter and check the flap operation. If the flap opens and closes smoothly, without binding, the mechanical portion of the unit is working.

NOTE: If the air temperature sensor or potentiometer is malfunctioning, the entire air flow sensor must be replaced.

DIGIJET AIR FLOW METER

Testing

1. Turn the ignition switch OFF. Unplug the air hose and the electrical connector from the air flow meter. Connect the ohmmeter to terminals 3 and 4 of the air flow meter. Resistance should be approximately 560 ohms. Terminals 6 and 9 should have the same resistance.
2. Connect the ohmmeter to terminals 2 and 3. Resistance should change when moving the sensor plate. The test result should be the same for terminals 7 and 9. Replace the air flow meter if it fails any resistance test.

DIGIJET AUXILIARY AIR REGULATOR

Testing

1. The engine must be cold to perform this test. Start the engine and let it run at idle speed, pinch the air regulator to intake manifold hose. The rpm should drop.
2. Run the engine at idle speed for about five minutes more, then repeat the same test, again the rpm should drop.
3. If there is no change in the rpm during these tests, unplug the electrical connector from the air regulator and check for voltage with the engine running. If there is voltage present, replace the auxiliary air regulator.

AUXILIARY AIR REGULATOR

The Auxiliary air regulator allows more air to bypass the throttle plate when the engine is cold, triggering a richer fuel mixture for better cold starting.

A rotating metal disc inside the valve contains an opening that lines up with the bypass hoses when the engine is cold. As the engine heats up, a bi-metallic spring gradually closes the opening by rotating the disc. The bi-metallic spring is heated by coolant temperature and a heater coil which is energized through the ignition circuit.

A double relay, usually located near the electronic control unit and grounded by a terminal of the control unit, controls the input to the fuel pump, cold start valve, injector position feed, control unit and the auxiliary air regulator.

Removal and Installation

1. Disconnect the air valve hoses.
2. Disconnect the air valve connector.
3. Disconnect the water bypass hose.
4. Remove the air valve attaching bolts and air valve.
5. Installation is the reverse of removal. Use a new gasket.

Testing

With the whole assembly at a temperature of about 20°C (about 68°F) and the electrical connectors and air hoses disconnected, visually check through the inside of the air lines to make sure that the diaphragm is partly open.

1. Using an ohmmeter, measure the resistance between the air valve terminals. Normal resistance is 29–49 ohms, depending on manufacturer's specifications.
2. Connect a voltmeter across the terminals of the connector and crank the engine.
3. If there is no voltage in the connector, look for a fault in the electrical system. If voltage is present, reconnect the valve and start the engine.
4. Check the engine rpm while pinching shut the air hose. At low temperature (below 140°F) the engine rpm should drop. After warmup, the engine speed should not drop more than 50 rpm.

Testing Air Mass Sensor

NOTE: Replace the air mass sensor as an assembly if the test results indicate a malfunction in any of the following procedures.

1. Ground the main relay terminal No. 21 and make sure the relay switches ON, a slight click should be heard when grounding.
2. Peel back the rubber boot from around the air mass sensor harness connector, but leave it connected to the sensors assembly.
3. Connect a voltmeter between terminal 9 and ground. The voltmeter should ready battery voltage (12 volts). Probe all terminals from the rear of the connector.
4. Connect the voltmeter between terminals 9 and 36; the reading should again be 12 volts.
5. If no voltage is present, check for an open circuit or broken wire in the power feed from the battery. If voltage is present, remove the ground connection from relay terminal No. 21 and proceed with testing. Leave the connector boot peeled back and probe all wire terminals from the rear of the wiring harness connector for all tests.

NOTE: Harness connectors can be damaged by test leads if probed from the front, causing a poor connection problem that did not exist before testing. Exercise caution during all electrical test procedures and never use excessive force during probing, removal or installation of wire harness connectors or components.

6. Connect an ohmmeter between terminals 6 and 7 on the air mass meter. Resistance should be about 4 ohms.
7. Connect the ohmmeter between terminals 6 and 14 and read the resistance valve. It should be between 0–1000 ohms (resistance varies depending on CO adjustment screw positioning). If values are as described, proceed with testing.
8. Connect a voltmeter between terminal 7 (+) and terminal 6 (–) on the air mass sensor connector.

9. Start the engine and note the voltage reading.

10. The voltage should increase with engine rpm. Slowly increase and decrease engine speed while watching the voltmeter and make sure the voltage changes up and down. Specific values are not as important as the fact that the needle (or digital readout) on the voltmeter swings back and forth as the rpm changes as described, proceed with testing.

11. Connect a voltmeter between terminal 8 (+) and 36 (–) to check the air mass sensor wire cleaning (burn-off) operation.

12. Start the engine and increase the engine speed to approximately 2500 rpm for a few seconds.

13. Switch off the engine. After about 5 seconds, the voltmeter should read approximately 1 volt for 1 second. Repeat this test a few times to verify the results.

14. If all tests are as described, remove the voltmeter and reposition the rubber boot cover around the air mass meter connector. Make sure the boot seals correctly to prevent moisture from corroding the electrical connectors.

AIR CONTROL VALVE

On the AFC system, with an air mass sensor, an air control valve is used to regulate the idle speed by bypassing air around the throttle valve. The amount of air bypassed is determined by a signal from the electronic control unit (ECU). Replacement of the air control valve is similar to the auxiliary air valve removal procedure.

Testing

1. Connect an ohmmeter between the fuel pump relay terminal 87 and the control unit connector terminal 10. The reading should be approximately 20 ohms.

2. Connect the ohmmeter between relay terminal 87 and the control unit connector terminal 23. The resistance value should again be about 20 ohms.

3. Remove the ohmmeter and reconnect the harness connectors, if removed. Start and warm up the engine.

4. Check the idle speed with a tachometer and compare the test results with the idle specification listed on the underhood emission control sticker.

5. Switch on the air conditioner (if equipped) and verify that the idle speed increases when the compressor is energized. If the idle does not increase, check for a sticking air control valve or failure of the A/C power circuit (shorted or open wire or microswitch).

6. Switch the engine OFF, then remove the connector from the coolant temperature sensor to simulate a cold engine.

7. Start the engine and verify that the high idle specification is obtained with a tachometer. Turn the ignition OFF and reconnect the coolant temperature sensor if the high idle is correct, then restart the engine and make sure the idle speed is once again at the normal (warm) value.

NOTE: If the air control valve is suspected of malfunction, install a new valve and repeat the test procedures. Adjust idle speed.

THROTTLE SWITCH

NOTE: On Digijet models, do not connect a test light to the throttle valve switch connectors if control unit is still connected.

The throttle switch forms part of the control for the fuel injection system, providing the ECU with information on throttle operating conditions. The switch is grounded at the intake manifold. The throttle valve switch is attached to the throttle chamber and actuates in response to accelerator pedal movement. This switch has two or three sets of contact points.

One set monitors the idle position and the other set monitors full throttle position. Some use additional contacts for mid-range operation. The idle contact closed when the throttle valve is positioned at idle and opens when it is at any other position. The idle contact compensates for after idle enrichment, and send the fuel shut-off signal.

The full throttle contact closes only when the throttle valve is positioned at full throttle (more than a 35 degree opening of the throttle valve). The contact is open while the throttle valve is at any other position. The full contact compensates for enrichment in full throttle.

On AFC systems with a Constant Idle Speed (CIS) feature incorporated into the injection circuit, a microswitch is used in place of the throttle switch. The microswitch is mounted so as to contact the throttle linkage at idle and signal the ECU as to what throttle position is being used. Some microswitches are set to be open at idle and some are closed. Use a test light to determine which type of microswitch is being used by checking for voltage while moving the throttle lever to open and close the contact lever. The microswitch is usually adjusted when setting the idle speed.

Adjustment

NOTE: A click should be heard when the throttle valve moves and the idle contact opens.

1. Make sure that the idle speed is correct. Check the underhood sticker for correct specification.

2. Disconnect the connector from the switch. The center pin is usually the 12 volt input terminal.

3. Connect an ohmmeter between terminals 2 and 18 of the switch.

4. Loosen the two screws holding the throttle plate switch.

5. with the engine off, rotate the switch clockwise until the ohmmeter indicates a closed circuit (idle contact closes).

6. At the exact point that the ohmmeter indicates a closed circuit, tighten the two screws holding the switch.

7. Check the adjustment.

Removal and Installation

1. Disconnect the electrical connector.

2. Remove the two screws and washers holding the switch to the intake manifold.

3. Remove the switch by slowly pulling it.

4. Reinstall in the reverse order and adjust the switch.

DECELERATION/IDLE SWITCH

Testing and Adjustment

1. Unplug the switch connector on the throttle body, then connect an ohmmeter to the switch contacts. The switch should show continuity with the throttle valve closed and fully open.

2. Run the engine at idle speed for a short time. Stop the engine and turn the ignition ON. Unplug the connectors from the switch and the full throttle enrichment switches. voltage between the connectors of the throttle valve idle switch should be ½ volt. If not, check for defective control unit or wiring.

3. To check the deceleration function of the switch, test results of Step 1 and 2 must be positive. Plug in all the throttle valve switch connectors. The temperature at the coolant sensor must be at 140°F (60°C) or more and resistance below 550 ohms.

4. Accelerate the engine slowly. At the same time, operate the switch by hand. The engine speed must fluctuate. If not, replace control unit.

FULL THROTTLE ENRICHMENT SWITCH

Testing

1. Unplug both throttle valve switches. Full throttle enrichment switch should have no continuity with throttle closed and continuity with throttle fully open.

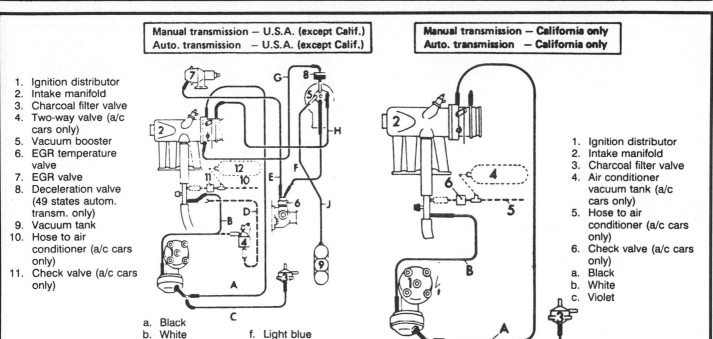

Manual transmission – U.S.A. (except Calif.)
Auto. transmission – U.S.A. (except Calif.)

Manual transmission – California only
Auto. transmission – California only

1. Ignition distributor
2. Intake manifold
3. Charcoal filter valve
4. Two-way valve (a/c cars only)
5. Vacuum booster
6. EGR temperature valve
7. EGR valve
8. Deceleration valve (49 states autom. transm. only)
9. Vacuum tank
10. Hose to air conditioner (a/c cars only)
11. Check valve (a/c cars only)

a. Black
b. White
c. Violet
d. Pink
e. Yellow
f. Light blue
g. Gray
h. Red
i. Light green

1. Ignition distributor
2. Intake manifold
3. Charcoal filter valve
4. Air conditioner vacuum tank (a/c cars only)
5. Hose to air conditioner (a/c cars only)
6. Check valve (a/c cars only)

a. Black
b. White
c. Violet

Golf model – typical

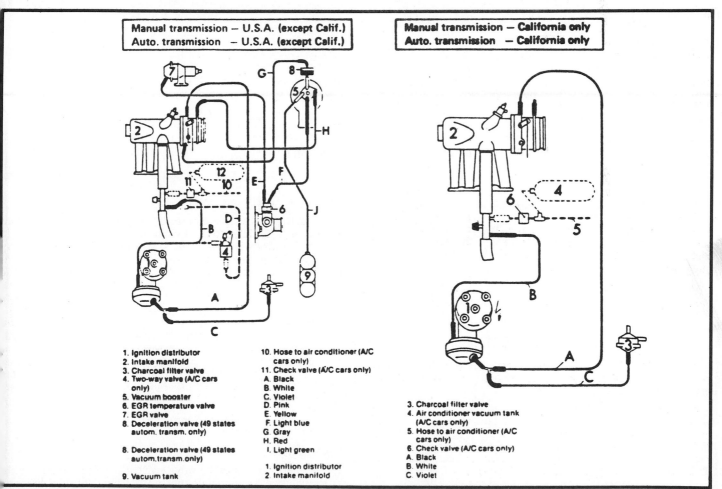

Manual transmission – U.S.A. (except Calif.)
Auto. transmission – U.S.A. (except Calif.)

Manual transmission – California only
Auto. transmission – California only

1. Ignition distributor
2. Intake manifold
3. Charcoal filter valve
4. Two-way valve (A/C cars only)
5. Vacuum booster
6. EGR temperature valve
7. EGR valve
8. Deceleration valve (49 states autom. transm. only)
8. Deceleration valve (49 states autom.transm.only)
9. Vacuum tank

10. Hose to air conditioner (A/C cars only)
11. Check valve (A/C cars only)
A. Black
B. White
C. Violet
D. Pink
E. Yellow
F. Light blue
G. Gray
H. Red
I. Light green

1. Ignition distributor
2. Intake manifold

3. Charcoal filter valve
4. Air conditioner vacuum tank (A/C cars only)
5. Hose to air conditioner (A/C cars only)
6. Check valve (A/C cars only)
A. Black
B. White
C. Violet

Volkswagon, Jetta, Golf and Scirocco vacuum circuits

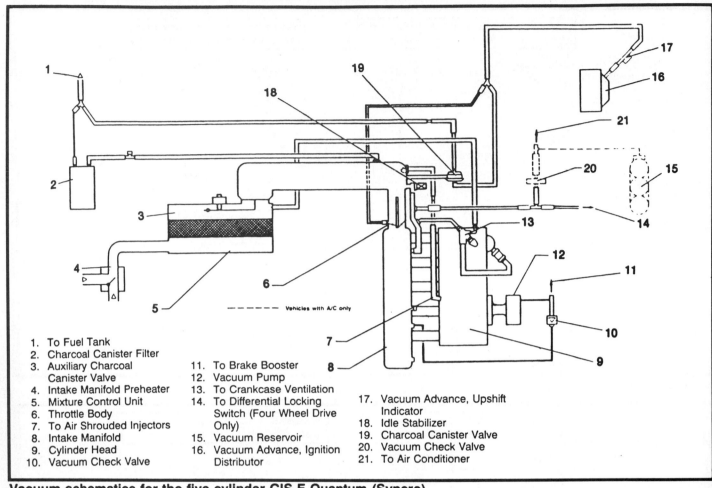

1. To Fuel Tank
2. Charcoal Canister Filter
3. Auxiliary Charcoal Canister Valve
4. Intake Manifold Preheater
5. Mixture Control Unit
6. Throttle Body
7. To Air Shrouded Injectors
8. Intake Manifold
9. Cylinder Head
10. Vacuum Check Valve
11. To Brake Booster
12. Vacuum Pump
13. To Crankcase Ventilation
14. To Differential Locking Switch (Four Wheel Drive Only)
15. Vacuum Reservoir
16. Vacuum Advance, Ignition Distributor
17. Vacuum Advance, Upshift Indicator
18. Idle Stabilizer
19. Charcoal Canister Valve
20. Vacuum Check Valve
21. To Air Conditioner

Vehicles with A/C only

Vacuum schematics for the five cylinder CIS-E Quantum (Syncro)

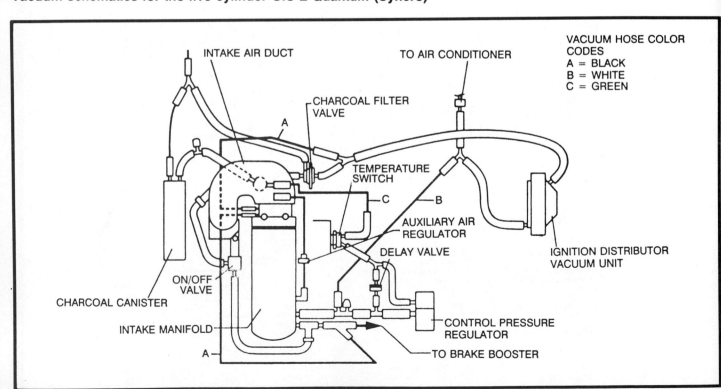

VACUUM HOSE COLOR CODES
A = BLACK
B = WHITE
C = GREEN

INTAKE AIR DUCT

TO AIR CONDITIONER

CHARCOAL FILTER VALVE

TEMPERATURE SWITCH

AUXILIARY AIR REGULATOR

DELAY VALVE

IGNITION DISTRIBUTOR VACUUM UNIT

CHARCOAL CANISTER

ON/OFF VALVE

INTAKE MANIFOLD

CONTROL PRESSURE REGULATOR

TO BRAKE BOOSTER

Vacuum schematics for the five cylinder CIS-E Quantum

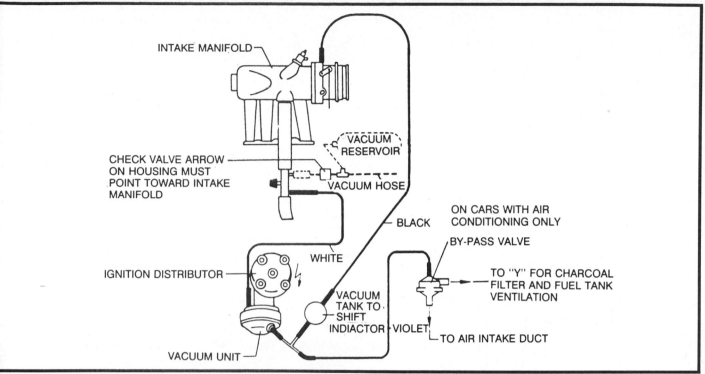

Vacuum schematics for the four cylinder CIS-E Quantum

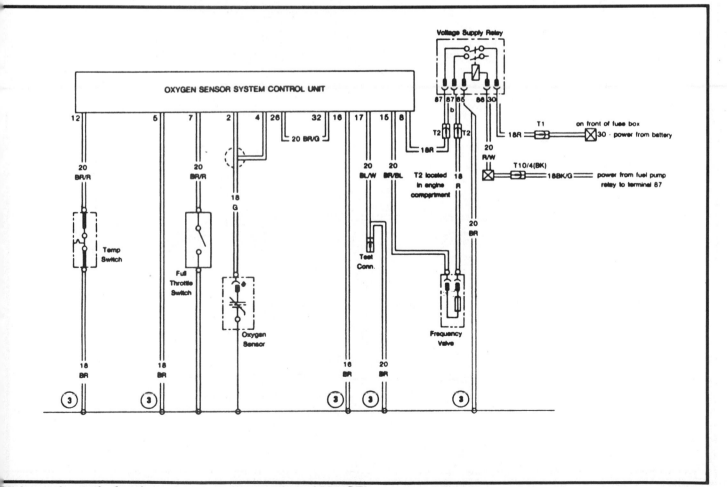

Wiring schematic for the oxygen sensor system—1984 GTI

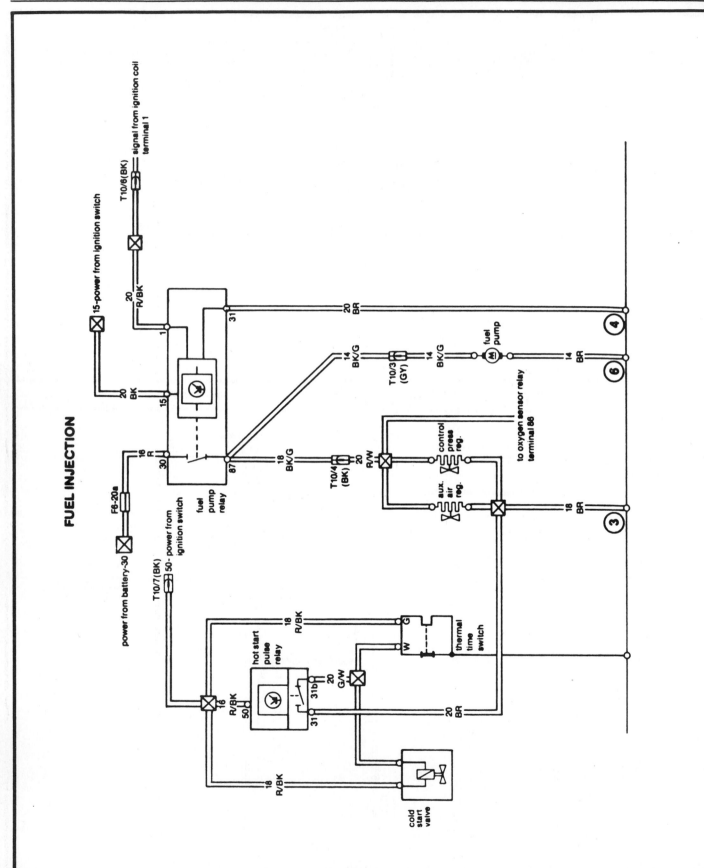

FUEL INJECTION

Wiring schematic for the oxygen sensor system–1984 Rabbit (fuel injected)

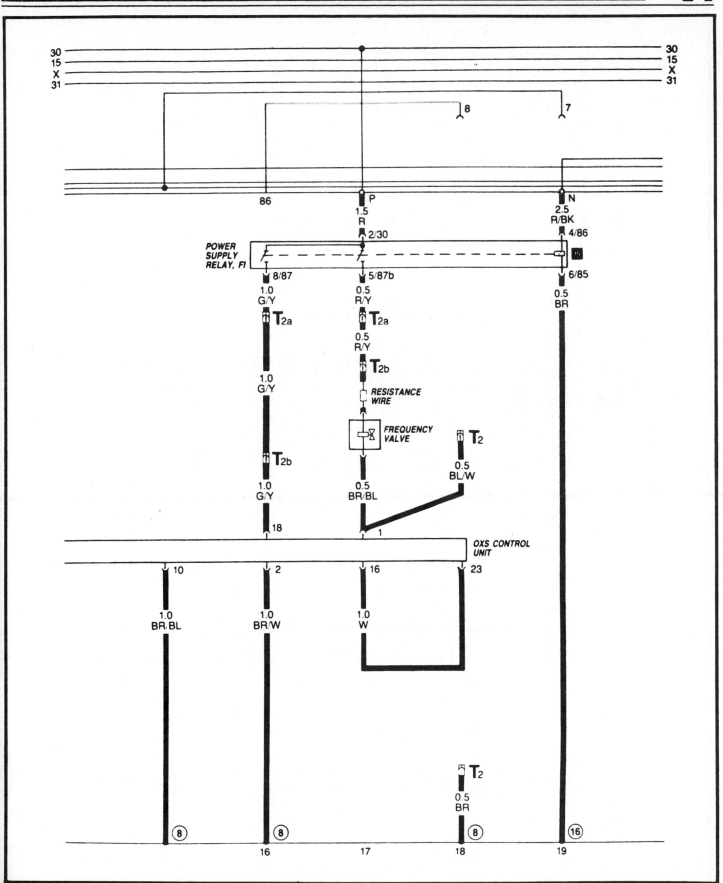

Wiring schematic for the oxygen sensor system—Scirocco

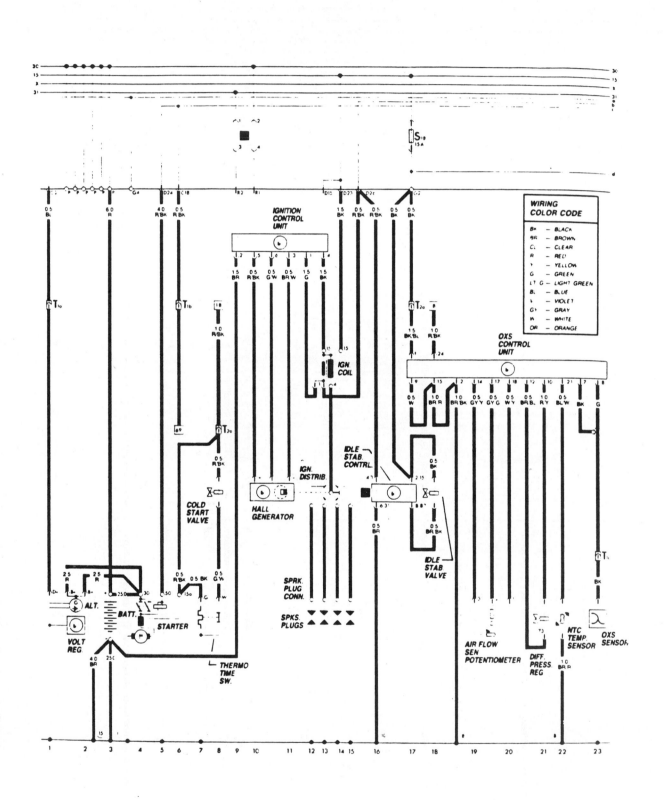

Wiring schematic for the oxygen sensor system—Jetta

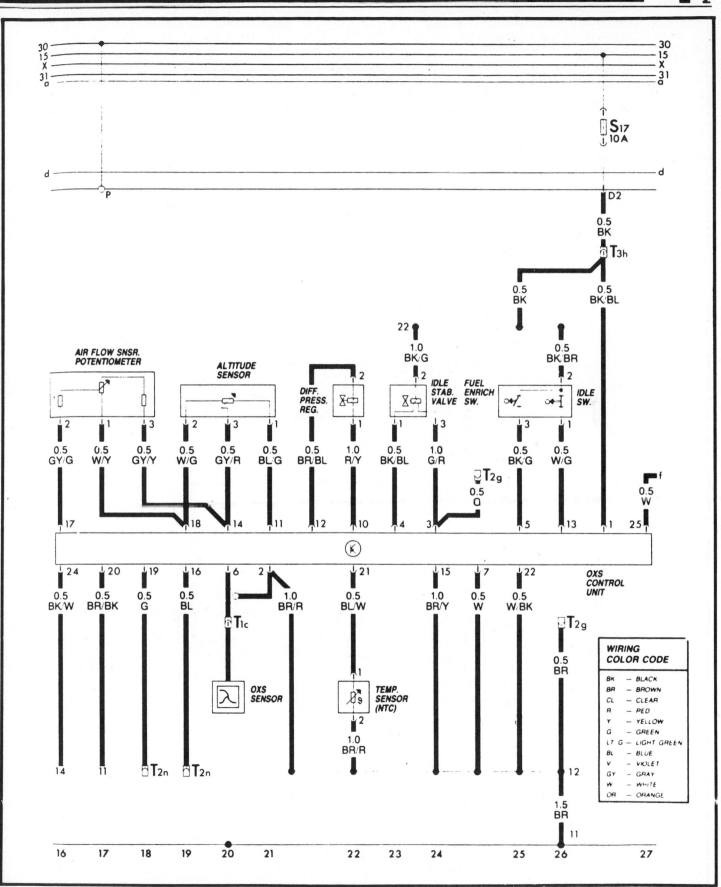

Wiring schematic for the oxygen sensor system — Quantum

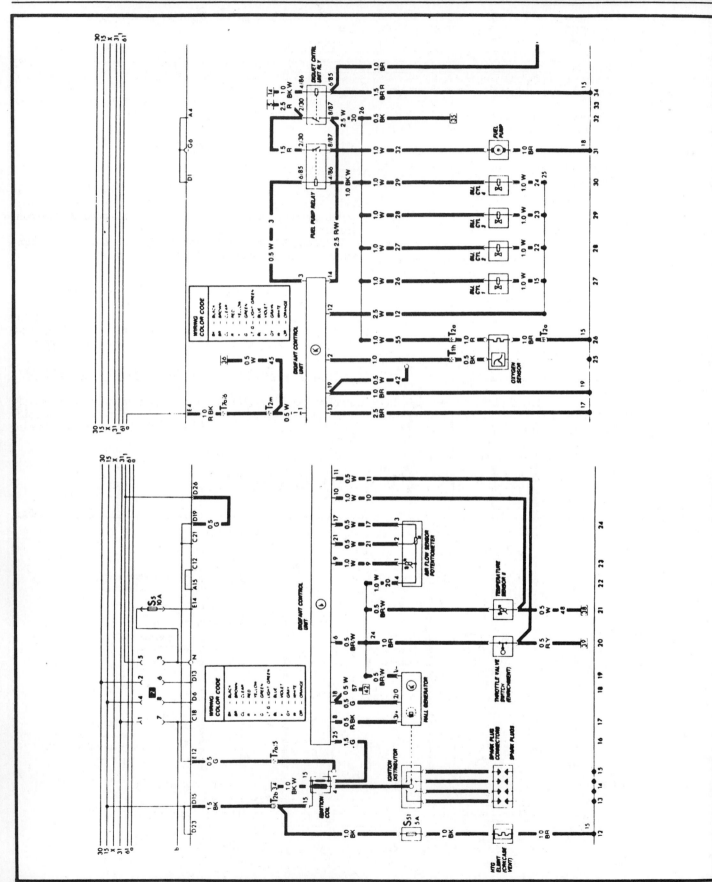

Wiring schematic for the Vanagon digijet fuel system

2. Run engine at idle for a short time. Stop engine and turn ignition ON. with both throttle valve switches unplugged, check for $\frac{1}{2}$ volt between connectors of full throttle enrichment switch harness. If not, check for defective wiring or control unit.

3. If the enrichment switch, wiring and control unit are good, check the full throttle enrichment by bringing the engine to normal operating temperature. connect a CO tester and tachometer to the engine.

4. Run the engine for about 2 minutes at idle speed. Increase the idle speed slowly until the tachometer reads about 4000 rpm. The CO should be between 0.3–1.1%.

5. With the engine at about 4000 rpm, operate the full throttle enrichment switch by hand for about 15 seconds. The CO must increase above 1.5%. If not, the control unit is defective.

RELAYS

Testing

1. The power supply and fuel pump relays are located in the engine compartment. They are both in a plastic box located on the firewall. The fuel pump relay is mounted on the right side of the box and power supply relay on the left.

NOTE: Do not connect test lamp to terminal 86 of fuel pump relay if control unit is plugged in.

2. Unplug all electrical connectors to injectors and check the power to relays by turning the ignition switch ON. Use test lamp to check for voltage at terminal 30 and 85 of both relays. The power supply relay should also have voltage at terminal 85. If not, check the wiring.

3. Terminal 87 of fuel pump relay should have voltage when the starter is operated. If not, check the wiring. If the wiring is good, check the relay. If the relay is good, replace the control unit.

POWER SUPPLY RELAY

Testing

1. Turn the ignition switch ON. Connect a test lamp to terminal 30 and 86. The test lamp should light. If not, check the wiring.

2. Connect a test lamp between terminal 86 and 87. If the test lamp does not light, replace the power supply relay.

FUEL PUMP

Testing

1. Connect a test lamp between terminal 30 and 96. The test lamp should light while cranking engine. If not, check the wiring to terminal 20 of control unit. If wiring is good, replace control unit.

2. Connect test lamp to terminal 87. Test lamp should light while cranking engine. If not, replace fuel pump relay.

DECELERATION/IDLE SWITCH

Close the throttle valve. Turn the adjusting screw so that the switch just closes. From this position, turn the adjusting screw exactly one turn farther in. Secure the screw with sealant.

FULL THROTTLE ENRICHMENT SWITCH

Loosen the switch retaining screw. Open the throttle valve fully. Move the switch until the cut-in position is reached. The roller should be nearly in center of the cam disk. Tighten the retaining screws.

DIGIFANT ENGINE CONTROL

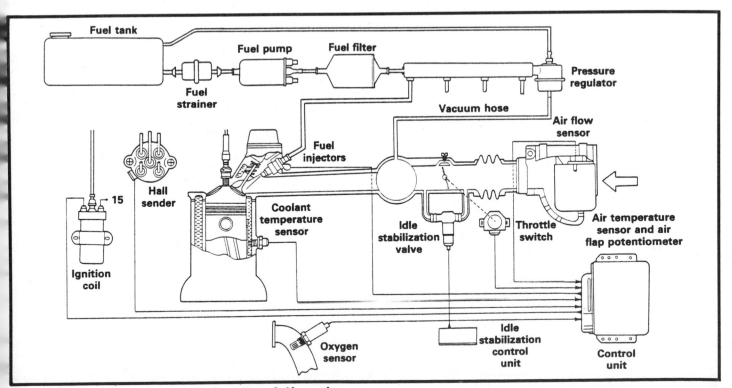

Digifant fuel and ignition control system 2.1L engine

General Information

The 2.1 liter engine is equipped with Digifant fuel and ignition control system. Digifant is a development of the Digijet fuel injection system combined with the map controlled digital ignition system. Through the use of a single control unit, all of the functions of the fuel system, ignition system and oxygen sensor system are carefully controlled to provide optimum mixture and ignition control for improvements in acceleration, deceleration and overall driveability.

The Digifant system features a larger throttle bore diameter, increased from 45mm–50mm. An idle stabilization system has been incorporated to further streamline the system and eliminate the need for a digital idle stabilizer and auxiliary air regulator. Fuel injection control is electronic and is based on the measurement of air entering the intake and on engine speed measured by the Hall sender. The coolant temperature sensor provides correction during engine starting and warm up.

The oxygen sensor, intake air temperature sensor and throttle switch provide the control unit with additional information to assure smooth performance under all driving conditions. A separate control unit is used for the idle stabilization valve. Ignition timing control is determined by an engine speed signal from the Hall sender and a load signal from the air sensor. A signal from the coolant temperature sensor provides a correction factor.

Components

ELECTRONIC CONTROL UNIT (ECU)

The Digifant electronic control unit incorporates all the functions of the fuel system and ignition system and provides both the actuation signal for the fuel injectors and optimum ignition timing point for all engine operating conditions. Injection duration opening signals are provided based on the following inputs:
- Engine speed
- Intake air volume
- Coolant temperature

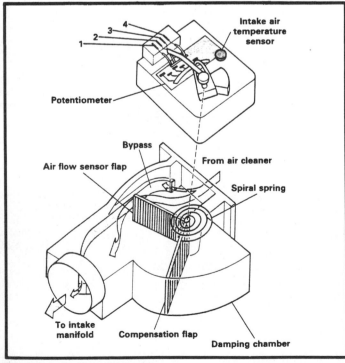

Digifant air flow sensor

- Oxygen content in the exhaust gas
- Battery voltage
- Throttle position
- Intake air temperature

COOLANT TEMPERATURE SENSOR

The coolant temperature sensor is a negative temperature coefficient resistor (NTC). The resistance signal it produces is used by the control unit to determine the amount of cold start and warm-up enrichment, ignition timing and idle stabilization during warm-up and when the oxygen sensor, idle stabilization and full throttle enrichment functions are activated.

FUEL PUMP

The fuel pump is a roller cell design. It is driven by a permanent magnet electric motor and is located near the fuel tank. Steel rollers are held in "cut-outs" on the rotor. Centrifugal force seals the rollers against the walls of the pressure chamber as the rotor spins. Fuel that is trapped between the rollers is forced out the delivery port. The pump is designed to be both cooled and lubricated by the fuel flowing through it. The pump delivers several times the amount of fuel needed to operate the engine at any time. Excess fuel is returned to the fuel tank via the fuel pressure regulator.

AIR FLOW SENSOR

The air flow sensor measures the amount of air entering the intake manifold and sends a voltage signal to the control unit. Intake air opens the air flow sensor flap which actuates the potentiometer to determine the voltage signal. This signal and the engine speed information supplied by the Hall sender are used as principal inputs for the determination of fuel injector opening duration and ignition timing points. A compensation flap connected to the air sensor dampens sudden movements of the air sensor flap due to oscillations of the intake air.

INTAKE AIR TEMPERATURE SENSOR

An intake air temperature sensor is mounted in the air flow sensor housing. It is a negative temperature coefficient (NTC) resistor, which means its resistance value drops as its temperature increases. The signal it supplies to the control unit is used to modify fuel injection rate depending on intake air temperature. The sensor can be tested by measuring the resistance value of the sensor and comparing the reading to a graph.

FUEL PRESSURE REGULATOR

The system pressure regulator maintains a constant fuel pressure to all injectors by regulating the quantity of fuel returned to the fuel tank. The regulator is connected to the intake manifold. It responds to manifold vacuum fluctuations, and thereby compensates for engine-load changes. When the engine is shut off, the regulator closes and seals to maintain residual fuel pressure in the injector lines for improved hot-start capability.

FUEL INJECTORS

Digifant fuel injectors are electronically controlled on/off valves. A solenoid actuates a needle valve allowing fuel to be forced through the injector nozzle. All four injectors open at the same time and inject fuel directly into the intake manifold near the intake valve. Injection quantity is controlled by the amount of time the injectors stay open. Injector opening time is regulated by the ECU, based on inputs from the various engine sensors.

NOTE: Digifant injectors (yellow body) are not interchangeable with AFC injectors (blue body).

THROTTLE SWITCH

Digifant uses a single throttle switch to signal the ECU when the throttle plate is in the fully closed (idle) or fully open (full load) position. The signal enables the ECU to determine that one of the three auxiliary functions (idle stabilization, deceleration fuel shut-off, or full load enrichment) is required and activate the appropriate circuit.

The throttle switch is an NOC switch, or normally open unless actuated. The contact arm is actuated by a cam with two eccentrics which attaches to the throttle plate shaft. One eccentric closes the contacts in the fully closed (idle stabilization or decel. fuel shut-off) position, and the other in the fully open (full load enrichment) position.

NOTE: The correct adjustment of the throttle switch is very important. If switch is misadjusted, engine may surge at idle or cut out during steady driving or light acceleration.

FUEL FILTERS

Two types of fuel filters are used on the Digifant system; one is a square plastic fuel strainer which is mounted before the fuel pump to protect it from foreign particles, while the main fuel filter is a metal cylinder which mounts behind the fuel pump. It has a finer filtering mesh to protect the injection components. Both are lifetime filters and do not require replacement under normal circumstances.

OXYGEN SENSOR

The oxygen sensor is made of a ceramic material called Zirconium dioxide. The inner and outer surfaces of the ceramic material are coated with platinum. The outer platinum surface is exposed to the exhaust gas, while the inner surface is exposed to the outside air.

The difference in the amount of oxygen contacting the inner and outer surfaces of the oxygen sensor creates a pressure differential which results in a small voltage signal in the range of 175–1100mV (0.175-1.1 V) being supplied to the ECU. The amount of voltage that is produced is determined by the fuel mixture.

The oxygen sensor is heated electrically to keep it at a constant operating temperature. This insures continuous and accurate reaction of the sensor during all operating conditions. The heated oxygen sensor has three wires, two for the heating element (ground and power) and a signal wire for the oxygen sensor. Power is supplied to the heating element whenever the ignition is on.

The oxygen sensor has a 60,000 mile replacement interval. A mileage counter will activate a warning light on the dash at 60,000 miles. At this time, the oxygen sensor should be replaced and the mileage counter reset.

IGNITION SYSTEM

The map controlled ignition system operates on the principle of a timing map which is programmed into the ECU Information on engine load, speed and coolant temperature are provided to the ECU in the form of voltage signals. In the ECU these signals are processed so that the ignition coil is controlled via terminal No. 1 in accordance with the programmed ignition map. The separate ignition control unit and digital idle stabilizer used in the past have been eliminated.

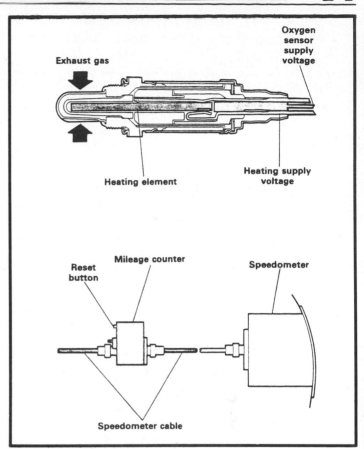

Digifant air flow sensor

An engine speed signal comes from the Hall sender in the distributor, and measurement of engine load is accomplished through a signal from the air sensor potentiometer. These two signals establish the ignition timing point. They are stored in the ignition map in the control unit's memory as 256 single operational points, 16 fixed points for each engine load point and 16 for each rpm point.

The engine coolant temperature sensor signals the control unit to determine ignition timing based on engine temperature. Throughout the engine warm-up phase, ignition timing is constantly being corrected. Once the engine reaches operating temperature, the timing is determined by the map.

IDLE STABILIZATION

The idle stabilization system used on the Digifant system insures that the idle speed remains constant at predetermined levels. The system controls the amount of air bypassing the throttle plate. If engine idle speed varies from the value stored in the control unit, the idle stabilizer valve will adjust the volume of air entering the engine at idle. This maintains idle speed within certain limits.

The idle stabilizer valve is operated by a control unit located in the engine compartment near the air cleaner intake hose. The control unit receives inputs from the following components:

- Throttle switch
- Coolant temperature sensor
- A/C compressor clutch
- Ignition coil terminal No. 1
- Automatic transmission selector switch
- Power Steering pressure switch

Entire electrical system can be checked by disconnecting multi-pin connector of control unit.

OHMMETER TO TERMINAL:	COMPONENTS	CHECKS/TEST CONDITIONS	SPECIFICATIONS
2 and 13	Oxygen Sensor	• Connector Disconnected and Grounded • Connector Connected	0 ohms ∞ ohms
6 and 9	Temp. Sensor I (Intake Air Temp.)	• Resistance	Corresponding with graph shown below
6 and 10	Temp. Sensor II (Coolant Temp.)	• Resistance	
6 and 11	Throttle Switch	• Idle Position • Full Throttle Pos.	0 ohms 0 ohms
6 and 17	Air Flow Sensor	• Resistance/Potentiometer	500-1000 ohms
12 and 14	Fuel Injectors	• Resistance	Approx. 3-5 ohms
17 and 21	Air Flow Sensor	• Resistance/Potentiometer	Ohms fluctuate as sensor plate is opened
Check at Components	Individual Fuel Injectors	Resistance	14 to 18 ohms
13 and Ground	Control Unit Ground Connection	Wiring	0 ohms
VOLTMETER TO TERMINAL:	**COMPONENTS**	**CHECKS**	**SPECIFICATIONS**
1 and 13	• Wiring From Starter • Starting Injection/Enrichment	• Voltage at Terminal 50 During Cranking	Cranking voltage
3 and 13 Bridged	Fuel Pump Relay	• Ignition ON	Fuel pump runs
13 and 14	Power Supply Relay	• Ignition ON	Battery voltage

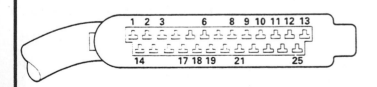

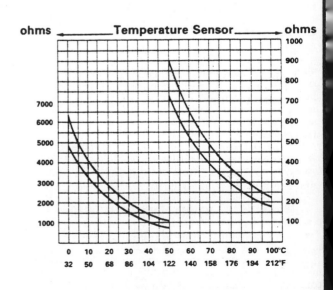

Digifant system check with Volt/Ohmmeter

With this system, the auxiliary air regulator and digital idle stabilizer are eliminated and any periodic idle adjustment is no longer required.

CRANKCASE EMISSION CONTROL

Crankcase vapors are drawn through a breather valve and vapor separator into the intake manifold where they are distributed to all cylinders. The breather valve operates via intake manifold vacuum. When manifold vacuum is high, such as at idle and during deceleration, the valve is closed as spring pressure on the valve seat is overcome. As manifold vacuum drops, such as highway speeds, the valve opens to allow more vapors to be admitted into the intake manifold.

A heating element is used in the crankcase vent line to prevent icing during cold engine operation. This element has a 5.5 mm hole in the restrictor plate. The element can be checked with an ohmmeter. Resistance should be between 4 ohms and 17 ohms at 25°C (77°F). The circuitry to operate the heating element is protected by an in-line, 5 amp fuse (SAE type) located in the wiring connector box in the engine compartment.

EVAPORATIVE EMISSION SYSTEM

Fuel vapors are collected in the expansion tanks. There, any liquid gasoline collects and flows back into the tank through the vent lines. Fuel vapors are drawn from the tops of the expansion tanks and flow to the carbon canister where they are stored when the engine is not running. After the engine is started the control valve is opened by throttle vacuum. Fresh air is drawn into the bottom of the canister, there it collects fuel vapors from the canister and is then drawn into the intake manifold.

Troubleshooting and Diagnosis

AIR FLOW SENSOR/INTAKE AIR TEMPERATURE SENSOR TEST

The following tests are to verify proper function of the air flow sensor, related wiring and connectors.
1. Make sure ignition switch is OFF.
2. Disconnect multi-pin connector from ECU.
3. Connect ohmmeter to terminals of multi-pin connector to test wiring and air flow sensor.
4. If readings do not meet specifications, disconnect electrical connector at air flow sensor.
5. Connect ohmmeter to terminals shown to connector pins of air flow sensor to test component. If okay, check wiring. If not, replace air flow sensor and retest.

COOLANT TEMPERATURE SENSOR TEST

The following checks are to verify proper function of the coolant temperature sensor, related wiring and connectors.
1. Make sure the ignition switch is OFF.
2. Disconnect multi-pin connector from ECU
3. Measure temperature of coolant temperature sensor with probe type thermometer.
4. Connect ohmmeter to terminals 6 and 9 of multi-pin connector of ECU and check the resistance.
5. If resistance is not within specifications, disconnect connector from coolant temperature sensor at sensor. Do not let connector contact exhaust manifold.
6. Connect ohmmeter to terminals of coolant sensor. Resistance should correspond to graph below. If not, replace sensor. If okay, check wiring.

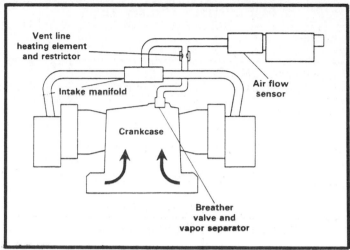

Digifant crankcase emission control

FUEL PUMP PRESSURE TEST

1. Connect pressure gauge US 1076 or VW 1318 (or equivalent) to fuel line T-piece. If using VW 1318 pressure gauge, the lever must be in a closed position.
2. Remove fuel pump relay and bridge terminals 30 and 87 with tool US 4480/3.
3. Run fuel pump and observe pressure. Pressure must be a minimum of 36 psi. If not, continue with next test.

FUEL PUMP VOLUME TEST

1. Be sure that the fuel tank is at least half full of fuel. Disconnect fuel return line at pressure regulator.
2. Attach about 4 feet of fuel line to the return line of the pressure regulator. Place other end of fuel line into a 1 liter measuring container.
3. Remove the fuel pump relay and bridge terminals 30 and 87 with tool US 4480/3.
4. Run the fuel pump for exactly 30 seconds. Delivery quantity should be at least 500cc.
5. If delivery quantity is not within specification, check the fuel flow from the tank before and after the fuel filters. If fuel flow from the tank is not obstructed, continue to with the next test.

FUEL PUMP ELECTRICAL TEST

1. Be sure that the battery is fully charged.
2. Connect an ammeter to the fuel pump, in series with a power supply to the fuel pump.
3. Remove the fuel pump relay bridge terminals 30 and 87 with tool US 4480/3.
4. Ammeter readings should be approximately 2.5–3.5 amps. Lower reading may indicate poor ground. Higher reading may indicate dragging pump motor, pump must be replaced.

FUEL PUMP POWER SUPPLY RELAY TEST

1. Position the ignition switch to the ON detent.
2. Check terminal 86 of the power supply relay with a voltmeter. It should read battery voltage.
3. Check terminal 87 of the power supply relay. It should read battery voltage.
4. If not, remove the power supply relay, check terminal 30 for battery voltage and terminal 85 for ground. If both are okay, replace power supply relay.

FUEL PUMP RELAY TEST

1. Check terminal 86 of the fuel pump relay for battery voltage. Check terminal 30 for battery voltage.
2. Remove the fuel pump relay and check terminal 85 for ground from terminal 3 of ECU while cranking. If no ground is indicated, check continuity from terminal 85 of the fuel pump relay holder to terminal 3 of ECU. If the continuity is okay, replace the ECU.
3. Reinstall the fuel pump relay. Turn the ignition OFF and then back ON and check terminal 87 for battery voltage. Battery voltage will only be indicated for about 5 seconds after switching on ignition.
4. If voltage is present, check the continuity from terminal 87 of the relay to the fuel pump, and from the fuel pump to ground. If the continuity is okay, replace the fuel pump.

FUEL PRESSURE REGULATOR TEST

1. Connect pressure gauge US 1076 or VW 1318, or equivalent, to the fuel line T-piece. If using VW 1318 pressure gauge, the lever must be in a closed position during the measurement procedure.
2. Run engine at idle speed and check pressure. With the vacuum hose on the pressure regulator connected, the pressure should be 33 psi. With the vacuum hose disconnected, the pressure should be 36 psi.

RESIDUAL PRESSURE TEST

1. Stop the engine, wait 10 minutes, then check the residual fuel pressure. Pressure should be 29–36 PSI.
2. If not, check the fuel pump check valve by clamping off the line from the fuel pump.
3. If not, check the fuel pressure regulator by clamping off the return line to the tank.
4. If not, check the fuel injectors by clamping off the lines from the injectors to the pressure regulator. If necessary, leak test the individual injectors.
4. Observe the pressure gauge while clamping off each of the above individual lines. If pressure drop ceases or slows dramatically, the problem is in the indicated component. Use care not to damage the lines with clamping device.

FUEL INJECTOR TEST

1. Remove the fuel injector in pairs (left bank or right bank). Leave the wires connected to the injectors.
2. Disconnect the electrical plugs from the injectors which are to remaine installed.
3. Hold the injectors in a jar or pan with paper towel in bottom of the jar or pan.
4. Operate the starter briefly. The spray pattern must be even and coneshaped.
5. Reinstall the fuel injectors, using new sealing rings.
6. Repeat the procedure for remaining pair of injectors.

INJECTION QUANTITY TEST

1. Disconnect the electrical plugs from the injectors.
2. Pull out the injector to be tested and place it in a graduated container.
3. Connect jumper wires to the injector to be tested, one from terminal 15 of ignition coil and one from ground.
4. Switch on ignition.
5. Remove the fuel pump relay bridge terminals 30 and 87 with tool US 4480, or equivalent. Run the pump for exactly 30 seconds. Delivery quantity must be a minimum of 87cc after 30 seconds. If not, replace injector and retest.
6. If still not to specifications, check fuel pump volume.

LEAK TEST

1. Remove electrical plugs at fuel injectors.
2. Remove injectors in pairs but leave connected to fuel ring line.
3. Turn ignition ON for about 5 seconds, this operates the fuel pump.
4. Check that no more than 2 drops of fuel leak from each injector in one minute.

COMPONENT TEST

1. Remove the electrical plugs at the fuel injectors.
2. Connect an ohmmeter across the injector terminals the reading should be approximately 14–18 ohms.

WIRING TEST

1. Touch the injectors while cranking the engine. You can feel the mechanical operation of the injector, and the function of the electro-magnetic solenoid.
2. If the injectors are not actuating, Disconnect all electrical plugs from fuel injectors.
3. Bridge the contacts of one plug with tool US 1115, or equivalent.
4. Operate the starter briefly, the diode must flicker. Repeat the above procedure on remaining plug contacts.
5. If the diode does not flicker, reverse test leads and repeat procedure to insure correct polarity of tester connections.
6. If not, turn the ignition off and remove the multi-pin connector plug from the ECU. Reconnect the electrical plugs to the fuel injectors.
7. Connect an ohmmeter to terminals 12 and 14 of the multi-pin connector plug. This will check the total resistance of all injectors including wiring to the ECU and power supply relay. The resistance reading should be approximately 3–5 ohms.
8. If the total resistance is within specification, replace the ECU. If the total resistance is not within specification, replace the harness.

NOTE: Since the internal resistance of the measuring instruments and the ambient temperature have a large influence on the readings, the test should be conducted with a digital multimeter.

THROTTLE SWITCH WIRING AND ECU CHECK

1. Be sure that the coolant temperature is above 60°C (140°F).
2. Turn the ignition switch to the ON position.
3. Disconnect the throttle switch electrical connector.
4. Check the voltage across the two female connectors at the wiring to ECU. Voltage should be approximately 5 volts.

NOTE: Do not use test a light for checking either voltage or throttle switch operation because damage to the circuitry of the ECU will result.

5. If voltage is not within specification, check the wiring and electrical connectors to the ECU for breakage or poor connection.
6. Reconnect the throttle switch and connect an ohmmeter between terminals 6 and 11 (4 and 7 for Digijet System) of the ECU multi-pin connector plug.
7. The reading should be approximately 0 ohms with the throttle in the fully closed or fully open position. If within specification, replace the ECU.

IDLE SWITCH

1. The results of the previous test must be satisfactory, before proceeding.
2. The Temperature at the coolant temperature sensor must be a minimum of 140°F and resistance of the sensor must be 550 ohms or less.
3. Disconnect the throttle switch connector.
4. Bridge the two female connectors of the wiring harness of the ECU together using bridge end of tool VW 1490 or equivalent.
5. Start the engine.
6. Raise the engine speed above 3000 rpm and then return to idle.
7. Operate the throttle valve by hand and slowly open the throttle valve slightly. Engine speed must fluctuate.
8. If not, replace the ECU. If okay, check the full throttle switch.

FULL THROTTLE SWITCH

1. The results of the previous test must be satisfactory, before proceeding.
2. The temperature at the coolant temperature sensor must be a minimum of 140°F and the resistance 550 ohms or less.
3. Connect a CO tester. Start the engine and let it idle for approximately two minutes.
4. Disconnect the throttle switch connector.
5. Slowly increase engine speed to approximately 4500 rpm. CO must read 0.3–0.1 % Vol.
6. With the engine speed at 4500 rpm bridge the female terminals of the throttle switch connector using the bridge end of tool VW 1490. The CO reading must increase in volume by approximately 1% or more.
7. If not, replace ECU. If okay, adjust the full throttle switch.

Adjustment

1. Disconnect the throttle switch connector.
2. Connect an ohmmeter to the two male connectors at the throttle switch (No.1).
3. Start the engine, the ohmmeter reading must be 0 ohms a idle.
4. Slightly open the throttle, the ohmmeter reading should go to infinity.
5. Slowly close the throttle to idle position. The ohmmeter reading must return to 0 ohms.

NOTE: Correct adjustment is very important. If the switch is misadjusted, the engine may surge or cut-out during steady or light throttle acceleration.

6. Stop the engine.
7. Using the accelerator pedal, open the throttle fully, the ohmmeter must read infinity.
8. If the ohmmeter readings are not correct, adjust the throttle switch.

THROTTLE SWITCH

Adjustment

1. Loosen the allen head retaining screw slightly (No. 2).
2. Open the throttle valve and than slowly close it.
3. Measure the switch point with a feeler gauge between the idle-stop and idle-stop screw (Gap A). At the point where the switch contacts close, Gap A must be between 0.002–0.004 in.
4. If not, correct by adjusting the position of the switch using an allen head cam-screw (No. 3). Do not tamper with the setting on the idle-stop screw.

5. Tighten retaining screw (No. 2). Recheck the adjustment using the engine rpm method above. If the ohmmeter readings are correct, reinstall the throttle switch connector and continue.
6. If not, replace the throttle switch.

OXYGEN SENSOR CHECK

1. Be sure that the engine is at operating temperature. Start the engine and allow it to idle for two minutes.
2. With the oxygen sensor connected, remove the hose from the pressure regulator. Plug the hose.
3. The CO should increase briefly, then drop in valve to 0.3–0.1 %. If not, proceed to determine whether the problem is with the oxygen sensor or with the ECU.
4. Turn off the engine. Disconnect oxygen sensor. The oxygen sensor must be disconnected with the ignition off, to cancel the meory in the electronic control unit (ECU).
5. Start the engine. Hold the disconnected oxygen sensor wire from ECU to gorund. The CO content must rise.
6. If not, check for continuity of the wiring to ECU terminals 2 and 13, using a volt/ohmmeter.
7. If continuity is okay, replace the ECU.

IGNITION SYSTEM CHECK

1. If spark is not present at terminal No.4 of the ignition coil when cranking, check for battery voltage at terminal 15 of the ignition coil with ignition switch in the ON position.
2. If not, trace the wiring and correct the fault.
3. If yes, connectt tool US 1115 to terminal 1 of the ignition coil and crank engine. The diode must flash while cranking.
4. If so, replace the ignition coil. If not, check the hall system.

HALL SYSTEM CHECK

Part A

1. Remove the wiring connector from the distributor.
2. Position the ignition switch in the ON position.
3. Measure the voltage at the outer terminals of the wiring connector. The reading should be a minimum of 5 volts. If voltage is present, go to Part B.
4. If voltage is not present at the outer terminals, remove the wiring connector from the fuel injection ECU and check for voltage across terminals 13 and 14.
5. If battery voltage is present, check for continuity between terminal 6 of the fuel injection ECU and the brown/white wire at the distributor wiring connector and terminal 8 of the ECU and the red/black wire at the distributor wiring connector.
6. If the wiring is okay, replace the fuel injection ECU and retest.

Part B

1. Reconnect the wiring connector to the distributor and peel back rubber boot.
2. Connect a voltmeter between the center terminal of the wiring connector and the positive terminal of the battery.
3. Crank the engine. The voltmeter reading should fluctuate. If not, replace the hall sender and retest.
4. If the voltage reading flucuates, check for continuity between the center terminal (green wire) of the distributor wiring connector and terminal 18 of ECU. If okay, replace the ECU.

IDLE STABILIZATION CHECK

Test One

1. Be sure that the engine is at operating temperature and the oil temperature at least 176°F.

2. Be sure that the throttle switch is connected and functioning properly.

3. All electrical accessories must be off during this checking procedure. The coolant fan should not be running when observing readings.

4. Connect multimeter US 1119, or equivalent, to the idle stabilization valve test adapter VW 1315A/2. Set the range of the meter to the 2 amp scale the readings will be in milliamperes.

5. Run engine at idle and observe the reading. Basic idle should be 430 ± 15 mA. If no, go to Idle Speed/CO Content-Checking and Adjusting.

6. If you have a fixed (non-fluctuating milliamp reading) and the idle is high (approximately 1100–1200 rpm), check for signal from terminal 1 of ignition coil at connector plug for idle stabilizer control unit. Connect US 1115 L.E.D. tester bewteen terminals 5 and 17 of connector plug. L.E.D. tester should flash while cranking.

7. If yes, replace the idle stabilization control unit and proceed. If no, repair the open circuit between terminal 1 of ignition coil and terminal 17 of idle stabilization control unit plug.

8. If you have no milliamp reading and idle is low and/or surging, check for power to the idle stabilization control unit from terminal 87 of the power supply relay. Connect US 1115 L.E.D. tester between terminals 5 and 14 of idle stabilization control unit plug. The L.E.D. tester should come on when the ignition is switched on.

9. If not, repair the open circuit between terminal 87 of the power supply relay and terminal 14 of idle stabilization control unit plug.

Test Two

NOTE: The following test should be done with a partner performing the specified operations while you observe the milliampere readings. The drive wheels should be raised off the ground during operations which require the vehicle to be in gear.

AUTOMATIC TRANSMISSION

1. Connect VW tool 1315/2 and US tool 1119 to the idle stabilizer valve, set meter to mA scale.

2. With the engine idling and the emergency brake firmly engaged, place the gearshift lever in drive. While observing multimeter the milliamp reading should increase.

3. If not, remove the idle stabilization control unit. Connect US tool 1119 between terminals 5 and 6 of the connector plug for the idle stabilization control unit and set it to the 2 volt range. Run the engine at idle. The reading should be 0 volts in park or neutral, 0.1 volt is acceptable, and increase to between 0.5–1.0 volt when placed in any drive gear.

4. If the system performs accordingly, replace idle stabilization control unit. If not, locate and repair the problem from neutral safety switch to terminal 6 of the connector plug for the idle stabilization control unit.

AIR CONDITIONING

1. With the engine idling, turn on the A/C while observing the multimeter. The milliamp reading should increase.

2. If not, remove the idle stabilization control unit. Connect US tool 1115 L.E.D. tester between terminals 2 and 5 of the connector plug for the idle stabilization control unit. Start the engine and switch the A/C on and off. The L.E.D. must light when A/C is off.

3. If it does replace idle stabilization control valve. If not, ensure that the A/C compressor clutch is functioning properly, repair, if necessary, and re-test. Check the wiring from the A/C compressor clutch to terminal 2 of connector plug for the idle stabilization unit.

POWER STEERING

1. With the engine idling, turn the steering wheel hard from the left stop or to the right stop while observing the multimeter. The milliamp reading should increase.

2. If not, remove the idle stabilization control unit. Connect US 1115 L.E.D. tester to terminals 5 and 15 of the connector plug. Start the engine and turn the wheels to the left or right stop. The L.E.D. tester must come on with wheels turned hard to stop.

3. If so, replace idle stabilization control unit. If not, check the operation of the power steering pressure switch. The switch must close with the engine running and the wheels turned hard to either the right or left stop.

4. If not, replace the power steering pressure switch. If yes, check the power steering pump pressure.

NOTE: The amount of increase in the milliamp readings for the preceding steps id dependent upon numerous factors. Of primary concern is that the milliamp readings do increase for each step, which indicates that the idle stabilization control unit is compensating for the prescribed load change. If the idle speed stabilization control unit is functioning properly, but the idle drops drastically or the engine stalls when a load is applied, the problem is with the idle stabilizer valve.

EVAPORATIVE EMISSION SYSTEM

Control Valve Check

1. Run engine at idle until normal operating temperature is reached.

2. Remove the white nylon purge line from the rubber boot at the right rear of the intake air distributor. Attach a hand operated vacuum pump to the open end of the purge line. Apply 5–10 in. of vacuum. The control valve should retain vacuum.

3. If not remove the purple vacuum line from the fitting on the throttle valve housing and install the vacuum gauge on the fitting. At idle, there must be less than 1 in. of vacuum available at fitting. If not, adjust the throttle valve stop screw.

4. Repeat the first two checks and see if the control valve retains vacuum at idle. Accelerate the engine by hand, the control valve must release vacuum.

5. If not, either the vacuum fitting on the throttle valve housing is plugged or the control valve is stuck in the closed position.

Leak Check

1. Remove the small hose "A" from the top of the charcoal filter. Connect it to leak tester US 4487.

2. Set the leak tester scale to 0. Use a soap and water solution as a leak test agent.

3. Pressurize the system with a hand pump to 3.3 cm of mercury. The system is functioning properly if the pressure is 2.54 cm or greater after 5 minutes. The system is leaking if the pressure drops below 2.54 cm after 5 minutes.

IGNITION TIMING

Adjustment

1. With the engine idling, disconnect the coolant temperature sensor and terminal 1 input to idle stabilization control unit. Do not let the connector hang down onto the exhaust manifold.

2. The engine speed will increase approximately 2000–2500 rpm. Manually increase the engine speed to this specification if necessary.

3. Timing specification is 5 ± 2 degrees BTDC. If out of specification adjust to 5 ± 1 degrees BTDC.

4. Reconnect the coolant temperature sensor and terminal 1 of the input idle stabilization control unit.

5. Increase the engine speed to 3500 rpm. Timing specification is 35 ± 5 degrees BTDC.

IDLE SPEED AND CO CONTENT

Adjustment

1. With ignition switch turned off, disconnect the oxygen sensor. The oxygen sensor must be disconnected with the ignition off in order to cancel a memory function in the ECU.

2. Connect a multimeter to the idle stabilization valve using test adapter VW 1315A/2. Set the range of meter to measure a minimum of 2 amps of current, readings will be in milliamperes.

3. Run the engine at idle and observe the reading. The reading should be 410–450 mA for the idle stabilizer, with an idle speed of approximately 880 + 50 rpm, with the coolant fan not running.

4. If not within specification, adjust by turning the idle screw on the throttle housing. Reconnect the no. 1 input to the idle stabilizer control unit.

5. Disconnect the harness plug from the idle stabilizer valve. The idle should remain relatively steady at 880 + 50 rpm.

6. Reconnect the harness plug to the idle stabilizer. Observe the CO reading. The CO content must be within specification.

7. To adjust the CO, remove screw caps as follows. Drill the CO adjusting screw cap using a 0.098 in. drill. Thread a 0.137 in. sheet metal screw into the drilled hole. Grasp the screw with a pliers, and pull out the cap.

8. Recheck the idle speed/milliampere adjustment and correct if necessary. Recheck the CO content and adjust if necessary.

9. Repeat this procedure until both idle setting, and CO content are within specifications. econnect the oxygen sensor. The CO% must return to normal specification of 0.3–1.1%. If not, Ckeck the oxygen sensor.

THROTTLE VALVE

Adjustment

NOTE: The stop screw is set at the factory and should not be moved. If the screw position has been altered, check and adjust as required.

1. Turn the adjusting screw out until a gap exists between the stop and the screw. Turn the screw in until it touches the stop.

2. In order to determine the exact point of contact with the screw stop, place a thin piece of paper between screw and the stop. Slide the paper and turn screw at same time until the screw pinches the paper.

3. Turn the screw clockwisean additional ½ turn. Check the idle speed and the CO content. Adjust if necessary.

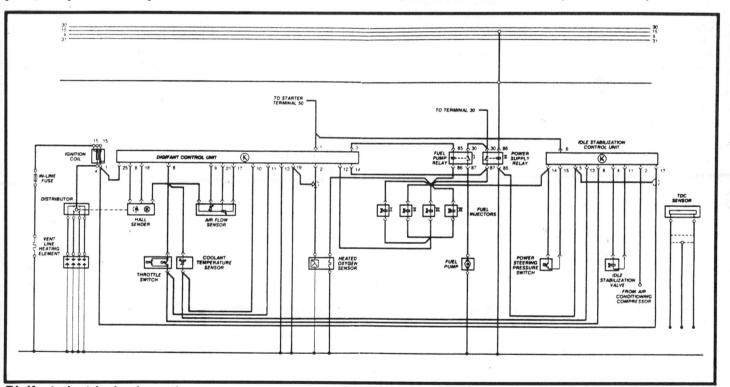

Digifant electrical schematic

DIGIFANT II

General Information

Digifant II is further development of the Digifant system. The Digifant II system uses a knock sensor. The control unit circuitry for the idle stabilization system is incorporated in the electronic control unit.

Throught the use of sophisticated electronic controls, all functions of the fuel and ignition systems are carefully controlled to provide a fuel efficient engine with good performance.

Component Inspection and Adjustment

CRANKCASE CONTROL VALVE

The crankcase emission control system is a closed system. Therefore, no crankcase emissions are discharged into the atmosphere. During operation the blow-by gases from the crankcase will be drawn from the valve cover to the throttle body. A crankcase emission control valve which is mounted to the valve cover regulates the amount of crankcase emissions entering the throttle body.

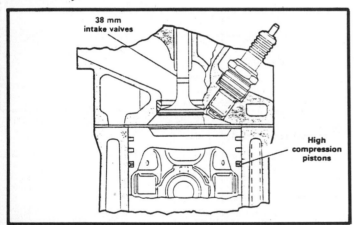

Cutaway view of a 1.8L engine, Digifant II

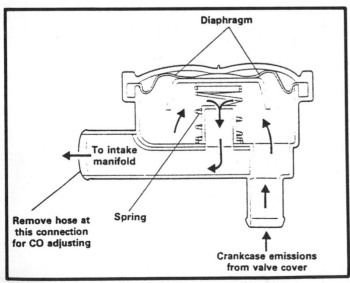

Digifant II crankcase emission control valve

When checking and adjusting CO content the hose from from the crankcase emission control valve is removed at the valve cover and the hose is plugged. The valve vents to atmosphere during checking and adjusting.

EXHAUST SYSTEM

Two exhaust systems are used. A single take down pipe on the 100 hp engine, and a double take down pipe on the 105 hp engine. The 100 hp engine take down pipe is made from hot aluminized steel and stainless steel for long life and freedom from corrosion. The swivel joint is similar to that which was used on vehicles with the CIS-E fuel injection.

The 105 hp engine has a double take down pipe and a larger exhaust manifold for better flow. This helps to improve the engine's torque and horsepower characteristics. The swivel joints on the 105 hp engine are made of corrugated stainless steel which connects the take down pipe to the exhaust manifold flange. This is the same part as used on the 16 valve engines.

ELECTRONIC CONTROL UNIT (ECU)

The heart of the Digifant II system is the new electronic control unit. The control unit incorporates all the functions of the fuel system and provides both the actuation signal for the fuel injectors and optimum ignition timing point for all engine operating conditions.

The control unit (ECU) receives the following inputs.
- Engine speed
- Intake air volume
- Coolant temperature
- Oxygen content in the exhaust gas
- Battery voltage
- Throttle position
- Intake air temperature

Digifant II therefore provides complete fuel injection and ignition control throughout the entire range of engine speed, load and temperature conditions. The injector opening time and ignition timing points are programmed in the control unit.

Fail safe functions are programmed into the control units memory so the system will continue to operate in the event of a fault in the coolant temperature sensor, oxygen sensor, or knock sensor. The ECU provides the ground for the fuel injectors. If the engine speed reaches 6500 rpm, the ECU interrupts the ground to the injectors, shutting off the fuel supply.

POWER SUPPLY RELAY

The power supply relay provides battery voltage to the ECU and fuel injectors.

FUEL PUMP RELAY

The fuel pump relay provides battery voltage to the fuel pump and the oxygen sensor heating element.

FUEL DELIVERY SYSTEM

The Digifant II fuel delivery system is similar to the system used with the CIS-E fuel injection system. However, the fuel pump pressure is reduced, and the fuel accumulator has been eliminated. The fuel pump is a roller cell design and is cooled and lubricated by the fuel flowing through it. The fuel pump has a check valve on the output side to help maintain residual pressure when the pump has been shut off. The fuel pressure regulator has a check valve as well which also aids in maintaining residual pressure.

The transfer pump in the fuel tank which supplies fuel to the reservoir is the same as used in the CIS-E fuel system. The fuel filter ia a lifetime fuel filter nd does not need replacing unless contaminated.

FUEL INJECTOR ASSEMBLY

The Digifant II fuel injector assembly includes, the injectors, the fuel pressure regulator, the service port for fuel pressure testing and injector wiring harness.

The complete assembly can be removed by removing the allen head mounting bolts. The injectors can be separated from the fuel rail by removing the "U" shaped clip.

The plastic injector inserts in the cylinder head have been changed to accept the new style injector. A 10mm wrench is needed to remove and install the inserts. When installing the inserts into the cylinder head, use D6 sealing compound or equivalent.

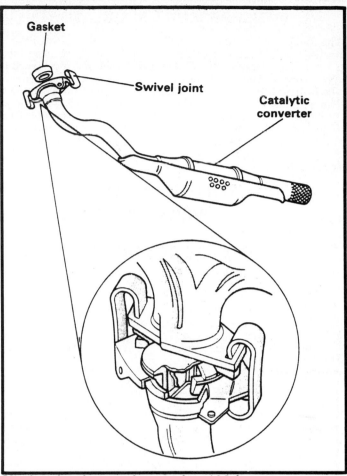

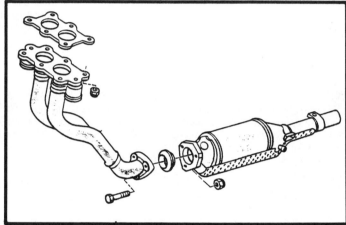

Double take down exhaust pipe 105 horsepower engine with Digifant II

Single take down exhaust pipe 100 horsepower engine with Digifant II

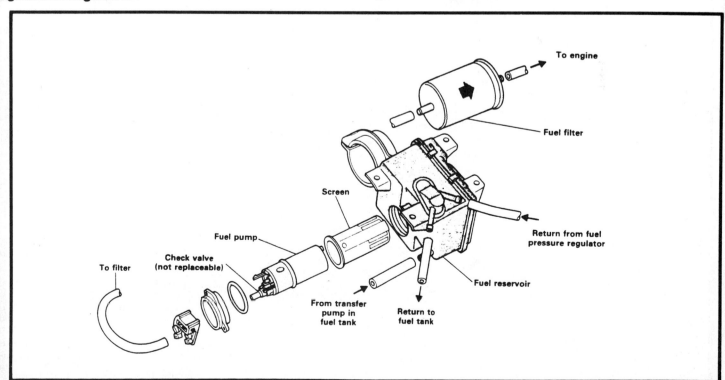

Digifant II fuel delivery system

FUEL PRESSURE REGULATOR

The fuel pressure regulator maintains approximately 2.5 bar of pressure at idle and up to 3.0 bar when the engine in under load. This is done by regulating th amount of fuel that is returned to the reservoir. The regulator mounts to the fuel injector assembly. A small filter screen is installed in the inlet of the regulator. The regulator has a vacuum hose that is connected to the intake manifold. The amount of vacuum supplied to the regulator helps control the amount of fuel that is returned to the fuel reservoir by moving the diaphragm inside the regulator. When the engine is shut off, the check valve closes and seals to maintain residual fuel pressure for restarting.

FUEL INJECTOR

Digifant II fuel injectors are electronically on/off valves. A solenoid actuates a needle valve allowing fuel to be forced through the injector nozzle. All four injectors open at the same time and inject fuel directly into the intake manifold near the intake valve. Injection quantity is controlled by the amount of time the injectors stay open. Injector opening time is regulated by the ECU, based on inputs from the various engine sensors.

The injectors are supplied 12 volts by the power supply relay. The ECU grounds the injector to control opening time. Internal resistance of each injector is 14–18 ohms. When checking all four injectors at the same time, the resistance should be 3.7–5.0 ohms.

AIR FILTER HOUSING

The Digifant II system is equipped with a vacuum operated preheat valve for the air intake system. The preheat valve is located on the air filter housing. A vacuum thermoswitch senses intake air temperature. The sensor controls the amount of vacuum to the preheat valve. The preheat valve regulates the amount of preheated air that is delivered to the intake manifold. Intake air is drawn into the filter housing behind the right headlight. The air flow sensor is bolted to th air filter housing.

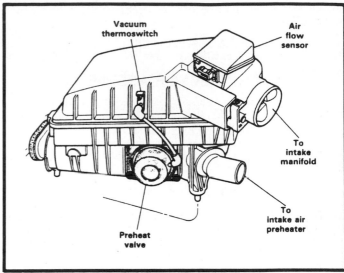

Digifant II air filter housing

AIR FLOW SENSOR

The air flow sensor measures the amount of air entering the intake manifold and sends a voltage signal to the control unit. Intake air opens the air flow sensor flap which actuates the potentiometer to determine the voltage signal. The signal and the engine speed information supplied by the Hall sender are used as the principal inputs for the determination of fuel injector opening duration and ignition timing points. A compensation flap is connected to the air sensor and dampens sudden movements of the air sensor flap due to oscillations of the intake air.

INTAKE AIR TEMPERATURE SENSOR

An intake temperature sensor is mounted in th air flow sensor

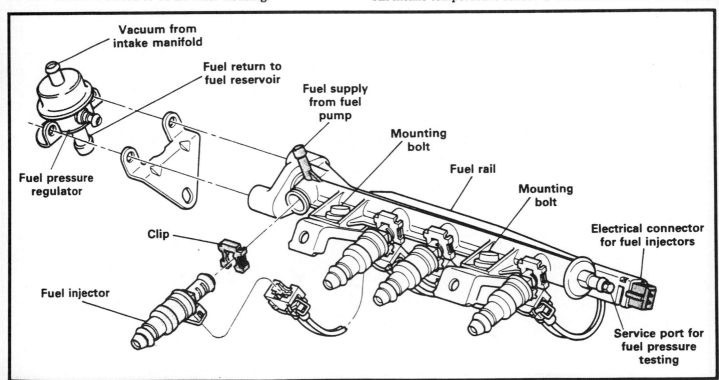

Digifant II fuel injector assembly

housing. It is a negative temperature coefficient (NTC) resistor, which means its resistance value drops as its temperature increases. The signal it supplies to the control unit is used to modify fuel injection rate depending on intake air temperature.

COOLANT TEMPERATURE SENSOR

The coolant temperature sensor is also a negative temperature coefficient resistor (NTC). The resistance signal it produces is used by the control unit to determine cold start enrichment. It also provides a signal to continue to enrich the mixture during engine warm up. The signals from this sensor also provide correction to ignition timing based on engine speed.

OXYGEN SENSOR

With Digifant II, a separate control unit and frequency value are not needed. The sensor is connected directly to the Digifant II ECU. The control unit uses the voltage signal from the oxygen sensor and adjusts th opening time of the injector to maintain proper air/fuel mixture. A heated oxygen sensor is used and is located at the front of the catalytic converter. Replacement inetrval for the oxygen sensor is every 60000 miles.

THROTTLE SWITCHES

The idle and full throttle switches are wired in parallel. The switchs are mounted on the throttle housing. A voltage signal is sent to the ECU when the throttle switch and throttle plates are closed. The switch opens when the throttle has been opened approximately 1°. The idle switch signal is used for, operation of idle stabilizer valve, operation of deceleration fuel shut off and activation of the special ignition timing map for deceleration. The full throttle switch closes about 10° before full throttle. This signal is used for full throttle enrichment.

IGNITION SYSTEM

The map controlled ignition system operates on the principle of a timing map which is programmed into the ECU. Information

on engine load, speed and coolant temperature are provided to the ECU in the form of voltage signals. In the ECU these signals are processed so that the ignition coil, is controlled via terminal #1 in accordance with the programmed ignition map.

An engine speed signal comes from the Hall sender in the distributor, and measurement of engine load is accomplished through a signal from the air sensor potentiometer. These two signals establish the ignition timing point. They are stored in the ignition map in the control units memory as 256 single operational points, 16 fixed points for each engine load point and 16 for each rpm point.

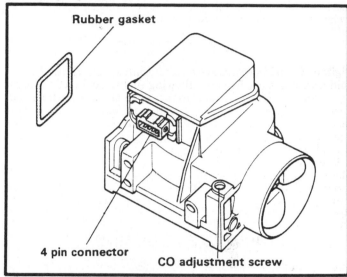

Digifant II air flow sensor

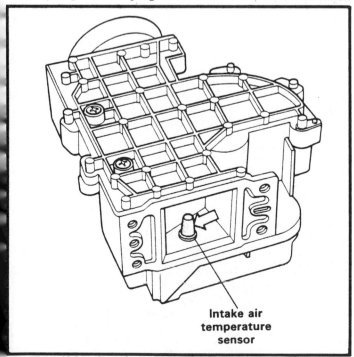

Digifant II intake air temperature sensor

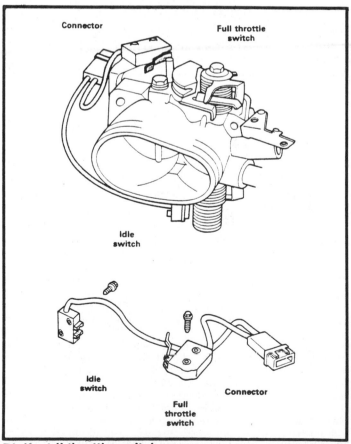

Digifant II throttle switches

The engine coolant temperature sensor signals the control unit to correct the ignition timing based on engine temperature. Throughout the engine warm-up phase, ignition timing is constantly being corrected. Once the engine reaches operating temperature, the timing is determined by the map. Ignition timing is also corrected through the use of a knock sensor.

KNOCK SENSOR

The knock sensor is attached to the left side of the cylinder block next to cylinder No. 2. It is a piezoelectric crystal encased in a metal and plastic housing.

Vibrations in the engine will cause the quartz crystal in the knock sensor to generate a small voltage. By monitoring this voltage, the ignition control unit can determine when ignition knock or detonation occurs. The ignition control unit will retard the ignition timing to prevent the ignition knock.

The construction of the knock sensor is slightly diffferent than previous versions. A steel bushing is located inside the sensor housing. This is to prevent the quartz crystal inside the sensor from being crushed or damaged by overtightening the installation bolt. The installation torque for this new sensor is 11–18 ft. lbs. No washers should be used on the installation bolt.

KNOCK SENSOR REGULATION

If a cylinder develops ignition knock, the Digifant II control unit will sense this through the knock sensor mounted on the engine block. The control unit will then retard the ignition timing 3.0 degrees for that cylinder. If the knocking stops, the ignition timing will be advanced in steps of 0.33 degrees back to the preprogrammed value.

If the knocking continues or recurs, the ignition timing can ber retarded up to 15 degrees for each cylinder. The difference between the two cylinders is limited to 9 degrees.

IGNITION DISTRIBUTOR

The ignition distributor has no centrifugal or vacuum advance. It contains a Hall sender which is operated by a trigger wheel. The trigger wheel has four apertures, one for each cylinder. The Hall sender sends a voltage signal to the ECU for each cylinder. From this signal, the control unit determines engine speed and crankshaft position.

IDLE STABILIZATION

The idle stabilization system used on the Digifant II system insures that the idle speed remains constant at predetermined levels. The system controls the amount of air bypassing the throttle plate. If the engine idle speed varies from the value stored in the control unit, the idle stabilizer valve will adjust the volume of air entering the engine at idle. This maintains idle speed within certain limits.

The idle stabilizer is operated by the ECU. The ECU receives inputs from the following components, the throttle switch, the coolant temperature switch, the A/C compressor clutch and the Hall sender. With this system any periodic idle adjustments are no longer needed.

The Digifant II ECU supplies the idle stabilizer with approximately 430 mA of current idle. If the idle speed drops below specification such as when the A/C compressor clutch is engaged, the current to the idle stabilizer is increased. The increase in current opens the valve further to allow additional air to bypass the throttle plate. This additional air maintains the correct idle speed during engine loads at idle.

Electrical current is passed through a set of electrical windings inside the valve. This creates a magnetic field which regulates the position of the valve plunger.

EVAPORATIVE EMISSION SYSTEM

The carbon canister stores fuel vapors from the fuel tank when the engine is shut off. During normal driving, fuel tank vapors are drawn into the throttle housing via the carbon canister control valve. The fuel vapors are drawn into the throttle housing via a 1.2mm orifice. At idle, the control valve is closed (low vacuum to control valve) and the carbon canister is not purged.

AUTOMATIC TRANSMISSION

Digifant II vehicles equipped with automatic transmission use a vacuum amplifier. The purpose of the amplifier is to increase vacuum at idle to the brake booster. The carbon canister vent line is not disconnected when checking or adjusting CO content.

MANUAL TRANSMISSION

Digifant II vehicles equipped with manual transmission use a vacuum amplifier. The purpose of the amplifier is to increase vacuum at idle to the brake booster. The carbon canister vent line is not disconnected when checking or adjusting CO content. It is important that these two vacuum hoses are not reversed.

IGNITION TIMING, IDLE SPEED AND CO

Adjustment

1. Be sure that the engine oil temperature is at least 80°C.
2. Connect VW 1367 engine tester, or equivalent, according to manufacturers specifications.
3. Connect exhaust probe EPA 75 or equivalent to CO receptacle.
4. Start engine and let idle for at least two minutes.
5. Be sure that all electrical accessories are turned off. be sure that the radiator fan is not running during the CO adjustment.
6. Check that the throttle switch is functioning properly. Remove and install throttle switch connector. Timing and idle speed must change.
7. Check that the idle stabilization system is functioning properly. With ignition switched on, idle stabilization valve must vibrate and hum.
8. Remove the connector at coolant temperature sensor.
9. Advance the engine speed to 2000–2500 rpm. If checking the timing it should be 4–8 degrees BTDC. If adjusting the timing it should be 6 ± 1 degrees BTDC.
10. Turn the engine off. Remove the hose for the crankcase emission control valve. Plug the hosee.
11. Start the engine and let it idle. Disconnect the coolant temperature sensor.
12. Advance the engine speed over 3000 rpm three times and then let engine idle.
13. Check the idle speed and CO content and adjust if necessary. The idle speed should be 800 ± 50 rpm. The CO% should be 0.7 ± 0.4%.
14. Reconnect the hose for the crankcase emission control valve. Reconnect the temperature coolant sensor.
15. After adjustment, advance the engine speed over 3000 rpm three times and return to idle. The idle speed and CO content must be within specifications.
16. If CO content increases when reconnecting the crankcase emission control valve, it is not due to improper CO adjustment. Oil dilution is the probable cause due to short distance driving. A short term solution is to change the engine oil.

IDLE STABILIZER

Checking

1. Be sure that the engine oil temperature at least 80°C.

2. Be sure that the coolant temperature sensor is functioning.

3. Check the idle speed adjustment.

4. Check for engine vacuum leaks.

5. Connect VW tool 1315 A/2 to the idle stabilizer.

6. Connect a multimeter to test leads of VW 1315 A/2. Set the meter to mA scale.

7. Start the engine.

8. Advance the engine speed to 3000 rpm three times and return to idle.

9. Measure the control current, it should be about 430 ± 30 mA and fluctuating.

10. Remove the connector from the coolant temperature sensor. The meater should read about 430 mA and stay constant.

11. When the engine is idling the control current for idle stabilization is dependent on engine speed. The current may fluctuate between 400–1000 mA due to the following engine conditions, a cold engine, the A/C on, the power steering to the lock position or any electrical accessories that are in the functioning position.

IGNITION MAP AND KNOCK SENSOR

Checking

1. Be sure that the engine oil temperature at least 80°C.

2. Be sure that the coolant temperature sensor is functioning.

3. Connect VW tool 1367, engine tester, according to the manufacturer's instructions.

4. Check and adjust ignition timing.

5. Start the engine and let idle for at least two minutes.

6. Remove the electrical connector on the coolant tenperature sensor.

7. Advance the engine speed to 2300 rpm.

8. Record the ignition timing.

9. Reconnect the coolant temperature sensor electrical connector.

10. Briefly raise the engine speed above 3000 rpm in order to store the knock sensor information in Digifant II ECU.

11. Advance the engine speed to 2300 rpm and recheck ignition timing. The timing should advance 30 ± 3 degrees from the initial setting. If the timing does not advance, 30 ± 3 degrees, check the knock sensor, torque, and wiring and also the coolant temperature sensor and wiring

COOLANT TEMTERATURE SENSOR

Checking

1. Disconnect the electrical connector from the coolant temperature sensor at the sensor.

2. Connect an ohmmeter to the terminals of the coolant sensor. Resistance should be within specification. If not, replace the sensor.

3. If within specification and problem still exists, check wiring.

AIR FLAP POTENTIOMETER

The air flap potentiometer is a variable resistor connected to the air flow sensor that provides a signal for determining fuel system enrichment. It is a internal component of air flow sensor.

AIR FLOW SENSOR

The air flow sensor measures the amount of air entering the intake manifold and sends a voltage signal to the electronic control unit. It is attached to the air filter housing.

COOLANT TEMPERATURE SENSOR

The coolant temperature sensor is used for measuring engine coolant temperature to determine cold running engine operation. It is located on the front side of the cylinder head between No. 3 and No. 4 cylinder.

ELECTRONIC CONTROL UNIT (ECU)

The ECU provides the proper actuation signal to the injectors and optimum ignition timing point based on inputs from other system components. It is located inside the engine compartment to the left side in the plenum.

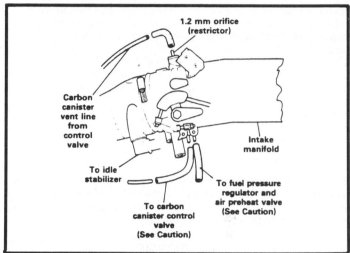

Digifant II vacuum hose layout manual transmission

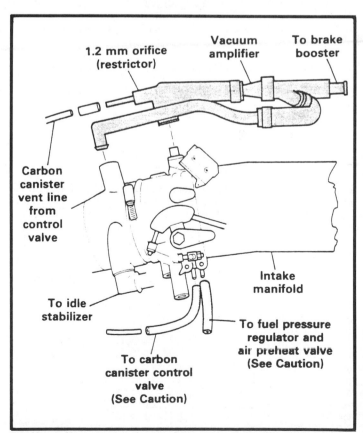

Digifant II vacuum hose layout automatic transmission

FUEL FILTER

The fuel filter, which removes foreign particles from the fuel system, is attached to the fuel reservoir in front of the fuel tank on the right side of the vehicle.

FUEL PUMP

The fuel pump is an electric pump which delivers fuel to the injectors. It is located inside the fuel reservoir.

FUEL PUMP RELAY

When energized by the power supply relay, the fuel pump relay provides battery voltage to the fuel pump and oxygen sensor heating element. It is located inside the relay panel.

FUEL SCREEN

The fuel screen is a strainer which removes foreign particles from the fuel system. It is located in front of the fuel pump, inside the fuel reservoir, inlet of each injector and inlet of fuel pressure regulator.

IDLE STABILIZATION VALVE

The idle stabilization valve is an electronically controlled valve used to maintain idle speed at a predetermined level by regulating intake air at idle. It is locatedon a rubber mount near the top of the intake manifold and valve cover.

INJECTOR

The injector is an electronically activated valve which directs a cone shaped mist of fuel into the intake port near each intake valve. They are located on intake manifold at cylinder head.

KNOCK SENSOR

The knock sensor is a piezoelectronic crystal whcih generates a small amount of voltage. This voltage signal which is sent to the ECU is used to correct ignition knock or detonation. It is located next to No. 2 cylinder on the engine block.

OXYGEN SENSOR

The oxygen sensor is used to detect the amount of oxygen in the exhaust gases. It threads into the catalytic converter housing on 105 hp.engine and into exhaust manifold on 100 hp. engine.

POWER SUPPLY RELAY

The power supply relay, when energized by the ignition switch, provides battery voltage to the ECU and fuel injectors. It is located in the relay panel.

PRESSURE REGULATOR

The pressure regulator is a diaphragm type regulator used to maintain system pressure at a given value. It is bolted to the left side of the fuel injector assembly.

TRANSFER PUMP

The transfer pump supplies the fuel pump reservoir with fuel from the tank. It is located inside the fuel tank and is attached to the fuel tank sending unit.

THROTTLE SWITCH

The throttle switch provides closed throttle and full throttle signals to ECU for idle stabilization, deceleration fuel shut-off, and full load enrichment. It is mounted to throttle valve housing.

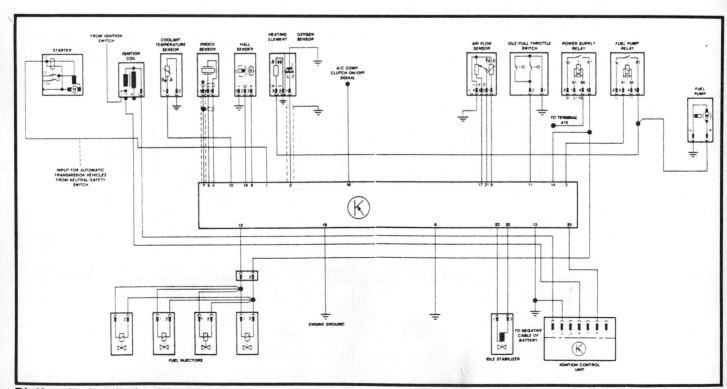

Digifant II electrical schematic

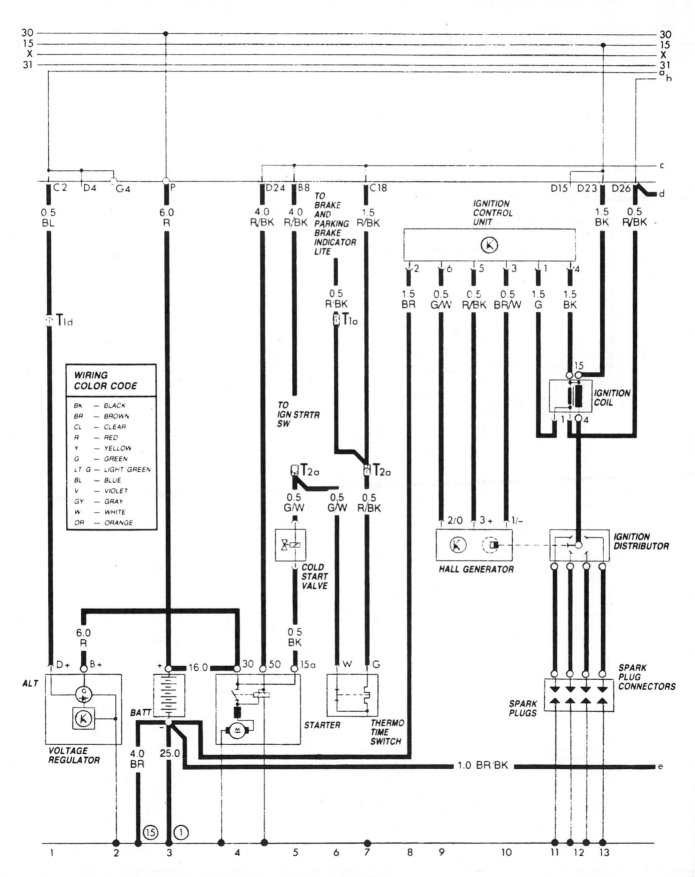

Electronic engine control wiring schematic—Jetta fuel injection

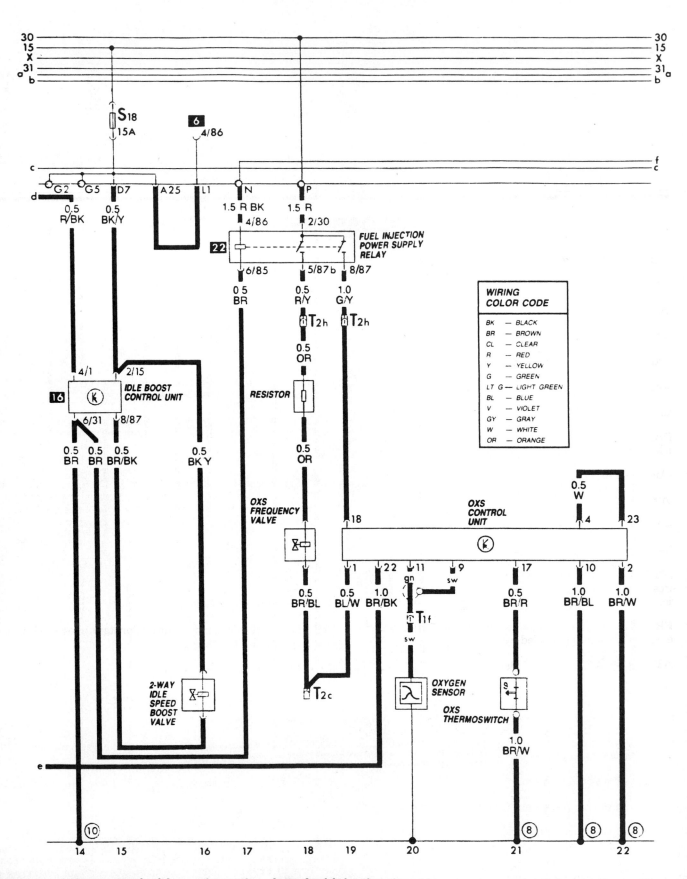

Electronic engine control wiring schematic—Jetta fuel injection (cont.)

GLOSSARY

AAV – Anti Afterburning Valve

AAP – Auxiliary Accelerator Pump

A/C – Air Conditioning

ACC – Air conditioner clutch compressor

ACT – Air Charge Temperature sensor

ACV – Air Control Valve

AI – Air Injection

AIR GAP – the distance or space between the reluctor tooth and pick up coil

AIS – Air Injection System

A/F – Air Fuel

AFC – Air Flow Controlled fuel injection

ALDL – Assembly Line Diagnostic Link

AMMETER – an electrical meter used to measure current flow (amperes) in an electrical circuit. Ammeter should be connected in series and current flowing in the circuit to be checked.

AMPERE (AMP) – the unit current flow is measured in. Amperage equals the voltage divided by the resistance

ARMATURE – See Reluctor For definition

A/T – Automatic Transmission

BALLAST RESISTOR – is a resistor used in the ignition primary circuit between the ignition switch and coil to limit the current flow to the coil when the primary circuit is closed. Can also be used in the form of a resistance wire.

BAC – Bypass Air Control System

BAR – Unit of pressure measurement. 1 bar is approx. 14.5 psi.

BID – Breakerless Inductive Discharge ignition system

BP – Barometric Pressure

BTDC – Before Top Dead Center

BVV – Bowl Vent Valve

BYPASS – system used to bypass ballast resistor during engine cranking to
increase voltage supplied to the coil

CALIBRATION ASSEMBLY – memory module that plugs into an on-board computer and contains instructions for engine operation

CANISTER – a container in an emission control system that contains charcoal to trap fuel vapors from the fuel system

CANP – Canister Purge solenoid that opens the fuel vapor canister line to the intake manifold when energized

CAPACITOR – a device which stores an electrical charge

CATALYST – special metals such as platinum and palladium that are contained within a catalytic converter. The catalyst contacts the hot exhaust gases and promotes more complete combustion of unburned hydrocarbons and reduction of carbon monoxide

CC – Catalytic converter

CCO – Converter clutch override

CHM – Cold Mixture Heater

CIS – Constant Injection System or Constant Idle Speed system manufactured by Bosch

CO – Carbon monoxide

CP – Crankshaft Position sensor

CPU – Central Processing Unit

CONDUCTOR – any material through which an electrical current can be transmitted easily

CONTINUITY – continuous or complete circuit. Can be checked with an ohmmeter

CYL SENSOR – Crankshaft Angle Sensor

DIELECTRIC SILICONE COMPOUND – non-conducting silicone grease applied to spark plug wire boots, rotors and connectors to prevent arcing and moisture from entering a connector

DIODE – an electrical devise that will allow current to flow in one direction only

DIS – Direct Ignition System

DSV – Deceleration Solenoid Valve

ECA – Electronic control assembly

ECC – Electronic Controlled Carburetor

ECCS – Electronic Concentrated Control System

ECI – Electronic Control Injection

ECIT – Electronic Control Ignition Timing

ECM – Electronic Control Module

ECS – Emission Control System

ECT – Engine coolant temperature sensor

ECU – Electronic Control Unit

EEC – Evaporative Emission Control

EFC – Electronic Fuel Control

EFE – Early Fuel Evaporation

EFI – Electronic Fuel Injection

EGI – Electronic Gasoline Injection

EGO – Exhaust Gas Oxygen sensor

EGR – Exhaust Gas Recirculation

EGRC – EGR control solenoid

EGRV – EGR vent solenoid

EICV – Electronic Idle Control Valve

EIS – Electronic Ignition System which uses a reluctor and a pick up coil along with a module to replace the ignition points and condenser

ELECTRONIC CONTROL UNIT (ECU) – ignition module, module, amplifier or igniter. See Module for definition

ESA – Electronic Spark Advance

ESC – Electronic Spark Control

ESV – Enrichment Solenoid Valve

EVP – EGR valve position sensor

FBC – Feedback Carburetor

FBCA – Feedback carburetor actuator

FBSV – Feedback Solenoid Valve

FCS – Fuel Control Solenoid

FCV – Float Chamber Ventilation System

FICB – Fast Idle Cam Breaker

GND or GRD – Ground or negative (-)

HAC – High Altitude Compensator

HALL EFFECT PICK-UP ASSEMBLY – used to input a signal to the electronic control unit. The system operates on the Hall Effect principle whereby a magnetic field is blocked from the pick-up by a rotating shutter assembly. Used by Chrysler, Bosch and General Motors

HC – Hydrocarbons. Any compound composed of hydrogen and carbon, such as petroleum products, that is considered a pollutant

HCV – Exhaust Heat Control Valve

HEGO – Heat Exhaust Gas Oxygen Sensor

IAS – Inlet Air Solenoid

IDM – Ignition Diagnostic Monitor

IGNITER – Term used by Japanese automotive and ignition manufacturers for the electronic control unit or module

IGNITION COIL – step-up transformer consisting of a primary and a secondary winding with an iron core. As the current flows in the primary winding stops, the magnetic field collapses across the secondary winding inducing the high secondary voltage. The coil may be oil filled or an epoxy design

IIA – Integrated Ignition Assembly

IMS – Inferred Mileage Sensor

INDUCTION – a means of transferring electrical energy in the form of a magnetic field. Principle used in the ignition coil to increase voltage

INFINITY – an ohmmeter reading which indicates an open circuit in which no current will flow

INJECTOR – a solenoid or pressure-operated fuel delivery valve used for fuel injection systems

I/O – Input/Output

INTERGRATED CIRCUIT (IC) – electronic micro-circuit consisting of a semi-conductor components or elements made using thick-flim or thin-flim technology. Elements are located on a small chip made of a semi-conducting material, greatly reducing the size of the electronic control unit and allowing it to be incorporated within the distributor

IMA Sensor – Idle Mixture Adjuster Sensor

ISC – Idle speed control device

ITS – Idle tracking switch. An input device that sends a signal to the control module to indicate throttle position

JSV – Jet Mixture Solenoid Valve

KDLH – Kick-Down Low Hold

KS – Knock Sensor. An input device that responds to spark knock caused by excessively advanced ignition timing

LED – Light Emitting Diode

LOS – Limited Operation Strategy

MAF – Mass Airflow Sensor. A device used to measure the amount of intake air entering the engine on some fuel injection systems

MAP – Manifold Air Pressure Sensor

MAS – Mixture Adjust Screw

M/C – Mixture Control

MCT – Manifold charge temperature sensor

MICROPROCESSORS – a miniature computer on a silicone chip

MIL – Malfunction Indicator Light

MODULE – Electronic control unit, amplifier or igniter of solid state or intergrated design which controls the current flow in the ignition primary circuit based on input from the pick-up coil.When the module opens the primary circuit, the high secondary voltage is induced in the coil

MPFI – Multi-Point Fuel Injection

MPS – Motor Postion Sensor

MS – Mechatro Spark Control

M/T – Manual Transmission

NDS – Neutral/Drive Switch

NGS – Neutral Gear Switch

NTS – Negative Temperature Coefficient Resistor

NOx – Nitrous Oxide. A compound formed during the engine combustion process when oxygen in the air combines with nitrogen to form photochemical smog

OCC – Output Cycling Check

OHM – the electrical unit of resistance to current flow

OHMMETER – the electrical meter used to measure the resistance in ohms.Self-powered and must be connected to an electrically open circuit or damage to the ohmmeter will result

OXYGEN SENSOR – used with the feedback system to sense the presence of oxygen in the exhaust gas and signal the computer which can reference the voltage signal to an air/fuel ratio

PA SENSOR – Atmospheric Pressure Sensor

PCV – Postive Crankcase Ventilation

PGM-FI – Programmed Fuel Injection System

PGM-IG – Programmed Ignition

PHENOMENA – Basis of symptons

PICK-UP COIL – inputs signal to the electronic control unit to open the primary circuit. Consists of a fine wire coil mounted around a permanent magnet. As the reluctor's ferrous tooth passes through the magnetic field an alternating current is produced,signaling the electronic control unit.Can operate on the principle of metal detecting,magnetic induction or Hall Effect. Is also referred to as a stator or sensor

PIP – Profile Ignition Pickup

POTENTIOMETER – a variable resistor used to change a voltage signal

PRIMARY CIRCUIT – is the low voltage side of the ignition system which consists of the ignition switch,ballast resistor or resistance wire,bypass,coil,electronic control unit and pick-up coil as well as the connecting wires and harnesses

PSPS – Power Steering Pressure Switch

PTC HEATER – Positive Temperature Coefficient Heater

PULSE GENERATOR – also called a pulse signal generator.Term used by Japanese and German automotive and ignition manufacturers to describe the pick-up and reluctor assembly.Generates an electrical pulse which triggers the electronic control unit or igniter

PULSE WIDTH – the amount of time the control unit energizes the fuel injectors to spray fuel into the intake manifold. Usually measured in milliseconds

PVS – Ported vacuum switch. A temperature-activated switch that changes vacuum connections when the coolant temperature changes

RAM – random access memory

RELAY – a switching device operated by a low-current circuit which controls the opening and closing of another circuit of higher current capacity

RELUCTOR – also called an armature or trigger wheel. Ferrous metal piece attached to the distributor shaft. Made up of teeth of which the number are the same as the number of engine cylinders.As the reluctor teeth pass through the pick-up magnetic field an alternating current is generated in the pick-up coil

RESISTANCE – the opposition to the flow of current through a circuit or electrical device,and is measured in ohms.Resistance is equal to the voltage divided by the amperage

ROM – read only memory

SAS – Speed Adjusting Screw

SCSV – Slow Cut Solenoid Valve

SECONDARY – the high voltage side of the ignition system,usually above 20,000 volts.The secondary includes the ignition coil, coil wire, distributor cap and rotor, spark plug wires and spark plug

SENSOR – also called the pick-up coil or stator. See pick-up coil for definition

SHUTTER – also called the vane. Used in a Hall Effect distributor to block the magnetic field from the Hall Effect pick-up. It is attached to the rotor and is grounded to the distributor shaft

SOLENOID – a wire coil with a movable core which changes position by means of electromagnetism when current flows through the coil

SPARK DURATION – the length of time measured in milliseconds(1/1000th second)the spark is established across the spark plug gap

SPFI – Single Point Fuel Injection

SPOUT – Spark Output

STATOR – another name for a pick-coil. See pick-up coil for definition

STI – Self-Test Input

STO – Self-Test Output

SWITCHING TRANSISTOR – used in some electronic ignition systems, it acts as a switch for high current in response to a low voltage signal applied to the base terminal

TA Sensor – Intake Air Temperature Sensor

TAB – Thermactor air bypass solenoid

TAD – Thermactor air diverter solenoid

TAS – Throttle Adjust Screw

TCCS – Toyota Computer Controlled System

TCP – Temperature Compensated Accelerator Pump

TDC – Top Dead Center

THERMISTOR – a device that changes its resistance with temperature

TK or TKS – throttle kicker solenoid. An actuator moves the throttle linkage to increase idle rpm

TPI – Tuned Port Injection

TP or TPS – Throttle Position Sensor

TRANSISTOR – a semi-conductor component which can be actuated by a small voltage to perform an electrical switching function

TRIGGER WHEEL – see Reluctor for definition

TW Sensor – Coolant Temperature Sensor

TVSV – Thermostatic Vacuum Switching Valve

TWC – Three-way catalyst, sometimes referred to as a dual catalytic converter. Combines two catalytic converters in one shell to control emissions of NOx HC and CO

VAF – Vane Airflow Meter

VAT – Vane Air Temperature

VB VOLTAGE – Battery Voltage

VECI – Vehicle Emission Control Information Label

VF VOLTAGE – Battery Voltage

VM – Vane Meter

VOLT – the unit of electrical pressure or electromotive force

VOLTAGE DROP – the difference in voltage between one point in a circuit and another, usually across a resistance. Voltage drop is measured in parallel with current flowing in the circuit

VOLTMETER – electrical meter used to measure voltage in a circuit. Voltmeters must be connected in parallel across the load or circuit

VREF – The reference voltage or power supplied by the computer control unit to some sensors regulated at a specific voltage

VV – Variable Venturi

VVC – Variable Voltage Choke

WOT – Wide open throttle switch

3475D